Industrial Organization

Industrial Organization: Markets and Strategies provides an up-to-date account of modern industrial organization that blends theory with real-world applications. Written in a clear and accessible style, it acquaints the reader with the most important models for understanding strategies chosen by firms with market power and shows how such firms adapt to different market environments. It covers a wide range of topics including recent developments on product bundling, branding strategies, restrictions in vertical supply relationships, intellectual property protection and two-sided markets, to name just a few. Models are presented in detail and the main results are summarized as lessons. Formal theory is complemented throughout by real-world cases that show students how it applies to actual organizational settings. The book is accompanied by a website containing a number of additional resources for lecturers and students, including exercises, solutions to exercises and slides.

Companion website at www.cambridge.org/belleflamme.

Paul Belleflamme is Professor of Economics at the Université catholique de Louvain, Belgium. He has published several articles in leading economics journals and teaches courses in the fields of industrial organization and managerial economics.

Martin Peitz is Professor of Economics at the University of Mannheim, Germany. He has published widely in leading economics journals and, with Paul de Bijl, is the author of *Regulation and Entry into Telecommunications Markets* (Cambridge University Press, 2003).

GH00498876

Industrial Organization

Markets and Strategies

Paul Belleflamme
Université catholique de Louvain

Martin Peitz
University of Mannheim

CAMBRIDGE
UNIVERSITY PRESS

CAMBRIDGE
UNIVERSITY PRESS

University Printing House, Cambridge CB2 8BS, United Kingdom

Published in the United States of America by Cambridge University Press, New York

Cambridge University Press is part of the University of Cambridge.

It furthers the University's mission by disseminating knowledge in the pursuit of education, learning and research at the highest international levels of excellence.

www.cambridge.org
Information on this title: www.cambridge.org/9780521681599

First published 2010
4th printing 2012

Printed in the United Kingdom by Bell and Bain Ltd, Glasgow

A catalogue record for this publication is available from the British Library

Library of Congress Cataloguing in Publication data
Belleflamme, Paul.
Industrial organization : markets and strategies / Paul Belleflamme, Martin Peitz. – 1st ed.
   p.   cm.
Includes index.
ISBN 978-0-521-68159-9 (pbk.)
1. Marketing.   2. Strategic planning.   I. Peitz, Martin.   II. Title.
HF5415.B4287   2010
658.4′012 – dc22   2009047718

ISBN 978-0-521-86299-8 Hardback
ISBN 978-0-521-68159-9 Paperback

Additional resources for this publication at www.cambridge.org/industrial_organization

Contents

Figures

Tables

Cases

Preface

A large part of economic transactions takes place through markets. On these markets, firms take decisions in response to prevailing market conditions that affect the well-being of market participants. Such decisions are relevant to the field of Industrial Organization (IO) and their analysis lies at the heart of this book. *Industrial Organization: Markets and Strategies* indeed aims at presenting the role of imperfectly competitive markets for private and social decisions.

Among the numerous decisions taken by firms is the *make-or-buy decision*, whereby firms compare the costs and benefits of manufacturing a product or service against purchasing it. Typically, the firm will prefer the 'make' option over the 'buy' option if the purchase price is higher than the in-house manufacturing cost or if outside suppliers are unreliable. Naturally, the firm must also have the necessary skills and equipment to meet its own product standards.

There is a clear analogy between this generic dilemma and the decision process that led us to write this book. As industrial organization teachers since the start of our academic careers, we have both long relied on existing textbooks to support our courses. Yet, through the years, our needs became different from the offers of outside suppliers. That is, the 'make' option started to become more tempting than the 'buy' option.

At the end of 2004 we firmly took our decision to 'make' a new textbook.[a] At that time (and this still holds today), we could not find on the market any textbook in industrial organization that suited the type of courses at the advanced undergraduate or master level we were teaching. We knew that many of our colleagues shared our views. Our objective was thus to produce a new text that would greatly simplify the work of teachers who, thus far, had to combine material from different books and look for applications to meet their students' needs. Naturally, benefits to teachers are meant to spill over to their students. Although we believe in formal modelling, we also believe that it is important not to overload students with techniques and to motivate the analysis with real-world cases. So, we endeavoured to write a book that blends up-to-date theoretical developments and real-life applications.

The concretization of our efforts currently lies in your hands. To convince you that the best option for you is the 'buy' decision, we propose three main reasons for which *Industrial Organization: Markets and Strategies* is your choice.

- We have produced a book that is easy to read, while maintaining a high level of rigour and conciseness. We intend to be exact and clearly state assumptions and results. As a consequence, you will be able to see easily where a new model starts, what are its assumptions and results, and what are the arguments that lead to those results.

- Our book covers a wide range of topics as it includes recent developments in the IO literature, as well as topical issues (related, e.g., to the digital economy).

- Many of the arguments made in IO theory are arguments at the margin; to formalize them we cannot rely on 'calculus-free theory'. Hence, we present and analyse

[a] As it took us four years to complete the redaction of this book, we can provide proof that we largely underestimated the costs of this 'make' decision. Firms, as analysed in this book, are not subject to such a bias.

simple and hopefully elegant models. We summarize the main results as lessons. We also illustrate the relevance of these models by relating them to real-world cases.

The **targeted audience** of the book is advanced Bachelor or Master students taking a course in industrial organization. The book is also a useful reference for an IO course at the Ph.D. level as well as for an advanced course for Business School teaching. In any case, to learn effectively from this book, students need to have a course of intermediate microeconomics or business economics in their academic background. Note that selected chapters of the book can also serve as support for courses in business and managerial economics, in management strategy, in strategic pricing, in economics of innovation, in the theory of competition policy or in oligopoly theory. It is also possible to focus on topics and cases to outline a course of industrial organization in the digital economy.

The specific features of the book help to address a number of **learning challenges** usually faced by industrial organization students.

- *Students often struggle to connect theory with practice*. The integration of real-world cases in the text, showing how theories relate to real applications, greatly reduces this problem. In addition, this helps students to understand better the relevance of topics.

- *Students often struggle to understand the working of models*. To address this issue, we carefully develop the models we present and we make their assumptions explicit. We want students to see models at work and we make sure that they do not spend their time uncovering hidden calculus.

- *Students may be overwhelmed by a large variety of models and lose track*. To avoid or, at least, reduce this risk, we have introduced a large number of lessons that guide the reader through the book and summarize the main insights of the analysis.

- *Students may become bored by constructed examples*. As a consequence, we draw many real-world cases from industries that students consider to be important, notably in consumer goods industries and in the digital economy. This makes students more involved and curious about how to address additional issues that appear in the cases.

- *Students often have trouble relating different topics with one another*. The book is carefully organized to make sure that students do not 'close' a topic (and forget its analysis) when moving to the next one. Each part of the book contains several chapters covering related topics and starts with a general introduction that gives a bird's-eye view of the part material and explains the links between the various chapters. Multiple cross-references between chapters are made throughout the text. As a result, students should acquire a deeper and more transversal understanding of the various issues of industrial organization.

- *The needs of different types of students may be in conflict*. In particular, students who want to dig deeper may have problems finding the right material, while those who simply want to read the textbook may be distracted by many references in the text or in footnotes. To solve this dilemma, we minimize the number of footnotes and provide access to the relevant literature through endnotes. Moreover, the bibliography is sorted by the parts in which the respective work is cited. Hence, the book adequately combines access to the scientific literature for those who need it, and uninterrupted reading for those who do not.

A number of **supplementary resources** accompany the book and help instructors teach and students learn. Exercises are posted on the textbook website. Solutions to these exercises are made available to instructors. Additional exercises can be uploaded by other researchers. On the website also slides are posted. These come in two different sets (two files per chapter). The first set provides a quick overview on the different topics. Instructors can use this set to motivate a particular topic, establish key insights, provide some intuition, and some reality check. The second set presents the most important models in-depth. Each instructor can make his or her preferred blend from the slides provided by the authors.

Students at Barcelona, Frankfurt, Liège, Louvain, Luxembourg, Manchester, Mannheim and Munich (from the advanced undergraduate to the Ph.D. level) have seen parts of this book at various stages of completion. We thank them for their feedback. Several people – colleagues and students – dedicated their precious time reading parts of this book and helped us to make this book a reality with comments and suggestions on previous drafts and exercises for the textbook website. At the risk of forgetting some of them, we want to mention Francesca Barigozzi (Bologna), Giuseppe De Feo (Glasgow), Estelle Derclaye (Nottingham), Vincenzo Denicolo (Bologna), Roman Inderst (Frankfurt), Heiko Karle (Brussels), Johannes Koenen (Mannheim), Florian Köpke (Mannheim), Christian Lambertz (Mannheim), Marco Marinucci (Louvain), Yann Ménière (Paris), Jeanine Miklós-Thal (Rochester), Volker Nocke (Mannheim), Pierre M. Picard (Luxembourg), Thomas Roende (Copenhagen), Isabel Ruhmer (Mannheim), Markus Reisinger (Munich), Maarten Pieter Schinkel (Amsterdam), Yossi Spiegel (Tel Aviv), Cecilia Vergari (Bologna), Georg von Graevenitz (Munich) and Xavier Wauthy (Brussels). We should add to this list the various anonymous referees who conscientiously reviewed and commented initial drafts of several chapters. We want to thank them all for their contributions, support and encouragement. Over the whole period, Chris Harrison from Cambridge University Press was supportive and, perhaps due to our incomplete information disclosure about the progress of the book, optimistic that this book project will come to a happy end. We kept going because we could not disappoint him after all these years. We thank the team at Cambridge University Press for their dedication to produce this book.

Part I
Getting started

Introduction to Part I: Getting started

A large part of economic transactions takes place through markets. Markets thus play a central role in the allocation of goods in the economy. Moreover, the existence and nature of markets affect production decisions. *Industrial Organization Markets and Strategies* is an attempt to present the role of imperfectly competitive markets for private and social decisions.

The array of issues related to markets and strategies is extremely large. To convince yourself, log in to the website of any newspaper or magazine, and start a search for these two key words: markets and strategies. The search engine will provide you with a long list of articles concerning a huge variety of sectors, companies and business practices. As an illustration, here follows a selection of recent articles that were returned by the *International Herald Tribune* search engine (www.iht.com) on 1 February 2009.[1]

'Pfizer Inc., the world's largest drugmaker, said Monday it is buying rival Wyeth for $68 billion in a deal that will quickly boost Pfizer's revenue and diversification and – if it works as advertised – help the company become more nimble.'

'Only a few years ago, debates about the future of banking across the Continent were dominated by talk of border-straddling "European champions" that could compete with U.S. giants. But now a different development looms: the disintegration of truly European banking as the financial crisis pressures banks to retrench and refocus on their home markets.'

'The shock waves from the global downturn are pushing a fragmented and once fast-growing Chinese retail sector to consolidate as sales slow and profit margins shrink. Global giants like Wal-Mart Stores and Carrefour will benefit from the consolidation, along with China's growing consumer class, but rapid expansion has caught some retailers overextended as their home markets collapse.'

'In moves that will help shape the online future of the music business, Apple said on Tuesday that it would remove anticopying restrictions on all of the songs in its popular iTunes store and allow record companies to set a range of prices for them.'

'The ancient Château d'Ermenonville and a circuit of others around Europe served for more than a dozen years as bases for executives from some of the biggest names in oil – Exxon Mobil; Royal Dutch Shell; Sasol, of South Africa; and Repsol YPF, of Spain – to fix prices of paraffin, the overlooked wax byproduct of crude oil, that is used in candles, paper cups, lip balm and chewing gum. The scheme drove up prices to consumers in a plot that probably touched most households, according to the European commissioner for competition, Neelie Kroes, whose office punished nine oil companies with more than half a billion euros in penalties.'

All these stories describe firms taking strategic decisions (e.g., acquisition of a competitor, repositioning of activities, change in product specification and pricing) that result from particular market conditions (e.g., European banks or Chinese retailers react to adverse demand shocks) and that affect the well-being of market participants (e.g., the acquisition is likely to improve Pfizer's performance, smaller Chinese retailers should suffer from the consolidation of the sector, European consumers were hurt by the collusive behavior of paraffin producers). Such decisions are relevant to the field of *Industrial Organization* and their analysis lies at the heart of this book.

Before we fully engage in the analysis of markets and strategies, we devote the first part of the book to a number of preliminaries. In Chapter 1, we provide a roadmap as well as some instructions about how to use the book. In Chapter 2, we present the players in a market, namely firms (that is, sellers) and consumers (that is, buyers). We elaborate on the hypothesis that firms maximize profits and that consumers maximize utility. A large part of the exposition can be seen as health warnings which should be kept in mind when consuming the book. We then start the analysis of market interaction and provide some prototypes of markets, ranging from perfectly competitive to monopolistic markets. This provides a first glance at firm strategy in market environments. While this is only a first look at such markets, it is hopefully useful material to refresh the knowledge that has been gained in some microeconomics lectures.

Once you have worked through these first two chapters, you will be ready to start the real thing.

1 What is *Markets and Strategies*?

In this short introductory chapter, we give a broad presentation of the book and indicate how we think it is best to use it. We start by explaining the title of the book: what do we mean by 'markets' and by 'strategies', and why do we associate the two terms? We argue that it is market power and the exercise of it that relate markets and strategies to one another. Next, we outline the approach that we adopt in this book: we believe in formal modelling, which explains that the book is theory-based; yet, we also believe that it is important not to overload readers with techniques and to motivate the analysis with real-life cases; our aim is thus to blend up-to-date theoretical developments and real-life applications in a rigorous and concise manner. Finally, we describe the level, the scope and the organization of the book.

1.1 Markets

Markets allow buyers and sellers to exchange goods and services in return for a monetary payment. Markets come in a myriad of different varieties. Examples are your local farmers' markets (local) and the market for passenger jets (global), the market for computer software (product) and software support (service), the market for electricity (homogeneous product) and markets for highly specialized steel (differentiated product). These markets may exist in physical or virtual space.

We mostly consider markets in which a small number of sellers set price or quantity strategically, as well as possible other variables, whereas buyers mostly come in large number so that they non-strategically react to supply conditions. The reverse situation applies to some procurement markets in which a small number of buyers faces a large number of sellers. We mainly use examples of markets in which buyers are final consumers; however, the formal investigation relies on certain characteristics of markets that also apply to other markets in which buyers are not final consumers but e.g. small retailers, service providers, or manufacturers.

Market power: what it means

Markets and Strategies, and the industrial organization literature at large, attempts to describe the interaction of firms as sellers, and consumers or other economic agents as buyers. The outcome of this interaction is a market allocation (i.e., an allocation of resources through free markets). This allocation depends on how the market operates. We want to predict these resulting allocations (positive analysis) and their efficiency or welfare properties. The latter can be used for normative analysis, e.g., to address the question about whether and how a government should intervene.

To address these questions, we have to make assumptions as to how markets operate. Here we may follow the perfectly competitive paradigm according to which both sides of the market are price-takers and simply post their supplies and demands. This paradigm appears to be well-suited for those industries in which there are only small entry barriers and many small firms compete against each other. In such a market, it can be seen as a good approximation to assume that firms indeed do not have any price-setting power, and that output decisions by an individual firm have a negligible effect on market price and thus on the profit-maximizing decisions of other firms.[a] Modern industrial organization literature largely ignores such perfectly competitive markets and, in this tradition, this book focuses on markets in which firms do have market power so that an incremental price increase above marginal costs does not lead to a loss of all (or most) of the demand.

If we are only interested in competition policy issues, neglecting perfectly competitive markets is essentially without loss of generality because antitrust authorities deal with concerns of market power and its abuse. If we look at the current landscape of important industries, we observe that firms such as Microsoft, Boeing, and Porsche clearly do have market power. For those firms, a small increase in price does not lead to a loss of all or most of the market share. Even small local retailers may enjoy market power in the sense that small price changes do not lead to drastic changes in demand. The reason is that although there are, e.g., many bakeries and butchers, they are located at different places and cater to different tastes. Here, product differentiation gives rise to market power. Alternatively, firms may offer identical products or services but consumers may not be perfectly informed. Then firms enjoy market power due to consumers being less than perfectly informed (or incurring search costs to obtain this information). Finally, consumers may be locked into long-term contracts or may have become accustomed to a particular product. Then a firm has some market power over these captive consumers due to consumer switching costs.[b]

Market power and its sources are at the core of *Markets and Strategies*. Because of market power, firms may want to invest in exploring their market environment and finding suitable instruments to improve their profits. Antitrust authorities may limit the set of actions that is available to firms by punishing certain types of behaviour or by interfering ex ante. For instance, mergers are only cleared if the antitrust authority does not foresee anticompetitive behavior as the result of the merger.

While market power appears at first sight to be a static concept, this view is misleading. Firms enjoy market power because other firms do not find it worthwhile to offer identical or similar products or services. In particular, fixed costs define a minimum level of output a firm has to achieve in the industry to make non-negative profits. However, the presence of other market characteristics alone may make it unattractive for firms to enter the industry. More generally, in some markets, only one or a small number of firms is viable. At this point, we want to discuss informally the number of firms in an industry.

---

[a] We review the competitive paradigm in some more detail in the next chapter.
[b] We systematically examine these different sources of market power in Part III of the book.

Natural monopoly and natural oligopoly

Consider a market with few firms and possibly only one firm as seller. If, in the latter case, the profit-maximizing monopolist makes positive profits and sells above marginal costs or, in a market with more than one firm, these firms make positive profits and sell above marginal costs, we may wonder whether additional firms may have an incentive to enter so that eventually profits are competed away. Note that post entry, the strategic situation is very different so that profits before entry are not a reliable source of information for the entrant firm. Rather, it has to predict profits that would occur after entry has taken place. It may well come to the conclusion that although current profit levels are high, entry would trigger fierce competition which therefore does not make it worthwhile to enter.

While entry may not be profitable so that there exists a natural monopoly due to demand and supply conditions, an alternative reason for the analysis of a market with a given number of firms is the scarcity of available necessary inputs. For instance, mining is limited to the presence of the natural resource of interest. In other cases, as we now discuss, the government limits the number of firms in the market.

Government-sponsored monopolies and oligopolies

From a competition policy perspective, the role of the government is to avoid the monopolization of the market. However, it should not be overlooked that the government sometimes does exactly the opposite, namely that it restricts entry of firms into the market so that the incumbent firms enjoy market power. The most extreme form are government-sponsored monopolies.

One justification for such monopolies are efficiency considerations based on fixed or sunk costs, or increasing returns more generally. In particular, since additional entry may lead to socially wasteful duplications of certain investments, additional firm entry may be privately profitable but socially undesirable. In such a case, the government may opt for a regulated monopoly and explicitly prohibit additional firm entry.

In some instances (e.g., due to resource constraints), it may be socially desirable to limit the number of firms to, say, three or four. An example can be found in spectrum auctions for mobile telephony. Here, the resource constraint is the available spectrum. The goal of the auction, then, is to efficiently distribute the spectrum that is made available.

A second and substantially different reason for granting an albeit temporary monopoly right can be found in investment incentives in new technologies. If innovations were not protected and could be immediately appropriated by other firms at zero or negligible costs, firms would not have strong incentives to invest in innovations. This is the rationale behind patent and copyright protection, or, more generally, intellectual property right protection.[c]

A third reason is the goal to create national champions motivated by the belief that national firms lead to higher welfare than foreign ones. Erecting international barriers of entry effectively limits competition (presuming that the government takes measures that favours the national firm). While such policies can be frequently observed in the real world, we do not analyse such policies in this book. We believe that this topic is better addressed in a course on international trade.

[c] See Part VII of the book.

Case 1.1 illustrates how a combination of the previous factors allowed Alcoa to enjoy a monopoly position in the aluminum market for a long period of time.

Case 1.1 Alcoa's natural monopoly[2]

The processes for extracting aluminum on a large scale were invented at the end of the nineteenth century. Because they were patented, a small number of companies were able to dominate the industry right from the start. Among these companies, the most successful was Alcoa (shorthand for 'The Aluminum Company of America'). Since the production of aluminum is capital intensive, it is subject to large economies of scale. This led Alcoa to manufacture intermediate or final aluminum products so as to develop adequate markets for its growing output. The production of aluminum is also intensive in energy (smelting requires a lot of electricity) and in raw materials (bauxite). Alcoa quickly understood the competitive advantage it could gain by controlling the procurement of these two crucial inputs. As for energy, Alcoa became in 1893 the first customer of the new Niagara Falls Power Company, signing up for hydroelectric power in advance of construction. As for the raw material, Alcoa progressively managed to stake out all the best sources of North American bauxite for itself. As a result of these strategies of downstream and upstream vertical integration (we study these strategies in Chapter 17), Alcoa managed to improve its productivity and increase its scale. These efficiency gains made entry more difficult and protected its leadership after initial patents had expired. Other factors explain the virtual monopoly position that Alcoa enjoyed until World War II: public policy, tariff protection, the failure of Alcoa's few potential competitors, and the limited checks of antitrust before World War I (see Appendix B for more on the latter factor).

1.2   Strategies

A large part of modern industrial organization (and most models presented in this book) considers firms as 'strategic players'. What do we mean by this term? This is what we explain in this section.

Analysing basic monopoly and oligopoly problems – decision theory vs. game theory

Game theory is concerned with situations where the players (the decision makers) strategically interact. In contrast, decision theory deals with situations where each decision maker can make his or her own choices in isolation, i.e., without concern for the actions taken by other decision-makers. Abusing terms, one can say that decision theory is a theory of 'one-person games', or of games where a single player plays against nature (thus taking uncertainty into account).

The basic monopoly problem can therefore be addressed by using the tools of decision theory. Indeed, a monopolist is by definition the only firm to be active in the market; moreover, if the environment is such that no entry is possible and if there is a large number of buyers, whose individual decisions have a negligible impact, the monopolist can make its one-shot decisions in complete isolation.

Things change as soon as other firms are present in the market, or could be present (i.e., if there is a threat of entry). Then, what these other firms do, or could do, affects the first firm's profits and it is thus wise for this firm to take this interaction into account in its decision process. That is, if other firms are present on the market, it is important to anticipate their actions; or, if other firms may enter the market, it is possible to take advance actions so as to discourage entry or to limit its negative effects. Similarly, if the firm remains the only seller but faces a single buyer, the bargaining power of this buyer has to be factored into the decision process. The analysis of such situations (i.e., oligopoly problems, monopolies threatened by entry or bilateral monopolies where a single seller faces a single buyer) belongs to the realm of game theory.

Firms as strategic players and the notion of equilibrium

To analyse markets in which firms interact strategically, we need a solution concept that provides predictions as to what will be the market outcome. The basic solution concept we use is the *Nash equilibrium*. Consider a price-setting duopoly. Here, the profit-maximizing price chosen by one firm depends on the price set by the other. We call this firm i's *best-response* b_i to the competitor's price p_j. By definition, in a Nash equilibrium, prices must be mutual best responses, i.e., $p_i^* = b_i(p_j^*)$, $i, j = 1, 2, i \neq j$. Note that this solution is not implied by the individual rationality assumption. Indeed, it is perfectly rational to set a different price as long as firm i believes that firm j sets a price different from p_j^*. The Nash equilibrium has the additional property that each player's belief about the intended play of the other player is confirmed. Thus, no player has an incentive to deviate given the competitor's equilibrium strategy. We can extend this notion to allow players to mix between different prices. In other words they choose a probability distribution of prices. If players can choose mixed strategies, we use the solution concept of *mixed-strategy Nash equilibrium.*

In richer economic environments, firms choose various actions over time, have private information about their type, make initially a choice that cannot be observed by others, or interact repeatedly for the foreseeable future. In all these cases, the set of Nash equilibria is typically too large. To obtain sharper predictions, we impose additional restrictions on the solution concept depending on the problem at hand.

Suppose firms choose actions over time and consider a particular set of strategies that form a Nash equilibrium. Then this equilibrium is said to be *subgame perfect* if it induces a Nash equilibrium in any subgame (even if this subgame is reached only off the equilibrium path). For instance, in a price setting oligopoly, one firm may be the first-mover and all other firms choose at a second stage. Here, the firm that is the first-mover anticipates the reaction of its competitors to its price change. The restriction to subgame perfect Nash equilibrium is the standard concept that is used in such applications, but it may nevertheless be criticized in situations where players are not fully forward looking.

In other economic environments, players may be of different types. For instance, in a price-setting duopoly each firm may be a low- or a high-quality firm. If this information is private information so that firms only know their own type but not the type of their competitor (while consumers later observe the true quality), beliefs about the other firm's type matter. Here we assume that players know the ex ante quality distribution so that their beliefs are correct from an ex ante point of view. The associated equilibrium concept is the one of *Bayesian Nash equilibrium*: in the price setting duopoly each firm maximizes its profits given its probability distribution over quality types of the competitor.

Private information can also be introduced into environments in which players choose sequentially. For instance a monopolist may sell a product whose quality is only known to the firm but not to consumers, who become the second player since their beliefs determine their purchasing decisions. In this case, the informed player moves first and may use its action to signal its type. In situations like these, we apply the *perfect Bayesian Nash equilibrium* concept. Here, uninformed players who choose later can use the observed action of the informed party to update their beliefs about the type of the firm. In the monopoly context, the firm may, for instance, choose a very high price to signal the quality of its product. For the reader who is not familiar with these concepts, we provide formal definitions of these concepts in Appendix A. In addition, the reader may want to consult a textbook in game theory.[3]

1.3   Models and material of *Markets and Strategies*

This book is theory-based. We are perfectly aware that there is also a great demand for a textbook that covers recent advances in empirical industrial organization. However, we decided to focus on theory (without ignoring empirical work) for two reasons: first, we find it important to start with theory at the advanced undergraduate level as guidance for empirical work; second, we find it difficult to provide the empirics at a level which is appropriate for advanced undergraduates. Concerning our second reason, we hope to be proved wrong soon and would be happy to see our theory-based textbook be complemented by a good textbook on the empirics of industrial organization.

It is our goal to present our book as a collection of topics which are then explored with the help of theoretical models. These models are deliberately simple so that we can rely on well-established concepts from game theory, which most of our readers will be familiar with. In particular, we try to avoid more debatable equilibrium refinement concepts. Most of our formal analysis relies on functional form specifications, e.g. we often specify the consumer side such that demand is linear. Such functional form assumptions are a mixed blessing: when highlighting an economic mechanism, we want to understand the general effects and do not want our results to rely on the specifics of the demand (and cost) functions. We try to avoid this criticism by providing a more general intuition for the results, which does not rely on the particular functional form and hope to be careful enough to address the most important robustness issues. Hence, we try to keep the cost of using functional form assumptions low while keeping the technical level of the exposition low. We are, however, aware that some of the models require somewhat more technical sophistication than others. Particularly demanding material is marked as such.

The main insights of our formal analyses are summarized as '*lessons*'. These lessons are less formal than propositions or theorems but, in our view, better allow the reader to take home the main message. Lessons are to be seen in the context of the models that are presented.

To better connect to the real world, we provide a number of '*cases*', which relate the general issue under investigation to a particular industry. Students from business schools should be warned that these do not, by any means, constitute full-blown case studies, but only sketch a few facts or findings from a particular industry, as illustrated by Case 1.1 above.

Our main text contains few footnotes that present additional remarks or observations. References and the occasional technical remarks are put into endnotes. So, if you are looking for detailed references to the scientific literature, do not forget to look at those endnotes; otherwise, we recommend not to interrupt your reading by consulting them. Each chapter (but this one) ends with a set of review questions and gives a very short guide to the most important work on which the exposition is based. Exercises are posted on our website. This allows us to continuously update them. They are, however, an integral part of the book. If you master the material of the book, you should be able to solve most of them.

1.4   Level, scope and organization of the book

Level

This book is aimed at advanced undergraduate students who take a course in Industrial Organization, Price Theory, or something similar. We presume that the reader is familiar with basic notions of calculus. The book can also partly be used for a more specialized course, which, to name a few topics, focuses on competition policy, asymmetric information and industrial organization, or innovation. This book is also aimed at courses at the Ph.D. level in economics and management. Here, it may be useful to complement the book with additional material such as research articles. Also, the book may be useful to practitioners in antitrust and strategy who want to catch up with some recent ideas.

Scope

Very broadly defined, the scope of the book is the analysis of all markets in which firms interact strategically. As illustrated by the numerous real-life situations presented in the book, this analysis spans a very large array of industries belonging to the secondary (manufacture of final goods) and tertiary (services) sectors of the economy, and also to what is sometimes called the 'quaternary sector', which consists of all intellectual activities.

Regarding the contents of the book (which we detail below), we want to stress that we depart from the majority of previous Industrial Organization (IO) textbooks by giving up the dichotomy between monopoly and oligopoly. Most books start with monopoly and then move to oligopoly (and, often, return to monopoly in between). We find it more appropriate to focus on content issues in the organization of the book. For each issue, we decide whether separating monopoly and oligopoly provides additional insights or not. For instance, price discrimination is first analysed in a context in which the behaviour of competitors is taken as given (monopoly) and then endogenized (oligopoly). Yet, most of the book considers strategic interaction and can thus be seen, like a large part of current IO theory, as applied oligopoly theory.

Organization

Markets and Strategies is organized in nine parts, each part being further divided into two to four chapters. Each part starts with a general introduction that gives a bird's-eye view of the part material; it is a verbal exposition, usually related to real-life situations, that informally describes the salient features of the analysis that follows and explains the organization and the links between the various chapters. The introduction ends with a summary of what the reader will learn from that part of the book. Each chapter starts with a short introduction that describes its contents. The chapter ends with several review questions and a quick guide to the relevant literature.

Here is a quick sketch of the book contents (we give a more detailed table of contents below). The book starts with two introductory parts. This part, **Part I**, helps the reader to *get started* by describing what the book is about and by defining a number of key concepts. **Part II** develops the *basic models of oligopolistic competition*. The goal is to understand how the nature of the strategic variable, namely price or quantity, and the timing of moves affect strategic interaction and, thereby, the extent of *market power*. The reader may already be familiar with some of these models through previous microeconomics or industrial organization courses. However, Part II also includes more advanced material including private cost information in oligopoly and dynamic firm entry and exit.

The next two parts describe how market power is acquired and exercised. **Part III** looks at *sources of market power*: product differentiation, advertising, and consumer inertia. **Part IV** examines how firms with market power design advanced *pricing strategies* to capture as much value as possible from their consumers.

The first four parts of the book mainly deal with search goods, i.e., products or services with features and characteristics that can be easily evaluated before purchase. In contrast, **Part V** examines *experience goods*, i.e., products and services with characteristics that can only be ascertained upon consumption because they are difficult to observe in advance. In such markets, consumers have less information than the producers about product quality, and therefore firms have to convince consumers that their products are of high quality. To this end, firms can use a variety of marketing instruments, which are studied in Part V.

The analysis made up until then is mostly positive in nature. **Part VI** turns to a more normative analysis by developing the theory of *competition policy*. It first explores two ways by which the number of firms in the market – and thus competition – may be reduced: either virtually when a number of firms act as if they were a single one, a behaviour known as *collusion*; or actually when *horizontal mergers* occur, which replace existing direct competitors by a new, bigger, entity. Next Part VI focuses on monopolization strategies, i.e. strategies by a single firm that hamper competition. It studies the potential *predatory behavior of incumbent firms* facing the threat of entry by other firms on their market. Finally, it analyses vertical arrangements between firms acting at successive stages of the value chain. In this context, *vertical mergers* are studied.

Parts VII and VIII examine how, in the long run, firms may act to modify a part of their environment that was considered as fixed up to then in the book, namely their technological possibilities. **Part VII** focuses on firms' investments in *research and development (R&D)*, which bring *innovation* to the market. It also explains what sets investments in R&D apart from other investments made by firms or individuals and why institutions such as *intellectual* *property* may be necessary to better align private and social incentives. While Part VII examines the early stages of the innovation process (i.e., the creation or invention of new knowledge), **Part VIII** is more concerned with the later stages, namely the design, adoption and diffusion of technologies. The focus is on so-called *network technologies*, i.e., technologies, such as software or communication devices, that become more valuable as they are more widely adopted. This is so because users of these technologies value compatibility, either with the technologies that other users adopt or between several pieces of complementary technologies that they adopt themselves. It follows that the design, adoption and diffusion of such technologies raise distinct and important issues compared to other types of technologies.

Parts VII and VIII contribute to the understanding of the specificities of what is called the 'information economy', the production and consumption of information. The last part of the book, **Part IX**, sheds additional light on the information economy by considering *market intermediation*. In many markets, intermediaries are necessary to make the transactions among buyers and sellers possible, or they contribute to add substantial value to these transactions. It is thus worth having a closer look at the *market micro-structure*, that is at the way markets are operated, by studying the strategies of intermediaries and what impacts they have.

The book contains two short appendices. **Appendix A** presents the basic tools of *game theory* that are used throughout the book. **Appendix B** gives a short description of *competition policy*, in its historical and legal aspects, thereby complementing Part VI.

Table of contents

2 Firms, consumers and the market

In this chapter, we introduce a number of concepts that will prove useful in the rest of the book. We also clarify the main assumptions underlying the analytical frameworks that we will use throughout the book. We start by describing the two types of actors who interact on markets, namely the firms and the consumers. How do we represent them? How are they assumed to behave? How do we measure their well-being? These are the questions we address in Section 2.1. We turn next to market interaction itself. In this book the form of market interaction we are interested in is imperfect competition. To delineate the scope of imperfect competition, it is useful to understand first two extreme market structures where interaction among firms is limited or nonexistent. Section 2.2 describes these two market structures, namely perfect competition and monopoly. Finally, in Section 2.3, we present ways to define a market and to measure its performance.

2.1 Firms and consumers

In this section, we describe how firms and consumers are usually modelled in the theory of industrial organization and throughout this book. In Subsection 2.1.1, we explain that firms are essentially associated to a program of profit maximization and we examine the component of profits that is specific to the firm, namely its cost function. Total revenues, the other component of profits, depend on the consumers' preferences (which determine demand) and on the type of market interaction; these two elements are respectively examined in Subsection 2.1.3 and in Section 2.2.

This simplified representation of the firm proves very useful when considering strategic interaction between firms, which is the main concern of this book. However, its main shortcoming is that it abstracts away all the relationships among the economic agents composing the firm. To assess the scope of the simplified representation of the firm, we look inside the black box of the firm in Subsection 2.1.2. Acknowledging that the firm may be composed of agents with different information and potentially conflicting objectives, we examine if and how those objectives can be aligned. We also study the determinants of the firm's boundaries: what does the firm decide to make and what does it prefer to buy?

In Subsection 2.1.3, we turn to the description of the consumers. Our focus is on final consumers (although we also consider firms as intermediate consumers in some parts of the book). Final consumers are usually supposed to be rational and price takers. Their decisions are then aggregated into demand functions. We discuss, however, alternative assumptions of consumer behaviour. Finally, in Subsection 2.1.4, we describe the specific assumptions we make in this book to assess economic allocations in imperfectly competitive markets.

2.1.1   **The firm**

We start our description of the firm by defining the various types of costs that enter a firm's profit function. We then discuss the hypothesis that firms maximize profits.

Opportunity costs

A basic lesson from microeconomics is that what a firm reports as costs are often not economic costs. This implies that conclusions about economic costs that are derived from reported cost data are questionable. Business people who use different cost concepts for their strategic decisions are therefore likely to make mistakes in their decision making. This is not to deny other cost concepts their role. In particular, it is often in the interest of a firm to shift costs over time and space to alter tax payments for the benefit of the firm. However, these cost accounting data are not helpful for decisions such as how to price a particular product or when to enter a particular market segment.

There are a number of general observations about the correct concept of economic costs. Economic costs refer to opportunity costs. This means that historic costs or factor costs are not the relevant costs. For instance, when a firm with scarce capacity of some production facility has to decide whether to produce a new product using this scarce capacity, the relevant economic costs have to include the profits that could be made from using the required capacity for its next best alternative use.

Cost functions, economies and diseconomies of scale and scope

In the analysis of markets, we typically take cost functions as the primitives of a firm. However, it is useful at this point to recall that cost functions are derived from a cost minimization problem. The cost function attaches a cost value to each output level, $C(q)$. This represents the minimal cost of the firm given the input prices and the production technology.

We typically assume that a firm's cost function is independent of the decision of other firms in the market. Note, however, that this is not necessarily the case. In particular, if the firms active in a particular market segment also compete for resources in the input market (and there are only a few firms in this input market), the output decision of a firm affects input prices, which not only feeds back into its own cost but also affects the costs of the other firms.

In intermediate microeconomics, the production technology of a firm is analysed. A single-product firm is said to enjoy *economies of scale* on a certain output range if it becomes less and less costly to produce on average one unit of output. In other words, average costs are decreasing. Conversely, a firm enjoys diseconomies of scale on a certain output range if it becomes more and more costly to produce on average one unit of output. In other words, average costs are increasing. Scale economies are important in the formation of an industry: in particular, the presence of scale economies favours a concentrated industry (as described in Case 1.1 above). However, in a short-term analysis any fixed costs are irrelevant and only marginal costs are relevant for firm decision making. Marginal costs may be constant, increasing, decreasing or U-shaped. The simplest formulation is to assume constant marginal costs of production. We will make this assumption in most of the models that we present in this book. This assumption, together with the presence of fixed costs implies that firms are subject to economies of scale.

A multiproduct firm may be able to lower its average costs of a particular product if it increases its product range (or if it increases the quantity of other products it already sells). In this case, we say that the firm enjoys *economies of scope*. In the opposite case, the firm has diseconomies of scope. Diseconomies of scale and scope can be motivated by technological and managerial constraints. In particular, large-scale multi-product production requires oversight, which in itself is costly and may in addition lead to behaviour that is not profit-maximizing from the firm's point of view.

Fixed and sunk costs

A firm may not only incur costs that can be attributed to each unit of output but, in addition, may have operation-independent costs. Once in business, a firm often incurs a fixed per period cost, which is independent of current output levels and only depends on earlier decisions such as capacity, geographic coverage, and output range. These *fixed costs* affect the profit level of the firm but do not affect, e.g., pricing decisions because the latter are guided by changes at the margin. Observed pricing schemes that apply a fixed markup over total average costs (and thus include fixed costs) are not profit-maximizing and will therefore not be considered in this book.

Besides fixed costs, firms from time to time incur initial costs, e.g., when they decide to enter a new geographic market or when they expand their product line. These costs are incurred once and, often, cannot be fully recovered when reversing the decision. The part of the costs that cannot be recovered are the *sunk costs* of the firm. Sunk costs are often exogenous from a firm's point of view. For instance, a retailer has to refurbish a retail outlet. Sometimes, these costs are determined by the government. For instance, a certain business may require a license that has to be purchased from the government and cannot be traded. In other cases, sunk costs are determined by the decisions of firms already active in the market. For instance, incumbent firms may have acquired a lot of reputation through advertising and other marketing measures. In this case, a firm may have to run an advertising campaign itself to convince consumers to switch to the product. Sunk costs are important to explain the formation of imperfectly competitive markets. However, we can abstract them away in the short-run analysis where the number of firms is taken as given. Only an analysis with an endogenous number of firms can make the effects of the level of sunk costs on competition explicit (as we will see in Chapter 4).

The profit-maximization hypothesis

A single-product firm is assumed to make profits $\pi(q)$ which depend on the quantity sold q. Consider for the sake of simplicity a firm with a single given product. Then, its profit are revenues $qP(q)$, where $P(\cdot)$ refers to the inverse demand of the firm, decreased by the costs $C(q)$ that the firm incurs. These costs C are the economic costs that the firm incurs. Hence, a firm's profit depending on its own quantity is $\pi(q) = qP(q) - C(q)$. This formulation ignores any other variable that may affect profits. In this book, we analyse a number of them, e.g. advertising, R&D efforts, and other efforts that affect inverse demand or costs. In addition, in a market context, we must be aware that the choices of competitors affect profits.

Firms are assumed to be profit maximizers. This is not to say that profit-maximizing behaviour is always the best approximation to observed market behaviour, but it provides arguably the natural benchmark for the analysis of firm behaviour. Since we are mostly concerned with firms with market power (and thus large firms), we are confident that profit-maximization is often a good behavioural assumption. In particular, if we are interested in competition policy, profit-maximizing behavior is the undisputed reference point that is used by antitrust authorities.[a]

Profit maximization can be seen as the natural objective of the owners of a firm. However, owners may have an objective function that not only contains profits but other objectives (or additional constraints). An example would be the owner of a media company who is not only interested in financial success but also has a particular world (or policy) view that he or she likes to promote. Another example is that the owner is also interested in market share or total revenue for personal reasons (by the way, this may be the implied objective function of a profit-maximizing firm that takes dynamic effects into account). One more example is that the owner has non-economic objectives such as to provide employment in his or her local community or takes particular interest in the well-being of some or all of his or her customers. While there certainly exist some good real-world examples that document deviation from the profit-maximization objective of owners, we still see profit maximization as the natural starting point of any analysis of industry and therefore maintain the profit-maximization hypothesis throughout the book.

Taking into account that most large companies are not owner-managed, we must address an additional important question: Is profit maximization a reasonable objective function of firms even if owners have this objective? We now turn to this question. Here our answer will be less confident.

2.1.2   Looking inside the black box of a firm

In this book, we mostly consider firms as single decision making units that maximize profits; this also holds for the industrial organization literature at large. While this is a helpful abstraction, it may be inappropriate. One reason is that in firms which are not owner-run, top management may have different objectives than the owners of a firm. Top management may have non-monetary incentives such as empire building. A good example is merger decisions, which may partly be explained by monetary and non-monetary incentives of top management to increase the scope of the firm, but which may not be in the interest of owners. Another reason is that many decisions are not taken by the top management but by middle management. Here, the incentives of the middle manager may be different from those of top management. The middle manager may not act in the interest of the whole firm but delegation may still be desirable for a number of reasons, in particular, because of asymmetric information problems within the firm and limited managerial span at the top management. Another reason for the effect of firm organization on firm decisions is dispersed information within a company together with strategic communication.[4]

We do not attempt to provide an overview of the theory of the firm, nor to provide an account of what determines the boundaries of the firm. We only take a quick look at the

---

[a] In a monopoly setting, the profit-maximization hypothesis can be more easily defended if the objective of a theory is to provide guidance to businesses.

relationship between the owner and the manager of a firm, ignoring the firm's interaction with other firms in the product market.[5] This allows us to obtain some insights as to whether firms are profit maximizers. Through performance-based pay, the owner can attempt to better align his and the manager's incentives. In a simple monopoly model, we uncover when interests of managers and owner can be aligned and when not.

A model of manager compensation and the manager–owner relationship

We consider a moral-hazard environment, in which shareholders do not observe the action by top management and have to design a wage contract or compensation scheme that can only be based on the observed profits.[6] The problem is that observed profits not only depend on the unobservable action by top management, but also on some unobservable random component. The owner (e.g., the community of shareholders) is assumed to be risk-neutral and thus maximizes the expected gross profit of the firm, π, minus the payment w to the manager. The owner observes gross profit π. Thus, he can make a wage contract or compensation scheme offered to the manager dependent upon π. Gross profit depends on some unobservable random event ε and the manager's effort $e \in [\underline{e}, \overline{e}]$. For a given random event ε, higher effort e results in higher profits π. We can write profits as $\pi(e, \varepsilon)$.

We analyse the following *principal–agent relationship*. The owner wants to induce the manager to choose the efficient effort level. However, he can only condition the pay on the contractible profit level π – here we ignore the possibility that the manager manipulates profits π. The owner's objective is to maximize his expected net profit

$$E_\varepsilon[\pi(e, \varepsilon) - w(\pi(e, \varepsilon))].$$

The manager's utility function is

$$u(\underset{+}{w}, \underset{-}{e}).$$

That is, a manager receives a higher utility if she receives a higher pay w. She also receives a higher utility if she exerts less effort. In addition, we assume that u is (weakly) concave in w – this amounts to income risk aversion; in the special case that u is linear in w the manager is risk-neutral with respect to income. The manager maximizes her expected utility

$$E_\varepsilon u(w(\pi(e, \varepsilon)), e).$$

The owner offers a wage contract $w(\cdot)$. Ex ante, there is a competitive supply of identical managers who have a reservation utility u_0. Therefore, choosing their best effort level given the proposed contract w must give the hired manager in expected terms at least her reservation utility – this is the *individual rationality* or *participation constraint* of the manager,

$$\max_e Eu(w(\pi(e, \varepsilon)), e) \geq u_0.$$

If the owner wants to induce a certain level of effort e^* from the manager, he must offer a contract that is '*incentive compatible*' so that the manager has an incentive to provide this effort level:

$$e^* = \arg\max_e Eu(w(\pi(e, \varepsilon)), e).$$

As a benchmark, we first consider the situation with full information; this means that the owner can perfectly infer the chosen effort level e (either by observing e directly or by observing ε). In this case, the owner can effectively choose his desired effort level e by imposing a large penalty in the wage contract for deviation from that level. This implies that *only* the participation constraint is relevant. For a given effort level e, denote random profits by $\tilde{\pi} \equiv \pi(e, \varepsilon)$. The owner's problem is then to maximize expected net payoff with respect to the wage offered, subject to the participation constraint of the manager:

$$\max_{w(\tilde{\pi})} E_{\tilde{\pi}}[\tilde{\pi} - w(\tilde{\pi})] \quad \text{s.t.} \ E_{\tilde{\pi}} u(w(\tilde{\pi}), e) \geq u_0.$$

This becomes a Lagrange problem as the constraint is binding: the owner will make the manager just indifferent between accepting the contract and quitting because all the bargaining power rests with the owner. Taking the first derivative of this Lagrange problem gives that $\partial_w u(w(\tilde{\pi}), e)$ is equal to a constant. Since the owner is risk-neutral but the manager is risk-averse, it is optimal for the owner to offer a wage for the manager that is independent of $\tilde{\pi}$. Therefore, *under full information the manager is fully insured.*

We compare this full insurance result to the case where the owner only observes π. Here, the owner has less control than under full information and he can obtain, at most, full information net profits $\pi - w(\pi)$. A full analysis of this model is quite complex. We restrict our analysis to two polar cases, an income risk-neutral manager and an infinitely income risk-averse manager.

Consider first an income risk-neutral manager. Recall that this is implied by a utility function that is linear in income. Let us assume that this utility function is additively separable in effort and income. The manager likes income and dislikes effort, which can be provided at a cost $z(e)$ to her. Thus we can write the utility function as $u(w, e) = w - z(e)$. In this case, we consider the solution under full information. Replacing income in the utility function, we can write the owner's objective function as

$$E(\pi - w) = E\pi - Eu(w, e) - z(e)$$
$$= E_\varepsilon \pi(e, \varepsilon) - z(e) - u_0,$$

where, in the second line, we use the fact that the manager's incentive constraint has to be satisfied and is binding in the solution to the owner's problem. Hence, under full information, the owner chooses

$$e^* = \arg\max_e E_\varepsilon \pi(e, \varepsilon) - z(e) - u_0.$$

Recall that under asymmetric information, the owner can only let the compensation scheme depend on observed profit π. Take the following wage contract:

$$w(\pi) = \pi - E_\varepsilon \pi(e^*, \varepsilon) + z(e^*) + u_0.$$

Clearly, if the manager chooses e^*, this compensation scheme satisfies the manager's participation constraint. According to this scheme, there is a fixed negative compensation $-E_\varepsilon \pi(e^*, \varepsilon) + z(e^*) + u_0$ and a variable compensation equal to profit π. Hence, the manager bears all the risk. Note that this is equivalent to a management buy-out in which the manager pays a price $p = E_\varepsilon \pi(e^*, \varepsilon) - z(e^*) - u_0$ for the firm.

The manager's objective function is

$$E_\varepsilon u(w(\pi(e, \varepsilon), e) = E_\varepsilon w(\pi) - z(e)$$

$$= E_\varepsilon \pi(e, \varepsilon) - z(e) + \underbrace{[-E_\varepsilon \pi(e^*, \varepsilon) + z(e^*) + u_0]}_{\text{does not depend on } e}.$$

Since the last term does not depend on effort e, and thus is a constant in the maximization problem, the solution to the manager's problem coincides with the solution to the owner's problem under full information. Hence, the manager's and the shareholders' incentives are perfectly aligned. We see thus that in the extreme case of a risk-neutral manager, the principal–agent problem can be solved and the profit-maximization hypothesis is fully justified.

Consider now the other polar case, an infinitely income risk-averse manager. In this case, the manager is mainly interested in a minimum guaranteed wage. Therefore, if $\min \widetilde{w}_1 > \min \widetilde{w}_2$, then she has the preference $(\widetilde{w}_1, e_1) \succ (\widetilde{w}_2, e_2)$. Suppose that the support of the distribution of profits is independent of the effort of the manager, but that the probability distribution does depend on effort. This means that even when exerting a lot of effort, the manager cannot exclude the possibility of failure or a bad outcome for the firm. Hence, independent of effort, a bad outcome may result, which would lead to the minimum wage. Therefore, the manager exerts minimal effort. The owner is unable to provide incentives to the manager that induce a higher effort level. He offers a constant wage (full insurance) such that the participation constraint of the manager is binding. Hence, with infinitely income risk-averse managers, the owner offers full insurance and cannot provide incentives to the manager to exert more than minimum effort. This implies that in such a world, a manager is likely to make erroneous decisions so that the firm may not implement the profit maximizing outcome.

For an intermediate degree of risk aversion, the owner will offer partial insurance, which consists of a fixed component and a performance-related payment.

Lesson 2.1   **In a principal–agent relationship between owner and manager with hidden effort, the manager bears the full risk if and only if he or she is risk neutral. Otherwise part of the risk is borne by the owner and the manager's incentives are not perfectly aligned with the owner's incentives.**

Note that there are other arguments according to which a manager may follow profit maximization in spite of the lack of explicit monetary incentives. We examine three arguments in turn: (i) manager reputation and future earnings, (ii) checks by the market, (iii) peer pressure.

First, managers do not have their position for life but rather depend on their market value in the market for managers. Clearly, since hiring decisions at the top level are made by shareholders, there is a premium on successful managers. This provides incentives for managers to maximize profit because of career concerns[b] and may lead to a management culture which is obsessed about effort. Managers who do not fit within this culture and provide less effort are then replaced by a new effort-obsessed manager. Then low profits are a signal

---

[b] This argument may be questioned in a stochastic environment because managers may be primarily concerned about their up-side potential and might therefore take too much risk.

about a low effort and from this, a manager's reputation might suffer. A loss in reputation is likely to reduce future earning possibilities of the manager.

Second, managers in traded companies should bear in mind that if their firm under-performs, they may become a take-over target because the firm has a higher potential value. The take-over is typically followed by a change of top management to carry out the changes that are deemed to increase the value of the firm.

Finally, there are also non-monetary objectives. For instance, a manager may be judged by his peers regarding his past performance. However, this does not give an unambiguous indi-cation that the manager will exert higher effort (and implement the correct decisions) because peer-groups may be biased in terms of other indicators such as market share and revenues.

The boundaries of the firm

Even if we take the firm as a single decision making unit, we have to address at which scale and scope the firm operates. In its activities, the firm should be guided by comparing the economic cost of internal provision of an activity and the economic cost of external provision. These costs should include the transaction costs a firm incurs. Such a comparison is straightforward if it is easy to allocate opportunity costs to the internal provision and if there exists a market with an established market price (or if the input can be procured through an auction). However, the external provision may result from bilateral trade (and bargaining between the firm and its supplier). Here, additional concerns have to be addressed. For instance, if the contract is incomplete and the potential partner is not trustworthy, the firm has to take the possibility of delays and quality problems by the external provider into account, which tends to make internal provision more attractive even if its production costs lie above those of the potential external provider.[7]

Clearly, in the real world, it is almost impossible to find single-product firms. Firms provide a range of products and vertically integrate activities. An obvious explanation for this integration is the shape of the production cost function, which makes the production of a whole product range or the integration of various production stages attractive – in other words, there are economies of scope. These economies of scope may also be present at the distribution stage so that technologically unrelated products are profitably produced and offered together (assuming that contractual arrangements are inferior).

A different reason for offering multiple products is the use of price and non-price strategies: if the firm is able to use sophisticated selling techniques, it may want to offer a whole product range even in the absence of any economies of scope. For instance, product bundling may be a profitable strategy for a firm, which requires it to have the appropriate portfolio of products; this is explored in Chapter 11. With respect to the vertical boundaries of the firm, vertical integration is also a way to avoid double marginalization. In addition, in vertical supply chains, integration is a means to avoid hold-up problems and post-contractual opportunism; we return to these issues in Chapter 17.

Related to economies of scope is the use of an essential facility. For instance, the wide applicability of a patent (and the difficulty to extract rents through a licensing agreement) may lead a firm to develop additional products. Perhaps more importantly, an intangible asset in the form of goodwill or reputation (in particular, among consumers) may make product line expansions profitable. Particular business practices such as umbrella branding can be explained by this; see Chapter 13.

The above arguments give reasons for horizontal and vertical integration. However, there are limits to the scope of the firm. These limits are due to the limited managerial span and the associated costs of an organization that are accelerating in the organization's size.

While throughout this book we sometimes recognize the multi-product nature of the firms and in one instance provide an explicit analysis of product line extension, we mostly simplify our analysis by postulating that firms produce a single product in the market under consideration.

2.1.3 Consumers and rational man

On the buyer side, we mostly phrase our analysis in terms of final consumers. However, in many of the applications, buyers can as well be firms that are active in downstream activities such as retailers.

Consumers as decision makers

We typically assume that consumers are rational in the sense that they choose what they like best. We do not deal with situations in which consumers systematically choose what is not in their best interest, given the information that is available at the point of time they have to take their decision.

While this assumption is widely made in economic models, it can easily be questioned. Certainly, consumers make errors from time to time. They may want to get a particular product, take the wrong one from the shelf by mistake or make the wrong click when ordering from an online retailer. Although consumers intend to choose what they like best, they may make non-systematic errors in their decision making. Economists can deal with this kind of error. Such errors (which are idiosyncratic across the population) lead to ex post heterogeneity between consumers. An example is the logit model that is analysed in Chapter 5.

More problematic are systematic errors. Psychologists, sociologists, marketing experts and economists also report systematic biases that cannot be reconciled with our utility maximizing hypothesis. While we are very well aware of the limitations of the utility-maximizing hypothesis, we do invoke it throughout this book. Having said this, we would like to point out that recent work by experimental economists shows that for instance other-regarding preferences are less pronounced in anonymous markets than say in bilateral (non-market) interactions. Since the vast majority of situations analysed in this book falls within the first category, we are confident that many of the analyses remain relevant (at least as a benchmark), even when modelling consumers in a more complex and realistic way. Recent advances that embed consumers with behavioural biases into market environments appear to be promising but not yet mature enough to be included in this book.[8]

Consumers and forward-looking behavior

In a dynamic context, consumer have to hold beliefs about the future course of action. For instance, if they consider buying clothes early in the season, they have to foresee how future offers and prices will look like. Again, we typically postulate that consumers are rational in the sense that they form expectations, given the information available to them at this point in time.[c] More demanding, we often use a notion of equilibrium according to which consumers find their beliefs confirmed. This can be defended as a consistency requirement according to which consumers do not systematically err when forming their beliefs.

Consumers and extrinsic uncertainty

Consumers often operate in an uncertain environment. They may be uncertain about the quality of a product or may not know particular product features. In such instances, consumers are typically assumed to be expected utility maximizers. We are well aware that there are well-documented deviations from expected utility maximization in the experimental literature. Nevertheless, we must hope that our model predictions are robust to those kind of deviations. Furthermore, we assume that consumers view this uncertainty in the same way, meaning that they have the same prior beliefs.

Consumers and intrinsic uncertainty – consumers as players

In some situations, not only firms are strategic players but also consumers (although they are still assumed to be small). If other consumers directly or indirectly affect a consumer's utility, this consumer has to form expectations about the behavior of other consumers. A good example are situations of technology adoption, as described in Chapter 20. Suppose, for the sake of the argument, that consumers cannot make their adoption decisions sequentially but that they have to make them simultaneously, and consider technologies, such as mobile telephones or word processing software, that are more useful if many people have adopted them. Then, the utility-maximizing decision of a consumer may depend on the adoption decision of the other consumers.

Utility and demand

Returning to the simple decision problem of a consumer under certainty, individual demand is derived as a solution to the utility maximization problem subject to a budget constraint. Suppose there are n products in the market. Then a consumer who chooses quantities $q = (q_1, \ldots, q_n)$ and a quantity q_0 of the Hicksian composite commodity[d] derives utility $u(q_0, q)$. Normalizing the price of the Hicksian composite commodity to 1, the utility maximization problem can then be written as $\max_{q_0,q} u(q_0, q)$ subject to the budget constraint $p \cdot q + q_0 \leq y$ where p is the price vector and y is income. If consumers have quasilinear preferences in the composite commodity, the maximization problem becomes $\max_{q_0,q} u(q) + q_0$ subject to $p \cdot q + q_0 \leq y$.

---

[c] Here, alternative formulations of consumer behaviour are a promising research area. New interesting insights are likely to arise, in particular in dynamic settings where consumers form habits and show time-inconsistent behaviour.

[d] The Hicksian composite commodity contains all other goods outside the market under consideration. Since we are interested in real prices, we can normalize the price of one unit of this basket to 1.

Under the assumption that preferences are locally nonsatiated (i.e., more is better) the budget constraint is binding and we must have $q_0 = y - p \cdot q$. Thus we can equivalently consider the utility maximization $\max_q u(q) + y - p \cdot q$. The solution to the system of first-order conditions $\partial u / \partial q_i = p_i$ gives the individual demand function.

In many models, we use particular specifications of individual demand. In particular, we often model consumers as having unit demand. This means that consumers buy one unit (or possibly zero units) of a product, possibly within a whole range of products. An example would be individual demand for cars, which, at any point in time, can be approximated to be of this type (the number of people who buy more than one unit is negligible).

The unit demand property implies that consumers face a discrete choice problem. If v_i denotes the (indirect) utility for one unit of product i, the choice problem of a consumer is simply $\max\{v_0, v_1, \ldots, v_n\}$, where v_0 denotes the value of not consuming in the market, which is often normalized to zero.

Alternatively, we often analyse models in which consumers have linear demand. Linear demand is generated by a linear–quadratic utility function, as we now show in the case of two goods, 1 and 2. A consumer's utility function is assumed to take the form

$$u(q_0, q_1, q_2) = aq_1 + aq_2 - \tfrac{1}{2}(bq_1^2 + 2dq_1q_2 + bq_2^2) + q_0,$$

where q_0 is the Hicksian composite commodity with a price normalized to 1. We assume that $b > |d|$, which implies that products are differentiated. Consumers maximize their utility $u(q_0, q_1, q_2)$ subject to the budget constraint $y = q_0 + p_1q_1 + p_2q_2$. From the first-order conditions, we find the individual inverse demand functions:

$$\begin{cases} p_1(q_1, q_2) = a - bq_1 - dq_2, \\ p_2(q_1, q_2) = a - bq_2 - dq_1. \end{cases}$$

Inverting the latter system and letting $\tilde{a} = a/(b+d)$, $\tilde{b} = b/(b^2 - d^2)$, and $\tilde{d} = d/(b^2 - d^2)$, we find that individual demand functions take the following form:

$$\begin{cases} q_1(p_1, p_2) = \tilde{a} - \tilde{b}p_1 + \tilde{d}p_2, \\ q_2(p_1, p_2) = \tilde{a} + \tilde{d}p_1 - \tilde{b}p_2, \end{cases}$$

for strictly positive quantities and zero otherwise. A few other specifications will appear later in this book.

To obtain aggregate demand, two alternative modelling choices are widely used. We may want to assume that any single consumer is representative of all other consumers so that aggregate demand is simply rescaled individual demand. One such example is the linear demand model from above which then also applies in the aggregate. Alternatively, we may want to model the feature that consumers have different tastes and thus disagree about the merits of a particular good. To obtain a downward sloping aggregate or market demand curve, consumers may all face a discrete choice problem such as the one depicted above and still aggregate demand will be nicely downward sloping. Suppose for instance that consumers face the option to buy either one unit of product 1 or one unit of product 2 (the outside option is assumed to be sufficiently unattractive). Suppose furthermore that the difference of gross willingness-to-pay for the product is uniformly distributed. Then, aggregate demand is linear in prices. The Hotelling model that is presented in the following chapter and widely applied to other issues in this book is such a specification. Note that for some aggregate demand representations, there is an underlying representative consumer model as well as a discrete choice problem. While this may give the impression that it is difficult to choose the appropriate demand model for a particular industry based on aggregate demand, we typically know a lot more about consumer behaviour, which allows us to make the choice between the different approaches.

2.1.4   Welfare analysis of market outcomes

Our approach, like the approach of industrial organization in general, is to focus on one market at a time. Strategic decisions by firms as well as policy decisions affect market outcomes such as price levels and output in this market. This potentially affects other markets, which in turn may generate feedback effects. We define the relevant market for our purposes and assume that such cross-market effects do not exist. Thus our models are *partial equilibrium* models, which treat costs, prices of products in other markets and income as given. By contrast, general equilibrium analysis would treat these variables as endogenous.

The partial equilibrium approach appears to be a useful approximation of a market that is not closely linked to other markets (so that substitutability or complementarity is weak, and vertical links are not present).[e] In addition, the market should be small compared to the overall economy so that income effects are small. If we use the particular specifications of the consumers' utility functions that utility functions are quasilinear or have a Cobb–Douglas-presentation, the partial equilibrium approach is justified.[9]

When it comes to adopt a more normative approach and to assess the efficiency of market outcomes, we need to define how well off firms and consumers are in any market outcome. As for firms, we simply use the sum of the firms' profits as a measure of their welfare. Measuring consumer welfare is more challenging. Throughout the book, we assume that changes in consumer welfare can be measured by the *consumer surplus*. The consumer surplus measures the net benefit a consumer enjoys from being able to purchase a good or service. It is computed as the difference between what the consumer is willing to pay and what the consumer actually pays for each unit consumed. As the willingness to pay is indicated by the demand curve and the payment actually required is the price, the consumer surplus corresponds to the surface of the area under the demand curve and above the market price. We illustrate this notion in Figure 2.1, for a linear demand function. At price $\bar{p}$, the consumer buys a quantity $\bar{q}$ and her consumer surplus corresponds to the triangle below the demand curve and above $\bar{p}$. Letting the inverse demand be given by $p = a - bq$, we easily compute the surface of this triangle as

$$CS(\bar{q}) = \tfrac{1}{2}b\bar{q}^2. \tag{2.1}$$

What Figure 2.1 does not include is the income effect resulting from a decrease in the price of the good. Indeed, as the price of the good falls while the consumer's income remains constant, the real income of the consumer increases, which may affect the consumption of the good. Implicit in the figure is the assumption that the income elasticity of demand for the good is zero. As indicated above, this assumption is reasonable when the market for the good is small compared to the overall economy. Then, income effects can largely be ignored and the consumer surplus becomes a good approximation of the welfare of an individual.

---

[e] Note that in other areas of economics (in particular, international economics and economic geography), specific general equilibrium models are used, in which some but not all of the feedback mechanisms are present.

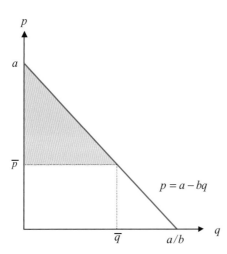

Figure 2.1 Consumer surplus

Two further difficulties arise when extending the single-consumer/single-good case to more than one good and to multiple consumers. For the extension to several goods, let us just mention that the absence of income effect in the demand functions allows us to generalize the single-good concept. As an illustration, take the utility function that we introduced in the previous subsection. We reproduce it here for convenience, together with the corresponding inverse and direct demand functions:

$$U(q_0, q_1, q_2) = q_0 + aq_1 + aq_2 - \tfrac{1}{2}(bq_1^2 + 2dq_1q_2 + bq_2^2),$$

$$\begin{cases} p_1(q_1, q_2) = a - bq_1 - dq_2, \\ p_2(q_1, q_2) = a - bq_2 - dq_1, \end{cases} \begin{cases} q_1(p_1, p_2) = \tilde{a} - \tilde{b}p_1 + \tilde{d}p_2, \\ q_2(p_1, p_2) = \tilde{a} + \tilde{d}p_1 - \tilde{b}p_2, \end{cases}$$

with $\tilde{a} = a/(b+d), \tilde{b} = b/(b^2 - d^2), \tilde{d} = d/(b^2 - d^2)$, and $b > d$. Note that the cross-partial derivatives of the demand functions are equal $(\partial q_1/\partial p_2 = \partial q_2/\partial p_1 = \tilde{d})$. Substituting the inverse demand functions for p_1 and p_2, one obtains as consumer surplus:

$$CS(q_0, q_1, q_2) = U(q_0, q_1, q_2) - (q_0 + p_1q_1 + p_2q_2)$$
$$= \tfrac{1}{2}\left(bq_1^2 + 2dq_1q_2 + bq_2^2\right). \tag{2.2}$$

In the limit case where $b = d$, the consumer takes goods 1 and 2 as perfect substitutes, meaning that q_1 and q_2 are quantities of the same homogeneous good. Then, letting $\bar{q} = q_1 + q_2$ measure the total quantity consumed, we observe that expression (2.2) boils down to expression (2.1). This illustrates how we can work with consumer surplus in the case of more than one product.

The extension to multiple consumers creates the difficulty that an aggregate measure of the welfare of all consumers is likely to be affected by redistributions of income between consumers. In this book, we take the income redistribution as given. We thus take the consumer surplus as a measure of aggregate consumer welfare. Furthermore, we take as our measure of *total welfare* the sum of the consumer surplus and of the firms' profits (which is also known as the producer surplus). This means that consumers and firms have the same weight in the measure of total welfare.

2.2   Market interaction

Our aim in this section is to understand how firms behave when they have market power. Our starting point in Subsection 2.2.1 is the benchmark of perfect competition where firms are price takers and have thus no market power. We move then to situations where a firm treats the market environment as given when taking its decision. This conduct is certainly reasonable for a firm that serves the whole market by itself; this is the monopoly case that we analyse in Subsection 2.2.2. This conduct is also reasonable for a dominant firm that shares the market with a set of small price-taking firms; this is the 'competitive fringe' situation that we examine in Subsection 2.2.3. Finally, we introduce the notion of imperfect competition in Subsection 2.2.4.

2.2.1   The perfectly competitive paradigm

In a perfectly competitive market, firms are price takers, in the sense that they take the market price as given. That is, each firm believes that its own individual decisions have no effect on the price of its product. The market price results from the combined actions of all firms and all consumers (summarized respectively by the market supply and demand curves). This representation only makes sense if there is a large number of firms on the market, the supply of each one being small relative to market demand for the product.

As a firm takes the market price as given, it perceives that it can sell any quantity at that price. Therefore, a perfectly competitive firm faces a horizontal demand curve and the marginal revenue generated by each additional unit of output produced and sold is just equal to the current market price. Like any firm, the perfectly competitive firm chooses output so as to maximize its profit. Profit is maximized for the output level that equates marginal cost and marginal revenue. Here, as marginal revenue is equal to the market price, we have that for each firm, profit maximization results in the equality between the price received for a unit of output and the marginal cost of producing that output.

Lesson 2.2   A perfectly competitive firm produces at marginal cost equal to the market price.

Formally, suppose that each firm faces an increasing cost function $C(q)$; marginal costs are written $C'(q)$. Letting p denote the market price, each firm maximizes its profit by producing the largest output q_c such that $C'(q_c) = p$. If the market price increases from p to $\widehat{p} > p$, then the profit-maximizing firm will increase its production to $\widehat{q}_c > q_c$ such that $C'(\widehat{q}_c) = \widehat{p}$. Hence, the increasing portion of the firm's marginal cost curve corresponds to its supply curve as it determines the level of output that the firm is willing to supply at any price.

2.2.2   Strategies in a constant environment ('monopoly')

We analyse here industries dominated by a single major player. We analyse how this 'monopolist' chooses prices when he produces either one or several products.

The monopoly pricing formula

Suppose, as a first approximation, that a firm can treat the market environment as given when taking its decision. This market environment is then described by a downward sloping inverse demand function $P(q)$ that depends negatively on the quantity the firm offers on the market. Suppose that the firm faces an increasing cost function $C(q)$. Marginal costs $C'(q)$ may be constant or upward sloping. Thus the monopoly problem is

$$\max_{q} \pi(q) = q P(q) - C(q).$$

The first-order condition of profit maximization is $q P'(q) + P(q) - C'(q) = 0$. The problem has a unique solution if the profit function is quasi-concave, which is implied by concavity of revenues and convexity of costs. Revenues are concave if $q P''(q) + 2P'(q) < 0$. Since $P' < 0$, a sufficient (but not necessary) condition is the concavity of the inverse demand function.

To better understand how the profit-maximizing quantity depends on demand and supply characteristics, it is useful to rewrite the first-order condition of profit maximization. It is equivalent to $P(q) - C'(q) = -q P'(q)$. Note that $-q P'(q)/P(q)$ is the inverse price elasticity of demand $1/\eta$ (expressed as an absolute value). Hence, by dividing both sides of the equation by $P(q)$, we can further rewrite the first-order condition as

$$\underbrace{\frac{P(q) - C'(q)}{P(q)}}_{\substack{\text{markup or} \\ \text{\textit{Lerner index}}}} = \underbrace{\frac{1}{\eta}}_{\substack{\text{inverse elasticity} \\ \text{of demand}}}. \tag{2.3}$$

This is the well-known *monopoly pricing formula*, also known as the *inverse elasticity rule*. On the left-hand side is the markup, which is the price–cost difference as a percentage of the price (also known as the Lerner index); on the right-hand side is the inverse elasticity of demand. According to the monopoly pricing formula, *the markup is higher the less elastic is demand*.

Lesson 2.3   **A profit-maximizing monopolist increases its markup as demand becomes less price elastic.**

In particular, as demand becomes infinitely inelastic the markup turns to infinity. Consider the polar opposite case that demand becomes infinitely elastic, i.e. $\eta \to \infty$. Then the price tends to marginal costs, which implies that the markup (and profit) tends to zero. As we have seen above, the latter situation holds under perfect competition. It demonstrates that firms only have market power if the demand they perceive is not infinitely elastic. Finally, we observe that instead of choosing quantity the monopolist may choose price so as to maximize $\pi(p) = pQ(p) - C(Q(p))$ with respect to p. In the monopoly model, setting price or setting quantity leads to the same results.

Monopoly pricing: several goods

We now extend the previous analysis to a multiproduct firm. For our purposes, it is sufficient to consider the two-product case. If neither demand nor costs are linked across markets, we can look at two maximization problems separately. This would lead to the same results as above, with the additional conclusion that the highest markup will be achieved for the product that has the smallest elasticity of demand. Yet, in general, demands and/or costs are linked. Let us thus write the demand functions as $q_1 = Q_1(p_1, p_2)$ and $q_2 = Q_2(p_1, p_2)$, and the cost function as $C(q_1, q_2)$. The maximization program then is

$$\max_{p_1, p_2} \pi = p_1 Q_1(p_1, p_2) + p_2 Q_2(p_1, p_2) - C(Q_1(p_1, p_2), Q_2(p_1, p_2)).$$

The first-order condition for product i generalizes the equality between marginal revenue (on the left-hand side) and marginal cost (on the right-hand side):

$$Q_i + p_i \frac{\partial Q_i}{\partial p_i} + p_j \frac{\partial Q_j}{\partial p_i} = \frac{\partial C}{\partial q_i} \frac{\partial Q_i}{\partial p_i} + \frac{\partial C}{\partial q_j} \frac{\partial Q_j}{\partial p_i}. \tag{2.4}$$

The multiproduct monopolist will depart from the single-product monopoly-pricing formula (2.3) because he will take into account the relationships between the demands and/or the costs of the two products. To see how, we consider two polar cases: first, we suppose that demands are linked but that costs are not; then, we suppose the reverse. In each case, we compare the monopolist's choice with what two independent firms (each responsible for one product) would decide.

Linked demands, unlinked costs. We assume here that costs can be 'separated' between the two activities: $C(q_1, q_2) = C_1(q_1) + C_2(q_2)$. Denote $C_i' = \partial C/\partial q_i$. Expression (2.4) can then be rewritten as

$$\left(p_i - C_i'\right) \frac{\partial Q_i}{\partial p_i} = -Q_i - \left(p_j - C_j'\right) \frac{\partial Q_j}{\partial p_i}.$$

Dividing both sides by $p_i(\partial Q_i/\partial p_i)$ and letting $\eta_i = -(p_i/Q_i)(\partial Q_i/\partial p_i)$ denote the own elasticity of product i's demand, one obtains

$$L_i \equiv \frac{p_i - C_i'}{p_i} = \frac{1}{\eta_i} + \frac{p_j - C_j'}{p_i} \frac{\partial Q_j/\partial p_i}{-\partial Q_i/\partial p_i}.$$

Compared to (2.3), the latter expression has an additional term on the right-hand side. This term has the sign of $\partial Q_j/\partial p_i$ (as p_j is set above C_j' and as $\partial Q_i/\partial p_i < 0$). There are two cases to distinguish. First, if products i and j are *substitutes* (i.e., $\partial Q_j/\partial p_i > 0$), then the additional term is positive, meaning that the Lerner index L_i is larger than the inverse elasticity of demand. This implies that the multiproduct monopolist sets higher prices than separate divisions. The multiproduct monopolist internalizes the competition effect between the two products and has therefore less incentives to decrease prices than two separate firms. This is the basic logic behind the comparison between duopoly and monopoly.

The second case is the exact opposite of the first: if products i and j are *complements* (i.e., $\partial Q_j/\partial p_i < 0$), then the additional term is negative and the Lerner index is smaller than the inverse elasticity of demand. Here, the multiproduct monopolist internalizes the positive demand effect between the two products and has more incentives to decrease prices than separate firms do. We will use the same argument in Chapter 19 when explaining the so-called 'tragedy of the anticommons' and its application to patents for complementary innovations. Note also that the monopolist could well have L_i or $L_j \leq 0$, i.e., charge a price *below* marginal cost for one product in order to take full advantage of the complementarity effect. One can find here the basic logic behind all the free stuff that consumers receive here and there, especially in the information economy (think of free software, video game demos, etc.). We will further examine this commercial practice in Chapter 8 when studying price discrimination; we will also see in Chapter 22 that pricing below marginal cost is common in two-sided markets.

Linked costs, unlinked demands. Assume now that $q_1 = Q_1(p_1)$ and $q_2 = Q_2(p_2)$, while the cost function has the general form $C(q_1, q_2)$. One potential link between the costs of the two products can come from *economies of scope*. Economies of scope are present when an increase in the production of one product reduces at the margin the cost of production of the other product, i.e., $\partial^2 C(q_1, q_2)/\partial q_i \partial q_j < 0$. To understand the impact of such economies on prices, let us rewrite expression (2.4) under the current assumptions. Because demands are independent, we have that $\partial Q_j / \partial p_i = 0$; it follows that

$$L_i = \frac{p_i - C_i'(q_i, q_j)}{p_i} = \frac{1}{\eta_i}.$$

What differs here with (2.3) is that the Lerner index for product i depends on q_j. Cost interdependences do not arise for separate firms (where $C'(q) = C_i'(q, 0)$) but will be internalized by the multiproduct monopolist. In particular, the monopolist realizes that by decreasing p_j, it increases q_j and, thereby, reduces $C_i'(q_i, q_j)$, which has the effect of increasing the markup for product i. Hence, in the presence of economies of scope, the multiproduct monopolist has an incentive to set lower prices than separate firms. Naturally, the reverse conclusion would apply in the presence of diseconomies of scope.

Lesson 2.4   A multiproduct firm that has monopoly power over several products sets lower prices than separate firms (each controlling a single product) when the products are complements or when there are economies of scope among the products. It sets higher prices when the goods are substitutes or when there are diseconomies of scope.

2.2.3   Dominant firm model

An important feature of the monopoly model is that the monopoly pricing formula states that the markup only depends on demand side characteristics. We extend this monopoly model by introducing a perfectly competitive segment. This perfectly competitive fringe limits the market power of the single firm with price-setting power. This firm may be called the dominant firm. While we may doubt the real-world relevance of a market with one large and many small players, the competitive fringe model provides the first step to endogenize the market environment that a firm with market power operates in.

Case 2.1 The market for generics[10]

After Merck's patent for the cholesterol-lowering drug Zocor expired, two generics producers, Israel-based Teva and India-based Ranbaxy, obtained a 180-day exclusivity on the generics market. (Another company entered into an agreement with Merck to sell an authorized generic version of Zocor). Merck responded to the entry of generics by drastically cutting its price.[f] Generics producers can be expected to compete head-on with each other (thus forming a competitive fringe) whereas the former patent holder offers a differentiated, since branded product that is established in the market. Typically this allows the former patent holder to charge much higher prices than generic producers; it may even increase its price as a response to patent expiry.

To present a particular competitive fringe model, we introduce a simple market environment which we will frequently use throughout this book, the Hotelling line along which consumers are located. Suppose two types of products (indexed by 1 and 2) are located at the extreme locations of the $[0, 1]$ interval. Letting l_i denote the 'location' of product i, we thus assume that $l_i \in \{0, 1\}$, $i = 1, 2$. Consumer locations x are uniformly distributed on the unit interval. Consumers incur a disutility from travelling to the location of the product that is linear in distance. They have mass M. A consumer's indirect utility is written as $r - \tau|l_i - x| - p_i$ if the consumer buys one unit of product i, where τ measures how easily one unit of a product of type 1 can be substituted by one unit of a product of type 2. Additional units of a product do not increase a consumer's utility. Furthermore, a consumer is interested in exactly one of the products. The willingness to pay r is taken to be the same across products. The analysis can be easily extended to introduce for instance a larger r for the dominant firm, a situation that would typically fit the situation of a market for a pharmaceutical whose patent has expired, as described in Case 2.1. Consumer x's purchasing decision solves $\max_{i=1,2}\{r - \tau|l_i - x| - p_i\}$. For prices such that both firms are active, there is exactly one indifferent consumer $\hat{x}$ who is defined by

$$r - \tau\hat{x} - p_1 = r - \tau(1 - \hat{x}) - p_2 \quad \text{or, equivalently,}$$

$$\hat{x} = \frac{1}{2} + \frac{p_2 - p_1}{2\tau}.$$

Hence, the demand of firm 1 consists of all consumers to the left of $\hat{x}$ and the demand of product 2 consists of all consumers to the right of $\hat{x}$.[g] For a mass M of consumers, the demand functions are

$$Q_i(p_i, p_j) = M\left(\frac{1}{2} + \frac{p_j - p_i}{2\tau}\right).$$

---

[f] According to some unnamed analysts, the rationale is that Merck attempts to keep more generics out of the market (an issue we will turn to in Chapter 16).

[g] This model is also called the *Hotelling model*. Variations of this model will reappear at various points in the book. In particular, in Chapter 5, we discuss the interpretation of product location and of consumer disutility; we also address product choice in such a model.

The product of type 2, located at 1, is in competitive supply (i.e., it is sold at marginal costs). We can think of a large group of small firms (a continuum, to be precise) that offer one unit each. These firms are heterogeneous in their costs and, in the aggregate, give rise to the cost function C. The product of type 1, located at 0, is sold by a single firm, firm 1. Hence, firm 1 enjoys some degree of market power which is, however, limited by the presence of the firms at the other location. We contrast two cases according to the form of the firms' cost function.

Constant marginal costs

Suppose first that firms have constant marginal costs c. Since product 2 is in competitive supply, $p_2 = c$. This implies that the price in the competitive fringe does not respond to the price set by firm 1. Hence we can write the profit-maximization problem of firm 1 as

$$\max_{p_1} \pi_1 = \max_{p_1} p_1 Q_1(p_1, c) - C(Q_1(p_1, c)) = \max_{p_1} (p_1 - c)M \left(\tfrac{1}{2} + \tfrac{c - p_1}{2\tau} \right).$$

This has the same structure as a monopoly pricing problem. The first-order condition of profit maximization can be written as

$$p_1 = c + \tau/2.$$

Hence, firm 1 sells at a price above marginal costs. Demand for firm 1 is $M/4$ in equilibrium and its profit is $(M\tau)/8$.

Increasing marginal costs

Our previous analysis was special in the sense that we did not consider the possibility of output-dependent marginal cost. We reconsider the competitive fringe model from above with the modification that costs at both locations take the form $C_i(q_i) = cq_i^2/2$.[h] This means that in the competitive segment, a larger output is accompanied by a higher price. Marginal costs are cq_i and the last unit is sold at these marginal costs, so that $p_2 = cQ_2(p_1, p_2)$. Thus, the price that prevails in the competitive fringe depends on the price set by firm 1:

$$p_2(p_1) = cM \left(\frac{1}{2} + \frac{p_1 - p_2}{2\tau} \right) \Leftrightarrow p_2(p_1) = \frac{cM(\tau + p_1)}{2\tau + cM}.$$

This defines a 'pseudo best response' of the competitive fringe: it says how the price in the competitive fringe reacts to the price set by firm 1. The price of the competitive fringe is increasing in the price of firm 1. Firm 1 takes this conduct by the competitive fringe into account; that is, it is aware that the competitive fringe will react to the dominant firm's price changes. This suggests sequential decision making similar to the oligopoly setting that will be analysed in Chapter 4. Firm 1 maximizes $\pi_1 = p_1 Q_1(p_1, p_2(p_1)) - (c/2)[Q_1(p_1, p_2(p_1))]^2$. Substituting for $p_2(p_1)$ we obtain

$$Q_1(p_1, p_2(p_1)) = \frac{M}{2\tau + cM} (\tau + cM - p_1).$$

[h] In the case of the competitive fringe, we may think of a continuum of heterogeneous, outcome-restricted firms whose aggregate cost function takes the form $C_2(q_2)$ and who compete in prices (see Section 3.1 on asymmetric Bertrand competition).

Again, we obtain a linear demand function. The novel feature is that the demand function firm 1 faces not only depends on demand-side characteristics (parameters M and τ in this model) but also on supply-side characteristics, namely the cost parameter c that applies to the competitive fringe. Here, an industry-wide change in costs (say from c to c') leads not only to a change in the cost function of firm 1 but also to a change of its demand function. Note also that, for a given price, a change of the mass of consumers M leads to a nonlinear change in demand for firm 1.

The profit-maximizing price of firm 1 is

$$p_1 = \frac{2(\tau + cM)^2}{4\tau + 3cM}.$$

Hence, demand of firm 1 is $M/4$ and its profit is

$$\pi_1 = \frac{M(\tau + cM)^2}{2(4\tau + 3cM)}.$$

Note that a change in technology that is used in the industry can be separated into two effects. First, the own-cost effect for firm 1 given its demand curve. An increase from c to c' tends to increase the price firm 1 charges and tends to decrease its profit. Second, such a cost change also shifts the pseudo best response of the competitive fringe outward. Furthermore, there is a positive feedback effect between prices from one segment to the other that tends to amplify the overall effect on the price of firm 1. Overall, prices increase when c rises.[i]

We can also evaluate the effect of a higher c on firm 1's profit. Here, a higher c increases both demand and costs; yet, it can be checked that the demand effect dominates the cost effect:

$$\frac{\partial \pi_1}{\partial c} = \frac{M^2(\tau + cM)(5\tau + 3cM)}{2(4\tau + 3cM)^2} > 0.$$

Hence, firm 1 benefits from higher industry costs even though the effect on its own costs tends to decrease profit. At first sight, this result may look surprising but the simple reason is that the supply curve of the competitive fringe rotates upward so that its price increases. This leads to larger inframarginal gains for the dominant firm (and also to a larger producer surplus in the competitive fringe) – the same qualitative finding would hold if the dominant firm was pricing competitively.

2.2.4 Imperfect competition

In the market structures presented so far, a firm can make its decision in isolation, either because it feels that its decision has no impact on the market (the perfectly competitive paradigm) or because it is the single, or the dominant, firm in the market. Outside these extreme settings, a restricted number of firms are active in the market and none of those firms can ignore that market outcomes depend on the combination of the decisions taken by all of them. As a result, firms would not be rational if they made their decisions in isolation. Instead, they must factor

---

[i] As we will analyse later in the next chapter, since both best responses are increasing in the other segment's price (so that prices are strategic complements in this competitive fringe model) and a larger c shifts both best responses outward, we have the monotone comparative statics result that a larger c leads to higher prices in the market.

into their maximization programme the fact that the other firms are also maximizing their own profits and that the profit levels are interdependent. As we explained above, game theory offers tools to solve such multi-personal decision problems. In particular, the concept of Nash equilibrium provides us with predictions as to what the market outcome will be.

There is no need to develop this issue further at this early stage. The parts of the book that follow starting with Part II are concerned with the study of imperfect competition.

2.3   Market definition and market performance

As we explained in the introductory chapter, market power is what relates markets and strategies to one another. Before we start analysing market power in the rest of this book, we must give ourselves ways to measure it (Subsection 2.3.2). And because market power is exercised on a particular market, we must first of all agree on how to define the boundaries of a market (Subsection 2.3.1).

2.3.1   How to define a market?

Market definition is the first step in the assessment of market power. Defining the market is necessary to identify the competitive constraints that a firm faces. It is also important to provide a framework for competition policy (e.g., to assess the effects of mergers on competition, as we will discuss in Chapter 15). To define a market, one typically starts by identifying the closest substitutes to the product (or service) that is the focus of the analysis. These substitutes exert the strongest competitive constraints on the behaviour of the firms supplying the product in question.

The conceptual framework currently used by competition authorities worldwide to establish which products are 'close enough' substitutes to be in the relevant market is known as the *hypothetical monopolist test*. The test defines as the relevant market the smallest product group (and geographical area) such that a hypothetical monopolist (or cartel) controlling that product group (in that area) could profitably sustain a Small and Significant Non-transitory Increase in Prices, or a *SSNIP* for short (the test is also known by this acronym).

Effectively, the test asks whether a hypothetical monopolist could sustain a price increase of 5–10% above competitive levels for at least one year (keeping constant the terms of sales of all other products).[j] If there exists a substitutable product to which a sufficient number of consumers would switch so as to make the price increase unprofitable, then the relevant market should be expanded to include that alternative product. The process is repeated until the point a SSNIP becomes sustainable.

One of the limits of the SSNIP test is that it focuses on demand-side substitutability: it is the consumers' switching possibilities that constrain the hypothetical monopolist's ability to raise prices. However, the hypothetical monopolist may also be prevented from sustaining a SSNIP by new firms starting to supply the product. In practice, if entry conditions are such that additional firms are able to supply a product at short notice and without incurring substantial

---

[j] The EU guidelines refer to 5–10% whereas the US guidelines refer to 5%.

sunk costs, then this supply-side substitutability (or entry threat) should lead to a widening of the relevant market. Case 2.2 illustrates this principle.

Case 2.2 Using supply-side substitutability to define the relevant market[11]

In the merger case *Torras/Sario*,[12] the European Commission (EC) took supply-side substitution into account when defining the market for the supply of paper for use in publishing. Various coatings can be used to produce papers of different grades. Consumers may not view different grades of paper as substitutes. Hence, relying only on demand-side substitutability, one would define the relevant market in a relatively narrow way. However, firms are able to produce different grades of paper using the same plant and raw materials. It may then be relatively easy for them to switch production between different grades. It follows that a hypothetical monopolist in one grade of paper might not profitably sustain a SSNIP because firms currently producing other grades would rapidly start supplying that grade. Acknowledging this supply-side substitutability, the EC widened the definition of the relevant market.

2.3.2   How to assess market power?

Once a market has been properly defined, it becomes possible to assess market power on that market. Market power can be defined as the ability to raise prices above the perfectly competitive level. The first way to measure market power is to look at the difference between price and marginal costs. As indicated above, the *Lerner index* (noted L) is defined as the markup, i.e., the difference between price and marginal costs as a percentage of the price,

$$L = \frac{p - C'}{p}.$$

The Lerner index is a snapshot of the intensity of competition. However, costs (and, in particular, marginal costs) are often not directly observable. This raises the question as to how the markup can be measured empirically. We tackle this issue in the next chapter. Let us just note for the moment that even if costs can be imputed from market outcomes, the Lerner index ignores dynamic considerations. For instance, the observation of a low price by one or several active firms does not necessarily mean that the market is very competitive because in some circumstances a firm profitably foregoes short-term gains to be able to raise margins in the future.[k]

Another way to try and capture the market power of firms is to look at *concentration indices*, which are statistics of the degree of concentration of the market. One such measure adds up the market shares of one or a certain number of firms; this is the *m-firm concentration ratio*:

$$I_m = \sum_{i=1}^{m} \alpha_i,$$

[k] This is so, for instance, when switching costs or network effects are present (see, respectively, Chapter 7 and Chapter 21).

where $\alpha_i = q_i/Q$ is firm i's market share and where firms are ordered by decreasing market share. If I_m is close to 1 for m small, this suggests that the market is quite concentrated and may therefore be a candidate for scrutiny by the antitrust authority. However, interpreting such a number is difficult since market conditions vary across markets and a market that is dominated by few firms may be quite competitive, whereas a market with many firms may be less competitive. Still, various I_m rules are used by antitrust authorities and regulators as a screening device. For instance, according to EU legislation a firm is called a dominant firm if its market share is $\alpha_1 \geq 0.4$, i.e. 40% of the relevant market. Clearly, since the outcome from the use of such a screening device is very important for a firm (because it determines, e.g., whether a firm is subject to certain types of regulation), the relevant market needs to be carefully defined.

While the m-firm concentration ratio adds market shares of a small number of firms in the market, the so-called *Herfindahl index* (also known as Herfindahl–Hirschman index) considers the full distribution of market shares. It is defined as the sum of squared market shares for all n firms active on the market:

$$I_H = \sum_{i=1}^{n} \alpha_i^2.$$

Arguably, the Herfindahl index provides a better measure of concentration as it captures both the number of firms and the dispersion of the market shares. One expects higher concentration if the number of firms decreases or if market shares become less dispersed. It is easily checked that the index does indeed increase if, keeping the dispersion fixed, the number of firms decreases or if, keeping the number of firms fixed, the dispersion of market shares increases. At one extreme, $I_H = 1$ if one firm serves the whole market. At the other extreme, $I_H = 1/n$ if there are n firms with identical market shares. Then, in a perfectly competitive market with many small firms (i.e., $n \rightarrow \infty$), the index has a value close to 0.

Expressing market shares in percentage terms, the index ranges from 0 to $100^2 = 10\,000$. The standards of US antitrust agencies define a market as unconcentrated if the index is below 1000, and as highly concentrated if the index is above 1800.[1] In the following case we report the Herfindahl index for some selected US manufacturing industries.

Case 2.3 How concentration differs across industries and over time

Table 2.1 reports Herfindahl indices (measured for the largest 50 companies) for the different industry groups composing the US manufacturing sector, in 1997 and in 2002. We observe that the indices vary across industry groups (from as low as 8.5, up to 797.6, on a scale going from 0 to 10 000) and across time, with some industry groups becoming more concentrated and other groups less concentrated. Note, however, that these numbers are reported at an aggregated industry level and are therefore often not useful for antitrust authorities.

---

[1] The European Commission prefers to focus on the level of the *change* of the index (that would result, e.g., from a proposed merger).

Table 2.1. *Herfindahl indices in the US manufacturing sector*

Industry Group	1997	2002	Variation
Transportation equipment mfg	797.6	574.7	−229.9
Beverage and tobacco product manufacturing	777.2	709.5	−67.7
Petroleum & coal products mfg	350	543.4	+193.4
Textile product mills	186.2	403	+216.8
Paper mfg	173.3	259.3	+86.0
Leather & allied product mfg	167.2	163.6	−3.6
Computer & electronic product mfg	136.6	135	−1.6
Electrical equipment, appliance, & component mfg	105.9	113.9	+8.0
Apparel mfg	100.6	105.7	+5.1
Primary metal mfg	97.4	149.6	+52.2
Textile mills	94.4	105.6	+11.2
Food mfg	91	118.7	+27.7
Chemical mfg	76.6	99.9	+23.3
Furniture & related product mfg	55.5	57.2	+1.7
Machinery mfg	55.4	71.3	+15.9
Wood product mfg	52.7	48.4	−4.3
Nonmetallic mineral product mfg	52.1	46.7	−5.4
Printing & related support activities	38.4	45.2	+6.8
Plastics & rubber products mfg	30.2	32	+1.8
Fabricated metal product mfg	8.5	10.2	+1.7

Source: US Economic Census Data – Manufacturing sector

While the Herfindahl index may be useful as a description for market concentration, it is unclear how it translates in general into market power. In particular, if we take into account that firms may face capacity constraints or that products are often differentiated, it should be apparent that the ability to sustain price above marginal costs and the market share of a firm are hardly linked. However, keeping those characteristics fixed, we may provide such a link. In the next chapter, we will propose a concrete specification, using the model of quantity competition (in Section 3.2); we will also present the empirical methods used to estimate market power (in Section 3.5).

Review questions

1. Explain why there is a trade-off between incentive and insurance considerations in a principal–agent relationship between owner and manager with hidden effort.

2. Discuss the factors that determine the vertical boundaries of a firm, that is, the factors behind the 'make-or-buy decision' of the firm.

3. Under which assumptions is the consumer surplus a reasonable measure of the consumer welfare in a particular market?

4. Explain, in your own words, the monopoly-pricing formula.

5. Describe the hypothetical monopoly test (or SSNIP test) that is used to define a market.

6. Give the definitions of the Lerner and Herfindahl indices. What are these measures used for?

Further reading

For a short reference to standard game-theoretic concepts see Appendix A of this book. A good introduction to game theory is provided by Gibbons (1992). A more elaborate treatment is Fudenberg and Tirole (1991). For a deeper investigation of what is inside the black box of the firm and of how the vertical boundaries of the firm are determined, see e.g. Grossman and Hart (1986), Hart and Holmström (1987), Holmström and Tirole (1989), or Holmström and Roberts (1998). For the foundations of partial equilibrium analysis and the use of consumer surplus as an appropriate measure of consumer welfare, see Chapter 3 in Vives (1999). For more on market definition, see Chapter 2 in Motta (2004).

Notes for Part I

1. See 'Pfizer to buy Wyeth for $68B; cut 8 000 jobs' (The Associated Press, 27 January 2009); 'Long encouraged to expand, European banks now pulling back' (by Carter Dougherty, 26 January 2009); 'Chinese retail sector faces consolidation' (by Kirby Chien, Reuters, 21 January 2009); 'Apple drops anti-copying measures in iTunes' (by Brad Stone, 6 January 2009); 'Oil companies carved up the market for paraffin in style' (by Doreen Carvajal and Stephen Castle, 11 December 2008).

2. For a thorough analysis of Alcoa's evolution, see Smith (1988).

3. For instance, Gibbons (1992) is a good choice. At a more advanced level, Fudenberg and Tirole (1991) treat a large number of topics.

4. The possible interaction between organizational design and product market competition has been largely ignored by the literature. For an information-based theory see Alonso, Dessein and Matouschek (2008).

5. Some work has looked at owner–manager relationships under imperfect competition. Examples are Fershtman and Judd (1987) and Schmidt (1997).

6. The analysis is based on Hart and Holmström (1987), as presented in Tirole (1988).

7. The property rights approach to the theory of the firm stresses that firm boundaries define the allocation of residual control rights. Suppose contracts are ex ante incomplete but can be completed ex post. Then residual control rights matter. Here, if a party to the contract is able to exercise residual control rights his or her ex post bargaining position is improved. This provides stronger incentive to make relationship-specific investments, i.e., investments that create a value within the relationship but lose that value if a relationship is broken. This applies to a large number of vertical supply relationships. This theory has been developed by Grossman and Hart (1986) and Hart and Moore (1990). It provides some rationale for extending firm scope. See also Holmström and Roberts (1998) and Holmström (1999). For a recent contribution, see Hart and Holmström (2008).

8. Interesting ongoing research considers behavioural anomalies on the consumer side and integrates them into models of industrial organization. A first guide to this growing literature is Ellison (2006).

9. See Vives (1999).

10. Based on Ching (2004) and Rupali Mukherjee, "Merck's Zocor price cut a mixed bag for drug cos", in *Times of India*, 29 June 2006.

11. Based on Office of Fair Trading (2004).

12. Case IV/M166 Torras/Sarrio OJ [1992] C58/00, [1992] 4 CMLR341.

References for Part I

Alonso, R., Dessein, W. and Matouschek, N. (2008). Organize to Compete. Mimeo.

Ching, A. (2004). A Dynamic Oligopoly Structural Model for the Prescription Drug Market After Patent Expiration. Mimeo.

Ellison, G. (2006). Bounded Rationality in Industrial Organization. In Blundell, R., Newey, W. and Persson, T. (eds.), *Advances in Economics and Econometrics: Theory and Applications, Ninth World Congress*. Cambridge: Cambridge University Press.

Fershtman, C. and Judd, K. (1987). Equilibrium Incentives in Oligopoly. *American Economic Review* 77: 927–940.

Fudenberg, D. and Tirole, J. (1991). *Game Theory*. Cambridge, MA: MIT Press.

Gibbons, R. (1992). *Game Theory for Applied Economists*. Princeton: Princeton University Press.

Grossman, S. and Hart, O. (1986). The Costs and Benefits of Ownership: A Theory of Vertical and Lateral Integration. *Journal of Political Economy* 94: 691–796.

Hart, O. and Holmström, B. (1987). The Theory of Contracts. In Bewley, T. (ed.), *Advances in Economic Theory, Fifth World Congress (Econometric Society Monographs)*. Cambridge: Cambridge University Press.

Hart, O. and Holmström, B. (2008). A Theory of Firm Scope. Mimeo.

Hart, O. and Moore, J. (1990). Property Rights and the Nature of the Firm. *Journal of Political Economy* 98: 1119–1158.

Holmström, B. (1999). Managerial Incentive Problems: A Dynamic Perspective. *Review of Economics Studies* 66: 169–182.

Holmström, B. and Tirole, J. (1989). The Theory of the Firm. Chapter 2 in Schmalensee, R. and Willig, R. (eds.), *Handbook of Industrial Organization, Part I*. Amsterdam: Elsevier Publishing.

Holmström, B. and Roberts, J. (1998). The Boundaries of the Firm Revisited. *Journal of Economic Perspectives* 12: 73–94.

Motta, M. (2004). *Competition Policy. Theory and Practice*. Cambridge: Cambridge University Press.

Office of Fair Trading (2004). *Market Definition. Understanding Competition Law*. London.

Schmidt, K. M. (1997). Managerial Incentives and Product Market Competition. *Review of Economic Studies* 64: 191–214.

Smith, G. D. (1988). *From Monopoly To Competition: The Transformations of Alcoa, 1888–1986*. New York: Cambridge University Press.

Tirole, J. (1988). *The Theory of Industrial Organization*. Cambridge, MA: MIT Press.

Vives, X. (1999). *Oligopoly Pricing: Old Ideas and New Tools*. Cambridge, MA: MIT Press.

Part II
Market power

Firms are assumed to maximize profits but the market environment limits their abilities to exploit consumers. Indeed, if we can believe the perfectly competitive paradigm, firms will end up selling at a price equal to marginal costs. In particular, if firms are price takers and small compared to the industry, they will not exert any market power.

But what happens if firms are not small compared to the industry they are operating in? This is certainly the case for heavy weights such as Coca Cola, Microsoft, Nokia, Mittal-Arcelor, Gazprom, Anheuser-Bush InBev and the like. These large firms have seized a significant share of their respective markets. They can thus hardly be described as price *takers*. Yet, as they face competition from a number of other firms, they cannot either be described as pure price *makers*, like the monopolies we studied in the previous chapter. While these large firms undeniably exert market power, so do their smaller competitors. Market power – i.e., the ability to 'make the price' or to sell at prices above marginal costs – is thus collectively shared in those industries in which a few firms compete with one another. Such industries are called *oligopolies* (from the Greek 'oligo', which means 'small number'). The vast majority of industries are oligopolies. The examples that spring to mind are the industries of these giant multinational firms that we mentioned above: soft drinks, software, mobile phones, steel, natural gas, beer, etc. But by simply looking around you, you will quickly realize that most of the goods and services you consume are produced, at least locally, by a small number of competing firms.

The distinctive feature of oligopolistic competition is that firms cannot ignore the behaviour of their competitors. Indeed, competitors do exist (this is not a monopoly) and they are not small (this is not perfect competition). It follows that firms' profits ultimately depend on the *combination* of the decisions taken by *all* the firms in the industry. Hence, firms' decisions cannot be optimal if they do not take this interdependence into account. Firms must incorporate in their decision making the anticipation of how their competitors are likely to act, *and* to react to their own decisions. Oligopolistic competition is thus synonymous with *strategic interaction*.

As an illustration of strategic interaction, consider the DVD-by-mail industry. Before 2004, Netflix (which was the first company to launch a subscription service in 1999) was almost the only firm active on the market. Yet, in 2004, Wal-Mart Stores and Blockbuster entered the market, taking aggressive actions. They undercut Netflix's prices and a sudden and bitter competition followed as Netflix reacted by reducing its prices too. What is interesting to note is that Netflix acknowledged that the rivals' actions took it by surprise. Netflix's CEO declared: 'We underestimated the likelihood and significance of competition ... We came to the view that if (competitors) were going to enter, they would have done it in 2002, when the market was smaller, or in 2003.'[1] Whether competition is potential (as before 2004) or actual (as after 2004), we see that firms cannot ignore it when they make their decisions.

Game theory provides us with the adequate tools to analyse situations of strategic interaction. We will use these tools extensively in this book.[a] However, the analysis of oligopolistic

[a] See Appendix A for a review of the basic concepts of game theory.

situations did not wait for the advent of game theory. Actually, it goes back to the nineteenth century and is associated with the names of Augustin Cournot (1801–77) and Joseph Bertrand (1822–1900). These two French engineers (the profession of economist did not really exist at their time) can be seen as the founding fathers of oligopoly theory or, it would be more correct to say, oligopoly *theories*. Indeed, there is no such thing as a unique and comprehensive oligopoly theory. This is best illustrated by the fact that Bertrand's main contribution (in 1883) was explicitly proposed as a critique to Cournot's theory (published in 1838). What we have instead is a collection of different oligopoly models. As will become quickly apparent, the basic models we review in this part of the book give a relatively large array of predictions regarding the relationship between market structure and market power in oligopolistic industries. Such variety of predictions may appear as disquieting at first glance, but it simply reflects that a great deal of variety also exists among industries. In other words, the different theories of oligopolistic behaviour should not be seen as competing, but rather as relevant in different industries or circumstances.

Our review of the basic oligopoly models starts in Chapter 3 with simple settings where firms are supposed to make a unique decision at a single point in time. The focus here is on how the nature of the strategic variable, namely price or quantity, affects strategic interaction and, thereby, the extent of market power. You probably already know the stark contrast between Cournot's and Bertrand's predictions regarding oligopolistic competition in homogeneous goods industries: while Cournot's analysis, based on quantity competition, concludes that oligopolistic firms enjoy a degree of market power that is inversely related to the number of firms operating in the industry, Bertrand's analysis, based on price competition, shows that market power vanishes completely as soon as two firms compete in the industry. In Chapter 3, we want to

understand how price and quantity competition differ, and which environments lead to which type of equilibrium behaviour. Referring to the DVD-by-mail case, one can think that firms compete in prices in that industry. It is indeed reported that the last weeks of 2004 saw a flurry of price cutting as Netflix, Blockbuster and Wal-Mart competed for consumers, in anticipation of the possible entry of Amazon.com in the market. This does not mean, however, that quantities are not an important strategic variable. Firms also compete in their ability to meet consumers' demand, which is traditionally more important for new releases than for back-catalogue movies. If firms want to meet this demand without having customers waiting too long, they must have a sufficient number of copies of the latest movies on hand.

In Chapter 4, we broaden the perspective by incorporating the time dimension. Firms do indeed make decisions at several points in time. We therefore need to understand how sequentiality (one firm decides before another) affects strategic interaction. We also want to look at what happens *before* and *after* strategic interaction takes place among a small number of firms: what brought this small number of firms (and not more or fewer of them) to enter the industry and to stay in it? In our example, Netflix was the first firm to propose the service of renting DVDs by mail. It can thus be seen as the 'leader' and Wal-Mart, Blockbuster and Amazon as the 'followers'. The followers seemed to benefit from the fact that they could observe Netflix's prices before setting their own price (and Netflix's underestimation of the entry threat certainly put the entrants in an even better position). After entry, price competition took place repeatedly through time. This gave rise to what the press dubbed the 'DVD price war'. One can conjecture that Wal-Mart, Blockbuster and Amazon factored this price war in their entry decision, as they had to forecast the expected profits that they could earn on this market.

What will you learn in this part of the book? You will get acquainted (or, probably, reacquainted) with a number of basic models of oligopoly theory, including the Cournot model, the Bertrand model with homogeneous products, the Bertrand model with differentiated products and linear demand, models with spatially differentiated products, and the Spence–Dixit–Stiglitz model of monopolistic competition. This will allow you to understand what market power means, how it affects (and is affected by) firms' behaviour and how it is measured. You will also be able to distinguish between strategic substitutes and strategic complements, simultaneous versus sequential strategy setting, exogenous versus endogenous entry, and exogenous versus endogenous sunk costs.

3 Static imperfect competition

Firms have various strategic options at their disposal. In the most basic models of strategic interaction, firms choose a single strategic variable, quantity or price, once. In many markets, firms are seen as price setters. It thus appears natural to start with the analysis of price-setting firms in an environment with a few firms; we do so in Section 3.1. In other markets, however, it seems more reasonable to assume that firms choose quantities rather than prices; we analyse quantity competition in Section 3.2. We then proceed to compare price and quantity competition. First, in Section 3.3, we show that quantity competition can sometimes be mimicked by a two-stage model in which firms choose their capacity of production and next, set their price; we also directly compare price and quantity competition in a unified model of product differentiation. Second, in Section 3.4, we bring the comparison of price and quantity competition to a more general level by introducing the concepts of 'strategic complements' and 'strategic substitutes'. Finally, in Section 3.5, we discuss the empirical investigation of industries with market power.

3.1 Price competition

We analyse here several models of price competition. We start with the standard Bertrand (1883) model where products are homogeneous. Then, we extend the model in two directions: first, we assume that firms have private information about their marginal costs of production; second, we consider differentiated products.

3.1.1 The standard Bertrand model

In the simplest version of the price-competition or Bertrand model, there are two firms with homogeneous products and identical constant marginal costs c. Both firms set price simultaneously to maximize profit. The firm with the lower price attracts all the market demand $Q(p)$, where p is the relevant price. Suppose that, at equal prices, the market splits somehow, say at α_1 and $\alpha_2 = 1 - \alpha_1$. Then firm i faces demand

$$Q_i(p_i) = \begin{cases} Q(p_i) & \text{if } p_i < p_j, \\ \alpha_i Q(p_i) & \text{if } p_i = p_j, \\ 0 & \text{if } p_i > p_j. \end{cases}$$

In this simple Bertrand model, there is a unique pure-strategy equilibrium in which both firms set price equal to marginal costs, $p = c$. To prove this result, it suffices to show that for all other price combinations, there is at least one firm that has an incentive to deviate. If $p_i > p_j > c$, firm i can increase its profits by setting $p_i' \in (c, p_j)$; if $p_i = p_j > c$, each

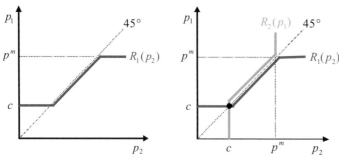

Figure 3.1 Reaction functions and equilibrium in the Bertrand duopoly (with homogeneous product, and identical and constant marginal costs)

firm can increase its profits by slightly undercutting the rival price; if $p_i > p_j = c$, firm j can increase its profits by increasing its price above c and below p_i.

Another useful way to show this result is to derive the firms' reaction functions. As the previous reasoning clearly shows, firm i's best response is to set a price p_i just below the price p_j of its rival so as to attract all consumers and maximize its profits. Naturally, this rule suffers two exceptions. First, for values of p_j less than the marginal cost c, firm i chooses $p_i = c$ as undercutting firm j would entail losses. Second, define p^m as the price that maximizes $(p - c) Q (p)$; that is, p^m is the monopoly price.[a] Then, for values of p_j larger than p^m, firm i chooses $p_i = p^m$ as a price just below p_j would not maximize profits. The left panel of Figure 3.1 depicts firm 1's reaction function, noted $R_1 (p_2)$, and the right panel superposes the two reaction functions, confirming that $p_1 = p_2 = c$ is the unique Nash equilibrium of the game. We note for future reference that the *reaction functions of Bertrand duopolists are (weakly) upward-sloping*: when one firm raises its price, the best response of the other firm is to raise its price too.[b]

The previous result is often called a paradox since we consider a market with just two firms and still the perfectly competitive outcome prevails. It shows that under some circumstances, the competitive pressure under duopoly can be sufficiently strong to give rise to marginal-cost pricing.

> **Lesson 3.1**   In the homogeneous product Bertrand duopoly with identical and constant marginal costs, the equilibrium is such that firms set prices equal to marginal costs and thus do not enjoy any market power.

The intuition behind this result is clear: firms cannot support prices above marginal cost because small price cuts can lead to large increases in quantity demanded and profits.[c]

Let us now introduce cost asymmetries in the Bertrand model. Firms might indeed have access to different technologies, resulting in different marginal costs of production. As

---

[a] We assume that $Q (p)$ is such that the monopoly profit function has a unique maximizer.
[b] With a continuous strategy space the reaction function is not well-defined (open set problem). The reaction function approximates the situation with a large but finite number of strategies.
[c] This result largely carries over to Bertrand oligopolies, with the qualification that there also exist Nash equilibria where at least two firms set the price equal to marginal cost (while the other firms may set the price above marginal cost).

we will describe in Part VII, this is typically what happens when a firm is granted a patent for the exclusive use of an improved technology. In particular, suppose that there are n firms in the market, which are ordered according to their marginal costs $c_i < c_{i+1}$, $i = 1, \ldots, n - 1$. Firms set price simultaneously. If two firms set the same price, the more efficient firm gets all the demand. Then, any price $p \in [c_1, c_2]$ is an equilibrium. Note, however, that if there is a small probability that the less efficient firm gets a small market share, firm 2 would not set a price $p < c_2$. Therefore, we select the equilibrium in which $p = c_2$ as the most reasonable equilibrium.[d] In the selected equilibrium, firm 1 enjoys positive profit, contrary to the symmetric pure price competition model. Firm 1 collects the efficiency gains compared to the next best alternative technology (i.e., the difference between c_2 and c_1).[e]

Note that in the equilibrium of the Bertrand game with symmetric costs, both firms use weakly dominated strategies: setting a higher price cannot make the firm worse off but, in a case where the competitor deviates from its Nash equilibrium strategy, such a deviation can be worthwhile. If a firm faces a competitor of unknown costs, it appears that the firm no longer has an incentive to set price equal to marginal costs. We turn to this setting next.

3.1.2   Price competition with uncertain costs

Suppose that each firm has private information about its marginal costs. In particular, the marginal costs of each firm are drawn independently from some distribution and firms learn the realization of their own cost parameter but not those of their competitors. When setting their prices, firms face a trade-off between margins and the likelihood of winning the competition for the best deal they offer to consumers. In this setting, we will show that firms typically set price above marginal costs, so that firms earn positive profits in equilibrium. This price–cost margin is decreasing in the marginal costs. This setting appears to be a natural next step in the analysis of price competition models. It delivers the result that even in the context of price competition with homogeneous goods, all firms in a market set price above marginal costs. The analysis is slightly involved and may therefore be skipped at a first reading.

We analyse this result in a simple setting with linear market demand and a uniform distribution of marginal costs.[2] Suppose that n firms face the market demand function $Q(p) = 1 - p$ and a marginal cost that is independently drawn from the uniform distribution on $[0, 1]$. Denote by $\widehat{p}_{-i}$ the lowest price charged by the competitors of firm i: $\widehat{p}_{-i} \equiv \min\{p_1, p_{i-1}, p_{i+1}, p_n\}$. Then firm i faces demand $q_i = 1 - p_i$ if $p_i < \widehat{p}_{-i}$, $q_i = (1 - p_i)/m$ if $p_i = \widehat{p}_{-i}$ where m is the number of firms that set the lowest price p_i, and $q_i = 0$ if $p_i > \widehat{p}_{-i}$. We solve for the symmetric Bayesian Nash equilibrium of this game, which is given by a function $p^*(\cdot)$ that maps marginal costs into prices. This function has the property that $p^*(1) = 1$ because the highest-cost firm will always set price equal to marginal cost. For this reason, we do not gain additional insights by considering a demand function of the type $a - p$ with $a > 1$. We look for a price function that is strictly increasing on $[0, 1]$ so that each cost type sets a different price.[f] Since a firm receives the same cost parameter as some of their competitors

---

[d] Formally speaking, all equilibria with $p < c_2$ are not trembling-hand perfect.
[e] It is implicitly assumed here that the difference $c_2 - c_1$ is not large enough for the optimal price that would be set by a monopoly producing at cost c_1 to fall below c_2; otherwise, firm 1 would set this monopoly price and not a price equal to c_2. In Part VII, we will say that the 'innovation' (represented by the cost reduction from c_2 to c_1) is supposed to be 'minor' or 'nondrastic'.
[f] The argument why this is the case is presented formally in the context of search models in Chapter 7.

with probability zero (and profits are bounded), we can restrict attention to situations in which firms have different cost parameters. Firm i's expected profit is

$$(p_i - c_i)(1 - p_i)\text{Prob}(p_i < \widehat{p}_{-i}),$$

because a firm of type c_i sells the product with probability $\text{Prob}(p_i < \widehat{p}_{-i})$. Due to the independence assumption, this probability is simply the product of the probabilities of setting the lowest price in all pairwise comparisons with the firm's competitors: $\text{Prob}(p_i < \widehat{p}_{-i}) = \text{Prob}(p_i < p^*(c_1)) \times \cdots \times \text{Prob}(p_i < p^*(c_{i-1})) \times \text{Prob}(p_i < p^*(c_{i+1})) \times \cdots \times \text{Prob}(p_i < p^*(c_n))$. For a firm of type c_i, we have $p_i = p^*(c_i)$ in equilibrium. Therefore, $p^{*-1}(p_j)$ denotes the marginal cost of a competitor who sets p_j and follows the equilibrium strategy. Since p^* is strictly increasing, we can write $\text{Prob}(p_i < p^*(c_j)) = \text{Prob}(p^{*-1}(p_i) < c_j)$ which, since c_j is uniformly distributed on $[0, 1]$, is equal to $1 - p^{*-1}(p_i)$. Consequently, $\text{Prob}(p_i < \widehat{p}_{-i}) = [1 - p^{*-1}(p_i)]^{n-1}$ and each firm solves the following maximization problem:

$$\max_{p_i} (p_i - c_i)(1 - p_i)[1 - p^{*-1}(p_i)]^{n-1}.$$

The first-order condition of profit maximization is

$$(1 + c_i - 2p_i)[1 - p^{*-1}(p_i)]^{n-1}$$
$$- (p_i - c_i)(1 - p_i)(n - 1)[1 - p^{*-1}(p_i)]^{n-2}\frac{\partial p^{*-1}(p_i)}{\partial p_i} = 0.$$

In a symmetric equilibrium, $p^*(c_i) = p_i$ and thus $c_i = p^{*-1}(p_i)$. We also note that the derivative of the inverse price-setting function is the inverse of the derivative. Hence, we can rewrite the above equation as

$$p^{*\prime}(c_i)(1 + c_i - 2p^*(c_i))[1 - c_i]^{n-1}$$
$$- (p^*(c_i) - c_i)(1 - p^*(c_i))(n - 1)[1 - c_i]^{n-2} = 0.$$

Dividing by $[1 - c_i]^{n-2}$ and rearranging gives the differential equation

$$p^{*\prime}(c_i) = \frac{(n - 1)(p^*(c_i) - c_i)(1 - p^*(c_i))}{(1 - c_i)(1 + c_i - 2p^*(c_i))}.$$

Suppose the solution to this equation is of the form $p^*(c_i) = a + bc_i$. Taking into account that $p^{*\prime}(c_i) = b$ and substituting, we obtain an equation in a, b, n and c_i. The only admissible solution is $a = 1/(n + 1)$ and $b = n/(n + 1)$. The price schedule is then given by

$$p^*(c_i) = \frac{1 + nc_i}{n + 1}. \tag{3.1}$$

To verify that this is indeed the unique equilibrium, we note that demand is

$$\text{Prob}(p_i < \widehat{p}_{-i}) = \left[\frac{(n + 1)(1 - p_i)}{n}\right]^{n-1}$$

for prices p_i with $1/(n + 1) < p_i < 1$. On this set of prices, firm i's maximization problem therefore is

$$\max_{p_i} (p_i - c_i)(1 - p_i)^n \left(\frac{n + 1}{n}\right)^{n-1}.$$

The unique solution to this problem is indeed given by Equation (3.1).

The equilibrium has a number of properties. First, all firms (except the firm with $c_i = 1$) set prices above marginal cost. The price–cost margin is increasing with the efficiency of the firm. Note also that the resulting equilibrium price $p^*(\widehat{c})$ that consumers pay, where $\widehat{c} = \min\{c_1, \ldots, c_n\}$, is decreasing with the number of firms even if the lowest cost in the market does not change. In other words, an increase in the number of firms leads to a more competitive outcome because it increases the competitive pressure in the market. In addition, it leads to a lower expected cost of the most efficient firm. This amplifies the effect of an increase in the number of firms on equilibrium price. Correspondingly, total industry output increases with the number of firms (although it is always one firm that is active). In the limit, as n turns to infinity, price converges to marginal costs. In this respect, the model delivers qualitatively similar results as the Cournot model (see Section 3.2). We summarize our main insight by the following lesson.

Lesson 3.2   **In the price competition model with homogeneous products and private information about marginal costs, firms set price above marginal costs and make strictly positive expected profits in equilibrium. More firms in the industry lead to lower price–cost margins, higher output and lower profits. As the number of firms converges to infinity, the competitive limit is reached.**

In contrast to a Cournot model (and price competition models with consumer search that will be analysed in Chapter 7), even though all active firms set price above marginal costs, only the most efficient firm makes strictly positive revenues. In other words, firms post prices above marginal costs but all except one firm do not generate any revenues at any point in time. While this appears to be often violated in real markets because of other market frictions (see, in particular, Part III), we believe that the model has some intuitive appeal: firms listing their products e.g. on Amazon Marketplace at a high price can only hope to make profits if more efficient firms happen to be absent. The present model provides a rationale as to why these high-cost firms are around in spite of this: more efficient supplies may have dried up so that only high-price alternatives remain available. If such markets operate over time and firms are repeatedly subject to cost shocks, the results of the model are compatible with price changes over time and a changing identity of the most efficient firm.

3.1.3   Price competition with differentiated products

While pure price competition takes away any margins that are not due to lower costs, competitors may avoid intense competition if they offer products that are not perfect substitutes. If products are only imperfect substitutes for one another, the market features product differentiation. In this case demand may respond smoothly to price changes. As we already saw in the previous chapter, Merck and other former patent holders do not set price equal to marginal costs and typically charge a premium over the price of generics. If reading this book gives you a headache and you decide to buy some Aspirin®, you may want to keep in mind that this is more costly than buying a pill that has the same chemical composition but is sold under a different name. Here, product differentiation is present even though the physical composition of the products is the same. Many firms also outside the pharmaceutical industries have long recognized the need to differentiate their products from competitors in order to increase their market power.[g] Our next case illustrates this behaviour.

Case 3.1 Bananas and oranges

Fruits such as bananas and oranges may look like a bad example to illustrate the idea of product differentiation. However, for more than 100 years, the Sunkist brand has been with us. Long ago, California citrus growers decided to sell their products in a distinct way and created the Sunkist trademark. This allowed them to advertise their products without being confused with competitors. Other firms have followed this example. For example, bananas with the Chiquita brand are sold at a premium. Sunkist and Chiquita managed to convince consumers that their brand offers certain features, such as taste and freshness, that competitors cannot guarantee.[3]

We now turn to a formal analysis of product differentiation and to this end, we use again the Hotelling line that we introduced in the dominant firm model of Chapter 2; this is the so-called Hotelling model. Suppose that two products (noted 1 and 2) are located at the extreme locations of the $[0, 1]$ interval. Firms have constant and identical marginal costs c of production and maximize profits $\pi_i = (p_i - c)Q_i(p_i, p_j)$. Consumers are uniformly distributed on the unit interval and incur a disutility from travelling to the location of the product, which is linear in distance. A consumer's indirect utility is written as $r - \tau|l_i - x| - p_i$ if the consumer buys one unit of product i. Additional units of this product do not increase a consumer's utility. Furthermore, a consumer is interested in exactly one of the products. Consumer x's purchasing decision solves $\max_{i=1,2}\{r - \tau|l_i - x| - p_i\}$. For prices such that both firms are active, there is exactly one indifferent consumer $\widehat{x}$ who is defined by

$$r - \tau\widehat{x} - p_1 = r - \tau(1 - \widehat{x}) - p_2 \text{ or, equivalently,}$$

$$\widehat{x} = \frac{1}{2} + \frac{p_2 - p_1}{2\tau}.$$

Hence, the demand of firm 1 consists of all consumers to the left of $\widehat{x}$ and the demand of firm 2 consists of all consumers to the right of $\widehat{x}$. For a mass 1 of consumers, demand functions are

$$Q_i(p_i, p_j) = \frac{1}{2} + \frac{p_j - p_i}{2\tau}.$$

Profit functions then become

$$\pi_i = (p_i - c)\left(\frac{1}{2} + \frac{p_j - p_i}{2\tau}\right).$$

The first-order condition of profit maximization is

$$\frac{\partial \pi_i}{\partial p_i} = \frac{1}{2\tau}\left(p_j - 2p_i + c + \tau\right) = 0.$$

[g] We investigate the incentives to differentiate products in Chapter 5.

Solving the previous equation for p_i, we derive firm i's reaction function:

$$p_i = \tfrac{1}{2}(p_j + c + \tau),$$

which is upward-sloping as in our previous model of Bertrand competition with homogeneous products.

At the intersection of the two reaction functions, we find the equilibrium prices: $p_i = p_j = c + \tau$. This demonstrates that due to product differentiation each firm faces a demand function that is not perfectly price-elastic. The more products are differentiated, i.e. the higher τ, the higher the price–cost margin of the firms in equilibrium.

Lesson 3.3   If products are more differentiated, firms enjoy more market power.

The above analysis was performed under the implicit assumption that all consumers prefer to purchase the product; that is, we did not consider the consumers' participation decision. Let us introduce the possibility to abstain from buying a product in the market, in which case the consumer's utility of the outside option is set equal to zero. Then, for τ sufficiently large, the participation constraint of some consumers is violated. It follows that for high values of τ, firms enjoy (local) monopoly power: each firm sets the monopoly price and ignores the presence of the other firm.

Duopolies with price competition not only appear in textbooks but do from time to time pop up in the real world, as the following case demonstrates.

Case 3.2 Airbus vs. Boeing and the market for wide-bodied aircrafts[4]

The market for large commercial jets is currently dominated by two firms: Boeing, of the United States, and Airbus, of Europe. It can therefore be described as a duopoly, and it is likely to remain a duopoly for years to come, in spite of its high profitability (the market is forecast to be worth $2.6 trillion over the next two decades). Potential entrants do exist. China and Russia need to replace the old Tupolevs and other Russian-built aircrafts that fly in both countries, but they do not want to rely on Boeing or Airbus without attempting to develop their own industries first. However, the two countries face enormous entry barriers: (i) new types of aircraft cost up to $10 billion to develop; (ii) it took decades for Boeing and Airbus to establish their safety and reliability records, while Russian and Chinese manufacturing suffer from a reputation of poor quality control.

Although this market provides a good example of a duopoly, it is less clear whether it is adequately described by price competition. The pure price competition models we have analysed so far fail to capture one important feature of this market, namely that capacity constraints may lead to delays. For instance, the Airbus A380 suffered a series of delays and was finally launched two years behind its original schedule. Boeing had also to delay the launch of its new 'Dreamliner' aircraft (B787) in 2007–8. This suggests that capacity constraints may play a role. We consider this issue formally in Section 3.3.

We extend the analysis to a setting of localized competition with n firms. Suppose firms are equidistantly located on a circle with circumference 1 and consumers are uniformly distributed on this circle. This is the so-called *Salop model*.[5] The consumers' decision making corresponds to the one in the Hotelling model: consumers buy at most one unit of the product and they buy it from the firm offering them the lowest 'generalized price', i.e., the price augmented by the transportation cost. We assume a unit transportation cost of τ. That is, consumer x's purchasing decision solves $\max_{k=i,i+1}\{r - \tau|l_k - x| - p_i\}$, where firms $k = i, i+1$ are the firms between which consumer x is located and where firm k's location is $l_k = k/n$. The consumer $\widehat{x}_{i,i+1}$ who is indifferent between firms i and $i+1$ is defined by

$$r - \tau\left(\widehat{x}_{i,i+1} - \tfrac{i}{n}\right) - p_i = r - \tau\left(\tfrac{i+1}{n} - \widehat{x}_{i,i+1}\right) - p_{i+1} \text{ or, equivalently,}$$

$$\widehat{x}_{i,i+1} = \frac{2i+1}{2n} + \frac{p_{i+1} - p_i}{2\tau}.$$

By analogy, we can identify the consumer who is indifferent between firm i and its left neighbour, firm $i - 1$, as

$$\widehat{x}_{i-1,i} = \frac{2i-1}{2n} + \frac{p_i - p_{i-1}}{2\tau}.$$

Firm i attracts all consumers located between $\widehat{x}_{i-1,i}$ and $\widehat{x}_{i,i+1}$. Because firms are located symmetrically, we focus on a symmetric equilibrium in which all firms charge the same price p. Hence, setting $p_{i-1} = p_{i+1} = p$ in the above expressions, we compute the demand for firm i as

$$Q_i(p_i, p) = \left(\frac{2i+1}{2n} + \frac{p_{i+1} - p_i}{2\tau}\right) - \left(\frac{2i-1}{2n} + \frac{p_i - p_{i-1}}{2\tau}\right)$$

$$= \frac{1}{n} + \frac{p - p_i}{\tau}.$$

Supposing that all firms have the same constant marginal costs of production c, we can write firm i's maximization programme as

$$\max_{p_i}(p_i - c)\left(\frac{1}{n} + \frac{p - p_i}{\tau}\right).$$

The first-order condition gives $1/n + (p - 2p_i + c)/\tau = 0$. Setting $p_i = p$ yields

$$p = c + \tau/n,$$

which is analogous to the result we obtained in the Hotelling model. An additional parameter, the number of firms, also affects the equilibrium outcome. A larger number of firms leads to closer substitutes on the circle. This increases the competitive pressure. As the number of firms turns to infinity, prices converge to marginal costs.

3.1.4   Asymmetric competition with differentiated products

In the previous models, firms did not produce the same product but these products were symmetric in the sense that each firm's incentives did not depend on whether it was called firm i or j. However, in some instances products are not only horizontally differentiated, but one product might also be of superior quality or offer additional features.

Suppose that firms operate in the same environment as in the previous Hotelling model but that a consumer's indirect utility is $v_i = r_i - \tau|l_i - x| - p_i$. Above, we had $r_1 = r_2$. Let us now assume that the willingness to pay for product 1 is greater than for product 2 at the ideal location l_i, i.e. $r_1 > r_2$, but that for some consumers, product 2 is more attractive than product 1, i.e. $r_2 + \tau > r_1$. Here, products are horizontally differentiated but product 1 is of superior quality or offers additional features that are of the same value to all consumers.[h] The indifferent consumer is given by

$$\hat{x} = \frac{1}{2} + \frac{(r_1 - r_2) - (p_1 - p_2)}{2\tau}. \tag{3.2}$$

Since $Q_1(p_1, p_2) = \hat{x}$ and $Q_2(p_1, p_2) = 1 - \hat{x}$, profit functions become

$$\pi_i = (p_i - c)\left(\frac{1}{2} + \frac{(r_i - r_j) - (p_i - p_j)}{2\tau}\right).$$

The first-order condition of profit maximization of firm i (on the range of prices such that demand is strictly positive for both firms) is

$$\frac{1}{2\tau}\left[p_j - 2p_i + c + \tau + (r_i - r_j)\right] = 0.$$

Solving the system of two linear equations, we obtain

$$\begin{cases} p_1^* = c + \tau + \frac{1}{3}(r_1 - r_2), \\ p_2^* = c + \tau - \frac{1}{3}(r_1 - r_2). \end{cases}$$

We observe that the high-quality firm, firm 1, sets a higher price; the price difference between firms is $p_1^* - p_2^* = (2/3)(r_1 - r_2)$. Hence in equilibrium demand for firm 1 is

$$Q_1(p_1^*, p_2^*) = \frac{1}{2} + \frac{r_1 - r_2}{6\tau},$$

and correspondingly for firm 2. Note that demand is strictly positive also for the low-quality firm (under our assumption that $r_2 + \tau > r_1$). However, the high-quality firm has larger demand than the low-quality firm in equilibrium.

To maximize welfare (measured as total surplus), prices must be equal to marginal cost. Introducing $p_1 = p_2 = c$ in expression (3.2), we obtain the socially optimal allocation

$$Q_1(c, c) = \frac{1}{2} + \frac{r_1 - r_2}{2\tau} > Q_2(c, c) = \frac{1}{2} + \frac{r_2 - r_1}{2\tau} > 0,$$

which shows that the ranking of demands also holds for the solution that maximizes welfare.

We can now ask whether the number of consumers served by firm 1 is socially sufficient. It is immediate to see that $Q_1(p_1^*, p_2^*) < Q_1(c, c)$: the equilibrium demand of firm 1 is too low from a social point of view. This is due to the fact that firm 1 sets a higher price than firm 2 under strategic price setting. This is a general feature of imperfect competition. Note that instead of considering a model in which firm i offers a more attractive product, we could analyse a situation in which firm i produces at lower costs. Our insight would be confirmed under this alternative assumption: the low-cost firm sells too few units from a welfare perspective.

---

[h] The distinction between horizontal and vertical product differentiation will be clarified in Chapter 5.

> **Lesson 3.4**   Under imperfect competition, the firm with higher quality or lower marginal costs sells too few units from a welfare perspective.

If a social planner wanted to correct this inefficiency, he would need to subsidize the high-quality (or low-cost) firm or to tax the low-quality (or high-cost) firm. This appears in contrast to government programmes that protect feeble firms.

3.2   Quantity competition

In this section, we analyse situations in which firms set quantities, as first analysed by Cournot (1838). The price clears the market and is thus equal to the inverse demand, $p = P(q)$ where q is total output in the industry. We may wonder where this price p comes from. In real markets, we typically observe some price setting, which makes it difficult to provide a literal interpretation of Cournot competition. However, the price setting is sometimes done on behalf of the firms by some auctioneer. If there is a small number of big players that provide most of the industry output, then these firms may commit themselves to bring a certain amount of a product to the market. The market clearing may be performed by an auctioneer (who, for simplicity, is assumed not to charge for market transactions) who finds the highest price at which all offered units are sold. The resulting equilibrium allocation is then equivalent to the outcome in the quantity-setting game.

We start our analysis of the Cournot model with the simple case of an oligopoly facing a linear demand for a homogeneous product and producing at constant marginal costs (Subsection 3.2.1). In order to gain further insights, we extend the initial setting by using general demand and cost functions (Subsection 3.2.2).

3.2.1   The linear Cournot model

We consider a homogeneous product market with n firms in which firm i sets q_i. Total output is then $q = q_1 + \cdots + q_n$. The market price is given by the linear inverse demand $P(q) = a - bq$ (with $a, b > 0$). Let us also suppose that the cost functions are linear: $C_i(q_i) = c_i q_i$ (with $0 \leq c_i < a \ \forall i = 1 \ldots n$). We first solve the model in the most general case for any number of potentially heterogenous firms ($c_i \neq c_j$ for any $i \neq j$). We use then this general analysis in two specific cases: in a duopoly ($n = 2$) and in a symmetric oligopoly ($c_i = c \ \forall i$).

Cournot oligopoly with heterogenous firms

Let us denote $q_{-i} \equiv q - q_i$ the sum of the quantities produced by all firms but firm i. The inverse demand can then be rewritten as

$$P(q_i, q_{-i}) = (a - bq_{-i}) - bq_i \equiv d_i(q_{-i}).$$

As firm i conjectures that the other firms do not modify their choice of quantity no matter what it decides itself to produce (this is known as the *Cournot conjecture*), the function $d_i(q_{-i})$ can

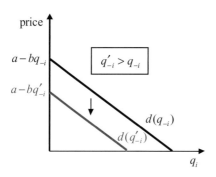

Figure 3.2 Residual demand for a Cournot oligopolist

be seen as the *residual demand* facing firm i. Clearly, if firm i expects the total quantity of the other firms to increase, it faces a lower residual demand, as illustrated in Figure 3.2.

Accordingly, firm i will produce a lower quantity. We now confirm this intuition analytically. Firm i chooses q_i to maximize its profits $\pi_i = (a - b(q_i + q_{-i}))q_i - c_i q_i$, which can also be written as $d_i(q_{-i})q_i - c_i q_i$, meaning that firm i acts as a monopolist on its residual demand. The first-order condition of profit maximization is expressed as

$$a - c_i - 2bq_i - bq_{-i} = 0 \tag{3.3}$$

or, solving for q_i, as

$$q_i(q_{-i}) = \tfrac{1}{2b}(a - c_i - bq_{-i}). \tag{3.4}$$

Expression (3.4) gives firm i's best response (or reaction) function. One checks that the best response function slopes downward: faced with a larger quantity produced by the rival firms (i.e., a larger q_{-i}), firm i optimally reacts by lowering its own quantity ($q_i(q_{-i})$ decreases). This is illustrated below, for the duopoly case, in Figure 3.3.

At the Cournot equilibrium, Equation (3.4) is satisfied for each of the n firms. In other words, each firm 'best responds' to the choices of the other firms. Summing the equations (3.4) derived for the n firms, we obtain

$$\sum_{i=1}^{n} q_i = \tfrac{1}{2b}\left(na - \sum_{i=1}^{n} c_i - b\sum_{i=1}^{n} q_{-i}\right).$$

By definition, $\sum_i q_i = q$ and it is easily understood that $\sum_i q_{-i} = (n-1)q$. Noting C for $\sum_i c_i$, we can rewrite the previous equation as

$$q = \tfrac{1}{2b}(na - C - b(n-1)q) \Leftrightarrow q^* = \frac{na - C}{b(n+1)}.$$

Introducing q^* (i.e., the total quantity produced at the Cournot equilibrium) into Equation (3.4), we find the quantity that firm i produces at the Cournot equilibrium (where $C_{-i} \equiv \sum_{j \neq i} c_j$):

$$q_i^* = \tfrac{1}{2b}\left(a - c_i - b\left(\frac{na - C}{b(n+1)} - q_i^*\right)\right) \Leftrightarrow q_i^* = \frac{a - (n+1)c_i + C}{b(n+1)} \Leftrightarrow$$

$$q_i^* = \frac{a - nc_i + C_{-i}}{b(n+1)}. \tag{3.5}$$

Evaluated at the equilibrium, the first-order condition (3.3) can be rewritten as $bq_i^* = a - b\left(q_i^* + q_{-i}^*\right) - c_i = P(q^*) - c_i$. It follows that firm i's equilibrium profits are computed as[i]

$$\pi_i^* = (P(q^*) - c_i)\, q_i^* = b\left(q_i^*\right)^2 = \frac{(a - nc_i + C_{-i})^2}{b\,(n+1)^2}. \tag{3.6}$$

We observe that π_i^* decreases with c_i and increases with C_{-i}, which allows us to state the following lesson.

Lesson 3.5   In the linear Cournot model with homogeneous products, a firm's equilibrium profits increase when the firm becomes relatively more efficient than its rivals (i.e., all other things being equal, when its marginal cost decreases or when the marginal cost of any of its rivals increases).

Implicit in the previous analysis was the assumption that the equilibrium is interior, in the sense that all firms find it optimal to be active at equilibrium. This is so if, for all firm i, we have $q_i^* \geq 0$, which is equivalent to $c_i \leq (1/n)(a + C_{-i})$. If we order firms according to their marginal costs ($c_i \leq c_{i+1}$, $i = 1 \ldots n-1$), the latter inequality is the most stringent for firm n. Hence, what the condition for an interior equilibrium says is that the less efficient firm cannot be 'too inefficient' relative to the rival firms (i.e., its marginal cost must be small enough).

Cournot duopoly

In order to illustrate the previous results, both analytically and graphically, we briefly redo the analysis in the duopoly case. Using expression (3.4), we can write the system of reaction functions:

$$\begin{cases} q_1 = \frac{1}{2b}\,(a - c_1 - bq_2), \\ q_2 = \frac{1}{2b}\,(a - c_2 - bq_1). \end{cases}$$

The solution of this system yields the following Nash equilibrium quantities:

$$q_1^* = \frac{a - 2c_1 + c_2}{3b} \quad \text{and} \quad q_2^* = \frac{a - 2c_2 + c_1}{3b}.$$

We let the reader compute the equilibrium profits and check that they correspond to the general formula given by expression (3.6). If we assume that $c_1 \leq c_2$, the condition for an interior equilibrium is $c_2 \leq (a + c_1)/2$.[j]

---

[i] As we will frequently use the linear Cournot model in the rest of the book, it is worth putting a bookmark at this page or, better, remembering expressions (3.5) and (3.6).

[j] The condition can also be interpreted as follows. If firm 1 was in a monopoly position, it would choose a quantity $q_1^m = (a - c_1)/(2b)$ and sell it at $p_1^m = (a + c_1)/2$. Yet, in the presence of firm 2, firm 1 is not able to set this monopoly price if $p_1^m \geq c_2$, which is equivalent to $c_2 \leq (1/2)(a + c_1)$. As already noted above, we will use a similar analysis in Chapter 18 when introducing the distinction between major and minor innovations.

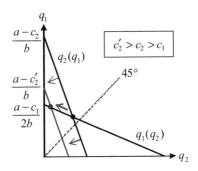

Figure 3.3 Cournot duopoly

Figure 3.3 nicely illustrates our previous results. First, the two firms' reaction functions are shown to be downward-sloping. Second, the assumption that $c_1 < c_2$ implies that at equilibrium, firm 1 produces a larger quantity (and achieves a larger profit) than firm 2. Third, keeping c_1 constant, we observe that firm 2's disadvantage widens when its marginal cost increases from c_2 to $c_2' > c_2$: firm 2's reaction function shifts down and the equilibrium moves up along firm 1's reaction function. Firm 2 remains active (i.e., $q_2^* \geq 0$) as long as the vertical intercept of firm 2's reaction function lies above the vertical intercept of firm 1's reaction function, or $(a - c_2')/b \geq (a - c_1)/(2b)$, which is equivalent to $c_2' \leq (a + c_1)/2$.

Symmetric Cournot oligopoly

Later in this book, we will frequently make the simplifying assumption that firms are ex ante symmetric in the sense that they all have the same cost structure. In the case of constant marginal costs, this amounts to assuming that $c_i = c$ for all i. Then, using expression (3.5), we derive the quantity produced by any firm at the Cournot equilibrium as

$$q_i^*(n) = \frac{a - c}{b(n + 1)}. \tag{3.7}$$

The total quantity and the market price are equal to

$$q^*(n) = \frac{n(a - c)}{b(n + 1)} \quad \text{and} \quad p^*(n) = a - bq^*(n) = \frac{a + nc}{n + 1}.$$

It follows that the markup (or Lerner index) at the equilibrium of the (symmetric linear) Cournot model is equal to

$$L(n) = \frac{p^*(n) - c}{p^*(n)} = \frac{a - c}{a + nc}.$$

If we let the number of firms (n) increase, we obtain the following comparative statics results: (i) the individual quantity decreases; (ii) the total quantity increases; (iii) the market price decreases; (iv) the markup decreases. Moreover, if we let the number of firms tend to infinity, we observe that the markup tends to zero, meaning that market power vanishes.

Lesson 3.6 **The (symmetric linear) Cournot model converges to perfect competition as the number of firms increases.**

The intuition for this result is simple: as the number of firms increases, each firm sees its influence on the market price diminish and is therefore more willing to expand its output. As a result, the market price decreases with the number of Cournot competitors. This result can be shown to hold in more general settings than the specific one considered here.[6]

3.2.2   Implications of Cournot competition

Let us now consider a general inverse demand function, $P(q)$, and general cost functions, $C_i(q_i)$. We then write firm i's profits as

$$\pi_i = P(q)q_i - C_i(q_i).$$

Each firm maximizes profits with respect to its own output. The first-order condition of profit maximization then is $P'(q)q_i + P(q) - C_i'(q_i) = 0$. Defining $\alpha_i = q_i/q$ as the market share of firm i and recalling that the inverse price elasticity of demand is $1/\eta = -P'(q)q/P(q)$, we can rewrite the first-order condition of profit maximization as

$$\frac{P(q) - C_i'(q_i)}{P(q)} = \frac{\alpha_i}{\eta}.$$

This is the basic *Cournot pricing formula*.

Lesson 3.7   In the Cournot model, the markup of firm i is larger the larger is the market share of firm i and the less elastic is market demand.

Hence, the Cournot model gives the empirically testable prediction that in a given market, a larger firm should have a larger markup. Assuming that costs are convex, $C''(q_i) \geq 0$, a sufficient condition for a Cournot equilibrium to exist is that $P'(q)q_i$ is decreasing in q_i. This condition is equivalent to

$$\frac{\partial^2 \pi_i}{\partial q_i \partial q_j} = P'(q) + q_i P''(q) \leq 0,$$

which is the condition of strategic substitutability, as will be defined below. If the cross derivative is indeed negative, then best response functions are downward sloping.

In the Cournot model with constant marginal costs ($C_i(q_i) = c_i q_i$), first-order conditions of profit maximization can be rewritten as

$$\frac{p - c_i}{p} = \frac{\alpha_i}{\eta}. \tag{3.8}$$

Equilibrium profits are $(p - c_i)\alpha_i Q(p)$ where p is the equilibrium price under Cournot competition. We can write industry-wide profits in two equivalent ways:

$$\sum_{i=1}^{n} \pi_i = \sum_{i=1}^{n}(p - c_i)q_i = \sum_{i=1}^{n}(p - c_i)\alpha_i q = \begin{cases} \left(p - \sum_{i=1}^{n}\alpha_i c_i\right)q, \\ \frac{pq}{\eta}\sum_{i=1}^{n}\alpha_i^2, \end{cases}$$

where the second line uses the first-order conditions, $p - c_i = \alpha_i p/\eta$. Equating the two alternative expressions and rearranging terms, we have

$$\frac{p - \sum_{i=1}^{n} \alpha_i c_i}{p} = \frac{\sum_{i=1}^{n} \alpha_i^2}{\eta} = \frac{I_H}{\eta}.$$

We recall from the previous chapter that I_H denotes the Herfindahl index, which measures the degree of concentration of the industry. We observe thus that *the average Lerner index (weighted by market shares) is proportional to the Herfindahl index*. This means that in the linear Cournot model, there is a one-to-one relationship between market power and concentration. To the extent that the linear Cournot model with constant marginal costs is a good description of real markets, this implies that calculating the Herfindahl index and estimating the price elasticity of demand allows for calculation of the average markup (or average Lerner index) in the market.

Lesson 3.8   In the linear Cournot model with homogeneous products, the Herfindahl index is an appropriate measure of market power since it captures the average markup in equilibrium.

3.3   Price versus quantity competition

Collecting the results of the previous two sections, we observe marked differences between price and quantity competition. Indeed, consider a market with linear demand, i.e. $Q(p) = a - p$. Suppose that two firms operate in this market and have the same constant marginal costs of production $c_1 = c_2 = c$. In the Bertrand model, we have that under simultaneous price setting $p_1 < p_2$ implies $\pi_2 = 0$ and $\pi_1 = (p_1 - c)(a - p_1)$, and the reverse for $p_1 > p_2$. At $p_1 = p_2$ with the tie-breaking rule that each firm attracts half of the demand, $\pi_1 = (1/2)(p_1 - c)(a - p_1)$ and $\pi_2 = (1/2)(p_2 - c)(a - p_2)$. The Bertrand equilibrium is then $p_1 = p_2 = c$. Output in this market is equal to output in a perfectly competitive market, $q_1^B = q_2^B = (a - c)/2$, and firms' profits are zero, $\pi_1^B = \pi_2^B = 0$. Contrast now these results with what obtains under Cournot competition. Here, setting $b = 1$ and $n = 2$ in expression (3.7), one easily finds that $q_1^C = q_2^C = (a - c)/3$. Cournot competitors thus produce less than Bertrand competitors. As a result, the markup is positive, $p^C - c = a - (q_1^C + q_2^C) - c = (a - c)/3 > 0$, and firms make positive equilibrium profits, $\pi_1^C = \pi_2^C = (a - c)^2/9 > 0$.

Lesson 3.9   In the homogeneous product case, price is higher, quantity is lower and profits are higher under quantity competition than under price competition.

In the rest of this section, we want to refine the previous statement by providing a deeper comparison of price and quantity competition. We will first relax one of the assumptions of the Bertrand model and suppose, more realistically, that firms may face limited capacities of production. In this framework, we will show that quantity competition can be mimicked by a two-stage model in which firms choose their capacity of production and next, set their price. Second, we will directly compare price and quantity competition in a unified model of product differentiation. Finally, we will try to identify industry characteristics to decide whether price or quantity competition is the appropriate modelling choice.

3.3.1   Limited capacity and price competition

The Bertrand model presumes that firms can serve any demand at constant marginal costs. This means that they do not face capacity constraints. For a large part of industrial production, the assumption of constant (or even decreasing) unit costs may be an appropriate assumption. However, this only holds as long as capacity is not fully utilized. Increasing output beyond capacity limits is often prohibitively costly so that in the short run, a firm has to respect these capacity choices. This critique of the Bertrand setting was first made by Edgeworth (1897). A concrete example related to retailing is that retailers have to order supplies well in advance; they then have to respect capacity limits at the price setting stage.[k] Case 3.3 provides another example.

Case 3.3 When capacity choices condition pricing decisions in the DVD-by-mail industry

Recall the case of the DVD-by-mail industry that we described in the introduction.[7] We mentioned the fact that at any point in time, demand for newly released movies is larger than for movies released, say, six months or one year before. To meet this larger demand, firms like Netflix or Blockbuster should hold an extra stock of copies of the latest movies. Yet, these copies are also more expensive. This has led firms to develop appropriate user interface and pricing schemes so as to steer subscribers toward renting back-catalogue movies instead of new releases. This illustrates that the choice of costly capacities precedes and conditions pricing decisions. A similar argument helps us understand why flights are much more expensive around Christmas: more people wish to travel at that period of the year but capacities are fixed (i.e., there is a fixed number of seats in any airplane and a given airport can accommodate a fixed number of airplanes per day). One also understands why the airline industry has invented the practice of 'yield (or revenue) management', which is a form of price discrimination (see Part IV) adapted to situations where capacities are fixed while demand is fluctuating (like, e.g., in air transport, in lodging or in the car rental business). The underlying principle of yield management can be summarized as setting the right prices so as to sell the right product, to the right client, at the right time. Again, capacity and price decisions are closely intertwined.

As an approximation for such markets, we consider that firms can pre-commit to a capacity of production before they engage in price competition. We will see that under a number of assumptions, this capacity-then-price model leads to the same outcome as the Cournot model of quantity competition. We will also discuss what happens when these assumption are relaxed.

---

[k] Think for instance of traditional retailing for clothing: firms have to order at the beginning of the season and are thus constrained later by this limit in capacity. Only in recent years some (mostly vertically integrated) clothing companies have increased their flexibility to the effect that retail outlets can react quickly to demand.

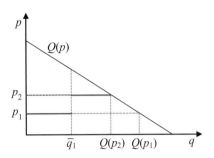

Figure 3.4 Efficient rationing with limited capacities

The model

To establish that result, we study the following two-stage game:[8] in stage 1, firms set capacities $\overline{q}_i$ simultaneously; in stage 2, firms set prices p_i simultaneously. It is assumed that the marginal cost of capacity is c and is incurred in the first stage; then, once capacity is installed, the marginal cost of production in the second stage is zero. In this setup, we characterize the subgame perfect equilibrium. This implies that at stage 1, firms are aware that their capacity choice may affect equilibrium prices. Firms not only know their own capacity choice but are also assumed to observe the competitors' capacity choice. For many industrial products, this is an appropriate assumption as factory sizes are known. The assumption may be more problematic in the retailer example but nevertheless be appropriate in some instances. For instance, if you think of a local farmers' market, the vendors can easily observe the capacity constraints of competitors.

When allowing for capacity constraints, it is well possible that one firm sets its price so low that the quantity demanded at that price exceeds its supply. This implies that some consumers have to be rationed. Suppose that there is a second firm on the market that offers the product at a higher price. Who will be served at the low price, who will not? At this point, we have to make an assumption on the rationing scheme. We assume that there is *efficient rationing*, i.e., consumers with higher willingness to pay are served first. We can provide two justifications for this particular rationing scheme. If there is rationing, products may be allocated according to who is first in the queue. Suppose each consumer demands 0 or 1 unit. Then consumers with a higher willingness to pay will be first in the queue. Alternatively, independently of the way a product in excess demand is allocated, there can be secondary markets that operate without costs; then, consumers with low willingness to pay will resell to consumers with high willingness to pay. Therefore, consumers with a high willingness to pay will never be rationed.[1]

Figure 3.4 illustrates efficient rationing. The first unit is purchased by the consumer with the highest willingness to pay, the second unit by the second-highest and so on. Hence, if firm 1 has capacity of $\overline{q}_1$ units, these units are sold to the $\overline{q}_1$ consumers with the highest willingness to pay. If $p_1 < p_2$ is such that quantity $\overline{q}_1$ is insufficient to serve all consumers, i.e. $Q(p_1) > \overline{q}_1$, some consumers are rationed and there is positive residual demand for firm 2 (this cannot be the case in the pure Bertrand model, in which capacity is never binding.).

We first want to analyse the price setting game for given capacities. Before doing so, it is helpful to observe that a firm never sets a very large capacity since capacity is costly. To be precise, a firm will never set a capacity such that its revenues are less than costs independently

---

[1] As consumers with a higher willingness to pay buy at the lowest price, consumer surplus is maximized under this rationing rule, which explains why it is called 'efficient' (see Levitan and Shubik, 1972).

of the decision of the competitor. Taking the linear demand $Q(p) = a - p$, the maximal revenue of a firm is $\max_q q(a - q) = a^2/4$; the quantity then is $q = a/2$. Costs at stage 1 have to be lower than maximal revenues, $c\bar{q}_i \leq a^2/4$. Hence the profit-maximizing capacity choice must satisfy

$$\bar{q}_i \leq a^2/(4c). \tag{3.9}$$

We now analyse the price-setting stage for capacities which satisfy the above inequality. If firm 1 offers the product at a lower price, firm 2 faces the following residual demand for product 2:

$$\widehat{Q}(p_2) = \begin{cases} Q(p_2) - \bar{q}_1 & \text{if } Q(p_2) - \bar{q}_1 \geq 0, \\ 0 & \text{else.} \end{cases}$$

Hence, for $p_1 < p_2$, profits are

$$\begin{cases} \pi_1 = (p_1 - c)\bar{q}_1, \\ \pi_2 = p_2 \widehat{Q}(p_2) - c\bar{q}_2 = p_2[Q(p_2) - \bar{q}_1] - c\bar{q}_2. \end{cases}$$

We now want to prove that *the equilibrium at the second stage of the game is such that both firms set the market-clearing price:* $p_1 = p_2 = p^* = a - \bar{q}_1 - \bar{q}_2$ (this price does indeed clear the market as it equalizes demand and supply, i.e., total capacity). This result holds provided that the demand parameter a is not too large; in particular, we impose the following condition:

(C1) $c < a < (4/3)c$.

To prove this result, we proceed as follows: supposing that $p_1 = p^*$, we need to show that $p_2 = p^*$ is a best response; that is, firm 2 cannot earn a larger profit by setting neither a lower, nor a larger price than p^*. First, it is easy to see that setting a lower price, $p_2 < p^*$, is not a profitable deviation. Indeed, at $p_1 = p_2 = p^*$, firm 2 sells all its capacity $\bar{q}_2$. By lowering its price, firm 2 would increase the demand for its product but would not be able to serve this additional demand because it is capacity constrained. Therefore, firm 2 would sell the same number of units as before but at a lower price, which would decrease its profit.

Second, knowing that firm 1 is capacity constrained, firm 2 could find it profitable to raise its price ($p_2 > p^*$). Indeed, due to firm 1's limited capacity, firm 2 can sell a positive volume at a price above p_1. This case requires some more reasoning than the previous one. Recall that firms have incurred the marginal cost c when installing their capacity in the first stage. Hence, in the second stage, they maximize their revenues (as the marginal production cost is zero). Provided that $p_1 < p_2$, firm 2's revenues are

$$p_2 \widehat{Q}(p_2) = \begin{cases} p_2(a - p_2 - \bar{q}_1) & \text{if } a - p_2 \geq \bar{q}_1, \\ 0 & \text{else.} \end{cases}$$

We have to show that the proposed equilibrium price p^* is located to the right of the maximum of this revenue function (as illustrated in Figure 3.5). If this holds, the proof is completed because increasing the price above p^* decreases profit, meaning that such a deviation is not profitable. The maximum of the revenue function is equal to $\bar{p}_2 = (a - \bar{q}_1)/2$. Then,

$$p^* > \bar{p}_2 \Leftrightarrow a - \bar{q}_1 - \bar{q}_2 > (a - \bar{q}_1)/2 \Leftrightarrow a > \bar{q}_1 + 2\bar{q}_2.$$

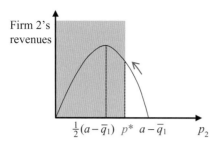

Figure 3.5 Setting $p_2 > p^*$ is not a profitable deviation

Invoking (3.9), we know that $\overline{q}_1 + 2\overline{q}_2 \leq (3/4)(a^2/c)$. Therefore, $a > \overline{q}_1 + 2\overline{q}_2$ is necessarily satisfied if

$$a > (3/4)(a^2/c) \Leftrightarrow a < (4/3)c,$$

which is guaranteed by condition (C1). Hence, it is not profitable to set $p_2 > p^*$, which completes our proof.

We can now insert these stage-2 equilibrium prices in the profit functions and thus obtain reduced profit functions for stage 1, which only depend on capacities:

$$\widetilde{\pi}_i(\overline{q}_1, \overline{q}_2) = (a - \overline{q}_1 - \overline{q}_2)\overline{q}_i - c\overline{q}_i.$$

We see that if we reinterpret capacities as quantities, the objective function is the same as in the Cournot model, in which prices are not set by firms but where, for any quantity choice, the price clears the market.

> **Lesson 3.10** In the capacity-then-price game with efficient consumer rationing (and with linear demand and constant marginal costs), the chosen capacities are equal to those in a standard Cournot market.

Discussion

We have to stress that Lesson 3.10 is drawn under a parameter restriction and for a particular rationing rule. What happens if we relax these assumptions? Note first that the key for the previous result to hold is that firm i has no incentive to increase its price above p^* when firm j sets $p_j = p^*$.[m] Under the efficient rationing rule, we have seen that firm i, ignoring its capacity constraint, would like to set $\bar{p}_i = (a - \overline{q}_j)/2$. Firm i will have sufficient capacity to satisfy residual demand at that price if $\bar{p}_i > p^*$. As we showed above, the parameter restriction we imposed excludes this possibility. In particular, this restriction guarantees that firms do not install capacities that are larger than $a/3$ (indeed, for $a < (4/3)c$, the upper bound on profitable capacities, $a^2/(4c)$, is below $a/3$). Note that $a/3$ is precisely the output firms produce at the Cournot equilibrium with no production costs. We can thus generalize our previous result by stating that *under efficient rationing, $p_1 = p_2 = p^*$ is the unique second-stage equilibrium*

---

[m] We know that firm i has no incentive to *lower* its price as this would induce an excess of total demand over total capacity, meaning that firm i could increase its price without losing sales.

when each firm's capacity is less than or equal to its Cournot best response to the other firm's capacity. Outside this region of capacity (which is possible when relaxing the parameter restriction, i.e., for $a > (4/3)c$), a pure strategy equilibrium fails to exist at stage 2: the only equilibria are in mixed strategies in which firms randomize prices over a common interval of prices. However, it can be shown that the first-stage capacity choices continue to correspond to the Cournot quantity equilibrium.[9]

Consider now an alternative rationing rule. Edgeworth (1897) proposed to allocate the cheapest units of the product randomly across consumers. Under this *proportional rationing rule*, all consumers have the same probability of being rationed.[n] Under this rule, the highest price charged is always the monopoly price p^m. Indeed, ignoring its capacity constraint, firm i maximizes $\alpha p_i Q(p_i)$, where α is the expected fraction of consumers that firm i serves. If $p^m < p^*$, firm i does not have sufficient capacity to satisfy residual demand at p^m and chooses then to set $p_i = p^*$. Given that $p^m = a/2$, the latter condition is equivalent to $\bar{q}_1 + \bar{q}_2 < a/2$, which is more demanding than the corresponding condition we obtained under the efficient rationing rule (actually, capacities sufficiently close to the upper bound given by (3.9) violate this condition as $a > c$ implies that $a^2/(2c) > a/2$). For capacities outside this region, the only equilibria are again in mixed strategies. Here, these mixed strategies are generally difficult to derive. However, it is possible to show that *under proportional rationing, the equilibrium tends to be more competitive than Cournot.*[10]

3.3.2   Differentiated products: Cournot versus Bertrand

While the purpose of the previous model was to show that quantity competition can be mimicked by a model with price competition at the last stage, the purpose of the present model is to compare the competitiveness between price and quantity competition. As indicated above in Lesson 3.9, the results are obvious in the homogeneous product case: quantity competition leads to higher prices, lower quantities and higher profits than price competition. These results are less obvious once we allow for product differentiation. Consider a simple duopoly model in which firms have constant marginal costs c_1 and c_2, respectively.[11] To obtain linear demand, we assume that there is a large number of identical consumers with a linear-quadratic utility function. In particular, suppose that the utility function takes the form

$$U(q_0, q_1, q_2) = aq_1 + aq_2 - \left(bq_1^2 + 2dq_1q_2 + bq_2^2\right)/2 + q_0,$$

where q_0 is the Hicksian composite commodity with a price normalized to 1.[o] We assume that $b > |d|$, which implies that products are differentiated. Consumers maximize their utility $U(q_0, q_1, q_2)$ subject to the budget constraint $y = q_0 + p_1q_1 + p_2q_2$. This gives rise to the following inverse demand functions

$$\begin{cases} P_1(q_1, q_2) = a - bq_1 - dq_2, \\ P_2(q_1, q_2) = a - dq_1 - bq_2, \end{cases}$$

---

[n] The proportional rule is clearly not efficient as some consumers may end up buying the good because they were offered the lower price although they would not have bought it at the higher price. From the point of view of the higher-priced firm, this rule yields a relatively high contingent demand, while the efficient rule yields the worst possible one.

[o] The Hicksian composite commodity contains all other goods outside the market under consideration. Since we are interested in real prices, we can normalize the price of one unit of this basket to 1.

for strictly positive prices and zero otherwise. Goods are substitutes if $d > 0$, they are independent if $d = 0$ and they are complements if $d < 0$. The ratio d/b can be interpreted as an inverse measure of the degree of product differentiation. It ranges from -1 when products are perfect complements to 1 when they are perfect substitutes; a value of zero means that products are independent. This system of two equations can be inverted (for $-1 < d/b < 1$) to obtain direct demand functions. Let $\tilde{a} = a/(b + d)$, $\tilde{b} = b/(b^2 - d^2)$, and $\tilde{d} = d/(b^2 - d^2)$. Demand functions then take the form

$$\begin{cases} Q_1(p_1, p_2) = \tilde{a} - \tilde{b}p_1 + \tilde{d}p_2, \\ Q_2(p_1, p_2) = \tilde{a} + \tilde{d}p_1 - \tilde{b}p_2, \end{cases}$$

for strictly positive quantities and zero otherwise. With quantity competition, firm i maximizes $(a - bq_i - dq_j - c_i)q_i$ taking q_j as given. With price competition, firm i maximizes $(\tilde{a} - \tilde{b}p_i + \tilde{d}p_j)(p_i - c_i)$ taking p_j as given.

Let us underline an important difference between quantity and price competition, which relates to the form of the best response functions. To see this, take the case of substitutable products (i.e., $d > 0$). Under quantity competition, the best response is downward sloping in q_j: $q_i(q_j) = (a - dq_j - c_i)/(2b)$. That is, facing an increase in firm j's quantity, firm i reacts by reducing its own quantity. Strategic choices move in opposite directions and, as we define it more generally below, quantities can then be said to be *strategic substitutes*. This confirms what we observed above in the Cournot duopoly with perfect substitutes (i.e., for $d = 1$). The opposite holds under price competition. The best response under price competition is upward sloping in p_j: $p_i(p_j) = (\tilde{a} + \tilde{d}p_j + \tilde{b}c_i)/(2\tilde{b})$. Here, facing an increase in firm j's price, firm i reacts by increasing its own price. Strategic choices move here in the same direction, meaning that prices are *strategic complements*. This is also what we observed in Section 3.1 when considering the standard Bertrand model and the Hotelling model.

Notice that in the presence of complementary products (i.e., for $d < 0$), the previous results are reversed: best response functions slope upward under quantity competition and downward under price competition, meaning that, in that case, quantities are strategic complements whereas prices are strategic substitutes. Admittedly, the terminology might induce some confusion, but it should already be clear by now that the concepts of strategic substitutability and strategic complementarity have to do with the the direction of strategic reactions, and not with the demand links between the products. Actually, as we will see below, these concepts go far beyond price and quantity competition as they can be applied to any type of strategic interaction.

We now compare the equilibrium under price and quantity competition. To simplify the exposition, we suppose that marginal costs are symmetric and equal to zero. A few lines of computation establish that equilibrium prices and quantities under quantity competition are $p_i^C = bq_i^C$ and $q_i^C = a/(2b + d)$, while equilibrium prices and quantities under price competition are $p_i^B = \tilde{a}/(2\tilde{b} - \tilde{d})$ and $q_i^B = \tilde{b}p_i^B$. To compare prices and quantities, we can rewrite p_i^B as $p_i^B = a(b - d)/(2b - d)$. Then

$$p_i^C - p_i^B = \frac{ab}{(2b + d)} - \frac{a(b - d)}{(2b - d)} = \frac{ab(2b - d) - a(b - d)(2b + d)}{(2b + d)(2b - d)}$$

$$= \frac{ad^2}{4b^2 - d^2} = \frac{a}{4(b^2/d^2) - 1} > 0.$$

Price competition always leads to lower prices and larger quantities than quantity competition. Hence, price as the strategic variable gives rise to a more competitive outcome than quantity as the strategic variable.

To understand this result, look at the slope of the perceived demand function in the two cases. Under price competition, the perceived demand function is $q_i = \tilde{a} - \tilde{b}p_i + \tilde{d}p_j$, with a slope (in absolute value) of $\tilde{b} = b/(b^2 - d^2)$. Under quantity competition, the perceived demand function is $q_i = a - (1/b)p_i - (d/b)q_j$, with a slope (in absolute value) of $1/b$. It is easily checked that $b/(b^2 - d^2) > 1/b$, meaning that a firm perceives a larger elasticity of demand when it takes the price of the rival as fixed rather than its quantity. It follows that firms quote lower prices under price competition than under quantity competition.

We also observe that the price difference depends on the degree of product differentiation d/b. The more differentiated the products, the smaller the difference between prices. As products become independent, $d/b \to 0$, the price difference turns to zero as in both environments both firms tend to behave as monopolists. Since firms produce too little from a social point of view, price competition is socially preferred to quantity competition. However, the profit comparison is less clear-cut. It depends on the sign of d. If products are substitutes, i.e. $d > 0$, quantity competition performs better than price competition from the firms' point of view. If products are complements, i.e. $d < 0$, price competition performs better.

3.3.3   What is the appropriate modelling choice?

One of the important basic insights of oligopoly theory is that the market outcome under imperfect competition depends on the variable, price or quantity, that is chosen for the analysis. From a real-world perspective, the difference between outcomes appears to be cumbersome. Since we want to explain market behaviour, we should better have a good idea as to what is the appropriate model of competition. Note first that this question is pointless in a monopoly setting. As we know from the monopoly analysis, if we fix the environment in which one firm operates, i.e., in particular if we fix the action of the competitor, profit maximization with respect to price gives the same result as profit maximization with respect to quantity. Thus, it is immaterial whether firms set price or quantity.

However, in an oligopoly setting, the difference between price and quantity competition materializes in the residual demand a firm faces given the action of the competitor. Suppose $\tilde{Q}_i(p_i)$ is the residual demand for firm i and $Q(p)$ is the market demand that a monopolist would face. Then, under price competition, price p_j is given. This means that the competitor is willing to serve any demand at price p_j. Then firm i's residual demand is $\tilde{Q}_i(p_i) = Q(p_i)$ if $p_i < p_j$ and $\tilde{Q}_i(p_i) = 0$ if $p_i > p_j$ (and demand is equally split for $p_i = p_j$). Hence, firm i's residual demand curve reacts very sensitively to price changes: it is perfectly elastic at $p_i = p_j$. Under quantity competition, quantity q_j is given. This means that irrespective of the price he will achieve, the competitor sells quantity q_j. Then firm i's residual demand is $\tilde{Q}_i(p_i) = \max\{Q(p_i) - q_j, 0\}$. Here, firm i's residual demand curve reacts less sensitively to price changes.

To choose between these two basic models of competition, we have to choose between two different ways in which firms behave in the market place: they either stick to a price and sell any quantity at this price or they stick to a quantity and sell this quantity at any price. The former option (i.e., price competition) appears to be the appropriate choice in case of unlimited capacity or when prices are more difficult to adjust in the short run than quantities. For instance, in the mail-order business, it is costly to print new catalogues or price-lists and, therefore, over some period of time, prices will remain fixed and quantities will adjust accordingly.

In contrast, the latter option (i.e., quantity competition) may be the more appropriate choice in case of limited capacities, even if firms are price setters. A formal explanation of this latter insight has been provided above in the capacity-then-price model, where quantities (seen as capacities) are more difficult to adjust than prices. For instance, this is the case in the package holiday industry: hotel rooms or aircraft seats are usually booked more than one year before a given touristic season and, therefore, prices adjust to sell the available capacities (using, e.g., 'last-minute discounts'). As illustrated in Case 3.4, technological progress may change the way firms behave in the market place and, thereby, the appropriate model to represent it.

Case 3.4 Digital revolution in the publishing industry

Digital technologies have turned 'publish on demand' (or print on demand, POD) into a common and accessible alternative (or supplement) to traditional publishing methods. POD systems allow publishers to print economically very small print runs of materials in book form, which make them particularly suitable for publications with low or fairly unpredictable demand. Compared to the traditional 'batch printing' approach, which requires books to be printed in large numbers so as to reduce unit cost, POD transfers costs from the fixed category to the variable category. Indeed, POD provides a cost-effective way of keeping the backlist going as books never go out of print (in contrast, batch printing induces lost sales or large reprint costs when books are out of print); furthermore, POD saves on storage or warehousing costs. The downside is that the actual cost of producing each individual book is rather more than the batch printing cost per unit. Comparing the publishing industry under the two technologies, it seems that the quantity competition model fits better with the batch printing technology (because prices will adjust to sell the existing capacity), and the price competition model with the POD technology (because quantity can be adjusted immediately at the announced prices).

Note that a similar 'digital revolution' is currently transforming the cinema industry. Digital technologies deeply change the way that films are made, produced and distributed. In particular, they allow the cost of distributing movies to be reduced dramatically, since moving a multi-gigabyte file containing picture and sound is much cheaper than shipping spools of 35mm film prints. As in the publishing industry, this makes it cheaper and easier to set up small cinemas and to let capacities quickly adjust to the fluctuations of the audience.

3.4   Strategic substitutes and strategic complements

The comparison of price and quantity competition with differentiated products has revealed that the two models lead to different conclusions about price–cost margins and thus market power. This comparison has also highlighted another difference between price and quantity competition models, namely in terms of how firms 'react' to actions taken by their competitors. Here, we provide a general presentation of the previous finding, which extends beyond the simple oligopoly models discussed so far, and which will be helpful in many situations with strategic interaction.[12] The analysis is based on a firm's reactions to the actions of its competitors, which are captured by the best response (or reaction) function. We are concerned with the slope of these best response functions.

Suppose that firm i has the objective function π_i which depends on some unspecified variables x_i $(i = 1, \ldots, n)$, where x_i is in the control of firm i and $x_{-i} = (x_1, \ldots, x_{i-1}, x_{i+1}, \ldots, x_n)$ is in the control of the other firms. Suppose that the variable is chosen from some compact interval of the real line. We say that the variables are *strategic complements* if, in the continuous and differentiable case, an increase in x_{-i} leads to a higher marginal product $\partial \pi_i / \partial x_i$. Formally, variables x_i are strategic complements if, for all i, we have $\partial \pi_i(x_i, x'_{-i})/\partial x_i \geq \partial \pi_i(x_i, x_{-i})/\partial x_i$ for all $x'_{-i} \geq x_{-i}$. If profits are twice differentiable, this is equivalent to $\partial^2 \pi_i(x_i, x_{-i})/\partial x_i \partial x_j \geq 0$ for all i. Strategic complementarity implies that the best response functions are upward sloping.[p]

We can also consider discrete variables. For simplicity, suppose that each variable x_i can only take two values, $x_i \in \{0, 1\}$. Formally, variables x_i are strategic complements if, for all i, we have $\pi_i(1, x'_{-i}) - \pi_i(0, x'_{-i}) \geq \pi_i(1, x_{-i}) - \pi_i(0, x_{-i})$ for all $x'_{-i} \geq x_{-i}$. The condition is formally equivalent to $\pi_i(1, x'_{-i}) + \pi_i(0, x_{-i}) \geq \pi_i(1, x_{-i}) + \pi_i(0, x'_{-i})$; that is, for $x_{-i} = 0$ and $x'_{-i} = 1$, variables are strategic complements if the sum of diagonal elements dominates the sum of off-diagonal elements.

In both the continuous and the discrete version, variables are *strategic substitutes* if the reverse inequalities hold. In particular, in the continuous version, strategic substitutability implies that best response functions are downward sloping. The two panels of Figure 3.6 illustrate the cases of strategic complements and substitutes in the model of price vs. quantity competition with differentiated products.[q]

The analysis of games with strategic complements is generally useful for three reasons. First, the existence of equilibrium is guaranteed (although there may exist multiple equilibria). Second, the set of equilibria has a smallest and a largest equilibrium. Third, games with strategic complements exhibit unambiguous comparative statics properties. While the first reason is of little relevance in models in which profits are quasi-concave, the second gives some structure on the equilibrium set in the presence of multiple equilibria. In the specification of the models that we are considering, we always have a unique equilibrium so that the second reason does not apply. However, the third reason is relevant: even if we do not obtain explicit solutions for equilibrium value, we are interested in the effect of changes in market environments on market outcomes. Let us return to the case with continuous variables. Consider a policy parameter γ and assume that an increase in this parameter globally increases marginal profits, $\partial^2 \pi_i(x_i, x_{-i}; \gamma)/\partial x_i \partial \gamma \geq 0$. Then, if variables are strategic complements, the smallest and

---

[p] In general, the continuity and differentiability of best response functions is not required: strategic complementarity corresponds to a situation in which best response functions are upward sloping (possibly with upward jumps).

[q] A health warning: while in many specifications of the Cournot model (e.g., the one with linear demand), quantities are strategic substitutes, this is not necessarily the case; correspondingly, for models with price competition. Indeed, we have seen in the previous section that the reverse applies if firms produce complementary instead of substitutable goods.

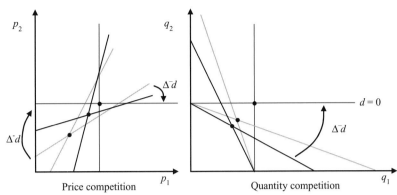

Figure 3.6 Reaction functions for price vs. quantity competition (when firms produce substitutable goods)

largest Nash equilibria have the property that a policy change from γ to γ', with $\gamma' > \gamma$, leads to an equilibrium in which both firms weakly increase their choices, $x^*(\gamma') \geq x^*(\gamma)$. Clearly, if there is a unique Nash equilibrium, we have the unique prediction that x^* weakly increases in γ.

Lesson 3.12   **If the firms' choices are strategic complements (i.e., if best response functions slope upwards) and if an increase in some parameter of the market environment raises marginal profits, then an increase in this parameter leads firms to increase their strategic choice at equilibrium.**

The intuition comes directly from the second partial derivatives. Strategic complementarity implies that for a given market environment γ, firm i optimally reacts to an increase in x_{-i} by increasing x_i. The condition $\partial^2 \pi_i(x_i, x_{-i}; \gamma)/\partial x_i \partial \gamma \geq 0$ says that given the behaviour of competitors x_{-i}, firm i optimally reacts to an increase in the policy parameter γ by increasing x_i. This means that an increase in γ leads to an outward shift of the best response function. Strategic interaction amplifies the effect of the policy change on x.

As an illustration, take the linear demand model of product differentiation that we analysed above. We showed that for substitutable products (i.e., for $d > 0$), prices are strategic complements. Now, if we let the degree of product differentiation increase (i.e., if we let the parameter d decrease), we observe that firms set higher prices at equilibrium. This is depicted in the left panel of Figure 3.6. Analytically, assuming that both firms have zero marginal costs, the profit function under price competition can be written as

$$\pi_i^B(p_i, p_j; d) = p_i(\tilde{a} - \tilde{b}p_i + \tilde{d}p_j) = p_i \frac{1}{b^2 - d^2}((b - d)a - bp_i + dp_j).$$

Then, we check that, around symmetric prices, an increase in product differentiation (i.e., a lower d) increases marginal profits:

$$\left.\frac{\partial^2 \pi_i^B(p_i, p_j; d)}{\partial p_i \partial d}\right|_{p_i = p_j = p} = \left.\frac{-a(b - d)^2 + (b^2 + d^2)p_j - 4bdp_i}{(b - d)^2(b + d)^2}\right|_{p_i = p_j = p}$$

$$= -\frac{(b - d)^2(a - p) + 2bd}{(b - d)^2(b + d)^2} < 0.$$

We should thus have that a decrease in d leads the firms to increase their equilibrium price choice: $p_i^B(d') > p_i^B(d)$ for $d' < d$. In this simple model, one can directly check the explicit solution for equilibrium prices and one observes indeed that $p_i^B = a(b-d)/(2b-d)$ is a decreasing function of d. For more complex models, monotone comparative statics results are powerful tools.[13]

3.5   Estimating market power

Markets differ in their degree of competitiveness. This may depend on the characteristics of the industry, on the conduct of firms (e.g. in their degree of collusion), and on the particular point in time the analysis is carried out. In general, a large price–cost margin is associated with a lack of competitive pressure. Following the theoretical models presented above, we consider markets in which products can be approximated to be homogeneous. Furthermore, we maintain the symmetry assumption that we invoked at various instances above.

Market demand is characterized by the demand equation

$$p = P(q, x),$$

where q is the total quantity in the market and x is a vector of exogenous variables that affects demand (but not costs). Marginal costs are supposed to be given by a function $c(q, w)$, where w is a vector of exogenous variables that affect (variable) costs.

One approach of empirically estimating market power is to postulate that various market structures can be nested in a single model.[14] Let marginal revenue be written as a function depending on a conduct parameter λ,

$$MR(\lambda) = p + \lambda \frac{\partial P(q, x)}{\partial q} q.$$

If $\lambda = 0$, the market is competitive, as would happen in the symmetric model of pure Bertrand competition. If $\lambda = 1$, we are in a monopoly situation and the firm fully takes into account the effect of a change of total output on price. In the n-firm symmetric Cournot model, we have $\lambda = 1/n$.

At equilibrium, marginal revenue is equal to marginal cost,

$$MR(\lambda) = p + \lambda \frac{\partial P(q, x)}{\partial q} q = c(q, w). \tag{3.10}$$

The basic model then consists of the demand equation and the equilibrium condition. It can be estimated non-parametrically (allowing for a flexible cost function).

How can we interpret the parameter λ? First, we may interpret λ literally as the firm's conjecture as to how strongly price reacts to its change in output. Clearly, in a monopoly world in which the firm knows the demand curve, it has to attribute $\lambda = 1$. However, in an oligopoly environment, it may expect competitors to adjust output so that $dq_{-i}/dq_i \neq 0$, where q_{-i} denotes the aggregate output of competitors. This is the basic property of the *conjectural variations approach*. It implies that in the n-firm symmetric quantitative competition model, λ may be different from $1/n$. Note that such conjectures are incompatible with Nash behaviour, which takes output of competitors as given. Consider a constant conjecture $\gamma = dq_{-i}/dq_i$.

The first-order condition of profit maximization in a market in which all firms hold constant conjectures γ can then be written as

$$p + (1 + \gamma)\frac{\partial P(q, x)}{\partial q}q_i = c(q, w).$$

Since in 'equilibrium' $q_i = q/n$, we obtain a relationship between the conjectural variation parameter γ and the conduct parameter λ: $\lambda = (1 + \gamma)/n$.

Thus we can infer from the observed or estimated conduct parameter λ and the observed number of firms n the conjectural variation parameter. We can thus see this exercise as the estimation of a static conjectural variation model. However, as pointed out above, conjectural variations different from zero are at odds with a game-theoretic static analysis. Alternatively, we can see conjectural variations as a short-cut for an explicit dynamic specification. In one such dynamic specification, firms compete in prices for two periods (products are symmetric but differentiated). Firms only observe their own realized demand; the demand intercept is unknown. Here, the first-period price can be used to manipulate the competitor's perception. This implies that a higher first-period price (leading to a lower first-period quantity q_i^1) makes the competitor choose a higher price in the second period (resulting in a lower second-period quantity q_j^2). Hence, $dq_j^2/dq_i^1 > 0.$[15]

A second interpretation is to be agnostic about the precise game being played. Rewriting the equilibrium condition, we have $p - c(q, w) = -\lambda(\partial P/\partial q)q$ or that the Lerner index satisfies

$$L = \frac{p - c(q, w)}{p} = -\lambda\frac{\partial P(q, x)}{\partial q}\frac{q}{p} = \frac{\lambda}{\eta},$$

where η is the price elasticity of demand. Here, λ can be interpreted as an index of market power.

Lacking cost data, the question is whether we can identify and thus estimate our index of market power λ. Suppose we have many observations of our endogenous variables p and q and our exogenous variables w and x. We then can write output as a function of exogenous variables w and x, $q = g_1(w, x)$. This equation is always identified. Since price is given by $p = P(q, x)$, we have $p = P(g_1(w, x), x) = g_2(w, x)$, which is also identified.[r] The equilibrium condition (3.10) is identified if there is a single marginal cost function $c(q, w)$ and a single index λ that satisfy this condition. Identification here is only a problem for some particular functional forms of demand, which, however, are often used in theoretical models (namely that demand is linear or has a constant-elasticity).

In the empirical estimation, one has to take care of two issues: the estimation of endogenous variables on the right-hand side and the feature that the index λ is a ratio of two estimated parameters. Once these two issues are properly taken care of, we have to interpret results. Following the second interpretation, we can simply treat λ as a continuous variable. Alternatively, we may explicitly test, e.g., the Cournot model and thus accept or reject the

---

[r] Recall that the identification problem in econometrics has to do with being able to solve for unique values of the parameters of the structural model from the values of the parameters of the reduced form of the model (the reduced form of a model being the one in which the endogenous variables are expressed as functions of the exogenous variables).

hypothesis that a particular market can properly be described as a Cournot market (so that λ takes a particular value).

Empirical estimates of λ or the Lerner index L have been obtained for a number of industries including textiles and tobacco. In his econometric study, Applebaum (1982) finds that textiles are priced close to marginal cost ($L = 0.07$), whereas tobacco enjoys a larger markup ($L = 0.65$) in his data set.[s] We return to the empirical estimation of market power in imperfectly competitive markets in later chapters, in particular, when considering differentiated product markets.

Review questions

1. How does product differentiation relax price competition? Illustrate with examples.

2. How does the number of firms in the industry affect the equilibrium of quantity competition?

3. When firms choose first their capacity of production and next, the price of their product, this two-stage competition sometimes looks like (one-stage) Cournot competition. Under which conditions?

4. Using a unified model of horizontal product differentiation, one comes to the conclusion that price competition is fiercer than quantity competition. Explain the intuition behind this result.

5. Define the concepts of strategic complements and strategic substitutes. Illustrate with examples.

6. What characteristics of a specific industry will you look for to determine whether this industry is better represented by price competition or by quantity competition? Discuss.

Further reading

The original literature on oligopoly theories dates back to the nineteenth and the early twentieth centuries. The seminal treatments of quantity and price competition are due, respectively, to Cournot (1838) and Bertrand (1883). Edgeworth (1897) introduced the notion of capacity constraints in price competition. Hotelling (1929) extended price competition by considering a spatial-differentiation model. This literature might be

---

[s] The author uses econometric production theory techniques in a framework which enables him to estimate the conjectural variation. The data are obtained from the US *Survey of Current Business*, over the period 1947–71.

difficult to read as it does not make use of the same vocabulary and concepts (in particular, the game-theoretical concepts) that are current nowadays. We prefer thus to refer you to Shapiro (1989), who provides a good and exhaustive introduction to oligopoly theory. For more on specific issues, see Spulber (1995) for price competition with uncertain costs, Kreps and Scheinkman (1983) on the capacity-then-price game, and Bulow, Geanakoplos and Klemperer (1985) for the concepts of strategic complements and substitutes.

4 Dynamic aspects of imperfect competition

So far in this part, we have only considered models that are *static*, in the sense that firms simultaneously take their decision at a single point in time.[a] This is clearly a simplified representation of reality but it helped us a great deal to understand the basic principles of oligopoly competition. Now, we want to extend the analysis by incorporating the time dimension. First, in Section 4.1, we examine situations in which firms do not take their decisions simultaneously but sequentially. One firm might indeed have the opportunity to choose its price or its quantity before the other firms in the industry, and it is important to investigate whether such opportunity benefits or hurts the firm. Second, in Section 4.2, we endogenize the number of firms in the industry; that is, assuming that the only impediment to entry is a fixed set-up cost, we analyse the entry decision that precedes price or quantity competition. Our main concern is to compare the number of firms that freely enter the industry, so as to exhaust all profit opportunities, with the number of firms that a social planner would choose. Third, in Section 4.3, we first distinguish endogenous from exogenous sunk cost industries and analyse how market size affects market concentration. We then sketch a stochastic dynamic model of firm turnover that allows us to analyse the effect of market size on the number of firms, their efficiency levels and firm turnover.

4.1 Sequential choice: Stackelberg

In the models of the previous chapter, firms were assumed to make their strategic decisions in a simultaneous way. The term 'simultaneous' does not have to be taken in its literal sense, though. What is meant by simultaneous decision making is not that decisions are made at the exact same moment, but rather that firms are not able to observe each other's decision before making their own. While this assumption is reasonable in a large number of market environments, there exist situations where some firms have the possibility to act before their competitors, who are then in a position to observe those firms' previous choices. Take the pharmaceutical industry as an illustration. Because of patent protection, firms set the price of their patented drugs before producers of generic drugs enter the market and set their own price.[b]

When decision making is sequential rather than simultaneous, a series of new issues arises. The first immediate question is to know whether it is preferable to be a *leader* or to be a *follower*. In other words, is it better to act first, and impose one's decision upon the competitors as a *fait accompli*? Or is it better to wait and see, and use the observation of the first mover's

---

[a] The only exception was the capacity-then-price model.

[b] See Chapters 18 and 19 for a complete treatment of patents and a closer look at the pharmaceutical industry.

decisions to inform one's own decision? The answer to this question mainly depends on the nature of the strategic variables and on the number of firms moving at different stages. To show this, we contrast sequential games where a single leader decides before either a single follower or an endogenous number of followers take their entry decision; we also contrast quantity and price competition.

Next, sequential decision making implicitly relies on the assumption that the first mover will not review its decision once the second mover has made its move. This supposes that the first mover has some form of *commitment* at its disposal. We need thus to discuss when and how such commitment is available for the firms.

4.1.1   One leader and one follower

Is it better for a firm to be a leader or a follower? We will say that there is a *first-mover advantage* if a firm gets a higher payoff in the game in which it is a leader than in the symmetric game in which it is a follower. Otherwise, we will say that there is a *second-mover advantage*. Because the way firms react to each other's decisions differs according to the nature of the strategic variable, sequentiality is likely to have different impacts under quantity and under price competition. This is why we distinguish the two cases.

Quantity competition

Let us start with the well-known von Stackelberg's (1934) critique of the Cournot equilibrium. Like Cournot, Stackelberg analyses a duopoly model where firms choose quantities. The difference with Cournot lies in the timing structure: instead of supposing that the two firms choose their quantity simultaneously, Stackelberg lets one firm (called the *leader*) choose its quantity before the other (called the *follower*). The solution concept changes as well: instead of looking for the Nash equilibrium of a one-stage game, one looks for the subgame perfect equilibrium of a two-stage game (of perfect information, with exogenously given first and second movers).

We examine the Stackelberg game (or leader–follower game) in a very simple framework. Let the inverse demand function be given by $P(q_1, q_2) = a - q_1 - q_2$, and suppose that both firms have identical constant marginal costs, which we set equal to zero. Without loss of generality, let firm 1 be the leader and firm 2, the follower. As we look for a subgame perfect equilibrium, we solve the game backwards and start with firm 2's problem. Given the quantity q_1 chosen by firm 1, firm 2 chooses its quantity q_2 to maximize its profits $\pi_2 = (a - q_1 - q_2)q_2$. From the first-order condition, one finds firm 2's reaction to the observed quantity of firm 1: $q_2(q_1) = (1/2)(a - q_1)$. We can now proceed to the first stage. The leader chooses its quantity q_1 to maximize its profits, anticipating the effect its choice will have on the follower's subsequent choice. That is, the leader's programme can be written as

$$\max_{q_1} \pi_1 = (a - q_1 - q_2(q_1))q_1 = \tfrac{1}{2}(a - q_1)q_1.$$

Here, the best response function of the follower is inserted in the objective function of the leader. This means that the leader correctly conjectures how the follower will respond to its choice q_1. This is in contrast to the Cournot model in which firm 1 takes the quantity choice of firm 2 as given. The profit-maximizing quantity choice is easily found as $q_1^L = a/2$ (with L for leader). Hence, the follower chooses $q_2^F = q_2\left(q_1^L\right) = a/4$ (with F for follower). The market price is then equal to $P(q_1^L, q_2^F) = a/4$, which allows us to compute the profits at the subgame perfect equilibrium:

$$\pi_1^L = \frac{a^2}{8} \quad \text{and} \quad \pi_2^F = \frac{a^2}{16}.$$

A first immediate conclusion follows from the comparison of these profit levels: as $\pi_1^L > \pi_2^F$ and firms are assumed to have the same cost function, each firm gets a higher payoff when being the leader rather than the follower. There is thus a *first-mover advantage*. A second set of results emerges when comparing the previous subgame perfect equilibrium with the Nash equilibrium of the (simultaneous) Cournot game. In the latter case, it is easily verified (using the analysis of the previous chapter) that both firms choose a quantity $q^C = a/3$ and earn profits equal to $\pi^C = a^2/9$ (with C for Cournot). We thus observe that, *compared to simultaneous quantity choices, the leader produces a larger quantity and makes larger profits, whereas the follower produces a lower quantity and makes lower profits.*

To understand the intuition behind these results, note that the leader has stronger incentives to increase its quantity when the follower observes and reacts to this quantity, than when the follower does not. To see this, start from the Nash equilibrium of the Cournot game $\left(q_1^C, q_2^C\right)$. As the first-order condition of profit-maximization is satisfied for firm 1, we necessarily have

$$P\left(q_1^C, q_2^C\right) + \frac{\partial P\left(q_1^C, q_2^C\right)}{\partial q_1} q_1 = 0. \tag{4.1}$$

Consider now the leader's problem in the sequential-move game. As the leader anticipates the follower's reaction, its marginal profit writes as

$$\frac{\partial \pi_1^L}{\partial q_1} = P\left(q_1, q_2\left(q_1\right)\right) + \frac{\partial P\left(q_1, q_2\left(q_1\right)\right)}{\partial q_1} q_1 + \frac{\partial P(q_1, q_2\left(q_1\right))}{\partial q_2} \frac{dq_2}{dq_1} q_1.$$

Let us now evaluate the leader's marginal profits at q_1^C. By definition of the Nash equilibrium, $q_2\left(q_1^C\right) = q_2^C$. Therefore, using (4.1), we see that the sum of the first two terms is equal to zero. We are thus left with

$$\left. \frac{\partial \pi_1^L}{\partial q_1} \right|_{q_1 = q_1^C} = \frac{\partial P\left(q_1^C, q_2^C\right)}{\partial q_2} \frac{dq_2}{dq_1} q_1^C > 0.$$

The positive sign follows from the facts that (i) the market price decreases with the follower's quantity ($\partial P/\partial q_2 < 0$) and (ii) quantities are strategic substitutes (which is synonymous to best response functions sloping downwards, $dq_2/dq_1 < 0$). Therefore, in the sequential move game, the leader increases its profits when expanding its quantity beyond the Cournot quantity. It inevitably follows that the follower will have no choice but to reduce its quantity below the Cournot one (and make lower profits), which explains the first-mover advantage.

We thus have the following ranking of profit levels for both firms:

$$\pi_i^L > \pi_i^C > \pi_i^F. \tag{4.2}$$

Although this result has been derived in a simple linear model with symmetric firms, it can be generalized to a much broader class of models (with nonlinear demand and costs, and asymmetric players).[16] We can thus draw the following general lesson.

Lesson 4.1	Consider a duopoly producing substitutable products and let one firm (the leader) choose its quantity before the other firm (the follower). At the subgame perfect equilibrium of this two-stage game, firms enjoy a first-mover advantage. Furthermore, the leader is better off and the follower is worse off than at the Nash equilibrium of the Cournot game (in which firms choose their quantity simultaneously).

Price competition

Crucial in the previous result was the fact that quantities are strategic substitutes: it is because the follower responds to an increase in the leader's quantity by reducing its own quantity that the leader finds it profitable to commit to a larger quantity than in the Cournot case. Hence, one suspects that the analysis changes in the presence of strategic complements, as is the case with price competition.[c] A quick look at the 'pure' Bertrand model suffices to convince us that there might be no first-mover advantage under price competition. Consider two firms setting sequentially their price for a homogeneous product. Suppose that both firms have constant marginal costs and that firm 1 is more efficient than firm 2: $c_1 < c_2$. As assumed above, all consumers buy from the cheapest firm and, in case of identical prices, the more efficient firm gets all the demand. We argued in Chapter 3 that in the simultaneous move game, $p = c_2$ is the most reasonable equilibrium.[d] Now, suppose that firm 1 sets its price p_1 before firm 2. In the second period, firm 2's reaction to p_1 is to set p_2 just below p_1 as long as $p_1 > c_2$ and to set $p_2 = c_2$ otherwise. In the first period, anticipating firm 2's reaction, firm 1 optimally chooses $p_1 = c_2$. Applying the same argument, we see that if we reverse the roles, we have firm 2 setting $p_2 = c_2$, followed by firm 1 setting $p_1 = c_2$. In sum, the prices set at the subgame perfect equilibrium of the two sequential games are the same as in the simultaneous game. Nothing changes and, in particular, there is no timing advantage in the sense that firms get the same profits whether they play as leader or as follower.

Naturally, the previous example is rather extreme because each firm's demand is totally discontinuous along the price diagonal. The latter feature disappears when products are differentiated. Then, one intuitively expects that price competition be characterized by a second-mover advantage. Here, it seems preferable to be the follower and keep the flexibility of undercutting the rival, rather than to be the leader and commit to one's strategic choice.

---

[c] We consider here substitutable products, for which best response functions slope downwards under quantity competition (strategic substitutability) and upwards under price competition (strategic complementarity). Recall that the opposite prevails if the products are complements. Actually, price competition with complementary (resp. substitutable) products is the dual problem of quantity competition with substitutable (resp. complementary) products. All the results we derive here for substitutable products can thus be easily transposed to the case of complementary products.

[d] Recall that this is so as long as the cost difference is not too large (so that the monopoly price corresponding to cost c_1 is larger than c_2).

Let us check that this intuition is correct in the case of symmetric firms. Let the (symmetric) demands by given by $Q_1(p_1, p_2)$ and $Q_2(p_1, p_2)$, and assume for simplicity that marginal costs are equal to zero. As above, we evaluate the marginal profit of the leader (say firm 1) at the prices that would prevail at the equilibrium of the simultaneous game. We write these prices p_1^B and p_2^B (with B for Bertrand); we also denote the follower's reaction to the leader's price by $p_2(p_1)$ and we know that $p_2^B = p_2(p_1^B)$. Hence,

$$
\left. \frac{\partial \pi_1^L}{\partial p_1} \right|_{p_1 = p_1^B} = \underbrace{Q_1\left(p_1^B, p_2^B\right) + p_1^B \frac{\partial Q_1\left(p_1^B, p_2^B\right)}{\partial p_1}}_{=0 \text{ by the FOC of the Bertrand game}} + \underbrace{p_1^B \frac{\partial Q_1\left(p_1^B, p_2^B\right)}{\partial p_2}}_{>0} \underbrace{\frac{dp_2}{dp_1}}_{>0}.
$$

We see here that because the leader's demand increases in the follower's price and because prices are strategic complements, the leader has an incentive to set a price exceeding p_1^B. Now, consider such a price $\bar{p}_1 > p_1^B$ and look at the firms' profits. Note first that with symmetric profit functions, we have that $p_2(\bar{p}_1) < \bar{p}_1$ for $\bar{p}_1 > p_1^B$ (this can be checked on Figure 3.6 above). The leader's profits can be written as $\pi_1^L = \pi(\bar{p}_1, p_2(\bar{p}_1))$ and the follower's profits as $\pi_2^F = \pi(p_2(\bar{p}_1), \bar{p}_1)$. Because $p_2(\bar{p}_1)$ is firm 2's best response to $\bar{p}_1$, we necessarily have that $\pi(p_2(\bar{p}_1), \bar{p}_1) > \pi(\bar{p}_1, \bar{p}_1)$. Also, because each firm's profit increases in the rival price and because $p_2(\bar{p}_1) < \bar{p}_1$, it follows that $\pi(\bar{p}_1, \bar{p}_1) > \pi(\bar{p}_1, p_2(\bar{p}_1))$. Combining the latter two inequalities, we conclude that $\pi(p_2(\bar{p}_1), \bar{p}_1) > \pi(\bar{p}_1, p_2(\bar{p}_1))$, i.e., that $\pi_2^F > \pi_1^L$ or that each firm (because of symmetry) gets a higher profit while being a follower, meaning that there is a second-mover advantage.

When firms are asymmetric, the previous conclusion still holds as long as the unit costs of the two firms are sufficiently close. Otherwise, for sufficiently different unit costs, it can be shown that only the high-cost firm has a second-mover advantage, whereas the low-cost firm has a first-mover advantage.[17]

> **Lesson 4.2**   Consider a duopoly producing substitutable products under constant unit costs, and let one firm (the leader) choose its price before the other firm (the follower). At the subgame perfect equilibrium of this two-stage game, at least one firm has a second-mover advantage.

4.1.2   One leader and an endogenous number of followers

The analysis so far was restricted to a leader–follower model with a single competitor. However, in some markets entry is endogenous and a leader faces a large and endogenous number of followers. Reconsider the case of a market for a drug whose patent expired. Here, the previous patent holder can be seen as the leader and generic producers that consider entering the market are the followers. In such markets, it has been reported that the leader cuts its price, possibly as an attempt to keep the number of entrants low. Instead of describing such a market by the dominant firm model from above, in which generic producers behave in a perfectly competitive and non-strategic way, a better approximation may be to view these generic producers as followers in an imperfectly competitive market environment. In the resulting two-stage leader–follower game with a large and endogenous number of firms entering at stage 2, it can be shown that the leader always acts more aggressively than the followers, in the sense that it always sets a larger quantity or a lower price than the followers.[18] As we have seen above, this is not the case in the leader–follower price-setting game with a single follower. The reason is that with a fixed number of firms, the leader is mainly concerned about the reactions of the other firms to its own choices. The qualitative feature then depends on whether variables are strategic substitutes or complements. By contrast, when entry is endogenous, the leader is also concerned about the effect of its own choices on the number of firms that enter. Here, an aggressive behaviour limits the number of firms that enter at stage 2. In order to capture a large market share, the leader is willing to accept a low markup.

4.1.3   Commitment

Implicit behind the sequential games we analysed above was the assumption that the leader can *commit* to its choice. The concept of commitment is certainly as old as military strategy but it was first really articulated, in the context of social sciences, by Schelling (1960). In a situation of conflicts between two parties, each party would like to influence the other party's behaviour in its favour. Threats and promises can be used to this end ('I'll punish you if you don't act the way I want' or 'I'll reward you if you act the way I want'). But, as Schelling argues, threats and promises are nothing more than cheap talk if they are not transformed into a commitment, i.e., if one does not find a way to become committed or obligated to carry out the threat or to keep the promise should it become necessary to do so. In other words, to influence someone else's choices, one needs to convince them that they will be punished if they do not act in the intended way (or that they will be rewarded if they do) because it will indeed be in one's best interest to inflict the punishment (or to grant the reward).

In the situations we study here, we understand that to achieve its goal, a commitment by one firm must be *visible*, *understandable* and *credible* for the competitors. The games we analysed are two-stage games of perfect information (which guarantees the visibility of the leader's move), played by rational players (which amounts to assuming that the follower correctly understands the leader's move). There remains the issue of credibility. In our modelling, it is captured by the limitation of the game to two stages. This implies in particular that the leader does not have the option to revise its initial choice at a later (third) stage of the game. In other words, the leader's choice is supposed to be irreversible. To understand the importance of this assumption, let us reconsider the quantity Stackelberg game (with inverse demand given by $p = a - q_1 - q_2$, and zero marginal costs for both firms). Recall that at the subgame perfect equilibrium, the leader produces a quantity $q_1^L = a/2$ and the follower, a quantity $q_2^F = a/4$. What would happen if we added a third (and final) stage to the game, in which the leader had the possibility to alter (at zero cost) its initial decision after observing the follower's decision? Would the previous result survive, in the sense that in the third stage, the leader would confirm its initial decision? The answer, obviously, is negative because $q_1 = a/2$ is not firm 1's best response to $q_2 = a/4$: as we saw above, the best response is $q_1 = (a - q_2)/2 = (3a)/8 < q_1^L$. Given the opportunity, the leader would reduce the quantity it initially claimed to produce.

We learn from this simple example that if the leader's move is reversible, the threat it carries (here, the threat is to grab a large share of the market) is not credible and, therefore, the leader's move loses all commitment power. Hence, the sequential timing structures we have considered only make sense if the leader is able, not only to act before the follower, but also (and as importantly) to make a move that it will credibly not reverse at a future date. The leader must therefore find a way to limit its future ability to modify its previous decisions. This is the well-known *paradox of commitment*: it is by limiting one's own options that one can manage to influence the opponent's course of actions in one's interest.[e]

Do we have irreversibility in the situations we considered above? Admittedly, how much to produce and what price to charge can be seen as decisions that are easy to reverse and that only have short-run impacts. So, the general stories we have told need some more compelling interpretation. As for the quantity Stackelberg game, we could understand it as a sequential choice of capacities rather than quantities. For instance, building a new plant, which cannot be easily redeployed outside its intended use, has a high commitment value. As for the price sequential game, external factors or previous technology choices might reduce a firm's ability to modify its prices. For instance, regulated firms often have to submit any proposed price change to the approval of the regulatory authorities (whereas their unregulated competitors can freely change their prices); a catalogue firm faces much higher costs of changing its prices than an Internet firm does. Contract provisions can also facilitate commitment on prices. One such provision is the *most-favoured customer clause*, whereby a firm commits to extend to the buyer the same price terms that it offers to its other customers. If one firm in a duopoly offers such a clause, this allows the firms to coordinate on a Stackelberg-like outcome, with the firm proposing the clause ending up as a leader in the pricing game.[19]

In the previous examples, firms make some additional decision (e.g., proposing a specific contract provision, choosing to sell through catalogue or on the Internet, etc.) in order to gain commitment value. We defer until Chapter 16 a full discussion of such 'strategic' choices (which precede and shape the 'tactical' decisions such as the choice of prices and quantities). We will provide a taxonomy of business strategies that will rely, as one can already guess now, on the distinction between strategic substitutes and complements. Indeed, we have contrasted above the case of quantity competition in which firms strive to be the leader and wish to commit to an 'aggressive' course of action by producing a large quantity, and the case of price competition in which firms prefer a follower's position and, if leading, commit to a 'soft' course of action by setting a high price.

4.2   Free entry: endogenous number of firms

Our analysis so far was limited to markets with a given number of firms. However, in a market economy, firms enter if they see profitable opportunities. Thus, an implicit assumption of our previous analysis has been that additional entry is prohibitively costly. Take the opposite view that there are no entry or exit barriers other than entry costs. In this case, we expect firms to enter as long as they can make economic profits. It is such a situation of free entry that we turn to now. Formally, we can analyse this as a two-stage game in which firms first enter and then decide on price or quantity. We call the subgame perfect equilibrium of this game the 'free-entry equilibrium'. We proceed by presenting two models of free entry with a finite number of firms. We first allow for free entry in the Cournot model and then turn to an extension of the

[e] History is rich with examples of army generals who crossed a river into the enemy's country and, after crossing the bridge, instructed that it be burnt so as to eliminate their troops' only method of retreat. Left with the simple alternative of winning or losing their lives, these armies generally won great victories.

Hotelling model, where firms can freely locate on a circle. Finally, we analyse a market with many small firms that, in contrast to perfect competition, all face downward sloping demand curves, a situation called monopolistic competition.

4.2.1   Properties of free-entry equilibria

Since firm entry (and exit) often requires time and is costly, we can view this analysis as applicable in the long term. Yet, if becoming active is costless, we may want to allow for entry even in the short term, which may be seen as a good approximation in some virtual markets (see also our analysis with uninformed consumers in Chapter 7). Clearly, in the long term, we should allow for entry and exit in an industry provided there are no long-run restrictions to entry and exit (see, however, the discussion of regulated industries in Chapter 2).

Our first task will be to consider an industry in which firms are not subject to shocks so that we can analyse the equilibrium number of firms in a two-stage model. Here, at stage 1, firms decide whether to enter and, at stage 2, they set their short-run strategic variable, which may be price or quantity. Consider an industry in which firms are symmetric so that each active firm makes $\pi(n)$ in equilibrium at stage 2, where n is the number of active firms in the industry. A standard property of oligopolistic markets is that profits are decreasing in the number of firms, $\pi(n) > \pi(n+1)$ for all n. If the firm has to pay an entry cost e at stage 1, then under free entry, the number of active firms n^e is determined by $\pi(n^e) - e > 0$ and $\pi(n^e + 1) - e < 0$. Ignoring integer constraints, we can simply write that n^e satisfies $\pi(n^e) - e = 0$. This implies that, everything else being equal, *an increase in fixed entry costs reduces the number of active firms*. Indeed, in many markets, entry costs can be seen as the main detriment to competition, as illustrated in Case 4.1.

Case 4.1 Entry in small cities in the US

Bresnahan and Reiss (1990, 1991) analyse homogeneous product markets in which the (equilibrium) number of firms changes in response to shifts in market demand. They analyse data from a set of separate, rural retail and professional markets in small US cities (with an average of 3740 inhabitants). The entry model is estimated by an ordered probit model where all firms in the market are treated as identical homogeneous competitors. While this restriction is not met in many markets, it appears to be appropriate in the markets under consideration because they do not offer much scope for spatial differentiation. The study shows that a firm enters a market if its profit margin is sufficient to cover its fixed costs of operating. Profit margins are driven down by additional entry.

The general perception is that society benefits from a larger number of active firms. Unambiguously, more competition exerts stronger pressure on price so that effectively consumers are better off. In differentiated product industries, an additional attractive feature of more (single-product) firms is an increase in product variety which directly increases consumer surplus, keeping prices fixed. However, total surplus considerations have to include the increase in costs stemming from more active firms. Indeed, decreasing average costs (on some set of quantities) are the main reason for a limited number of active firms. In particular, the duplication of entry costs is to the detriment of society. Hence, using the total surplus criterion, we may wonder whether the unregulated market provides a socially excessive or insufficient number of firms in the market. The following subsections develop a number of imperfect competition models to address this question.

4.2.2   The Cournot model with free entry

Suppose that firms must incur fixed set-up costs $e > 0$ upon entry and compete à la Cournot once they have entered the market. We want to compare the number of entrants at the free-entry equilibrium with the number that a second-best social planner would choose. By second-best, we mean that the planner is assumed to be able to control entry but not the behaviour of firms once they are in the market.[20]

The second stage of the game is the Cournot model that we examined in Section 3.2. Recall that we consider a homogeneous product market with n firms. The market price is given by the inverse demand, $P(q)$, where q denotes total output. We assume that all firms have the same cost function $C(q_i)$. At the symmetric equilibrium, each firm produces the same quantity $q(n)$, which is a function of the number of firms active on the market. Then, when n firms have entered the market, the equilibrium profits per firm are equal to $\pi(n) = P(nq(n))q(n) - C(q(n)) - e$. Our analysis continues under three rather weak assumptions: (A1) individual equilibrium output decreases with the number of firms; (A2) aggregate equilibrium output increases with the number of firms; and (A3) equilibrium price remains above marginal costs whatever the number of firms.

Ignoring for now the integer constraint on the number of firms, the free-entry equilibrium number of firms, n^e, satisfies the zero-profit condition: $\pi(n^e) = 0$. On the other hand, to compute the socially optimal number of firms, we must maximize social welfare, given the Cournot behavior of the firms. That is, the socially optimal number of firms, n^*, is the number of firms that solves

$$\max_{n} W(n) \equiv \int_0^{nq(n)} P(s)\,ds - nC(q(n)) - ne.$$

We have thus that n^* satisfies the first-order condition of welfare maximization: $W'(n^*) = 0$. Differentiating $W(n)$ with respect to the number of firms, we find

$$W'(n) = P(nq(n)) \left[n\frac{\partial q(n)}{\partial n} + q(n)\right] - C(q(n)) - nC'(q(n))\frac{\partial q(n)}{\partial n} - e$$

$$= \pi(n) + n\left[P(nq(n)) - C'(q(n))\right]\frac{\partial q(n)}{\partial n}. \tag{4.3}$$

The latter expression shows that the marginal impact of an additional entrant on social welfare is made of two components: first, the new entrant contributes directly to social welfare through its profits; second, the entrant indirectly affects welfare by altering the behaviour of the firms that are already active on the market. In particular, if a *business-stealing effect* is present, existing firms react to the new entry by contracting their output levels: $q(n+1) < q(n)$ for all n. Ignoring the integer constraint, the business-stealing effect implies thus that $\partial q(n)/\partial n < 0$. Assuming that the equilibrium price remains above marginal costs whatever the number of firms on the market, it follows that the second term in expression (4.3) is negative: entry induces an aggregate output reduction of $n(\partial q(n)/\partial n)$, which in turn causes a reduction of social welfare of $[P(nq(n)) - C'(q(n))]n(\partial q(n)/\partial n)$. We can thus conclude that because of the business-stealing effect,

$$\pi\,(n) > W'(n),$$

meaning that *the evaluation of the desirability of entry is higher for the marginal entrant than for the social planner.*

We thus expect that the free-entry equilibrium number of firms will be too large from a welfare perspective: $n^e > n^*$. To complete the argument, we still need to show that profits per firm fall as n increases. Differentiating $\pi\,(n)$ with respect to n, we obtain

$$\pi'\,(n) = \left[P\,(nq\,(n)) - C'\,(q\,(n))\right]\frac{\partial q(n)}{\partial n} + q\,(n)\,P'\,(nq\,(n))\,\frac{\partial(nq(n))}{\partial n}.$$

The business-stealing effect and our assumption that the equilibrium price remains above marginal costs imply that the first term is negative. As for the second term, it is also negative if we assume that the (postentry) equilibrium aggregate output increases with the number of firms active on the market: $\partial\,(nq\,(n))\,/\partial n$.

Let us now collect our results. By definition, $W'\,(n^*) = 0$; combined with the finding that $\pi\,(n) > W'\,(n)$, it follows that $\pi\,(n^*) > 0 = \pi\,(n^e)$ (by definition of the free-entry equilibrium number of firms). Because $\pi'\,(n) < 0$, the latter inequality implies that $n^e > n^*$.

Lesson 4.3   **Because of the business-stealing effect, the symmetric Cournot model with free entry exhibits socially excessive entry.**

We want now to address the relevance of these assumptions by considering a specific framework. To this end, we come back to the symmetric Cournot model with linear cost and demand functions that we analysed in Section 3.2. Recall that the inverse demand is given by $P\,(q) = a - bq$ and that all firms have the same constant marginal costs of production; variable costs are $C\,(q_i) = cq_i$ with $c < a$. The equilibrium quantity is found as

$$q\,(n) = \frac{a-c}{b\,(n+1)}.$$

It is immediate to see that $\partial\,(q\,(n))\,/\partial n < 0$, meaning that assumption (A1) is satisfied in the present case. We check that assumptions (A2) and (A3) are satisfied too:

$$\frac{\partial(nq(n))}{\partial n} = \frac{\partial}{\partial n}\left(\frac{n(a-c)}{b(n+1)}\right) = \frac{a-c}{b(n+1)^2} > 0,$$

$$p\,(n) - c = a - c - bn\frac{(a-c)}{b(n+1)} = \frac{a-c}{n+1} > 0\ \forall n.$$

We can now express individual profits and social welfare at the Cournot equilibrium for a given number of firms:

$$\pi(n) = \frac{1}{b}\left(\frac{a-c}{n+1}\right)^2 - e,$$

$$W\,(n) = \frac{n\,(n+2)}{2b}\left(\frac{a-c}{n+1}\right)^2 - ne.$$

Ignoring the integer constraint, we find the free-entry equilibrium and the second-best number of firms as follows:

$$\pi(n^e) = 0 \Leftrightarrow (n^e + 1)^2 = \frac{(a-c)^2}{be},$$

$$W'(n^*) = 0 \Leftrightarrow (n^* + 1)^3 = \frac{(a-c)^2}{be}.$$

A quick comparison of the latter two equalities confirms Lesson 4.3. For instance, if it is socially optimal to have three firms in the industry ($n^* = 3$), than seven firms will actually enter at the free-entry equilibrium (as $(7 + 1)^2 = (3 + 1)^3$). This example also shows that even in the presence of integer constraints, socially excessive entry is an issue. To avoid socially excessive entry, society may opt for entry regulation. Examples of entry regulation is the auctioning of entry permits as in the case of broadcasting or mobile telephony. Here, the motivation for restricted entry is, however, the scarcity of spectrum. As shown above, the argument can be made for entry restriction even in the absence of such scarcities.

It can also be shown that the result of excessive entry can be reversed when the integer constraint is fully taken into account. It is important to note, however, that entry may be insufficient only in special circumstances and never by more than one firm. That is, the general result when taking the integer constraint into account is $n^e \geq n^* - 1$.[21] To illustrate this point, suppose that parameters are such that $8/3 \leq (a-c)^2/be < 4$. The second inequality implies that $\pi(1) < 0$, meaning that no firm enters the industry; on the other hand, it follows from the first inequality that $W(1) > 0$, meaning that a monopoly is the socially optimal outcome. Hence, in that special case (and in that case only), $n^* = 1 > n^e = 0$.[f]

4.2.3   Price competition with free entry

To analyse free entry followed by price competition, we return to the Salop circle that was introduced in Chapter 3: we assume that firms and consumers are located around a circle instead of an interval. In particular, we assume that a unit mass of consumers are uniformly distributed on a circle with a circumference equal to 1. Firms are also located on the circle and consumers travel to their preferred firm along the circle.[g] As above, we consider a two-stage game: in the first stage, firms decide whether or not to enter the market (entry entails a fixed setup cost of e); in the second stage, the firms that have entered set a price for their product and consumers make their purchasing decision.

As for the first stage, because our focus is on entry, we leave aside the location decision and assume instead that it is exogenously imposed upon firms that they must locate equidistantly from one another. So, assuming that n firms enter the market, the distance between two neighbouring firms is equal to $1/n$. Recall that, at equilibrium, firms set prices $p(n) = c + \tau/n$ and sell to $1/n$ consumers. We can now turn to the first stage of the game. As above, the free-entry equilibrium number of firms is determined by the zero profit condition

---

[f] It is easily checked that for $4 \leq (a-c)^2/be < 9$, $n^e = n^* = 1$ and for $(a-c)^2/be > 9$, $n^e > n^*$.

[g] A geographical interpretation of this model is a city such that all shops are located along a peripheral highway, on which consumers have to travel because the city centre is very hard to cross. An interpretation in terms of product space is the choice of airline schedules on a 24-hour clock.

(abstracting again from the integer constraint):

$$\pi\left(n^e\right) = 0 \Leftrightarrow (p-c)\frac{1}{n^e} - e = 0 \Leftrightarrow \frac{\tau}{\left(n^e\right)^2} = e$$

$$\Leftrightarrow n^e = \sqrt{\frac{\tau}{e}}.$$

It follows that the price at the free-entry equilibrium is equal to

$$p = c + \sqrt{\tau e}.$$

We observe that if the setup cost e increases, fewer firms enter the market and the market price is higher; also, if the transportation cost τ increases, the larger product differentiation allows more firms to enter and to charge higher prices.

Let us now derive the number of firms that a social planner would allow in the market. In this model, whether the planner is able to control the firms' pricing decision or not does not really matter. Indeed, because all consumers are identical and have an inelastic demand, the profit margin is nothing but a transfer from the consumers to the firms. The planner selects thus the number of firms so as to minimize total costs, i.e., the sum of the firms' fixed setup costs and of the consumers' transportation costs. That is, the socially optimal number of firms, n^*, is the number of firms that solves

$$\min_n TC\left(n\right) \equiv ne + \tau\left(2n\int_0^{1/(2n)} s\, ds\right) = ne + \frac{\tau}{4n}.$$

Differentiating with respect to the number of firms, we find

$$TC'\left(n^*\right) = 0 \Leftrightarrow e - \frac{\tau}{4\left(n^*\right)^2} = 0$$

$$\Leftrightarrow n^* = \frac{1}{2}\sqrt{\frac{\tau}{e}} = \frac{1}{2}n^e.$$

We observe thus that at the free-entry equilibrium, twice as many firms enter than it would be socially optimal.[22]

Lesson 4.4   **In the Salop circle model, the market generates socially excessive entry.**

The result is therefore qualitatively the same as in the above Cournot model. To understand the result, note that entry entails mixed welfare effects. On the one hand, there is a positive effect due to lower prices (as in the Cournot model) or to more variety and hence, lower consumer transportation costs (in the Salop model).[h] On the other hand, there is a negative effect coming from the duplication of fixed costs. Note that private and social incentives to enter diverge: a firm's entry is motivated by the expectation that operating profits are above fixed costs. It is irrelevant for this firm whether revenue comes from 'stealing the business' from competitors or from generating new business. The social planner, however, is interested

[h] As already indicated, lower prices are welfare neutral in the Salop model because they do not affect the quantity consumed.

only in revenues from new business, which comes from lower price, and not in revenue coming from business stealing (note that it is also concerned with a better match of consumers to products). The possible dominance of the business-stealing effect explains why too many firms may enter the market and why regulation of entry may be welfare-improving (e.g., by taxing entry through a licensing fee). The following case documents socially excessive entry.

Case 4.2 Socially excessive entry of radio stations in the US

Berry and Waldfogel (1999) estimate a differentiated product market with entry. A commercial radio station's revenue equals the annual advertising revenue per listener, which is the price set by the radio station, times the number of listeners. More radio stations and thus more product variety are viable the larger the number of listeners in one geographic market. Thus metropolitan areas with large population support more radio stations than smaller ones. The authors use data on advertising prices, number of stations and radio listening in 135 US metropolitan areas. They estimate the function that captures the population share that are listeners and the inverse demand function for advertising.[23] These two functions provide an estimate of how revenues vary with the number of radio stations. New radio stations are substitutes for existing ones. Because of the business-stealing effect private benefits of entry may exceed social benefits. Using the free-entry assumption, the authors infer the distribution of fixed station costs. The estimates of revenues and fixed costs are then used to calculate the surplus of radio stations and advertisers. The number of stations under free entry is then compared to the number in the social optimum (in a second-best sense, i.e. where the planner can only control the number of stations). The number of radio stations under free entry is found to be socially excessive. Relative to the social optimum, the welfare loss of free entry is calculated to be 40 per cent of industry revenue.

4.2.4 Monopolistic competition

The industries we have looked at so far comprise a small number of firms. Yet, there also exist industries comprising many firms, each offering a differentiated product. Such industries correspond to a market structure referred to, by Chamberlin (1933), as monopolistic competition. *Monopolistic competition* exhibits the following four features, the first three relating to perfect competition and the fourth to monopoly (hence this hybrid denomination): (1) there is a large number of firms, each producing a single variety of a differentiated product; (2) each firm is negligible, in the sense that firms do not interact directly through strategic interdependence but only indirectly through aggregate demand effects; (3) there are no entry or exit barriers so that economic profits are zero; (4) each firm faces a downward-sloping demand curve and therefore enjoys market power. The markets for restaurants, clothing, shoes and service industries in large cities can be viewed as sharing these features.

We introduce here a model that shares these four features and is usually presented under the common label of *S-D-S model*. (This model is named this way because it is due to Spence, 1976, and Dixit and Stiglitz, 1977). This model features two additional differences with the Salop circle model that we just analysed. First, on the Salop circle, each firm competes for consumers only with its direct neighbours (i.e., with the firms offering similar products); in contrast, we will now assume that each product competes for sales with all other products. The second difference relates to the modelling of consumers: the Salop model relies on a continuum of consumers with heterogenous tastes for the available products; the present model assumes instead that there exists a single, representative, consumer who loves variety and who consumes therefore a little bit of every available product.[i] Perhaps the most important difference is that the entry of an additional firm does not make existing products closer substitutes.

Consider a representative consumer with utility function

$$U = q_0^{1-\gamma} \widetilde{q}^{\gamma} \quad \text{with} \quad 0 < \gamma < 1.$$

In this formulation, q_0 is the quantity consumed of a unique nondifferentiated good (which is chosen as numéraire) and $\widetilde{q}$ is the quantity of a composite differentiated good defined by an index of the CES (constant-elasticity-of-substitution) type:

$$\widetilde{q} = \left(\sum_{i=1}^{n} q_i^{\frac{\sigma-1}{\sigma}} \right)^{\frac{\sigma}{\sigma-1}}, \tag{4.4}$$

where q_i is the quantity consumed of variety i, n the number of available varieties, and $\sigma > 1$ is the elasticity of substitution between any two varieties.

The representative consumer maximizes U subject to the budget constraint $q_0 + \widetilde{p}\widetilde{q} \leq y$, where $\widetilde{p}$ is the price index of the differentiated good (to be defined below) and y is the consumer's income. As the consumer exhausts her budget, we can use $q_0 = y - \widetilde{p}\widetilde{q}$ to rewrite the consumer's maximization programme as

$$\max_{\widetilde{q}} U = (y - \widetilde{p}\widetilde{q})^{1-\gamma} \widetilde{q}^{\gamma}.$$

The first-order condition yields

$$\frac{\partial U}{\partial \widetilde{q}} = \widetilde{q}^{\gamma-1} (y - \widetilde{p}\widetilde{q})^{-\gamma} \left[\gamma (y - \widetilde{p}\widetilde{q}) - (1-\gamma) \widetilde{p}\widetilde{q} \right] = 0$$

$$\Leftrightarrow \widetilde{p}\widetilde{q} = \gamma y.$$

From the previous expression, we see that the consumer spends a constant share of her budget, γy, on the differentiated good. Now, to find the quantity consumed of each variety, we have to maximize (4.4) with respect to q_i, subject to $\sum_{i=1}^{n} p_i q_i \leq \gamma y$. The Lagrangian for this problem writes as $L = \widetilde{q} + \lambda \left(\gamma y - \sum_{j=1}^{n} p_j q_j \right)$. The first-order conditions are the following:

$$\frac{\partial L}{\partial q_i} = \frac{\partial \widetilde{q}}{\partial q_i} - \lambda p_i = 0 \Leftrightarrow \widetilde{q}^{1/\sigma} q_i^{-1/\sigma} = \lambda p_i \Leftrightarrow q_i = \widetilde{q}\lambda^{-\sigma} p_i^{-\sigma},$$

$$\frac{\partial L}{\partial \lambda} = \gamma y - \sum_{j=1}^{n} p_j q_j = 0 \Leftrightarrow \sum_{j=1}^{n} p_j q_j = \gamma y.$$

Combining these two equalities, we obtain

$$\sum_{j=1}^{n} p_j \left(\widetilde{q}\lambda^{-\sigma} p_j^{-\sigma} \right) = \gamma y \Leftrightarrow \widetilde{q}\lambda^{-\sigma} = \frac{\gamma y}{\sum_j p_j^{-(\sigma-1)}}.$$

[i] We will come back to these various modelling choices when studying models of (horizontal and vertical) product differentiation in Chapter 5.

Introducing the latter expression into the expression for q_i yields the demand function of the representative consumer for variety i:

$$q_i = \left(\tilde{p}^{\sigma-1}\gamma y\right) p_i^{-\sigma}. \tag{4.5}$$

We observe that the demand for a particular variety is a function of the prices of all varieties. If the firm producing variety i charges a larger price than the other firms, the representative consumer purchases less of variety i, but the demand for this variety remains positive because of the consumer's love for variety. The demand functions respect thus the second and fourth features of monopolistic competition.

The price index $\tilde{p}$ is obtained by introducing (4.5) into (4.4) and by using the fact that $\tilde{p}\tilde{q} = \gamma y$:

$$\tilde{q} = \left(\sum_{i=1}^{n}\left(\left(\tilde{p}^{\sigma-1}\gamma y\right) p_i^{-\sigma}\right)^{\frac{\sigma-1}{\sigma}}\right)^{\frac{\sigma}{\sigma-1}} = \tilde{p}^{\sigma}\tilde{q}\left(\sum_{i=1}^{n} p_i^{-(\sigma-1)}\right)^{\frac{\sigma}{\sigma-1}}$$

$$\Leftrightarrow \tilde{p} = \left(\sum_{j=1}^{n} p_j^{-(\sigma-1)}\right)^{-1/(\sigma-1)}.$$

Note that if all prices are identical and equal to p, then $\tilde{p} = pn^{-1/(\sigma-1)}$, which is a decreasing function of the number n of varieties since $\sigma > 1$.

The demand elasticity for product i is[j]

$$\eta_i = -\frac{\partial q_i}{\partial p_i}\frac{p_i}{q_i} = \sigma \left(\tilde{p}^{\sigma-1}\gamma y\right) p_i^{-\sigma-1}\frac{p_i}{\left(\tilde{p}^{\sigma-1}\gamma y\right) p_i^{-\sigma}}$$

$$= \sigma.$$

Firm i chooses its profit-maximizing price according to the inverse-elasticity rule (see Section 2.3). Assuming that all firms have the same constant marginal cost c, we have

$$\frac{p_i - c}{p_i} = \frac{1}{\sigma} \Leftrightarrow p_i = \frac{\sigma}{\sigma-1}c.$$

Note that price is independent of total expenditure in the market. We can then compute the equilibrium quantity and profits for a given number of varieties:

$$q_i(n) = \frac{\sigma-1}{\sigma}\frac{\gamma y}{nc} \quad \text{and} \quad \pi_i(n) = \frac{\gamma y}{n\sigma} - e.$$

Finally, we can turn to the first stage of the game and determine the free-entry equilibrium number of firms by imposing the zero-profit condition:

$$\pi_i(n^e) = 0 \Leftrightarrow n^e = \frac{1}{\sigma}\frac{\gamma y}{e}.$$

The equilibrium number of firms (and thus of varieties) increases with the budget share that the representative consumer allocates to the differentiated good (γy), decreases with the fixed

---

[j] As announced above, σ also measures the elasticity of substitution between two varieties. Note first that $q_i/q_j = (p_i/p_j)^{-\sigma}$: the relative demand for two varieties is independent of the prices of the other varieties. It follows that the elasticity of substitution is $-\partial \ln(q_i/q_j)/\partial \ln(p_i/p_j) = \sigma$.

set up cost (e), and decreases with the elasticity of substitution between varieties (σ). At the free-entry equilibrium, each firm produces a quantity $q(n^e) = (\sigma - 1)e/c$.

Let us now derive the social optimum. We continue to take a second-best perspective by assuming that the planner can regulate entry but not output. Suppose also that the planner finances the fixed entry costs (ne) by a lump-sum tax on the consumer's income; the disposable income is then equal to $y - ne$. Using the above results, we know that the consumer allocates a share γ of her disposable income to the differentiated good: $\tilde{p}\tilde{q} = \gamma(y - ne)$. Because $p_i = \frac{\sigma}{\sigma-1}c$ for all firms, the price index is given by $\tilde{p} = \frac{\sigma}{\sigma-1}cn^{-1/(\sigma-1)}$ and because of symmetry, the consumer chooses the same quantity q of each variety, which implies that $\tilde{q} = qn^{\sigma/(\sigma-1)}$. Hence, $\tilde{p}\tilde{q} = \frac{\sigma}{\sigma-1}cnq$. Using the fact that $\tilde{p}\tilde{q} = \gamma(y - ne)$, we find that

$$q = \frac{\sigma - 1}{\sigma}\frac{\gamma(y - ne)}{nc} \quad \text{and} \quad \tilde{q} = \frac{\sigma - 1}{\sigma}\frac{\gamma(y - ne)}{c}n^{\frac{1}{\sigma-1}}.$$

We also know that the consumer chooses $q_0 = (1 - \gamma)(y - ne)$. The consumer's utility rewrites thus as

$$U = q_0^{1-\gamma}\tilde{q}^{\gamma} = [(1 - \gamma)(y - ne)]^{1-\gamma}\left[\frac{\sigma - 1}{\sigma}\frac{\gamma(y - ne)}{c}n^{\frac{1}{\sigma-1}}\right]^{\gamma}$$

$$= K \cdot n^{\frac{\gamma}{\sigma-1}}(y - ne),$$

where $K \equiv (1 - \gamma)^{1-\gamma}\left(\frac{\sigma-1}{\sigma}\frac{\gamma}{c}\right)^{\gamma}$. Because the firms' total gross profits do not depend on the number of firms (it is equal to $\gamma y/\sigma$) and because the fixed entry costs (ne) are financed by a lump-sum tax on the consumer's income, the socially optimal number of firms is found by maximizing the consumer's utility with respect to n:

$$\frac{\partial U}{\partial n} = K\left(\frac{\gamma}{\sigma-1}n^{\frac{\gamma}{\sigma-1}-1}(y - ne) - en^{\frac{\gamma}{\sigma-1}}\right) = 0$$

$$\Leftrightarrow n^* = \frac{1}{\sigma - (1 - \gamma)}\frac{\gamma y}{e} > n^e = \frac{1}{\sigma}\frac{\gamma y}{e}.$$

We observe thus that under the present specification, monopolistic competition yields insufficient entry from a social viewpoint. However, under different specifications of the S-D-S model, one can obtain the opposite result. The tension between private and social incentives arises because additional entry may not be profitable but the total surplus added may be above costs so that entry is socially insufficient. However, since parts of the profit are diverted away from competitors, entry may as well be socially excessive. We therefore close our analysis with the following general lesson.

Lesson 4.5   In models of monopolistic competition (and models of imperfect competition more generally), the market may generate excessive or insufficient entry. Whether too many or too few firms enter depends on how much an entrant can appropriate of the surplus generated by the introduction of an additional differentiated variety.

4.3   Industry concentration and firm turnover

In this section, our first goal is to clarify the distinction between endogenous and exogenous sunk cost industries and to analyse how market size affects market concentration. We then sketch a stochastic dynamic model of firm turnover that allows us to analyse the effect of market size on the number of firms, their efficiency levels and firm turnover.

4.3.1   Exogenous versus endogenous sunk costs

The underlying assumption of our analysis of entry was that firms, in order to enter an industry, have to pay a cost e up-front, which cannot be recovered upon exiting the market. This cost e is called an exogenous sunk cost. (It is called exogenous because it is a parameter in the model that is not affected by decisions.) Depending on demand and cost conditions, the equilibrium number of firms was determined. We then answered the question as to whether the market provides socially excessive or socially insufficient entry. We now turn to a different question, namely how the number of firms (and the concentration in an industry) changes as market conditions change. We first answer this question within our previous framework, assuming exogenous sunk costs. We then reconsider the issue when firms can partly endogenize fixed costs.

Exogenous sunk costs and industry concentration

All the above presented models with entry have the property that larger entry costs e lead to a smaller equilibrium number of firms and that an increase in market size (which acts multiplicatively on market demand for a given market size) leads to a larger equilibrium number of firms. An increase in market size allows more firms to profitably enter an industry. As market size increases, it becomes more likely that an additional firm would gain sufficient profits after entry to cover the sunk costs it incurs upon entry. This reduces industry concentration. Hence, when the market grows without bound, the industry becomes fragmented. This is most easily seen in the Cournot model: as e tends to zero, the equilibrium number of firms tends to infinity. Similarly, as the market size tends to infinity, the equilibrium number of firms tends to infinity as well. This feature can be seen as a general feature of industries in which firms of similar quality face exogenous sunk costs. Using concentration measures such as the Herfindahl index or an n-firm concentration measure such as C_4 or C_6, theory predicts that these measures are decreasing in market size.

> **Lesson 4.6**   **In industries with exogenous sunk costs, industry concentration decreases and approaches zero as market size increases.**

For empirical analyses across sectors and geographical areas, a particular model (such as a specific Cournot model) appears to be too restrictive, since a particular model with specific parameter values most likely cannot capture the multitude of different market characteristics that differ across various geographic markets. Therefore, Sutton (1991) proposes to consider the lower bound of concentration. This picks the lowest concentration measure for a number of observations with the same or similar market size. Theory then predicts that this lower bound is close to zero for market size sufficiently large. This has been documented for a number of industries, e.g. hair salons in the US.[24]

The insight that a larger market size leads to less concentration is at odds with empirical observations in some other industries. Studying such industries over time, these can be characterized by a large increase in market demand over time together with a persistently high concentration in the industry (e.g. measured by the Herfindahl index). Also, provided that distinct geographic markets can be identified, there is a persistently high concentration across these markets of varying size. Both observations contradict economic theory based on exogenous sunk costs.

It may appear hard to imagine that any increase in input costs (and other 'exogenous' costs) could neutralize the effect of larger market size. This begs the question as to how economic theory and empirical observations can be reconciled. For this we develop a theory that presumes that fixed costs are partly endogenous as opposed to exogenous.[25]

A quality-augmented Cournot model

To incorporate investments in quality, we consider a quality-augmented Cournot model.[26] In this model, after the entry stage, firms invest in quality s_i and afterward compete in quantities. In particular, suppose that consumers have a Cobb–Douglas utility function of the form $u(q_0, q) = q_0^{1-\gamma}(sq)^{\gamma}$. Then consumers spend a fraction γ of their income y on the good that is offered by Cournot competitors. Suppose that there is a measure M of consumers in the market. This denotes the market size. Total consumer expenditure in the market is $M\gamma y$. For all n active firms, we must have that the price–quality ratio is the same across firms, i.e., $p_i/s_i = p_j/s_j \equiv \lambda$ for all i, j active. Hence, industry revenues satisfies

$$R = \sum p_i q_i = \lambda \sum s_i q_i.$$

Rewriting this equation, we have

$$\lambda \equiv R \Big/ \left(\sum s_i q_i \right). \tag{4.6}$$

Note that λ depends on firm i's quantity,

$$\frac{d\lambda}{dq_i} = -\frac{Rs_i}{\left(\sum s_i q_i \right)^2} = -\frac{s_i}{R}\lambda^2.$$

A firm maximizes its profit $M\pi$ where π is the profit per unit mass of consumers,

$$M\pi = (p_i - c)q_i = (\lambda s_i - c)q_i.$$

Taking the first-order condition with respect to q_i we have

$$\frac{d\pi_i}{dq_i} = (\lambda s_i - c) + s_i q_i \frac{d\lambda}{dq_i} = 0.$$

Substituting and rearranging, we obtain

$$\lambda s_i - c = \frac{s_i^2 q_i}{R} \lambda^2 \text{ or, equivalently,}$$

$$\frac{R}{\lambda} - \frac{cR}{\lambda^2 s_i} = s_i q_i. \tag{4.7}$$

Summing over all these n rewritten first-order conditions, we have

$$\frac{nR}{\lambda} - \frac{cR}{\lambda^2} \sum_i \frac{1}{s_i} = \sum_i s_i q_i,$$

which, as follows from (4.6), is equal to R/λ since total revenues is equal to total expenditure. Substituting, dividing by R and multiplying by λ, we find that

$$n - \frac{c}{\lambda} \sum_i \frac{1}{s_i} = 1.$$

Rearranging this equation, we get

$$\lambda = \frac{c}{n-1} \sum_i \frac{1}{s_i}. \tag{4.8}$$

We can now use this expression and substitute for λ in the rewritten first-order condition (4.7):

$$s_i q_i = \frac{R}{\frac{c}{n-1} \sum_i \frac{1}{s_i}} - \frac{cR}{\left(\frac{c}{n-1} \sum_i \frac{1}{s_i}\right)^2 s_i}$$

$$\Leftrightarrow s_i q_i = \frac{R}{c} \left(\frac{n-1}{\sum_i \frac{1}{s_i}} - \frac{(n-1)^2}{\left(\sum_i \frac{1}{s_i}\right)^2 s_i} \right)$$

$$\Leftrightarrow q_i = \frac{R}{c} \frac{n-1}{s_i \sum_i \frac{1}{s_i}} \left(1 - \frac{(n-1)}{s_i \sum_i \frac{1}{s_i}} \right). \tag{4.9}$$

This gives us a necessary and sufficient condition for all firms to make positive sales, namely that the term in brackets is positive for all firms. If a particular firm i is the firm with the lowest quality, we must have

$$\frac{1}{n-1} \sum_i \frac{1}{s_i} > \frac{1}{s_i}.$$

Hence, qualities are not allowed to be too different. We observe that the equilibrium quantity is independent of quality if all firms set the same quality. This is due to our Cobb–Douglas utility specification according to which total expenditure in the market is fixed.

To obtain profit functions for the stage at which firms set qualities, we have to substitute for price. Using Equation (4.8) and the definition of λ, we find that the equilibrium price-cost margin of firm i satisfies

$$p_i - c = \left(\frac{s_i}{n-1} \sum_i \frac{1}{s_i} - 1 \right) c.$$

Using this expression for price–cost margin and the expression for demand in (4.9), we can write equilibrium profits at the quantity competition stage as

$$(p_i - c)q_i = \left(\frac{s_i}{n-1} \sum_i \frac{1}{s_i} - 1 \right) \frac{n-1}{s_i \sum_i \frac{1}{s_i}} \left(1 - \frac{n-1}{s_i \sum_i \frac{1}{s_i}} \right) R$$

$$= \left(1 - \frac{n-1}{s_i \sum_i \frac{1}{s_i}} \right)^2 R.$$

If we include entry costs e and the fixed costs for producing quality, $C(s)$, then in a symmetric equilibrium for given quality $s_i \equiv s$, the net profit of a firm is equal to $(p^*(n) - c)q^*(n) - e - C(s) = R/(n^2) - e - C(s) = M\gamma y/(n^2) - e - C(s)$. This implies that as market size M explodes, the number of firms turns to infinity and illustrates our previous lesson that in a two-stage entry-then-quantity-competition model, there is no strictly positive lower bound of concentration.

Endogenous sunk costs and industry concentration

Let us now analyse stages 1 and 2 of the three stage game in which, first, firms decide whether to enter, second, which quality to develop, and, third, which quantity to produce. We consider stage 2 after n firms have entered the industry.

If all other firms have set quality $\hat{s}$, firm i's profit (gross of the entry cost) is

$$\left(1 - \frac{n-1}{s_i \left(\frac{1}{s_i} + \frac{n-1}{\hat{s}} \right)} \right)^2 R - C(s_i) = \left(1 - \frac{1}{\frac{1}{n-1} + \frac{s_i}{\hat{s}}} \right)^2 R - C(s_i).$$

While the result we will derive holds more generally, we confine ourselves to a particular cost function $C(s_i) = \alpha s_i^\beta$. In symmetric equilibrium with $s_i = \hat{s} \equiv s^*$, we must have

$$2 \left(1 - \frac{1}{\frac{1}{n-1} + 1} \right) \frac{\frac{1}{s^*}}{\left(\frac{1}{n-1} + 1 \right)^2} R = \alpha \beta (s^*)^{\beta-1}$$

or, equivalently,

$$\frac{(n-1)^2}{n^3} R = \frac{\alpha \beta}{2} (s^*)^\beta.$$

Thus equilibrium quality is

$$s^* = \sqrt[\beta]{\frac{2R}{\alpha \beta} \frac{(n-1)^2}{n^3}},$$

which is increasing in the industry revenues $R = M\gamma y$. This implies that as market size M increases, firms compete more fiercely in quality. At least some of the profits are competed away by increasing qualities, which lead to higher investments but leave industry revenues unaffected.

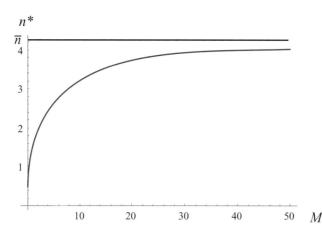

Figure 4.1 Equilibrium number of firms in an endogenous sunk cost industry

The net profit of a firm is thus

$$\frac{M\gamma y}{n^2} - e - \frac{2}{\beta}\frac{(n-1)^2}{n^3}M\gamma y = \frac{M\gamma y}{n^3}\left(n - \frac{2}{\beta}(n-1)^2\right) - e.$$

For profits to be positive, it must be the case that $n - \frac{2}{\beta}(n-1)^2$ is positive. For instance, if $\beta = 3$, this expression is positive for $n \leq 3$. Note that this expression is independent of market size M. Hence, even as M explodes, there is an upper bound on the number of firms that the industry can sustain in equilibrium (and thus there is a positive lower bound on concentration).

The upper bound on the number of firms is given by $\bar{n} \leq 1 + \frac{1}{4}(\beta + \sqrt{\beta}\sqrt{8 + \beta})$. Figure 4.1 gives the equilibrium number of firms in a particular example (where we assume parameter values $\beta = 5$, $e = 0.2$ and $\gamma y = 1$). We observe that the equilibrium number of firms is increasing with market size but cannot exceed four even as the market size becomes infinitely large. This shows that the market has the property of a natural oligopoly because only a small number of firms can be sustained, independently of market size.[k]

When market size increases, the market becomes more valuable, which makes firms invest more in quality. The incentives to invest in quality are driven by strategic reasons: it gives firms a better position at the quantity-competition stage. In equilibrium, all firms invest the same amount, so that their relative position remains unchanged.

Lesson 4.7   In markets with endogenous sunk costs, even as the size of the market grows without bounds, there is a strictly positive upper bound on the equilibrium number of firms.

This shows that the existence of endogenous costs that are sunk at the final competition stage can significantly change the relationship between market size and concentration.

[k] Note that in this section we have elaborated on a Cournot model with quality investment; however, the insight that only a small number of firms can be supported in an industry can also be made in models with price competition and differentiated products. In those models only a small number of firms can possibly be sustained in equilibrium even absent an escalation of investment costs as market size increases, i.e. sunk costs do not need to be endogenous. We will analyse such markets in Chapter 5.

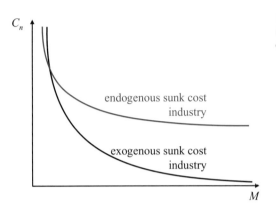

Figure 4.2 The lower bound of concentration in endogenous versus exogenous sunk cost industries

Endogenous sunk costs here arise from fixed investments that increase the value of the firm's product to customers, such as advertising or improvements in product quality due to product innovations. Alternatively, these costs lower the marginal cost of production, such as process innovations. The model can be rewritten to allow for this alternative interpretation. Thus the theory applies more generally to sunk investments that increase the price–cost margin on each unit of the product sold.

As discussed above, when comparing various geographic markets of an industry or following an industry over time, an empirical investigation faces the challenge that not only market size but also other factors may differ. Hence, for a similar market size, one may observe industries with very different degrees of concentration. Sutton (1991) therefore develops his theory with the goal to establish that endogenous sunk cost industries show a strictly positive lower bound of concentration; he does not claim that there is a functional relationship between market size and concentration. The difference between such a lower bound for endogenous versus exogenous sunk cost industries is illustrated in Figure 4.2. Here C_n refers to a concentration measure, e.g. the market share of the four or six largest firms or the Herfindahl index. Our previous lesson thus can be reformulated as follows: *in industries with endogenous sunk costs, there is a lower bound of market concentration that decreases in market size, but there is a strictly positive minimal concentration that holds for any market size.*

Sutton (1991) and various follow-up studies provide empirical support to the view that, due to endogenous sunk costs, many industries are highly concentrated, independently of market size. A key feature of these industries is that firms make important fixed investments in advertising or R&D.[27] Here we provide a particularly intriguing example: the concentration of supermarkets in the US.

Case 4.3 Endogenous sunk costs for supermarkets in the US[28]

Ellickson (2007) analyses market concentration of US supermarkets in 1998 (defined as stores selling a full line of food products and making more than $2 million of annual sales). Since a large revenue share of supermarkets comes from perishable products, scale economies across the whole US market are not very relevant and there is the hope that a disaggregated analysis can shed some light on the issue as to whether endogenous sunk costs are relevant in this market. However, it is a priori not clear that the US can indeed be divided into separate geographic markets with respect to supermarkets. Interestingly, most supermarket chains use very similar locations for their distribution centre. Ellickson then identifies 51 distribution markets; using his definition of distribution markets, he finds that on average around 82 per cent of revenues of a store comes from products that are supplied by a distribution centre in the same distribution market to which the store is assigned.

Ellickson finds that the distribution markets are highly concentrated and dominated by four to six supermarket chains, independently of the size of the particular distribution market. Is this due to endogenous sunk costs? To answer this question, we first have to find out what is the relevant quality variable in this environment. Since consumers prefer supermarkets that offer a larger variety, the quality of a supermarket is captured by the available number of products as a measure of product variety. A supermarket chain can make two types of investment to increase variety: it can increase shelf space by building larger stores and it can increase the number of products for given shelf space. For the latter, it has to better manage its distribution systems e.g. by installing advanced logistical software, optical scanners and specialized sorting equipment. This allows the chain to continuously replenish products in its stores. Investments in distribution systems have become important since the 1980s. As a result of both types of investment and larger shelf space, the average number of products in a store has increased from around 14 000 in 1980 to 22 000 in 1994, and to 30 000 in 2004. Second, it is observed that investment costs are mostly incurred within each distribution market and scale economies across these markets cannot be seen as a source of concentration. While some smaller supermarkets survive, the dominance of four to six chains in each distribution market suggests that the supermarket industry is best characterized as an endogenous sunk cost industry in which larger market size leads to an escalation in investments in distribution systems and store space.

4.3.2   Dynamic firm entry and exit

While static models can provide us with predictions concerning the number of firms that are active in an industry, they are unable to generate entry and exit dynamics in the market. We would expect market entry in growing industries and market exit in declining industries. However, many industries are characterized by simultaneous entry and exit.[29] Two industry features generate simultaneous entry and exit: first, firms are heterogeneous (e.g. with respect to their marginal costs) and second, their prospects change over time, e.g. because they are subject to idiosyncratic cost shocks. To understand simultaneous entry and exit it is useful to focus on a stationary environment. In such a setting we compare stationary equilibria across such environments: this yields, e.g., cross-country predictions or predictions about outcomes before and after an unexpected supply or demand shock has hit an industry. In particular, we want to understand how market size affects the number of active firms and turnover rates.

To this end we sketch a stochastic dynamic model of a monopolistically competitive industry, i.e. an industry with many small firms facing downward sloping demand.[30] In this model there is no positive lower bound of concentration, i.e., we return to the analysis of exogenous sunk cost industries. Before we start, let us state a health warning: the analysis below is rather general because particular distributional assumptions and demand specifications do not make the analysis more compact; for some readers, the material may become too technical.

Considering small firms allows us to analyse equilibrium distributions of active firms. Firms are thus a continuum and their 'number' is a measure. Firms differ by their realized marginal cost c and whether they were active in the previous period. Realized marginal cost of a new firm at date t is drawn from the $[0, 1]$ interval according to some distribution function G. Established firms (which were active in the previous period) inherit their marginal cost from $t - 1$ with probability α. With the remaining probability $1 - \alpha$, they draw again their cost parameter according to the same distribution as new firms. The parameter α measures the persistency of technology (or of input prices due to contractual restrictions).

There are many consumers giving rise to a market of size M. Time t is discrete. Firms maximize the discounted sum of expected profits over an infinite horizon; the common discount factor is δ. Per-period equilibrium profits per unit mass of consumers are denoted by π, which depends on the realized marginal costs and the set of firms that is active. Inactive firms receive their outside option, which is assumed to be equal for all firms and is normalized to zero.

In each period, the market operates as follows. At stage 1, potential entrants decide whether or not to enter. If a firm enters, its entry cost e is sunk at this stage. It is only after the entry stage, at stage 2, that firms learn their realization of marginal costs. At stage 3, new and established firms decide whether to exit the market and become inactive. At stage 4, firms pay fixed cost f and compete in the imperfectly competitive market. We will not specify a particular competition game but assume that equilibrium profits satisfy a number of properties.

A firm's equilibrium profit $M\pi$ (gross of fixed costs) at the competition stage in a market of size M depends on the firm's realized marginal cost and on the number and the distribution of efficiency levels of competing firms. The population of firms can be described as a measure μ.[31] Hence, we can write equilibrium profits of a firm of type c as $M\pi(c; \mu) - f$. We make a number of assumptions on profits π. First, we assume that firms with lower marginal costs make strictly higher profits (when positive); this appears to be a natural assumption that should be met by any reasonable oligopoly model. Second, we introduce a partial ordering $\succeq$ on the set of measures μ: if for all admissible c we have that $\pi(c; \mu) \geq \pi(c; \mu')$, we say that μ is preferred to μ' (i.e. $\mu \succeq \mu'$). We require that if there are more firms at each efficiency level under the measure μ' than under the measure μ, then $\mu \succeq \mu'$. The meaning here is that competition is less intense under the measure μ so that a firm's profits are higher (e.g. because there are fewer or less efficient competing firms). We assume that measures μ are completely ordered under $\succeq$ so that if a low-cost firm is doing better under measure μ than under measure μ', this also holds for a high-cost firm (that has positive likelihood in the measure μ). Finally, we require π to be continuous.[32]

Two additional assumptions are needed. Suppose that firms prefer μ to μ'. First, more efficient firms are assumed to gain more in absolute terms from a change from μ' to μ than less efficient firms, i.e., $\pi(c; \mu) - \pi(c; \mu')$ is strictly decreasing in c for all types c that are present under μ. Note that this is equivalent to equilibrium output per firm being increasing in μ (where μ is ordered according to $\succeq$). Second, *less* efficient firms are assumed to gain in relative terms: consider a rather inefficient firm; this firm gains relatively more compared to a more efficient firm under the measure μ instead of μ'. To be precise, $\pi(c; \mu)/\pi(c; \mu')$ is strictly increasing in c for all types c that are present under μ. Note that this is equivalent to equilibrium price being increasing in μ. For instance, the Cournot model and the differentiated product model with linear demand and price-setting firms satisfy all assumptions (both have to be specified for a continuum number of firms).[33]

In this model, we want to understand the properties of stationary equilibria. In a stationary equilibrium, the number and distribution of firms (i.e., μ) is constant over time. First, consider the decision of a firm at the exit stage. For this we compare the value of the firm when it exits, which is normalized to zero, to the value when it stays in the market. In the latter case, it makes profit $M\pi(c;\mu) - f$ in the present period. In the next period, it either inherits its costs from the previous period (with probability α) or it draws its cost parameter again from the distribution G. Hence, the value of a firm of type c at the exit stage is

$$V(c) = \max\{0, \overline{V}(c)\} \text{ where}$$

$$\overline{V}(c) = M\pi(c;\mu) - f + \delta \left[\alpha V(c) + (1-\alpha) \int_0^1 V(z)G(dz) \right].$$

We define c^* as the largest solution such that $V(c) > 0$ for all $c < c^*$. Hence, a firm of type $c > c^*$ optimally exits the market whereas a firm of type $c < c^*$ stays. In a stationary equilibrium with entry, $V(c^*) = 0$.

At the entry stage, a potential entrant achieves expected value $V^e = \int_0^1 V(c)G(dc) - e$. In a stationary equilibrium with entry, firms enter as long as their expected value is strictly positive; hence, $V^e = 0$. This implies that for $c < c^*$, we have to solve $\overline{V}(c) = M\pi(c;\mu) - f + \delta[\alpha\overline{V}(c) + (1-\alpha)e]$ which is equivalent to $\overline{V}(c) = [M\pi(c;\mu) - f + \delta(1-\alpha)e]/(1 - \delta\alpha)$. For $c > c^*$ the value function in case of entry is $\overline{V}(c) = M\pi(c;\mu) - f + \delta(1-\alpha)e$. Hence, the condition for the firm's optimal exit can be written as

$$M\pi(c^*;\mu) - f + \delta(1-\alpha)e = 0. \tag{4.10}$$

We observe that current profit for the indifferent type c^* is negative. This means that a firm stays in the market even if its current profit is negative (but not too negative) because it has a positive option value of staying in the market. This positive option value stems from the fact that it will obtain better cost realizations with positive probability in the future.

At the entry stage, the potential entrant's value can be rewritten as

$$V^e = \int_0^1 V(c)G(dc) - e$$

$$= \int_0^{c^*} \overline{V}(c)G(dc) - e$$

$$= \int_0^{c^*} \frac{M\pi(c;\mu) - f + \delta(1-\alpha)e}{1 - \delta\alpha} G(dc) - e.$$

The free entry condition thus becomes

$$\int_0^{c^*} [M\pi(c;\mu) - f + \delta(1-\alpha)e]G(dc) - (1 - \delta\alpha)e = 0. \tag{4.11}$$

A new firm that exits at a cost realization $c \geq x$ and decides optimally thereafter is said to follow an exit policy x. Its value is

$$\overline{V}(x;\mu) = \int_0^x \overline{V}(c)G(dc) - e.$$

The free entry condition can then be rewritten as $\overline{V}(c^*;\mu) = 0$. The optimal exit policy is thus determined by

$$\frac{\partial}{\partial x}\overline{V}(c^*;\mu) = 0. \tag{4.12}$$

The stationary equilibrium is then characterized by the solution to Equations (4.10), (4.11) and (4.12). Restricting the analysis to equilibria with strictly positive firm turnover, it can be shown that it is unique. The equilibrium distribution of active firms takes the same shape as the distribution function G that is truncated at c^* and rescaled. Since firms less efficient than c^* exit, we can write the measure of active firms as $\mu([0, c^*])$. If m denotes the mass of new firms, we denote by $\tau = m/\mu([0, c^*])$ the turnover rate, which, in stationary equilibrium, can be written as

$$\tau = (1-\alpha)\frac{1 - G(c^*)}{G(c^*)}.$$

We can now address the question stated at the beginning: *what is the effect of market size on the number of active firms and the turnover rate?* In a free entry equilibrium, the measure of active firms $\mu([0, c^*(M)])$ and market size M are positively related. For any given distribution of active firms and any given exit policy, an increase in market size raises the value of each active firm. Essentially, there is a market expansion effect, with prices being fixed. Hence, the measure of active firms has to increase with market size M. However, in response to an increase in M, the mass of active firms increases, which leads to a downward pressure on price. This price competition effect works differently for more versus less efficient firms: the percentage decrease in profits is stronger for less efficient firms since their markup is lower. Consider an increase in market size from M to M'. Then the firm with marginal cost $c^*(M)$ would have a negative value in the larger market of size M'. Hence, the marginal active firm in the larger market must be more efficient than in the smaller market, $c^*(M) > c^*(M')$. The competitive pressure increases with the size of the market. Consequently, firm turnover τ and market size M are positively correlated.

Lesson 4.8   In monopolistically competitive markets, an increase in market size leads to a larger total number of firms in the market. It also leads to a distribution of active firms in which only particularly efficient firms stay in the market and the turnover rate is higher. Thus firms tend to be younger in larger markets.

An implication of this result is that market integration will lead to much more concentrated distribution of costs: less efficient firms that remained active in a small market prefer to exit after market integration. Overall, market integration leads to more firm turnover not only in a transition phase but in the new stationary equilibrium. For a new firm, it is thus less likely that the firm is successful, i.e. that it receives a cost draw that makes entry worthwhile. However, due to the increase in market size, active firms obtain higher volumes.

A related result concerns fixed costs. The above theory predicts that firms tend to be younger in markets with higher fixed costs. The reason is that firms have to be more efficient to stay in the market. Hence, for an existing firm that draws a new cost parameter, it becomes more likely that it exits the market. The resulting higher firm turnover then implies that firms are younger on average.[1]

The result also allows us to compare (regional) markets that differ in market size and fixed costs. Think of the following. Do you need a haircut? What kind of hair salon should you find in a small or in a large town? Case 4.4 tells you what to expect in Sweden.

Case 4.4 Entry and exit of hair salons in Sweden

Asplund and Nocke (2006) consider hair salons in Sweden. In particular, they compare the age distribution of hair salons across local markets. Hair salons are a good candidate to provide a suitable data set. Local markets can indeed be seen as independent: who would travel a long distance to get a haircut somewhere else? Also, this is a service that is physically provided and there are no virtual haircuts, competition from the Internet can thus be ignored. This industry has a number of other features that make it a good candidate to test the above theory. First, entry and exit are not isolated events: this is an industry with high firm turnover rates. Second, the number of firms in any given (even small) market is large so that the assumption of monopolistic competition may seem adequate (which is compatible with the view that this is an exogenous sunk cost industry). Third, there are very few chains in Sweden so that complications due to multiple outlets do not need to be considered.

Local markets are defined according to postal areas. Market size of each market is proxied by the population (which is somewhat problematic in areas where there is a lot of commuting out or in). Concerning the fixed costs, it seems inappropriate to assume that they are the same across markets, in particular since rents for the salon differ between areas. To capture this additional heterogeneity across markets, land values are taken as a proxy for rents. A random sample of 1030 hair salons is analysed. This sample is split into subsamples according to market size (small or large). For the effect of market size, the empirical hypothesis is that the estimated age distribution function of firms with large market size lies above the estimated age distribution of firms with small market size. In Sweden, this hypothesis is confirmed by the data. Also, regression results show that market size has highly statistically significant negative effect on firm age. This is robust to the inclusion of various control variables (that reflect additional sources of heterogeneity across markets).

---

[1] Note that an increase of the entry costs e has a negative effect on firm turnover, in contrast to an increase of the fixed cost f.

Review questions

1. Why is there generally a first-mover advantage under sequential quantity competition (with one leader and one follower) and a second-mover advantage under sequential price competition? Explain by referring to the concepts of strategic complements and strategic substitutes.

2. When firms only face fixed setup costs when entering an industry, how is the equilibrium number of firms in the industry determined? Is regulation possibly desirable (to encourage or discourage entry)? Discuss.

3. What is the difference between endogenous and exogenous sunk costs? What are the implications for market structure?

4. Which market environments lead to simultaneous entry and exit in an industry?

Further reading

The seminal analysis of sequential quantity competition (with one leader and one follower) is due to von Stackelberg (1934). For a generalized analysis of sequential quantity and price competition, see, respectively, Amir and Grilo (1999) and Amir and Stepanova (2006). For our analysis of free-entry, we followed Mankiw and Whinston (1986) for the extension of the Cournot model, Salop (1979) for the model of localized price competition on a circle, and Spence (1976) and Dixit and Stiglitz (1977) for the model of monopolistic competition. The book by Sutton (1991) is the seminal contribution to the analysis of endogenous sunk cost industries. An updated account is provided by Sutton (2007). The model of dynamic entry and exit is due to Asplund and Nocke (2006).

Notes for Part II

1. Source: DVD price wars: How low can they go? By John Borland and Evan Hansen, 5 November 2004, CNET News.com (last consulted 1 October 2007).

2. The analysis goes back to Hansen (1988) in an auction-theoretic setting. For a general analysis of the Bertrand game, see Spulber (1995). For a derivation of expressions in the uniform-linear case, see e.g. Lofaro (2002).

3. The Sunkist story is nicely told in Arens (2004).

4. Based on 'China and Russia take on the might of Boeing and Airbus', *The Times*, 20 March 2007.

5. This model is has become widely used since Salop (1979).

6. For instance, Amir and Lambson (2000) study the symmetric case wherein all firms have the same twice continuously differentiable and non-decreasing cost function, and demand is continuously differentiable and downward-sloping. They show that the equilibrium price falls with an increase in the number of Cournot competitors if, for all Q, $p'(Q) < c(q)$ for all q in $[0, Q]$.

7. Source: DVD price wars: How low can they go? By John Borland and Evan Hansen, 5 November 2004, CNET News.com (last consulted 1 October 2007).

8. This is due to the seminal analysis by Kreps and Scheinkman (1983).

9. See Kreps and Scheinkman (1983).

10. See Davidson and Deneckere (1986) for a characterization of mixed strategies under proportional rationing.

11. The analysis is based on Singh and Vives (1984).

12. We follow here the seminal analysis of Bulow, Geanakoplos and Klemperer (1985).

13. On the theory of supermodular games, see Vives (1990) and Milgrom and Roberts (1990). For recent applications in industrial organization see e.g. Vives (2005).

14. This approach has been suggested by Just and Chern (1980), Bresnahan (1982) and Lau (1982). For an in-depth analysis of this and alternative approaches, we refer the reader to Perloff, Karp and Golan (2007), from which we heavily borrow. See also Bresnahan (1989).

15. For a formal analysis of this point see Riordan (1985). In a signalling context with private information about costs, Mailath (1989) shows qualitatively similar results.

16. Amir and Grilo (1999) show that log-concavity of the (inverse) demand function alone (i.e., regardless of the cost function) leads to ranking (4.2). One would need a log-convex demand and production being costless for at least one firm to have $\pi_i^L > \pi_i^N$.

17. Amir and Stepanova (2006) prove these results under very general conditions as they remove the common assumptions of concavity of profits in own action (or continuity and single-valuedness of the reaction curves), and of existence and uniqueness of the Bertrand equilibrium. They generalize thereby the previous analyses of Gal-Or (1985) and Dowrick (1986).

18. For a detailed analysis see Etro (2008).

19. See Cooper (1986).

20. We follow here Mankiw and Whinston (1986).

21. See Mankiw and Whinston (1986).

22. It can be shown that excessive entry also obtains when assuming quadratic (or other forms of) transportation costs.

23. The former is obtained from a nested logit model of the consumers' decision to listen. The nested logit model is explained in Chapter 5.

24. See Ellickson (2007).

25. The seminal contribution on endogenous sunk cost industries is due to Sutton (1991). This book has been reviewed by Bresnahan (1992) and Schmalensee (1992). For a recent overview, see Sutton (2007).

26. The model is presented in Chapter 3 in Sutton (1991) and Appendix B in Sutton (2007).

27. Apart from Sutton's pioneering work, we would like to mention the empirical investigations on manufacturing industries by Robinson and Chiang (1996) and Lyons, Matraves and Moffat (2001), on pharmaceuticals by Matraves (1999), and on banking by Dick (2007).

28. All the material reported in this case is from Ellickson (2007).

29. For an overview see Caves (1998). For instance, Dunne, Roberts and Samuelson (1988) is an important empirical contribution.

30. Our analysis follows Asplund and Nocke (2006), who provide more detail and analysis. Related work is by Hopenhayn (1992) who considers firm turnover in a perfectly competitive market. Related analyses in monopolistically competitive markets are provided by Das and Das (1997) and Melitz (2003). Imperfect competition models in which integer constraints have to be taken into account are less tractable. For a framework for such models, see Amir and Lambson (2003); for the Cournot analysis see Amir and Lambson (2000).

31. To be precise, this is a Borel measure.

32. To do so, we have to endow the set of measures μ with the topology of weak convergence.

33. However, the CES demand model, which has been presented in the previous section, does not satisfy the last assumption.

References for Part II

Amir, R., and Grilo, I. (1999). Stackelberg versus Cournot Equilibrium. *Games and Economic Behavior* 26: 1–21.

Amir, R., and Lambson, V. E. (2000). On the Effects of Entry in Cournot Markets. *Review of Economic Studies* 67: 235–254.

Amir, R., and Lambson, V. E. (2003). Entry, Exit, and Imperfect Competition in the Long Run. *Journal of Economic Theory* 110: 191–203.

Amir, R., and Stepanova, A. (2006). Second-Mover Advantage and Price Leadership in Bertrand Duopoly. *Games and Economic Behavior* 55: 1–20.

Applebaum, E. (1982). The Estimation of the Degree of Oligopoly Power. *Journal of Econometrics* 9: 283–299.

Arens, W. F. (2004). *Contemporary Advertising*. 9th edn. McGraw-Hill.

Asplund, M. and Nocke, V. (2006). Firm Turnover in Imperfectly Competitive Markets. *Review of Economic Studies* 73: 295–327.

Berry, S. and Waldfogel, J. (1999). Free Entry and Social Inefficiency in Radio Broadcasting. *Rand Journal of Economics* 30: 397–420.

Bertrand, J. (1883). Théorie Mathématique de la Richesse Sociale. *Journal des Savants*, 499–508.

Bresnahan, T. F. (1982). The Oligopoly Solution Concept is Identified. *Economics Letters* 10: 87–92.

Bresnahan, T. F. (1989). Empirical Studies of Industries with Market Power. In Schmalensee, R. and Willig, R. (eds.), *Handbook of Industrial Organization.* Vol. 2. Amsterdam: North-Holland. pp. 1011–1057.

Bresnahan, T. F. (1992). Sutton's Sunk Costs and Market Structure: Price Competition, Advertising, and the Evolution of Concentration: Review Article. *Rand Journal of Economics* 23: 137–152.

Bresnahan, T. F., and Reiss, P. C. (1990). Entry in Monopoly Markets. *Review of Economic Studies* 57: 531–553.

Bresnahan, T. F. and Reiss, P. C. (1991). Entry and Competition in Concentrated Markets. *Journal of Political Economy* 99: 977–1009.

Bulow, J., Geanakoplos, J. and Klemperer, P. (1985). Multimarket Oligopoly: Strategic Substitutes and Complements. *Journal of Political Economy* 93: 488–511.

Caves, R. (1998). Industrial Organization and New Findings on the Turnover and Mobility of Firms. *Journal of Economic Literature* 36: 1947–1982.

Chamberlin, E. (1933). *The Theory of Monopolistic Competition*. Cambridge, MA: Harvard University Press.

Cooper, T. (1986). Most-Favored Pricing Policy and Tacit Collusion. *Rand Journal of Economics* 17: 377–388.

Cournot, A. (1838). *Recherches sur les Principes Mathématiques de la Théorie de la Richesse*. Paris: Calmann-Lévy (new edition 1974).

Das, S. and Das, S. P. (1997). Dynamics of Entry and Exit of Firms in the Presence of Entry Adjustment Costs. *International Journal of Industrial Organization* 15: 217–241.

Davidson, C. and Deneckere, R. (1986). Long-run Competition in Capacity, Short-run Competition in Price, and the Cournot Model. *Rand Journal of Economics* 17: 404–415.

Dick, A. (2007). Market Size, Service Quality and Competition in Banking. *Journal of Money, Credit and Banking* 39: 49–81.

Dixit, A. K. and Stiglitz, J. E. (1977) Monopolistic Competition and Optimum Product Diversity. *American Economic Review* 67: 297–308.

Dowrick, S. (1986). Von Stackelberg and Cournot Duopoly: Choosing Roles. *Rand Journal of Economics* 17: 251–260.

Dunne, T., Roberts, M. J. and Samuelson, L. (1988). Patterns of Firms Entry and Exit in U.S. Manufacturing Industries. *Rand Journal of Economics* 19: 495–515.

Edgeworth, F. (1897). La Teoria Pura del Monopolio. *Giornale degli economisti* 40: 13-31. Reprinted in English as The Pure Theory of Monopoly. In *Papers Relating to Political Economy*, Vol. I, London: Macmillan: 111–142.

Ellickson, P. (2007). Does Sutton Apply to Supermarkets? *Rand Journal of Economics* 38: 43–59.

Etro, F. (2008). Stackelberg Competition with Endogenous Entry. Forthcoming in *Economic Journal*.

Gal-Or, E. (1985). First Mover and Second Mover Advantages. *International Economic Review* 26: 649–653.

Hansen, R. G. (1988). Auctions with Endogenous Quantity. *Rand Journal of Economics* 19: 44–58.

Hopenhayn, H. (1992). Entry, Exit, and Firm Dynamics in the Long Run. *Econometrica* 60: 1127–1150.

Hotelling, H. (1929). Stability in Competition. *Economic Journal* 39: 41–57.

Just, R. E. and Chern, W. E. (1980). Tomatoes, Technology, and Oligopsony. *Bell Journal of Economics and Management Science* 11: 584–602.

Kreps, D. and Scheinkman, J. (1983). Quantity Precommitment and Bertrand Competition Yield Cournot Outcomes. *Bell Journal of Economics* 14: 326–337.

Levitan, R. and Shubik, M. (1972). Price Duopoly and Capacity Constraints. *International Economic Review* 13: 111–122.

Lau, L. J. (1982). On Identifying the Degree of Competitiveness from Industry Price and Output Data. *Economics Letters* 10: 93–99.

Lofaro, A. (2002). On the Efficiency of Bertrand and Cournot Competition under Incomplete Information. *European Journal of Political Economy* 18, 561–578.

Lyons, B., Matraves, C. and Moffatt, P. (2001). Industrial Concentration and Market Integration in the European Union. *Economica* 68: 1–26.

Mailath, G. (1989). Simultaneous Signaling in an Oligopoly Model. *Quarterly Journal of Economics* 104: 417–427.

Mankiw, N. G. and Whinston, M. D. (1986). Free Entry and Social Inefficiency. *Rand Journal of Economics* 17: 48–58.

Matraves, M. (1999). Market Structure, R&D and Advertising in the Pharmaceutical Industry. *Journal of Industrial Economics* 47: 169–194.

Melitz, M. (2003). The Impact of Trade on Intra-Industry Reallocations and Aggregate Industry Productivity. *Econometrica* 71: 1695–1725.

Milgrom, P. and Roberts, J. (1990). Rationalizability, Learning and Equilibrium in Games with Strategic Complementarities. *Econometrica* 58: 1255–1277.

Perloff, J. M., Karp, L. S. and Golan, A. (2007). *Estimating Market Power and Strategies*. Cambridge: Cambridge University Press.

Riordan, M. (1985). Imperfect Information and Dynamic Conjectural Variation. *Rand Journal of Economics* 16: 41–50.

Robinson, W. T. and Chiang, J. (1996). Are Sutton's Predictions Robust?: Empirical Insights into Advertising, R&D, and Concentration. *Journal of Industrial Economics* 64: 389–408.

Salop, S. (1979). Monopolistic Competition with Outside Goods. *Bell Journal of Economics* 10: 141–156.

Schelling, T. C. (1960). *The Strategy of Conflicts*. Cambridge, MA: Harvard University Press.

Schmalensee, R. (1992). Sunk Costs and Market Structure: A Review Article. *Journal of Industrial Economics* 40: 125–134.

Shapiro, C. (1989). Theories of Oligopoly Behavior. In Schmalensee, R. and Willig, R. (eds.), *Handbook of Industrial Organization*. Vol. 1. Amsterdam: North-Holland.

Singh, N. and Vives, X. (1984). Price and Quantity Competition in a Differentiated Duopoly. *Rand Journal of Economics* 15: 546–554.

Spence, M. (1976). Product Selection, Fixed Costs, and Monopolistic Competition. *Review of Economic Studies* 43: 217–235.

Spulber, D. (1995). Bertrand Competition when Rivals' Costs are Unknown. *Journal of Industrial Economics* 41: 1–11.

Sutton, J. (1991). *Sunk Costs and Market Structure: Price Competition, Advertising, and the Evolution of Concentration*. Cambridge MA: MIT Press.

Sutton, J. (2007). Market Structure: Theory and Evidence. In Armstrong, M. and Porter, R. (eds.), *Handbook of Industrial Organization*. Vol. 3. Amsterdam: North-Holland.

Vives, X. (1990). Nash Equilibrium with Strategic Complementarities. *Journal of Mathematical Economics* 19: 305–321.

Vives, X. (2005). Games with Strategic Complementarities: New Applications to Industrial Organization. *International Journal of Industrial Organization* 23: 625–637.

von Stackelberg, H. (1934). *Marktform und Gleichgewicht*. Vienna: Springer.

Part III
Sources of market power

Introduction to Part III: Sources of market power

Consider the banking deposit market. If you have some savings, you are most probably one of the many agents active on the supply side of this market. Indeed, on this market, households and non-financial firms supply deposit funds, banks demand these funds and an interest rate plays the role of price. Even if banks are on the demand and not on the supply side, it only requires a little bit of imagination to apply the insights of Chapter 3 to analyse how banks compete for deposit funds. In particular, following the prediction of the Bertrand model, we can expect that if deposits are a homogeneous product, price competition among banks will drive the deposit rates that banks pay up to the loan rates that they charge, thereby eliminating their intermediation margin and their profits. It appears, however, that this prediction does not correspond to the reality: banks do manage to secure a positive intermediation margin and can therefore be said to possess market power.[a]

In this part of the book, we want to understand where market power comes from, be it in the banking sector or in any other oligopolistic market. As we will see, market power may result from the conduct of the firms and/or from the environment of the market. Starting with firms' conduct, we describe how market power results from a well-blended *marketing mix*. The three key variables of the marketing mix are Price, Product and Promotion.[b] While we defer the study of elaborated pricing strategies (known as price discrimination) to Part IV, we examine here how the choice of prices is determined by the earlier choice of the other two *P*'s. In Chapter 5, we focus on decisions related to *product differentiation*. The way product differentiation relaxes price competition has already been demonstrated in Chapter 3. But our previous model was very preliminary as it treated product positioning as exogenous. Here, we want to analyse how firms choose to differentiate their products. In our banking example, banks relax competition on deposits by differentiating their services; for instance, increasing the number of branches or allowing customers to make transactions on the Internet increases the quality of the service. We will argue that two main conflicting forces are at play when firms choose the degree of product differentiation: on the one hand, differentiation relaxes price competition but on the other hand, it may reduce the demand that faces the firm.

In Chapter 6, we turn to the promotion or *advertising* strategies. To try and increase their market power, banks devote substantial resources to advertise their products and services.[c] They do so with different objectives in mind: they may want to provide their customers with information about new products or services (e.g., 'Call 1-800 ING

---

[a] Maudos and Nagore (2005) compute Lerner indices of market power for the banking sectors of 58 countries (taking average values for the period 1995–99). There are important differences among countries: market power is high (a Lerner index over 30%) in Ghana (39%), Latvia (36%), Nepal (33%), or Jamaica (31%), while it is low (below 10%) in the Netherlands (9%), Luxembourg (8%), Ireland (7%), or Panama (6%). A comparison between the main economic areas shows that market power is higher in the USA (23%) and Japan (20%) than in the European Union (15%).

[b] With these '3 *P*'s' is usually associated a '4th *P*', namely Place, which refers to the choice and management of the distribution channels. We will consider decisions of this sort in Chapter 17.
[c] Örs (2006) reports that 'in 2004, U.S. commercial banks have spent an estimated $9.6 billion on advertising, which corresponds to 9.5% of industry net income'.

Direct. Hang up richer'); they may also want to persuade customers to purchase their products instead of the rival ones (e.g., 'At Keytrade Bank, benefit from the highest interest rates on the market'); finally, they may want to promote the consumption of their advertised products by associating them with values that customers might share (e.g., 'Dexia, the bank for sustainable development'). The latter three objectives correspond respectively to the *informative*, *persuasive* and *complementary* views on advertising. We will first examine how pricing and advertising decisions are intertwined in a monopoly setting. We will then move to oligopoly settings and show, basically, that advertising may make markets more or less competitive depending on the role advertising has and on the form that it takes. In this chapter, we will also take a normative point of view and try to shed some light on an old debate: is advertising a waste of resources or can it improve society's welfare?

Besides the correct choice of the marketing mix, firms can also increase their market power by exploiting exogenous elements pertaining to their market environment. Chapter 7 focuses on a number of reasons for which the purchasing behaviour of the consumers may exhibit a form of *inertia*. A first reason is the potential lack of information on the consumer side about the existence of products or about their prices. We examine situations where some consumers are better informed than others, which allow them to obtain a better deal. This explains why in a number of industries, prices for essentially the same product may be different across firms at the same point in time, or different for the same firm at different points in time, a phenomenon known as *price dispersion*. It is the presence of less-informed consumers that allows firms to secure positive profits even if they sell homogeneous products. This property holds even when consumers can decide on whether they want to acquire additional information through costly *search*.

In our banking example, the previous explanation echoes the fact that you might find it difficult or time-consuming to compare the deposit rates (and to read the associated small prints) of competing banks. It may also well be the case that, even if you have spotted that another bank offers a higher interest rate, it turns out that moving your accounts from your actual bank to this other bank (which entails a number of administrative chores) completely offsets the advantage of the higher rate. In other words, you may find yourself 'locked in' by your previous bank choice. In the second section of Chapter 7, we analyse *switching costs* of this sort, which drive consumers to purchase repeatedly from the same firm. Clearly, switching costs give firms market power on those consumers who are locked in. Yet, such market power comes with a price: firms have to compete fiercely to attract the consumers entering the market, especially if these consumers are forward-looking and anticipate that they will be exploited later on. Hence, one understands why, in markets characterized by switching costs, prices often follow an increasing sequence through time. For instance, it is quite likely that you joined your bank because it was offering attractive deals for students or because your parents were offered some bonus if they opened an account for you. It is equally likely that you no longer benefit from these advantages today. If you fit this profile, you have a live illustration of this practice commonly known as 'bargain-then-rip-off'. You might also have received dedicated offers from other banks encouraging you to switch to them (combining some welcome gift with promises to make the switch as easy as possible).[d] Such practice of *customer poaching*

[d] For instance, one can read the following on Citibank's UK website (last consulted on 10 July 2007): '*Transferring your account away from your current bank might seem daunting but with Citibank it couldn't be easier. With our Managed Account Transfer process we take care of transferring all your standing orders and Direct Debits, making your transition to Citibank as smooth and hassle-free as possible.*'

is also common in these markets. One of the main issues of the last two sections of Chapter 7 is to examine under which conditions switching costs and customer poaching make markets more or less competitive.

What will you learn in this part of the book?
You will become familiar with the various sources of market power. You will be able to understand how or why oligopolistic firms manage to set equilibrium prices above marginal costs? How? By choosing the right marketing mix; for instance, by positioning their products and by promoting them in the best way possible, given the choices of their competitors. Why? Because some consumers lack information about the existing products or find it too costly to acquire this information. Also because consumers face switching costs and prefer to purchase repeatedly from the same vendor. In the process, you will learn the difference between horizontal and vertical differentation, you will be able to make the distinction between different views of advertising, and you will get acquainted with the concepts of switching costs and price dispersion.

5 Product differentiation

In most markets for consumer goods, there do not exist identical products from the viewpoint of consumers. Even if physical properties are hardly distinguishable, branding may achieve that products are differentiated. A number of questions ensue as to how to apprehend product differentiation. How do consumers perceive products and services? To what extent do different consumers share the same perceptions? How similar are the demand curves of various individuals? Do consumers care for variety? The answers to these questions, and hence the modelling choices of the analyst, depend on the nature of the products or services under consideration. Think for instance of the car market, which has been the object of a number of empirical studies. Here, the assumption that consumers buy a single car, but that the population of consumers has heterogeneous tastes, is a natural assumption to make. For other consumer goods, neither discrete choice nor unit demand are natural assumptions to make. If you think of beer or carbonated soft drinks, the discrete choice assumption is often an appropriate assumption to make but consumers not only differ in their brand preference but also in their individual demand curves. In the case of wine, we believe that neither unit demand nor discrete choice are good approximations of actual consumer behaviour and therefore, are bad modelling assumptions: a large share of consumers actually enjoy some variety and buy variable amounts of quantity.

In this chapter, we first address these questions by discussing some general approaches to differentiated products (Section 5.1). Then, we analyse discrete-choice models of horizontal and vertical product differentiation (respectively in Sections 5.2 and 5.3). In Section 5.2 we elaborate on the Hotelling model with linear and quadratic transportation costs, which have become standard workhorses in the industrial organization literature. The product positioning of a firm is guided by its attempt to provide a product that fits most tastes but, on the other hand, to avoid competition from the other firms by offering more specialized products. We elaborate on this trade-off. In Section 5.3 we focus on the observable quality choice by firms. Here, we add to our discussion of entry into product markets from Chapter 4 by showing that even negligible scale economies is sufficient for the property that only a small number of firms is viable in a market. We then turn to the empirical estimation of product differentiation (in Section 5.4), which provides some very basic approaches to estimate differentiated product markets.[e]

---

[e] This chapter is also connected to Chapter 9, where we consider quality choice of a multi-product firm. Also Chapter 12 is complementary in nature because it covers the important case that product quality is not directly observable by consumers.

5.1   Views on product differentiation

Whether or not products (that are described by certain features or characteristics) are differentiated depends on consumer preferences. One source of product differentiation is heterogeneity among consumers. Consumer preferences are specified on the underlying characteristics space. This approach is often called the characteristics approach.[1] It has the advantage that, e.g., new product introduction and product modifications can be analysed without ambiguities. Such ambiguities may arise if preferences are only defined over products. In addition, consumers typically are assumed to make a discrete choice among products (and possibly an outside option), i.e. they decide which brand or product to buy and do not mix between different products. This approach is therefore called the *discrete choice approach*. Most models in this approach have the additional property that consumers buy zero or one unit of the product; however, also models with variable demand and discrete choice can be analysed. An alternative approach is to model each consumer with a variable demand for all products but to assume that all consumers are identical. This is called the *representative consumer approach*.

In Chapter 3, we have seen an example for each of the latter two approaches. The model in which consumers' ideal points are distributed on an interval belongs to the class of models that follows the discrete choice approach. The linear demand model (in which we compared price to quantity competition) belongs to the class of models that follows the representative consumer approach; an alternative functional form specification that we used e.g. in Chapter 4 are CES utility functions. Also preferences in these representative consumer models can be specified on an underlying characteristics space.[2] The idea here is that a product is a bundle of different characteristics. A consumer has preferences over these bundles. Prices for products can then be expressed relative to the performance of a product in each of its characteristics dimensions. Each characteristic gives utility so that consumption decisions are determined by marginal utility being equal to the implicit price of the characteristic. While this approach has regained attention in recent empirical demand analyses, we decided not to return to it in this book.[3]

Within the class of discrete choice models we can, in addition, distinguish between *horizontal* and *vertical* product differentiation. Loosely speaking, we are in a situation of horizontal product differentiation when each product would be preferred by some consumers; in contrast, if everybody would prefer one over the other product, products are vertically differentiated. A first definition of horizontal versus vertical product differentiation would thus be the following (where, for simplicity, we consider a duopoly): *if for equal prices consumers do not agree on which product is the preferred one, products are horizontally differentiated; if on the contrary, for equal prices, all consumers prefer one over the other product, products are vertically differentiated.*

According to this definition, only demand-side characteristics matter. While such a definition connects to the loose notion of variety versus quality, such a definition is not very helpful in distinguishing different types of market structures. For this, also the technology or cost side has to be included. We therefore find the following modified definition useful according to which *we are in a situation of vertical product differentiation if all consumers prefer one over the other product if prices are set at marginal costs.* Clearly, profits and therefore equilibrium prices are affected by the cost side and thus affect market performance. As we show in the subsection on natural oligopolies, market structure critically depends on whether products are vertically differentiated according to this second definition.

However, let us note that, although the distinction between horizontal and vertical differentiation is useful for research purposes, it is not easy to draw this distinction in practice. Indeed, as illustrated in Case 5.1, many real-world products or services combine elements of the two types of differentiation, as they are defined by more than one characteristic (all consumers may prefer to have more of each characteristic, which indicates vertical differentiation, but they may differ in how they value different characteristics, which indicates horizontal differentiation).

Case 5.1 Coffee differentiation[4]

Examples for horizontal and vertical product differentiation are even found in some markets for raw materials, which at first glance may look like the perfect example of a homogeneous product market. Take coffee (for those who prefer tea, the phenomenon is less recent). Coffee drinkers in rich countries have been made aware (or, depending on your view, made believe) by specialty roasters including mass phenomena like 'Starbucks' that origin and type of coffee matter for taste. This trend has led to prizes for the best coffee in various competitions and protected trademarks (and even disputes along the vertical supply chain about these trademarks). This suggests that, while the commodity market still plays an important role for coffee producers, some growers have definitely left this market and stepped up the ladder of vertical product differentiation (and, in addition, have horizontally differentiated). Take for instance Fazenda Esperança, who won first prize in Brazil's Cup of Excellence competition for the 2006 harvest. It made close to US$2000 per bag (of 60 kg), more than ten times the commodity price in an online auction in January 2007 (the winning bidders came from Japan and Taiwan).

5.2   Horizontal product differentiation

We reexamine markets with differentiated products that we analysed in Chapter 3. In this (and the following) section we take into account that product specifications and design are part of the firms' strategy sets. We start with a simple model where firms only choose their product location (the price is assumed to be constant and the same for all firms). We next turn to a richer setting in which firms choose first their location and then their price; we show how the location decisions, and, equivalently, product differentiation, depends on the specifics of the market.

5.2.1   A simple location model

A first simple model of product differentiation that abstracts from the pricing issue considers the product location choice of the firms for constant prices. Such a situation describes well certain industries in which prices are regulated and in which firms only have non-price strategies available. For instance, in Europe, many professions are subject to price regulation so that they face a fixed price $\bar{p}$. Suppose therefore that firms have to decide to which consumer tastes to tailor their product on offer. In particular, suppose that consumers are uniformly distributed on the interval $[0, 1]$ and have mass 1. The consumer's location describes her ideal point in the product space. The literal interpretation is that consumers are located in a linear city (e.g., the main road of a village). They prefer that the product (at location l_i) be located close by. They incur a linear transportation cost $t(|x - l_i|) = \tau |x - l_i|$, where the transportation cost parameter τ measures the substitutability between any given pair of products. The smaller τ the better consumers can substitute between any given products l_i and l_j. While transportation costs are the literal interpretation in our model, the model captures many different aspects of product differentiation. For instance, a particular dish may differ in its spiciness, a wine in its sweetness, a newspaper in its political orientation etc. In all these cases, the function t should be understood as an opportunity cost that a consumer incurs if a product in the market does not represent her ideal variety. Consumer x derives utility $v_i(x) = r - \tau |x - l_i| - \overline{p}$, where r is the reservation value of the consumer for a product located at l_i and $\overline{p}$ is the regulated price. We assume that r is sufficiently large such that all consumers purchase.

Firms incur constant marginal costs of production, which are less than the regulated price $c < \overline{p}$. Firms decide where to locate on the line and consumers then decide from which firm to buy. For any locations $l_1 < l_2$, there is a consumer who is indifferent between the two offerings. This consumer is located in the centre between the two firms, $\hat{x} = (l_1 + l_2)/2$. All consumers to the left (resp. right) of the indifferent consumer buy rather from firm 1 than from firm 2 (resp. from firm 2 than from firm 1). Thus the demand of firm 1 is $Q_1(l_1, l_2) = (l_1 + l_2)/2$ and the demand of firm 2 is $Q_2(l_1, l_2) = 1 - (l_1 + l_2)/2$.

Firms maximize profits with respect to their product location given the location of the competitor. Profits of firm i are given as

$$\pi_i(l_i, l_j) = \begin{cases} (\overline{p} - c)(l_i + l_j)/2 & \text{if } l_i < l_j, \\ (\overline{p} - c)/2 & \text{if } l_i = l_j, \\ (\overline{p} - c)[1 - (l_i + l_j)/2] & \text{if } l_i > l_j. \end{cases}$$

Formally speaking, we solve for the Nash equilibrium of the simultaneous location game. *The unique equilibrium has the property that both firms locate at the centre, i.e.* $l_1 = l_2 = 1/2$. First note that no firm has an incentive to deviate. Any firm that deviates will serve less than half the market. Note also that for any different locations, $l_1 \neq 1/2$ and $l_2 \neq 1/2$, at least one firm has an incentive to deviate because if firm i is located for instance to the left of $1/2$, firm j has an incentive to move slightly to the right of firm i. But this cannot be an equilibrium either because firm i increases its profit by locating at the same place as firm j. Hence, the only location equilibrium implies that firms locate both at the centre.

The main insight of the model is that although firms can differentiate their products, they choose not to. Firms maximize market share in this model and this leads them to locate at a point where they can best cater to consumer tastes. This is a general finding which generalizes to general distribution functions of consumer locations and general (increasing) transportation costs functions.

Lesson 5.1   If duopolists choose product locations (but do not set prices), they offer the same products, i.e., they choose not to differentiate their products.

Note that from a social point of view there is an excessive sameness because total transport would be minimized at locations 1/4 and 3/4. The introduction of competition here does not improve welfare since the number of firms is irrelevant if location is not affected. In the presence of fixed costs, society is actually better off with a single firm rather than two firms. If the single firm can offer the product at two locations, then a merger actually improves welfare because the monopolist chooses the socially efficient location.

Our lesson is robust to the functional form of the transport cost function. However, the result of minimal differentiation is not robust in other dimensions. In particular, with three firms minimum differentiation is not an equilibrium outcome. Moreover and more interestingly, we have restricted the analysis to fixed prices and want to check the robustness of our lesson in the context of price setting in a duopoly context.

5.2.2 The linear Hotelling model

We now turn to a model of horizontal product differentiation in which firms choose prices in addition to locations. We want to find out whether our insight about minimum differentiation also holds if prices are set by the firms.

As before, consumers have a reservation value r for their ideal product. A consumer of type x is located at some point x on the interval $[0, 1]$. Consumers buy up to one unit from one of the firms. Firm i is located at l_i somewhere on the interval $[0, 1]$, it charges price p_i, and consumers have to travel to the firm if they decide to visit it. For the moment we maintain the assumption that consumers incur a linear transportation cost $t(|x - l_i|) = \tau |x - l_i|$, where the transportation cost parameter τ measures the substitutability between any given pair of products. If a consumer of type x buys product i, she then derives utility $v_i(x) = r - \tau |x - l_i| - p_i$.

As in the previous model, we assume that consumers are uniformly distributed on the interval $[0, 1]$ and are of mass 1. In such a market, we analyse a duopoly in which firms first simultaneously decide which location to pick (or, equivalently, which product to produce) and secondly, they simultaneously set prices. In this two-stage game, we want to characterize subgame perfect equilibria. Firms are assumed to incur constant marginal costs of production c.

To analyse this market, we first consider the pricing game for given locations. Without loss of generality, we can label firms such that $l_1 \leq l_2$. Suppose firms are situated at different locations and that the price difference is sufficiently small such that some consumers prefer product 1 whereas others prefer product 2. Then there exists a consumer $\widehat{x} \in [l_1, l_2]$ who is indifferent between the two products. This indifferent consumer is given by $r - \tau(\widehat{x} - l_1) - p_1 = r - \tau(l_2 - \widehat{x}) - p_2$. We can solve for $\widehat{x}$ and obtain

$$\tau(l_1 + l_2) - (p_1 - p_2) = 2\tau\widehat{x} \Leftrightarrow \widehat{x} = \frac{l_1 + l_2}{2} - \frac{p_1 - p_2}{2\tau}.$$

In particular, if firms set symmetric locations (i.e., if $l_1 = 1 - l_2$) and set the same price, the indifferent consumer is located at $1/2$ and each firm obtains half of the demand. But what do we mean by the price difference being 'sufficiently small'? The admissible price difference is determined by the conditions for $\widehat{x}$ to lie between l_1 and l_2 indeed. That is,

$$\begin{cases} \widehat{x} \geq l_1 \Leftrightarrow p_1 \leq p_2 + \tau(l_2 - l_1), \\ \widehat{x} \leq l_2 \Leftrightarrow p_1 \geq p_2 - \tau(l_2 - l_1). \end{cases}$$

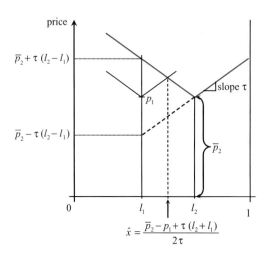

Figure 5.1 Consumer choice in the linear Hotelling model

What happens if one of these conditions is not met? Start by supposing that the first condition holds with equality: $p_1 = p_2 + \tau (l_2 - l_1)$, so that the indifferent consumer is exactly located at firm 1's location ($\hat{x} = l_1$). Now consider any consumer at the left of l_1, say $\tilde{x} = l_1 - \varepsilon$ (with $0 < \varepsilon \leq l_1$). Because of linear transport costs, this consumer is also indifferent between product 1 and product 2:

$$v_1(\tilde{x}) = r - \tau(l_1 - \tilde{x}) - p_1$$
$$= r - \tau(l_1 - \tilde{x}) - (p_2 + \tau(l_2 - l_1))$$
$$= r - \tau(l_2 - \tilde{x}) - p_2 = v_2(\tilde{x}).$$

The intuition is that compared to the consumer located at l_1, the consumer located at $\tilde{x}$ incurs the same extra transport cost when consuming either product 1 or product 2; hence, if the former is indifferent between the two products, so is the latter.[f] Now, given p_2, if firm 1 slightly decreases its price, all consumers to the left strictly prefer product 1. However, if firm 1 slightly increases its price, all consumers including those to the left of l_1 strictly prefer product 2. That is, for $p_1' > p_2 + \tau (l_2 - l_1)$, firm 1 will receive zero demand: $Q_1 (p_1', p_2; l_1, l_2) = 0$. There is thus a discontinuity at prices such that a consumer at l_1 is indifferent between product 1 and product 2. The same reasoning applies for the other condition. It is thus only for prices respecting the above two conditions that all consumers located to the left of $\hat{x}$ will buy from firm 1 and all consumers located to the right will buy from firm 2. Consumer choice is illustrated in Figure 5.1.

We can then write profits as the price–cost difference times demand:

$$\pi_1 (p_1, p_2; l_1, l_2) = \begin{cases} 0 & \text{if } p_1 > p_2 + \tau (l_2 - l_1), \\ (p_1 - c) \left(\frac{l_1 + l_2}{2} + \frac{p_2 - p_1}{2\tau} \right) & \text{if } |p_1 - p_2| \leq \tau (l_2 - l_1), \\ (p_1 - c) & \text{if } p_1 < p_2 - \tau (l_2 - l_1). \end{cases}$$

[f] This no longer holds when transport costs are quadratic rather than linear: even if the extra distance is the same for the two products, the extra cost is larger for product 2 because transport costs increase with distance. Consumer $\tilde{x}$ therefore strictly prefers product 1. This explains why the demand discontinuities disappear under quadratic transport costs, as we show in the next subsection.

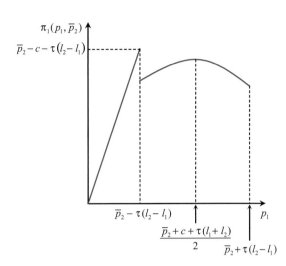

Figure 5.2 Profit function in the linear Hotelling model

The profit function is illustrated in Figure 5.2. Note that if the competitor is located in the interior of the interval (i.e., $l_2 < 1$), firm 1's profit function has a downward jump. The reason is the discontinuity we identified in the demand function: because of linear transport costs, too large a price difference leads all consumers to buy from the same firm. In particular, as p_1 is increased, firm 1 starts by attracting all consumers but shares the market with firm 2 as soon as $p_1 \geq p_2 - \tau (l_2 - l_1)$. This explains the downward jump in the profit function, as depicted in Figure 5.2 (there is a second downward jump when p_1 becomes larger than $p_2 + \tau (l_2 - l_1)$ as firm 1's demand drops to zero). Technically speaking, π_1 has two local suprema and is not quasi-concave in p_1. Therefore, simply solving first-order conditions is prone to errors. It is only when both firms are located at the extremes that profit functions are quasi-concave, so that the solutions to the first-order conditions must be global maximizers. Hence, if we fix locations to be at the extremes, we have a simple duopoly model, in which first-order conditions characterize equilibria. We will use this particular specification at various points in this book.

Here, we want to elaborate on the possibility that locations are not necessarily at the extremes. Then, although profit functions are not quasi-concave, we can still use the first-order conditions if locations are not too close. In such a situation, profit functions have two local suprema but the one characterized by the first-order conditions is a global maximizer, given the appropriate choice of the competitor. If first-order conditions implicitly define the firms' best responses, we have that undercutting by a discrete amount in order to capture all consumers must not become profitable for firm 1 given some (high) price of firm 2. However, firm 1's best reply $p_1 (p_2)$ jumps down to $p_2 - \tau (l_2 - l_1)$ at some critical value of p_2 (unless $l_2 = 1$) so that the first-order conditions can no longer be used to characterize best-responses. Note that this implies that in this game, prices are not strategic complements.

The pricing game can be characterized as follows. *(i) For $l_1 = l_2$ the unique price equilibrium is given by $p_1^* = p_2^* = c$. (ii) For $l_1 \neq l_2$ there exists a price equilibrium if and only if $(2 + l_1 + l_2)^2 \geq 12 (2 + l_1 - 2l_2)$ and $(4 - l_1 - l_2)^2 \geq 12 (2 + 2l_1 - l_2)$. Furthermore, whenever the price equilibrium exists, it is unique and characterized by*

$$p_1^* (l_1, l_2) = c + \tfrac{\tau}{3} (2 + l_1 + l_2) \quad and \quad p_2^* (l_1, l_2) = c + \tfrac{\tau}{3} (4 - l_1 - l_2).$$

To preclude undercutting from being profitable, the two firms need to be located sufficiently far apart.

We now turn to the location stage. We first observe that since at stage 1 a firm can always decide to locate close to the competitor, there does not exist a subgame perfect equilibrium.[5] However, we may argue that firms can only gradually relocate their products and that therefore, for our purposes, it would be sufficient to show that at some locations, firms do not have a tendency to relocate. The problem is that on the whole range of locations for which a price equilibrium exists, there is a tendency to move closer. This means that firms have a tendency to move into the region in which a price equilibrium does not exist. This can be called 'instability in competition' and shows that in a model in which firms can decide which type of product to produce and in which price is set strategically, it is not a priori clear that firms decide to differentiate their products. Indeed, profit functions may be badly behaved so that the model does not provide us with a prediction on where firms locate.

> **Lesson 5.2**   Although product differentiation relaxes price competition, models of imperfect competition in which firms choose product characteristics do not necessarily generate predictions concerning prices and product choices. Firms may have an incentive to offer better substitutes to generate more demand, which may lead to instability in competition.

5.2.3   The quadratic Hotelling model

We will now analyse a modification of the previous model which generates drastically different results. Consider the previous model with the only difference that the transportation cost function is a quadratic function of distance, $t\left(|x - l_i|\right) = \tau\left(x - l_i\right)^2$.

The indifferent consumer $\widehat{x}$ satisfies $p_1 + \tau\left(\widehat{x} - l_1\right)^2 = p_2 + \tau\left(\widehat{x} - l_2\right)^2$. She can be explicitly expressed as a function of prices, locations and parameter τ by rewriting the indifference condition:

$$p_1 + \tau\widehat{x}^2 - 2\tau\widehat{x}l_1 + \tau l_1^2 = p_2 + \tau\widehat{x}^2 - 2\tau\widehat{x}l_2 + \tau l_2^2 \Leftrightarrow$$

$$2\tau\widehat{x}(l_2 - l_1) = \tau(l_2^2 - l_1^2) - (p_1 - p_2) \Leftrightarrow$$

$$\widehat{x}(p_1, p_2) = \frac{l_1 + l_2}{2} - \frac{p_1 - p_2}{2\tau(l_2 - l_1)}.$$

Because transport costs are now quadratic, we no longer observe the discontinuities that we had with linear transport costs. The firms' demands are linear in both prices, for all location pairs such that $\widehat{x} \in [0, 1]$. Firm 1 chooses p_1 to maximize $\pi_1 = (p_1 - c)\widehat{x}(p_1, p_2)$, while firm 2 chooses p_2 to maximize $\pi_2 = (p_2 - c)\left[1 - \widehat{x}(p_1, p_2)\right]$. Solving the system of the two first-order conditions, one finds that *there exists a unique price equilibrium for each location pair $l_1 \leq l_2$, given by*

$$p_1^*(l_1, l_2) = c + \tfrac{\tau}{3}(l_2 - l_1)(2 + l_1 + l_2) \text{ and}$$

$$p_2^*(l_1, l_2) = c + \tfrac{\tau}{3}(l_2 - l_1)(4 - l_1 - l_2).$$

Note that these prices converge to c (the competitive outcome) when the interfirm distance $l_2 - l_1$ tends to zero. Since the marginal consumer is located at $\hat{x}\left(p_1^*, p_2^*\right) = (2 + l_1 + l_2)/6$, firms' payoffs for the first-stage game (using the expressions of $p_1^*(l_1, l_2)$ and $p_2^*(l_1, l_2)$, and assuming without loss of generality that $l_1 \leq l_2$) are

$$\hat{\pi}_1(l_1, l_2) = \tfrac{1}{18}\tau(l_2 - l_1)(2 + l_1 + l_2)^2 \text{ and}$$

$$\hat{\pi}_2(l_1, l_2) = \tfrac{1}{18}\tau(l_2 - l_1)(4 - l_1 - l_2)^2.$$

If firm locations are confined to the unit interval, then $\partial\hat{\pi}_1/\partial l_1 < 0$ for all $l_1 \in [0, l_2)$ and $\partial\hat{\pi}_2/\partial l_2 > 0$ for all $l_2 \in (l_1, 1]$. *In the subgame perfect equilibrium of the two-stage game with quadratic transportation costs, firms choose $l_1^* = 0$ and $l_2^* = 1$.* Contrary to Hotelling's belief, spatial competition does not lead to minimum differentiation. This is in sharp contrast to the pure locational competition model with fixed prices, which leads to the two-firm minimum differentiation result. Firms differentiate in order to build some monopoly power vis-à-vis the consumers situated in their vicinities.

In general, there are always two forces at play: on the one hand, firms want to differentiate themselves from competitors to enjoy market power and on the other hand, firms want to locate where they can best meet consumers' preferences. The first force, which we will call the *competition effect*, drives competitors apart; the second force, which we will call the *market size effect*, brings them together.

In the present model, the first force is sufficiently strong to lead to what has been (quite misleadingly) called maximal differentiation. However, this is an artefact of our particular assumption about the distribution of consumer tastes,[6] the shape of the transportation cost function, and the feasible product range. With respect to the feasible product range, we assumed that firms have to locate within the $[0, 1]$ interval. Consider the case that firms can locate anywhere on the real line. To show that the first force does not always dominate the second force, we only have to show that location pairs do not tend to $-\infty$ and $+\infty$. Indeed, it is straightforward to show that firms will locate at $-1/4$ and $5/4$, that is, firms further relax price competition compared to the case in which they were restricted to locate in the $[0, 1]$-interval but, eventually, the first and the second force have equal strength which limits the degree of product differentiation in equilibrium.

> **Lesson 5.3** With endogenous product differentiation, the degree of product differentiation is determined by balancing the competition and the market size effect. According to the former effect, firms have incentives to increase product differentiation; according to the latter effect, firms have incentives to reduce product differentiation.

As we have seen in the case of linear transport costs, firms have the tendency to move closer to the centre; with the quadratic specification, firms tend to locate rather 'far' apart to relax competition. The trade-off between relaxing competition and catering to consumer tastes is inherent to all models of spatial competition. However, if we extend the model such that firms enjoy some market power even if they choose the same location, firms may actually not have an incentive to locate apart in the product space so that the market size effect dominates everywhere.[7]

While the Hotelling model is tractable with two firms, introducing additional products makes the analysis increasingly difficult. The reason is that along an interval one cannot hope for symmetric allocations. A solution to this technical problem is to connect the ends of the interval so that firms and consumers are located on the circle – this model is widely known as the Salop model. Here, a natural candidate for an equilibrium is an equilibrium with equidistant locations, which in a world with free entry, has been analysed in Chapter 4.[8] It should be remarked that with equidistant locations a price equilibrium exists also for linear transportation costs (see the analysis of free entry in Chapter 4).

5.3   Vertical product differentiation

We now turn to situations of vertical differentiation where all consumers agree that one product is preferable to another product. We start by analysing a similar two-stage game as in the previous section: firms first position their product and then compete in price. Next, we reconsider the issue of natural monopolies and oligopolies that we already examined in the previous chapter. We show here that with vertically differentiated products, even a negligible amount of scale economies may suffice to limit entry to a single firm or a small number of them.

5.3.1   Quality choice

Product differentiation may not correspond to idiosyncratic tastes concerning the different products. There may exist dimensions in the space of product characteristics along which all consumers agree that one product is more desirable than the other. In this case, we refer to the *quality* of a product. Suppose that the quality of the product can be described by some number $s_i \in [\underline{s}, \overline{s}] \subset \mathcal{R}_+$. Consumers agree that high quality is better than low quality but they are heterogeneous in the way they value quality. To capture this heterogeneity, we introduce a preference parameter for quality $\theta \in [\underline{\theta}, \overline{\theta}] \subset \mathcal{R}_+$. Consumers with a large θ are those consumers who value quality improvements more strongly, i.e., they are more sensitive to quality changes. Again, we consider discrete choice and unit demand, i.e., each consumer chooses one unit of one of the products in the market. Consumers are distributed uniformly on $[\underline{\theta}, \overline{\theta}]$ and consumers are of mass $M = \overline{\theta} - \underline{\theta}$. The utility function describing the population of consumers thus has the property

$$\frac{\partial^2 u\,(\theta, s, \ldots)}{\partial s \partial \theta} > 0.$$

We capture this effect by a simple multiplicative interaction between preference parameter and quality.[9] Suppose that the direct utility for one unit of good i is $u_i = q_0 + \theta\,(s_i - \overline{s})$. If a consumer does not buy in the market, she only consumes the outside good q_0 and her utility is assumed to be $u_0 = q_0 - r - \theta\overline{s}$. Each consumer faces the budget constraint $y = r + \theta\overline{s}$. Hence, the indirect utility function for the discrete choice problem is

$$v(p, y; \theta) = \max[0, \max_i v_i(p, y; \theta)],$$

where the conditional indirect utility is

$$v_i(p, y; \theta) = r - p_i + \theta s_i.$$

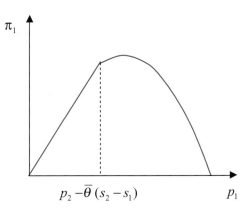

Figure 5.3 Profit function under vertical differentation

Firms are assumed to have the same constant marginal cost of production independent of quality; without loss of generality, let us assume that this cost is equal to zero. First suppose that firms set prices simultaneously, taking the qualities as given. Firm 1 produces quality s_1 and firm 2 produces quality s_2, with the convention that $s_1 < s_2$. (We address below the quality choice by the two firms prior to price competition.) In the analysis, we assume that prices are set such that $p_1, p_2 < r$ in equilibrium, which holds if r is sufficiently large. This implies that all consumers buy in the market. (If we set r sufficiently small, e.g. equal to zero, some consumers with a low reservation value necessarily do not buy in the market.) For given qualities $s_1 < s_2$, there is a consumer $\widehat{\theta}$ who is indifferent between buying product 1 and product 2. For this, note that all consumers prefer high quality but if high quality asks for a premium, some consumers choose the low-quality product. The indifferent consumer satisfies $r - p_1 + \widehat{\theta} s_1 = r - p_2 + \widehat{\theta} s_2$. Solving for $\widehat{\theta}$ gives

$$\widehat{\theta} = \frac{p_2 - p_1}{s_2 - s_1} \text{ for } \widehat{\theta} \in \left[\underline{\theta}, \overline{\theta}\right].$$

That is, the indifferent consumer is determined by the ratio of price and quality differences. Consumers of type $\theta > \widehat{\theta}$ buy the high-quality product s_2 whereas consumers of type $\theta < \widehat{\theta}$ buy the low-quality product. Profit functions, which depend on prices and qualities, are then of the form

$$\pi_1(p_1, p_2; s_1, s_2) = \begin{cases} 0 & \text{if } p_1 > p_2 - \underline{\theta}(s_2 - s_1), \\ p_1\left(\frac{p_2 - p_1}{s_2 - s_1} - \underline{\theta}\right) & \text{if } p_2 - \overline{\theta}(s_2 - s_1) \le p_1 \le p_2 - \underline{\theta}(s_2 - s_1), \\ p_1\left(\overline{\theta} - \underline{\theta}\right) & \text{if } p_1 < p_2 - \overline{\theta}(s_2 - s_1). \end{cases}$$

Firm 1 has to sell at a lower price than firm 2 in order to be able to attract some consumers. In this model, demand changes continuously with price changes for given qualities because, as firm 1 lowers its price more and more, consumers find that the utility gain from the lower price more than offsets the utility loss from lower quality in comparison to its competitor. Figure 5.3 illustrates the shape of firm 1's profit function.[10]

Again we are interested in the pricing and product choice of two competing firms. For this, we analyse the two-stage game in which, first, firms simultaneously set quality and, secondly, they simultaneously set prices. We want to characterize the subgame perfect equilibria of this game.

At stage 2, quality choices are given and we analyse price competition for given qualities. Solving the system of first-order conditions of profit maximization (with respect to prices), we obtain

$$p_1^* = \tfrac{1}{3} \left(\overline{\theta} - 2\underline{\theta} \right) (s_2 - s_1),$$
$$p_2^* = \tfrac{1}{3} \left(2\overline{\theta} - \underline{\theta} \right) (s_2 - s_1).$$

Note that this expression is valid only for interior solutions. For this, we impose the parameter restriction $\overline{\theta} > 2\underline{\theta}$. Otherwise, firm 1 cannot make positive profit in equilibrium.

Equilibrium prices depend only on the quality difference. It is not surprising to observe that the price of the high-quality firm is increasing with the quality difference. This implies that a higher quality of the high-quality firm leads to a higher price of that firm. Conversely, a higher quality of the low-quality firm leads to a lower price of the high-quality firm. This is due to more intense competition between the two firms. Perhaps more surprisingly, the price of the low-quality firm is also increasing with the quality difference. As a corollary, a higher quality of the low-quality firm leads to a lower price of that firm. Thus, as long as the low-quality firm has a quality less than the quality of the other firm, its profit is decreasing with quality. This result is due to our assumption that all consumers are active so that effectively a firm with the lowest quality available is still attractive in the market. The negative effect on price is also due to the increased competitive pressure. Although a higher quality makes the low-quality firm more attractive, its ability to charge a premium is reduced due to increased competitive pressure and the latter effect dominates the former. Finally, we observe that a low-quality firm gains from a higher quality of its competitor because competition becomes less intense.

We can now substitute for prices in the profit function and obtain reduced-form profit functions which only depend on quality. For $s_1 < s_2$, we have

$$\widetilde{\pi}_1 (s_1, s_2) = \tfrac{1}{9} \left(\overline{\theta} - 2\underline{\theta} \right)^2 (s_2 - s_1) \text{ and}$$
$$\widetilde{\pi}_2 (s_1, s_2) = \tfrac{1}{9} \left(2\overline{\theta} - \underline{\theta} \right)^2 (s_2 - s_1).$$

At stage 1, firms set qualities anticipating the resulting equilibrium prices. Thus, because $\widetilde{\pi}_1$ and $\widetilde{\pi}_2$ increase with the quality difference, $(s_1, s_2) = (\underline{s}, \overline{s})$ or $(\overline{s}, \underline{s})$ are the equilibrium quality choices of the game in which firms set qualities simultaneously and have profit functions $\widetilde{\pi}_i$. If firms first set qualities sequentially and then prices simultaneously, the first mover would choose the highest available quality $\overline{s}$ and the second mover would set the lowest available quality $\underline{s}$. In this model, the incentive to relax price competition is so strong that both firms benefit from the low-quality firm setting a lower quality. As already mentioned above, this result is due to the particular model. The more general message is that competing firms have at least some incentive to relax price competition by offering vertically differentiated products (as illustrated in Case 5.2).[g]

Lesson 5.4   **In markets in which products can be vertically differentiated, firms offer different qualities in equilibrium. This allows them to relax price competition.**

---

[g] Another question in the context of quality differentiation is whether a single firm has an incentive to produce more than one quality. We will address this question in Chapter 9.

Case 5.2 Product positioning in the VLJ industry: the 'battle of bathrooms'[11]

Very light jets (VLJ) are small jet aircrafts that are lighter than (and cost about half the price of) what are commonly termed business jets, and typically seat between 3 and 7 passengers plus one crew member. They are designed for short-haul flying, typically city-to-city trips. In 2007, there were two main competitors in this point-to-point air taxi industry: Magnum Jet and DayJet. The two companies have chosen planes from different manufacturers: Magnum's plane of choice is the Adam Aircraft A700, while DayJet's choice is the Eclipse 500. Because there are marked differences between these two aircrafts, the decisions of DayJet and Magnum Jet can be interpreted as a form of vertical differentiation of their services. Indeed, compared to the Eclipse 500, the Adam A700 is more expensive ($2.2 million versus $1.5 million) but has more cabin space (7 cubic metres versus 4.5 cubic metres). Moreover, the Adam A700 has a lavatory whereas the Eclipse 500 does not. Considering the media hype that surrounded the announcement of the Eclipse 500 certification, this 'bathroom issue' appears to be a major source of differentiation. Each side tries to convince potential consumers that they made the right choice. On the Magnum/Adam side, one quips: 'You are not going to get women on a plane unless it has a lavatory,' (Jim Burns, founder of Magnum Air) or 'People are not going to get on a plane without a bathroom, or at least they're not going to do it more than once.' (Rick Adam, CEO of Adam Aircraft). On the DayJet/Eclipse side, one replies that they heard from extensive market research that 'having no bathroom on board was not an issue for short, 60 or 90-minute trips. Given the choice of driving six hours or taking connecting flights, time-conscious business travelers simply find the bathroom question a non-issue. What is an issue for them is spending two days of travel for a two-hour meeting.' (Ed Iacobucci, CEO of DayJet Corp.). The future will tell us about the real impact of the 'battle of bathrooms' on the distribution of market shares in the air-taxi industry.

5.3.2   **Natural oligopolies**

In many oligopolistic markets, there are natural bounds to the number of firms in the market. As we have explored in the previous chapter, the number of firms in the market is determined by the entry process. Here, treating the number of firms as a continuous variable, the least efficient firm is indifferent between entry and no entry. Taking integer constraints into account (i.e., the fact that the number of firms in a small market should be taken as a natural number), all active firms can make strictly positive profits in an equilibrium with endogenous entry because the 'free' entry condition simply states that entry by an additional firm is not profitable. The number of active firms is then determined by technology and demand characteristics. The conventional view is that due to pronounced scale economies on a range of quantities, only a small number of firms is active in an oligopolistic market. Indeed, the situation that on top of constant marginal costs a firm has to incur fixed costs (which are sunk at the entry stage) is one particular example of scale economies. Clearly, the number of firms is determined not by technology alone but in combination with demand characteristics of the market under consideration.

The purpose of this subsection is to show that under particular demand characteristics, any negligible amount of scale economies is sufficient to make entry profitable for only a limited number of firms. In the extreme, a natural monopoly may arise even though entry costs are arbitrarily small.[12] With this result in mind, let us reconsider the duopoly model of vertical product differentiation from above: consumer types θ are uniformly distributed on the interval $[\underline{\theta}, \overline{\theta}]$ and obtain utility $\theta s_i - p_i$ from one unit of product i that has quality s_i and is sold at price p_i. Firms have zero marginal costs and set prices simultaneously. Suppose that there is an equilibrium in which both firms have positive demand. Recall that in the duopoly setting equilibrium prices are

$$p_1^* = \tfrac{1}{3} \left(\overline{\theta} - 2\underline{\theta} \right) (s_2 - s_1),$$
$$p_2^* = \tfrac{1}{3} \left(2\overline{\theta} - \underline{\theta} \right) (s_2 - s_1).$$

Hence, for both firms to have positive demand in equilibrium, we must have $\overline{\theta} > 2\underline{\theta}$. If the reverse inequality holds, so that consumers have rather similar tastes for quality, $\overline{\theta} \leq 2\underline{\theta}$, the low-quality firm does not serve any consumers in equilibrium even when charging zero price, given p_2^*. If the pricing decision is preceded by an entry stage with entry costs $e > 0$, which can be arbitrarily small, the low-quality firm has no incentive to enter the market. Even if firms can choose their qualities, there is no room for more than one firm in this market to operate profitably. This means that the market constitutes a natural monopoly. With sequential entry, there exists a unique subgame perfect equilibrium in which the firm that is first in deciding whether to enter chooses maximal quality $\overline{s}$ and no other firm enters. The firm then sets the unrestricted monopoly price.

Lesson 5.5   **Markets with vertical product differentiation may be natural monopolies, i.e. only one firm can enter profitably although entry costs are arbitrarily small.**

Such a result cannot arise under horizontal product differentiation since in a market with horizontal product differentiation, there always exist profitable niches. An example is the model in which firms are equidistantly located on a circle. Assuming that firms relocate under additional entry, there is a symmetric equilibrium in which firms make strictly positive profits gross of entry costs for any finite number of firms. As the entry cost decreases, more and more firms enter the industry. Ignoring the integer constraint, the free entry condition $\pi(n^*) - e = 0$ determines the equilibrium number of firms n^*. The property that more firms enter as the entry cost decreases even holds if incumbent firms do not relocate in response to entry. However, in this case the analysis is more involved and free entry does not lead to zero profits of all firms.

We continue to analyse the extension of the vertical differentiation model to an n-firm oligopoly. We order the firms such that $s_i < s_{i+1}$. Firm i's profit (gross of entry costs) is

$$\pi_i (p; s) = p_i \left(\widehat{\theta}_i - \widehat{\theta}_{i-1} \right)$$

where $\widehat{\theta}_0 = \underline{\theta} > 0$, $\widehat{\theta}_i = \frac{p_{i+1} - p_i}{s_{i+1} - s_i}$ for all $i = 1, \ldots, n-1$, and $\widehat{\theta}_n = \overline{\theta}$ when all consumers buy in the market so that the market is fully covered.

When all firms are active, the first-order conditions of profit maximization are given by

$$
\begin{cases}
X_1 \equiv \widehat{\theta}_1 - \underline{\theta} = \dfrac{p_1^*}{s_2 - s_1}, \\[2mm]
\vdots \\[2mm]
X_i \equiv \widehat{\theta}_i - \widehat{\theta}_{i-1} = \dfrac{p_i^*}{s_{i+1} - s_i} + \dfrac{p_i^*}{s_i - s_{i-1}}, \\[2mm]
\vdots \\[2mm]
X_n \equiv \overline{\theta} - \widehat{\theta}_{n-1} = \dfrac{p_n^*}{s_n - s_{n-1}}.
\end{cases}
$$

For all firms to be active we must have

$$
0 < p_1^* < p_2^* < \cdots < p_n^*.
$$

Demand for firm $i = 2, \ldots, n - 1$ is

$$
X_i = \frac{p_i^*}{s_{i+1} - s_i} + \frac{p_{i-1}^*}{s_i - s_{i-1}} + \frac{p_i^* - p_{i-1}^*}{s_i - s_{i-1}} > \frac{p_i^* - p_{i-1}^*}{s_i - s_{i-1}} = \widehat{\theta}_{i-1}
$$

Since $X_i = \widehat{\theta}_i - \widehat{\theta}_{i-1}$, we must have $\widehat{\theta}_i > 2\widehat{\theta}_{i-1}$. For the firm with the lowest quality, we must have $X_1 > 0$. This implies that $\widehat{\theta}_1 > \underline{\theta}$. Finally, for the firm with the highest quality, demand is

$$
X_n = \frac{p_n^*}{s_n - s_{n-1}} = \frac{p_n^* - p_{n-1}^*}{s_n - s_{n-1}} + \frac{p_{n-1}^*}{s_n - s_{n-1}} > \frac{p_n^* - p_{n-1}^*}{s_n - s_{n-1}} = \widehat{\theta}_{n-1}
$$

Since $X_n = \overline{\theta} - \widehat{\theta}_{n-1}$, we must have $\overline{\theta} > 2\widehat{\theta}_{n-1}$. Combining all these inequalities, we find that $\overline{\theta} > 2^{n-1}\underline{\theta}$ as a condition for all firms to be active. By contrast, if $\overline{\theta} \leq 2^{n-1}\underline{\theta}$ not all n firms can capture a positive market share at positive prices. In this case, the market exhibits a finiteness property, i.e. it only supports a finite number of firms and the market constitutes a natural oligopoly.

In the more general case with quality dependent marginal costs of production, profits are

$$
\pi_i = (p_i - c(s_i))\left(\widehat{\theta}_i - \widehat{\theta}_{i-1}\right).
$$

Here it can be shown that the sufficient condition for the finiteness property to hold is that $c'(s) \notin \left[\underline{\theta}, \overline{\theta}\right]$ for all $s \in [\underline{s}, \overline{s}]$. This condition is equivalent to $\max_s c'(s) < \underline{\theta}$ and $\min_s c'(s) > \overline{\theta}$. In the case of two products, this condition implies that all consumers agree which of the two products is preferred when priced at marginal costs. This corresponds to our second definition of vertical product differentiation. In such a market, not all firms can find a profitable niche and only a finite number of firms enters even as entry costs converge to zero.

5.4   Empirical analysis of product differentiation

In the formal analysis of imperfect competition, we typically start with a formulation of individual choice and then derive restriction on aggregate demand. Empirical work that uses structural estimations often relies on these restrictions. In what follows, we provide a general discussion of the approach of random utility models (which lead to discrete choice by individual consumers) and then present a particular specification that has proved useful in empirical work. Here, we will be interested in pricing issues and take product specifications as given.

5.4.1   Probabilistic choice and the logit model

In discrete choice models of product differentiation, it is important to have customers choosing differently (in a particular way) in order to make aggregate demand 'smooth'. Often this is formalized by assuming that customers are heterogeneous in some aspects that are relevant to their choice (an interpretation which is taken in most of this book). Instead of viewing customers as heterogeneous by nature, one may propose that customers (at least in certain subgroups) are the same before some random variable is realized. After this realization customers are different from each other and heterogeneity results from randomness. As discussed below, the distinction between probabilistic choice and heterogeneous deterministic choice seems to be partly a matter of labelling.

Following probabilistic choice theory, customers are identical *ex ante* (statistically identical) but are *ex post* different due to different realizations of random variables.[13] Modelling customer behaviour as probabilistic is motivated by experimental evidence from the psychology literature. In a controlled experiment, an individual must make repeated choices between two alternatives under 'similar' circumstances; sometimes one and sometimes the other will be chosen. Also, intransitivities in choices seem to occur rather frequently.

Probabilistic choice theory can explain such behaviour that reflects fluctuations that are inherent in the process of evaluating alternatives. Individual behaviour is specified as stochastic. The resulting randomness at the individual level can be modelled by random utility (or random preferences) or by random decision rules. Let us look at an example of random utility. Starting with a deterministic indirect utility function for a homogeneous good, $v = r - p$, randomness is introduced as an additive term: $v_i = r - p_i + \epsilon_i = \bar{v}_i + \epsilon_i$ where $E\epsilon_i = 0$ and $\bar{v}_i$ is the 'observable' or 'measured' utility, which reflects the preferences of a subpopulation for good i in expectation. There are two different interpretations for probabilistic modelling of individual behaviour reflected by ϵ_i. According to the first explanation, individuals behave probabilistically while according to the second, they behave completely deterministically but are observed as if they were acting probabilistically. We present the two explanations in Case 5.3.

Case 5.3 Probabilistic modelling of individual behaviour and Apple's iPhone[14]

In 2007 Apple entered the market for mobile telephones with the iPhone. This new product, which Apple regards as revolutionary, has experienced mixed reactions by consumers. Whereas long queues formed when the product was introduced in the market, other consumers reacted less enthusiastically. Even controlling for differences in observable characteristics, consumers in this market appear to be ex post heterogeneous. Below, we present two complementary explanations for individual behaviour that appears to be probabilistic at the individual level.

First, we discuss the interpretation according to which individuals behave in an intrinsic probabilistic way. In the words of the psychology literature, individual choice can be seen as the result of the following procedure: (step 1) a certain *stimulus* ϵ_i provokes a *sensation* v_i or a *psychological state*, which is seen as a realization of a random variable; (step 2) the response of an individual then depends upon the comparison of sensations. This explanation is based upon the observation that, for a given stimulus, there is some qualitative fluctuation from one occasion to the next. Similarly, an individual might not take into account some of the characteristics and/or make an 'error' in evaluating particular characteristics of a good. Examples are new products such as the iPhone in 2007, whose characteristics are difficult to assess so that consumers make errors in their judgements of the relative merits of this product compared to competing products.

Second, we discuss the interpretation of probabilistic choice that is due to the modeller's lack of information. That is, ϵ_i is interpreted as an uncertainty due to the lack of knowledge available to the observer, which, e.g., is a firm that tries to cater to the tastes of a subpopulation of consumers. Here, ϵ_i takes into account idiosyncratic taste differences inside the subpopulation. Probabilistic choices do not reflect a lack of rationality in consumers as decision makers but reflect a lack of information with respect to characteristics of alternatives or decision makers on the part of the observer. According to this interpretation, consumers belonging to a particular subpopulation are indistinguishable from each other for the observer but behave differently although each single consumer behaves deterministically. Hence, unobserved heterogeneity can be modelled as probabilistic choice. In particular, an observer might not be able to describe the state in which a consumer has to take her decision. State-dependent utility can be modelled as probabilistic if customers are in different states and the observer does not know the state of the world. Sources of this lack of knowledge can be unobservable characteristics, unobservable variation in individual utilities (e.g. state-dependent utilities where the state is not observable), measurement errors (amount of observable characteristics not perfectly known), and functional misspecification.

In what follows, we will give a couple of examples of binary discrete choice models followed by an analysis of a popular multinomial choice model, the *multinomial logit*. In a binary discrete choice model, consumers face two alternatives 1 and 2. These can be seen as two substitute products offered to consumers. Denote e_i the realization of ε_i. Since consumers maximize their utility, a consumer with realizations e_i and e_j chooses product i if $\bar{v}_i - \bar{v}_j > e_j - e_i$. Note that instead of working with a random utility specification, one can work alternatively with a random choice rule. In particular, consumers compare utilities $v_i = \bar{v}_i$ and choose good i if $v_i - v_j > e$, where e is the realization of a random variable ε (with $E\varepsilon = 0$). Thus if $\varepsilon = \varepsilon_2 - \varepsilon_1$, the resulting choices of this model coincides with the choices made according to the random utility model.

Our first example specifies ε to be uniformly distributed on the interval $[-L, L]$. Then the probability density is $f(e) = 1/(2L)$ if $e \in [-L, L]$ and zero otherwise. Thus, (probabilistic) demand for good i is 0 if the observable utility of good i is relatively low, namely if $\bar{v}_i - \bar{v}_j \leq -L$. It is 1 if the observable utility of good i is relatively high, namely if $\bar{v}_i - \bar{v}_j \geq L$. It takes values between 0 and 1 for intermediate values, namely demand is $\frac{1}{2} + \frac{\bar{v}_i - \bar{v}_j}{2L}$ if $-L < \bar{v}_i - \bar{v}_j < L$. For given product characteristics, we can take the linear or the quadratic Hotelling model as a special case of such a linear probabilistic demand model (where one has to take asymmetric density function if product characteristics are asymmetric).

While a linear model is attractive for computational reasons, such models do not perform well in empirical analysis. A particular non-uniform density that has been applied successfully to empirical problems is to assume that $\varepsilon = \varepsilon_2 - \varepsilon_1$ is logistically distributed. That is, the distribution function has the form $F(e) = 1/[1 + \exp\{-e/\mu\}]$. Note that the family of logistic distributions can be parametrized in μ, where a larger μ increases the variance of the distribution. Normalize the mass of consumers to 1. Probabilistic demand then is of the form

$$Q_1 = \frac{1}{1 + \exp\{-(\bar{v}_1 - \bar{v}_2)/\mu\}} = \frac{\exp\{\bar{v}_1/\mu\}}{\exp\{\bar{v}_1/\mu\} + \exp\{\bar{v}_2/\mu\}}.$$

This particular model of consumer choice is called the *binomial logit model* and can be applied to duopoly markets or to situations in which the focus is on the behaviour of a particular firm.

If we appropriately specify the random component ε_i of each product or alternative that is available, we can extend the analysis to a market with more than two products. Suppose there are n products available in the market. We have to specify the joint distribution of $(\varepsilon_i)_{i=1,\ldots,n}$. We assume that the ε_i are independently and identically distributed (i.i.d.) according to the double exponential distribution

$$F(e_i) = \text{Prob}(\varepsilon_i \leq e_i) = \exp\left\{-\exp\left\{-\left(\tfrac{e_i}{\mu} + \gamma\right)\right\}\right\}$$

where γ is Euler's constant ($\gamma \approx 0.5772$) and μ is a positive constant. This particular double exponential distribution has the property that its mean is 0 and variance $\pi^2\mu^2/6$ where $\pi \approx 3.141$. The corresponding density function is

$$f(e_i) = \tfrac{1}{\mu} \exp\left\{-\left(\tfrac{e_i}{\mu} + \gamma\right)\right\} \exp\left\{-\exp\left\{-\left(\tfrac{e_i}{\mu} + \gamma\right)\right\}\right\}.$$

Under our assumption with respect to the random term ε_i, choice probabilities and thus probabilistic demand is given by the following expression:

$$Q_i = \frac{\exp\{\bar{v}_i/\mu\}}{\sum_{j=1}^{n} \exp\{\bar{v}_j/\mu\}}.$$

This formula is the *multinomial logit*. Note that for $n \geq 3$, choice probabilities are given by the multinomial logit if and only if ε_i are double exponential, provided that the ε_i are i.i.d. and the cumulative distribution function is strictly increasing on R.[15]

An axiomatic justification for the distributional assumption in the multinomial logit can be obtained as follows. Denote A the choice set and denote A_k the expanded choice set in which each alternative contains k times the number of units of A. Then, under the assumption that the ε_i^k are i.i.d. for $k = 1, 2, \ldots$ (where ε_i^k is the random variable associated with product i in the set A_k) and that the cumulative distribution function is strictly increasing on R, then choice probabilities are invariant to any expansion of the choice set, i.e. $Q_i(A) = Q_i(A_k)$ if and only if ε_i^k are double exponential.

An additional justification of the multinomial logit is based on two axioms: (i) independence of irrelevant alternatives (i.e., eliminating a strictly dominated alternative from the choice set does not affect choice probabilities) and (ii) path independence (i.e., if choices are sequenced by first choosing subsets and then choosing within these subsets, such sequencing does not affect choice probabilities). In a probabilistic choice model, these axioms are satisfied if and only if choice probabilities and thus demand are equal to those of the multinomial logit.[16]

5.4.2   Empirical analysis of horizontal product differentiation

To empirically estimate models of product differentiation (where product characteristics are assumed to be given), we elaborate on the logit model of demand from above to bring it closer to the data. Suppose that consumers can choose between n products in the market and an outside good with the utility $\bar{v}_0$ normalized to zero.[17] Set for simplicity $\mu = 1$. We then can write market shares as

$$\alpha_i = \frac{\exp\{\bar{v}_i\}}{1 + \sum_{j=1}^{n} \exp\{\bar{v}_j\}}.$$

All consumers have the same mean utility level $\bar{v}_i$ and this mean utility level is assumed to take the form

$$\bar{v}_i = \beta x_i + \xi_i - \gamma p_i, \tag{5.1}$$

where x_i is the vector of observed product characteristics and β is the corresponding vector of parameters. The variable ξ_i contains the influence of all unobserved characteristics and can be interpreted as the mean utility derived from unobserved characteristics. Finally, γ is the parameter associated to price. Then

$$\log \alpha_i - \log \alpha_0 = \beta x_i + \xi_i - \gamma p_i. \tag{5.2}$$

In this transformed market share equation, market shares are linear in unobserved product characteristics. If we consider ξ_i as an error term, we can estimate demand parameters (β, γ) from this structural model (using appropriate instrumental variables to control for the correlation between unobserved product characteristics and prices).

So far we have only considered the demand side. On the supply side, suppose that firms set prices according to the prediction of a Nash equilibrium in prices. Note that equilibrium prices respond to costs and costs are not directly observable. However, costs are affected by product characteristics, part of which are observable to us. Denote the vector of relevant observable product characteristics on the cost side by w_j. Then we assume that the constant marginal cost of production is of the form $c_i = \kappa w_i + \omega_i$, where ω_i is the mean cost derived from unobservable characteristics and κ is the vector of parameters associated to the observable characteristics. Profits of firm i are $\pi_i = (p_i - c_i) M \alpha_i$. Assuming that a price equilibrium exists and is uniquely determined by the first-order condition, we obtain as the relevant pricing equation,

$$(p_i - c_i) \frac{\partial \alpha_i}{\partial p_i} + \alpha_i = 0.$$

This equation can be rewritten as

$$p_i = c_i + \frac{\alpha_i}{|\partial \alpha_i / \partial p_i|} = \kappa w_i + \frac{\alpha_i}{|\partial \alpha_i / \partial p_i|} + \omega_i$$

$$= \kappa w_i + \frac{1}{\gamma} \frac{\alpha_i}{\partial \alpha_i / \partial \bar{v}_i} + \omega_i.$$

In the logit model, $\partial \alpha_i / \partial \bar{v}_i = \alpha_i (1 - \alpha_i)$ so that the pricing equation becomes

$$p_i = \kappa w_i + \frac{1}{\gamma} \frac{1}{1 - \alpha_i} + \omega_i, \tag{5.3}$$

where parameters κ and γ have to be estimated. If we consider ω_i as an error term, we can jointly estimate Equations (5.2) and (5.3).

While the logit model serves well as a first model to analyse a differentiated product industry, the underlying assumptions and the implied properties make it unsuitable for many empirical implementations.[18] Note that own- and cross-price elasticities of the logit take the form

$$\eta_{ij} = \frac{\partial \alpha_i}{\partial p_j} \frac{p_j}{\alpha_i} = \begin{cases} -\gamma p_i (1 - \alpha_i) & \text{if } i = j, \\ \gamma p_j \alpha_j & \text{otherwise.} \end{cases}$$

We make two observations. First note that in various markets with many products, the market share for each product is small so that $\gamma(1 - \alpha_i)$ is more or less constant across products. This implies that own-price elasticities are more or less proportional to prices, i.e., the price elasticity of demand is small if the price is low and large if the price is large. Hence, the lower-priced firm must enjoy a higher markup. The result is due to the assumed linearity in price. This means that the particular functional form assumption implies a particular property of own-price elasticities, which in some markets, however, is violated.

A second property of the logit concerns cross-price elasticities. Since the error terms ε_i are i.i.d. across products, the logit implies a peculiar substitution pattern among products. Suppose that we consider choice probabilities in the absence of one of the n products. Then introducing this additional product does not affect relative market shares.

5.4.3   Empirical analysis of vertical product differentiation

A similar approach can be used to estimate vertical differentiation models.[19] Consider consumer j consuming product i. Her utility function is given by $v_{ij} = \theta_j s_i - p_i + \epsilon_i = \bar{v}_{ij} + \epsilon_i$ (where, as above, $E\epsilon_i = 0$ and $\bar{v}_{ij}$ is the 'observable' utility). Here, s_i measures the quality of product i and θ_j is a scalar random variable that represents the value attached by consumer j to quality. Recall that in the vertical differentiation model, consumers agree that more quality is preferable but disagree about the value of quality. Assume further that the quality index of product i can be decomposed into the sum of observed characteristics (x_i) and of unobserved characteristics (ξ_i): $s_i = \beta x_i + \xi_i$, where β is the vector of parameters corresponding to the observed characteristics. Now, we can order the products by increasing level of quality (i.e., we let $s_0 < s_1 < \cdots < s_n$) and normalize the unit of quality so that θ_j has mean one. It follows that the mean utility has still the same expression as in (5.1):

$$\bar{v}_i = \beta x_i + \xi_i - \gamma p_i, \text{ with } \gamma \equiv 1.$$

Note that θ_j is effectively a single random coefficient that interacts with observed *and* unobserved characteristics. It follows that what we obtain here can be seen as the exact opposite of the logit model, as summarized in the following table.

Logit model	Vertical differentiation model
As many consumer characteristics, as there are products.	Only one consumer characteristic, θ_j, the 'taste' for quality.
All products are strict substitutes.	Only products that are adjacent in the quality ladder are substitutes.

The common point between the two models is that they both place strong assumptions on the pattern of estimated cross-price elasticities. We now examine richer models to estimate horizontal product differentiation.

5.4.4   Nested logit and other extensions

The restriction on substitution patterns that is imposed by the logit model can be a serious limitation for applications. Take for instance the car market. Here, it is very unlikely that a product introduction in a particular segment, e.g. family van, has the same effect on the market share of a car in that segment as on an SUV. One possibility is to postulate that there are no substitution effects between the segments and to proceed with the estimation for each segment. An intermediate possibility is to group different cars together in a single nest and to use the *nested logit* model, according to which consumers select among nests and then within the nests. The resulting demand function then restricts substitution patterns within each segment but allows for different substitution patterns for products within compared to products across nests. Cross-price elasticities between products belonging to different nests are positive but lower than within nests.

Estimating the demand side involves estimating

$$\log \alpha_i - \log \alpha_0 = \beta x_i + \xi_i - \gamma p_i + \sigma \log(\bar{\alpha}_{i|g}),$$

where the last term is an endogenous extra term compared to the logit model. This extra term depends on a substitution parameter σ and on the market share of product i within group g. The set of products in group g is denoted by I_g. The conditional market share is

$$\bar{\alpha}_{i|g} = \exp \left[\frac{(\beta x_i + \xi_i - \gamma p_i)/(1 - \sigma)}{\sum_{i \in I_g} \exp[(\beta x_i + \xi_i - \gamma p_i)/(1 - \sigma)]} \right].$$

Parameters β, γ and σ can be estimated using instrumental variable regressions. Also the pricing equation (5.3) has to be adjusted to account for the nesting structure. The nested logit approach has proved to be useful in a variety of industries, including the car industry.

Case 5.4 Nested logit in the US car market

Goldberg (1995), using micro data from the Consumer Expenditure Survey for the US automobile market, estimates nested logit models to capture consumers' sequential choice which appears to be characteristic for the decision to buy a car. The US automobile industry is modelled as a differentiated product oligopoly. She then uses her estimation results in counterfactual simulations to explore two trade policy issues, voluntary export restraints and exchange rate pass-through.

In other situations, we can consider the consumer choice problem when they have already decided on a particular manufacturer product. Thus we are abstracting from competition between manufacturers and focus on competition between retailers who offer this particular product. In the physical world, one would have to consider big ticket items because otherwise the opportunity cost to visit a particular retailer is non-negligible. However, consumers who visit Internet retailers have arguably lower costs to select between competing offers.[h] Here, we are considering differentiation among competing internet retailers. Also in this case, the nested logit may provide on the one hand sufficient flexibility and on the other hand sufficient structure to analyze data. This approach is suited to detect differentiation due to branding, i.e. a situation in which product characteristics (here, characteristics of the retailer) are not observable to consumers, so that the reputation of the firm matters.[i]

Case 5.5 Nested logit for Internet bookshops: brand matters

Smith and Brynjolfsson (2001) analyse click-through data (not actual purchases) from Internet shopbots which provide information on price and service levels offered by competing Internet retailers for given manufacturer products. In their data set, they observe more than 20 000 consumers over more than two months in their clicking behaviour for books. Books appear to be an appropriate product category because it appears to be a reasonable assumption that consumers first choose a particular book on a particular shopbot (EvenBetter.com) and second choose among the competing offers for the selected book. The empirical analysis only considers the second step. The consumer model here is that consumers first decide whether to go for a branded retailer who charges a premium (Amazon, Barnes & Noble and Borders) or to go for more competitive offerings among lesser known rivals. Second, consumers are to make their choice of retailer and third the type of delivery. The decision tree is depicted in Figure 5.4. Clearly consumers using a shopbot are likely to be more price-sensitive than consumers who directly go to the

---

[h] However, also on the Internet we can observe price dispersion even after controlling for differences between retailers. This can be formalized by analyzing consumer search models; see Chapter 7.
[i] For a formal analysis of branding and reputation under asymmetric information, see Chapter 13.

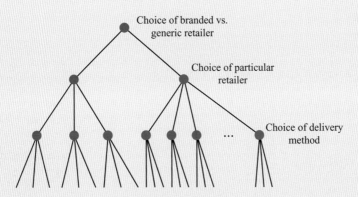

Figure 5.4 The consumer choice problem on Internet shopbots

website of one of the Internet retailers. However, the attempt is to understand the behaviour of these consumers. If these consumers are willing to pay a premium for branded retailers, this should be seen as particular strong evidence that retailer brands are valuable. Smith and Brynjolfsson find that customers strongly prefer offers from the three branded retailers after controlling for observable characteristics such as price and delivery time. This result obtains in the multinomial logit in which the choice of a branded retailer is captured through a dummy. As we have seen, the multinomial logit places strong restrictions on price elasticities. Hence, the question arises whether the result is driven by these restrictions. To address this concern, the authors analyse various specifications of the nested logit to confirm their key qualitative finding: retailer brands are valuable on Internet shopbots. This challenges the view that the Internet undermines the role of brands.

While nesting appears to work in markets in which there is a natural way to form such nests, in other markets there is no natural way of doing so. Here, one needs a more flexible demand system without resorting to the modeller's ex ante knowledge about demand. Recent empirical work has therefore used random coefficient models that allow the full interaction between consumer and product characteristics: according to the random coefficient model, the parameter β is consumer-specific. These random coefficient models have the drawback that the market share equation is difficult to calculate and estimation typically proceeds by simulation.[20]

Review questions

1. In which industries is product differentiation important? Provide two examples.

2. What makes firms locate close to each other in the product space? And what makes them differentiate themselves from their competitors?

3. When is vertical product differentiation present in an industry? Discuss demand and cost characteristics.

4. Does the number of firms in an industry with constant marginal costs necessarily converge to infinity as the entry cost turns to zero? Explain.

5. Why are we interested in empirically estimating models of product differentiation? (After all, to understand the intensity of competition in the short run, we only need to know the Lerner index.)

Further reading

The analysis of horizontal product differentiation goes back to Hotelling (1929). For the analysis with endogenous prices see d'Aspremont, Gabszewicz and Thisse (1979). Vertical product differentiation models have been proposed by Gabszewicz and Thisse (1979) and Shaked and Sutton (1982). Natural oligopolies have been analysed by Gabszewicz and Thisse (1980) and Shaked and Sutton (1983). For an elaborate treatment of discrete choice models, we recommend Anderson, de Palma and Thisse (1992). For those who want some further reading on formal results on equilibrium existence in discrete choice models, we recommend Caplin and Nalebuff (1991). Do you want to learn more about empirical work? A seminal paper in the field is Berry, Levinsohn and Pakes (1995). Nevo (2000) provides an accessible guide towards empirical implementation.

6 Advertising and related marketing strategies

Every day, consumers in developed countries are subjected to hundreds of advertising messages. Advertising is indeed everywhere around us: on television, in our print magazines and newspapers, in our mail, on the Internet, on billboards in the streets, etc. It is estimated that $285.1 billion have been spent on advertising in the United States in 2006. To put this number in perspective, this represents 2.2% of US GDP, a spending of $952 per capita, and 48% of the world spending on advertising. The 100 top US marketers account for 37% of the total advertising spending. On the top of the list, Procter and Gamble (P&G) alone was responsible for $4.9 billion of US ad spending. Again, to put this number in perspective, this represents 16.62% of P&G's North-American sales (and 7.18% of their worldwide sales) in 2006. Actually, P&G is no exception: advertising expenditures represent a substantial proportion of sales in many consumer goods industries, and this proportion tends to be larger in those industries (such as detergents, cigarettes and beer) where products are highly substitutable and competition between brands is very intense.[a]

In this chapter, we want to understand to what end and to what effect firms devote resources to advertising. We first investigate how advertising affects consumers (Section 6.1). Then, we look again at the marketing mix. This time, we take Products as given but we examine how the combination of the other two *P*'s – Promotion and Price – is chosen by the firms. We first perform the analysis in a monopoly setting (Section 6.2). This further allows us to discuss the welfare effects of advertising (Section 6.3). Finally, we analyse advertising decisions in oligopoly settings (Section 6.4).[b]

6.1 Views on advertising

Firms would not use advertising if consumers were not responding to it. This truism immediately poses the following basic question: why do consumers respond to advertising? Economists have expressed three distinct views about this question.[21] According to the first view, advertising is *persuasive* in that it alters consumers' tastes; advertising therefore amplifies product differentiation and consumers' loyalty to a particular brand. The second view holds that advertising is *informative*: advertising provides consumers with information about the existence, prices and characteristics of products, either directly or indirectly. The indirect channel refers

---

[a] See the advertising/sales ratios given in Table 6.2 for a confirmation; see also the other statistics given in Case 6.1 for a broader view of advertising spending. All these statistics come from *Advertising Age Data Center, 2007 Marketer Profiles Yearbook* (25 June 2007).
[b] We return to advertising in later chapters. In Chapter 12, we analyse the indirectly informative view of advertising; in Chapter 22, we look at advertising in media markets from a two-sided market perspective.

to the idea that a firm's willingness to spend resources on advertisement can be interpreted as a signal that the quality of this firm's product is high (we will develop this kind of argument further in Chapter 12). Finally, the third view contends that advertising is *complementary* to the advertised product. Here, advertising does not modify consumers' preferences and it does not matter whether it conveys information or not; what is central is that advertising enters as one argument into the consumers' utility function and it does so in a complementary fashion with the advertised product. Compatible with this view is that an individual consumes 'social images' or 'self-images' by combining particular products together with their advertisements. For instance, having a particular brand of sport shoes will give you the 'benefit of being cool' if (i) you actually possess these shoes, and (ii) the ad links these shoes to a cool image for your relevant peer group.[22]

As all three views seem relevant, one could be tempted to mesh them into a single explanation. However, one needs to realize that these views entail radically different positive and normative implications. In particular, the normative implications of persuasive and informative views are completely at odds with each other. The persuasive view suggests that advertising makes demand less elastic (as consumers become more loyal) and, therefore, results in higher prices and may make entry more difficult. The informative view suggests that advertising allows consumers to make better informed decisions. If consumers become informed about the existence of a product this tends to make demand more elastic, which then increases competition. So, advertising is often seen as welfare-reducing under the persuasive view, but as welfare-increasing under the informative view. As for the complementary view, it stands somewhere in the middle: advertising is seen as largely uninformative but it may nevertheless be beneficial through its direct valuation by the consumers (its implications for market allocation are the same as under the persuasive view). Similar conclusions emerge if consumers are already informed about the existence of products but are not yet informed about product characteristics.

Economists have thus subjected these various views to theoretical and empirical scrutiny. In the next sections, we present some main theoretical contributions, starting with the positive and normative theory in a monopoly setting and moving then to oligopoly situations. Before that, we shed some light on the empirical investigations.

Case 6.1 US 2006 media spending on advertising[23]

Out of the $285.1 billion that was spent on advertising in the United States in 2006, 47% ($135 billion) came from 'unmeasured disciplines' (i.e., marketing services such as sales promotion, digital communications and direct marketing), while the other 53% ($150 billion) came from media spending measured by ad-tracking services. In the latter category, television accounted for the largest share (43.6%), with the press being the second largest medium (19.9% for newspapers and the same share for magazines), followed by the radio (7.4%), the Internet (6.5%) and outdoor ads (2.6%). Noteworthy is the fact that Internet spending grew by 17.3% and local newspapers spending decreased by 3.1% compared to 2005.

The split of the media spending by advertising category gives the following ranking: 1. Automotive (13.2%). 2. Retail (12.8%). 3. Telecom (7.3%). 4. Medicine and remedies (6.1%). 5. General services (5.8%). 6. Financial services (5.8%). 7. Food, beverages and candy (4.8%). 8. Personal care (3.8%). 9. Airlines, hotels and car rentals (3.6%). 10. Movies, recorded video and music (3.6%). Other (33.1%).

Empirically distinguishing different types of advertising

While advertising can have different roles and economic theory can help us understand the strategic effects and allocative consequences of these different types of advertising, it is an empirical question as to whether at a particular moment in a given market, advertising was more or less of one of those types. This identification issue can be addressed in a number of different ways. One approach is to look at advertising spots and try to classify them according to the different types.[24] While there is some hope to identify directly informative advertising, it seems impossible to distinguish between, e.g., indirectly informative and persuasive advertising. An alternative approach is to find industries that are subject to a shock (e.g., that a certain type of advertising becomes legal) and to analyse the effect of advertising on market outcomes.

Yet another approach is to look at implied purchasing behaviour. Directly informative advertising should be valuable for inexperienced consumers but of little value for experienced consumers. We may also argue that even indirectly informative advertising for experience goods (i.e., goods whose quality or suitability can only be observed after purchase) has this property. While it takes a consumer some time to become informed, after a sufficient amount of consumption experiences, she improves her understanding of the (ex ante) unobservable characteristics (if she recalls her experience). Thus, indirectly informative advertising also affects utility mainly of inexperienced consumers but not those who are experienced. In contrast, one may argue that persuasive advertising or complementary advertising tend to affect experienced and unexperienced consumers symmetrically. This leads to the *testable hypothesis that informative advertising affects the demand of inexperienced consumers more strongly than of experienced consumers*. This has been analysed in the Yoplait 150 case.

Case 6.2 Yoplait 150[25]

If consumer behaviour can be monitored for a certain period of time, it is interesting to analyse the effect of advertising on demand in the case of a newly introduced product. This was the case for Yoplait 150, the first low-calorie, low fat yogurt introduced by Yoplait (the second-largest yogurt manufacturer in the US) into the US market in April 1987. For a 15-month time period, there exist scanner data in two geographical areas for around 2000 households in each (covering more than 80% of relevant retailers) – scanner data record consumer purchases through supermarket UPC scanners. Combining scanner data with available price data, it was possible to reconstruct which set of prices a household was facing in each shopping situation. These data were complemented by each household's TV advertising exposure (for 50% of households) so that one can individually link the advertising of a product, here Yoplait, to the advertising exposure of an individual household. In the Yoplait 150 case, it was thus possible to link observable household characteristics and advertising to individual demand.

One concern with many products is intertemporal effects on the consumption side through stockpiling behaviour. However, due to the limited storability of yogurt, this is of limited concern in the Yoplait 150 case.

Solving a fully dynamic model of consumer behaviour is complicated since consumers can learn from past consumption experiences. Instead one can estimate a reduced form equation of the discrete choice between buying and not buying Yoplait 150. Suppose

$$q_{it} = \begin{cases} 1 & \text{if } X_{it}\beta_1 - \gamma p_{it} + \varepsilon_{1it} > Z_{it}\beta_2 + \varepsilon_{2it} \\ 0 & \text{else,} \end{cases}$$

where q_{it} is the purchasing decision (1 when Yoplait 150 is bought and 0 else) of consumer i on shopping trip t. Ignoring dynamic effects, $X_{it}\beta_1 - \gamma p_{it} + \varepsilon_{1it}$ would represent the expected utility from purchasing Yoplait 150. (In a dynamic context, this expression approximates the value function conditional on buying Yoplait 150.) In this expression, X_{it} contains all explanatory variables except price: advertising, various household characteristics and several lagged variables capturing previous shopping behaviour.

The key variable for interpretation is the interaction between advertising and past purchases, which allows us to distinguish the effect of advertising on experienced versus inexperienced consumers. Assuming that the ε's are i.i.d. double exponentially distributed, we obtain the binary logit model (see Section 5.4). However, estimation results may not be reliable because the i.i.d. assumption is likely to be violated. This is the case if consumers have time-persistent unobservable tastes for Yoplait 150 (or yogurt in general). Including unobservables μ_i, consumer choice is $q_{it} = 1$ if $X_{it}\beta_1 + \mu_i - \gamma p_{it} + \varepsilon_{1it} > Z_{it}\beta_2 + \varepsilon_{2it}$. These unobservables can be treated as random effects. While we do not describe the more involved estimation procedure with random effects, we report estimation results for both types of estimations; Table 6.1 gives the key findings.[26]

Table 6.1. *Informative advertising in the Yoplait 150 case*

Variable	Logit	Random effect
Advertising/inexperienced	2.04073 (0.72313)	2.30566 (0.77561)
Advertising/experienced	0.90371 (0.63504)	0.43304 (1.21180)
t-statistic on difference	1.47662	1.58703

Note, however, that we have suppressed all other explanatory variables except the two we are interested in. The estimation results show that inexperienced consumers are significantly more likely to purchase Yoplait 150 as a reaction to advertising than experienced consumers. Furthermore, advertising does not significantly increase the purchasing probability of experienced consumers. This supports the view that in the Yoplait 150 case, advertising was predominantly informative.

6.2   Price and non-price strategies in monopoly

Before returning to the strategic interaction between firms, we take another look at the monopoly pricing problem. We enrich this problem including a second, non-price variable. In addition to price, the monopolist may have to take a number of decisions, e.g. how much to invest in improved quality, how many added features to add to the basic product (this is a bundling decision), or how much to spend on advertising the product. For concreteness, we will elaborate on the advertising decision of the firm. However, instead of including advertising expenditure A in the analysis we may include the R&D expenditure or the expenditure for bundled added features.

The basic property of increasing expenditure along any of these dimensions is that this will lead to a demand increase. Hence, the firm can, through some payment, shift demand.

6.2.1   Price–Advertising decisions: the Dorfman–Steiner model

Apart from the strategic variable price p, firms often have non-price strategic variables at their disposal which allows them to shift demand. In a monopoly setting, we consider advertising expenditure A which translates into advertising 'frequency', for instance the number of advertising minutes on TV.[27] We consider actions $(p, A) \geq 0$. In the present monopoly setting, the solution does not depend on the timing of decisions. In particular, it is irrelevant to the solution whether the monopolist has to choose the advertising expenditure before or at the same point when the price decision is made. Demand as a function of price and advertising expenditure, $Q(p, A)$, decreases with price and increases in advertising expenditure, $Q_p \equiv \partial Q/\partial p < 0$ and $Q_A \equiv \partial Q/\partial A > 0$. This implies that consumers respond to more advertising by increasing their demand.[c] The firm faces variable costs of production $C(Q(p, A))$ with $C' > 0$. The firm's profits are then given by $\Pi(p, A) = pQ(p, A) - C(Q(p, A)) - A$.

The firm then maximizes profits $\Pi(p, A)$ with respect to p and A. For a given advertising expenditure A, we obtain again the monopoly pricing formula (assuming that the solution to the first-order conditions is a global maximizer):

$$\frac{\partial \Pi}{\partial p} = (p - C') Q_p + Q = 0 \Leftrightarrow \frac{p - C'}{p} = -\frac{Q}{pQ_p} = \frac{1}{\eta_{Q,p}}. \tag{6.1}$$

[c] We propose below two specific formulations of the function $Q(p, A)$. But so far, as the model does not explain why consumers respond to advertising, we can use it as a positive theory of monopoly pricing and advertising, but not as a normative tool. The normative analysis is deferred to Section 6.3.

In addition, the firm has to determine its profit-maximizing advertising expenditure:

$$\frac{\partial \Pi}{\partial A} = (p - C') Q_A - 1 = 0$$

$$\Leftrightarrow \frac{p - C'}{p} = \frac{1}{Q_A}\frac{1}{p} = \frac{Q}{AQ_A}\frac{A}{pQ} = \frac{1}{\eta_{Q,A}}\frac{A}{pQ}, \tag{6.2}$$

where $\eta_{Q,A} = AQ_A/Q$ is the advertising elasticity of demand. Expressions (6.1) and (6.2) give two different values to the markup $(p - C')/p$. Equating these two values, we obtain

$$\frac{1}{\eta_{Q,p}} = \frac{1}{\eta_{Q,A}}\frac{A}{pQ} \Leftrightarrow \frac{A}{pQ} = \frac{\eta_{Q,A}}{\eta_{Q,p}}. \tag{6.3}$$

Thus Equation (6.3) determines the profit-maximizing advertising expenditure as a percentage of revenue by an elasticity rule:

$$\underbrace{\frac{\text{advertising expenditure}}{\text{revenue}}}_{\text{advertising intensity}} = \frac{\text{advertising elasticity of demand}}{\text{price elasticity of demand}}.$$

Lesson 6.1   **A monopolist sets its advertising intensity equal to the ratio of the advertising elasticity of demand over the price elasticity of demand.**

Hence, if demand is relatively more sensitive to changes in the advertising expenditure compared to changes in price, the advertising expenditure is a large fraction of its revenues. Therefore, we would expect high advertising intensity in industries in which consumer demand is very elastic with respect to the advertising efforts of a firm. Table 6.2 reports advertising intensities for the top 10 US marketers.

Table 6.2. *Advertising intensities for the top 10 US marketers*

Marketer	A	pQ	Intensity
Procter & Gamble Co.	4898	68 222	7.18%
AT&T	3345	63 055	5.30%
General Motors Corp.	3296	207 349	1.59%
Time Warner	3089	44 224	6.98%
Verizon Communications	2822	88 144	3.20%
Ford Motor Co.	2577	160 100	1.61%
GlaxoSmithKline	2444	42 534	5.75%
Walt Disney Co.	2320	34 285	6.77%
Johnson & Johnson	2291	53 324	4.30%
Unilever	2098	49 548	4.23%

A: US ad spending in 2006 ($ millions)
pQ: worldwide sales in 2006 ($ millions)

6.2.2   **A closer look at how advertising affects demand**

The above model was silent about how the advertising expenditure increases demand. Here, we want to be more specific and propose two ways of building a demand function $Q(p, A)$ with $Q_A > 0$.[28]

Persuasive advertising

The first way follows what is often attributed to the persuasive view by assuming that advertising increases the consumers' willingness to pay and thereby the demand facing the monopolist. Take a continuum of consumers of mass equal to one. Each consumer buys at most one unit of the monopolist's product. Consumers are heterogeneous in their intrinsic valuation of the product, denoted by θ. We assume that θ is uniformly distributed over the interval $[0, 1]$. Persuasive advertising has the effect of 'inflating' the consumers' intrinsic valuation of the product; more precisely, what consumer θ is effectively willing to pay for one unit of the product is $g(A)\theta$, with $g(0) = 1$ and $g'(A) > 0$. So, at price p, the consumers who are willing to purchase the product are such that $g(A)\theta \geq p$ or $\theta \geq p/g(A)$, which yields a demand of

$$Q(p, A) = 1 - p/g(A).$$

The price elasticity of demand is easily computed as $\eta_{Q,p} = p/(g(A) - p)$, which clearly decreases with A (since $g'(A) > 0$). It follows that a larger advertising expenditure translates into a less elastic demand, which corresponds to the prediction of the persuasive view (which, however, is indistinguishable from the complementary view or the informative view when consumers better learn the fit between product characteristics and tastes).

Case 6.3 Advertising Heinz ketchup[29]

According to demand estimates using scanner data, Heinz advertising has a greater positive effect on those consumers who already have a relatively high willingness to pay. For those readers who have seen Heinz advertising, this may not come as a surprise because Heinz puts emphasis in its advertising on differentiating its brand by stressing the 'thickness' of the ketchup. This is a product characteristic that may be highly valued by some consumers but not others. Consumers who most value this 'thickness' have the highest willingness to pay for Heinz; advertising that focuses on this aspect may raise the willingness to pay for those consumers. If this is the case, advertising reduces the price elasticity of demand.

Informative advertising

In contrast, the second way pertains to the informative view as the increase in demand follows from a better information of the consumers about the *existence* of the product sold by the monopolist.[30] Suppose that there are N consumers in the market, with the same individual decreasing demand function, $d(p)$, for the monopolist's product. Initially, all consumers are unaware of the existence of this product. It is only by receiving an ad that they can get to know the product. The monopolist chooses to send a number A of advertising messages. These messages cannot be targeted to any particular consumer, so that each consumer has the same probability of receiving a message. The consumers who do not purchase are those who have not received an ad. The latter event occurs with probability $\left(1 - \frac{1}{N}\right)^A$, which can be approximated by $e^{-A/N}$ when N is sufficiently large. Total demand is thus given by

$$Q(p, A) = N\left(1 - e^{-A/N}\right)d(p) \equiv G(A)d(p).$$

Note that $G'(A) = e^{-A/N} > 0 > G''(A) = -(e^{-A/N})/N$. The proponents of the informative view expect advertising to make demand more elastic. In this simple monopoly model, however, $\eta_{Q,p} = pd'(p)/d(p)$ is insensitive to the number of advertising messages sent. At least, advertising does not decrease the elasticity of demand, as advocated by the persuasive view. To have informative advertising increase the elasticity of demand, we will consider competition in a differentiated products industry, as we discuss later in this chapter.

6.3   Some welfare economics of advertising

Is advertising socially desirable? Very polarized positions have characterized this long-standing debate. To shed some light on this difficult question, we develop here a formal treatment of the welfare effects of advertising in a monopoly setting, ignoring effects that arise due to imperfect competition.[31] Our starting point is the general model we used in the previous section. Recall that the monopolist chooses the price of its product, p, and its advertising expenditure, A, so as to maximize its profit, $\Pi(p, A) = pQ(p, A) - C(Q(p, A)) - A$, where $Q(p, A)$ is the demand function, which decreases in price and increases in advertising expenditure, $Q_p < 0$ and $Q_A > 0$. For a given (p, A), we can then define social welfare as

$$W(p, A) = \Pi(p, A) + \int_p^{r(A)} Q(p, A)\,dp,$$

where $r(A)$ satisfies $Q(r(A), A) = 0$ (that is, $r(A)$ is the maximum price consumers are willing to pay; it may vary with advertising).

To measure the welfare effects of advertising, we take the following steps: (i) we start with the monopoly solution (p_m, A_m) defined by Equations (6.1) and (6.2); (ii) we change advertising to some nearby level A; (iii) we assume that the monopolist reacts with its profit-maximizing price $p_m(A)$; (iv) we compute the change in welfare. Translated in mathematical terms, we want to evaluate

$$\left.\frac{dW(p_m(A), A)}{dA}\right|_{A=A_m} = \left\{\frac{d\Pi(p_m(A), A)}{dA} + Q(r(A), A)r'(A)\right.$$
$$\left.\left. - Q(p_m(A), A)p'_m(A) + \int_{p_m(A)}^{r(A)} Q_A(p, A)\,dp\right\}\right|_{A=A_m}.$$

The first term is equal to zero because, under (6.1) and (6.2), advertising does not have a first-order effect on profit. The second term is also equal to zero by the very definition of $r(A)$. The previous expression can thus be rewritten as

$$\left.\frac{dW(p_m(A), A)}{dA}\right|_{A=A_m} = -Q(p_m, A_m)p'_m(A_m) + \int_{p_m}^{r(A_m)} Q_A(p, A_m)\,dp. \qquad (6.4)$$

The first term in (6.4) has been highlighted by Dixit and Norman (1978). They show that, whether welfare is calculated on the basis of the pre- or the post-advertising demand curve, the change in welfare due to a slight increase in advertising, starting from the monopoly solution, is equal to the monopoly quantity ($Q(p_m, A_m)$) multiplied by the opposite of the variation in the monopoly price resulting from the increase in advertising ($-p'_m(A_m)$). That is, if advertising raises the monopoly price, then it reduces the consumer surplus and, thereby, social welfare. But it can be argued that Dixit and Norman do not take the right perspective by measuring the impact of advertising relative to a fixed standard (be it the pre- or the post-advertising demand). One should instead compare the consumer surplus under the pre-advertising demand curve with the consumer surplus under the post-advertising demand curve. This is where the second term in (6.4) comes in. This term accounts for the additional consumer surplus that advertising generates on the infra-marginal units (i.e., the units below the pre-advertising quantity $Q(p_m, A_m)$) as demand shifts under the increase in advertising. This second term is positive as it represents a social benefit from advertising, which arises regardless of whether the price increases or decreases. Combining the two terms, we can draw the following lesson.

Lesson 6.2   **If additional advertising does not cause the monopolist to raise its price (i.e., if $p'_m(A_m) \leq 0$), then the monopolist supplies too little advertising, as an increase in advertising above the monopoly level would be welfare-improving. On the other hand, when advertising increases price, it induces two conflicting effects on welfare and the net effect is ambiguous.**

The previous lesson leaves us with the question of the direction of the price change induced by additional advertising; that is, we still need to ascertain the sign of $p'_m(A_m)$. As we now show, the direction of the price change depends on the nature of advertising and on the monopoly's cost function. Note that the following discussion is rather technical.

By definition, $p_m(A)$ is the solution to the first-order condition $\partial \Pi / \partial p = 0$. Totally differentiating the latter equation, we have

$$\frac{\partial^2 \Pi}{\partial p^2} dp + \frac{\partial^2 \Pi}{\partial p \partial A} dA = 0 \Leftrightarrow \frac{dp}{dA} = \frac{\partial^2 \Pi / \partial p \partial A}{-\partial^2 \Pi / \partial p^2}.$$

As the second-order condition for profit maximization imposes that $\partial^2 \Pi / \partial p^2 < 0$, it follows that sign $\{p'_m(A)\} = $ sign $\{\partial^2 \Pi / \partial p \partial A\}$. Now, to find $\partial^2 \Pi / \partial p \partial A$, we differentiate (6.1) with respect to A:

$$\frac{\partial^2 \Pi}{\partial p \partial A} = Q_A + (p - C') Q_{pA} - C'' Q_A Q_P. \tag{6.5}$$

Let us go back to the two examples we developed in Section 6.2. In the second example, illustrating the informative view of advertising, we obtained the following demand function: $Q(p, A) = N(1 - e^{-A/N}) d(p) \equiv G(A) d(p)$. It follows that $Q_p = G(A) d'(p) < 0$, $Q_A = G'(A) d(p) > 0$, and $Q_{pA} = G'(A) d'(p) < 0$. Introducing these values in (6.5) and rearranging terms, we have

$$\frac{\partial^2 \Pi}{\partial p \partial A} = G'(A)\left[d(p) + (p - C')d'(p)\right] - C''Q_A Q_P = -C''Q_A Q_P.$$

The second equality follows from (6.1): $d(p) + (p - C')d'(p) = 0$. As $Q_A Q_P < 0$, we thus have that sign $\{p'_m(A)\} = $ sign $\{C''\}$: advertising does not increase the monopoly price if $C'' \leq 0$, i.e., if the marginal cost is constant or decreasing. We can thus complement Lesson 6.2: *when advertising is informative, monopoly advertising is socially insufficient if marginal cost is constant or decreasing.*

Consider now the first example, representative of persuasive advertising. In that example, the demand function was given by $Q(p, A) = 1 - p/g(A)$, with $g'(A) > 0$. To simplify the exposition, we suppose that marginal cost is constant and equal to c, and we set $g(A) = \alpha A$. In that case, the first-order condition (6.1) becomes

$$\frac{\partial \Pi}{\partial p} = \frac{\alpha A - 2p + c}{\alpha A} = 0 \Leftrightarrow p_m(A) = \frac{\alpha A + c}{2}.$$

It is clear that $p'_m(A) > 0$: *persuasive advertising raises the monopoly price*. So, here, we have that the two terms in (6.4) have opposite signs. However, it can be shown that, in this specific example, the net effect is still positive. Therefore, *even if persuasive advertising increases the monopoly price, the monopolist may provide too little advertising from a social point of view*. The latter conclusion also holds for complementary advertising (i.e., when advertising facilitates social prestige).

6.4   Advertising and competition

In oligopolistic markets, advertising inevitably affects competition. Of course, the question of interest is whether advertising toughens or softens competition. From the above discussion about the different views on advertising, we already guess that the answer to this question is ambiguous. Advertising can play a constructive as well as a combative role.[d] Advertising plays a *constructive role* when it informs consumers about the existence, characteristics and prices of products, or when it increases the perceived differences between brands. Then, advertising increases total demand and/or product differentiation and is therefore likely to soften price competition. In contrast, advertising plays a *combative role* when it mainly helps firms steal each other's business. Then, advertising is likely to toughen price competition. This is the general intuition. But we will see below, considering in turn instances of informative and persuasive advertising, that things can be more complicated when we go down to the detailed working of particular markets.

6.4.1   Informative advertising

Advertising can provide consumers with direct information about the existence, the characteristics and/or the prices of products available on the market. Even when advertising does not

---

[d] The terminology is due to Marshall (1919). The debate on the social value of advertising had already started in the nineteenth century (see e.g. Marshall, 1890).

contain information of this kind, or when the information is not verifiable, advertising may still play an indirect informative role (see Chapter 12). Here, we focus on the direct informative role of advertising.

In some markets, consumers are not aware of products and therefore have either to search or be exposed to advertising. Suppose that it is up to the firms to inform consumers about products via advertising; that is, individual consumer search is assumed to be prohibitively costly.[e] If consumers learn about the existence of a good, they buy it if their reservation price exceeds the price and if they prefer this product to other products they are informed about. Clearly, if a consumer does not know other products, the firm as the sole provider is in a monopoly position with respect to this buyer. However, since firms are assumed not to be able to monitor the information consumers have received, firms have to keep in mind that other consumers do know about other goods and, therefore, that a higher price may mean lower sales. Increasing the advertising expenditure leads to more informed consumers of the particular product, which means that a better advertising technology leads to more informed consumers and higher profits. This indeed holds in the monopoly setup, i.e., in markets in which the behaviour of other firms can be taken as given. But with imperfect competition, more advertising leads to more consumers who are informed about the existence of *several* products. This tends to lead to more intense competition. Overall, a better advertising technology may lead to lower profits of the firms.

We formalize this intuition with the help of the Hotelling model with linear transport costs where two firms are located at the extreme points of the unit interval.[32] There is a unit mass of consumers who are uniformly distributed over this interval. The notation is as before: a consumer x has utility $u = r - \tau x - p_1$ if he buys one unit of good 1 and $u = r - \tau (1 - x) - p_2$ if he buys one unit of good 2. Among consumers who know about both products, there is an indifferent consumer $\widehat{x}$ who is given by

$$r - \tau \widehat{x} - p_1 = r - \tau (1 - \widehat{x}) - p_2 \Leftrightarrow \widehat{x} = \tfrac{1}{2} - \tfrac{1}{2\tau} (p_1 - p_2).$$

Then if all consumers knew both products, demand for good 1 would be

$$Q_1(p_1, p_2) = \widehat{x} (p_1, p_2) = \tfrac{1}{2} - \tfrac{1}{2\tau} (p_1 - p_2)$$

and demand for good 2, $Q_2(p_1, p_2) = 1 - \widehat{x} (p_1, p_2)$.

However, only a share λ_i of consumers know about the existence of product i. We assume that the probability that a consumer is informed is independent of the location, so that advertising is not targeted and independent of the fact whether a consumer knows about the competitor's product. Then, there are $\lambda_i \lambda_j$ consumers who know about the existence of both goods. Consumers in this group are fully informed. There are $\lambda_i (1 - \lambda_j)$ consumers who know of the existence only of product i but not of product j.

There are thus three types of consumers: fully informed consumers who know both products, partially informed consumers who know one of the two products, and uninformed consumers who know none. Uninformed consumers do not buy. Partially informed consumers have to decide whether to buy the good they know: in the case where a consumer knows good i, she buys if $r - \tau - p_i \geq 0$. For simplicity, we assume that r is large enough so as to guarantee

---

[e] In the next chapter, we make the alternative assumption that search is not too costly.

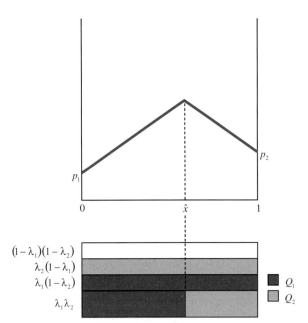

Figure 6.1 Demand with informative advertising

that the latter inequality is met, meaning that it is individually rational for all consumers to buy at least one of the goods.

Firms simultaneously set prices and the number of advertisements. To inform a share λ_i of consumers about the existence, characteristics and price of product i, a firm incurs costs of $A(\lambda_i)$, $A' > 0$, $A'' > 0$. For the sake of simplicity, we assume that A takes the quadratic form $A(\lambda_i) = a\lambda_i^2/2$. If advertising was associated with low cost, firms would inform all consumers. To exclude this possibility we assume that $a > \tau/2$.

Thus, $(1 - \lambda_1)(1 - \lambda_2)$ is the share of uninformed consumers, $\lambda_1(1 - \lambda_2)$ is the share of consumers informed about product 1 but not about product 2, $\lambda_2(1 - \lambda_1)$ is the share of consumers informed about product 2 but not about product 1, and $\lambda_1\lambda_2$ is the share of fully informed consumers. Demand for firm 1 is then of the form

$$Q_1(p_1, p_2, \lambda_1, \lambda_2) = \lambda_1 \left[(1 - \lambda_2) + \lambda_2 \hat{x}(p_1, p_2) \right]$$
$$= \lambda_1 \left[(1 - \lambda_2) + \lambda_2 \tfrac{1}{2\tau}(\tau - p_1 + p_2) \right].$$

Similarly for firm 2. Figure 6.1 illustrates the demand of the two firms. The upper part of the figure identifies the indifferent consumer $\hat{x}$. Demand among consumers who know both products splits accordingly.

More informative advertising from both firms first leads to a larger share of fully informed consumers. This implies, as we now show, that more informative advertising raises the price elasticity of demand (which confirms the prediction of the informative view). Consider a symmetric situation, i.e., $p_1 = p_2 \equiv p$ and $\lambda_1 = \lambda_2 \equiv \lambda$. The price elasticity of demand is

$$\eta_{p_1, Q_1} = \left(\frac{-\lambda_1\lambda_2}{2\tau} \right) \frac{p_1}{Q_1(p_1, p_2, \lambda_1, \lambda_2)},$$

which, evaluated at symmetric prices, becomes

$$\eta_{p_1,Q}\big|_{p_1=p_2=p} = -\frac{1}{2\tau}\frac{\lambda_2 p}{(1-\lambda_2)+\frac{\lambda_2}{2}} = -\frac{1}{2\tau}\frac{\lambda_2 p}{1-\frac{\lambda_2}{2}} = -\frac{\lambda_2 p}{(2-\lambda_2)\tau}.$$

Set $\lambda = \lambda_2$. It then follows that more informative advertising, which leads to a higher share of consumers who are informed of each product, raises the price elasticity of demand, $(\partial|\eta_{p,Q}|)/(\partial\lambda) > 0$. The reason is that, as λ increases, segments without a competitor become smaller relative to segments with a competitor, which leads to more intense competition.

We now turn to the equilibrium analysis. Firm 1's profit maximization problem is

$$\max_{p_1,\lambda_1} (p_1 - c)\, Q_1\,(p_1, p_2, \lambda_1, \lambda_2) - A\,(\lambda_1).$$

Correspondingly for firm 2. We characterize the Nash-equilibrium in pure strategies. Recall that a Nash equilibrium $(p_1^*, p_2^*, \lambda_1^*, \lambda_2^*)$ satisfies

$$(p_1^*, \lambda_1^*) = \arg\max_{p_1,\lambda_1} \pi_1\,(p_1, p_2^*, \lambda_1, \lambda_2^*) \text{ and}$$

$$(p_2^*, \lambda_2^*) = \arg\max_{p_2,\lambda_2} \pi_2\,(p_1^*, p_2, \lambda_1^*, \lambda_2)$$

The first-order conditions of profit maximization can be written as

$$\frac{\partial \pi_1}{\partial p_1} = \lambda_1 \left[(1-\lambda_2) + \lambda_2 \frac{1}{2\tau}(\tau - 2p_1 + p_2 + c)\right] = 0$$

$$\Leftrightarrow p_1 = \frac{p_2 + c + \tau}{2} + \frac{(1-\lambda_2)}{\lambda_2}\tau \tag{6.6}$$

and

$$\frac{\partial \pi_1}{\partial \lambda_1} = (p_1 - c)\left[(1-\lambda_2) + \lambda_2 \frac{1}{2\tau}(\tau - p_1 + p_2)\right] - a\lambda_1 = 0$$

$$\Leftrightarrow \lambda_1 = \frac{1}{a}(p_1 - c)\left[1 - \lambda_2 + \lambda_2 \frac{1}{2\tau}(p_2 - p_1 + \tau)\right]. \tag{6.7}$$

With respect to the price reaction as given by Equation (6.6), recall that $p_1 = \frac{1}{2}(p_2 + c + \tau)$ is the reaction function if all consumers were informed. Hence, if $\lambda_j < 1$, firm i sets a higher price given p_j than with full information of all consumers. This means that the elasticity of demand is lower than with full information. With respect to the advertising reaction as given by Equation (6.7), note that the marginal cost of advertising, $a\lambda_1$, is equal to the marginal revenue of advertising, where the latter is simply the product of the profit margin $p_1 - c$ and the probability that a sale takes place.

We are now in the position to characterize the symmetric equilibrium, i.e., $p_1^* = p_2^* = p^*$ and $\lambda_1^* = \lambda_2^* = \lambda^*$.[f] Substituting into the reaction functions (6.6) and (6.7), we have

$$p^* = \frac{p^* + c + \tau}{2} + \frac{1-\lambda^*}{\lambda^*}\tau \Leftrightarrow p^* = c + \tau + 2\frac{1-\lambda^*}{\lambda^*}\tau$$

$$\Leftrightarrow p^* = c + \frac{2-\lambda^*}{\lambda^*}\tau. \tag{6.8}$$

---

[f] Note that, for given λ's, profit functions are concave in the vicinity of the solution to the first-order conditions that come from maximizing profit with respect to price. Hence, we characterize local maxima. For prices to be global maximizers, r must not be too large. Otherwise, a firm could profitably deviate by setting a much larger price and serve only consumers who are not informed about its competitor's product.

We also solve for the equilibrium share of consumers that receive advertising by some firm i (which depends on the equilibrium price and will be rewritten below):

$$\lambda^* = \frac{1}{a}(p^* - c)\left(1 - \lambda^* + \frac{\lambda^*}{2}\right) = \frac{1}{a}(p^* - c)\left(1 - \frac{\lambda^*}{2}\right).$$

Substituting for p^* using the equilibrium value given by Equation (6.8), we further rewrite:

$$\lambda^* = \frac{\tau}{a}\frac{2 - \lambda^*}{\lambda^*}\left(1 - \frac{\lambda^*}{2}\right) \Leftrightarrow \frac{2a}{\tau}(\lambda^*)^2 = (2 - \lambda^*)^2$$

$$\Leftrightarrow \sqrt{\frac{2a}{\tau}}\lambda^* = 2 - \lambda^* \Leftrightarrow \left(1 + \sqrt{\frac{2a}{\tau}}\right)\lambda^* = 2$$

$$\Leftrightarrow \lambda^* = \frac{2}{1 + \sqrt{2a/\tau}}. \tag{6.9}$$

The expression on the right-hand side of Equation (6.9) gives the equilibrium share of consumers who are informed through advertising depending on exogenous parameters of the model. We can use this expression and substitute into Equation (6.8) to obtain equilibrium prices that only depend on exogenous parameters,

$$p^* = c + \tau\frac{2 - \frac{2}{1+\sqrt{2a/\tau}}}{\frac{2}{1+\sqrt{2a/\tau}}} = c + \tau\left[\left(1 + \sqrt{2a/\tau}\right) - 1\right]$$

$$= c + \tau\sqrt{2a/\tau} = c + \sqrt{2a\tau}.$$

To summarize the analysis we state the following result. *In the informative advertising model presented above, in equilibrium, firms set prices $p_1^* = p_2^* = c + \sqrt{2a\tau}$ and inform the share $\lambda_1^* = \lambda_2^* = 2/\left(1 + \sqrt{2a/\tau}\right)$ of consumers.*
Finally, we report equilibrium profits,

$$\pi_1^* = \pi_2^* = \frac{2a}{\left(1 + \sqrt{2a/\tau}\right)^2}.$$

We are now in a position to make a number of observations with respect to the equilibrium with informative advertising. The need to inform consumers affects equilibrium prices. First, it is immediate to see that $p^* > c + \tau$ since $a > \tau/2$. This shows that the price is higher than $c + \tau$, which would be the equilibrium price if all consumers were fully informed. The reason is that a lower elasticity of demand implies a higher markup. Second, we observe that more product differentiation leads to a higher price, $(\partial p^*)/(\partial \tau) > 0$ and this effect is stronger than in the situation in which all consumers are fully informed. Third, a decrease in the cost of advertising a leads to a lower price, $(\partial p^*)/(\partial a) > 0$. Here, advertising is informative and more advertising reduces the number of consumers who lack information about the existence of the competitor's products. This leads to more intense competition and thus reduces price.[33]
The amount of advertising is, in equilibrium, affected by the cost of advertising and the degree of product differentiation. First, as advertising becomes cheaper, there is more advertising (measured by the number of informed consumers), $(\partial\lambda^*)/(\partial a) < 0$. Second, the more differentiated the products, the more firms advertise, $(\partial\lambda^*)/(\partial \tau) > 0$. The reason is that more production differentiation relaxes price competition. Thus, if the situation increasingly

resembles a monopoly environment, the firm has stronger incentive to advertise because the negative competition effect that arises from advertising is avoided.

Since prices and advertising decisions are affected by the degree of product differentiation and the advertising cost, profits are also affected. First, we observe that profits increase with the degree of product differentiation, measured by the parameter τ. Formally, $\partial \pi_i^*/\partial \tau > 0$. This is hardly surprising since a larger τ reduces the elasticity of demand and thus increases the market power of each firm. Second, we observe that profits increase as advertising becomes more costly, $\partial \pi_i^*/\partial a > 0$. This result may look surprising at first sight because the direct (non-strategic) effect is negative: in particular, for given p and λ, higher a leads to lower profits. Also, in a monopoly environment, a higher advertising cost would lead to lower profits. However, with imperfect competition, there is an opposite strategic effect which dominates: higher advertising costs lead to lower shares of informed consumers λ. In particular, for each firm the share of fully informed consumers is smaller. Thus demand is less elastic, which translates into higher prices.

Lesson 6.3   **Due to strategic effects of informative advertising, higher advertising costs translate into more market power. Firms' profits can therefore be higher in a market with higher advertising costs.**

The prediction of the model may be tested in a market which experiences an industry shock in the form of lower advertising costs. For instance, the rise of Internet search engines may have lowered advertising costs. The prediction of the model then would be that with the presence of Internet search engines, firms' profits are actually lower than before.

Another application would be restrictions of advertising and industry lobbying in favour of these restrictions. The idea here is that a high a serves as a collusive device. In particular, industry representatives may lobby for restrictions on the type and frequency of advertising that are allowed. In the extreme case, if consumers have some local information, firms may lobby to prohibit advertising. This may help to explain the advertising restrictions that are self-imposed by certain professions (such as lawyers or accountants).

6.4.2   Persuasive advertising

The persuasive view contends that advertising changes the preferences of the consumers. In the monopoly setting that we considered above, such advertising had the effect of shifting the monopolist's demand outward. In an oligopoly setting, the key question is whether an increase in one firm's demand comes at the expense of another firm's demand or not. If the answer is yes, then advertising only leads to a shift of demand between brands. Advertising entails a business-stealing effect, which raises the possibility that advertising may be excessive.[g] In particular, firms may be caught in a prisoners' dilemma type of situation, where at equilibrium, all firms invest equally in advertising, which leaves market shares and gross profits unchanged but reduces net profits by the advertising costs. In contrast, there may be situations where persuasive advertising results in a global expansion of demand, or in an increase in market

---

[g] Due to business stealing, informative advertising may also be socially excessive.

power, that benefits all firms in the industry. In such a case, the prediction is that the level of advertising obtained in equilibrium may be too low. As discussed above, it is not easy to assess empirically the relative importance of these two effects. Depending on the industry studied, one can conclude whether advertising affects primarily the level of market demand rather than the distribution of market shares, or the opposite.[h]

In this section, we study three distinct ways in which persuasive advertising may affect preferences. To present them, we rely once more on the Hotelling model with linear transport costs where two firms are located at the extreme points of the unit interval.[34] In the basic model, consumers are uniformly distributed on the interval [0, 1] and a consumer with identity $x \in [0, 1]$ has utility $u = r - \tau x - p_1$ if he buys one unit of good 1 and $u = r - \tau (1 - x) - p_2$ if he buys one unit of good 2. We now allow the reservation value (r), the distribution of consumers or the transport cost parameter (τ) to be influenced by advertising. This enables us to model three potential effects of persuasive advertising: respectively, an increase in consumer willingness to pay, a change in the distribution of consumer tastes, or an increase in perceived product differences. We examine advertising competition in these three cases. In Section 6.2, we considered that advertising and pricing decisions were made simultaneously; this assumption makes sense when the main role of advertising is to inform consumers about the existence, the characteristics and/or the price of the product. In the case of persuasive advertising aiming at changing consumers' preferences, it seems more legitimate to assume that advertising decisions are longer-term decisions that are carried out with a strategic view to affecting the environment in which the pricing game is played. We therefore analyse a two-stage game where advertising decisions precede pricing decisions. As for advertising, we stick to the notation of the previous model of competitive informative advertising and denote by λ_i firm i's advertising intensity. Also, we still assume for simplicity that the cost of advertising intensity λ_i is equal to $a\lambda_i^2/2$.

Advertising increases willingness to pay

Advertising may affect consumers' preferences by enhancing the value of the product in the eyes of the consumer (this is what we assumed in the monopoly model of Section 6.2). Here, a simple way to model this effect is to assume that the reservation values may differ across goods, with

$$r_i(\lambda_i) = r + \beta \lambda_i,$$

where β is a positive parameter. That is, by spending λ_i in advertising, firm i raises the consumers' willingness to pay for its product. Then, given advertising intensities (λ_1, λ_2) and prices (p_1, p_2), the indifferent consumer is such that $r + \beta \lambda_1 - \tau \hat{x} - p_1 = r + \beta \lambda_2 - \tau (1 - \hat{x}) - p_2$, or

$$\hat{x}(p_1, p_2; \lambda_1, \lambda_2) = \frac{1}{2} + \frac{p_2 - p_1}{2\tau} + \beta \frac{\lambda_1 - \lambda_2}{2\tau}.$$

It is clear from the latter expression that, at given prices, a firm can increase its market share by advertising more than its rival. In the second stage, firm 1 maximizes

---

[h] Roberts and Samuelson (1988) reach the first conclusion in their study of cigarette advertising, whereas Kelton and Kelton (1982) reach the opposite conclusion in their study of the brewing industry.

$\pi_1 = (p_1 - c)\hat{x}(p_1, p_2; \lambda_1, \lambda_2)$. From the first-order condition, we derive firm 1's reaction function: $p_1 = \frac{1}{2}(c + \tau + p_2 + \beta\lambda_1 - \beta\lambda_2)$. Proceeding in a similar way, we find firm 2's reaction function as $p_2 = \frac{1}{2}(c + \tau + p_1 + \beta\lambda_2 - \beta\lambda_1)$. We thus observe that, all other things equal, when a firm increases its advertising intensity in the first stage, it commits to set its own price higher, and also forces the rival firm to set its price lower in the second stage. Computing the Nash equilibrium prices and profits, we find

$$p_i(\lambda_i, \lambda_j) = c + \tau + \tfrac{1}{3}\beta(\lambda_i - \lambda_j),$$

$$\pi_i(\lambda_i, \lambda_j) = \tfrac{1}{18\tau}(3\tau + \beta(\lambda_i - \lambda_j))^2.$$

In the first stage, firm i chooses λ_i to maximize $\pi_i(\lambda_i, \lambda_j) - (a/2)\lambda_i^2$. The first-order condition is $\frac{\beta}{9\tau}(3\tau + \beta(\lambda_i - \lambda_j)) - a\lambda_i = 0$. Because second-order conditions require that $9a\tau > 2\beta^2$, we have that each firm reacts to an increase in the rival's advertising by decreasing its own advertising (in other words, advertising intensities are strategic substitutes): $\lambda_i = [\beta/(9a\tau - \beta^2)](3\tau - \beta\lambda_j)$. Solving for the Nash equilibrium, we find

$$\lambda_1^* = \lambda_2^* = \beta/(3a).$$

It follows that $p_1^* = p_2^* = c + \tau$ as in the initial Hotelling model. Because both firms choose the same advertising intensity, they increase the willingness to pay for their product in a symmetric way and, thereby, they neutralize each other: equilibrium prices are not affected by advertising. Equilibrium profits are computed as

$$\pi_1^* = \pi_2^* = \frac{\tau}{2} - \frac{\beta^2}{18a} < \frac{\tau}{2}.$$

Firms are made worse off by their ability to make persuasive advertising. As in the model with informative advertising, firms would welcome an increase in advertising costs (larger a) or a reduction in the 'persuasive power' of advertising (lower β). Actually, if firms could cooperate at the advertising stage, they would altogether refrain from advertising. Indeed, acting cooperatively, they would face the following maximization programme:

$$\max_{\lambda_1, \lambda_2}(\pi_1 + \pi_2) = \frac{(3\tau + \beta\lambda_1 - \beta\lambda_2)^2}{18\tau} + \frac{(3\tau + \beta\lambda_2 - \beta\lambda_1)^2}{18\tau} - \tfrac{1}{2}a(\lambda_1^2 + \lambda_2^2).$$

Evaluating the first-order condition at symmetric advertising intensities gives

$$\frac{\partial(\pi_1 + \pi_2)}{\partial\lambda_i}\bigg|_{\lambda_1 = \lambda_2 = \lambda} = -\lambda a < 0,$$

meaning that the optimal choice is $\lambda_1 = \lambda_2 = 0$. We can find in the latter result a second explanation as to why some professional associations are in favour of legislation that forbid advertising for their profession.[i]

---

[i] Recall the first explanation we drew from our analysis of informative advertising: restrictions on advertising (or higher advertising costs) were seen as a collusive device, allowing firms to keep a larger share of consumers uninformed and, thereby, to relax price competition.

Advertising changes the distribution of consumer tastes

A firm may also use persuasive advertising to mould consumers' preferences so as to convince them that what they *really* want is its product and not the rival one. To capture this idea in the model, we let advertising transform the initial uniform distribution of the consumers into a different distribution. To be precise, we take the following symmetric distribution function:

$$F(x; \lambda_1, \lambda_2) = (1 + \lambda_1 - \lambda_2)x - (\lambda_1 - \lambda_2)x^2, \tag{6.10}$$

with continuous density

$$f(x; \lambda_1, \lambda_2) = (1 + \lambda_1 - \lambda_2) - 2(\lambda_1 - \lambda_2)x.$$

If both firms make the same advertising expenditure λ, we keep the initial uniform distribution: $F(x; \lambda, \lambda) = x$ and $f(x; \lambda, \lambda) = 1$. If firm 1 advertises more than firm 2, $\lambda_1 > \lambda_2$, then we have a concave distribution, which is biased towards firm 1. Conversely, if $\lambda_1 < \lambda_2$, then the distribution is convex and biased towards firm 2. For instance, density $f(x; 1, 0) = 2 - 2x$ favours firm 1, while the density $f(x; 0, 1) = 2x$ favours firm 2.

The demand for firm 1 is given by $F(\hat{x}; \lambda_1, \lambda_2)$ and the demand for firm 2 by $1 - F(\hat{x}; \lambda_1, \lambda_2)$, where $\hat{x} = \frac{1}{2} + \frac{p_2 - p_1}{2\tau}$ identifies the indifferent consumer. Using expression (6.10), we have

$$Q_1(p_1, p_2; \lambda_1, \lambda_2) = (1 + \lambda_1 - \lambda_2)\left(\frac{1}{2} + \frac{p_2 - p_1}{2\tau}\right) - (\lambda_1 - \lambda_2)\left(\frac{1}{2} + \frac{p_2 - p_1}{2\tau}\right)^2.$$

Because of the relative complexity of the latter demand function, we consider here that firms choose advertising intensities and prices simultaneously and we invoke symmetry to considerably simplify the problem. Firm 1 solves the following programme:

$$\max_{\lambda_1, p_1} \pi_1(p_1, p_2; \lambda_1, \lambda_2) = (p_1 - c)Q_1(p_1, p_2; \lambda_1, \lambda_2) - \frac{a}{2}\lambda_1^2.$$

The first-order condition with respect to p_1 is

$$\frac{\partial \pi_1}{\partial p_1} = Q_1 + \frac{\partial Q_1}{\partial p_1}(p_1 - c) = 0.$$

At the symmetric equilibrium, $\lambda_1 = \lambda_2 = \lambda$, which implies that $Q_1 = \hat{x}$ and $\partial Q_1/\partial p_1 = -1/(2\tau)$. It follows that the reaction functions are exactly the same as in the Hotelling model, yielding the usual equilibrium prices, $p_1^* = p_2^* = c + \tau$. The first-order condition with respect to λ_1 is

$$\frac{\partial \pi_1}{\partial \lambda_1} = \frac{\partial Q_1}{\partial \lambda_1}(p_1 - c) - a\lambda_1 = \left(\frac{1}{4} - \left(\frac{p_2 - p_1}{2\tau}\right)^2\right)(p_1 - c) - a\lambda_1 = 0.$$

Using the fact that $p_1^* = p_2^* = c + \tau$, we can rewrite the latter equation as $\frac{1}{4}\tau - a\lambda_1 = 0$, which implies that $\lambda_1^* = \lambda_2^* = \tau/(4a)$.[j]

As in the case where advertising increases willingness to pay, both firms advertise but end up neutralizing each other. Advertising expenditures are thus a mere cost for the firms, which are trapped in a prisoners' dilemma. Equilibrium profits are (assuming that $16a > \tau$ to

---

[j] When solving the two-stage game, we find almost the same result: prices are still equal to $c + \tau$, but the equilibrium advertising expenditure is lower: $\lambda^* = \tau/(6a)$.

guarantee positive profits)

$$\pi_1^* = \pi_2^* = \frac{1}{2}\tau - \frac{\tau^2}{32a} < \frac{1}{2}\tau.$$

We can draw the following lesson from the two cases we just analyzed.

Lesson 6.4 **When firms invest in persuasive advertising that increases the willingness to pay for their product or that changes the distribution of consumer tastes in their favour, advertising expenditures are simply a form of wasteful competition: if firms could cooperate, they would agree not to advertise.**

Advertising increases perceived product differences

Advertising may finally lead consumers to attach more importance to those differences that already exist between the two products. In the Hotelling model, the transportation cost parameter τ is an inverse measure of the substitutability between any given pair of products. That is, a larger value of τ means that products are seen as more differentiated. So, a simple way to capture the idea that persuasive advertising increases perceived product difference is to have

$$\tau(\lambda_1, \lambda_2) = \tau + \beta\lambda_1 + \beta\lambda_2.$$

As for the second-stage pricing game, we can simply replicate the analysis of the Hotelling model by changing the transport cost:

$$p_1(\lambda_1, \lambda_2) = p_2(\lambda_1, \lambda_2) = c + \tau + \beta\lambda_1 + \beta\lambda_2,$$
$$\pi_1(\lambda_1, \lambda_2) = \pi_2(\lambda_1, \lambda_2) = \tfrac{1}{2}(\tau + \beta\lambda_1 + \beta\lambda_2).$$

At the first stage, firm i chooses λ_i to maximize $\frac{1}{2}(\tau + \beta\lambda_i + \beta\lambda_j) - \frac{a}{2}\lambda_i^2$. The first-order condition is simply $\beta/2 - a\lambda_i = 0$, which gives $\lambda_1^* = \lambda_2^* = \beta/(2a)$. It follows that prices and profits at the subgame perfect equilibrium are respectively given by[k]

$$p_1^* = p_2^* = c + \tau + \frac{\beta^2}{a} \quad \text{and} \quad \pi_1^* = \pi_2^* = \frac{\tau}{2} + \frac{3\beta^2}{8a}.$$

In this case, because persuasive advertising increases product differentiation, it allows firms to relax price competition and to make higher profits. Note that advertising has a public good nature, which leads each firm to free-ride on the other firm's effort. Indeed, if firms were choosing advertising intensities cooperatively in the first stage, they would advertise more (it is easily checked that they would choose $\lambda = \beta/a$) and achieve even higher profits.

Lesson 6.5 **Firms invest in persuasive advertising that increases perceived product differences to relax price competition and, thereby, achieve higher profits. Because advertising is a public good in that case, firms would even be better off by coordinating their advertising decisions.**

[k] We assume that $r > c + \frac{3}{2}\tau + \frac{3}{2}\frac{\beta^2}{a}$, which makes sure that the market is still covered after the increase in perceived product differentiation (or that advertising does not allow firms to become local monopolists).

The previous result explains why some industry associations find it profitable to carry out coordinated advertising or promotion campaigns. Such joint campaigns are even more likely when advertising is also informative, as illustrated in Case 6.4.

Case 6.4 Joint advertising campaign to promote private healthcare

The following announcement was posted on www.privatehealth.co.uk in December 2005 (emphasis added). 'For the first time ever, a group of insurers and independent hospitals *have combined* to launch a major television and newspaper advertising campaign *to promote the benefits of private healthcare*. Six of Britain's leading private hospitals and health insurance companies *have joined forces* to champion the benefits of private healthcare. AXA PPP healthcare, BMI Healthcare, BUPA Hospitals, BUPA Health Insurance, Norwich Union Healthcare and Standard Life Healthcare are backing a one million pound, one month national press campaign with strong positive messages about the industry and its contribution to the health of the nation.'

One simple explanation for such announcements is that advertising is used to increase industry demand. A different explanation, advanced by the previous model, is that advertising increases the visibility of different insurers, which raises the perceived differences between them. This suggests that either the persuasive view or the direct informative view is relevant. According to the latter, consumers learn about true differences between insurers; according to the former, consumers are made to believe that such differences exist.

While we have framed the possibly anticompetitive effect of advertising in the context of persuasive advertising, it would be misleading to attribute to informative advertising a procompetitive effect in general. Indeed, by informing consumers about product-specific characteristics, firms can increase the degree of observed product differentiation and thus relax competition.

Review questions

1. Which industries advertise a lot? Give two examples and discuss the likely reasons for high advertising expenditures.

2. Discuss the difference between persuasive advertising and advertising as a complement.

3. Consider informative advertising about a product's existence. Does an increase in the advertising cost function necessarily lead to lower profits? Discuss.

4. Discuss possible effects of persuasive advertising under imperfect competition.

Further reading

The basic monopoly model of advertising goes back to Dorfman and Steiner (1954). The welfare economics of advertising have been advanced by Dixit and Norman (1978). On the strategic effects of informative advertising see Grossman and Shapiro (1984). Our analysis of persuasive advertising is based on Bloch and Manceau (1999) and von der Fehr and Stevik (1998). Ackerberg (2001) analyses how to empirically distinguish between informative and persuasive advertising. Bagwell (2007) provides a detailed account of the economics literature on advertising.

7 Consumer inertia

The first two chapters of Part III examined how firms choose two main elements of the marketing mix, namely product positioning and advertising, in order to gain market power. In that sense, market power was endogenous as it resulted from the firms' strategic choices. In this chapter, strategic choices of this kind are absent as we mostly consider sources of market power that are exogenous to the firms' conduct. In a nutshell, what confers market power to the firms is the presence of some form of inertia in the purchasing behaviour of the consumers. As we will observe throughout this chapter, such inertia may come from different sources and may enable firms to deploy various strategies.

In Section 7.1, we consider environments in which firms sell identical products and do not make any advertisement. We show that firms can nevertheless enjoy market power if consumers are imperfectly informed about the existence and prices of available products. Not only are prices above marginal costs, but also prices may differ across firms and/or across time, a phenomenon known as price dispersion. We further show that such price dispersion may persist even when consumers incur costs to search for information about products and prices.

In Section 7.2, we consider markets where switching firms is costly for the consumers, which induces them to purchase repeatedly from the same firm. This gives firms market power over those consumers who have purchased from them in the past. Because this form of consumer lock-in results either from environmental factors (such as learning costs) or from the firms' conduct (e.g., by offering discounts to their past customers), we have here a mixture of endogenous and exogenous market power. More importantly, because market power results from consumers' past choices, the problems we analyse in this section are inherently dynamic.

Finally, in Section 7.3, we study another dynamic problem that arises in markets where firms are able to identify from whom consumers have bought in the past. In such markets, firms may decide to offer special discounts as an attempt to 'poach' the customers of their competitors. In this section, as in the previous one, we are interested in the impacts on competition: we will examine under which conditions switching costs and poaching make markets more or less competitive.

7.1 Uninformed consumers and search costs

In the previous chapter, we considered situations where consumers (i) did not know about the existence, characteristics or price of existing products, and (ii) obtained 'passively' the relevant information through the firms' informative advertising. Here, we maintain the first feature (at least some consumers lack information) but we modify the second: instead of being passive, information acquisition is now active in the sense that consumers can *search* for the information themselves.[a] However, one important result of this section is that the existence of positive search costs for at least some consumers allows firms to exert market power, even in homogeneous product markets with price-setting firms. More strikingly, we also describe equilibria that exhibit not only average prices above marginal cost but also *price dispersion*. Such price dispersion invalidates the so-called 'law of one price' that the standard Bertrand model of Chapter 3 predicted, and also meets the facts: empirical studies consistently report the existence of price dispersion in many homogeneous markets and attribute it not only to hidden product heterogeneities but also to information costs (costs of searching for price information on the consumer side, or costs of transmitting this information on the firm side).[b]

Before presenting this empirical literature (in Subsection 7.1.3), we review several lines of theoretical research examining the drivers of price dispersion. We start with situations where a share of the consumers is (exogenously) uninformed about the prevailing prices (Subsection 7.1.1). We move then to environments where consumers optimally decide whether to search for the information or not (Subsection 7.1.2). Note that in Chapter 23, we will extend the previous analyses to examine the effects of price comparison search engines, also known as shopping robots or 'shopbots'.

7.1.1   Price dispersion

In many industries, we observe price dispersion, meaning that at any point in time prices for essentially the same product are different across firms. One explanation is that some consumers are better informed than others and that the better informed consumers obtain a better deal than the less informed. We will look at two situations. In the first situation, suppose there are two firms, one firm focuses on the locked-in uninformed consumers, whereas the other firm, apart from selling to its own locked-in consumers, sells to all informed consumers. While the first firm enjoys a large markup but sells few units, the second firm sacrifices on its margin but sells many units. We can call this type of price dispersion *spatial price dispersion*. In the second situation, all firms randomize over price. Then for all prices over which firms randomize, profits must be equalized. We call this type of price dispersion *temporal price dispersion*.

Spatial price dispersion

Spatial price dispersion occurs in a situation where multiple sellers contemporaneously offer a homogeneous product at different prices. Formally, firms do not randomize over prices but choose asymmetric pure strategies. Hence, whereas some firm can be called a high-price firm,

---

[a] Clearly, in reality, search and advertising coexist: both consumers and firms spend resources to find each other in the marketplace. We separate the two in order to identify better their respective effects. For analyses of the interaction between search and advertising activities, see Anderson and Renault (2006) and Janssen and Non (2007). For an alternative route, see also our analysis of information gatekeepers in Chapter 23 based on Baye and Morgan (2001), where firms and consumers spend resources in the information transmission process.

[b] Recall that a homogeneous product market may also exhibit price dispersion if costs are private information (see Chapter 3). A distinguishing feature of models with consumer search is that more than one firm is active. For a combination of a search model with private information about costs, see MacMinn (1980).

another can be called a low-price firm. Consumers know that one firm is always the low-price firm but some of them do not know which one.

We analyse a duopoly market with two types of consumers.[35] One group of consumers consists of informed consumers who know all the prices (e.g., because they read the informative price advertising in the newspaper or because they use a price search engine on the Internet). The other consumers are uninformed in the sense that they only know the price of the store they go to frequently or that is located in their neighbourhood, without considering offers at other stores (this may be a physical store or a website). In other words, some consumers search and switch without any friction from one store to the other, whereas others have prohibitively high search or switching costs. A high-priced store only attracts uninformed consumers from its 'neighbourhood'.

Since products are homogeneous, a consumer who knows the two products buys the lowest-priced product. We assume that consumers have unit demand and a finite reservation price r, which differs across consumers. Suppose that a share λ^I of consumers is informed about both products and a share $1 - \lambda^I$ is uninformed (i.e., they only know one of the products). In the context of physical retailing, the interpretation is that the latter consumers only know the price of their neighbourhood store but not of the other store. Assuming symmetry, the share of uninformed consumers per firm is $\lambda^U = (1 - \lambda^I)/2$. Firms have constant marginal costs of production c. Denote $Q(p)$ the market demand of consumers. Suppose that the demand function of the uninformed consumers does not differ from the demand by informed consumers and suppose that the monopoly pricing problem is well-defined, i.e. there is a unique solution $p^m = \arg\max_p (p - c)Q(p)$. Then a firm that sells only to uninformed consumers makes profit $\pi^U = \lambda^U(p^m - c)Q(p^m)$. Clearly, a firm will never make lower profits in any equilibrium. Suppose that firm 2 follows this strategy and sets $p_2 = p^m$. Clearly, firm 1 setting $p = p^m - \varepsilon$ cannot be an equilibrium because firm 2 would have an incentive to undercut the competitor to sell to all informed consumers itself. For any price p set by firm 1, we must therefore ask whether firm 2 has an incentive to undercut. Reversely, firm 1 will never settle for an outcome in which its profit is less than π^U. Hence, we must have

$$\lambda^U(p^m - c)Q(p^m) = (\lambda^U + \lambda^I)(p_1 - c)Q(p_1).$$

This defines a price $\widetilde{p}_1$ and has the property that both firms make the same profit (albeit at different prices) and firm 2 does not have an incentive to deviate from this strategy. But does firm 1 have an incentive to deviate? If it increases its price but keeps it below p^m, it will still serve all informed consumers but make a higher profit per consumer. Thus we have found that *in the present model, in which firms simultaneously set prices, there does not exist an equilibrium in pure strategies* (we will analyse mixed strategy in a slightly modified model below).

Suppose now that, say, firm 1 is the first mover and firm 2 the second mover. In other words, we are reconsidering the Stackelberg model of Chapter 4. Then for any price $p_1 > \widetilde{p}_1$, firm 2 has an incentive to undercut. To start with the obvious, there is a (subgame perfect) equilibrium in which firm 1 sets p^m and firm 2 sets a price slightly less than p^m. In this equilibrium, firm 1 makes profit π^U and firm 2 makes profit $(\lambda^U + \lambda^I)(p^m - c)Q(p^m)$. Hence, the more flexible firm 2 performs better. Since firm 2 enjoys higher profits, this situation features a second-mover advantage.

There is another subgame perfect equilibrium, which is more interesting for our purposes because it exhibits price dispersion. In this equilibrium, firm 1 sets $p_1 = \tilde{p}_1$ and firm 2 sets $p_2 = p^m$. Note that given p_1, firm 2 has no incentive to deviate. Also firm 1 has no incentive to change its price at stage 1. Setting a lower price cannot increase profits since it cannot increase the number of consumers. Setting a higher price than p_1 triggers the use of an undercutting strategy by firm 2. In this equilibrium, consumers can purchase a homogeneous good but do so at different prices.

Lesson 7.1   **A homogeneous product market with informed and uninformed consumers and sequential price setting may exhibit spatial price dispersion; that is, one firm consistently charges a high price and the other a low price. Due to limited consumer information, uninformed consumers end up paying on average a higher price than informed consumers.**

Temporal price dispersion

As in the previous model, we analyse a market with two groups of consumers.[36] One group of consumers consists of informed consumers, the other consumers are uninformed. High-priced stores only attract uninformed consumers from their neighbourhood. Reducing the price leads (in expectations) to a larger quantity demanded. In a situation of price dispersion, the loss due to price reduction is exactly offset by the positive effect on demand and costs. Since informed consumers tend to buy at a lower price, there is a sort of price discrimination between informed and uninformed consumers.[c] Although all firms sell the same good, the law of one price does not hold: some consumers buy at a high price, others at a lower. While our focus in the previous analysis was on asymmetric pure-strategy equilibria (referred to as 'spatial' price dispersion) here we consider mixed strategies (referred to as 'temporal' price dispersion) in a situation with simultaneous price setting.

We consider a monopolistically competitive market in which there is free entry. Products are homogeneous. Thus a consumer who knows a certain set of products buys the lowest-priced product within this set. We assume that consumers have unit demand and a finite reservation price r. Suppose that, as in the previous model, a share λ^I of consumers is informed and a share $1 - \lambda^I$ is uninformed. There are n identical firms, where n is determined by the free-entry condition $\pi^e(n) = 0$. Consequently, there are $\lambda^U = (1 - \lambda^I)/n$ uninformed consumers per firm (assuming that firms are fully symmetric). Firms have the cost function $C(q)$ with strictly decreasing average (total) costs $C(q)/q$. This is an increasing returns-to-scale property which is satisfied, e.g., if there are a positive fixed cost and constant marginal costs of production, $C(q) = cq + f$. Firms cannot discriminate between informed and uninformed consumers.

---

[c] Related to our remark on vertical product differentiation, 'price discrimination' occurs at the level of the industry. The novel feature here is that this discrimination is due to information asymmetries across consumers (in contrast, in the product-differentiation models in Chapter 5, we assumed that all consumers observe the prices of all products).

Suppose there is a sequence of entry decisions of firms. At a final stage all firms that decided to enter set prices simultaneously. At this stage we allow for random prices, i.e. probability distributions over prices. A strategy at stage 2 is a probability distribution over $\mathcal{R}_+$ denoted by $F(p)$. We want to characterize the equilibrium probability distribution. This means that we want to characterize the symmetric mixed strategy equilibrium of the game. We proceed in seven steps.

(1) Denote

$$\underline{p} = \frac{C(\lambda^I + \lambda^U)}{\lambda^I + \lambda^U}.$$

That is, $\underline{p}$ is equal to the average cost a firm incurs when it serves all its potential consumers (i.e., the informed consumers, λ^I, and its share of uniformed consumers, λ^U). A firm necessarily makes losses for $p < \underline{p}$ because it can not recover costs even in the most favourable circumstances (when all informed consumers buy from it). In any Nash equilibrium, we must have that almost surely firms do not set prices below $\underline{p}$, i.e., $F(p) = 0$ for $p < \underline{p}$.

(2) We must have $F(p) = 1$ for $p > r$. For $p > r$, a firm faces no demand. If other firms chose prices above r with positive probability, a firm could make strictly positive profit by setting its price, e.g., equal to r. Hence, Nash equilibrium strategies must be probability distributions on $[\underline{p}, r]$.

(3) There does not exist a symmetric equilibrium where all firms charge the same price; in other words, there do not exist symmetric pure strategy Nash equilibria and *any symmetric Nash equilibrium must exhibit price dispersion*. The reasons for this are the following. On the one hand, if all firms set $p = \underline{p}$ with probability 1, firms would make losses which violates the zero-profit condition. On the other hand, for any price in $(\underline{p}, r]$, the Bertrand undercutting argument applies; that is, a firm can increase profit by undercutting its competitors.

(4) There cannot be any mass point in the equilibrium strategy. A mass point means that a particular price is chosen with strictly positive probability by all firms. This would imply a strictly positive probability of a tie. Then for $p > \underline{p}$, the undercutting argument applies (also a mass point at $\underline{p}$ can be ruled out because then, with positive probability, more than one firm would set price equal to $\underline{p}$ and thus would make losses).

(5) To determine expected profits, note first that in a symmetric equilibrium, every firm uses the same strategy $F(p)$. Hence, at price p the probability of being the cheapest firm is $(1 - F(p))^{n-1}$. If a firm succeeds in making the best offer, it attracts all informed consumers and its profits in this case of success (subscript s) are $\pi_s(p) = p(\lambda^U + \lambda^I) - C(\lambda^U + \lambda^I)$. On the other hand, if a firm fails in making the best offer, it can only sell to its corresponding share of consumers that is uninformed λ^U and its profits in case of failure (subscript f) are $\pi_f(p) = p\lambda^U - C(\lambda^U)$. Thus, expected profits take the form

$$E_p(\pi_i) = \int_{\underline{p}}^{r} \left\{ \pi_s(p)(1 - F(p))^{n-1} + \pi_f(p) \left[1 - (1 - F(p))^{n-1} \right] \right\} f(p)dp.$$

(6) We are now in a position to determine the equilibrium probability distribution over prices. In a mixed-strategy equilibrium, each price with positive likelihood $f(p) > 0$ must be such that the expected profit conditional on this price be zero, i.e., $\pi_s(p)(1 - F(p))^{n-1} + \pi_f(p)[1 - (1 - F(p))^{n-1}] = 0$. This expression can be rewritten as

$$1 - F(p) = \left(\frac{\pi_f(p)}{\pi_f(p) - \pi_s(p)} \right)^{\frac{1}{n-1}}.$$

Thus we have an explicit expression for the equilibrium distribution of prices on its support. The right-hand side is strictly decreasing in p due to the fact that average costs are strictly decreasing.

(7) As a final step, we show that the support of the equilibrium price distribution is the full range $[\underline{p}, r]$. To see this, note that prices slightly above $\underline{p}$ must be included, thus $F(\underline{p} + \varepsilon) > 0$ for any $\varepsilon > 0$; otherwise, undercutting would be profitable (because price would still be strictly above average costs with the firm serving all informed consumers). Also note that prices slightly below r must be included, thus $F(r - \varepsilon) < 1$ for any $\varepsilon < 0$. Suppose the contrary, namely $F(\hat{p}) = 1$ with $\hat{p} < r$. At $\hat{p}$, only uninformed consumers buy and $\hat{p}\lambda^U - C(\lambda^U) = 0$. Then $r\lambda^U - C(\lambda^U) > 0$ and a deviation to price $p = r$ with probability 1 is profitable. We can summarize our analysis as follows: *the only symmetric equilibrium distribution of prices chosen by each firm is characterized by*

$$F(p) = \begin{cases} 0 & \text{for } p < \underline{p}, \\ 1 - \left(\frac{\pi_f(p)}{\pi_f(p) - \pi_s(p)} \right)^{\frac{1}{n-1}} & \text{for } p \in [\underline{p}, r], \\ 1 & \text{for } p > r. \end{cases}$$

Lesson 7.2   **If firms compete in a market with informed and uninformed consumers, the market may exhibit temporal price dispersion; that is, at equilibrium, firms randomize over prices.**

Note that $\pi_f(r) = 0$ and $\pi_s(\underline{p}) = 0$. These two equations then determine n and $\underline{p}$. If the cost function takes the form $C(q) = cq + f$, the free entry condition $\pi_f(r) = 0$ is equivalent to

$$n = \tfrac{1}{f}(r - c)(1 - \lambda^I).$$

We observe that the equilibrium number of firms increases if the market becomes more profitable, i.e., if the fixed costs f decreases, if the difference between willingness-to-pay and marginal cost $r - c$ increases, or if the share of uninformed consumers $1 - \lambda^I$ increases.

Substituting the expression for n into $\pi_s(\underline{p}) = 0$ and solving for $\underline{p}$, we obtain

$$(\underline{p} - c)\left(\lambda^I + \frac{1 - \lambda^I}{n} \right) - f = 0 \Leftrightarrow (\underline{p} - c)\left(\lambda^I + \frac{f}{r - c} \right) = f$$

$$\Leftrightarrow \underline{p} = c + \frac{f}{\lambda^I + \frac{f}{r-c}}.$$

Hence, the lower bound of the support of the equilibrium price distribution increases with the size of the fixed costs f, with the difference between willingness-to-pay and marginal cost $r - c$, and with the share of uninformed consumers $1 - \lambda^I$. In the limit where all consumers are uninformed, the support shrinks to the single point r, where all firms enjoy monopoly power over $1/n$ of the consumer population.

7.1.2   Consumer search

In the previous models with informed and uninformed consumers, the information acquisition of consumers was exogenous. However, we have many examples in which consumers can decide on whether they want to acquire additional information through costly search. A first important remark is that this does not challenge the previous results. In particular, the equilibrium of the spatial and temporal price dispersion models can be shown to persist when consumers optimally decide to acquire information. Indeed, we can see information as being provided by some third-party 'clearing house' that lists the prices charged by the firms in the market (e.g., a specialized magazine which displays the prices different firms charge for a similar product, or a price comparison search engine, also known as 'shopbot', i.e., a software program that compiles a large database of products sold at online stores). In the model, the value of information (noted V_I) is given by the difference between the expected price paid by those consumers who do access the clearing house and the expected price paid by those who do not. Suppose now that consumers differ in the cost they face to access the clearing house: some have a high cost, z_H, while others have a low cost, z_L. Then, provided that $z_L \leq V_I < z_H$, the group of consumers with cost z_L will optimally use the clearinghouse (thereby becoming 'informed' and paying lower average prices), while the other group will not (thereby staying 'uninformed' and paying larger average prices).[37] Hence, if consumers differ in their information acquisition cost, the price-dispersion equilibrium derived above persists when not only firms, but also consumers, are optimizing.

In other environments, however, consumers do not have access to clearing houses (where the entire list of prices can be accessed for a fixed cost) but rather have to incur an incremental cost to obtain each additional price quote. This is so if they have to visit or phone physical stores, or if they have to search, one by one, the websites of virtual sellers. In such cases, consumers have to form expectations over the prevailing prices since their search efforts depend on expected gains from lower prices. Again, we consider homogeneous products where the only market imperfection is the potential lack of information about existence and prices on the consumer side. Consumers can engage in costly search and thus obtain additional information. We are interested in equilibrium configurations, where, on average, consumers do not regret their decision to search. Formally, we will analyse Bayesian Nash equilibria.

The Diamond paradox

As a starting point, consider an oligopoly in which firms produce a homogeneous product at constant marginal cost c. Consumers learn without cost about the existence and price of a product by one firm (and each firm is equally likely to be drawn). Consumers can decide to learn additional information at an opportunity cost z. We do not need to specify the nature of the search process and the distribution of z in the population; the only relevant assumption we need at this point is that there is a lower bound of search costs $\underline{z} > 0$. We simply assume that a consumer who engages in search learns about the existence and the price of at least one other product.

Suppose that the monopoly problem is well-defined, i.e., there is a unique solution to $\arg\max_p (p - c)Q(p)$. Firms set prices simultaneously and we are interested in the equilibrium outcome in this market. Recall that if search was costless, prices would be equal to marginal cost. Does this result survive with small search costs? The answer is obviously 'no'. If all other firms set prices equal to marginal cost, a firm could slightly increase its price without losing consumers because consumers upon observing this price anticipate that search is not worthwhile. While price equal to marginal cost will not result with positive search costs, the question remains whether equilibrium prices will at least become close to marginal cost as the search cost turns to zero. Again, the answer is 'no'. Worse, firms will fully exploit their market power, as stated in the next lesson.

Lesson 7.3   **If all consumers have positive search costs, oligopolistic firms will set price equal to the monopoly price.**

This is known as the *Diamond paradox* and shows that the Bertrand result crucially depends on the assumption that consumers can acquire information without cost.[38] Note that this is the unique Bayesian Nash equilibrium. First, let us see that setting the monopoly price is indeed an equilibrium. In this equilibrium, consumers expect firms to set the monopoly price. A firm which deviates by setting a lower price certainly makes those consumers happier that learnt about it in the first place, but since the other consumers do not learn about it, this will not attract additional consumers. Given their beliefs, consumers have an incentive to abstain from costly search, so that a deviation by a firm is not rewarded by consumers.

This argument would also hold for deviations from any symmetric prices. However, if $p < p^m$ each firm has an incentive to slightly increase its price above that price p (holding consumer beliefs constant). Therefore, $p < p^m$ does not constitute an equilibrium. Clearly, a price $p > p^m$ cannot be an equilibrium because a deviation to p^m is always profitable (it may even attract additional consumers). Overall, we find that search can substantially alter equilibrium outcomes. In the following, we will look a bit deeper into this issue.

Sequential search

In real-world markets, consumers can often engage in sequential search, i.e., after observing the price of a good at one store they can decide whether to buy or to continue shopping around.[d] In such a situation, we can imagine that these consumers shopping around exert some price discipline on firms, since they will only stop searching if the expected gain from further search is more than offset by the expected search cost. Also, with sequential search, the market should exhibit price dispersion. In addition, firms may never set prices close to the monopoly price.

While a short description of sequential search appears to be intuitive, a formal analysis is rather involved.[39] We therefore restrict ourselves to describing how a sequential search

---

[d] Alternatively, consumers can search in a non-sequential way, i.e., they decide how many prices to observe before purchasing from the store with the lowest observed price. See Baye, Morgan and Scholten (2006) for a review of non-sequential (or fixed sample size) search and a comparison with sequential search.

model works that has some similarities to the model with uninformed consumers that we have developed above. Note that with uninformed consumers, the highest price that occurs with positive likelihood is the monopoly price; so, this price constitutes an upper bound on the distribution of prices that can be observed in the market. With sequential search, this monopoly price may no longer be feasible since consumers can acquire price information, so that they may never buy from a firm that sets the monopoly price. This suggests that the upper bound on the distribution of prices that can be observed in the market has to be endogenously determined.

Suppose that a share of consumers is always informed, i.e., is observing all prices and will buy from the cheapest firm. The other consumers are initially uninformed: they observe the price from one firm (e.g. the store in the consumers' neighbourhood) and can acquire additional price information at some cost per additional search. After each additional search, they can decide to stop searching and choose the cheapest product in the sample. After each search, these consumers have to compare their expected gain from one additional search to the search cost. If the net effect is positive, they continue searching; otherwise they buy according to their demand function. Firms set their prices as the result of a realization from a probability distribution. They are aware of the fact that some consumers search sequentially. In Bayesian Nash equilibrium, consumers base their decision on the expected price distribution. Firms take search behaviour derived from this distribution as given and set a profit-maximizing price. Clearly, each price with a positive likelihood must give the same expected payoff. Suppose there is a fixed number of firms with constant marginal costs of production. As the number of initially uninformed consumers vanishes, the price distribution becomes more and more concentrated. In the limit, all firms set the perfectly competitive price. Conversely, as the number of informed consumers vanishes, firms set prices close to the monopoly price. For situations in between, firms set prices in the range between the competitive price and the maximum of the monopoly price and a price that makes search consumers stop searching.

7.1.3   Empirical investigation of price dispersion

The predictions of the theoretical models we have just reviewed have been largely confronted to the data (both in online and offline markets for homogeneous products). Much of the empirical literature has examined whether search intensity is correlated with levels of price dispersion, controlling for factors outside of the models that might also influence price dispersion (such as subtle product heterogeneities).[40]

To measure price dispersion, the obvious starting point is to use the price distribution $F(p)$ predicted by the theoretical models. One can then compute the variance in prices. However, the variance is not suitable for comparing levels of price dispersion through time or across markets. One needs a standardized measure such as the coefficient of variation, which divides the standard deviation by the mean. A large number of empirical analyses of price dispersion use this measure. An alternative measure that is also often used is the sample range, i.e., the difference between the largest and the lowest observed prices in the sample. Finally, one can gauge price dispersion by measuring the value of information, i.e., the difference between the average observed price and the lowest observed price; the larger this difference, the more dispersed the prices, and also the more consumers can gain by using, e.g., the services of a clearing house or a shopbot (on this, see Chapter 23).

As for search intensity, it can be proxied by variables that affect either the benefits or the costs of search. Theoretical models predict that the benefits of search are larger for items that account for a larger share of the consumer's budget, or that are purchased with a higher frequency. It is thus expected that more search will be exercised for such items, resulting in lower levels of price dispersion. As for search costs, they are generally unobservable. Yet, by comparing environments (or periods of time) for which search costs are likely to be different, one can assess the influence of search costs on price dispersion; one such experiment consists in comparing online versus offline markets, starting from the premise that search is more expensive in the latter markets than in the former. Case 7.1 presents some of the results obtained along these various lines of research.

Case 7.1 Does search intensity affect price dispersion?

Dispersion and the benefits of search. Stigler (1961) was the first to test the hypothesis that price dispersion should be lower for items that account for a large share of the searcher's budget. His results provide casual evidence in support of this hypothesis: the coefficient of variation for coal (which represents a small percentage of the overall government budget) is 14.7%, whereas that for an automobile (which makes up a large share of a household's budget) is 1.7%. More recently, Aalto-Setälä (2003) examines the dispersion in prices for homogeneous groceries in Finland and shows that one of the variables that increases relative price dispersion the most is low budget share of the product. As for the hypothesis that markets with more repetitive or experienced buyers should be characterized by more search, Sorensen (2000) provides an elegant test. He looks at the market for prescription drugs, in which the purchase frequency of a particular drug can be measured by the dosage and the duration of the therapy. As the benefits of search are likely to be larger for frequently purchased drugs, there should be more search, and thus less price dispersion, for those drugs. This is indeed what the data reveal. For instance, price ranges for one-time prescriptions are estimated to be 34% larger than those for prescriptions that must be purchased monthly.

Dispersion and the costs of search. As indicated above, because search costs are largely unobservable, a common strategy has been to compare levels of price dispersion in online versus offline markets (where search costs are arguably larger). Interestingly, the numerous papers that have adopted that strategy have produced a mixed set of findings: for some products, online markets give rise to less price dispersion, but the opposite prevails for other products. After reflection, this is not surprising insofar as the theoretical literature is also ambiguous about the impact that lower search costs have on levels of price dispersion. However, taking a historical perspective, it clearly appears that despite the reductions in information costs over the past century (due to the widespread adoption of the automobile, the telephone, the Internet, etc.), price dispersion in homogeneous product markets is still very present (and does not even seem to have decreased). You can have an indication of price dispersion on the Internet, on a weekly basis, by consulting www.Nash-equilibrium.com, a website designed by Michael R. Baye, John Morgan and Patrick Scholten.

7.2 Switching costs

In many markets, consumers make decisions with long-term effects. For instance, a client who has opened an account with a bank faces opportunity costs if he switches to a competitor. Such costs are called *switching costs* and give firms market power over those consumers who are locked-in. In a dynamic context, firms and consumers are often aware of such lock-in effects. While firms have market power over consumers once they are locked-in, at an earlier stage they are aware of how valuable these consumers are when trying to attract them once they enter the market. At this earlier stage, firms are competing fiercely with the idea to milk consumers later. Hence, a priori it is not clear whether the market with switching costs will be more or less competitive than a market without switching costs.

In this section, we want to shed light on this issue. To this end, we propose two formal two-period models and examine in turn the competitive effects of exogenous and endogenous switching costs (Subsections 7.2.1 and 7.2.2). We also discuss how switching costs can be identified and measured in specific industries (Subsection 7.2.3).

7.2.1   Competitive effects of switching costs

The key property of switching costs is that consumers who have bought from a particular supplier in the past put a premium on continuing to purchase from the same supplier. Typically, switching costs result from some firm-specific investment that the consumer cannot transfer to another supplier. Therefore, repeat purchases lead to economies of scale on the consumer side. As detailed in Case 7.2, switching costs can come in different varieties, depending on the specificities of the industry.

Case 7.2 Examples of switching costs[41]

Transaction costs: changing suppliers may simply require time and effort or be disruptive if seller–customer specific information is lost in the process (e.g., changing bank accounts, insurances, travel agency, telephone service or, for firms as customers, accountancy and legal services, etc.).

Contractual costs: firms may succeed in creating switching costs by getting customers to agree to contracts that lock the consumer in for a certain period (e.g., contracts offered by mobile phone operators with a certain minimum term) or by creating schemes inducing repeat purchase (e.g., discount coupons or 'loyalty'-programmes such as frequent-flyer programs or point collection for banks).

Compatibility costs: in many situations, consumers value the compatibility of their current and future purchases with the equipment they already own; this is the case for many 'systems' made of complementary products (e.g., video games console, operating systems and applications, etc.), and for the combined purchase of original equipment – or durables – and replacement parts – or consumables (e.g., printers and ink cartridges, electric toothbrushes and replacement heads, etc.).[e]

Learning costs: the specific investment incurred by the consumer may take the form of specific knowledge, or more generally, human capital; switching brand or supplier would mean spending time and energy to learn how to use the new brand (e.g., a new software) or how to interact with the new supplier (e.g., a health insurance).

Uncertainty costs: for 'experience goods', the quality or suitability can only be observed after purchase; a consumer who has found a suitable good may then be reluctant to switch to an unknown competing brand, even if this brand is less expensive (this might explain why a large proportion of consumers continue to buy their cars from the same car manufacturer).[f]

Psychological costs: for 'credence goods', the quality may not be observable even after purchase; because the quality of the good or service is taken on trust, the customer may be reluctant to switch to another supplier she has not yet learned to trust (think, e.g., of the relationship you have with your dentist).

Shopping costs: the previous examples were indicating a form of scale economies resulting from purchasing the same product repeatedly from the same supplier; there might also exist 'economies of scope' when purchasing different products from the same supplier at the same point in time; if a broad portfolio of brands can be bought at the same shop, the consumer can save transaction costs.

As stated above, consumer switching costs give rise to consumer lock-in. Thus, firms increase their price-setting power and we expect higher prices once consumers are locked-in. Since firms realize that consumers are more valuable when consumer switching costs are present in the market, firms may compete aggressively for new consumers. It is thus unclear what are the competitive effects of switching costs.

Monopoly

While switching costs affect pricing decisions already in a monopoly model, the overall effect of switching costs is neutral, that is, the average price and the allocation remains unaffected. This can be seen as follows: consider a setting with two periods and unit demand. Consumer switching costs make the outside option less attractive in the second period when the consumer is locked-in (she essentially has to pay a penalty when not consuming the product on offer). In the first period, the consumer knows that she has to pay a price that increases by the switching cost compared to the situation without consumer switching costs. This reduces the willingness-to-pay in the first period exactly by the level of the switching cost z. Hence,

---

[e] We take a closer look at such markets in our analysis of bundling in Chapter 11 and network effects in Chapter 20.
[f] Colombo *et al.* (2000) report that among 20 000 new car buyers in France in 1989, almost half purchased their car from the same supplier as before. This may be seen as an indication of brand loyalty resulting in consumer switching costs. However, to the extent that consumers have heterogeneous time-invariant tastes over different car brands before their initial purchase, product differentiation (as analysed in Section 4.2) is an alternative explanation for the high probability of staying with the same supplier.

denoting the monopoly price in the absence of switching costs by p^m, the consumer pays $p^m - z$ in the first period and $p^m + z$ in the second period.

Imperfect competition

To study competitive effects, we analyse a two-period duopoly model with consumer switching costs, which will shed some light on the question of what determines whether or not consumer switching costs make the market more competitive.[42] In period 1, all consumers are inexperienced. They buy a differentiated product according to their preferences while anticipating the potential lock-in effect in period 2. After period 1, a share λ_n of consumers (who are randomly drawn) leave the market and are replaced by the same number of new consumers. In period 2, all remaining consumers from period 1 in the turf of firm A face a switching cost z for buying from firm B and vice versa. Thus, second-period profits depend on first-period prices because they depend on first-period market shares. In period 1, firm i maximizes the sum of profits over both periods (i.e., for simplicity, there is no discounting). We can write

$$\pi_i \left(p_i^1, p_j^1, p_i^2, p_j^2 \right) = \pi_i^1 \left(p_i^1, p_j^1 \right) + \pi_i^2 \left(p_i^1, p_j^1, p_i^2, p_j^2 \right).$$

We again use the linear Hotelling model to describe product differentiation. Consumers of mass 1 are uniformly distributed on the interval $[0, 1]$. Product A is located at 0 and product B at 1. A consumer of type x incurs a disutility of $-x$ if he purchases a unit of product A and $-(1 - x)$ if he purchases a unit of product B. Firms have constant marginal costs c. As we want to consider only situations with full participation (or full market coverage), we assume that the reservation price of consumers, r, is sufficiently high.[g]

In period 2, there are two groups of consumers. A share λ_n of consumers are new in the market and thus do not have consumer switching costs; the remaining share, $\lambda_o = 1 - \lambda_n$, are old consumers. We contrast two scenarios concerning the preferences of old consumers for the competing brands (i.e., their location x on the unit line). In the first scenario, it is assumed that old consumers keep their preferences from one period to the next. In contrast, in the second scenario, it is assumed that preferences in the two periods are unrelated. In the latter case, there are two sources of uncertainty for the first-period consumers: (i) they do not know if they will still purchase in period 2, and (ii), if they stay in the market, they do not know what will be their future relative valuation of the two products (for instance, if the firms are airlines, unforeseen travel obligations may modify the consumer's preferences for the two airlines).[h]

Scenario 1. Old consumers inherit their type from period 1

We analyse the game by first deriving the equilibrium in period 2 for any given first-period market shares α_A and α_B (with $\alpha_A = 1 - \alpha_B$ as we assume full market coverage). Thus, all consumers with $x \in [0, \alpha_A]$ have bought from firm A in the first period, whereas all consumers

---

[g] With respect to the models we used in the previous subsections, we make the following minor modifications: (i) we set $\tau = 1$, (ii) firms are now denoted A and B, leaving the superscript 1 and 2 to denote the time periods.

[h] We separate the two scenarios to simplify the exposition. We draw the main insights from the first scenario, which we develop in detail. The second scenario is slightly more complicated and is left for motivated readers. Note that we could very well consider a more general model where the group of old consumers is further divided into two subgroups, those who keep their preferences and those who draw a new preference parameter in period 2, as analysed in Klemperer (1987b).

with $x \in [\alpha_A, 1]$ have bought from firm B. As we assume here that the share of consumers who stay in the market in period 2 keep the type they had in period 1, the question is whether these consumers will continue to buy from the same firm in period 2. Suppose that consumer x bought from firm A in period 1. She will still buy from firm A in period 2 provided that $r - x - p_A^2 \geq r - z - (1 - x) - p_B^2$, where the net utility for B's product is decreased by the switching cost z. The above inequality can be rewritten as

$$x \leq \tfrac{1}{2} \left(1 + p_B^2 - p_A^2 + z \right) \equiv \hat{x}_A.$$

Similarly, consumer x buys from firm B in both periods if $r - (1 - x) - p_B^2 \geq r - z - x - p_A^2$, or

$$x \geq \tfrac{1}{2} \left(1 + p_B^2 - p_A^2 - z \right) \equiv \hat{x}_B = \hat{x}_A - z.$$

It is clear that if the price difference $p_B^2 - p_A^2$ is sufficiently small and the switching cost sufficiently large, old consumers do not revise their purchasing decision. More precisely, this is so if $\hat{x}_B = \hat{x}_A - z \leq \alpha_A \leq \hat{x}_A$, which can be rewritten as $z \geq \left| \left(p_A^2 + \alpha_A \right) - \left(p_B^2 + \alpha_B \right) \right|$. We will see below that the latter condition is indeed met at equilibrium.

As for the share λ_n of consumers who enter the market in period 2, they do not face any switching cost and thus buy from firm A if their preference parameter x is such that $r - x - p_A^2 \geq r - (1 - x) - p_B^2$, or $x \leq \tfrac{1}{2} \left(1 + p_B^2 - p_A^2 \right)$. It follows that the second-period demand of firm A is

$$q_A^2 \left(p_A^2, p_B^2 \right) = \lambda_o \alpha_A + \lambda_n \tfrac{1}{2} \left(1 + p_B^2 - p_A^2 \right).$$

A firm has substantial market power over old consumers who inherited their tastes from the first period. Indeed, with only such consumers and a sufficiently large z, both firms would ask the monopoly price in period 2 (we make this statement precise below). However, firms compete for the new consumers. The first-order condition of profit maximization in period 2 is

$$\frac{\partial \pi_A^2}{\partial p_A^2} = q_A^2 + \left(p_A^2 - c \right) \frac{\partial q_2^A}{\partial p_A^2} = 0.$$

For $\lambda_n > 0$, we can solve for p_A^2 and find firm A's reaction function:

$$p_A^2 \left(p_B^2 \right) = \frac{\lambda_o}{\lambda_n} \alpha_A + \tfrac{1}{2} \left(1 + c + p_B^2 \right).$$

Proceeding similarly for firm B and solving for the Nash equilibrium, one obtains[i]

$$p_A^2 = c + \tfrac{1}{\lambda_n} \left(1 + \tfrac{1}{3} (2\alpha_A - 1)(1 - \lambda_n) \right),$$

$$q_A^2 = \tfrac{1}{2} \left(1 + \tfrac{1}{3} (2\alpha_A - 1)(1 - \lambda_n) \right), \tag{7.1}$$

$$\pi_A^2 = \tfrac{1}{2\lambda_n} \left(1 + \tfrac{1}{3} (2\alpha_A - 1)(1 - \lambda_n) \right)^2,$$

and correspondingly for firm B.

---

[i] This defines a pure-strategy equilibrium at stage 2 provided that $|\alpha_A - \alpha_B| < z$ using the equation of sales from above. For $\lambda_n > 0$ sufficiently large, this constitutes the unique equilibrium. Note that, in contrast to the search models analysed in the previous section, products are differentiated so that a pure strategy equilibrium exists.

It is useful to take a closer look at the equilibrium outcome at stage 2 in the case where first-period market shares are symmetric, i.e. $\alpha_A = \alpha_B = 1/2$. In that case, second-period equilibrium prices are characterized by $p_A^2 = p_B^2 = c + 1/\lambda_n$.[j] This implies that period 2 demand also splits evenly and that profits are $\pi_A^2 = \pi_B^2 = 1/(2\lambda_n)$. To understand why profits are decreasing in the share of new consumers, we compare this outcome with two extreme cases: (1) independent preferences across periods, i.e. $\lambda_n = 1$; (2) unchanged preferences across periods, i.e. $\lambda_n = 0$. In the former case, prices are equal to prices in a market without switching costs. Using the Hotelling model with linear transportation costs that we analysed in Section 5.2 (with $\tau = 1$), we have $p_A^2 = p_B^2 = c + 1$, $q_A^2 = q_B^2 = 1/2$, and $\pi_A^2 = \pi_B^2 = 1/2$.

In the latter case ($\lambda_n = 0$), our previous analysis (using the above first-order conditions) does not apply. Here, all consumers have bought in period 1 what they also tend to like in period 2; in addition, there are positive consumer switching costs. Hence, (because of symmetry) firms choose joint-profit-maximizing prices: for $r \geq c + 1$, we have $p_A^2 = p_B^2 = r - 1/2$ under symmetry ($\alpha_A = \alpha_B$). This is a global maximizer under some restriction on r. We observe that firms set a price that is higher than in a market without switching costs (assuming that $r \geq c + 3/2$, which is the condition for market coverage in the market without switching costs).

We now turn to the *strategic interaction in the first period*. In the first period, each firm maximizes its joint profit in periods 1 and 2 (recall that there is no discounting). Profits are

$$\pi_A \left(p_A^1, p_B^1 \right) = \pi_A^1 \left(p_A^1, p_B^1 \right) + \tilde{\pi}_A^2 \left(\alpha_A \left(p_A^1, p_B^1 \right) \right)$$

and correspondingly for firm B. The first-order condition is

$$0 = \frac{\partial \pi_A}{\partial p_A^1} = \frac{\partial \pi_A^1}{\partial p_A^1} + \underbrace{\frac{\partial \tilde{\pi}_A^2}{\partial \alpha_A}}_{+} \underbrace{\frac{\partial \alpha_A}{\partial p_A^1}}_{-}.$$

We observe that there is a second-period indirect effect of a price change in period 1. This is due to the fact that market share is valuable, so that a price increase in period 1 has a negative repercussion in period 2. It follows that, at profit maximum, we must have $\partial \pi_A^1 / \partial p_A^1 > 0$. Thus, everything else equal, each firm competes more aggressively than it would do in the absence of second-period profits. However, this finding comes with an important warning. It does not imply that firms necessarily compete more aggressively than in the absence of switching costs. The latter statement is an equilibrium statement so that everything else is not equal, in particular, the competitor sets a different price.

As a benchmark case, we can analyse a situation in which *consumers are myopic*, in the sense that they do not foresee that they will be locked-in in the following period. The first-period demand is determined exactly as in the model without consumer switching costs. Since future market share is valuable, we obtain the unambiguous result that *first-period prices are lower than in the absence of switching costs*.

Things are less clear once we take into account that *consumers are forward-looking* (and that expectations are rational). Forward-looking consumers know that they will be partially

---

[j] The finding is similar to the informative advertising model analysed in Subsection 6.4.1 when taking advertising as given because consumers who are locked-in play the same role as consumers who only know about the existence of one product.

locked-in in the second period and thus have to be 'animated' to buy in the first place. In their first-period purchasing decision, they must predict second-period prices. Since a first-period price cut increases market share, it foretells a second-period price rise. Consequently, forward-looking consumers are less attracted by a first-period price cut and first-period demand is less elastic than in an otherwise identical market without switching costs. Reduced-form profit functions at the first stage (which only depend on first-period prices) have the form

$$\tilde{\pi}_A \left(p_A^1, p_B^1 \right) = \left(p_A^1 - c \right) \alpha_A \left(p_A^1, p_B^1 \right) + \tfrac{1}{2\lambda_n} \left(1 + \tfrac{1}{3} \left(2\alpha_A - 1 \right) \left(1 - \lambda_n \right) \right)^2.$$

To proceed, we have to compute first-period market shares $\alpha_i \left(p_A^1, p_B^1 \right)$. Suppose that consumers are rational and forward-looking. If consumer x buys from firm A in period 1, she knows that she has a probability $(1 - \lambda_n)$ of staying in the market in period 2 (with the same taste parameter as before) and to buy again from firm A; with the complementary probability λ_n, she exits the market and does not get any surplus. Hence, her expected surplus is equal to $v_A^e (x) = \left(r - x - p_A^1 \right) + (1 - \lambda_n) \left(r - x - p_A^2 (\alpha_A) \right)$. Similarly, buying from B in period 1 gives an expected surplus of $v_B^e (x) = \left(r - (1 - x) - p_B^1 \right) + (1 - \lambda_n) \left(r - (1 - x) - p_B^2 (\alpha_A) \right)$. The indifferent consumer is therefore located at $\hat{x}$, such that $v_A^e (\hat{x}) = v_B^e (\hat{x})$, or

$$\hat{x} = \tfrac{1}{2} + \tfrac{1}{2(2-\lambda_n)} \left(p_B^1 - p_A^1 + (1 - \lambda_n) \left(p_B^2 (\alpha_A) - p_A^2 (\alpha_A) \right) \right).$$

Using the second-period solution (7.1), we can write the second-period price difference as $p_B^2 (\alpha_B) - p_A^2 (\alpha_A) = 2 (1 - \lambda_n) (1 - 2\alpha_A) / (3\lambda_n)$. Because all consumers located to the left of $\hat{x}$ buy from firm A in period 1, we have $\alpha_A = \hat{x}$. Therefore, combining the latter two equations, we have

$$\alpha_A = \tfrac{1}{2} + \tfrac{1}{2(2-\lambda_n)} \left(p_B^1 - p_A^1 + (1 - \lambda_n) \tfrac{2(1-\lambda_n)}{3\lambda_n} \left(1 - 2\alpha_A \right) \right) \Leftrightarrow$$

$$\alpha_A \left(p_A^1, p_B^1 \right) = \tfrac{1}{2} \left(1 + Z (\lambda_n) \left(p_B^1 - p_A^1 \right) \right), \quad \text{where } Z (\lambda_n) \equiv \tfrac{3\lambda_n}{2+2\lambda_n - \lambda_n^2}.$$

Note that $Z' (\lambda_n) > 0$, $Z (0) = 0$ and $Z (1) = 1$. So, if some consumers stay ($\lambda_n < 1$), so that $Z (\lambda_n) < 1$, first-period market share is less responsive to price changes than when there are no consumer switching costs. Reduced-form first-period profits that only depend on first-period prices then take the form

$$\tilde{\pi}_A \left(p_A^1, p_B^1 \right) = \left(p_A^1 - c \right) \tfrac{1}{2} \left(1 + Z (\lambda_n) \left(p_B^1 - p_A^1 \right) \right)$$

$$+ \tfrac{1}{2\lambda_n} \left(1 + \tfrac{1}{3} Z (\lambda_n) (1 - \lambda_n) \left(p_B^1 - p_A^1 \right) \right)^2.$$

Taking the first-order conditions of profit maximization and using symmetry, we can characterize the equilibrium. Firms set the following prices along the equilibrium path:

$$\begin{cases} p_A^1 = p_B^1 = c + \tfrac{1}{3} (4 - \lambda_n) \\ p_A^2 = p_B^2 = c + \tfrac{1}{\lambda_n} \end{cases}$$

Equilibrium profits are given by

$$\pi_A = \pi_B = \tfrac{1}{2} \left(\tfrac{1}{3} (4 - \lambda_n) \right) + \tfrac{1}{2} \tfrac{1}{\lambda_n} = \tfrac{4\lambda_n - \lambda_n^2 + 3}{6\lambda_n}.$$

We observe that $p_A^2 - p_A^1 = \frac{1}{3\lambda_n}(1 - \lambda_n)(3 - \lambda_n) > 0$. That is, *firms sell at a discount in the first period*, $p_A^1 < p_A^2$. The reason is that consumers anticipate that they will be locked-in in the second period and thus have to be offered a carrot in the first period. We also observe that prices and profits are decreasing in the share of new consumers, λ_n.

To establish the effect of consumer switching costs on the competitiveness of the market, it is useful to compare the previous equilibrium with the prices that would be set if there were no switching cost (or if all period 2 consumers were new consumers, i.e., $\lambda_n = 1$). In the latter case, we showed above that prices would be equal to $c + 1$ in both periods. Here, we easily see that $p_A^2 = p_B^2 > p_A^1 = p_B^1 > c + 1$: *switching costs make firms better off in both periods and reduce competitive pressure*. We summarize some properties of the subgame perfect equilibrium in the following lesson.

Lesson 7.4   Consider a market which opens for two periods and in which old consumers inherit their second-period tastes from the first period and face switching costs. Then firms sell at a discount in the first period but still at a higher price than the one that would prevail absent switching costs and switching costs relax price competition.

Scenario 2. Old consumers newly draw their type in period 2

It is important to stress that the previous conclusions are driven by our assumption that old consumers have the same taste parameter in the two periods. If we assume instead that old consumers staying in the market newly draw their taste parameter in period 2, then firms will have much less monopoly power over old consumers. As the analysis of the model becomes more complicated, we state here the main results for the reader who would prefer to skip the following analytical developments. Redoing the previous analysis, we obtain that *switching costs make firms worse off in the first period* since $p_A^1 = p_B^1 < c + 1$ and that they do not make firms better off in the second period since $p_A^2 = p_B^2 = c + 1$. Intuitively, market share in period 1 is valuable so that firms compete fiercely in period 1. However, for symmetric market shares, the outcome in period 2 is the same as in the absence of consumer switching costs. Hence, consumer switching costs increase competitive pressure. That leads us to our next lesson (again we refer to properties of the subgame perfect equilibrium).

Lesson 7.5   Suppose that old consumers newly draw their taste parameter in the second period and face switching costs. Then firms sell at a discount in the first period; the first-period price is below and the second-period price is equal to the price that would prevail absent switching costs. In other words, switching costs intensify price competition.

These two model versions have shown us that it depends on the details of consumer behaviour whether the presence of consumer switching costs makes the market more or less competitive. Therefore, if a regulator or competition authority finds that there are substantial consumer switching costs, this does not necessarily imply that firms enjoy a lot of market power. In other words, the particular market in question has to be carefully investigated before reaching the verdict that consumer switching costs are a concern for the public authority involved.

We now formally establish the results stated in Lesson 7.5. The methodology is exactly the same as in the first scenario but the analysis is more involved because old consumers have to form expectations about their future tastes. Readers may choose to skip this part. We start again by deriving the demand for firm A in the second period. For the new consumers, it is the same as in Scenario 1: they buy from firm A if their taste parameter is lower than $\frac{1}{2}\left(1 + p_B^2 - p_A^2\right)$. As for old consumers, their choice depends on the (unrelated) realizations of their taste parameter in the two periods. Take a consumer whose taste parameter in period 1 is below α_A, meaning that this consumer buys from firm A in period 1. Using our previous analysis, we know that this consumer will continue buying from firm A in period 2 if her newly drawn taste parameter is below $\hat{x}_A = \frac{1}{2}\left(1 + p_B^2 - p_A^2 + z\right)$. Take now a consumer who bought from firm B in period 1 (i.e., her taste parameter was above α_A); then this consumer would switch to the product of firm A in period 2 if her newly drawn taste parameter is below $\hat{x}_B = \frac{1}{2}\left(1 + p_B^2 - p_A^2 - z\right)$. Switching occurs if second-period prices and switching costs are such that $0 < \hat{x}_B = \hat{x}_A - z < \hat{x}_A < 1$. These conditions can be rewritten as $\left|p_B^2 - p_A^2\right| < 1 - z$, which requires $z < 1$. So, for $z < 1$, there are prices such that there are consumers who previously bought from a particular firm in period 1 and are indifferent in period 2. It follows that firm A's second-period demand is given by

$$q_A^2\left(p_A^2, p_B^2\right) = \lambda_n \tfrac{1}{2}\left(1 + p_B^2 - p_A^2\right)$$
$$+ \lambda_o\left(\alpha_A \tfrac{1}{2}\left(1 + p_B^2 - p_A^2 + z\right) + \alpha_B \tfrac{1}{2}\left(1 + p_B^2 - p_A^2 - z\right)\right)$$
$$= \tfrac{1}{2}\left[1 + p_B^2 - p_A^2 + (1 - \lambda_n)(2\alpha_A - 1)z\right].$$

Similarly, $q_B^2\left(p_A^2, p_B^2\right) = \tfrac{1}{2}\left[1 + p_A^2 - p_B^2 - (1 - \lambda_n)(2\alpha_A - 1)z\right]$.

Firm A chooses p_A^2 to maximize $\pi_A^2 = \left(p_A^2 - c\right)q_A^2\left(p_A^2, p_B^2\right)$ while firm B chooses p_B^2 to maximize $\pi_B^2 = \left(p_B^2 - c\right)q_B^2\left(p_A^2, p_B^2\right)$. Solving for the Nash equilibrium, one obtains

$$p_A^2 = c + 1 + \tfrac{1}{3}(2\alpha_A - 1)(1 - \lambda_n)z,$$
$$q_A^2 = \tfrac{1}{2}\left(1 + \tfrac{1}{3}(2\alpha_A - 1)(1 - \lambda_n)z\right),$$
$$\pi_A^2 = \tfrac{1}{2}\left(1 + \tfrac{1}{3}(2\alpha_A - 1)(1 - \lambda_n)z\right)^2,$$

and correspondingly for firm B.

Assuming forward-looking consumers, we can now express the reduced-form profit function at the first stage:

$$\tilde{\pi}_A\left(p_A^1, p_B^1\right) = \left(p_A^1 - c\right)\alpha_A\left(p_A^1, p_B^1\right) + \tfrac{1}{2}\left(1 + \tfrac{1}{3}(2\alpha_A - 1)(1 - \lambda_n)z\right)^2.$$

As in Scenario 1, we need to compute first-period market shares $\alpha_i\left(p_A^1, p_B^1\right)$. The indifferent consumer, $\hat{x}$, is such that the sum of the difference in her first-period surpluses from buying from one versus the other firm, and of the difference in her expected second-period surpluses is equal to zero. The first-period surplus difference is simply given by $\left(r - \hat{x} - p_A^1\right) - \left(r - (1 - \hat{x}) - p_B^1\right) = 1 - 2\hat{x} + p_B^1 - p_A^1 \equiv \Delta_S^1$. Things are more complicated for the second period since consumers do not know which will be their taste parameter. Note first that each consumer has a probability $(1 - \lambda_n)$ of staying in the second period. Now, the expected surplus in period 2 from buying from firm A in period 1 can be written as

$$(1 - \lambda_n)\left[\int_0^{\hat{x}_A} \left(r - p_A^2(\alpha_A) - x\right) dx + \int_{\hat{x}_A}^1 \left(r - z - p_B^2(\alpha_B) - (1 - x)\right) dx\right].$$

That is, if the newly drawn type is below $\hat{x}_A$, the consumer buys again from A; otherwise, she buys from B and incurs the switching cost z. By analogy, the expected surplus in period 2 from buying from firm B in period 1 is

$$(1 - \lambda_n)\left[\int_0^{\hat{x}_B} \left(r - z - p_A^2(\alpha_A) - x\right) dx + \int_{\hat{x}_B}^1 \left(r - p_B^2(\alpha_B) - (1 - x)\right) dx\right].$$

We can now compute the difference between the two expected surpluses, and it turns out that the resulting expression is greatly simplified:

$$\Delta_S^2 = (1 - \lambda_n)\left(p_B^2(\alpha_B) - p_A^2(\alpha_A)\right) z$$
$$= \tfrac{2}{3}(1 - 2\alpha_A)(1 - \lambda_n)^2 z^2,$$

where the second line is obtained by replacing $p_A^2(\alpha_A)$ and $p_B^2(\alpha_B)$ by their respective equilibrium values.

As $\hat{x}$ is defined by $\Delta_S^1 + \Delta_S^2 = 0$ and $\hat{x} = \alpha_A$, we can write

$$0 = 1 - 2\alpha_A + p_B^1 - p_A^1 + \tfrac{2}{3}(1 - 2\alpha_A)(1 - \lambda_n)^2 z^2 \Leftrightarrow$$

$$\alpha_A\left(p_A^1, p_B^1\right) = \tfrac{1}{2}\left(1 + Y(\lambda_n)\left(p_B^1 - p_A^1\right)\right), \text{ where } Y(\lambda_n) \equiv \tfrac{3}{3 + 2z^2(1-\lambda_n)^2}.$$

Note that $Y'(\lambda_n) > 0$, $Y(0) = 3/(3 + 2z^2) > 0$ and $Y(1) = 1$. As in Scenario 1, if some consumers stay ($\lambda_n < 1$), so that $Y(\lambda_n) < 1$, first-period market share is less responsive to price changes than when there are no consumer switching costs. However, in contrast to Scenario 1, an absence of new consumers ($\lambda_n = 0$) leaves the market share responsive to price changes. Firms have less market power on old consumers because they may have different tastes in period 2 than in period 1.

Now, we can express the reduced-form first-period profits as a function of first-period prices only:

$$\tilde{\pi}_A\left(p_A^1, p_B^1\right) = \left(p_A^1 - c\right)\tfrac{1}{2}\left(1 + Y(\lambda_n)\left(p_B^1 - p_A^1\right)\right)$$
$$+ \tfrac{1}{2}\left(1 + \tfrac{1}{3}Y(\lambda_n)(1 - \lambda_n)\left(p_B^1 - p_A^1\right)z\right)^2.$$

Taking the first-order conditions of profit maximization and using symmetry, we can characterize the equilibrium. Firms set the following prices along the equilibrium path:

$$\begin{cases} p_A^1 = p_B^1 = c + 1 - \tfrac{2}{3}(1 - \lambda_n)(1 - z + \lambda_n z)z, \\ p_A^2 = p_B^2 = c + 1. \end{cases}$$

So, we check the results stated in Lesson 7.5: first-period prices are below the price that firms would set in the absence of switching costs, while second-period prices are just equal to this price.[k] Clearly, the combination of switching costs and of old consumers who newly draw their taste parameter makes competition fiercer. Note that the effects on equilibrium first-period prices (and thus on equilibrium profits) of a change in the share of new consumers or in the level of switching costs are not clear. Simple derivations reveal:

$$
\begin{cases}
\text{if } z < \frac{1}{2(1-\lambda_n)}, & \text{then } \frac{\partial p^1}{\partial \lambda_n} > 0 \quad \text{and} \quad \frac{\partial p^1}{\partial z} < 0, \\
\text{if } z > \frac{1}{2(1-\lambda_n)}, & \text{then } \frac{\partial p^1}{\partial \lambda_n} < 0 \quad \text{and} \quad \frac{\partial p^1}{\partial z} > 0.
\end{cases}
$$

It is only when switching costs are large enough to start with that firms see their profits improve when switching costs increase or when the share of new consumers decreases. Otherwise, because old consumers newly draw their type and face thus less 'expected lock-in' than in the first scenario, higher switching costs or a higher share of old consumers deteriorate firms' profits at the margin.

7.2.2   Coupons and endogenous switching costs

In the previous analysis, switching costs were assumed to be exogenous: they were independent of the firms' or consumers' decisions (as is the case, e.g., with learning or transaction costs). However, as illustrated in Case 7.2, firms may succeed in creating switching costs by rewarding 'loyal' customers and thereby encouraging repeat purchase. For instance, firms may offer coupons (i.e., a discount in absolute value) for consumers who bought from them in the past. Switching costs become then *endogenous* as they are proposed by the firms and accepted by the consumers.[l]

General presentation

To analyse competition with 'coupon-induced' switching costs, we slightly modify the model we used so far. Regarding consumers, we assume that they all change preferences from period 1 to period 2 (and that they ignore their second-period taste in period 1). As for firms, they make an additional decision in period 1: on top of choosing the price for their product in period 1, p_i^1, they also choose a coupon $\gamma_i \geq 0$ that their loyal customers will enjoy in period 2. We assume that firms cannot commit to their second-period price in period 1; so, they choose p_i^2 ($i = A, B$) in period 2.[43]

Because consumers redraw their taste parameter in the second period, the model presents the same technical difficulties as the previous one. We therefore choose to first state the main result and then to derive it, leaving up to the reader to decide whether to follow the derivations or to skip them.

---

[k] Recall that we assume here that $z < 1$.

[l] Firms also use coupons simply to promote their products. Promotions are a form of short-run non-price competition that is (at least) as important as advertising and coupons constitute the lion's share of the promotion budgets. Nevo and Wolfram (2002) report the following numbers: 'In 1996, manufacturers of consumer packaged goods distributed 268.5 billion coupons, of which 5.3 billion (2%) were redeemed. The average face value for coupons redeemed by consumers in 1996 was 69 cents, so consumers used coupons worth approximatively $3.5 billion.' Coupons can also be a tool to allow price discrimination, as will be discussed in Chapter 9.

Lesson 7.6 Suppose that all consumers stay in the market for two periods and newly draw their taste parameter in the second period. Firms find it profitable to create switching costs by announcing coupons in the first period that loyal customers can redeem in the second period. Coupons relax price competition: first- and second-period prices are higher than in the absence of coupons (although loyal customers pay a lower price in the second period).

The intuition for these results goes as follows. The presence of switching costs, induced by the announced coupons, segments the second-period market into two groups with different demand elasticities, according to their first-period choices. This means that each firm can charge a higher price to its loyal customers without fearing that they switch to the other firm. Although it becomes obviously harder to poach customers from the other firm, each firm tries to do so and, therefore, refrains from exploiting its loyal customers: the price charged to poached customers is above $c + 1$ (i.e., the price that would prevail in the absence of coupons), while the net price paid by loyal customers is below $c + 1$. Because loyal consumers are a majority in period 2, it follows that period 2 is more competitive than in the absence of coupons. Yet, the lower second-period profits are more than compensated by higher first-period profits: consumers agree to pay higher prices in period 1, as they anticipate that their loyalty will be rewarded in the second period. So, *overall, coupons decrease the competitiveness of markets.*

Case 7.3 Coupons in the ready-to-eat breakfast cereals market

Nevo and Wolfram (2002) provide some empirical evidence supporting the theoretical analysis. They built a data set with information on shelf prices and available coupons for 25 ready-to-eat breakfast cereals (in up to 65 US cities from early 1989 to late 1992). They find that lagged coupons are positively correlated with current sales, which is the idea we just explored: coupons are a tool to encourage repeat purchase.

Formal analysis

We now prove the claim that was made in Lesson 7.6.

We start by deriving the demand for firm A in the second period. Recall that we assume here that all consumers already consumed in period 1 (i.e., there are no new consumers) and have redrawn their taste parameter at the start of period 2. As before, let α_A denote firm A's market share in period 1 (which leaves a market share of $\alpha_B = 1 - \alpha_A$ to firm B as we assume full market coverage). Take a consumer whose taste parameter in period 1 is below α_A, meaning that this consumer bought from firm A in period 1. If she buys from A again, she will be rewarded for her loyalty and pay $p_A^2 - \gamma_A$; on the other hand, if she buys from B, she will not be able to redeem any coupon and she will pay the full price p_B^2. Loyalty to firm A is the preferred course of action if $r - x - \left(p_A^2 - \gamma_A\right) \geq r - (1 - x) - p_B^2 \Leftrightarrow x \leq \hat{x}_A = \frac{1}{2}\left(1 + p_B^2 - p_A^2 + \gamma_A\right)$.[m] Similarly, a former customer of firm B remains loyal if her new taste parameter is larger than $\hat{x}_B = \frac{1}{2}\left(1 + p_B^2 - p_A^2 - \gamma_B\right)$. As $\gamma_A, \gamma_B \geq 0$, we have that $\hat{x}_B \leq \hat{x}_A$. To proceed, let us assume that switching occurs in period 2, which is the case if $0 < \hat{x}_B \leq \hat{x}_A < 1$ or $\gamma_B - 1 < p_B^2 - p_A^2 < 1 - \gamma_A$. (We will check below that these conditions are met at the symmetric equilibrium of the game.) Then, in period 2, a share $\alpha_A \hat{x}_A$ of consumers buys from firm A at the discounted price $p_A^2 - \gamma_A$, while another share $(1 - \alpha_A)\hat{x}_B$ buys at the full price p_A^2. Hence, firm A's second-period maximization problem can be written as

$$\max_{p_A^2} = \alpha_A \frac{1}{2}\left(1 + p_B^2 - p_A^2 + \gamma_A\right)\left(p_A^2 - \gamma_A - c\right)$$

$$+ (1 - \alpha_A)\frac{1}{2}\left(1 + p_B^2 - p_A^2 - \gamma_B\right)\left(p_A^2 - c\right).$$

From the first-order condition, we find firm A's reaction function:

$$p_A^2\left(p_B^2\right) = \frac{1}{2}\left(c + 1 + p_B^2 + 2\alpha_A \gamma_A - (1 - \alpha_A)\gamma_B\right).$$

We can proceed in a similar way for firm B and then solve the system made of the two reaction functions to find the second-period equilibrium prices:

$$p_A^2 = c + 1 + \alpha_A \gamma_A \quad \text{and} \quad p_B^2 = c + 1 + \alpha_B \gamma_B.$$

We observe that second-period prices increase both in the firm's first-period market share and in the coupon it has announced. The equilibrium profit for firm A in period 2 is easily computed as

$$\pi_A^2 = \frac{1}{2} - \frac{1}{2}\alpha_A(1 - \alpha_A)\gamma_A(\gamma_A + \gamma_B).$$

Assuming forward-looking consumers, we can now express firm A's maximization problem in period 1:

$$\max_{p_A^1, \gamma_A} \tilde{\pi}_A(p_A^1, p_B^1, \gamma_A, \gamma_B) = \left(p_A^1 - c\right)\alpha_A + \frac{1}{2} - \frac{1}{2}\alpha_A(1 - \alpha_A)\gamma_A(\gamma_A + \gamma_B).$$

As above, we need to compute firm A's first-period market share α_A, which depends on p_i^1 and γ_i. The indifferent consumer, $\hat{x}$, is such that the sum of the difference in her first-period surpluses from buying from one versus the other firm (noted Δ_S^1), and of the difference in her expected second-period surpluses (noted Δ_S^2) is equal to zero. The first-period surplus difference is simply given by $\Delta_S^1 = \left(r - \hat{x} - p_A^1\right) - \left(r - (1 - \hat{x}) - p_B^1\right) = 1 - 2\hat{x} + p_B^1 - p_A^1$. The expected surpluses in period 2 from buying from firm A or from firm B in period 1 respectively can be written as

$$S_A^2 \equiv \int_0^{\hat{x}_A} \left(r - \left(p_A^2 - \gamma_A\right) - x\right) dx + \int_{\hat{x}_A}^1 \left(r - p_B^2 - (1 - x)\right) dx$$

$$S_B^2 \equiv \int_0^{\hat{x}_B} \left(r - p_A^2 - x\right) dx + \int_{\hat{x}_B}^1 \left(r - \left(p_B^2 - \gamma_B\right) - (1 - x)\right) dx.$$

[m] This expression is almost identical to the corresponding one in the previous model; the only difference is that the exogenous switching cost z is replaced by the endogenous switching cost (i.e., the foregone coupon) γ_A.

A few lines of computations establish that

$$\Delta_S^2 = S_A^2 - S_B^2 = \tfrac{1}{4}\left((\gamma_A + \gamma_B)^2 + 2(\gamma_A - \gamma_B)\right) - \tfrac{1}{2}(\gamma_A + \gamma_B)^2\,\alpha_A.$$

Using the fact that $\hat{x} = \alpha_A$, we can solve $\Delta_S^1 + \Delta_S^2 = 0$ to find

$$\alpha_A\left(p_A^1, p_B^1, \gamma_A, \gamma_B\right) = \frac{4\left(1 + p_B^1 - p_A^1\right) + (\gamma_A + \gamma_B)^2 + 2(\gamma_A - \gamma_B)}{2\left(4 + (\gamma_A + \gamma_B)^2\right)}. \tag{7.2}$$

The first-order conditions for profit-maximization in period 1 are

$$\begin{cases} \frac{\partial \tilde{\pi}_A}{\partial p_A^1} = \alpha_A + \left(p_A^1 - c\right)\frac{\partial \alpha_A}{\partial p_A^1} - \tfrac{1}{2}(1 - 2\alpha_A)\gamma_A(\gamma_A + \gamma_B)\frac{\partial \alpha_A}{\partial p_A^1} = 0, \\[2mm] \frac{\partial \tilde{\pi}_A}{\partial \gamma_A} = \left(p_A^1 - c\right)\frac{\partial \alpha_A}{\partial \gamma_A} - \tfrac{1}{2}\alpha_A(1 - \alpha_A)(2\gamma_A + \gamma_B) \\[2mm] \qquad\qquad - \tfrac{1}{2}(1 - 2\alpha_A)\gamma_A(\gamma_A + \gamma_B)\frac{\partial \alpha_A}{\partial \gamma_A} = 0, \end{cases}$$

where the values of $\partial \alpha_A / \partial p_A^1$ and $\partial \alpha_A / \partial \gamma_A$ are obtained by differentiating expression (7.2). We focus on symmetric equilibrium, so that $p_A^1 = p_B^1 = p$, $\gamma_A = \gamma_B = \gamma$ and so, $\alpha_A = 1/2$. It follows that $\partial \alpha_A / \partial p_A^1 = -1/(2(1 + \gamma^2))$ and $\partial \alpha_A / \partial \gamma_A = 1/(4(1 + \gamma^2))$, which allows us to rewrite the first-order conditions as

$$\begin{cases} \frac{\partial \tilde{\pi}_A}{\partial p_A^1} = \tfrac{1}{2} - (p - c)\frac{1}{2(1 + \gamma^2)} = 0 & \Leftrightarrow \frac{p-c}{1+\gamma^2} = 1, \\[2mm] \frac{\partial \tilde{\pi}_A}{\partial \gamma_A} = (p - c)\frac{1}{4(1 + \gamma^2)} - \tfrac{1}{8}(3\gamma) = 0 \Leftrightarrow \frac{p-c}{1+\gamma^2} = \frac{3\gamma}{2}. \end{cases}$$

It is then immediate that

$$\gamma_A = \gamma_B = \tfrac{2}{3} \quad \text{and} \quad p_A^1 = p_B^1 = c + \tfrac{13}{9}.$$

Using the latter expressions, one finds the equilibrium second-period prices:

$$p_A^2 = p_B^2 = c + \tfrac{4}{3},$$

which are lower than the first-period prices.[n] As for the firms' profits, they are equal to $\tilde{\pi}_A = \tilde{\pi}_B = 10/9$. In the absence of coupons, the game would be similar, in each period, to the Hotelling model with linear transportation costs that we analysed in Section 5.2; that is, we would have $p_i^1 = p_i^2 = c + 1$ and $\tilde{\pi}_i = 1$. We observe thus that coupons allow firms to increase their profits. We also observe that prices in both periods are higher than in the absence of coupons, although loyal customers pay a lower price in period 2 ($p_i^2 - \gamma_i = c + 2/3 < c + 1$). Finally, we check that loyal consumers are a majority in period 2 ($\hat{x}_A = 1 - \hat{x}_B = 5/6$). This establishes the results stated in Lesson 7.6.

7.2.3   Estimating switching costs

There exist several methods to identify and measure switching costs, using either econometric or non-econometric tools.[44] The econometric methods for identifying and measuring switching costs are either direct or indirect. The *direct econometric methods* rely on choice modelling to estimate the values that consumers place on the different attributes of a product. These estimations can then be used either to compare the choice probabilities of old and new

[n] We still need to check that, as we assumed, switching does occur in period 2. It is so if $\gamma_B - 1 < p_B^2 - p_A^2 < 1 - \gamma_A$, or $-1/3 < 0 < 1/3$, which is satisfied.

customers, or to quantify the impact on consumer choices of a product characteristic that is expected to create switching costs (e.g., a loyalty card program) or to be related directly to switching costs (e.g., compatibility with some original equipment). Provided that adequate steps are taken to control for unobserved consumer heterogeneity,[o] these direct methods allow the identification, measurement and direct evaluation of the impacts of switching costs; their main drawback, however, comes from their 'data intensive' nature: information on individual consumer behaviour is required, which is difficult and expensive to obtain. As we show in Case 7.4, the direct methods are based on the probabilistic choice models described above in Section 5.4.

In contrast, *indirect econometric methods* use aggregate market data (which are easier to acquire) but lead to more questionable analyses as they rely on strong assumptions and involve complex econometrics issues. Two strategies are available when using aggregate data. A first strategy is to estimate cross price elasticities of consumption of a particular brand between periods. Small elasticities would indicate that past and future consumption have little impact on current consumption, which would suggest that switching costs are low. Note that large elasticities do not necessarily imply higher switching costs as they might also reflect other effects (e.g., the endogeneity of tastes because of fashion). The second strategy consists in testing the predicted effects on prices of a change in switching costs. As a preliminary, one needs then to identify variables that directly measure switching costs and/or events that directly affect the level of switching costs. For instance, the introduction of number portability in mobile telecommunications markets is meant to facilitate customer switching across operators (as it allows customers to keep their phone number); estimating its impact on prices (or margins) therefore permits an indirect estimation of the magnitude of switching costs in these markets.

Among the *non-econometric methods*, the first that springs to mind consists in measuring the actual level of customer switching in a particular market. However, the level of switching conveys little information by itself as actual switching behaviour and switching costs are not necessarily negatively correlated. Indeed, it is possible to observe a low level of switching in the presence of low switching cost (because prices adjust to prevent customers from switching),[p] as well as a high level of switching in the presence of high switching costs (because, e.g., old customers switch to benefit from the better deals offered to new customers). Qualitative information (about why customers do not switch) may help refine the analysis but such information should also be treated with caution. A more promising non-econometric method consists in comparing old and new customers of a particular brand or product. When price discrimination between old and new customers is not possible, the relevant comparison is in terms of choices: do old customers of a particular brand choose that same brand proportionately more than new customers? On the other hand, when price discrimination is possible, the relevant comparison is in terms of prices: do old customers of a particular brand pay a higher price than new customers?[q]

---

[o] As Goldfarb (2006) puts it: 'The core problem is to separate the direct effect of past choices ("true state dependence") from serially correlated unobservables ("spurious state dependence").'

[p] As remarked earlier, this may be simply due to product differentiation.

[q] Such discrimination may serve as a self-selection device among consumers of different tastes, which is not due to consumer switching costs. See the subsection on behaviour-based price discrimination in Chapter 10, and, in particular, the section coming next on customer poaching.

Case 7.4 **Direct econometric methods to estimate switching costs in the market for mobile telephony**

We described above in Section 5.4 probabilistic choice and the logit model. Recall that this approach is based on the idea that any good or service can be described by a set of attributes that are likely to affect consumers' choices. From this assumption, one constructs a utility function that relates attribute levels, prices and individual characteristics to the utility enjoyed. Including a stochastic component in this utility function turns the analysis into one of probabilistic choice. As we showed above, assuming a particular distribution of the stochastic error allows us to express the probability that a particular choice is made in terms of the logistic distribution (the resulting model is the binary logit model if the choice is between two options, or the multinomial logit model when there are more than two options).

We now explain how to use probabilistic choice models in order to estimate switching costs. The main idea is to compare the choice probabilities of new versus current customers. Absent switching costs, all consumers (new or current) sharing the same preferences should make the same choice; yet, if current customers tend to choose the same alternative as the one they chose in the past with a higher probability than new customers, then this may indicate the presence of switching costs. To test this prediction, define the utility of consumer i when choosing product j as follows $v_{ij} = \beta x_{ij} + \delta z_{ij} + \mu w_{ij} + \varepsilon_{ij}$, where x is a vector of observed product characteristics, z is a vector of individual characteristics, w is a vector of dummy variables which take the value 1 if consumer i chose product j in the previous period (and zero otherwise), ε is the stochastic component, and β, δ and μ are the corresponding vectors of parameters. It is the vector of parameters μ that allows us to identify the existence of switching costs for each product and to quantify their magnitude. For instance, if the estimation of the model reveals that μ_k is statistically greater than zero, then it can be concluded that the purchase of product k in the previous period increases the probability of choosing product k again in the current period, which is indicative of switching costs for that particular product.

Using a methodology of this type, Lee *et al.* (2006) estimate the switching costs and consumers' valuation of the number portability service in the Korean mobile communications market. They conclude (i) that the switching costs have been lowered considerably since number portability has been in force, but that (ii) a significant level of switching costs still remains despite number portability.

7.3   Customer poaching

In this section, we complement the analysis of dynamic market power that we started in the previous section. Our previous analysis of endogenous switching costs was relevant for markets where firms use coupons to make their own customers buy again from them. Here, we consider markets where firms make distinct offers to their rivals' past customers in order to attract them. This practice is known as *consumer poaching*. Recent examples include telephone companies which make offers that only apply to 'new' customers, that is, those customers who are not yet customers of the firm (see Case 7.5 for another illustration).

Practising such customer poaching requires firms to keep records of their customers. For subscription services and Internet transactions, customers typically have to reveal their identity and thus may allow the firm to condition its price on the behaviour of customers.[r] In this sense, customer poaching is a particular case of behaviour-based price discrimination, which is a topic of the following part of the book, where we will return to behaviour-based price discrimination in a monopoly context. We analyse customer poaching in this part of the book because it nicely relates to the analysis of switching costs and allows us to address dynamic issues in a simple model of product differentiation, highlighting that the strategic analysis of market power leads to insights that are not obvious without rigorous analysis.

Policy makers in general and competition authorities in particular may be concerned about customer poaching leading to higher overall prices or, if this is not the case, at least to higher prices for certain groups of customers. We will investigate these concerns in a two-period model with horizontal product differentiation, in which firms can set different prices in the second period depending on whether or not consumers have bought the product in the first period.

Case 7.5 Pay-to-switch in the business automation software market[45]

There are two major competitors on the market for business automation software (which encompasses an array of programs for accounting, purchasing, order taking and sales): SAP and Oracle. As it was lagging behind SAP, Oracle started in 2005 to expand via the acquisition of smaller rivals, such as PeopleSoft and Siebel. SAP's reaction was to implement its so-called 'safe passage' programme, aimed at companies worried about future support and development for PeopleSoft's or Siebel's products after the companies' acquisition by Oracle. As part of the offer, SAP offered Siebel US customers a credit of up to 75% of their Siebel licensing fees toward the purchase of comparable SAP software. SAP introduced similar discounts to PeopleSoft customers and extended the offer to companies running software from J. D. Edwards and Retek, both of which Oracle also swallowed.

The model

We consider a market with two firms, which set prices in two periods (period 1 and period 2).[46] Suppose that products are horizontally differentiated and that firms cannot affect their degree of product differentiation. In particular, we take the simple Hotelling specification that we used in the previous models: firms are located at the extremes of the unit interval and consumers are uniformly distributed on this interval (with a total mass of 1). Consumers have unit demand

[r] However, if customers' IP addresses change, an unconditional price may have to be posted in advance. For instance, Amazon was considering using conditional prices but abandoned the plan after consumer complaints.

in each period. The per-period utility of consumer x is $r - x - p$ if a product is located at 0 and sold at price p, and $r - (1 - x) - p$ if a product is located at 1 and sold at price p, where r is assumed to be sufficiently large so that all consumers prefer to participate in the market. Firms have constant marginal costs of production c.

We analyse the following strategic situation. *Stage 1a.* Firms simultaneously set first-period prices p_A^1 and p_B^1, respectively. *Stage 1b.* Consumers decide which firm to buy from. *Stage 2a.* Firms simultaneously set second-period prices. If it can identify previous customers, firm i sets prices p_{iA}^2 to customers who bought from firm A in the previous period and p_{iB}^2 to the remaining consumers. Otherwise, $p_{iA}^2 = p_{iB}^2 = p_i^2$. *Stage 2b.* Consumers decide which firm to buy from given the prices that apply.

In period 1, firms maximize expected profits where second-period profits are discounted with discount factor δ. At stage 1b, consumers may simply maximize per-period utility and thus behave myopically, or they may be forward-looking. We analyse the subgame perfect equilibrium of three variations of the model: (i) where firms cannot observe the identity of consumers so that $p_{iA}^2 = p_{iB}^2 = p_i^2$; (ii) where firms do observe the identity of customers and where consumers are myopic; and (iii) where firms observe the identity of customers and all consumers maximize expected discounted utility (and thus are forward-looking).

Firms cannot observe consumers' identities

The first variation is a straightforward single repetition of the single-shot Hotelling model. By backward induction, the equilibrium of the one-shot game will be played along the equilibrium path of the two-stage game. Equilibrium prices are $p_A^{t*} = p_B^{t*} = c + 1, t = 1, 2$. In both periods the market splits at $\hat{x}^t = 1/2$. Hence, the equilibrium profit for both firms is $\hat{\pi} = 1/2 + \delta/2$. Because of the symmetry assumption, the allocation is efficient.

Period 2 equilibrium when firms can observe consumers' identities

Consider now the possibility that firms set different prices p_{iA}^2 and p_{iB}^2 in period 2. Note that after period 1, the market splits at $\hat{x}^1$ such that all consumers to the left (resp. right) buy from firm A (resp. firm B). We start our analysis by investigating competition in period 2 taking $\hat{x}^1$ as given. Then, if both firms poach some customers from their competitor, there exist indifferent consumers $\hat{x}_A^2$ and $\hat{x}_B^2$. Consumer $\hat{x}_A^2$ is a consumer who bought in period 1 from firm A (and thus belongs to segment A) and is indifferent between staying with firm A and switching to firm B. Here, segment A is the home segment for firm A and the foreign segment for firm B. Similarly, consumer $\hat{x}_B^2$ is a consumer who bought in period 1 from firm B (and thus belongs to segment B) and is indifferent between staying with firm B and switching to firm A. Figure 7.1 illustrates period-2 demand in this model.

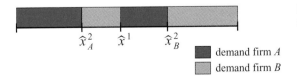

$\hat{x}_A^2 \qquad \hat{x}^1 \qquad \hat{x}_B^2$

■ demand firm A
□ demand firm B

Figure 7.1 Period-2 demand in the model with customer poaching

Firm A's and B's profit maximization problems respectively are

$$\max_{p^2_{AA}, p^2_{AB}} (p^2_{AA} - c)\widehat{x}^2_A + (p^2_{AB} - c)(\widehat{x}^2_B - \widehat{x}^1),$$

$$\max_{p^2_{BA}, p^2_{BB}} (p^2_{BA} - c)(\widehat{x}^1 - \widehat{x}^2_A) + (p^2_{BB} - c)(1 - \widehat{x}^2_B).$$

Note that consumers to the left of $\widehat{x}^1$ can only buy at prices p^2_{AA} and p^2_{BA}, while consumers to the right of $\widehat{x}^1$ can only buy at prices p^2_{BB} and p^2_{AB}. Therefore, market segments A and B are completely separated from each other and pricing decisions in one segment are independent of the other segment. The indifferent consumer in segment A is $\widehat{x}^2_A = 1/2 + (p^2_{BA} - p^2_{AA})/2$. Similarly, $\widehat{x}^2_B = 1/2 + (p^2_{BB} - p^2_{AB})/2$. Consider first segment A. Here, the maximization problems are $\max_{p^2_{AA}} (p^2_{AA} - c)\widehat{x}^2_A$ and $\max_{p^2_{BA}} (p^2_{BA} - c)(\widehat{x}^1 - \widehat{x}^2_A)$, for firms A and B respectively. The system of first-order conditions of profit maximization is

$$\begin{cases} 1 + p^2_{BA} - 2p^2_{AA} + c = 0, \\ 2\widehat{x}^1 - 1 + p^2_{AA} - 2p^2_{BA} + c = 0. \end{cases}$$

Solving this system we obtain

$$p^2_{AA} = c + \tfrac{1}{3}(2\widehat{x}^1 + 1) \quad \text{and} \quad p^2_{BA} = c + \tfrac{1}{3}(4\widehat{x}^1 - 1).$$

The analysis in segment B is very similar and we obtain second-period equilibrium prices

$$p^2_{AB} = c + \tfrac{1}{3}[4(1 - \widehat{x}^1) - 1] \quad \text{and} \quad p^2_{BB} = c + \tfrac{1}{3}[2(1 - \widehat{x}^1) + 1].$$

Substituting into the expressions for $\widehat{x}^2_A$ and $\widehat{x}^2_B$ we have

$$\widehat{x}^2_A = \tfrac{1}{2} - \tfrac{1}{3}\widehat{x}^1 \quad \text{and} \quad \widehat{x}^2_B = \tfrac{1}{2} + \tfrac{1}{3}\widehat{x}^1.$$

We can already make a number of interesting observations. For any $\widehat{x}^1 \in (0, 1)$, we have that $p^2_{AA} > p^2_{AB}$. Thus each firm is poaching its competitor's customers. In particular, if the market has split symmetrically in period 1 so that $\widehat{x}^1 = 1/2$, equilibrium prices in period 2 are $p^2_{AA} = p^2_{BB} = c + 2/3$ and $p^2_{AB} = p^2_{BA} = c + 1/3$. This means that there is not only customer poaching but also that customers who do not switch pay a lower price than in an environment in which firms do not condition on past behaviour (where they would pay $c + 1$). The market allocation in period 2 then is described by $\widehat{x}^2_A = 1/3$ and $\widehat{x}^2_B = 2/3$. Thus consumers with $x \in [0, 1/3)$ stay with firm A, those with $x \in (1/3, 1/2)$ switch to firm B, those with $x \in (1/2, 2/3)$ switch to firm A, and those with $x \in (2/3, 1]$ stay with firm B.

Lesson 7.7   Customer poaching is an equilibrium phenomenon. It leads not only to lower prices for those consumers who switch firms, but also to lower prices for those consumers who do not, compared to a situation in which conditioning on past consumer behaviour is not possible. Consequently, firms make lower profits in the second period.

Ignoring effects in period 1, we therefore find that consumer surplus increases under discrimination whereas total surplus decreases because the efficient allocation is that all consumers with $x < 1/2$ buy from firm 1 while all consumers with $x > 1/2$ buy from firm 2. Thus, the recommendation of a competition authority as to whether or not to ban price discrimination depends clearly on the standard it has adopted.

To understand why prices are lower than without discrimination, note that a firm that is fishing for customers who previously bought from the competitor is in a better situation if it can discriminate, because it does not suffer inframarginal losses from a price reduction on its previous customers. This makes the firm price more competitively. Using the comparative statics results with strategic complements that we have established in the previous chapter, we observe that each firm's best response in the foreign segment shifts downward. Since best responses are upward sloping, the equilibrium price of both firms in that segment is lower.

We also observe that while we presented a model with horizontal product differentiation, market segments look like exhibiting vertical product differentiation because the home product appears to be superior to the foreign product. Indeed, for $\widehat{x}^1 = 1/2$, we see that if both firms set prices equal to marginal costs, all consumers would stay. Thus the definition of vertical product differentiation is satisfied.[s]

Period 1 equilibrium when firms can observe consumers' identities

Let us now turn to the first period. Clearly, in a symmetric equilibrium, $\widehat{x}^1 = 1/2$ and our insights in this special case hold in the subgame perfect equilibrium of the two-stage game. In the first period, firm A maximizes expected discounted profits

$$\pi_A = \pi_A^1 + \delta\pi_A^2 = (p_A^1 - c)\widehat{x}^1 + \delta\left[(p_{AA}^2 - c)\widehat{x}_A^2 + (p_{AB}^2 - c)(\widehat{x}_B^2 - \widehat{x}^1)\right]$$
$$= (p_A^1 - c)\widehat{x}^1 + \delta\left[\left(\left[c + \tfrac{1}{3}(2\widehat{x}^1 + 1)\right] - c\right)\left(\tfrac{1}{2} - \tfrac{1}{3}\widehat{x}^1\right)\right.$$
$$\left. + \left((c + \tfrac{1}{3}[4(1 - \widehat{x}^1) - 1]) - c\right)\left((\tfrac{1}{2} + \tfrac{1}{3}\widehat{x}^1) - \widehat{x}^1\right)\right].$$

Similarly, for firm B. These reduced-form profit functions only depend on first-period prices. We can then analyse the remaining question as to whether and in which way the possibility of customer poaching in the second period affects competition in the first period. For this, we consider specifications of consumer behaviour. The particular specification we choose affects how the indifferent consumer $\widehat{x}^1$ is affected by price changes.

We start by assuming that *consumers are myopic*. In this case, the indifferent consumer in period 1, $\widehat{x}^1$, solves $r - \widehat{x}^1 - p_A^1 = r - (1 - \widehat{x}^1) - p_B^1$. Hence, $\widehat{x}^{1m} = 1/2 + (p_B^1 - p_A^1)/2$. Substituting this expression in the profit functions, we can solve for the Nash equilibrium in the two-stage game and obtain that $p_A^1 = p_B^1 = c + 1$, which is the same price as without discrimination. Hence, if consumers are myopic, firms make the same profits in period 1 and lower profits in period 2 than without discrimination.

Let us now turn to the case that *consumers are forward-looking*. The rational consumer who is indifferent in period 1 foresees that if she chooses product A in period 1, she will switch to product B in period 2, whereas if she chooses product B in period 1 she will switch to

---

[s] The model also shows that whether a differentiated product market features horizontal or vertical product differentiation may depend on the strategies that are available to firms. In the present context, the possibility of discrimination gives rise to two separate vertically differentiated markets, whereas if discrimination is banned, the market features horizontal product differentiation also in the second period.

product A in period 2. Thus, the indifferent consumer is defined by

$$r - \widehat{x}^1 - p_A^1 + \delta\left[r - (1 - \widehat{x}^1) - p_{BA}^2\right] = r - (1 - \widehat{x}^1) - p_B^1 + \delta\left(r - \widehat{x}^1 - p_{AB}^2\right).$$

At stage 1b, we substitute for the equilibrium values at stage 2 and obtain

$$\widehat{x}^1 = \frac{1}{2}\frac{3(1 + p_B^1 - p_A^1) + \delta}{3 + \delta}.$$

Note that first-period demand reacts less sensitively to first-period price changes than in an environment with myopic consumers,

$$\left|\frac{\partial \widehat{x}^1}{\partial p_A^1}\right| = \frac{1}{2}\frac{3}{3 + \delta} < \frac{1}{2} = \left|\frac{\partial \widehat{x}^{1m}}{\partial p_A^1}\right|.$$

Therefore, equilibrium prices are greater than with myopic consumers. Here, consumer myopia is good for consumers and bad for firms. We can explicitly calculate equilibrium prices as

$$p_A^1 = p_B^1 = c + 1 + \frac{\delta}{3}.$$

Compared to the situation where firms are unable to observe consumers' identities, we find that firms set a higher price in the first period ($p_i^1 = c + 1 + \delta/3 > c + 1$) and lower prices in the second period ($p_{ij}^2 = c + 1/3 < p_{ii}^2 = c + 2/3 < c + 1$). The discounted total price is the same for those consumers who do not switch ($p_i^1 + \delta p_{ii}^2 = (c + 1)(1 + \delta)$) and strictly lower for the ones who switch ($p_i^1 + \delta p_{ij}^2 = (c + 1)(1 + \delta) - \delta/3$). Hence, forward-looking consumers are globally made better off by consumer poaching. The reverse applies for firms. Computing the discounted equilibrium profits, we find indeed that firms achieve lower profits under consumer poaching:

$$\pi_i = \pi_i^1 + \pi_i^2 = \left(\frac{1}{2} + \frac{\delta}{6}\right) + \delta\frac{5}{18} = \frac{1}{2} + \frac{4\delta}{9} < \widehat{\pi} = \frac{1}{2} + \frac{\delta}{2}.$$

We conclude with the following lesson:[47]

Lesson 7.8   Customer poaching with forward-looking consumers relaxes price competition in the first period but intensifies it in the second period. In total, firms would be better off if they could agree not to poach each other's customers. On the opposite, poaching makes consumers globally better off.

Review questions

1.   What is the effect of search cost on equilibrium prices? In particular, what happens if all consumers have positive search costs?

2.   Provide two examples of industries in which search costs are likely to be important, and two examples of industries exhibiting switching costs.

3. Many markets exhibit price dispersion. In light of the theoretical analysis presented in this chapter, how can one explain such a phenomenon? Relate your discussion to the analysis in Chapter 3 in which firms have private information about costs.

4. How can one (i) measure price dispersion, and (ii) empirically estimate switching costs?

5. Does an increase in switching costs lead to more relaxed or more intense competition? Discuss.

6. How do markets work in which firms poach customers?

Further reading

Spatial price dispersion is analysed in Salop and Stiglitz (1977). Our analysis of temporal price dispersion is based on Varian (1980). The Diamond paradox is due to Diamond (1971). For further reading on sequential search, see the seminal paper by Stahl (1989). Sorensen (2000) provides an empirical analysis of price dispersion in the prescription drug industry. Baye, Morgan and Scholten (2006) provide an overview on the economics of search and price dispersion. Our analysis of consumer switching costs is based on Klemperer (1987a and 1987b). Switching costs are determined endogenously by Caminal and Matutes (1990). Klemperer (1995) and Farrell and Klemperer (2007) provide valuable overviews on the literature of consumer switching costs. Our analysis of customer poaching draws on Fudenberg and Tirole (2000).

Notes for Part III

1. This approach goes back to Hotelling (1929) and, in a different vein, Lancaster (1966), among others.

2. This has been advocated by Lancaster (1966).

3. The empirical approach has been put forward by Rosen (1974). However, it requires perfect competition, a continuum of products and perfect observability of characteristics. Dispensing with all these requirements, Bajari and Benkard (2005) show how this idea can be put to work in a setting that is most relevant for imperfectly competitive markets. They apply their approach to estimating personal computer demand.

4. Based on 'Excellence in a cup', *The Economist*, 7 January 2007, p. 58.

5. The non-existence result has been shown by d'Aspremont, Gabszewicz and Thisse (1979).

6. Anderson, Goeree and Ramer (1997) show that a tighter density leads to less product differentiation.

7. See de Palma *et al.* (1985).

8. See Salop (1979). While such a model is less suited to analyse the degree of product differentiation (what would be the meaning of minimal versus maximal product differentiation?), it is well suited to address issues of firm entry and to derive comparative statics results in a free entry world (see Chapter 4). In an alternative specification with quadratic transport costs, it can be shown that the configuration with equidistant locations constitutes a subgame-perfect equilibrium in the location-then-price game (see Economides, 1989).

9. Gabszewisz and Thisse (1979) and Shaked and Sutton (1982) were the first to analyse vertically differentiated oligopolies. The present formulation uses the widely adopted specification by Tirole (1988). For an analysis of the underlying consumer preferences, see Peitz (1995).

10. As a technical remark, firm 1's profit function π_1 is quasi-concave in p_1 and continuous in (p_1, p_2). Furthermore, we can restrict attention to prices at which consumers do better than not to consume in the market. A sufficient condition is to consider prices $p_i \in [0, r + \overline{\theta}\,\overline{s}]$. Therefore, we can apply Kakutani's fixed point theorem to show the existence of equilibrium.

11. Based on 'Battle of bathrooms: Era of very light jets starts with basics', by Joe Sharkey, *The New York Times*, 28 August 2006, and on 'No throne room on Eclipse VLJ: Real issue or media hype?', by Karen Di Piazza, *CharterX.com*, 1 September 2006.

12. The seminal contributions on this issue are Gabszewicz and Thisse (1980) and Shaked and Sutton (1982). We follow the exposition in Anderson, de Palma, and Thisse (1992).

13. The exposition draws on Anderson, de Palma and Thisse (1992, Chapter 2).

14. For more on the first interpretation, see Thurstone (1927) and Quandt (1956). For more on the second interpretation, see Manski (1977).

15. See Yellott (1977, p. 135).

16. See Luce (1959).

17. For a general result on equilibrium existence and uniqueness in the logit world, see Konovalov and Sandor (2005).

18. See, e.g., Nevo (2000).

19. We follow here Berry (1994, pp. 250–51).

20. Important contributions include Berry, Levinsohn and Pakes (1995) and Nevo (2001).

21. This section draws on Bagwell (2007).

22. See Becker and Murphy (1993) for more on the complementary view.

23. Source: *Advertisng Age Data Center. 2007 Marketer Profiles Yearbook.* 25 June 2007.

24. For instance, Resnik and Stern (1978) examine television advertising and find that it contains little direct information.

25. This case is based and freely draws on the analysis in Ackerberg (2001).

26. It draws on Table 5 in Ackerberg (2001); see the article for more details.

27. The first formal analysis is due to Dorfman and Steiner (1954).

28. These examples are proposed by Bagwell (2007).

29. This case is based on Erdem, Keane and Sun (2008).

30. This approach has been suggested by Butters (1977).

31. This unified treatment is due to Bagwell (2007), who nicely surveys and discusses the normative theory of monopoly advertising.

32. The model is due to Grossman and Shapiro (1984). The particular specification has been analysed by Tirole (1988, Chapter 7).

33. This confirms Stigler (1961).

34. This analysis mixes insights from von der Fehr and Stevik (1998) and Bloch and Manceau (1999).

35. Our presentation is inspired by, but different from, Salop and Stiglitz (1977) who consider a market with free entry in which firms face U-shaped average cost curves. They show that on a set of parameters there exists an equilibrium in which some firms sell at the competitive price (at minimum average costs) while others sell at a higher price.

36. We follow here the model of sales of Varian (1980).

37. This is already contained in the analysis of Salop and Stiglitz (1977). As Baye, Morgan and Scholten (2003) point out, this situation can be seen as a consequence of the so-called 'digital divide' if accessing the clearing house is viewed as being able to compare prices on the Internet.

38. See Diamond (1971).

39. For a formal model see Stahl (1989).

40. For a broad review of this literature, see Baye, Morgan and Scholten (2006, Section 3). We summarize here their main findings.

41. See Klemperer (1995) and Office of Fair Trading (2003).

42. We combine here insights from Klemperer (1987a and b, 1995).

43. This model was proposed by Caminal and Matutes (1990). They also analyse the case where firms can commit to their second-period prices.

44. We follow here the survey made in Section 6 of Office of Fair Trading (2003), as well as the Annex B to this report.

45. Based on 'SAP entices Siebel customers with big discounts', by Alorie Gilbert, CNET News.com, 10 October 2005. Arguably, consumer switching costs are relevant in this case. In our formal analysis below, we abstract from such costs.

46. The analysis is inspired by and largely based on Fudenberg and Tirole (2000). For a related analysis that however considers only the second period (because decisions in the first period are taken as given), see Schaffer and Zhang (2000). For an extension of customer poaching to a model with switching costs, see the analysis of the banking industry by Bouckaert and Degryse (2004).

47. This is essentially Proposition 2 in Fudenberg and Tirole (2000).

References for Part III

Aalto-Setälä, V. (2003). Explaining Price Dispersion for Homogeneous Grocery Products. *Journal of Agricultural & Food Industrial Organization* 1 (Article 9): 1–14.

Ackerberg, D. (2001). Empirically Distinguishing Informative and Prestige Effects of Advertising. *Rand Journal of Economics* 32: 316–333.

Anderson, S. P., de Palma, A. and Thisse, J.-F. (1992). *Discrete Choice Theory of Product Differentiation.* Cambridge, MA and London: MIT Press.

Anderson S. P., Goeree, J. K. and Ramer R. (1997). Location, Location, Location. *Journal of Economic Theory* 77: 102–127.

Anderson, S. P. and Renault, R. (2006). Advertising Content. *American Economic Review* 96: 93–113.

Bagwell, K. (2007). The Economic Analysis of Advertising. In Armstrong, M. and Porter, R. (eds.), *Handbook of Industrial Organization, Vol. 3.* North-Holland: Amsterdam.

Bajari, P. and Benkard, L. (2005). Demand Estimation With Heterogeneous Consumers and Unobserved Product Characteristics: A Hedonic Approach. *Journal of Political Economy* 113: 1239–1276.

Baye, M. R. and Morgan, J. (2001). Information Gatekeepers on the Internet and the Competitiveness of Homogeneous Product Markets. *American Economic Review* 91: 454–474.

Baye, M. R., Morgan, J. and Scholten, P. (2003). The Valuation of Information in an Online Consumer Electronics Market. *Journal of Public Policy and Marketing* 22: 17–25.

Baye, M. R., Morgan, J. and Scholten, P. (2006). Information, Search, and Price Dispersion. Forthcoming in Hendershott, T. (ed.), *Handbook on Economics and Information Systems,* Elsevier.

Becker, G. S. and Murphy, K. M. (1993). A Simple theory of Advertising as a Good or Bad. *Quarterly Journal of Economics*: 942–964.

Berry, S. (1994). Estimating Discrete Choice Models of Product Differentiation. *Rand Journal of Economics* 25: 242–262.

Berry, S., Levinsohn, J. and Pakes, A. (1995). Automobile Prices in Market Equilibrium. *Econometrica* 63: 841–890.

Bloch, F. and Manceau, D. (1999). Persuasive Advertising in Hotelling's Model of Product Differentiation. *International Journal of Industrial Organization* 17: 557–574.

Bouckaert, J. and Degryse, H. (2004). Softening Competition by Inducing Switching in Credit Markets. *Journal of Industrial Economics* 52: 27–52.

Butters, G. (1977). Equilibrium Distributions of Sales and Advertising Prices. *Review of Economic Studies* 44: 465–491.

Caminal, R. and Matutes, C. (1990). Endogenous Switching Costs in a Duopoly Model. *International Journal of Industrial Organization* 8: 353–374.

Caplin, A. and Nalebuff, B. (1991). Aggregation and Imperfect Competition: On the Existence of Equilibrium. *Econometrica* 59: 25–59.

Colombo, R., Ehrenberg, A. and Sabavala, D. (2000). Diversity in Analyzing Brand-Switching Tables: The Car Challenge, *Canadian Journal of Marketing Research* 19: 26–36.

d'Aspremont, C., Gabszewicz, J. J. and Thisse, J.-F. (1979). On Hotelling's 'Stability in Competition'. *Econometrica* 47: 1145–1150.

de Palma, A., Ginsburgh, V., Papageorgiou, V. V. and Thisse, J.-F. (1985). The Principle of Minimum Differentiation Holds under Sufficient Heterogeneity. *Econometrica* 53: 767–781.

Diamond, P. (1971). A Model of Price Adjustment. *Journal of Economic Theory* 3: 156–168.

Dixit, A. and Norman, V. (1978). Advertising and Welfare. *Bell Journal of Economics* 9: 1–17.

Dorfman, R. and Steiner, P. O. (1954). Optimal Advertising and Optimal Quality. *American Economic Review* 44: 826–836.

Economides, N. (1989). Symmetric Equilibrium Existence and Optimality in Differentiated Products Markets. *Journal of Economic Theory* 47: 178–194.

Erdem, T., Keane, M. and Sun, B. (2008). The Impact of Advertising on Consumer Price Sensitivity in Experience Goods Markets. *Quantitative Marketing and Economics* 6: 139–176.

Farrell, J. and Klemperer, P. (2007). Coordination and Lock-In: Competition with Switching Costs and Network Effects. In Armstrong, M. and Porter, R. (eds.). *Handbook of Industrial Organization, Vol. 3.* Amsterdam: North-Holland.

Fudenberg, D. and Tirole, J. (2000). Customer Poaching and Brand Switching. *Rand Journal of Economics* 31: 634–657.

Gabszewicz, J.-J. and Thisse, J.-F. (1979). Price Competition, Quality and Income Disparities. *Journal of Economic Theory* 20: 340–354.

Gabszewicz, J. J. and Thisse, J.-F. (1980). Entry and Exit in a Differentiated Industry. *Journal of Economic Theory* 22: 327–338.

Goldberg, P. (1995). Product Differentiation and Oligopoly in International Markets: The Case of the U.S. Automobile Industry. *Econometrica* 63: 891–951.

Goldfarb, A. (2006). State Dependence at Internet Portals. *Journal of Economics and Management Strategy* 15: 317–352.

Grossman, G. M. and Shapiro, C. (1984). Informative Advertising with Differentiated Products. *Review of Economic Studies* 51: 63–81.

Hotelling, H. (1929). Stability in Competition. *Economic Journal* 39: 41–57.

Janssen, M. C. W. and Non, M. C. (2007). Advertising and Consumer Search in a Duopoly Model. *International Journal of Industrial Organization*. In Press.

Kelton, C. and Kelton, D. (1982). Advertising and Intraindustry Brand Shift in the U.S. Brewing Industry. *Journal of Industrial Economics* 30: 293–303.

Klemperer, P. (1987a). Markets with Consumer Switching Costs. *Quarterly Journal of Economics* 102: 375–394.

Klemperer, P. (1987b). The Competitiveness of Markets with Consumer Switching Costs. *Rand Journal of Economics* 18: 138–150.

Klemperer, P. (1995). Competition when Consumers Have Switching Costs: An Overview with Applications to Industrial Organization, Macroeconomics, and International Trade. *Review of Economic Studies* 62: 515–539.

Konovalov, A. and Sandor, Z. (2005). On Price Equilibrium with Multi-Product Firms. Mimeo.

Lancaster, K. (1966). A New Approach to Consumer Theory. *Journal of Political Economy* 74: 132–157.

Lee, J., Kim, Y., Lee, J.-D. and Park, Y. (2006). Estimating the Extent of Potential Competition in the Korean Mobile Telecommunications Market: Switching Costs and Number Portability. *International Journal of Industrial Organization* 24: 107–124.

Luce, R. D. (1959). *Individual Choice Behavior: A Theoretical Analysis*. New York: Wiley.

MacMinn, R. D. (1980). Search and Market Equilibrium. *Journal of Political Economy* 88: 308–327.

Manski, C. (1977). The Structure of Random Utility Models. *Theory and Decision* 8: 229–254.

Marshall, A. (1890). *Principles of Economics*. London: MacMillan and Co.

Marshall, A. (1919). *Industry and Trade: A Study of Industrial Technique and Business Organization, and of their Influences on the Conditions of Various Classes and Nations*. London: MacMillan and Co.

Maudos, J. and Nagore, A. (2005). Explaining Market Power Differences in Banking: A Cross-Country Study. Mimeo. Instituto Valenciano de Investigaciones Economicas.

Nevo, A. (2000). A Practitioner's Guide to Estimation of Random-coefficients Logit Models of Demand. *Journal of Economics and Management Strategy* 9: 513–548.

Nevo, A. (2001). Measuring Market Power in the Ready-to-eat Cereal Industry. *Econometrica* 69: 307–342.

Nevo, A. and Wolfram, C. (2002). Why Do Manufacturers Issue Coupons? An Empirical Analysis of Breakfast Cereals. *Rand Journal of Economics* 33: 319–339.

Office of Fair Trading (2003). Switching Costs. Part One: Economic Models and Policy Implications. Economic Discussion Paper 5. London, UK.

Örs, E. (2006). The Role of Advertising in Commercial Banking. CEPR Discussion Paper No. 5461.

Peitz, M. (1995). Utility Maximization in Models of Discrete Choice. *Economics Letters* 49: 91–94.

Quandt, R. E. (1956). A Probabilistic Theory of Consumer Behavior. *Quarterly Journal of Economics* 70: 507–536.

Resnik, A. and Stern, B. (1978). An Analysis of the Information Content in Television Advertising. *Journal of Marketing* 41: 50–53.

Roberts, M. and Samuelson, L. (1988). An Empirical Analysis of Dynamic Nonprice Competition in an Oligopolistic Industry. *Rand Journal of Economics* 19: 200–220.

Rosen, S. (1974). Hedonic Prices and Implicit Markets: Product Differentiation in Pure Competition. *Journal of Political Economy* 82: 34–55.

Salop, S. C. (1979). Monopolistic Competition with Outside Goods. *Bell Journal of Economics* 10: 141–156.

Salop, S. C. and J. Stiglitz (1977). Bargains and Rip-offs: A Model of Monopolistically Competitive Price Dispersion. *Review of Economic Studies* 44: 493–510.

Shaffer, G. and Zhang, Z. J. (2000). Pay to Switch or Pay to Stay: Preference-based Price Discrimination in Markets with Switching Costs. *Journal of Economics and Management Strategy* 9: 397–424.

Shaked, A. and Sutton, J. (1982). Relaxing Price Competition through Product Differentiation. *Review of Economic Studies* 49: 3–13.

Shaked, A. and Sutton, J. (1983). Natural Oligopolies. *Econometrica* 51: 1469–1483.

Smith, M. and Brynjolfsson, E. (2001). Consumer Decision-Making at an Internet Shopbot: Brand Still Matters. *Journal of Industrial Economics* 49: 541–558.

Sorensen, A. (2000). Equilibrium Price Dispersion in Retail Markets for Prescription Drugs. *Journal of Political Economy* 108: 833–850.

Stahl, D. O. (1989). Oligopolistic Pricing with Sequential Consumer Search. *American Economic Review* 79: 700–712.

Stigler, G. (1961). The Economics of Information. *Journal of Political Economy* 69: 213–225.

Thurstone, L. L. (1927). A Law of Comparative Judgment. *Psychology Review* 34: 273–286.

Tirole, J. (1988). *The Theory of Industrial Organization*, Cambridge, MA: MIT Press.

Varian, H. R (1980). A Model of Sales. *American Economic Review* 70: 651–659.

von der Fehr, N.-H. M. and Stevik, K. (1998). Persuasive Advertising and Product Differentiation. *Southern Economic Journal* 65: 113–126.

Yellott, J. I. (1977). Generalized Thurstone Models of Ranking: Equivalence and Reversibility. *Journal of Mathematical Psychology* 22: 48–69.

Part IV
Pricing strategies and market segmentation

Introduction to Part IV: Pricing strategies and
market segmentation

Consider the book you have in your hands and
suppose, for now, that this is the only IO textbook
on the market, so that we, the authors, are in a
monopoly position. To introduce this part, we want
to illustrate here how the profit we (or, more
correctly, our publisher) can make by selling our
book depends on the *information* we have about
our potential consumers, and on the range of
instruments we can use to design our tariffs. With
limited information and instruments, the best we can
do is to set a 'one-size-fits-all', uniform, price for all
our potential consumers. However, more information
and instruments allow us to increase our profit.

Regarding the *information* about the
consumers, it is not enough to know that
consumers differ in their willingness to pay for our
book; the crucial issue is to know who is willing to
pay what. Armed with such knowledge, we can
increase profit by setting different prices to different
consumers, a practice generally known as *price
discrimination*, presuming that resale is not possible
or sufficiently costly. In some situations, the
consumers' willingness to pay can be directly
inferred from some observable characteristics.
Ideally, we would like to know exactly how much
each potential consumer is willing to pay for the
book; we would then make a personalized
take-it-or-leave-it offer to each of them by quoting a
price just below the consumer's reservation price;
we would thereby appropriate the entire consumer
surplus. More realistically, we can use market data
analysis to segment our market in several groups,
with the consumers in each group sharing some
common characteristics and correlated willingness

to pay. For instance, we can segment the market on
a geographical basis and sell the book at different
prices, say, in the US and in Europe if market
research reveals that those two markets exhibit
different demand functions.[a] In other situations,
however, there is no direct way to segment the
market based on some observable characteristics.
In such cases, we can still increase our profit by
using an incentive compatible mechanism whereby
consumers reveal their willingness to pay to us. For
instance, we can publish two versions of the book:
one 'high-end' version (hard-back and in colour) and
one 'low-end' version (paperback in black and
white); if we price correctly the two versions,
consumers with a high willingness to pay will reveal
themselves by purchasing the high-end version
rather than the low-end version. In Chapters 8 and
9, we detail these three forms of price discrimination
and their implications for sellers and for consumers.

An alternative, or complementary, way to
increase our profit consists in using more tariff
instruments. The possibility of selling different
versions of the same product is a first example of
using more instruments than just prices. A product
that is sold over several periods makes it possible
for a firm to set different prices over time. This
increases the number of price instruments and one
may expect that a firm cannot do worse than setting
only a price in the first period. However, if a firm
cannot commit to a price path over the whole time
horizon, it may have an incentive to lower its price in
subsequent periods. Under some conditions, a
monopolist loses its market power because it
competes with future selves. Fortunately for us, new
catalogues for academic books come out only once

---

[a] Actually, they do (see Case 8.3 below).

a year and we very much hope that you do not want to wait for a cheaper copy until next year (and our publisher says that it will not lower its price in any case). But what do we know about intertemporal pricing of durable goods in general? This is an issue that we explore in Chapter 10. We also study another intertemporal pricing strategy that consists in conditioning price on the time of purchase or on the consumer's past behaviour. For instance, we could make the price of our book depend on whether the consumer has bought other books from our publisher in the past. Or, if the book is sold on the Internet, we could lower the price for a consumer who has previously visited the web page of the book but who decided against purchasing.

Finally, we could set a special price for a bundle containing the book, a CD-ROM with extra material and an instructor's manual, while still selling one or several of the three items separately. We could also charge for the variable usage of the web site associated to the book. These practices of 'bundling' and 'tying' are examined in Chapter 11.

Assuming that we can commit ourselves to a particular pricing stategy, it is intuitive that, as long as we stay in a monopoly position, more information and a wider range of tariff instruments can only lead us to higher profits (we can indeed do no worse than with a uniform price). Unfortunately for us, there are other excellent IO books out there, competing for the same market. In such an *oligopoly* context, it is no longer so clear that more information and more instruments translate into higher profits. Actually, the reverse may even be true. Intuitively, if our competitors behave like us and use the information they have about the consumers to set discriminatory prices, competition might be exacerbated for some groups of consumers and profits may end up falling below the profits we would all obtain if we were using uniform prices. For each type of price discrimination and tariff instrument, we will examine the implications of imperfect competition. We will also adopt a broader point of view and study the welfare effects of these various practices.

What will you learn in this part of the book?
You will first get to know a large array of price (and non-price) strategies that firms may resort to in order to segment markets and, potentially, extract more consumer surplus by effectively selling at different prices to different consumers. You will learn that price discrimination can take various forms according to how well a firm knows its consumers' willingness to pay and which type of tariff instruments it can use. You will also learn that the effects that these various forms of price discrimination have on profits and on welfare depend crucially on the degree of competition in the industry. In monopolistic industries, more information and a wider range of tariff instruments can only increase the firm's profits (at the expense of consumer surplus, the effect on welfare being ambiguous). In oligopolistic industries (or in monopoly markets in which the monopolist lacks commitment power), however, it is much less clear whether more information and more instruments translate into higher profits. The positive surplus-extracting effect of price discrimination may be offset by its negative competition-enhancing effect.

8 Group pricing and personalized pricing

This chapter is organized as follows. In Section 8.1, we start by defining formally the three types of price discrimination, which we will refer to as personalized pricing, group pricing and menu pricing. We cover the latter type in the next chapter. Here, we consider jointly the first two types because, as we will argue, personalized pricing is nothing but an extreme form of group pricing, where the market segmentation is so fine that each separate 'group' consists of a single consumer. Both practices rely on the existence of observable and verifiable indicators of the consumers' willingness to pay. Coupled with the absence of resale among consumers (i.e., arbitrage), this allows the firms to make a specific and unique price offer to each separate group of consumers.[b] The better the information about consumers, the finer the partition of the consumers into groups and the larger the possibilities for firms to extract consumer surplus. If the firm is a monopoly, as we assume in Section 8.2, this is clearly the only effect at play. We thus observe that the discriminating monopolist's profits increase with the quality of the information it has about the willingness to pay of its consumers.

In an oligopoly setting, however, the previous conclusion may not hold because a second effect comes into play. As we show in Section 8.3, price discrimination gives firms more flexibility to respond to their rivals' actions, which tends to exacerbate price competition and, thereby, to lower profits. Choosing to discriminate becomes thus a strategic decision. As we show below, the balance between the two contrasting forces (surplus extraction and fiercer competition) depends on the quality of the information about consumers and on the relative importance of the different groups of consumers.

8.1 Price discrimination

In this section, we first propose a general typology of price discrimination practices. We then describe how firms manage to segment the market into well-recognized groups of consumers and sometimes, to acquire information about individual reservation prices.

8.1.1 Price discrimination: a typology

To introduce Chapters 8 and 9, let us formally define what is meant by *price discrimination*. Price discrimination implies that two varieties of a good are sold (by the same seller) to two

---

[b] In contrast, when groups cannot be identified, the only possibility for selling at different prices to different consumers is to propose to all consumers the same menu of price offers among which they self-select. This is the practice of menu pricing that we consider in the next chapter.

buyers at different net prices, the net price being the price (paid by the buyer) corrected for the cost associated with the product differentiation.[1] Under what conditions is such a practice feasible? First, firms must enjoy some market power, so that they are in a position to set prices. Second, consumers are not able (or find it too costly) to engage in *arbitrage*. Arbitrage refers either to the transfer of the good itself between consumers (i.e., one consumer buys the good at the low price and resells it to another consumer just below the high price), or to the transfer of demand between different packages aimed at different consumers (see Chapter 9).[c]

Following Pigou (1920), it is customary to distinguish three different types of price discrimination, according to the information that firms have about buyers. The most favourable case for the firm is when it has complete information about individual preferences. The firm is then able to charge an individualized price for each buyer and for each unit purchased by each buyer, thereby extracting all of the consumer surplus. In Pigou's taxonomy, this practice is known as *first-degree price discrimination* (or *perfect discrimination*). Shapiro and Varian (1999) propose the more descriptive term of *personalized pricing*.

When the firm does not know exactly each consumer's willingness to pay, it may still manage to extract a fraction of the consumer surplus by relying on some indicators (such as age, occupation, location) that are related to the consumers' preferences. If the firm can observe a buyer's characteristics, then it can charge different prices as a function of these characteristics. This type of price discrimination is referred to as *third-degree price discrimination* in Pigou's taxonomy, or as *group pricing* in Shapiro and Varian's. This practice is common in the software industry: e.g., office software are often sold at different prices to home users and to professionals, students enjoy special discounts on a range of software products.

It is often argued that personalized pricing cannot be applied in practice because of the enormous amount of information it requires. However, firms are now able to use information technologies in order to improve their knowledge of consumers' preferences and, thereby, to approach personalized price offers. That is, by collecting and processing an increasing amount of information about consumers' willingness to pay, firms are able to refine the group segmentation, tending to the ideal situation where each group consists of a single consumer. Personalized pricing can thus be seen as an extreme form of group pricing. We therefore examine the two practices together in this chapter.

When buyers' characteristics are not directly observable, the firm still has the option to use self-selecting devices in order to extract some consumer surplus. The idea is to discriminate between heterogeneous buyers by targeting a specific package (i.e., a selling contract that includes various clauses in addition to price) for each class of buyers. The firm faces then the problem of designing the menu of packages in such a way that each consumer indeed chooses the package targeted for her. Pigou describes this practice as *second-degree price discrimination*, whereas Shapiro and Varian refer to it, more descriptively, as *menu pricing* or versioning. (Menu pricing is the topic of Chapter 9.) Case 8.1 nicely illustrates the distinction between group and menu pricing; it also shows that the airline industry widely resorts to price discrimination practices.

---

[c] Avoiding the first form of arbitrage is particularly easy and inexpensive when firms sell personal services; this explains why price discrimination is a common practice in such industries.

Case 8.1 **Price discrimination in airline fares**

The willingness to pay for an airline ticket on a given route and date is likely to vary considerably among consumers (according to how urgent and predictable the decision to fly is, according to whether the consumers are bearing the cost themselves or not, ...). Moreover, arbitrage opportunities are limited because the flight itself is a non-durable service. Finally, the marginal cost of a passenger is negligible as long as the full capacity of the airplane is not reached. For all these reasons, airlines have long devoted resources to implement price discrimination. Airlines price discriminate by offering discount fares to consumers who satisfy various restrictions. Purchase restrictions mainly belong to two categories. On the one hand, some restrictions intend to foster self-selection, which corresponds to menu pricing. For instance, the restriction may specify the number of days in advance that purchase is required, add surcharges for one-way tickets or require a Saturday-night stayover; the objective is to bring travellers to reveal their private information about their value of time. Also, business and economy class tickets differ in prices and along several dimensions (comfort, flexibility, refund policy, etc.), which is a form of discrimination based on quality or versioning. On the other hand, other restrictions intend to segment the market on the basis of observable passengers' characteristics (such as family, age, student or various events) and correspond to group pricing.

Interestingly, European low cost carriers (or LCCs, such as Ryanair or easyJet) have eliminated completely both types of restrictions. In particular, they issue 'point-to-point' tickets whose price does not systematically depend on the day of departing or of returning; they also offer 'no-frills' flights with no class distinction for seats. However, airlines still practice intertemporal price discrimination (see Chapter 10) as the fare may depend on how long before departure the booking is made. They also practice a form of geographical group pricing, as explained in Case 9.2 below. Note that recently a number of flag carriers including BA scrapped the Saturday-night rule according to which a lower-priced ticket is only available if a Saturday night is included (which was introduced as an attempt to distinguish business from non-business travel). This may be taken as evidence that competition has worked against price discrimination.

8.1.2   **'Know thy customers'**

Personalized pricing has long been viewed as unworkable, essentially because sellers were not practically able to gather enough detailed information about individual willingness to pay. Spatial economics was the only field in which pricing regimes akin to personalized pricing were explored: in a spatial setting where the distance between sellers and buyers is observable and where products are costly to transport across locations, prices can be adjusted so as to include freight charges to the location of the buyer (so-called 'delivered prices') and thus differ across buyers.

Recent developments in information technologies have fuelled a rapid growth of computer-mediated transactions (e-commerce) and have increased the practicality of more personalized pricing regimes in non-spatial settings. The current technologies have made a finer segmentation of consumer markets not only widely possible, but also commercially feasible. Indeed, information technologies have dramatically decreased the transaction costs of both gathering personal information about Internet users and of monitoring their purchasing habits, as well as the amount of time and effort required for changing online prices. Sellers can acquire precise information about their consumers through different sources: (i) directly through repeated interaction with the buyers, (ii) via telemarketing or direct-mail surveys, (iii) from credit card reports, or (iv) from web-based marketing firms (such as Double Click or I-Behaviour). Case 8.2 illustrates how firms analyse and use customer information to their advantage.

Case 8.2 Data mining

The main idea behind data mining is to gather large amounts of customer information and to analyse it so as to identify trends indicative of customers' wants and needs. Customer-loyalty cards provide a great deal of useful information as they allow sellers to learn not only what is selling but also who is buying it. However, gathering information is one thing; using this information in a profitable way is another thing. It is only in recent years that improvements in both hardware and software, together with the rise of e-commerce, have enabled firms to exploit all the potential of data mining. Having matured, data mining is now advancing on three fronts: (i) the use of data in real time in order to adjust prices, (ii) the use of historical data in order to predict future trends, and (iii) the analysis of 'unstructured' data, such as text on the web. As for the first direction (which is the one that directly relates to first- and third-degree price discrimination), a survey published in *The Economist*[2] reports the following example. 'The traditional British pub seems like an unlikely place to find the latest in data mining. But some pub chains now change the prices of different drinks from day to day, using software that assesses the impact that 'happy hour' offers have on sales. If discounting a particular beer boosts sales one day, it is likely to remain discounted the next – and if not, something else will be tried. As well as being much faster than traditional data mining, this kind of thing requires many other elements to be in place, such as the capacity to track inventory accurately and re-price products dynamically.'

8.2   Group and personalized pricing in monopoly

We use a very simple model to understand how a monopolist increases its profits when it obtains more refined information about its consumers' reservation prices. Suppose we have a unit mass of consumers with unit demand for the monopolist's product. A consumer's valuation (i.e., her reservation price) for the product, noted θ, is drawn from the uniform distribution over the interval $[0, 1]$. At price p, consumers with $\theta \geq p$ purchase one unit of the product and the other consumers stay out of the market. Therefore, under our assumptions, the total quantity demanded is $q = 1 - p$. Suppose for simplicity that the producer's marginal cost is equal to zero. Then, if the firm is to set a uniform price, it chooses p so as to maximize $p(1 - p)$.

The optimal uniform price is easily found as $p^u = 1/2$. For this price, we compute the firm's profits, the consumer surplus and the deadweight loss respectively as

$$\pi^u = \tfrac{1}{4}, CS^u = \tfrac{1}{8}, DL^u = \tfrac{1}{8}.$$

The optimum under a uniform price is depicted in the left panel of Figure 8.1. The monopolist has two reasons for being dissatisfied with this situation. First, more profits could be made on consumers with $\theta > 1/2$ as they are willing to pay more than p^u. Second, profits could also be made on consumers with $\theta < 1/2$ if a lower price could be charged to them. However, this is pure wishful thinking because the firm has no other option than to set a single price when all it knows about consumers is their overall distribution.

Suppose now that the monopolist acquires customer-specific information and, thereby, a more accurate estimate of how much each consumer values its product. In particular, the information partitions the $[0, 1]$ interval into N subintervals of equal length and allows the monopolist to charge different prices to different groups of consumers. The larger N, the more precise the information; as N goes to infinity, prices can be personalized.

Consider first $N = 2$. Now, facing a particular consumer, the monopolist knows whether this consumer's valuation lies between 0 and 1/2, or between 1/2 and 1. The firm sets a price p_1 for the first segment where demand is given by $q_1 = 1/2 - p_1$, and a price p_2 for the second segment where demand is given by $q_2 = \max\{1/2, 1 - p_2\}$. As segments are of size 1/2, prices must be such that $0 \le q_i \le 1/2$ $(i = 1, 2)$. Because of our assumption of constant marginal costs, the monopolist's problem is easy to solve as the two segments are separated both in terms of demand and in terms of costs.[d] We can thus solve the two problems separately and we easily find the optimal prices as $p_1 = 1/4$ and $p_2 = 1/2$. The corresponding profits, consumer surplus and deadweight loss are (where we indicate in brackets the number of segments)

$$\pi\,(2) = \tfrac{1}{4} + \tfrac{1}{16} > \pi^u,$$

$$CS\,(2) = \tfrac{1}{8} + \tfrac{1}{32} > CS^u,$$

$$DL\,(2) = \tfrac{1}{32} < DL^u.$$

As depicted in the right panel of Figure 8.1, we observe that going from one group to two groups makes both the monopolist and the consumers better off. In this specific example, nothing changes for consumers in the second segment $(1/2 \le \theta \le 1)$ as they still all buy at a price of 1/2. Changes only occur for the other segment where some of the consumers now buy (and so, enjoy some surplus). As we now show, when the quality of the information improves (i.e., when the number of subintervals increases), the monopolist's profits increase at the expense of the consumer surplus (and of the deadweight loss).

---

[d] In contrast, when costs depend on the *total* quantity produced (e.g., because marginal cost is increasing), decisions on the two segments cannot be separated. The problem can then be solved according to the following two-step procedure. First, for a given quantity produced, it must be that marginal revenue is equal across segments (otherwise, it would be possible to increase profits by transferring units from one segment to the other). Second, the optimal global quantity is determined by equating the common marginal revenue and the marginal cost. Applying the inverse elasticity rule, it is then straightforward to show that a lower markup prevails in the market segment with a larger price elasticity. We establish this point formally below, when examining geographic price discrimination. Note that this point is reminiscent of what we studied in Chapter 2 when considering a multi-product monopolist.

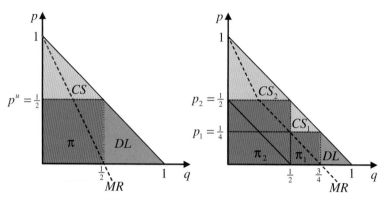

Figure 8.1 Uniform pricing (left) vs. group pricing with two segments (right)

When the monopolist is able to identify N segments, the mth segment (with $1 \leq m \leq N$) has length $1/N$ and its boundaries are $\frac{m-1}{N}$ and $\frac{m}{N}$. If the price charged on this segment is p_m, demand is given by $q_m = m/N - p_m$. As indicated above, constant marginal costs allow us to solve the monopolist's problem on this segment independently of the other segments. The unconstrained optimal price is $p_m = m/2N$. Demand at this price is $q_m = m/2N$, which cannot be larger than the segment size, i.e., $1/N$. Therefore, the condition to have an interior solution is $m/2N < 1/N \Leftrightarrow m < 2$. We conclude that an interior solution obtains on the first segment only: $p_1 = q_1 = 1/2N$, and the profit, consumer surplus and deadweight loss are respectively given by:

$$\pi_1(N) = \left(\tfrac{1}{2N}\right)^2, CS_1(N) = DL_1(N) = \tfrac{1}{2}\left(\tfrac{1}{2N}\right)^2.$$

For all segments $2 \leq m \leq N$, the monopolist sets a price so as to cover the whole segment: $p_m = \frac{m-1}{N}$ and $q_m = \frac{1}{N}$. We have then

$$\pi_m(N) = \tfrac{1}{N}\left(\tfrac{m-1}{N}\right), CS_m(N) = \tfrac{1}{2}\left(\tfrac{1}{N}\right)^2, DL_m(N) = 0, m = 2, \ldots, N.$$

Summing over the N segments, we have

$$\pi(N) = \left(\tfrac{1}{2N}\right)^2 + \sum_{m=2}^{N} \tfrac{1}{N}\left(\tfrac{m-1}{N}\right) = \tfrac{2N^2-2N+1}{4N^2} = \tfrac{1}{2} - \tfrac{2N-1}{4N^2},$$

$$CS(N) = \tfrac{1}{2}\left(\tfrac{1}{2N}\right)^2 + (N-1)\tfrac{1}{2}\left(\tfrac{1}{N}\right)^2 = \tfrac{4N-3}{8N^2},$$

$$DL(N) = \tfrac{1}{8N^2}.$$

Differentiating the latter expressions with respect to N, we observe that, unambiguously, the firm's profits increase with the quality of information, while the deadweight loss decreases. As for the consumer surplus, the first derivative has the sign of $(3 - 2N)$; that is, we confirm what we noted above: the consumer surplus increases when going from $N = 1$ to $N = 2$ (uniform pricing to pricing over two segments) but decreases afterward. As N goes to infinity, profits tend to $1/2$ and both the consumer surplus and the deadweight loss tend to zero, as depicted in Figure 8.2. We summarize our findings as follows.

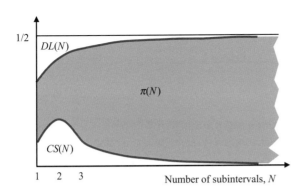

Figure 8.2 Effect of increased segmentation on the division of welfare under monopoly group pricing

Lesson 8.1   **As the information about the consumers' reservation prices becomes more precise, the discriminating monopolist increases its profits. The consumer surplus first increases but then decreases. In the limit case of personalized prices, the monopolist captures the entire surplus and the deadweight loss completely vanishes.**

Note that in terms of efficiency, personalized pricing (or first-degree, or perfect, price discrimination) by a monopolist is equivalent to perfect competition: it implements the first-best since the last unit is sold at marginal cost. However, in distributive terms, the two allocations are completely at odds with each other: the whole social surplus goes to the firm under personalized prices, but to the consumers under perfect competition.

8.3   Group and personalized pricing in oligopolies

We now extend the previous analysis to settings where a number of competing firms may decide to engage in group, or even personalized, pricing. A natural extension of the previous model is to have two firms, located at both ends of the Hotelling line, offering the same product and having access to information allowing them to segment the consumer space. We first analyse such a model of localized competition. We move next to settings of international group pricing, where firms segment markets along geographical boundaries.

8.3.1   Group pricing and localized competition

We develop now a location model of oligopolistic group pricing and we address the following questions: (i) What are the firms' incentives to acquire customer-specific information of a given quality? (ii) How do these incentives evolve as the quality of information improves?

The model

We extend the linear Hotelling model that we introduced in Chapter 3.[3] Two firms, labelled 1 and 2, are located at the two endpoints of the unit interval; they sell competing brands

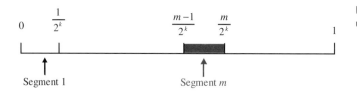

Figure 8.3 Partition of the unit interval

(at zero marginal cost) to a unit mass of consumers who have unit demands and are uniformly distributed on [0, 1]. Consumers have a reservation value r for their ideal product and incur a linear transportation cost, τ, per unit of distance. So, a consumer located at $x \in [0, 1]$ derives utility $v_1 = r - \tau x - p_1$ when buying from firm 1 and utility $v_2 = r - \tau (1 - x) - p_2$ when buying from firm 2. We assume that r is large enough, so that each consumer will buy.

The location of a particular consumer indicates her respective valuation for the two brands. In the standard Hotelling model, firms have no means to identify the location of any consumer. Here, we extend the analysis by letting firms acquire customer-specific information that allows them to classify the consumers into different segments and, thereby, to imperfectly estimate their location. As in the monopoly setting above, we assume that the information partitions the unit interval into N subintervals of equal length. To simplify the analysis, we further assume that $N = 2^k$, $k = 0, 1, 2, \ldots$, where k can be seen as a measure of the quality of the information: the larger k, the finer the consumers' segmentation and the sharper the estimate of their valuation for the two brands. Figure 8.3 depicts the partition of the unit interval.

Both firms have access to information of quality k; we compare situations with (exogenously) increasing values of k. That is, we examine what happens when firms have access to more data about consumer characteristics (such as gender, age, income group, geographical location, ...) and/or to more sophisticated techniques to process these data (as illustrated in Case 8.2). The game we analyse has three stages: first, given information of quality k, firms decide whether to acquire it or not; second, firms choose their regular prices; third, the firm(s) with information target(s) specific discounts to the consumer segments.[e]

Pricing decisions

We start by analysing the last two stages of the game. There are four subgames to consider according to the firms' decisions regarding the acquisition of information in the first stage.

Neither firm acquires information. In this case, both firms set a regular price in stage 2 and stage 3 is not reached. As shown in Chapter 3, the indifferent consumer is defined by $\hat{x}$ such that $r - \tau \hat{x} - p_1 = r - \tau (1 - \hat{x}) - p_2$, which yields $\hat{x}(p_1, p_2) = (\tau - p_1 + p_2)/(2\tau)$. As all consumers located at the left of $\hat{x}$ buy from firm 1, firm 1 chooses p_1 to maximize $p_1 \hat{x}(p_1, p_2)$. Its reaction function is obtained from the first-order condition for profit maximization: $R_1(p_2) = \frac{1}{2}(\tau + p_2)$. As for firm 2, it serves all consumers located at the right of $\hat{x}$ and thus chooses p_2 to maximize $p_2 [1 - \hat{x}(p_1, p_2)]$, which yields the following reaction

---

[e] The pricing decision is modelled as a two-step process for the following reasons. First, firms typically adjust their regular prices slower than the choice of targeted discounts. Second, if the two decisions are made simultaneously, it can be shown that there is no pure-strategy equilibrium in the subgames where only one firm has information.

function: $R_2(p_1) = \frac{1}{2}(\tau + p_1)$. The Nash equilibrium in price is found at the intersection of the two reaction functions: $p_1 = p_2 = \tau$. It follows that $\hat{x} = 1/2$ and that the firms' profits are equal to (where the superscript NI, NI indicates that each firm is in a 'no information' situation):

$$\pi^{NI,NI} = \tfrac{1}{2}\tau.$$

Both firms acquire information. In this subgame, both firms choose their regular price in stage 2 and their promotions in stage 3. As they both know in which of the $N = 2^k$ segments each consumer is located, they are able to charge different prices for different segments. Let p_{1m} and p_{2m} denote the prices firm 1 and 2 respectively charge in segment m. As represented in Figure 8.3, segment m (with $m \in \{1, \ldots, 2^k\}$) can be expressed as the interval $[(m-1)/2^k, m/2^k]$.

As cost and demand conditions allow the firms to treat each segment separately, we can solve for the price equilibrium in each segment independently of the other segments. Consider segment m and suppose that, at the price equilibrium, both firms sell positive quantities. This means that there exists in segment m a consumer who is indifferent between the two firms. Repeating our previous analysis, this consumer is easily identified as $\hat{x}_m = (\tau - p_{1m} + p_{2m})/(2\tau)$. It follows that firm 1 chooses p_{1m} to maximize $\pi_{1m} = p_{1m}(\hat{x}_m - (m-1)/2^k)$, and firm 2 chooses p_{2m} to maximize $\pi_{2m} = p_{2m}(m/2^k - \hat{x}_m)$. We leave it as an exercise to the reader to check that the equilibrium prices are

$$p_{1m} = \frac{\tau(2^k - 2m + 4)}{3 \times 2^k} \quad \text{and} \quad p_{2m} = \frac{\tau(2m + 2 - 2^k)}{3 \times 2^k},$$

which gives us the identity of the indifferent consumer:

$$\hat{x}_m = \frac{2^k + 4m - 2}{6 \times 2^k}.$$

It remains to be checked under which conditions this indifferent consumer does indeed strictly belong to segment m (meaning that both firms sell positive quantities). The following two conditions must be met:

$$\begin{cases} \hat{x}_m > \frac{m-1}{2^k} \Leftrightarrow m < 2^{k-1} + 2 \equiv m^+(k), \\ \hat{x}_m < \frac{m}{2^k} \Leftrightarrow m > 2^{k-1} - 1 \equiv m^-(k). \end{cases}$$

The latter conditions are always met when $k = 0$ (no segmentation) and $k = 1$ (two segments), meaning that both firms sell positive quantities in each segment. For $k \geq 2$, one observes that the firms compete head-to-head only in the two middle segments (i.e., segments $m^-(k) + 1 = 2^{k-1}$ and $m^-(k) + 2 = m^+(k) - 1 = 2^{k-1} + 1$).[f] In these two segments, poaching occurs in equilibrium: one firm manages to attract some of the other firm's 'loyal' consumers (e.g., some consumers located at the left of 1/2 end up buying from firm 2).

In segments 1 to $m^-(k)$, firm 2 prefers to charge a zero price and to leave the whole segment demand to firm 1, which acts then as a constrained monopolist. That is, facing $p_{2m} = 0$,

---

[f] For instance, when $k = 3$, there are 8 segments, $m^-(3) = 3$ and $m^+(3) = 6$, meaning that it is only in segments 4 and 5 that both firms have positive demands.

firm 1 sells to all consumers in segment m as long as $p_{1m} + \tau\left(m/2^k\right) \leq \tau\left[1 - \left(m/2^k\right)\right]$; the profit-maximizing price on this segment is thus $p_{1m} = \tau(2^k - 2m)/2^k$. Conversely, firm 2 acts as a constrained monopolist in segments $m^+(k)$ to 2^k, where it sets $p_{2m} = \tau(2m - 2^k - 2)/2^k$.

Summing the firms' equilibrium profits over all segments and invoking symmetry, we can compute the profits firms obtain when they both use the information, which we denote by $\pi^{I,I}(k)$.[4] It can then be shown that $\pi^{I,I}(k)$ *exhibits a U-shape as a function of k and is always below* $\pi^{NI,NI}$, the profits when neither firm acquires the information. The U-shape results from the interplay between two conflicting forces: higher competition and surplus extraction. The first effect dominates when the quality of information is low. In the segments where both firms sell a positive quantity, an information refinement intensifies price competition and prices fall. However, as the quality of information improves, the second effect starts to dominate. Firms are more able to identify the preferences of the consumers and to know where they are immune to the other firm's competition; the number of segments on which a firm acts as a constrained monopolist increases and thereby, the firm's ability to extract more surplus by raising prices.

To establish that $\pi^{I,I}(k) < \pi^{NI,NI} = \frac{1}{2}\tau$, we examine what happens if we let k tend to infinity. In that case, we assume that the quality of information is so high that firms can identify the exact valuation of each individual consumer. Firm i's strategy is then to set a price schedule $p_i(.)$ for each consumer location x. As the two firms set *personalized prices*, they engage in Bertrand competition in each and every location. Because firms have different costs (except for $x = 1/2$), it is the firm with the lowest cost that prevails; it does so by setting a price equal to the other firm's marginal cost; otherwise, it charges the lowest price it can, which is its own marginal cost. Let us assume that at equal prices, consumers buy from the closest firm (so that we avoid an open set problem). Hence, it follows that the firms' reaction functions are given by $p_1^*(x) = p_2^*(x) = \max\{\tau x; \tau(1 - x)\}$. In words, to profitably serve a consumer located at x, firm 1 must set $p_1(x)$ such that $\tau x \leq p_1(x) \leq p_2(x)$. The lowest price firm 2 can charge is its own cost of serving this consumer, i.e., $\tau(1 - x)$. It follows that firm 1 can always make a profit on consumers such that $\tau(1 - x) > \tau x$ or $x < 1/2$. For these consumers, firm 1 charges $p_1(x) = \tau(1 - x)$ and realizes a profit of $\pi_1(x) = \tau(1 - x) - \tau x = \tau(1 - 2x)$. We compute the equilibrium profits as

$$\pi^{I,I}(\infty) = \int_0^{1/2} \tau(1 - 2x)\,dx = \int_{1/2}^1 \tau(2x - 1)\,dx = \tfrac{1}{4}\tau,$$

which is indeed lower than $\pi^{NI,NI} = \frac{1}{2}\tau$.

Only one firm acquires the information. In the remaining two subgames, only one firm possesses information. Both firms set their regular price in stage 2 and the firm with the information chooses specific discounts in stage 3 once it has observed the regular price of the rival firm. Suppose firm 1 has the information (the other case is treated in a symmetric way). At stage 3, after observing firm 2's regular price p_2, firm 1 chooses its promotional prices p_{1m} (with $m = 1, \ldots, 2^k$). In segment m, firm 1 maximizes $p_{1m}q_{1m}$, where $q_{1m} = (\tau - p_{1m} + p_2)/(2\tau) - (m - 1)/2^k$ is the demand it faces in that segment. Let $p_{1m}^*(p_2)$ denote the solution to this maximization problem.

We can now turn to firm 2's problem in stage 2. In segment m, the demand addressed to firm 2 is $q_{2m} = m/2^k - \left[\tau - p^*_{1m}(p_2) + p_2\right]/(2\tau)$. Firm 2 chooses p_2 to maximize

$$\pi_2^{I,NI} = p_2 \sum_{m=1}^{2^k} q_{2m}.$$

As firm 2 lacks the necessary information to treat the various segments independently, it is no longer possible to solve for the equilibrium in each segment separately. Therefore, the problem becomes significantly more complex to solve. Nonetheless, it is possible to fully characterize the solution to this problem.

The solution can be seen as an asymmetric version of what we obtained in the subgame where both firms possess the information. In particular, the set of segments can again be divided into three groups. Going from left to right, we have that firm 1 acts as a constrained monopolist in the first group of segments; then comes a group of segments where both firms have positive demand; finally, in the last group of segments, it is firm 2 that acts as a constrained monopolist. There are, however, two main differerences with the previous case: first, the informed firm is a constrained monopolist on a larger number of segments than the uninformed firm; second, competition takes place in segments located in the second half of the interval, meaning that it is only the informed firm that is able to poach some 'loyal' consumers from its rival.[g] As an illustration, for $k = 3$ (8 segments), firm 1 attracts all consumers in segments 1 to 5, some consumers in segments 6 and 7 and leaves all consumers in segment 8 to firm 2.

It can also be shown that the uninformed firm's profits monotonically decrease with the quality of information. The informed firm's profits, however, are non-monotonic in k. The same two forces of higher competition and surplus extraction are at play here. When the quality of information is low ($k = 1, 2$), profits fall below the non-discrimination case (i.e., $\frac{1}{2}\tau$) because of the other firm's aggressive reaction: knowing that the rival has committed credibly to price discriminate, the uninformed firm lowers its regular price significantly. It is only when information becomes more precise ($k \geq 3$) that the informed firm is able to extract sufficiently more surplus, so as to take advantage of the information benefits in spite of the uninformed firm's defensive reaction.

Again, we examine what happens at the limit of *personalized prices*. Firm 2 sets a regular price p_2 at stage 2 and firm 1 sets the price schedule $p_1(x)$ at stage 3. Firm 1 attracts a consumer located at x as long as $p_1(x) \leq p_2 + \tau(1 - x)$. It follows that firm 1's optimal price schedule in stage 3 is given by $p_1(x) = \max\{p_2 + \tau(1 - x); \tau x\}$. Given this price schedule, firm 2 is left with consumers such that

$$p_2 + \tau(1 - x) < \tau x \Leftrightarrow x < \tfrac{1}{2} + \tfrac{p_2}{2\tau} \equiv \hat{x}(p_2).$$

At stage 2, firm 2's problem is thus to choose p_2 so as to maximize $\pi_2 = p_2(1 - \hat{x}(p_2)) = p_2(\tau - p_2)/(2\tau)$. Therefore, firm 2's optimal price is $p_2^* = \tau/2$ and $\hat{x}(p_2^*) = 3/4$; that is, the informed firm manages to poach half of the other firm's loyal consumers (i.e., those consumers

---

[g] These results hold for all $k \geq 2$ (for $k = 1$, both firms are active in the two segments; yet, firm 2 poaches fewer consumers than firm 1).

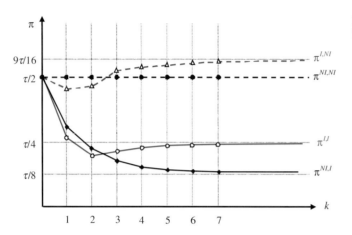

Figure 8.4 Profits of a typical firm at stage 1

located between $1/2$ and $3/4$). The equilibrium profits are computed as follows:

$$\pi_1^{I,NI} = \int_0^{3/4} \left(\tfrac{\tau}{2} + \tau\,(1 - 2x) \right) dx = \tfrac{9}{16}\tau \equiv \pi^{I,NI}\,(\infty),$$

$$\pi_2^{I,NI} = \tfrac{\tau}{2}\tfrac{1}{4} = \tfrac{\tau}{8} \equiv \pi^{NI,I}\,(\infty).$$

Interestingly, the informed firm eventually obtains larger profits than in the non-discrimination case.

Information acquisition decision

We can now move to the first stage of the game where the two firms decide simultaneously whether to acquire the information or not. We plot in Figure 8.4 the equilibrium profit as a function of the quality of the information (k) that a firm obtains in the various subgames (where $\pi^{I,I}$ and $\pi^{NI,NI}$ denote the profit when, respectively, both firms possess the information or neither of them does; $\pi^{I,NI}$ corresponds to the case where the firm has the information while the rival has not, and the other way round for $\pi^{NI,I}$).

Comparing the profit levels, we observe that the equilibrium of stage 1 depends on the quality of information. When information is of a relatively low quality, namely for $k = 1$ and $k = 2$, not acquiring the information is a dominant strategy for the firms (as $\pi^{NI,NI} > \pi^{I,NI}$ and $\pi^{NI,I} > \pi^{I,I}$). The reverse conclusion holds when the quality of information is relatively high, namely for $k \geq 3$. Here, acquiring the information is a dominant strategy (as $\pi^{NI,NI} < \pi^{I,NI}$ and $\pi^{NI,I} < \pi^{I,I}$). That is, when information is sufficiently precise, firms use it at equilibrium. Yet, so doing, they get trapped into a prisoner's dilemma-type situation as they would be better off if they could both refrain from using the information (we have indeed that $\pi^{NI,NI} > \pi^{I,I}$).

To understand these results, recall that in this duopoly setting, customer-specific information generates two effects for the firm that acquires it: a *surplus extraction effect* (the firm is able to extract more surplus from each consumer) and a *competition effect* (the rival firm reacts by pricing lower). When the quality of information is low, the competition effect dominates and firms prefer to credibly commit to set a uniform price, by not acquiring the information. When the quality of information improves, the surplus extraction effect becomes stronger and it is a dominant strategy for the firms to acquire the information and price discriminate. We summarize the main insights we can draw from this analysis as follows.

> **Lesson 8.2**   In a competitive setting, customer-specific information impacts firms in two conflicting ways. On the one hand, it allows firms to extract more surplus from each consumer. On the other hand, it exacerbates price competition. When the quality of information is sufficiently large, the former effect dominates the latter. Then, firms use the information and price discriminate at equilibrium. However, they may well be better off if they could jointly agree not to use the information.

8.3.2   Personalized pricing and location decisions

Up to now, we have considered that the firms' respective locations were fixed at the two extremes of the unit interval. Here, we endogenize the location decisions by letting firms choose where to locate before engaging in price competition.[5] As the emphasis is on location choice, we do not consider the full information acquisition game; we focus instead on the situation where both firms have acquired a very precise information that allows them to charge personalized prices.

As above, a strategy for firm i, located at $l_i \in [0, 1]$, is to set a price schedule $p_i(.)$ for each consumer location x. We assume that $p_i(.)$ is a measurable function on $[0, 1]$ which satisfies $p_i(.) \geq \tau |x - l_i|$ almost everywhere (call that set $\mathcal{P}_i$). Firm 1's profit function can be written as follows:

$$\pi_1 (p_1(.), p_2(.); l_1, l_2) = \int_{M_1} (p_1(x) - \tau |x - l_1|) \, dx$$

where

$$M_1 = \{x \in [0, 1] \mid p_1(x) < p_2(x) \text{ or } (p_1(x) = p_2(x) \text{ and } |x - l_1| < |l_2 - x|)\}.$$

We are looking for a non-cooperative price schedule equilibrium in pure strategies; that is, a pair $(p_1^*(.), p_2^*(.))$ of price schedules such that

$$\pi_i (p_i^*(.), p_j^*(.); l_1, l_2) \geq \pi_i (p_i(.), p_j^*(.); l_1, l_2) \quad \text{for all } p_i(.) \in \mathcal{P}_i; \quad i = 1, 2, \quad j \neq i.$$

Using the same argument as above with fixed location, we understand that the price schedule equilibrium is given by

$$p_1^*(x) = p_2^*(x) = \max \{\tau |x - l_1|, \tau |x - l_2|\}.$$

Letting $\overline{m} = (l_1 + l_2)/2$, we have that firm 1 sells to consumers located on $[0, \overline{m}]$. Its profits are computed as the difference between the other firm's and its own total transportation cost on the interval $[0, \overline{m}]$, as depicted in Figure 8.5.

We are now in a position to solve the location choice game. In order to maximize profits, a firm must choose a location generating the largest decrease in total transportation costs. Indeed, firm 1's profits can be expressed as follows: $\pi_1 =$ (total transportation cost of firm 2 as a monopolist) $-$ (total transportation cost of the two firms together). Hence, if both

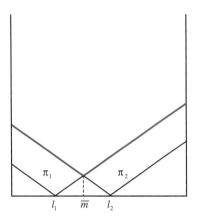

Figure 8.5 Firm's profits under perfect price discrimination for given locations

firms locate at the transportation cost minimizing points, $l_1 = 1/4$ and $l_2 = 3/4$ (as shown in Chapter 5), no firm can increase its profits by deviating. This obtains in the unique subgame perfect equilibrium.

> **Lesson 8.3**   When both firms set personalized prices and locations are endogenous, firms choose the socially optimal locations.

8.3.3   Geographic price discrimination

The existence of price differences for the same products across countries or across regions is an issue that has attracted a lot of attention from economists. Macroeconomists wonder whether such differences invalidate the law of one price or the purchase parity power. Microeconomists wonder whether there is evidence of price discrimination. Answering the latter question requires separating the influence of cost differences and margin differences as the sources of price differences. Margin differences mainly result from differences in price elasticities across market segments. A monopoly which can prevent resale arbitrage will certainly price discriminate across segments with different price elasticities of demand. As hinted above (see Section 8.2), a monopoly will set the highest price in the segment with the lowest elasticity. Before we establish this point formally, we come back to the textbook example that we developed in the introduction to this part of the book.

> **Case 8.3 International price discrimination in the textbook market**
>
> Cabolis *et al.* (2006) investigate differences in book prices between the United States and other countries. They find that general audience books are similarly priced internationally, but that textbooks are substantially more expensive in the US (often more than double the price). Because most of the textbooks in their sample are printed in the US, they can rule out cost factors (either printing or transportation costs) as the source of differentials of this magnitude (also differences in tax rates can be excluded as the relevant explanation). It

follows that price differentials must be due to differences in markups, and thereby demand. According to the authors, the most convincing explanation for such a different demand in the US is cultural: for most courses in the US, a single comprehensive textbook is used as the 'required' main reference for students; in contrast, European students are provided with a list of textbooks, which supplement the material given by the instructor, with no obligation to buy any of them. Hence, the willingness to pay for textbooks is typically higher in the US, which explains that publishers can impose larger markups. As for preventing resale arbitrage, publishers often explicitly indicate 'NOT FOR SALE IN THE US' on the cover of the international editions of their textbooks. Moreover, it is a copyright infringement for someone to buy an international textbook (e.g., on a bookselling website such as Amazon or eBay) and to resell it outside its intended country (only personal use is permitted).

Monopoly group pricing: the basic argument

Suppose that the monopolist can sell its product on k separate markets. Let $Q_i(p_i)$ denote the distinct downward-sloping demand curve for market i (where the monopolist sets a price p_i). Let $C(q)$ denote the monopolist's total cost, with $q = \sum_{i=1}^{k} q_i$ and $q_i = Q_i(p_i)$ is the quantity demanded on market i. The monopolist chooses the vector of prices $(p_1, p_2, \ldots, p_k)$ that maximizes its profits:

$$\Pi(p_1, p_2, \ldots, p_k) = \sum_{i=1}^{k} p_i Q_i(p_i) - C\left(\sum_{i=1}^{k} Q_i(p_i)\right).$$

This problem is a straightforward extension of the monopoly problem we presented in Chapter 2: it is as though the monopolist was producing k different products with independent demands and (possibly) dependent costs. As we saw in Chapter 2, the markup (i.e., the price–cost difference as a percentage of the price) is given by the inverse-elasticity rule; this holds for any market segment i:

$$\frac{p_i - C'(q)}{p_i} = \frac{1}{\eta_i},$$

where $\eta_i = -p_i Q_i'(p_i)/Q_i(p_i)$ is the elasticity of demand on market segment i and $C'(q)$ is the marginal cost of producing the aggregate quantity q. It is immediate from the above expression that if $\eta_i > \eta_j$, then $p_i < p_j$. In words:

Lesson 8.4   **A monopolist optimally charges less in market segments with a higher elasticity of demand.**

Does this result carry through in oligopoly settings? For sure, international price differences do exist in oligopolistic markets and these differences can be explained, to some extent, by differerent price elasticities, as illustrated in Case 8.4.

Case 8.4 International price discrimination in the car market

The European car market is characterized by a large and persistent price dispersion across countries. Using a panel data set extending from 1980 to 1993 for 5 countries, Goldberg and Verboven (2001) demonstrate that there exist significant differences in quality-adjusted prices across countries, with systematically higher prices in Italy and the UK (prices can differ up to 30% of the car price between two countries). To explain the sources of such differences, they use a multiproduct oligopoly model with product differentiation. The model identifies three sources: price elasticities (generating different markups), costs and import quota constraints. The first source, which is indicative of geographical price discrimination, seems to be the main explanation for higher prices in Italy: a strong bias for domestic brands generates high markups for the domestic firm (i.e., Fiat). As for the higher UK prices, they are mainly attributed to better equipped cars and/or differences in the dealer discount practices.

To check whether the European monetary union and the adoption of the euro had the effect of reducing the cross-country price differences, the same authors perform a similar analysis over the period 1993–2003 (Goldberg and Verboven, 2004). They consider 15 countries, among which 12 joined Euroland in 1999 and officially adopted the euro in 2002, while the remaining 3 stayed outside the monetary union. Overall, their results suggest a big role for exchange rate stability in reducing international price dispersion and a smaller role for a common currency. They find, however, that price differentials remain surprisingly high after the euro. Despite the single currency, the European car market is far from integrated. This lack of integration can be attributed to the selective and exclusive distribution system that has been in place since 1985. This system allows car manufacturers to select authorized dealers through qualitative and quantitative criteria, and to assign them territorial exclusivity (see Chapter 17 for more on such so-called 'vertical restraints'). This system can be blamed for limiting the cross-border arbitrage opportunities (even though the adoption of the euro makes price comparisons easier) and, thereby, for facilitating geographical price discrimination.

In September 2002, the European Union stopped tolerating this system and replaced it by a new regulation with more flexibility (car manufacturers are still allowed to impose selectivity or territorial exclusivity on their dealers, but not both at the same time). The objective was to promote competition between dealers of the same brand and to reduce price dispersion. To assess the potential effects of this policy change, Brenkers and Verboven (2006) estimate a differentiated products demand system for new cars and specify a model of oligopoly pricing under the pre-2002 distribution regime. Then, they evaluate the possible competitive effects from the creation of international intrabrand competition (cross-border trade), which will result in a reduction of international price discrimination. Their findings are the following: (i) a reduction in international price discrimination mainly redistributes consumer gains across countries; (ii) it has a positive but modest effect on total welfare; (iii) the effects on the manufacturers' profits are either small or positive. According to the latter finding, the possibility to engage in international price discrimination would not be the main profit motive for the selective and exclusive distribution system; price differences would just appear as unintended side effects.

Although geographical price discrimination exists in oligopolistic industries, we can think of strategic motives which could lead oligopolists not to exploit demand differences across segments and set instead the same uniform price on all segments. Think for example of a chain-store retailer which serves several, geographically separated, local markets. The issue we want to study here is whether the retailer prefers to price discriminate across local markets (so as to adapt to diverging local conditions) or to adopt a uniform pricing policy (i.e., to set common prices that apply across all their stores). If the retailer is in a monopoly position on all local markets, we know that price discrimination is the profit-maximizing conduct.[h] However, if rival firms are present on some local markets, a common price policy might be profitable for strategic reasons; the basic intuition is that committing to set the same price everywhere may help softening price competition on the competitive market segments and, thereby, increasing profits.[i] We now build a simple model to understand what drives chain-store retailers to opt for discriminatory or for uniform prices.[6]

A model of oligopolistic international pricing

We consider the following simple setting with three independent markets (indexed by 1, 2 and 3) and two chain-store retailers (indexed by 1 and 2). Retailer 1 is a monopolist on market 1, retailer 2 is a monopolist on market 2, and the two retailers compete on market 3. We can see the 'duopoly market' 3 as a large/affluent market, which supports competition, whereas the two 'monopoly markets' 1 and 2 are smaller/poorer markets, which cannot accommodate more than a single retailer. We assume that there is no cost or demand connection between markets. For simplicity, we set all costs to zero on all markets. As far as demand is concerned, we reflect the differences in market sizes by modelling demand on the three markets in the following way.

On the duopoly market, market 3, consumers see the retailers' products as imperfect substitutes. To model this, we suppose (as we did in Chapter 3) that there is a large number of identical consumers with the linear-quadratic utility function

$$U(q_0, q_{13}, q_{23}) = aq_{13} + aq_{23} - \left(bq_{13}^2 + 2dq_{13}q_{23} + bq_{23}^2\right)/2 + q_0,$$

where q_{i3} is the quantity sold by retailer i ($i = 1, 2$) on market 3, and q_0 is the Hicksian composite commodity with a price normalized to 1. For the sake of this example, we set $a = b = 1$ and $d = 1/2$. Consumers maximize their utility $U(q_0, q_{13}, q_{23})$ subject to the budget constraint $y = q_0 + p_{13}q_{13} + p_{23}q_{23}$. This gives rise to the following inverse demand functions (for strictly positive prices and zero otherwise): $p_{13} = 1 - q_{13} - \frac{1}{2}q_{23}$ and $p_{23} = 1 - q_{23} - \frac{1}{2}q_{13}$. Inverting this system of two equations, we obtain the direct demand functions (for strictly positive quantities and zero otherwise):

$$\begin{cases} q_{13} = \frac{2}{3}\left(1 - 2p_{13} + p_{23}\right), \\ q_{23} = \frac{2}{3}\left(1 - 2p_{23} + p_{13}\right). \end{cases}$$

---

[h] We should keep in mind that this result was obtained under a number of assumptions. In particular, it was assumed that resale is not possible or too costly.
[i] We will elaborate on commitment strategies of this sort in Chapter 16.

As for the monopoly markets 1 and 2, we assume that they are identical and that the inverse demand is given by $p_i = \alpha - q_i$ ($i = 1, 2$), with $\alpha < 1$. The only difference between the monopoly and the duopoly markets is thus in terms of the demand intercept, which is lower in the monopoly markets ($\alpha < 1$), to capture the idea that these markets are *a priori* less attractive for firms than the contested duopoly market. Otherwise, the slope of the inverse demand functions (the own-price effect) is the same across markets.

We analyse the following two-stage game. In the first stage, the two retailers simultaneously choose between local pricing (i.e., to set p_i and p_{i3}, with possibly $p_i \neq p_{i3}$) and uniform pricing (i.e., to set $\bar{p}_i (= p_i = p_{i3})$ on markets i and 3). In the second stage, firms compete in price according to the pricing strategy chosen in the first stage.

At stage 2, firm i's maximization problem depends on its first-stage pricing choice. Under *local pricing*, firm i's problem is

$$\max_{p_i, p_{i3}} \pi_i^L = (\alpha - p_i)p_i + \tfrac{2}{3}(1 - 2p_{i3} + p_{j3})p_{i3}.$$

Solving for the first-order conditions, we find the following: on its local market, the firm sets the monopoly price ($p_i = \alpha/2$), and on the contested market, the firm sets its price according to the reaction function

$$p_{i3} = R_i^L(p_{j3}) = \tfrac{1}{4} + \tfrac{1}{4}p_{j3}. \tag{8.1}$$

Under *uniform pricing*, firm i's problem is

$$\max_{\bar{p}_i} \pi_i^L = \left[(\alpha - \bar{p}_i) + \tfrac{2}{3}(1 - 2\bar{p}_i + p_{j3})\right]\bar{p}_i.$$

From the first-order condition, we find the firm's reaction function

$$\bar{p}_i = R_i^U(p_{j3}) = \tfrac{2+3\alpha}{14} + \tfrac{1}{7}p_{j3}. \tag{8.2}$$

There are three different subgames to solve at stage 2: (i) both firms price locally (subgame LL), (ii) both firms price uniformly (subgame UU), and (iii) one firm prices locally and the other firm prices uniformly (subgames LU and UL). To guarantee interior solutions in all subgames, we impose $\alpha \geq 1/4$.

When *both firms price locally*, profit-maximizing prices on the monopoly markets are $p_1 = p_2 = \alpha/2$, while equilibrium prices on the duopoly market are defined by: $p_{13}^{LL} = R_1^L(p_{23}^{LL})$ and $p_{23}^{LL} = R_2^L(p_{13}^{LL})$. Solving the latter system of equations, one finds $p_{13}^{LL} = p_{23}^{LL} = 1/3$. By symmetry, we have that the firms obtain the same profits at the equilibrium of subgame LL: $\pi^{LL} = \tfrac{1}{4}\alpha^2 + \tfrac{4}{27}$.

When *both firms price uniformly*, the equilibrium uniform prices are found by solving the system of two equations $\bar{p}_1^{UU} = R_1^U(\bar{p}_2^{UU})$ and $\bar{p}_2^{UU} = R_2^U(\bar{p}_1^{UU})$; that is, $\bar{p}_1^{UU} = \bar{p}_2^{UU} = \tfrac{1}{4}\alpha + \tfrac{1}{6}$. The corresponding equilibrium profits are $\pi^{UU} = \tfrac{7}{432}(2 + 3\alpha)^2$.

Finally, when *one firm prices locally (say firm i) and the other prices uniformly (say firm j)*, firm i chooses $p_i = \alpha/2$ on its monopoly market and reacts on market 3 according to $R_i^L(\bar{p}_j)$, whereas firm j chooses its common price according to $R_j^U(p_{i3})$. The Nash equilibrium is such that $p_{i3}^{LU} = R_i^L(\bar{p}_j^{LU})$ and $\bar{p}_j^{LU} = R_j^U(p_{i3}^{LU})$. Solving, we get $p_{i3}^{LU} = \tfrac{1}{18}\alpha + \tfrac{8}{27}$, and $\bar{p}_j^{LU} = \tfrac{2}{9}\alpha + \tfrac{5}{27}$. We can then compute the equilibrium profits: firm i's profits are $\pi^{LU} = \tfrac{1}{4}\alpha^2 + \tfrac{1}{2187}(16 + 3\alpha)^2$ and firm j's profits are $\pi^{UL} = \tfrac{7}{2187}(5 + 6\alpha)^2$.

In the following table, we compare the equilibrium prices in the three subgames for three different parameters of the monopoly markets.

Subgame		Local markets			Contested market		
		$\alpha = \frac{1}{2}$	$\alpha = \frac{2}{3}$	$\alpha = \frac{4}{5}$	$\alpha = \frac{1}{2}$	$\alpha = \frac{2}{3}$	$\alpha = \frac{4}{5}$
LL		*0.25*	0.33	**0.40**	*0.33*	0.33	**0.33**
UU		*0.29*	0.33	**0.37**	*0.29*	0.33	**0.37**
LU, UL	L	*0.25*	0.33	**0.40**	*0.32*	0.33	**0.34**
	U	*0.30*	0.33	**0.36**	*0.30*	0.33	**0.36**

First, we observe that for $\alpha = 2/3$, firms set the exact same price (namely $1/3$) whatever the market and whatever the subgame. So, even when firms opt for local pricing, there is no actual price discrimination. This is so because at $\alpha = 2/3$, the advantage of the local markets (they are less competitive) is just offset by their disadvantage (they are smaller). When local markets are smaller than this pivotal size (e.g., for $\alpha = 1/2$), we observe that under local pricing, prices are lower on the local markets than on the contested market. The opposite prevails when local markets are larger than the pivotal size (e.g., for $\alpha = 4/5$).

We are now in a position to analyse the pricing policy choices. The first-stage game is depicted in the following matrix.

	Local pricing	Uniform pricing
Local pricing	π^{LL}, π^{LL}	π^{LU}, π^{UL}
Uniform pricing	π^{UL}, π^{LU}	π^{UU}, π^{UU}

Which Nash equilibrum obtains depends on the sign of two key profit differences: $\pi^{LL} - \pi^{UL}$ (which measures a firm's incentive to price locally when the other firm prices locally as well) and $\pi^{UU} - \pi^{LU}$ (which measures a firm's incentive to price uniformly when the other firm prices uniformly as well). When the first (resp. second) difference is positive, both firms price locally (resp. uniformly) at equilibrium; when both differences are negative, the equilibrium is such that one firm prices locally and the other firm prices uniformly. Figure 8.6 depicts the two differences and represents the equilibria. There are four zones to consider: (i) for $1/4 \leq \alpha \leq 2/3$, both firms choose local pricing; (ii) for $2/3 \leq \alpha \leq 914/1263 \approx 0.724$, both firms choose uniform pricing; (iii) for $914/1263 \leq \alpha \leq 298/393 \approx 0.758$, one firm chooses uniform pricing and the other, local pricing; (iv) for $298/393 \leq \alpha < 1$, both firms choose local pricing.

To understand the intuition behind these results, we analyse how profits change when a firm goes from local pricing to uniform pricing. Suppose first that $\alpha < 2/3$, which means that the disadvantage local markets have in terms of size is not compensated for by the advantage they have in terms of lower competition. In that case, if firm 1 prices locally, it sets $p_1 < p_3$. Otherwise, if it prices uniformly, it chooses $\bar{p} \in (p_1, p_3)$. That is, firm 1 increases the price on its monopoly market, which lowers its profits on that market (since the profit-maximizing price

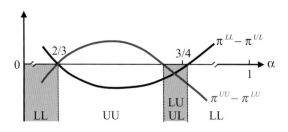

Figure 8.6 Pricing policy choices at equilibrium

is p_1). On the other hand, firm 1 decreases the price on the contested market. Because prices are strategic complements, firm 2 reacts by decreasing its price too, which has a negative effect on firm 1's profits. We therefore conclude that the firm has nothing to gain by moving from local to uniform pricing, whatever the choice of the other firm. Local pricing is a dominant strategy for $\alpha < 2/3$.

Suppose now that $\alpha > 2/3$. Here, moving from local to uniform pricing entails a lower price on the local market and a larger price on the contested market. It is still true that any move away from the monopoly price on the local market decreases profits there. Yet, increasing the price on the contested market triggers a favourable reaction from the opponent (as it increases its price too) and raises profits on that market. Uniform pricing can then be seen as a credible way to raise prices, and thus to soften competition, on the contested market. As long as the local market is not too large, the latter effect dominates the former one and uniform pricing becomes the dominant strategy. However, as α increases, the first negative effect grows relatively larger. So, we first have a situation where moving from local to uniform pricing still pays when the opponent prices locally (i.e., $\pi^{UL} > \pi^{LL}$), but does not pay when the opponent prices uniformly (i.e., $\pi^{UU} > \pi^{LU}$). Finally, for α close to 1, uniform pricing is dominated whatever the opponent's pricing policy.

There are thus two areas where both firms choose price discrimination at equilibrium. However, there is a striking difference between these two areas. For $\alpha < 2/3$, local pricing is a dominant strategy and is also the most profitable option. In contrast, for $\alpha \geq 0.758$, local pricing is still a dominant strategy but is no longer the most profitable option. It can indeed be checked that for $\alpha > 2/3$, $\pi^{UU} > \pi^{LL}$. Firms are thus in a prisoners' dilemma: they both price discriminate although they would be better off if they could commit to set a uniform price.

We summarize our findings in the following lesson.

Lesson 8.5   Chain-store retailers are often in a monopoly position on small markets but compete with other retailers on larger markets. Despite the differences between the markets (and the absence of arbitrage), the retailers might refrain from price discriminating and set instead a uniform price on all markets. The reason is that uniform pricing acts as a credible way to raise prices, and thus to soften competition, on the contested markets.

We have thus shown that depending on market conditions, chain-store retailers may decide to price uniformly or locally. Casual observation reveals that the two strategies are indeed adopted. For instance, some firms like IKEA commit to price uniformly at all their points of sales in a given country by publishing all prices in a nationally distributed catalogue.

On the other hand, Case 8.5 gives evidence of asymmetric equilibria, where, within the same sector, some firms price locally and other firms price uniformly.

Case 8.5 Pricing by supermarkets in the United Kingdom[7]

From April 1999 to July 2000, the UK Competition Commission carried out an extensive investigation of the supply of groceries from multiple grocery retailers (i.e., supermarket chains controlling 10 or more stores). Among the 15 leading supermarket groups, 8 were found to price uniformly while 7 adjusted prices to local conditions, such variation not being related to costs. For these 7 retailers, the Commission found that in general only a limited number of products had their price adjusted. As for the extent of the price differences, it was reported that 'the average level of difference between the minimum and maximum prices for each product varies across companies from 4.3 to 19.2 per cent, although the price range for individual products can be very much more, with prices as much as doubling in some stores compared with others' (Competition Commission, p. 126). The Commission was concerned that local pricing may reflect the fact that shops were able to exploit local market power. Therefore, it considered remedying this potential problem by imposing national pricing or by requiring that prices be published on the Internet. However, simulation results led the Commission to conclude that such remedies were either undesirable, disproportionate or presented practical difficulties. Hence, the Commission made no recommendation for remedial action in respect of local pricing. This seems much in line with the insights that we can draw from the model we developed above. It is clear that consumers of different markets are affected in opposite ways when going from uniform to local pricing. It is therefore not surprising that the impacts on global welfare are ambiguous.

Review questions

1. In which industries do we observe group pricing? Provide two examples.

2. Does an increase in competition lead to more or less (third-degree) price discrimination? Discuss.

3. How does the ability to geographically price discriminate affect location decisions of firms?

4. What is an empirical regularity concerning international price discrimination?

Further reading

The analyses of group pricing under oligopoly follows first Liu and Serfes (2004) and then Capozza and van Order (1978) and Thisse and Vives (1988). An elaborate discussion of price discrimination is provided by Phlips (1983). A more recent, selective overview (covering mostly topics of the following chapters) is provided by Armstrong (2007). For an empirical analysis of international price discrimination we refer to Goldberg and Verboven (2001).

9 Menu pricing

In this chapter, we start by emphasizing the difference between menu pricing and group pricing (Section 9.1). We then provide a formal analysis of menu pricing by a monopolist. We derive the conditions under which menu pricing leads to higher profits than uniform pricing; we also perform the same analysis in terms of welfare (Section 9.2). Finally, we turn to the analysis of menu pricing in oligopolistic settings; we consider in turn quality- and quantity-based menu pricing (Section 9.3).

9.1 Menu pricing versus group pricing

The previous chapter described situations where the sellers are able to infer their buyers' willingness to pay from some observable and verifiable characteristics of those buyers (like age, gender, location, etc.). In many situations, however, there exists no such reliable indicator of the buyers' willingness to pay. How much a consumer is willing to pay is their private information. The only way for a seller to extract more consumer surplus is then to bring the consumer to reveal this private information. To achieve this goal, the seller must offer his product under a number of 'packages' (i.e., some combinations of price and product characteristics). The key is to identify some dimensions of the product that are valued differently across consumers, and to design the product line so as to emphasize differences along those dimensions. The next step consists in pricing the different versions in such a way that consumers will sort themselves out by selecting the version that most appeals to them. Such practice is known as menu pricing, versioning, second-degree price discrimination, or nonlinear pricing. A few examples are given in Case 9.1.

Case 9.1 Examples of menu pricing in the information economy

The dimension along which information goods are versioned is usually their *quality*, which is to be understood in a broad sense (for instance, the quality of a software might be measured by its convenience, its flexibility of use, the performance of the user interface, ...). For instance, 'nagware' is a form of shareware that is distributed freely but displays a screen encouraging users to pay a registration fee, or displaying ads. In this case, annoyance is used as a discriminating device: some users will be willing to pay to turn off the annoying screen. Versioning of information goods can also be based on *time*, following the tactic of delay. For example, new books often appear first in hardcover and later as less expensive paperbacks. Similarly, movies can first be viewed in theaters; a few months later, they are released on DVD, and are shown on premium cable television; eventually, they are broadcast on terrestrial television. The price of these choices usually declines with the viewing date. Finally, versioning can be based on *quantity*: software site licences often provide discounted royalties as the number of networked machines or users grow; online databases offer discounts based on number of users or on usage by a particular user (measured by the number of searches performed, the quantity downloaded or printed, etc.); music performance licences use factors like the number of square metres in a bar or store, or the size of the audience for a radio or TV station to set quantity-based royalties; magazine and newspaper subscriptions feature quantity discounts.[8]

The situation whereby the uninformed party (here the seller) brings the informed parties (here the buyers) to reveal their private information is generally known as a *screening problem*; the seller is in the position of a mechanism designer who seeks to maximize her profit by finding the optimal nonlinear tariff that ensures incentive compatibility, that is, making sure that consumers do not imitate the behaviour of other consumers with lower valuation for the good (a practice known as 'personal arbitrage'). Menu pricing can thus be seen as a particular area of application of mechanism design theory. The goal of *mechanism design* is to obtain some outcome as a function of agents' preferences, taking account of the fact that agents are rational and may lie about their preferences. Therefore, mechanism design is at the crossroads of game theory and social choice (game theory teaches us how to analyse the strategies agents will follow in a particular game, while social choice teaches us how to choose some outcome given a set of agents' preferences).[9]

Before turning to a formal analysis of menu pricing, we want to stress that it is not always obvious to draw a clear line between menu and group pricing. Even if there exist different versions of the same product, which are available to any consumer, consumers still have to be aware of the existence of these versions and/or make the effort to compare the different offerings. If the latter is true for only a limited number of consumers, then the firm should not be concerned with personal arbitrage and can thus apply group pricing rather than menu pricing. Case 9.2 shows evidence along these lines.

Case 9.2 Geographical pricing by low cost carriers

As we mentioned in Case 8.1 above, European Low Cost Carriers (or LCCs, such as Ryanair or easyJet) have abandoned many price discrimination practices that are commonly used in the airline industry. The price of their 'point-to-point' tickets does not systematically depend on the day of departing or of returning; they also offer 'no-frills' flights with no class distinction for seats. Yet, LCCs sometimes engage in a form of geographical price discrimination on their own website. Bachis and Piga (2006) show indeed that airlines may charge, at the same time and for the same flight, fares expressed in different currencies that violate the Law of One Price. Their data are taken from the websites of six European LCCs and pertain to both UK domestic flights and flights connecting the UK with the main continental European countries. A simple example illustrates the nature of the price discrimination tactic employed by the LCCs in their sample. 'Consider a flight from London to Madrid. Normally, this corresponds to the first leg of a round trip by a British traveller, and to the return leg of a Spanish traveller who has just visited the UK. The location of the first leg determines the currency used by the LCCs to show the final fares, so the Spanish traveller will be offered a fare in Euro while the British one in Sterling. If the booking occurs at the same time, and in the absence of price discrimination, the ratio of the two fares should be very close to the prevailing exchange rate and the Law of One Price should hold. However, about 23% of the almost two million observations in our dataset report a difference between the two fares of at least 7 British Sterling or more.' (Bachis and Piga, 2006, p. 2) It is important to note that the two fares are, in principle, accessible to any consumer, meaning that LCCs do not artificially segment the market by making a particular fare only available for a particular group of consumers. Therefore, the practice resembles more menu pricing than group pricing. Yet, as the two fares do not appear simultaneously on the same screenshot, only customers who are aware of this practice and who make the extra effort of consulting different screenshots will effectively compare prices. It turns out that very few consumers do control for arbitrage opportunities.

9.2   A formal analysis of monopoly menu pricing

We focus here on the case of menu pricing based on different quality levels (but we show at the end of the section how the initial model can be easily reinterpreted as a model of discrimination based on time or on quantity). We derive the conditions under which menu pricing leads to higher profits than uniform pricing. We perform the same analysis in terms of welfare and apply our results to the specific case of information goods.[10]

9.2.1   Quality-dependent prices

We assume that all consumers prefer higher quality and lower prices but that they differ in their relative valuations of these two attributes. We define a consumer's indirect utility as

$$v = \begin{cases} U\left(\theta, s\right) - p & \text{if consumer buys one unit of quality } s \text{ at price } p, \\ 0 & \text{if he does not buy,} \end{cases}$$

where $s \geq 0$ is the quality of the product, $p \geq 0$ is its price, and θ is the consumer's taste parameter. As all consumers value higher quality, we assume that $U\left(\theta, s\right)$ is an increasing function of s. As for the distribution of tastes θ, we assume for simplicity that it is concentrated at two points: there are two types of consumers, indexed by $i = 1, 2$, in respective proportions $1 - \lambda$ and λ.[a] We take $\theta_2 > \theta_1$ and accordingly, we refer to type 1 as the 'low type' and to type 2 as the 'high type'. We assume that high-type consumers care more about quality

---

[a] The results presented here continue to hold in settings with continuous distributions of consumers along θ such that the probability density function is positive everywhere.

than low-type consumers: for any quality level s, $U(\theta_2, s) > U(\theta_1, s)$. Furthermore, we also assume that high-type consumers value more any *increase* in quality than low-type consumers: for any $s_2 > s_1$,

$$U(\theta_2, s_2) - U(\theta_2, s_1) > U(\theta_1, s_2) - U(\theta_1, s_1). \tag{SC}$$

This condition is the standard *single-crossing property* according to which higher types exhibit a greater willingness to pay for every increment in quality. As we will see, this condition is necessary for menu pricing to be possible.

The monopolist is able to produce two exogenously given qualities s_1 and s_2, with $s_2 > s_1$, at respective constant unit costs c_1 and c_2 (with $c_i < U(\theta_1, s_i)$ to make the problem non-trivial). The question is whether the monopolist will choose to price-discriminate by offering the two qualities priced appropriately, or whether he will prefer to offer a single quality. In the latter case, let us assume that the monopolist always prefers to offer the high quality s_2. A sufficient condition for the monopolist to select the high quality is

$$U(\theta_1, s_2) - U(\theta_1, s_1) > c_2 - c_1, \tag{HQ}$$

according to which the value low-type consumers attribute to an increase in quality is larger than the cost difference between the two qualities. Then, the monopolist has two options: either he charges the high price equal to $U(\theta_2, s_2)$ and sells to high-type consumers only, or he lowers the price to $U(\theta_1, s_2)$ and sells to all consumers. The former option is more profitable if the proportion of high types, λ, is large enough, namely if

$$\lambda > \frac{U(\theta_1, s_2) - c_2}{U(\theta_2, s_2) - c_2} \equiv \lambda_0.$$

The profit from selling only the high-quality can thus be written as

$$\Pi_s = \begin{cases} \lambda(U(\theta_2, s_2) - c_2) & \text{if } \lambda \geq \lambda_0, \\ U(\theta_1, s_2) - c_2 & \text{if } \lambda < \lambda_0. \end{cases}$$

Under menu pricing, the monopolist must find the profit-maximizing price pair (p_1, p_2) that induces type i consumers to select quality s_i. There are two concerns: participation (each consumer must do at least as well consuming the good as not consuming it) and self-selection (or incentive compatibility, each type of consumer must prefer their consumption to the consumption of the other type of consumer). For the low-type group, the participation and incentive compatibility constraints respectively read as

$$U(\theta_1, s_1) - p_1 \geq 0 \Leftrightarrow p_1 \leq U(\theta_1, s_1), \tag{PC1}$$
$$U(\theta_1, s_1) - p_1 \geq U(\theta_1, s_2) - p_2 \Leftrightarrow p_1 \leq p_2 - [U(\theta_1, s_2) - U(\theta_1, s_1)]. \tag{IC1}$$

Similarly for the high-type group:

$$U(\theta_2, s_2) - p_2 \geq 0 \Leftrightarrow p_2 \leq U(\theta_2, s_2), \tag{PC2}$$
$$U(\theta_2, s_2) - p_2 \geq U(\theta_2, s_1) - p_1 \Leftrightarrow p_2 \leq p_1 + [U(\theta_2, s_2) - U(\theta_2, s_1)]. \tag{IC2}$$

Of course, the monopolist wants to choose p_1 and p_2 to be as large as possible. It follows that, in general, one of the first two inequalities and one of the second two inequalities will be binding. Intuitively, we can guess that what matters is participation of the low type and self-selection of the high type; we expect thus (PC1) and (IC2) to bind. Let us demonstrate this. Suppose first, by contradiction, that (PC2) is binding. Then (IC2) implies that

$p_2 \le p_1 + p_2 - U(\theta_2, s_1)$ or $U(\theta_2, s_1) \le p_1$. Using the assumption that high types care more about quality, we can write $U(\theta_1, s_1) < U(\theta_2, s_1) \le p_1$, which contradicts (PC1). It follows that (PC2) is not binding and that (IC2) is binding; that is, $p_2 = p_1 + [U(\theta_2, s_2) - U(\theta_2, s_1)]$.

Now consider (PC1) and (IC1). If (IC1) were binding, we would have $p_1 = p_2 - [U(\theta_1, s_2) - U(\theta_1, s_1)]$. Using the binding (IC2), the latter equality can be rewritten as $p_1 = p_1 + [U(\theta_2, s_2) - U(\theta_2, s_1)] - [U(\theta_1, s_2) - U(\theta_1, s_1)]$, which implies $U(\theta_1, s_2) - U(\theta_1, s_1) = U(\theta_2, s_2) - U(\theta_2, s_1)$. As menu pricing supposes $s_2 > s_1$, this contradicts our initial assumption (SC). It follows that (IC1) is not binding and that (PC1) is binding, so

$$p_1^* = U(\theta_1, s_1), \text{ and}$$
$$p_2^* = U(\theta_2, s_2) - [U(\theta_2, s_1) - U(\theta_1, s_1)]. \tag{9.1}$$

Because $U(\theta_2, s_1) > U(\theta_1, s_1)$, we observe that $p_2^* < U(\theta_2, s_2)$: the monopolist is not able to extract full surplus from high-type consumers.

Lesson 9.1   **Consider a monopolist who offers two pairs of price and quality to two types of consumers. Prices are chosen so as to fully appropriate the low-type's consumer surplus. High-type consumers obtain a positive surplus (the so-called 'information rent') because they can always choose the low-quality offering instead.**

Under personalized pricing consumers do not hold private information and also high-type consumers would obtain zero surplus. More generally, if there remains some heterogeneity within each group, group pricing does not allow for the full extraction of consumer surplus but the firm does not need to pay an information rent.

When is menu pricing optimal?

We need now to compare profits when the monopolist only sells the high quality and when it price discriminates by selling both qualities. In the latter case, profits are given by

$$\Pi_m = (1 - \lambda)[U(\theta_1, s_1) - c_1] + \lambda[U(\theta_2, s_2) - (U(\theta_2, s_1) - U(\theta_1, s_1)) - c_2].$$

Consider first the case where the proportion of high-type consumers is large enough, so that the monopolist sells to them only when it produces a single quality ($\lambda \ge \lambda_0$). Then, menu pricing modifies profits as follows:

$$\Delta\Pi = \Pi_m - \Pi_s = (1 - \lambda)(U(\theta_1, s_1) - c_1) - \lambda(U(\theta_2, s_1) - U(\theta_1, s_1)).$$

Menu pricing involves two opposite effects. First, it increases profits through *market expansion*: low-type consumers now buy the low quality, which yields a margin of $U(\theta_1, s_1) - c_1$ per consumer. Second, it decreases profits because of *cannibalization*: high-type consumers still buy the high quality but now, at a price reduced by $U(\theta_2, s_1) - U(\theta_1, s_1)$. The net effect is positive provided that high-type consumers are not too numerous:

$$\Delta\Pi > 0 \Leftrightarrow \lambda < \frac{U(\theta_1, s_1) - c_1}{U(\theta_2, s_1) - c_1} \equiv \bar{\lambda}. \tag{9.2}$$

The latter condition is compatible with our starting point if and only if $\bar{\lambda} > \lambda_0$, which is equivalent to

$$\frac{U(\theta_2, s_2) - c_2}{U(\theta_2, s_1) - c_1} > \frac{U(\theta_1, s_2) - c_2}{U(\theta_1, s_1) - c_1}.$$

Let us now examine the other case (i.e., $\lambda < \lambda_0$). Here, the monopolist sells the high quality at a low price to everyone if he decides to sell only one quality. The change in profits induced by menu pricing is then given by

$$\Delta \Pi = \Pi_m - \Pi_s = (1 - \lambda)\left[(U(\theta_1, s_1) - c_1) - (U(\theta_1, s_2) - c_2)\right]$$
$$+ \lambda\left[(U(\theta_2, s_2) - U(\theta_2, s_1)) - (U(\theta_1, s_2) - U(\theta_1, s_1))\right].$$

There are again two opposite effects: (i) profit from low-type consumers decreases (because they buy the low quality instead of the high quality, which is detrimental for the monopolist according to assumption (HQ)), but (ii) profit from high-type consumers increases (they continue to buy the high quality but pay now a higher price according to assumption (SC)). Here, the net effect is positive as long as high-type agents are numerous enough:

$$\Delta \Pi > 0 \Leftrightarrow \lambda > \frac{U(\theta_1, s_2) - U(\theta_1, s_1) - (c_2 - c_1)}{U(\theta_2, s_2) - U(\theta_2, s_1) - (c_2 - c_1)} \equiv \underline{\lambda}. \tag{9.3}$$

For this condition to be compatible with our starting point, we need $\lambda_0 > \underline{\lambda}$, or

$$\frac{U(\theta_2, s_2) - c_2}{U(\theta_2, s_1) - c_1} > \frac{U(\theta_1, s_2) - c_2}{U(\theta_1, s_1) - c_1}, \tag{9.4}$$

which is the exact same condition as in the previous case. Condition (9.4) says that going from low to high quality increases surplus *proportionally more* for high-type consumers than for low-type consumers. We can therefore conclude:

Lesson 9.2   **Menu pricing is optimal (i) if the proportion of high-type consumers is neither too small nor too large, and (ii) if going from low to high quality increases surplus proportionally more for high-type consumers than for low-type consumers.**

Distortion of quality

In the previous analysis, we assumed that qualities were given and that the only task left to the monopolist was to choose prices. Suppose now that the monopolist can also choose which quality to offer. If menu pricing is the optimal conduct, then the monopolist will choose to offer two different qualities. But which qualities exactly? To answer this question, we slightly modify the previous model as follows. Let $c(s)$ denote the monopolist's cost (per unit of output) of producing quality s. Assume that $c'(s) > 0$ and $c''(s) > 0$: it is more expensive and increasingly more expensive to produce higher quality. The monopolist knows from expressions (9.1) how to price given qualities to extract maximum profits. So, the remaining problem is to select s_1

and s_2 so as to maximize:

$$\Pi = (1 - \lambda)[U(\theta_1, s_1) - c(s_1)]$$
$$+ \lambda[U(\theta_2, s_2) - (U(\theta_2, s_1) - U(\theta_1, s_1)) - c(s_2)].$$

Under conditions (9.4), the solution to this problem is given by

$$\frac{\partial \Pi}{\partial s_1} = (1 - \lambda)\left(\frac{\partial U(\theta_1, s_1)}{\partial s_1} - c'(s_1)\right) - \lambda\left(\frac{\partial U(\theta_2, s_1)}{\partial s_1} - \frac{\partial U(\theta_1, s_1)}{\partial s_1}\right) = 0$$

$$\Leftrightarrow c'(s_1) = \frac{\partial U(\theta_1, s_1)}{\partial s_1} - \frac{\lambda}{1 - \lambda}\left(\frac{\partial U(\theta_2, s_1)}{\partial s_1} - \frac{\partial U(\theta_1, s_1)}{\partial s_1}\right),$$

$$\frac{\partial \Pi}{\partial s_2} = \frac{\partial U(\theta_2, s_2)}{\partial s_2} - c'(s_2) = 0 \Leftrightarrow c'(s_2) = \frac{\partial U(\theta_2, s_2)}{\partial s_2}.$$

We observe that the first-order condition for high quality coincides with the solution of the first best (in which the firm identifies consumers and does not need to respect incentive constraints), whereas, compared to the first best, there is an additional negative term on the right-hand side of the first-order condition for low quality. This means that the monopolist distorts low quality downward compared to the first best. We conclude from the latter two equations that the monopolist uses lower-quality as a market-segmentation technique. More precisely, we draw the following lesson.

Lesson 9.3   **When a monopolist optimally chooses different qualities to implement menu pricing, high-type consumers are offered the socially optimal quality, while low-type consumers are offered a quality that is distorted downward compared to the first best.**

Welfare effects of menu pricing

We now turn to the welfare analysis, assuming again that qualities s_1 and s_2 are given and cost, respectively, c_1 and c_2 per unit. Social welfare is computed as the sum of consumer surplus and the monopolist's profit. From the above analysis, we easily compute the following:

$$W_s = \begin{cases} \lambda(U(\theta_2, s_2) - c_2) & \text{if } \lambda \geq \lambda_0, \\ U(\theta_1, s_2) - c_2 + \lambda[U(\theta_2, s_2) - U(\theta_1, s_2)] & \text{if } \lambda < \lambda_0. \end{cases}$$

$$W_m = (1 - \lambda)(U(\theta_1, s_1) - c_1) + \lambda(U(\theta_2, s_2) - c_2).$$

The change in welfare induced by menu pricing can then be computed as $\Delta W = W_m - W_s$, with

$$\Delta W = \begin{cases} (1 - \lambda)(U(\theta_1, s_1) - c_1) > 0 & \text{if } \lambda \geq \lambda_0, \\ -(1 - \lambda)[U(\theta_1, s_2) - U(\theta_1, s_1) - (c_2 - c_1)] < 0 & \text{if } \lambda < \lambda_0. \end{cases}$$

We observe that welfare increases when $\lambda \geq \lambda_0$. In that case, menu pricing expands the market as low-type consumers are sold the low quality, whereas they are left out of the market when only the high quality is sold. In contrast, welfare decreases when $\lambda < \lambda_0$. Here, the monopolist chooses to cover the whole market when it sells only the high quality; so, under menu pricing, low-type consumers are sold the low quality instead of the high one, although, according to condition (HQ), what they are willing to pay for higher quality is larger than the extra cost of producing higher quality; gains of trade are thus left unexploited and welfare is lower.

Lesson 9.4   **Menu pricing improves welfare if selling the low quality leads to an expansion of the market; otherwise, menu pricing deteriorates welfare.**

9.2.2   Information goods and damaged goods

Let us now make specific assumptions about consumers' utility and about the cost of producing quality. It is common to assume linear utility of the following form: $U(\theta, s) = \theta s$; the indirect utility is then given by $U = \theta s - p$. In that case, condition (9.4) can be rewritten as

$$\frac{\theta_2 s_2 - c_2}{\theta_2 s_1 - c_1} > \frac{\theta_1 s_2 - c_2}{\theta_1 s_1 - c_1} \Leftrightarrow \frac{c_2}{s_2} > \frac{c_1}{s_1}.$$

That is, the average cost of quality (c_i/s_i) must be increasing for menu pricing to be profitable when utility is a linear function of product quality. A corollary is that menu pricing is not profitable when the marginal cost of production is invariant with product quality (i.e., $c_1 = c_2 = c$), which is the case for most information goods (for which c is often close to zero).

However, as shown in Case 9.1, menu pricing is a common practice for information goods. One way to reconcile our model with the facts is to assume that consumers' utility is not linear in product quality.[b] Assume, for example, that $U(\theta, s) = k + \theta s$, with $k \geq 0$. This formulation could be justified as follows. The product comprises several dimensions: consumers are heterogeneous regarding one particular dimension; this is along that dimension that the monopolist differentiates the two versions of the product, s_1 and s_2; as for the other dimensions, consumers are homogeneous and k is their common valuation. Now, condition (9.4) rewrites as

$$\frac{k + \theta_2 s_2 - c_2}{k + \theta_2 s_1 - c_1} > \frac{k + \theta_1 s_2 - c_2}{k + \theta_1 s_1 - c_1} \Leftrightarrow k > \frac{c_1 s_2 - c_2 s_1}{s_2 - s_1}. \tag{9.5}$$

For the case of information goods, with $c_1 = c_2 = 0$, we see that the condition is satisfied as long as $k > 0$. Then, menu pricing is profitable when the proportion of high-type consumers is neither too small nor too large:

$$\frac{\theta_1}{\theta_2} < \lambda < \frac{k + \theta_1 s_1}{k + \theta_2 s_1},$$

which is obtained from conditions (9.2) and (9.3).

Interestingly, condition (9.5) can even be satisfied in cases where $c_1 > c_2$, i.e., when the monopolist actually incurs an extra cost in order to produce the low-quality version. This extreme form of menu pricing is referred to as a *damaged good strategy*: firms intentionally

---

[b] As we will see in the next section, another way to obtain equilibrium price discrimination under linear costs and utility is to introduce competition in the market.

damage a portion of their goods in order to price discriminate.[c] This strategy is widely used in software markets: initially, the producer develops a complete full-featured version and then introduces additional low-quality versions by disabling a subset of features or functionalities from the flagship version.[d]

A series of motivations can be invoked to explain this prevalence of menu pricing in the software industry. First, it must be noted that the cost of creating multiple versions is relatively low. Second, price discrimination is an obvious objective because the heterogeneity in the consumers' valuations for a particular software is likely to be large. Third, very cheap low-quality versions can be seen as 'fighting brands' targeted at consumers with a low willingness to pay, who could be tempted to substitute a pirated version for the legitimate product (see Chapter 19 for more on the issue of information goods piracy). Finally, complementarity between different versions might explain why software manufacturers often provide a read-only (or play-only) version and a full version of the same product. Here, the degraded version is designed to view and print (or play) contents written in a specific format, but is not capable of producing the contents in the specific format (think of Acrobat Reader, RealPlayer, Mathematica Reader, or various Microsoft Office – Word, Excel, PowerPoint – Viewers). In terms of prices, manufacturers usually offer the viewer or player almost free of charge by allowing consumers to download it from the Internet. Yet, to be able to create and edit contents (as well as viewing or playing them), users need to purchase the corresponding full version, which is sold at a positive price. This price structure makes sense because the seller might find it profitable to give away for free a degraded version of the software in order to build the network of the full version. We are indeed in the presence of indirect network effects: the more users are able to read a particular format, the more users are eager to write in this format, and conversely. So, one way to increase the willingness to pay for the full version (which contains the write function) is to broaden the base of 'readers', which is achieved by giving free access to the read-only version.[11] We will return to network effects in Parts VIII and IX. Case 9.3 presents other examples of damaged goods outside the software industry.

Case 9.3 Damaged goods and fighting brands[12]

Striking examples of damaged goods are (i) Sony 60′ recordable MiniDisc (MD), (ii) Sharp DV740U DVD player, and (iii) IBM LaserPrinter E. (i) Sony MDs come in two formats – 60′ and 74′ discs – which are sold at different prices; yet, the two formats are physically identical: a code in the table of contents identifies a 60′ disc and prevents recording beyond this length, even though there is room on the media. (ii) Among the many DVD players that Sharp sells, those with model numbers DVE611 and DV740U are almost similar, except that the DV740U device does not allow the user to play output

---

[c] Arguably, marginal costs may remain unchanged and quality degradation may come at a fixed cost. The argument equally applies to an increase in fixed costs.

[d] Sundararajan and Ghose (2005) use a 7-month, 108-product panel of software sales from Amazon.com to estimate quality degradation associated with software versioning. They find degradations ranging from as little as 8% to as much as 56% below the quality of the corresponding flagship version.

encoded in the PAL format on an NTSC television (PAL and NTSC are the TV standards prevailing respectively in Europe and in North America). Actually, the DV740U has the ability to play PAL output, but this is made impossible by using a different plastic cover on the remote so as to hide a critical button. (iii) The LaserPrinter E was identical to the original LaserPrinter, except for the fact that its software limited its printing to five rather than ten pages per minute. In the first two examples, price discrimination seems to be the main motive to introduce the damaged version. However, this is not so clear in the case of IBM LaserPrinterE. It appears indeed that IBM introduced the damaged version following Hewlett-Packard's entry into the low-end segment of the market with its LaserJet IIP (whose quality was inferior to IBM's orginal LaserPrinter). This suggests that IBM saw the damaged good not so much as a price discrimination tool than as a 'fighting brand', designed to compete on the newly opened low-end market. The creation by British Airways (BA) of the 'no-frills' subsidiary Go can be understood along the same lines, as it followed the entry by the low-cost carrier easyJet on the UK market. It is possible that BA only started to find it profitable to serve the low-end segment of the market once it was opened up by the entry of easyJet.

9.2.3   Extension to time- and quantity-dependent prices

We now show how simple transformations allow us to reinterpret the previous problem in terms of time- or quantity-dependent prices. In the previous formulation, suppose that utility is linear, $U(\theta, s) = \theta s$, and let $c(s_i)$ denote the cost of producing one unit of quality s_i.

Time-dependent prices

As indicated in Case 9.1, a common menu pricing tactic is delay (as is the case for new books, which appear first in hardcover and later as less expensive paperbacks). Products are introduced on the market at successive dates and at declining prices. The idea is to discriminate between the consumers who value the products very highly and are very impatient and those to whom the product is less valuable or who are less impatient. We thoroughly examine this form of intertemporal price discrimination in the next chapter. Here, we just show how the above problem can easily be transformed into an intertemporal problem. Let $s_i = e^{-rt_i}$, where t_i is interpreted as the date when the good is produced and delivered, and r is the interest rate. The monopolist needs then to find release dates t_1 and t_2 that solves the following problem:

$$\max_{t_1, t_2} \Pi = (1 - \lambda)\left[\theta_1 e^{-rt_1} - c(e^{-rt_1})\right] + \lambda\left[\theta_2 e^{-rt_2} - (\theta_2 - \theta_1)e^{-rt_1} - c(e^{-rt_2})\right].$$

Here, the monopolist chooses two production/delivery dates, t_i $(i = 1, 2)$ targeted at the two types of consumers with unit demands.[e] The discounted prices are $\theta_1 e^{-rt_1}$ for delivery at the 'late' date t_1 and $\theta_2 e^{-rt_2} - (\theta_2 - \theta_1)e^{-rt_1}$ for delivery at the 'early' date $t_2 \leq t_1$. At these

---

[e] It is implicitly assumed that the monopolist can credibly commit to these two dates. We return to the issue of commitment at length in the next chapter.

prices, the low-type (i.e., patient) consumers are indifferent between not participating and buying later and the high-type (i.e., impatient) consumers are indifferent between buying sooner or later.

Quantity-dependent prices

Quantity is another aspect that could define the package bought by the consumer, and thereby serve as a basis for menu pricing. In such cases, unit price depends on quantity purchased (but not on the identity of the consumer). This type of menu pricing is also known as *nonlinear pricing*. One particular version of nonlinear pricing are *two-part tariffs* which are widely used by utilities such as telephone, gas, or electricity. Also, several goods combine a base product (e.g. razor, printer, fax machine) for which you pay once and for all, and consumables (e.g. razor blades, paper, ink, respectively) whose total cost depends on the quantity consumed). Similarly, many sport club memberships involve a fixed and a variable part.

Suppose consumers can buy a certain allowance, i.e., quantity q_i at a price p_i. Again, it is possible to transform the above problem into a corresponding problem where discrimination is based on quantity. Let $q_i = c(s_i)$. Then $s_i = c^{-1}(q_i)$; denote this inverse function as $V(q_i)$. Since there is a monotonic relationship between s_i and q_i, we can again rephrase the monopolist's problem in terms of the new decision variable q_i:

$$\max_{q_1, q_2} \Pi = (1 - \lambda)\left[\theta_1 V(q_1) - q_1\right] + \lambda\left[\theta_2 V(q_2) - (\theta_2 - \theta_1)V(q_1) - q_2\right].$$

In this version, q_i is interpreted as the quantity to be purchased by consumers of type i. This is equivalent to the problem of a monopolist with a constant marginal cost of production (scaled here to unity) facing two types of consumers. Their utility functions have the form $U(q_i, i) = \theta_i V(q_i)$ for $i = 1, 2$.

9.3   Menu pricing under imperfect competition

As indicated in Case 8.1, airline travel is a canonical example of menu pricing. It is also an industry where imperfect competition prevails on many of the routes and casual observation reveals that competition does not make menu pricing disappear. Although the previous monopoly analysis gives us useful insights about the surplus-extracting potential of menu pricing, it remains silent as to how menu pricing is affected by – and affects – competition. We want now to fill this gap by considering two models of competitive menu pricing: in the first model, we consider price discrimination based on different qualities and in the second model, we look at two-part tariffs (i.e., quantity-based price discrimination). In both cases, we model competition by using the linear Hotelling model of Chapter 3: two firms, labelled 1 and 2, are located at the extreme points of the unit interval and consumers are uniformly distributed on this interval.

Before doing so, we want to take a look at the empirical evidence on menu pricing. A number of empirical studies have attempted to assess how competition affects the incentives to price discriminate. In Case 9.4, we ask how price discrimination can be measured and identified, and we review some of the empirical studies.

Case 9.4 Empirical studies of price discrimination[13]

To understand how price discrimination can be empirically identified, let us take a simple framework in which a firm sells two products, 1 and 2. Suppose $p_1 > p_2$ and write $\Delta p = p_1 - p_2$. This price difference can be decomposed as the sum of a cost difference $\Delta c = c_1 - c_2$ and a margin difference $\Delta m = m_1 - m_2$: $\Delta p = \Delta c + \Delta m$. Price discrimination is said to exist if the margin difference Δm is the main source of the observed price difference Δp. The definition is simple enough but it is far from obvious how to distinguish between margin differences and cost differences. A first methodological approach consists in using direct cost information. For instance, Clerides (2002) uses information about production technologies to estimate the production costs of hardback and softback books. According to his estimates, only 5% of the average price difference between the two types of books can be attributed to a cost difference, which demonstrates the existence of price discrimination. In the absence of direct cost information, the alternative is to use a model of pricing behaviour in order to infer the margin difference. Using this approach, Verboven (2002) finds evidence of menu pricing in the market for gasoline and diesel cars in Europe. Consumers can choose between two engine types: a 'low-quality' gasoline engine and a 'high-quality' diesel engine (the higher quality comes from lower fuel consumption and less expensive fuel due to lower taxes). According to their annual mileage, consumers have heterogeneous willingnesses to pay for this higher quality. Gasoline cars are thus targeted at low-mileage drivers and diesel cars, at high-mileage drivers. Estimates show that on average 75% to 90% of the price difference between the two types of cars can be explained by margin differences.

As for the effects of competition on price discrimination, empirical studies seem to suggest that competition tends to reinforce price discrimination. For instance, Borenstein (1991) studies the competitive retail gasoline market. He shows that the positive difference between the margins on unleaded gas and on leaded gas reduced after the number of competing stations offering leaded gas went down. Borenstein and Rose (1994) analyse a similar question for the US airline industry. Because there are usually more than two different prices on a given airline/route, they measure price dispersion (instead of the price difference Δp). They show that price dispersion is positively related to the number of competitors on a given route.

9.3.1   Competitive quality-based menu pricing

In this model,[14] firms 1 and 2 can both sell a high-end and a low-end version of the same product, of respective qualities s_H and s_L (with $s_H > s_L$) and at respective prices p_{iH} and p_{iL} (with $i = 1, 2$). The model therefore combines *vertical* differentiation (as two different qualities are available) and *horizontal* differentiation (as the two firms are located at the extreme points of the Hotelling line). Consumers differ in the two dimensions. As far as the vertical (quality) dimension is concerned, we assume that the consumers differ in their marginal utility of income, noted α: the wealthier the consumer, the lower her marginal utility of income and so, the lower the value of α. Hence, wealthier consumers are less price sensitive. We assume that a unit mass of consumers have $\alpha = \alpha_h$ and a unit mass of consumers have $\alpha = \alpha_l$. Hence, assuming $\alpha_h < \alpha_l$, we refer to group h the 'high' types and to group l as the 'low' types. Consuming one unit of quality K ($K = H$ or L) from firm i ($i = 1$ or 2) yields the following utility to a consumer of group k ($k = h$ or l): $s_K - \alpha_k p_{iK}$.[f] Regarding the horizontal dimension, consumers differ according to their 'location' on the product line, which measures how well the two firms' products match their tastes. For simplicity, we normalize the transportation cost of both groups to unity; so, a consumer located at $x \in [0, 1]$ incurs a disutility of x when buying from firm 1, and of $(1 - x)$ when buying from firm 2.[g] Consumers buy at most one unit of one of the two versions of the product; if they do not buy, their utility is set to zero. In sum, the net utility of a consumer of group k ($k = h$ or l) who is located at $x \in [0, 1]$ is given by:

$$
U_k(x) = \begin{cases}
s_H - \alpha_k p_{1H} - x & \text{if buying quality } H \text{ from firm 1,} \\
s_H - \alpha_k p_{1H} - (1 - x) & \text{if buying quality } H \text{ from firm 2,} \\
s_L - \alpha_k p_{1L} - x & \text{if buying quality } L \text{ from firm 1,} \\
s_L - \alpha_k p_{1L} - (1 - x) & \text{if buying quality } L \text{ from firm 2,} \\
0 & \text{if not buying.}
\end{cases}
$$

Concerning costs, we assume that firms can produce the two versions at the same constant marginal cost, which we normalize to zero for simplicity. As argued above, this assumption fits in particular information goods such as software and music files. With such constant costs and linear utility, we have demonstrated in the previous section that a monopoly does not find it profitable to price discriminate. However, in the present competitive context, we will show that menu pricing can emerge as an equilibrium strategy. To do so, we build an example by giving specific values to the parameters: we set

$$\alpha_l = 5, \alpha_h = 1, s_H = 3 \text{ and } s_L = 2.$$

We now want to show that under this configuration of parameters, the pricing game between the two firms has two equilibria in pure strategies: (i) there is *a 'discriminatory' equilibrium* in which both firms offer the two versions, and the consumers self-select with the high types buying the high-end version and the low types buying the low-end version; (ii) there is also *a 'non-discriminatory' equilibrium* in which firms only produce the high-end version. We characterize the two equilibria in turn.

Discriminatory equilibrium

The high-type consumer who is indifferent between buying the high-end version from either firm is identified by x_h such that $s_H - \alpha_h p_{1H} - x_h = s_H - \alpha_h p_{2H} - (1 - x_h)$; that is,

---

[f] If we divide throughout by α_k and let $\theta_k = 1/\alpha_k$, we obtain the linear formulation that we used in the previous section: $\theta_k s_K - p_{iK}$. Under this formulation, consumers differ in their valuation of quality but have the same marginal utility of income. As $\alpha_h < \alpha_l$, $\theta_h > \theta_l$, meaning that 'high types' value quality more than 'low types'. Here, we assume instead (but equivalently) that consumers differ in their marginal utility of income but value quality in the same way.

[g] Implicit in this formulation is that high-type consumers, because of their lower marginal utility of income, are both more likely to buy the high-end version *and* less sensitive to price differences between the firms. This looks like a reasonable assumption if high types are seen as wealthier consumers.

$x_h = \frac{1}{2}[1 + \alpha_h (p_{2H} - p_{1H})]$. Similarly, the low-type consumer who is indifferent between the low-end versions of firms 1 and 2 is identified by $x_l = \frac{1}{2}[1 + \alpha_l (p_{2L} - p_{1L})]$. If we leave aside the incentive compatibility constraints, there is no connection between the two markets; it is thus as though the firms were playing two separate Hotelling games, one involving selling version H to high types and the other involving selling version L to low types. Formally, firm 1 maximizes $\pi_1 = p_{1H}x_h + p_{1L}x_l$ and firm 2 maximizes $\pi_2 = p_{2H}(1 - x_h) + p_{2L}(1 - x_l)$. The Nash equilibrium prices are easily found as:

$$p_{1H}^* = p_{2H}^* = \frac{1}{\alpha_h} = 1 \equiv p_H^*,$$

$$p_{1L}^* = p_{2L}^* = \frac{1}{\alpha_l} = \frac{1}{5} \equiv p_L^*.$$

The corresponding profits are equal to

$$\pi_1^* = \pi_2^* = \frac{1}{2}1 + \frac{1}{2}\frac{1}{5} = \frac{3}{5} \equiv \pi^*.$$

However, we still need to check whether these prices satisfy the incentive compatibility constraints. First, we have to make sure that high types prefer version H to version L. They do if $s_H - \alpha_h p_H^* \geq s_L - \alpha_h p_L^*$, which is true in our example as $3 - 1 > 2 - \frac{1}{5}$. Second, low types must also prefer version L to version H. This is so if $s_L - \alpha_l p_L^* \geq s_H - \alpha_l p_H^*$, which is satisfied as $2 - 5\frac{1}{5} > 3 - 5$.

As long as firms sell the high-end version to high types and the low-end version to low types, they cannot increase profits by unilaterally deviating to other prices than p_H^* and p_L^*. Yet, they could deviate by selling the high-end version to both types of consumers.[h] So, supposing that firm 2 sticks to the above strategy (i.e., $p_{2H} = p_H^*$ and $p_{2L} = p_L^*$), let us examine whether firm 1 is able to increase profits by selling version H at price p_{1H} to consumers of both groups. The indifferent high-type consumer is identified as before: $x_h = \frac{1}{2}[1 + \alpha_h(p_H^* - p_{1H})]$. As for low types, the indifference condition is now $s_H - \alpha_l p_{1H} - \tilde{x}_l = s_L - \alpha_l p_L^* - (1 - \tilde{x}_l)$, or $\tilde{x}_l = \frac{1}{2}[1 + (s_H - s_L) + \alpha_l(p_L^* - p_{1H})]$. It follows that firm 1's profits are bounded above by

$$\bar{\pi}_1(p_{1H}) = \frac{1}{2}p_{1H}\left[1 + \alpha_h\left(p_H^* - p_{1H}\right)\right]$$

$$+ \frac{1}{2}p_{1H}\left[1 + (s_H - s_L) + \alpha_l\left(p_L^* - p_{1H}\right)\right]$$

$$= \frac{1}{2}p_{1H}[(2 - p_{1H}) + (3 - 5p_{1H})] = \frac{1}{2}p_{1H}(5 - 6p_{1H}).$$

The price that maximizes $\bar{\pi}_1$ is readily computed as $p_{1H} = 5/12$. Substituting into the profit function, we obtain that profits are at most $25/48 \simeq 0.521$, which is less than $\pi^* = 3/5 = 0.6$.

Since the deviation is not profitable, we have established that there exists an equilibrium where firms set the prices (p_L^*, p_H^*), and consumers buy from the closest firm and self-select between the two versions.

---

[h] Other possible deviations are: (i) selling H to low types and selling L to high types; (ii) selling L only. The former deviation is not feasible as high types will strictly prefer buying H whenever the low types are willing to buy H. As for the latter deviation, if it is profitable to sell L at price p_{1L} to some consumers, then it is even more profitable to sell H at $p_{1L} + (s_H - s_L)/\alpha_l - \varepsilon$ to the same consumers; so, it is not necessary to consider this deviation separately.

> **Lesson 9.5**   Consider a market in which a monopolist optimally decides to choose uniform pricing. Introducing a competitor in this market may lead to price discrimination by both firms.

Noteworthy is the fact that under the present configuration of parameters, the incentive compatibility constraints all turn out to be nonbinding. So, competition in menu pricing becomes relatively simple as it amounts to analysing competition on two separate segments; in that sense, menu pricing has the flavour of group pricing, but not quite since (i) all consumers have access to all goods and (ii) low types buy a lower-quality good. Effectively, we are in a situation that is equivalent to personalized pricing, as analysed before.

Non-discriminatory equilibrium

Let us now show that there exists another equilibrium in which both firms sell the high-end product to both types of consumers (at respective prices p_{1H} and p_{2H}). In this situation, the indifferent high-type consumer is still identified by x_h, whereas the indifferent low-type consumer is now given by $\hat{x}_l = \frac{1}{2}[1 + \alpha_l (p_{2H} - p_{1H})]$. Firm 1's maximization programme is thus

$$\max_{p_{1H}} \pi_1 = p_{1H} (x_h + \hat{x}_l) = p_{1H} [1 + \bar{\alpha} (p_{2H} - p_{1H})],$$

where $\bar{\alpha} = (\alpha_h + \alpha_l)/2$ is the average marginal utility of income (in our example, $\bar{\alpha} = 3$). From the first-order condition, we derive firm 1's reaction function: $p_{1H} (p_{2H}) = (1 + \bar{\alpha} p_{2H})/(2\bar{\alpha})$. Invoking the symmetry of the model, we find the Nash equilibrium prices and profits as

$$\hat{p}_H = \frac{1}{\bar{\alpha}} = \frac{1}{3}, \quad \text{and} \quad \hat{\pi} = \frac{1}{\bar{\alpha}} = \frac{1}{3}.$$

Here, incentive compatibility is obviously not an issue since a single version is offered. So, as long as both firms only sell version H, they have no reason to set a price other than $\hat{p}_H$. Yet, they can deviate by changing their selling strategy altogether. Two deviations may be profitable: (i) selling version H to high types and nothing to low types; (ii) selling version H to high types and version L to low types (as in the previous case). We need to show that none of these two deviations is profitable.

Suppose first that firm 2 sets $\hat{p}_H$ and that firm 1 deviates by selling version H to high types only (at price p_{1H}). Low types do not buy from firm 1 if the most eager low-type consumer (i.e., the consumer located at 0) prefers to buy from firm 2: $s_H - \alpha_l p_{1H} < s_H - \alpha_l \hat{p}_H - 1 \Leftrightarrow p_{1H} > \hat{p}_H + (1/\alpha_l) = 1/3 + 1/5 = 8/15$. In this case, firm 1 chooses p_{1H} to maximize $\pi_{1H} = \frac{1}{2} p_{1H} [1 + \alpha_h (\hat{p}_H - p_{1H})] = \frac{1}{6} p_{1H} [4 - 3p_{1H}]$. The unconstrained maximum is $p_{1H} = 2/3 > 8/15$, which implies that indeed no low-type consumer buys from firm 1. The best deviation is obtained by setting $p_{1H} = 8/15$, which yields profit:

$$\pi_{1H} = \frac{1}{6}\frac{2}{3}\left(4 - 3\frac{2}{3}\right) = \frac{2}{9} < \frac{3}{9} = \hat{\pi}.$$

We observe thus that this deviation is not profitable.

Suppose next that firm 1 deviates by selling version H to high types (at p_{1H}) and version L to low types (at p_{1L}). If incentive compatibility constraints were not an issue, firm 1 could simply select the optimal price for each group. The high-type indifferent consumer is identified as usual: $x_h = \frac{1}{2}[1 + \alpha_h(\hat{p}_H - p_{1H})]$. The indifferent low-type consumer is such that $s_L - \alpha_l p_{1L} - \bar{x}_l = s_H - \alpha_l \hat{p}_H - (1 - \bar{x}_l)$, or $\bar{x}_l = \frac{1}{2}[1 - (s_H - s_L) + \alpha_l(\hat{p}_H - p_{1L})]$. Firm 1 will thus choose p_{1H} and p_{1L} to maximize

$$\pi_1(p_{1H}, p_{1L}) = \frac{1}{2}p_{1H}[1 + \alpha_h(\hat{p}_H - p_{1H})]$$
$$+ \frac{1}{2}p_{1L}[1 - (s_H - s_L) + \alpha_l(\hat{p}_H - p_{1L})]$$
$$= \frac{1}{6}p_{1H}(4 - 3p_{1H}) + \frac{5}{6}p_{1L}(1 - 3p_{1L}).$$

The profit-maximizing prices are easily found as $p_{1H}^* = 2/3$ and $p_{1L}^* = 1/6$, and the corresponding profits are

$$\pi_1(p_{1H}^*, p_{1L}^*) = \frac{7}{24} \simeq 0.292 < \hat{\pi} = \frac{1}{3}.$$

Without even checking for the incentive compatibility constraints (which could only make things worse if they were not satisfied), we can conclude that this second deviation is not profitable either and, therefore, that both firms charging $\hat{p}_H$ and selling version H to both groups of consumers is an equilibrium.[15]

Summary

We have shown the possibility of multiple equilibria in a game where firms compete with menu pricing. For the same set of parameters, there is an equilibrium involving both firms to price discriminate and another equilibrium involving them not to. There is thus a form of complementarity in practicing menu pricing: each firm optimally mimics the choice of the rival firm. To understand why this occurs, note first that it is more profitable to sell the high-end version to both groups (because everyone is willing to pay more for that version and it costs the same to produce it), unless the profit-maximizing prices for the high-end version differ largely between the two groups. The latter situation will prevail if the rival firm price discriminates. Indeed, the firm's unconstrained best-response prices for the two groups of consumers will be far apart and it will then be optimal to discriminate as well. On the other hand, if the rival firm charges the same price for both groups, then the firm's unconstrained best-response prices will be the same for both groups and it will be optimal to choose an intermediate price and sell the high-end version to everyone.

In the discriminatory equilibrium, version H is sold to high types at price $p_H^* = 1$ and version L is sold to low types at price $p_L^* = 1/5$; firms achieve a profit of $\pi^* = 3/5$. In the non-discriminatory equilibrium, firms sell version H to both types at price $\hat{p}_H = 1/3$ and make a profit of $\hat{\pi} = 1/3$. We thus have that profits are higher in the discriminatory equilibrium.[i] This contrasts markedly with the results we obtained previously for group and personalized pricing. Recall that in the duopoly setting we examined, we always had a unique equilibrium and when the equilibrium involved price discrimination, firms were in a prisoner's dilemma because they would have been better off were they not discriminating. Here, price discrimination

---

[i] This result holds true for the whole region of parameters in which the two equilibria coexist.

and uniform pricing equilibria coexist, with discrimination yielding higher profits to both firms.

Lesson 9.6   **Quality-based menu pricing in a duopoly context may involve equilibrium multiplicity: either both firms price discriminate or none does. Contrary to group and personalized pricing in a duopoly, firms may prefer to coordinate on the situation where they both price discriminate. Contrary to monopoly menu pricing, incentive compatibility constraints may not be binding.**

Extension

In the above model, we have assumed that when the two versions are sold, all consumers observe all prices. However, there are many instances where only the price of the low-end version of the product is advertised. Businesses then try to make consumers 'upgrade' to the high-end version by selling additional 'add-ons' at higher prices at the point of sale, as illustrated in Case 9.5.

Case 9.5 Add-on pricing

If you have ever booked a rented car at an airport, you probably know this business tactic: the agent at the desk must have proposed you to rent a larger car than the one you had booked and to add an extra insurance, both 'for only small additional fees'. Later on, having arrived at the hotel, you might also have realized that the quoted price for your room did not include Internet access, mini-bar items, in-room movies and the like. Typically, you would not have been able to learn the prices of these add-ons beforehand.

Is there a rationale for such firm behaviour? One can repeat the previous analysis to study this practice of 'add-on pricing'.[16] It is assumed that firms only advertise the price of the low-end version and that consumers must incur a small sunk cost to learn the price of the high-end version. One important conclusion from this analysis is that add-on pricing can raise equilibrium profits by creating an adverse selection problem that softens price competition.[j] Intuitively, if a firm undercuts on price, the pool of consumers it will attract will contain a disproportionate share of low-type consumers. This is not a problem when firms offer a single version (there is selection but not adverse selection since low types' money is as good as high types' money). In contrast, when firms offer both versions and the price of the high-end version is not advertised, the selection becomes adverse: because of the unobservability, there is a large gap between the prices of the two versions and firms do not want to attract too many low types who do not consume the add-ons. Hence, firms have lower incentives to cut prices, making equilibrium profits go up.

---

[j] We study adverse selection problems systematically in Chapter 12.

9.3.2 Competitive quantity-based menu pricing

To examine competitive nonlinear quantity-based pricing, we use the following model.[17] Two firms, labelled 1 and 2, compete by setting two-part tariffs of the form $T_i(q) = m_i + p_i q$, where m_i is a fixed fee and p_i is a variable fee. As described above, such two-part tariffs are used in a large variety of contexts. For instance, in telephony, the fixed fee can be viewed as a subscription fee for telephone services and the variable fee as the price per minute of communication. As in the previous model, we assume that the firms are located at the two endpoints of the unit interval (firm 1 at 0 and firm 2 at 1). They sell competing brands (produced at a constant marginal cost of c) to a unit mass of consumers. Consumers are uniformly distributed on $[0, 1]$ and are supposed to be one-stop shoppers (i.e., they buy from at most one firm).[k] Instead of supposing as before that consumers have unit demands, we assume now that they can consume any quantity from the firm they decide to patronize. Let $u(q)$ denote a consumer's gross utility (excluding transport costs and payments to the firm) if she buys a quantity q. So, when a consumer faces a variable fee p, the quantity consumed q is such that $u'(q) = p$. Inverting the latter expression, we obtain the demand function $q(p)$, which we assume to be decreasing in p. All consumers of firm i buy the same quantity and their net surplus (still excluding transport costs) is $w(p_i, m_i) = v(p_i) - m_i$, where $v(p_i)$ is given by

$$v(p_i) = \max_q \{u(q) - p_i q\} \text{ with } v'(p_i) = -q.$$

Consumers enjoy a fixed surplus r from consumption and incur a linear transportation cost, τ, per unit of distance. So, a consumer located at $x \in [0, 1]$ derives net utility $r - \tau x + w(p_1, m_1)$ when buying from firm 1 and net utility $r - \tau(1 - x) + w(p_2, m_2)$ when buying from firm 2. We assume that r is large enough, so that all consumers choose to participate in the market with the relevant range of tariffs. Denote $w_1 = w(p_1, m_1)$ and $w_2 = w(p_2, m_2)$. Then, the indifferent consumer is such that

$$r - \tau \hat{x} + w_1 = r - \tau(1 - \hat{x}) + w_2 \Leftrightarrow \hat{x}(w_1, w_2) = \frac{1}{2\tau}(\tau + w_1 - w_2).$$

Let us now analyse the pricing game between the two firms. Competition in variable and fixed fees (p_i and m_i) can equivalently be viewed as competition in variable fee and net surpluses (p_i and w_i). Then, as $m_i = v(p_i) - w_i$, firm 1 maximizes

$$\max_{p_1, w_1} \Pi_1 = \frac{1}{2\tau}(\tau + w_1 - w_2)[(p_1 - c)q(p_1) + v(p_1) - w_1],$$

where the first term is the mass of consumers buying from firm 1 and the second term is the per consumer profit. The first-order condition for profit maximization with respect to p_1 is

$$\frac{\partial \Pi_1}{\partial p_1} = 0 \Leftrightarrow q(p_1) + q'(p_1)(p_1 - c) + v'(p_1) = 0.$$

Since $v'(p_1) = -q(p_1)$, the condition boils down to $q'(p_1)(p_1 - c) = 0$. As $q'(p_1) < 0$ and applying the same argument to firm 2, we have that

$$p_1^* = p_2^* = c.$$

---

[k] This assumption is quite realistic in markets where competition with two-part tariffs prevails: customers purchase only one firm's product or service so as to save fixed fees.

Hence, because of marginal cost pricing, the equilibrium involves efficient consumption. Next, the first-order condition with respect to w_1 is

$$\frac{\partial \Pi_1}{\partial w_1} = 0 \Leftrightarrow [(p_1 - c)q(p_1) + v(p_1) - w_1] - (\tau + w_1 - w_2) = 0.$$

Using the previous result ($p_1^* = c$) and invoking the symmetry of the model (which implies that $w_1 = w_2$ at the equilibrium), we can rewrite the latter condition as $v(p_1) - w_1 - \tau = 0$. Recalling that $m_i = v(p_i) - w_i$ and using the same argument for firm 2, we obtain that

$$m_1^* = m_2^* = \tau.$$

At the equilibrium, each firm makes a profit equal to $\Pi_1^* = \Pi_2^* = \tau/2$. We denote the equilibrium industry profit under nonlinear tariffs as $\Pi_{NL} = \tau$.

We record the following result.

Lesson 9.7   If two firms compete over the Hotelling line with two-part tariffs and if all consumers are served over the relevant range of tariffs, then firms offer tariffs $T(q) = \tau + cq$ where τ is the consumer's transport cost parameter and c is the firms' marginal cost of production.

This occurs in the unique symmetric equilibrium. Here, the variable fee is equal to the firms' marginal cost. A general condition for this result is that the demand of the marginal consumer be equal to the average demand. This condition is fulfilled under the particular utility functions we use here (because, as we have seen, all consumers purchase the same amount whatever their location). The same condition also ensures that a monopoly using two-part tariffs will price at marginal cost.[18] An important implication of this analysis is that our standard work-horse, the Hotelling model with unit demand can be seen as a short-cut for competition in two-part tariffs (where the reservation value is $r + v(c)$).

Note that in our analysis we have restricted ourselves to homogeneous consumers. One can extend the model to include unobserved heterogeneity:[19] consumers have private, product-specific information about their tastes. If this vertical taste parameter does not interact with the horizontal parameter, firms offer cost-based two-part tariffs, as in the present setting. This means that there is no screening in equilibrium. Here the firms' incentive to compete dominates any benefit that could arise from screening. This is a situation in which the belief that more competition leads to less price discrimination is correct.

A corollary of the previous result is that *competition with two-part tariffs improves welfare compared to competition with linear tariffs*. Indeed, two-part tariffs induce marginal-cost pricing, whereas linear prices drive firms to set positive price–cost margins since there is no other way to generate profit. It is not clear, however, how this increase in welfare is split between the firms and the consumers. As this issue is a bit technical to analyse, we state our result upfront.

> **Lesson 9.8** Competition based on two-part tariffs rather than on linear tariffs increases industry profits and welfare. Yet, if welfare is concave in linear prices, the increase in industry profits is larger than the increase in welfare, which implies that consumers are harmed by nonlinear pricing.

The reader may want to skip the formal analysis below that formally establishes Lesson 9.8.

We introduce some additional pieces of notation. Let $\pi_i(p_i) \equiv (p_i - c)\,q(p_i)$ denote per consumer profit under linear price p_i, and for a candidate equilibrium price p, define

$$s(k) \equiv v(c + k(p - c)),$$

where k is a scalar. Hence, $s(0) = v(c)$ and $s(1) = v(p)$. Noting $s_k(k)$ the derivative of $s(k)$ with respect to k, we have $s_k(k) = (p - c)\,v'(c + k(p - c))$. Recalling that $v'(p_i) = -q(p_i)$, we have then the following equality:

$$\pi(c + k(p - c)) = k(p - c)\,q(c + k(p - c)) = -k s_k(k).$$

In particular, $\pi(p) = -s_k(1)$.

Suppose firm j chooses $p_j = p$. For p to be a symmetric equilibrium price, it must be that $p_i = p$ maximizes firm i's profit, which can be written as

$$\Pi_i = \tfrac{1}{2\tau}(\tau + v(p_i) - v(p))\,\pi_i(p_i).$$

Letting $p_i = c + k(p - c)$, we can use the notation we just introduced to perform the analysis in terms of the scalar k rather than the price p. Firm i's profit can be rewritten as

$$\Pi_i = \tfrac{1}{2\tau}(\tau + s(k) - s(1))(-k s_k(k)),$$

and it is necessary that $k = 1$ maximizes this expression for p to be a symmetric equilibrium. The first-order condition gives

$$-k(s_k(k))^2 - (\tau + s(k) - s(1))(s_k(k) + k s_{kk}(k)) = 0.$$

If we evaluate the condition at $k = 1$, we have

$$-(s_k(1))^2 - \tau(s_k(1) + s_{kk}(1)) = 0 \Leftrightarrow -s_k(1) = s_{kk}(1) + \tfrac{1}{\tau}(s_k(1))^2.$$

Recalling that $\pi(p) = -s_k(1)$, we can express industry profit at the symmetric equilibrium with linear prices in two different ways:

$$\Pi_L = -s_k(1) \text{ and} \tag{9.6}$$

$$\Pi_L = s_{kk}(1) + \tfrac{1}{\tau}(s_k(1))^2. \tag{9.7}$$

Now, as we assumed that $q'(p_i) < 0$, we have that $s_{kk}(1) > 0$. So, using (9.7), we have that $\Pi_L > \tfrac{1}{\tau}(s_k(1))^2$. But, using (9.6), we also have that $\tfrac{1}{\tau}(s_k(1))^2 = \tfrac{1}{\tau}\Pi_L^2$. Combining these two results, we find that

$$\Pi_L > \tfrac{1}{\tau}\Pi_L^2 \Leftrightarrow \Pi_L < \tau = \Pi_{NL}.$$

Hence, we conclude that profits are higher when nonlinear pricing is employed rather than linear pricing.

Let us now turn to consumers. At some price $\hat{p} = c + k(p - c)$, welfare is the sum of consumer surplus ($v(\hat{p})$) and of industry profit ($\pi(\hat{p})$). Using the previous equivalences, we can rewrite welfare as a function of the scalar k: $W(k) \equiv s(k) - ks_k(k)$. Under two-part tariffs, $\hat{p} = c$ (i.e., $k = 0$) and so $W_{NL} = W(0)$; under linear pricing, $\hat{p} = p$ (i.e., $k = 1$) and so $W_L = W(1)$. Suppose that total welfare is concave in linear prices and thus is concave in k. This implies in particular that $W(k)$ lies below its tangent at $k = 1$. It also follows that the welfare difference between two-part tariffs and linear pricing, $\Delta W = W_{NL} - W_L = W(0) - W(1)$, satisfies

$$\Delta W \leq -W'(1) = s_{kk}(1).$$

Now, using (9.6) and (9.7), we know that $s_{kk}(1) = \Pi_L - \frac{1}{\tau}\Pi_L^2 = \frac{\Pi_L}{\tau}(\tau - \Pi_L)$. Furthermore, we have just shown that $\Pi_L < \tau$, which implies that $\Pi_L/\tau < 1$ and thus that $s_{kk}(1) = (\Pi_L/\tau)(\tau - \Pi_L) < \tau - \Pi_L$. Combining the previous results, we obtain that

$$W_{NL} - W_L < \Pi_{NL} - \Pi_L \Leftrightarrow CS_{NL} \equiv W_{NL} - \Pi_{NL} < CS_L \equiv W_L - \Pi_L,$$

meaning that consumers in aggregate are worse off when nonlinear tariffs are used.

To understand the previous results, let us compare how prices are fixed in the two cases. With nonlinear pricing, lowering the fixed fee has two opposite effects: (i) it induces a loss of profit on existing consumers, and (ii) it attracts profitable consumers from the other firm. The optimal fixed fee balances these two forces. By contrast, with linear pricing, lowering price has the same two effects, but also an additional positive effect: with elastic demands, a lower price expands demand from each type of consumer and thus entails a gain in average profit per consumer. As a result, there is more incentive to lower prices with linear pricing, which explains why consumers do better. Yet, as welfare is unambiguously higher under two-part tariffs because the variable fee is equal to marginal cost, it must be that industry profits are larger too.

Review questions

1. Suppose a firm can target two groups of consumers by a menu of prices with different qualities but that it can also offer different prices to different consumer groups. What should it do?

2. When does menu pricing dominate uniform pricing in monopoly? Discuss the countervailing effects.

3. How does competition affect the use of menu pricing? Discuss.

4. What are the effects of competition on quantity-based menu pricing?

Further reading

Our formal analysis of menu pricing under monopoly is based on Salant (1989). Deneckere and McAfee (1996) initiated work on damaged goods. A good introdution into the empirics of price discrimination is provided by Verboven (2006). For an analysis of competitive quality-based menu pricing see Ellison (2005), and of competitive quantity-based menu pricing see Armstrong and Vickers (2001, 2006).

10 Intertemporal price discrimination

In many markets, firms offer the same product in different periods and consumers buy only one item over the whole time horizon. This description of consumer behaviour fits particularly well for *durable goods* such as cars, washing machines (and other household appliances), computers and software (which does not wear out at all unless obsolescence is artificially imposed). It also fits for particular items that can be ordered in advance, such as a holiday package, a plane ticket and a concert ticket. While our insight derived in the first two sections of this chapter only applies to durable goods, we then obtain results that also apply to ticket sales.

In the case of durable goods, consumers derive the benefit from the purchase of the good over a number of periods. Also, consumers can decide on the timing of their purchase. An example is furniture consumers may want to replace. They may buy the piece immediately and replace the old piece; or they keep their old piece for some more time and thus postpone the purchase of the desired piece. Suppose a firm sells a product over a number of periods and that both firm and consumers have discount factor δ. If the firm sells the product in the first period only at a uniform price, it makes the standard monopoly profit (see Chapter 2). If the firm can sell the product over several periods, we may think that this opens up the possibility of price discrimination, which is beneficial for the firm. Whether this conjecture is correct depends on a number of circumstances, as we will explore in this chapter.

An important issue is whether a firm can commit to future prices and if the answer is negative, what kind of prices consumers expect. Clearly, even if a firm preannounces future prices, we must ask whether the firm has an incentive to deviate at some later point. Therefore, as a starting point, we consider the situation in which the firm lacks any commitment power and sets the period t price in that period, not earlier (Section 10.1). We then redo the analysis under the assumption that the firm has an instrument that gives it commitment power over future prices (Section 10.2). Finally, we study the related topic of behaviour-based price discrimination, i.e. the practice whereby firms base the price they charge a consumer on their purchasing history (Section 10.3).

10.1 Durable good monopoly without commitment

A monopolist who sells a product at various instances in time may be thought to be in a better position to extract surplus from consumers than a monopolist who only sells once, because, as already pointed out above, selling at various points in time opens up the possibility of intertemporal price discrimination. As we will see, we can give some logic to this reasoning, only to subsequently question its applicability to many markets of consumer goods. To this end, we will contrast a model with a small number of consumers (here: two) and a model with a large number of consumers (here: a continuum).

10.1.1   Small number of consumers

It is useful to start with a simple model. Suppose a durable product can be sold over two periods and consumers derive utility from a unit of this product only in these two periods. This means that the product becomes obsolete after period 2, independently of the time of purchase. Denote δ the intertemporal discount rate. A monopolist sells the product over two periods at constant unit costs $c < 1/2$ to two consumers. Consumer 1 would be willing to pay $r_H = 1$ in each period for consumption in that period (relative to the outside option of not consuming in that period, which is equal to zero). Hence, if she buys the product in period 1, she is willing to spend $1 + \delta$ in period 1 (for consumption in both periods) and if she buys the product in period 2 she is willing to spend 1 in period 2. Consumer 2 would be willing to pay only half of what consumer 1 is willing to pay, $r_L = 1/2$. If the monopolist were to sell the product only in period 1, it would sell only to buyer 1 at price $1 + \delta$. Its profit then is $1 + \delta - c$. If it sold to both buyers (at price $(1 + \delta)/2$), it would only make a profit of $1 + \delta - 2c$.

If the firm sells in both periods, it will sell to consumer 1 in the first period and to consumer 2 in the second period. If consumer 1 has bought in the first period, it will set its second-period price equal to $p^2 = 1/2$. It may still extract the full surplus from consumer 1 in the first period by setting the price equal to $1 + \delta$ minus some negligible amount. Thus, if consumer 1 and consumer 2 buy in the respective periods, the monopolist's present discounted value of profit is $1 + \delta - c + \delta(1/2 - c)$, which is greater than the profit of a monopolist which can only sell in period 1. However, we may wonder why consumer 1 buys in period 1 since she has the possibility of delaying its purchase to period 2. At the above mentioned prices, such a deviation would indeed be profitable since her present value of utility would be $\delta(1 - 1/2)$ which is greater than a negligible amount. However, we have overlooked that the monopolist offered the product in period 2 at $p^2 = 1/2$, *conditional on selling one unit in period 1*. If consumer 1 postpones her purchase, the monopolist can rethink its pricing strategy. Indeed in this case, it is profit maximizing to set the price equal to $p^2 = 1$ since $1 - c > 1 - 2c$. This implies that consumer 1 does not gain from delaying her purchase.

> **Lesson 10.1**   A durable good monopolist (who cannot commit to future prices) may be able to increase profits through intertemporal price discrimination compared to a situation in which it is only active in the first period.

The above analysis may be criticized as being very special. In particular, we assumed that consumer 2 had a sufficiently lower willingness to pay compared to consumer 1 and that there were only few (namely two) buyers. We will see that we can extend the argument to essentially any distribution of willingness to pay and the argument (in a modified form) still holds. However, limiting the analysis to a small number of buyers is restrictive and results are markedly different if we turn to a large number of consumers.

Let us consider the issue whether the distribution of willingness to pay matters. Generalizing the previous example, we assume that consumer 2 is willing to spend at most r_L per period (with $r_L < r_H = 1$). Note first that if $r_L \leq c$, the monopolist never finds it profitable to sell to consumer 2. The best option in this case is to sell to consumer 1 only, in period 1, at price $p^1 = 1 + \delta$.

On the other hand, if $r_L > c$, then the monopolist has a wider range of options. If the monopolist only sells in period 1, the alternative is either to sell only to consumer 1 at price $1 + \delta$, which yields profits equal to $1 + \delta - c$, or to sell to both consumers at price $(1 + \delta)r_L$, in which case profits are equal to $2(1 + \delta)r_L - 2c$. Selling to both consumers is preferable if $2(1 + \delta)r_L - 2c > 1 + \delta - c$, which is equivalent to $r_L > \frac{1}{2}(1 + \delta + c)/(1 + \delta)$. In sum, the profits if selling in period 1 only are given by

$$
\pi^{\text{one}} = \begin{cases} 2(1+\delta)r_L - 2c & \text{if } r_L > \frac{1}{2}\left(1 + \frac{c}{1+\delta}\right), \\ 1 + \delta - c & \text{if } r_L \leq \frac{1}{2}\left(1 + \frac{c}{1+\delta}\right). \end{cases}
$$

Consider now the possibility of selling in periods 1 and 2. What is crucial for the monopolist is the decision of consumer 1. Consumer 1 prefers to buy immediately in period 1 rather than to delay her purchase until period 2 if

$$
1 + \delta - p^1 \geq \delta\left(1 - p^2\right). \tag{10.1}
$$

The value of p^2 in condition (10.1) depends on what the two consumers decide. Suppose first that consumer 1 does not buy in period 1; this means that consumer 2 does not buy either. In that case, the monopolist has two possibilities in period 2: he either sets $p^2 = 1$ and only consumer 1 buys, or he sets $p^2 = r_L$ and the two consumers buy. The first option is preferable if $1 - c \geq 2(r_L - c)$, which is equivalent to $r_L \leq (1 + c)/2$. Suppose this is the case; then $p^2 = 1$ and condition (10.1) becomes $1 + \delta - p^1 \geq 0$; or $p^1 \leq 1 + \delta$. It follows that the firm sets prices $p^1 = 1 + \delta$ and $p^2 = r_L$. The present discounted value of profit then is $1 + \delta - c + \delta(r_L - c)$. Suppose now that $r_L > (1 + c)/2$. Here, the firm would sell to both consumers and $p^2 = r_L$, which is correctly anticipated by consumer 1; condition (10.1) becomes $1 + \delta - p^1 \geq \delta(1 - r_L)$, or $p^1 \leq (1 + \delta) - \delta(1 - r_L)$. This implies that the monopolist can no longer extract the full surplus from consumer 1. With $p^1 = 1 + \delta r_L$ and $p^2 = r_L$, the present discounted value of profit is equal to $1 + \delta r_L - c + \delta(r_L - c)$. We can summarize the profits (in present discounted value) when selling in both periods as follows:

$$
\pi^{\text{two}} = \begin{cases} 1 + \delta r_L - c + \delta(r_L - c) & \text{if } r_L > \frac{1}{2}(1 + c), \\ 1 + \delta - c + \delta(r_L - c) & \text{if } r_L \leq \frac{1}{2}(1 + c). \end{cases}
$$

We now want to compare π^{two} to π^{one} to see when it is more profitable to sell in both periods, even when the firm has the possibility to commit itself to sell in period 1 only. Continuing to assume that $r_L > c$, we have to distinguish between three regions of parameters.

1. Suppose first that consumer 2 has a rather low valuation, i.e., $c < r_L \leq \frac{1}{2}\left(1 + \frac{c}{1+\delta}\right)$. This interval is non-empty as long as $c \leq \frac{1+\delta}{1+2\delta}$. It is easily seen that $\pi^{\text{two}} = 1 + \delta - c + \delta(r_L - c) > \pi^{\text{one}} = 1 + \delta - c$, meaning that the monopolist prefers to sell in both periods and is able to extract the full surplus.

2. Take now the other end of the spectrum and suppose that consumer 2 has a very high valuation, i.e. $\frac{1}{2}(1+c) < r_L < 1$. Here, the opposite conclusion holds: the monopolist prefers to commit to sell in period 1 only. One checks indeed that

$$\pi^{\text{one}} - \pi^{\text{two}} = [2(1+\delta)r_L - 2c] - [1 + \delta r_L - c + \delta(r_L - c)]$$

$$= 2r_L - 1 - (1-\delta)c > 0 \Leftrightarrow r_L > \tfrac{1}{2}(1 + c - \delta c),$$

with the latter inequality being implied by $r_L > \frac{1}{2}(1+c)$.

3. For intermediate valuations of consumer 2, i.e., for $\frac{1}{2}\left(1 + \frac{c}{1+\delta}\right) < r_L \le \frac{1}{2}(1+c)$, the relevant comparison is between $\pi^{\text{two}} = 1 + \delta - c + \delta(r_L - c)$ and $\pi^{\text{one}} = 2(1+\delta)r_L - 2c$. Intertemporal discrimination is preferred by the monopolist if

$$\pi^{\text{two}} \ge \pi^{\text{one}} \Leftrightarrow r_L \le \frac{1 + \delta + (1-\delta)c}{2+\delta} \equiv \bar{r}_L.$$

Some additional computations establish that

$$\bar{r}_L > \tfrac{1}{2}\left(1 + \tfrac{c}{1+\delta}\right) \Leftrightarrow c < \tfrac{1+\delta}{1+2\delta} \quad \text{and} \quad \bar{r}_L < \tfrac{1}{2}(1+c) \Leftrightarrow c > \tfrac{1}{3}.$$

Collecting the previous results, we find that a monopolist that sells to two buyers over two periods chooses intertemporal price discrimination as its profit-maximizing strategy, when committing to sell in period 1 only is possible, in the following regions of parameters:

$$\begin{cases} 0 \le c \le \tfrac{1}{3} & \text{and} \quad c < r_L \le \tfrac{1}{2}(1+c), \\ \tfrac{1}{3} < c \le \tfrac{1+\delta}{1+2\delta} & \text{and} \quad c < r_L \le \tfrac{1}{2+\delta}(1 + \delta + (1-\delta)c). \end{cases}$$

We observe that price discrimination is chosen if consumer 2 has an 'intermediate' valuation and if the marginal cost is not too large (regions 1 and 3). Moreover, because $(1+\delta)/(1+2\delta)$ decreases with δ, we see that a lower discount factor tends to make intertemporal pricing more attractive for the firm. Outside these two regions of parameters, the monopolist does not price discriminate and sells only in period 1 (either to consumer 1 only if $r_L \le c$, or to both consumers in the remaining region of parameters). Figure 10.1 depicts the monopolist's optimal conduct.[a] From a welfare point of view, the downside of discrimination is a lower total surplus since the postponed purchase is associated with unrealized gains.

Lesson 10.2 **In a market with two consumers, the firm may prefer intertemporal pricing to selling to both consumers in the first period because the firm can fully discriminate between both consumers. Consumer surplus is reduced to zero in this case.**

The analysis can be extended to any number of periods and finite number of buyers. If the number of consumers remains the same but there is discounting (and possibly pricing) for an infinite number of periods, the argument becomes slightly more sophisticated and profits weakly increase under intertemporal pricing. With infinitely many periods, a consumer of

---

[a] We can also observe on the figure that with $r_L = 1/2$ and $c < 1/2$, intertemporal pricing is the optimal strategy for all admissible values of δ, which confirms the conclusion of our initial example.

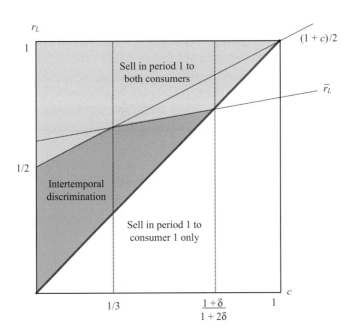

Figure 10.1 Optimal intertemporal pricing in the presence of two consumers

type r is willing to pay $r/(1-\delta)$ in any given period, provided she did not buy before. The profit-maximizing intertemporal pricing strategy then takes the form of setting $p^t = 1/(1-\delta)$ if none of the two consumers purchases and $p^t = r/(1-\delta)$ if only consumer 1 has purchased in the previous period. Equilibrium profit is then $1/(1-\delta) + \delta r_L/(1-\delta) - (1+\delta)c = (1+\delta r_L)/(1-\delta) - (1+\delta)c$. A sufficient condition for intertemporal pricing to dominate an offer to sell only in period 1 (to both consumers) is $1 + \delta r_L > 2r_L$, which is satisfied if δ is sufficiently large. A qualitatively similar result holds for more than two buyers although the condition on the discount factor tends to become more demanding.

10.1.2   Large number of consumers

The above analysis gives reasons to believe in intertemporal pricing of a durable good as a price-discrimination strategy that increases profits compared to selling in a single period. Let us examine whether this conclusion carries over to settings with large numbers of buyers.

We first slightly modify our numerical example from the previous subsection. We still suppose that there are two periods and a single firm sells the product at price p^1 in period 1 and at price p^2 in period 2. As before, a buyer of type H is willing to spend at most $r_H = 1$ per period on the product and a buyer of type L is willing to spend at most $r_L = 1/2$ per period on the product. The difference from the previous example is that there is a continuum of buyers of each type, with each group assumed to be of size 1. As before, if the monopolist were to sell the product only in period 1, it would sell only to type 1 at price $1 + \delta$. Its profit then is $1 + \delta - c$ whereas, if it sold to both types, it would only make a profit equal to $1 + \delta - 2c$.

If the firm sells in both periods, it will sell to type-H consumers in the first period and to type-L consumers in the second period. If type-H consumers have bought in the first period, it will set its second-period price equal to $p^2 = 1/2$. This is also the price a type-H consumer expects when postponing her purchase because now, in contrast to our earlier analysis, the firm cannot condition on individual deviations by type-H consumers, since an individual consumer is negligible and does not affect the aggregate level of purchases that is observed by the firm. Thus, from the period-1 perspective, a type-H consumer can obtain a net utility of $\delta(1 - 1/2) = \delta/2$. This implies that the first period price cannot exceed $p^1 = (1 + \delta) - \delta/2 = 1 + \delta/2$. The present discounted value of profit is therefore $p^1 \times 1 + \delta p^2 \times 1 - (1 + \delta)c = 1 + \delta/2 + \delta/2 - (1 + \delta)c = (1 + \delta)(1 - c)$, which is less then the profit the firm would obtain if it committed to sell in period 1 only (i.e., $1 + \delta - c$). Thus, with a continuum of consumers of two types, committing to a uniform price is more profitable than intertemporal pricing as a discrimination strategy.

> **Lesson 10.3** **With a continuum of consumers, a durable good monopolist cannot increase profits through intertemporal price discrimination compared to a situation in which it is only active in the first period.**

The restriction to two types may look restrictive. We therefore consider a modified model with a continuum of different types.[20] Consumers derive in each period a value r from one unit of the good. In the consumer population, r is uniformly distributed on the unit interval, $r \sim U[0, 1]$. The firm and consumers have the same discount rate δ. Hence, a consumer is willing to pay $(1 + \delta)r$ for the good in period 1. If the firm could sell the product in period 1 only, it would set the monopoly price $(1 + \delta)/2$ and would make profit $(1 + \delta)/4$. Suppose the firm did so in the first period and that all consumers with a valuation above the price buy in period 1 (i.e., consumers with $r \geq 1/2$) but that the good can also be sold in the second period. In the second period, the firm would face residual demand $Q^2(p^2) = 1/2 - p^2$. In period 2, the firm then would set its profit-maximizing price equal to $p^2 = 1/4$. However, in period 1, all consumers should foresee that they will be able to purchase the product at this price in period 2. Consider the consumer of type $r = 1/2 + \varepsilon$, $\varepsilon > 0$. To buy in period 1 gives utility $(1 + \delta)(1/2 + \varepsilon) - (1 + \delta)/2 = (1 + \delta)\varepsilon$. If the consumer postpones the purchase, she obtains utility $\delta[(1/2 + \varepsilon) - 1/4] = \delta(1/4 + \varepsilon)$. Hence for ε sufficiently small, this consumer would do better to postpone her purchase. Hence, the proposed situation cannot constitute a profit-maximizing situation. The reason is that the monopolist faces competition from his own product in the second period. This leads to a downward pressure on price.

We now formally analyse the two-period problem. For prices p^1, p^2 there is a consumer $\hat{r}$ who is indifferent between buying in period 1 and in period 2. This consumer is given by $(1 + \delta)\hat{r} - p^1 = \delta(\hat{r} - p^2)$. Hence,

$$\hat{r} = p^1 - \delta p^2.$$

Consumers with a lower r buy in period 2, consumers with a higher r buy in period 1. Suppose that consumers above $\hat{r}$ have bought in period 1. Residual demand is then $\hat{r} - p^2$. Thus in period 2, the firm's price will be $\arg\max_{p^2} p^2(\hat{r} - p^2) = \hat{r}/2$. In period 1, $\hat{r}$ is given by the expression above and we can write the firm's decision problem in period 1, anticipating the outcome in period 2, as

$$\max_{p^1} p^1(1 - \hat{r}) + \delta p^2(\hat{r} - p^2).$$

Since the second-period price will satisfy $p^2 = \hat{r}/2 = (p^1 - \delta p^2)/2$, we can replace $p^2 = p^1/(2 + \delta)$. This shows that the firm will set the price in period 2 at less than half the first-period price. Consumers in period 1 anticipate that the firm will set the price according to this formula. Thus the consumer who is indifferent between buying in period 1 or waiting until period 2 is given by

$$\hat{r} = p^1 - \delta\tfrac{1}{2+\delta}p^1 = \tfrac{2}{2+\delta}p^1.$$

Hence, the profit-maximization problem in period 1 becomes

$$\max_{p^1} p^1 \left(1 - \tfrac{2}{2+\delta}p^1\right) + \delta\tfrac{1}{2+\delta}p^1 \left(\tfrac{2}{2+\delta}p^1 - \tfrac{1}{2+\delta}p^1\right)$$

$$= \max_{p^1} p^1 \left(1 - \tfrac{2}{2+\delta}p^1 + \delta\tfrac{1}{2+\delta}\tfrac{1}{2+\delta}p^1\right) = \max_{p^1} p^1 \left(1 - \tfrac{4+\delta}{(2+\delta)^2}p^1\right).$$

It follows that the profit-maximizing first-period price is

$$p^1 = \frac{(2+\delta)^2}{2(4+\delta)}.$$

Inserting this price into the first-period profit function, we obtain equilibrium profit

$$\pi = \frac{(2+\delta)^2}{4(4+\delta)}.$$

Comparing first-period price and profit to the situation in which the firm can commit to sell in period 1 only, we obtain the following result (note that $(2+\delta)^2 < (1+\delta)(4+\delta)$):

Lesson 10.4 In the two-period durable good problem with a continuum of consumers and without commitment, the monopolist obtains lower profit and sets a lower first-period price than in a situation in which it can commit to sell in period 1 only.

While we have assumed that the firm announces p^2 in period 2, we can include the possibility to announce prices p^1 and $\hat{p}^2$ initially. However, even if the firm announces some price for the second period in period 1, it maintains the flexibility to lower its price later on. The firm will meet all demand for any price above marginal costs. In other words, the price that is announced initially does not give commitment power.

Our two-period model can be extended to include many periods. When periods become sufficiently small, the *Coase conjecture* applies: the firm loses all price-setting power. That is, the monopoly setting leads to an outcome that converges to the perfectly competitive outcome. To obtain the perfectly competitive outcome in the monopoly setting sounds surprising but the intuition is that the monopolist solves a sequence of maximization problems. Since, absent commitment, future actions cannot be controlled, the current monopolist cannot avoid the competition that is generated by its future self. This result still holds as consumers become more patient as long as there is a minimum unit of account (so that the number of prices essentially becomes finite).[21]

The argument that in a durable good monopoly a single firm generates competitive pressure by competing with itself extends to subsequent quality improvements. It is important for the analysis of market power in highly concentrated durable goods industries, as illustrated in Case 10.1.

Case 10.1   Durable good monopoly and the Microsoft case

In 1998, the US Department of Justice (DoJ) accused Microsoft of an antitrust violation because of Microsoft's inclusion of its web browser in its operating system. Other issues and claims were raised in the trial that followed, among which were predatory behaviour and exclusionary agreements. In January 1999, Richard Lee Schmalensee (Dean of the Sloan School of Management of the MIT) presented his testimony on behalf of Microsoft. One of his main conclusions was that 'Microsoft does not have monopoly power in the PC operating system market alleged by Plaintiffs . . . Microsoft cannot and has not excluded entry by others. It has maintained its leadership in providing operating systems for Intel-compatible computers through its superior foresight, skill, and efficiency. Microsoft cannot control prices except in the trivial sense in which every owner of intellectual property, from book authors to chip designers, can do so. Current and future competition from numerous sources has constrained Microsoft from charging a monopoly price for Windows.' To support this thesis, Schmalensee argued that when assessing market power, one should not look at static competition but at dynamic competition. Dynamic competition is particularly strong in microcomputer software because there is a 'race to improve and disclose'. In this respect, Schmalensee said in his testimony (point 65, emphasis added): 'Market forces create strong pressures to improve the software product. These improvements result in "upgrades" to the product. In some cases these upgrades consist of relatively minor improvements, but in other cases they consist of radical changes in the look, feel, and functionality of the product. Two major market forces are at work here. First, *software products are durable goods*, so the producer can make additional sales only as a result of selling to people who have not previously bought the product or by selling upgrades to previous customers. Selling upgrades to their installed base of users has historically been an important source of revenue for software firms. In the case of Microsoft, more than 35 percent of Office revenues comes from upgrades rather than new sales.'

An important issue in determining price–cost margins in the durable good monopoly is whether our earlier two-consumer model or the continuum model is more realistic. We would argue that for consumer goods, the continuous approximation appears to be more convincing. Indeed, if we start in a setting with a finite number of prices and a finite number of consumers, as the number of buyers increases the firm loses commitment power. In particular, for a large number of buyers and sufficient heterogeneity of consumer valuations r, the outcome resembles the one of a market with a continuum of different types. To the extent that the durable good problem does not concern final consumers but retailers and, more generally, intermediaries, we should, however, not discard the possibility that intertemporal pricing is a profitable strategy even without commitment.

10.2   Durable good monopoly with commitment

In the previous analysis, it was assumed that the firm did not to have an instrument available that would give it commitment power over price p^2 (or future prices more generally). However, several mechanisms and business practices can be used to (partially or totally) restore the firm's commitment ability. First, a solution in terms of *pricing* consists in renting the good instead of selling it. Indeed, if the monopolist rents rather than sells, it has no incentive to decrease price below the monopoly price, for the price cut would not only apply to future consumers but also to existing ones. Under renting, existing customers can renegotiate terms at each period and are therefore guaranteed to face the same conditions as later buyers. Other solutions to the commitment problem rely on *contracts*. For instance, return policies, money-back guarantees or repurchase agreements (whereby the monopolist repurchases the good if a lower price is ever observed in the market) make it costly to lower the price in the next period and achieves thereby the desired commitment not to lower prices in the future. The monopolist can also achieve commitment through *reputation*. For instance, a firm that is active in many markets can build a reputation for sticking to its preannounced price. A deviation from this price in one market would lead to losses in other markets because consumers would also expect deviations in these other markets. The *technology* of production can serve as another commitment mechanism: e.g., capacity restrictions prevent the monopolist from expanding output (and thus from reducing prices) or renting the factory makes the flow costs of staying in the market expensive. In a similar vein, the monopolist might be able to limit the durability of its product by hastening its obsolescence; this strategy of *planned obsolescence* might be achieved directly by shortening the useful life of the product or indirectly by introducing new versions of the product over time. The latter practice is particularly suited for software (for it is basically the only way to make it wear out). It also seems to be used in textbook markets, as illustrated in Case 10.2.

Case 10.2 Planned obsolescence of textbooks[22]

To avoid the 'self-competition' imposed by the durability of their product, firms may decide to introduce a new version of the product, so as to make the used units economically obsolete. Yet, periodic introduction of new versions may be motivated by other reasons: demand for existing versions may decline because the technology or the information content become outdated; the firm may face a more intense competition from new rival products. It is then a matter of empirical investigation to identify the relative importance of these alternative explanations. Using a new data set containing information on new and used textbook transactions for 1996–2000, Iizuka (2007) examines the extent to which the publishers of textbooks used in economics courses introduce new editions to 'kill off' used units. The author constructs a variable that captures the extent of competition between used and new units and examines how this affects the timing of textbook revision; he also includes various product and market attributes in the estimation (such as the age of the textbook, textbook categories, physical characteristics of the textbook, market size, and rival firm's revision decision). He finds that, at the aggregate level, textbook publishers introduce new textbooks more frequently when the share of used textbooks increases, holding all other factors constant. This result is consistent with the view that publishers introduce new editions to kill off used units and does not appear to be affected by competition among the textbooks in the same category (there is no evidence that a rival firm's revision decision increases the likelihood of revising one's own textbook). Interestingly, the accumulation of used books is found to have more impact for 'applied' than for 'principles' textbooks.

In what follows, we show that intertemporal price discrimination (taking the form of introductory offers or of clearance sales) allows the monopolist to increase profits over uniform pricing if capacities are fixed (and limited), but not if capacities are flexible. This demonstrates how capacity restrictions can solve the commitment problem facing the durable good monopoly.

10.2.1   Fixed capacity

Suppose a firm faces a binding capacity constraint $\bar{q}$. A firm may want to use an intertemporal pricing strategy to sell its good among a heterogeneous consumer population with unit demand. The monopolist produces at zero cost and may set prices and capacities for two periods. In the case of excess demand in one period, consumers are rationed randomly.[b] For the sake of simplicity we assume that there is no discounting. A good example is the (advance) sale of tickets for a particular event. A firm may provide a limited quantity at a low price in advance, we call this an *introductory offer*. Alternatively, a firm may initially sell at a high price and commit to sell the remaining units at a low price. We call this latter strategy a *clearance sale* strategy. As we will show, such intertemporal pricing strategies may dominate uniform pricing. We will also illustrate the revenue equivalence between clearance sales and introductory offers when demand is certain.

There are two types of consumers: a mass λ^H of high-valuation consumers and a mass λ^L of low-valuation consumers. For simplicity, we set the total mass of low and high types to 1, and so $\lambda^L = 1 - \lambda^H$. Without loss of generality, we can then restrict attention to quantities $\bar{q} \leq 1$. A high-type consumer has willingness to pay $r_H = 1$ for one unit and a low-type consumer has willingness to pay r_L. Consider the single-price revenue or profit function

$$\pi(q) = \begin{cases} q & \text{if } q \leq \lambda^H, \\ r_L q & \text{if } q \in (\lambda^H, 1], \end{cases}$$

where q is the quantity sold. Observe that, $\pi(q)$ has a downward jump at $q = \lambda^H$ and is thus not concave.

Let us construct a concave function $\bar{\pi}(q)$ which weakly lies above $\pi(q)$ and is constructed by taking convex combinations of the two local maxima at λ^H and 1 (see

---

[b] According to random rationing, each consumer who wants to buy a product has the same probability of being served, independently of her willingness to pay. The argument that we present here does not strictly require random (or proportional) rationing. However, it breaks down under efficient rationing.

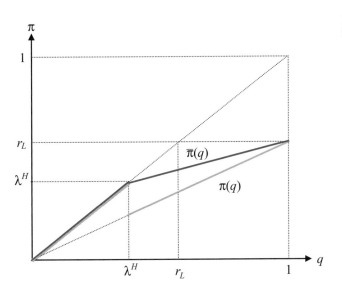

Figure 10.2 'Concavified' profit function

Figure 10.2). This 'concavified' profit function thus is

$$\bar{\pi}(q) = \begin{cases} q & \text{if } q \leq \lambda^H, \\ \left(1 - \frac{q - \lambda^H}{1 - \lambda^H}\right)\lambda^H + \left(\frac{q - \lambda^H}{1 - \lambda^H}\right)r_L & \text{if } q \in (\lambda^H, 1]. \end{cases}$$

It will turn out that a monopolist can obtain profits $\bar{\pi}(q)$ by using the appropriate intertemporal pricing strategy.

Note that the monopolist's profit of charging a uniform price of 1 is $\pi(\lambda^H)$, and that from charging a uniform price of r_L is $\pi(\bar{q})$. Clearly, if the maximum quantity the monopolist can sell is not larger than the number of high-type consumers, i.e., $\bar{q} \leq \lambda^H$, then the best the monopolist can do is to charge the uniform price $p = 1$. Suppose now that $\bar{q} \in (\lambda^H, 1)$. In this case, we have $\bar{\pi}(\bar{q}) > \max_{q \leq \bar{q}} \pi(q) = \max\{\pi(\lambda^H), \pi(\bar{q})\}$ if and only if $r_L > \lambda^H$. We now want to show that the monopolist can obtain the revenue $\bar{\pi}(\bar{q})$ by either using a clearance sale or an introductory offer strategy. Hence, if $\bar{q} \in (\lambda^H, 1)$ and $r_L > \lambda^H$, the monopolist can do better than charging a uniform price.

Clearance sales

Here, high-value consumers face a complicated task since their utility-maximizing decision may depend on the behaviour of other consumers. Clearly, if no consumer bought in the first period, the probability of obtaining the good in the second period is (weakly) higher than if all high-value consumers did buy in the first period. Consistent consumer behaviour is described by a consumer Nash equilibrium. In many situations, multiple equilibria exist. Whenever this is the case, we select the equilibrium that is most favourable for the firm. In other words, we assume that the firm is able to coordinate consumers on its preferred equilibrium. Then, suppose that all high-value consumers buy in the first period. No high-value consumer has an incentive to deviate given capacity and second-period price $p^2 = r_L$ if $1 - p^1 = \phi^*(1 - r_L)$

where $\phi^* = [\bar{q} - \lambda^H]/[1 - \lambda^H]$ is the probability of obtaining the good in period 2; this follows from the assumption of random rationing. Hence, the monopolist optimally charges the price $p^1 = (1 - \phi^*) + \phi^* r_L$. In period 2, the monopolist charges a price of r_L and sells $\bar{q} - \lambda^H$ units. His revenue is thus

$$\lambda^H \left[(1 - \phi^*)1 + \phi^* r_L\right] + \left[\bar{q} - \lambda^H\right] r_L = (1 - \phi^*)\lambda^H + \left[\bar{q} - \lambda^H + \lambda^H \phi^*\right] r_L$$
$$= (1 - \phi^*)\lambda^H + \phi^* r_L$$
$$= \bar{\pi}(\bar{q}).$$

Introductory offers

Here, the monopolist charges a first-period price of r_L and commits to the first-period capacity $k_1 = \phi^*$. In $t = 2$, he charges the price 1, and sells $(1 - \phi^*)\lambda^H$ units. His revenue is thus

$$(1 - \phi^*)\lambda^H + \phi^* r_L = \bar{\pi}(\bar{q}).$$

Under introductory offers, a mass $(1 - \phi^*)\lambda^H$ of consumers purchase the good at price 1. Under clearance sales, a mass λ^H of consumers buy at a convex combination of the high price 1 and the low price r_L, where the weight of the high price is equal to the probability of being rationed in the second period, $1 - \phi^*$. Therefore, profits that can be associated with high price are $(1 - \phi^*)\lambda^H$ under both strategies. A similar argument holds for the low price. We can thus conclude the following.

Lesson 10.5   Under fixed and limited capacity, and under demand certainty, both clearance sales and introductory offers allow the monopolist to 'concavify' its single-price revenue function and lead to the same revenue, which may be greater than with uniform pricing.

10.2.2   Flexible capacity

We now consider the possibility that the firm can adjust capacity at an initial stage without cost.[23] We still assume that the total mass of consumers with positive valuation is equal to 1, so that $\lambda^L = 1 - \lambda^H$. Consider first *uniform pricing* (i.e., $p^1 = p^2$). The profit-maximizing uniform price is equal to 1 if $\lambda^H \geq r_L$, and equal to r_L if $\lambda^H \leq r_L$. The maximal profit from uniform pricing is thus given by

$$\pi^U = \max \left\{\lambda^H, r_L\right\}.$$

Next, consider *introductory offers* (i.e., $p^1 < p^2$). The only candidate equilibrium prices are $p^1 = r_L$ and $p^2 = 1$, and total capacity $\bar{q} \geq 1$. The profit with this pricing strategy – as a function of first-period capacity $\bar{q}_1$ – is then given by

$$\pi^{IO}(\bar{q}_1) = r_L \bar{q}^1 + (1 - \bar{q}^1)\lambda^H,$$

which is linear in $\bar{q}^1$. That is, the optimal choice of first-period capacity is either $\bar{q}^1 = 0$ or $\bar{q}^1 = 1$; in either case, the monopolist effectively charges a uniform price. Hence, the introductory offer strategy is (weakly) dominated by uniform pricing.

Finally, consider the *clearance sales* pricing strategy (i.e., $p^1 > p^2$). Clearly, it is optimal to set $p^2 = r_L$, $\bar{q}^1 = \bar{q} \in [\lambda^H, 1]$, and p^1 such that the high types are just indifferent between buying in period 1 (without being rationed), and buying in period 2 (and being rationed with probability $1 - [\bar{q} - \lambda^H]/[1 - \lambda^H])$. The high type's indifference condition writes as

$$1 - p^1 = \frac{\bar{q} - \lambda^H}{1 - \lambda^H}\left(1 - p^2\right),$$

where $p^2 = r_L$. The profit-maximizing first-period price (as a function of total capacity $\bar{q}$) is then given by

$$p^1(\bar{q}) = \frac{1 - \bar{q}}{1 - \lambda^H} + \frac{\bar{q} - \lambda^H}{1 - \lambda^H}r_L,$$

and the profit by

$$\pi^{CS}(\bar{q}) = p^1(\bar{q})\lambda^H + r_L(\bar{q} - \lambda^H).$$

Since the clearance sales profit is linear in $\bar{q}$, and we assumed $\lambda^H \leq \bar{q} \leq 1$, the optimal capacity $\bar{q}$ is either $\bar{q} = \lambda^H$ or $\bar{q} = 1$. However, if $\bar{q} = \lambda^H$, then all capacity is sold at price 1, and this strategy is equivalent to setting a uniform price of 1. If, on the other hand, $\bar{q} = 1$, then $p^1 = p^2 = r_L$, which is a uniform pricing strategy. Hence, the uniform pricing strategy (weakly) dominates the clearance sales strategy as well. This can also be deduced from Figure 10.2: when q can be freely chosen, the firm obtains its global profit maximum either at λ^H or 1. In this case, π and $\bar{\pi}$ coincide and the optimal intertemporal pricing strategy degenerates to a uniform pricing strategy.

Lesson 10.6 If capacity can be adjusted without cost, there is no rationale to intertemporally price discriminate in market in which demand is certain and in which consumers do not learn over time.

This result can be shown to hold more generally. Intertemporal price discrimination can only be optimal if capacity costs are not linear and the single-price revenue function is not single-peaked.

10.2.3   Intertemporal pricing and demand uncertainty

The attractiveness of intertemporal pricing is increased in the presence of demand uncertainty. We substantitate this statement in two different market environments. The first environment is characterized by aggregate demand uncertainty, in the sense that the firm's demand is subject to shocks. In the second environment, aggregate demand is assumed to be independent of the realized state of the world, but there is uncertainty for individual consumers.

Aggregate demand uncertainty

Many markets that feature intertemporal pricing also exhibit an aggregate demand that is subject to shocks. We explore the role of demand uncertainty for the use of intertemporal pricing strategies in a simple numerical example. In particular, this will provide us with a better understanding of the logic underlying clearance sales.[24]

Suppose there are two states of the world, a good demand state and a bad demand state, which occur with probabilities $\rho(G)$ and $\rho(B)$, respectively. Consumers have unit demand and may either have a high or a low valuation for the good. High types have a valuation of $r_H = 3$, and low types a valuation of $r_L = 1$, independently of the demand state. The monopolist produces at zero cost and may set prices and capacities for two periods. In the case of excess demand in one period, consumers are rationed randomly. There is no discounting. We consider three examples, which differ by the masses of the two types of consumers in the two demand states, as summarized in the following table.

	Good demand state		Bad demand state	
	High type	Low type	High type	Low type
Example 1	2	0	0	1
Example 2	2	$\frac{1}{2}$	0	$\frac{3}{2}$
Example 3	2	2	0	3

Example 1 In the good demand state, there is a mass 2 of high valuation consumers, but no low types. In the bad demand state, there are no high types, and a mass 1 of low types. A consumer who learns that he has a high valuation can thus infer that the demand state must be good. The optimal selling policy is a clearance sale with a total capacity of (slightly less than) 2, a first-period price of 3 and a second-period price of 1. All high types will then purchase the good in the first period (anticipating that they would be rationed with probability one if they were to wait for clearance sales to occur in the second period), while all low types will purchase the good in the second period. This yields an expected profit of (almost) $\rho(G) \times 6 + \rho(B) \times 1$. It is straightforward to verify that this clearance sales policy dominates uniform pricing: a uniform price of 3 would yield a profit of only $\rho(G) \times 6$, while a uniform price of 1 would yield an expected profit of only $\rho(G) \times 2 + \rho(B) \times 1$. The clearance sales policy also performs better than the best introductory offer policy, which involves a first-period capacity of 1, a first-period price of 1, and a second-period price of 3. This yields an expected profit of only $\rho(G) \times 4 + \rho(B) \times 1$ since, in the good demand state, half of the high types are able to purchase the good at the low first-period price, while the remaining high types are rationed and purchase the good at the high second-period price. In this example, the monopolist can extract all of the surplus by using clearance sales. Such perfect price discrimination is, however, often infeasible.

Example 2 Suppose parameters are as in the first example, but suppose there is an additional mass $1/2$ of low-type consumers in each demand state. The optimal selling policy is as in the first example, yielding an expected profit of $\rho(G) \times 6 + \rho(B) \times 3/2$. While some consumers with positive valuation do not purchase the good in the good demand state, this clearance sales policy effectively implements the optimal state-contingent pricing policy, which involves a price of 3 in the good demand state, and a price of 1 in the bad demand state. Hence, as in the first example, the monopolist could not further increase its profit by learning the demand state in advance (before setting prices and capacity).

Example 3 Suppose parameters are as in the first example, but suppose there is an additional mass 2 of low-type consumers in each demand state. By choosing the same clearance sales policy as in the previous examples, the monopolist would obtain an expected profit of $\rho(G) \times 6 + \rho(B) \times 2$. Alternatively, it may choose a clearance sales policy with a total capacity of 3, a first-period price of 2, and a second-period price of 1. Here, the first-period price is less than the high type's valuation of 3 since by postponing the purchasing decision until the second period, a high type is not rationed with probability 1 but with probability $1/2$. Expected profit is then $\rho(G) \times (2 \times 2 + 1 \times 1) + \rho(B) \times 3 \times 1 = \rho(G) \times 5 + \rho(B) \times 3$. Hence, this clearance sales policy performs better than the first if and only if the bad demand state is sufficiently likely.

The optimal clearance sales policy dominates uniform pricing: a uniform price of 3 yields an expected profit of $\rho(G) \times 6$, while a uniform price of 1 results in an expected profit of $\rho(G) \times 4 + \rho(B) \times 3$. Clearance sales also perform better than introductory offers. To see this, consider the best introductory offer policy, which consists in setting a first-period capacity of 3, a first-period price of 1, and a second-period price of 3. This policy results in an expected profit of $\rho(G) \times 9/2 + \rho(B) \times 3$. While this introductory offer policy may dominate uniform pricing, it is always dominated by a clearance sales policy (namely the one with an overall capacity of 3).

The examples demonstrate that due to demand uncertainty, intertemporal pricing strategies such as introductory offers and clearance sales can dominate uniform pricing even in an environment in which there are no capacity costs ex ante. Critical for the use of clearance sales is the possibility to commit to total capacity and a second-period price. Critical for the use of introductory offers is the possibility of limiting the supply of the product in the first period. Whenever both types of strategies are feasible, one can show in the simple two-type model that the optimal sales strategy may be a clearance sales strategy but never an introductory offer strategy. This also implies that the revenue equivalence under demand certainty fails to hold under aggregate demand uncertainty.

Lesson 10.7   Even if capacity can be adjusted ex ante without cost, intertemporal price discrimination can be profit maximizing under aggregate demand uncertainty.

This insight is derived under the assumption that within a 'season' capacity adjustments are prohibitively costly. As such costs change in an industry over time, this gives a clear indication that price discrimination should disappear as within-season adjustments become less costly, as argued in Case 10.3.

Case 10.3 Zara and the clothing industry

Demand for clothing is subject to a large degree of demand uncertainty due to varying
weather conditions and changes in tastes. However, before a new season starts, retailers
have to order stocks for the new selection. Restocking during the season used to be
difficult. For instance for the US in the 1980s, Pashigian (1988) reports a mean lead time of
about 35 weeks for US orders from the Far East, and of more than 14 weeks for domestic
orders. As a consequence, retailers often face stocks they have to clear before the new
collection arrives. They do so with the help of season or clearance sales. More recently,
flexible manufacturing and advances in the use of IT have reduced this lead time. This has
allowed vertically integrated clothing companies – Zara being the prime example –
to replenish stocks rapidly. Interestingly, Zara uses clearance sales less frequently.

Uncertainty for individual consumers

The previous results rest on the assumption that consumers do not learn about their valuations
over time. A different market environment has to be considered if consumers obtain better
knowledge about their valuation for the product over time. This may apply to many ticket
purchases where consumers are initially uncertain whether e.g. the particular date fits them
well. Then, even if within 'season' adjustments of capacity are feasible at no cost (so that
the firm cannot commit ex ante to a limited capacity), intertemporal price discrimination may
be the profit-maximizing strategy: a firm may want to distinguish between different types of
consumers who have different valuations of the good and whose valuation for the product is
revealed over time.

   The simplest illustration of this result is probably to consider a two-period, two-type
model with no discounting in which there is only uncertainty for individual consumers but in
which aggregate demand is independent of the realized state of the world.[25] Suppose that a
share λ of consumers do not face any uncertainty about their valuation and thus effectively
know it from the beginning. We denote this valuation by r. Suppose that this is also the expected
valuation of the remaining share of consumers but that with probability $1/2$ the valuation is
$r + d$ and with the same probability it is $r - d$. These consumers learn their valuation only after
the first period. We assume that the consumers' underlying random variables are independent
of one another so that in period 2 a share λ of consumers has valuation r, a share $(1 - \lambda)/2$
has valuation $r + d$, and the remaining share $(1 - \lambda)/2$ has valuation $r - d$.

   Suppose that a firm faces unit cost $c < r$. Hence, if the firm sells the product only
in period 1, it optimally sets $p^1 = r$. Selling in period 1 only allows the firm to extract the
full expected surplus because all consumers are assumed to have the same expected valuation.
If the firm sells in period 2 only, it sets its price p^2 equal to r or $r + d$. Clearly, the former
option performs worse than selling at $p^1 = r$ in period 1 only. So we concentrate on the latter
strategy. The firm's profit in this case is $(1 - \lambda)(r + d - c)/2$. For c sufficiently close to r, the
firm can reach a higher profit by selling in period 2 instead of period 1. The exact condition is
that $d > \frac{1+\lambda}{1-\lambda}(r - c)$. The reason is that the firm would rather sell only in the good state to ex
ante uninformed consumers if $c > r - d$, which is a necessary condition for selling in period

2 only to dominate selling in period 1 only. However, since the firm loses ex ante informed consumers when it increases its price above r, the condition is much more demanding. If the reverse holds, the firm prefers to sell in period 1 only rather than in period 2 only.

A possibly optimal intertemporal pricing strategy is to set $p^1 = r$ and $p^2 = r + d$. Note that in this case, those consumers who face uncertainty are indifferent between buying in period 1 or 2 and the firm makes profit $\lambda(r - c) + (1 - \lambda)(r + d - c)/2$. Clearly, this dominates selling in period 2 only. It possibly also dominates selling in period 1 only. Indeed, $\lambda(r - c) + (1 - \lambda)(r + d - c)/2 > r - c$ reduces to $d > r - c$ or, equivalently, $c > r - d$. Hence, whenever it is better for the firm to sell in period 2 only rather than in period 1 only, intertemporal pricing leads to higher profits. Intertemporal pricing rather than selling in period 1 only is profit maximizing if and only if the valuation of ex ante uncertain consumers in the negative realization is less than the unit cost.

> **Lesson 10.8** **A firm may optimally use intertemporal pricing as a price discrimination device in an environment in which the firm can perfectly predict its demand but in which not all consumers can perfectly predict their valuation at the beginning.**

We note that in this setting, the firm has unlimited capacity and does not need to commit to production in the beginning. Here, the driving force is the presence of different consumer types which make screening profitable for the firm. By delaying her purchasing decision to period 2, a consumer can condition her purchase on her realized valuation. She thus avoids having bought the product when her valuation turns out to be low. Finally, we note that buying in period 2 is equivalent to a contract that is signed in period 1 before the individual uncertainty is resolved, but that allows the consumer to obtain a full refund at zero opportunity costs.

10.3   Behaviour-based price discrimination

Price discrimination is behaviour-based when prices are based on purchasing history. In the e-commerce world, sellers are able to monitor consumer transactions, typically through the use of 'cookies'. A cookie is a unique identifier which is sent by a website for storage by the consumer's web browser software. The cookie contains information about the current transaction and persists after the session has ended. As a result, at the next visit of the website by the consumer, the server can retrieve identification and match it with details of past interactions, which allows the seller to condition the price offers that he makes today on past behaviour. In other words, cookies make behaviour-based price discrimination feasible. Note that other technologies can be used toward the same objective: static IP addresses, credit card numbers, user authentication, and a variety of other mechanisms can be used to identify user history.

To account for such possibility, we extend the previous model with a continuum of consumer types but consider now a non-durable good so that consumption occurs in the period of purchase.[26] As above, there are two periods ($t = 1, 2$) and consumers may want to buy in any period; a consumer's willingness to pay in each period is given by $r \sim U[0, 1]$;

the consumers and the firm share the same discount factor δ; the firm faces a zero marginal cost of production. The firm cannot commit to future prices but it can make the second-period price conditional on whether the consumer has purchased in the first period, i.e. the firm sets $(p^1, p^2(p^1), \tilde{p}^2(p^1))$, where $\tilde{p}^2$ is offered to consumers who did not buy in the first period.

Consider the second period, supposing that all consumers $r \in [\hat{r}, 1]$ have bought in period 1. Then, provided that $\hat{r} \geq 1/2$, the profit-maximizing price for consumers who bought in period 1 is $p^2 = \hat{r}$. The other consumers are offered the product at $\tilde{p}^2 = \hat{r}/2$. In period 1, the indifferent consumer satisfies $\hat{r} - p^1 + \delta(\hat{r} - p^2) = \delta(\hat{r} - \tilde{p}^2)$. Substituting for profit-maximizing second-period prices, we have $\hat{r} - p^1 = \delta\frac{1}{2}\hat{r}$, or $\hat{r} = \frac{2}{2-\delta}p^1$. Hence,

$$p^2 = \tfrac{2}{2-\delta}p^1 > p^1 \quad \text{and} \quad \tilde{p}^2 = \tfrac{1}{2-\delta}p^1 < p^1,$$

which implies that $\tilde{p}^2 < p^1 < p^2$: consumers who bought (resp. did not buy) in period 1 are offered the product in period 2 at a higher (resp. lower) price than in period 1.

In the first period, the firm maximizes its profit, which we can rewrite as a function of $\hat{r}$ only:

$$p^1(1 - \hat{r}) + \delta p^2(1 - \hat{r}) + \delta \tilde{p}^2(\hat{r} - \tilde{p}^2)$$
$$= \tfrac{2-\delta}{2}\hat{r}(1 - \hat{r}) + \delta\hat{r}(1 - \hat{r}) + \delta\tfrac{1}{4}\hat{r}^2$$
$$= \tfrac{2+\delta}{2}\hat{r}(1 - \hat{r}) + \delta\tfrac{1}{4}\hat{r}^2.$$

The first-order condition of profit maximization is

$$\tfrac{2+\delta}{2}(1 - 2\hat{r}) + \delta\tfrac{1}{2}\hat{r} = 0 \Leftrightarrow \tfrac{2+\delta}{2} = \left(2 + \tfrac{\delta}{2}\right)\hat{r} \Leftrightarrow \hat{r} = \tfrac{2+\delta}{4+\delta},$$

which is greater than $1/2$, as postulated. Hence, prices are

$$p^1 = \frac{4 - \delta^2}{2(4 + \delta)}, \quad p^2 = \frac{2 + \delta}{4 + \delta}, \quad \tilde{p}^2 = \frac{2 + \delta}{2(4 + \delta)},$$

with the property that $p^1 < 1/2$. The firm's profit is

$$\pi = \frac{(2 + \delta)^2}{4(4 + \delta)}.$$

Lesson 10.9   A firm that sells a good over two periods and cannot commit to future prices conditions its second-period price on purchase history.

If the firm was able to commit to future prices, it would not be in its interest to make prices conditional upon purchasing history. Indeed, with commitment, it is profit maximizing to set the price equal to $1/2$ in each period. This yields a higher profit of $(1 + \delta)/4$. The logic is related to the standard commitment problem in a durable good environment, as we will show next.

The present model can be interpreted as a model of renting a durable good, where the rental price can be conditioned upon previous consumer behaviour. Here, the consumer who rents foresees that he will be charged a higher price in the second period. In the durable good problem without commitment, the firm would make profit equal to $\frac{1}{4}(2 + \delta)^2/(4 + \delta)$ as has been shown earlier. This is the same profit as in the rental model in which the firm uses behaviour-based price discrimination. Thus, the difference between rental and sale of a durable good disappears if the firm is able to price discriminate between previous buyers and non-buyers. Indeed, the discounted price for renting the products in the two periods is the same as the price for purchasing the durable good. Prices and quantities coincide in the two models. This shows the equivalence of the buying and renting models.

Lesson 10.10 **If a durable good monopolist operates in a market that opens for two periods and is able to condition its rental price on rental history, selling or renting out a durable good is revenue equivalent.**

To better understand the equivalence, note that since the firm and consumers have the same discount rate, the firm and consumers who buy in period 1 are only interested in the expected payment for the good in period 1 (which may be paid in period 1 and give the right to consume it in both periods, or which may be rented over the two periods). Consumers who do not buy in period 1 constitute residual demand (which is priced according to $\hat{r}/2$ in our linear demand model) in the durable and the non-durable good model. Consumers foresee the prices in period 2 and thus a price p^1 leads to an expected discounted payment, which is linear in p^1. Then it does not matter whether the firm rents the good and extracts the payment $p^1 + \delta p^2$ or whether it charges this amount upfront as a durable good monopolist.[c]

The previous model was based on the assumption that consumers cannot prevent the firm from observing their purchase history. In a number of situations, however, consumers can take defensive measures. For instance, no one is forced to join a loyalty programme and it is possible to set one's browser to reject cookies or to erase them after a session is over.[d] If consumers have the possibility to hide their previous behaviour (possibly at some cost), they can pretend that they are visiting a website for the first time. Therefore, as usual in menu pricing, sellers are bound to offer buyers some extra benefits in order to prevent them from hiding their identity.[27]

Behaviour-based price discrimination is also relevant under oligopoly, as has been analysed in Chapter 7. Such price discrimination may be used to poach customers from competitors. The main insight in this context was that the possibility of discrimination makes competition more intense after initial customer bases have been built. However, this tends to reduce competitive pressure at the stage where the initial customer base is determined, leading to high initial prices.[28]

[c] The revenue equivalence does not hold in a market that opens for more than two periods.

[d] According to the Jupiter Research 2004 survey, an increasing number of people are blocking cookies or deleting them to protect their privacy or security: nearly 58% of online users deleted the small files; as many as 39% may be deleting cookies from their primary computer every month. (Sharma, D. C., CNET News.com, 16 March 2005).

Review questions

1. If a durable good monopolist cannot commit to future prices, does the number of consumers matter? Explain.

2. Does a durable good monopolist have an incentive to set its prices flexibly in each period? Discuss.

3. Why would a monopolist deviate from uniform pricing and set non-constant prices? And what selling policies may it choose?

4. What happens if a firm can set individualized prices depending on previous purchases?

Further reading

For the basic analysis of the two-period durable good monopoly, we refer to Bulow (1982). An elaborate analysis on the importance of the number of consumers is provided by von der Fehr and Kühn (1995). Intertemporal price discrimination with demand certainty is explored by Wilson (1988) and, with demand uncertainty, by Nocke and Peitz (2007). A rather informal introduction to ticket pricing is provided by Courty (2003). More on behaviour-based price discrimination can be found in Fudenberg and Villas-Boas (2007).

11 Bundling

Just as inducing self-selection by offering a menu of versions enhances the monopolist's ability to extract surplus, so can selling different products as a combination package. Two such techniques are bundling and tying. The practice of *bundling* consists in selling two or more products in a single package (bundling is said to be 'pure' when only the package is available, or 'mixed' when the products are also available separately). The distinguishing feature of bundling is that the bundled goods are always combined in fixed proportions. In contrast, the related practice of *tying* (or *tie-in sales*) is less restrictive in that proportions might vary in the mix of goods.

Economists have given different explanations for bundling and tying. First, some explanations are too transparent to merit formal treatment. In the case of perfectly complementary products, such as matching right and left shoes, no one questions the rationale of bundling: there is virtually no demand for separate products and bundling them together presumably conserves packaging and inventory costs. In other cases where products are not necessarily complements, various cost efficiencies might provide a basis for profitable bundling. In many instances the opportunity cost for consumers to combine various components typically exceeds the assembling cost of the manufacturer (take, e.g., a personal computer). Also, in the business of services, the cost structure is often characterized by a high ratio of fixed to variable costs and a high degree of cost sharing, which makes it cost effective to use the same facilities, equipment and personnel to offer multiple services as a single 'package' (think of 'all-inclusive' holiday packages).

More interestingly, even in the absence of cost efficiencies, there are demand-side incentives that makes bundling and tying profitable strategies. On the one hand, bundling and tying can be used as entry-deterrent strategies; the recent case brought against Microsoft by the European Commission follows this line of argument. We defer the analysis of this motivation for bundling to Chapter 16. On the other hand, bundling and tying can serve as an effective tool for sorting consumers and price discriminate between them. This is the motivation that we study in this chapter. As in the previous chapters, we first gain useful insights by considering bundling and tying in a monopoly setting (Sections 11.1 and 11.2). We turn then to an analysis of bundling in competitive settings (Section 11.3). Case 11.1 illustrates how common the practices of bundling and tying are in the information economy.

Case 11.1 **Examples of bundling in the information economy**

CONTENT. (i) Subscription to cable television is typically to a package of channels together, rather than to each channel separately; similarly for subscription to magazines, for CDs (which can be seen as bundles of different songs) or for newspapers (which can be seen as a bundle of news, arts, lifestyle and sports content). (ii) Software companies sell individual products but also offer packages (or 'suites') consisting of several applications (e.g., Microsoft Office suite). (iii) As for software platforms, many tasks that used to be performed by stand-alone applications have become integrated into other applications (e.g., spell checkers, which were originally sold separately from word processors) or into the software platform itself. (iv) Movie distributors frequently force theaters to acquire 'bad' movies if they want to show 'good' movies from the same distributor.

INFRASTRUCTURE. (i) Computer systems are comprised of many components. Typically, the microprocessor, memory, and other components are combined to create a hardware platform such as a PalmOne Zire PDA, a Nokia mobile phone handset, or an Xbox game console. (ii) Audio equipment usually can be bought as separate components or as a complete system. (iii) Photocopier manufacturers offer bundles that include the copier itself as well as maintenance; they also offer the alternative of buying the copier and servicing separately. (iv) A classic example of tying was the practice adopted by IBM in the era of punch-card computers: IBM sold its machines with the condition that the buyer use only IBM-produced tabulating cards. A current example involves computer printers (ink cartridges are generally specific to a particular model of a particular manufacturer).

11.1   A formal analysis of monopoly bundling

Bundling can be thought of as a form of second-degree price discrimination. First, when a bundle is sold at a lower price than the sum of the prices of the components, the strategy resembles nonlinear pricing with quantity discounts (it is as if one component was sold at its individual price and the other component at a discounted price, equal to the difference between the bundle price and the individual price of the first component). Second, bundling is a 'twisted' form of menu pricing: instead of increasing the menu of prices to better cater for consumer heterogeneity, bundling amounts to setting a unique price for several goods in order to reduce consumer heterogeneity.

This can be illustrated in an example with two consumers with negatively correlated valuations.[29] Suppose two products are either sold separately or as a bundle to two consumers. Each product is produced at zero cost and consumers demand up to one unit of each product. Consumer 1 has a valuation of 3 for product 1 and 2 for product 2, while consumer 2 has the reverse valuations. Then under separate selling, the firm sells each product at price 2 and obtains a profit equal to 8. Under pure bundling the firm can increase the price for the bundle to 5 and both consumers still buy. Hence, since consumer valuations are negatively correlated, bundling is profit increasing. As the following analysis reveals, bundling is profitable even if valuations are uncorrelated.[30]

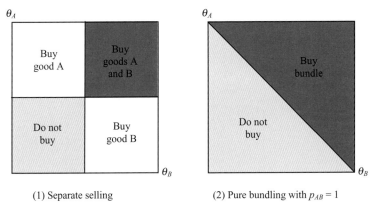

(1) Separate selling   (2) Pure bundling with $p_{AB} = 1$

Figure 11.1 Separate selling vs pure bundling

Consider a monopoly firm producing two goods A and B at zero cost.[31] A unit mass of consumers have preferences over the two goods. Each consumer is identified by a couple (θ_A, θ_B), where θ_A and θ_B are the consumer's respective valuations for goods A and B. Consumers are distributed with density $f(\theta_A, \theta_B)$. For simplicity, we assume that (θ_A, θ_B) is uniformly distributed over the unit square. That is, the valuations for A and B are independent and uniform over $[0, 1]$. We also assume that a consumer's valuation for the bundle is equal to the sum of her separate valuations for the component goods. This assumption of *strict additivity* is justified for independently valued goods. However, it is restrictive for interrelated goods: when goods are complements (resp. substitutes), the valuation for the bundle is larger (resp. lower) than the sum of the separate valuations for the component goods. We will return to the case of interrelated goods below.

We compare three strategies for the monopolist: separate selling (the goods are sold separately), pure bundling (only bundles containing the two goods are sold), and mixed bundling (the goods are both sold as a bundle and separately).

11.1.1 Pure bundling as a device to offer a discount

Consider first *separate selling*. If the two goods are sold separately, they are priced independently and the profit maximizing prices are easily found as $p_A^s = p_B^s = 0.5$. Then, under separate selling, the firm's profits are equal to

$$\pi^s = 0.25 + 0.25 = 0.5.$$

Consider now *pure bundling*. When selling goods A and B as a bundle, the monopolist can replicate the previous solution by setting the price of the bundle equal to the sum of the optimal prices under separate selling; that is, $p_{AB} = p_A^s + p_B^s = 1$. Profits are then the same as under separate selling, but the identity of the buying consumers changes. This is best seen by comparing the two panels of Figure 11.1.

What is important to note is that there are now more marginal consumers than in the case of separate selling (taking into account that a marginal consumer here buys a unit of each of the two products). It follows that the monopolist has larger incentives to decrease the bundle price than to decrease the separate prices. To see this, consider a price reduction of ε

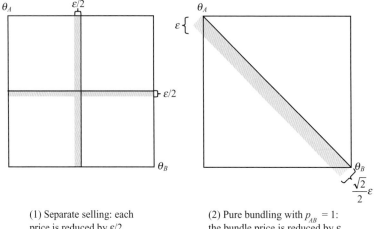

(1) Separate selling: each
price is reduced by $\varepsilon/2$

(2) Pure bundling with $p_{AB} = 1$:
the bundle price is reduced by ε

Figure 11.2 Effect of price reduction under separate selling and pure bundling

for the bundle (from $p_{AB} = 1$) and compare it to a corresponding price reduction of $\varepsilon/2$ for each product (from $p_i^s = 0.5$). The comparison is shown graphically in Figure 11.2. Under separate selling, the monopolist sells $\varepsilon/2$ additional units of good A and $\varepsilon/2$ additional units of good B, i.e. the equivalent of $\varepsilon/2$ additional bundles. Under pure bundling, for small ε, the number of additional bundles sold can be approximated by $\sqrt{2}(\sqrt{2}/2)\varepsilon = \varepsilon$. Hence, for a corresponding price reduction, twice as many additional bundles are sold under pure bundling.

From the above argument, we understand that the monopolist can reach higher profits by setting $p_{AB} < 1$. For a given price p_{AB}, the consumers who do not buy are those with $\theta_A + \theta_B < p_{AB}$; there are $\frac{1}{2}(p_{AB})^2$ of them. Therefore, the demand at price p_{AB} is equal to $1 - \frac{1}{2}(p_{AB})^2$ and the profit-maximizing price is found by solving: $\max p_{AB} \left(1 - \frac{1}{2}(p_{AB})^2\right)$. The first-order condition yields $1 - 3/2(p_{AB})^2 = 0$. The profit-maximizing price of the bundle is

$$p_{AB}^b = \sqrt{\tfrac{2}{3}} \approx 0.82 < 1.$$

Hence, the monopolist chooses a price which is lower than the combined price under separate selling and achieves thereby higher profits:

$$\pi^b = \tfrac{2}{3}\sqrt{\tfrac{2}{3}} \approx 0.544 > 0.5.$$

> **Lesson 11.1** **If consumers have heterogeneous but uncorrelated valuations for two products, then the monopolist increases its profits under pure bundling compared to separate selling. It increases its demand by selling the bundle cheaper than the combined price under separate selling.**

Noteworthy is the fact that pure bundling works although the two products are independently valued. As hinted above and as we will discuss formally below, it would work even better, though, if the values for the two products were negatively correlated.

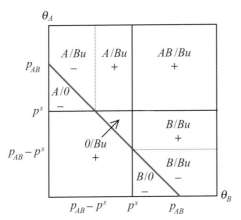

Figure 11.3 Consumer surplus under pure bundling vs. separate selling

'X/Y' means that the consumer buys X under separate selling and Y under pure bundling; '+' ('−')means that pure bundling increases (decreases) consumer surplus with respect to separate selling.

Let us now examine how going from separate selling to pure bundling affects consumers. As depicted in Figure 11.3, some consumers are made better off and others are made worse off. Basically, *the consumers who have a relatively high valuation for both goods prefer pure bundling, while those who have a high valuation for one good and a low valuation for the other prefer separate selling.* The consumers who prefer pure bundling can be divided into three groups: (i) consumers with $\theta_A, \theta_B \geq p^s$ buy both goods anyway but do it at a discount under pure bundling; (ii) consumers with $\theta_i \geq p^s$ and $\theta_j \geq p_{AB} - p^s$ buy one more good under pure bundling and increase their surplus as $\theta_A + \theta_B - p^b_{AB} \geq \theta_i - p^s$; (iii) consumers with $\theta_A + \theta_B \geq p^b_{AB}$ and $\theta_A, \theta_B < p^s$ buy nothing when goods are sold separately but buy the bundle under pure bundling. The consumers who prefer separate selling can be divided into two groups: (i) consumers with $\theta_A + \theta_B \geq p^b_{AB}$ and $\theta_i < p^b_{AB} - p^s$ buy one more good under pure bundling but reduce their surplus as $\theta_i - p^s \geq \theta_A + \theta_B - p^b_{AB}$; (ii) consumers with $\theta_i \geq p^s$ and $\theta_A + \theta_B < p^b_{AB}$ buy one good when goods are sold separately but nothing under pure bundling.

Computing aggregate consumer surplus, we observe that it is higher under pure bundling. Indeed, we have:

$$CS^s = \int_{p^s}^1 (\theta_A - p)\, d\theta_A + \int_{p^s}^1 (\theta_B - p)\, d\theta_B = (1 - p^s)^2 = \tfrac{1}{4},$$

$$CS^b = \int_0^{p^b_{AB}} \left(\int_{p^b_{AB}-\theta_B}^1 (\theta_A + \theta_B - p^b_{AB})\, d\theta_A \right) d\theta_B$$

$$+ \int_{p^b_{AB}}^1 \left(\int_0^1 (\theta_A + \theta_B - p^b_{AB})\, d\theta_A \right) d\theta_B$$

$$= 1 - p^b_{AB} + \tfrac{1}{6} \left(p^b_{AB} \right)^3 = 1 - \tfrac{8}{27} \sqrt{6} \approx 0.27 > \tfrac{1}{4}.$$

Since bundling increases the number of consumers who are served, it is of little surprise that, on aggregate, consumers are made better off by pure bundling compared to separate selling.

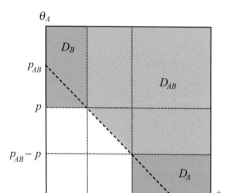

Figure 11.4 Demand under mixed bundling

11.1.2   Mixed bundling

If the firm practices mixed bundling, it sells products A and B separately (at respective prices p_A and p_B) in addition to the bundle consisting of A and B (at price p_{AB}). Then, consumers who are indifferent between buying product $k = A, B$ and not buying are of type $\widehat{\theta}_k = p_k$. Consumers who are indifferent between product k and the bundle AB satisfy $\theta_k - p_k = \theta_A + \theta_B - p_{AB}$. Hence, we can write $\widetilde{\theta}_B = p_{AB} - p_A$ and $\widetilde{\theta}_A = p_{AB} - p_B$. We restrict the analysis to symmetric situations such that $p_A = p_B \equiv p$. As long as the bundle is offered at a discount ($p_{AB} < 2p$), the demand for product A (and for product B) and the demand for the bundle are respectively given by (see Figure 11.4):

$$D_A (p, p_{AB}) = D_B (p, p_{AB}) = (1 - p)(p_{AB} - p),$$

$$D_{AB} (p, p_{AB}) = (1 - p_{AB} + p)^2 - \tfrac{1}{2}(2p - p_{AB})^2.$$

Hence, the profit function for prices such that demand for products A, B and AB is positive and $p_A = p_B = p$ is

$$\pi(p_A, p_B, p_{AB}) = 2p\left[(1 - p)(p_{AB} - p)\right]$$
$$+ p_{AB}\left[(1 - p_{AB} + p)^2 - \tfrac{1}{2}(2p - p_{AB})^2\right].$$

The first-order condition with respect to p gives $\partial \pi / \partial p = 2(2 - 3p)(p_{AB} - p) = 0$. It follows that

$$p_A^m = p_B^m = \tfrac{2}{3} \approx 0.67.$$

Taking the first-order condition with respect to p_{AB} and evaluating it at $p = 2/3$, one finds $\tfrac{7}{3} - 4p_{AB} + \tfrac{3}{2}p_{AB}^2 = 0$. Among the two roots of this equation, we keep the one that meets our initial assumption, $p_{AB} < 2p$, i.e.

$$p_{AB}^m = \tfrac{1}{3}(4 - \sqrt{2}) \approx 0.86.$$

Therefore, the monopolist's profits under mixed bundling are

$$\pi^m \equiv \pi\left(\tfrac{2}{3}, \tfrac{2}{3}, \tfrac{1}{3}(4 - \sqrt{2})\right) \approx 0.549.$$

Here, the bundle is sold at a discount since $p_A^m + p_B^m > p_{AB}^m$. Note that the goods sold individually are more expensive than under separate selling: $p_k^m > p_k^s$. The intuition for this result is that demand reacts less sensitively to price changes of p_A and p_B for given p_{AB} under mixed bundling than in the case of separate selling. Note also that the bundle is more expensive than under pure bundling: $p_{AB}^m > p_{AB}^b$. Here the intuition is similar: demand reacts less sensitively to a price change of p_{AB} for given p_A and p_B under mixed bundling than in the case of pure bundling.

> **Lesson 11.2**   Mixed bundling allows the monopolist to increase its profits even further than pure bundling. Under mixed bundling, the bundle is more expensive than under pure bundling and the individual components are more expensive than under separate selling.

Going from pure bundling to mixed bundling affects consumers in diverse ways. Redoing the same type of analysis as above, we can identify three groups of consumers that are made worse off, and two groups that are made better off. Computing aggregate consumer surplus under mixed bundling, CS^m, and comparing it to the values we obtained in the other two cases, we can show that consumers are globally worse off under mixed bundling than under pure bundling, but better off than under separate selling: $CS^b > CS^m > CS^s$.[a]

> **Lesson 11.3**   Consumers may be worse off under mixed bundling than under pure bundling.

Now, adding the firm's profit to consumer surplus, we can compute welfare under the three regimes and we obtain the following ranking: $W^b = 0.819 > W^m = 0.804 > W^s = 0.75$. We observe thus that *pure bundling yields the largest welfare among the three regimes*. However, this conclusion depends on the assumptions that underlie our analysis: (i) the products are independently valued, (ii) the consumers' valuations for the two products are not correlated and are distributed uniformly, (iii) the marginal cost of production is equal to zero. The latter assumption is crucial. Indeed, if the goods were produced at a positive marginal cost, it could be the case that under pure bundling, some consumers would buy a product although their valuation for that product is below the marginal cost of production. Mixed bundling would correct this inefficiency by inducing such consumers to buy a single product rather than the bundle, which tends to improve welfare compared to pure bundling.

11.1.3   Extensions

We now extend the previous analysis in several directions. First, we consider cases where the joint consumption of the two products enhances (or reduces) the perceived value within each consumer; products are then said to be 'interrelated'. Second, we assume that the consumers'

---

[a] The exact value is $CS^m = \frac{5}{27} + \frac{4}{81}\sqrt{2} \approx 0.255$.

valuations for the two products are correlated rather than independent. Finally, we extend the analysis to more than two component products.

Interrelated products

When the monopolist sells complementary products, the value consumers attach to the bundle is larger than the sum of the values they attach to the component products, and conversely for substitutable products. To model this, let us write the gross valuation for the bundle as $\theta_{AB} = (1 + \gamma)(\theta_A + \theta_B)$, where $\gamma > 0$ for complements, $\gamma < 0$ for substitutes and $\gamma = 0$ for independently valued products (like in the previous setting). As a motivating example for the case of $\gamma > 0$, think of the Microsoft Office suite that combines (among others) Word and Excel. Because it is possible to create links between the two applications and because the commands are very similar, the bundle is, per se, more attractive for consumers than separate products. This seems to reinforce the profitability of pure bundling with respect to separate sales. However, it can be shown that the advantage that pure bundling has over separate selling tends to decrease as the synergies between the two products become stronger. Establishing this argument is a bit tedious and we leave it as an exercise for the motivated reader (see the exercises on the accompanying web page). We just give here the main intuition: as complementarity between the two products increases, less and less consumers are interested in consuming one product in isolation; therefore, most consumers buy either the two products or nothing, meaning that separate selling becomes equivalent to pure bundling.[b]

Correlated values

We have shown above that pure bundling improves profit over separate selling when the two products are independently valued. We also saw that bundling works even better when the values for the two products are negatively correlated. Let us now show that bundling indeed works better under negative than under positive correlation. To introduce correlated values, we assume that the valuation for A is uniformly distributed over $[0, 1]$ and that the valuation for B is obtained from the valuation for A in the following way: $\theta_B = \rho \theta_A + (1 - \rho)(1 - \theta_A)$, with $0 \leq \rho \leq 1$. If $\rho = 1$, then $\theta_B = \theta_A$: the two values are perfectly positively correlated (all of the consumers lie along the 45-degree line); if $\rho = 0$, then $\theta_B = 1 - \theta_A$: the two values are perfectly negatively correlated (all of the consumers lie along the opposite diagonal, $\theta_A + \theta_B = 1$). Let us contrast these two extreme cases.

Consider first *separate selling*. As far as product A is concerned, the demand comes from the consumers with a value of θ_A larger than p_A, whatever the value of ρ. Therefore, $D_A(p_A) = 1 - p_A$ and the optimal price for the monopolist is $p_A^s = 1/2$. The same analysis applies for product B when $\rho = 1$ (since $\theta_B = \theta_A$): $p_B^s = 1/2$. When $\rho = 0$, the consumers who buy B are such that $\theta_B = 1 - \theta_A \geq p_B$, or $\theta_A \leq 1 - p_B$. Hence, $D_B(p_B) = 1 - p_B$ and, again, $p_B^s = 1/2$. So, in the two extreme cases of perfect positive or negative correlation, the monopolist sets the same prices for the separate products and earns a profit of $\pi^s = 2 \times 1/2 \times 1/2 = 1/2$. There is, however, one important difference between the two cases since the identity of the buyers changes: when $\rho = 1$, the consumers with $1/2 \leq \theta_A \leq 1$ buy

---

[b] The two regimes are certainly equivalent for $\gamma > 1$ (i.e., when joint consumption more than doubles the sum of the values attached to separate components) as no consumer decides to buy isolated products.

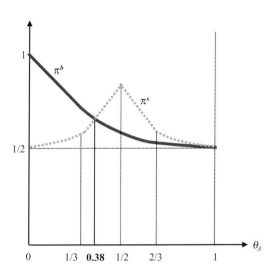

Figure 11.5 Separate selling vs. pure bundling with correlated values

both products; in contrast, when $\rho = 0$, the consumers with $0 \leq \theta_A \leq 1/2$ buy product A and those with $1/2 \leq \theta_A \leq 1$ buy product B.

Consider now *pure bundling*. Under the assumption of strict additivity, the valuation for the bundle is $\theta_A + \theta_B$, which is equal to $2\theta_A$ for $\rho = 1$ and to 1 for $\rho = 0$. In the former case (perfect positive correlation), the demand for the bundle is $D_{AB}(p_{AB}) = 1 - \frac{1}{2}p_{AB}$; the optimal price is then equal to $p_{AB}^b = 1$. All consumers with $\theta_A \geq 1/2$ buy the bundle and profit is then equal to $\pi^b(1) = 1/2 = \pi^s$: *pure bundling leaves profit unchanged when values are perfectly positively correlated.* The reason is simple: the consumers who buy the bundle are exactly the same as those who buy the two products under separate selling; bundling does not expand demand. In contrast, in the latter case (perfect negative correlation), all consumers value the bundle at 1. Hence, the monopolist sets $p_{AB}^b = 1$, sells to the whole market and makes a profit of $\pi^b(0) = 1 = 2\pi^s$: *pure bundling gives twice as much profit as separate selling when values are perfectly negatively correlated.* Here, bundling dramatically increases demand: all consumers buy only one product when products are sold separately, whereas they all buy both products when they are sold as a bundle. Performing the comparison for all values of $\rho \in [0, 1]$, it can be shown that pure bundling outperforms separate selling only if $\rho < \sqrt{1/7} \simeq 0.38$, as illustrated in Figure 11.5.[32]

Lesson 11.4   **Profits are higher under pure bundling than under separate selling if and only if the correlation between the values for the two products is negative, or sufficiently weak if positive.**

The intuition for this result should be clear by now. By selling a bundle at a lower price, the monopolist attempts to attract consumers who place a relatively low value on either of the two products but who are willing to pay a reasonable sum for the bundle. When the two products are sold separately, these consumers would buy a single product, but if the products are sold as a bundle, they would buy the bundle and, therefore, acquire a product they would not have purchased otherwise. This strategy works, however, provided that the reservation

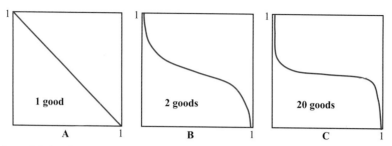

Demand for bundles of 1, 2 and 20 goods with i.i.d. valuations uniformly distributed over [0,1]. The vertical axis measures price per good; the horizontal axis measures the quantity of bundles as a fraction of total population. (Source: Bakos and Brynjolfsson, 1999)

Figure 11.6 Bundling an increasing number of goods

prices for the individual products are sufficiently different. If so, bundling reduces variation in reservation prices and, thereby, enables the monopolist to capture more of the product's value.

Larger number of products

In our initial analysis, we assumed that the valuation for the two products, (θ_A, θ_B), was uniformly distributed over the unit square. Let us assume now that θ_A and θ_B are independently distributed uniformly over the unit interval. If sold separately, each product generates a linear demand curve, like in Panel A of Figure 11.6. If the monopolist sells the two products as a bundle, the valuation for the bundle will go from zero (for those consumers who value both goods at zero) to two (for those consumers who value both goods at one). The total area under the demand curve for the bundle will be just equal to the sum of the areas under the separate demand curves. However, the shape of the demand curve changes: it is more elastic around a bundle price of 1 (i.e. a price of $1/2$ per product) and less elastic near bundle prices of 2 or 0. If the monopolist adds more goods to the bundle, this effect becomes even more pronounced (as illustrated in Panels B and C of Figure 11.6).

This result is very general and follows from the law of large numbers.[33] As more products are added to the bundle, the distribution for the valuation of the bundle is more concentrated around the mean of the underlying distribution. Since the demand function for the bundle is derived from the cumulative distribution function, it becomes more elastic around the mean and less elastic near the extremes (this is true even if the valuations for the separate components are drawn from different distributions). As a result, the profit differential between pure bundling and separate selling grows larger as more goods are aggregated into the bundle. Indeed, because the demand function for the bundle becomes flatter for a larger set of quantities, the monopolist is able to capture an increasing fraction of the total area under the demand curve, which reduces both the consumer surplus and the deadweight loss with respect to separate selling.

Lesson 11.5   As more products are included in a bundle, the demand curve for the bundle becomes flatter. This tends to reduce consumer surplus and deadweight loss.

As we discussed above, the profitability of bundling tends to disappear as marginal costs of production increase (we have assumed so far that marginal costs are zero). This is even more true for larger bundles. So, the above argument works well for goods with zero (or near zero) marginal costs, such as information goods. The fact that software 'suites' tend to include an increasing number of applications may be seen as an illustration. Interestingly, the previous result can be extended to other types of aggregation. For instance, software applications are often sold under *site licensing* (which amounts to selling multiple copies to install in a multi-user location); this can be seen as aggregation across consumers. Similarly, *subscriptions* (to a newspaper, a magazine, a website, . . .) are a form of aggregation over time. Again, these examples involve information goods, whose marginal cost is very low.

11.2   Tying and metering

Tying can be viewed as a price discrimination device because it enables the monopolist to charge more to consumers who value the good the most. Here, the value consumers place on the primary product (e.g., the printer) depends on the frequency with which they use it, which is itself measured by their consumption of the tied product (e.g., the ink cartridges). Those who most need the primary product will consume more of the secondary product and, thereby, pay a higher effective price. That is, tying is used for metering purposes and it is metering that serves as a basis for price discrimination.[c]

We develop here a particularly simple model to illustrate how metering can be used to price discriminate between different consumer types.[34] Consider a monopoly that produces printers and ink cartridges. There is a unit mass of consumers who differ in the quantity q of ink cartridges they need in a certain period of time (where $q = Q/k$, with Q being the number of copies consumers make and k measures how many copies can be printed with one ink cartridge). For simplicity, assume that q is uniformly distributed on the unit interval. Let p_p and p_c denote the prices the monopoly sets for, respectively, the printer and the cartridges. Consumers have the alternative to outsource printing; let γ denote the constant cost of outsourcing k copies; this includes the financial cost of outsourcing and the time and hassle associated with not having the printer on site. It determines the consumers' willingness to pay for printers and cartridges. A consumer will purchase a printer if and only if

$$p_p + p_c q \leq \gamma q \Leftrightarrow q \geq \frac{p_p}{\gamma - p_c} \equiv \hat{q},$$

where it is assumed that $p_p \geq 0$ and $p_c < \gamma$ (i.e., as the printer cannot be subsidized, $p_p \geq 0$, no consumer would buy it if cartridges were more expensive than external printing services, $p_c \geq \gamma$). It follows that the quantity demanded of printers and of cartridges are respectively

---

[c] Firms may also use tying to leverage market power from one market to another. Explicit tied sales are *per se* illegal in the US; in the European Union, tying may be considered as an exclusionary abuse under Article 82 of the Treaty (we return to this in Chapter 16 and in Appendix B). This may explain why the tied sale is often implicit rather than explicit. For instance, printer manufacturers patent the shape of their toner cartridges. Thus, although consumers are not contractually forced to purchase a toner cartridge along with the printer, they are not left with any other option as competitors may not be allowed to or be able to sell compatible cartridges.

given by

$$Q_p(p_p, p_c) = 1 - \hat{q} = 1 - \frac{p_p}{\gamma - p_c},$$

$$Q_c(p_p, p_c) = \int_{\hat{q}}^1 q\, dq = \frac{1}{2}\left(1 - \left(\frac{p_p}{\gamma - p_c}\right)^2\right).$$

Assuming for simplicity that the marginal cost of producing printers and cartridges is zero, we can write the monopolist's profit as

$$\pi = p_p\left(1 - \frac{p_p}{\gamma - p_c}\right) + p_c\frac{1}{2}\left(1 - \left(\frac{p_p}{\gamma - p_c}\right)^2\right). \tag{11.1}$$

As a benchmark, consider the case where the monopoly is not allowed to meter and is thus forced to charge $p_c = 0$. Then the monopoly chooses p_p to maximize $\pi = p(1 - (p/\gamma))$. The profit-maximizing price is easily found as $p = \gamma/2$. The indifferent consumer is thus given by $\hat{q} = 1/2$ and profits are equal to $\pi = \gamma/4$.

Suppose now that $p_c > 0$ is allowed. Before solving for the profit-maximizing prices, let us show that the monopoly can adjust prices so as to increase its profit while keeping the consumer $\hat{q} = 1/2$ indifferent. To keep the consumer indifferent, we must have $1/2 = \frac{p_p}{\gamma - p_c}$, which is equivalent to $p_c = \gamma - 2p_p$. Substituting into the profit function (11.1), we obtain $\pi = \frac{1}{2}p_p + \frac{3}{8}(\gamma - 2p_p)$. The first-order derivative with respect to p_p is equal to $1/2 - 3/4 < 0$, which shows that the monopolist indeed gains by decreasing p_p (and increasing p_c so as to keep the consumer indifferent). Doing so, the monopolist keeps demand constant, but makes all customers with demands above $\hat{q}$ pay more. The monopolist has thus an incentive to price discriminate by making customers with a larger demand (who are identified through metering) pay a higher price.

Actually, in this simple model, the monopolist finds it profitable to push this logic to the extreme by setting the price of printers as close as possible to zero and the price of cartridges as close as possible to the external cost γ. To show this formally, we consider the first-order condition of profit maximization (11.1) with respect to p_p:

$$\frac{d\pi}{dp_p} = \left(1 - \frac{2p_p}{\gamma - p_c}\right) - p_c\frac{p_p}{(\gamma - p_c)^2} = 0 \Leftrightarrow p_p = \frac{(\gamma - p_c)^2}{(2\gamma - p_c)}. \tag{11.2}$$

Take now the derivative of profit with respect to p_c and evaluate it at the value we have just found for p_p:

$$\frac{d\pi}{dp_c}\Bigg|_{p_p = \frac{(\gamma - p_c)^2}{(2\gamma - p_c)}} = \left\{-p_p^2\frac{1}{(\gamma - p_c)^2} + \frac{1}{2}\left(1 - \left(\frac{p_p}{\gamma - p_c}\right)^2\right) - p_c\frac{p_p^2}{(\gamma - p_c)^3}\right\}\Bigg|_{p_p = \frac{(\gamma - p_c)^2}{(2\gamma - p_c)}}$$

$$= \frac{1}{2} - \frac{3}{2}\frac{(\gamma - p_c)^2}{(2\gamma - p_c)^2} - p_c\frac{\gamma - p_c}{(2\gamma - p_c)^2} = \frac{\gamma^2}{2(2\gamma - p_c)^2} > 0$$

Hence, the monopolist sets p_c as large as possible, say $p_c^* = \gamma - \varepsilon$ (with ε arbitrarily small). Using (11.2), the optimal printer price is found as $p_p^* = \varepsilon^2/(\gamma + \varepsilon)$. At these prices, almost all consumers decide to buy the printer and cartridges from the monopolist. The total quantity of cartridges consumed is just below $1/2$ and profits are thus just below $\gamma/2$, which is almost twice what the monopolist could achieve in the absence of metering (i.e., when it is forced to set $p_c = 0$).[d]

Lesson 11.6   A monopolist can profitably use tying as a metering device to obtain a larger payment from consumers who use the tied product more intensively. The monopolist charges a low price for the primary product and a high price for the usage of the tied product.

There are many well-known examples of this practice: on top of printers (and copying machines) and toner cartridges, think of razors and blades, or Polaroid cameras and films. The firm may even sell the primary product below costs (as used to be the case for the sale of mobile handsets). Case 11.2 illustrates that the same logic applies when an ancillary product is sold after the purchase of a single unit good, as is the case for popcorn purchased after entering a venue charging admission.

Case 11.2 Why does popcorn cost so much at the movies?[35]

Popcorn purchased after entering a movie theater is generally priced much higher than in grocery stores. This could be explained by the restriction, or even absence, of choice that consumers face once they have entered the theater. Price discrimination through metering could provide another explanation: theaters optimally choose to shift profits from admission tickets to concessions because they can 'meter' the surplus extracted from a customer by how much of the aftermarket good they demand. According to this explanation, one should find a positive correlation between willingness to pay for movies and demand for concessions. To test whether this explanation is valid, Hartmann and Gil (2008) analyse a data set with approximately five years of weekly attendance, box office revenue and concession revenue for a chain of 43 Spanish movie theaters. They use low attendance in a particular week as a proxy for customer types with a greater willingness to pay for movies. This corresponds to the intuitive idea that low attendance weeks only attract customers with a higher valuation for the theater than the average attendee. Hence, a negative relationship between attendance and concessions sales per attendee would support the hypothesis of metering price discrimination. The empirical analysis indeed confirms that there is a robust negative correlation between concession demand per attendee and attendance. Further support comes from the finding that concession sales are also lower when more students and seniors arrive at the theater (and pay lower prices as a result of third-degree price discrimination).

[d] The exact profit is $\frac{1}{2}\gamma^2/(\gamma + \varepsilon)$.

11.3   Competitive bundling

In many markets bundling is used by several competing firms. When one thinks of bundling in imperfectly competitive markets, the first motivation that comes to mind is entry deterrence. As we explained above, we defer the treatment of this issue to Chapter 16. Here, we focus on the price discrimination motivation and the new question we investigate is how the surplus extraction gains of bundling balance with its competitive effects. As we will see, the answer depends on the nature of the available products. We contrast two settings. In the first one, the two goods are independent, one is produced by a duopoly and the other by a competitive industry. In this setting, bundling softens price competition because it allows firms to differentiate their products. By contrast, in the second setting, the two goods are perfect complements: they are the components of a system. Two firms each offer a differentiated version of each component. Here, bundling intensifies competition because it reduces variety and leads to lower prices through the internalization of the complementarity link between the two components.

11.3.1   Bundling as a way to soften price competition

When firms produce a homogeneous product and compete in prices, they may use bundling as a way to differentiate their products and, thereby, reduce price competition in their primary market. To formalize this idea, we extend the model of Section 11.1 in the following way.[36] We still have a unit mass of consumers who have preferences over goods A and B and who are each identified by a couple (θ_A, θ_B) drawn from the uniform distribution over the unit square. In contrast with the previous setting, we assume now that (i) good A is produced by two firms (noted 1 and 2) at marginal cost $c_A < 1$, and (ii) good B is produced by a perfectly competitive industry at marginal cost $c_B < 1$. Firms 1 and 2 are also able to produce good B; however, they will not decide to produce good B separately, as there is no profit to be made on that market. The issue is thus whether they might have an incentive to bundle good B with good A.

We analyse the following two-stage game. In the first stage, the two firms choose their marketing strategy. There are three possible actions: sell good A only (specialization), sell the bundle AB only (pure bundling), or sell both good A and the bundle (mixed bundling). In the second stage, firms set the price(s) for the product(s) they have decided to sell.

Starting with the second stage, it is quickly seen that in five out of the nine subgames, the unique Nash equilibrium (in pure strategies) is such that both firms earns zero profit. This is certainly the case when both firms choose the same marketing strategy: if they both specialize (i.e., produce A only), Bertrand competition drives prices down to c_A and profits to zero; similarly, if they both choose pure bundling, equilibrium prices are equal to $c_A + c_B$ and profits are again zero; finally, the two previous results are combined when they both choose mixed bundling. Moreover, in the two subgames where one firm specializes while the other firm opts for mixed bundling, there is Bertrand competition for good A, which is thus priced at c_A, and since perfect competition prevails on market B, the bundle price cannot exceed $c_A + c_B$; so, again, both firms earn zero profit. We are thus left with the four subgames where one firm chooses pure bundling, while the other chooses either specialization or mixed bundling.

Consider first the situation where one firm (say firm 1) specializes and the other sells only the bundle. Let p_A be the price of good A and p_{AB}, the price of the bundle. For a consumer to buy the bundle, four conditions have to be met. The consumer must prefer buying the bundle

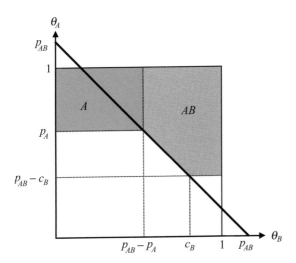

Figure 11.7 Bundling in a duopoly

over (C1) buying only good A, (C2) buying B only (at the perfect competition price c_B), (C3) buying A and B separately, and (C4) buying nothing. Formally,

$$\theta_A + \theta_B - p_{AB} \geq \theta_A - p_A \Leftrightarrow \theta_B \geq p_{AB} - p_A \tag{C1}$$

$$\theta_A + \theta_B - p_{AB} \geq \theta_B - c_B \Leftrightarrow \theta_A \geq p_{AB} - c_B \tag{C2}$$

$$\theta_A + \theta_B - p_{AB} \geq \theta_A + \theta_B - p_A - c_B \Leftrightarrow p_{AB} \leq p_A + c_B \tag{C3}$$

$$\theta_A + \theta_B - p_{AB} \geq 0 \Leftrightarrow \theta_A \geq p_{AB} - \theta_B. \tag{C4}$$

Note that condition (C3) imposes that the bundle be sold at a discount (i.e., cheaper than the sum of the prices of the separate components).

For a consumer to buy good A only, condition (C1) has to be reversed: $\theta_B \leq p_{AB} - p_A$. As condition (C3) is necessary to have an equilibrium in this subgame, we have that $p_{AB} - p_A \leq c_B$, which implies that the consumers who prefer A over the bundle do not get any utility from good B (since $\theta_B < c_B$). Hence, the remaining condition is that buying A only is better than buying nothing: $\theta_A \geq p_A$. Figure 11.7 depicts these various conditions and allows us to identify the demands for good A and for the bundle AB:

$$D_A(p_A, p_{AB}) = (1 - p_A)(p_{AB} - p_A),$$

$$D_{AB}(p_A, p_{AB}) = (1 - p_A)(1 - p_{AB} + p_A)$$
$$+ \tfrac{1}{2}(2 + p_A - p_{AB} - c_B)(c_B - p_{AB} + p_A).$$

At stage 2, firm 1 chooses p_A to maximize $\pi_A = (p_A - c_A) D_A(p_A, p_{AB})$. The first-order condition is $3p_A^2 - 2(1 + c_A + p_{AB})p_A + p_{AB} + c_A + c_A p_{AB} = 0$. This polynomial admits two positive roots. So, for a given value of p_{AB}, there are two values of p_A that satisfy the condition. However, it can be shown that for $p_{AB} \geq 1$, the largest root corresponds to a value of p_A above 1, which has to be rejected. As for the firm producing the bundle, it chooses p_{AB} to maximize $\pi_{AB} = (p_{AB} - c_A - c_B) D_{AB}(p_A, p_{AB})$. The first-order condition gives $\tfrac{3}{2}p_{AB}^2 - (4 + c_B + c_A) p_{AB} + 1 - \tfrac{1}{2}p_A^2 + 3c_B + p_A - \tfrac{1}{2}c_B^2 + 2c_A = 0$. Here, it can be shown that for any p_A, the largest root of this polynomial corresponds to a value of p_{AB} above 2, which has to be rejected.

Hence, for $p_{AB} > 1$, the reaction functions of the two firms are

$$R_A(p_{AB}) = \frac{1+c_A+p_{AB}}{3} - \frac{1}{3}\left[(1-p_{AB})(1-c_A)+(p_{AB}-c_A)^2\right]^{\frac{1}{2}},$$

$$R_{AB}(p_A) = \frac{4+c_A+c_B}{3} - \frac{1}{3}\left[4c_B^2 + 2c_Bc_A - 10c_B + c_A^2 - 4c_A + 10 + 3p_A^2 - 6p_A\right]^{\frac{1}{2}}.$$

A Nash equilibrium is then defined as a couple $\left(p_A^*, p_{AB}^*\right)$ such that $p_A^* = R_A\left(p_{AB}^*\right)$, $p_{AB}^* = R_{AB}\left(p_A^*\right)$, $p_A^* < 1$, $1 < p_{AB}^* < 2$, and $p_{AB}^* \leq p_A^* + c_B$. There does not exist a Nash equilibrium for all configurations of parameters. For instance, if $c_B = 0$, there is no demand for good A to be sold separately (see Figure 11.7 for a confirmation).

We will not try here to characterize the conditions the parameters must satisfy for an equilibrium to exist. Let us just examine one example. For $c_A = 1/4$ and $c_B = 3/4$, the reaction functions intersect at $\left(p_A^*, p_{AB}^*\right) = (0.529, 1.213)$ and we check that $p_A^* + c_B = 1.279 > p_{AB}^* = 1.213$. Computing equilibrium profits, we have that $\pi_A^* \approx 0.09 > \pi_{AB}^* \approx 0.05$. Actually, each firm would like the other to bundle products so that price competition is reduced. Note also that in this equilibrium, bundling entails two sources of welfare losses: (i) there is a deadweight loss in the A market as price is set above marginal cost (some consumers with $\theta_A > c_A$ do not buy good A); (ii) there is also a deadweight loss in the B market as some consumers with $\theta_B < c_B$ consume good B via the bundle.

We have thus shown that there may exist equilibria where one firm specializes, the other firm chooses pure bundling and both firms make positive profits. We still have to consider the two subgames where one firm chooses pure bundling (AB) and the other, mixed bundling ($A\&AB$). As the bundle is sold by both firms, its price is driven down to marginal cost because of Bertrand competition. Therefore, the firm that has chosen pure bundling makes zero profit. As for the other firm, it makes positive profit at equilibrium: $\pi_{A\&AB}^* > 0$. Yet, it can be shown that $\pi_{A\&AB}^* < \pi_A^*$; that is, facing a firm that offers the bundle only, it is more profitable to specialize in good A rather than to sell both A and the bundle. The intuition is clear: mixed bundling undermines the differentiation role played by bundling for it creates a fiercer price competition for the bundle. It follows that *mixed bundling is a weakly dominated strategy in this setting*,[e] which contrasts with what we observed in the monopoly model of the previous section.

Lesson 11.7 Consider a homogeneous primary good produced by a duopoly and a secondary good produced competitively. In equilibrium, one firm specializes in the primary good and the other bundles the two goods. Both make positive profits although they produce homogeneous goods and compete in price. Bundling acts here as a product differentiation device, which reduces price competition in the primary market. Bundling reduces welfare.

11.3.2   When bundling intensifies price competition

We consider now a situation where goods A and B are perfect complements (i.e., they do not provide any utility unless consumed together).[37] Actually, the two goods can be seen as the

---

[e] This is so as long as an equilibrium exists in the corresponding second-stage subgames.

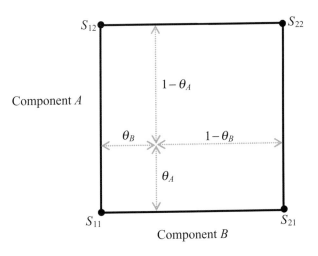

Figure 11.8 Preferences for systems

components of a *system* (think of, e.g., a home stereo system, a camera with its lenses, a computer made of a central unit and a monitor, ...). There are two firms, 1 and 2; each of them produce the two components (at zero marginal cost, to simplify the analysis). Equivalent components produced by the two firms are differentiated. To model this differentiation, we still assume that consumers are identified by a couple (θ_A, θ_B) drawn from the uniform distribution over the unit square, but we give another meaning to this couple: it now corresponds to the location of the consumer in a two-dimensional Hotelling model and represents this consumer's ideal specification of the components. Supposing that components are compatible,[f] consumers can choose among four possible systems: two 'pure' systems (made of components produced by the same firm), S_{11} and S_{22}, and two 'hybrid' systems (made of components produced by different firms), S_{12} and S_{21}. As represented in Figure 11.8, the four systems are located at the four corners of the unit square: starting from the bottom-left corner and going clockwise, we have S_{11}, S_{12}, S_{22}, and S_{21}. So, for a consumer located at (θ_A, θ_B), θ_A (resp. $1 - \theta_A$) measures the disutility (i.e., the transportation cost) of buying component A from firm 1 (resp. firm 2), and likewise for θ_B regarding component B. Letting r measure every consumer's reservation price for one unit of her ideal system, we have that a consumer located at (θ_A, θ_B) derives a net surplus of $r - \theta_A - (1 - \theta_B) - p_A^1 - p_B^2$ if she buys component A from firm 1 (at price p_A^1) and component B from firm 2 (at price p_B^2). Net surpluses from other systems are defined accordingly.

As in the previous section, we consider a two-stage game in which the two firms choose first their marketing strategy (separate selling, pure bundling or mixed bundling) and then their prices. A full-fledged analysis of this model is cumbersome and would drag us into unnecessary complications. We will therefore restrict ourselves to stating the main results and explaining the intuition behind them.

---

[f] Either compatibility can be enforced unilaterally (e.g., by building an adaptor or a converter) or it requires the agreement of both firms. Here, to focus on the effects of bundling, we abstract away firms' decisions about compatibility (see Matutes and Régibeau, 1988 and 1992 for more). We suppose that compatibility prevails because otherwise, separate selling and mixed bundling would be equivalent to pure bundling (since consumers could only choose between firm 1's pure system and firm 2's pure system). We will come back to system goods and to compatibility issues in Chapters 20 and 21.

A first important result is that *the pure bundling strategy is dominated by the separate selling strategy*. This follows from the combination of two effects. First, going from pure bundling to separate selling increases variety: under pure bundling, consumers have to choose between S_{11} and S_{22}, whereas under separate selling, they can 'mix and match' by assembling two more systems (S_{12} and S_{21}). If r is not too large, the market will not be fully covered. Hence, the increase in variety will allow some consumers to find a system closer to their specification. That is, at given prices, some consumers who were not consuming under pure bundling, will consume one of the hybrid systems under separate selling. Industry demand is thus shifted upward. However, this effect disappears when firms find it profitable to serve the whole market (which happens for larger values of r).

The second effect relates to the pricing of complementary products: firms have larger incentives to cut prices under pure bundling than under separate selling. Indeed, under pure bundling, reducing the price of one component increases the demand for both components in the system; therefore, the firm internalizes the complementarity between the demands for the two components. In contrast, under separate selling, if (say) firm 1 cuts the price of its component A, it expands the demand for system S_{11} (and thus for its own component B) but also the demand for system S_{12} (and thus for the rival's component B). So, firm 1 does not fully internalize the complementarity link between the two components. Prices will thus be lower under pure bundling than under separate selling. The consequences on profits, however, depend on whether the market is covered or not. If the market is not covered (r is relatively small), firms are local monopolies and pure bundling allows them to fully internalize the complementarity effects, thereby securing larger profits. However, as discussed above, separate selling increases variety and it can be shown that the latter effect dominates the former, so that the net effect is in favour of separate selling. On the other hand, when the market is covered (r is relatively large), firms compete directly and pure bundling intensifies competition since the internalization of the complementarity effects leads to lower prices (and thus to an aggressive reaction from the rival firm). As this is the only effect playing in this case (since the increased variety effect disappears in a covered market), we conclude again that pure bundling gives lower profits than separate selling.

Let us now compare mixed bundling to separate selling. From the previous discussion, one could think that mixed bundling is an ideal strategy as it allows the firm to take advantage of both the increase in system variety and the internalization of the complementarity effects. However, things are a bit more complicated for other effects come into play. Again, the intensity and the balance of these effects depend on the coverage of the market. When the market is partially covered, a firm that has chosen mixed bundling does indeed fully internalize the complementarity effects for its pure system; yet, because it also sells the components separately, it has lower incentives to internalize the complementarity effects for the hybrid systems. It follows that given the rival prices, a firm that has chosen mixed bundling will charge a higher price for its pure system and lower prices for its individual components than a firm that has chosen separate selling. Thus, the bundling firm free-rides on the non-bundling firm's effort to expand the demand for the hybrid systems through lower-priced components. This explains why choosing mixed bundling is a dominant strategy. However, it can be shown that firms would be better off if they could commit on not bundling components. This prisoners' dilemma type of situation is reminiscent of what we already observed for group and personalized pricing in Chapter 8. As described in Case 11.3, the convergence between TV, telephone and broadband has given rise to a situation of this kind.

When the market is fully covered whatever the firms' decisions regarding bundling, there is an additional effect that discourages firms to unilaterally choose mixed bundling. We still have that the pure system is cheaper and the separate components are more expensive if sold by a bundling firm rather than by a non-bundling firm. However, when firms are direct competitors, this triggers more aggressive responses from the rival firm (because the cheaper bundle also steals business from the rival's pure system), which backfires on the bundling firm's own system. When the reservation price is sufficiently large, separate selling is then the dominant strategy.[g]

Lesson 11.8   **When two competing firms sell compatible components of a system, separate selling always dominates pure bundling. If consumers have a relatively low reservation price for their ideal system, both firms end up choosing mixed bundling but they would be better off if they could agree to adopt separate selling instead. If the reservation price is relatively high, both firms select separate selling at the equilibrium. In general, bundling of perfectly compatible components intensifies competition.**

Case 11.3 Triple play[38]

Because pictures, sound and data are now all processed, stored and transmitted digitally, the traditional technical boundaries between the information, communication and entertainment industries have collapsed. This digital convergence allows telephone companies and cable operators alike to offer so-called 'triple-play' bundles that include telecommunications, television and access to the Internet. As a result, once separated firms are now competing directly with one another. In this new competitive arena, bundling appears as a crucial strategic tool. The strategic motivation for using bundling appears indeed as the strongest, for triple-play bundling allows very little direct gains: (i) on the demand side, strict additivity of consumers' valuations appears as a realistic assumption (the complementarity between TV, broadband access and telephone is low, if not inexistent; moreover, there is little evidence that consumers save on subscription costs when buying a bundle rather than mixing and matching); (ii) on the production side, triple play does not seem to increase efficiency (the economies of scope in the joint supply of the three services are rather low). So, triple-play bundling should be viewed as a way for firms that are installed incumbents in their native market to invade neighbouring markets. Yet, this gives rise to a prisoner's dilemma: triple play is a dominant strategy (as soon as one firm adopts triple-play bundling, competitors have no other choice than to follow suit) but firms would arguably be better off if they could collectively refrain from bundling (which would be made possible, for instance, if bundling products was legally prohibited).

[g] It can be shown that there is a small range of reservation prices r for which the equilibrium of the game is such that one firm chooses mixed bundling and the other firm chooses separate selling.

Review questions

1. What is the meaning of pure and mixed bundling? Give a real-world example for each practice.

2. What is the intuition that bundling (pure or mixed) can increase profits compared to separate selling?

3. How can bundling reduce competition?

4. Can bundling increase competition? Explain.

Further reading

For a general analysis of monopoly bundling we refer to McAfee, McMillan and Whinston (1989). Bundling a large number of products is analysed in Bakos and Brynjolfsson (1999). With respect to imperfect competition, Chen (1997) explores how bundling can soften competition. On the other hand, as analysed by Matutes and Régibeau (1992), competitive bundling may increase competition.

Notes for Part IV

1. This definition is adapted from Phlips (1983, p. 6). As Phlips argues, this definition seems more acceptable than the standard definition, which identifies price discrimination as the practice of setting different prices for the same good. Indeed, one often observes that it is not the same product, but differentiated products, that are sold at discriminatory prices.

2. 'A golden vein', *The Economist*, 10 June 2004.

3. We follow here Liu and Serfes (2004) where the reader will find all the details of the computations. We also follow Thisse and Vives (1988) for the case of personalized prices.

4. The exact expression for this profit function (as well as for the other subgames) can be found in Liu and Serfes (2004).

5. See Capozza and Van Order (1978). See also Thisse and Vives (1988).

6. We extend here the setting proposed by Dobson and Waterson (2005). The previous examples are also drawn from this article.

7. This case draws from Competition Commission (2000).

8. See Meurer (2001).

9. For a general introduction to mechanism design, see e.g. Myerson (1989).

10. We adapt the framework proposed by Salant (1989), which unifies the analyses of Mussa and Rosen (1978), Stokey (1979), and Spence (1977, 1980).

11. See Csorba and Hahn (2006) for a formal analysis.

12. This case compiles examples and analyses proposed by Deneckere and McAfee (1996), Johnson and Myatt (2003) and McAfee (2007).

13. This case borrows from the survey of Verboven (2006).

14. We follow here Ellison (2005).

15. To be exhasutive, we should show that there is no equilibrium where the firms sell version H to the high types and version L to the low types, but at different prices than $p_{1H}^* = 2/3$ and $p_{1L}^* = 1/6$. For a proof, see Ellison (2005).

16. See Ellison (2005).

17. We follow here Armstrong and Vickers (2001, 2006).

18. However, this result does not hold if firms have different costs, if some consumers do not buy from either firm, or if the transportation cost is not a shopping cost. See Rochet and Stole (2002) and Yin (2004) for further details.

19. See Armstrong and Vickers (2001).

20. The durable good problem with two periods has been analysed by Bulow (1982).

21. See von der Fehr and Kühn (1995).

22. This case is based on Iizuka (2007).

23. This analysis draws on Wilson (1988).

24. These examples are taken from Nocke and Peitz (2007).

25. For a more elaborate analysis, see Nocke and Peitz (2008) and Möller and Watanabe (2008). The analysis of partial refund contracts by Courty and Li (2000) is closely related. See also Gale and Holmes (1993).

26. This analysis is based on Fudenberg and Villas-Boas (2007) and Armstrong (2007).

27. See Acquisti and Varian (2005) for an analysis along these lines.

28. For a formal analysis of behaviour-based discrimination in a duopoly context, see Pazgal and Soberman (2008).

29. The argument is due to Stigler (1968).

30. By continuity, this result extends to moderately positively correlated valuations.

31. We follow here Nalebuff (2004) and McAfee, McMillan and Whinston (1989).

32. See Belleflamme (2006).

33. See Bakos and Brynjolfsson (1999).

34. The analysis draws from Appendix B in Nalebuff (2003).

35. This case is based on Hartmann and Gil (2008).

36. We follow here Chen (1997).

37. This model is due to Matutes and Régibeau (1992).

38. This case draws from Crampes and Hollander (2006).

References for Part IV

Acquisti, A. and Varian, H. R. (2005). Conditioning Prices on Purchase History. *Marketing Science* 24: 367–381.

Armstrong, M. (2007). Recent Developments in the Economics of Price Discrimination. In Blundell, R., Newey, W. and Persson, T. (eds.), *Advances in Economics and Econometrics 3: Theory and Applications (Ninth World Congress)*. Cambridge: Cambridge University Press.

Armstrong, M. and Vickers, J. (2001). Competitive Price Discrimination. *Rand Journal of Economics* 32: 579–605.

Armstrong, M. and Vickers, J. (2006). Competitive Nonlinear Pricing and Bundling. Mimeo.

Bachis, E. and A. Piga (2006). On-line International Price Discrimination with and without Arbitrage Conditions. Mimeo.

Bakos, Y. and Brynjolfsson, E. (1999). Bundling Information Goods: Pricing, Profits, and Efficiency. *Management Science* 45: 1613–1630.

Belleflamme, P. (2006). Versioning Information Goods. In Illing, G. and Peitz, M. (eds.), *Industrial Organization and the Digital Economy*. Cambridge, MA: MIT Press.

Borenstein, S. (1991). Selling Costs and Switching Costs: Explaining Retail Gasoline Margins. *Rand Journal of Economics* 22: 354–369.

Borenstein, S. and Rose, N. (1994). Competition and Price Dispersion in the U.S. Airline Industry. *Journal of Political Economy* 102: 653–683.

Brenkers, R. and Verboven, F. (2006). Liberalizing a Distribution System: The European Car Market. *Journal of the European Economic Association* 4: 216–251.

Bulow, J. (1982). Durable Goods Monopolist. *Journal of Political Economy* 90: 314–332.

Cabolis, C., Clerides, S., Ioannou, I. and Senft, L. (2007). A Textbook Example of International Price Discrimination. *Economics Letters* 95: 91–95.

Capozza, D. R. and Van Order, R. (1978). A Generalized Model of Spatial Competition. *American Economic Review* 68: 896–908.

Chen, Y. (1997). Equilibrium Product Bundling. *Journal of Business* 70: 85–103.

Clerides, S. (2002). Book Value: Intertemporal Pricing and Quality Discrimination in the U.S. Market for Books. *International Journal of Industrial Organization* 20: 1358–1408.

Competition Commission (2000). *Supermarkets: A Report on the Supply of Groceries from Multiple Stores in the United Kingdom*. Cm4842, London: TSO.

Courty, P. (2003). Some Economics of Ticket Resale. *Journal of Economic Perspectives* 17: 85–97.

Courty, P. and Li, H. (2001). Sequential Screening. *Review of Economic Studies* 67: 697–717.

Crampes, C. and Hollander, A. (2006). Triple Play Time. Mimeo.

Csorba, G. and Hahn, Y. (2006). Functional Degradation and Asymmetric Network Effects. *Journal of Industrial Economics* 54: 253–268.

Deneckere, R. J. and McAfee, R. P. (1996). Damaged Goods. *Journal of Economics and Management Strategy* 5: 149–174.

Dobson, P. and Waterson, M. (2005). Chain-store Pricing across Local Markets. *Journal of Economics and Management Strategy* 14: 93–119.

Ellison, G. (2005). A Model of Add-on Pricing. *Quarterly Journal of Economics* 120: 585–637.

Fudenberg, D. and Villas-Boas, J. M. (2007). Behavior-based Price Discrimination and Customer Recognition. In Hendershott, T. J. (ed.), *Economics and Information Systems*. Amsterdam: Elsevier.

Gale, I. and Holmes, T. (1993). Advance-purchase Discounts and Monopoly Allocation of Capacity, *American Economic Review* 83, 135–146.

Goldberg, P. K. and Verboven, F. (2001). The Evolution of Price Dispersion in the European Car Market. *Review of Economic Studies* 68: 811–848.

Goldberg, P. K. and Verboven, F. (2004). Cross-country Price Dispersion in the Euro Era: A Case Study of the European Car Market. *Economic Policy* 40: 484–521.

Hartmann, W. R. and Gil, R. (2008). Why Does Popcorn Cost So Much At the Movies? An Empirical Analysis of Metering Price Discrimination. Mimeo.

Iizuka, T. (2007). An Empirical Analysis of Planned Obsolescence. *Journal of Economics and Management Strategy* 16: 191–226.

Johnson, J. P. and Myatt, D. P. (2003). Multiproduct Quality Competition: Fighting Brands and Product Line Pruning. *American Economic Review* 93: 748–774.

Liu, Q. and Serfes, K. (2004). Quality of Information and Oligopolistic Price Discrimination. *Journal of Economics and Management Strategy* 13: 671–702.

Matutes, C. and Régibeau, P. (1988). Mix and Match: Product Compatibility without Network Externalities. *Rand Journal of Economics* 19: 221–234.

Matutes, C. and Régibeau, P. (1992). Compatibility and Bundling of Complementary Goods in a Duopoly. *Journal of Industrial Economics* 40: 37–54.

McAfee, P. (2007). Pricing Damaged Goods. *Economics: The Open-Access, Open-Assessment E-Journal* 1, 2007–1.

McAfee, R. P., McMillan, J. and Whinston, M. (1989). Multiproduct Monopoly, Commodity Bundling, and Correlation of Values. *Quarterly Journal of Economics* 104: 371–383.

Meurer, M. J. (2001). Copyright Law and Price Discrimination. 23 *Cardozo Law Review* 55.

Möller, M. and Watanabe, M. (2008). Advance Purchase Discounts versus Clearance Sales. Mimeo.

Mussa, M. and Rosen, S. (1978). Monopoly and Product Quality. *Journal of Economic Theory* 18: 301–317.

Myerson, R. B. (1989). Mechanism Design. In Eatwell, J., Milgate, M. and Newman, P. (eds.). *The New Palgrave: Allocation, Information, and Markets*. New York: Norton, 191–206.

Nalebuff, B. (2003). Bundling, Tying, and Portfolio Effects. Department of Trade and Industry working paper #1.

Nalebuff, B. (2004). Bundling as an Entry Barrier. *Quarterly Journal of Economics* 119: 159–187.

Nocke, V. and Peitz, M. (2007). A Theory of Clearance Sales. *Economic Journal* 117: 964–990.

Nocke, V. and Peitz, M. (2008). Advance-purchase Discounts as a Price-Discrimination Device. Mimeo.

Pashigian, B. P. (1988). Demand Uncertainty and Sales: A Study of Fashion and Markdown Pricing. *American Economic Review* 78: 936–953.

Pazgal, A. and Soberman, D. A. (2008). Behavior-based Discrimination: Is it a Winning Play and If So When? *Marketing Science* 27: 977–994.

Phlips, L. (1983). *Economics of Price Discrimination. Four Essays in Applied Price Theory.* Cambridge: Cambridge University Press.

Pigou, A. C. (1920). *The Economics of Welfare*. London: Macmillan.

Rochet, J.-C. and Stole, L. (2002). Nonlinear Pricing with Random Participation. *Review of Economic Studies* 69: 277–311.

Salant, S. W. (1989). When is Inducing Self-selection Suboptimal for a Monopolist? *Quarterly Journal of Economics* 104: 391–397.

Shapiro, C. and Varian, H. (1999). *Information Rules: A Strategic Guide to the Network Economy*. Boston, MA: Harvard Business School Press.

Spence, A. M. (1977). Non-linear Prices and Welfare. *Journal of Public Economics* 8: 1–18.

Spence, A. M. (1980). Multi-product Quantity-dependent Prices and Profitability Constraints. *Review of Economic Studies* 47: 821–841.

Stigler, G. (1968). *The Organization of Industry*. Homewood, IL: Irwin.

Stokey, N. L. (1979). Intertemporal Price Discrimination. *Quarterly Journal of Economics* 93: 355–371.

Sundararajan, A. and Ghose, A. (2005). Software Versioning and Quality Degradation? An Exploratory Study of the Evidence. Mimeo.

Thisse, J.-F. and Vives, X. (1988). On the Strategic Choice of Spatial Price Policy. *American Economic Review* 78: 122–137.

Verboven, F. (2002). Quality-based Price Discrimination and Tax Incidence – the Market for Gasoline and Diesel Cars in Europe. *Rand Journal of Economics* 33: 275–297.

Verboven, F. (2006). Price Discrimination: Empirical Studies. Forthcoming in *The New Palgrave: A Dictionary in Economics*, MacMillan.

von der Fehr, N.-H. and Kühn, K.-U. (1995), Coase Versus Pacman: Who Eats Whom in the Durable Good Monopoly? *Journal of Political Economy* 103: 785–812.

Wilson, C. (1988). On the Optimal Pricing Policy of a Monopolist. *Journal of Political Economy* 96: 164–176.

Yin, X. (2004). Two-part Tariff Competition in Duopoly. *International Journal of Industrial Organization* 22: 799–820.

Part V
Product quality and information

Introduction to Part V: Product quality and information

So far in this book, we have mainly been dealing with *search goods*, i.e., products or services with features and characteristics that can be easily evaluated before purchase. In contrast, this part of the book examines products and services with characteristics that can only be ascertained upon consumption because they are difficult to observe in advance. We talk here of *experience goods*.[a]

Managing experience goods is the day-to-day concern of large firms selling consumer goods, such as Nestlé, Procter&Gamble, or Unilever. These firms frequently introduce new branded products. They are always interested in not only making consumers aware of the product (e.g., through advertising as we have analysed in Chapter 6) but also in convincing consumers that the new product satisfies their wants. Perhaps the main challenge when launching a new product is that consumers do not observe the quality of the product, as is typically the case with experience goods. Similarly, firms that enter an otherwise perfectly competitive industry with a patented product (or, alternatively open new markets with a proprietary technology) often produce an experience good.

These markets are characterized by *asymmetric information* as consumers have less information than the producers about product quality. In such markets, firms have to convince consumers that their products are of high quality. To this end, firms can use a variety of marketing instruments. This is the topic of the following two chapters. We mostly focus on markets in which a single firm has market power; situations in which multiple firms have market power are more challenging and will not be systematically analysed in this context.

In Chapter 12, we analyse the basic problem of asymmetric information. Adverse selection may lead to a breakdown of quality in the market. If a firm has initially to invest in quality, the effect of asymmetric information on quality provision is ambiguous. In response to an asymmetric information problem, the firm may also choose from an arsenal of marketing devices. Here, we focus on price and advertising signals of quality, both in isolation and in combination. Suppose that, e.g., Nestlé plans to introduce a new upmarket instant coffee (if this is not a contradiction by itself). Nestlé may then initially deviate with its price from the full information price in order to convince consumers of the high quality. Alternatively or in addition, it may buy advertising time for the new product simply as an attempt to convince consumers that the product is worth a try. The idea is that signalling costs are lower for high quality than for low quality, which makes price and advertising signals credible. In particular, repeat purchase considerations (but also cost considerations) can give rise to different deviation costs. For instance, Nestlé may want to introduce its premium instant coffee at a price above the full information price as an attempt to communicate to consumers that the product is of excellent quality.

[a] This typology is due to Nelson (1970), who identifies a third category of goods, namely *credence goods*, for which quality is difficult or impossible for the consumer to ascertain, even after consumption. Many forms of medical treatments fall into this category.

Chapter 13 goes beyond the price/ advertising signals and explores additional strategies that may be chosen by a firm. Here, we consider guarantees and warranties, branding over time (in the presence of a moral hazard problem), and umbrella branding. In the presence of short-lived products like instant coffee, the warranty aspect does not play a role but Nestlé may offer a money-back guarantee if a consumer does not like the product. Nestlé also relies on its brand to keep the product going because lapses (or quality deviations) today may be punished by consumers for a while in the future, as some soft drink and mineral water producers have learnt. Here, the rational punishment by consumers can provide the proper incentives to maintain its quality and monitor the production process. Finally, as is evident for a firm such as Nestlé, a firm can attempt to transfer trust and goodwill not only over time but also across products. In that case, the use of umbrella branding opens up additional punishment strategies for consumers, which may give stronger incentives to firms to reveal their quality and invest in quality provision. If you do not like instant coffee what about some Nestlé instant tea?

As evidence of these different tactics, here are some quotes from a document entitled 'Nestlé Quality Policy' that Nestlé has posted on its website:[b]

SUCCESS IS BUILT ON QUALITY. Quality is the cornerstone of our success. Every day, millions of people around the world show their confidence in us by choosing Nestlé products. This confidence is based on our quality image and a reputation for high standards that has been build up over many years.... A Nestlé brand name on a product is a promise to the customer that it is safe to consume, that it complies with all regulations and that it meets high standards of quality. Customers expect us to keep this promise every time.... The effort is worth it. Companies with high quality standards make fewer mistakes, waste less time and money and are more productive. They also make higher profits.

What will you learn in this part of the book?
You will become familiar with asymmetric information problems, in which the firm (which is the informed party) chooses its marketing strategy (e.g., price, advertising, warranty or branding) to inform consumers about product quality. This is an application of signalling games to the study of firm strategy in experience goods markets. You will also get some insights into the modelling of firm reputation, an important issue in the understanding of the role of branding.

[b] See www.nestle.com; last visited on February 1, 2009.

12 Asymmetric information, price and advertising signals

A classic example of asymmetric information problems is the market for used cars. The current owner has private information about product characteristics whereas buyers only have a vague idea. This asymmetric information problem may result in the breakdown of the market: only lemons (i.e., used cars of a poor quality) may be offered for sale or, worse, all sellers may withdraw from the market. Alternatively, if sellers can disclose their information, asymmetric information may result in full information disclosure, so that the asymmetric information is solved. What is the likely outcome and why? This is what we explore in Section 12.1. We start by analysing hidden information problems, where firms do not control the quality of their product but observe the realization of quality, whereas consumers cannot observe quality before buying the product. We also examine hidden action problems that arise when firms are able to invest in the quality of their products; in that case, we explore the impact asymmetric information has on the private investment incentives.

When producers, like car manufacturers, are not able to credibly disclose some relevant information, they will try to use strategic variables to convince consumers that their products are of high quality. In Section 12.2, we focus on advertising and price signalling in a monopoly setting. Wasteful advertising and prices which are distorted away from their full information level may serve as a means to make consumers believe in high product quality. We first analyse the two signals separately and then we investigate how they can be used jointly. Finally, in Section 12.3, we examine how imperfect competition affects the use of prices as a signal of quality. In particular, we show that a high price can signal product quality also under competition.

12.1 Asymmetric information problems

When consumers do not observe product quality or other characteristics whereas firms do, market participants face a situation of asymmetric information. In particular, if quality or other characteristics are not controlled by the firm but are realizations of some random variable, we are confronted with a *hidden information* problem. Otherwise, that is, if the firm chooses quality or product characteristics itself, market participants face a *hidden action* problem. We consider the two types of problems in turn.

12.1.1 Hidden information problem

To describe the basic hidden information problem, we build the following simple model. Suppose that a single seller offers a product of two potential levels of quality. Throughout this chapter and the next, we will denote quality by the index s, which can take the value L or H according to whether quality is 'low' or 'high'. This describes the seller's type. We represent the seller's opportunity cost by c_s, $s \in \{L, H\}$. High quality is assumed to be more costly than low quality, $c_H > c_L$. On the demand side, there is a unit mass of buyers who are assumed to be identical and have unit demand. The valuation of each buyer is assumed to be r_s. By definition, $r_H > r_L$: all consumers prefer a higher quality.

Suppose that $r_s > c_s$; that is, for each quality level, the consumers' valuation is larger than the seller's opportunity cost. Hence, if there is full information about product quality, the seller can profitably sell the product to buyers, whatever the actual quality of the product. However, as we are dealing with experience goods, it is more reasonable to assume that only the seller observes its product quality, whereas buyers know that with probability λ the product is of high quality and with the remaining probability is of low quality. Then the expected utility for buyers is $\lambda r_H + (1 - \lambda)r_L$, provided that both seller types are active. Case 12.1 illustrates how circumstances may drive consumers to revise their expectation of the quality of second-hand cars.

Case 12.1 Why did prices plunge on the Mumbai second-hand car market after July 2005?[1]

On 26 July 2005, Mumbai (formerly known as Bombay, the economic capital city of India) was struck by a great deluge. For the next couple of days, tens of thousands of cars were stranded in the rain, many of them being submerged in water. These cars were later towed to the nearest service centre for reparation. However, consumers were aware that water damages were likely to have long-lasting consequences and that additional use might, in the future, aggravate the internal damage that was currently unobservable (e.g., water might have entered the engine or any other part, and got mixed with the fuel; similarly, if seats and covers had simply been machine dried, they could start smelling after some time). Therefore, consumers rationally factored these likely additional future expenses into their costs. In other words, they revised their expectation of quality downward, which explains why the second-hand market for cars dropped by at least 15%.

To formally analyse asymmetric information problems, we consider the following three-stage game: at the first stage, Nature draws the seller's product quality from some known distribution and its realization is observed by the seller but not by buyers; at the second stage, the seller decides whether and which price to post; at the third stage, consumers form beliefs about the firm's product quality and make their purchasing decision.

Adverse selection

Since buyers are homogeneous, the seller can extract the full expected surplus from buyers. Hence, if both firm types are active (i.e., if consumers expect that the seller would offer its product for sale whatever the actual realization of quality), there is a perfect Bayesian equilibrium in which the firm sets the same price independent of quality, $p = \lambda r_H + (1 - \lambda)r_L$

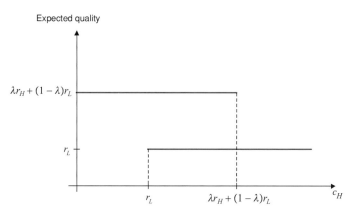

Figure 12.1 Expected quality under asymmetric information

and all consumers buy.[c] If this is the case, the information uncertainty is not resolved – an equilibrium in which the information uncertainty is not resolved is a *pooling equilibrium*. However, the allocation is welfare maximizing since all potential gains from trade are realized.

Note that a high-quality firm is only willing to sell its product if $p > c_H$. Suppose instead that $p < c_H$, which can be rewritten as $\lambda(r_H - c_H) + (1 - \lambda)(r_L - c_H) < 0$. In that case, the high-quality firm cannot recover its opportunity cost and therefore does not participate. (This condition holds if $r_L < c_H$ and if low quality is sufficiently likely.) The only equilibrium with $\lambda(r_H - c_H) + (1 - \lambda)(r_L - c_H) < 0$ is therefore of a different nature. Consumers realize that a high-quality seller does not have an incentive to participate in this environment and their expected utility goes therefore down to r_L. In equilibrium, the low-quality seller sets price $p = r_L$ whereas the high-quality seller does not post a price. Thus in this market, only low quality survives, which depicts a situation of *adverse selection*.[2]

Let us now return to the opposite case in which $p > c_H$ and show that the adverse selection problem may nevertheless arise. To see this, suppose that consumers hold beliefs that only a low-quality firm makes offers. Then, to sell any product, the firm has to set a price at or below r_L. Thus if $c_H > r_L$, there is an equilibrium in which the high-quality firm does not sell, which confirms the consumers' beliefs.

To summarize, Figure 12.1 depicts the average quality in equilibrium. For sufficiently low c_H, namely if $c_H < r_L$, there are only perfect Bayesian equilibria in which the firm sets the same price p independent of quality. For intermediate values of opportunity costs such that $c_H \in [r_L, \lambda r_H + (1 - \lambda)r_L]$, there are two types of (pure-strategy) equilibria, one in which only the low-quality type is active and the other in which both are. For high levels of c_H, the firm only stays in the market if it is of low quality.

> **Lesson 12.1**   **In markets in which product quality is exogenous but unobservable, high-quality products may not be offered for sale.**

If there is a continuum of quality levels, asymmetric information may lead to a complete *unravelling of the market*, so that only the lowest quality survives in the market. This

---

[c] See the Game Theory Appendix for the definition of a perfect Bayesian Nash equilibrium.

essentially means that there is almost a complete breakdown of the market. In other markets, different identifiable types of sellers offer different compositions of high- and low-quality products. This provides an indirect test for asymmetric information, as illustrated in Case 12.2.

Case 12.2 Adverse selection in the second-hand car market[3]

The second-hand car market is a natural testing ground for adverse selection. Genesove (1993) analyses wholesale auctions for second-hand cars in the US in 1989 in which sellers can be distinguished by type. Either the seller is a new car dealer (NCD), that is, he or she also sells new cars, or a used car dealer (UCD) who only sells used cars. The seller type is observable to buyers and thus allows them to condition their bid on this type. Buyers, i.e., potential bidders, can inspect the car in question but this inspection is superficial so that asymmetric information is likely to be still at play. Sellers offer some of their cars at such an auction to manage their stocks. A key difference between UCDs and NCDs is their composition of cars. In particular, both types will have trade-ins (these are used cars which have been turned in as part payment for another car), but NCDs have a much higher share of these. In addition, UCDs and NCDs have different compositions of trade-ins, NCDs are likely to have above average trade-ins compared to UCDs. Furthermore, retail demand is different for the two types. In particular, UCDs have demand for used cars that are close substitutes for new cars. Thus the portfolio of NCDs is likely to consist of used cars that are close substitutes for new cars. This does not hold for UCDs. These reasons suggest that there is a premium for cars sold by NCDs compared to UCDs. There is indeed weak empirical evidence for such a premium: NCDs enjoy a 3 percent premium over UCDs (which corresponded to around 115 US$ at the mean price at that point in time).[d] A further distinction between cars can be based on whether a car is the first time sold or whether it had several owners. If one-owner cars enjoy a premium over several owner cars, this can be seen as evidence for adverse selection because, e.g., a car that is sold for the second time was already adversely selected the first time it was sold so that the average quality of a two-owner car is below the one of a one-owner car. The data confirm that one-owner cars sell at a higher price: they enjoy a 9 percent premium (which is statistically significant). To summarize, the data indicate that adverse selection is an important phenomenon in the second-hand car market.

Information revelation

In some markets a seller may decide to credibly reveal its private information.[e] We must then ask: What are the incentives for a firm to provide information on product characteristics? In the case of two qualities, a high-quality producer has an incentive to reveal its quality to consumers, whereas a low-quality producer would like to keep this information private. However, because consumers know that a high-quality producer always provides information,

---

[d] However, the coefficient in the estimation turned out to be statistically insignificant.
[e] Intermediaries often help sellers to reveal this information. For a detailed analysis see Chapter 23.

they correctly anticipate that a product whose quality has not been revealed must be of low quality. Such an unravelling argument can be made even for a continuum of quality levels. Hence, if it is not costly to release information, all firms will do so in equilibrium.[4] Case 12.3 presents some evidence of such behaviour.

Case 12.3 Selling used products over eBay

Information asymmetries are particularly pronounced for used products such as used cars.[5] Some sellers have addressed these problems by offering warranties for used cars; others allow for detailed inspections. Perhaps more surprising is that eBay has proved to be a successful platform to sell used cars. One explanation for its success is that it allows sellers to disclose information. As has been tested empirically, this voluntary information disclosure reduces the information asymmetry in the market. Obtaining information on voluntary information disclosure in a large dataset is not trivial. However, some standardized checks can provide proxies for the degree of information disclosure, for instance, the number of bytes used to reveal information, the number of photos included, and text search for particular words such as 'rust' and 'no rust'. This provides information on top of the information that has to be provided. It can then be checked that these various information measures have a positive effect on price. However, if consumers are willing to pay more, this must mean that they obtain better cars. We can therefore infer that information about features that are valuable to buyers is more likely to be disclosed by sellers.

12.1.2   Hidden action problem

Our analysis of asymmetric information so far has been restricted to hidden information. If the realization of quality is not an exogenous event but is instead controlled by the firm, we speak of a situation of *hidden action*. In such a framework, we describe first how hidden action generates a moral hazard problem. We ask then whether the problem still holds if firms have the possibility to make a risky investment in quality and if the investment level but not the outcome can be observed by the consumers.

Moral hazard

We use the same setup as above, except that the first stage of our three-stage game changes: it is not Nature but the firm itself that chooses its quality (and as before, the firm sets its price at stage 2, and buyers form beliefs about product quality and make their purchasing decision at stage 3).

To assess the impact of asymmetric information, we first analyse the benchmark of full information. Under full information, the firm chooses high quality if it yields a larger margin, i.e., if $r_H - c_H > r_L - c_L$; the firm chooses low quality if the reverse inequality holds. Note that this implements the first best allocation (this is due to the fact that the firm fully extracts all surplus).

Now, if the quality choice is a hidden action, the firm has no means to convince consumers that its product is of high quality. If for some price weakly less than r_H, consumers believe that the product is of high quality, the low-quality firm can always mimic the behaviour of the high-quality firm at stage 2. Therefore, the high-quality firm cannot at the same time derive profits above $r_L - c_H$ and separate itself from a low-quality firm. Consequently, in the unique equilibrium of the game, the firm produces low quality. Here, the hidden action creates a *moral hazard problem*.

Lesson 12.2   **In markets in which firms choose quality, firms tend to provide too low quality from a social point of view.**

Risky investments in quality

In the remainder of this chapter, we analyse whether there are ways to overcome adverse selection and moral hazard problems. Before doing so, we may ask whether a risky investment in quality (where the investment is observable to consumers) results in the same type of quality trap as above.[6] Clearly, the situation we envisage now potentially allows consumers to obtain information about the expected quality in the market since consumers observe the investment level and have a clear understanding of the relationship between investment spending and expected quality. Case 12.4 gives an example of such investment in quality improvement.

Case 12.4 Quality management systems

The type of investment we have in mind can be exemplified by a firm's effort to meet standards for quality management systems, such as ISO 9000. The ISO 9000 certification does not guarantee the quality of end products and services; rather, it certifies that consistent business processes are being applied. That is, it proves that the firm (actually, any type of organization) has put in place the necessary processes (i.e., a quality management system) 'to fulfil the customer's quality requirements, and applicable regulatory requirements, while aiming to enhance customer satisfaction, and achieve continual improvement of its performance in pursuit of these objectives' (taken from www.iso.org). Cole (1998, p. 68) confirms this view by suggesting that firms may make ISO 9000 'their primary instrument for signaling quality to their customers'. However, firms may also seek certification simply in compliance with requirements of major customers or regulators. To disentangle the relative importance of these two motivations, Anderson *et al.* (1999) estimate a probit model of ISO 9000 certification. They show that the signalling motivation is indeed important: the desirability of communicating quality outcomes to external parties provides incremental explanatory power for the certification decision (even after including compliance motivations for seeking certification). Quality management systems seem thus to correspond to the type of investments we refer to in this section.

The probability that the product is of high quality is denoted by λ. A higher probability λ requires a larger investment $I(\lambda)$. We view this investment as a commitment to meet on average a certain reliability of the product. Suppose that $I' > 0$ and $I'' > 0$ and, in particular, $I(\lambda) = (k/2)\lambda^2$. We assume the same parameter restrictions as above including $r_L > c_L$ so that under full information, low quality is put on the market. Thus, under full information, the firm's maximization problem is $\max_\lambda \lambda(r_H - c_H) + (1 - \lambda)(r_L - c_L) - (k/2)\lambda^2$. Solving the first-order condition of profit maximization, we obtain as the probability for high quality $\lambda^f \equiv [(r_H - c_H) - (r_L - c_L)]/k$.

Consider now the situation in which consumers observe the firm's investment I but not the realization of quality. We start with the situation where consumers expect both qualities to be put on the market. Then the expected utility is $\lambda r_H + (1 - \lambda)r_L$, which is the price the firm will set at stage 2. Hence, expected profits at stage 1 are

$$\lambda[\lambda r_H + (1 - \lambda)r_L - c_H] + (1 - \lambda)[\lambda r_H + (1 - \lambda)r_L - c_L] - (k/2)\lambda^2$$

$$= \lambda(r_H - c_H) + (1 - \lambda)(r_L - c_L) - (k/2)\lambda^2.$$

Hence, the objective function of the firm is the same as under full information and the solution to this problem, denoted by λ^a is equal to λ^f.

However, at stage 2, the firm may not be interested in offering high quality on the market, while it is always willing to do so under full information (under our assumption that $r_H > c_H$). This indeed holds true if $r_H - c_H > 0 > \lambda r_H + (1 - \lambda)r_L - c_H$, where the latter expression is the price–cost margin of a high-quality firm under asymmetric information (a necessary condition for the latter inequalities to hold is that $r_L < c_H$). Then $I(\lambda^a)$ cannot be the profit-maximizing investment decision. Instead the firm may want to invest more so that at stage 2, it is committed to stay also with the high-cost (high-quality) product. (Alternatively, it does not invest at all.) For this, it has to invest at least $I(\widetilde{\lambda})$, where $\widetilde{\lambda} = (c_H - r_L)/(r_H - r_L)$. Indeed, $\lambda \geq \widetilde{\lambda}$ implies that $\lambda r_H + (1 - \lambda)r_L - c_H \geq 0$. Hence, the profit-maximizing investment at stage 1 is $I(\widetilde{\lambda})$ (where $\widetilde{\lambda} > \lambda^a$) if expected profits are positive at stage 1, that is, if $\widetilde{\lambda}(r_H - c_H) + (1 - \widetilde{\lambda})(r_L - c_L) - (k/2)\widetilde{\lambda}^2 > 0$. Here, the adverse selection effect that makes the full-information investment level unsustainable may lead to *overinvestment* compared to full information.

A numerical example (which gives parameter values to all parameters except k) illustrates when more investment under asymmetric than under full information occurs. Take the following parameter values: $r_H = 1$, $r_L = 1/3$, $c_H = 1/2$ and $c_L = 1/4$ (so that $r_H - c_H = 1/2$ and $r_L - c_L = 1/12$). Under full information, the firm would choose its investment such that $\lambda^f = 5/(12k)$. As we have seen above, under asymmetric information and provided that consumers expect that products are sold on the market independent of the realization of the random variable, the firm would invest such that $\lambda^a = \lambda^f$. However, for a high-quality firm to make positive operating profits, the price must exceed costs, i.e., $\lambda r_H + (1 - \lambda)r_L - c_H \geq 0$, which becomes $\lambda \geq \widetilde{\lambda} \equiv 1/4$ under our parameter values. Hence, the firm will indeed implement λ^a if $\lambda^a \geq \widetilde{\lambda}$. Otherwise, if the firm implemented λ^a, consumers would know that a high-quality firm would not participate, so that their beliefs about product quality would not be confirmed. Consumers expect a sufficiently high probability that the product is of low quality, which reduces their willingness to pay. Hence, the firm cannot charge a sufficiently high price to cover its cost in case it is of high quality. One possibility for the firm is to increase its investment expenditure so as to increase the probability of high quality. In expectations, quality is higher than under full information if $\tilde{\lambda} = 1/4 > 5/(12k) = \lambda^f$, which is equivalent to $k > 5/3$. To be an equilibrium strategy also at the investment stage, expected profits must be positive, i.e. $\lambda(1/2) + (1 - \lambda)(1/12) - (k/2)\lambda^2 \geq 0$. Evaluated at $\lambda = 1/4$, this is equivalent to $k \leq 6$. Hence, there is a range for parameter values k such that the firm invests more under asymmetric than under full information (this range is $(5/3, 6]$).

> **Lesson 12.3** **If consumers observe investments in the reliability of products but not reliability itself, a firm may actually invest more in reliability (or quality) under asymmetric information than under full information.**

It is perhaps useful to restate the argument in words. We have seen that for given beliefs, investment incentives are not affected by consumer information. However, taking into account the participation constraint of a high-quality firm, investments under given beliefs may be insufficient to make selling high quality worthwhile. Thus λ^a cannot be the equilibrium belief at the investment level $I(\lambda^a)$. To make the participation of the high-quality firm worthwhile, the firm has to distort its investment upward in order to convince consumers that a high-quality outcome is more likely, in which case they are willing to pay more. To summarize, *we should not conclude that asymmetric information about product quality automatically reduces the incentives to provide higher quality; the reverse may actually be true.*

12.2   Advertising and price signals

We concluded the previous section by showing that asymmetric information may induce a firm to overinvest in the quality or the reliability of its product. A different argument is that a firm may use resources that do not provide any direct benefit to consumers. A firm, however, may use the corresponding expenditure to convince consumers of its merits. We now turn to this type of argument in the context of advertising. Recall that we already alluded to this argument in Chapter 6 when mentioning that advertising may be informative in an indirect way. Advertising may thus serve as a signal of quality. We also show in this section that prices may be used as another signal of quality, either on their own or in combination with advertising.

12.2.1   Advertising signals

In many markets for experience goods, we observe firms spending large amounts of resources on advertising and other marketing activities, which lack an apparent message or news. Here, we investigate how such public money burning, as exemplified by big advertising campaigns, can convince consumers that quality is high.

Basic intuition

Suppose that a firm does not have warranties as a policy at its disposal. (Warranties will be analysed in the next chapter; one reason may be that due to the moral hazard problem on the consumer side, the firm has opted not to offer particular warranties.) We may then want to know whether a firm can use other strategies such as advertising (as considered in this subsection) or distorted prices (as considered in the next subsection) to signal the quality of its product. The explanation we want to give here is that large advertising expenditures can indirectly reveal information about the products, namely they can signal to consumers that such a firm is of high quality. For such a signalling device to work, consumers must believe that such advertising expenditures come from a high-quality firm, and such beliefs must be confirmed by the actual equilibrium play of the firm.

There are three channels by which a signalling device can work. *Repeat purchases* by consumers constitute a first channel. This is the channel we examine in this subsection. The key insight is that signals work if there is a repeat business effect, so that gains from adopting a certain strategy are different for a high- and a low-quality firm. In environments in which repeat purchases are absent, there are two other channels for signalling: *cost differences for various qualities* and *information differences among consumers*. We analyse these other two channels in the next subsection when considering price signals.

So, considering repeat purchases and abstracting from cost and information differences, signalling works as follows. If consumers do not learn about the product over time and are all completely uninformed about the product's quality, a high-quality firm does not have a credible and profitable signalling strategy since any attempt by a high-quality firm to overcome the asymmetric information problem it faces can be mimicked by the low-quality type. However, if the firm can also sell (at some later point) to consumers who have become informed about product quality, it may have an incentive to spend resources as a signal of product quality. The idea here is that a low-quality firm would be discovered at some point, thus losing its sales. This means that the expected change in profits from cheating for a low-quality firm is possibly less pronounced than the expected change in profits from telling the truth for a high-quality firm. We want to analyse this argument in detail.

The model

To consider not only situations in which low quality is characterized by a higher breakdown probability but to allow for other quality differences, we simply assume that high quality gives a utility of r_H, whereas low utility gives a utility of r_L, as in the previous section. Also, to make clear that our result in this subsection only relies on the repeat purchase effect, and relies neither on differences in costs nor on some consumers being informed, we assume that unit costs of low and high quality are the same, $c_L = c_H = c$ and that all consumers face the same asymmetric information problem. To make the problem interesting, we assume that $r_H > c$, but we do not make any assumption with respect to the low-quality product.

A firm sells a product of given quality for two periods. Each product is useful only for the period in which it is sold. Consumers learn the quality of the product after period 1 if they have purchased the product in period 1. For simplicity, there is no discounting between periods. Under *full information*, a high-quality firm does not advertise, sells its product at a price $p^1 = p^2 = r_H$ in the two periods, and makes profit $2r_H - 2c$. A low-quality firm sells at $p^1 = p^2 = r_L$ and makes profits $\pi_L = 2r_L - 2c$ if $r_L > c$. Otherwise, it does not sell and makes zero profit.

Under *asymmetric information*, we consider the following timing. First, the firm learns its type but consumers do not. Then, the firm sets its first-period price and it possibly takes some action that can be publicly observed by consumers but that does not directly affect demand. To fix ideas, we assume that the firm spends some amount of resources on advertising; the action is thus to choose some advertising expenditure and we denote this variable by A. After observing first-period price and advertising, consumers decide whether to buy. If a consumer buys (and consumes the product), it observes the product quality. In the second period, the firm sets its second-period price and afterwards consumers buy. Since advertising expenditures cannot be rational in the second period, we only need to consider advertising in the first period. We analyse separating perfect Bayesian Nash equilibria. In most of the analysis, we restrict attention to belief systems in which only the advertising level but not the price can affect beliefs.

In a separating equilibrium, described by equilibrium actions p^1, p^2, A and beliefs $\mu(A)$, we must have that a high-quality firm does not have an incentive to mimic low quality, as well as the reverse. In addition, we have to check participation constraints. Here, we implicitly assume that beliefs are constant in price so that only advertising signals are viable, if at all.

Suppose now that a high-quality firm spends A on advertising. Then a low-quality firm that spends the same amount of advertising is believed to be of high quality, $\mu(A) = 1$, i.e., the probability that a product is of high quality is believed to be 1. However, after period 1, consumers find out that the product quality is low and are only willing to pay r_L. Hence, a low-quality firm that mimics the behaviour of a high-quality firm makes profit $\pi'_L = r_H + r_L - 2c - A$, provided that $r_L > c$. Otherwise the profit would be $r_H - c - A$.

Case 1: the low quality is profitable. We first investigate the potential role of advertising if $r_L > c$. In the separating equilibrium, the low quality firm does not advertise and makes profit $\pi_L = 2r_L - 2c$, while a high-quality firm advertises and makes a profit of $\pi_H = 2r_H - 2c - A$. A deviation by the high-quality firm would be to not advertise; in that case, it would make profit $\pi'_H = r_L + r_H - 2c$, as it would be perceived to be of low quality in the first period. Incentive compatibility requires thus that $\pi_H \geq \pi'_H$ or $A \leq r_H - r_L$. As for the low-quality firm, it does not find it profitable to mimic the behaviour of a high-quality firm provided that $\pi_L \geq \pi'_L$ or $A \geq r_H - r_L$. We see that the two incentive constraints cannot be met simultaneously. It follows that in this setting, advertising does *not* constitute a viable signal. The reason is that although we presented a model with repeat purchase, the advertising decision does not affect differences of second-period profits. Thus no repeat purchase effect is present.

We offer two justifications as to why advertising can be a signal of product quality in this simple model. In the previous analysis, consumers were fully rational. In particular, we have assumed that a consumer who is deceived by a low-quality firm is willing to buy its product in period 2 at the price r_L. It seems, however, quite convincing to assume that a consumer's willingness to pay in period 2 not only depends on the observed quality but also on her feeling whether she was cheated. To take an extreme case, consumers may boycott a firm that they trusted in period 1 and that has failed them. Then the low-quality firm's deviation profit is now only $\pi'_L = r_H - c - A$ because it is no longer able to sell in period 2. In this case, the low quality firm's incentive constraint is violated for $A > \hat{A} \equiv (r_H - r_L) - (r_L - c)$. Profits of the high-quality firm remain unchanged. Hence, a high-quality firm can credibly signal quality by spending $A \in [\hat{A}, r_H - r_L]$. Selecting the separating equilibrium with the lowest signalling cost, we have that a high-quality firm set $A = \hat{A}$. Due to the 'revenge' consumers take when deceived, the second-period profits of the low-quality firm depend on its first-period action. In other words, there is a repeat purchase effect that makes advertising a signal of product quality.

Case 2: the low quality is not profitable. We now turn to a second justification, which arises in the fully rational model under the alternative parameter constellation that $r_L < c$. In this case, low quality will not be active in separating equilibrium. Equilibrium profits therefore are $\pi_H = 2r_H - 2c - A$ (as before) and $\pi_L = 0$. The deviation profit of the low-quality firm is $\pi'_L = r_H - c - A$ since the firm is only active if it is perceived to be of high quality. Hence for $A > \tilde{A} = r_H - c$ the low-quality firm's incentive constraint is satisfied. Recall that consumers learn the firm's product quality after period 1 only if they have purchased the product in period 1. This affects the deviation profit of the high-quality firm because in period 1, nobody buys at $p > r_L$ so that $\pi'_H = 0$ in this case. Alternatively, for $p < r_L$, a purchase is beneficial for consumers even if the product is of low quality. Hence, for $p < r_L$ the high-quality firm's profit is at most $\pi''_H = r_L + r_H - 2c$, and the maximal deviation profit is $\max\{0, (r_H - c) - (c - r_L)\}$, which is strictly less than $r_H - c$. Equilibrium profits are up to $\pi_H = 2r_H - 2c - \tilde{A} = r_H - c > 0$. Again a repeat business effect is present because now the second-period profits of the *high-quality* firm depend on its first-period action (provided that $r_L + r_H - 2c < 0$).

Lesson 12.4   **Advertising and other strategies in which a firm publicly 'burns money' can be a credible means for a firm to communicate to consumers that it is of high quality. In particular, such a strategy can be successful if a repeat purchase effect is present.**

The predictions of the previous lesson are, unfortunately, difficult to test in practice, as explained in Case 12.5.

Case 12.5 **Empirical examination of advertising as a signal of quality**

Although the signalling role of advertising has received a lot of attention in the theoretical literature, there are relatively few studies of its empirical relevance. This lack of systematic empirical studies has certainly to do with the difficulty of collecting comprehensive data sets containing various types of product characteristics along with producer and consumer information. Moreover, as explained by Horstmann and MacDonald (2003), the following data and methodology problems have to be addressed when testing the signalling role of advertising. First, a common strategy to test the signalling hypothesis consists in finding the positive correlations among quality, advertising and price predicted by the theoretical models. To do so, one must quantify the notion of quality that is appropriate for the signalling model; that is, one needs to find product information that is relevant to consumers but is available only to the firm. Common measures based on previous consumer experience, on observable product characteristics or including an assessment of 'value for money', do not meet this requirement; neither do publicly available quality indices. A second problem occurs when the data contain a mix of new and established products. In that case, one needs to account for consumer experience with the product in order to build a correct test of the signalling hypothesis. Third, the use of cross-section data including significant product and/or firm heterogeneity makes the interpretation of correlation coefficients unclear if one fails to control adequately for this heterogeneity.

Given these difficulties, it does not really come as a surprise that the results of the existing empirical studies are quite inconclusive, although they seem to be somewhat supportive of the signalling hypothesis.[7]

In the previous analysis, we have focused on an action A as a signal of high quality. Note, however, that consumers may base their beliefs on price and the firm may alternatively set a price below marginal costs to signal high quality. Consider the case that firms cannot advertise but in which the price may contain information about product quality. Note that any price below c would lead to losses for a low-quality firm. Thus consumers may hold beliefs that any price below c must come from a high-quality firm. A firm that sets a price below marginal costs can thus signal that it is of high quality. Take this price to be $c - \varepsilon$. Hence, the high-quality firm makes profit $\pi_H = c - \varepsilon + r_H - 2c = r_H - c - \varepsilon$. Since ε can be arbitrarily small, the high-quality firm can make profits up to $r_H - c$. Hence, in this simple model, a low price in the first period can be used as a signal of high quality.

> **Lesson 12.5** **A price below marginal costs can be a credible strategy for a firm to communicate to consumers that it is of high quality because it allows the firm to benefit from repeat purchases.**

In our simple model, we have seen that instead of advertising in the first period the firm can equivalently lower its price. The equivalence of the low price and the advertising signal is due to our assumption that all consumers are identical and have unit demand. If the firm faces a downward-sloping demand curve, the equivalence breaks down and the analysis becomes more complex. Price may be used in combination with advertising to signal product quality. Whether the price is distorted above or below the full information price depends on the particularities of the model. The direction of the distortion and the viability of advertising signals depends on costs and the effect of advertising on demand.

12.2.2   Price signals

While we so far have singled out the repeat purchase effect as an explanation for the possibility of signalling, we will now focus on price signalling and analyse two single-period models in which price can signal product quality. Before doing so, it is useful to consider a general framework in which demand possibly depends on price p, expected quality s^e and true quality s.

General framework

Suppose that there is a single firm with market power that faces a demand curve $Q(p, s^e, s)$.[f] The firm's profit is $(p - c(s))Q(p, s^e, s)$. If its quality is low ($s = s_L$) denote the full information profit-maximizing price as $p_L = \arg\max_p (p - c(s_L))Q(p, s_L, s_L)$. Accordingly, a low-quality firm has no incentive to mimic a high-quality firm if its full information profit exceeds the profits it can possibly obtain mimicking the behaviour of a high-quality firm, where consumers believe that only high-quality firms set price p. This inequality reads

$$(p_L - c(s_L))Q(p_L, s_L, s_L) \geq (p - c(s_L))Q(p, s_H, s_L),$$

if p is the signalling price chosen by a high-quality firm. Denote $\widehat{p}_H$ as a solution to $(p_L - c(s_L))Q(p_L, s_L, s_L) = (\widehat{p}_H - c(s_L))Q(\widehat{p}_H, s_H, s_L)$, which may not be uniquely defined. The high-quality firm has to distort its full information price $p_H = \arg\max_p (p - c(s_H))Q(p, s_H, s_H)$ if the low-quality firm has an incentive to mimic at this price. We consider minimal deviations $\widehat{p}_H$. The high-quality firm has a (strict) incentive to use a price-signalling strategy if profits with price signalling are greater than maximal profits under the belief that the firm is of low quality, i.e.,

$$(\widehat{p}_H - c(s_H))Q(\widehat{p}_H, s_H, s_H) \geq \max_p (p - c(s_H))Q(p, s_L, s_H).$$

Note that this reasoning also applies to a repeat purchase model where the above profit function is a reduced profit function.

We now elaborate on the general price-signalling model in two specific applications. What makes price signalling viable differs in the two models. In the first model, it is the presence of a share of fully informed consumers, whereas in the second model, it is the difference in the cost of producing high and low quality. Before that, we briefly describe in Case 12.6 what disastrous consequences may result from a failure of prices to signal high quality, i.e., when low-quality firms manage to mimic the behaviour of high-quality ones.

Case 12.6 When low quality poses as high quality

Bangladesh was hit with devastating floods in July and August 2007. In his description of the aftermath of the flood, Maswood Alam Khan (General Manager of the Bangladesh Krishi Bank) writes the following (emphasis added): 'Millions of people in 38 of 64 districts of our country are passing hellish moments; thousands are afflicted with diseases like diarrhoea, typhoid, pneumonia, jaundice and skin infections. Refugees may fall sick with malaria, dengue fever and other fatal diseases. . . . The weak women and children are

---

[f] We do not explicitly consider other firms in this market, which is admissible if these other firms set prices that are not affected by the actions of the firm under consideration (as would be the case with a competitive fringe that produces at marginal costs) or, trivially, if there is no other firm in the market.

losing out to the adult and strong men in their fight to grab whatever miniscule relief materials are trickling down to relief camps. In addition, *unscrupulous businesspersons are selling adulterated medicines at higher than normal prices lest buyers should doubt the genuineness of medicines, if offered at lower prices.*' ('Facing aftermath of the flood', *The Independent*, Bangladesh, August 2007).

A model with a share of fully informed consumers

In the first model, high- and low-quality products are produced at the same marginal cost and demand is perfectly inelastic. Price signalling is viable if a share of consumers is fully informed. We will show that if this share is sufficiently large, the firm can actually separate with full information prices. For a smaller share, it has to lower its price below the full information level. Here, the informed consumers generate an information spillover: uninformed consumers obtain information through the firm's price because they know that some other consumers have better information and act according to this information.

Suppose the same model as in the previous subsection with the following two modifications: (i) there is only one selling period so that there are no repeat purchases, and (ii) a share λ of consumers is fully informed about the firm's product quality. Suppose furthermore that $r_L > c$. Under full information, the high-quality firm would set $p_H = r_H$ and the low-quality firm would set $p_L = r_L$.

We first show that for λ sufficiently large, there is a separating equilibrium in which the high-quality firm realizes its full information profit. Hence, we have to show that prices $p_H = r_H$ and $p_L = r_L$ can be supported in equilibrium. In such an equilibrium, consumers believe that a firm that sets its price equal to r_H must be of high quality and the profits are $\pi_H = r_H - c$ for the high-quality firm and $\pi_L = r_L - c$ for the low-quality firm. Clearly, the high-quality firm does not have an incentive to deviate. Consider a deviation by the low-quality firm. The only potentially profit-maximizing deviation is to mimic the behaviour of the high-quality firm. In this case its profit would be $\pi'_L = (1 - \lambda)(r_H - c)$. The incentive constraint of the low-quality firm is thus satisfied if $\pi_L \geq \pi'_L$ or

$$r_L - c \geq (1 - \lambda)(r_H - c) \Leftrightarrow \lambda \geq \tilde{\lambda} = \frac{r_H - r_L}{r_H - c}.$$

Hence, *if the share of informed consumers is sufficiently large, i.e., $\lambda \geq \tilde{\lambda}$, the high-quality firm can signal its product quality through the full-information price.*

Yet, if the share of informed consumers is smaller, full-information prices cannot be supported in equilibrium. To satisfy the incentive constraint of the low-quality firm, the high-quality firm has to set a price $\hat{p}_H < r_H$. At this signalling price, consumers believe the product to be of high quality, for higher prices the firm is believed to be of low quality. Under these beliefs, the high-quality firm does not have an incentive to deviate from $\hat{p}_H$ as long as $\hat{p}_H \geq r_L$ and then, it makes profit $\pi_H = \hat{p}_H - c$. In a separating equilibrium, the low-quality firm's profit is still $\pi_L = r_L - c$. If the low-quality firm mimics the high-quality firm, its profits are $\pi'_L = (1 - \lambda)(\hat{p}_H - c)$. The incentive constraint of the low-quality firm is thus satisfied if

$$r_L - c \geq (1 - \lambda)(\hat{p}_H - c) \Leftrightarrow \hat{p}_H \leq c + \frac{r_L - c}{1 - \lambda}.$$

We observe that the upper bound on $\widehat{p}_H$ is increasing in λ. Note that at $\lambda = 0$, we have that the incentive constraint becomes $\widehat{p}_H \leq r_L$. *In the model in which a share λ of consumers knows the product quality ex ante, the separating equilibrium that maximizes the firm's profit takes the form that $p_L = r_L$ and*

$$\widehat{p}_H = \begin{cases} c + \frac{r_L - c}{1 - \lambda} & \text{for } \lambda \in [0, \frac{r_H - r_L}{r_H - c}) \\ r_H & \text{for } \lambda \in [\frac{r_H - r_L}{r_H - c}, 1] \end{cases}.$$

The price is increasing with λ until it reaches the full information price p_H.[g] This again illustrates that the firm suffers from the asymmetric information problem and that a larger share of informed consumers alleviates it. For our purposes we have obtained the following key insights:

Lesson 12.6   If some consumers know the product quality, the firm can set a higher price for high compared to low quality, and use this price to signal its quality to the remaining share of uninformed consumers. As the share of informed consumers increases, the price of the high-quality firm reaches the corresponding full-information price. Above a critical size of informed consumers, signalling is feasible with full-information prices.

A model with cost differences between high and low quality

In the second model, all consumers face the same asymmetric information problem. However, there are cost differences between high and low quality, and consumers have variable demand. We show that in this model, price can be used as a signal of product quality. In the following subsection, we will then show that under certain conditions price in combination with advertising is a more attractive signalling strategy for the high-quality firm than price alone, because advertising allows the firm to reduce its price distortion. Such an argument could also be presented if a repeat purchase effect is included.[8]

Suppose that a firm produces low quality at marginal cost c_L and high quality at c_H, with $c_L, c_H < 1$. The firm's demand is assumed to be

$$Q(p; s^e) = \tfrac{1}{2}(1 + s^e - p).$$

In this example, demand is independent of true quality since consumers purchase only once and no consumer has any private information on the product's quality.[h]

Consider first the *market under full information*. Suppose that the firm is of recognized low quality, $s = s_L = 0$. Then the firm maximizes $\max_p (p - c_L) Q(p; s_L)$. The first-order condition of profit maximization can be written as $1 + c_L - 2p = 0$. Hence, $p_L = (1 + c_L)/2$

---

[g] Note that for λ sufficiently small the firm would prefer to be in the pooling equilibrium in which it sets the same price irrespective of quality. We leave it to the interested reader to apply equilibrium selection arguments to select between pooling and separating equilibria.

[h] This demand follows, e.g., from the following competitive fringe model. The firm is located at 0 of the [0, 1]-interval. A competitive fringe of low quality is assumed to be located at 1. Consumers obtain indirect utility $u_i = r + s_i - p - \tau |l_i - x|$. In what follows we assume that the firm never serves all consumers. A sufficient condition is that $(s_H - s_L) < \tau + c$. Setting without loss of generality $s_L = 0$ and assuming that $\tau = 1$, one obtains the demand function.

and the corresponding profit is $\pi_L(p_L; s_L) = (1 - c_L)^2/8$. Suppose now that the firm is of recognized high quality, $s = s_H$. Then the firm maximizes $\max_p (p - c_H) Q(p; s_H)$. The first-order condition of profit maximization can be written as $1 + c_H + s_H - 2p = 0$. Hence, $p_H = (1 + c_H + s_H)/2$ and the corresponding profit is $\pi_H(p_H; s_H) = (1 - c_H + s_H)^2/8$.

Consider now *asymmetric information*: the firm's quality is not observed but consumers form beliefs about product quality conditional on the price they observe. We are interested in characterizing the separating equilibrium with the smallest price distortion relative to the full-information price. In a separating equilibrium, the low-quality firm sets its price equal to the full-information price p_L. Thus profit for s_L is $\pi_L = (1 - c_L)^2/8$. Suppose that above some price $\widehat{p}_H$, consumers believe the product to be of high quality. The profit of a high-quality firm is then

$$\pi_H(\widehat{p}_H; s_H) = \tfrac{1}{2}(\widehat{p}_H - c_H)(1 + s_H - \widehat{p}_H).$$

If a low-quality firm mimics the behaviour of a high-quality firm, its profit would be equal to

$$\pi_L(\widehat{p}_H; s_H) = \tfrac{1}{2}(\widehat{p}_H - c_L)(1 + s_H - \widehat{p}_H).$$

We are now in the position to analyse the separating conditions. We start with the incentive constraint of the low-quality firm. We must have that it is not profitable to mimic the equilibrium behaviour of the high-quality firm, i.e., $\pi_L \geq \pi_L(\widehat{p}_H; s_H)$. This condition is $\tfrac{1}{8}(1 - c_L)^2 \geq \tfrac{1}{2}(\widehat{p}_H - c_L)(1 + s_H - \widehat{p}_H)$ or, equivalently,

$$\widehat{p}_H^2 - (1 + c_L + s_H)\widehat{p}_H + \tfrac{1}{4}\left[(1 - c_L)^2 + 4(1 + s_H)c_L\right] \geq 0.$$

Note that

$$\sqrt{(1 + c_L + s_H)^2 - (1 - c_L)^2 - 4(1 + s_H)c_L} = \sqrt{s_H^2 + 2(1 - c_L)s_H}.$$

Hence, to satisfy the incentive constraint, the price for the high-quality product thus has to satisfy

$$p \leq p_L^- \equiv \tfrac{1}{2}(1 + c_L + s_H) - \tfrac{1}{2}\sqrt{s_H^2 + 2(1 - c_L)s_H}$$

or

$$p \geq p_L^+ \equiv \tfrac{1}{2}(1 + c_L + s_H) + \tfrac{1}{2}\sqrt{s_H^2 + 2(1 - c_L)s_H}.$$

Variables p_L^- and p_L^+ are well-defined. The firm of type s_L has no incentive to deviate if the firm of type s_H sets a price $\widehat{p}_H \in (-\infty, p_L^-] \cup [p_L^+, \infty)$.

Let us now turn to the incentive constraint of the high-quality firm. Suppose the firm sets a price p and is believed to be of high quality. Its profit is

$$\pi_H(p; s_H) = \tfrac{1}{2}(p - c_H)(1 + s_H - p).$$

If the firm simply sets its profit-maximizing price under the assumption that it is believed to be of low quality (i.e., that it cannot convince consumers that it is of high quality), it sets its price to maximize $(p - c_H) Q(p; s_L)$. This price is $(1 + c_H)/2$, which gives profit $(1 - c_H)^2/8$. Hence, for price signalling to be profitable, we must have $\tfrac{1}{2}(p - c_H)(1 + s_H - p) \geq \tfrac{1}{8}(1 - c_H)^2$ or, equivalently,

$$p^2 - (1 + c_H + s_H)p + \tfrac{1}{4}\left[(1 - c_H)^2 + 4(1 + s_H)c_H\right] \leq 0.$$

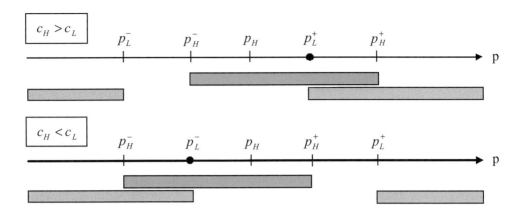

Figure 12.2 Price distortion to signal high quality

Note that a necessary condition is $p > c_H$. Since

$$\sqrt{(1 + c_H + s_H)^2 - (1 - c_H)^2 - 4(1 + s_H)c_H} = \sqrt{s_H^2 + 2(1 - c_H)s_H},$$

the separating constraint is satisfied for prices p with

$$p_H^- \equiv \tfrac{1}{2}(1 + c_H + s_H) - \tfrac{1}{2}\sqrt{s_H^2 + 2(1 - c_H)s_H} \le p$$

$$\le \tfrac{1}{2}(1 + c_H + s_H) + \tfrac{1}{2}\sqrt{s_H^2 + 2(1 - c_H)s_H} \equiv p_H^+.$$

Combining the two incentive constraints, we have that signalling prices must satisfy $p \in [p_H^-, p_H^+]$ and either $p \in (-\infty, p_L^-]$ or $p \in [p_L^+, \infty)$. Therefore, for signalling to be an equilibrium phenomenon, we must have that $p_H^+ > p_L^+$ or $p_L^- > p_H^-$. Observe that

$$p_H^+ - p_L^+ = \tfrac{1}{2}(c_H - c_L) + \tfrac{1}{2}f(s_H) \quad \text{and} \quad p_L^- - p_H^- = -\tfrac{1}{2}(c_H - c_L) + \tfrac{1}{2}f(s_H),$$

$$\text{where } f(s_H) \equiv \sqrt{s_H^2 + 2(1 - c_H)s_H} - \sqrt{s_H^2 + 2(1 - c_L)s_H}.$$

It can be shown that (i) both $f(s_H)$ and $f'(s_H)$ have the same sign as $(c_L - c_H)$, and (ii) $f(s_H)$ tends to $(c_L - c_H)$ as s_H tends to infinity. It follows that: (i) if $c_H = c_L$, then $p_L^- = p_H^-$ and $p_L^+ = p_H^+$; (ii) if $c_H > c_L$, then $p_H^+ > p_L^+$ and $p_L^- < p_H^-$; (iii) if $c_H < c_L$, then $p_H^+ < p_L^+$ and $p_L^- > p_H^-$. As represented on Figure 12.2, for $c_H > c_L$ (resp. $c_H < c_L$), it is the price p_L^+ (resp. p_L^-) that lies within the interval that defines prices that are compatible with the incentive constraint of the high-quality firm.

Collecting the previous findings, we can conclude the following. When high quality costs more than low quality ($c_H > c_L$), the firm can signal its type by setting a sufficiently *high* price. In particular, selecting the equilibrium with the least-cost distortion, we find that the high price p_L^+ is a signal of product quality. Conversely, if low quality costs more ($c_H < c_L$), the firm can signal its type by setting a sufficiently *low* price, namely p_L^-. It is also clear that if the two qualities are equally costly to produce ($c_H = c_L$), the high-quality firm cannot signal its type.

It remains to be investigated when the high-quality firm actually has to distort its price. For $c_H > c_L$, this is the case if $p_L^+ > p_H$, and for $c_H < c_L$, the condition is $p_L^- < p_H$. The two conditions can be rewritten as

$$\sqrt{s_H^2 + 2(1 - c_L)s_H} > |c_H - c_L|,$$

which is satisfied if the marginal cost difference is not too large with respect to the level of high quality s_H. Put differently, if the marginal cost difference is sufficiently large, the high-quality firm can set its full-information price p_H as a signal of high quality. Reversely, if it is sufficiently small the high-quality firms has to distort its price to signal its quality.

Lesson 12.7   In an environment with asymmetric information about a firm's product quality, if marginal production costs depend on quality, a firm can signal its product quality with price. Signalling is possibly costly, i.e., the firm sets a price that is different from its full-information price.

We do not elaborate on the full set of separating equilibria. Game theory has provided us with tools to select among equilibria. There are good reasons to focus on those signalling equilibria in which the price distortion (in its effect on profits) is minimal. However, this still does not give us a unique prediction. In addition, there exist pooling equilibria in which price does not contain any information along the equilibrium path. To select between separating and pooling equilibria, one approach is to rule out 'unreasonable' out-of-equilibrium beliefs, as has been proposed e.g. with the 'intuitive criterion'. We decided not to discuss such equilibrium refinements in this book.[9]

The following case illustrates that price signalling is observed on the Bordeaux wine market (which seems to exhibit some features of the two specific models we just analysed).

Case 12.7 Price signalling for Bordeaux wines[10]

Wine (as most food products) certainly belongs to the category of experience goods because its quality can rarely be ascertained before actual consumption. When considering wines from the well-known Bordeaux region of France, one needs to distinguish between 'primeur' and 'bottled' wine: the wine is first sold as primeur several months after the harvest, while it is still in barrels; then, almost a year after, the wine is eventually bottled. As consumers' willingness to pay depends on their expectations about wine quality, it can be conjectured that producers might be willing to signal quality on the market for bottled wine through the primeur price.

Ali and Nauges (2007) test this conjecture, using an unbalanced panel data set of 1153 wines produced by 132 Bordeaux châteaux over fifteen vintages. To this end, they measure the impact of primeur price on subsequent bottled wine prices, while checking for the effects of current quality and reputation. They show that a 10% increase in the primeur price increases the subsequent prices of bottled wine by 3%. Taken along with the finding that current quality, as measured by Robert Parker's ratings, also has a very small impact on bottled wine prices, they conclude that the primeur price acts as a quality signal for consumers.

Note that the Bordeaux wine market presents characteristics pertaining to the two environments we have just considered. On the one hand, there seems to be a sufficiently high share of informed buyers acting in the market, so as to make price signalling viable, as indicated in Lesson 12.6. Yet, potential buyers are not fully informed about wine quality, since wine is not yet finished at the time of primeur sales. They thus have to form quality expectations using information such as the climatic conditions that prevailed during the grape-growing season and the reputation of the *château* (we consider the role of reputation in the next chapter). On the other hand, it is more costly to produce high-quality than low-quality wine and therefore, only high primeur prices can provide an effective signal of high quality, as explained in Lesson 12.7.

12.2.3   Joint price and advertising signals

We return to a two-period model to investigate whether a monopolist wants to use a two-dimensional signal in the form of price and advertising as a signal of product quality.[11] Hence, we consider a situation in which the firm sets its price p^1 and an advertising expenditure A in the first period, and its price p^2 in the second period. In contrast with our earlier analysis of a two-period model, demand is now sensitive to price changes. This, as we will see, destroys the equivalence of price and advertising signals but makes, under some conditions, a two-dimensional signalling strategy the preferred option of the firm. The idea of such signalling in a two-period model is that repeated purchases are more likely in the case of positive former experience (stemming from high quality). This implies that stimulating initial purchases is valuable especially for products with high quality.

The model we consider has the following features. Consumers with unit demand have different willingness-to-pay. Hence, the firm faces a downward sloping demand curve. A strategy of the firm is to set in period 1 price p^1 and A, conditional on its type s_L or s_H. Based on this observation, consumers form beliefs $\mu(p, A) \in [0, 1]$, which is the expected probability that the product is of high quality. We can define as product quality the probability that consumers are satisfied with the product quality (which is assumed to be the same realization in periods 1 and 2). High quality thus means that it is more likely that consumers are satisfied. If a consumer is satisfied she obtains a gross rent of r_H and otherwise she obtains zero. In period 2, there is only demand among those consumers who have already bought in period 1 and were satisfied with the product. Since consumers are fully informed in period 2, there is no role for advertising in the second period.

Discounting second-period profits by $\delta \in (0, 1]$, we write profits as a function of first-period price and advertising, consumer beliefs and product quality,

$$\pi\,(p, A, \mu, s) = \pi^1\,(p, A, \mu, s) + \delta\widetilde{\pi}^2\,(p, \mu, s).$$

Here, $\tilde{\pi}$ is a reduced profit function in which the profit-maximizing second-period price has been substituted. In this simple model, first-period advertising has no direct effect on second-period profits; however, through consumer beliefs μ, second-period profits may depend indirectly on advertising. We have $\partial\tilde{\pi}^2/\partial p < 0$ and $\partial\tilde{\pi}^2/\partial\mu > 0$. The key property is that second-period profits of a high-quality firm react more sensitively to price than those of a low-quality firm. In line with our previous analysis, we call this effect the *repeat-business effect*:

$$|\partial\tilde{\pi}^2(p, \mu, s_L)/\partial p| < |\partial\tilde{\pi}^2(p, \mu, s_H)/\partial p|. \tag{RB}$$

The intuition for this property is that, for any given μ, fewer consumers buy in the second period if the first-period price rises. Lost consumers are more painful for producers of high quality (since under high quality, a high share of consumers would be content and repeat the purchase). However, there may be a countervailing cost-effect: namely, lost consumers are less painful for producers of high quality if $c_H > c_L$ (so that the profit margin for high quality is lower than for low quality). Hence, the property (RB) holds if $c_H \leq c_L$ or if $c_H - c_L > 0$ is sufficiently small.

Suppose that advertising is demand-neutral, the only direct effect on profits (i.e. keeping beliefs μ constant) stems from the effect on costs, $\partial\pi/\partial A = -1$. Therefore, a positive level of advertising in the first period can only be profit maximizing if there is a positive indirect effect on profits through a change of consumer beliefs $\mu(p, A)$. As remarked before, we do not need to consider advertising in the second period since it does not influence demand directly and there does not remain a possibility for signalling.

In any separating equilibrium, a firm of low quality sets $A = 0$. Consider a separating equilibrium with lowest costs. The firm of low quality sets

$$p^m(s_L) \equiv \arg\max_p \underbrace{\pi^1(p, 0, 0, s_L) + \delta\tilde{\pi}^2(p, 0, s_L)}_{=\pi(p,0,0,s_L)}.$$

We denote the profit of the low-quality firm in a separating equilibrium by $\pi^m(s_L) \equiv \pi(p^m(s_L), 0, 0, s_L)$.

The high-quality firm solves the maximization problem

$$\max_{p,A} \pi(p, A, 1, s_H)$$

subject to $\pi(p, A, 1, s_L) \leq \pi^m(s_L)$. To separate itself from the low-quality firm, it has to set a positive level of advertising, $A > 0$. Denote λ the Lagrange multiplier in the Lagrangian. The first-order condition with respect to A can be written as:

$$\pi_A(p, A, 1, s_H) = \lambda\pi_A(p, A, 1, s_L).$$

Since advertising is demand-neutral, we have $\pi_A(p, A, 1, s_H) = \pi_A(p, A, 1, s_L)$ which implies that $\lambda = 1$. The first-order condition with respect to p can be written as

$$\pi_p(p, A, 1, s_H) - \pi_p(p, A, 1, s_L) = 0,$$

which is equivalent to

$$\pi_p^1(p, A, 1, s_H) - \pi_p^1(p, A, 1, s_L) = \delta\left[\tilde{\pi}_p^2(p, 1, s_L) - \tilde{\pi}_p^2(p, 1, s_H)\right]. \tag{12.1}$$

For $A > 0$ to be profit maximizing, (12.1) must be satisfied.

We distinguish two cases. Suppose first that *high quality is more costly than low quality*, $c_H > c_L$. In this case, π_p^1 increases in quality and the left-hand side of (12.1) is positive. We also observe that $\tilde{\pi}_p^2$ decreases in quality; this is the repeat-business effect (RB) from above. Hence, also the right-hand side of (12.1) is positive. The monopolist is thus able to signal high quality through $A > 0$ and a distorted price.

If, by contrast, *high quality is less costly than low quality*, $c_H \leq c_L$, first-period marginal profit π_p^1 (weakly) decreases in quality so that the left-hand side of (12.1) cannot be positive, whereas the right-hand side remains positive. Therefore, condition (12.1) cannot be satisfied and advertising is not part of the signalling strategy.

> **Lesson 12.8**   With repeat purchases and variable demand, the monopolist can use advertising as part of his signalling strategy only if $c_H > c_L$.

Some additional intuition may be useful. An upward distortion of the first-period price above $p^m(s_H)$ reduces quantity sold and revenues. If high quality is more costly than low quality, $c_H > c_L$, this distortion is less painful for a producer of high quality than for a producer of low quality. However, a price increase also decreases second-period revenue since there is a smaller number of consumers who were served in period 1 (and satisfied with the product). This second-period effect, which has been isolated as the repeat-business effect, is more painful for a producer of high quality since consumers would have had a positive experience of the product with higher probability. The profit-maximizing first-period price p will then be chosen such that (12.1) just holds so that the two effects cancel each other out (together with the constraint for A). If $c_L \leq c_H$, the high quality is signalled through a low price $p < p^m(s_H)$ and $A = 0$. Here a separating equilibrium may exist even if $c_H = c_L$.

12.3   Price signalling under imperfect competition

In the remaining part of this chapter, we address the issue of price signalling in the context of imperfect competition.[12] We analyse a market in which two firms compete in prices and, at the same time, face an asymmetric information problem so that they may want to use price as a signal of product quality. Firms have private information about their quality. Hence, not only consumers but also competitors do not know their type. However, consumers can update their beliefs about quality because they observe prices, but a competitor does not have this option available.

In particular, consider the representative consumer model with linear-quadratic utility, as has been presented in Chapter 3. Here, we have to present a quality-augmented version. Quality of product i is $s_i = 0$ if the product is of low quality and $s_i = 1$ if the product is of high quality; the probability that a firm is of high quality is λ with $0 < \lambda < 1$. Consumers hold perceptions s_i^e. Each consumer chooses the quantity of products 1 and 2 and the quantity of the outside good whose price is normalized to zero, given prices p_1, p_2 and perceived qualities s_1^e and s_2^e. We can write the indirect utility as $v(q_1, q_2) = q_0 + u(q_1, q_2)$ where

$$u(q_1, q_2) = [a - (1 - s_1^e)\delta]q_1 + [a - (1 - s_2^e)\delta]q_2 - (bq_1^2 - dq_1q_2 + bq_2^2)$$

and q_0 is the quantity of the outside good. Using the budget constraint, we can write $q_0 = y - p_1 q_1 - p_2 q_2$ and we can maximize the indirect utility to obtain linear inverse demand functions of the form

$$P_i(q_i, q_j) = a - (1 - s_i^e)\delta - bq_i - dq_j, \quad j \neq i.$$

Note that product quality enters through the intercept of the inverse demand function: this intercept is equal to a if product i is of high quality ($s_i^e = 1$) and is reduced to $a - \delta$ if product i is of low quality ($s_i^e = 0$). Inverting the linear system, we obtain demand functions

$$Q_i(p_i, p_j) = \tilde{a} - \tilde{b}(1 - s_i^e)\delta + \tilde{d}(1 - s_j^e)\delta - \tilde{b}p_i + \tilde{d}p_j,$$

where $\tilde{a} = a/(b + d)$, $\tilde{b} = b/(b^2 - d^2)$, and $\tilde{d} = d/(b^2 - d^2)$. We normalize the unit cost of low quality to zero, $c_L = 0$, while the unit cost of high quality is assumed to be $c_H = k > 0$. Suppose that high quality is socially desirable so that $\delta > k$. Given the competitor's price and perceived quality, a firm's profit depends on its price, its perceived quality and its true quality, i.e.,

$$\pi_i(p_i, s_i, s_i^e; p_j, s_j^e) = (p_i - ks_i)Q_i(p_i, p_j).$$

We are interested in equilibria in which the price of each firm signals quality. Since the market is symmetric, we restrict attention to symmetric equilibrium. Hence, we must look for symmetric separating perfect Bayesian equilibria with $p_L^* \equiv p_{1L}^* = p_{2L}^* \neq p_{1H}^* = p_{2H}^* \equiv p_H^*$. When a firm sets its price, it does not know the competitor's type and it has to use the following information. With probability λ, the competitor is of high quality. In equilibrium, it sets in this case price p_H^* and consumers believe it to be of high quality. With the remaining probability $1 - \lambda$, the competitor is of low quality. In equilibrium it then sets price p_L^* and consumers believe it to be of low quality. Given the equilibrium strategy of firm j, firm i's expected profit is thus

$$E_j \pi_i(p_i, s_i, s_i^e; p_j, s_j^e) = (p_i - ks_i)E_j\left[\tilde{a} - \tilde{b}(1 - s_i^e)\delta + \tilde{d}(1 - s_j)\delta - \tilde{b}p_i + \tilde{d}p_s^*\right]$$

where expectations are taken with respect to the competitor's true type. Hence,

$$E_j \pi_i(p_i, s_i, s_i^e; p_j, s_j^e) = (p_i - ks_i)\{\lambda[\tilde{a} - \tilde{b}(1 - s_i^e)\delta + \tilde{d}(1 - s_j)\delta - \tilde{b}p_i + \tilde{d}p_H^*]$$
$$+ (1 - \lambda)[\tilde{a} - \tilde{b}(1 - s_i^e)\delta + \tilde{d}(1 - s_j)\delta - \tilde{b}p_i + \tilde{d}p_L^*]\}$$
$$= (p_i - ks_i)[\tilde{a} - \tilde{b}(1 - s_i^e)\delta + \tilde{d}(1 - s_j)\delta - \tilde{b}p_i + \tilde{d}Ep^*],$$

where $Ep^* = \lambda p_H^* + (1 - \lambda)p_L^*$. Here, regardless of its true type, a firm would like to be perceived as a high-quality firm, everything else given; at the same time, a firm would like to be a low-quality firm, everything else given. Hence, as we already know from the monopoly model, a low-quality firm will not distort its price in a separating equilibrium. A low-quality firm chooses its full-information best response whereas any high-quality firm has to distort its price. There is an important difference, though, with the monopoly model. In the monopoly model, the presence of asymmetric information does not change the outside option for consumers; therefore, a low-quality firm sets the same price under asymmetric information as under full information. This is not the case under competition because here, in equilibrium, the firm best responds to the competitor's expected equilibrium price which, under asymmetric information, is different from the full-information equilibrium price.

We can shorten firm i's maximization to $(p - ks_i)\widetilde{b}(Z(s_i^e) - p_i)$ where $Z(s_i^e) = [\widetilde{a} - \widetilde{b}(1 - s_i^e)\delta + \widetilde{d}(1 - \lambda)\delta + \widetilde{d}Ep^*]/\widetilde{b}$. Under two parameter restrictions, it can be shown that, for each type, there are prices that give positive expected profits, and that realized demand is always positive. To establish a separating equilibrium, we have to consider four situations: (1) the low-quality firm is perceived to be of low quality and thus maximizes $p_i\widetilde{b}(Z(s_L) - p_i)$ with respect to p_i; (2) the high-quality firm is perceived to be of high quality and in this case, the high-quality firm maximizes $(p_i - k)\widetilde{b}(Z(s_H) - p_i)$ on the set of prices under which the firm is perceived as of high quality; (3) the low-quality firm is perceived to be of high quality and chooses its price accordingly; (4) the high-quality firm is perceived to be of low quality and thus maximizes $(p_i - k)\widetilde{b}(Z(s_L) - p_i)$.

In situation (1), the low-quality firm sets price $p_L^* = (Z(s_L) + c_L)/2$ and obtains profit $\widetilde{b}(Z(s_L) - c_L)^2/4$. If the high-quality firm was perceived to be of low quality, it would obtain profit $\widetilde{b}(Z(s_L) - c_H)^2/4$. The separating price of the high-quality firm, p_H^*, therefore must satisfy that profits of a high-quality firm with price p_H^* be greater or equal to $\widetilde{b}(Z(s_L) - c_H)^2/4$, i.e. $(p_H^* - c_H)\widetilde{b}(Z(s_H) - p_H^*) \geq \widetilde{b}(Z(s_L) - c_H)^2/4$. In addition, a deviation to $p^*(s_H)$ must not be profitable for the low-quality firm, i.e. $(p_H^* - c_L)\widetilde{b}(Z(s_H) - p_H^*) \leq \widetilde{b}(Z(s_L) - c_L)^2/4$. Solving these two inequalities, one obtains that the equilibrium price of a high-quality firm must satisfy

$$p_H^* \in \left[\tfrac{1}{2}\left\{ Z(s_H) + c_L + [(Z(s_H) - c_L)^2 - (Z(s_L) - c_L)^2]^{\frac{1}{2}} \right\}, \right.$$

$$\left. \tfrac{1}{2}\left\{ Z(s_H) + c_H + [(Z(s_H) - c_H)^2 - (Z(s_L) - c_H)^2]^{\frac{1}{2}} \right\} \right].$$

The lower bound is above the best-response of a high-quality firm whose type is known. Hence, *there is an upward distortion of the price.* Selecting the equilibrium with lowest distortion, we have to take the lower bound of the interval so that the incentive constraint of the low-quality firm is binding.

To summarize the analysis until now, the separating equilibrium with minimal distortion is characterized by (recalling that c_L is set to zero) $p_H^* = \{Z(s_H) + [(Z(s_H) + Z(s_L))(Z(s_H) - Z(s_L))]^{\frac{1}{2}}\}/2$ and $p_L^* = Z(s_L)/2$. We are not yet done since $Z(s_L)$ and $Z(s_H)$ depend on Ep^*. To make this dependence explicit, we write $x = Ep^*$, $Z_H(x) = Z(s_H)$ and $Z_L(x) = Z(s_L)$. Since $x = Ep^* = \lambda p_H^* + (1 - \lambda)p_L^*$, we have to solve the fixed point problem

$$x = \lambda\tfrac{1}{2}\left\{ Z_H(x) + [(Z_H(x) + Z_L(x))(Z_H(x) - Z_L(x))]^{\frac{1}{2}} \right\} + (1 - \lambda)\tfrac{1}{2}Z_L(x).$$

Solving this equation is a bit cumbersome but can be done.[13]

The first result that emerges from the analysis is that if high quality is more costly than low quality, a high price can signal high quality also under imperfect competition. This price lies above the best-response price to Ep^* of a high-quality firm whose type is known. Interestingly, a low-quality firm has more demand in equilibrium than a high-quality firm. This is socially undesirable and would not occur under full information. It can then be shown that separating prices are above full-information prices, both for low- and high-quality firms. Suppose that, at an earlier stage (however, after they know their type), firms can decide whether to reveal information about product quality. Then it can be shown that there are parameter values for which both types of firm prefer not to reveal this information. This is in contrast to results under monopoly where asymmetric information hurts the high-quality firm. We summarize this discussion by the following lesson.

Lesson 12.9   **A high price can signal product quality also under competition. If high quality is costly, a high-quality firm distorts its price upward. Equilibrium prices are greater than prices under full information. Equilibrium profits may be greater than in the same market under full information for low-quality and high-quality firms. The asymmetric information problem may therefore persist even if firms can reveal their private information to consumers without costs.**

The last result suggests a stronger role for public policy than the analysis under monopoly has suggested. Since firms may have an incentive to hide their private information, firms may need to be obliged by law to reveal this information or other means, such as minimum quality standards or public quality checks, may be required. However, the effect of such policy interventions can be ambiguous and must be explored carefully before being implemented.

Review questions

1. If a firm faces asymmetric information and it has to invest in R&D to increase the probability of high quality, does this information lead to more or less investment? Discuss the effects that play a role.

2. What is the role of advertising spending in experience good markets? Are spending caps welfare increasing?

3. If a firm can choose price and advertising to convince consumers of high quality, do there exist circumstances under which the firm prefers not to use one of those two instruments? Discuss.

4. Consider a market in which product quality does not affect marginal costs. Do repeat purchases facilitate or hinder advertising signals?

Further reading

The seminal paper on adverse selection is by Akerlof (1970). The first signalling models are due to Spence (1973) in the context of the labour market. Here, we focus on applications to advertising and pricing. The idea that advertising can be indirectly informative is due to Nelson (1974). The seminal analysis of price and advertising signals under monopoly is due to Milgrom and Roberts (1986). Our analysis of price signalling in oligopoly follows Daughety and Reinganum (2008). The survey by Bagwell (2007) illuminates the issue of price and advertising signals.

13 Marketing tools for experience goods

In the previous chapter, we have looked at advertising and prices as two strategic variables that might be used to overcome asymmetric information problems. In this chapter, we will look at additional instruments that belong to the toolbox of a firm, such as a car manufacturer, which is confronted with asymmetric information. We focus on two broad classes of instruments, namely warranties (in Section 13.1) and branding (in Section 13.2).

Warranties can be an effective tool to separate high from low-quality products. A potential drawback is that consumers may not handle products with care if they hold a full warranty. This leads to a double moral hazard problem and makes this option possibly rather unattractive.

Branding is another important tool for producers of experience goods. It is an essential success factor for many companies since they want to be recognized over time and across products. Firms can then rely on their brand that stems from repeated interaction over time and on the use of one brand for several products so that consumers can correlate their beliefs about product quality across products – this latter practice is known as umbrella branding. An additional insight is that competition may substantially affect the logic of branding.

13.1 Warranties

Warranties are an everyday feature of experience goods. For instance, cars, consumer electronics and appliances typically come with warranties. Warranties establish liability between the manufacturer and the buyer in the event that an item fails (i.e., if the item is unable to perform satisfactorily its intended function when properly used). Usually, the warranty contract specifies both the performance that is to be expected and the redress available to the buyer if a failure occurs. Warranties serve many purposes. These include protecting manufacturers and buyers, assuring buyers against items which do not perform as promised, and helping dispute resolution between buyer and manufacturer. To meet these objectives, public authorities have formulated legislation imposing minimal warranties.

We focus here on another important purpose of warranties: we analyse them as a means of information disclosure by the firm. Thus we consider individual actions by firms that go beyond warranty policies that are required by government. The idea is simple. Since a firm has private information about its product quality, it can calculate the expected cost of adopting a particular warranty policy. A generous warranty policy (e.g., a 5 year unlimited warranty) is less costly for the firm if its product is more reliable (and thus is of higher quality). Therefore, we would expect that firms can use warranties to signal that a product is reliable. In

Subsection 13.1.1, we formally investigate this issue in a monopoly environment.[14] In Subsection 13.1.2, we extend the first model to add investments in quality control in a moral hazard environment.

13.1.1   Warranties as a reliability signal

Suppose that a firm offers a product that breaks down within a given time interval with probability $1 - \lambda$. In this case, the consumer's utility is set equal to zero. Her willingness-to-pay for a product that works properly is set equal to $r > 0$. The consumer may abstain from buying the product. In this case, her utility is assumed to be u_0, which we set equal to zero as well. Hence, if a consumer believes that the product breaks down with probability $1 - \lambda$, she will buy the product if $\lambda r - p \geq u_0 = 0$ where p is the price of the product.

There is a unit mass of homogeneous consumers. There are two types of firms: firms within the first group have a smaller break-down probability than firms within the second group, $\lambda_1 > \lambda_2$. The firm knows its type, consumers do not. Suppose that a firm has type λ_1 with probability ρ and type λ_2 with probability $(1 - \rho)$. Thus the expected utility of consumers is $(\rho\lambda_1 + (1 - \rho)\lambda_2)r - p$. Absent warranties (and presuming that both types of firms offer their product), the firm will therefore set its price $p = (\rho\lambda_1 + (1 - \rho)\lambda_2)r$ independently of its type (if we assume that marginal costs are lower than this price). Formally speaking, this is a pooling equilibrium since prices do not depend on the firm's private information. The firm cannot reveal its quality through price since a λ_2-type cannot be prevented from mimicking a λ_1-type.

To keep the analysis as simple as possible, we assume that production costs of a unit is independent of the breakdown probability and is denoted by c. We can now consider full warranties. If the firm introduces a full warranty, this is supposed to mean that it replaces a defect product by a new product (and if the new product fails again, it is again replaced and so on until the product really works). The expected cost of introducing a warranty is then c/λ_1 for a λ_1-type and c/λ_2 for a λ_2-type.[a] Thus the expected profit of a firm that charges price p and offers a full warranty is $p - c/\lambda$.

We consider now the game in which after learning its type at stage 1, the firm sets a price and a warranty policy at stage 2. The warranty policy can only take the extreme forms of no warranty or full warranty, $\omega \in \{0, 1\}$. Consumers observe the warranty policy and the price but not the firm's type. On the basis of their observations, they update their beliefs about the firm's type and make their purchasing decision at stage 3. We are interested in separating equilibria in which a λ_1-firm behaves differently from a λ_2-firm.[b] In particular, we claim that warranties are only offered by λ_1-types (i.e., 'high-quality' firms).

Since firm types are correctly identified by consumers, a product that is offered without warranty is believed to be of the λ_2-type. Thus a consumer is willing to pay $\lambda_2 r$ if no warranty is offered and the firm of type λ_2 will set its price equal to this expected utility, $p_2 = \lambda_2 r$. The firm's profit is $\lambda_2 r - c$, which is assumed to be positive. If the product comes with a warranty, consumers will believe that this product is offered by a firm of type λ_1. (However, beliefs do not affect expected utility here because a product that breaks down

---

[a] In order to have a functioning product with probability 1, the incurred cost for a product with breakdown probability $1 - \lambda$ is $c(1 + (1 - \lambda) + (1 - \lambda)^2 + (1 - \lambda)^3 + \cdots) = c\sum_{i=0}^{\infty}(1 - \lambda)^i = c/\lambda$.
[b] More precisely, these are perfect Bayesian equilibria in which actions are conditioned on type, and beliefs are not constant in actions.

is assumed to be immediately replaced without any cost for the consumer). Consumers are willing to pay r in this case. Hence, $p_1 \leq r$.

We now have to show under which conditions none of the two types has an incentive to deviate. Consider first a λ_2-firm. A deviation for this firm would give $p_1 - c/\lambda_2$. Hence, a deviation is not profitable at p_1 if $\lambda_2 r - c \geq p_1 - c/\lambda_2$ which is equivalent to $p_1 \leq \lambda_2 r + [(1 - \lambda_2)/\lambda_2] c$. Consider next a λ_1-firm. Here, a deviation is not profitable if $p_1 - c/\lambda_1 \geq \lambda_2 r - c$ which is equivalent to $p_1 \geq \lambda_2 r + [(1 - \lambda_1)/\lambda_1] c$. We observe that for both types of firms, the respective incentive constraints are satisfied if

$$\lambda_2 r + \frac{1 - \lambda_2}{\lambda_2} c \geq p_1 \geq \lambda_2 r + \frac{1 - \lambda_1}{\lambda_1} c.$$

A λ_1-type firm then chooses the price that is its most profitable strategic choice. Clearly, this price cannot exceed the consumers' willingness-to-pay r. We therefore have the following result: *Under the assumption that $\lambda_2 r > c$, there exists a separating equilibrium according to which a λ_1-type firm chooses warranty $\omega = 1$ and a price $p_1 = \min\{r, \lambda_2 r + [(1 - \lambda_2)/\lambda_2] c\}$.*[c] *The λ_2-type firm does not offer any warranty and sets a price $p_2 = \lambda_2 r$.*

If the breakdown probability $1 - \lambda_2$ is sufficiently large, the high-quality firm extracts the full surplus r. Otherwise, the firm cannot extract the full surplus because the incentive constraint of the λ_2-type would be violated. In both cases, a warranty $w = 1$ is a signal of high reliability of the product.

Lesson 13.1   **Firms may use warranties as a signal to consumers that their product is relatively reliable.**

Warranties as signals appear to be a significant feature for products in which breakdown is an important quality aspect about which there is asymmetric information. However, consumers must have confidence that the product will be still around after a while, that the warranty is credible (no hassle), and that it is important enough to keep track of the record. (To show that the latter condition is often not satisfied, ask yourself who will keep the receipt of the purchase of a particular light bulb that has a 10-year warranty?)

Case 13.1 Warranties in the market for new cars

In the car industry, several manufacturers have offered warranties that deviate from the industry average. Generous warranties supposedly increase the quality perception consumers hold about different brands. In the past, several manufacturers which encountered quality problems not only overhauled their product lines but also increased warranty coverage. A case in point is the recent success of Hyundai in the US market. As of 2006, Hyundai offered a 10-year or 100 000-mile powertrain protection plus a 5-year or 60 000-mile bumper-to-bumper protection. On top of this comes a 5-year unlimited

---

[c] Here, we implicitly assume that a high-quality firm makes positive profits, i.e. $p_1 - c/\lambda_1 \geq 0$. This is satisfied if $\lambda_2 r + [(1 - \lambda_2)/\lambda_2] c \geq c/\lambda_1$. A sufficient condition is thus $\lambda_2 r - c \geq 0$.

roadside assistance on all new vehicles. This warranty not only limits the risks consumers incur when buying, holding the quality as given. In addition, this warranty could be interpreted by consumers as saying that Hyundai had overcome quality problems of the past and offers in effect high-quality cars. 'The warranty lured customers who might have been skeptical about buying a Hyundai, and, after their purchase, they were convinced Hyundai produced good quality. As a result, Hyundai sales have soared and repeat customers are increasing.' (Michelle Krebs, 'General Motors is changing perception, reality and warranties', *ContraCostaTimes.com*, 22 September 2006.)

13.1.2   Warranties and investment in quality control

In many markets, a firm may invest in its technology and quality control so as to reduce the probability that its product is faulty. To study such a situation, we consider a moral hazard instead of an adverse selection environment. First, we consider that moral hazard is only on the firm side, as consumers do not observe the investment in quality control. Second, we take into account that moral hazard can also be on the consumer side as the care a consumer exercises in using the product may also affect the probability that the product breaks down.

Moral hazard on the firm side

We modify the model of the previous subsection as follows. A firm chooses its price, the reliability of its product, which represents its quality, $s = \lambda$ and its compensation policy $w \in [0, 1]$, which may fully or partially compensate consumers for a faulty product. Under full compensation ($w = 1$), the consumer obtains r, and under partial compensation she obtains wr. Hence, a consumer's expected indirect utility when buying the product is $\lambda r + (1 - \lambda)wr - p$ and 0 otherwise.

A firm's cost is increasing and strictly convex in the probability that the product works properly. For simplicity, we assume that the cost of producing a product of quality s takes a quadratic form, $C(s) = \gamma s^2$. The firm obtains profit $p - (1 - \lambda)wr - \gamma s^2$. The firm sets its price so as to make consumers indifferent between buying and not buying, $p = \lambda r + (1 - \lambda)wr$. Since $\lambda = s$, we can write the firm's profit as $\lambda r + (1 - \lambda)wr - (1 - \lambda)wr - \gamma \lambda^2 = \lambda r - \gamma \lambda^2$, which is independent of w. The first-order condition of profit maximization with respect to λ, $r - 2\gamma\lambda = 0$, determines the optimal quality level $\lambda^* = r/(2\gamma)$. This is the first-best solution to the investment problem.

The question is whether this solution survives under moral hazard, i.e., we have to show that a firm that sets λ^*, w, and $p^* = \lambda^* r + (1 - \lambda^*)wr = [r^2 + (2\gamma - r)wr]/(2\gamma)$ does not have an incentive to deviate. First, observe that a firm that does not offer any refund, i.e. $w = 0$, sets its price equal to $p^* = r^2/(2\gamma)$ and makes profit $r^2/(2\gamma) - \gamma[r/(2\gamma)]^2 = r^2/(4\gamma)$. Clearly, such a firm can increase its profit by setting the same price but $s = \lambda = 0$. Hence, without warranties or refunds, the moral hazard problem cannot be solved, the firm does not invest in quality, and it makes zero profit.

Take the opposite extreme of a full refund $w = 1$. In this case, $p^* = r$ and the firm makes profit $r^2/(4\gamma)$. Suppose that a firm deviates and does not provide any quality. Then, its profit is $p^* - r = r - r = 0$, which is clearly not profitable. Also, other deviations are not profitable. This shows that refund policies can provide the incentives for a firm to provide high quality, meaning low breakdown probabilities. In this simple model, even the first best can be implemented. If only partial refund policies could be implemented, $w \in [0, \overline{w}]$, the firm would underinvest in product reliability but the moral hazard problem could at least be partially solved.

> **Lesson 13.2** **Warranties and return policies can provide incentives to firms to invest in product reliability when the firm's investment decision cannot be observed by consumers.**

Moral hazard also on the consumer side

The fact that full warranties do best in relaxing the incentive constraint of the firm and thus provide the best means to solve the firm's moral hazard problem begs the question why, in reality, we often do not observe full but limited warranties. One answer to this question is that so far we have neglected that the way a consumer uses its product may affect the probability that the product breaks down and that the type of warranty or return policy may affect the way a consumer treats the product.

Hence there is a moral hazard problem on the firm *and* on the consumer side, a situation of *double moral hazard*. We extend our model as follows.[15] Suppose that a product's reliability λ is not only affected by the firm's quality choice s but also by the care with which consumers treat the product. This is represented by the variable $e \in [0, 1]$, which relates to the effort consumers exert. Suppose that $\lambda(s, e) = s + \alpha e$ and that providing effort on the consumer side is costly with a disutility of the form $D(e) = \delta e^2$. A consumer's expected utility is thus

$$v(p, s, w, e) = (s + \alpha e)r + (1 - s - \alpha e)wr - p - \delta e^2$$

if she buys and exerts effort e; it is zero if she does not buy. The firm's expected profit is

$$\pi(p, s, w, e) = p - (1 - s - \alpha e)wr - \gamma s^2.$$

In the *first best*, $v(p, s, w, e) + \pi(p, s, w, e)$ is maximized where the first-order conditions $\partial \lambda / \partial e = D'(e)$ and $\partial \lambda / \partial s = C'(s)$ are satisfied. In our specification, these conditions are $\alpha r = 2\delta e$ and $r = 2\gamma s$ so that $e = \alpha r / (2\delta)$ and $s = r/(2\gamma)$ in the first best.

Under *asymmetric information*, consumers choose their effort so as to maximize their utility given their beliefs $\hat{s}$ about quality and the observed price and warranty. The solution of the consumer problem satisfies the first-order condition $\alpha r - \alpha wr - 2\delta e = 0$. Solving for e, we obtain $e = \alpha(1 - w)r/(2\delta)$. We observe three properties of this solution. First, *the consumers' effort level depends negatively on the degree of compensation or the extent of the warranty*. This is very intuitive: a product with a full warranty does not give any incentive to consumers to provide effort to carefully use the product. Second, the privately optimal effort level does not depend on the perceived quality. This property is due to our formulation of λ. If cross-derivatives with respect to s and e were different from zero, this would no longer be the case. Hence, this second observation is due to our particular specification and not general. Third, *for $w > 0$, there is a social underprovision of effort on the consumer side*.

The firm sets its variables knowing that consumers will make their effort choice $e = \alpha(1 - w)r/(2\delta)$. As pointed out above, in general, also consumer beliefs about s would enter here but due to our specification of an additive structure of λ, only the firm's compensation policy affects the consumers' effort choice. The firm therefore sets p, s and w so as to maximize $p - [1 - s - \alpha^2(1 - w)r/(2\delta)]w\,r - \gamma s^2$.

For given w, the profit-maximizing quality satisfies $wr = 2\gamma s$ so that $s = wr/(2\gamma)$. Again the additivity in $\lambda(s, e)$ leads to such a simple solution. Here, for $w < 1$, there is social underprovision of quality. When w is announced, consumers believe that the firm offers quality $\widehat{s}(w) = wr/(2\gamma)$. The firm extracts the full surplus under the constraints that s and e are determined as characterized above. The objective function when choosing w can therefore be written as

$$\lambda(s, e)r - \delta s^2 - \gamma e^2 = [wr/(2\gamma) + \alpha^2(1 - w)r/(2\delta)]r$$
$$- \delta[wr/(2\gamma)]^2 - \gamma[\alpha(1 - w)r/(2\delta)]^2,$$

which is quadratic in w and can be explicitly solved. In particular, if $\gamma = \delta$, we obtain $w = 1/(1 + \alpha^2)$, which is strictly between 0 and 1 for $\alpha > 0$. This means that the firm does not offer full compensation because such a compensation policy does not provide incentives to consumers to exert effort. The solution for w can then be inserted in the expressions for e and s which then also only depend on the parameters of the model.

> **Lesson 13.3**   If the firm and consumers are subject to a moral hazard problem, the firm only provides partial compensation for a faulty product.

13.2   Branding

Branding is a key element of a firm's effort to differentiate its product from competitors and to provide information about quality and intended 'meaning' of the product. In particular, the use of trademarks allows firms to provide this information at a lower cost because they avoid or, at least, reduce confusion with competing products. While the importance of brands is closely linked to the arrival of mass production and mass media, branding is as old as early civilizations in the Bronze Age: brands as a means of providing information about horizontal and vertical product characteristics can be traced back more than 4000 years, as illustrated in Case 13.2.

> **Case 13.2 The birth of brands in the Indus valley**[16]
>
> The Sumerian and Akkadian economies of the third and second millennia BCE belonged to a set of societies that traded extensively with each other and covered an area from Egypt in the West to the Indus Valley in the East. The Indus Valley or Harappan civilization, located in present-day India, flourished together with Mesopotamian societies. The

Harappan cities were home to craftsmen. These craftsmen worked in stone and bronze and produced little square seals of tigers, Brahma bulls, elephants, and other animals. According to Indianologist Stanley Wolpert, these seals were 'probably made for merchants who used them to "brand" their wares' (Wolpert, 2000).

Information about product differentiation characteristics can be easily analysed in the context of product differentiation, which has been the focus of Chapter 5. In this section we focus on the quality dimension of brands. In our previous analysis in this part of the book, the firm used instruments such as advertising, price and warranties to signal its quality to consumers. So far, we always assumed that quality was given or chosen ex ante. However, when a firm regularly updates its product features and suppliers, it repeatedly faces the problem that consumers may not trust it. As we will show in this section, the mere possibility that a firm will always be around the next period, opens up the possibility that it is trusted. This can be achieved by building a reputation of high quality as examined in Subsection 13.2.1 in a monopoly setting, and in Subsection 13.2.2 in an oligopoly setting. Brand names also allow consumers to correlate their beliefs about product quality across periods, but also across products if the same brand is extended to several products of the same firms. We study this practice of *umbrella branding* in Subsection 13.2.3.

Before turning to the formal analysis of branding, we argue in the following case that brand names can have an effect on demand, but that it is not easy to isolate this effect in practice.

Case 13.3 Twin cars and brand names[17]

As we show in this section, branding can be used to provide information about product quality and solve the moral hazard problem. But how can we test this prediction in practice? Products with different brand names most often have different physical characteristics as well. It is therefore difficult to disentangle the respective effects of the brand name and of other product characteristics. There exist, however, categories of products that escape this problem. For instance, 'twin cars' have essentially the same physical attributes (they are usually made in the same plant) but carry different brand names. Such twin cars can be produced by the same manufacturer (e.g., in the mid 1980s, Ford produced the twin Ford Thunderbird and Mercury Cougar, while Chrysler produced the twin Plymouth Valiant and Dodge Dart), or by different manufacturers, which engage in the development and production of a common car model, then selling it as separate models of different brands. The latter strategy was followed by many car producers in Europe in the 1990s in order to enter the MPV (multi-purposes vehicle) segment (e.g., the Citroen Evasion, Fiat Ulysses, Lancia Zeta and Peugeot 806 were equivalent models, and so were the Ford Galaxy, Seat Alhambra and Volkswagen Sharan).

Because of their technical equivalence, twin cars can serve as the basis of a natural experiment to examine how brand names affect demand. Sullivan (1998) examines how price differences among second-hand twin cars are related to different brand names.

She finds for the US automobile market that the relative price of second-hand twin car pairs is significantly different from unity, concluding that consumers do not perceive twin models as being perfect substitutes. This suggests that car buyers use information about parent brand quality to infer the quality of models under the parent brand. However, it appears that this conclusion cannot be extended to the primary car market. Lado *et al.* (2004) perform a similar analysis on the primary Spanish MPV car market and their results contradict Sullivan's analysis. They find indeed that brand premia are not significantly different for brands belonging to the same twin car, but they may differ for brands producing different cars.

13.2.1   Intertemporal branding and reputation

As the effects of reputation and branding are inherently intertemporal, we analyse an infinite horizon model in which the firm chooses quality in each period.[18] In each period, the firm sets the quality s and the price p of its product. Consumers observe the price before purchase but not the quality, which is only observed after purchase. In each period, they have utility $r_H - p$ for a product of high quality, $r_L - p$ (with $r_L \geq 0$) for a product of low quality, and 0 if they do not buy. Both firm and consumers, discount future periods with discount factor $\delta < 1$. The firm's production costs are c_H and c_L, respectively, with $c_H > c_L$. We assume that $r_H - c_H > r_L - c_L$. This implies that under full information, the firm would set high quality in each period and the first-best allocation would be implemented.

   The firm faces a moral hazard problem that cannot be solved in a single-period model, as we have seen in Section 13.1. However, we claim that under some conditions, there are equilibria in the model with repeated moral hazard, in which the firm always produces high quality. The reason for the existence of such equilibria is that consumer beliefs can be conditioned on past firm behaviour. In particular, consumers may believe that, independent of its prices, a firm that offered low quality at some point in the past will also offer low quality in the present. Such beliefs make deviations from high quality to low quality at any point in time very costly for the firm because it will no longer be able to sell its product at price r_H.

   We may say that a firm has the *reputation* for high quality if it never produced low quality in the past. This implies that consumers give a firm in the first period the benefit of the doubt and presume that it is of high quality. Along the proposed equilibrium path, the firm produces high quality in each period and sells the product at $p = r_H$. Hence, the present discounted value of profit is

$$\pi^* = r_H - c_H + \delta(r_H - c_H) + \delta^2(r_H - c_H) + \cdots = (r_H - c_H)/(1 - \delta).$$

Consider now a deviation by the firm. It may decide to produce low quality at some point in time t. If it does so, it can cheat in period t and sell low quality at $p = r_H$. However, from $t + 1$ onward, it can only sell at r_L since consumers expect low quality. Therefore, in future periods, it will also produce low quality. This deviation strategy gives a present discounted value of profit equal to

$$\pi' = r_H - c_L + \delta(r_L - c_L) + \delta^2(r_L - c_L) + \cdots = (r_H - c_L) + (r_L - c_L)\delta/(1 - \delta).$$

Such a deviation is not profitable if $\pi^* \geq \pi'$ which is equivalent to

$$[(r_H - c_H) - (r_L - c_L)]\delta/(1 - \delta) \geq c_H - c_L. \tag{13.1}$$

The right-hand side is the short-term gain which stems from lower production cost, whereas the left-hand side is the long-term reputation loss from deviation in period t. This reputation loss is greater than the short-term gain if there is a high efficiency gain from high quality (i.e. $(r_H - c_H) - (r_L - c_L)$ large), if there is little discounting (i.e. δ close to 1) or if the reduction in production costs from producing low instead of high quality is small (i.e. $c_H - c_L$ small). We find that there are equilibria in which the firm produces high quality in all periods if condition (13.1) holds.

Reputation matters in these equilibria because consumers believe that payoff-irrelevant past behaviour matters for present behaviour. Such equilibria are therefore often called *bootstrap equilibria*.[d] If consumers did not hold such beliefs, it would not be possible to support the provision of high quality. While our constructed equilibrium may look attractive, it critically relies on consumer beliefs and very different outcomes can be supported through different belief systems.

> **Lesson 13.4** **Suppose that a firm repeatedly faces the moral hazard problem whether to offer high quality. If consumers use past firm behaviour as a guide for future behaviour and, in particular, if they no longer trust firms that offered low quality in the past, the firm may always provide high quality.**

While we did not introduce an explicit cost of branding (e.g., because consumers have to be made aware that a brand is sold over time), even costly branding is a profitable strategy to solve the moral hazard problem. One can also extend the analysis to consider a mix of moral hazard and adverse selection. Suppose that in each period, the quality of a firm is the realization of a random variable. A firm may then decide to sell a product under the same name of a previously sold high-quality product or to sell it under no (or a different) name. If consumers trust brands that in the past delivered high quality, a firm does not have an incentive to destroy its reputation and therefore only uses its trusted brand for products of high quality, in order to benefit from the brand value in the future.[19] Applying this argument directly requires that consumers repeatedly interact with the same seller. Alternatively, consumers may communicate with each other. This communication may be facilitated by an intermediary, an issue we will look into in Chapter 23.

13.2.2   Reputation and competition

The subsection on intertemporal branding highlighted that a firm can preserve its reputation over time. The insight was obtained in a simple market environment in which a single firm repeatedly faced a moral hazard problem. We may want to ask whether the result is robust to competition. At the same time, there are two directions in which one would like to extend the analysis: first, a firm subject to a moral hazard problem may also face adverse selection (in a

---

[d] With respect to the punishment, we explore similar behaviour by competitors in the context of cartels in Chapter 14.

market in which, in contrast with the discussion above, the firm cannot withhold a product with a bad outcome since the product's outcome cannot be observed before the product is traded) and, secondly, the firm may not perfectly control the quality of the product, in the sense that a firm that exerts effort can only reduce the probability of a bad outcome but not avoid it.[20]

Monopoly setting

We first discuss such an extension in the context in which the firm enjoys market power. Consider a market in which a firm faces an adverse selection and a moral hazard problem, and consumers cannot perfectly distinguish between different types and actions of the firm in each period $t = 0, 1, 2, \ldots$. Such a situation is called a situation of *imperfect monitoring*. More specifically, suppose that a firm can be of two types: it can be an apt ($\theta = 1$) or an inapt firm ($\theta = 0$), with an initial share $\lambda_0 \in (0, 1)$ of apt firms in the market. Suppose, in addition, that the firm (i.e., the owner–manager) can exert effort $e \in \{0, 1\}$ at cost $c \in (0, 1)$ per consumer. The probability that consumers experience a good outcome is equal to γ if the firm is apt and has provided effort, i.e., if $e \cdot \theta = 1$; this probability is $\beta < \gamma$ if the firm is inapt or did not provide effort, i.e., if $e \cdot \theta = 0$. A good outcome provides utility normalized to $r_H = 1$ and a bad outcome, utility normalized to $r_L = 0$. Hence, if consumers observe the firm's type and effort decision, their expected gross surplus would be γ if $(\theta, e) = (1, 1)$ and 0 otherwise. Clearly, in such a market, only an apt firm may have an incentive to provide costly effort.

We now want to understand whether there is an equilibrium in which an apt firm always exerts effort. Note that the firm's revenue varies continuously with consumers' expectation about the likelihood that the apt firm chooses effort. In an equilibrium in which the apt firm always chooses effort, the frequency with which a good outcome is observed converges almost surely to γ. Hence, consumers who observe such a frequency become convinced that the firm in the market is apt. Since consumers are convinced that this firm always exerts effort, consumers' beliefs and thus their actions become insensitive to bad realizations. A bad outcome is attributed to bad luck and a firm looses its incentive to provide effort. Consequently, an equilibrium in which the firm repeatedly provided effort does not exist.[21] This shows that *the reputation mechanism explored in the previous section breaks down in such a context.*

Competitive setting

The negative result under monopoly raises the following question: in which markets can reputation be sustained in a repeated moral hazard problem? Introducing competition between (many) firms provides a positive answer to this question, as we will explore below. The general message thus is that *competition may actually help to solve the moral hazard problem.*

Let us continue with the description of further details of the model. There is a continuum of infinitely lived consumers in the market (of measure 1). Each consumer buys from exactly one firm, while each firm can serve a continuum of consumers. All consumers of a firm have the same experience when consuming its product, i.e., they observe either a good or a bad outcome. After observing the outcome, consumers can stay (i.e., be loyal) with the firm or decide to switch. In each period, consumers have the option to buy or to take the outside option: they can buy in a perfectly competitive market in which only inapt firms are present. In this outside market high effort is enforced. Hence, the outside option takes value β, which is the expected value of an inapt firm that provides effort. (Note that a consumer who does not buy is treated as a switching consumer next period.) We assume that a loyal consumer does not gather any information on other firms in the market. However, she maintains all the available information, namely past prices and observed outcomes, for the whole past since she switched last time. When a consumer switches, the consumer loses all this information but she observes the full price distribution of all firms in the market.

In each period, we thus have the following timing of moves: (1) firms set prices, (2) loyal consumers decide whether to buy and switching consumers decide whether and from which firm to buy, (3) firms decide whether to exert effort, (4) outcomes occur, (5) consumers stay or exit and (6) firms that do not maintain loyal consumers exit. An important assumption is that firms learn their own outcomes but not the outcomes of their competitors. They also observe the price distribution as well as their number of loyal consumers and consumers who buy. In such a market, we analyse Markovian perfect Bayesian equilibria; 'Markovian' here means that consumers condition their buying decision only on observed prices and their beliefs about the firms' types, and that a firm sets its price depending on consumers' beliefs and the composition of consumers.

We want to show that an equilibrium exists in which all apt firms exert effort and characterize its properties. In such an equilibrium, consumers punish a firm with a bad outcome by switching. This implies that a firm with a bad outcome exits from the market. Note that in every period, not only a fraction of inapt firms but also a fraction of apt firms exit the market, although it is common knowledge that the fraction of inapt firms vanishes over time. Since a bad outcome is more likely to occur if the firm is inapt, the share of apt firms that remain in the market increases over time (in the postulated equilibrium in which apt firms always exert effort). The share of apt firms evolves according to

$$\lambda_t = \frac{\gamma \lambda_{t-1}}{\gamma \lambda_{t-1} + \beta(1 - \lambda_{t-1})} \quad \text{for } t \geq 1. \tag{13.2}$$

The number of consumers per firm that has not yet exited increases over time according to

$$n_t = \frac{n_{t-1}}{\gamma \lambda_{t-1} + \beta(1 - \lambda_{t-1})} \quad \text{for } t \geq 1 \tag{13.3}$$

where initially $n_0 = 1$. To support an equilibrium in which all apt firms exert effort, the short-term deviation gain must be smaller than the long-term loss. Denote V_t the per-consumer equilibrium value of an apt firm that always provides effort. For a deviation not to be profitable, we must have

$$V_t = p_t - c + \gamma \delta \frac{n_{t+1}}{n_t} V_{t+1} \geq p_t + \beta \delta \frac{n_{t+1}}{n_t} V_{t+1} \text{ for all } t \geq 0, \tag{13.4}$$

which is equivalent to

$$c \leq (\gamma - \beta) \delta \frac{n_{t+1}}{n_t} V_{t+1}. \tag{13.5}$$

In addition, consumers must prefer to buy in the market, i.e., the net surplus must exceed the outside option, $\gamma \lambda_{t-1} + \beta(1 - \lambda_{t-1}) - p_t \geq \beta$, which is equivalent to $p_t \leq (\gamma - \beta)\lambda_{t-1}$, and the equilibrium price must be profit maximizing given consumers' beliefs. Focusing on zero profit equilibria, firms are only willing to exert effort in period 0 if $p_0 - c + \gamma \delta n_1 V_1 \geq 0$.

Since also inequality (13.5) must hold for $t = 0$, we observe that the price in the initial period must be negative. Because of the normalization of costs, this means that not only firms that exert effort but also firms that do not must sell their product below costs.

We restrict attention to equilibria in which, in each period, the apt firm is indifferent to the provision of effort so that (13.5) is satisfied with equality and gives an expression for V_t depending on n_{t-1} and n_t, $V_t = c/[(\gamma - \beta)\delta(n_t/n_{t-1})]$. The resulting sequence satisfies the property that no price can be lowered without violating some incentive constraint of the apt firm (given its other prices and market sizes).

Substituting the expression for V_t and V_{t+1} into (13.4) characterizes the equilibrium price in period t,

$$p_t^* = \frac{c}{\delta(\gamma - \beta)} \left(\frac{n_{t-1}}{n_t} - \beta\delta \right).$$

Using expression (13.3), we obtain

$$p_t^* = \frac{c}{\delta(\gamma - \beta)} \left(\gamma \frac{\lambda_{t-1}}{\lambda_t} - \beta\delta \right).$$

After using (13.2), the latter expression becomes

$$p_t^* = \frac{c}{\delta(\gamma - \beta)} [(\gamma - \beta)\lambda_{t-1} + \beta(1 - \delta)],$$

which is an increasing sequence in t. Using $V_0 = 0$, one obtains $p_0^* = -[\beta/(\gamma - \beta)]c$ and we note that $p_0 < p_1$. Future higher prices provide incentives to an apt firm to exert effort because effort increases the expected length of stay in the market. We thus have characterized the equilibrium price path. The equilibrium in which all apt firms exert effort exists if the cost of providing effort is sufficiently small. The following lesson summarizes the main insight of this analysis.

Lesson 13.5   **Competition may solve a repeated moral hazard problem in situations in which, under monopoly, the reputation mechanism would break down.**

We make two remarks on the constructed equilibrium. First, we analysed equilibria in which consumers always punish firms with a bad outcome. There are other equilibria, in which consumers are willing to forgive. Such equilibria have the feature that firms charge different prices depending on their history.

Second, the equilibrium has the feature that fewer and fewer firms remain in the market, so that the number of consumers per firm n_t increases. It does so at a geometric rate so that $n_t V_t$ diverges. This feature is due to the fact that firms exit but that other firms cannot enter. An extended model with firm entry corrects for this undesirable feature, while confirming the main insight.[22]

13.2.3   Umbrella branding

An *umbrella brand* is a brand that covers an array of diverse products, which are more or less related. Umbrella branding is a standard business practice for products with experience good attributes. The main reason why umbrella branding works is that consumers make inferences from the characteristics observed in one product to the characteristics of others. Perhaps most important is that consumers can draw inferences from experience about the quality of a product sold under the same umbrella brand. For instance, if a consumer has a negative experience with a product, she may be less inclined to buy another product of the same brand. A firm can thus try to link the expected quality of one product to the customers' experience with another product.[e] If this is the case, an umbrella brand carries information.

Case 13.4 Virtues of the Virgin brand

When you fly into space (unlikely) or drink a cola while reading a book (more likely), you may knowingly use the products and services of the same firm. Technologically, the provisions of these products and services have nothing in common and still they are offered under the same brand. The Virgin brand is perhaps the ultimate example of umbrella branding. According to their website, Virgin has 33 divisions operating under the Virgin name. These span diverse industries including travel, tourism, telecommunications, media, bottled drinks, health and finance with products and services all united under the umbrella Virgin brand. Industry-specific brands are e.g. Virgin Atlantic, Virgin Books, Virgin Drinks, Virgin Spa, Virgin Earth, Virgin Fuels, Virgin Games, Virgin Life Care, Virgin Media, Virgin Mobile, Virgin Money, Virgin Life Care and Virgin Vacations. The Virgin empire's origins can be traced to a music record shop in London that was started by Richard Branson in 1972. He soon expanded into other businesses related to the music business before entering completely different industries. Virgin believes that what ties these disparate businesses together are common perceptions about the values of the products and services sold under the umbrella Virgin brand. Or, as Richard Branson, founder of Virgin, puts it, 'consumers understand that all the values that apply to one product – good service, style, quality, value and fair dealing – apply to others' (*Time Magazine*, 24 June 1996). It is possibly the reverse argument that drove Richard Branson to turn to Zavvi Entertainment Group (a management buyout vehicle) to take the loss-making chain Virgin Megastores off his hands in 2007.[f]

We consider a model according to which a firm simultaneously decides about the product quality of its two products and the use of umbrella branding, where it is assumed that umbrella branding is associated with a higher cost.[23] A product is sold for two periods to a homogeneous group of consumers with unit demand. After the first period, there is a

---

[e] Such a strategy requires the firm to be able to judge the product quality before the product is launched on the market. It also requires that at least a share of the consumers of one product must also be potential consumers of the other products sold under the same umbrella brand. Otherwise, umbrella branding becomes meaningless (provided that one consumer does not punish a firm because of the experience of another consumer).

[f] In some cases, even common ownership no longer holds. While Branson initially was partial or sole owner of all companies that use the Virgin brand, subsequently some companies were sold off. For instance, Virgin Music is now part of EMI. Using the same brand across companies raises additional questions that we do not address here.

positive probability that consumers will detect low quality.[g] We analyse those pure-strategy equilibria in which the firm absorbs all the expected surplus. The basic insight is that a firm has a stronger incentive to provide high quality under umbrella branding because there is a positive probability that a deviation will be punished in the second period, not just with respect to the product one has the bad experience with, but also with respect to the other.[h]

Description of the model

Consider a market in which a firm produces and sells two experience goods for two periods. The firm decides for each product whether to produce low or high quality, $s_i \in \{s_L, s_H\}$. The firm is committed to maintaining the same quality level over two periods. The same production technology is used for both periods, hence quality remains the same over periods. Producing one unit of high quality (over both periods) entails a total cost of $c_1 = c_2 = c$. High-quality products never break down, whereas low-quality products break down with probability $1 - \lambda_1 = 1 - \lambda_2 = 1 - \lambda$. The consumers' willingness to pay for a product that does not break down is $r_1 = r_2 = r_H \equiv r$ in each period. For a product that breaks down, the willingness to pay is $\underline{r}_1 = \underline{r}_2 = \underline{r}$. To simplify our analysis, we set $r_L = (1 - \lambda)\underline{r} + \lambda r = 0$. In this specification, production costs of a high-quality product are independent from the quality of the other product. Similarly, consumer valuations for one high-quality product are independent of the quality of the other product. Hence, in a world without asymmetric information, there are no demand or supply-side economies of scope and any interdependencies between the two products come from consumer beliefs.

Consumers of mass 1 demand up to one unit of each product in each period. The indirect utility for high-quality product $i = 1, 2$ in period $t = 1, 2$ is $u_i^t = r - p_i^t$, where p_i^t is the price to be paid. For low quality, u_i^t is equal to $-p_i^t$ if the consumer buys and to 0 otherwise. A consumer derives a total utility of $u_1^1 + u_2^1 + u_1^2 + u_2^2$. If both products are sold in both periods, the firm's profits (gross of any costs of umbrella branding) are $p_1^1 + p_2^1 + p_1^2 + p_2^2 - C(s_1) - C(s_2)$, where $C(s_i)$ is equal to c if high quality is provided; otherwise it is zero. Hence under perfect information, if $r \geq c$, the firm chooses $s_i = s_H$ and $p_i^t = r$ for both products and both periods; its profits are then $4r - 4c$. If $r < c$, then $s_i = s_L$ and $p_i^t = 0$, and profits are zero. Since the firm absorbs all of the surplus, it implements the first-best allocation under perfect information. In other words, any deviations from the first-best are here due to the asymmetric information problem faced by the firm and are not due to its market power.

Timing of the game

We analyse the following three-period game (solving for pure-strategy perfect Bayesian Nash equilibria).

---

[g] For concreteness, one may bear in mind a technical product, where low-quality products break down with some probability. Also in the services sector, consumers are unlikely to detect cheap quality with certainty.
[h] The model allows us to separate umbrella branding and the incentives to provide quality from other issues; in particular, price cannot signal product quality.

$t = 0$: The firm decides whether to use umbrella branding. Then it chooses the qualities of both products, i.e., (s_H, s_H), (s_H, s_L), (s_L, s_H), or (s_L, s_L).

$t = 1$: Consumers observe whether the firm uses umbrella branding, but they do not observe the quality of any of the products. The firm makes 'take it or leave it' offers p_1^1 and p_2^1 for products 1 and 2 to each consumer. Consumers form beliefs and accept both, one or neither of the two offers.

$t = 2$: If the product is of low quality, consumers detect the quality of the product they purchased in period 1. The firm makes take-it-or-leave-it offers p_1^2 and p_2^2 for products 1 and 2 to each consumer. Consumers update beliefs and accept both, one or neither of the two offers.

The firm's choice of quality cannot immediately be observed by the consumers. Hence, in the first period, they lack any hard information about product quality. In the second period, if a product is of low quality, they receive a negative realization with probability $1 - \lambda$ and thus detect low quality before making a second purchase. They use this information to update their beliefs in period 2.

Our construction can be motivated as follows. Consumers may have to regularly replace a product, that is, in periods 1 and 2. The firm, due to technological choices, is committed to offer the same product in both periods. Then, $1 - \lambda$ represents the detection probability of low quality. If consumers realize that the product is not working properly or is of low quality, they adjust expectations accordingly.

We analyse equilibria in which consumers do not use prices in their belief formation. Effectively, the firm is able to extract the full expected surplus from consumers. This allows us to focus on the quality dimension in the use of umbrella branding and amounts to the equilibrium selection that is most favourable for the firm.

Independent selling

Consider a situation in which, from observing the quality of one product, consumers do not make inferences about the quality of the other products. One reason may be that consumers are not aware that the products are produced by the same firm since they are sold under different brands. Another possible reason is that there are two non-intersecting groups of consumers that consume each of the products (with the same umbrella brand) and that do not communicate. In this case, both products can be treated separately.

If the moral hazard problem is solved in the absence of umbrella branding, then, in $t = 1$, the consumer's expected value of the product is simply r. If the product does not work well in $t = 1$, then the expected value drops to zero in $t = 2$. If the product works well, then consumers keep their beliefs about quality. Because the firm makes take-it-or-leave-it offers, it can set the price equal to the expected valuation of the consumers. Hence, if it decides to produce high quality, expected profits amount to $\pi_H = 2r - 2c$. If it deviates and produces low quality, expected profits are $\pi'_H = r + \lambda r$. A deviation is not profitable if $\pi_H \geq \pi'_H$ or $(1 - \lambda)r \geq 2c$. Hence, for $2c \leq (1 - \lambda)r$, the moral hazard problem can be solved by a one-product firm which then produces high quality s_H, whereas for higher marginal costs, it produces low quality s_L.

We observe that for $2c \leq (1 - \lambda)r$, there also exists an equilibrium in which the firm chooses low quality but that this equilibrium is Pareto-dominated by the equilibrium with high quality. This means that for small and large costs c, the first-best is implemented: for $2c \leq (1 - \lambda)r$, the firm chooses the socially optimal high quality; for $c \geq r$, the firm chooses the socially optimal low quality. For an intermediate range, $(1 - \lambda)r < 2c < 2r$, the firm chooses low quality, although the first-best would be to provide high quality. Hence due to moral hazard, quality is socially underprovided.

Umbrella branding

We now turn to the two-product case and show that umbrella branding alleviates the moral hazard problem. In order to correlate beliefs about product quality across products, the consumers must at least know that the firm produces two products. This is achieved by putting the products under the same umbrella brand. The firm now has four different options. It can produce both products in high quality (s_H, s_H), product 1 in high quality and product 2 in low quality (s_H, s_L), the reverse (s_L, s_H), and, finally, both products in low quality (s_L, s_L).

We are interested in the following question: for which parameter constellation can the provision of high quality be supported as an equilibrium outcome? Clearly, in such an equilibrium, low quality can never be observed along the equilibrium path, and off-equilibrium beliefs need to be specified. If beliefs are correlated across products, consumers may believe that if one product defaults, the other product is also of low quality. In this case, prices drop to zero in the second period. Depending on the production choices, expected profits amount to

$$\pi_{HH} = 2r + 2r - 4c,$$

$$\pi_{HL} = \pi_{LH} = 2r + 2\lambda r - 2c,$$

$$\pi_{LL} = 2r + 2\lambda^2 r.$$

We see that $\pi_{HH} \geq \pi_{LL}$ iff $2c \leq (1 - \lambda^2)r = (1 - \lambda)(1 + \lambda)r$. Furthermore, $\pi_{HH} \geq \pi_{HL}$ iff $c \leq (1 - \lambda)r$, which is implied by $2c \leq (1 - \lambda)(1 + \lambda)r$. To sum up, an equilibrium with (s_H, s_H) can be supported for $2c \leq (1 - \lambda)(1 + \lambda)r$. Recall that under uncorrelated beliefs (i.e., without the use of an umbrella brand), it could be supported only for $2c \leq (1 - \lambda)r$.[i]

Next, consider pure-strategy equilibria in which only low quality is chosen. Here, consumers believe that if one product is detected to be of low quality, the other product is perceived to be of low quality as well. Expected profits are then $\pi_{HH} = -4c$, $\pi_{HL} = \pi_{LH} = -2c$ and $\pi_{LL} = 0$. As a result, it is always optimal to provide low quality, and an equilibrium with (s_L, s_L) can be supported for every parameter constellation with $c > 0$. Note that this equilibrium action can also be supported by uncorrelated beliefs.

Selecting the Pareto-dominant equilibrium, umbrella branding does not improve upon independent selling for $2c \leq (1 - \lambda)r$. Umbrella branding does improve upon independent

---

[i] If c is sufficiently small, other off-equilibrium beliefs, which also support (s_H, s_H), can be found.

selling if $(1 - \lambda)r < 2c \leq (1 - \lambda)(1 + \lambda)r$. If $2c > (1 - \lambda)(1 + \lambda)r$, low quality is provided even under an umbrella brand, hence umbrella branding is neutral to quality provision.

When umbrella branding supports high-quality provision, the firm gains $4r - 4c$ with the umbrella, while it would obtain zero profit for sufficiently high marginal costs if it opted for independent branding. Hence, the umbrella brand is used whenever $(1 - \lambda)r < 2c \leq (1 - \lambda)(1 + \lambda)r$. We summarize our above findings by the following proposition. *Suppose that the firm and consumers coordinate on Pareto-dominant equilibria. Then umbrella branding is chosen if the inequalities $(1 - \lambda)r < 2c \leq (1 - \lambda)(1 + \lambda)r$ hold, i. e., for medium detection probability $(1 - \lambda)$, medium cost differential c, and/or medium value differential r.*

The model thus gives the following predictions (choosing the Pareto-dominant equilibrium if there is more than one): the firm chooses low quality and no umbrella branding for sufficiently high costs of quality provision and sufficiently low detection probabilities; it chooses high quality and no umbrella branding for sufficiently low costs of quality provision and sufficiently high detection probabilities; and it chooses high quality and umbrella branding for an intermediate range of costs. Clearly, umbrella branding can only play a role when the firm is vulnerable to quality defections. Umbrella branding then provides a safeguard to consumers, since a defection can be more severely punished.

Lesson 13.6   **If beliefs can be correlated across products, the region of parameter constellations where high-quality provision can be supported as an equilibrium action expands. Hence, umbrella branding can mitigate the moral hazard problem.**

Empirical work has looked at whether consumers react to the use of umbrella brands. Such effects can be studied in controlled laboratory experiments but perhaps more interesting is the confirmation from field data that umbrella branding is related to reputation concerns.

Case 13.5 Umbrella branding in the market of oral hygiene products

To disentangle economies of scope in production from reputation effects, one has to consider umbrella brands in which one product is not technologically related to the other but for which the two products are likely to be linked in the eyes of consumers. One such example is toothpaste and toothbrush. Indeed, Erdem (1998) uses panel data for exactly those two types of oral hygiene products. Some of the two products whose purchases are tracked over time share the same brand name in both product categories. Her regression results are consistent with the interpretation that consumers are uncertain about quality levels, and experience does not provide perfect information. The main finding is that consumers' expected product qualities are highly correlated if products are sold under an umbrella brand.

Review questions

1. What is the simple logic of warranties as a quality signal? What limits the attractiveness of warranties as a signal for high-quality firms?

2. Describe the basic moral hazard problem in the context of quality provision? How can reputation for high quality be sustained?

3. Why may the reputation mechanism break down under monopoly? Why can the reputation mechanism be reinforced by competition?

4. Why should consumers trust umbrella brands more than separate brands? Discuss the out-of-equilibrium behaviour of consumers.

Further reading

Spence (1977) provides a formal argument that warranties can be used as a signal. A double moral hazard problem in the context of warranties has been analysed by Cooper and Ross (1985). Klein and Leffler (1981) show that intertemporal branding is a solution to the repeated moral hazard problem. Hörner (2002) highlights the role of competition in preserving reputation. Umbrella branding as a signal has been explored by Wernerfelt (1988) and Cabral (2000) among others. Here, we analyse the hidden action problem as in Hakenes and Peitz (2008). For a guide to the literature on seller reputation see Bar-Isaac and Tadelis (2008).

Notes for Part V

1. See 'Things you need to know about second-hand cars', *Economic Times*, 2 September 2005.

2. The seminal paper on adverse selection is by Akerlof (1970).

3. This case is based on Genesove (1993).

4. This argument is due to Milgrom (1981).

5. For an empirical investigation, see Lewis (2007).

6. This analysis is based on Belleflamme and Peitz (2007).

7. See Archibald *et al.* (1983), Moorthy and Zhao (2000), Caves and Greene (1996), Nichols (1998), Thomas *et al.* (1998), Horstmann and MacDonald (2003).

8. The seminal paper is Milgrom and Roberts (1986).

9. Graduate text books on game theory or microeconomics more generally address equilibrium refinements in signalling games, see e.g. Fudenberg and Tirole (1991) and Mas-Colell, Whinston and Green (1995). In particular, the intuitive criterion proposed by Cho and Kreps (1987) is frequently chosen for equilibrium selection.

10. This case is based on Ali and Nauges (2007).

11. The seminal paper is Milgrom and Roberts (1986). We follow the expostion of Bagwell (2007).

12. The analysis is based on Daughety and Reinganum (2008). For a related analysis of the Hotelling model with quality uncertainty and endogenous product locations, see Bester (1998).

13. We refer to the appendix in Daughety and Reinganum (2008) for details. Readers who go through their proof should be aware of the slightly different notation.

14. For a more elaborate analysis of the signalling role, see Spence (1977). Alternatively, Heal (1977) offers insurance to buyers as a rationale for warranties and Grossman (1981) provides a model in which warranties can be both, signal and insurance.

15. Our analysis is inspired by Cooper and Ross (1985). For an analysis that includes prices as signals, see Lutz (1989).

16. This case is based on Moore and Reid (2008), which contains additional examples from early civilizations.

17. This case is based on Sullivan (1998) and Lado *et al.* (2004).

18. The seminal papers on this are Klein and Leffler (1981) and Shapiro (1983).

19. A formal analysis along these lines is provided by Choi (1998).

20. This subsection is based on Hörner (2002). For earlier work on repeated moral hazard under competition see Allen (1984). For an analysis of the effect of market structure (in particular, the number of firms) on the incentives to provide high quality see Kranton (2003). She finds that competition for consumers can eliminate the price premium that is needed to induce firms to maintain a reputation for high-quality production.

21. This argument is due to Holmstrom (1999).

22. Such a model is analysed in Hörner (2002).

23. The analysis is based on Hakenes and Peitz (2008). For a related earlier contribution in an adverse selection context, see in particular Wernerfelt (1988). Other important contributions, again in an adverse selection setting, include Cabral (2000) and Mikóls-Thal (2008). These latter consider environments in which umbrella branding is not fully revealing because, in equilibrium, a two-product firm with two low-quality products imitates the behaviour of a firm with two high-quality products with positive probability.

References for Part V

Akerlof, G. (1970). The Market for 'Lemons': Quality Uncertainty and the Market Mechanism. *Quarterly Journal of Economics* 84: 488–500.

Ali, H. H. and Nauges, C. (2007), The Pricing of Experience Goods : The Example of En Primeur Wine. *American Journal of Agricultural Economics* 89: 91–103.

Allen, F. (1984). Reputation and Product Quality. *Rand Journal of Economics* 15: 311–327.

Anderson, S. W., Daly, J. D. and Johnson, M. F. (1999). Why Firms Seek ISO 9000 Certification: Regulatory Compliance or Competitive Advantage? *Production and Operations Management* 8: 28–43.

Archibald, R., Haulman, C. and Moody, C. (1983). Quality, Price, Advertising and Published Quality Ratings. *Journal of Consumer Research* 9: 347–356.

Bagwell, K. (2007). The Economic Analysis of Advertising. In Armstrong, M. and Porter, R. (eds.), *Handbook of Industrial Organization. Vol. 3*. North-Holland: Amsterdam.

Bar-Isaac, H. and Tadelis, S. (2008). Seller Reputation. *Foundations and Trends in Microeconomics* 4: 273–351.

Belleflamme, P. and Peitz, M. (2007). Asymmetric Information and Overinvestment in Quality. Mimeo.

Bester, H. (1998). Quality Uncertainty Mitigates Product Differentiation. *Rand Journal of Economics* 29: 828–844.

Cabral, L. M. B. (2000), Stretching Firm and Brand Reputation. *Rand Journal of Economics* 31: 658–673.

Caves, R. E. and Greene, D. P. (1996). Brands' Quality Levels, Prices, and Advertising Outlays: Empirical Evidence on Signals and Information Costs. *International Journal of Industrial Organization* 14: 29–52.

Cho, I.-K. and Kreps, D. (1987). Signaling Games and Stable Equilibria. *Quarterly Journal of Economics* 102: 179–221.

Choi, J. P. (1998). Brand Extension as Information Leverage. *Review of Economic Studies* 65: 655–670.

Cole, R. E. (1998), Learning from the Quality Movement: What Did and What Didn't Happen? *California Management Review* 41: 43–73.

Cooper, R. and Ross, T. W. (1985). Product Warranties under Double Moral Hazard. *Rand Journal of Economics* 16: 103–113.

Daughety, A. and Reinganum, J. (2008). Imperfect Competition and Quality Signaling. *Rand Journal of Economics* 39: 163–183.

Erdem, T. (1998). An Empirical Analysis of Umbrella Branding. *Journal of Marketing Research* 35: 339–351.

Fudenberg, D. and Tirole, J. (1991). *Game Theory*. MIT Press.

Genesove, D. (1993). Adverse Selection in the Wholesale Used Car Market. *Journal of Political Economy* 101: 644–665.

Grossman, S. J. (1981). The Informational Role of Warranties and Private Disclosure about Product Quality. *Journal of Law and Economics* 24: 461–483.

Hakenes, H. and Peitz, M. (2008). Umbrella Branding and the Provision of Quality. *International Journal of Industrial Organization* 26: 546–556.

Heal, G. (1977). Guarantees and Risk Sharing. *Review of Economic Studies* 44: 549–560.

Holmström, B. (1999). Managerial Incentive Problems: A Managerial Perspective. *Review of Economic Studies* 66: 169–182.

Hörner, J. (2002). Reputation and Competition. *American Economic Review* 92: 644–663.

Horstmann, I. and MacDonald, G. (2003). Is Advertising a Signal of Product Quality? Evidence from the Compact Disc Player Market, 1983–1992. *International Journal of Industrial Organization* 21: 317–345.

Klein, B. and Leffler, K. (1981). The Role of Market Forces in Assuring Contractual Performance. *Journal of Political Economy* 89: 615–641.

Kranton, R. (2003). Competition and the Incentives to Produce High Quality. *Economica* 70: 385–404.

Lado, N., Licandro, O. and Perez, F. (2004). How Brand Names Affect the Price Setting of Carmakers Producing Twin Cars?. Economics Working Papers ECO2004/01, European University Institute.

Lewis, G. (2007). Asymmetric Information, Adverse Selection and Seller Disclosure: The Case of eBay Motors. Mimeo.

Lutz, N. (1989). Warranties as Signals under Consumer Moral Hazard. *Rand Journal of Economics* 20: 239–255.

Mas-Colell, A., Whinston, M. and Green, J. (1995). Microeconomic Theory. MIT Press.

Miklós-Thal, J. (2008). On the Signalling and Feedback Effects of Umbrella Branding. Mimeo.

Milgrom, P. (1981). Good News and Bad News: Representation Theorems and Applications. *Bell Journal of Economics* 12: 380–391.

Milgrom, P. R. and Roberts, J. (1986). Price and Advertising Signals of Product Quality. *Journal of Political Economy* 94: 796–821.

Moore, K. and Reid, S. (2008): The Birth of Brand: 4000 Years of Branding History. *Business History* 50: 419–432.

Moorthy, S. and Zhao, H. (2000). Advertising Spending and Perceived Quality. *Marketing Letters* 11: 221–233.

Nelson, P. (1970). Information and Consumer Behavior. *Journal of Political Economy* 78: 311–329.

Nelson, P. (1974). Advertising as Information. *Journal of Political Economy* 82: 729–754.

Nichols, M. W. (1998). Advertising and Quality in the U.S. Market for Automobiles. *Southern Economic Journal* 64: 922–939.

Shapiro, C. (1983). Premiums for High Quality Products as Returns to Reputations. *Quarterly Journal of Economics* 98: 659–679.

Spence, M. (1973). Job Market Signaling. *Quarterly Journal of Economics* 87: 355–374.

Spence, M. (1977). Consumer Misperception, Product Failure and Product Liability. *Review of Economic Studies* 44: 561–572.

Sullivan, M. W. (1998). How Brand Names Affect the Demand for Twin Automobiles. *Journal of Marketing Research* 35: 154–165.

Thomas, L., Shane, S. and Weigelt, K. (1998). An Empirical Examination of Advertising as a Signal of Product Quality. *Journal of Economic Behavior and Organization* 37: 415–430.

Wernerfelt, B. (1988). Umbrella Branding as a Signal of New Product Quality. *Rand Journal of Economics* 19: 458–466.

Wolpert, S. (2000). *A New History of India*. 6th Edition. Oxford, UK: Oxford University Press.

Part VI
Theory of competition policy

Introduction to Part VI: Theory of competition policy

So far in this book, our approach has been mostly positive: we have been concerned with describing and explaining the workings of imperfectly competitive markets. The first chapters helped us to understand what market power is, where it comes from and how it is exerted. In some specific situations, we also compared the outcome that results from the interaction among firms with the social surplus-maximizing outcome. Yet, such comparisons did not give rise to recommendations for a competition authority.

In this part of the book, we change our perspective and adopt a normative approach: now that we understand what is, we can express views about what ought to be, that is, we provide guidance for competition policy. To the extent that competition authorities follow the rules spelled out under this normative approach, this analysis is again helpful to address positive questions: it may help explain why firms choose certain actions when they foresee the reaction of competition authorities.

The basic postulate for competition policy is that competition is desirable as it is a fundamental force to deliver economic efficiency. The problem, as we have already noticed in the previous chapters, is that firms may be tempted to suppress competition as it makes their lives easier. It is thus necessary to edict and enforce a set of rules in order to maintain competition. This is exactly how Neelie Kroes, the European Commissioner for Competition Policy until 2009, defines her role:[1]

The Single Market [i.e., the integrated European market] is a precious achievement, and the best way to keep it functioning effectively is to ensure competition between companies. My job is about acting as a referee of this process. If we think of the European economy as football match: I set and enforce the rules of the game, in conjunction with the other Commissioners. We make sure it is a fair match, and that there is punishment for people and companies that break the rules and spoil the game for others.

The rules of the game are commonly known as competition policy. Different referees act in different jurisdictions: in the European Union, the European Commission is the referee for all competition issues that transcend national borders (otherwise, national competition authorities are in charge); in the United States (where the term 'antitrust policy' is preferred), two agencies act as referees, the Department of Justice and the Federal Trade Commission. On both sides of the Atlantic (as well as in most developed nations), competition policy is nowadays largely informed by the economic theory of industrial organization.[a] Our objective in Part VI is thus to develop the economic approach to competition policy. To this end, we first want to pursue the analysis of the previous chapters and identify the channels through which particular business practices may be harmful for competition. Then, we want to use this knowledge to analyse how such practices can be prevented.

What kind of foul play should the referees watch for in the competition game? Neelie Kroes defines her missions as follows:[2]

---

[a] The economic approach to competition policy has not always been favoured, though. We refer you to Appendix B for a historical perspective on the development of antitrust policy in the US and in Europe.

(i) 'ensure companies do not fix prices or carve up markets', (ii) 'stop mergers and take-overs that restrict competition', and (iii) ensure that companies do not 'block new companies from succeeding'.

We tackle the first item on this list in Chapter 14. We study *collusive behaviours*, such as price-fixing or market sharing, whereby firms within an industry eliminate the competition that is existing (or ought to exist) between them. Our goal in this chapter is to understand how these collusive practices emerge and can be sustained over time. We also investigate how these practices can be detected and fought. In this respect, the European Commission has significantly improved its record since the turn of the twenty-first century, by detecting and punishing collusive practices in sectors as diverse as car glass, elevators and escalators, candle waxes, vitamins or synthetic rubber. Neelie Kroes does not hide how proud she is of this record:[3]

During my time as Competition Commissioner I have prohibited more than a dozen cartels on markets worth hundreds of billions of Euros. I do not know of a single person who wants us to stop this fight.

In Chapter 15, we partly tackle the second item on the list, namely the analysis of mergers between direct competitors, or *horizontal mergers*. A priori, horizontal mergers tend to decrease welfare as they reduce the number of independent decision makers on the market. On the other hand, mergers may increase efficiency through a number of synergies (such as cost reductions due to the elimination of overlapping functions, etc.). We therefore need to assess how these two countervailing forces affect the profitability of mergers for the merging parties, and the desirability of mergers for the consumers, the non-merging firms and society as a whole. The competition authorities' responsibility is to stop proposed mergers (which are thus deemed as profitable by the merging parties) that are likely to be welfare-detrimental, as exemplified by the European Commissioner for Competition Policy:

If there were no merger control rules, some mergers would cause customers to be denied the choice of goods and services, while paying higher prices. When we prohibited Ryanair's acquisition of Aer Lingus in 2007, it was because of the real risk of higher prices for consumers taking 14 million journeys each and every year to and from Ireland.

The last item on the list refers to the idea that firms could block other firms from succeeding. Such exclusionary practices are called 'abuse of dominant position' in the European competition law, or 'monopolization' in the US antitrust law. The last two chapters of Part VI examine exclusionary behaviour in two different types of situations. Chapter 16 considers situations where *strategic incumbent firms* make entry on their market impossible, or at least difficult, for other firms. To do so, incumbent firms have to commit to some course of action that would harm rival firms if they decide to enter the market. Such commitment relies on a costly and irreversible investment that takes place prior entry. What type of investment in what type of situation? This is the main question we address in this chapter. We first provide a general taxonomy of entry-related strategies. We consider next a number of specific strategies, which affect either cost or demand variables. The bundling of products may belong to the latter category: by bundling products A and B, a firm that has a monopoly position in market A may be able to extend its domination to market B. This is the exclusionary conduct that Microsoft has been found guilty of by the European Commission in 2004, as we detail it below in Case 16.5. Here is what Neelie Kroes stated about this famous case in 2007:[4]

Microsoft cannot abuse its Windows monopoly to exclude competitors in other markets. Microsoft can improve its products, but the Court [of First Instance] confirmed that there was no technical benefit to building its media player into its operating system in the way that it did. Consumers did not benefit. Consumers only paid the price through reduced choice and less innovation on the market as a whole. This is an important precedent, not just for this particular product on this particular market.

Exclusionary practices may also arise in *vertically related markets*, i.e., in markets for intermediate products that occupy successive steps in the value chain of some final product or service. Here, we return to the question about the effects of mergers. When a firm decides to merge vertically, either 'upstream' with one of its input suppliers, or 'downstream' with one of its retailers, the merged entity may foreclose the access to inputs or to customers to its rivals. Such exclusionary effects have, however, to be balanced with potential efficiency effects of vertical mergers, in particular the elimination of successive margins. We address these issues in Chapter 17. We show how vertical mergers differ from horizontal mergers. We also examine the potential exclusionary and efficiency effects of various vertical restraints, such as resale-price maintenance or exclusive dealing contracts. These issues are also at the heart of competition policy, as illustrated by one last quote of Neelie Kroes about the improvement of competition in European energy markets:[5]

In 2005 I decided to carry out a detailed sector inquiry under competition rules to understand better why the ongoing drive to more openness in these markets had neither delivered greater choice and cost reflective prices for consumers, nor resulted in anywhere near a truly integrated European energy market. The problems this sector inquiry brought into the spotlight are: first, highly concentrated markets which former incumbent suppliers still dominate; second, vertical foreclosure since companies use their control over the supply pipes and cables to keep rival suppliers out of the market . . .

What will you learn in this part of the book?
While this part of the book largely addresses competition policy issues (cartels, collusion, mergers, exclusionary conduct), it also enriches the set of market environments that are analysed in this book. To name a few, you will become acquainted with supergame strategies in repeated market interaction, you will explore the relevance of commitment strategies, and you will learn about situations of vertical oligopoly, where the market consists of an upstream and a downstream sector.

14 Cartels and tacit collusion

Collusive (or price-fixing) agreements, whereby firms in an industry avoid competing with one another, play an important role in antitrust analysis. In this chapter, we focus on two important aspects of collusion. First, we shed some light on the incentives of firms to stay inside or outside of an *explicit cartel*; that is, we focus on cartel formation. Here, cartel members are assumed to jointly take their decisions. For such explicit cartels to work, firms must enter into (long-term) binding agreements so as to form a joint profit-maximizing entity. The main issues here are the formation and the stability of such cartels: what is their optimal and equilibrium size? We study these issues in Section 14.1.

Second, we analyse how cartels and other forms of collusion can be sustained in the absence of binding agreements. Here, collusion emerges as the noncooperative equilibrium of a situation of repeated competition. Because firms noncooperatively adopt strategies that lead to a coordinated outcome, collusion is said to be *tacit*.[b] Since cartels are illegal, such tacit collusion is of particular importance for firms belonging to a cartel. For collusion to work, firms must have a correct 'understanding' of how other colluding firms will react to their behaviour. Therefore, the main issue in this second approach is the sustainability of tacit collusion: what is the set of prices that can be sustained in a noncooperative equilibrium when competition is repeated over time? We examine this issue in Section 14.2.

There is a consensus that collusive agreements are welfare-reducing and should therefore be forbidden.[c] Note that price-fixing cartels stand out as one of the few areas in antitrust policy in which the inflexible 'per se' approach has not been challenged and replaced by a 'rule-of-reason' approach (as is the case, e.g., for the vertical restrictions examined in Chapter 17). As there is an agreement about what to do, the main issue is how to do it: how can antitrust authorities detect collusion and how should they fight it? This is what we study in Section 14.3.

---

[b] Tacit comes from Latin *tacitus*, past participle of *tacere*, which means *'to be silent'*.
[c] It is nevertheless possible to provide arguments according to which price-fixing (perhaps not all the way up to monopoly level, but above the noncooperative solution) may actually be *beneficial* for society. One argument is that the noncooperative solution sustains too few firms and thus too little product variety in the market. Collusion, by increasing price-cost margins, leads to higher industry profits and, in effect, more entry. This additional entry may be socially desirable to ameliorate the previous social underprovision of the number of products. In addition, if a cartel not only shares information but in addition relocates capacities to more efficient use (which often will involve side-payments), overall production costs are reduced, which tends to raise welfare. In spite of these arguments, the general idea is that collusive agreements in the market place are bad for society.

14.1   Formation and stability of cartels

Although most competition laws forbid price-fixing agreements, explicit cartels continue to form and operate in a vast array of industries. As illustrated in Case 14.1 (to which we will return several times throughout this chapter), cartels may last and maintain discipline over a long period of time. In this section we discuss cartels with explicit agreements and we address the issue of cartel formation and stability. This is important because in many markets, not all participants on the seller side collude, but only a subset of firms may form a cartel. In that case, we examine how such a cartel forms and what conditions keep a cartel member's incentives to stay in this group.

Case 14.1   The vitamin cartels

The worldwide market for bulk vitamins is estimated to be worth EUR 3.25 billion as of 1999. In Europe, sales of bulk vitamins were EUR 800 million in 1998 (with vitamins E, A and C accounting respectively for about EUR 250, 150 and 120 million). Production of vitamins is highly concentrated: the largest firm, Hoffmann-La Roche, has a market share of 40 to 50%, BASF has 20 to 30% and Aventis, 5 to 15%. The three largest firms combined thus control between 65 and 95% of this market.[6] While slow and costly plant construction, as well as economies of scale in the production technology, foster concentration on the production side, the buyer side is more fragmented as bulk vitamins are bought by a large number of different companies, e.g. producers of various food products, pharmaceutical companies and animal feed manufacturers. However, some buyers are likely to be large enough to enjoy some bargaining power in the form of lower prices.

On 21 November 2001, the European Commission imposed a then record fine of EUR 855.22 million on eight companies for participating in secret market-sharing and price-fixing cartels affecting vitamin products.[7] Overall, the Commission assessed the existence of eight distinct cartels involving different vitamins between September 1989 and February 1999. This European case followed an investigation by the United States Department of Justice, which in 1999 had already led to Hoffmann-La Roche pleading guilty and paying a US dollar 500 million criminal fine for leading a worldwide conspiracy to raise and fix prices and allocate market shares for certain vitamins sold in the United States and elsewhere.[d] In this context, BASF too pleaded guilty and paid US dollar 225 million in fines. In addition, there were large payments in civil settlements.

The European Commission found that overall 13 European and non-European companies participated in the cartels. The three main companies involved were Hoffmann-La Roche in Switzerland, BASF in Germany and Takeda Chemical Industries in Japan.[e] Overall the cartels involved the vitamins A, E, B1, B2, B5, B6, C, D3, Biotin (H), Folic Acid (M), Beta Carotene and carotinoids. The first cartel arrangements were

---

[d] The fine represented the largest fine that the US Department of Justice obtained in a criminal case up until then (see US Department of Justice, 1999).

[e] The other ten involved companies were Aventis in France (formerly Rhône-Poulenc), Daiichi Pharmaceutical in Japan, Eisai in Japan, Merck in Germany, Kongo Chemical in Japan, Lonza in Germany, Solvay Pharmaceuticals in the Netherlands, Sumitomo Chemical in Japan, Sumika Fine Chemicals in Japan and Tanabe Saiyaku in Japan.

formed in the vitamin A and E markets, where they were also maintained for the longest time, ending in February 1999. Hoffmann-La Roche was active in every vitamin market concerned and BASF in all but two markets.

According to the European Competition Commissioner Mario Monti, the vitamin cartel was 'the most damaging series of cartels the Commission has ever investigated due to the sheer range of vitamins covered, which are found in a multitude of products from cereals, biscuits and drinks to animal feed, pharmaceuticals and cosmetics'. He concluded that 'the companies' collusive behaviour enabled them to charge higher prices than if the full forces of competition had been at play, damaging consumers and allowing the companies to pocket illicit profits'.[8]

When firms within an industry form a cartel, they eliminate the competition that was existing between them. This leads them to reduce their joint output or to increase their prices. As this collusive behaviour also benefits the firms outside the cartel, the formation of a cartel can be seen as a public good. One can therefore conjecture that firms will tend to free-ride on the cartels formed by other firms, making cartels highly unstable. However, as we now show, the stability of a cartel depends on the institutional procedures of group and network formation that govern the formation of this cartel.

We contrast three procedures.[9] In the first procedure, firms decide simultaneously whether or not to participate in a single industry-wide cartel; it is implicitly assumed that cartel membership is open, in the sense that firms cannot exclude other firms from the cartel. In contrast, the second procedure allows for the endogenous formation of multiple cartels in a sequential way and with exclusive membership; here, each firm anticipates how its decision will affect the behaviour of firms choosing actions subsequently in the game. Finally, the third procedure relies on bilateral market-sharing agreements, whereby pairs of firms refrain from competing on each other's territory; the collection of these bilateral agreements then constitutes a collusive network.

We compare the three procedures in an industry described by the following simple market structure: n symmetric firms produce a homogeneous good at constant marginal cost c; they compete à la Cournot and face an inverse demand given by $p = a - q$, where q is the total quantity produced. We will also indicate how the results may change under different market structures (e.g., when products are differentiated).

14.1.1   Simultaneous cartel formation

We start by considering a very simple game in which firms decide simultaneously whether or not they want to join a single cartel. If a firm joins the cartel, it jointly chooses with the other cartel members the quantity that maximizes their joint profits.[10] Otherwise, the firm remains independent and chooses the quantity that maximizes its own profits. Suppose that a cartel of k firms, with $1 < k \leq n$, is formed. The Cournot game is thus played among $(n - k)$ independent firms and the cartel made of the other k firms. As all $(n - k + 1)$ players are symmetric (they have the same constant marginal cost c and face the same demand), we recall from Chapter 3 that each player gets profits equal to $[(a - c)/(n - k + 2)]^2$ at the Cournot equilibrium. Because of symmetry, we assume that inside the cartel, the division of profits is equitable. Hence, for a given cartel size k, profits for firms inside and outside the cartel are respectively given by

$$\pi^{in}(k) = \frac{(a-c)^2}{k(n-k+2)^2} \quad \text{and} \quad \pi^{out}(k) = \frac{(a-c)^2}{(n-k+2)^2}.$$

Now, for the cartel to be stable, it must be that no cartel member has an incentive to unilaterally leave the cartel, which is equivalent to

$$\pi^{in}(k) \geq \pi^{out}(k-1) \Leftrightarrow \frac{(a-c)^2}{k(n-k+2)^2} \geq \frac{(a-c)^2}{(n-k+3)^2}.$$

The latter condition can be rewritten as follows:

$$(n-k+3)^2 \geq k(n-k+2)^2 \Leftrightarrow$$

$$(n-k)^2 + 6(n-k) + 9 \geq k(n-k)^2 + 4k(n-k) + 4k \Leftrightarrow$$

$$(1-k)(n-k)^2 + (6-4k)(n-k) + (9-4k) \geq 0.$$

It is easily seen that for $k \geq 3$, which supposes $n \geq 3$, all the terms of the above inequality are negative. This implies that the condition is always violated, meaning that whatever the size of the cartel, each member has an incentive to leave it. For $k = 2$, the condition becomes $-n^2 + 2n + 1 > 0$, which is never satisfied for $n > 2$. If $n = 2$, the only possible cartel comprises all firms (i.e., $k = n = 2$) and the above inequality is then satisfied. We have thus proved the following result.

Lesson 14.1   **Consider the formation of a single cartel on a Cournot market with homogeneous goods and constant marginal costs. If there are at least three firms in the industry, all firms remain independent. If there are just two firms in the industry, the two firms form a cartel.**

The intuition for this result is simple: because the formation of the cartel induces positive externalities on the firms outside the cartel (through the higher market price), all firms prefer to free-ride on the public good provided by cartel members. In the linear Cournot model with constant marginal costs, this free-riding incentive is so strong that it prevents the formation of any cartel.

However, when firms produce horizontally differentiated goods, competition is relaxed and so is the free-riding incentive.[f] To examine the effects of product differentiation on cartel stability, suppose that each of the n firms in the industry produces a differentiated variety at a constant marginal cost c. Consider the following inverse demand functions $p_i = a - q_i - \gamma \sum_{j \neq i} q_j$, where $\gamma \in [0, 1]$ measures the strength of product substitutability.[g]

Two important results emerge from the analysis of the cartel formation game in this model. First, it is possible to show that, unless $n = 2$, the full cartel is not stable, whatever the degree of product substitutability – the reader may want to check this. There is always an incentive for an individual firm to free-ride on the cartel comprising all the other firms: for $n \geq 3$, $\pi^{out}(n-1) > \pi^{in}(n)$ for all $\gamma \in (0, 1]$.

---

[f] To be sure, in the extreme case of perfectly differentiated goods, cartelization would make no difference as firms would be monopolies; firms would therefore be indifferent between being inside or outside the cartel.

[g] As shown in Chapter 3, these inverse demand functions are derived from the maximization of a quadratic utility function of a representative consumer having a taste for variety.

Second, partial cartels may be stable, as illustrated by the following example. Let $n = 3$, $\gamma = 1/2$ and $a - c = 1$. We want to show that the cartel formation game has a Nash equilibrium in which two firms form a cartel while the third firm remains independent. In this situation, firms in the cartel (say firms 1 and 2) choose quantities q_1 and q_2 so as to maximize their joint profits $\Pi_{12} = \left(1 - q_1 - \frac{1}{2}(q_2 + q_3)\right) q_1 + \left(1 - q_2 - \frac{1}{2}(q_1 + q_3)\right) q_2$. As the two firms are symmetric, the maximum is such that $q_1 = q_2 \equiv q_{12}$, and the joint profits can be rewritten as $\Pi_{12} = 2\left(1 - \frac{3}{2}q_{12} - \frac{1}{2}q_3\right) q_{12}$. From the first-order condition, we derive the cartel's reaction function as $q_{12}(q_3) = \frac{1}{6}(2 - q_3)$. The independent firm chooses q_3 to maximize $\pi_3 = \left(1 - q_3 - \frac{1}{2}(q_{12} + q_{12})\right) q_3$. Again, we obtain the reaction function from the first-order condition: $q_3(q_{12}) = \frac{1}{2}(1 - q_{12})$. Solving for the system of the two reaction functions, we find the equilibrium quantities $q_{12} = 3/11$ and $q_3 = 4/11$. Computing the equilibrium profits, we have $\pi_1 = \pi_2 = \pi^{in}(2) = 27/242$ and $\pi_3 = \pi^{out}(2) = 32/242$. Observe that the free-riding effect is still present as the outsider obtains a larger profit than the insiders.

There are two requirements for the cartel to be stable: first, no cartel member has an incentive to leave the cartel; second, no outside firm finds it profitable to join the cartel. The first requirement refers to the *internal stability* of the cartel, and the second to its *external stability*.[11] Checking first for internal stability, we must compute the profits a firm would obtain by leaving the cartel. In that case, the three firms would be independent and each firm would choose its quantity q_i to maximize $\pi_i = \left(1 - q_i - \frac{1}{2}(q_j + q_k)\right) q_i$. The first-order condition gives $1 - 2q_i - \frac{1}{2}(q_j + q_k) = 0$. Invoking symmetry, each firm produces the same quantity q at the equilibrium and the latter condition becomes: $1 - 3q = 0$. Hence, $q = 1/3$ and equilibrium profits are $\pi^{out}(1) = 1/9$. Internal stability is fulfilled as long as $\pi^{in}(2) \geq \pi^{out}(1)$, which is true as $27/242 \simeq 0.1116 > 1/9 \simeq 0.1111$.

To check for external stability, we must compute the profits firm 3 would obtain by joining firms 1 and 2 in the cartel. In that case of full collusion, the three firms choose their common quantity q so as to maximize $\Pi_{123} = 3\left(1 - q - \frac{1}{2}(2q)\right) q = 3(1 - 2q)q$. The profit-maximizing quantity is easily found as $q = 1/4$, which results in per firm profits of $\pi^{in}(3) = 1/8$. Hence, there is no incentive for the outside firm to join the cartel if $\pi^{out}(2) \geq \pi^{in}(3)$, which is satisfied as $32/242 \simeq 0.132 > 1/8 = 0.125$.

When products are sufficiently differentiated, competition is less intense and, as a result, outside firms do not benefit so much from the formation of a cartel. In other words, the free-riding incentive is reduced with respect to the case of homogeneous goods. In our example, the reduction is strong enough to dissuade one of the two cartel members to leave the cartel; on the other hand, free-riding is still attractive enough to dissuade the outside firm to join the cartel.

> **Lesson 14.2** Consider the formation of a single cartel on a Cournot market with differentiated goods. If goods are sufficiently differentiated, it is possible to find stable cartels comprising not all firms but a strict subset of them.

14.1.2 Sequential cartel formation

We now allow for the formation of multiple cartels. In such a case, the profit of each firm will depend on the entire cartel structure. Hence, each firm will have to anticipate the other firms' reaction when deciding whether to join a cartel or not. To take this forward-looking behaviour into account, we assume here that the production stage (i.e., the Cournot game) is preceded by a sequential game of cartel formation.[12] This sequential game is defined by an exogenous specification of the ordering of the firms that determines the order of move. It proceeds as follows. The first firm in the ordering proposes the formation of a cartel (to which it belongs) and all the prospective members of this cartel sequentially respond in turn to the proposal (note that the sequence of all firms is initially determined according to some exogenous rule). If they all agree, the proposed cartel is formed in the order initially determined. If at least one firm rejects the first proposal, the cartel is not formed and it is the first firm that rejected the offer that makes a counteroffer and proposes a cartel to which it belongs. If all firms accept the first proposal, the cartel is formed and these firms withdraw from the game. The first among the remaining firms then makes a proposal and the game proceeds. To make sure that cartels will eventually be formed (with, possibly, all firms remaining separate) and the Cournot game will ensue, it is assumed that there is no discounting in the cartel formation game but that firms receive zero profits if the game is played infinitely.[h]

The game has complete information and infinite horizon; we therefore use the solution concept of a *stationary perfect equilibrium*.[i] Note the differences with the previous setting: cartel formation is now sequential (rather than simultaneous) and membership is exclusive (rather than open). Moreover, as the game is only played among the remaining firms once a cartel has been formed, this sequential cartel formation embodies a high degree of commitment of the firms.

The stationary perfect equilibrium of this game has a very simple structure: at each period *the first firms in the sequence choose to remain independent and to free-ride on the cartel that the last firms will eventually form*. To find the critical cartel size, we need to compare the profits a firm obtains in a cartel of a given size, $\pi^{in}(k)$, with the profits each firm obtains when they all remain independent, $\pi^{out}(1)$. Firms prefer to form a cartel than to remain independent if

$$\pi^{in}(k) \geq \pi^{out}(1) \Leftrightarrow \frac{(a-c)^2}{k(n-k+2)^2} \geq \frac{(a-c)^2}{(n+1)^2}.$$

Developing the latter condition, we have

$$(n+1)^2 \geq k(n-k+2)^2 \Leftrightarrow (k-1)\left(-k^2 + (2n+3)k - (n+1)^2\right) \geq 0.$$

Solving for k, we have that[13]

$$\pi^{in}(k) > \pi^{out}(1) \Leftrightarrow k > \frac{1}{2}\left(2n+3 - \sqrt{4n+5}\right).$$

Let k^* denote the first integer following $\frac{1}{2}\left(2n+3 - \sqrt{4n+5}\right)$. Then, the first $n - k^*$ firms indeed prefer to remain independent. However, the last k^* firms will choose to form a cartel

---

[h] When firms are ex ante identical (as is assumed here), Bloch (1996) shows that a simpler finite game generates the exact same cartel structures as the ones obtained at the stationary perfect equilibria of the infinite game. In this finite game, the first firm announces an integer k_1, corresponding to the size of the cartel it wants to see formed, firm $k_1 + 1$ announces an integer k_2 etc. until the total number n of firms is exhausted. An equilibrium of the finite game determines a sequence of integers adding up to n, which completely characterizes the cartel structure as all firms are ex ante identical.

[i] Stationarity requires that strategies only depend on the payoff-relevant part of the history (i.e., here, the cartel structure formed by the previous players and the ongoing offer).

as it is no longer profitable for a firm to stay out and free-ride on the cartel formed by the others. In this specification we show that the minimal profitable cartel size is larger than 80% of the firms in the industry:

$$k^* - \frac{80}{100}n = \frac{1}{10}\left(2n + 15 - 5\sqrt{4n + 5}\right) = \frac{1}{10}\frac{(2n + 15)^2 - 25(4n + 5)}{2n + 15 + 5\sqrt{4n + 5}}$$

$$= \frac{1}{10}\frac{4(n - 5)^2}{2n + 15 + 5\sqrt{4n + 5}} \geq 0.$$

It follows that there will always be at most one cartel formed at equilibrium.

Lesson 14.3   **Consider a Cournot market with homogeneous goods. In the unique equilibrium of the sequential cartel formation game, the first $(n - k^*)$ firms remain independent while the last k^* firms form a cartel, with k^* being larger than 80% of the firms in the industry.**

Recall that in the simultaneous cartel formation game, any firm has an incentive to leave the cartel. Here, the sequentiality allows firms to commit to stay out of the cartel, which makes it possible for a cartel to form at equilibrium. In that respect, the cartel formed in this sequential way has the attributes of a complete merger of the firms. A horizontal merger can indeed be seen as a cartel requiring the unanimity of its members: if one member disagrees, the cartel does not form (i.e., the merger is not implemented). We will show in the next chapter that the '80% rule' stated in Lesson 14.3 also applies to horizontal mergers of symmetric firms in a Cournot industry.

14.1.3   Network of market-sharing agreements

In the previous two situations, collusion resulted from the formation of multilateral agreements. Here, we instead consider *bilateral* collusive agreements. In particular, we talk about *market-sharing agreements* of the following form: if two firms are active on different geographical markets or serve distinct consumer segments, they may collude by signing a market-sharing agreement, whereby they both refrain from competing on the other firm's territory (we return to such agreements, and give illustrations, in the next section). At the industry level, the collection of such bilateral market-sharing agreements constitutes a collusive structure.

We refer to this collusive structure as a *collusive network*. A network is represented by a graph g on the set N of firms. A graph is a set of pairwise links, denoted ij, between firms i and j. Here, the link ij is formed if firms i and j sign a market-sharing agreement. The larger is the number of firms, the more complex are the potential networks. It is therefore very hard to characterize the formation of a network as the result of a noncooperative game of link formation. Hence, we just focus here on the issue of network stability. We say that network g is stable if no pair of firms has an incentive to form a new link, and no firm has an incentive to unilaterally destroy an existing link.[14] Applied to the present situation, a collusive network is stable if no pair of firms finds it profitable to sign a new market-sharing agreement, and no firm has an incentive to renege on an existing market-sharing agreement.

Suppose that the n firms are initially present on different geographical markets and that each market is characterized by Cournot competition over homogeneous goods. As above, we assume that the inverse demand (on each market) is given by $p = a - q$, and that all firms have the same constant marginal cost of production c. For a given collusive network g, let $n_i(g)$ denote the number of firms active on market i. The total profit of firm i (initially installed on market i) can then be written as

$$\Pi_i(g) = \frac{(a-c)^2}{(n_i(g)+1)^2} + \sum_{j \text{ with } ij \notin g} \frac{(a-c)^2}{(n_j(g)+1)^2},$$

where the first term is the Cournot equilibrium profit that firm i obtains in its home market, and the second term is the sum of profits firm i obtains in all the foreign markets in which it is present (i.e., the markets of the firms with which it has not signed a market-sharing agreement). Denoting by $g + ij$ the graph obtained by adding link ij to graph g, we can use the previous definition to compute firm i's *incentive to form an agreement* with firm j as

$$\Pi_i(g+ij) - \Pi_i(g) = \underbrace{\left[\frac{(a-c)^2}{n_i(g)^2} - \frac{(a-c)^2}{(n_i(g)+1)^2}\right]}_{\text{less competition on } i\text{'s market}} - \underbrace{\frac{(a-c)^2}{(n_j(g)+1)^2}}_{\text{lost access to } j\text{'s market}}. \quad (14.1)$$

There are two conflicting effects at work when forming a new agreement. On the one hand, firm i benefits from the reduction of competition on its own market (as firm j has withdrawn); on the other hand, firm i foregoes access to market j and the profits it was making there. (These are the only two effects as the other markets $k \neq i, j$ are left unaffected by the market-sharing agreement between firms i and j.)

We first examine the *stability of the empty network*, i.e., the situation in which no market-sharing agreement is signed and no collusion occurs. In the absence of any agreement, all n firms are present on all markets. Hence, using expression (14.1) and writing g_0 for the empty network, we compute the benefit that two firms would have to sign an agreement as

$$\Pi_i(g_0+ij) - \Pi_i(g_0) = \frac{(a-c)^2}{n^2} - 2\frac{(a-c)^2}{(n+1)^2} = \frac{(a-c)^2\left(-n^2+2n+1\right)}{n^2(n+1)^2}.$$

It is quickly seen that $\left(-n^2+2n+1\right)$ is positive for $n = 2$ and negative for $n \geq 3$. It follows that for $n \geq 3$, no pair of firms has an incentive to form a new link, meaning that the empty network is stable for $n \geq 3$.

Suppose now that two firms in a non-empty network g have an incentive to sign an agreement: $\Pi_i(g) - \Pi_i(g-ij) \geq 0$ and $\Pi_j(g) - \Pi_j(g-ij) \geq 0$, or

$$\begin{cases} \frac{(a-c)^2}{(n_i(g)+1)^2} \geq \frac{(a-c)^2}{(n_i(g)+2)^2} + \frac{(a-c)^2}{(n_j(g)+2)^2}, \\ \frac{(a-c)^2}{(n_j(g)+1)^2} \geq \frac{(a-c)^2}{(n_j(g)+2)^2} + \frac{(a-c)^2}{(n_i(g)+2)^2}. \end{cases}$$

We note first that because of symmetry, this system of inequalities can only be satisfied if $n_i(g) = n_j(g)$: a market-sharing agreement can only be concluded among two firms with the same number of competitors on their home markets. Indeed, if one market had a smaller number of competitors, the firm on the other market would have no incentive to form an agreement, as the profit it makes on the foreign market would already be larger than the profit it makes on its home market. Second, setting $n_i(g) = n_j(g) = x$, the two inequalities can be rewritten as

$$\frac{(a-c)^2}{(x+1)^2} \geq 2\frac{(a-c)^2}{(x+2)^2} \Leftrightarrow (x+2)^2 \geq 2(x+1)^2 \Leftrightarrow 2 - x^2 \geq 0.$$

As $x = 1$ is the only strictly positive number that satisfies the latter inequality, it follows that if a non-empty network is formed, it must be such that each firm is a monopoly on its home market ($n_i(g) = 1$). In other words, *the only non-empty stable network is the complete network*, in which all pairs of firms sign market-sharing agreements, resulting in full collusion. Any firm would indeed have an incentive to defect from any network of smaller size.

Lesson 14.4   **If collusive networks are negotiated bilaterally, they may lead to full collusion, with every firm a monopolist on its own market.**

As the empty network is also stable (except for $n = 2$), we see that the free-riding incentives remain strong. However, they do not prevent the formation of full collusion. As above, when products are differentiated, competition is reduced and with it, the incentives to sign market-sharing agreements. Different stable network architectures might then emerge (e.g., a network with one isolated firm and all other ($n - 1$) firms signing agreements with one another).

14.2   Sustainability of tacit collusion

In this section, we consider situations where collusion is reached in a 'tacit', noncooperative, way. Firms do not necessarily resort, e.g., to explicit quota agreements to discipline collusion. Instead, all that is needed is some 'meeting of the minds' between colluding firms and a common understanding that deviation from the collusive 'tacit agreement' will be met by some form of punishment. However, the analysis is also highly relevant for explicit agreements: sustainability is necessary for cartels that are reached in a cooperative way as long as punishments cannot be legally binding.

We start by analysing a simple repeated game framework to understand what this 'meeting of the minds' exactly means (Subsection 14.2.1). We then extend the basic setting in two directions: we first ask how punishments should optimally be designed to promote collusion and second how multimarket contact can make collusion easier to sustain (Subsections 14.2.2 and 14.2.3). We close this section with two more advanced topics, analysing how demand fluctuations and the unobservability of firms' actions impact the sustainability of tacit collusion (Subsections 14.2.4 and 14.2.5).

14.2.1   Tacit collusion: the basics

Consider a number of firms (say two, for simplicity) that offer perfect substitutes produced at constant marginal costs c. Suppose that instead of competing just once, the two firms repeatedly compete over time. That is, at each period $t = 1, 2, \ldots T$, the firms repeat the 'static' game we analysed in Chapter 3 by simultaneously choosing the price, or the quantity, of their product. They observe the rival's action after each period. A strategy is then a list of actions (a contingent plan) that tells the firm what to choose in each period as a function of past prices or quantities (that is, the history of the game). Strategies can take complicated forms; in particular, the action prescribed at some period may depend on the observed actions (of all players) at all previous periods. Future periods are discounted by the factor δ and thus present discounted profits are $\sum_{t=0}^{T} \delta^t \pi_i^t(\sigma_1^t, \sigma_2^t)$, where π_i^t is firm i's profit in period t, σ_i^t is firm i's action in that period (with $\sigma_i = p_i$ or $\sigma_i = q_i$ according to whether we consider price or quantity competition) and T is the last period (the 'horizon') of the repeated game.

The question we want to investigate is whether firms can design strategies that allow them to reach a situation of tacit collusion, whereby they share the monopoly profit in each and every period. In what follows, we first show that whether the horizon is finite or infinite makes a crucial difference. We then compare price and quantity competition and examine the impact of the number of firms on the sustainability of tacit collusion.

Finite vs. infinite horizon

Suppose that the static game that firms play has a unique Nash equilibrium. We first want to show that *tacit collusion is not possible when competition is repeated over a finite number of periods* (that is, when competition stops at some finite date T). Since there is a known end date to the game, we can use backward induction to solve the game for its subgame perfect equilibria. Consider thus the last period (period T). At this period, firms only care about their current profits as nothing ensues: the Nash equilibrium is thus the one of the static game and each firm earns the level of profits at this equilibrium (denoted by π^n). Moving back to the penultimate period ($T-1$), we now have that firms maximize their flow of profits over the last two periods. Yet, from our previous result, we know that whatever action they choose in period $T-1$, this will not affect the profits they obtain in the subsequent period (i.e., π^n); therefore, the Nash equilibrium in period $T-1$ is thus again the Nash equilibrium of the static game. The same argument carries on up to the first period. We have thus learned the following lesson.

Lesson 14.5   If competition is repeated over a finite number of periods, firms play according to the (unique) Nash equilibrium of the static game in each period. Tacit collusion cannot emerge.

Consider now an *infinite horizon* ($T = \infty$). This is not to say that firms compete until the end of time; it just means that there is no known end date to the game: at each period, there is a probability that firms will compete one more time. The first thing to note is that the subgame perfect equilibrium we described for the finite horizon case is still an equilibrium here. Think of the strategy that tells the firm to choose, in each period and irrespective of what happened in the past, the action corresponding to the Nash equilibrium of the static game. Clearly, if firm i follows this strategy, it is firm j's best response to follow this strategy as well. The Nash equilibrium of the static game is thus repeated infinitely and no tacit collusion takes places. What is interesting is that this situation is no longer the only equilibrium. In particular, tacit collusion may emerge at the subgame perfect equilibrium of the (infinitely) repeated game.

To see this, consider the so-called *grim trigger strategy*. According to this strategy, firm *i* starts by choosing the action that maximizes total profits (i.e., the sum of firm 1's and firm 2's profits). Firm *i* keeps on choosing this action as long as both firms have done so in all previous periods. We are then in the *cooperation phase*. However, if one firm deviates (i.e., chooses any other action), this deviation 'triggers' the start of the *punishment phase*: from the next period on, and forever after, both firms choose the action that corresponds to the Nash equilibrium of the static game.

We define the following per period profit levels: when both firms play the cooperative action, they both obtain $\pi^c = \pi^m/2$ (where π^m is the per-period monopoly profit); when one firm plays the cooperative action and the other optimally deviates, the deviating firm obtains π^d; at the Nash equilibrium of the static game, both firms obtain π^n. Naturally, we have $\pi^d > \pi^c > \pi^n$. Since firms maximize their flow of profits over all the periods of the game, they will compare the immediate gain from deviation with future losses resulting from the other firm's punishment. As we will now show formally, this trade-off (and thus the feasibility of tacit collusion) depends (i) on the magnitude of the deviation and the punishment profits, with respect to the collusive profits, and (ii) on the firms' discount factor.

Since there is no terminal period to the game, we cannot solve it by backward induction. We proceed differently by supposing that one firm (say firm 2) follows the grim trigger strategy and by investigating under which conditions firm 1's best response is to follow the grim trigger strategy as well. Suppose first that we are in the punishment phase. Firm 2 then plays the action corresponding to the Nash equilibrium of the static game (now and forever) and, obviously, firm 1's best response is to play the same action at each period. Hence, firm 1 finds it best to follow the trigger strategy.[j] Consider now the cooperative phase. If firm 1 follows the grim trigger strategy, it will obtain π^c in all subsequent periods (as the punishment phase will never be triggered). In present discounted value, firm 1 will obtain

$$V^C = \pi^c + \delta\pi^c + \delta^2\pi^c + \cdots = \frac{\pi^c}{1 - \delta}.$$

On the other hand, if firm 1 deviates, it will obtain π^d in the current period and π^n in all subsequent periods as the punishment phase will start. In present discounted value, deviation would give

$$V^D = \pi^d + \delta\pi^n + \delta^2\pi^n + \cdots = \pi^d + \delta\pi^n/(1 - \delta).$$

Hence, firm 1 prefers to follow the grim trigger strategy if and only if

$$V^C \geq V^D \Leftrightarrow \frac{\pi^c}{1 - \delta} \geq \pi^d + \frac{\delta}{1 - \delta}\pi^n$$

$$\Leftrightarrow \frac{\delta}{1 - \delta}(\pi^c - \pi^n) \geq \pi^d - \pi^c,$$

---

[j] This makes the punishment credible. Hence, it can be played in subgame perfect equilibrium off the equilibrium path.

where the left-hand side is the discounted long-term losses induced by the punishment and the right-hand side is the short-term gain from deviation. Solving for δ, we can rewrite the previous condition as

$$\delta \geq \frac{\pi^d - \pi^c}{\pi^d - \pi^n} \equiv \delta_{\min}, \tag{14.2}$$

where $\delta_{\min}$ lies strictly between 0 and 1. We conclude the following.

Lesson 14.6   When competition is repeated over an infinite horizon, tacit collusion can be sustained by the grim trigger strategy as long as firms have a large enough discount factor.

The intuition is clear: firms must put sufficient weight on future losses to offset the temptation of securing an immediate gain by deviating; the minimum weight is lower (and thus tacit collusion is more likely) when deviation pays less (i.e., when the difference $\pi^d - \pi^c$ decreases) and punishment hurts more (i.e., when the difference $\pi^c - \pi^n$ increases). Note that this result hinges on the fact that firms are able to observe deviations from the collusive outcome and then start the punishment phase. In Subsection 14.2.5, we examine what changes when deviations are only imperfectly observable.

If condition (14.2) is met, then there exists a subgame perfect equilibrium in which firms share the monopoly profit in each period. Note that there are plenty other equilibria in the game. Actually, we can use the exact same argument to show that, if δ is large enough, any profit level $\tilde{\pi} \in [\pi^n, \pi^m/2]$ can be achieved by each firm in each period by setting the corresponding action $\tilde{\sigma}$ such that $\pi(\tilde{\sigma}, \tilde{\sigma}) = \tilde{\pi}$. Thus, this infinitely repeated game presents us with an embarrassment of riches; this result is commonly referred to in the literature as the *Folk theorem*.[15]

Application to price competition

Consider the simple Bertrand competition model with constant and identical marginal costs of production that we introduced in Chapter 4. If firms set the same price, the market is assumed to split evenly. Thus, if both firms collude and set the monopoly price p^m, they make in each period a profit of $\pi^c = \pi^m/2$. At any point in time, the largest short-term gain is achieved by slightly undercutting the rival's price by some arbitrarily small amount. Then deviation profits are $\pi^d = \pi^m - \varepsilon$. Since the total profit loss from setting a price slightly below p^m is negligible, we can drop ε in the analysis below. After a deviation has occurred, each firm sets the Nash equilibrium price c and makes zero profit: $\pi^n = 0$. Substituting for these values into the expression of the minimum discount factor (14.2), we obtain the following:

$$\delta_{\min}^{\text{Bert}} = \frac{\pi^d - \pi^c}{\pi^d - \pi^n} = \frac{\pi^m - (\pi^m/2)}{\pi^m - 0} = \frac{1}{2}.$$

To illustrate the Folk theorem, note that if firms set $\tilde{p} \in [c, p^m]$, then total profit is $\pi(\tilde{p}) = \tilde{\pi}$, with $\tilde{\pi} \in [0, \pi^m]$. In that case, the collusive profit is $\pi^c = \tilde{\pi}/2$, deviation through undercutting yields $\pi^d = \tilde{\pi}$, while in the punishment phase, each firm still obtains $\pi^n = 0$. Therefore, the minimum discount factor for sustaining collusion is the same as in the case where both firms set the monopoly price. We can thus state the following result.

Lesson 14.7   In the infinitely repeated Bertrand price-setting duopoly game, any profit level between zero and the monopoly profit can be supported in a subgame perfect equilibrium if the discount factor is sufficiently large, $\delta \geq 1/2$.

Let us extend this simple example to the situation in which n firms operate in the market. Deviation profits remain unchanged ($\pi^d = \pi^m$) but total collusive profits have to be shared among n firms ($\pi^c = \pi^m/n$). Therefore, the condition that a deviation from the fully collusive outcome is not profitable becomes

$$V^C \geq V^D \Leftrightarrow \frac{1}{1-\delta}\frac{\pi^m}{n} \geq \pi^m \Leftrightarrow \delta \geq 1 - \frac{1}{n} \equiv \delta_{\min}^{\text{Bert}}(n).$$

The critical discount factor $\delta_{\min}^{\text{Bert}}(n)$ is increasing in n. This means that collusion becomes more difficult to sustain (in the sense that it requires less discounting) as the number of firms in the market increases. This suggests that collusion is more likely to be observed in markets in which a small number of firms are active.

Lesson 14.8   In the infinitely repeated Bertrand price-setting game, the set of discount factors that can support collusion is larger the smaller the number of firms in the market.

As has been pointed out above, though cartels rely on explicit agreements, firms cannot appeal to courts to enforce these agreements (as they are illegal) and must therefore rely on self-enforcing mechanisms. Thus, the previous finding equally applies to cartels, like the vitamin cartels that we described in Case 14.1.

Case 14.2 The vitamin cartels (2)

The sustainability of the vitamin cartels was fostered by three key factors. First, the production of vitamins is highly concentrated and associated with high entry costs, thus coordination among a small number of manufacturers could be effective and a strong firm could enforce existing agreements as well as threaten to punish deviating firms. Second, bulk vitamins are a homogeneous product with clear quality and product standards giving the transparency necessary to run a cartel successfully. Third, demand can be considered relatively inelastic giving rise to a strong incentive to increase prices above the competitive level.

It has been observed that cartelization led to an increase in prices. Even more pronounced were price drops at the end of the cartelization period: it has been reported that price drops of 50% occurred for most cartelized vitamins shortly after announcement of the guilty pleas in the US.[16] While prices are easily observable, the profitability and long-term effects of cartelization are more difficult to observe. In particular, demand and supply factors may have changed over time. Thus, it is unclear what the industry would have looked like in the absence of the cartel.[k]

Application to quantity competition

We now analyze the linear n-firm Cournot model with constant and identical marginal costs of production: the inverse demand is given by $P(q) = a - q$ and all firms have marginal costs of production c. The monopoly quantity is easily found as $q^m = (a - c)/2$, resulting in collusive profits

$$\pi^c = \pi^m / n = \frac{1}{4n}(a - c)^2. \tag{14.3}$$

We also recall from Chapter 3 that the Cournot Nash equilibrium profits in this linear model are

$$\pi^n = \frac{1}{(n + 1)^2}(a - c)^2.$$

If all other firms choose a quantity q, the best deviation is the quantity z that maximizes $z(a - c - z - (n - 1)q)$. From the first-order condition, we find $z = (1/2)(a - c - (n - 1)q)$. Substituting for this value in the profit function, we obtain

$$\pi^d(q) = \tfrac{1}{4}(a - c - (n - 1)q)^2. \tag{14.4}$$

Hence, if the other firms play the collusive quantity $q^m / n = (a - c)/(2n)$, we have

$$\pi^d = \frac{(n + 1)^2}{16n^2}(a - c)^2.$$

We now have all the elements to compute the minimum discount factor that allows firms to sustain the monopoly outcome. Using expression (14.2), we obtain

$$\delta_{\min}^{\text{Cour}}(n) \equiv \frac{\pi^d - \pi^c}{\pi^d - \pi^n} = \frac{\frac{(n+1)^2(a-c)^2}{16n^2} - \frac{(a-c)^2}{4n}}{\frac{(n+1)^2(a-c)^2}{16n^2} - \frac{(a-c)^2}{(n+1)^2}} = \frac{(n + 1)^2}{n^2 + 6n + 1}.$$

It can be checked that $\delta_{\min}^{\text{Cour}}(n)$ increases with n. For instance, in a duopoly, the minimum discount factor is $9/17 \approx 0.53$; if there are three firms in the market, the value increases to $4/7 \approx 0.57$; for ten firms, we reach $121/161 \approx 0.75$, and so on and so forth. Therefore, as under price competition, *collusion is harder to sustain the larger the number of firms in the market*. In the limit as $n \longrightarrow \infty$, the critical discount factor converges to 1.

---

[k] In general, a more detailed understanding of the effects of cartelization on industry performance would be desirable. In their survey of the empirical analysis of cartels in a wide number of industries, Levenstein and Suslov (2006) conclude that cartels 'appear to increase prices and profits, but more careful studies with explicit counterfactual analysis would make a significant contribution to our understanding of the full economic effects of collusion'.

Note that in this linear example, collusion is easier to sustain under price competition than under quantity competition when the market is a duopoly: $\delta_{\min}^{\text{Bert}}(2) = 0.5 < \delta_{\min}^{\text{Cour}}(2) \simeq 0.53$. However, the opposite result prevails when there are at least three firms in the market; one can indeed check that for $n \geq 3$, $\delta_{\min}^{\text{Bert}}(n) > \delta_{\min}^{\text{Cour}}(n)$. It is not surprising that the comparison between the two types of competition leads to ambiguous results insofar as both the gain from deviation $(\pi^d - \pi^c)$ and the impact of punishment $(\pi^c - \pi^n)$ are larger under price competition than under quantity competition. For $n = 2$, the stronger punishment makes collusion easier to sustain under price competition; for $n \geq 3$, the stronger incentive to deviate makes collusion harder to sustain under price competition.

To sum up, we have shown in this subsection that firms can sustain collusion in an infinitely repeated interaction provided the future is a sufficiently strong component of the stream of profits. We have also shown that this general insight holds not only for the simple price competition game but for oligopoly games more generally. So far, we restricted the analysis to grim trigger strategies. However, firms may want to use different strategies, raising the question which are the best strategies in such an infinitely repeated game in order to support full or partial collusion. We turn to this issue in the following subsection.

14.2.2   Optimal punishment of deviating firms

We concluded the previous subsection by comparing the sustainability of tacit collusion under price and quantity competition. One important difference between the two settings arises from the strength of punishment. Under price competition, reversion to the Nash equilibrium generates zero profits for all firms, which provides the most severe credible punishment.[17] In contrast, under quantity competition, reversion to the Nash equilibrium gives rise to positive profits. It seems thus possible to design more severe punishment schemes enabling the firms to sustain collusive outcomes over a larger set of discount factors. On the other hand, the punishment must be credible, in the sense that firms must find it optimal to abide by it. With regard to the grim trigger strategy, the reversion to the Nash equilibrium forever ensures this credibility. With more severe punishments, credibility can be restored by shortening the punishment phase and eventually coming back to the collusive outcome, so as to reward firms that punish a deviator.

To formalize the basic idea, we consider the following *stick-and-carrot strategies*, in which deviators are punished for only one period:

(i)   Start the game by playing the collusive output q^*, as prescribed by the collusive agreement.

(ii)   Cooperate as long as the collusive output has been observed in all preceding periods.

(iii)   If one of the players deviates from the collusive agreement at period t, play $\hat{q}$ at period $t + 1$(punishment phase) and return to the collusive agreement at period $t + 2$.

(iv)   If one of the players chooses a quantity $q \neq \hat{q}$ during the punishment phase, start the punishment phase again at the following period.

With this strategy, the punishment has a simple two-phase stick-and-carrot structure: the profit reduction following a deviation is used as a stick, while the promise to return to the collusive outcome after just one period constitutes the carrot. In the following we explain how this strategy is used to sustain collusion in general; we then use the specific example of a linear Cournot duopoly to show how the stick-and-carrot strategy expands the firms' ability to sustain collusive outcomes.

General analysis

It can be shown that in the set of stationary symmetric strategies the stick-and-carrot strategy is optimal when the quantity $\hat{q}$ is chosen to maximize the scope for collusion.[18] For a given discount factor δ, we need to characterize the best collusive sustainable output q^* and the punishment output $\hat{q}$. The punishment output $\hat{q}$ is set to minimize the deviator's profit under the constraint that deviations from the punishment do not pay for any of the firms.

To carry out the general analysis, we need some additional notation. We consider n firms that produce a homogeneous good at constant marginal cost c. The inverse demand is given by $P(q)$. We assume that there is a unique monopoly quantity defined by $q^m = \arg\max_q q(P(q) - c)$, and that $q(P(q) - c)$ is monotonically increasing until q^m and monotonically decreasing after q^m. Monopoly profits are denoted $\pi^m = q^m(P(q^m) - c)$. If $q_i = q^m/n$ for all i, then each firm obtains the collusive profit $\pi^c = \pi^m/n$. We also suppose that the static Cournot oligopoly game has a unique symmetric pure strategy equilibrium, with quantities $q^n \neq q^m/n$ and profit π^n. If all other firms choose a combined quantity $(n-1)q$, let $\pi^d(q)$ denote the profit obtained by a firm that responds optimally to each competitor's quantity q. Formally,

$$\pi^d(q) = \max_z z(P(z + (n-1)q) - c).$$

We also define $\pi(q)$ as the profit obtained by a firm when all firms produce the same quantity q:

$$\pi(q) = q(P(nq) - c).$$

By definition, $\pi(q^m/n) = \pi^m/n$. Notice also that, at the symmetric Cournot equilibrium, $\pi(q^n) = \pi^d(q^n) = \pi^n$.

Using this notation, we express the present discounted value of complying with the punishment as $V^P \equiv \pi(\hat{q}) + [\delta/(1-\delta)]\pi(q^*)$. That is, in the period that follows the deviation, both firms choose the punishment output $\hat{q}$, which gives them profits equal to $\pi(\hat{q})$, and from there on, they return to the collusive agreement by choosing both the collusive output q^*, which gives them the collusive profits $\pi(q^*)$. On the other hand, a deviation from the punishment would yield $\pi^d(\hat{q}) + \delta V^P$. That is, deviation yields immediate profits of $\pi^d(\hat{q})$, which stems from the best-response to the rival's output $\hat{q}$, and triggers a new start of the punishment phase, which generates a stream of profits given by V^P. Hence, no deviation occurs as long as $V^P \geq \pi^d(\hat{q}) + \delta V^P$, which is equivalent to

$$\delta\left[\pi(q^*) - \pi(\hat{q})\right] \geq \pi^d(\hat{q}) - \pi(\hat{q}). \tag{14.5}$$

This *credibility condition* is easily interpreted: the cost of not complying with the punishment, which stems from the one-period delay before returning to the collusive outcome, must be larger than the immediate gain of deviating from the punishment. For the punishment to be the harshest possible, condition (14.5) must hold as equality. That is, $\hat{q}$ is found as the solution to $\delta \left[\pi \left(q^* \right) - \pi \left(\hat{q} \right) \right] = \pi^d \left(\hat{q} \right) - \pi \left(\hat{q} \right)$.

It must also be checked that it does not pay to deviate from the cooperative phase. We only need to look one period ahead as firms return to the collusive outcome after one period of punishment. Complying with the collusive agreement yields $(1 + \delta) \pi \left(q^* \right)$, while deviating yields $\pi^d \left(q^* \right) + \delta \pi \left(\hat{q} \right)$, i.e., the profits resulting from the best-deviation from q^* followed by the profits obtained in the punishment phase. Hence, firms abide by the collusive agreement as long as $(1 + \delta) \pi \left(q^* \right) \geq \pi^d \left(q^* \right) + \delta \pi \left(\hat{q} \right)$, or equivalently

$$\delta \left[\pi \left(q^* \right) - \pi \left(\hat{q} \right) \right] \geq \pi^d \left(q^* \right) - \pi \left(q^* \right). \tag{14.6}$$

This *sustainability condition* has a similar interpretation as the previous credibility condition: the cost of deviation (incurred next period) must be larger than the immediate gain of deviation.

Full collusion is sustainable if condition (14.6) is satisfied for $q^* = q^m / 2$ and with $\hat{q}$ being the most severe punishment obtained by solving (14.5) with equality. Otherwise, only partial collusion can be sustained, and the best collusive output is found as the solution q^* to $\delta \left[\pi \left(q^* \right) - \pi \left(\hat{q} \right) \right] = \pi^d \left(q^* \right) - \pi \left(q^* \right)$.

Application to the linear Cournot duopoly

We return to the special case that $P \left(q \right) = a - q$ and that duopolists have the same constant marginal cost c. We use the definition of $\pi \left(q \right)$ and we set $n = 2$ in expressions (14.3) and (14.4) to find

$$\pi \left(q^* \right) = \tfrac{1}{8} \left(a - c \right)^2, \quad \pi \left(\hat{q} \right) = \left(a - c - 2\hat{q} \right) \hat{q}, \quad \text{and} \quad \pi^d \left(\hat{q} \right) = \tfrac{1}{4} \left(a - c - \hat{q} \right)^2.$$

Then, condition (14.5) holding as equality can be rewritten as

$$\delta \left[\tfrac{1}{8} \left(a - c \right)^2 - \left(a - c - 2\hat{q} \right) \hat{q} \right] = \tfrac{1}{4} \left(a - c - \hat{q} \right)^2 - \left(a - c - 2\hat{q} \right) \hat{q}.$$

This quadratic form in $\hat{q}$ admits two roots. As punishment requires expanding output, we select the largest root.[1] This is admissible as long as the market price remains above zero, i.e., $p = a - 2\hat{q} \geq 0$, or $\hat{q} \leq a/2$. Making the computations, we find the following:

$$\hat{q} \left(\delta \right) = \begin{cases} \frac{2(3 - 2\delta) + \sqrt{2\delta}}{2(9 - 8\delta)} \left(a - c \right) & \text{for } \delta < \tfrac{1}{2} \left(\tfrac{a + 2c}{a + c} \right)^2, \\ \tfrac{1}{2} a & \text{for } \delta \geq \tfrac{1}{2} \left(\tfrac{a + 2c}{a + c} \right)^2. \end{cases}$$

For which range of discount factors is full collusion sustainable? For $q^* = q^m / 2 = (a - c)/4$, we compute that $\pi^d \left(q^* \right) = 9 \left(a - c \right)^2 / 64$. Hence, condition (14.6) becomes

$$\delta \left[\tfrac{1}{8} \left(a - c \right)^2 - \left(a - c - 2\hat{q} \left(\delta \right) \right) \hat{q} \left(\delta \right) \right] \geq \tfrac{9}{64} \left(a - c \right)^2 - \tfrac{1}{8} \left(a - c \right)^2 = \tfrac{1}{64} \left(a - c \right)^2.$$

Start with $\delta \geq \tfrac{1}{2} \left(\tfrac{a + 2c}{a + c} \right)^2$. Then $\hat{q} \left(\delta \right) = a/2$, and the condition simplifies to[m]

$$\delta \left[\tfrac{1}{8} \left(a - c \right)^2 + \tfrac{1}{2} ac \right] \geq \tfrac{1}{64} \left(a - c \right)^2 \Leftrightarrow$$

$$\delta (a + c)^2 \geq \tfrac{1}{8} \left(a - c \right)^2.$$

---

[1] The other root never satisfies the sustainability condition.
[m] We assume here that $c < a/2$, so that the best response to $\hat{q} = a/2$ is a positive quantity; otherwise, the best response is zero, which implies that $\pi^d \left(\hat{q} \right) = 0$ and that the condition is less stringent.

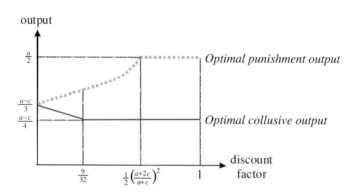

Figure 14.1 Stick-and-carrot strategy in the linear Cournot duopoly

Hence, condition (14.6) becomes $\delta \geq \frac{1}{8} \left(\frac{a-c}{a+c} \right)^2$ which is implied by condition (14.5) in this case, namely $\delta \geq \frac{1}{2} \left(\frac{a+2c}{a+c} \right)^2$.

For $\delta < \frac{1}{2} \left(\frac{a+2c}{a+c} \right)^2$, we ease the computations by setting $x \equiv \sqrt{2\delta}$, so that $\delta = x^2/2$. Using this change of variable and introducing the appropriate value of $\hat{q}(\delta)$, we can rewrite condition (14.6) as

$$\frac{x^2}{2} \left[\frac{1}{8} (a-c)^2 - \left(a - c - 2\frac{2(3-x^2)+x}{2(9-4x^2)} (a-c) \right) \frac{2(3-x^2)+x}{2(9-4x^2)} (a-c) \right] \geq \frac{1}{64} (a-c)^2 \Leftrightarrow$$

$$\frac{x^2}{2} \left[\frac{1}{8} - \left(1 - 2\frac{2(3-x^2)+x}{2(9-4x^2)} \right) \frac{2(3-x^2)+x}{2(9-4x^2)} \right] \geq \frac{1}{64}$$

which further simplifies to

$$\frac{x^2}{16(3-2x)^2} \geq \frac{1}{64} \Leftrightarrow \delta = \frac{x^2}{2} \geq \frac{9}{32}.$$

We thus find that full collusion is sustainable as long as $\delta \geq 9/32 \simeq 0.28$.

What happens for discount factors smaller than $9/32$? As indicated above, full collusion (i.e., each firm producing half the monopoly output, $(a - c)/4$) can no longer be sustained. However, partial collusion (i.e., each firm producing more than $(a - c)/4$ but less than the Nash equilibrium output, $(a - c)/3$) can be sustained. To find the best collusive output and the corresponding punishment output, we must solve the system made of conditions (14.5) and (14.6) holding as equalities. In our linear example, this system admits two solutions. The first solution is, without any surprise, the Nash equilibrium of the static game: $q^* = \hat{q} = (a - c)/3$. Obviously, this solution does not allow firms to sustain collusion. The second solution is the optimal stick-and-carrot strategy:

$$q^* = \tfrac{1}{27} (9 - 8\delta)(a - c) \quad \text{and} \quad \hat{q} = \tfrac{1}{27} (9 + 8\delta)(a - c).$$

Notice that the collusive output q^* ranges from the Nash output for $\delta = 0$ to half the monopoly output for $\delta = 9/32$, while the punishment output ranges from the Nash output for $\delta = 0$ to the value $\hat{q}(\delta)$ we found above for $\delta = 9/32$. Figure 14.1 represents the optimal stick-and-carrot strategy $(q^*, \hat{q})$ for all discount factors in the linear Cournot duopoly model.

Collecting our previous results, we can conclude the following.

> **Lesson 14.9**   In the infinitely repeated Cournot quantity-setting game, the set of discount factors that can support full collusion is larger when firms use the optimal punishment of the stick-and-carrot strategy rather than the reversion to the Nash equilibrium of the grim trigger strategy.

14.2.3   Collusion and multimarket contact

Up to this point we have assumed that firms repeatedly interact in the same market. However, in many real-world cases, firms face largely the same competitors in several markets. This leads to the question as to whether multimarket contact facilitates collusion. Identifying the type of environments in which collusion is likely to occur is important for antitrust authorities, as they can only dedicate limited resources to the detection of collusive behaviour.

Multimarket contact has contrasting effects on the sustainability of collusion: on the one hand, it makes deviation from a collusive outcome more profitable (as firms can deviate on all markets at the same time); but on the other hand, it also makes deviation more costly (as deviators would also be punished on all markets). These two opposite effects cancel out when markets are identical, firms are identical and technology exhibits constant returns to scale. In this case, multimarket contact does not facilitate collusive behaviour. However, when one of these conditions is not met, firms may use multimarket contact to pool their incentive constraints across markets and thereby improve their ability to sustain collusive outcomes. Below we analyse different settings that illustrate this point.[19] Case 14.3 gives some evidence that multimarket contact does indeed facilitate collusion.

> **Case 14.3 Multimarket contact in the US airline industry[20]**
>
> The airline industry appears as an ideal candidate for the empirical testing of the effects of multimarket contact on pricing. First of all, firms in the airline industry do indeed compete with each other on several markets. Those markets are easily identified as different city-pair routes. Second, theory predicts (as we show below) that multimarket contact may facilitate collusion (i) when firms differ in their production costs across markets, or (ii) when markets themselves differ. Both conditions are relevant in this industry. Cost differences among firms are likely to result from the hub and spoke model, which gives a significant cost advantage to the carrier operating the hub.[n] As for market differences, one observes significant cross-route differences both in the number of operating firms and the rate at which demand is growing. Finally, based on documented evidence, industry experts have claimed that airlines have long lived by the 'golden rule', whereby airlines refrain from pricing aggressively in a given route for fear of retaliation in another jointly contested route.

[n] According to this model, an airline uses a central airport (the hub) as a transfer point to get passengers from one city to another (the spokes).

To test the effects of multimarket contact, Evans and Kessides (1994) analyse time-series and cross-sectional variability of airline fares in the 1000 largest city-pair routes between 1984 and 1988. Their estimation of a fixed-effects price equation indicates that multimarket contact has a statistically significant and quantitatively important effect on price: fares are, on average, higher on routes where the competing carriers have extensive interroute contacts. As an illustration, they estimate that moving from the route in their sample with the 25th percentile in contact to a route with the 75th percentile increases prices by 5.1% (which corresponds to an increase of a round-trip ticket price by almost $13 on the median ticket price in 1988).

Differences between markets

Suppose that each market is characterized by repeated (Bertrand) price competition. As we have seen above, the optimal punishment in this case consists in reverting to the static Bertrand solution forever. Before exploring the effects of multimarket contact, let us look more closely at the factors that influence collusion on each market taken separately. We have already shown above that collusion becomes harder to sustain as the number of firms on the market increases. This is because the gain from deviation increases while the punishment remains the same. A similar intuition underlies the result that a lower frequency of interaction or of price adjustments hinders collusion. Indeed, if firms have to wait longer before interacting again or before adjusting their prices, the punishment following a deviation will come later, thereby allowing the deviator to benefit longer from its cheating behaviour.

To see this, suppose that n firms compete only every k periods (i.e., they interact in periods 1, $k + 1$, $2k + 1$, etc.). In that case, the present discounted values of abiding by the collusive agreement and of deviating are respectively given by $V_1^C = (\pi^m/n) + \delta^k (\pi^m/n) + \delta^{2k} (\pi^m/n) + \cdots = (\pi^m/n)/(1 - \delta^k)$ and $V_1^D = \pi^m$. Suppose alternatively that firms interact in each period but have to fix their prices for k periods (i.e., the price set in period 1 remains valid up to period k; a new price is then set in period $k + 1$ and so forth). Here, we have that $V_2^C = (\pi^m/n)/(1 - \delta)$ and $V_2^D = \pi^m (1 + \delta + \delta^2 + \cdots + \delta^{k-1}) + \delta^k \times 0 = \pi^m (1 - \delta^k)/(1 - \delta)$.

The two conditions for the sustainability of collusion, $V_1^C \geq V_1^D$ and $V_2^C \geq V_2^D$, boil down to the same inequality: $1 - \delta^k \leq 1/n$. Therefore, the fully collusive outcome is sustainable if and only if

$$\delta \geq \left(1 - \frac{1}{n} \right)^{1/k}.$$

As already argued above, this threshold increases with n. The new result is that the threshold also increases with k. Hence, collusion is easier to sustain in fast-moving markets than in markets where transactions are irregular.

Lesson 14.10   Firms find it harder to sustain collusion when they interact less frequently or when price adjustments are less frequent.

To see the effects of multimarket contact, suppose now that two firms compete not only in one but in two markets. Suppose also that the two markets differ along some dimension. In our first illustration, firms interact more frequently on one market than on the other; in our second, one market is more competitive than the other.

Different frequency of interaction Suppose that firms can change prices more frequently in market 1 than in market 2. To give a concrete specification, suppose that firms can change prices in every period in market 1 ($k = 1$) and only in even periods in market 2 ($k = 2$). The implicit discount factor between periods is δ. Considering markets separately and applying the above analysis, we find that the threshold on the discount factor is $1/2$ in market 1 and $\sqrt{1/2} \approx 0.707$ in market 2. Hence, if $0.5 \leq \delta < 0.707$, collusion is sustainable in market 1 but not in market 2, when considering the two markets separately. This would indeed be the result if we had two different sets of firms in the two markets.

Multimarket contact opens up the possibility that a deviation in market 2 can be (immediately) punished in market 1. With full collusion, discounted profits are $\pi^m/(1-\delta)$. A firm that undercuts makes monopoly profits in market 1 for one period and in market 2 for two periods. Thus the discounted deviation profit is $\pi^m + (1+\delta)\pi^m = (2+\delta)\pi^m$. Such a deviation is not profitable if $2 + \delta \leq 1/(1-\delta)$, which is equivalent to $\delta^2 + \delta - 1 \geq 0$ or $\delta \geq (\sqrt{5}-1)/2 \approx 0.618$. This illustrates how the pooling of incentive constraints across the two markets facilitates collusion.

Different number of firms We can repeat the analysis by supposing instead that the two markets differ in their number of firms (but are identical otherwise). Suppose that firms A and B are both present in markets 1 and 2, and that firm C is present on market 2 only. Supposing that interaction takes place in every period and considering the two markets separately, we have that for $1/2 \leq \delta < 2/3$, collusion can be sustained in market 1 (where there are two firms) but not in market 2 (where there are three firms and where the threshold on the discount factor is thus $1 - (1/3) = 2/3$). However, firms A and B can take advantage of their multimarket contact to sustain collusion on both markets. The idea is to induce firm C to collude by leaving it a larger market share on market 2, while using the interaction on market 1 as a disciplining device. More precisely, let s denote firm C's share of market 2. Firm C does not deviate as long as $s\pi^m/(1-\delta) \geq \pi^m$, or $s \geq 1 - \delta$. So, firms A and B will leave a share of $1 - \delta$ to firm C and keep a share $\delta/2$ for each of them. Considering the profits to be made on the two markets, A and B prefer not to deviate as long as

$$\frac{1}{1-\delta}\left[\frac{\pi^m}{2} + \frac{\delta\pi^m}{2}\right] \geq 2\pi^m \Leftrightarrow \delta \geq \frac{3}{5}.$$

This new threshold lies between $1/2$ and $2/3$. Hence, for $\delta \in [3/5, 2/3]$, firms A and B are able to sustain collusion in both markets although they would not be able to collude on market 2 were they only active on that market. The reason is that a discount factor strictly larger than $1/2$ gives some slack enforcement power in market 1, which the firms can then use to discipline collusion in market 2.

So, whatever the nature of the differences between markets, the message is the same.

> **Lesson 14.11**   **With multimarket contact on different markets, collusion may become sustainable in several markets, even tough deviations would be profitable if firms were active only in one of the markets.**

Differing firms: market-sharing agreements

Reciprocal market-sharing agreements, whereby firms refrain from entering each other's territory, are commonly observed in many industries, as illustrated in Case 14.4 below. Such agreements are likely to occur in situations where firms have separate home markets and incur a transportation cost to serve the other market, or where firms face a fixed cost of production. We develop an example corresponding to the first situation: markets are identical but firms differ in the sense that the 'home' firm has a lower marginal cost than the 'foreign' firm. We show that in a Bertrand model with homogeneous products, multimarket contact may again facilitate collusion in the presence of such cost differences. In particular, collusion is easier to sustain under market-sharing agreements than when firms are present on both markets and assign production quotas.[21]

Case 14.4 Market-sharing agreements in Europe and the US[22]

Market-sharing agreements have long been held under suspicion by antitrust authorities. In one of the earliest cases litigated under the Sherman Act, the Addyston Pipes Case of 1899, the Supreme Court struck down a group of iron pipe producers which rigged prices on certain markets, and reserved some cities as exclusive domains of one of the sellers.[23] In recent years, the globalization of markets and the deregulation of industries that used to be regulated on a territorial basis (airlines, local telecommunication services and utilities) have increased the scope for explicit or implicit market-sharing agreements.

   The European Commission has been particularly aware of the potential risk of market sharing, as firms that used to enjoy monopoly power in some territories seem reluctant to compete on the global European market. In a landmark case against Solvay and ICI in 1990, the European Commission has established that the two companies had operated a market-sharing agreement for many years by confining their soda-ash activities to their traditional home markets, namely continental Western Europe for Solvay and the United Kingdom for ICI. It was also found that over many years, all the soda-ash producers in Europe accepted and acted upon the 'home market' principle, under which each producer limited its sales to the country or countries in which it had established production facilities.[24] In the United States, the Telecommunications Act of 1996 was specifically designed to encourage regional operators to enter each other's market. It appears today that both industries are still dominated by a handful of dominant companies, each with highly clustered regional monopolies.

   Antitrust authorities reacted by issuing new guidelines that emphasize market-sharing agreements as an alternative form of collusion. For example, in its 1999 merger guidelines, the Irish Competition Authority states that: 'As an alternative to a price-fixing cartel, firms ... may divide up the country between them and agree not to sell in each other's designated area. ... At its simplest, a market-sharing cartel may be no more than an agreement among firms not to approach each other's customers or not to sell to those in a particular area. This may involve secretly allocating specific territories to one another or agreeing on lists of which customers are to be allocated to which firm.' (Irish Competition Authority, 1999).

We consider again two markets (1 and 2) and two firms (A and B). Suppose that firm A is installed in market 1, while firm B is installed in market 2. Each firm produces a homogeneous good at constant marginal cost c and faces a transportation cost of τ to move one unit of output from its 'home' market to the 'foreign' market. Suppose also that demand on both markets is given by $Q(p) = a - p$. The monopoly price for the home firm is equal to $p^m(c) = (a + c)/2$. To ensure that competition between the two firms is viable, we assume that the marginal cost of the foreign firm is smaller than the monopoly price: $c + \tau < (a + c)/2$, or $2\tau < a - c$.

As a benchmark, we first examine the optimal collusive outcome that would prevail if firms were only competing in one market. As we assume Bertrand competition, the optimal punishment consists for both firms in setting their price equal to c in every future period following a deviation; the home firm makes all the sales and both firms earn zero discounted profits. Let s_h and s_f denote the respective market shares of the home and the foreign firm (by definition, $s_h + s_f = 1$). If the collusive price is $p \geq c + \tau$, a deviating firm with cost c_i will slightly undercut and achieve an immediate profit equal to $\pi^d(p, c_i) = (p - c_i)(a - p)$, where $c_i = c$ for the home firm and $c_i = c + \tau$ for the foreign firm. Hence, both firms abide by the collusive agreement as long as

$$\begin{cases} \text{(home firm)} \ \frac{1}{1-\delta} s_h (p - c)(a - p) \geq (p - c)(a - p) \Leftrightarrow s_h \geq 1 - \delta, \\ \text{(foreign firm)} \ \frac{1}{1-\delta} s_f (p - c - \tau)(a - p) \geq (p - c - \tau)(a - p) \Leftrightarrow s_f \geq 1 - \delta. \end{cases}$$

We can sum the two conditions and conclude that only if $\delta \geq 1/2$ the firms can sustain collusive prices above $c + \tau$. It must be noted, however, that a large enough market share must be allocated to the inefficient foreign firm to keep it from deviating; in particular, it must be that $s_f \geq 1 - \delta$.

Consider now the two-market setting. We focus on symmetric collusive outcomes whereby both firms set the same price p on both markets and the home firm receives a share s_h. For a given $p \geq c + \tau$, it is easy to see that the best collusive outcome involves $s_h = 1$, which implies that each firm completely withdraws from the foreign market.[o] Then, the best collusive price is $p^m(c) = (a + c)/2$. It follows that the present discounted value of abiding by the market-sharing agreement is

$$V^C = \frac{1}{1 - \delta} \frac{(a - c)^2}{4}.$$

The best deviation consists in entering the foreign market and undercutting the home firm, thereby obtaining an immediate profit of $(p^m(c) - c - \tau)(a - p^m(c))$; meanwhile, the firm

---

[o] The collusive profit is $\pi^c(s_h) = s_h (p - c)(a - p) + (1 - s_h)(p - c - \tau)(a - p) = (a - p)(p - c - \tau + \tau s_h)$, which increases with s_h.

keeps the monopoly profit on its home market. As before, the punishment that follows the deviation yields a continuation profit of zero. So, the present discounted value of deviation is

$$V^D = \frac{(a-c)^2}{4} + \frac{(a-c)(a-c-2\tau)}{4}.$$

Therefore, a market-sharing agreement specifying that each firm sets $p^m(c)$ on its home market and does not enter the foreign market can be sustained if $V^C \geq V^D$, or

$$\frac{\delta}{1-\delta} \frac{(a-c)^2}{4} \geq \frac{(a-c)(a-c-2\tau)}{4} \Leftrightarrow \delta \geq \frac{1}{2} \frac{a-c-2\tau}{a-c-\tau}.$$

It is clear that the latter threshold is smaller than $1/2$, which shows the following result.

Lesson 14.12   **The optimal market-sharing agreement can be sustained over a larger set of discount factors than the most profitable collusive outcome that firms can achieve when they are present on both markets.**

14.2.4   Tacit collusion and cyclical demand

Many markets are characterized by demand fluctuations. We therefore extend the single-market analysis by considering two demand states. From the point of view of the firm, demand is either good, $Q_G(p)$, or bad, $Q_B(p)$, with $Q_G(p) > Q_B(p)$ for all p. The former situation can be associated with a boom phase of the industry and the latter with a recession phase. To the extent that there is a comovement between the industry under consideration and the economy in general, industry demand expands in an economic boom.

In this subsection, we maintain the assumption that firms observe the state of the demand.[25] They are thus able to detect any deviation from the collusive behaviour by any other firm. For the sake of simplicity, suppose that the good demand state occurs with probability $1/2$. The realization of demand is independent over time.[26] In each period, firms learn the state of demand before prices are set.

We want to describe a collusive outcome that can be supported as a (subgame perfect) equilibrium and is the most preferred outcome by the firms. This means that we look for a pair of prices (p_B, p_G) such that (1) p_B is set in the bad demand state and p_G is set in the good demand state, (2) deviations from (p_B, p_G) are not profitable, and (3) the equilibrium is such that there does not exist another equilibrium which is preferred by both firms. The expected present discounted profit along the equilibrium path is

$$V^C = \sum_{t=0}^{\infty} \delta^t \left(\frac{1}{2} \frac{Q_B(p_B)}{2}(p_B - c) + \frac{1}{2} \frac{Q_G(p_G)}{2}(p_G - c) \right)$$

$$= \frac{1}{1-\delta} \left(\frac{1}{2} \frac{Q_B(p_B)}{2}(p_B - c) + \frac{1}{2} \frac{Q_G(p_G)}{2}(p_G - c) \right).$$

To support the preferred equilibrium firms use trigger strategies so that the punishment for deviation is maximal. Recall that this means that after a deviation from (p_B, p_G) firms set the competitive (Nash equilibrium) price c forever.

Full collusion

We start by providing the conditions needed to sustain the fully collusive outcome in equilibrium. In fact, it is only a simple extension of the result in a world with demand certainty. The fully collusive outcome consists in both firms charging the respective monopoly price p_s^m in state $s = 1, 2$. That is $p_s^m = \arg\max_{p_s} \pi_s(p_s) = \arg\max_{p_s}(p_s - c)Q_s(p_s)$. Let $\pi_s^m \equiv (p_s^m - c)Q_s(p_s^m)$ denote the monopoly profit in state s. Expected present discounted profit for prices (p_B^m, p_G^m) can be written as

$$V^m = \frac{1}{1-\delta} \frac{(\pi_B^m + \pi_G^m)}{4}. \tag{14.7}$$

A deviation in state s leads to (almost) the monopoly profit in that period and to zero profits in all future periods. Thus, like in the analysis with demand certainty, a deviation leads to a short-term gain and a long-term loss. The upper bound for expected present discounted profit of a deviation is thus $V_s^D = \pi_s^m$ in state s. Along the equilibrium path, the firm would make profit $\pi_s^m/2$ in state s.

For a deviation to be not profitable, one must have

$$V_s^D \le \frac{\pi_s^m}{2} + \delta V^m \Leftrightarrow \frac{\pi_s^m}{2} \le \delta V^m. \tag{14.8}$$

Using (14.7), we can rewrite (14.8) as

$$\frac{\pi_s^m}{2} \le \frac{\delta}{1-\delta} \frac{\pi_B^m + \pi_G^m}{4} \Leftrightarrow 2(1-\delta)\pi_s^m \le \delta\pi_B^m + \delta\pi_G^m.$$

Note that since $\pi_B^m < \pi_G^m$, condition (14.8) is more stringent in the good demand state as deviation is more profitable while the severity of the punishment is independent of the demand state. Collusion is thus sustainable as long as $\pi_G^m/2 \le \delta V^m$. Here, the punishment entails the loss of an average of high and low profits, so that the punishment is less severe than if the good demand state persisted, as would be the case with demand certainty. In other words, *the fully collusive outcome is more difficult to sustain than under demand certainty*. In the good demand state, the inequality simplifies to $2\pi_G^m \le \delta\pi_B^m + 3\delta\pi_G^m$. Solving for δ, we obtain a critical value δ^0 above which the fully collusive outcome can be supported,

$$\delta \ge \delta^0 \equiv \frac{2\pi_G^m}{\pi_B^m + 3\pi_G^m} = \underbrace{\frac{1}{1 + \dfrac{\pi_B^m + \pi_G^m}{2\pi_G^m}}}_{\in\left(\frac{1}{2}, 1\right)}.$$

This critical value lies within the interval $(1/2, 2/3)$.

Lesson 14.13   **Under demand uncertainty, the critical discount factor above which the fully collusive outcome can be sustained is larger than under demand certainty.**

As we have seen, a firm is more tempted to undercut when the demand state is good. (Recall that condition (14.8) holds if and only if it holds in the good demand state.) This suggests that for lower discount factors, full collusion cannot be sustained in the good demand state, whereas it can be sustained in the bad demand state. We now turn to this type of partial collusion.

Partial collusion

We now provide conditions such that a partially collusive outcome can be sustained in equilibrium. To this end, we consider discount factors $\delta \in \left[\frac{1}{2}, \delta^0\right)$. We choose (p_1, p_2) so as to maximize expected profits subject to the undercutting constraints (i.e., incentive constraints). That is, we solve the problem

$$\max_{p_B, p_G} \frac{1}{1-\delta} \left(\frac{1}{2} \frac{\pi_B(p_B)}{2} + \frac{1}{2} \frac{\pi_G(p_G)}{2} \right)$$

subject to

$$\frac{\pi_B(p_B)}{2} \leq \frac{\delta}{1-\delta} \left(\frac{1}{2} \frac{\pi_B(p_B)}{2} + \frac{1}{2} \frac{\pi_G(p_G)}{2} \right), \tag{14.9}$$

$$\text{and} \quad \frac{\pi_G(p_G)}{2} \leq \frac{\delta}{1-\delta} \left(\frac{1}{2} \frac{\pi_B(p_B)}{2} + \frac{1}{2} \frac{\pi_G(p_G)}{2} \right). \tag{14.10}$$

It is still true that the temptation to undercut is higher when the demand state is good. This implies that the binding constraint is (14.10). Constraint (14.9) can thus be ignored. Taking this into account and rearranging terms, we can rewrite the problem as

$$\max_{p_B, p_G} \pi_B(p_B) + \pi_G(p_G) \quad \text{subject to} \quad \pi_G(p_G) \leq K\pi_B(p_B),$$

where $K \equiv \delta/(2 - 3\delta)$ with $K \geq 1$ for $\delta \geq 1/2$. Note that the constraint is relaxed if π_B is increased. Since maximal profit in the bad demand state is $\pi_B(p_B^m) = \pi_B^m$, the high-demand price $\widetilde{p}_G$ is then chosen so as to satisfy $\pi_G(p_G) = K\pi_B^m$. This implies that for $\delta \in \left[\frac{1}{2}, \delta^0\right)$, firms partially collude with $(p_B^m, \widetilde{p}_G < p_G^m)$: in the bad demand state, firms charge the monopoly price; in the good demand state firms set prices more aggressively than under monopoly.

In particular, the result is compatible with $p_G < p_B^m$, in which case firms price lower in the good than in the bad demand state (but this is only a possibility not an implication of the model). In other words, the model can generate lower prices after a positive demand shock and countercyclical prices and markups.[27]

Lesson 14.14 When full collusion cannot be sustained, firms may partially collude by setting the respective monopoly price in the bad demand state and setting a price lower than the respective monopoly price in the good demand state. This result is compatible with countercyclical prices and markups.

A number of empirical observations can be related to the model. In the market for a particular drug, namely antibiotic tetracycline, pure discipline among firms broke down when the Armed Service Medical Procurement Agency placed a large order in October 1956, which can be interpreted as a positive demand shock.[28] Also, it has been observed that the price of cement tends to move countercyclically.[29] The suspicion is that a cartel cannot sustain full collusion in a good demand state.

14.2.5   **Tacit collusion with unobservable actions**

We now present a model (of price competition) in which firms do not directly observe deviations from the collusive outcome.[30] Firms cannot make direct inferences about deviation from market outcomes because we postulate that there is uncertainty in the market which is not generated by actions taken by the firms. In particular, our key assumption is that firms do not observe their rivals' prices but infer them (imperfectly) from their own demand. Furthermore, firms do not observe the state of demand before each period.

For simplicity, we consider collusion among two firms. As before, products are perfect substitutes produced at c and there are two demand states, a good and a bad one. In the bad demand state, demand is assumed to be zero, whereas in the good demand state, there is positive demand at $p = c$, i.e., $Q(c) > 0$, and demand is strictly decreasing (at prices with strictly positive demand, $Q(p) > 0$).

The high-demand state occurs with probability $(1 - \alpha)$. To avoid complications, we assume that realization of demand is i.i.d. over time. Denote the monopoly price in the good demand state by p^m and the corresponding monopoly profit by π^m. If a firm cannot sell at a particular point in time, it does not know whether this is due to the fact that demand is zero or because the rival prices lower so that it does not obtain any demand. In such a situation, the firm facing zero demand has to solve a non-trivial signal extraction problem: if demand is zero, there is no reason to suspect that the competitor deviated from the collusive outcome, whereas if the demand state is good and the competitor deviated from the collusive price such behaviour should be punished.[p]

Consider the infinitely repeated Bertrand game under demand uncertainty, in which future profits are discounted by δ. We propose the following intertemporal strategies for both firms:

1. Start with the collusive phase and charge price p^m until one firm makes zero profit (which along the equilibrium path, occurs in the low demand state).

2. If one firm makes zero profits, this triggers a punishment phase for $T \in \mathbb{N}_+ \cup \{\infty\}$ periods in which each firm charges c. After T periods firms return to step 1.

Clearly such strategies lead to higher profits than atemporal profits under Bertrand competition, which would be zero. We have to show that such strategies constitute equilibrium strategies. We construct T such that the expected present discounted value is maximized under some constraints that guarantee that the strategies constitute an equilibrium.

In the punishment phase, a deviation is not profitable for any of the two firms since its profits cannot become strictly positive. Consider the collusive phase. Let V^C denote the expected present value of a firm's profit from date t presuming that the game is in the collusive phase. With probability $(1 - \alpha)$, the demand state is good so that firms share monopoly profits and continue in the collusive phase. With the remaining probability, profits are zero and firms

---

[p] Note the following: In a situation in which at least one firm faces zero demand, it is common knowledge that at least one firm makes zero profit.

enter the punishment phase, where V^P denotes the corresponding expected present value.[q] Hence,

$$V^C = (1-\alpha)\left(\tfrac{1}{2}\pi^m + \delta V^C\right) + \alpha(0 + \delta V^P). \tag{14.11}$$

The present value when entering the punishment phase is determined by the sum of zeros for T periods, which is the length of the punishment phase, and the present value in the collusive phase discounted by δ^T because after T periods firms return to the collusive phase; that is,

$$V^P = \underbrace{0 + 0 + \cdots + 0}_{T \text{ periods}} + \delta^T V^C. \tag{14.12}$$

Firms must not have an incentive to deviate in the collusive phase. Therefore, the collusive profit V^C must be higher than the profit it earns if it slightly undercuts the other firm. In the latter case a firm obtains the full monopoly profit but then finds itself in the punishment period for T periods. Hence, the incentive constraint reads

$$V^C \geq (1-\alpha)(\pi^m + \delta V^P) + \alpha\delta V^P.$$

Using equation (14.11), one can rewrite the condition as

$$(1-\alpha)\delta(V^C - V^P) \geq (1-\alpha)\tfrac{1}{2}\pi^m, \tag{14.13}$$

where the left-hand side is the expected long-term loss from the deviation, and the right-hand side is the expected short-term gain from deviation. Hence, to avoid undercutting, V^P must be sufficiently lower than V^C. This means that the punishment must be sustained for sufficiently many periods. To obtain explicit conditions for our parameters, we need to solve the system of equations given by (14.11) and (14.12). Substituting the value of V^P into (14.11), we obtain the value in the collusive phase

$$V^C = (1-\alpha)\left(\tfrac{1}{2}\pi^m + \delta V^C\right) + \alpha\delta^{T+1}V^C$$
$$\Leftrightarrow \left[1 - (1-\alpha)\delta - \alpha\delta^{T+1}\right]V^C = (1-\alpha)\tfrac{1}{2}\pi^m$$
$$\Leftrightarrow V^C = \frac{(1-\alpha)\tfrac{1}{2}\pi^m}{1 - (1-\alpha)\delta - \alpha\delta^{T+1}}. \tag{14.14}$$

Plugging this value into (14.12), gives the value when entering the punishment phase,

$$V^P = \delta^T \frac{(1-\alpha)\tfrac{1}{2}\pi^m}{1 - (1-\alpha)\delta - \alpha\delta^{T+1}}. \tag{14.15}$$

We can now substitute expressions (14.14) and (14.15) into the incentive constraint (14.13):

$$(1-\alpha)\delta\left(1 - \delta^T\right)\frac{(1-\alpha)\tfrac{1}{2}\pi^m}{1 - (1-\alpha)\delta - \alpha\delta^{T+1}} \geq (1-\alpha)\tfrac{1}{2}\pi^m$$
$$\Leftrightarrow (1-\alpha)\delta - (1-\alpha)\delta^{T+1} \geq 1 - (1-\alpha)\delta - \alpha\delta^{T+1}$$
$$\Leftrightarrow 2(1-\alpha)\delta + (2\alpha - 1)\delta^{T+1} \geq 1. \tag{14.16}$$

---

[q] Since we are analyzing a stationary game, V^P and V^C do not need a time index.

The highest profits for the firms are thus the maximum of the expected present value subject to the constraint that no firm has an incentive to undercut in the collusive phase: max V^C subject to (14.16). Note that V^C decreases in T, as can be seen from (14.14). Therefore the solution to this problem is the lowest possible T that satisfies the incentive constraint (14.16). Clearly, not to punish, i.e. $T = 0$, always violates the incentive constraint. This means that a positive length of punishment phase is needed.

Whether collusion can be sustained with punishment depends also on the probability of the bad demand state. In particular, if the bad demand state is sufficiently likely, collusion breaks down. To see this, suppose that $\alpha \geq 1/2$. Consider constraint (14.16) which we can rewrite as

$$2(1-\alpha)\delta(1-\delta^T) + \delta\delta^T \geq 1.$$

For $\alpha \geq 1/2$, the left-hand side of the inequality is weakly less than $\delta(1-\delta^T) + \delta\delta^T = \delta < 1$, which is a contradiction. Hence, the above proposed strategies do not constitute an equilibrium for $\alpha \geq 1/2$ and collusion cannot be sustained.

The left-hand side of the inequality increases with T only if $\alpha < 1/2$ and is maximal for $T = \infty$. To make at least maximal punishment ($T = \infty$) sustainable, one must have $2(1-\alpha)\delta \geq 1$, which is equivalent to

$$(1-\alpha)\delta \geq 1/2. \tag{14.17}$$

That is, for a given discount factor δ, the good demand state must be sufficiently likely (i.e., $1 - \alpha$ must be large enough). Similarly, for a given $\alpha < 1/2$, the discount factor must be sufficiently close to 1. If $(1-\alpha)\delta > 1/2$, the optimal length of punishment is given by the lowest T that satisfies (14.16). In sum, *if $(1-\alpha)\delta > 1/2$, there is an equilibrium with the property that phases of collusion and phases of punishment alternate, where each punishment phase is initiated by a bad realization of demand within a collusion phase.* We summarize our analysis with the following lesson:

Lesson 14.15   **Even if firms cannot observe deviations of other firms from equilibrium play, collusion can still be supported to some extent. However, the conditions for collusion to be sustainable are stricter than in a world in which deviations can be immediately observed and punished. In addition, profits are lower.**

14.3   Detecting and fighting collusion

In the previous two sections, we have tried to understand under which conditions collusive conduct (be it tacit or explicit) is viable and sustainable. This does not tell us, however, how to use this knowledge to design policy enforcement. A priori, detecting and fighting collusion seem to be fraught with difficulty. We have indeed seen in the previous section that collusive outcomes can be sustained even without explicit agreements. We may therefore ask why competition authorities mainly try to uncover explicit agreements such as price-fixing cartels if firms have other means to sustain collusion.

The answer to the latter question is that tacit collusion without explicit agreements may be hard to sustain because firms may lack information to detect deviations from the collusive outcome and because firms have to coordinate their actions (to select a collusive outcome among the multiple noncooperative equilibria, and to use an appropriate punishment strategy). Compared to tacit collusions, cartels allow for better monitoring of other firms. In particular, managers may exchange price and output levels between firms so that deviations from collusion can be more easily detected, as illustrated in Case 14.5.

Case 14.5 The vitamin cartels (3)

The different vitamins cartels (see the description in Case 14.1) all operated similarly. Regular meetings allowed to monitor and enforce agreements by the cartel members. In particular, information on sales volumes and prices of the companies were exchanged monthly or quarterly. In addition, 'a formal structure and hierarchy at different levels of management, often with overlapping membership at the most senior levels' was established.[31]

Another argument for explicit collusion is that in the presence of demand uncertainty, information sharing within a cartel may be required for firms to be able to observe price or output decisions of other firms. As we have seen in Subsection 14.2.5, if firms face stochastic demand and do not directly observe the other firms actions, they often have to tackle a signal extraction problem and may misinterpret the action of other firms. To avoid the complete breakdown of collusion, firms must punish actions that, in the absence of the information problem, would not have to be punished. As a consequence, firms make lower profits and the conditions for some type of collusion to be feasible at all are more demanding than in the absence of the signal extraction problem. Thus monitoring and information sharing can help to sustain (full) collusion.[32] In addition, in a formal cartel, the coordination on particular actions is easier to achieve. This tends to increase equilibrium profits. Unfortunately, there is no good theory around that allows us to address the advantages of formal agreements over implicit understanding with respect to the coordination problem.[33] Nevertheless, the analysis of the two previous sections leads to the following lesson:

Lesson 14.16 **Without the information sharing within a cartel, collusion is more likely to be infeasible. Even if it is feasible, collusion may not be supported over the whole time-horizon but firms may alternate between collusive and punishment phases (of varying length) in which they switch between a high and a low price.**

The previous discussion suggests that communication is central to collusion. Because of the importance of communication between firms, collusion might leave significant pieces of evidence: permanent records of meetings or agreements (on paper, fax, emails or hard-drive of computers) may have been kept, telephone conversations may have been tapped. In the absence of such evidence, detecting and legally proving the existence of a cartel is extremely difficult, as we explain in Subsection 14.3.1. Competition authorities have thus designed policies so as to encourage cartel members to bring evidence to the authorities by themselves. We examine these so-called 'leniency programs' in Subsection 14.3.2.

The difficulty in detecting collusion

In Chapter 3, we have described several ways to measure price–cost margins in a given industry. One might be tempted to use high price–cost margins as evidence of collusion. Yet, this approach is mistaken: a high price–cost margin simply indicates market power, and we have seen in Part III that there are various sources of market power absent collusion (e.g., product differentiation, advertising, search and switching costs). Therefore, it is not true that a high price–cost margin proves collusion. By the way, the reverse statement is not true either: collusion does not necessarily imply a 'high' price–cost margin. To see this, think of symmetric firms competing à la Bertrand; absent collusion, the price–cost margin would be equal to zero; with collusion, firms might achieve some positive margin, but this margin could be equivalent to the one that would prevail in a noncolluding industry with limited capacity. In that case, an observer who wrongly thinks that the relevant benchmark is one with limited capacity would infer from the observed price–cost margin that there is no collusion.

Hence, to detect collusion, we should not only look at the level of the price–cost margin. What should raise suspicions about collusion is a sharp increase in the price–cost margin, because, if market conditions do not change, such an increase is difficult to rationalize in the absence of a cartel. The question then is: How can collusion be detected? Four methods have been described in the literature.[34] A first method asks whether the observed firms' behaviour is consistent or not with properties or behaviour that are supposed to hold under a wide class of competitive models. A second method tests for structural breaks in the behaviour of firms, based on the idea that a discrete change in firms' pricing functions might be due to the formation of a cartel (or to its demise). These two methods, however, do not provide any evidence of collusion; they just show that observed behaviour does not seem to correspond to what can be expected from competition. They are thus used primarily as screening methods.

In contrast, the third and fourth methods can serve verification purposes. The third one asks whether the behaviour of suspected colluding firms differs from that of competitive firms. If only a subset of firms in the industry colludes and if these firms can be identified, the comparison between colluding and competitive firms can be directly carried out. Otherwise, one can resort to comparison across markets (when firms collude in some markets but not in others) or across periods (before and after the suspected date of formation of the cartel). Finally, the fourth method examines which model better fits the data, a collusive or a competitive model.

Arguably, these four methods suffer from two general problems. First, the necessary data to identify firms' behaviour are often not available: cost is often unobservable and, in many cases, price and quantity data may not be publicly available. In consequence, competition authorities have to get the relevant data from the firms suspected of collusion. This places them at an informational disadvantage since firms have a clear incentive to misreport their private information so as to disguise a collusive behaviour as a competitive one. The authorities are thereby likely to suffer from what has been coined the *indistinguishability theorem*.[35]

Here is a simple illustration of this problem. Suppose that the industry consists of n symmetric firms: they produce a homogeneous good at the same constant marginal cost c and face the linear inverse demand $P(q) = a - q$. If firms compete à la Cournot, we are familiar by now with the following result: the Nash equilibrium of this linear Cournot model is such that each firm produces $q^n = (a - c)/(n + 1)$, resulting in a price of $p^n(c) = (a + nc)/(n + 1)$. If all firms collude, they will jointly produce the monopoly output, $q^m = (a - c)/2$ and the the market price will be $p^m(c) = (a + c)/2$. Suppose now that the competition authorities can estimate the demand intercept a, but cannot exactly observe the firms' marginal cost. All the authorities know is that the true cost c lies somewhere in the interval $[c^-, c^+]$, with $c^+ < a$. Indistinguishability follows if the lowest possible collusive price, $p^m(c^-)$, lies below the highest possible competitive price, $p^n(c^+)$; this is equivalent to[r]

$$\frac{a + c^-}{2} < \frac{a + nc^+}{n + 1} \Leftrightarrow c^+ - c^- > \frac{n - 1}{2n}(a - c^-).$$

When the latter inequality is satisfied, firms are able to misreport their cost so as to hide their collusive behaviour without arousing suspicions from the authorities. To put some specific numbers to the example, suppose that $n = 3$, $a = 10$, $c^- = 3$, and $c^+ = 7$. One can check that the above inequality is satisfied with these numbers. Now assume that the true cost is $c = 4$. Then, if firms collude, the observed price is equal to $p^m(4) = 14/2 = 7$. Since the authorities do not know this true value, firms can simply lie and artificially inflate their cost so as to make the observed price compatible with competitive conduct. In particular, by reporting a cost of 6 (which is credible as $c^- < 6 < c^+$), firms would induce the authorities to believe that the observed price results from Cournot competition (as $p^n(6) = 28/4 = 7$) and not from collusion (as $p^m(6) = 8$).

Even if the data about cost, price and quantity are available, all detection methods have to face the additional problem that the estimation of firms' behaviour may be extremely sensitive to the specification of the models. Case 14.6 illustrates the seriousness of this problem.

Case 14.6 The Joint Executive Committee[36]

The *Joint Executive Committee* was a cartel that railroads created in the late nineteenth century to coordinate the rate charged for transporting grain in the US from Chicago to the East Coast. As the cartel preexisted the first antitrust regulations issued in the US (the Sherman Act), firms had no reason to conceal their coordinated activities and the cartel is thus very well documented. The agreement involved allocation of market shares but prices were set individually by the railroads. This opened the possibility of secret price cuts which, combined with demand fluctuations, endangered the stability of the cartel. This is in line with the predictions of the theory. We showed indeed in Subsection 14.2.5 that there is an equilibrium with the property that phases of collusion and phases of punishment alternate, where each punishment phase is initiated by a bad realization of demand within a collusion phase.

Porter (1983) and Ellison (1994) have tested this hypothesis and tried to assess how successful the cartel was in raising prices during collusion phases. The two authors came to rather different conclusions: according to Porter's estimate, railroads reached price–cost margins consistent with Cournot behaviour; in contrast, Ellison obtains an estimate close to full collusion. This difference in the results may be attributed to differences in the chosen specifications: Ellison extended Porter's analysis by allowing for auto-correlated demand (a high demand today is more likely to generate a high demand tomorrow) and by assuming that the probability of being in a collusion phase tomorrow depends on whether firms are currently in a phase of collusion or of punishment.

---

[r] It is easily checked that this inequality is compatible with $c^+ < a$.

We can sum up the previous discussion as follows.

Lesson 14.17   In the absence of hard evidence of communication among colluding firms, collusion is hard to detect because data on cost, price and quantity are often unavailable or are manipulated. Moreover, even if data are available, the estimation of the firms' behaviour may be extremely sensitive to the specification of the model.

14.3.2   Leniency and whistleblowing programs

An important aspect for antitrust authorities and courts that investigate alleged cartels is to find evidence for the existence of a cartel that sustains prices above the industry's competitive level. Following the US example, the European Union and other developed countries have introduced *corporate leniency* programmes, by which they provide reduced sentences to firms that cooperate with the antitrust authority or the courts and provide evidence on the existence of a cartel and its inner working. These corporate leniency programmes are also extended to individual informants, or *whistleblowers*, by shielding them from criminal sanctions (including jail). These incentives contribute to accomplish the main objective of law enforcement by making cartels less stable and thus reducing the likelihood that a cartel is formed in the first place. An additional objective is the break-up of existing cartels. Here, the social gain from breaking up the cartel has to be compared with the prosecution cost.

The vitamin cartels provide again an illustration of the implementation of leniency programmes.

Case 14.7 The vitamin cartels (4)

For violation of article 81 of the European Community Treaty and Article 53 of the European Economic Area Agreement, eight companies were fined while the remaining five companies evaded their fines as the respective cartels had become time-barred in 2001. The largest fines were awarded to Hoffmann-La Roche with EUR 462 million, BASF with EUR 296.16 million and Takeda Chemical Industries with EUR 37.05 million. As reflected in the size of their fines, Hoffmann-La Roche and BASF were considered the joint leaders and instigators of the cartels with their strong market shares empowering them to implement the anticompetitive agreements. Aventis on the other hand was the first company to cooperate both with the US Department of Justice and the European Commission and thus received significantly lower fines. Other cartel members that cooperated with those authorities during the investigations also obtained reduced fines according to their level of cooperation. Yet, despite the vitamin cartels being detected and punished both in the US and Europe, the incentive to form new cartel arrangements apparently remained and led to another fine in 2004 for animal feed vitamins, where EUR 66.34 million were imposed on Akzo Nobel, BASF and UCB (see European Commission, 2004).

While many cartels involve bulk commodities, some cartel cases concern branded consumers goods, as the following case illustrates. This case exemplifies that cooperation by one of the cartel members was key for uncovering an illegal cartel and fining their members.

Case 14.8 The beer cartel in the Netherlands[37]

According to the findings of the European Commission, four Dutch beer brewers formed a cartel on the beer market in the Netherlands, a branded consumer good market, which is normally not seen as a prime candidate for collusion. The cartel coordinated prices and price changes (at the wholesale level). It operated in two market segments: the segment in which consumption is on the premises (bars, restaurants, hotels) and the retail segment, which are mostly supermarkets in the Netherlands. In the former segment brewers coordinated rebate policies. Occasionally, brewers also allocated customers in both market segments, which amounts to market-sharing agreements.

In 2007 the European Commission fined the three leading Dutch brewers Heineken, Grolsch and Bavaria a total of around EUR 274 million for operating this cartel between at least 1996 and 1999. Essential information came from InBev, which was also participating in the cartel (InBev provided information on similar cartels in other European countries). The information provided by InBev led to surprise inspections. The Commission obtained evidence in the form of handwritten notes taken at the unofficial meetings of the cartel members and the proof of dates of secret meetings. Under the Commission's leniency program, InBev did not have to pay fines.

The model

To evaluate the effects of leniency and whistleblowing programmes, we extend the tacit collusion setting developed in Section 14.2.[38] As before, we define the following per period (gross) profit levels: when both firms collude, they both obtain π^c; when one firm colludes and the other optimally deviates, the deviating firm obtains π^d; if both firms compete, they obtain π^n. We now add another player in the game, namely the competition authority. Its objective is to maximize consumer surplus and its instruments are the following: (i) it can impose fines on colluding firms, and (ii) it can reduce fines (or give a reward) to firms or individuals bringing evidence of collusion.

Regarding evidence of collusion, we make the following assumptions. First, as discussed above, we realistically assume that collusion cannot occur without communication among the firms and that communication generates hard evidence (memos, reports of meetings, etc.). This evidence can be found by the competition authority if it audits the industry. We assume that audit takes place with probability ρ. The evidence can also be brought to the competition authority by a firm or by one of its employees (as in Cases 14.7 and 14.8). It is further assumed for simplicity that the evidence disappears at the end of the period. Let F denote the maximal fine imposed by the authority. In expectation, this fine is assumed to be too small to deter collusion, $\pi^c - \rho F > \pi^n$ (the expected net profit from collusion is larger than the profit from competition).

To take communication into account, we add an initial stage to the repeated game we considered in Section 14.2. In this initial stage, firms decide whether or not to communicate (about prices, quotas, punishments, etc.). If they both choose to communicate, communication takes place, evidence is generated and the repeated game ensues; that is, each firm chooses either to collude or to deviate and compete; each firm may in addition decide to report the evidence of collusion to the competition authority. In all other cases, i.e., if at least one firm prefers not to communicate, there is no communication and thus no collusion; both firms have no other choice than to compete.

No revelation mechanism

As a benchmark, consider first the case where the competition authority can only rely on audits to detect collusion. The profits firms can obtain in that case are as follows. If at least one firm does not communicate, they both earn π^n. If both firms communicate, they both earn $\pi^c - \rho F$ when they both collude. If one firm deviates, it increases its profit to $\pi^d - \rho F$. Collusion can be sustained if the discounted profit from colluding is larger than the profit obtained when deviating, followed by eternal competition:[s]

$$\frac{1}{1-\delta}(\pi^c - \rho F) \ge (\pi^d - \rho F) + \frac{\delta}{1-\delta}\pi^n,$$

which is equivalent to

$$\frac{\delta}{1-\delta}[(\pi^c - \rho F) - \pi^n] \ge (\pi^d - \rho F) - (\pi^c - \rho F), \qquad (14.18)$$

where the left-hand side is the discounted loss from punishment and the right-hand side is the immediate gain from deviation.

Leniency programme

Consider now a corporate leniency programme whereby a firm that reports evidence of collusion is granted a 'reward' R by the competition authority. We will discuss below whether this reward is a mere reduction of the maximal fine F ($R \le 0$) or is actually a positive transfer ($R > 0$). As firms want to deter reporting, they will punish it in the same way they punish a deviation. As a result, if a firm decides to report, it will deviate as well. Clearly, denouncing is attractive only in the presence of some leniency; that is, the reward must be larger than the expected fine: $R > -\rho F$ (which is of course satisfied when the reward is positive). What changes with respect to the benchmark we just analysed is the profit for a reporting/deviating firm: it increases from $\pi^d - \rho F$ to $\pi^d + R$. The condition for the sustainability of collusion then becomes

$$\frac{\delta}{1-\delta}[(\pi^c - \rho F) - \pi^n] \ge (\pi^d + R) - (\pi^c - \rho F),$$

---

[s] Firms optimally use the grim trigger strategy. Recall also that evidence is assumed to disappear after one period; therefore, in the punishment phase that starts in the next period, firms earn π^n (and not $\pi^n - \rho F$).

which is more stringent than (14.18) when $R > -\rho F$. Reversing the inequality, we can compute the minimum reward R_{min} that the competition authority must offer to induce a firm to report collusion:

$$R \geq R_{min} = \frac{\delta}{1-\delta}\left[(\pi^c - \rho F) - \pi^n\right] - \left[\pi^d - (\pi^c - \rho F)\right].$$

If the minimal reward R_{min} is zero or negative, then leniency (whereby the reporting firm pays only a limited fine, or no fine at all) suffices to deter collusion. This is the case as long as the discount factor is not larger than $[\pi^d - (\pi^c - \rho F)]/(\pi^d - \pi^n)$. Otherwise, R_{min} is positive, meaning that the competition authority has actually to pay a reward to the reporting firm.

> **Lesson 14.18**   Reducing fines for firms that report incriminating evidence may deter collusion. However, for some cartels, competition authorities have to grant sufficiently large, positive rewards to deter collusion.

Several concerns may arise about the implementation of these, potentially large, rewards. First, large rewards may not be credible if the competition authority is budget constrained; however, the fines paid by the other firms can be used to reward the informant. Second, public opinion may oppose the idea of granting rewards to guilty firms. This problem could be circumvented by secretly bargaining with the informant, but this would seriously undermine the predictability and credibility of the whole leniency programme. In practice, leniency programmes usually deny amnesty to ring-leaders. However, as the previous argument shows, offering rewards to any cartel member, including the instigator, improves collusion deterrence. A third issue is that large rewards could generate additional incentives to collude, for instance by inducing firms to 'take turns' for reporting collusion. To counter this, competition authorities grant leniency only to the first informants.

Whistleblowing programme

The corporate leniency programme can be adequately complemented by a programme that grants a positive reward, noted B, to employees reporting incriminating evidence. Here, the idea is that firms will have to bribe informed employees to prevent them from disclosing information; this will make collusion less profitable and thus, harder to sustain. To show how useful such a programme can be, we consider a situation where full corporate leniency does not suffice to deter collusion, i.e., $R_{min} > 0$. Suppose that collusion requires that k employees be in the know, and that employees stay with the firm for one period only.[t] It follows that if a firm wants to prevent its employees from denouncing it would have to pay a total bribe of kB (in each period).

---

[t] The whistleblowing programme would even be more effective if employees stayed longer with the firm.

Assume first that the whistleblowing programme is the only instrument that the competition authority can use. In that case, a deviating firm is still exposed to prosecution and must compensate its informed employees. Hence, both the collusion and the deviating profits are reduced by the total bribe. It follows that collusion *cannot be sustained* if

$$\frac{\delta}{1-\delta}[(\pi^c - \rho F - kB) - \pi^n] < (\pi^d - \rho F - kB) - (\pi^c - \rho F - kB),$$

which is equivalent to

$$R_{\min} = \frac{\delta}{1-\delta}[(\pi^c - \rho F) - \pi^n] - [\pi^d - (\pi^c - \rho F)]$$

$$< \frac{\delta kB}{1-\delta} - \rho F.$$

We observe that the latter condition becomes less stringent, meaning that collusion is easier to deter, when the individual reward B, the number of informed employees k or the discount factor increase.

Assume now that the competition authority can combine corporate leniency and individual whistleblowing. If an informing firm can benefit from, say, full leniency, a deviating firm prefers reporting over bribing its informed employees; the profit of a deviating firm is thus π^d and the condition for collusion not to be sustainable becomes

$$\frac{\delta}{1-\delta}[(\pi^c - \rho F - kB) - \pi^n] < \pi^d - (\pi^c - \rho F - kB) \Leftrightarrow R_{\min} < \frac{kB}{1-\delta}.$$

Importantly, we observe that the competition authority may not manage to destroy collusion when it uses the leniency and whistleblowing programmes separately, but may succeed when it uses the two instruments in combination. This would occur when

$$\max\left\{\frac{\delta kB}{1-\delta} - \rho F, 0\right\} < R_{\min} < \frac{kB}{1-\delta}.$$

Lesson 14.19   **Corporate leniency and individual whistleblowing programmes are complementary in the fight against collusion.**

Review questions

1. Contrast the conditions for cartels to be stable when they form in a simultaneous versus sequential way.

2. Explain how a collusive outcome may emerge noncooperatively as the equilibrium of a repeated game. Discuss how the horizon of the game, the number of firms, the frequency of interaction and multimarket contact affect the sustainability of collusion.

3.   Explain why tacit collusion is harder to sustain when demand fluctuates and when the rivals' actions cannot be observed.

4.   Explain why competition authorities encourage colluding firms and their employees to report incriminating evidence through leniency and whistleblowing programmes.

Further reading

To compare the different procedures of cartel formation, we have followed the survey by Bloch (2002). A seminal analysis of cartel stability is due to d'Aspremont *et al.* (1983). Friedman (1971) was the first to model tacit collusion through 'supergames'. Abreu (1986, 1988) extended this analysis by examining optimal punishment schemes. The seminal analyses of tacit collusion under unobservable actions, demand fluctuations and multimarket contact are respectively due to Green and Porter (1984), Rotemberg and Saloner (1986), and Bernheim and Whinston (1990), respectively. Our analysis of leniency and whistleblowing programmes follows Aubert, Rey, and Kovacic (2006). Recent surveys about the design of these programmes and about the detection of collusion are found, respectively, in Spagnolo (2008) and Harrington (2008).

15 Horizontal mergers

Horizontal mergers (that is, mergers between direct competitors) in concentrated industries are an important issue for competition authorities. In this chapter, we explore whether mergers are profitable and/or welfare enhancing. Merger control in the US has a long tradition going back to the Clayton Act from 1914, according to which mergers that lead to a substantial lessening of competition are forbidden. The current approach is outlined in the 1992 Horizontal Merger Guidelines. Merger control in the European Union was introduced in 1990 (before, individual member states were in charge) and substantially revised in the 2004 Horizontal Merger Guidelines. We refer you to Appendix B for a few more details on the legal aspects of competition policy.

Although the empirical evidence on the profitability of mergers that actually took place is mixed, we should not observe (in expectation) unprofitable mergers under the assumption that managers maximize the net value of the firm. Thus, from an antitrust perspective, the worrying cases are profitable but welfare-reducing mergers. Mergers that are at the same time profit-increasing and welfare-reducing only occur in imperfectly competitive markets: mergers among competing firms with market power tend to reduce competition and thus have anticompetitive price effects. However, this does not imply that mergers are necessarily welfare-reducing because a merger may realize efficiency effects. Efficiency gains may stem from (1) production reshuffling among the plants that belong to the merged firm so that relatively efficient plants that were underutilized before the merger turn out larger volumes, or production is adjusted to local demand with the effect that transport costs are reduced, (2) scale economies at a single plant (even if other plants use the same technology), (3) synergies by pooling certain functions, and (4) larger innovative capacity leading to future efficiency gains. A merger assessment then requires to trade off welfare-reducing price effects with welfare-increasing gains in productive efficiency – this is called the *Williamson trade-off*.[39]

The final decision reached by the competition authority or the courts depends on the objective function that is used. In this chapter, we take total surplus as the relevant welfare measure. Note, however, that antitrust authorities tend to use consumer surplus as the relevant criterion. Applying this latter criterion typically raises the threshold for the efficiency gain that makes a merger socially desirable, since gains in profits that are due to higher prices are ignored.

We start in Section 15.1 by analysing the profitability of mergers in Cournot industries, using simple specifications. In Section 15.2, we then turn to the welfare analysis of mergers in Cournot industries. In Section 15.3, we extend the previous analyses in several directions: we consider successive mergers, entry-inducing mergers, mergers in industries in which firms compete in prices and the impact of mergers on tacit collusion. Finally, in Section 15.4, we examine how merger analyses are conducted empirically. To give some idea of the importance of the merger phenomenon, Case 15.1 presents some data on mergers and acquisitions in Europe.

Case 15.1 Mergers and acquisitions in Europe[40]

According to the Thomson Financial Securities Data, 87 804 mergers and acquisitions (M&As, for short) were recorded for Europe in the period 1993–2001. In monetary terms, the total value of these deals adds up to US$ 5.6 trillion.[a] This nine-year period has been called the 'fifth merger wave' in Europe. The fourth wave took place between 1983 and 1989. In comparison, the fifth wave is more than eight times as large (in number of deals and in total value) as the fourth wave. The impressive growth of M&A activity can be explained by the challenges brought about by the development of the single European market and the introduction of the Euro in the 1990s, a period characterized by deregulation in various industries and increased regional competition. This drove mostly domestically oriented firms to resort to mergers as a survival strategy. Moreover, the introduction of the Euro eliminated all currency risks within the Eurozone, which reduced the home bias of investors. Indeed, one third of the intra-European M&As of the period 1993–2001 were cross-border deals.

15.1   Profitability of simple Cournot mergers

We start our analysis of merger profitability by considering simple models. The common assumption in this section is that firms behave, before and after the merger, as Cournot competitors. We first consider mergers between two or several firms in the absence of efficiency gains. We then examine how efficiency gains affect the profitability of mergers.

15.1.1   Mergers between two firms

Suppose for the moment that there are only two firms in the market for a homogeneous product. Firm 1 can make a take-it-or-leave-it offer for acquiring firm 2. If firm 2 rejects the offer, firms make duopoly profits. Thus, firm 2 accepts an offer at least as high as its profit in duopoly. Firm 1 can therefore make an offer that is acceptable to firm 2 if monopoly profit $\pi^m = \pi(1)$ is greater than industry profits in duopoly $2\pi(2)$. Clearly, this property is satisfied in the market for a homogeneous product, meaning that *a merger to monopoly is always profitable*.

---

[a] A trillion is a million million, or 10^{12}. To give an order of magnitude, the nominal GDP of the European Union was US$ 16.8 trillion in 2007, according to IMF statistics.

However, for mergers which fall short of a merger to monopoly, the issue is less clear-cut. Suppose there are n identical firms in a symmetric product market that compete in quantities (or capacities). We can write $\pi_i(n) = \pi(n)$ as the firm's equilibrium profit in a market with n firms. Suppose that there are no synergy effects of a merger so that the production possibilities of the industry are unaffected. If firms have constant marginal costs of production c and products are homogeneous, a merger does not give a relative advantage to the merged firm and a merger is equivalent to buying a firm and closing it down.[b]

To analyse correctly the incentive to merge, we need to compare profits at the post-merger and pre-merger equilibria. We consider a single merger between two firms. For notational convenience, suppose that firm n is taken over by firm 1. In general, a merger has the effect that not only the equilibrium profit of each firm decreases with the number of firms, i.e. $\pi_i(n) < \pi_i(n-1)$ for all i and n but that industry profits decline with the number of competitors, $n\pi(n) < (n-1)\pi(n-1)$. Clearly, for a single merger to be profitable, one must have that $2\pi(n) < \pi(n-1)$. The other firms in the industry will always gain from the merger. The merging firms internalize their previous rivalry once they are placed under common control; this drives them to reduce output, which increases the market price and benefits the firms outside the merger. As a result, the takeover of firm n by firm 1 generates a positive external effect on the other firms. (Recall that we observed the same type of external effect in the previous chapter with the formation of cartels.) As a response to the merger, the other firms increase output, which is detrimental to the merging firm's profit.

We formally investigate a merger between two firms in a market with linear demand of the form $P(q) = a - q$ and constant marginal costs c.[41] We will show that a merger is profitable only if the market is very concentrated (provided that no firms can enter the industry). Recall the analysis of Cournot competition. The first-order condition of profit maximization is $a - q - q_i - c = 0$. Summing over all firms and solving for q, one obtains

$$q = \frac{n}{n+1}(a-c).$$

Cournot equilibrium profits are

$$\pi(n) = \pi_i(n) = \frac{(a-c)^2}{(n+1)^2}.$$

In this simple model the condition that a single merger is profitable, i.e. $2\pi(n) \le \pi(n-1)$, is satisfied if and only if

$$2\frac{(a-c)^2}{(n+1)^2} \le \frac{(a-c)^2}{n^2},$$

which is equivalent to $2n^2 \le (n+1)^2$ or $n^2 - 2n - 1 \le 0$. This inequality is satisfied only for $n = 2$ but not for any $n \ge 3$. Hence, in this simple example a single merger between two firms is not profitable if at least three firms are present in the market.[c] We can draw the following lesson.

---

[b] However, with increasing marginal costs, the merged firm could do better than the other firms. We consider this possibility below.

[c] This result is reminiscent of what we observed in the previous chapter when analysing the stability of collusive networks made of bilateral market-sharing agreements. We used the same argument to conclude that the empty network (in which all firms are present on all markets) is always stable.

> **Lesson 15.1** **Under Cournot competition, mergers of two firms are unlikely to be profitable if the market is fragmented but they are more likely to be profitable if the market is concentrated.**

Note that it is exactly in the cases where markets are concentrated (so that a merger is likely to be profitable) that antitrust authorities are concerned about the potentially negative welfare effects of a merger. We will turn to the welfare effects of mergers in the next section.

It is important to note that the above result is derived under several restrictive assumptions: (1) only two firms merge, (2) there are no increasing marginal costs of production and, in particular, there are no capacity constraints (or, in other words, capacities can be easily adjusted after a merger), (3) a merger does not affect the efficiency of production, (4) only a single merger is feasible, (5) no additional firms can enter and (6) firms are Cournot competitors. In the rest of this section, we relax the first three assumptions. Relaxing each of the other three assumptions necessitates longer developments; we leave this to Section 15.3.

15.1.2   Mergers between several firms

In this subsection we ask whether a merger of k firms is profitable in an industry with n firms. Using the previous specification, equilibrium profits in the pre-merger n-firm Cournot model are (with the subscript ea meaning 'ex ante')

$$\pi_{ea} = \left(\frac{a-c}{n+1}\right)^2. \tag{15.1}$$

If there is a merger among k firms, there remain $n - k + 1$ independent decision makers in the market (the $(n - k)$ 'outside firms' and the new merged entity). Replacing n by $(n - k + 1)$ in the previous formula, we find that equilibrium profits in the post-merger Cournot equilibrium are (with the subscripts I and O referring, respectively, to the insiders and the outsiders to the merger):

$$\pi_I = \pi_O = \left(\frac{a-c}{n-k+2}\right)^2.$$

A merger among k firms is profitable as long as the post-merger profit of the merged entity is at least as large as the sum of the pre-merger profits of the merging firms:

$$\pi_I \geq k\pi_{ea} \Leftrightarrow \left(\frac{a-c}{n-k+2}\right)^2 - k\left(\frac{a-c}{n+1}\right)^2 \geq 0.$$

The latter condition can be rewritten as

$$(n+1)^2 \geq k(n-k+2)^2 \Leftrightarrow (k-1)\left(-k^2 + (2n+3)k - (n+1)^2\right) \geq 0.$$

We already derived the same condition in the previous chapter when analysing the sequential formation of cartels. We recall that it is equivalent to

$$k > \tfrac{1}{2}\left(2n + 3 - \sqrt{4n+5}\right) \equiv \hat{k},$$

which means that *the merger is profitable if it involves a sufficiently large number of firms.* In particular, we can show that the threshold $\widehat{k}$ is larger than 80% of the firms in the industry (actually, $\widehat{k}/n = 80\%$ for $n = 5$ and $\widehat{k}/n > 80\%$ for any other n). This means that in this example, a merger with an initial market share below 80% cannot be profitable.[d] We therefore conclude the following.

Lesson 15.2   **Mergers between multiple firms are profitable for Cournot competitors only if a highly concentrated market results.**

The intuition behind this result should be clear by now. The profitability of the merger depends on two opposite forces. On the one hand, by internalizing previous rivalry, the merged entity reduces its quantity and, thereby, increases its profit. On the other hand, the outside firms react by increasing their quantity (as quantities are strategic substitutes in a Cournot industry), which reduces the profitability of the merger. For the first effect to dominate, the number of outside firms must be small enough.

Clearly, the conclusion would be totally different in the presence of strategic complementarity. We will indeed show in Section 15.3 that in a Bertrand industry, the reaction of the outside firms is favourable – and not detrimental – to the merged entity. The previous conclusion also hinges on our assumption that the merger entails no efficiency gain, an assumption that we now relax.

15.1.3   Efficiency-increasing mergers

When the merger confers an advantage to the merged entity with respect to the outside firms, the merged firm does not reduce its production as much as absent these advantages (it may even increase it). Hence, the outside firms do not increase their production so much in reaction (they may even decrease it), meaning that the adverse effect that we identified above will be less pronounced (or even become a positive effect). In consequence, more mergers should become profitable in the presence of efficiency gains. We verify this conjecture by modelling two different types of efficiency gains: scale economies and synergies.

Scale economies

In the previous model, the merged entity did not differ from the outsiders as it continued to have access to the same technology. In particular, the merged entity did not take advantage of having access to the combined productive capacity of the merging partners. This was an

---

[d] There are clear parallels between the formation of mergers and the formation of cartels. Here, a merger is profitable (and therefore forms) if it makes the merging firms globally better off; in other words, the merger requires unanimity of the merging firms, in the sense that if one firm 'deviates' (by rejecting the proposal), the merger does not take place. A similar condition applies when a cartel is formed as the result of a sequential game because the sequentiality allows firms to commit to stay out of the cartel. In contrast, in the case of simultaneous cartel formation, an individual deviation does not entail the dissolution of the cartel: the other firms who decided to join remain in the cartel, which makes the deviation more attractive (we saw indeed that such cartels would not form in a Cournot industry of the type we consider here).

immediate consequence of the assumption that average costs are constant. Alternatively, we can make the following assumptions:[42] (i) each firm owns a certain amount of capital, (ii) when some firms merge, the merged entity owns their combined capital stock; (iii) each firm's marginal cost increases linearly with that firm's output; (iv) the larger the firm's capital stock, the lower the slope of the marginal cost curve. Under these assumptions, the merged entity has a lower marginal cost curve than either of the constituent firms. In addition, since the marginal cost of each rival firm rises with its output, the ability of rival firms to expand in response to the merger is not as great as in the prior model with constant marginal cost. As a result, horizontal mergers are much more likely to be profitable under these alternative assumptions.

As above, we consider Cournot competition in an industry that initially comprises n symmetric firms and where inverse demand is given by $P(q) = a - q$. What differs is the form of the firms' cost function. Let K denote the capital stock of each firm, and c and h be some positive parameters. Then, firm i's cost function is given by

$$C(q_i, K) = cq_i + \frac{h}{2}\frac{1}{K}q_i^2.$$

Marginal cost is then $c + (h/K)q_i$ and we see that it rotates about the intercept as the stock of capital, K, changes. To simplify the exposition, we write from now on $\kappa \equiv h/K$.

We start by deriving the Cournot equilibrium before the merger. Equating marginal revenue to marginal cost for a typical firm i, we find: $a - 2q_i - q_{-i} = c + \kappa q_i$. At the symmetric equilibrium, each firm produces the same quantity q_{ea}. Then, replacing q_i by q_{ea} and q_{-i} by $(n-1)q_{ea}$ in the latter equation and solving for q_{ea}, we have $q_{ea} = (a-c)/(n+\kappa+1)$. Substituting into the profit function, we find the pre-merger (ex ante) equilibrium profits:

$$\pi_{ea} = \frac{(\kappa+2)(a-c)^2}{2(n+\kappa+1)^2}.$$

Consider now the merger between (for simplicity) two firms. Because the merging partners pool their capital stocks, the merged entity benefits from a lower marginal cost than the outside firms. The cost function of the merged entity (noted I) is indeed given by $C(q_I, 2K) = cq_I + (\kappa/4)q_I^2$, and the marginal cost is $c + (\kappa/2)q_I$. The first-order condition for profit maximization of the merged entity yields $(a - 2q_I - q_{-I}) - (c + (\kappa/2)q_I) = 0$. At the post-merger equilibrium, each of the $(n-2)$ identical outside firms produces the same quantity, noted q_O. It follows that $q_{-I} = (n-2)q_O$ and the latter equation can be rewritten as

$$a - c - \left(2 + \tfrac{\kappa}{2}\right)q_I - (n-2)q_O = 0. \tag{15.2}$$

For a typical outside firm i, the first-order condition for profit maximization yields $(a - 2q_i - q_{-i}) - (c + \kappa q_i) = 0$. At the equilibrium, $q_i = q_O$ and $q_{-i} = (n-3)q_O + q_I$. Substituting into the latter equation, we have

$$a - c - q_I - (n-1+\kappa)q_O = 0. \tag{15.3}$$

Solving the system (15.2)–(15.3), we find the equilibrium quantities

$$q_I = \frac{2(\kappa+1)(a-c)}{\kappa^2 + (n+3)\kappa + 2n} \quad \text{and} \quad q_O = \frac{(\kappa+2)(a-c)}{\kappa^2 + (n+3)\kappa + 2n},$$

which allows us to compute the equilibrium profits of the merged entity as

$$\pi_I = \frac{(\kappa + 4)(\kappa + 1)^2 (a - c)^2}{(\kappa^2 + (n + 3)\kappa + 2n)^2}.$$

We can now examine under which condition a merger of two firms is profitable. Profitability of the merger requires that $\pi_I \geq 2\pi_{ea}$, or

$$\frac{(\kappa + 4)(\kappa + 1)^2 (a - c)^2}{(\kappa^2 + (n + 3)\kappa + 2n)^2} \geq 2 \frac{(\kappa + 2)(a - c)^2}{2(n + \kappa + 1)^2}.$$

Developing, we find that the latter inequality is equivalent to

$$\kappa^3 - 2(n - 5)\kappa^2 + (2n - 3n^2 + 17)\kappa - 4(n^2 - 2n - 1) \geq 0.$$

We recover the previous model with constant marginal costs by setting $h = 0$. In that case, $\kappa = h/K = 0$ and the condition becomes $n^2 - 2n - 1 \leq 0$. As we have seen above, this inequality is only satisfied for $n = 2$, meaning that two-firm mergers are not profitable as soon as there are more than two firms in the industry. Now, with $h > 0$, the condition can be satisfied for larger values of n provided that κ be large enough. For instance, it can be checked that if there are initially ten firms in the industry, a merger between two firms is profitable if $\kappa \geq 22.4$. Recalling that $\kappa = h/K$, the condition says that a merger is more likely to be profitable if marginal costs are sufficiently increasing (large h) and/or if firms are sufficiently constrained by their capital stock (small K) so that a merged entity is substantially 'larger' than the merging partners. We summarize these findings in the following lesson.

> **Lesson 15.3** **Fixed asset combinations and increasing marginal costs enlarge the scope for profitable mergers in Cournot industries.**

Synergies

We now move away from scale economies and increasing marginal costs back to a model with constant marginal costs. Efficiency gains are modelled by assuming that the merger reduces the (constant) marginal cost of production of the merged firm, say from c to $c - x$. As for the outside firms, the marginal cost of production remains at c. The general idea is that the merger makes it possible to exploit the synergies that exist among the merging firms, and this allows the merged entity to produce in a more efficient way. To keep the analysis interesting, we suppose that this cost advantage of the merged entity is not large enough to exclude the outside firms from the market; we make this condition explicit below.

Let us derive the post-merger Cournot equilibrium supposing that k of the n firms decide to merge. The merged entity chooses the quantity q_I that maximizes $\pi_I = [(a - q_I - q_{-I}) - (c - x)]q_I$. The first-order condition yields $a - c + x - 2q_I - q_{-I} = 0$. Suppose that, at the post-merger equilibrium, each of the $(n - k)$ identical outside firms produces the same quantity, denoted by q_O. It follows that $q_{-I} = (n - k)q_O$ and the first-order condition that characterizes the merged firm's reaction to q_{-I} can be rewritten as

$$a - c + x - 2q_I - (n - k)q_O = 0. \tag{15.4}$$

A typical outside firm i chooses the quantity q_i that maximizes $\pi_i = [(a - q_i - q_{-i}) - c]q_i$. The first-order condition of profit maximization can be written as $a - c - 2q_i - q_{-i} = 0$. At the post-merger equilibrium, $q_j = q_O$ for each outsider $j \neq i$; hence, $q_{-i} = (n - k - 1)q_O + q_I$. Since in (symmetric) equilibrium all outsiders including firm i set q_O, we have that the outsiders' (equilibrium) reaction to q_I is given by

$$a - c - q_I - (n - k + 1)q_O = 0. \tag{15.5}$$

We find the Nash equilibrium by solving the system of equations (15.4) and (15.5) in q_I and q_O,

$$q_I = \frac{a - c + (n - k + 1)x}{n - k + 2} \quad \text{and} \quad q_O = \frac{a - c - x}{n - k + 2}. \tag{15.6}$$

To make sure that the outside firms remain in the market after the merger, we assume that

$$\phi \equiv \frac{x}{a - c} < 1.$$

The ratio ϕ measures the cost reduction as a percentage of $(a - c)$. Then, equilibrium profits are easily calculated as

$$\pi_I = \left(\frac{a - c + (n - k + 1)x}{n - k + 2}\right)^2 \quad \text{and} \quad \pi_O = \left(\frac{a - c - x}{n - k + 2}\right)^2. \tag{15.7}$$

Recalling that the pre-merger profits are given by expression (15.1), we can now examine the condition for the merger among k firms to be profitable:

$$\pi_I \geq k\pi_{ea} \Leftrightarrow \left(\frac{a - c + (n - k + 1)x}{n - k + 2}\right)^2 \geq k\left(\frac{a - c}{n + 1}\right)^2$$

$$\Leftrightarrow \frac{a - c + (n - k + 1)x}{n - k + 2} \geq \sqrt{k}\left(\frac{a - c}{n + 1}\right)$$

$$\Leftrightarrow \phi \geq \frac{(n - k + 2)\sqrt{k} - (n + 1)}{(n - k + 1)(n + 1)} \equiv \phi_p(k, n). \tag{15.8}$$

Hence, for the merger to be profitable, the synergies (expressed as a fraction of the 'size' of the market, $a - c$) must be larger than some threshold $\phi_p(k, n)$. As an illustration, mergers between two firms (which we showed to be unprofitable in the absence of synergies) are profitable if $\phi \geq \phi_p(2, n) = [(\sqrt{2} - 1)n - 1]/(n^2 - 1)$. For instance, with three firms in the industry, the necessary cost reduction is 3% of the market size; it is equal to 4.5% for $n = 5$ and decreases for larger values of n. More generally, it can be checked that $\phi_p(k, n) < 1$ and that $\phi_p(k, n)$ is a concave function of k: it starts from a positive value at $k = 2$, then increases, reaches a maximum, decreases and becomes negative for k larger than $\hat{k}$ (where $\hat{k}$ is the minimal number of firms we derived above that makes a merger profitable in the absence of synergies; see Figure 15.1 below for an illustration with $n = 9$).

Lesson 15.4   **Mergers between Cournot competitors that do not result in a highly concentrated market are profitable only if they entail sufficiently large synergies.**

At $\phi = \phi_p(k, n)$, the cost reduction is just large enough to exactly balance the two opposite forces that affect the profitability of the merger: the positive effect stemming from the internalization of competition among the merging firms and the negative effect stemming from the reaction of the outside firms; the efficiency gains have the double advantage of reinforcing the positive effect and of reducing the negative effect.

15.2   Welfare analysis of Cournot mergers

While we have concentrated on the profitability of mergers so far, antitrust authorities should only be concerned with a merger if it is detrimental to welfare. Therefore, we have to conduct a welfare analysis. We use the total surplus criterion, i.e., the sum of the consumer surplus (CS) and total profits; total profits are defined as the combined sum of the profits of the merging firms (belonging to the subset I of 'insiders'), Π_I and of the firms outside the merger (belonging to the subset O of 'outsiders'), Π_O. Thus welfare is $W = CS + \Pi_I + \Pi_O$. The competition authority is concerned with the welfare change induced by the merger: $\Delta W = \Delta CS + \Delta \Pi_I + \Delta \Pi_O$.

As we have seen in the previous section, the internalization of competition drives the merged entity to decrease its production; yet, the efficiency gains work in the opposite direction. The net effect on price is thus ambiguous and so is the net effect on welfare. What we can conjecture is that, although the merger reduces competition, it may increase total surplus if the efficiency gains are large enough. This is the conclusion that competition authorities sometimes reach, as illustrated in Case 15.2.

Case 15.2 The 'efficiency defence' in the Superior Propane case[43]

In 1998, *Superior Propane Inc.* and *ICG Propane Inc.* were the two largest distributors of propane in Canada. When the two companies announced their intention to merge, Canada's Commissioner of Competition (who is the head of the Competition Bureau) immediately filed an application before the Competition Tribunal seeking an order to dissolve the merger. The Commissioner indeed argued that the merger would substantially lessen competition in 66 of 74 local markets for the supply of propane. In 16 markets the merged entity would even have a pure monopoly or near monopoly (with a market share ranging from 97% to 100%). The Tribunal accepted the Commissioner's argument and concluded that the merger substantially lessened competition. Using econometric estimates of industry cost and demand functions, the deadweight loss resulting from reduced competition was estimated at C$6 million per year over a ten-year horizon. On the other hand, the Tribunal also accepted evidence for cost efficiencies of C$29 million per year over the same horizon. Hence, applying the total surplus criterion, the Tribunal decided that the merger should be permitted. Note, however, that the Court of Appeal rejected the unqualified application of the total surplus standard, requiring instead that a larger weight be placed on consumer surplus.

To examine the interplay between the competition-reducing effect of mergers and their potential efficiency gains, we first exploit the model with synergies that we just analysed in the previous section. We then turn to a general welfare analysis of Cournot mergers.

15.2.1   Linear Cournot model with synergies

Recall the model of the previous section. Inverse demand is given by $P(q) = a - q$, k firms merge, the constant marginal cost of the merged entity is $c_I = c - x$, while the constant marginal cost of the $(n - k)$ outsiders is $c_O = c$. We compute the cost reduction that would leave the quantity of the merged firm unchanged:

$$q_I = kq_{ea} \Leftrightarrow \frac{a - c + (n - k + 1)x}{n - k + 2} = k\frac{a - c}{n + 1}$$

$$\Leftrightarrow \phi = \frac{k - 1}{n + 1} \equiv \phi_c(k, n),$$

where $\phi \equiv x/(a - c)$, as above. At $\phi = \phi_c(k, n)$, the quantity expansion resulting from the synergies exactly compensates the quantity reduction due to the internalization of competition within the merged entity. As the output of the merged entity equals the combined pre-merger output of the merging firms, the outside firms do not modify their equilibrium choice and total quantity is thus left unchanged. By the same token, the market price remains at its pre-merger level and consumers are thus not affected by the merger. Hence, the threshold $\phi_c(k, n)$ also gives us the minimal synergies for the merger to make consumers better off. Comparing $\phi_c(k, n)$ to the profitability threshold $\phi_p(k, n)$ derived in expression (15.8), we observe that

$$\phi_c > \phi_p \Leftrightarrow \frac{k - 1}{n + 1} > \frac{(n - k + 2)\sqrt{k} - (n + 1)}{(n - k + 1)(n + 1)}$$

$$\Leftrightarrow (n - k + 1)(k - 1) + (n + 1) = k(n - k + 2) > (n - k + 2)\sqrt{k},$$

which is clearly satisfied. We can therefore draw the following lesson.

Lesson 15.5   **There exist levels of synergies that make mergers profitable but, at the same time, detrimental to consumers.**

For $\phi_p < \phi < \phi_c$, mergers are profitable but decrease consumer surplus. A competition authority that takes the consumer surplus as the relevant criterion would thus decide to block the formation of such mergers.

Let us now examine what happens if total surplus is taken as the relevant welfare measure. Total surplus is computed as the sum of consumer surplus and the firms' profits. Having linear demand with slope -1, consumer surplus is equal to half the square of total

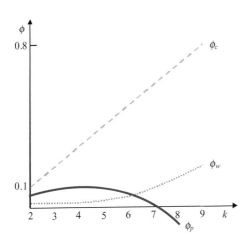

Figure 15.1 Levels of synergies necessary for a Cournot merger to be profitable (ϕ_p), to enhance welfare (ϕ_w) or consumer surplus (ϕ_c)

quantity. Before the merger, total quantity is equal to $n\,(a-c)/(n+1)$. After the merger, total quantity is obtained from expression (15.6):

$$q_I + (n-k)\,q_O = \tfrac{a-c+(n-k+1)x}{n-k+2} + (n-k)\,\tfrac{a-c-x}{n-k+2} = \tfrac{(a-c)(n-k+1)+x}{n-k+2}.$$

Using the latter expression, together with (15.1) and (15.7), we can compute the pre- and post-merger levels of the total surplus:

$$W^{pre} = \tfrac{1}{2}\left(\tfrac{n(a-c)}{n+1}\right)^2 + n\left(\tfrac{a-c}{n+1}\right)^2,$$

$$W^{post} = \tfrac{1}{2}\left(\tfrac{(a-c)(n-k+1)+x}{n-k+2}\right)^2 + \left(\tfrac{a-c+(n-k+1)x}{n-k+2}\right)^2 + (n-k)\left(\tfrac{a-c-x}{n-k+2}\right)^2.$$

The computations to derive the cost reduction necessary for the merger to improve welfare are lengthy and thus omitted here. What we find is $W^{post} > W^{pre}$ provided that

$$\phi \geq \frac{-(n+1)(n-k+3)+(n-k+2)\sqrt{n^2-2k^2+4kn+6k}}{(n+1)(2n^2+2k^2+6n-4kn-6k+3)} \equiv \phi_w(k,n).$$

In Figure 15.1, we fix the number of firms in the industry to $n=9$ and we represent the various thresholds for different values of k. We observe that $\phi_w(k,n) < \phi_c(k,n)$, which is not a surprise as mergers (even without synergies) increase total profits in the industry; competition authorities accept mergers more readily when they are concerned with total surplus rather than with consumer surplus only. The comparison between $\phi_w(k,n)$ and $\phi_p(k,n)$ is less clear-cut: for $2 \leq k \leq 6$, we have that $\phi_p(k,n) > \phi_w(k,n)$, meaning that any profitable merger increases total surplus.[e] In contrast, for $7 \leq k \leq 9$, the ranking of the two thresholds is reversed, $\phi_p(k,n) < \phi_w(k,n)$, which implies that welfare-reducing mergers could

---

[e] For $\phi_p(k,n) > \phi > \phi_w(k,n)$, a merger would increase welfare although firms do not find it profitable to merge. In such situations, it would be (second-best) optimal to subsidize firms to merge, where second-best here refers to the situation that the social planner optimally determines the conditions for the merger but does not directly intervene at the competition stage.

form. As the same pattern would be observed for arbitrary values of n, we can conclude the following.

Lesson 15.6 **Suppose that mergers among Cournot competitors induce synergies. When a merger does not make the market too concentrated, profitability of the merger is a sufficient condition for welfare improvement. However, if the merger results in a highly concentrated market, it could be profitable and welfare-detrimental at the same time.**

We derived this result in a very specific setting. In the next subsection, we extend the welfare analysis of mergers to much more general settings.

15.2.2   General welfare analysis

A profitable merger among the insiders (i.e., such that $\Delta \Pi_I > 0$) is necessarily welfare-increasing if its 'external effect' on consumers and outsiders is positive, i.e., if $\Delta CS + \Delta \Pi_O > 0$. Although the latter condition is not necessary (a merger could enhance welfare in spite of a negative external effect if it is sufficiently profitable for the insiders), it has an important practical interest. The estimation of the external effect requires much less information than the estimation of the overall welfare effect. There is indeed no need to assess the change in insiders' profits, which is typically hard to observe as it depends on internal synergies (e.g., the exact magnitude of x in the previous model might not be observable). What matters for consumers and outsiders is the change in the equilibrium output of the insiders.

In this spirit we now analyse the welfare effects of Cournot mergers by deriving general conditions for positive external effects.[44] Suppose that revenues satisfy $P'(q) + q_i P''(q) < 0$, where q denotes industry output.[45] Suppose furthermore that the cost function of each firm is convex, $C_i'' \geq 0$. Under these two assumptions, we can restrict attention to first-order conditions of profit maximization because profits are concave. First-order conditions of profit maximization are

$$\frac{\partial \pi_i}{\partial q_i} = P(q) - \frac{\partial C_i}{\partial q_i} + P'(q)q_i = 0,$$

which implies that the ratio of price–cost margins of two firms is equal to their ratio of market shares,

$$\frac{P(q) - \frac{\partial C_i}{\partial q_i}}{P(q) - \frac{\partial C_j}{\partial q_j}} = \frac{q_i}{q_j} = \frac{s_i}{s_j}.$$

We can now analyse the effect of a merger on consumer surplus and the outsiders' profit,

$$CS + \Pi_O = \int_0^q P(q)dq - P(q)q + \sum_{i \in O}[P(q)q_i - C_i(q_i)].$$

Denote $\lambda_i \equiv -dq_i/dq$; this function defines firm i's equilibrium response to a total output change dq caused by a change in production of some firms. Under some additional conditions,[f] we show below that *in a Cournot industry, a merger within a subset of firms has a positive external effect on consumers and on other firms if*

$$s_I < \sum_{i \in O} \lambda_i s_i, \tag{15.9}$$

evaluated at the output by insiders before the merger, q_I^{initial}.

Condition (15.9) provides an upper bound on the combined share of the merging firms for their merger to generate positive external effects. The intuition is as follows. If the combined share of the merging firms is small, they will not find it profitable to restrict output much, if at all. When they do restrict output, the outsiders react by expanding their output. As a result, output is shifted towards larger firms that have lower pre-merger marginal costs. Such a shift is beneficial from a welfare point of view. We record this result in the following lesson.

> **Lesson 15.7**   In a Cournot industry, a merger within a subset of firms (the 'insiders') has a positive external effect on the other firms (the 'outsiders') and on consumers if the combined (pre-merger) share of the insiders is below some threshold, which depends on the way outsiders react at equilibrium to the change in total output generated by the merger. If there exists a positive external effect, a profitable merger is welfare-increasing.

We now show the result formally. The proof, which proceeds in four steps, can be skipped by less technically oriented readers.

(i) Note first that the best-response of firm i, $r_i = dq_i/dq_{-i}$ (where $q_{-i} = q - q_i$), satisfies that $r_i \in (-1, 0)$. This implies that $-\lambda_i \equiv dq_i/dq < 0$.[g]

(ii) We next evaluate an infinitesimal change of $CS + \Pi_O$,

$$dCS + d\Pi_O = P(q)dq - P'(q)qdq - P(q)dq$$

$$+ \sum_{i \in O} P'(q)q_i dq + \sum_{i \in O} \left[P(q) - \frac{\partial C_i}{\partial q_i} \right] dq_i$$

$$= -P'(q)qdq + P'(q) \sum_{i \in O} q_i dq + \sum_{i \in O} \left[P(q) - \frac{\partial C_i}{\partial q_i} \right] dq_i$$

$$= -P'(q)qdq + P'(q)q_O dq + \sum_{i \in O} -P'(q)q_i dq_i,$$

---

[f] Namely, demand and cost functions in the industry satisfy $P'' \geq 0$, $P''' \geq 0$ and $C_i''' \leq 0$.

[g] To see this note that $r_i dq_{-i} = dq_i$. Thus $r_i dq_{-i} + r_i dq_i = dq_i + r_i dq_i$. We also have that $r_i dq_{-i} + r_i dq_i = r_i dq$. The equality $r_i dq = dq_i + r_i dq_i$ is equivalent to $dq_i/dq = r_i/(1 + r_i) \equiv -\lambda_i$ with $\lambda_i > 0$. This holds since $r_i < 0$ and $1 + r_i > 0$ (as $r_i > -1$).

where, in the last equality, we have used the first-order condition of profit maximization. This expression can be further rewritten as

$$dCS + d\Pi_O = (-q + q_O)P'(q)dq + \sum_{i \in O} -P'(q)q_i \frac{dq_i}{dq}dq$$

$$= -q_I P'(q)dq + \sum_{i \in O}[-P'(q)]q_i(-\lambda_i)dq$$

$$= P'(q)dq \left(\sum_{i \in O} \lambda_i q_i - q_I \right).$$

(iii) We can then evaluate the welfare effect of a merger that leads to a reduction of output among insiders from q_I^{initial} to q_I^{final} as

$$\Delta CS + \Delta \Pi_O = \int_{q_I^{\text{initial}}}^{q_I^{\text{final}}} \frac{dCS + d\Pi_O}{dq_I}dq_I = \int_{q_I^{\text{final}}}^{q_I^{\text{initial}}} -\frac{dCS + d\Pi_O}{dq_I}dq_I$$

$$= \int_{q_I^{\text{final}}}^{q_I^{\text{initial}}} [-P'(q)]\frac{dq}{dq_I} \left(\sum_{i \in O} \lambda_i q_i - q_I \right) dq_I.$$

(iv) Since $-P'(q) > 0$ and $dq/dq_I > 0$ (as follows from (i)), we have that $\sum_{i \in O} \lambda_i q_i - q_I > 0$ implies that $\Delta CS + \Delta \pi_O > 0$. Hence, if $\sum_{i \in O} \lambda_i q_i - q_I > 0$ evaluated at q_I^{initial} and $d \left(\sum_{i \in O} \lambda_i q_i - q_I \right)/dq_I \leq 0$, we indeed have $\sum_{i \in O} \lambda_i q_i - q_I > 0$ for all $q_I \in [q_I^{\text{final}}, q_I^{\text{initial}}]$ and the result follows. It can be shown that the second inequality $d \left(\sum_{i \in O} \lambda_i q_i - q_I \right)/dq_I \leq 0$ is satisfied if $P'' \geq 0$, $P''' \geq 0$ and $C_i''' \leq 0$.

We can use this general result to evaluate welfare effects in the linear demand model with constant marginal costs that we have analysed first. In that case, it is easy to check that $\lambda_i = 1$. The (sufficient) condition for the merger to induce a positive external effect becomes

$$\sum_{i \in O} s_i - s_I > 0 \Leftrightarrow (1 - s_I) - s_I > 0 \Leftrightarrow s_I < 1/2.$$

That is, the insiders cannot have a combined market share larger than half of the market. However, we have shown above that the profitability of the merger requires a combined market share above 80% of the market. Therefore, we see that with linear demand and constant marginal costs, the merger only increases welfare if it is highly unprofitable.

15.3   Beyond simple Cournot mergers

In this section, we extend the analysis of the previous two sections in four directions. First, we examine what happens when more than a single merger can take place. Second, we incorporate the idea that mergers could trigger entry into the industry. Third, we analyse mergers between producers of differentiated products that compete in prices rather than in quantities. Finally, we relax an implicit assumption that we made so far, namely that mergers do not alter the fundamental mode of market competition: a merger may facilitate collusion among the remaining firms; this possibility should thus be taken into account when assessing the profitability and the welfare impacts of mergers.

15.3.1   Successive mergers

If more than one merger is feasible, firms have to anticipate that future mergers may occur, which may make an initially unprofitable merger eventually profitable. This implies that due to the miscoordination among firms, an industry may show no signs of merger activity. If, e.g. due to an exogenous event, firms start to believe that other firms may also want to engage in mergers, the industry may exhibit a series of mergers, which may be called a *merger wave*. The first mergers of this wave may only be profitable under the presumption that other mergers may occur. In that case, the most optimistic or best-placed firm may take the initiative and convince other firms that consolidation is in the interest of all firms. As illustrated in the following case, this scenario seems to fit fairly well the situation of the US airline industry at the beginning of 2008.

Case 15.3 Potential consolidation in the US airline industry[46]

In February 2008, two major airlines in the US, Delta Airlines and Northwest Airlines, announced their plan to merge. Experts conjectured that other major airlines were likely to follow suit with merger plans of their own, starting a merger wave in the airline industry. Indeed, at the same period, the *Associated Press* reported that United Airlines and Continental were also in serious merger discussions while, according to *The Wall Street Journal*, Continental had been in discussions with American Airlines as well.

What seemed clear from the declarations of airline executives was that mergers were conditional on one another. Two major airlines needed to merge for the other airlines to follow suit. Subsequent mergers would occur as a reaction to the increased market share of the first merger. However, airline executives were content with the status quo if the first merger did not take place. It thus seemed that a merger did not appear to be profitable until another pair of carriers merged. This may explain why airline consolidation has not happened yet.

Similar considerations as those concerning merger profitability affect the welfare analysis of mergers. Merger policy that is based on the evaluation of a single merger can be criticized as short-sighted. Indeed, a merger among a number of firms changes the conditions under which firms outside this merger operate. Consider a group of firms which do not belong to a proposed merger. This group of firms may consider a merger itself. However, as we just discussed, the profitability of this second merger may depend on whether the originally proposed merger goes ahead. Potentially, if an antitrust authority approves a merger, other perhaps even more welfare-increasing mergers may no longer be profitable and thus not proposed, or loose their welfare-enhancing feature and may thus be blocked. In other words, an antitrust authority may take erroneous decisions if it neglects the long-term consequences.

While this appears to be a major problem of current antitrust practice, there is a surprisingly simple response to this concern of dynamic inconsistency. Presuming that antitrust authorities try to maximize consumer surplus (not total surplus), which at least on paper is what most antitrust authorities are expected to do, it can be shown for a wide class of Cournot games (results are essentially robust for some price-setting models) that the antitrust authority does not make any errors basing its decision only on short-term effects and ignoring effects on future mergers.[47]

This result hinges on a form of complementarity between mergers that change consumer surplus in the same direction. In particular, *if two mergers increase consumer surplus in isolation, they also increase consumer surplus when they take place together*. To show this, we use the linear Cournot model with synergies presented in Section 15.1. Consider two disjoint sets, I_1 and I_2, of merging firms. There are k_j firms in set I_j and the synergies resulting from the merger allow the merged entity to reduce its constant marginal cost from c to $c - x_j$. Suppose that $k_1 + k_2 < n$, so that there remain some outsiders even if both mergers have taken place.

As we discussed above, a merger makes consumers better off if it increases the total quantity produced. In Chapter 3, we derived the total equilibrium quantity in a linear Cournot model. Let us quickly redo this analysis here. Suppose as before that inverse demand is given by $P(q) = a - q$. The first-order condition for profit maximization of a typical Cournot competitor i with constant marginal cost c_i is $a - c_i - 2q_i - q_{-i} = 0$. Summing over all firms, we obtain $na - \sum_{i=1}^{n} c_i - 2q - (n-1)q = 0$, and solving for q, we get

$$q = \frac{na - C}{n + 1} \quad \text{with} \quad C \equiv \sum_{i=1}^{n} c_i.$$

We can now use this formula to express conditions for a merger to increase total quantity and therefore consumer surplus. Before any merger takes place, there are n firms in the industry and they all have the same marginal cost c; hence, $C_{ea} = nc$ and total quantity is

$$q_{ea} = \frac{n(a - c)}{n + 1}.$$

If only firms in set I_j merge, there are $(n - k_j + 1)$ firms in the industry and the sum of marginal costs is equal to $C_j = (n - k_j + 1)c - x_j$. Total quantity after the merger of the firms in I_j is thus

$$q_j = \frac{(n - k_j + 1)(a - c) + x_j}{n - k_j + 2}.$$

Hence, the merger within the set I_j, taking place in isolation, increases consumer surplus if $q_j \geq q_{ea}$, or[h]

$$\frac{x_j}{a - c} \geq \frac{k_j - 1}{n + 1}. \tag{15.10}$$

Now, if two mergers take place, we obtain the following: the number of firms in the industry is $(n - k_1 - k_2 + 2)$, the sum of marginal costs is $C_{12} = (n - k_1 - k_2 + 2)c - x_1 - x_2$, and total quantity is

$$q_{12} = \frac{(n - k_1 - k_2 + 2)(a - c) + x_1 + x_2}{n - k_1 - k_2 + 3}.$$

The two mergers combined increase consumer surplus if $q_{12} \geq q_{ea}$, or

$$\frac{x_1 + x_2}{a - c} \geq \frac{k_1 + k_2 - 2}{n + 1}. \tag{15.11}$$

---

[h] This is the threshold that we denoted $\phi_c(k, n)$ in Section 15.2.

It is readily seen that if condition (15.10) is met for both sets of firms, so is condition (15.11) as it is nothing but the sum of the other two conditions. This proves our claim that if two mergers increase consumer surplus in isolation, so do they when they occur together. Moreover, we showed in Section 15.2 that, in this model, a merger that does not decrease consumer surplus is necessarily profitable. So, conditional on one merger being proposed (because it is profitable) and approved (because it increases consumer surplus), the second merger remains profitable and beneficial to consumers. This finding helps us understand better why the competition authority can use a myopic policy, as summarized in the following lesson.

> **Lesson 15.8** In environments where multiple disjoint mergers can be proposed over time, an antitrust authority that is concerned with the maximization of (discounted) consumer surplus can use a myopic policy that approves mergers if they do not decrease consumer surplus at the time of approval.

15.3.2   Mergers and entry

The profitability of a merger should be questioned if entry can occur. Consider the possible merger to monopoly among duopolists and suppose that under free entry, a duopoly prevailed before the merger takes place.[48] This holds if firms incur fixed costs f which satisfy $\pi(2) > f > \pi(3)$, where $\pi(n)$ denotes per firm equilibrium profit gross of any fixed costs when n firms are active in the industry. Let us reconsider the merger decision of firms. In the absence of entry, merger to monopoly is even more profitable since now, in addition, the fixed cost of one firm can be avoided: $\pi(1) > 2\pi(2) \Rightarrow \pi(1) - f > 2\pi(2) - 2f$.

Consider now an infinitely repeated Cournot game with a merger stage at the beginning. In period 1, firm 1 can make a take-it-or-leave-it offer to the other firm, who accepts or rejects the offer. If such an offer is successful, a potential entrant decides whether to enter (and this decision becomes effective after Δt periods). Firms set quantities in period 1 and then subsequently in periods 2, 3, . . . This is repeated infinitely and firms are assumed to choose their quantity noncooperatively in each period (Markov perfect strategies). This rules out the kind of collusive behaviour that was analysed in the previous chapter. Firms maximize discounted profits, where the discount factor is δ. If no merger takes place, each firm's discounted profits are

$$V(2) = \tfrac{1}{1-\delta}(\pi(2) - f).$$

Hence, if firm 1 wants to make a successful take over bid, it has to offer at least $V(2)$. Firm 1 would then become temporarily a monopolist, namely for $\Delta t - 1$ periods. Since entry into the market is profitable, a potential entrant would enter as soon as it is ready, namely after Δt periods.

If $\Delta t = \infty$, we are back in the situation in which entry is impossible and thus a merger to monopoly is necessarily profitable. Consider the opposite case that $\Delta t = 0$. Then, after placing a successful takeover bid of $V(2)$, firm 1 will encounter a new competitor in the market so that its expected profit will be also $V(2)$, gross of the payment made for the takeover. Thus its profit will be zero, which is less than the discounted duopoly profit. This means that if the entry threat is immediate, there does not exist any rationale for a merger. This reasoning shows that *entry barriers are at the heart of the competitive effects of mergers.*

With a delay of entry of Δt periods, firm 1's profit after a successful merger is

$$V(1) = \sum_{t=0}^{\Delta t-1} \delta^t [\pi(1) - f] + \sum_{t=\Delta t}^{\infty} \delta^t [\pi(2) - f].$$

A merger is profitable if $V(1) -$ acquisition cost $> V(2)$. Since the acquisition cost is $V(2)$, we must have $V(1) > 2V(2)$. Take $\Delta t = 1$ so that a successful take-over gives rise to a temporary monopoly for one period. A merger is profitable if

$$\pi(1) - f > 2 \sum_{t=0}^{\infty} \delta^t [\pi(2) - f] - \delta \sum_{t=0}^{\infty} \delta^t [\pi(2) - f] = (2 - \delta) \frac{\pi(2) - f}{1 - \delta}.$$

Expanding this inequality and isolating the discount factor, we find the following condition for merger profitability:

$$\delta < 1 - \frac{\pi(2) - f}{\pi(1) - \pi(2)} \equiv \bar{\delta}.$$

It is easily seen that $\pi(2) > f$ implies that $\bar{\delta} < 1$, and $\pi(1) + f > 2\pi(2)$ implies that $\bar{\delta} > 0$. Therefore, if firms are sufficiently impatient (i.e., δ close to 0), a merger is still profitable. However, if firms are sufficiently patient (i.e., δ close to 1), the merger to monopoly is not profitable because the merger only temporarily gives rise to a monopoly position.

Lesson 15.9   If a merger only temporarily leads to a smaller number of firms because there is subsequent entry, a merger in a Cournot model is not profitable when firms are sufficiently patient.

15.3.3   Mergers under price competition

If firms are not Cournot competitors but set prices in a differentiated product market, there are much stronger incentives to merge. Indeed under Cournot competition, outsiders choose a higher output after a merger, which reduces the profit of the merging firm. With price competition, firms compete less aggressively after a merger. That is, outsiders set a higher price. The merging firm then benefits from these higher prices. Thus, with price competition, there is a rationale for mergers even in a non-concentrated industry. To illustrate this insight, we take the (slightly modified) linear demand model from Chapter 5. Demand for product i is assumed to be

$$Q_i(p_1, \ldots, p_n) = a - p_i + d\bar{p}_{-i},$$

where $\bar{p}_{-i} \equiv \sum_{j \neq i} p_j/(n - 1)$ denotes the average price that is charged for all products other than i. Suppose that firms face zero marginal costs so that profits of a firm selling product i are $\pi_i(p) = p_i Q_i(p)$ where $p = (p_1, \ldots, p_n)$. Solving for p_i in the first-order condition, we obtain the best-response

$$p_i = \tfrac{1}{2} \left(a + d\bar{p}_{-i} \right). \tag{15.12}$$

As is common in price competition models with product differentiation, best responses are upward sloping and prices are strategic complements. In the pre-merger competition, there is a unique equilibrium which is symmetric. Since $p_i = \overline{p}_{-i}$ we obtain the equilibrium price

$$p_{ea}^* = \frac{a}{2 - d}.$$

Suppose that two firms merge and call this merged, two-product firm, I. Since its two products are symmetric, firm I maximizes its profits by setting the same price p_I for its two products. All other firms remain single-product firms that face the same environment. Hence, there are one two-product firm and $(n - 2)$ one-product firms in the market. In equilibrium, the single-product firms all set the same price p_O^*.

Given symmetric prices p_O, the profits of firm I are $\pi_I = 2p_I(a - p_I + d\frac{1}{n-1}(p_I + (n - 2)p_O))$. The best-response to p_O is implicitly defined by the first-order condition

$$a - 2p_I + 2d\tfrac{1}{n-1}p_I + d(n - 2)\tfrac{1}{n-1}p_O = 0.$$

(At the equilibrium, p_I is replaced by p_I^* and p_O by p_O^*.) The two-product firm internalizes the positive effect of a price change for one of its products on the demand for the other product. Therefore, it prices less aggressively than a single-product firm. In other words, the best-response of the two-product firm is shifted outward compared to the pre-merger situation. Together with the property that prices are strategic complements, this implies that equilibrium prices of the merged two-product firm and the one-product firms after the merger are larger than the pre-merger prices – this is a rather general property under price competition, which is not due to the particular specification we are analysing here. Since the two-product firm prices less aggressively than the competing one-product firms, we must have $p_I^* > p_O^* > p_{ea}^*$.[i]

To explicitly calculate prices in our model, we turn to the maximization problem of a one-product firm. Here we can take the best response (15.12) from above where $\overline{p}_{-i} = \frac{1}{n-1}(2p_I + (n - 3)p_O)$. Hence, in equilibrium we must have

$$p_O^* = \tfrac{1}{2}\left[a + d\tfrac{1}{n-1}\left(2p_I^* + (n - 3)p_O^*\right)\right].$$

We thus have to solve a system of two linear equations in p_I^* and p_O^*. The solution is given by

$$p_I^* = \frac{a(n - 1)(n - 1 + \frac{d}{2})}{(2 - d)(n - 1)^2 - d^2},$$

$$p_O^* = \frac{a(n - 1)^2}{(2 - d)(n - 1)^2 - d^2}.$$

It is easily checked that indeed $p_I^* > p_O^* > p_{ea}^*$, as has been argued above.

Lesson 15.10   If firms have differentiated products and compete in prices, a merger between two firms leads to higher prices for all firms.

---

[i] Compare to the comparative statics results for strategic complements as analysed in Chapter 3.

Since the competitors of the merged firm set higher prices than before the merger, profits of the merged firm increase even if there are no efficiency gains from the merger.[49] This implies that, in contrast to quantity competition, there are strong private incentives to merge absent any efficiency gains, whereas, as we have seen earlier, absent efficiency gains mergers under quantity competition are profitable only if the industry is initially very concentrated.

With price competition a merger is necessarily welfare-reducing if there are no efficiency gains. If, however, a merger (for instance) reduces marginal costs, then it may be welfare-increasing. In particular, it may be the case that due to the reduction in marginal costs, the best-response of the merged firm shifts *inward* after the merger. In this case, equilibrium prices will be unambiguously lower for all firms, so that consumer welfare is increased (the condition for total welfare to increase is more likely to be satisfied since profit increases are counted as well).

15.3.4   Coordinated effects

We have dealt so far with the so-called *unilateral effects* of mergers, i.e., the consequences of a merger under the assumption that firms compete both before and after the merger. We should not overlook, however, the possibility that a merger could increase the incentives of the remaining firms to engage in tacit collusion. The so-called *coordinated effects* of mergers refer to that possibility.[j] Case 15.4 shows that competition authorities do indeed reject mergers on the grounds of coordinated effects.

Case 15.4 Coordinated effects in the Nestlé–Perrier merger[50]

In Europe, the first case of application of the concept of collective (joint or oligopolistic) dominance (which is the European terminology for coordinated effects) is the Nestlé–Perrier merger. In 1992, Nestlé, a player on the French bottled-water market with its brands Vittel and Hepar, notified the European Commission (EC) of its intention to acquire Perrier. At that time, the market had an annual volume of 5.25 billion litres and consisted of three major firms: Perrier, BSN and Nestlé, with respective market shares of 36%, 23% and 17%. The remaining 24% were left to a very fragmented competitive fringe. As such, the merger of Nestlé and Perrier would have given the merged entity a dominant position (with 53% of the market). The EC rejected the merger invoking unilateral effects: the merger would have established a dominant firm with too much market power.

As a consequence, the two merging firms agreed to sell Volvic (a major mineral source of Perrier) to BSN. As Volvic's share of the market was 15%, they argued that the post-merger market would become a balanced duopoly, with two entities ('Nestlé + Perrier – Volvic' and 'BSN + Volvic') having a market share of 38% each. Yet, the EC rejected the modified merger again invoking, this time, coordinated effects: it was feared that the

---

[j] This terminology comes from the US merger guidelines. In the EU, a distinction is made between *non-coordinated effects* (which include unilateral effects and single-firm dominance) and *collective dominance effects* (which correspond to coordinated effects).

merger would establish 'oligopolistic' dominance. The EC judged that the potential for collusion was very high for the following reasons: (i) two main players would be of similar size, nature and cost structure; (ii) monitoring each others' prices was relatively easy; (iii) the demand for water was relatively price inelastic; (iv) there were high barriers to entry. Actually, looking at the prospects for collusion, the first merger proposition appeared as less objectionable. Indeed, in the absence of Volvic's reselling, Nestlé–Perrier would have had much more spare capacity than BSN. This implies that Nestlé–Perrier would have had large incentives to cut prices and BSN very low retaliation possibilities. Hence, the transfer of Volvic's spare capacity would have facilitated collusion.

Finally, Nestlé made a third proposition that involved, on top of selling Volvic to BSN, selling off a variety of its brands (Vichy, Thonon, Pierval, St Yorre, etc), as well as 3 billion litres of water capacity to a third party. The EC accepted this solution.

Using the analysis of the previous chapter, we identify two main ways in which a merger may affect the sustainability of tacit collusion. On the one hand, a merger decreases the number of firms in the market, which makes tacit collusion easier to sustain, as we showed in Chapter 14. On the other hand, a merger may affect the degree of symmetry among the remaining firms. For instance, in the presence of synergies, the merged entity may become a more efficient producer than the outside firms. Similarly, in differentiated good industries, the merged entity may own a larger set of brands or varieties than the outsiders. Asymmetries among firms have several implications on the sustainability of tacit collusion. First, it might be more difficult to define the common collusive price as, e.g., more efficient firms will prefer lower prices than less efficient ones. Second, the allocation of production quotas is also harder to agree upon as equal sharing would typically be inefficient when some firms are more efficient than others. Finally, even if the previous two problems are solved, it remains that low-cost firms have more incentives to renege on a collusive agreement because deviation pays more and punishment hurts less for them. So, we can draw the following general lesson.

Lesson 15.11 **A merger may exert two conflicting effects on the sustainability of collusion: a positive effect through the reduction in the number of firms and a negative effect if it increases the asymmetry among firms.**

We build a very simple model to illustrate how these two effects come into play. Suppose that there are initially n symmetric firms in the industry. They produce a homogeneous good at the same constant marginal cost c and compete in prices. Suppose for simplicity that demand is perfectly price-inelastic: all consumers have a unit demand and the same reservation price r. So, for any price below r, firms can sell a total quantity q. In this initial situation, the best collusive price is $p_m = r$ and tacit collusion is sustainable if and only if firms prefer to abide by the collusive agreement rather than to undercut the rivals (which secures an immediate gain of the whole market but is followed by zero profits thereafter because of punishment). As we saw in Chapter 14, this condition is equivalent to

$$\frac{1}{1-\delta}(r-c)\frac{q}{n} \geq (r-c)q \Leftrightarrow \delta \geq 1 - \frac{1}{n} \equiv \delta_{pre}.$$

Suppose now that k firms merge (with $2 \leq k < n$) and, because of synergies, benefit from a lower marginal cost of production, namely $c - x$. Suppose also that the collusive agreement still defines equal market shares. The outsiders (which keep a marginal cost equal to c) are then willing to sustain collusion if

$$\frac{1}{1 - \delta} (r - c) \frac{q}{n - k + 1} \geq (r - c)q \Leftrightarrow \delta \geq 1 - \frac{1}{n - k + 1}.$$

Hence, from the outsiders' point of view, collusion is more attractive as the collusive profits are increased (because they are equally shared among a lower number of firms), while the gain from deviation and the consequences of punishment remain the same. As for the merged entity, it is willing to sustain collusion as long as

$$\frac{1}{1 - \delta} [r - (c - x)] \frac{q}{n - k + 1} \geq [r - (c - x)]q + \frac{\delta}{1 - \delta} [c - (c - x)]q.$$

Because the lowest punishment price of the outsider is $p = c$, the merged entity can still make positive profits in the punishment phase, which makes deviation more attractive. Hence, the condition is clearly more stringent. The condition can be simplified to

$$[r - (c - x)] \frac{1}{n - k + 1} \geq (1 - \delta)[r - (c - x)] + \delta x$$
$$= [r - (c - x)] - \delta(r - c).$$

Thus the merged entity does not deviate if

$$\delta \geq \left(\frac{n - k}{n - k + 1} \right) \left(\frac{r - c + x}{r - c} \right) \equiv \delta_{post}.$$

We can now assess whether the merger facilitates or hinders tacit collusion by comparing the pre- and post-merger minimal discount factors. In particular, the merger facilitates tacit collusion if

$$\delta_{post} < \delta_{pre} \Leftrightarrow \left(\frac{n - k}{n - k + 1} \right) \left(\frac{r - c + x}{r - c} \right) < 1 - \frac{1}{n} \Leftrightarrow \frac{x}{r - c} < \frac{k - 1}{n(n - k)}.$$

That is, if the synergies are not too large, the firms remain similar enough after the merger and the positive effect stemming from increased concentration dominates, making collusion easier to sustain. Note that the latter condition becomes less stringent as the merger involves more firms (i.e., as k increases).

As the previous analysis suggests, it is difficult to estimate the impact of mergers on the scope for tacit collusion in theory, as conflicting effects may partially off-set each other. Estimating this impact in practice seems even more difficult. Quantitative and econometric methods may be of some help to evaluate *ex post* the likelihood of collusion in some industry, but what is needed here is an *ex ante* evaluation of how a merger could affect this likelihood and no good method has been proposed so far to tackle this challenging issue.[51] As for the estimation of unilateral effects, a variety of methods exists, to which we turn in the following section.

15.4   Empirical merger analyses

Three different approaches have been proposed to evaluate the unilateral effects of horizontal mergers: event studies, direct price comparisons and merger simulations. We describe briefly the first two approaches and spend some more time on the third approach.[52]

15.4.1   Event studies and direct price comparisons

Event studies refer to the analysis of stock market performance of merging firms and outsiders following a merger announcement and the eventual investigation and subsequent decision of the competition authority. The idea is to learn the potential effects of a merger from the reactions of the stock market. For instance, an increase in the equity value of the merging firms and of the outsiders could be seen as an indication that the merger is likely to result in higher prices and thus, higher profits in the industry, at the expense of consumers. It can be objected, however, that it is not clear when stock market participants learn about a merger announcement and, more importantly, what they learn from it (the announcement may simply inform about the good health of the industry, which is likely to generate higher returns for all firms). Moreover, a high variance of stock returns is often observed for large outsiders that only obtain a relatively small share of their profits from the market where the merger is announced, which casts doubt on the relevance of event studies for assessing unilateral effects of mergers.[53]

Another method for assessing the *ex post* effects of a merger is the *direct comparison of prices* before and after the merger. Looking retrospectively at the actual effects of mergers may be useful for two reasons: first, it can help competition authorities to identify the characteristics that are likely to make a merger anticompetitive or efficiency-enhancing; second, *ex post* analyses may be used to assess the performance of *ex ante* analyses, such as the merger simulations that we discuss in the next subsection. Unfortunately, this type of analysis is still rare.[54]

15.4.2   Merger simulations

There are essentially two steps in any merger simulation. First, one must collect pre-merger market information (such as ownership structure, cost and price data) so as to estimate direct and cross price elasticities, and to calibrate a one-shot noncooperative oligopoly model that matches the critical features of the industry under review. The second step consists then in using the calibrated model to calculate the post-merger equilibrium, taking into account the change in the ownership structure.

Although there exist basic simulation tools with low data requirements, the currently used models are very sophisticated and, thereby, are capable of incorporating a number of complex market facts. In particular, Almost Ideal Demand System (AIDS) and nested logit models can be used to analyse markets with differentiated consumer products.[k] Actually, merger simulations are particularly useful in these markets, because the traditional tools of merger analysis, such as market shares and concentration indices, are quite problematic to use

---

[k] The AIDS model is due to Deaton and Muellbauer (1980). For a description of the nested logit model, see Chapter 5.

in such context. Merger simulations are also useful to quantify and disentangle the impacts a merger is likely to have on concentration and efficiencies. Impacts of proposed merger remedies can be estimated likewise.

Merger simulations have thus a number of important advantages; unfortunately, they also have serious limitations. First, price predictions are always subject to modelling error (due to imperfect assumptions or from sampling error in the statistical estimation of model parameters). Second, in their current form, merger simulations focus on the immediate price and output effects of mergers; hence, they leave aside longer-term potential impacts of the merger, such as those related to entry, product repositioning or other modifications of the marketing mix. Finally, merger simulations usually assume that the firms' behaviour does not change as a result of the merger (e.g., pre- and post-merger competition is modelled as a Bertrand game). However, as discussed at the end of the previous section, firms may be able to sustain tacit collusion after the merger, while they were not able to do so beforehand. Retrospective direct price comparisons can be used to test the predictive power of prospective merger simulations and assess how serious their limitations are. Yet, as indicated above, the economic literature contains only a few such analyses.[1]

The econometric literature on merger analysis has been growing over the last decade. Various models have been used (Cournot, Bertrand, auctions, etc.) to study mergers in various industries. For instance, Froeb, Tardiff and Werden (1996) simulate hypothetical mergers of Japanese long-distance carriers using a logit model that incorporates brand characteristics. Nevo (2000) estimates a random coefficients model to study the effects of mergers in the US ready-to-eat cereal industry. Werden and Froeb (2002) simulate the proposed merger of two brewers in Sweden. Pinkse and Slade (2004) also study mergers in the brewing industry, using a distance metric approach. Froeb, Tschantz, and Crooke (2003) simulate the merger of parking lots using a logit model. The following two cases consider applications of the nested logit, the first concerning mobile telephony and the second concerning truck manufacturing.

Case 15.5 Merger simulation in mobile telephony in Portugal

Grzybowski and Pereira (2007) assess the unilateral effects on prices of a merger in the Portuguese mobile telephony market, which was proposed in February 2006. There were, at the time, three major operators on the Portuguese mobile telephony market: Tmn, Vodafone and Optimus, with respective revenue market shares of 50%, 37% and 13%. The proposed merger was between Tmn and Optimus. It naturally raised antitrust concerns as it would have reduced the number of competitors from three to two and have increased the level of concentration substantially. To simulate the unilateral effects of the proposed merger, the authors use aggregate quarterly data from 1999 to 2005 to estimate an aggregate nested logit model (see Chapter 5 for a description). Marginal cost estimates are obtained by using estimates of the price elasticities of demand and by assuming that firms

---

[1] Peters (2006) examines how well simulation methods would have predicted the actual price changes that followed six airline mergers in the 1980s. The main result is that merger simulations seem to capture important elements of the price changes but the predictions remain imperfect.

play a static price competition game. Estimates of the price elasticities of demand and of the marginal costs are then used to simulate the merger. The results indicate that 'the merger would lead to significant price increases, even in the presence of substantial cost efficiencies. On average, industry prices would increase by 7–10% without cost efficiencies, and by 6–10% with a 10% a marginal cost reduction. One firm could increase the price by as much as 13–22%. On average, without marginal cost efficiencies, the consumer surplus would decrease by about 2–4%.' (p. 206)

Case 15.6 The proposed merger between the European truck manufacturers Volvo and Scania

Ivaldi and Verboven (2005), based on their study for the European Commission, analyse the effects of the merger between Volvo and Scania, two truck manufacturers, in the EU. They apply a nested logit model to panel data on list prices and horsepower for two types of trucks for each of the seven major truck manufacturers in 16 different European countries in 1997 and 1998. The simulation results suggest a serious anticompetitive price effect of the merger: it predicted a price increase of 10–23% for rigid trucks and 7–13% for tractor trucks produced by merging parties. According to the study, predicted efficiency gains are dominated by 'consumer' loss due to price increases.

　　This study was criticized by the party representing Volvo, see Hausman and Leonard (2005). In the end, the European Commission did not base its ruling on the commissioned study, instead it rather relied on traditional analyses establishing that the merger would create a dominant position for the new entity.

Review questions

1. Explain why mergers that do not involve efficiency gains are rarely profitable in Cournot industries.

2. What is the main advantage of assessing the welfare impact of a merger by looking at its 'external effect'? Explain in words the condition under which this external effect is positive.

3. Taking successive mergers and entry into account, discuss whether and, if yes, how merger analysis has to be reconsidered.

4. Explain the fundamental differences between mergers in Cournot and in Bertrand industries.

5. What is meant by the 'coordinated effects' of a merger. Discuss.

Further reading

Seminal papers analysing the profitability of Cournot mergers are Salant, Switzer and Reynolds (1983) – who state the '80% rule' – and Perry and Porter (1985) – who study efficiency-increasing mergers. A major contribution to the welfare analysis of Cournot mergers is Farrell and Shapiro (1990). When going beyond simple Cournot mergers, we mainly followed Nocke and Whinston (2007) to deal with successive mergers, Pesendorfer (2005) to consider entry, Deneckere and Davidson (1985) to study Bertrand mergers, and Compte, Jenny and Rey (2002) to account for coordinated effects. As for empirical merger analyses, recent surveys can be found in Whinston (2006) and in Werden and Froeb (2008).

16 Strategic incumbents and entry

If natural (or innocent) entry barriers in an industry are sufficiently large, entry is said to be *blockaded* for additional firms.[55] In some markets, entry barriers are at a level that only a single firm can enter. In such a situation, the single incumbent firm can behave as a monopolist without fearing entry. In contrast, for lower entry barriers, entry is a threat that the incumbent cannot ignore. Facing potential entry, the incumbent will thus react strategically with a view either to make entry unprofitable or, at least, to minimize the harm that entry causes. Entry is said to be *deterred* in the former case, and *accommodated* in the latter.

Because an incumbent is already established in the industry, it has the advantage of being able to act before a potential entrant decides whether or not to enter. However, acting before is not sufficient to influence the entrant's decision: the incumbent must also act in a credible way. We already raised this issue in Chapter 4 when analysing the Stackelberg game. In the present context, a threat to make the entrant's life impossible or hard if it enters can only be effective if this threat is turned into a commitment. That is, the incumbent's action must modify its incentives in such a way that if entry was to happen, it would be in the incumbent's best interest to carry out the threat.[56]

To achieve such commitment, the incumbent will invest prior to entry and in an irreversible way in some strategic variable that will affect its future conduct and, thereby, the profits the entrant could attain upon entry. It may also affect directly the entry cost so that this cost becomes endogenous.[57] In Section 16.1, we show how the incumbent's investment decision depends on the strategic effect of this investment and on the type of product market competition. Combining these two dimensions with the two potential attitudes with respect to entry (deterrence or accommodation), we propose a taxonomy of entry-related strategies. Next, we apply this taxonomy to a number of specific examples of investments that an incumbent can make when facing the possibility of entry. In Section 16.2, we examine strategies affecting cost variables, namely investments in capacity, investments in R&D and strategies designed to raise the entrant's costs. In Section 16.3, we turn to strategies affecting demand variables. Here, we show how brand proliferation, bundling decisions and manipulation of an installed base of customers in the presence of switching costs can be used as entry deterrence tools. All these actions may be seen as anticompetitive and are thus subject to antitrust investigations.

Finally, we extend the previous analyses in two directions: imperfect information in Section 16.4, and multiple incumbents in Section 16.5. Regarding the former, we argue that limit pricing can deter entry when the entrant is uncertain about the cost level of the incumbent. As for the latter, we examine whether entry deterrence can be achieved, noncooperatively, by a group of established firms.

16.1   Taxonomy of entry-related strategies

The incumbent's investment decision in anticipation of the possibility of entry depends on the strategic effect of this investment and on the type of product market competition. To show this dependence, we analyse the following two-stage game between one incumbent firm (indexed by 1) and one potential entrant (indexed by 2).[58] At the first stage, the incumbent chooses the level of some irreversible investment, denoted by K_1. At the second stage, after observing K_1, the entrant decides whether or not to enter and then product market decisions are taken. In particular, if the entrant enters, a duopoly results; otherwise, the incumbent remains in a monopoly position. Payoffs are described as follows.

- If the potential entrant decides to enter, the two firms simultaneously make their second-stage decisions, σ_1 and σ_2. Typically, this decision is either a price ($\sigma_i = p_i$) or a quantity ($\sigma_i = q_i$). Profits are given by $\pi_1(K_1, \sigma_1, \sigma_2)$ and $\pi_2(K_1, \sigma_1, \sigma_2)$, where by convention π_2 includes entry costs (if any). It is assumed that profit functions are such that a unique and stable Nash equilibrium exists in stage 2 for any K_1; we denote this equilibrium $\{\sigma_1^*(K_1), \sigma_2^*(K_1)\}$.

- If the potential entrant does not enter, it makes zero profit, while the incumbent obtains $\pi_1^m(K_1, \sigma_1^m(K_1))$, where $\sigma_1^m(K_1)$ is the monopoly choice in stage 2, expressed as a function of the first-stage investment.

As for the first stage, we assume that both $\pi_1(K_1, \sigma_1^*(K_1), \sigma_2^*(K_1))$ and $\pi_1^m(K_1, \sigma_1^m(K_1))$ are strictly concave in K_1, and that the functions $\sigma_1^*(K_1)$ and $\sigma_1^m(K_1)$ are differentiable. A strategic incumbent chooses its first-stage investment K_1 either to deter entry, or to accommodate it in the least harmful way. In the case of *entry deterrence*, the incumbent's objective is to choose K_1 such that $\pi_2(K_1, \sigma_1^*(K_1), \sigma_2^*(K_1)) \leq 0$. In the case of *entry accommodation*, the incumbent chooses K_1 so as to maximize its own profit, $\pi_1(K_1, \sigma_1^*(K_1), \sigma_2^*(K_1))$, taking as given that firm 2 has entered, i.e. $\pi_2(K_1, \sigma_1^*(K_1), \sigma_2^*(K_1)) > 0$.

In both cases, we want to compare the investment level at the subgame perfect equilibrium of the two-stage game with a hypothetical 'non-strategic' investment level. Such 'non-strategic' choice could be made by a 'myopic' incumbent that does not internalize the effects of its investment on the entrant's second-stage decisions. Alternatively, the incumbent would choose 'non-strategically' if its investment was not observable by the entrant. We take this benchmark in order to define the notions of strategic *overinvestment* and *underinvestment*. In particular, we talk of overinvestment when the strategic level exceeds the non-strategic level, and of underinvestment otherwise.

16.1.1   Entry deterrence

Consider first the case where the incumbent chooses its investment level so as to make entry unprofitable. We rule out the possibility that the monopoly choice of K_1 is sufficient to deter entry.[a] We thus focus on situations where the incumbent must distort its investment choice.

---

[a] In this case, entry would be *blockaded* (using the terminology we introduced above) and there would not be any strategic interaction, which presents no interest for our analysis.

As distortion is costly, the incumbent will choose the investment level that is just sufficient to deter entry, i.e., K_1 is chosen such that

$$\pi_2\left(K_1, \sigma_1^*(K_1), \sigma_2^*(K_1)\right) = 0.$$

To see in which direction the level of K_1 must be distorted, we compute the impact of a change in K_1 on the entrant's profit. That is, we totally differentiate π_2 with respect to K_1:

$$\frac{d\pi_2}{dK_1} = \frac{\partial \pi_2}{\partial K_1} + \frac{\partial \pi_2}{\partial \sigma_1} \frac{\partial \sigma_1^*(K_1)}{\partial K_1} + \frac{\partial \pi_2}{\partial \sigma_2} \frac{\partial \sigma_2^*(K_1)}{\partial K_1}.$$

Note that $\sigma_2^*(K_1)$ is such that $\frac{\partial}{\partial \sigma_2} \pi_2\left(K_1, \sigma_1^*(K_1), \sigma_2^*(K_1)\right) = 0$ because of the envelope theorem. The previous expression can thus be rewritten as

$$\underbrace{\frac{d\pi_2}{dK_1}}_{\text{Total effect}} = \underbrace{\frac{\partial \pi_2}{\partial K_1}}_{\text{Direct effect}} + \underbrace{\frac{\partial \pi_2}{\partial \sigma_1} \frac{d\sigma_1^*(K_1)}{dK_1}}_{\text{Strategic effect (SED)}}. \tag{16.1}$$

There are two channels through which the incumbent's investment can affect the entrant's profit. First, it can have a *direct effect* ($\partial \pi_2/\partial K_1$). The direct effect can be of any sign. For instance, suppose that the incumbent's investment is advertising. As we have seen in Chapter 6, if advertisement is persuasive, firm 1 will increase its market share at the expense of firm 2 (hence, $\partial \pi_2/\partial K_1 < 0$); in contrast, if advertisement is informative, it might expand aggregate demand and, thereby, benefit firm 2 (hence, $\partial \pi_2/\partial K_1 > 0$). On the other hand, if the incumbent invests in capacity (as we will analyse in the next section), the entrant's profit will not be directly affected ($\partial \pi_2/\partial K_1 = 0$). The incumbent's investment can also have an indirect or *strategic effect*: by changing its ex ante decision, the incumbent modifies its ex post behaviour ($d\sigma_1^*(K_1)/dK_1$), which affects firm 2's profit in a proportion given by $\partial \pi_2/\partial \sigma_1$.

We say that the investment makes the incumbent *tough* if the total effect on the entrant's profit ($d\pi_2/dK_1$) is negative. Conversely, if the total effect is positive, then the investment makes the incumbent *soft*. Naturally, as the objective of entry deterrence is to reduce the entrant's profit to zero, the incumbent wants to look aggressive. So, if the investment makes him tough ($d\pi_2/dK_1 < 0$), the incumbent has an incentive to overinvest. This is the so-called 'top dog strategy'. The opposite prevails when the investment makes the incumbent soft; in that case, in order to look aggressive, the incumbent must underinvest. This is the so-called 'lean and hungry look'.

Lesson 16.1   If investment makes the incumbent *tough* (i.e., if investment decreases the entrant's profit), then the incumbent must behave as a *top dog* to deter entry: he must overinvest (be strong or big) to look aggressive. Conversely, if investment makes the incumbent *soft* (i.e., if investment increases the entrant's profit), then the incumbent must adopt a *lean and hungry look* to deter entry: he must underinvest (be weak or small) to look aggressive.

16.1.2   Entry accommodation

Deterring entry may happen to be too costly for the incumbent (we will determine when this is so more precisely in the specific examples below). In this case, firm 1 takes entry as given and shifts its focus from the entrant's profits towards its own. That is, it no longer chooses K_1 to make π_2 negative but to maximize π_1. Hence, to derive the incumbent's incentive to invest, we now totally differentiate $\pi_1(K_1, \sigma_1^*(K_1), \sigma_2^*(K_1))$ with respect to K_1. Noting as above that $\sigma_1^*(K_1)$ is such that $\frac{\partial}{\partial \sigma_1} \pi_1(K_1, \sigma_1^*(K_1), \sigma_2^*(K_1)) = 0$, we have:

$$\underbrace{\frac{d\pi_1}{dK_1}}_{\text{Total effect}} = \underbrace{\frac{\partial\pi_1}{\partial K_1}}_{\text{Direct effect}} + \underbrace{\frac{\partial\pi_1}{\partial\sigma_2}\frac{d\sigma_2^*(K_1)}{dK_1}}_{\text{Strategic effect (SEA)}}.$$

The total effect can again be split into two effects. The *direct effect* is the profit-maximizing effect, that exists even if K_1 has no effect on firm 2. Therefore, we can neglect this effect when comparing our results with the benchmark situation, since it appears in both cases. It is the *strategic effect* that makes the difference. It results from the influence of firm 1's investment on firm 2's second-stage behaviour $(d\sigma_2^*(K_1)/dK_1)$, which affects firm 1's profit in proportion to $\partial\pi_1/\partial\sigma_2$. In the present case, we say that the incumbent should overinvest if the strategic effect is positive; it should underinvest otherwise.

What determines the sign of SEA, the strategic effect in the entry accommodation case? Presuming that the reaction function of firm 2 does not directly depend on K, we can show that it depends (i) on the sign of the strategic effect in the entry deterrence case (SED), and (ii) on the strategic substitutability or complementarity of the firms' second-stage choices. We proceed in three steps.

1. Assuming that the firms' second-stage choices have the same nature, we have that $\partial\pi_1/\partial\sigma_2$ and $\partial\pi_2/\partial\sigma_1$ have the same sign, implying that

$$\text{sign}\left(\frac{\partial\pi_1}{\partial\sigma_2}\frac{d\sigma_2^*(K_1)}{dK_1}\right) = \text{sign}\left(\frac{\partial\pi_2}{\partial\sigma_1}\frac{d\sigma_2^*(K_1)}{dK_1}\right).$$

2. Using the chain rule, we have

$$\frac{d\sigma_2^*(K_1)}{dK_1} = \left(\frac{d\sigma_2^*}{d\sigma_1}\right)\left(\frac{d\sigma_1^*}{dK_1}\right).$$

3. Combining the latter two expressions, we can write

$$\text{sign}\underbrace{\left(\frac{\partial\pi_1}{\partial\sigma_2}\frac{d\sigma_2^*(K_1)}{dK_1}\right)}_{\text{SEA}} = \text{sign}\underbrace{\left(\frac{\partial\pi_2}{\partial\sigma_1}\frac{d\sigma_1^*}{dK_1}\right)}_{\text{SED}} \times \text{sign}\underbrace{\left(\frac{d\sigma_2^*}{d\sigma_1}\right)}_{\substack{\text{slope of firm 2's}\\\text{reaction curve}}} \quad (16.2)$$

There are thus four possible cases. To link entry deterrence and entry accommodation more easily, let us suppose that in the entry deterrence case, the direct effect is negligible (or zero), in the sense that the sign of the total effect $(d\pi_2/dK_1)$ is determined by the sign of the SED in expression (16.1). This means, using our previous terminology, that investment makes firm 1 tough (soft) if SED is negative (positive).

Consider first that second-stage choices are *strategic substitutes*. As we explained in Chapter 3, this implies that reaction curves are downward sloping (as is usually the case when firms compete in quantities). Hence, from expression (16.2), we see that SEA has the reverse sign of SED. We thus have the following relationships:

$$\begin{cases} \text{investment makes firm 1 tough} \rightarrow \text{SED} < 0 \rightarrow \text{SEA} > 0 \rightarrow \text{overinvest}, \\ \text{investment makes firm 1 soft} \rightarrow \text{SED} > 0 \rightarrow \text{SEA} < 0 \rightarrow \text{underinvest}. \end{cases}$$

We observe thus that *entry accommodation and entry deterrence call for the same conduct when second-stage choices are strategic substitutes*. That is, if investment makes the incumbent tough, he should overinvest, i.e., follow the top dog strategy, whether he chooses to deter entry or to accommodate it. Intuitively, a commitment to be aggressive both reduces the entrant's profit (which is good for deterrence) and increases the incumbent's profit because of the entrant's 'friendly' reaction (which is good for accommodation). The reverse applies when the investment makes the incumbent soft. Here, deterrence and accommodation both call for underinvestment, i.e., the lean and hungry look.

It is easy to see that the previous equivalence is broken under *strategic complements*. Now, because reaction curves are upward sloping, expression (16.2) tells us that SEA has the same sign as SED, and thus

$$\begin{cases} \text{investment makes firm 1 tough} \rightarrow \text{SED} < 0 \rightarrow \text{SEA} < 0 \rightarrow \text{underinvest}, \\ \text{investment makes firm 1 soft} \rightarrow \text{SED} > 0 \rightarrow \text{SEA} > 0 \rightarrow \text{overinvest}. \end{cases}$$

So, when deterrence calls for overinvestment (top dog), accommodation calls for underinvestment. This accommodation strategy is called the '*puppy dog strategy*', which consists in being weak or small to look inoffensive. By the same token, when deterrence calls for underinvestment (lean and hungry look), accommodation calls for overinvestment. This is called the '*fat cat strategy*', which consists in being big to look inoffensive. The intuition is clear. Under strategic complementarity and accommodation, the commitment to be aggressive reduces the incumbent's profits as the entrant reacts in an aggressive way. Therefore, the incumbent wants to look inoffensive, so as to trigger a favourable response from the entrant.

We collect all our previous results in the following lesson.

Lesson 16.2 **The optimal business strategies for entry deterrence (D) and for entry accommodation (A) are summarized in the following table.**

	Investment makes the incumbent	
	tough	soft
Strategic substitutes	*(D and A)* Top Dog	*(D and A)* Lean and Hungry
Strategic complements	*(D)* Top Dog *(A)* Puppy Dog	*(D)* Lean and Hungry *(A)* Fat cat

In Case 16.1, we illustrate the taxonomy by examining how Kodak first deterred and eventually accommodated Fuji's entry in the US photographic film market (we will return to this case twice more in this chapter).

Case 16.1 Kodak vs Fuji – Act I[59]

The US consumer market for photographic film was mostly dominated by a single firm, Eastman Kodak Company (Kodak), up to the 1970s. It was only in 1980 that Fuji Photo Film of Japan (Fuji) managed to successfully enter the market: Fuji reached a 5% market share in that year and strengthened its foothold in the following years. As it appears that Fuji's entry was first deterred and then accommodated by Kodak, it is important to understand why and how this happened.

To this end, Kadiyali (1996) studied the two firms' pricing and advertising strategies for entry, deterrence and accommodation. She collected quarterly firm-level time series data on quantities, prices, advertising dollars, and costs of factors and materials for both the pre-entry (1970–9) and post-entry (1980–90) periods. Using these data, she estimated a simultaneous-equation system of firm-level optimization rules for pricing and advertising choices, and firm-level demand and cost functions. She did this first for the pre-entry monopoly market and second, for the post-entry duopoly market. In the latter case, she estimated a menu of market structure hypotheses in order to uncover the competitive regime underlying the observed market outcome data (in the spirit of the 'new empirical IO' framework that we described in Chapter 3). The final step consisted in using the pre- and post-entry descriptions of the market to create a third picture that explains the links and similarities between them.

The empirical result is that Kodak deterred Fuji's entry in the 1970s and that Kodak and Fuji jointly deterred further entry in the 1980s. We defer the explanation of these conducts to Cases 16.6 and 16.8. We focus here on the explanation of entry accommodation. The analysis reveals that by 1980, Kodak was compelled to accommodate Fuji, as it suffered from both demand and cost disadvantages relative to Fuji. To show this, the author first solved for the equilibrium where Kodak sets prices and advertising to deter Fuji's entry. She then compared Kodak's hypothetical profits under this scenario with its actual profits in 1980. The conclusion is that Kodak's profits would indeed have been lower if it had not accommodated Fuji's entry.

The remaining issue is to determine Kodak's accommodation strategy. The estimates of demand and costs reveal that one firm's price and advertising were strategic complements for the other firm. Hence, we know that an incumbent accommodating entry is better off not acting in an aggressive way, so as to avoid an aggressive reaction from the entrant (which would have been especially harmful as Fuji enjoyed both demand and cost advantages at that time). The analysis confirms that Kodak adopted a conciliatory stance in both its pricing and advertising strategies. In terms of pricing, a commitment to low prices makes the incumbent tough and therefore, according to the above taxonomy, the appropriate conduct is to 'underinvest' (puppy dog strategy). As Kadiyali reports, Kodak's pre-entry average price was $3.53 per roll, which, given marginal-cost estimates, implied a profit of $0.74 per roll. Kodak's post-entry price and margin were $2.06 and $1.28 per roll (note that the marginal cost dropped from $2.79 per roll before entry to $0.78 after entry; this suggests that Fuji's entry might have spurred Kodak to invest more in R&D in an effort to lower its own costs down to Fuji's level). At the same time, Fuji's price was

$1.66 per roll. Clearly, Kodak could have cut its price (given Fuji's lower price and its own profit margin), but decided against it in accordance with a puppy dog strategy. As for advertising, the analysis reveals that investment made Kodak soft: advertising contributed mainly to expand the market and it was estimated that an increase in Kodak's advertising budget benefited Fuji proportionally more than it benefited Kodak. Applying the taxonomy in this case tells us that the fat cat strategy is appropriate (overinvest to appear inoffensive). Kodak clearly adopted this strategy as its post-entry advertising budget was 3.2 times its pre-entry budget in real dollar terms.

In the next two sections, we apply the previous taxonomy to a number of specific examples, in which the 'investment' K_1 takes on various meanings.

16.2   Strategies affecting cost variables

While the incumbent's strategic options are often multiple, we present here a number of selected strategic actions an incumbent firm may take to affect post-entry competition and thus entry itself. We start with actions related to cost variables, either the incumbent's own cost or the entrant's cost. We consider actions related to demand variables in the next section.

16.2.1   Investment in capacity as an entry deterrent

In this part of the analysis, we focus on installed capacity as a strategic variable. The idea is that an incumbent firm, by installing capacity early on, credibly conveys to its potential competitor that it will have low marginal costs and thus be a tough competitor to deal with. This may convince a potential entrant that it will not recover its entry costs. In this case, the incumbent can maintain its monopoly position in spite of the threat of entry. In particular, for an intermediate level of entry costs, the incumbent may strategically distort its investment upward. Note that in practice many investment decisions are lumpy and thus automatically give commitment. However, in other cases, capacity is related to contracts with upstream suppliers. Here, the incumbent may sign long-term supply contracts that are costly to revise. It may also sign long-term labour contracts which make part of the labour costs a fixed cost that cannot be avoided.

To relate the present analysis to our previous taxonomy, note that we analyse a situation where investment makes the incumbent tough and where firms compete in quantities in the second stage (strategic substitutability). We will check that the incumbent chooses to follow the *top dog strategy*, whether he deters or accommodates entry.

We analyse the following multi-stage game between an incumbent firm (indexed by 1) and a potential entrant (indexed by 2).[60] At stage 1, the incumbent sets capacity $\overline{q}_1$. At stage 2, the entrant decides upon entry and the active firms, i.e., the incumbent and the entrant if it decided to enter, set additional capacity and produce a quantity that is not larger than the installed capacity; that is, the incumbent sets $\Delta \overline{q}_1 \geq 0$ and $q_1 \leq \overline{q}_1 + \Delta \overline{q}_1$, and the entrant sets $\Delta \overline{q}_2 \geq 0$ and $q_2 \leq \Delta \overline{q}_2$. The products of the two firms are assumed to be homogeneous and the inverse demand has the linear form $P(q) = 1 - q = 1 - q_1 - q_2$.

We assume the following cost structure. Let e denote the sunk costs paid at stage 2 in case of entry; let k denote the marginal cost of an expansion in capacity; and let c denote the marginal cost of production. Accordingly, the incumbent's cost function at stage 1 is given by

$$C_1^1(\bar{q}_1) = k\bar{q}_1.$$

At stage 2, the variable costs of the incumbent and the entrant are respectively given by

$$C_1^2(q_1, \Delta\bar{q}_1) = cq_1 + k\Delta\bar{q}_1,$$
$$C_2^2(q_2) = cq_2 + k\Delta\bar{q}_2.$$

To understand this cost structure, we can think of production requiring the input of both capital and labour, the cost of one unit of capital being k and the cost of one unit of labour being c. If the incumbent wishes to produce more than its installed capacity $\bar{q}_1$, it must hire the additional capacity $\Delta\bar{q}_1$ at cost k per unit and it must also hire the corresponding additional labour at cost c per unit.

If firm 2 has decided to enter at stage 1, the firms play a Cournot duopoly at stage 2. The incumbent's profit function is $\pi_1 = (1 - q_1 - q_2 - c)q_1 - k\Delta\bar{q}_1$. Suppose firm 1 installs additional capacity at stage 2, i.e. $\Delta\bar{q}_1 > 0$. To be profit-maximizing it must make its total capacity, $\bar{q}_1 + \Delta\bar{q}_1$, available on the market. Any additional unit sold requires additional capacity. Hence, if the incumbent wishes to produce more than the capacity installed in stage 1, $q_1 > \bar{q}_1$, it has to acquire additional capacity and the marginal cost is $(c + k)$. Suppose now that firm 1 does not install additional capacity so that $q_1 \leq \bar{q}_1$. The marginal cost of production then is c. The first-order derivative of profits with respect to q_1 is thus

$$\frac{\partial \pi_1}{\partial q_1} = \begin{cases} 1 - 2q_1 - q_2 - c - k & \text{for } q_1 > \bar{q}_1, \\ 1 - 2q_1 - q_2 - c & \text{for } q_1 \leq \bar{q}_1. \end{cases}$$

It follows that the incumbent's best-response function takes the following form:

$$q_1(q_2) = \begin{cases} \frac{1}{2}(1 - q_2 - c - k) & \text{for } q_1 > \bar{q}_1, \\ \frac{1}{2}(1 - q_2 - c) & \text{for } q_1 \leq \bar{q}_1. \end{cases}$$

As depicted in the left panel of Figure 16.1, there are two possible curves: the upper curve becomes the reaction function if there is spare capacity (i.e. for $q_1 \leq \bar{q}_1$), and the lower curve if capacity has to be extended (i.e. for $q_1 > \bar{q}_1$). Note that at the capacity level $\bar{q}_1$, the incumbent's best-response at stage 2 is not affected by small changes of the competitor's quantity, namely for quantities between $\tilde{\tilde{q}}_2 = 1 - c - k - 2\bar{q}_1$ and $\tilde{q}_2 = 1 - c - 2\bar{q}_1$. This can be illustrated by considering the incumbent's profit function for different values of q_2, as done in Figure 16.2.

As for the entrant, the profit function is given by $\pi_2 = (1 - q_1 - q_2 - c)q_2 - k\Delta\bar{q}_2 - e$. Because the entrant has no initial capacity, $q_2 = \Delta\bar{q}_2 > 0$ and the first-order condition for profit maximization is

$$\frac{\partial \pi_2}{\partial q_2} = 1 - q_1 - 2q_2 - c - k = 0.$$

Solving for q_2 in the latter expression, we find firm 2's candidate best-response to firm 1's quantity:

$$q_2(q_1) = \frac{1}{2}(1 - q_1 - c - k). \tag{16.3}$$

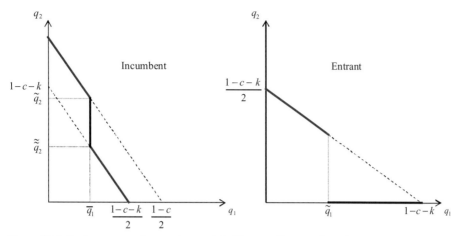

Figure 16.1 Best responses in an entry model with capacity commitment

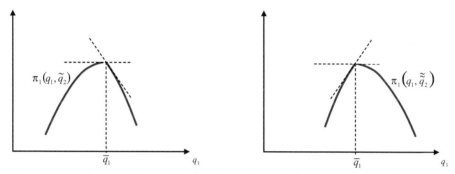

Figure 16.2 The incumbent's profit function in an entry model with capacity commitment.

This quantity is firm 2's actual best-response as long as it generates non-negative net profits:

$$\pi_2(q_1) = (1 - q_1 - q_2(q_1) - c - k) q_2(q_1) - e$$
$$= \tfrac{1}{4}(1 - q_1 - c - k)^2 - e \geq 0,$$

which is equivalent to

$$q_1 \leq \widetilde{q}_1 \equiv 1 - c - k - 2\sqrt{e}.$$

We assume that $e < \tfrac{1}{4}(1 - c - k)^2$ so that $\widetilde{q}_1 > 0$ (otherwise, entry would not even be profitable if the entrant could become a monopoly). In short, the potential entrant optimally chooses to enter and produce the positive quantity given by (16.3) as long as the incumbent's quantity does not exceed $\widetilde{q}_1$, and to stay out of the market otherwise (which amounts to produce nothing and to save the sunk entry cost e). The right panel of Figure 16.1, depicts the entrant's reaction function.

The second-stage equilibrium takes place at the intersection of the two firms' reaction functions. Which intersection obtains depends on where the two functions 'jump'. The entrant's reaction function jumps down to zero at $\widetilde{q}_1$ (i.e., at the output of firm 1 above which entry is not profitable, which is itself a decreasing function of the entry cost e). As for firm 1's reaction

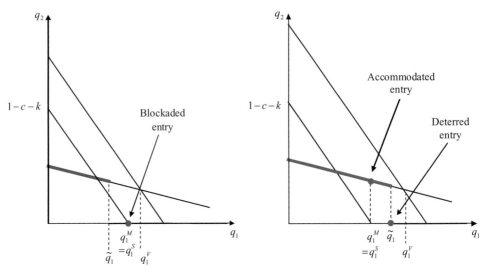

Figure 16.3 Possible equilibria in an entry model with capacity commitment

function, the jump is endogenous as it depends on the incumbent's initial choice of capacity $\bar{q}_1$. That is, the incumbent has the option of choosing which reaction function it presents in the post-entry duopoly by committing to a level of installed capacity.

There are three possibilities to consider. The first possibility corresponds to the case of *blockaded entry*. In that case, entry is not profitable although the incumbent behaves as an unconstrained monopolist. What would be the choices of an unconstrained monopolist? It would install a capacity $\bar{q}_1$ at cost $k\bar{q}_1$ and then produce up to this capacity at cost $c\bar{q}_1$. Therefore, an incumbent monopolist chooses q_1 to maximize $\pi_1 = (1 - c - k - q_1)q_1$, which gives

$$q_1^M = \tfrac{1}{2}(1 - c - k).$$

Entry is blockaded if the monopoly output is larger than the output $\tilde{q}_1$ under which entry becomes profitable: $q_1^M > \tilde{q}_1$, which is equivalent to

$$e > e^+ \equiv \tfrac{1}{16}(1 - c - k)^2.$$

This possibility is depicted in the left panel of Figure 16.3.

The second possibility is the exact opposite of the first. It corresponds to the case where *entry is inevitable*. Firm 2 always finds it profitable to enter because it knows that the maximum amount firm 1 is willing to produce is below $\tilde{q}_1$. What is this maximum amount? If firm 2 enters, the best Nash equilibrium from the point of view of firm 1 is on the upper part of firm 1's reaction function, i.e., the curve corresponding to the case where unlimited initial capacity would be available (meaning that marginal cost is c rather than $c + k$; see Figure 16.1). The Nash equilibrium is the solution of the following system of equations: $q_1 = \tfrac{1}{2}(1 - q_2 - c)$ and $q_2 = \tfrac{1}{2}(1 - q_1 - c - k)$. Solving for q_1, we find

$$q_1^V = \tfrac{1}{3}(1 - c + k).$$

Facing firm 2's entry, the incumbent does not find it profitable to produce more than q_1^V. Therefore, in stage 1, it will not find it profitable either to install a larger capacity than q_1^V. In other words, capacity levels above q_1^V are not credible threats of entry deterrence and firm 2 has thus no reason to fear them (which confirms the incumbent in its decision not to install such levels). Hence, if firm 2 can achieve positive profits at this Nash equilibrium, it will certainly enter. This is so if $\tilde{q}_1 > q_1^V$, which is equivalent to[b]

$$e < e^- \equiv \tfrac{1}{9} (1 - c - 2k)^2 .$$

Now, knowing that entry is inevitable, firm 1 will exploit its first-mover advantage to limit the scale of entry. To maximize its profit in the face of entry, firm 1 will behave as a Stackelberg leader. As we described it in Chapter 4, the incumbent anticipates the entrant's reaction when choosing its capacity in stage 1. That is, firm 1 sets q_1 to maximize

$$\pi_1 = (1 - c - k - q_1 - q_2 (q_1)) q_1 = \tfrac{1}{2} (1 - c - k - q_1) q_1.$$

The maximum is easily found as

$$q_1^S = \tfrac{1}{2} (1 - c - k) .$$

In this linear model, a Stackelberg leader happens to choose the same capacity (and output) as a monopolist: $q_1^S = q_1^M$. Note that q_1^S will be firm 1's choice in this situation provided $q_1^S \leq q_1^V$. It can be checked that this is so as long as the cost of capacity expansion is large enough (precisely if $k \geq (1 - c)/5$, which also guarantees that $e^+ > e^-$).

The last possibility corresponds to the case where *entry is neither blockaded nor inevitable*, i.e., $q_1^M = q_1^S \leq \tilde{q}_1 \leq q_1^V$ or $e^- \leq e \leq e^+$. This case is probably the most interesting as entry depends on the incumbent's initial capacity choice. The incumbent has indeed two options: it can either *accommodate* or *deter* entry. Entry accommodation corresponds to our previous case: firm 1 behaves as a Stackelberg leader and chooses capacity q_1^S, which yields a profit of

$$\pi_1^A = \tfrac{1}{2} \left(1 - c - k - q_1^S \right) q_1^S = \tfrac{1}{8} (1 - c - k)^2 .$$

To deter entry, firm 1 must install a larger capacity since $\tilde{q}_1 > q_1^S$. This has the negative effect of lowering the market price but the positive effect of keeping the entrant at bay. In that case, firm 1's profit is computed as

$$\pi_1^D (e) = (1 - c - k - \tilde{q}_1) \tilde{q}_1 = 2\sqrt{e} \left(1 - c - k - 2\sqrt{e} \right) .$$

It can be checked that $\pi_1^D (e)$ is an increasing function of the entry cost e for $e \leq e^+$. Intuitively, entry is easier to deter when it is more costly. Hence, the incumbent prefers deterrence over accommodation if the entry cost is large enough. Some computations establish that on the relevant range of entry costs, $\pi_1^D (e) > \pi_1^A$ for $e > e^*$, with

$$e^* \equiv \tfrac{(2-\sqrt{2})^2}{64} (1 - c - k)^2 .$$

The latter threshold is clearly smaller than $e^+ = \tfrac{1}{16} (1 - c - k)^2$. Depending on the value of k, e^* can be larger or smaller than $e^- = \tfrac{1}{9} (1 - c - 2k)^2$.[c] In the former case ($e^* > e^-$), the

---

[b] We suppose here that $k < (1 - c)/2$. Otherwise, $\tilde{q}_1 < q_1^V$ even for $e = 0$ (in that case, even free entry would not take place because the incumbent's advantage in terms of marginal cost would be too large).
[c] To be precise, $e^* > e^-$ for $k > 0.44 (1 - c)$. As we have assumed that $(1 - c)/5 < k < (1 - c)/2$, both cases are possible.

incumbent chooses to accommodate entry for $e^- \leq e < e^*$ and to deter it for $e^* \leq e \leq e^+$; in the latter case, the incumbent always chooses to deter entry. The two options are illustrated in the right panel of Figure 16.3.

We can summarize our analysis as follows.

> **Lesson 16.3** In an entry model with capacity commitment, the incumbent's conduct depends on the cost of entry, e. For small entry costs ($e < e^*$), the incumbent prefers to accommodate entry and behave as a Stackelberg leader. For intermediate entry costs ($e^* \leq e \leq e^+$), the incumbent chooses to deter entry by expanding its capacity. For large entry costs ($e > e^+$), the incumbent can behave as an unconstrained monopolist as entry is blockaded.

Case 16.2 explains the difficulties in testing the predictions of the previous lesson, and how these difficulties can be overcome in some settings.

> **Case 16.2 Entry deterrence in hospital procedure markets**[61]
>
> Empirically testing whether firms invest in capacity to deter entry requires to estimate the ex ante threat of entry and the investments that would have been made absent strategic motives. Because each of these parameters can be a challenge to estimate, it is not surprising that the literature on this topic is rather limited.[62] Testing becomes easier in settings where potential entrants are easy to identify, and where investment trends and deviations thereof can be observed. This happens to be the case in markets for inpatient surgical procedure, which are a primary output of the hospital industry.
>
> Dafny (2005) focuses on electrophysiological studies (EP), a procedure to identify and correct cardiac arrhythmias. He explicitly models the demand and supply for this procedure and uses this model to illustrate the incentives to invest strategically in volume-increasing assets or activities, focusing on incumbents' ability to deter entry through this channel.
>
> The empirical test used to investigate whether the entry deterrence motive affects investment decisions is based on the following insight.[63] Investment levels are likely to increase monotonically with market potential if firms act non-strategically. However, if firms act in a strategic way, they should invest more in markets of intermediate attractiveness because entry deterrence is unnecessary in very small markets and impossible in very large ones. Note that if entry costs are inversely proportional to market potential, this is also what Lesson 16.3 suggests. Hence a non-monotonic relationship between investment and market size constitutes evidence of a strong entry-deterrence motive.
>
> Dafny observes such a non-monotonic relationship: in the year following an announced reimbursement increase for EP (which raised the threat of entry), incumbents in moderately attractive markets generated a volume growth that was statistically significantly greater than that in unattractive or very attractive markets.

The remaining issue is whether entry deterrence is anticompetitive. A priori, the answer seems ambiguous: actual competition does not take place but potential competition forces the incumbent to expand its capacity. To get some insight, we consider intermediate entry costs ($e^* \leq e \leq e^+$) and we compare the market price that prevails when entry is deterred with the one that would prevail if entry was accommodated. When entry is deterred, the incumbent remains a monopoly and produces $\tilde{q}_1 = 1 - c - k - 2\sqrt{e}$. The market price under deterrence is then

$$p^d = 1 - \tilde{q}_1 = c + k + 2\sqrt{e}.$$

If entry had been accommodated, firms would play as in the Stackelberg game. That is, the incumbent would produce $q_1^S = \frac{1}{2}(1 - c - k)$, and the entrant would react by producing $q_2^S = \frac{1}{2}\left(1 - q_1^S - c - k\right) = \frac{1}{4}(1 - c - k)$. Hence, the market price under accommodation would be

$$p^a = 1 - q_1^S - q_2^S = \frac{1}{4}(1 + 3c + 3k).$$

Comparing the two expressions, we observe that the market price is lower under deterrence than under accommodation if

$$p^d < p^a \Leftrightarrow e < \frac{1}{64}(1 - c - k)^2 \equiv e^c.$$

Observing that $(2 - \sqrt{2})^2 \simeq 0.343$, it is clear that $e^c \in [e^*, e^+]$. We can thus conclude the following:

Lesson 16.4 **Suppose that entry costs are such that the incumbent prefers to deter entry. Then, if entry costs are not too large, consumer surplus is higher if entry is deterred instead of being accommodated. The opposite prevails for larger entry cost.**

We could also compare total surplus under deterrence and accommodation and we would reach a similar conclusion: because entry deterrence forces the incumbent to increase its capacity beyond the accommodation level, deterrence can turn out to be welfare-improving.

16.2.2   Investment as an entry deterrent reconsidered

We consider now a simple model of R&D competition (an issue we will return to in Chapter 18).[64] Let K_1 be some investment that allows firm 1 to lower its average (and marginal) cost of production in the first stage. We write $\bar{c}(K_1)$, with $\bar{c}'(K_1) < 0$. The incumbent's first-period profits are $\pi^m(\bar{c}(K_1))$, which is an increasing function of K_1.

In the second period, the incumbent and the entrant compete in R&D, and potentially in prices. Regarding R&D, each firm spends resources x_i to increase its chances to find an innovation that allows constant average cost c. The R&D technology in the second period is stochastic: firm i's probability of finding the innovation is given by $\mu_i(x_i)$, with $\mu_i'(0) = \infty$, $\mu_i' > 0$, and $\mu_i'' < 0$ (which represents decreasing returns to scale in R&D).

The innovation is said to be drastic (or major) in the sense that if only one firm finds it, this firm is able to drive the other firm out of the market. The innovating firm then obtains profits $\pi^m(c)$. If both firms find the innovation, they are both able to produce a homogeneous good at the same cost; price competition then drives their profits down to zero. Finally, if no firm finds the innovation, the incumbent keeps its first-period profit $\pi^m(\overline{c}(K_1))$, whereas the entrant stays out of the market (because it has no technology to fall back on) and makes zero profit. We obtain thus the following expected profits in the second period, given entry and given K_1:

$$\begin{cases} \pi_1 = \mu_1(1-\mu_2)\pi^m(c) + (1-\mu_1)(1-\mu_2)\pi^m(\overline{c}(K_1)) - x_1, \\ \pi_2 = \mu_2(1-\mu_1)\pi^m(c) - x_2. \end{cases}$$

The incumbent chooses x_1 to maximize π_1 and the entrant choose x_2 to maximize π_2. The first-order conditions for a Nash equilibrium are

$$\begin{cases} \mu_1'[\pi^m(c) - \pi^m(\overline{c}(K_1))](1-\mu_2) = 1, \\ \mu_2'\pi^m(c)(1-\mu_1) = 1. \end{cases}$$

As we assume that $\mu_i' > 0$ and $\mu_i'' < 0$, we see in both first-order conditions that x_i and x_j have to move in opposite directions to maintain the equality. In other words, reaction curves are downward sloping, or R&D expenditures are strategic substitutes (if one firm spends more, the other reacts by spending less).

It remains to be seen whether first-period investment makes the incumbent tough or soft. An increase in K_1 reduces the first-period marginal cost and thereby increases $\pi^m(\overline{c}(K_1))$. This means that the incumbent's fall-back position in the second period improves if it fails to find the innovation. Hence, a larger value of K_1 *lowers* the incumbent's incentive to innovate: investment makes the incumbent *soft*.[65] Yet, this is precisely what the incumbent wants to avoid. Since R&D expenditures are strategic substitutes, firm 1 wants to commit to play more aggressively and increase its incentive to innovate. Therefore, it will tend to reduce K_1, i.e., to *underinvest* in the first period.

This model illustrates thus the *lean and hungry look* strategy in the case of entry accommodation. Moreover, because K_1 has no direct effect on π_2, we know that it is also the appropriate strategy to deter entry.

16.2.3   Raising rivals' costs

The strategies we have considered so far in this section were turned towards the incumbent's own cost function. The incumbent's goal was to find a credible way to shift his second-stage reaction function so as to deter entry or to accommodate it in the most profitable way. Clearly, accommodation or deterrence can also be achieved by acting directly on the entrant's cost function. For instance, the incumbent could sabotage the entrant's production facilities, or lobby the government to raise taxes on imported products so as to deter the entry of foreign competitors. Here, the direct effect of the incumbent's investment on the entrant's profit (i.e. $\partial \pi_2 / \partial K_1$) would be sufficiently negative to allow the incumbent to deter entry without having to commit to a costly course of action. Such strategies are clearly anticompetitive and are too transparent to need further analysis.

More interesting are cost-raising strategies that force the incumbent to raise his own costs as well. These include lobbying efforts that, if successful, e.g., increase labour costs (or the cost for imported inputs). For example, with the liberalization of the German postal market, the incumbent Deutsche Post was pushing for minimum wage legislation in this sector to apply also to newcomers.[d] There is now a trade-off between the harm the incumbent does to the potential entrant and the harm it does to itself. Analyses of this trade-off can be performed in models with one incumbent and a competitive fringe.[66] Using a model of this type, we showed in Chapter 2 that the dominant firm does indeed have an incentive to increase the cost of the competitive fringe even though this increases its own cost in the same way.

Here, we want to recast the analysis of cost-raising strategies within the framework we have used in this section. Using our previous notation, we have both $\partial \pi_2 / \partial K_1 < 0$ and $\partial \pi_1 / \partial K_1 < 0$. Thus, our previous taxonomy proves ill-suited to characterize strategies of this kind. In particular, we will see that the nature of the second-stage competition is of a lesser importance: all other things being equal, raising the rival's cost deteriorates the rival's position whether the firms' actions are strategic substitutes or complements. What is clear anyway is that using such strategies is a form of *overinvestment* since a non-strategic incumbent would not deliberately increase its own cost. Intuitively, an incumbent would accept to hurt itself only if it could hurt the rival relatively more in the process.

As above, we consider a two-stage game. At the first stage, firm 1 chooses the level of some 'investment', K_1, that has the effect of raising its own (constant) marginal cost, as well as the (constant) marginal cost of the entrant: both $c_1 (K_1)$ and $c_2 (K_1)$ are increasing functions of K_1. At the second stage, firm 2 decides to enter and product market decisions are made (in a duopoly if the entrant enters, and in a monopoly otherwise).

Let us denote the second-stage equilibrium profits by $\pi_i^* (c_i (K_1), c_j (K_1))$. Whatever the nature of second-stage competition, firm i's equilibrium profit increases with its rival's marginal cost and decreases with its own marginal cost. The marginal rate of substitution between these two effects can be expressed by the following ratio:

$$\rho_i \equiv \frac{\partial \pi_i^* / \partial c_j}{-\left(\partial \pi_i^* / \partial c_i\right)} > 0. \tag{16.4}$$

For a cost-raising strategy to have an entry-deterring effect, it is necessary that the effect of K_1 on π_2^* be negative:

$$\frac{d \pi_2^*}{d K_1} = \underbrace{\frac{\partial \pi_2^*}{\partial c_1}}_{+} \underbrace{\frac{\partial c_1}{\partial K_1}}_{+} + \underbrace{\frac{\partial \pi_2^*}{\partial c_2}}_{-} \underbrace{\frac{\partial c_2}{\partial K_1}}_{+} < 0 \Leftrightarrow \frac{\partial c_2 / \partial K_1}{\partial c_1 / \partial K_1} > \rho_2. \tag{16.5}$$

In the case of entry accommodation, the incumbent chooses a cost-raising strategy if it increases its own profit:

$$\frac{d \pi_1^*}{d K_1} = \underbrace{\frac{\partial \pi_1^*}{\partial c_1}}_{-} \underbrace{\frac{\partial c_1}{\partial K_1}}_{+} + \underbrace{\frac{\partial \pi_1^*}{\partial c_2}}_{+} \underbrace{\frac{\partial c_2}{\partial K_1}}_{+} > 0 \Leftrightarrow \frac{\partial c_2 / \partial K_1}{\partial c_1 / \partial K_1} > \frac{1}{\rho_1}. \tag{16.6}$$

As long as $\rho_1 \rho_2 < 1$, we have that condition (16.6) is more stringent than condition (16.5). This implies that if the cost-raising strategy does not have an entry-deterring effect, it will certainly not be chosen when the incumbent prefers to accommodate entry.

---

[d] Due to their lower market penetration their services are likely to be more labour intensive. Minimum wage legislation then affects them much more than the incumbent.

This conclusion seems reasonable as it turns out that $\rho_i < 1$ for a large class of models. Consider for instance the model of horizontal product differentiation that we introduced in Chapter 3, with the linear inverse demand schedule $p_i = a - q_i - dq_j$ ($i, j \in \{1, 2\}, i \neq j$). Under Cournot competition, firm i chooses its quantity q_i to maximize $\pi_i = (a - q_i - dq_j - c_i)q_i$. From the first-order condition, we derive firm i's reaction function: $q_i(q_j) = \frac{1}{2}(a - c_i - dq_j)$. Proceeding in a similar way for firm j, we find $q_j(q_i) = \frac{1}{2}(a - c_j - dq_i)$. Solving for the Nash equilibrium, we obtain

$$q_i^{C*} = \frac{(2 - d)a - 2c_i + dc_j}{4 - d^2}. \tag{16.7}$$

It is easily checked, using the first-order condition, that the equilibrium profit is simply the square of the equilibrium quantity. Hence, we find $\rho_i = d/2 < 1$ for all $d \in [0, 1]$. Repeating the analysis with price competition, we would find $\rho_i = d/(2 - d^2) < 1$ for all $d \in [0, 1]$. We can thus safely conclude the following.

Lesson 16.5 **Cost-raising strategies (i.e., strategies that raise the rival's cost but also the incumbent's) are more likely to be used to deter entry than to accommodate it.**

Case 16.3 illustrates how incumbents sometimes use the regulatory process to increase rivals' costs and thereby deter entry by presumably more efficient competitors.

Case 16.3 Regulatory entry deterrence in the professions[67]

Professional regulations on business structure and practices exist for many professions in many countries. Some of these regulations place restrictions on the entry to certain professions. Entry restrictions can be either qualitative or quantitative. Qualitative restrictions ensure that only those with appropriate qualifications and expertise have access to the profession, thereby safeguarding quality of service. Quantitative restrictions are mainly designed to guarantee access to important services. For instance, many countries impose entry controls in the form of quantitative limits (based on geographic and/or demographic criteria) for the notary and pharmacy professions.

These regulations are usually set by governments or by self-regulatory bodies. In the latter case (but, due to lobbying, also in the former), subgroups of professionals may be tempted to influence the regulatory process to increase rivals' costs and thereby deter rivals' entry. To test the presence of such 'strategic regulatory entry deterrence', Haas-Wilson (1989) examines the US ophthalmic industry in the period 1970–85. In her data she identifies whether regulation is in place in a particular US state at a given point in time. Her hypothesis is that self-employed optometrists have managed to deter entry of their larger commercial rivals in some geographic areas by obtaining regulations constraining commercial operations (namely commercial practice restrictions regarding employment, trade name, advertising, location and branch office). The model distinguishes entry according to the subgroup of the firm (i.e., whether or not the optometrist is self-employed). In the empirical model the frequency of entry is a function of the incentives to enter the industry. These depend on subgroup-specific entry barriers. The estimations reveal that the three largest chains opened 1.5 to 1.7 fewer stores per year in fully regulated versus nonregulated states. The results suggest thus that cost-raising strategies can be used to restrict entry into the market without the need to lower price.

In Chapter 17, where we consider vertically related markets, we will analyse a number of similar strategies. In particular, we will examine how exclusive contracts may be used as entry-deterring strategies.

16.3   Strategies affecting demand variables

An incumbent can also react to the threat of entry by committing to reduce the demand that is available for the entrant. Several variables of the marketing mix can be used to achieve this objective. In this section, we focus on product positioning, bundling and switching costs. In terms of product positioning, an incumbent may decide to increase the number of varieties it puts on the market so as to leave fewer niches that an entrant could occupy. We study this practice of 'brand proliferation' in Subsection 16.3.1. Regarding bundling, the basic idea we develop in Subsection 16.3.2 is the following: an incumbent controlling two products and facing entry on the market of one of them may find it profitable to offer the two products as a bundle so as to make entry less profitable. Finally, in Subsection 16.3.3, we examine the incumbent's incentives to build an earlier base of customers when threatened by entry in a market with switching costs.

16.3.1   Brand proliferation

Businesses typically offer a variety of products. They may do so for various reasons: to take advantage of economies of scale and scope in production, to exploit possible demand complementarities or to mitigate asymmetric information problems. However, offering a variety of products may also be the strategy of choice due to the threat of entry. An incumbent firm may indeed offer a product range beyond what would be privately optimal if it was protected from competitors. That is, due to the threat of entry by competitors, the incumbent may decide to increase its product range with the intent to keep competitors outside the market for a certain range of products.

To see this argument, suppose that an incumbent firm can produce a base product which is located at position zero in some product space. In addition, it may want to install a modification of this product, which serves as an imperfect substitute to the base product. Denote the corresponding monopoly profits by $\pi^m(1)$ and $\pi^m(2)$, respectively (where 1 and 2 refer to the number of products marketed by the firm). Suppose that $\pi^m(1) > \pi^m(2)$. Hence, it is privately optimal to produce a single product in the protected monopoly.

Consider now the following three-stage game. At stage 1, firm 1 decides whether to offer only the base product or both products. At stage 2, a competitor may enter and offer a product that directly competes with the second, modified product. For the sake of the argument, let us suppose that the latter two products are perfect substitutes. If the competitor enters it has to pay the entry cost e. At stage 3, firms simultaneously set prices. Consumers make purchasing decisions and firms collect profits.

If entry takes place at stage 2, firms will set prices in equilibrium at stage 3 such that profits $\pi_i^d(k)$ are obtained, where i is the index of the firm and k is the number of products offered by the incumbent. The entrant's profits at stage 2 are therefore $\pi_2^d(1) - e$ (which we assume to be positive) if it competes against a single-product incumbent, whereas they are $0 - e$ if it competes against a two-product firm because it competes head-on with the second of the incumbent's products. Clearly, entry in the latter case is not profitable. This gives the incumbent the possibility of deterring entry by offering both products. Such deterrence is profitable if $\pi^m(2) > \pi_1^d(1)$. If this inequality is satisfied, there is a unique subgame perfect equilibrium in which firm 1 uses brand proliferation to deter entry.

Lesson 16.6   An incumbent firm may use brand proliferation to deter entry.

The ready-to-eat breakfast cereal industry provides an illustration of the use of brand proliferation to deter entry, as described in Case 16.4.

Case 16.4   Entry deterrence in the ready-to-eat cereal industry[68]

The production of ready-to-eat (RTE) breakfast cereal has been highly concentrated in the US from the 1940s to the early 1970s. The four major manufacturers (Kellogg, General Foods, General Mills and Quaker Oats) were making at least 85% of sales, and this number was up to 95% when including the next two largest producers. During this period, there was no single entry of significant importance into this industry. It was only in the early 1970s that several large firms were able to enter the industry thanks to a sharp increase in demand that had not been well anticipated by most of the established firms.

The lack of noticeable entry over a long period of time into a profitable and growing industry can only be attributed to the presence of some barrier to entry. None of the 'usual suspects' – such as economies of scale, capital requirements, product differentiation, patents, or control of raw material sources – seems sufficient to explain that large food processing firms (like Colgate) did not find it profitable to enter during that period, although they did afterwards when the demand grew unexpectedly. For instance, the minimum efficient firm size was estimated to be a 3–5% market share, which does not appear as insurmountable.

This leaves brand proliferation as a potential explanation for the lack of entry. Indeed, it turns out that, although no new *firm* entered, new *brands* were regularly introduced by incumbent firms. Schmalensee (1978) reports that the six leading producers introduced over 80 brands between 1950 and 1972. It is precisely in 1972 that the Federal Trade Commission issued a complaint over the four top producers, alleging that 'these practices of proliferating brands, differentiating similar products and promoting trademarks through intensive advertising result in high barriers to entry into the RTE cereal market' (quoted by Schmalensee, 1978).

Our insight that the incumbent may use brand proliferation as an entry deterrence relies on the implicit assumption that exit from the industry is sufficiently costly. With sufficiently small exit costs, our conclusions are altered drastically, as we are now going to argue.[69] Suppose that between stages 2 and 3 (say at stage 2.5), both firms have the option to withdraw the modified product at an exit cost x. Provided that both firms decided to offer their products and then have the possibility to revise their decision, the pay-off matrix at this intermediate step is the one of Table 16.1.

Table 16.1. *Payoffs in the brand proliferation game*

		Firm 2	
		Stay	Exit
Firm 1	Stay	$\pi_1^d(2), 0$	$\pi^m(2), -x$
	Exit	$\pi_1^d(1) - x, \pi_2^d(1)$	$\pi^m(1) - x, -x$

Since the entry costs are sunk at this stage it is a dominant strategy for the entrant to stay. Given that the entrant stays, the profit-maximizing decision for the incumbent depends on the level of exit costs. Note that $\pi_1^d(2) < \pi_1^d(1)$ because, in the former case, intense competition among the modified products negatively affects the profits of the incumbent's base product. In other words, the presence of the incumbent's modified product exerts a negative effect on the incumbent's profits with respect to its base product (a form of 'cannibalization'). Therefore, if the exit cost is not too high, i.e., if it is such that $x < \pi_1^d(1) - \pi_1^d(2)$, the incumbent will withdraw its modified product. This implies that brand proliferation as an entry-deterring strategy is not credible for intermediate levels of exit costs. It is only if the incumbent can commit not to exit that brand proliferation survives as an entry deterrent.

Lesson 16.7   **If the incumbent can withdraw its product at sufficiently low cost from a segment in which it faces a direct competitor, brand proliferation is not a credible strategy for entry deterrence.**

16.3.2   Bundling and leverage of market power

In Chapter 11, we already examined the practice of bundling, which consists in selling two or more products in a single package. Bundling was presented there as an effective tool for sorting consumers and price discriminate between them. Here, we consider another potential motivation for bundling products, namely entry deterrence. The basic idea is the following. Suppose that an incumbent firm is a monopolist in the market for product A but faces potential competition in the market for product B. By bundling products A and B, the incumbent may reduce the demand addressed to a rival firm producing product B and thereby, make entry unprofitable or induce exit from the industry.

We check this conjecture by analysing the following model.[70] Suppose firm 1 has a protected monopoly for product A. For product B, we consider a homogeneous product market

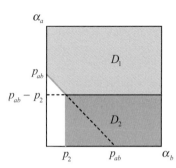

Figure 16.4 Demand in the duopoly model with bundling by firm 1

on which firms 1 and 2 can be active. Consumers have valuations α_a and α_b for products A and B respectively, which are supposed to be uniformly and independently distributed on the $[0, 1]$ interval. The willingness-to-pay is thus uniformly distributed on the unit square. Suppose that good B can be produced by any firm at zero marginal costs and fixed costs are $f > 0$. Hence, the market for good B (considered in isolation) is a natural monopoly because at most one firm can operate profitably under price competition.

Suppose that in the status quo firm 1 serves the market for product A and firm 2 the market for product B. In the status quo, firm 1 sets price $p_1 = 1/2$ and makes profit $1/4$. Similarly, firm 2 sets price $p_2 = 1/2$ and makes profit $1/4 - f$. Suppose now that firm 1 considers entering the market of firm 2. To be precise, at stage 1a, firm 1 decides whether to enter market B and if it does so, whether to sell products A and B separately or as a pure bundle. As a response, firm B can exit the market at stage 1b before engaging in price competition. At stage 2, firms set prices simultaneously.

Selling separately is not necessarily profitable in equilibrium. Consider equilibria of the subgame which start after firm 1's entry into market B. Suppose firm 2 stays in the market. Then, if firm 1 also stayed Bertrand competition would drive prices down to marginal costs. In such a situation, firm 1 would have to bear the fixed cost f without any positive profit margin in market B. It is thus profitable for firm 1 to exit. This justifies firm 2's decision to stay and firm 1 is better off not to enter market B to start with.

Alternatively, firm 1 may decide to sell products A and B as a bundle at price p_{ab}. In the situation with bundling, the consumers who decide to buy product B alone are such that (i) $\alpha_b - p_2 \geq \alpha_a + \alpha_b - p_{ab} \Leftrightarrow \alpha_a \leq p_{ab} - p_2$ (product B only is preferred to the bundle), and (ii) $\alpha_b - p_2 \geq 0 \Leftrightarrow \alpha_b \geq p_2$ (product B only is preferred to no consumption). Hence, firm 2's demand is $(1 - p_2)(p_{ab} - p_2)$, as illustrated in Figure 16.4 by the area D_2. (Note that in the figure valuations for product B are on the horizontal axis.)

Hence, the first-order condition of profit maximization for firm 2 is

$$(1 - 2p_2)(p_{ab} - p_2) - p_2(1 - p_2) = 0$$

and the best response can be written as

$$p_2^{br} = \frac{1 + p_{ab}}{3} - \frac{1}{3}\sqrt{1 - p_{ab} + p_{ab}^2}.$$

The consumers who buy the bundle are characterized by: (i) $\alpha_a + \alpha_b - p_{ab} \geq \alpha_b - p_2 \Leftrightarrow \alpha_a \geq p_{ab} - p_2$ (the bundle is preferred to product B only), and (ii) $\alpha_a + \alpha_b - p_{ab} \geq 0$ (the bundle is preferred to no consumption). Firm 1 thus faces demand $(1 - p_{ab} + p_2) - p_2^2/2$

(see region D_1 in Figure 16.4). The first-order condition of profit maximization of firm 1 is $p_2^2/2 - p_2 + 2p_{ab} - 1 = 0$ and the best response can be written as

$$p_{ab}^{br} = \frac{1 + p_2 - p_2^2/2}{2}.$$

Solving the system of first-order conditions gives equilibrium prices at stage 2: $p_{ab}^* \approx 0.61$ and $p_2^* \approx 0.24$. Equilibrium profits at stage 2 are $\pi_1^* \approx 0.369 - f$ and $\pi_2^* \approx 0.067 - f$, respectively. Compared to the status quo one obtains a change in profits of

$$\Delta \pi_1 \approx 0.119 - f,$$
$$\Delta \pi_2 \approx -0.183.$$

Hence, we observe that entering with a bundle is profitable for firm 1 independently of the possibility of exit of firm 2 if $f < 0.119$. In the full game, entry with a bundle can induce exit of firm 2 for an intermediate range of fixed costs. Namely, if $0.067 < f < 0.119$, in the unique subgame perfect equilibrium, firm 1 enters with a bundle at stage 1a, firm 2 exits at stage 1b and the firm sets the monopoly price for the bundle p_{ab}^m, that has been characterized in Chapter 11. For smaller fixed costs $f < 0.067$, firm 1's bundling decision does not induce exit and prices are p_{ab}^* and p_2^*. The analysis provides the following lesson:

Lesson 16.8   **A firm with market power in one market may be able to use pure bundling to leverage its market power into another second market and induce exit by firms operating in this second market.**

The reason to bundle a product here focuses on the market with potential competition. However, it is well conceivable that in a longer-term analysis, the monopoly position of firm 1 in market A is at risk if a competitor establishes itself successfully in market B.[71] In this case, firm 1 may forego short-term profit goals ($\Delta \pi_1$) and the use of technological bundling may allow firm 1 to induce exit of firm 2 in market B. If being successful in market B is prerequisite for entry in market A, firm 1's successful attempt to induce exit in market B protects its monopoly position in market A in the long term. Even if potential competitors can attack firm 1 in either market, due to limited resources and coordination failures a bundling strategy that leads to monopoly in markets 1 and 2 may be the best long-term strategy for firm 1. An additional argument can be made for bundling to improve the prospects of firm 1 which may be challenged in its 'home' market A. Bundling may be used as a commitment device for spending in R&D in market A, which effectively reduces the probability of entry in this market.[72] Such dynamic considerations have been important in one of the most exciting recent antitrust cases.

Case 16.5 The European Microsoft case[73]

In 2004, the European Commission found that Microsoft had leveraged its market power from its primary market for PC operating systems (OS) into the secondary, complementary market for work group server OS (workgroup servers are low-end servers that link with PC clients). In the primary market, Microsoft controlled over 90% of the market with Windows. In the secondary market, Microsoft's market share rose from 20% in the late 1990s to over 60% in 2001.

The Commission argued that at least part of this spectacular increase was due to anticompetitive actions and in particular, to Microsoft's deliberate restriction of the interoperability between Windows PCs and non-Microsoft work group servers. To be effective, the OS of work group servers must indeed work well with Windows, which runs on more than 90% of the PC. This requires the support of Microsoft since it controls the interfaces. Hence, Microsoft had the ability to reduce the interoperability of rival work group server OS. The Commission argued that Microsoft also had the incentives to do so. The dynamic incentives were particularly strong as Microsoft was concerned that customers could start running applications directly on servers, thereby reducing their reliance on the PC OS functionality. Hence, a strong presence of rivals in the server OS market could threaten Microsoft's monopoly position in the PC OS market. Microsoft had thus a clear interest in reducing the attractiveness of rival work group server OS by denying them interoperability with Windows. Network effects (see Chapter 20) did the rest of the job: as rival server OS lost market share, application developers shifted away from writing for them; customers (who value an OS for the variety of applications that are compatible with it) followed suit, which further decreased the developers' interest for non-Microsoft OS.

The restriction of interoperability can be seen as a form of virtual bundling between Microsoft's PC OS and work group server OS. In the parallel case on the Windows Media Player (a decoding software for media content), bundling was not virtual but real. Here, the Commission alleged that by bundling Windows Media Player with its Windows OS, Microsoft leveraged the market power derived from the PC OS into the market for encoding software for media content.

For these two cases, Microsoft was fined EUR 497 million and imposed behavioural remedies including compulsory licensing of intellectual property and forced unbundling. In 2007, Microsoft was fined a further EUR 280 million for delaying compliance with the remedy requiring the provision of technical information on the Windows interface in order to facilitate interoperability.

The conclusions in Chapter 11 are in stark contrast to the findings in this section. In a monopoly setting, we have seen that bundling may lead to expanded demand and a welfare-improving allocation relative to separate selling. In this section, we have pointed out potentially anticompetitive effects in an environment with potential entry. While we do not have a clear checklist to identify situations in which bundling is welfare-reducing, we can identify a number of factors which should raise concerns about the use of bundling. These factors are a large degree of market power in at least one of the markets, high levels of fixed or entry costs, the absence of other strong firms in related markets, a positive correlation of willingness-to-pay across products and the use of pure instead of mixed bundling.

16.3.3   Switching costs as an entry deterrent

We considered switching costs in Chapter 7. Recall that the key property of switching costs is that consumers who have bought from a particular firm in the past put a premium on continuing to purchase from the same firm. Typically, switching costs result from some firm-specific investments that the consumer cannot transfer to another supplier (e.g., investments in learning, in compatible equipment, in trust). In our previous analysis, we showed that the effects of switching costs on competition are ambiguous: depending on the specificities of the industry, switching costs may relax or intensify price competition.

Here, we examine how switching costs affect entry conditions and we reach another ambiguous conclusion. We consider an incumbent firm that sells a product exhibiting switching costs and that faces the potential entry of a competing firm. The question we ask is whether the incumbent has an incentive to expand (i.e., to overinvest in) or to contract (i.e., to underinvest in) its installed base of customers if it wants to deter entry. The answer is ambiguous because switching costs exert two opposite forces on entry. On the one hand, by expanding its customer base, the incumbent makes it more costly for the entrant to attract customers and, thereby, reduces the profitability of large-scale entry. Entry deterrence calls then for overinvestment (top dog strategy). On the other hand, switching costs may make small-scale entry more profitable if the incumbent cannot price discriminate between old and new buyers. In this case, an incumbent with a large installed base prefers to set a large price in order to 'skim' its locked-in consumers. As it sets the same price for unattached consumers, it makes it easier for an entrant to compete on that segment of the market. If this second force dominates, entry deterrence calls for underinvestment (lean and hungry look).

To illustrate these two forces, we come back to the model we introduced in Chapter 7.[74] Consumers of mass 1 are uniformly distributed on the interval $[0, 1]$. In the first period, only the incumbent, firm 1, is active. It is located at 0 and produces good 1 at zero marginal cost. Firm 2 has the possibility to enter in period 2. If it enters, its location is exogenously fixed at the other extreme of the interval; its marginal cost of production is also equal to zero. A consumer of type x incurs a disutility of $-x$ if she purchases a unit of product 1 and $-(1 - x)$ if she purchases a unit of product 2. Moreover, a consumer who has bought from the incumbent in period 1 incurs a switching cost of z if she buys from the entrant in period 2. We assume that all consumers stay in the market from one period to the next and newly draw their taste parameter in period 2.[e] Finally, to guarantee full participation, we assume that the reservation price of consumers, r, is sufficiently high.

Suppose that a share $0 < K_1 \leq 1$ of consumers have bought from the incumbent in period 1. In line with our taxonomy of entry-related strategies, we focus on the potential second-period competition and we are interested in signing the derivatives of the firms' equilibrium profits with respect to the 'investment' K_1, which is here the size of the incumbent's installed base of customers.

We first analyse the consumers' behaviour. A consumer located at x in period 2 and who has not bought from firm 1 in period 1 decides to buy from 1 in period 2 as long as $p_1 + x \leq p_2 + (1 - x)$, or $x \leq (1/2)(1 + p_2 - p_1) = \hat{x}$, where p_1 and p_2 are the prices set, respectively, by the incumbent and the entrant in period 2. On the other hand, if the consumer bought from firm 1 in period 1, she is more inclined to continue to do so in period 2 as switching to the entrant would cost her z; the condition to buy from firm 1 in period 2 becomes: $p_1 + x \leq p_2 + (1 - x) + z$, or $x \leq (1/2)(1 + p_2 - p_1 + z) = \hat{x} + (z/2)$. We

---

[e] The analysis would not change in any fundamental way if we assumed instead that a share of consumers leaves the market at the end of period 1 and is replaced by new ones, or that a share of consumers keeps their taste parameter in period 2.

can now turn to the price game that is played in period 2 if firm 2 enters. We consider two cases according to the importance of the switching costs.

Small switching costs

Consider first the case where the switching cost is not too large so that $\hat{x} + (z/2) \le 1$ (we make this condition precise below). In this case, the entrant manages to make some consumers switch at equilibrium. As consumers newly draw their type in period 2, there is a probability K_1 that the consumer ending up at location x bought from firm 1 in period 1 (and a probability $(1 - K_1)$ that she did not). Hence, the incumbent's and entrant's second-period profits are respectively given by

$$\pi_1 = p_1 \left(K_1 \left(\hat{x} + \tfrac{z}{2} \right) + (1 - K_1) \hat{x} \right) = p_1 \left(\tfrac{1}{2} (1 + p_2 - p_1) + K_1 \tfrac{z}{2} \right),$$
$$\pi_2 = p_2 \left(K_1 \left(1 - \hat{x} - \tfrac{z}{2} \right) + (1 - K_1)(1 - \hat{x}) \right) = p_2 \left(\tfrac{1}{2} (1 + p_1 - p_2) - K_1 \tfrac{z}{2} \right).$$

From the first-order conditions for profit maximization, we find the incumbent's and the entrant's best-response functions:

$$p_1 (p_2) = \tfrac{1}{2} p_2 + \tfrac{1}{2} (1 + K_1 z) \quad \text{and} \quad p_2 (p_1) = \tfrac{1}{2} p_1 + \tfrac{1}{2} (1 - K_1 z).$$

Note that an expansion of the incumbent's installed base shifts the incumbent's best-response outward and the entrant's best-response inward. That is, a larger K_1 commits the incumbent to set larger prices and forces the entrant to set lower prices in period 2. This is because more consumers have to incur a switching cost if they buy from the entrant, which deteriorates the entrant's position on that segment of the market.

Equilibrium prices and profits are then easily found as

$$\begin{cases} p_1 = 1 + \tfrac{1}{3} K_1 z, & \pi_1 (K_1) = \tfrac{1}{18} (3 + K_1 z)^2, \\ p_2 = 1 - \tfrac{1}{3} K_1 z, & \pi_2 (K_1) = \tfrac{1}{18} (3 - K_1 z)^2. \end{cases}$$

We observe that, in this case, increasing the first-period installed base (K_1) is profitable both for entry accommodation (as π_1 increases in K_1) and for entry deterrence (as π_2 decreases in K_1). The top dog strategy of overinvestment is thus indicated in both instances.[f]

For this argument to be valid, we still need to check that our initial conditions are met. We compute that $\hat{x} + (z/2) = \tfrac{1}{6} (3z - 2z K_1 + 3)$, which is below one as long as $(3 - 2K_1) z \le 3$. The latter condition is satisfied, for instance, if we suppose that a non-strategic incumbent would optimally set $K_1 = 1/2$ and if $z < 3/2$.[g] Then, what our result says is that for such values of the switching cost, the incumbent has an incentive to increase K_1 above $1/2$.

Large switching costs

Consider now situations where z is large enough for $\hat{x} + (z/2) > 1$. Here, none of the previous firm 1's buyers switch to the entrant in period 2. Then, the incumbent's and entrant's

---

[f] Even though prices are strategic complements, the incumbent chooses a top dog strategy under accommodation because switching costs make the high period-1 investment profitable under accommodation.
[g] We also check that $\hat{x} > 0$ for these values.

second-period profits are respectively given by

$$\pi_1 = p_1 \left(K_1 + (1 - K_1) \hat{x} \right) = p_1 \left(K_1 + (1 - K_1) \tfrac{1}{2} (1 + p_2 - p_1) \right),$$
$$\pi_2 = p_2 \left((1 - K_1)(1 - \hat{x}) \right) = p_2 (1 - K_1) \tfrac{1}{2} (1 + p_1 - p_2).$$

The incumbent's and the entrant's best-response functions are now:

$$p_1 (p_2) = \tfrac{1}{2} p_2 + \tfrac{1 + K_1}{2(1 - K_1)} \quad \text{and} \quad p_2 (p_1) = \tfrac{1}{2} p_1 + \tfrac{1}{2}.$$

In contrast with the previous case, the entrant's reaction is now unaffected by the size of the incumbent's installed base as the entrant can only compete for the unattached consumers.

A few lines of computation yield the equilibrium prices and profits:

$$\begin{cases} p_1 = \frac{3 + K_1}{3(1 - K_1)}, & \pi_1 (K_1) = \frac{1}{18} \frac{(3 + K_1)^2}{1 - K_1}, \\ p_2 = \frac{3 - K_1}{3(1 - K_1)}, & \pi_2 (K_1) = \frac{1}{18} \frac{(3 - K_1)^2}{1 - K_1}. \end{cases}$$

We observe now that both π_1 and π_2 are increasing functions of K_1. Although a larger K_1 reduces the number of consumers the entrant has access to, it also allows the entrant to charge higher prices as the incumbent does so as well. At equilibrium, the second positive effect dominates the first negative one. As a result, entry accommodation and entry deterrence call here for contrasted conducts: the incumbent should overinvest to accommodate entry (top dog strategy) but underinvest to deter entry (lean and hungry look).

As above, this argument is valid as long as the initial conditions are met at equilibrium. We have

$$\hat{x} + (z/2) = \frac{1}{6(1 - K_1)} (3z + 3 - 3zK_1 - 5K_1) > 1 \Leftrightarrow z > \frac{3 - K_1}{3(1 - K_1)}.$$

If we continue to assume that a myopic incumbent would set $K_1 = 1/2$, the latter inequality is satisfied for $z > 5/3$. We have thus illustrated the following result.

Lesson 16.9   Switching costs affect entry conditions in two opposing ways: on the one hand, they hamper large-scale entry that seeks to attract existing customers of the incumbent; on the other hand, they induce the incumbent to harvest its base of consumers with high prices, thereby relaxing price competition for unattached consumers and making entry easier on that segment.

16.4   Limit pricing under incomplete information

An important antitrust concern is the behaviour of incumbent firms to set low prices in order to avoid or delay entry. Such limit pricing raises the question of whether a temporarily low price can indeed discourage another firm from entry. The deterrence story here relies on a connection between a low price today and an unfavourable environment for the entrant tomorrow. This is illustrated by the switching cost model in the previous section, in which an installed base can be increased by lowering the pre-entry price. If, however, price is a short-run variable that can be changed at no or little cost and does not affect future demand, a low price today may be irrelevant for the entrant's entry decision. Indeed, if the entrant can perfectly predict profits after entry, the entrant will ignore today's price.

The limit pricing story, however, becomes relevant in the presence of asymmetric information. We will analyse the possibility of limit pricing in markets in which, prior to entry, the potential entrant is uncertain about the cost structure of the incumbent, while the demand function is assumed to be public information.[75]

Consider a two-period model. Before the first period, the cost of the incumbent is realized. In the first period, the incumbent operates as a protected monopolist. After learning its cost, the incumbent sets its quantity $q^1(c)$, which determines the first-period price $p^1(c)$. The entrant observes the price and may infer the incumbent's cost from the price. Period 2 is divided into two subperiods. First, the entrant decides whether to enter and pay the fixed cost e which is sunk at this point; we write $\varepsilon = 1$ if entry takes place and $\varepsilon = 0$ otherwise. The entry strategy is denoted by $\varepsilon(p^1)$. Second, after the entry decision, the entrant learns the incumbent's marginal cost. Then firms compete in quantities in case of entry, whereas the incumbent remains a monopolist if entry did not take place.

A key feature of the analysis is the following: since the marginal cost of the incumbent determines its subsequent behaviour, the entrant may be in a situation that entry is profitable if the incumbent has high costs c_H, while entry is not profitable ex ante if the incumbent costs are low, c_L. Therefore, a high-cost incumbent may hide its type by using a pooling strategy. In consequence, the entrant cannot infer the incumbent's cost structure and may not want to enter the market.[h]

The specifics of the model are as follows. Suppose that the prior probability of high costs is μ. Marginal costs satisfy $c_H < 1/2$ and $c_L = 0$. The entrant is always of low cost. Firms face the inverse demand curve $P(q) = 1 - q$ in each period and maximize the sum of profits.

Suppose entry did not take place. Then the incumbent sets the second-period quantity $q_I^2(c; \varepsilon = 0) = (1 - c)/2$. Otherwise, firms compete à la Cournot and equilibrium quantities are

$$q_I^2(c_H; \varepsilon = 1) = \tfrac{1}{3}(1 - 2c_H) \quad \text{and} \quad q_E^2(c_H; \varepsilon = 1) = \tfrac{1}{3}(1 + c_H)$$

if the incumbent has high cost and

$$q_I^2(c_L; \varepsilon = 1) = q_E^2(c_L; \varepsilon = 1) = \tfrac{1}{3}$$

if the incumbent has low cost.

If the entrant knew that the incumbent is of high cost, its equilibrium profit would be $\pi_E^2(c_H; 1) = (1 + c_H)^2/9$. If, on the contrary, the entrant knew that the incumbent is of low cost its equilibrium profit would be $\pi_E^2(c_L; 1) = 1/9$. Hence, for entry cost e with $(1 + c_H)^2/9 > e > 1/9$, the entrant does not enter if it knows that the incumbent is of low cost, whereas it enters if it knows that the reverse holds. This is the interesting parameter constellation.

What happens if the entrant does not know the incumbent's costs when making its entry decision? It then uses prior beliefs to calculate expected profits. Expected profits net of the entry cost are negative if $\mu[(1 + c_H)^2/9] + (1 - \mu)(1/9) - e < 0$. Hence, in the range of entry costs $[e^-, e^+]$ with $e^- = 1/9$ and $e^+ = \mu[(1 + c_H)^2/9] + (1 - \mu)(1/9)$, an informed

---

[h] To analyse this game, we consider perfect Bayesian equilibria.

entrant enters with probability μ (i.e., when the incumbent turns out to have high costs) whereas an uninformed entrant does not enter.

We can now characterize pooling equilibria in which the high-cost incumbent imitates the low-cost incumbent in the first period. Consider the following strategies. In period 1, the incumbent sets $q_I^1(c) = 1/2$, which is the single-period monopoly output of the low-cost incumbent. The potential entrant's entry strategy is $\varepsilon(p^1) = 1$ if $p^1 > 1/2$ (i.e., $q_I^1 < 1/2$) and $\varepsilon(p^1) = 0$ if $p^1 \leq 1/2$. The entrant believes that an incumbent with $q_I^1 < 1/2$ has high costs with probability 1, whereas an incumbent with $q_I^1 \geq 1/2$ has high costs with probability μ. Given its beliefs, the entrant should not enter. It remains to be checked that a high-cost incumbent does not have an incentive to deviate from $q_I^1 = 1/2$. Along the proposed equilibrium path, the incumbent makes first-period profit $(1 - 2c_H)/4$ and second-period profit $(1 - c_H)^2/4$. Alternatively, the incumbent can set $q_I^1 = (1 - c_H)/2$, which triggers entry in period 2. Hence, the deviation profit is first-period monopoly profit $(1 - c_H)^2/4$ plus second-period duopoly profit $(1 - 2c_H)^2/9$. Hence, a deviation is not profitable if

$$\frac{1 - 2c_H}{4} \geq \frac{(1 - 2c_H)^2}{9}$$

or, equivalently, $1/4 \geq (1 - 2c_H)/9$ which is always satisfied. This shows that the high-cost incumbent deliberately lowers its first-period price below its one-shot monopoly price to avoid entry in the second period.[i]

Lesson 16.10   If the entrant is uncertain about the incumbent's costs and would enter if it knew that the incumbent had high cost, a high-cost incumbent can mimic the low-cost incumbent in the monopoly period and thus avoid entry thereafter. Such a strategy is the equilibrium strategy of the incumbent for particular beliefs held by the entrant and an intermediate level of entry costs.

In Case 16.6, we illustrate the previous lesson by taking another look at the US photographic film market that we already described above.

Case 16.6 Kodak vs. Fuji – Act II

Recall from Case 16.1, that Fuji did not enter the US photographic film market before 1980, despite the price–cost margin that Kodak enjoyed in the 1970–9 period. A plausible explanation for this is that Kodak was limit pricing and limit advertising to deter entry. As

---

[i] A full analysis of this limit pricing model is more involved since a large number of equilbria exists. In particular, there are separating equilibria in which the *low-cost* firm sets a larger quantity (and thus a lower price than its one-shot monopoly price), whereas the high-cost firm sets its one-shot monopoly price in the first period and thus triggers entry along the equilibrium path. Considering separating equilibria, entry occurs exactly when it would have occured if the entrant was ex ante informed about the incumbent's costs. The only effect of asymmetric information is the lower first-period price of the low-cost incumbent. Thus asymmetric information increases total surplus.

argued in the present section, if Fuji had imperfect information on either market demand or Kodak's costs, Kodak could choose low prices and high advertising budgets to indicate low costs of production.[76] This practice of using limit pricing and advertising leads to low price and advertising elasticities. According to Kadiyali's (1996) estimates, Kodak's price and advertising elasticities were indeed low during the 1970–9 period. Although the author was not able to verify if Kodak's low cost or Fuji's low demand opportunities resulted from other causes (nor to distinguish between separating or pooling equilibria), the observed low price and advertising elasticities are symptomatic of limit pricing and advertising.

Another channel by which low prices today deter entry exists if there are intertemporal demand linkages. These demand linkages can be created by incumbent firms as in the case of loyalty programmes. The theory would then suggest that an incumbent firm should lower its prices when the threat of entry arises. Hence, as illustrated in the previous section, a deterrence theory based on consumer switching costs also leads to low prices as a response to potential entry. The following case provides evidence that is consistent with this theory.

Case 16.7 Entry deterrence in the airline industry: the threat by Southwest Airlines

Goolsbee and Syverson (2008) investigate how incumbents in the US airlines industry responded to the threat of entry by Southwest Airlines. Southwest Airlines had an episode of fast expansion where it started to operate at additional airports. Operating a new airport implies that new routes become available where Southwest now operates in airports on both sides of a route instead of only on one side. This makes it much easier to serve such routes and dramatically raises the likelihood that Southwest will start serving those routes soon in the future. Hence, particular routes are identified where the probability of future entry rises sharply.

Goolsbee and Syverson find that incumbent airlines cut fares of a particular route significantly when they are threatened by Southwest's entry into this route. Furthermore, their findings suggest that the largest price changes by incumbents are restricted to routes that were concentrated beforehand. As a consequence incumbents experience short-run increases in their passenger loads at the times of such fare cuts. The empirical findings are consistent with theories that predict low prices as a response to entry due to longer-term loyalty among current customers. According to loyalty-based theories fare cuts by incumbents that happen before Southwest enters a particular route create some longer-term loyalty among their customers. By locking in a customer base before actual entry occurs, the major carriers could dampen the competitive impact of Southwest's actual entry if and when it does occur.[j]

---

[j] This idea is related to the use of long-term contracts as a barrier to entry, as discussed in the next chapter, or when there are switching costs, as discussed above. We note that loyalty programmes such as frequent-flyer miles endogenously lead to consumer switching costs.

16.5   Entry deterrence and multiple incumbents

All the situations we have considered so far in this chapter involved a monopolist incumbent (or a group of colluding incumbents) reacting to the potential entry of a single entrant. In this section, we move away from this one incumbent/one entrant framework and examine situations with several incumbents and/or entrants. The issue we want to study is the possibility of free riding in entry deterrence. If entry can be successfully deterred by a proper subset of the incumbents, then incumbents outside that subset freely benefit from the other firms' investments. Hence, investments in entry deterrence acquire the nature of a public good for the group of incumbent firms and, as usual with public goods, underinvestment may result. That is, incumbents acting in a noncooperative way may invest less in entry deterrence than they would do if they could coordinate their actions.

The free rider problem in entry deterrence has been examined in various settings. We develop a simple example to show that the number of entrants is critical for the underinvestment result to be observed.[77] We consider a homogeneous product industry with two incumbent firms (labelled 1 and 2) and contrast two cases: in the first case, there is a single potential entrant (labelled 3) and in the second case, there are two potential entrants (labelled 3 and 4). The game has three stages. In the first stage, the two incumbents choose their capacities $\bar{q}_1$ and $\bar{q}_2$, respectively. In the second stage, upon observing $\bar{q}_1$ and $\bar{q}_2$, the entrant(s) decide whether to enter and if so, choose their capacity. In the third stage, the active firms play a capacity-constrained Cournot game. More precisely, after having invested in sunk capacity, firms have a constant marginal cost of production of c up to their capacity level, and are unable to produce more than this. As for the inverse demand, we assume that it is given by $P(q) = a - q$. We denote by $\alpha \equiv a - c$ for the demand intercept net of the constant marginal cost.

To simplify the analysis, suppose that only two capacity levels are available: $\bar{q}_H$ and $\bar{q}_L$ (with $\bar{q}_H > \bar{q}_L$) with associated fixed costs f_H and f_L (with $f_H > f_L$). Think of firms having to choose between a small plant of capacity $\bar{q}_L$ that costs f_L, and a large plant with capacity $\bar{q}_H$ that costs f_H. We are interested in situations where entry prevention requires the joint effort of the two incumbents. So, we restrict the attention to parameter configurations such that the incumbents both need to install capacity $\bar{q}_H$ if they want to remain a duopoly. If none or only one of the incumbents installs $\bar{q}_H$, we assume the following: (i) if there is a single entrant, it always enters; (ii) if they are two entrants, both enter if the two incumbents choose $\bar{q}_L$ but only one enters if one incumbent chooses $\bar{q}_H$.

The first stage of the game can be represented by the symmetric pay-off matrix of Table 16.2.

Table 16.2. *Payoffs in the noncooperative entry deterrence game*

		Firm 2	
		$\bar{q}_L$	$\bar{q}_H$
Firm 1	$\bar{q}_L$	π_{LL}, π_{LL}	π_{LH}, π_{HL}
	$\bar{q}_H$	π_{HL}, π_{LH}	π_{HH}, π_{HH}

In this framework, underinvestment in entry deterrence, i.e., both incumbent firms choose $\bar{q}_L$, is associated with the joint satisfaction of the following three conditions: (1) $\pi_{LL} \geq \pi_{HL}$: allowing entry is a Nash equilibrium; (2) $\pi_{HH} < \pi_{LH}$: preventing entry is not a Nash equilibrium; and (3) $\pi_{HH} > \pi_{LL}$: incumbents' total profits are higher preventing than allowing entry.

Consider first the case with a *single potential entrant*. As mentioned above, we assume that firm 3 stays out if firms 1 and 2 both choose $\bar{q}_H$, and enters otherwise. Combining the second and third conditions for underinvestment, we must have that $\pi_{LH} > \pi_{LL}$, i.e., that an incumbent choosing $\bar{q}_L$ is better off when the other incumbent chooses $\bar{q}_H$ rather than $\bar{q}_L$. In the present setting, this inequality can be rewritten as

$$[\alpha - \bar{q}_L - \bar{q}_H - \bar{q}_3(\bar{q}_L, \bar{q}_H)]\bar{q}_L - f_L > [\alpha - 2\bar{q}_L - \bar{q}_3(\bar{q}_L, \bar{q}_L)]\bar{q}_L - f_L \Leftrightarrow$$

$$\bar{q}_3(\bar{q}_L, \bar{q}_L) - \bar{q}_3(\bar{q}_L, \bar{q}_H) > \bar{q}_H - \bar{q}_L,$$

where $\bar{q}_3(\cdot, \cdot)$ denotes firm 3's optimal capacity choice according to the incumbents' choices. As easily seen, the latter inequality can never be satisfied (as $\bar{q}_3(\bar{q}_L, \bar{q}_L) - \bar{q}_3(\bar{q}_L, \bar{q}_H)$ is at best equal to $\bar{q}_H - \bar{q}_L$). It follows that *underinvestment is not possible when there is a single potential entrant*.

We now construct an example to show that *underinvestment may occur when there are two potential entrants*. As indicated above, we assume that 2, 1 or 0 entries occur if 0, 1 or 2 incumbents install the large capacity. We assume also that parameters are such that, upon entry, entrants choose to install the small capacity. Here, the inequality $\pi_{LH} > \pi_{LL}$ may well be satisfied as two firms enter in case LL but only one in case LH. The inequality can indeed be rewritten as

$$[\alpha - \bar{q}_L - \bar{q}_H - \bar{q}_L]\bar{q}_L - f_L > [\alpha - 2\bar{q}_L - 2\bar{q}_L]\bar{q}_L - f_L \Leftrightarrow 2\bar{q}_L > \bar{q}_H.$$

For instance, take $\bar{q}_H = 19$ and $\bar{q}_L = 10$ and, to meet the other conditions, set $\alpha = 100$, $f_H = 1170$ and $f_L = 595$. With these values, we check that entrants never install the large capacity and we compute the following incumbents' equilibrium profits: $\pi_{LL} = (\alpha - 4\bar{q}_L)\bar{q}_L - f_L = 5$, $\pi_{LH} = (\alpha - 2\bar{q}_L - \bar{q}_H)\bar{q}_L - f_L = 15$, $\pi_{HL} = (\alpha - 2\bar{q}_L - \bar{q}_H)\bar{q}_H - f_H = -11$, and $\pi_{HH} = (\alpha - 2\bar{q}_H)\bar{q}_H - f_H = 8$. We observe thus that the incumbents face a prisoner's dilemma: as choosing a small capacity is a dominant strategy ($\pi_{LL} = 5 > \pi_{HL} = -11$ and $\pi_{LH} = 15 > \pi_{HH} = 8$), both firms do so, which makes entry profitable for firms 3 and 4; however, the incumbents would be better off if they both installed $\bar{q}_H$, thereby preventing firms 3 and 4 from entering ($\pi_{HH} = 8 > \pi_{LL} = 5$).

To see why underinvestment arises, note that if one incumbent were to install a large capacity, this by itself would deter one entrant. Then, the other incumbent would have an incentive to install a small capacity and not deter the other entrant (as $\pi_{LH} = 15 > \pi_{HH} = 8$); yet, this would decrease the profit of the first incumbent below what it can gain by installing a small capacity (as $\pi_{HL} = -11 < \pi_{LL} = 5$). As a result, the two incumbents end up installing a small capacity and entry takes place.

The comparison of the two cases allows us to identify a general requirement for a model of noncooperative entry deterrence to exhibit a free-rider problem: the total return to investing in entry deterrence need not occur at a single critical point. This requirement is never met when there is a single entrant, but may be met when there are multiple entrants. This is the case in our numerical example as investment by a single incumbent already deters one of the two entrants. We conclude the following.

Lesson 16.11   **Multiple incumbents may not be able to deter entry if they do not coordinate their investment decisions.**

Naturally, a way to solve the free-riding problem is for the incumbents to collude in their choice of investments in entry deterrence, as illustrated in Case 16.8 that takes a last look at the Kodak–Fuji duopoly.

Case 16.8 Kodak vs. Fuji – Act III

Recall from Case 16.1 that Fuji entered the US photographic film market in 1980. Kadiyali (1996) claims that the limit pricing and advertising observed in the pre-entry period (see Case 16.6) persisted in the post-entry market. She bases her claim on three observations. First, in the post-entry period, both Kodak and Fuji had very low own-price elasticities (which means low real prices) and very low own-advertising elasticities (which implies high levels of advertising, given the diminishing impact of advertising on demand). Second, compared to the pre-entry levels, prices were indeed low and advertising levels much higher. Finally, no further entry occurred in this market although the price–cost margins for Kodak and Fuji were $1.28 and $1.35 per roll, respectively.

What is interesting to note here is that the two firms seem to have joined forces in order to deter entry. We explained above that Kadiyali estimated several market structure hypotheses in order to uncover the competitive regime underlying the observed market outcome data for the post-entry period (1980–90). Her estimates indicated that Kodak and Fuji were tacitly colluding in the choice of both price and advertising. By performing several simulations, Kadiyali showed that collusion was needed to keep prices low enough to deter entry but higher than would be achieved in a more competitive, less profitable, equilibrium. In other words, there would have been too little investment in entry deterrence (from the incumbents' point of view) if Kodak and Fuji had not cooperated.

Review questions

1.   Explain why entry deterrence and entry accommodation call for the same strategy when product decisions are strategic substitutes, and for opposing strategies when product decisions are strategic complements. Illustrate with some examples.

2. Why, and in what circumstances, would an incumbent firm facing potential entry find it profitable to expand its production capacity above the level that a monopolist ignoring entry would choose?

3. Explain under which conditions an incumbent firm is able to use brand proliferation to deter entry.

4. Why is incomplete information crucial for limit pricing to serve as an entry deterrent? Explain.

5. Is there a free-riding problem when several incumbents try to deter entry? Discuss.

Further reading

The first analyses of an incumbent's behaviour in the face of entry defended what has been later called the 'Sylos Postulate' (see Bain (1956), Modigliani (1958) and Sylos-Labini (1962)). This postulate asserts that potential entrants expect incumbents to maintain their price or output constant at a level that deters entry (i.e., a 'limit price' or a 'limit output') whether or not it is profitable for them to do so. We did not develop this postulate in this chapter as it clearly ignores both the strategic interaction between firms and the dynamic aspects of entry. Indeed, taking these two considerations into account, one realizes that it is not always profitable for incumbents to adopt entry-deterring prices and, even when deterrence is feasible, accommodating entry might yield superior profits. It follows that entrants could reasonably expect incumbents to adjust ex post when confronted with the fact of a rival's entry. Such expectation seems particularly reasonable when incumbents' choices are easily reversible, as is the case with the choice of prices or quantities.

   Subsequent work within this framework therefore concentrated on refining the concept of strategic investment to deter entry, in particular by the introduction of the concept of perfectness, or credibility, into the entry game. We largely covered two analyses that belong to this tradition: the model of Dixit (1980), which focuses on capacity rather than production, and the taxonomy presented by Fudenberg and Tirole (1984), which explores systematically the framework of an investment-then-entry two-stage game. As for the specific entry-deterrent strategies, our exposition is related to Schmalensee (1978) and Judd (1985) for brand proliferation, Whinston (1990) and Peitz (2008) for bundling, Klemperer (1987) for switching costs. Still in the same tradition are analyses of multiple incumbents/multiple entrants settings. We followed Waldman (1991); other contributions are surveyed in Kovenock and Suddhasatwa (2005). Finally, the limit-pricing story regained its relevance when Milgrom and Roberts (1982a,b) reconsidered it in settings where the entrant is imperfectly informed about the profitability of entry. Other important contributions to this issue are Matthews and Mirman (1983) and Harrington (1986).

Because of the difficulties related to estimating the threat of entry and to building the counterfactual state of the world in which entry did or did not occur, the empirical literature on strategic reactions to entry is rather limited. We covered a number of papers in the various cases of this chapter. A rapid survey of the empirical literature can be found in Conlin and Kadiyali (2006). For surveys of the theoretical literature, see Neven (1989) and Wilson (1992).

17 Vertically related markets

Firms that sell products usually require inputs, which are produced by other firms in an upstream industry (which again may require inputs from other firms). This leads to a vertical supply chain that is needed to produce a final product. Up until now, we have analysed various forms of competition at one level of the vertical supply chain. This approach is appropriate if inputs are provided in a perfectly competitive way under constant marginal costs. In this case, the input price is equal to the marginal cost that is incurred upstream and this input price does not vary with input supply. However, inputs are often also provided by firms with market power. We then have to take the whole vertical supply chain into account to understand how markets function. For instance, can upstream firms deny competitors access to their distribution channel, e.g., because they have signed an exclusive dealing contract with their retailers? Also, what are the effects of vertical mergers?

We start in Section 17.1 with the traditional double marginalization problem within a monopoly context and explore the consequences of allowing contracts between the upstream and downstream firm that differ from linear pricing. In Section 17.2, we analyse the role of resale-price maintenance and exclusive territories. In Section 17.3, we address the role of exclusive dealing contracts. Finally, in Section 17.4, we analyse a model with an oligopolistic industry upstream and downstream. We examine the effects of vertical mergers in such markets.

17.1 The double-marginalization problem

A pricing inefficiency in vertically related markets stems from the so-called double-marginalization problem. The idea is the following: in a market with firms operating only at one level of a vertical supply chain, retail prices are higher than in a market with vertically integrated firms because a downstream firm applies a margin to the wholesale price which includes the margin of an upstream firm. The inefficiency arises because the retailer does not take into account the externality exerted on the upstream firm by changing the retail price. We first formally develop this insight within a monopoly context. We next examine contractual solutions to this problem. Finally, we consider the impact of double marginalization on the provision of retailing services.

17.1.1 Linear pricing and double marginalization

We start by analysing the double-marginalization problem within a monopoly context.[78] Suppose that market demand is linear, $Q(p) = a - bp$. Marginal costs are constant and equal to

$c < a/b$. The upstream firm, which is called *manufacturer*, does not sell directly but through a single downstream firm, which is called *retailer*. The producer sets the wholesale price w at stage 1. At stage 2, the retailer, who, for simplicity, is assumed not to incur any costs, observes the wholesale price and sets the retail price p.

We solve this pricing problem by backward induction. The retailer maximizes its profits, $\max_p (p - w)(a - bp)$. Hence, for a given wholesale price w the retailer sets

$$p(w) = \frac{a + bw}{2b}.$$

A price w thus gives rise to market demand

$$a - b\frac{a + bw}{2b} = \frac{a}{2} - \frac{bw}{2}$$

and the retailer's profit is

$$\frac{(a - bw)^2}{4b}.$$

The manufacturer takes the profit-maximizing behaviour of the retailer into account. He thus takes the market demand depending on w, which comes from the retailer's profit maximization. His maximization problem is

$$\max_w (w - c) \left(\frac{a}{2} - \frac{bw}{2} \right).$$

The first-order condition of profit maximization can be written as $a + bc - 2bw = 0$ which is equivalent to

$$w = \frac{c}{2} + \frac{a}{2b}.$$

The corresponding retail price is

$$p^* = \frac{3}{4}\frac{a}{b} + \frac{c}{4}.$$

A vertically integrated firm would solve $\max_p (p - c)(a - bp)$ and thus set its price equal to $p^m = a/(2b) + c/2$. We check easily that $a/b > c$ implies that $p^m < p^*$. This shows that a vertical merger is welfare-increasing. What is the underlying reason? The retailer ignores that a higher price–cost margin downstream also reduces profits upstream. By contrast, under vertical integration, this effect is internalized.

Lesson 17.1   In a vertically related industry with an upstream and a downstream monopolist in which each firm maintains the price-setting power of its product, the retail price is above the monopoly price set by a vertically integrated firm.

Is there any empirical evidence of double marginalization? The next case provides supporting evidence.

Case 17.1 Double marginalization in US cable TV[79]

Double marginalization is possibly an issue in cable television because the standard business practice in this industry is to charge for programming per subscriber, which corresponds to a linear price. In this market, vertically integrated cable systems operators produce their own programming. They coexist with operators who do not produce content. Evidence in the US market is consistent with the presence of double marginalization. In particular, vertically integrated operators have a larger subscriber base. It has further been documented that vertically integrated cable systems operators are more likely to carry their own premium programming than to rely on programming by other upstream firms.

The empirical evidence concerns more complex markets than the one analysed above. This requires a couple of remarks. Our first remark concerns the role of competition. While the double marginalization is most pronounced in successive monopoly, the basic insight remains relevant under imperfect competition. If the upstream market operates as an oligopoly, these firms' equilibrium prices contain a markup, which downstream firms treat as part of their marginal costs. If the downstream market also operates as an oligopoly, these downstream firms will apply their markup on their marginal costs, which again implies double marginalization. As one layer of the market loses its market power, the double marginalization becomes less pronounced. In the extreme, if inputs for the downstream firms are in perfectly competitive supply, double marginalization is no longer an issue because upstream firms are unable to sell at a positive markup. We elaborate on this in the subsection on vertical oligopoly below.

Our second remark is that the double-marginalization problem can be alleviated or even be avoided through the use of more sophisticated contracts that differ from linear contracts, as we will see next.

17.1.2   Contractual solutions to the double-marginalization problem

A simple way to mimic the monopoly solution of the vertically integrated firm is to agree to a profit-sharing agreement. For instance, if both firms agree to split any downstream profits according to shares α and $(1 - \alpha)$ and the retailer purchases the product at marginal costs c, the vertically integrated solution is implemented.

While this suggests an easy solution to the double marginalization problem, its applicability can be questioned. In particular, if a retailer's price is not easily observable for the manufacturer and the retailer sells products by different sellers, the retailer's profits or revenues are not easily observable. By contrast, if the retailer exclusively sells products by one seller, the latter can easily calculate the former's revenues. Hence, to the extent that the manufacturer has to give a certain profit level to the retailer but has otherwise the full bargaining power, he can set the wholesale price equal to marginal costs and make his profits through revenue sharing.

An additional problem arises if the retailer has nonobservable marginal costs. Profit sharing would give incentives to the retailer to misrepresent her costs. A simple alternative is to agree to revenue sharing (together with the wholesale price equal to marginal production costs). Clearly, since the retailer's costs are not considered, it has an incentive to sell too few products. Thus informational problems between the two parties would lead to a divergence from the vertically integrated solution.

In our simple setting without information problems, two-part tariffs can implement the vertically integrated solution. The two-part tariff consists of a wholesale price per unit and a fixed fee. The manufacturer optimally sets the wholesale price equal to marginal manufacturer costs. The manufacturer now makes profits from a fixed fee which is levied upon the retailer. The profit-maximizing level is equal to the profit of the retailer gross of this fee so that the upstream firm absorbs all profits. Such a fee can be understood as a franchise fee.

This result holds under the assumptions that there is a single retailer and that the manufacturer is fully informed. However, at least one of these assumptions is often violated in practice. Suppose there are several retailers that operate as monopolists in their respective market and that differ in the volumes they can sell and the upstream manufacturer cannot tell them apart. The manufacturer has to set the fixed fee equal to the gross profit of the smallest retailer to ensure that all retailers participate. If it increases the fixed fee, it will not serve some retailers. In this situation, the manufacturer may optimally set its unit price above marginal costs to extract profits from all retailers. By doing so, it will extract more profits from large retailers than from small retailers. In this case, the double-marginalization problem reappears. However, if the information about, e.g., market size of each monopolistic retailer is not private information, the manufacturer may price discriminate between different types of retailers. In the extreme, i.e., if there is perfect discrimination, two-part tariffs and other nonlinear prices can indeed solve the double-marginalization problem.

> **Lesson 17.2** **Nonlinear pricing and other contracts can solve to the double-marginalization problem.**

A different solution lies in the use of resale-price maintenance (i.e., a practice by which an upstream firm mandates prices downstream), which will be analysed below in competitive environments. In our simple monopoly context from above, resale-price maintenance leads to the same allocation as vertical integration. Hence, while we have found theoretical solutions to the double-marginalization problem, it is an open question whether they are feasible in practice. In particular, the presence of local monopolists in the downstream market who can become active in resale may make it optimal for the manufacturer not to use nonlinear pricing. So far we have investigated only pricing issues. An additional issue is that manufacturers' profits often depend on investments in services, an issue we turn to next.

17.1.3 Double marginalization and retail services

In a retailing context, downstream firms often provide complementary services; for instance, they explain to consumers the functioning of a product and thus increase the consumers' willingness-to-pay, or they hold excess sales staff to keep lines short. From the view point of the manufacturer, such effort provision constitutes a moral hazard problem because the manufacturer would like to compensate the retailer for such efforts but does not observe them.

Let us first abstract from any competition between retailers and assume that market demand is a function $Q(p, s)$, which depends on the retail price and the service level or quality provided by the retailer. To provide service s, the retailer incurs a cost $\psi(s)$ per unit of output. Under vertical integration, the manufacturer/retailer maximizes $(p - c - \psi(s))Q(p, s)$, where c are the constant marginal costs of production. Denote the solution of this vertically integrated structure by p^m and s^m.

Consider now the situation that manufacturer and retailer are not vertically integrated and that the manufacturer is restricted to set a linear wholesale price. The manufacturer maximizes $(w - c)Q(p(w), s)$ with respect to w at stage 1 and the retailer maximizes $(p - w - \psi(s))Q(p, s)$ with respect to p and s at stage 2. To obtain positive profit, the manufacturer must set $w > c$. With respect to the retail price, we have again a double-marginalization problem. In addition, the retailer distorts its service provision compared to the vertically integrated solution: the retailer does not take into account that an increase in services also increases the manufacturer's profit. If the manufacturer can use a two-part tariff, it can obtain the solution of the vertically integrated structure. For this it sets $w = c$ and extracts the retailer's surplus through the fixed charge. However, resale-price maintenance alone will not solve the problem any longer because the manufacturer would not only need to control the price but also the service level.

17.2   Resale-price maintenance and exclusive territories

The previous section exclusively focused on vertical externalities. In particular, we considered price distortions in a market with vertically nonintegrated monopolists. Clearly, one way to enforce optimal prices from the viewpoint of the upstream firm, is to mandate prices downstream, an activity called *resale-price maintenance* (RPM). The downstream price resulting from RPM would allow a positive margin for the retailer so as to ensure that the downstream firm remains active. We will focus on the role of RPM in imperfectly competitive retail markets. Furthermore, in imperfectly competitive markets, it may be desirable for manufacturers to grant exclusive territories to their retailers.

17.2.1   Resale-price maintenance

Resale-price maintenance gives the manufacturer power over price and thus potentially eliminates competition between retailers. However, in markets in which retailers's investments are of little relevance, one may wonder whether resale-price maintenance inflicts any social harm. Manufacturers have an incentive to keep retailer margins small and competition at the manufacturer level may be sufficiently strong to keep retail prices down.

However, in many markets in which products are not sold directly by manufacturers, there is arguably a much bigger role for retailers beyond the reduction of transaction costs. Retailers engage in costly service provision and manufacturers are aware that their pricing strategy should not destroy retailers' investment strategy. To formally investigate the role of RPM in this context, consider a market with a single manufacturer (upstream firm) and two competing retailers $i = 1, 2$ (downstream firms) which both carry the manufacturer's product.[80] These retailers are horizontally differentiated on the Hotelling line (with linear transport costs) and compete in price (unless RPM is in place) and service. Consumers are heterogeneous with respect to their horizontal location and the service dimension, which can be interpreted as an opportunity cost of time. With a finite reservation price, this implies that those consumers who are located far away from the product and have a high opportunity cost of time do not purchase any product.

Denote the retail price by p_i and the service level (or quality of retail services) by s_i. The demand for the manufacturer's good at retailer i is then a function $Q_i(p_1, p_2, s_1, s_2)$. Each retailer makes profit

$$\pi_i(p_1, p_2, s_1, s_2) = (p_i - w)Q_i(p_1, p_2, s_1, s_2) - K(s_i)$$

where w is the wholesale price and $K(s_i)$ the cost of providing service level s_i. Manufacturer's profit is $(w - c)(q_1 + q_2)$.

In a setting without RPM, the manufacturer simply sets a linear non-discriminatory wholesale price w. We will then contrast this solution to a contract offered by the manufacturer that sets not only a wholesale price but also a price floor for the retail price. For comparison, consider also producer surplus, i.e. the total profit of the industry,

$$PS(p_1, p_2, s_1, s_2) = (p_1 - c)Q_1(p_1, p_2, s_1, s_2) + (p_2 - c)Q_2(p_1, p_2, s_1, s_2)$$
$$- K(s_1) - K(s_2). \tag{17.1}$$

Total industry profits are maximized only if $\partial PS/\partial p_i = 0$ and $\partial PS/\partial s_i = 0$. Using (17.1), retailer i's profit can be written as

$$\pi_i(p_1, p_2, s_1, s_2) = PS(p_1, p_2, s_1, s_2) - (w - c)Q_i(p_1, p_2, s_1, s_2)$$
$$- (p_j - c)Q_j(p_1, p_2, s_1, s_2) - K(s_j).$$

For a given wholesale price (which has been set at the first stage of a two-stage game), each retailer maximizes its profits with respect to p_i and s_i. First-order conditions are

$$\frac{\partial \pi_i}{\partial p_i} = \frac{\partial PS}{\partial p_i} - (w - c)\frac{\partial Q_i}{\partial p_i} - (p_j - c)\frac{\partial Q_j}{\partial p_i} = 0,$$

$$\frac{\partial \pi_i}{\partial s_i} = \frac{\partial PS}{\partial s_i} - (w - c)\frac{\partial Q_i}{\partial s_i} - (p_j - c)\frac{\partial Q_j}{\partial s_i} = 0.$$

Note that retailers implement the solution that maximizes total profits of the full vertical structure if the last two terms in both first-order conditions cancel out to zero. The second term captures the vertical externality with respect to price and service level that has been analysed in the previous section. The third term captures a horizontal externality, which is due to the imperfect competition between retailers: each retailer ignores the effect of a price and service change on the demand of its competitor. Suppose the manufacturer can possibly set w such that the two externalities exactly offset each other. For this to hold, using symmetry and rearranging, we must have

$$\frac{\frac{\partial Q_i}{\partial p_i}}{\frac{\partial Q_i}{\partial p_i} + \frac{\partial Q_j}{\partial p_i}} = \frac{\frac{\partial Q_i}{\partial s_i}}{\frac{\partial Q_i}{\partial s_i} + \frac{\partial Q_j}{\partial s_i}}. \tag{17.2}$$

If this does not hold with equality, because retailers are either more sensitive to price competition or to retail service competition, RPM affects retail prices and services, as the following lesson states.

Lesson 17.3   **The use of resale-price maintenance by a manufacturer leads to higher retail prices and more retail services if consumers are more sensitive to price competition than to service competition. Conversely, this leads to lower prices and fewer retail services if consumers are less sensitive to price competition than to service competition.**

In the model specified above, it can be shown that Equation (17.2) cannot hold: the left-hand side of (17.2) is larger than the right-hand side. This is due to the property of the model that some consumers do not buy and that, for a given consumer location, the marginal consumer cares less for services the larger their distance to the product in the product space. This implies that an increase in services by the retailer is less effective in stealing business from the competitor than a reduction in price. Hence, in this particular model retailers are biased towards price competition and the manufacturer can improve by setting a price floor that is binding in equilibrium. If the manufacturer can use two-part tariffs, it can obtain the full profit of the vertically integrated solution.[a] This demonstrates the use of RPM to implement the vertically integrated solution. While RPM can be used to correct for vertical and horizontal externalities, welfare results are ambiguous. This is hardly surprising in the present model since the manufacturer has monopoly power.

Another important issue for a retailer engaging in promotional efforts is that other retailers may free-ride on its activities. In such a market an additional horizontal externality is present. If consumers first seek advice about the usefulness of a product and then shop around for the best price, a retailer has little incentive to invest in services. The manufacturer who confronts this problem can use resale-price maintenance to avoid destructive price competition which would wipe out these investment incentives (alternatively it may use exclusive territories).[81] Here, RPM protects the profit margin of the retailer. Since the retailer cannot be undercut, consumers have no reason to become 'disloyal'. One of the services of the retailer may be to provide information about product quality that is unobservable to consumers. In such a situation of asymmetric information the retailer may signal to consumers that a particular product is of high quality by recommending the product or offering after-sales warranties. RPM can provide incentives to provide the right signals to consumers. Absent this vertical restraint, if a retailer offered his service so that consumers could infer the product quality of the manufactured good, some consumers, after learning the product quality, could buy from a cheaper retailer, who does not provide this service. This would undermine the incentives for the retailer to offer this costly service.[b]

---

[a] An alternative solution for the manufacturer is to use exclusive territories. Here, the manufacturers separates the market into two independent vertical monopolies, as has been analysed in the previous section. In this case the manufacturer can use two-part tariffs to implement the vertically integrated solution (under the assumption that the manufacturer is fully informed). We will analyse a different issue in the context of exclusive territories below.
[b] We will return to the aspect of quality certification by intermediaries in Chapter 23.

The argument that investment incentives of the retailer will be eroded in the absence of RPM has been emphasized in the context of the German book market, as the following case illustrates.

Case 17.2 RPM for German books in Germany[82]

Until 2002, booksellers and publishers in Germany were part of a voluntary contractual agreement according to which booksellers were not allowed to offer rebates on the price that was fixed by the publisher, while publishers were not allowed to supply to booksellers who had not signed the agreement (this agreement goes back to 1888). At the end of the twentieth century, about 90% of the books (in terms of turnover) in the German book trade were sold under this agreement. In 2002, resale-price maintenance became mandatory by law in the German book trade. However, it is forbidden per se for essentially all other sectors (the exception has been defended by Germany at the European level as a measure to protect its cultural diversity). What makes the book trade so special (in Germany)? Proponents of RPM in the German book trade claim that booksellers play an important role to cater to the diverse tastes of readers. In the absence of RPM, traditional booksellers would be driven out of the market, which would lead to less informed purchases and, in effect, to less variety offered by publishers. Whether this is indeed true is an open question. Interestingly, Switzerland, another majority German speaking country, had RPM in place, but changed track in 2007.

While the investment aspect may provide a justification in favour of RPM, another possibly anticompetitive effect of RPM should be pointed out: RPM can affect the sustainability of a cartel in the upstream market. This, at least, has been argued by the US Supreme Court. One argument is that cartels become less stable if wholesale prices cannot be observed by other cartel members.[83] Then it becomes difficult to distinguish between retail price changes due to cost changes in the downstream market and those due to individual deviations by cartel members. RPM eliminates this retail price variation and thus leads to more uniform retail prices. Consequently, under RPM, price deviations by cartel members are easier to detect and thus facilitate collusion between cartel members.

17.2.2   Exclusive territories

Manufacturers may distribute their products under an agreement that grants exclusive territories to particular downstream firms. Everything else given, this increases market power of downstream firms. We may wonder why upstream firms could be interested in granting market power to downstream firms since this may reduce the profits they can make upstream. One argument is that exclusive territories may increase downstream investment in services since it protects part of the rents that are generated through the investment. Otherwise, competitors may free-ride on the 'public good' that is provided by the retailer. An example is the product information that is provided by the sales staff of one retailer. For instance, if a car dealer invests in its sales staff to provide important pre-purchase information, other car dealers who sell products without these services but at a lower price may undermine the investment incentives. Contracts that involve exclusive territories can be observed in a variety of industries, in

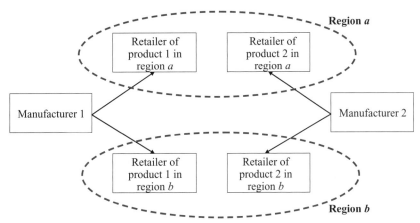

Figure 17.1 A two-region model with exclusive territories

particular, if the product is distributed within a franchise agreement. However, it may run foul of antitrust authorities if the manufacturer that is involved enjoys significant market power. Case 17.3 takes a closer look at the distribution system in the car industry.

Case 17.3 Exclusive territories in European car dealerships[84]

In the European Union, cars were seen as a product unlike others and therefore received special treatment by the European Commission. According to the block exemption that was granted to car manufacturers until 2002, car manufacturers were allowed to operate distribution systems that were both exclusive and selective. They were exclusive in two ways: they protected dealers through exclusive territories, and they required dealers to essentially exclusively sell a single brand. They were selective by insisting that dealers meet certain criteria in order to qualify for (and retain) the franchise. In 2002, a new regulation was introduced with the aim to increase competition. Car manufacturers can apply a so-called exclusive distribution system, i.e., exclusive territories, or, alternatively, choose a selective distribution system (they cannot have both). A selective distribution system permits the car manufacturers to choose their authorized partners, but the latter must be permitted to actively sell into other territories. This system is called quantitative if selection criteria directly limit the number of dealers. This is the system currently chosen by almost all car manufacturers. Note that this allows for multi-brand dealers.

We may wonder why upstream firms have an incentive to offer rents downstream, in particular, if we abstract from investment decisions downstream. Here, an important argument is that even though exclusive territories create market power downstream and thus lead to reduced output in the industry, it may be in the interest of upstream firms to offer them nevertheless because this makes upstream demand less elastic and thus reduces competition upstream.

We develop this idea in a two-product, two-region price-competition model with identical linear market demand in each region, as illustrated in Figure 17.1.[85] Suppose that there is one retailer (i.e. downstream firm) for each product in each region. Suppose furthermore that retailers do not face any transport costs selling in the other region. This implies that, absent exclusive territories, there is pure Bertrand competition between retailers of the same product, and retailer in region $k \in \{a, b\}$ selling product $i \in \{1, 2\}$ sells the product at its unit cost. The unit cost is equal to the wholesale price, w_i, plus the unit cost of retailing, which, for simplicity, is set equal to zero. We thus have $p_{ia} = p_{ib} = w_i$. We effectively have a perfectly competitive retailing sector and the two upstream firms set their price as in a standard duopoly model. With demand in region k of the form $\alpha_k(1 - p_{ik} + dp_{jk})$ (with $i \neq j \in \{1, 2\}$, $k \in \{a, b\}$, $\alpha_a + \alpha_b = 1$, and $0 \leq d < 1$), each upstream firm maximizes $w_i(1 - w_i + dw_j)$ with respect to w_i, where marginal costs are assumed to be constant and identical across upstream firms and are set equal to zero. In equilibrium, $p^* = w^* = 1/(2 - d)$ and each upstream firm makes profit $\pi^c = 1/(2 - d)^2$.

Suppose now that manufacturers grant exclusive territories to each of their retailers. Since retailers can obtain strictly positive profits under this arrangement, they are willing to sign contracts which give them exclusivity in their region under the condition that they do not sell in the other region. The timing is then as follows. First, manufacturers set their wholesale price. Second, after learning the wholesale price of their own supplier, retailers set retail prices simultaneously (note that in the absence of exclusive territories it is irrelevant whether retailers learn the wholesale price of the product they do not carry). Hence, in region k of size α_k, the retailer of product i maximizes $\alpha_k(p_{ik} - w_i)(1 - p_{ik} + dp_{jk})$. The first-order condition of profit maximization is $1 - 2p_{ik} + dp_{jk} + w_i = 0$. As retailer i does not observe the competing retailer j's input price, it has to form an expectation about that price. Because the same applies to both retailers, each retailer believes that the competing retailer within the same region faces the symmetric equilibrium wholesale price w^*. Thus, solving for each retailer, we obtain retail prices

$$p_{ik}(w_i, w^*) = \frac{2}{4 - d^2}\left[1 + d\frac{1 + w^*}{2} + w_i\right].$$

If $w_i = w^*$, this simplifies to

$$p_{ik}(w^*, w^*) = \frac{1 + w^*}{2 - d}. \tag{17.3}$$

Since this hold in both regions, manufacturer i maximizes $w_i[1 - p_{ik}(w_i, w^*) + dp_{jk}(w^*, w^*)]$ (since regions are symmetric we do not distinguish between the two regions). The first-order condition is

$$1 - p_{ik}(w_i, w^*) - w_i\frac{\partial p_{ik}(w_i, w^*)}{\partial w_i} + dp_{jk}(w^*, w^*) = 0.$$

Since, in equilibrium, $w_i = w^*$ and since $\partial p_{ik}(w_i, w^*)/\partial w_i = 2/(4 - d^2)$, we have

$$1 - \frac{1 - d}{2 - d}(1 + w^*) - w^*\frac{2}{4 - d^2} = 0$$

which is equivalent to

$$w^* = \frac{2 + d}{4 - d - d^2}.$$

Substituting this expression into (17.3) we obtain the equilibrium retail price

$$p^* = \frac{6 - d^2}{(2 - d)(4 - d - d^2)}.$$

We immediately observe that, due to double marginalization, $p^* > p^c$. Manufacturers' equilibrium profits are $\pi^* = w^*[1 - (1 - d)p^*]$, which, using the expressions from above, becomes

$$\pi^* = \frac{2+d}{2-d}\frac{2}{(4-d-d^2)^2}.$$

A few lines of computation establish that the profit π^* with exclusive territories is larger than the profit π^c without exclusive territories as long as d is large enough (precisely, if $0.78 < d < 1$). That is, upstream firms are better off with exclusive territories if the two products are close enough substitutes, meaning that the competition between retailers within the same region is strong. We can thus state the following lesson.

> **Lesson 17.4**   **Manufacturers may make higher profits if they sell through exclusive territories than if they do not. Retailers are also better off. However, consumers suffer and total surplus is reduced.**

Although retailers obtain a positive share of producer rents, offering exclusive territories can be profitable for manufacturers because demand at the upstream level becomes less sensitive to price, which makes manufacturers less aggressive.[86] While our result has been shown in a very special model, the main insight is robust to a number of variations. Also, under some stronger assumptions, it can be shown that even a unilateral move to the use of exclusive territories can be profitable for a manufacturer.

17.3   Exclusive dealing

Exclusive dealing clauses as part of contracts between upstream and downstream firms were largely seen as anticompetitive according to the antitrust doctrine that prevailed in the first half of the twentieth century in the US. Starting in the 1950s, this view was challenged by the Chicago Law School, which argued that a downstream firm which foresees that more attractive terms are available under competition will demand a compensation from the proposing upstream firm for signing a long-term contract with an exclusivity clause.[87] The Chicago Law School thus showed that the traditional reasoning was illogical and argued that exclusive dealing, when observed in practice, must be due to efficiency gains. As the following case illustrates, cost advantages from exclusive dealing may indeed be substantial, at least for beer in Chicago.

> **Case 17.4 Beer distribution in Chicago**[88]
>
> The American beer industry is highly concentrated. Take market shares in 1994: Anheuser Busch produced 45% of the beer that was shipped in the USA, Miller, 22%, Coors, 10%. Imported beers, treated together, accounted for about 5% of the market. Around this time,

Anheuser Busch offered its distributors extended credit and increased marketing support in return for exclusivity. Asker (2004) empirically analyses the foreclosure motive versus the efficiency motive using data from the Greater Chicago area. Here, the vertical industry structure is regulated by state law: it is a three-tier system where the brewer sells to distributors who sell on to retailers. Another feature of the American beer market is that distributors are granted exclusive territories. Although 'retail' price maintenance (referring to the price paid by retailers to distributors) is prohibited, brewers recommend and monitor the price paid from retailers to distributors, so that they essentially set both the input and the output price of their distributors.

Asker (2004) uses a detailed description of the Greater Chicago distribution networks of 12 beer brewers and merges this with sales from Dominick's Finer Foods, a large Chicago supermarket chain. These beer brewers make up more than 90% of all beer sales of this supermarket chain. Data include the wholesale price paid by the chain and the price paid by consumers, which allows for tracking the sale of beer through the vertical chain. Here, the vertical chain contains in addition to the 12 brewers, 42 distributors who serve the 71 stores that are included in the data set. Brewers are modelled as the price setters of the price paid by the supermarket chain to the distributors. Using scanner data, demand functions (together with first-order conditions of the brewers which take into account that the supermarket chain set profit-maximizing retail prices) are estimated using a random coefficient logit model (see Chapter 5).

Asker finds that brewers that use exclusive dealing contracts enjoy a cost advantage of between 9 cents and 14 cents per bottle compared to brewers that do not use such contracts. This advantage is substantial given the fact that the average wholesale cost of a bottle of beer is 50 cents. In addition, he finds evidence that exclusive distributors offer an increased level of service, which results in additional sales. The key question is what are the sources of these cost advantages: are they due to anticompetitive or efficiency effects? Welfare consequences of exclusive dealing are shown to be drastically different under either one of these two types of effects.

While the Chicago critique makes the correct point that the incentives of the downstream firm have to be considered, it can be challenged in a market with imperfect competition because in the presence of exclusivity clauses, the market conditions the downstream firm encounters are different from those in an environment in which exclusivity clauses are illegal. Thus, under certain conditions, the traditional view can be restored: exclusive dealing may deter entry and lead to a welfare loss. As a consequence, a simple per se legality or illegality of exclusive dealing clauses is inappropriate and a rule-of-reason approach in which the economic effects are carefully studied appears to be more promising.

Our main goal of this section is to understand the economic rationales as to why exclusive dealing can be anticompetitive or efficiency-enhancing. However, to set the stage we have to lay out the Chicago critique (which is unrelated to selling beer in Chicago), which challenged earlier conventional wisdom that exclusive dealing is necessarily anticompetitive. While our exposition focuses on exclusive dealing and similar practices such as boycotts, insights that are obtained from our analysis apply more generally to loyalty discounts and other practices in which an upstream firm effectively offers different terms to different market participants, a point that is well understood by competition authorities.

17.3.1   **Anticompetitive effects of exclusive dealing contracts? The Chicago critique**

Courts in the US were traditionally hostile to the use of exclusive dealing contracts. The fact that a firm with a large market share used exclusive contracts was viewed with suspicion. Also the European Commission agreed with the view that exclusive dealing can be anticompetitive, as the following case exemplifies.

Case 17.5 Selling spices in Belgium[89]

In the 1970s, only four producers (Brooke Bond Liebig (Liebig), India, Ducros and Topo) together had a revenue share of around 85 percent of total revenues in the market for spices; the largest firm, Liebig, had a market share of 39 per cent in 1976. Spices were sold through food stores and large self-service stores (including supermarkets and hypermarkets), all selling spices as part of a wide variety of food products. The three largest supermarkets chains at that point, GB-Inno-BM, Delhaize Frères et Cie Le Lion and Sarma Penney, contributed almost 60 percent to Liebig's sales in Belgium. According to their agreement with Liebig, these three chains exclusively sold spices by Liebig (except for own brand spices), charged the retail price set by Liebig (resale-price maintenance) and displayed Liebig spices prominently. Liebig in return granted annual rebates, sales incentives and guaranteed a minimum profit (as agreed with the chain). The European Commission found that although supermarket chains could sell their own brand in addition to Liebig's spices, the agreement restricted inter-brand competition because no other brands other than Liebig and the own brand could be sold. The financial rewards (rebates, RPM and minimum profit) were seen as an implicit compensation to the supermarket chains for the exclusion of competing brands from their shelves.

But are exclusive dealing contracts anticompetitive? The so-called Chicago Law School questioned the claim that strong incumbent upstream firms can use exclusive dealing clauses (usually applied to downstream firms such as retailers) to vertically foreclose the market to potential entrants. To clarify this point, consider a market with two sellers, an incumbent and an entrant, who offer purchasing contracts for a homogeneous product. There is a buyer, who can be interpreted as a retailer that operates as a monopolist in its markets and can extract all the surplus from final consumers. This buyer is assumed to have demand $Q(p)$. The incumbent faces constant marginal cost of production c_I, while the entrant is more efficient and has marginal costs $c_E < c_I$. The entrant also has to pay an entry cost e. Let us assume that entry occurs if no exclusive dealing clause is signed, i.e., $(c_I - c_E)Q(c_I) > e$. This implies that entry is efficient. The timing is as follows. First, the incumbent offers the buyer a payment m in return for signing a legally binding exclusive dealing contract. The buyer decides whether to accept or reject this contract. After observing whether exclusive dealing will prevail, a potential entrant decides whether to enter. The incumbent observes whether entry has occurred and firms in the market set prices simultaneously.

If the potential entrant did not enter, the incumbent would set its monopoly price $p^m = \arg\max_p (p - c_I)Q(p)$ and obtain monopoly profit $\pi^m = (p^m - c_I)Q(p^m)$. If the entrant does enter, there is asymmetric Bertrand competition between the two firms so that the price is equal to c_I. The incumbent makes zero sales and the entrant obtains profit $(c_I - c_E)Q(c_I)$. Hence, for obtaining exclusivity, the incumbent is willing to pay up to π^m to the buyer up-front. However, the buyer suffers a loss from accepting exclusivity because he has to pay the price p^m instead of c_I. The buyer's loss from confronting the incumbent as a monopolist instead of competition between incumbent and entrant is $\Delta CS = \int_{c_I}^{p^m} Q(p)dp$.

Since $\Delta CS > \pi^m$ (where $\Delta CS - \pi^m$ is the deadweight loss from monopoly pricing), the buyer cannot be compensated by the incumbent to accept the exclusive dealing clause at a payment $m \leq \pi^m$. Hence, it is not profitable for the incumbent to induce the buyer to accept exclusive dealing. This shows that in the present setting, exclusive dealing cannot be anticompetitive. Actually, following the logic of this model, since there are no efficiency gains from exclusive dealing, it will not be observed in equilibrium. We have thus formalized the claim of the Chicago Law School that exclusive dealing cannot be used for anticompetitive purposes. Note that in our setting, the incumbent can make a take-it-or-leave-it offer to the buyer. However, our insight can be generalized to any distribution of bargaining power between incumbent and buyer (maintaining the assumption that bargaining is efficient and that fixed payments can be made). Our present analysis did not elaborate on the possibly efficiency-enhancing effect of exclusive dealing; this will be the topic in a later subsection. Before doing so, we will scrutinize the general claim by the Chicago Law School that exclusive dealing does not constitute anticompetitive behaviour.

17.3.2   Vertical integration and long-term contracts as partial deterrence devices

In this subsection, we raise our first objection to the general claim that exclusive dealing clauses cannot be anticompetitive. We proceed by modifying our previous model and show that vertical integration leads to socially insufficient entry. We then show that long-term exclusive dealing contracts can achieve the same outcome as vertical integration.[90]

Consider the market from the previous subsection, where we now set the willingness-to-pay for all consumers to be identical and equal to 1, and the entrant's entry cost e arbitrarily small. Furthermore, we assume that there is unit demand, i.e., $Q(p) = 1$. The incumbent has a constant marginal cost of production $c_I = 1/2$, whereas the entrant's marginal cost c_E takes a realization between 0 and 1. Everybody knows that c_E is uniformly distributed between 0 and 1. The socially optimal allocation in this case would be that the buyer obtains the good from the incumbent if $c_I < c_E$ and from the entrant if $c_I > c_E$. The novel feature is that, initially, the incumbent does not know the entrant's cost parameter (it will be drawn later). This will drastically affect our results.

Let us first consider the model with entry in the absence of vertical integration or long-term contracting. The marginal cost of the entrant takes some value between 0 and 1, which at the pricing stage is observed by all parties. Competition has the same form as in the asymmetric Bertrand model. Therefore, the equilibrium price is $1/2$ if $c_I > c_E$ and c_E if

$c_I < c_E$. Hence, the incumbent's expected profit is

$$\int_{c_I}^{1} (c_E - c_I) dc_E = \int_{1/2}^{1} c_E dc_E - \frac{1}{4} = \frac{1}{8}.$$

The entrant's expected profit is

$$\int_{0}^{c_I} (c_I - c_E) dc_E = \frac{1}{4} - \int_{0}^{1/2} c_E dc_E = \frac{1}{8}.$$

The expected price is

$$\int_{0}^{1} \max\{c_I, c_E\} dc_E = \frac{1}{4} + \frac{1}{2}\frac{3}{4} = \frac{5}{8}.$$

so that the expected net buyer surplus is $1 - 5/8 = 3/8$.

Suppose now that buyer and incumbent can vertically integrate before the entrant's cost is observed and it enters (at an arbitrarily small cost e). Suppose furthermore that now the integrated firm obtains the power to make a take-it-or-leave-it offer to the entrant before the entrant's cost is observed. We are not defending an interpretation of the effect of vertical integration as interesting by itself but later implement this outcome through long-term exclusive dealing contracts.

The vertically integrated firm chooses the price it offers the entrant such that it minimizes its expected cost of obtaining the product (either internally at cost $c_I = 1/2$ or externally through the entrant). In this case, access by the entrant to the buyer is difficult, i.e., the entrant needs to have very low costs. The buyer can buy internally at price $c_I = 1/2$ or offer a price p to the (upstream) entrant. This is a take-it-or-leave-it offer so that the entrant accepts if $p \geq c_E$. The price offer p is set such that the expected cost of obtaining the product is minimized,

$$\min_{p} p \text{ Prob}\{c_E \leq p\} + \frac{1}{2}\text{Prob}\{c_E > p\}.$$

Since c_E is uniform on $[0, 1]$, we have that Prob$\{c_E \leq p\} = p$ and Prob$\{c_E > p\} = 1 - p$. The minimization problem becomes

$$\min_{p} p^2 + \frac{1}{2}(1 - p).$$

The first-order condition of cost minimization is

$$2p - \frac{1}{2} = 0 \Leftrightarrow p = \frac{1}{4}.$$

Hence, the buyer who owns the incumbent firm offers $p = 1/4$ to the entrant. Consequently, there is insufficient entry: if $c_E \in (1/4, 1/2)$, entry does not take place but would be socially efficient. In this sense, vertical integration constitutes an entry barrier. In other words, there is a 25% chance that socially desirable entry does not take place.

Lesson 17.5 Vertical integration between an upstream seller and a downstream seller may lead to an inefficient allocation because the integrated firm uses its market power to offer too low a price for the product of the outside seller.

We are now in a position to analyse the effect of long-term exclusive dealing contracts between incumbent seller and buyer.[c] We consider the following timing of events: at $t = 1$, the seller proposes a contract to the buyer; at $t = 2$, the buyer accepts or rejects the contract; at $t = 3$, the entrant observes its costs and then decides whether to enter; at $t = 4$, there is price competition between sellers if the contract was rejected at $t = 2$; otherwise, the contract applies to the incumbent, whereas the entrant sets its price.

We will now show that the nonintegrated incumbent achieves the same allocation through a long-term contract as with vertical integration and that this is indeed its profit-maximizing strategy. Consider the following contract: the incumbent offers the product at price $3/4$ and sets a penalty for a breach of contract equal to $1/2$; this corresponds to liquidated damages.

Suppose the buyer accepts this contract. Conditional on the buyer signing the contract, we can then analyse the entrant's strategy. The entrant makes an offer to the buyer (who is already signed up). The buyer accepts any offer up to what it would have to pay if it honours the contract minus liquidated damages. Hence, it accepts any price

$$p \le \frac{3}{4} - \frac{1}{2} = \frac{1}{4}.$$

This implies that at stage 4, the entrant sets its price equal to $1/4$ provided that it covers its cost. At stage 3, the entrant becomes active if its costs are weakly less than $1/4$. The allocation then is the same as under vertical integration.

Two things remain to be checked. First, the buyer must have an incentive to sign the contract and secondly, it must be profitable for the incumbent seller to propose such a contract.

Let us analyse the incentive of the buyer to sign the contract. If the buyer rejects the contract and entry takes place, both firms are assumed to compete in prices (Bertrand competition). Clearly, entry takes place only if $c_E \le 1/2$. Hence, under competition, the entrant sells the product at a price equal to $c_I = 1/2$. Entry does not take place if $c_E > 1/2$. In this case, the incumbent's monopoly position allows him to extract the full surplus. This implies that the expected price paid by the buyer is

$$\text{Prob}\left(c_E \le \frac{1}{2}\right) \cdot \frac{1}{2} + \text{Prob}\left(c_E > \frac{1}{2}\right) \cdot 1 = \frac{1}{2} \cdot \frac{1}{2} + \frac{1}{2} \cdot 1 = \frac{3}{4}.$$

This is the same expected price if it signs the contract. Therefore, the buyer has no incentive to reject the contract proposed by the incumbent. Since under vertical integration the sum of the incumbent seller's profit and the buyer's net surplus is maximized and the entrant's profit is the same under the two solutions (the solution under vertical integration and the solution under the proposed long-term contract), the proposed contract maximizes the incumbent seller's expected profit.

[c] As in the asymmetric pure Bertrand model in Chapter 3, the following tie-breaking rule holds: if both firms set the same price, the consumer buys from the more efficient firm.

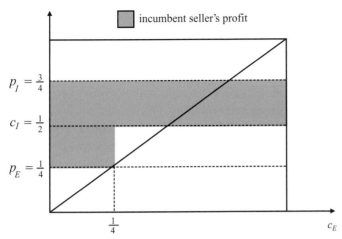

Figure 17.2 Exclusive dealing contracts as a barrier of entry: the incumbent seller's profit

To see that the incumbent is indeed better off with the long-term contract than without it, we calculate profits. With the proposed contract the incumbent seller makes expected profit

$$(p - c_I)\text{Prob}\left(c_E \geq \frac{1}{4}\right) + \quad \text{penalty} \times \text{Prob}\left(c_E < \frac{1}{4}\right)$$

$$= \left(\frac{3}{4} - \frac{1}{2}\right)\frac{3}{4} + \frac{1}{2}\frac{1}{4} = \frac{5}{16}.$$

We note that the contract has the property that profits turn out to be higher if the entrant has a low cost realization so that there is a breach of contract.

The profit is represented in Figure 17.2. If, alternatively, the incumbent seller did not propose any contract at stage 1, it would sell at c_E whenever $c_I \leq c_E$. The expected profit in that case is

$$\int_{\frac{1}{2}}^{1} \left(c_E - \frac{1}{2}\right) dc_E = \frac{1}{8},$$

which is clearly less than 5/16. We thus have shown that *in the model with uncertain costs of the entrant seller, the incumbent seller offers an exclusive contract before entry takes place that will be signed by the buyer. This contract implements the allocation under vertical integration and thus constitutes a barrier of entry.*

The general lesson from this analysis is that exclusive dealing can be anticompetitive. This contradicts the thinking of the Chicago Law School according to which exclusive dealing clauses are only used if there are efficiency gains from doing so. We summarize with the following lesson.

Lesson 17.6   **Under imperfect competition, exclusive dealing contracts that are signed before entry takes place can constitute a barrier of entry. In effect, there is too little entry from a welfare perspective.**

17.3.3   **Full exclusion and multiple buyers**

We have seen that due to imperfect competition and contract design which includes liquidated damages, an incumbent firm can exclude a more efficient rival. However, this exclusion was not always possible. We return to the basic setting in which a potential entrant has known costs $c_E < c_I$. Suppose that the entrant enjoys increasing returns so that its average cost is decreasing (or that it faces a U-shaped average cost function). This means that if a sufficiently large number of buyers sign up an exclusive dealing contract with the incumbent, the entrant cannot offer attractive terms to the remaining buyers. Effectively, by signing up with the incumbent, buyers exert a negative externality on other buyers. The incumbent thus avoids entry if it manages to convince a sufficiently large number of buyers to sign the exclusive dealing contract.[91]

Buyer (mis-)coordination

Our first insight concerns the possibility of buyer miscoordination. To show the potentially anticompetitive effect of exclusive dealing, it is sufficient to extend the basic setting that we presented for illustration of the Chicago critique by considering two buyers instead of one. Each buyer has the same demand curve $Q(p)$. Buyers (which again can be seen as monopoly retailers) simultaneously decide whether to sign the exclusive dealing contract, where the incumbent is assumed to offer the same contract to both buyers.

Suppose that in the absence of exclusive dealing contracts, entry by the more efficient firm takes place, i.e., $2(c_I - c_E)Q(c_I) > f$. However, let us assume that an entrant who sells to one buyer only cannot recover its entry costs at price c_I, i.e., $(c_I - c_E)Q(c_I) < f$. Hence, if the incumbent can sign the exclusive dealing contract with one buyer, entry is not viable.

Recall that the incumbent is willing to pay up to π^m to each buyer. Suppose that buyer 2 signs and let us investigate the behaviour of buyer 1. In such a situation, entry will not take place and the incumbent will set the monopoly price p^m independent of whether buyer 1 signs. Therefore, for any positive payment, buyer 1 has an incentive to sign. Since this argument applies symmetrically to buyer 2, we have found an equilibrium in which the incumbent offers a positive payment to both buyers for obtaining exclusivity, both buyers sign and entry by the efficient firm does not take place. Such a subgame perfect equilibrium has the feature that buyers suffer a coordination failure.

Lesson 17.7   Due to buyer miscoordination, an incumbent firm can possibly make buyers sign exclusive dealing clauses. Here, the incumbent firm is better off with these clauses in place and the more efficient rival firm is excluded from the market.

There exists another equilibrium in which buyers do coordinate their decisions. In this case, we are back to the original setting in which exclusive dealing clauses are not anticompetitive and will not arise in equilibrium. Hence, while we have learnt that exclusive dealing can be anticompetitive if buyers end up in an equilibrium which makes them both worse off, there remains some ambiguity as to whether this will indeed be the case since it requires miscoordination.

Discriminatory contracts

Consider now the possibility that the incumbent can propose discriminatory contracts. For instance, it may offer buyer 1 a contract that it finds impossible to resist. In this way, the incumbent can make sure that entry does not take place and that it obtains monopoly rents from buyer 2. Suppose the incumbent offers $\Delta CS = \int_{c_I}^{p^m} Q(p)dp$ plus some very small amount to buyer 1 for signing an exclusive dealing contract, while not making any contractual offer to buyer 2. Clearly, buyer 1 will accept this offer under our assumption that $(c_I - c_E)Q(p) < f$, i.e., entry will not take place. The incumbent is better off making such an offer rather than not making any offer if $2\pi^m - \Delta CS > 0$. It is easily verified that this inequality holds if demand is for instance linear. Such a 'divide-and-conquer' strategy is more costly for the incumbent than relying on buyer miscoordination but has the advantage for the incumbent that the entrant is excluded in *any* equilibrium following this contract offer.

> **Lesson 17.8** **By offering discriminatory contracts an incumbent firm can induce a subset of buyers to strictly prefer exclusive dealing and thus monopolize other buyers without paying them for signing exclusive dealing contracts. The rival firm is then effectively excluded from the market.**

This argument applies beyond the two-buyer specification. The incumbent only has to target a sufficiently large set of buyers. While 'convincing' these buyers leads to a net loss per attracted buyer, the incumbent obtains monopoly profits on the remaining set of buyers who were not targeted. If the second effect dominates the first, the incumbent strictly prefers exclusion through such discriminatory contracts to no exclusion. To implement discriminatory offers, the incumbent may condition its offers on observable characteristics of buyers. Alternatively, it may implement them by limiting the total number of buyers to which such an offer applies. This latter possibility suggests to take a closer look at the possibility that the incumbent can sequentially make contract proposals to buyers.

Sequential contract proposal

Suppose now that the incumbent can propose contracts sequentially and that such sequencing of contract proposal comes at negligible cost. As we will argue now, such sequential contracting is more profitable for the incumbent than a divide-and-conquer strategy. To see this, suppose that the incumbent first offers a contract to buyer 1 and then to buyer 2. We maintain the assumption that $(c_I - c_E)Q(p) < f$, so that an entrant needs both buyers to be profitable. Under the assumption $2\pi^m - \Delta CS > 0$ from above, it is thus profitable to offer a contract to buyer 2 that it prefers over rejecting the contract in case buyer 1 rejects the contract (this directly follows from the analysis of divide-and-conquer strategies). Buyer 1 foresees that if it rejects the contract, the incumbent will make sure that buyer 2 signs it. Since this forecloses the market, buyer 1 is willing to sign any contract that leaves a non-negative net surplus for itself. Once buyer 1 has signed, buyer 2 also signs any contract that does not make it worse off than not buying at all. Hence, the incumbent can exclude the entrant at zero cost and buyers do not benefit at all from the presence of a more efficient potential entrant.

To summarize the main insight of this and the previous subsection, efficient entrants may not be able to make it in the market if incumbent firms can use exclusive dealing contracts. Hence, *exclusive dealing may be anticompetitive in markets in which incumbents enjoy a high degree of market power*. But as mentioned in the beginning, there can be efficiency rationales in defence of the use of exclusive dealing. In the next subsection, we take a closer look at one particular efficiency argument.

17.3.4   Exclusive contracts and investment incentives

The value of a product or service is determined by investments at the seller and buyer (read retailer) level. Here, we focus on the relevance of investments at the retailer level that affect the value of a product. What kind of investments matter? For instance, a seller may train the sales staff of a retailer. Under an exclusive dealing contract, there are no other sellers that would benefit from such a training; hence, the investment only affects the value of a product within the buyer–seller relationship but there are no external effects. By contrast, in the absence of exclusive dealing, the other seller may reap some of the benefit from the investment because the sales staff may use their newly acquired skills to increase the sales of this alternative seller instead of the seller whose investment has lead to these improved skills in the first place. The investment may affect cost levels (e.g., by making sales staff more efficient) or the value of the product (e.g., because the training of the sales staff improves the match between final customers and product version and thus increases the willingness-to-pay).

To formally analyse this issue, suppose there is an incumbent seller (I), a buyer (B), and possibly an external source, an entrant seller (E).[92] Incumbent seller and buyer can sign an exclusive dealing contract. Then the incumbent seller or the buyer decides about an investment, which is not contractible. Depending on this investment, buyer and seller make a joint surplus that is to be divided among them. In the absence of exclusive dealing, the buyer is free to buy from an external source. In contrast, with exclusive dealing, the buyer needs to get the agreement of the incumbent seller to use the external source instead. To fix ideas, suppose that the entrant seller does not have any bargaining power, e.g., because there are several perfectly competitive entrant sellers offering their services. Concerning incumbent seller and buyer, we suppose that the two parties evenly split the surplus that is achieved on top of the disagreement value; this is the so-called Nash bargaining solution. The disagreement values are the payments that the parties would collect if they did not agree.

Let us first understand that an exclusive dealing contract does not affect investment levels if the investment does not affect the surplus obtained by contracting with the external source, i.e., if it leaves disagreement profits unchanged. An exclusive dealing contract is denoted by $x = 1$, whereas a nonexclusive dealing contract is denoted by $x = 0$. The incumbent's cost is c_I, and it requires the incumbent's relation-specific investment $A_I(c_I) \geq 0$, which is decreasing and strictly convex on $[\underline{c}_I, \overline{c}_I]$; the product has value r. The entrant seller's product has also value r and due to its lack of bargaining, the entrant accepts a contract that covers its costs c_E with $c_E < r$. Note that if $c_E < c_I$, incumbent seller and buyer can profitably renegotiate an exclusive dealing contract. However, the incumbent is compensated for waving the exclusive dealing contract and thus affects the ex post surplus among buyer and incumbent seller. The incumbent seller's surplus drives its ex ante investment incentive. We may then be tempted to claim that the use of exclusive contracts enhances the incumbent seller's investment incentives.[93] The reasoning here is that the incumbent seller affords a larger share of surplus in the ex post bargaining under exclusivity. Hence, ex ante investment incentives are strengthened. While this may sound convincing, the claim is wrong.

The total surplus in the market depends on which of the sellers is more efficient; it is given by $TS(c_I) = \max\{r - c_I, r - c_E\}$. Denote the disagreement profits by $v_I^0(c_I, x)$ and $v_E^0(c_I, x)$, respectively. Hence, the incumbent seller's *ex post* profit is $v_I^0(c_I, x) + [TS(c_I) - v_I^0(c_I, x) - v_E^0(c_I, x)]/2 - A_I(c_I)$.

We want to compare the investment choice under exclusive to the one under nonexclusive contracts. Consider first the nonexclusive contract $x = 0$. The disagreement profit of the incumbent seller is 0. The buyer can extract the full rent from the external source and thus has disagreement profit $v_E^0(c_I, x) = r - c_E$. Both disagreement profits are independent of c_I. The buyer's profit is $(r - c_E) + \max\{(r - c_I) - (r - c_E), 0\}/2$ and the incumbent seller's profit is $\max\{(r - c_I) - (r - c_E), 0\}/2 - A_I(c_I)$. The profit maximizing investment level $A_I(c_I)$, if different from zero, is determined by the solution of $TS'(c_I)/2 = A'(c_I)$ to c_I. Since the incumbent captures only half the surplus that is generated through the investment, it underinvests.

Consider now the investment level under exclusion. In this case, the disagreement profit of both the incumbent seller and the buyer are equal to zero, since the buyer cannot source externally without the agreement of the incumbent seller. Gross of the investment cost, the incumbent seller and the buyer obtain $\max\{(r - c_I), 0\}/2$. Since also with exclusion, disagreement levels are independent of the incumbent seller's investment, its investment choice is not affected by the presence of exclusive dealing. Note that the incumbent seller's profit is larger under exclusion; however, this additional profit $(r - c_E)/2$ is independent of the investment level. Clearly, the buyer is willing to sign the exclusive dealing contract for the payment of this amount. Otherwise, that is, if the payment is less, it would do better under non-exclusion.[d, 94]

Lesson 17.9 In a bargaining environment in which incumbent seller and buyer share any surplus above their disagreement profits and in which profits of any entrant seller are held down to zero, exclusive dealing does not affect the incumbent seller's investment incentives, provided that this investment does not affect the surplus that can be generated by contracting with the entrant seller instead.

The main objective of this analysis is to show that exclusive dealing can be efficiency-enhancing because it protects investments by the incumbent seller. To this effect, suppose that there are positive spillovers, i.e., also c_E depends negatively on the investment level. Hence, when reducing c_I the incumbent seller also reduces c_E. We therefore write $c_E(c_I)$ with $c_E' > 0$. Under an exclusive contract, the incumbent seller's profit is as before

---

[d] A qualitatively different result emerges if we consider a market in which exclusion cannot be renegotiated, e.g., because exclusion is accompanied by technological constraints that are implemented ex ante and that do not allow to source externally. If $c_E < c_I < r$, total surplus is $\widetilde{TS}(c_I) = r - c_I$, while disagreement profits are zero. In this case $\widetilde{TS}'(c_I) = -1 < 0 = TS'(c_I)$. Hence, the possibility arises that the incumbent seller has a stronger investment incentive under a nonrenegotiable exclusive contract than in the absence of exclusion.

$\max\{(r - c_I), 0\}/2 - A_I(c_I)$. However, with the nonexclusive contract, the incumbent seller now obtains $\max\{(r - c_I) - (r - c_E(c_I)), 0\}/2 - A_I(c_I)$. The profit-maximizing investment level $A_I(c_I)$, if different from zero, is now determined by solving $(-1 + c_E'(c_I))/2 = A'(c_I)$ in c_I. For any given cost $c_I \in [\underline{c}_I, \overline{c}_I]$, the left-hand side is greater than $TS'(c_I)/2 = -1/2$ under exclusion. This implies that the incumbent seller has a stronger incentive to invest under exclusion.

The general argument is that if third parties can free-ride on the investment of the upstream firm, the upstream firm has weaker incentives to invest. Exclusive dealing clauses can protect investment incentives and can thus be seen as efficiency-enhancing. Clearly, in real-world cases there can be a tension between the possibility of vertical foreclosure and efficiency-enhancing investments, as the following case illustrates.[95]

Case 17.6 Spontaneous ice cream purchases in Germany[96]

For quick consumption, part of the industrial ice cream is sold in individual portions, typically close to cashiers and at visible places in supermarkets and the like. In 1990, this market segment was highly concentrated with Langnese-Iglo's market share above 50%, Schöller at more than 25% and the rest spread around 12 other manufacturers, each with a market share of less than 10%. In this market, manufacturers often use exclusive dealing clauses. They come in two forms. The manufacturer can provide retailers with one or several freezer cabinets (on loan) under the condition that the retailer does not store any other products than the ones by the manufacturer in it; call this freezer exclusivity. The manufacturer can also require the retailer not to sell any competitors' products in the shop. While one can distinguish between these two clauses, in practice this distinction is immaterial if installing more than one freezer is not an option (as in small shops). The competition concern in this market is that large manufacturers can use exclusivity clauses to foreclose entry. This is of particular concern for manufacturers who do not have other strong brands in their portfolio which the retailer would like to carry. However, there are also clear reasons to believe that efficiency concerns should be taken seriously into account because one cannot expect manufacturers to invest in freezers which are installed in the shops if retailers can use these freezers for products of any other manufacturer and, in particular, direct competitors. This suggests that at least freezer exclusivity should be allowed. However, the European Commission decided differently in 1992 and prohibited Langnese-Iglo and Schöller from using any of the exclusivity clauses. This decision was later confirmed by the courts.

17.4   Vertical oligopoly and vertical mergers

While the majority of antitrust merger cases concerns horizontal mergers, there is a number of important merger cases in which vertical aspects play a key role.[e] Vertical mergers raise

[e] Famous cases are e.g. Brown Shoe Co. vs. United States (1962) as discussed below, Civic Aeronautics Board (1984), and GE/Honeywell (2001).

antitrust concerns for two set of reasons, exclusionary effects and collusive effects. However, there are often arguments why a vertical merger may be efficiency increasing, in particular, because it avoids double marginalization and because it internalizes externalities with respect to investment activities between upstream and downstream firms. In this section, we will take a look at exclusionary effects and then address coordinated effects. Before doing so, we present the Cournot model in the context of vertical oligopoly, i.e., there are several upstream and downstream firms which set quantities.[97]

17.4.1   Vertical oligopoly

Many downstream industries use inputs from upstream industries which are also organized oligopolistically. The double-marginalization problem analysed under monopoly continues to be an issue under oligopoly. While this basic insight is general, the precise workings of vertically related oligopolies can be intricate. One issue which we will abstract from is that a downstream firm that increases output not only faces a low retail price but also has to pay a higher input price due to an increase of input demand.[98]

We consider a Cournot industry with an upstream and a downstream sector. In the upstream sector, $n^u \geq 1$ symmetric firms produce a homogeneous intermediate good at constant marginal costs $c > 0$. In the downstream sector, the intermediate good constitutes an input and $n^d \geq 1$ symmetric firms transform one unit of input into one unit of a homogeneous final good at constant marginal costs; if downstream firms are retailers, the one-to-one conversion naturally holds. Marginal costs in the downstream sector are normalized to zero. Inverse demand $P(q)$ is downward sloping, $P'(q) < 0$ and $q = \sum_{i=1}^{n} q_i$.[99]

Firms play a two-stage game. At the first stage, upstream firms set upstream quantities simultaneously. The market-clearing input price (from the point of view of downstream firms), denoted by w, is determined by equating the total amount of output supplied by the upstream firms with the demand of the downstream firms. At the second stage, downstream firms set quantities in the final good market. Here, downstream firms are assumed not to have market power in the upstream sector (and thus take w as given).[100] The equilibrium concept is subgame perfect Nash equilibrium.

Let us first look at the general specification before turning to the linear-demand specification. Solving the game by backward induction we can write the profit function of downstream firm i as

$$\pi_i(q_i, q_{-i}) = q_i (P(q) - w),$$

where $q_{-i} = q - q_i$. The resulting first-order condition of profit maximization is

$$\frac{\partial \pi_i}{\partial q_i} = P(q) - w + q_i P'(q) = 0.$$

Noting that at a symmetric equilibrium we have $q_i = q/n^d$ for $i = 1, \dots, n^d$, we can rewrite the first-order condition and obtain[101]

$$w = P(q) + \frac{q P'(q)}{n^d}. \tag{17.4}$$

Using (17.4), we can derive the profit function of upstream firm j. Denote the aggregate quantity produced by the upstream firms as x, where $x = \sum_{j=1}^{n^u} x_j$ and $x_{-j} = x - x_j$

and note that in equilibrium $q = x$. Thus, the profit function of upstream firm j can be written as

$$\pi_j(x_j, x_{-j}) = x_j \left(\left(P(x) + \frac{x P'(x)}{n^d} \right) - c \right). \tag{17.5}$$

This yields the first-order condition

$$\frac{\partial \pi_j}{\partial x_j} = \left[P(x) + \frac{x P'(x)}{n^d} + x_j P'(x) \frac{1 + n^d}{n^d} + \frac{x_j x P''(x)}{n^d} \right] - c = 0.$$

Using the fact that in a symmetric equilibrium $n^u x_j = n^d q_i = q$, we can conclude that aggregate quantity in this two-layer industry is given by

$$\left[P(q^\star) + \frac{q^\star P'(q^\star)}{n^d} + \frac{(1 + n^d) q^\star P'(q^\star)}{n^d n^u} + \frac{(q^\star)^2 P''(q^\star)}{n^d n^u} \right] - c = 0. \tag{17.6}$$

In equilibrium with strictly positive quantity, Equation (17.6) has to be satisfied.[102] Note that due to the vertical structure not only elasticities but also changes in elasticity enter the equation.

Let us now consider the linear case $P(q) = a - bq$, which allows us to explicitly solve for equilibrium market prices. We analysed the Cournot equilibrium of the downstream market in Chapter 3. Recall that for a given wholesale price w the equilibrium quantity is

$$q = \frac{n^d}{n^d + 1} \frac{a - w}{b}.$$

so that the retail price satisfies

$$p = a - bq = \frac{a + n^d w}{n^d + 1} > w,$$

as $a > w$. The wholesale price is

$$w = a - b \frac{n^d + 1}{n^d} q.$$

Since, in equilibrium, $q = x$ the profit function of upstream firm j in the linear demand case is

$$\pi_j(x_j, x_{-j}) = x_j \left(a - b \frac{n^d + 1}{n^d} x - c \right).$$

The first-order condition of profit maximization is thus

$$a - b \frac{n^d + 1}{n^d} (2 x_j + x_{-j}) - c = 0.$$

Summing up over all n^u upstream firms, we obtain

$$n^u a - b \frac{n^d + 1}{n^d} (n^u + 1) x - n^u c = 0,$$

which is equivalent to

$$x = \frac{n^d}{n^d + 1} \frac{n^u}{n^u + 1} \frac{a - c}{b}.$$

Due to double marginalization, total output is thus lower than in an industry in which the input is supplied competitively at marginal costs (as in that case, output would be equal to

$(a - c)/b)$. In subgame perfect equilibrium, wholesale and retail prices are

$$w^* = \frac{1}{n^u + 1}a + \frac{n^u}{n^u + 1}c,$$

$$p^* = \frac{n^u + n^d + 1}{(n^u + 1)(n^d + 1)}a + \frac{n^d}{n^d + 1}\frac{n^u}{n^u + 1}c.$$

We observe that in vertical oligopoly the retail price is larger and the total quantity smaller than under downstream oligopoly and upstream perfect competition. Also, the retail prices under vertical oligopoly react less sensitively to a change in marginal costs c. Clearly, keeping the number of downstream firms fixed, the double-marginalization problem becomes less pronounced as the number of upstream firms increases.

Lesson 17.10 **The double-marginalization problem persists in vertical oligopoly. Compared to a perfectly competitive upstream industry it is the more pronounced the more concentrated the upstream market.**

17.4.2   Exclusionary effects of vertical mergers

Vertical mergers can have efficiency-enhancing as well as anticompetitive effects. One concern about vertical mergers is that they effectively foreclose the access to inputs. Foreclosure here means that inputs are not – or only at a higher price – available to nonintegrated downstream rivals. Another concern is the foreclosure to customers. Anticompetitive harm is understood, by today's antitrust authorities, as a situation where consumers are hurt (meaning that consumer surplus is reduced). However, in the 1960s and 1970s, the mere fact that rival's might be hurt was seen as sufficient reason to prohibit vertical mergers (even in industries that are not very concentrated).

Case 17.7 Vertical merger in the US shoe industry[103]

Two US shoe companies, Brown Shoe and Kinney, wanted to merge their activities. Brown Shoe was the number 4 shoe manufacturer with a market share of 4 per cent, and the number 3 shoe retailer. Kinney was the largest shoe retailer with a market share less than 2 percent. It was also a manufacturer (number 12). In 1962, the US Supreme Court prohibited this merger on the ground that it foreclosed competitors from the market and thus put rivals at a disadvantage.

According to this view, the antitrust authorities should intervene if competitors are hurt. This approach came under attack in the 1970s since it rules out vertical mergers even if efficiency-enhancing effects (such as the avoidance of double marginalization or non-price efficiencies) lead to final consumers being better off. In other words, the role of competition authorities should not be to protect competitors but to protect competition. In particular, while antitrust authorities should be concerned with foreclosure, the possibility of foreclosure is not a sufficient condition for intervention.

The model

We focus on input foreclosure: vertical integration may lead to higher input (or wholesale) prices for competitors.[104] The higher price may be due to vertically integrated firms not selling inputs on the market or, at least, restricting their supply. This means that vertical integration can be used as a tool to increase the rivals' costs. As we have seen in the previous chapter, the analysis of raising-the-rivals'-costs strategies depends very much on whether market interaction is in strategic substitutes or strategic complements. We start with a setting with strategic substitutes. More specifically, we postulate that the upstream and downstream markets are homogeneous oligopolies, where firms are Cournot competitors. Suppose that first upstream and then downstream firms simultaneously set quantities, as has been the case in the previous subsection.[105]

Consider a market in which n^u firms compete upstream and n^d firms compete downstream. Inverse demand takes a linear form, $P(q) = a - bq$. Considering vertical mergers by k upstream and k downstream firms, there remain $n^u - k$ nonintegrated upstream firms and $n^d - k$ nonintegrated downstream firms.[f] Here vertically integrated firms are assumed not to be able to commit to quantity in the upstream market but can rather flexibly adjust production according to demand conditions in the downstream market. While the marginal cost of a vertically integrated firm is c, downstream firms face an input price of w per unit, which is determined by the market.

Note that the upstream component of the vertically integrated firm could sell to other downstream firms. However, this would lower the wholesale price and thus the cost-advantage a vertically integrated firm enjoys downstream. In this setting the profit-maximizing choice of a vertically integrated firm depends on its conjectures about the response of total quantity upstream and downstream in response to its activity on the input market. Here, we assume that if a vertically integrated firm sells an extra unit of the input, it presumes that all other upstream manufacturers do not change their quantity. Consequently, total quantity by downstream firms has to increase by this extra unit. To capture also the profit margin in the downstream market, it would do better selling the unit downstream itself than sell it as an input to some downstream firm. We also assume that if a vertically integrated firm buys one unit of input from some other upstream firm, it presumes that the total quantity of inputs increases by one unit (i.e. the wholesale price remains constant). Then it is better for the firm to produce this extra unit itself than to buy it from another firm. These assumptions are in accordance with the vertical oligopoly model presented in the previous subsection and imply that vertically integrated firms neither sell nor buy in the wholesale market.[106] Hence, even if $w > c$, vertically integrated firms do not sell inputs on the market because they anticipate that this feeds into higher total output thus reducing the retail price p. Alternatively, we may assume that vertically integrated firms can commit neither to sell nor to buy inputs to the downstream industry. In particular,

---

[f] While the occurence of k simultaneous vertical mergers may appear to be highly unlikely, we should think of this as the outcome of a vertical merger wave (which stops when additional mergers are no longer profitable or are prohibited by antitrust authorities).

the use of specific technologies or the lumpy decision to enrol on a trading platform for inputs can provide such a commitment.

Downstream equilibrium

Profits for nonintegrated downstream firms are $\pi^D = q_i(P(q) - w) = q_i(a - bq - w)$; profits for integrated firms are $\pi^I = q_i(P(q) - c)$. First-order conditions of profit maximization can be rewritten as

$$q_i = \frac{a - c - bq_{-i}}{2b} \quad \text{for } i = 1, \ldots, k,$$

$$q_j = \frac{a - w - bq_{-j}}{2b} \quad \text{for } j = k + 1, \ldots, n^d.$$

In equilibrium, $q^I = q_i$ for all $i = 1, \ldots, k$ and $q^{NI} = q_j$ for all $j = k + 1, \ldots, n^d$. Hence, $q_{-i} = (k - 1)q^I + (n^d - k)q^{NI}$ and $q_{-j} = kq^I + (n^d - k - 1)q^{NI}$ in the above equations, which can then be rewritten as

$$\begin{cases} (n^d - k)q^{NI} + (k + 1)q^I = \frac{a-c}{b}, \\ (n^d - k + 1)q^{NI} + kq^I = \frac{a-w}{b}. \end{cases}$$

Solving the system of two equations, equilibrium quantities in the downstream market at the given wholesale price w are

$$q^I = \frac{1}{b(n^d + 1)} \left[a - c + (n^d - k)(w - c) \right], \tag{17.7}$$

$$q^{NI} = \frac{1}{b(n^d + 1)} \left[a - w - k(w - c) \right]. \tag{17.8}$$

Due to double marginalization, $w > c$ and $q^I > q^{NI}$. Hence, the cost-advantage of a vertically integrated firm depends on the degree of market power of upstream manufacturers.

Upstream equilibrium

Solving (17.8) for the wholesale price we have that the wholesale price is equal to

$$w = \frac{a + kc}{k + 1} - b \frac{n^d + 1}{k + 1} q^{NI}. \tag{17.9}$$

At the upstream level, $n^u - k$ nonintegrated firms compete in quantities. Total input by non-integrated firms is $x_j + (n^u - k - 1)x^{NI}$ given that all other nonintegrated upstream firms choose x^{NI}. Since $x_j + (n^u - k - 1)x^{NI} = (n^d - k)q^{NI}$, we can write the wholesale price as a function of x_j:

$$w = \frac{a + kc}{k + 1} - b \frac{n^d + 1}{k + 1} \frac{x_j + (n^u - k - 1)x^{NI}}{n^d - k}.$$

Each nonintegrated upstream firm solves

$$x^{NI} = \arg\max_{x_j} \frac{1}{k + 1} \left(a - c - b \frac{n^d + 1}{n^d - k} \left[x_j + (n^u - k - 1)x^{NI} \right] \right) x_j.$$

In equilibrium, upstream production is

$$x^{NI} = \frac{n^d - k}{n^d + 1} \frac{1}{n^u - k + 1} \frac{a - c}{b}.$$

Since $(n^u - k)x^{NI} = (n^d - k)q^{NI}$, we have

$$q^{NI} = \frac{n^u - k}{n^d - k} x^{NI} = \frac{n^u - k}{n^u - k + 1} \frac{1}{n^d + 1} \frac{a - c}{b}.$$

Substituting this expression into Equation (17.9), we obtain the equilibrium wholesale price

$$w = \frac{a + kc}{k + 1} - \frac{a - c}{k + 1} \frac{n^u - k}{n^u - k + 1}$$

$$= c + \frac{a - c}{(k + 1)(n^u - k + 1)}.$$

Impacts of vertical mergers

We first observe in the latter expression that w is increasing in k if and only if $k > n^u/2$. In words, the wholesale price that nonintegrated downstream competitors have to pay increases with vertical integration if at least $n^u/2$ firms with upstream activities are already vertically integrated. This demonstrates the possibility of foreclosure in a market in which vertical integration eliminates the double-marginalization problem.

However, an open question is whether final customers gain or lose from vertical integration. Higher input prices for nonintegrated firms tend to be also bad news for final customers. For this we have to study the effect of vertical integration on retail prices.

Concerning the vertically integrated firm's quantity, we can calculate

$$x^I = q^I = \frac{1}{b(n^d + 1)} [a - c + (n^d - k)(w - c)]$$

$$= \frac{1}{b(n^d + 1)} \left[a - c + (n^d - k) \frac{a - c}{(k + 1)(n^u - k + 1)} \right]$$

$$= \frac{1}{n^d + 1} \left[1 + \frac{n^d - k}{(k + 1)(n^u - k + 1)} \right] \frac{a - c}{b}.$$

The equilibrium retail price is thus given by

$$p = a - b[kx^I + (n^u - k)x^{NI}]$$

$$= a - \frac{1}{n^d + 1} \left[k \left(1 + \frac{n^d - k}{(k + 1)(n^u - k + 1)} \right) + (n^u - k) \frac{n^d - k}{n^u - k + 1} \right] (a - c)$$

$$= a - \frac{1}{n^d + 1} \left[k + \frac{n^d - k}{n^u - k + 1} \left(\frac{k}{k + 1} + (n^u - k) \right) \right] (a - c)$$

$$= c + \frac{1}{n^d + 1} \left[1 + \frac{n^d - k}{(k + 1)(n^u - k + 1)} \right] (a - c).$$

We can now answer whether vertical integration leads to higher or lower retail prices. Let us treat k as a continuous variable. Then we compute the derivative of the retail price with respect to k as

$$\frac{dp}{dk} = \frac{(a-c)}{(n^d+1)(k+1)^2(n^u-k+1)^2}\left[-k^2+2n^dk-\left(n^u+n^dn^u+1\right)\right].$$

The sign of the derivative is given by the sign of the polynomial of degree 2 in k. Two cases have to be distinguished. First, if $n^d \leq n^u + 1$, then the polynomial admits no real root and is always negative, meaning that more vertical integration (i.e., an increase in k) decreases the retail price. Second, if $n^d > n^u + 1$, then the polynomial admits two roots: $k^+ = n^d + \sqrt{(n^d+1)(n^d-n^u-1)}$ and $k^- = n^d - \sqrt{(n^d+1)(n^d-n^u-1)}$. It is easily seen that $k^+ > n^d$ (and thus cannot be reached as $k < n^u < n^d$) and $0 < k^- \leq n^u$. It follows that the polynomial is negative for $0 \leq k < k^-$ and positive for $k^- < k \leq n^u$. In sum, two conditions must be met for an additional vertical merger to increase the retail price: (i) there must be strictly more firms downstream than upstream ($n^d > n^u + 1$), and (ii) the level of vertical integration must already be sufficiently large ($k > k^-$).

Note also that it can be checked that $k^- > n^u/2$, meaning that it takes a larger number of vertical mergers to increase the retail price than to increase the wholesale price. For an illustration, set $n^u = 10$ and $n^d = 15$; then $n^u/2 = 5$ and $k^- = 7$. If we increase the number of vertical mergers from 0 to 10, we observe that (i) the wholesale and retail prices decrease up to $k = 5$, (ii) the wholesale price increases while the retail price still decreases when going to $k = 6$ and $k = 7$, and (iii) both prices increase when increasing k above 7.

We summarize our analysis with the following lesson.

Lesson 17.11   **Vertical integration may raise the costs of nonintegrated downstream rivals. A higher wholesale price may or may not lead to higher retail prices.**

Profitability of vertical mergers

Note that we thus have identified that vertical integration can be a tool to increase the rivals' costs: nonintegrated downstream firms have to pay a higher input price. As we have shown, this may lead to higher retail prices so that final consumers are worse off even though the vertically integrated firm avoids inefficiencies due to double marginalization. However, one open question is whether vertical integration is profitable for the firms involved. Calculations are rather involved and we only want to mention that conditions are very demanding for vertical integration to be profitable unless all downstream firms have vertically integrated. To conclude this part of the analysis, we have formalized the notion that vertical mergers can lead to foreclosure in the sense that rival firms have to pay a higher input price after a vertical merger. However, such mergers may not hurt consumers (since retail prices may fall) and often are not profitable for the firms involved in the merger, unless one side of the market becomes fully vertically integrated.

Also in a price competition setting vertical integration can be used to reduce competition in the upstream market.[107] Suppose that an upstream duopoly sells a homogeneous product to differentiated downstream firms at a wholesale price w. If the vertically integrated firm withdraws from the input market, it increases the market power of the nonintegrated upstream firm. Increased market power leads to higher input prices and thus to less aggressive behaviour by downstream rivals of the integrated firm. Strategic complementarity implies that downstream prices of all nonintegrated firms are larger than in the absence of integration. Unless the countervailing effect of eliminating double marginalization is too strong, consumers suffer from higher retail prices and integration is profit increasing.

Here, we have looked at an isolated vertical merger. The induced cost difference in the downstream market can be avoided by counter mergers of other nonintegrated downstream and upstream firms leading to a vertical merger wave. This suggests that this may not be the end of a story in a full-fledged analysis of mergers. However, this requires that willing partners in the other sector are available after a vertical merger. Even if those partners are available, later vertical mergers may not deliver the same increase in operating profits and thus may not be attractive, including any costs of organizing the vertical merger.[108]

While our focus has been on input foreclosure, vertical merger analyses are also concerned with the possibility of customer foreclosure according to which nonintegrated upstream firms are denied access to its distribution or retail channel. This reduces the non-integrated upstream rivals' possibilities to sell their product. We can apply our insights from the analyses of exclusive dealing clauses. These considered markets in which the distribution channel of the downstream firm is essential. The lesson is clear: Vertical integration which effectively leads to upstream competitors being denied access to the distribution channel of the vertically integrated firm can have anticompetitive effects.

In addition to solving double-marginalization problems several non-price efficiencies can explain the success of vertically integrated firms. For instance, a vertically integrated firm may better coordinate the logistics of upstream and downstream activities. Also, it may be superior in providing investment incentives even though contractual relationships may be quite successful, as has been discussed in the previous section.

While exclusionary effects of vertical mergers have to be taken seriously into account in highly concentrated industries, one should not be overwhelmed by the possibility of anti-competitive outcomes due to vertical integration. Vertical integration must not only foreclose nonintegrated competitors, it must also be anticompetitive and it must be profitable for the firms involved. Efficiency gains may make vertical integration attractive from a social point of view.

Case 17.8 Vertical integration in cements and ready-mixed industries in the US[109]

An empirical analysis of the cements and ready-mixed concrete industries by Hortaçsu and Syverson (2007) provides support for an efficiency defence of vertical mergers. The data cover the period from 1963 to 1997 in which the two industries experienced two periods of integration. The first vertical merger wave took place in the first half of the 1960s. As a response, following a rather naive foreclosure theory, the courts ruled against those mergers. As a consequence of the Chicago Law School, the rationale for foreclosure was questioned. This has been made explicit by the Federal Trade Commission which, in 1985, explicitly relaxed its enforcement policy regarding vertical mergers in the two industries. As a consequence, the fraction of cement plants that were part of vertically integrated firms rose from 32.5 to 49.5 percent in the period 1982 to 1992 (the fraction of sales rose from 49.5 to 75.1 percent).

Are vertical mergers anticompetitive? Final prices would rise as a result of vertical mergers if the anticompetitive concerns were warranted. By contrast, lower retail prices suggest that vertical mergers are consumer-surplus increasing. Hortaçsu and Syverson do not find evidence for anticompetitive mergers. They observe that greater vertical integration in a market corresponds to the expansion of larger, more productive integrated firms: these integrated firms increase market share to the detriment of less efficient producers, which are higher priced. However, once having controlled for firm size and productivity impacts, vertical integration itself hardly explains plant- and market-level outcomes. Efficiencies thus appear not to be linked to vertical integration itself. Efficiency is rather linked to firm size in the downstream market. These more efficient firms simply tend to be vertically integrated.

This leaves us with one more concern about vertical integration: coordinated effects.

17.4.3   Coordinated effects of vertical mergers

Vertical mergers may have negative welfare consequences due to coordinated effects: vertical integration may improve the viability of collusion among competing firms.[110] In line with the analysis in Chapter 15, a vertical merger is said to facilitate collusion if it reduces the critical discount factor above which the monopoly outcome can be sustained using trigger strategies – recall that this involves the infinite reversion to the Nash equilibrium of the static game following a deviation by one of the firms.

A key reason for vertical integration facilitating collusion is the *outlets effect*: vertical integration by an upstream firm reduces the number of outlets through which its rivals can sell when deviating. This generally reduces their profit from cheating and thus facilitates collusion. Counteracting the outlets effect is the *punishment effect*. If an upstream firm integrates with a downstream firm, these profits now become part of the profit of the merged entity. Thus the merged entity can expect to make more profits in the non-cooperative punishment phase than the upstream firm would make alone. However, absent any changes in market share, the merged entity will make the same profit as a stand-alone upstream firm when monopoly profits are sustained by collusion upstream. So, for a given collusive market share, the merged entity suffers less than a stand-alone upstream firm from a switch from collusive to punishment phases, and is correspondingly more tempted to cheat on any collusive agreement. It can be shown that *the outlets effect outweighs the punishment effect so that the net effect of a vertical merger is to facilitate collusion.*

This result can be shown in a rather general setting. For simplicity, we confine ourselves to a particular numerical example to make this point.[111] Suppose that the maximal industry profit in the market under consideration is 100, and that there are 5 upstream and 5 downstream firms. Upstream firms can set nonlinear prices to extract rents from downstream firms. If firms in the upstream market collude (symmetrically), they can make 20 each. To obtain this profit, downstream firms must be induced to set the price equal to the monopoly price of the vertically integrated structure and all rents must be extracted upstream.

If firms do not collude in this homogeneous product market, the five upstream firms are supposed to obtain zero profits; downstream firms are assumed to make profits of 10. This will constitute the punishment outcome after a deviation by one of the firms is detected. Hence, a deviating upstream firm faces the trade-off of an immediate gain of $100 - 20 = 80$ versus a loss of 20 in each subsequent period if upstream firms use grim trigger strategies. Hence, for a sufficiently large discount factor a deviation is not profitable: $80 - [\delta/(1 - \delta)]20 \leq 0$ or, equivalently, $\delta \geq 8/10$.

We will now argue that vertical integration can lead to a critical discount factor less than 0.8. In other words, collusion can more easily be supported if an upstream firm integrates with a downstream firm. Consider that one upstream and one downstream firm have vertically integrated and that the integrated firm deviates. Now the integrated firm can make strictly positive profits after collusion has broken down. Suppose that this punishment payoff is equal to 10, which stems from the firm's downstream activities. Since deviation profits are larger than in the absence of collusion, it becomes more difficult to support collusion. This can be called the punishment effect. For vertical integration to facilitate collusion, the integrated firm must obtain a larger share of total producer surplus under collusion. Let it obtain 30 (20 from the sales of its integrated downstream activities and 10 from sales to the four nonintegrated downstream firms). Hence, a deviation of the integrated firm is not profitable if $(100 - 30) - [\delta/(1 - \delta)](30 - 10) \leq 0$ or $\delta \geq 7/9$.

The key question now is for which discount factors the nonintegrated firms do not have an incentive to deviate from the collusive outcome. To avoid further complications, we assume that the integrated firm does not adjust its output. This holds if downstream prices are set at the same time upstream offers are being made. If a nonintegrated upstream firm deviates from the collusive strategy, it cannot profitably sell to the integrated firm because the latter internalizes that it then would forego profits from its integrated activities. Hence, the short-term profit of a deviating nonintegrated firm is only 80 in the presence of an integrated firm. This reduction of the nonintegrated firm's deviation rents tends to make collusion more easily supported. We have called this the outlets effect because the deviating nonintegrated firm can sell through fewer 'outlets'. There is a countervailing effect though: under collusion, the nonintegrated firms can only share a profit of 70 among 4, which gives 17.5 per firm. According to this punishment effect, the long-term loss for a deviating nonintegrated upstream firm is less in the situation with vertical integration. The outlets effect dominates the punishment effect if $(80 - 17.5) - [\delta/(1 - \delta)]17.5 \leq 0$ or, equivalently, $\delta \geq 25/32 \approx 0.78125$. Since this number is less than 8/10, we have shown that vertical integration facilitates collusion: there are discount factors such that collusion can be sustained only if there is vertical integration in the industry. For such discount factors all upstream firms in the industry benefit from vertical integration.

Lesson 17.12   Downstream vertical integration reduces the number of outlets through which upstream rivals can sell and thus reduces profits if deviating from a collusive outcome. Vertical integration may then facilitate collusion.

If downstream firms set their prices after the upstream offers have become available, the analysis becomes more involved and additional effects come into play. However, the lesson that vertical integration can facilitate collusion remains robust.

Review questions

1. Suppose that an industry consists of two upstream monopolists who exclusively sell at a linear price to one downstream duopolist each. What would be the effect of vertical integration (so that each upstream monopolist owns its retail outlet) on the final good price?

2. What are possible efficiency-defences of the use of resale-price maintenance?

3. For which reasons can it be profitable for manufacturers to grant exclusive territories to their retailers?

4. Provide two reasons why the Chicago school argument on exclusive dealing (namely that, whenever exclusive dealing is observed, it must be welfare improving) is wrong.

5. Should competition authorities prohibit vertical mergers that lead to higher input prices?

6. What are possible coordinated effects of vertical mergers?

Further reading

For work on resale-price maintenance we follow Winter (1993); other important works include Mathewson and Winter (1984) and Jullien and Rey (2007). For work on exclusive territories, see Rey and Stiglitz (1995). Key contributions to the analysis of exclusive dealing are Aghion and Bolton (1987), Rasmussen, Ramseyer and Wiley (1991), Bernheim and Whinston (1998), and Segal and Whinston (2000a, 2000b). More work is surveyed by Rey and Vergé (2008). Our exposition on exclusionary effects of vertical mergers follows mostly Salinger (1988). Other important contributions include Ordover, Saloner and Salop (1990) and Chen (2001). On coordinated effects of vertical mergers, see Nocke and White (2007). Surveys on vertical integration which are targeted at competition policy audiences are provided by Church (2008) and Riordan (2008).

Notes for Part VI

1. See Neelie Kroes' personal web page at ec.europa.eu/commission_barroso/kroes/whatido_en.html. Last consulted 29 December 2008.

2. The first two quotes come from Neelie Kroes' personal web page. The last quote comes from Kroes (2008).

3. This quote and the next come from Kroes (2008).

4. See Kroes (2007a).

5. See Kroes (2007b).

6. See European Commission (2001a).

7. See European Commission (2001b).

8. See European Commission (2001b, p. 1).

9. We follow here Bloch (2002).

10. Note that these models can be seen as merger games in which firms can disintegrate.

11. This typology is due to d'Aspremont et al. (1983).

12. This model is proposed by Bloch (1996).

13. The polynomial in the second bracket has two roots: $(1/2)(2n + 3 \pm v(4n + 5))$. The larger root is clearly larger than n, while the smaller root can be shown to be positive.

14. This notion of pairwise stability has been introduced by Jackson and Wolinsky (1996). The analysis of networks of bilateral market-sharing agreements is due to Belleflamme and Bloch (2004).

15. See, e.g., Friedman (1971, 1977).

16. For details on prices see Connor (2001).

17. Under cost asymmetries things are more tricky. See Miklos-Thal (2008).

18. See Abreu (1986, 1988).

19. We follow here the seminal analysis of Bernheim and Whinston (1990).

20. This case is based on Evans and Kessides (1994).

21. Belleflamme and Bloch (2008) show that this result is only partly true when firms compete in quantities.

22. This case draws from Belleflamme and Bloch (2004).

23. See Scherer and Ross (1990), pp. 318–319.

24. See Official Journal L 152, 15/06/1991, pp. 1–15.

25. The analysis is based on Rotemberg and Saloner (1986).

26. Allowing for correlated demand would substantially complicate the analysis without affecting our main insights.

27. Note that the Rotemberg–Saloner model is not the only explanation of countercyclical markups. Another explanation is that demand may be less elastic during recessions leading to higher markups in monopolistic or imperfectly competitive markets in the absence of collusion; see e.g. Stiglitz (1984) and Bils (1989). Also capital market imperfections can generate countercyclical markups; see e.g. Chevalier and Scharfstein (1996). According to this explanation, firms have low cash flows and greater difficulties in obtaining external funding during recessions. As a response, firms try to boost current profits by increasing price and care less about building market share.

28. See Scherer (1980).

29. See Rotemberg and Saloner (1986).

30. The analysis is based on Green and Porter (1984).

31. See European Commission (2001b, p. 2). The members of the cartel thus were able to allocate sales quotas, effectively cementing their market shares, and to agree on target prices including simultaneous price increases. The actions of the different cartels were also coordinated between each other and sometimes even the same management personnel of the companies was involved. Hoffmann-La Roche as the largest vitamin producer played a leading role, for example in the negotiations held in Japan and the Far East it represented all European manufacturers. Together with BASF it was alleged to also have convinced the Japanese vitamin producer Eisai to participate in the cartels.

32. Cartel members may be able to effectively communicate private information to each other, e.g. about cost levels. If firms talk to each other, they can agree how to split the market. This may allow them to increase productive efficiency because the cartel tends to assign a larger market share to members who happen to have lower costs. For a dynamic analysis see Athey and Bagwell (2001).

33. The game theoretic analysis of cheap talk is closest to this issue. For a discussion of its applicability to the analysis of cartels see Whinston (2006).

34. We follow here Harrington (2008).

35. See Harstad and Phlips (1994).

36. This case draws from Kühn (2001) and Harrington (2008).

37. This case is based on European Commission (2007).

38. This extension is due to Aubert, Rey and Kovacic (2006).

39. See Williamson (1968).

40. The data presented here come from Martynova and Renneboog (2006).

41. This part of the analysis is based on Salant, Switzer and Reynolds (1983).

42. We follow here Perry and Porter (1985).

43. This case is based on Baldanza (2002) and Ross and Winter (2005).

44. The analysis is based on Farrell and Shapiro (1990).

45. This implies that quantities are strategic substitutes.

46. This case draws from The Domino Effect: Will Airlines Follow One Another in the Consolidation Game? Knowledge@Wharton, 20 February 2008.

47. This result is formally established by Nocke and Whinston (2007).

48. The analysis is based on Pesendorfer (2005).

49. This result is due to Deneckere and Davidson (1985).

50. This case draws on Compte, Jenny and Rey (2002).

51. Compte, Jenny and Rey (2002), Kühn (2004) and Vasconcelos (2005) are the few exceptions that attempt to provide theoretical and empirical underpinnings for estimating coordinated effects of mergers.

52. This section draws on Whinston (2006) and on Werden and Froeb (2008).

53. This point is made by McAfee and Williams (1988). Event studies have been initiated by Eckbo (1983) and Stillman (1983).

54. For a recent survey of this literature, see Weinberg (2007).

55. The terminology is due to Bain (1956).

56. See Schelling's (1960) analysis of conflicts.

57. For an analysis of industries with endogenous sunk costs see Sutton (1991).

58. We follow here Fudenberg and Tirole (1984).

59. Cases 16.1, 16.6 and 16.8 draw from Kadiyali (1996).

60. The analysis is based on Dixit (1980).

61. This case follows Dafny (2005).

62. Conlin and Kadiyali (2006) briefly survey this literature.

63. This test was introduced by Ellison and Ellison (2007).

64. We follow here Fudenberg and Tirole (1984).

65. This result holds if the equilibrium is stable in the second period (i.e. best-response dynamics converge to the equilibrium if the starting point is sufficiently close to the equilibrium) and requires that $\mu_1'' \mu_2''(1 - \mu_1)(1 - \mu_2) > (\mu_1' \mu_2')^2$. One can show that a research technology such as $\mu_i(\sigma) = \min(1, b\sqrt{s})$, with b small, meets this requirement.

66. See, e.g., Salop and Scheffman (1983, 1987).

67. This case draws from Haas-Wilson (1989) and European Commission (2005).

68. This case is based on Schmalensee (1978).

69. This argument is formally analysed in Judd (1985).

70. Our analysis draws from Whinston (1990), using the specification in Peitz (2008). A related argument is made by Nalebuff (2004) according to which bundling reduces a competitor's profits if it decides to enter. However, in the Nalebuff model, this statement is only valid under a different timing of events.

71. The following arguments have been formalized by Carlton and Waldman (2002).

72. See Choi and Stefanadis (2001).

73. For a detailed analysis of this case, see Kühn and Van Reenen (2009). We summarize the main facts here.

74. Klemperer (1987) was the first to examine how the threat of entry affects an incumbent's behaviour in markets with switching costs. His model, based on quantity competition, is slightly different from the one we use here but the argumentation is very similar.

75. The analysis is based on Milgrom and Roberts (1982a,b); e.g. Motta (2004) provides a similar specification to ours. Interesting variations of the nature of asymmetric information are provided by Harrington (1986) and Matthews and Mirman (1983).

76. Bagwell and Ramey (1988) and Bagwell (2007) examine the conditions under which an incumbent firm prices and advertises so as to deter entry that otherwise would be profitable.

77. We follow here Waldman (1991). For a useful survey of the literature, see the introduction in Kovenock and Suddhasatwa (2005).

78. The double-marginalization problem was first addressed by Sprengler (1950).

79. For an empirical analysis, see Waterman and Weiss (1996).

80. The analysis is based on Winter (1993).

81. The argument has been made informally by Telser (1960). For a formal analysis in a differentiated product market, see Mathewson and Winter (1984); see also Mathewson and Winter (1998).

82. For more information see Schulz (2005), who also provides a relevant theoretical analysis.

83. This has been argued by Mathewson and Winter (1998). See Jullien and Rey (2007) for a formal analysis. For an analysis that RPM facilitates collusion if there is a downstream firm that is a common retailer to several upstream firms, see Bernheim and Whinston (1985).

84. The European Union maintains a very informative website on the block exemption at http://ec.europa.eu/competition/sectors/motor_vehicles/overview_en.html (last visited February 2009). A report by London Economics (2006), which was commissioned by the European Commission, evaluates the impact of this new regulation on market outcomes. For an empirical investigation see Brenkers and Verboven (2006).

85. The following analysis is based on Rey and Stiglitz (1995).

86. An alternative interpretation of the formal analysis is the following. Suppose that there is a single region and that firms are vertically integrated. This corresponds to our analysis in the absence of exclusive territories. If firms disintegrate, each manufacturer has its independent retailer. This can be called

vertical separation. Our results then say that in spite of the double-marginalization problem that is avoided under vertical integration, vertical separation can be profitable for manufacturers. This insight has been obtained by Bonanno and Vickers (1988). Yet another interpretation is to consider a horizontal merger in the downstream sector. Although this increases market power downstream, manufacturers possibly benefit from such a merger.

87. See Posner (1976) and Bork (1978).

88. This case is based on Asker (2004). For complementary evidence, see Sass (2005).

89. For more details, see Russo *et al.* (2009).

90. We use Tirole's (1988) version of the seminal contribution by Aghion and Bolton (1987).

91. This subsection follows Rasmussen *et al.* (1991) and Segal and Whinston (2000a).

92. The analysis is based on Segal and Whinston (2000b). For an alternative model, see Besanko and Perry (1993). In the latter, sellers offer differentiated products and compete in prices. They face a perfectly competitive retailing sector. Seller investments affect the distribution cost of the product, as illustrated by the training of the sales staff. However, an investment is assumed to spill over into lower distribution costs of the competing products. It can then be shown that without exclusion, sellers invest less. Furthermore, welfare may be reduced by prohibiting exclusive dealing.

93. This claim has been made by Klein (1988).

94. Another caveat of our previous analysis may be the particular assumption on the bargaining outcome. Alternatively, consider so-called outside option bargaining according to which the total surplus is shared evenly as long as none of the disagreement values binds; otherwise, the binding party's profit is set equal to this disagreement profit and the other party keeps the remaining surplus. Under this bargaining, the incumbent seller would actually invest less under exclusion than under non-exclusion. See Segal and Whinston (2000b) for details.

95. For a useful discussion, see Ornstein (1989).

96. For a more detailed account, see Motta (2004) who also elaborates on the appropriate market definition, an aspect we do not focus on here.

97. Good and very readable overviews on vertical mergers are provided by Church (2004, 2008) and Riordan (2008).

98. Note that an increase in input prices also occurs in perfectly competitive industries with an upward sloping supply curve for inputs. However, in this case, the strategic interaction between upstream firms can be safely ignored and the input price is equal to marginal cost.

99. For simplicity, we assume that $P(q)$ is thrice continuously differentiable and that $c > \lim_{q \to \infty} P(q)$.

100. See e.g. Greenhut and Ohta (1979) and Salinger (1988). This property approximately holds if the upstream sector serves a large number of independent downstream markets so that a quantity change by a firm in one of these downstream markets has a negligible effect on the price of its input. One example is where a large number of local retail markets that are served by the upstream firms and whose demand is independent of one another. To make the property hold exactly, we have to assume that upstream firms sell to a continuum of (identical) downstream sectors. Let us then consider one such representative downstream sector.

101. We need to make sure that the solution to the first-order condition uniquely determines q. We assume that $n^d P'(q) + q P''(q) < 0$. This guarantees that the solution to the first-order conditions is unique and, thus, that the inverse demand function faced by the upstream firms is unique as well. To make sure that the unique solution to the first-order conditions is indeed a maximizer for each downstream firm given $q_{-i} = [(n^d - 1)/n^d]q$ we assume that $q/n^d = \arg\max_{q_i} \pi_i(q_i, [(n^d - 1)/n^d]q)$, where q solves the first-order conditions. For a related discussion see Kolstad and Mathiesen (1987) and Gaudet and Salant (1991).

102. To make sure that such a solution exists and is unique, we make the assumption that $(n^d + 1)(n^u + 1)P'(q) + (n^d + n^u + 3)q P''(q) + q^2 P'''(q) < 0$. This is the counterpart to the assumption for the downstream sector. To make the problem interesting we must also have that $\lim_{q \to 0} P(q) > c$ because otherwise no firm would produce a positive quantity. Finally, we have to assume that each upstream firm's profits are in fact maximized at q^*/n^u given $x_{-j} = [(n^u - 1)/n^u]q^*$, i.e. $q^*/n^u = \arg\max_{x_j} \pi_j(x_j, [(n^u - 1)/n^u]q^*)$.

103. The US Supreme Court decision is archived as Brown Shoe Co. vs. United States, 370 U.S. 294 (1962).

104. Other economic analyses have shown possibly anticompetitive effects of input foreclosure by vertical integration. In an important contribution, Hart and Tirole (1990) argue that an upstream monopolist cannot credibly commit to supply only one downstream firm if supply contracts between upstream and downstream firm are unobservable and unverifiable. Restricting attention to non-discriminatory contracts but allowing the contracts to be nonlinear, the upstream firm can extract all downstream surplus under symmetry downstream. The gross surplus is equal to downstream oligopoly profit. Here, vertical integration provides a solution to the commitment problem because it allows the firm to collect the monopoly profits. For discussion and extensions, see Rey and Tirole (2007).

105. The analysis follows Salinger (1988).

106. With respect to selling inputs the vertically integrated firms hold so-called Cournot conjectures, while with respect to buying inputs the vertically integrated firms hold so-called Bertrand conjectures. Under different conjectures vertically integrated firms may want to become active in the wholesale market. See Gaudet and Long (1996) and Schrader and Martin (1998). For a

model with price competition with differentiated products in the downstream market, see Häckner (2003).

107. See Ordover, Saloner, and Salop (1990).

108. For additional contributions, see Choi and Yi (2000) and Chen (2001).

109. This case freely borrows from Hortaçsu and Syverson (2007).

110. We follow closely Nocke and White (2007). For a related analysis see Normann (2007).

111. The example is borrowed from Nocke and White (2007).

References for Part VI

Abreu, D. (1986). Extremal Equilibria of Oligopolistic Supergames. *Journal of Economic Theory* 39: 191–225.

Abreu, D. (1988). On the Theory of Infinitely Repeated Games with Discounting. *Econometrica* 56: 383–396.

Aghion, P., and Bolton, P. (1987). Contracts as a Barrier to Entry. *American Economic Review* 77: 388–401.

Asker, J. (2004). Measuring Advantages from Exclusive Dealing. Mimeo.

Athey, S. and Bagwell, K. (2001). Optimal Collusion with Private Cost Shocks. *Rand Journal of Economics* 32: 428–465.

Aubert, C., Rey, P. and Kovacic, W. E. (2006). The Impact of Leniency and Whistle-Blowing Programs on Cartels. *International Journal of Industrial Organization* 24: 1241–1266.

Bagwell, K. (2007). Signaling and Entry Deterrence: A Multi-dimensional Analysis. Mimeo. Forthcoming in *Rand Journal of Economics*.

Bagwell, K. and Ramey, G. (1988). Advertising and Limit Pricing. *Rand Journal of Economics* 19: 59–71.

Bain, J. (1956). *Barriers to New Competition: Their Character and Consequences*. Cambridge, MA: Harvard University Press.

Baldanza, A. F. (2002). Anti-competitive, Efficiency-enhancing Mergers and the Efficiencies Defence: The Superior Propane Decision. *Antitrust/Competition & Marketing Law Bulletin*, May: 1–6.

Belleflamme, P. and Bloch, F. (2004). Market Sharing Agreements and Collusive Networks. *International Economic Review* 45: 387–411.

Belleflamme, P. and Bloch, F. (2008). Sustainable Collusion on Separate Markets. *Economics Letters* 99: 384–386.

Bernheim, B. D. and Whinston, M. D. (1985). Common Marketing Agency as a Device for Facilitating Collusion. *Rand Journal of Economics* 16: 269–281.

Bernheim, B. D., and Whinston, M. D. (1990). Multimarket Contact and Collusive Behavior. *Rand Journal of Economics* 21: 1–26.

Bernheim, B. D. and Whinston, M. (1998). Exclusive Dealing. *Journal of Political Economy* 106: 64–103.

Besanko, D. and Perry, M. K. (1993). Equilibrium Incentives for Exclusive Dealing in a Differentiated Products Oligopoly. *Rand Journal of Economics* 24: 646–667.

Bils, M. (1989). Pricing in a Customer Market. *Quarterly Journal of Economics* 104. 699–718.

Bloch, F. (1996). Sequential Formation of Coalitions in Games with Fixed Payoff Division. *Games and Economic Behavior* 14: 537–556.

Bloch, F. (2002). Coalitions and Networks in Industrial Organization. *Manchester School* 70: 36–55.

Bonanno, G. and Vickers, J. (1988). Vertical Separation, *Journal of Industrial Economcs* 36: 257–265.

Bork, R. H. (1978). *The Antitrust Paradox: A Policy at War with Itself*. New York: Basic Books.

Brenkers, R. and Verboven, F. (2006). Liberalizing A Distribution System: The European Car Market. *Journal of the European Economic Association* 4: 216–251.

Carlton, D. and Waldman, M. (2002). The Strategic Use of Tying to Preserve and Create Market Power in Evolving Industries. *Rand Journal of Economics* 33: 194–220.

Chen, Y. (2001). On Vertical Mergers and their Competitive Effects. *Rand Journal of Economics* 32: 667–685.

Chevalier, J. and Scharfstein, D. S. (1996). Capital-Market Imperfections and Countercyclical Markups: Theory and Evidence. *American Economic Review* 86: 703–725.

Choi, J.-P. and Yi, S.-S. (2000). Vertical Foreclosure with the Choice of Input Specifications. *Rand Journal of Economics* 31: 717–743.

Choi, J. P. and Stefanadis, C. (2001). Tying, Investment, and the Dynamic Leverage Theory. *Rand Journal of Economics* 32: 52–71.

Church, J. (2004). The Impact of Vertical and Conglomerate Mergers on Competition. Report prepared for DG Competition, European Commission.

Church, J. (2008). Vertical Mergers. *Issues in Competition Law and Policy* 2: 1455–1501.

Compte, O., Jenny, F. and Rey, P. (2002). Capacity Constraints, Mergers, and Collusion. *European Economic Review* 46: 1–29.

Conlin, M. and Kadiyali, V. (2006). Entry-Deterring Capacity in the Texas Lodging Industry. *Journal of Economics & Management Strategy* 15: 167–185.

Connor, J. M. (2001). *Global Price Fixing: Our Customers Are the Enemy (Studies in Industrial Organization)*. Berlin: Springer.

Dafny, L. S. (2005). Games Hospitals Play: Entry Deterrence in Hospital Procedure Markets. *Journal of Economics and Management Strategy* 14: 513–542.

d'Aspremont, C., Gabszewicz, J. J., Jacquemin, A. and Weymark J. A. (1983). On the Stability of Collusive Price Leadership. *Canadian Journal of Economics* 16: 17–25.

Deaton, A. and Muellbauer, J. (1980). An Almost Ideal Demand System. *American Economic Review* 70: 312–336.

Deneckere, R. and Davidson, C. (1985). Incentives to Form Coalitions with Bertrand Competition. *Rand Journal of Economics* 16: 473–486.

Dixit, A. K. (1980). The Role of Investment in Entry-Deterrence. *Economic Journal* 90: 95–106.

Eckbo, B. E. (1983). Horizontal Mergers, Collusion, and Stockholder Wealth. *Journal of Financial Economics* 11: 241–273.

Ellison, G. (1994). Theories of Cartel Stability and the Joint Executive Committee. *Rand Journal of Economics*. 25: 37–57.

Ellison, G. and Ellison, S. F. (2007). Strategic Entry Deterrence and the Behavior of Pharmaceutical Incumbents Prior to Patent Expiration. Mimeo, MIT Department of Economics.

European Commission (2001a). Commission decision of 21 November 2001, Case COMP/E-1/37.512 – Vitamins, http://eur-lex.europa.eu/LexUriServ/site/en/oj/2003/l_006/l_00620030110en00010089.pdf

European Commission (2001b). Press release IP/01/1625, 21 November 2001, http://europa.eu/rapid/pressReleasesAction.do?reference=IP/01/1625

European Commission (2004). Press release IP/04/1454, 9 December 2004, http://europa.eu/rapid/pressReleasesAction.do?reference=IP/04/1454

European Commission (2005). Progress by Member States in Reviewing and Eliminating Restrictions to Competition in the Area of Professional Services. COM(2005) 405 final.

European Commission (2007). Press release IP/07/509, 18 April 2007, http://europa.eu/rapid/pressReleasesAction.do?reference=IP/07/509

Evans, W. S. and Kessides, I. N. (1994). Living by the 'Golden Rule': Multimarket Contact in the U.S. Airline Industry. *Quarterly Journal of Economics* 109: 341–366.

Farrell, J. and Shapiro, C. (1990). Horizontal Mergers: An Equilibrium Analysis, *American Economic Review* 80: 107–126.

Friedman, J. (1971). A Noncooperative Equilibrium for Supergames. *Review of Economic Studies* 28: 1–12.

Friedman, J. (1977). *Oligopoly and the Theory of Games*. Amsterdam: North-Holland.

Froeb, L. M., Tardiff, T. J. and Werden, G. J. (1996). The Demsetz Postulate and the Welfare Effects of Mergers in Differentiated Products. In McChesney, F. S. (ed.), *Economic Inputs, Legal Outputs: The Role of Economists in Modern Antitrust*. Chichester: Wiley.

Froeb, L. M., Tschantz, S. and Crooke, P. (2003). Bertrand Competition with Capacity Constraints: Mergers Among Parking Lots. *Journal of Econometrics* 113: 49–67.

Fudenberg, D. and Tirole, J. (1984). The Fat-Cat Effect, the Puppy-Dog Ploy and the Lean and Hungry Look. *American Economic Review* 74: 361–366.

Gaudet, G. and Long, N. V. (1996). Vertical Integration, Foreclosure, and Profits in the Presence of Double Marginalization. *Journal of Economics and Management Strategy* 5: 409–432.

Gaudet, G. and Salant, S. W. (1991). Uniqueness of Cournot Equilibrium: New Results from Old Methods. *Review of Economic Studies* 58: 399–404.

Goolsbee, A. and Syverson, C. (2008). How Do Incumbents Respond to the Threat of Entry? Evidence from the Major Airlines. Mimeo, forthcoming in *Quarterly Journal of Economics*.

Green, E. and Porter, R. (1984). Non-cooperative Collusion Under Imperfect Price Information, *Econometrica* 52: 87–100.

Greenhut, M. L. and Ohta, H. (1979). Vertical Integration of Successive Oligopolists. *American Economic Review* 69: 137–141.

Grzybowski, L. and Pereira, P. (2007). Merger Simulation in Mobile Telephony in Portugal. *Review of Industrial Organization* 31: 205–220.

Haas-Wilson, D. (1989). Strategic Regulatory Entry Deterrence An Empirical Test in the Ophthalmic Market. *Journal of Health Economics* 8: 339–352.

Häckner, J. (2003). Vertical Integration and Competition Policy. *Journal of Regulatory Economics* 24: 213–222.

Harrington, J. (1986). Limit Pricing When the Potential Rival is Unsure of its Cost Function. *Econometrica* 54: 429–437.

Harrington, J. (2008). Detecting Cartels. In Buccirossi, P. (ed), *Handbook in Antitrust Economics*. Cambridge, MA: MIT Press.

Harstad, R. M. and Phlips, L. (1994). Informational Requirements of Collusive Detection: Simple Seasonal Markets. Mimeo. (Reproduced in Phlips, L. (1995), *Competition Policy: A Game-Theoretic Perspective* (Chapter 8). Cambridge: Cambridge University Press.)

Hart, O. and Tirole, J. (1990). Vertical Integration and Market Foreclosure. *Brookings Papers on Economic Activity: Microeconomics*. Special Issue: 205–286.

Hausman, J. and Leonard, G. K. (2005). Using Merger Simulation Models: Testing the Underlying Assumptions, *International Journal of Industrial Organization* 23: 693–698.

Hortaçsu, A. and Syverson, C. (2007). Cementing Relationships: Vertical Integration, Foreclosure, Productivity, and Prices. *Journal of Political Economy* 115: 250–301.

Ivaldi, M. and Verboven, F. (2005). Quantifying the Effects from Horizontal Mergers in European Competition Policy. *International Journal of Industrial Organization* 23: 669–691.

Jackson, M. and Wolinsky, A. (1996). A Strategic Model of Social and Economic Networks. *Journal of Economic Theory* 71: 44–74.

Judd, K. (1985). Credible Spatial Preemption. *Rand Journal of Economics* 16: 153–166.

Jullien, B. and Rey, P. (2007). Resale Price Maintenance and Collusion. *Rand Journal of Economics* 38: 983–1001.

Kadiyali, V. (1996). Entry, its Deterrence, and its Accommodation: a Study of the U.S. Photographic Film Industry. *Rand Journal of Economics* 27: 452–478.

Klein, B. (1988). Vertical Integration as Organizational Ownership: The Fisher Body-General Motors Relationship Revisited. *Journal of Law, Economics and Organization* 4: 199–213.

Klemperer, P. (1987). Entry Deterrence in Markets with Consumer Switching Costs. *Economic Journal* 97: 99–117.

Kolstad, C. D. and Mathiesen, L. (1987). Necessary and Sufficient Conditions for Uniqueness of a Cournot Equilibrium. *Review of Economic Studies* 54: 681–690.

Kovenock, D. and Suddhasatwa, R. (2005). Free Riding in Noncooperative Entry Deterrence with Differentiated Products. *Southern Economic Journal* 72: 119–137.

Kroes, N. (2007a). *Introductory remarks on CFI ruling on Microsoft's abuse of dominant market position*. Press conference, Brussels, 17 September 2007.

Kroes, N. (2007b). *Improving competition in European energy markets through effective unbundling*. Fordham Corporate Law Institute's Annual Seminar 2007, New York, 27 September 2007.

Kroes, N. (2008). *In defence of competition policy*. Opening remarks at conference 'Competition policy, growth and consumer purchasing power', Brussels, 13 October 2008.

Kühn, K.-U. (2001). Fighting Collusion: Regulation of Communication Between Firms. *Economic Policy* 32: 167–197.

Kühn, K.-U. (2004). The Coordinated Effects of Mergers in Differentiated Products Market. Mimeo. University of Michigan Law School.

Kühn, K.-U. and Van Reenen, J. (2009). Interoperability and Market Foreclosure in the European Microsoft Case. In Lyons, B. (ed.), *Cases in European Competition Policy: The Economic Analysis*. Cambridge: Cambridge University Press.

Levenstein, M. and V. Suslow (2006), What Determines Cartel Success? *Journal of Economic Literature* 44: 43–95.

Martynova, M. and Renneboog, L. (2006). Mergers and Acquisitions in Europe. In Renneboog, L. (ed.), *Advances in Corporate Finance and Asset Pricing*. Amsterdam: Elsevier.

Marvel, H. (1982). Exclusive Dealing. *Journal of Law and Economics* 25: 1–25.

Mathewson, F. and Winter, R. (1984). An Economic Theory of Vertical Restraints. *Rand Journal of Economics* 15: 27–38.

Mathewson, F. and Winter, R. (1998). The Law and Economics of Resale Price Maintenance. *Review of Industrial Organization* 13: 57–84.

Matthews, S. and Mirman, L. (1983). Equilibrium Limit Pricing: The Effects of Private Information and Stochastic Demand. *Econometrica* 51: 981–995.

McAffee, R. P. and Williams, M. A. (1988). Can Event Studies Detect Anticompetitive Mergers? *Economics Letters* 28: 199–203.

Miklos-Thal, J. (2008). Optimal Collusion and Cost Asymmetries. Mimeo.

Milgrom, P. and Roberts, J. (1982a). Limit Pricing and Entry under Incomplete Information: An Equilibrium Analysis. *Econometrica* 50: 443–460.

Milgrom, P. and Roberts, J. (1982b). Predation, Reputation and Entry Deterrence. *Journal of Economic Theory* 27: 280–312.

Modigliani, F. (1958). New Developments on the Oligopoly Front. *Journal of Political Economy* 66: 215–232.

Motta, M. (2004). *Competition Policy. Theory and Practice.* Cambridge: Cambridge University Press.

Nalebuff, B. (2004). Bundling as an Entry Deterrent. *Quarterly Journal of Economics* 119: 159–187.

Neven, D. J. (1989). Strategic Entry Deterrence: Recent Developments in the Economics of Industry. *Journal of Economic Surveys* 3: 213–234.

Nevo, A. (2000). Mergers with Differentiated Products: the Case of the Ready-to-eat Cereal Industry. *Rand Journal of Economics* 31: 395–421.

Nocke, V. and Whinston, M. D. (2007). Sequential Merger Review. Mimeo.

Nocke, V. and White, L. (2007). Do Vertical Mergers Facilitate Upstream Collusion? *American Economic Review* 96: 1321–1339.

Normann, H.-T. (2007). Vertical Integration, Raising Rivals Costs and Upstream Collusion. forthcoming in *European Economic Review*.

Ordover, J. A., Saloner, G. and Salop, S. C. (1990). Equilibrium Vertical Foreclosure. *American Economic Review* 80: 127–142.

Ornstein, S. (1989). Exclusive Dealing and Antitrust. *Antitrust Bulletin* 34: 65–98.

Peitz, M. (2008). Bundling may Blockade Entry. *International Journal of Industrial Economics* 26: 41–58.

Perry, M. K. and Porter, R. H. (1985). Oligopoly and the Incentive for Horizontal Merger. *American Economic Review* 75: 219–227.

Pesendorfer, M. (2005). Mergers under Entry. *Rand Journal of Economics* 36: 661–679.

Peters, C. (2006). Evaluating the Performance of Merger Simulations: Evidence from the U.S. Airline Industry. *Journal of Law and Economics* 49: 627–649.

Pinkse, J. and Slade, M. E. (2004). Mergers, Brand Competition, and the Price of a Pint. *European Economic Review* 48: 617–643.

Porter, R. H. (1983). A Study of Cartel Stability: The Joint Executive Committee, 1880-1886. *Bell Journal of Economics* 14: 301–314.

Posner, R. (1976). *Antitrust Law: An Economic Perspective*. Chicago: University of Chicago Press.

Rasmussen, E. B., Ramseyer, J. M. and Wiley Jr., J. S. (1991). Naked Exclusion. *American Economic Review* 81: 1137–1145.

Rey, P. and Stiglitz, J. (1995). The Role of Exclusive Territories in Producers' Competition. *Rand Journal of Economics* 26: 431–451.

Rey, P. and Tirole, J. (2007). A Primer on Foreclosure. In Armstrong, M. and Porter, R. (eds.), *Handbook of Industrial Organization*. Vol III. Elsevier.

Rey, P. and Vergé, T. (2008). Economics of Vertical Restraints. In Buccirossi, P. (ed.), *Handbook of Antitrust Economics*. MIT Press.

Riordan, M. (2008). Competitive Effects of Vertical Mergers. In Buccirossi, P. (ed.), *Handbook of Antitrust Economics*. MIT Press.

Ross, T. W. and Winter, R. A. (2005). The Efficiency Defense in Merger Law: Economic Foundations and Recent Canadian Developments. *Antitrust Law Journal* 72: 471–505.

Rotemberg, J. and Saloner, G. (1986). A Supergame-Theoretic Model of Price Wars During Booms. *American Economic Review* 76: 390–407.

Russo, F., Schinkel, M. P., Guenster, A. M. and Carree, M. (2009). *European Commission Decisions on Competition: Landmark Antitrust and Merger Cases from an Economic Viewpoint*. Cambridge: Cambridge University Press.

Salant, S., Switzer, S. and Reynolds, R. (1983). Losses from Horizontal Merger: The Effects of an Exogenous Change in Industry Structure on Cournot-Nash Equilibrium. *Quarterly Journal of Economics* 98: 185–199.

Salinger, M. (1988). Vertical Mergers and Market Foreclosure. *Quarterly Journal of Economics* 103: 345–356.

Salop, S. C. and Scheffman, D. T. (1983). Raising Rivals' Costs. *American Economic Review* 73: 267–271.

Salop, S. C. and Scheffman, D. T. (1987). Cost-Raising Strategies. *Journal of Industrial Economics* 36: 19–34.

Sass, T. (2005). The Competitive Effects of Exclusive Dealing: Evidence from the U.S. Beer Industry. *International Journal of Industrial Organization* 23: 203–225.

Schelling, T. C. (1960). *The Strategy of Conflicts*. Cambridge, MA: Harvard University Press.

Scherer, F. M. (1980). *Industrial Market Structure and Economic Performance*. Boston: Houghton-Mifflin.

Scherer, F. M. and Ross, D. (1990). *Industrial Market Structure and Economic Performance*. Boston: Houghton-Mifflin.

Schmalensee, R. (1978). Entry Deterrence in the Ready-to-Eat Breakfast Cereal Industry. *Bell Journal of Economics* 9: 305–327.

Schrader, A. and Martin, S. (1998). Vertical Market Participation. *Review of Industrial Organization* 13: 321–331.

Schulz, N. (2005). Resale Price Maintenance and the Service Argument: Efficiency Effects, Working Paper.

Segal, I. and Whinston, M. (2000a). Naked Exclusion: Comment. *American Economic Review* 90: 296–309.

Segal, I. and Whinston, M. (2000b). Exclusive Contracts and Protection of Investments. *Rand Journal of Economics* 31: 603–633.

Spagnolo, G. (2008). Leniency and Whistleblowers in Antitrust. In P. Buccirossi (ed.), *Handbook of Antitrust Economics*. Cambridge, MA: MIT Press.

Sprengler, J. (1950). Vertical Integration and Antitrust Policy. *Journal of Political Economy* 58: 347–352.

Stiglitz, J. (1984). Price Rigidities and Market Structure. *American Economic Review* Papers and Proceedings 74: 350–355.

Stillman, R. (1983). Examining Antitrust Policy Towards Horizontal Mergers. *Journal of Financial Economics* 11: 225–240.

Sutton, J. (1991). *Sunk Costs and Market Structure*. Cambridge, MA: MIT Press.

Sylos-Labini, P. (1962). *Oligopoly and Technical Progress*. Cambridge, MA: Harvard University Press.

Telser, L. (1960). Why Should Manufacturers Want Fair Trade? *Journal of Law and Economics* 3: 86–105.

Tirole, J. (1988). *The Theory of Industrial Organization* Cambridge, MA: MIT Press.

US Department of Justice (1999), Press release, 20 May 1999, www.usdoj.gov/atr/public/ press_releases/1999/2450.pdf

Vasconcelos, H. (2005). Tacit Collusion, Cost Asymmetries, and Mergers. *Rand Journal of Economics* 1: 39–62.

Waldman, M. (1991). The Role of Multiple Potential Entrants/Sequential Entry in Noncooperative Entry Deterrence. *Rand Journal of Economics* 22: 446–453.

Waterman, D. and Weiss, A. A. (1996). The Effects of Vertical Integration between Cable Television Systems and Pay Cable Networks. *Journal of Econometrics* 72: 357–395.

Weinberg, M. (2007). The Price Effects of Horizontal Mergers: A Survey. Mimeo.

Werden, G. J. and Froeb, L. M. (2002). Calibrated Economic Models Add Focus, Accuracy, and Persuasiveness to Merger Analysis. In Swedish Competition Authority. *The Pros and Cons of Merger Control*.

Werden, G. J. and Froeb, L. M. (2008). Unilateral Competitive Effects of Horizontal Mergers. In Buccirossi, P. (ed) *Handbook of Antitrust Economics*. Cambridge, MA: MIT Press.

Whinston, M. (1990). Tying, Foreclosure, and Exclusion. *American Economic Review* 80: 837–869.

Whinston, M. (2006). *Lectures on Antitrust Economics*. Cambridge, MA: MIT Press.

Williamson, O. E. (1968). Economies as an Anti-Trust Defence: The Welfare Trade-Off. *American Economic Review* 58: 18–36.

Wilson, R. (1992). Strategic Models of Entry Deterrence. In Aumann, R. J. and Hart, S. (eds.), *Handbook of Game Theory, Vol. 1*. NewYork: Elsevier Science Publishers.

Winter, R. (1993). Vertical Control and Price versus Non-Price Competition. *Quarterly Journal of Economics*: 61–76.

Part VII
R&D and intellectual property

Introduction to Part VII: R&D and intellectual property

On 27 February 2006, GlaxoSmithKline (GSK) announced that the European Commission had granted approval of *Rotarix*™ in the European Union (EU), allowing active vaccination of infants from the age of six weeks, against the highly contagious rotavirus (which causes gastroenteritis). This vaccine had been developed since 1997 by GSK Biologicals for a *research and development (R&D)* expenditure estimated between EUR 500 and 800 million. On the same day, Yahoo filed a lawsuit against wireless content company MForma, charging this company and a group of ex-Yahoo employees there with theft of trade secrets. According to the lawsuit, the group of seven former Yahoo employees copied large amounts of confidential business and technical data when they left the Web portal company, and brought it to use in their new positions at MForma. Still on that very same day, Ben Franzen (an artist from Atlanta) and Kembrew McLeod (an assistant professor of communications studies at the University of Iowa) presented their documentary, called 'Copyright Criminals', which gathers interviews of musicians, artists, lawyers, scholars, music industry executives and others about the rise of sampling and remix culture. The authors believe that creativity is better served by letting artists freely borrow from others. A few hours before, France's highest court ('Cour de Cassation') ruled that the right to make a personal copy ('copie privée') of cinematographic works on DVD can be restricted by copyright holders when duplication 'could cause an unjustified damage to the legitimate interests of authors'.

What do these events have in common, except that they occurred on the same day? They all involve intangible assets, which consist of human knowledge and ideas and to which a legal entitlement, called *intellectual property* (IP) is usually attached. Intangible assets of this kind become increasingly crucial in our economies. According to a survey on patents and technology published in *The Economist* in October 2005, '[a]s much as three-quarters of the value of publicly traded companies in America comes from intangible assets, up from around 40% in the early 1980s'. One can read in the same survey that technology licensing revenue accounts for an estimated $100 billion worldwide and that this figure is growing fast. Firms are increasingly seeking patents, attempting to extend their scope, granting more licenses, litigating more and transforming their business models around intellectual property. At the same time, highly reliable open source software are collectively produced by a decentralized crowd of developers who do not seek any immediate monetary compensation for their efforts; commercial software vendors are contributing to these projects and, even more paradoxically, they do sometimes initiate open source projects by releasing part of their proprietary source code.

Similar contrasting trends are observed in the entertainment industries (music, cinema, videogames, . . .). For instance, on 22 February 2006, the Belgian Federal Police raided and seized one of eDonkey2000's largest indexing servers (these servers have been very popular for users running eMule, eDonkey and other eDonkey2000 based file-sharing applications, with around 1.3 million users online on average sharing over

170 million files). On this occasion, Dan Glickman, Chairman and CEO of the Motion Picture Association (MPA) declared: 'This is a major victory in our fight to cut off the supply of illegal materials being circulated on the Internet via peer-to-peer networks.' On the other hand, Creative Commons, a nonprofit group aimed at carving out ways to share creative works, is expanding from the realm of copyright into patents and scientific publishing. Creative Commons has built a licensing system that allows content creators to decide which usage rights to their work to grant others.

These contrasting examples raise the following questions: *Why is intellectual property used and diffused in such contrasting ways? Who are the winners and who are the losers in these different situations? What is best for society as a whole?* These questions appear as all the more important now that intellectual property stands at the heart of industrial and economic policy. In March 2000, in the so-called *Lisbon Agenda*, the EU Heads of States and Governments agreed to make the EU 'the most competitive and dynamic knowledge-driven economy by 2010'. At national and regional levels, governments also take special measures to boost the economy through a substantial increase in the public funding of both fundamental and applied research, based on the observation that *innovation* is one of the main sources of economic growth.

The importance and prevalence of the previous issues call for careful analyses of the mechanisms and institutions governing the production, use and diffusion of intellectual property. In this respect, the economic approach appears as fundamental as it focuses on markets, incentives and strategic interaction. In this part of the book, we aim at developing a rigorous economic analysis of a large set of issues surrounding intellectual property, R&D and innovation.

Part VII is concerned with activities generating information and knowledge. These activities suffer from a generic problem of appropriability, because they entail externalities, indivisibilities and uncertainty. As a result, investments in information and knowledge are quite different from other investments made by firms or individuals. In particular, markets generally fail to provide the right incentives to make these investments. Institutions need thus to be put in place in order to improve the provision of information and knowledge. The most prominent of these institutions is the protection of intellectual property (IP). In Chapter 19, we explain its economic rationale and describe two of its main forms: patents and copyright. We also examine a number of important issues related to the protection of IP. Which mix of length and breadth should patents have? What are the perverse effects of the patent system (duplication of efforts in patent races, 'sleeping patents', patent filing for defensive reasons, etc.)? Is the patent system appropriate for sequential and cumulative innovations? How do licensing and patent pooling affect the optimal design of the IP system? What are the effects of digital technologies and the Internet on the protection of IP?

In Chapter 18, we examine the two-way relationship between market structure and the incentives for R&D, focusing first on the profit incentive to innovate and then considering the strategic incentives to innovate in situations where firms compete in R&D. We also compare the pros and cons of various forms of cooperative R&D relative to noncooperative R&D for firms competing in a product market.

The two chapters differ in the line of analysis they pursue: Chapter 18 is more positive, while Chapter 19 is more normative. As a result, the two chapters also differ with respect to the balance between theory and cases: Chapter 18 is more 'theory intensive', while Chapter 19 is more 'case intensive'. In particular, Chapter 19 provides the reader with insights on R&D and intellectual property in industries like pharmaceuticals, software and digital music.

What will you learn in this part of the book?
You will first enlarge the perspective of the previous parts by incorporating innovation into the picture. You will see how firms use innovation as a strategic weapon, either on their own or in cooperation with some of their competitors. You will also understand why firms' investments in R&D are often insufficient, but may sometimes be excessive from society's point of view. You will then learn how to organize your thoughts about a number of topical issues related to innovation policy. In particular, you will understand the role of the patent system, and you should be able to form your own opinion about the proposed reforms of this system.

18 Innovation and R&D

In this chapter, our goal is to examine the interplay between market structure and innovation. This is clearly a two-way relationship: on the one hand, firms' incentives to invest in R&D depend on the structure of the product market they are acting in (i.e., on the number of rival firms and on the way they compete); on the other hand, firms are likely to use R&D to shape the structure of their market (e.g., by using R&D to increase their market share or to keep potential competition at bay). As the two effects are complex and intertwined, we simplify the analysis by assuming that firms can somehow appropriate the return from their R&D investments (we analyse how they actually manage to do so in the next chapter). We also break down the analysis into separate issues.

First, in Section 18.1, we assess how market structure affects the incentives for conducting R&D, which are measured by the profit increase that the innovator gains from the innovation. First, incentives to innovate are compared in the two market structures where strategic considerations are absent, namely monopoly and perfect competition. It is shown that the latter generates larger incentives to innovate than the former. Next, we extend the analysis to include strategic interaction by considering oligopolies. We reach an ambiguous result: a higher intensity of competition may increase or decrease the incentives to innovate depending on the initial starting point, the size of the innovation and the way competition is increased.

In Section 18.2, we reverse our point of view by investigating how innovation may influence market structure. First, we reconsider a monopolist's incentives to innovate in situations where a competing firm threatens to enter the market. We show that the incumbent firm is often keener to invest in R&D than the entrant. Monopoly is thus likely to prevail over time, which indicates that innovation does indeed drive market structure. Second, we enrich the previous analysis by incorporating explicitly the time dimension. Indeed, a firm's main motivation when investing in R&D is often to be the first to come up with an innovation. In such a *race* to be the first innovator, firms have to decide about the timing of their R&D investments. In this dynamic framework, we reconsider the comparison between the R&D decisions of an incumbent and of an entrant. We also examine the possibility that such races might exacerbate incentives to invest in R&D in such a way that total investments exceed the socially desirable level.

Finally, in Section 18.3, we consider other strategic aspects of R&D investments that arise when firms anticipate the effects their R&D investments will have on the product market competition. Here, the questions of interest are the following. Do firms invest more or less when they recognize the strategic nature of their R&D decisions? Should firms be allowed to coordinate their decisions at the R&D stage? How do the answers to the previous two questions depend on the public good nature of R&D?

Nature of technical progress

Before we enter into the detailed analyses, it is important to note that the three sections of this chapter differ not only by the issues they address but also by the assumptions they make about the nature of technical progress. As will be made explicit below, we assume in Section 18.1 that R&D investment determines (instantaneously and for sure) the size of the innovation and that only a single firm ends up using the innovation. In contrast, Section 18.2 assumes some form of 'tournament technical progress' where the timing of innovation is uncertain and depends on the R&D investments of all firms, and where the size of the innovation is fixed. Finally, Section 18.3 resembles Section 18.1 in that the tournament aspect and uncertainty are left aside but differs in two major aspects: first, the size of the innovation depends on the intensity of the firm's R&D investment (and potentially on the other firms' investments as well) and second, firms have the simultaneous opportunity to achieve competing innovations.

This variety of settings may seem confusing at first glance. However, it is motivated by the fact that the innovation process itself differs widely across situations and industries. In this respect, it is useful to distinguish between two types of innovative environments.[1] On the one hand, when the creation of knowledge addresses a known need, it seems logical to assume that *ideas are common knowledge*. In other words, any good idea is likely to be had and implemented by someone else. In this environment, discovery is seen as the result of some exogenously given production function that transforms R&D inputs into an invention of a certain quality, or into a probability of finding a new product or process. This environment corresponds to what is assumed in Sections 18.2 and 18.3. On the other hand, there are also instances where the need had not been identified prior to someone thinking of the idea. It is then natural to assume that *ideas are scarce*, in the sense that there exists no substitute idea that would address the same economic need (or that each idea occurs to a single, random person). This environment fits more the framework assumed in Section 18.1. We will return to this distinction throughout our analysis.

18.1   Market structure and incentives to innovate

In his classic work, *Capitalism, Socialism, and Democracy* (1943), Schumpeter stressed the link between market structure and R&D. His first contention was about the necessity of tolerating the creation of monopolies as a way to encourage the innovation process. This argument is nothing but the economic rationale behind the legal protection of intellectual property that we develop in the next chapter. Schumpeter's second conjecture was that large firms are better equipped to undertake R&D than smaller ones. The best way to support this conjecture is probably to say that large firms have a larger *capacity* to undertake R&D, insofar as they can deal more efficiently with the three market failures observed in innovative markets: externalities, indivisibilities and uncertainty.[a] As far as externalities are concerned, large firms are likely to have less competitors able to imitate their innovation. In terms of indivisibilities, large firms are more qualified to exploit increasing returns in R&D. Finally, regarding uncertainty, large firms are more diversified and, hence, more willing to take risks.

---

[a] We detail these three market failures in Chapter 19.

However, it is not clear whether large firms, because of their monopoly power, also have larger *incentives* to undertake R&D.

To assess the effect of market structure on the incentives for R&D, we proceed in three steps. First, we focus on the *profit incentive* to innovate, leaving aside any strategic consideration. Basically, we want to answer the following question: which market structure, monopoly, oligopoly or perfect competition, provides firms with the highest incentives to undertake R&D? Second, we introduce some *strategic incentives* to innovate by considering either potential competition (between an incumbent and a potential entrant) or actual competition (between oligopolists). Further strategic motivations will be considered in the next two sections.

As a preliminary to our analysis, let us define a number of concepts that will be used throughout Part VII. First, we make a distinction between product and process innovation. A *process* innovation is the generation, introduction and diffusion of a new production process (with the products remaining unchanged). A *product* innovation is the generation, introduction and diffusion of a new product (with the production process being unchanged).

We will mainly focus here on process innovations and we will often represent them in our models simply through a reduction of the marginal costs of production for a given product. Why do we leave product innovations aside? Firstly because we have already addressed product introduction and product positioning in Chapter 5. Secondly because it can be argued that a product innovation is nothing but an extreme case of a process innovation. That is, the new product already existed but was simply too expensive to produce; so, it took a process innovation to make the new product available.

As for process innovations, it is useful to classify them according to their impact on the market structure. A process innovation is said to be *drastic* (or *major*) if it reduces costs to such an extent that it allows the innovator to behave as a monopolist without being constrained by price competition in the industry. Otherwise, the innovation is said to be *nondrastic* (or *minor*); in this case, the innovator may gain some cost advantage over its rivals but competition constrains the innovator.

Figure 18.1 illustrates the distinction. Consider the market for a homogeneous product. A number of firms produce this product at constant marginal cost c_0 and compete in prices. Suppose that some firm discovers a process innovation that reduces the marginal cost of production. In the left panel of the figure, the innovation reduces the cost from c_0 to c_d. One observes that the cost reduction is so large that the monopoly price corresponding to the new cost c_d, $p^m(c_d)$, falls below c_0. In that case, the innovator can fix the monopoly price without fear of competition from the other firms and the innovation is thus drastic. The right panel illustrates the case of a nondrastic innovation: innovation reduces marginal cost only to c_{nd} and because $p^m(c_{nd}) > c_0$, the innovator cannot behave as a monopolist and is constrained by the price competition of the rival firms.

18.1.1   Monopoly versus perfect competition: the replacement effect

To assess the profit incentive to innovate, we can ask the following question, in line with the seminal analysis of Arrow (1962): how much is a firm willing to pay for an innovation that it would be the only one to use? Here, we implicitly refer to a creative environment in which ideas

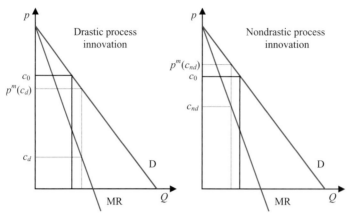

Figure 18.1 Drastic and nondrastic process innovations

are scarce. For simplicity, consider a nondrastic (minor) process innovation that is protected by a patent of infinite length. This process innovation lowers the constant marginal cost of a particular good from c_0 to $c_1 < c_0$. To assess how much a firm would pay to acquire this innovation (knowing that it will become its sole user), we use the graphic analysis depicted in Figure 18.2.

Consider first an initial *competitive situation*. Prior to the innovation, the quantity q_0^c is sold at price c_0 and all firms earn zero profit. The firm that obtains the new technology produces at cost c_1 and, as the innovation is nondrastic, this firm is constrained to charge $p = c_0 - \varepsilon$ (with ε arbitrarily small) instead of the monopoly price p_1^m (as the other firms are able to charge a price as low as $c_0 < p_1^m$). As the innovator sells the quantity q_0^c, its profit is equal to $\pi^c = q_0^c(c_0 - c_1)$. That is, the per-period value placed by a competitive firm on the innovation is represented in Figure 18.2 by the surface of the rectangle $c_0 D F c_1$, i.e., by the sum of areas 1 and 2.[b]

Consider now an initial *monopoly situation*. We assume that the monopolist faces no threat of entry and is thus the only firm which can benefit from the innovation. Prior to the innovation, the monopolist produces at cost c_0 and its optimum is to sell a quantity q_0^m at price p_0^m. Its profit is equal to $\pi_0^m = q_0^m(p_0^m - c)$. This profit can be measured in Figure 18.2 in two alternative ways. First, it can be measured by the area of the rectangle with base q_0^m and height $(p_0^m - c)$. Equivalently, recalling the principles of integration, profit can be measured by the area below the marginal revenue curve and above the marginal cost curve (as this area corresponds to the difference between total revenues and total costs); that is, the monopolist's profit with cost c_0 is also measured by the area of the triangle $A c_0 B$. After lowering its cost to c_1, the monopolist finds it optimal to sell a quantity q_1^m at price p_1^m, resulting in a profit equal to $\pi_1^m = q_1^m(p_1^m - c)$. Applying our second way to measure profit, we have that the monopolist's profit after the innovation corresponds to the area of the triangle $A c_1 E$. We can now gauge the

[b] Given that the innovator is awarded a patent of unlimited duration, the incentive to innovate in the competitive situation is given by the total present value of the flow of profits. That is, denoting the interest rate by r, $V^c = \sum_{t=0}^{\infty}(1+r)^{-t}\pi^c = (1/r)(1+r)\pi^c$ (using discrete time discounting) or $V^c = \int_0^{\infty} e^{-rt}\pi^c \, dt = (1/r)\pi^c$ (using continuous time discounting).

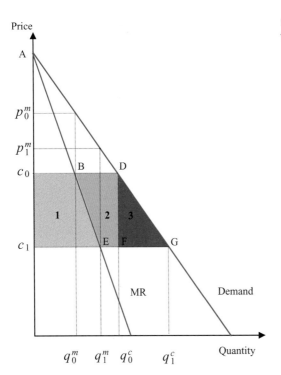

Figure 18.2 Incentives to innovate as a function of market structure

per period value placed by a monopoly on the innovation as the profit increase $\pi_1^m - \pi_0^m$. In Figure 18.2, this value is equal to the difference between the triangles Ac_1E and Ac_0B, which is given by area 1 (i.e., area c_1c_0BE). Recalling that a competitive firm is willing to pay up to the areas 1 *and* 2, we reach the following conclusion.

> **Lesson 18.1   A competitive firm places a larger value on a minor process innovation than a monopoly does.**

The intuition behind this result is quite straightforward and comes from the comparison of the pre-innovation situations: prior to the innovation, the monopolist already earns a positive profit, whereas the competitive firm just recoups its costs. This is known as the *replacement effect*: for the competitive firm, the innovation creates a brand new profit opportunity but for the monopolist, the innovation just 'replaces' an existing profit by a larger one. Note that the same argument applies even more clearly for the case of a drastic innovation. Here, the (per period) incentives to innovate for a competitive firm and for a monopolist are respectively given by π_1^m and $\pi_1^m - \pi_0^m$.

As illustrated in Case 18.1, the replacement effect can also explain why a firm that is active on several markets tends to direct its R&D investments more towards the markets on which it faces more competition.

Case 18.1 Microsoft's incentives to innovate

Arrow's argument about the replacement effect can be extended to a multiproduct firm. Following the argument, a multiproduct firm would have higher incentives to innovate on the market segments where it faces competition than on those segments where it enjoys significant market power. The following quote, taken from an analysis of Microsoft's launch of the Xbox in 2005, perfectly illustrates the previous conjecture. 'It is surely no coincidence that Microsoft's hidden ability to innovate has become apparent only in a market in which it is the underdog and faces fierce competition. Microsoft is far less innovative in its core businesses, in which it has a monopoly (in Windows) and a near monopoly (in Office). But in the new markets of gaming, mobile devices and television set-top boxes, Microsoft has been unable to exploit its Windows monopoly other than indirectly – it has financed the company's expensive forays into pasture new.'[2]

It is worth noting that the value the competitive firm places on the innovation still falls short of the social value of the innovation. Indeed, a benevolent social planner would be willing to pay up to the increase in social surplus that the innovation generates. The per-period social value of the innovation is represented in Figure 18.2 by the difference between the areas of triangle $c_1 A G$ (social surplus under cost c_1) and triangle $c_0 A D$ (social surplus under cost c_0), that is, by the sum of areas 1, 2 and 3. The reason is that the competitive firm fails to appropriate the increase in consumer surplus (i.e., area 3).

18.1.2   Incentives to innovate in oligopolies

As oligopolies are intermediate market structures between the two extremes of monopoly and perfect competition, one could be tempted to infer from the previous argument that incentives to innovate in oligopolies stand somewhere between the low incentives of the monopolist and the high incentives of the perfectly competitive firm. However, this conjecture turns out to be wrong. To show this, we reconsider our initial question (i.e., how much is a firm willing to pay for an innovation that it would be the only one to use?) and examine how its answer is affected by the intensity of competition.

There is no obvious way to address this issue as the intensity of competition can be measured in different ways: either by the number of firms on the market, or by the degree of product substitutability, or by the nature of competition (as we showed in Chapter 3, price competition leads to more competitive outcomes than quantity competition). Here, we take the number of firms as a measure of the intensity of competition. Using the simple linear Cournot model with n firms introduced in Chapter 3, we want to show that *the profit incentive to innovate may follow an inverse U-shape as the number of firms in the industry increases.* As a consequence, Cournot competition with an adequate number of firms may lead to larger incentives to innovate than both perfect competition and monopoly.[3]

Suppose that n firms compete à la Cournot on the market of a homogeneous product. Suppose further that both the demand and the cost functions are linear. Specifically, we take $P(q) = a - q$ (with $a > 0$ and $q = \sum_i q_i$) and $C_i(q_i) = c_i q_i$ (with $0 \leq c_i < a \; \forall i = 1 \ldots n$). In Chapter 3, we showed that firm i's equilibrium profits at the Cournot equilibrium are equal to

$$\pi_i^* = \left(\frac{a - nc_i + \sum_{j \neq i} c_j}{n+1} \right)^2 . \tag{18.1}$$

Initially, all firms produce at cost $c_i = c_0$. An independent research lab finds a process innovation that reduces the constant marginal cost of production from c_0 to $c_1 < c_0$. We assume that the innovation is nondrastic. That is, the monopoly price corresponding to c_1 is larger than the initial cost c_0: $(a + c_1)/2 > c_0$, which is equivalent to $c_0 - c_1 < a - c_0$. In the latter inequality, $c_0 - c_1$ measures the absolute size of the innovation (i.e., the cost reduction) and $a - c_0$ measures the size of the initial market (i.e., the difference between the largest price consumers are willing to pay, a, and the pre-innovation marginal cost). We can thus measure the *relative size of the innovation* by the ratio

$$\psi \equiv \frac{c_0 - c_1}{a - c_0} \quad \text{with} \quad 0 < \psi < 1.$$

The pre-innovation profit, π_{pre}, is easily computed by setting $c_i = c_j = c_0$ in expression (18.1). As for the post-innovation situation, we are only interested in the profit accruing to the innovator, which we note π_{post}; we also compute it easily by setting $c_i = c_1$ and $c_j = c_0$ ($\forall j \neq i$) in expression (18.1). Accordingly, we have

$$\pi_{pre} = \left(\frac{a - c_0}{n+1} \right)^2 \quad \text{and} \quad \pi_{post} = \left(\frac{a - nc_1 + (n-1) c_0}{n+1} \right)^2 .$$

We measure the profit incentive to innovate as the extra profit that accrues to the innovator with respect to the pre-innovation situation: $PI \equiv \pi_{post} - \pi_{pre}$. After some manipulations and emphasizing that the profit incentive depends on the number of firms, we have

$$PI(n) = \frac{n}{(n+1)^2}(2 + n\psi)\psi(a - c_0)^2.$$

We want now to assess how the profit incentive to innovate changes as the number of firms in the industry increases. To this end, we compute

$$PI(n+1) - PI(n) = \left[\frac{n+1}{(n+2)^2}(2 + (n+1)\psi) - \frac{n}{(n+1)^2}(2 + n\psi) \right] \psi(a - c_0)^2$$

$$= \frac{(2n^2 + 4n + 1)\psi - 2(n^2 + n - 1)}{(n+2)^2(n+1)^2} \psi(a - c_0)^2.$$

We understand from the latter expression that *an increase in the number of firms raises the profit incentive to innovate if the relative size of the innovation is large enough.* Formally, defining

$$\hat{\psi}(n) \equiv \frac{2(n^2 + n - 1)}{2n^2 + 4n + 1},$$

we have that $PI(n+1) > PI(n)$ if and only if $\psi > \hat{\psi}(n)$. We note that $\hat{\psi}(n)$ increases with n and tends to 1 as n tends to infinity. Therefore, there exists a finite size of the Cournot industry that maximizes the profit incentive to innovate. In particular, monopoly leads to the largest incentive to innovate if $PI(2) < PI(1)$ or $\psi < \hat{\psi}(1) = 2/7 \simeq 0.286$; duopoly leads to the largest incentive to innovate if $\hat{\psi}(1) \simeq 0.286 < \psi < \hat{\psi}(3) = 10/17 \simeq 0.588$; and so on and so forth.

> **Lesson 18.2**   In a Cournot industry with a homogeneous product, the market structure that gives the largest profit incentive to innovate is monopoly when the innovation size is not too large; it is oligopoly otherwise (and the 'ideal' number of firms in the industry increases with the innovation size).

To understand the previous result, note that an increase in the number of firms in the industry has two opposite effects on the profit incentive to innovate. On the one hand, there is a competition effect: a larger number of firms reduces profits both for the innovating and for the non-innovating firms. On the other hand, there is a competitive advantage: the larger n, the larger the number of rival firms producing in a less efficient way. The coexistence of these two conflicting forces explains why the incentive to innovate first increases and then decreases as the industry gradually expands.

18.2   When innovation affects market structure

The previous section was dealing with creative environments where ideas are scarce. It was thus appropriate to represent the innovation process as external to the industry under review and to measure how much a given firm in the industry is willing to pay for an innovation. In contrast, in creative environments in which ideas are common knowledge, several firms have the simultaneous opportunity to achieve competing innovations. Innovation therefore becomes a competitive tool in itself and its effects on the market structure need to be assessed.

To this end, we reconsider incentives to innovate in a monopoly when the threat of entry is taken into account. We want to identify who between the incumbent firm and the entrant is the most likely to innovate. The answer to this question will indeed indicate how innovation affects market structure: simply put, if the incumbent innovates, monopoly persists but if the entrant innovates, entry takes place and the industry becomes a duopoly. We address this issue first in a simple static setting where the innovation process is certain (Subsection 18.2.1) and next, in a more realistic dynamic setting where the innovation process is uncertain (Subsection 18.2.2). Finally, in Subsection 18.2.3, we consider dynamic R&D competition between two symmetric firms and compare their R&D decisions with the choice of a social planner; the concern here is that R&D competition might give firms too large incentives to invest in R&D from a social point of view.

18.2.1   Monopoly threatened by entry: the efficiency effect

We consider here that two firms can acquire a given innovation: an incumbent monopoly as well as a potential entrant. If both firms are active in the market they are assumed to make duopoly profit π^d. One can imagine that the innovation has been discovered by a third firm which cannot (or prefers not to) exploit it itself and auctions it to the highest bidder. The question is thus: who, between the incumbent and the entrant, will place the highest bid for the innovation?

Clearly, each firm is willing to bid up to the difference between the profit it would make if it gets the innovation and the profit it would make if it does not. For the potential entrant, the situation is quite similar to what we had in the previous section: if the potential entrant does not obtain the innovation, it stays out of the market and earns zero profit; on the other hand, with the innovation, the entrant becomes a duopolist with a cost advantage; we denote its profit by $\pi^d(c_1, c_0)$. Hence, the value of the innovation for the entrant is its discounted duopoly profit $V_E = (1/r)\pi^d(c_1, c_0)$, where r is the continuous time discount factor.

Things are a bit more complicated for the incumbent as it has to take into account what happens if the entrant is the one who successfully innovates. In that case, the incumbent would become a duopolist with a cost disadvantage and would earn a profit equal to $\pi^d(c_0, c_1)$. On the other hand, if the incumbent successfully innovates, it avoids entry and earns the monopoly profit $\pi^m(c_1)$. As a result, the incumbent places the following value on the innovation: $V_I = (1/r)\left[\pi^m(c_1) - \pi^d(c_0, c_1)\right]$.

Comparing the two values, we see that the incumbent has a higher incentive to acquire the innovation if the following condition is met:

$$V_I > V_E \Leftrightarrow \pi^m(c_1) > \pi^d(c_0, c_1) + \pi^d(c_1, c_0). \tag{18.2}$$

This condition is satisfied when the products sold by the two firms are close substitutes. In that case, a monopoly with a low cost earns a higher profit than two noncolluding duopolists can earn together, especially if one of them produces at a higher unit cost. This is so because the monopolist is always able to mimic the choices made by the duopolists; so, if it chooses otherwise, it is because such choices can be improved upon in terms of profit. However, the previous argument might no longer hold if the entrant is bringing a significantly differentiated product to the market. If consumers enjoy variety, the entry of a differentiated product might increase the size of demand in such a way that the inequality in (18.2) is reversed. This is also explained by the fact that the incumbent has less to lose from entry when the entrant's product is not a close substitute (in the limit, if the two products are completely differentiated, $\pi^d(c_0, c_1) = \pi^m(c_0)$ and $\pi^d(c_1, c_0) = \pi^m(c_1)$, and the replacement effect is the only effect at play).

> **Lesson 18.3** **A monopoly threatened by entry is willing to pay more for a minor innovation than a potential entrant who can produce a close substitute to the monopolist's product.**

The fear of losing its monopoly position provides the incumbent with a stronger incentive, a property known as the *efficiency effect*.[4] It follows that in industries where entry represents an important threat, incumbent firms use innovation as a tool to prolong their monopoly situation over time. We have thus here an illustration of how innovation affects market structure.

18.2.2   Asymmetric patent races: replacement and efficiency effects

The previous analysis abstracted away two important dimensions of R&D competition, namely *time* and *uncertainty*. Indeed, it was implicitly assumed that an investment in R&D translated immediately, and with certainty, into some process innovation. In many situations, however, the innovation process is uncertain and the real objective of R&D competition is to be the first to come up with an innovation (so as to outperform the rival firms). R&D competition takes thus the form of a *race for a patent*. In such a race, firms have to decide not only about the intensity of their R&D investment (so as to increase their chances to find the innovation) but also about the timing of their R&D investments (so as to be the first to innovate).

To enrich our analysis of the effect of R&D competition on market structure, we examine here an asymmetric patent race between an incumbent firm and an entrant.[5] Recall the elements we have gathered so far. On the one hand, we invoked the *replacement effect* to argue that monopoly power acts as a strong disincentive to innovate. On the other hand, we predicted the persistence of monopoly on the basis of the *efficiency effect*: in a static setting, a monopolist threatened by entry is willing to pay more for an innovation than a potential entrant. Our goal is now to study the interplay between these two effects in the framework of a patent race. Therefore, we use the same setup as in the previous subsection. Recall that the innovation allows firms to reduce the marginal cost of production from c_0 to $c_1 < c_0$, and that profits (per unit of time; we assume continuous time) are given as in the following table.

		After innovation	
	Before innovation	Incumbent obtains patent	Entrant obtains patent
Incumbent	$\pi^m(c_0) \equiv \pi_0^m$	$\pi^m(c_1) \equiv \pi_1^m$	$\pi^d(c_0, c_1) \equiv \pi_{01}^d$
Entrant	0	0	$\pi^d(c_1, c_0) \equiv \pi_{10}^d$

At each point in time, firm k spends some amount x_k on R&D. We assume a 'memoryless' stochastic process of the Poisson type. This means that a firm's probability of success only depends on its current R&D at any point in time and not on the accumulated stock of investment in R&D. This assumption allows us to abstract away issues related to dynamic investment problems and to diffusion of knowledge. The probability of success is formalized as a (twice continuously differentiable) hazard function $h(x)$ which is strictly concave and satisfies some boundary condition so that we only need to consider interior solutions. To be precise, (i) $h(0) = 0$, (ii) $h' > 0$, (iii) $h'' < 0$, (iv) $\lim_{x \to \infty} h'(x) = 0$, and (v) $\lim_{x \to 0} h'(x) = \infty$. A strategy for firm k consists in specifying its research expenditure for each point in time. Hence, it sets a function $x_k(\cdot)$. Since h is independent of the competitor's history and the competitor's history is payoff-irrelevant, x_k may depend on time only. Yet, since the stochastic process is memoryless, time has no effect. Indeed, at each date t, if neither firm has made a discovery, the game starting at this moment is identical to the initial game. It follows that the equilibrium strategies are constant over time.

We start by deriving the probability that no firm has made a discovery before some date t. Assuming that the patent race starts at date 0, we can use the Poisson process to determine the probability that firm k has been successful by date t.[c] Noting $\tau(x_k)$ the date of success given R&D expenditure x_k, we have that $\text{Prob}\{\tau(x_k) \le t\} = 1 - e^{-h(x_k)t}$. Therefore, the probability

---

[c] A *Poisson process* is a stochastic process that is defined in terms of the occurrence of events (e.g., the arrival of customers in a simple queuing system or the number of web page requests at a server). Its main property is 'memorylessness': the number of arrivals occurring in any bounded interval of time after some date t is independent of the number of arrivals occurring before date t.

that at date t none of the two firms succeeded is equal to $e^{-(h(x_I)+h(x_E))t}$ (where the subscripts I and E refer, respectively, to the incumbent and to the entrant). We can now compute the present discounted value of the expected profit over time for the two firms, respectively noted $V_I(x_I, x_E)$ and $V_E(x_I, x_E)$.

$$V_I = \int_0^\infty e^{-rt} e^{-(h(x_I)+h(x_E))t} \cdot \left(\pi_0^m - x_I + h(x_I)\frac{\pi_1^m}{r} + h(x_E)\frac{\pi_{01}^d}{r} \right) dt$$

$$= \frac{\pi_0^m - x_I + (h(x_I)/r)\pi_1^m + (h(x_E)/r)\pi_{01}^d}{r + h(x_I) + h(x_E)},$$

$$V_E = \int_0^\infty e^{-rt} e^{-(h(x_I)+h(x_E))t} \cdot \left(h(x_E)\frac{\pi_{10}^d}{r} - x_E \right) dt = \frac{(h(x_E)/r)\pi_{10}^d - x_E}{r + h(x_I) + h(x_E)}.$$

Let us decompose the firms' expected profits. In the absence of an innovation, the incumbent realizes a profit of $(\pi_0^m - x_I)dt$. With 'probability' $h(x_I)dt$, the incumbent is first to innovate and derives a discounted profit (discounted to date t) of π_1^m/r. In these first two instances, the entrant does not make any profit. Finally, with 'probability' $h(x_E)dt$, the potential entrant is first to innovate and obtains π_{10}^d/r, leaving the incumbent with π_{01}^d/r.

A Nash equilibrium is a pair (x_I^*, x_E^*) such that x_j^* maximizes V_j^* given x_k^* ($j \neq k \in \{I, E\}$). Using a standard fixed point argument, we can prove that a Nash equilibrium exists. Moreover, because of the strict concavity of h, we can assert that the Nash equilibrium is continuous in c and in π_0^m.

The question of interest is, of course, to compare x_I^* and x_E^*. The persistence of monopoly would obtain if $x_I^* > x_E^*$, meaning that the incumbent invests more in R&D than the entrant and is therefore more likely to be the first to innovate (and thus to remain a monopolist). Actually, the answer to this question depends on the combination of the two effects we mentioned above. On the one hand, the *efficiency effect* suggests that the incumbent has more incentives to innovate, as the net flow profit it receives by preempting the entrant (i.e., $\pi_1^m - \pi_{01}^d$) is larger than what the entrant gains by being first (i.e., π_{10}^d). On the other hand, the *replacement effect* is also present here because the marginal productivity of R&D expenditure for the incumbent decreases with its initial profits:

$$\frac{\partial}{\partial \pi_0^m} \left(\frac{\partial V_I}{\partial x_I} \right) < 0.$$

The intuition behind this finding is that, by increasing x_I, the incumbent moves the discovery date forward and hastens its own replacement. In contrast, the entrant does not forego a flow profit when innovating. It is not clear which effect will dominate.

Lesson 18.4 **In a patent race, it is in general ambiguous whether the incumbent or the entrant has a stronger incentive to invest.**

Yet, considering extreme situations, we can be sure that it is not always the same effect that dominates. If we consider a *nondrastic innovation* (as we have mainly done so far), making h almost linear would lead to a situation where the efficiency effect dominates: at equilibrium, the incumbent engages in more R&D than the entrant ($x_I^* > x_E^*$). In such a case, R&D is high, discovery is made early and the incumbent is concerned with the possibility of innovation by the entrant, whereas the replacement effect is not important. On the other hand, if we consider instead a *drastic innovation*, then we can prove that the replacement effect dominates: at equilibrium, the incumbent does *less* R&D than the entrant ($x_I^* < x_E^*$). Indeed, if the entrant discovers a drastic innovation, it becomes a de facto monopolist and hence, the efficiency effect disappears. This result lends credence to Schumpeter's conjecture about *creative destruction* (i.e., the idea that innovation leads one monopoly to replace another).

Case 18.2 illustrates the ambiguity mentioned in Lesson 18.4. It is impossible to say nowadays who will win the race to fuel the car of the future: one among the incumbent automobile manufacturers or some newcomer?

Case 18.2 The race for cleaner cars

The threats of global warming caused by the rising emissions of greenhouse gases exert an increasing pressure on automobile manufacturers to make cleaner cars. It is indeed estimated that surface transportation generates about a quarter of the man-made carbon emissions (and in this category, cars, buses and trucks are much larger pollution sources than ships and trains). In the traditional car industry, Toyota seems to have taken the lead of the race with its gasoline–electric hybrid, the Prius. Other carmakers have developed cars powered by hydrogen fuel cells (which make electricity by mixing the gas with oxygen), but mass production of such cars is not announced before 2010. Despite its very large R&D spending, the car industry could well be unseated by disruptive technologies proposed by firms outside the industry. For instance, Tesla Motors, a Silicon Valley upstart (funded by prominent entrepreneurs such as the founders of PayPal and Google), has come up with an all-electric sports car; because this car is largely made of lightweight composites, it is greener than a Prius, while being faster than a Ferrari.[6]

18.2.3   Socially excessive R&D in a patent race

As we will argue in the next chapter, there is a general presumption that markets provide too little incentive to introduce new innovations, which justifies the legal protection of IP. It must be noted, however, that IP protection might sometimes go one step too far by providing *too much* incentive to do R&D. Because of their 'winner-takes-all' nature, patent races might well lead to socially wasteful duplication of efforts.

To show this, we use a simplified version of the model of the previous subsection. Suppose that two firms consider incurring a fixed cost of f to establish a research division, in the hope of finding a new product. This hope is translated by a probability of success equal to ρ. If one firm only finds the new product, it will obtain the monopoly profit π^m on the product market; this monopoly is guaranteed by a patent sufficiently broad to prevent imitation. If both firms find the new product, they will both market it and each firm will obtain the duopoly profit π^d.

We want to determine the Nash equilibrium of the game in which the two firms simultaneously decide whether or not to invest in R&D. With the previous information, we can compute the expected profits depending on the firms' investment decisions. If a firm does not invest in R&D, it does not enter the new market and its profit is therefore set to zero. If a firm does invest in R&D, its expected profit depends on whether the rival firm also invests or not. If the rival firm does not invest, then the firm active in R&D will incur the cost f and get the monopoly profit with probability ρ: its expected profit is thus given by $\rho\pi^m - f$. On the other hand, if the rival firm also invests in R&D, the firm will get the monopoly profit if it is the only one to be successful, or the duopoly profit in case both firms are successful; as the respective probabilities of these two events are $\rho(1-\rho)$ and ρ^2, each firm's expected profit is equal to $\rho(1-\rho)\pi^m + \rho^2\pi^d - f$. The normal form of the game is represented in the matrix of Table 18.1.

Table 18.1. *Expected profits in a patent race*

	Investment (I)	No investment (NI)
I	$\rho(1-\rho)\pi^m + \rho^2\pi^d - f, \rho(1-\rho)\pi^m + \rho^2\pi^d - f$	$\rho\pi^m - f, 0$
NI	$0, \rho\pi^m - f$	$0, 0$

We easily see that the Nash equilibrium involves investment by both firms provided that

$$\rho(1-\rho)\pi^m + \rho^2\pi^d - f \geq 0 \Leftrightarrow f \leq \rho(1-\rho)\pi^m + \rho^2\pi^d \equiv f_2^{priv}.$$

Let us now adopt a public policy perspective and ask when it is socially optimal to have both firms investing in R&D. Abstracting away the potential gain in consumer surplus that the development of the new product could generate, we simply take aggregate profit as an indicator of social welfare. This would indeed be correct if firms extracted the full surplus. In the monopoly case this holds if all consumers have the same willingness to pay or if the monopolist can perfectly price discriminate. In a duopoly, consumers typically obtain a positive surplus. However, a special case in which also under duopoly consumers obtain zero surplus is the following situation: if both firms are successful with probability 1/2 each firm is equally likely to be the first and, in this case, to make the monopoly profit.

From Table 18.1, we observe that expected aggregate profits are larger when two firms invest in R&D rather than a single firm if and only if

$$2\left(\rho(1-\rho)\pi^m + \rho^2\pi^d - f\right) \geq \rho\pi^m - f$$
$$\Leftrightarrow f \leq \rho(1-\rho)\pi^m + \rho^2\pi^d - \rho^2\left(\pi^m - \pi^d\right) \equiv f_2^{publ}.$$

As $f_2^{publ} = f_2^{priv} - \rho^2(\pi^m - \pi^d)$ and as $\pi^m > \pi^d$, it appears clearly that $f_2^{publ} < f_2^{priv}$. Therefore, when the fixed cost f of establishing a research division lies between f_2^{publ} and f_2^{priv}, both firms invest in R&D at the Nash equilibrium although it would be socially preferable if only one firm did so. Put simply, there is 'too much' R&D for such values of f. What makes private and public incentives diverge is the fact that firms do not take into account the negative effect their R&D effort has on the rival firm's profits. So, facing a relatively low cost of R&D, they find it optimal to invest in R&D even though the other firm invests as well. Yet, from the industry point of view, the cost of R&D duplication (i.e., the cost f of an additional research division) is larger than the expected benefits stemming from the increase in the probability of finding the new product.

> **Lesson 18.5** Since a firm ignores the effect of its R&D efforts on the rival's profits, imperfectly competitive firms tend to overinvest.

18.3   R&D cooperation and spillovers

In this section, we continue to consider innovative environments where ideas are common knowledge. That is, we have in mind industries such as automobiles in which new models are continually being developed, meaning that all firms in the industry have the simultaneous opportunity to achieve competing innovations. In terms of the modelization of the innovative process, we leave aside the tournament and uncertain aspects of innovation that we considered in Section 18.2 and we come back instead to what we assumed in Section 18.1, i.e., that R&D investments result immediately and for sure into an innovation. This simplification allows us to analyse more deeply a series of issues pertaining to the *strategic use of R&D* and to *R&D cooperation*. To this end, we depart from the setting used in Section 18.1 in several ways. First, we recognize that R&D is like any form of investment in that it precedes the production stage; as a result, we take into account the issues of strategic commitment that inevitably arise in considering R&D decisions. Therefore, we place firms in a symmetric position by allowing them all to invest in R&D (as is realistic when ideas are common knowledge rather than scarce). Second, we note that R&D exhibits many of the attributes of a public good (see Chapter 19) and, hence, we model the fact that R&D by one firm typically leads to *spillovers* which benefit other firms.[d] Finally, we incorporate in our setting the possibility for firms to cooperate on R&D decisions and, thereby, to internalize spillovers. Such form of cooperation is indeed widespread and is widely allowed, if not encouraged, by public authorities (see Case 18.3 below). These different aspects of R&D (strategic behaviour, spillovers, cooperation) have been widely studied.[7]

We will base our discussion on a model that has the merits of allowing us to disentangle the separate influence of strategic behaviour and of R&D cooperation, and to treat in a unified way the cases where the firms' decisions on the product market are strategic substitutes or strategic complements.

We consider an industry of two symmetric firms ($i = 1, 2$), which compete in a two-stage game. At the first stage, firms simultaneously conduct process R&D and choose R&D expenditures $r(x_i)$ to reduce their marginal costs by x_1 and x_2, respectively. We assume that R&D activities exhibit decreasing returns to scale, i.e., $r' > 0$ and $r'' > 0$ for x_i strictly less

---

[d] Spillover levels vary drastically across industries. They are often inversely related to the level of patent protection. For instance, low-tech mature industries (e.g., paper) exhibit low effective patent protection and, hence, high spillovers; conversely, R&D intensive industries (e.g., such as pharmaceutical drugs and software) exhibit high effective patent protection and low spillovers. See Griliches (1990).

than $c/2$.[8] At the second stage, upon observing x_1 and x_2, firms compete in the product market with substitutable products. Noting σ_i firm i's strategic choice in the second-stage, the analysis encompasses both quantity competition ($\sigma_i = q_i$) and price competition ($\sigma_i = p_i$).

We assume that marginal production costs are independent of output but decreasing in R&D, both that of the firm itself and, through spillover effects, of its rivals:

$$c_i(x_i, x_j) = c - x_i - \beta x_j, \tag{18.3}$$

where $\beta \in [0, 1]$ is the spillover coefficient. The parameter β measures the extent to which firm i benefits from R&D undertaken by firm j: when β is equal to zero, R&D is a private good as R&D expenditures benefit only the firm undertaking them; at the other extreme ($\beta = 1$), R&D is a pure public good as a firm fully benefits from the other firm's R&D.

We can write each firm's profits as follows:

$$\tilde{\pi}_i = \pi_i[c_i(x_i, x_j), \sigma_i, \sigma_j] - r(x_i).$$

In the latter expression, π_i denotes the firm's net revenue from production and sales; it depends on the firm's unit production costs and on its own and rival firm's second-stage strategic choices.

Regarding competition on the product market, each firm's first-order condition sets equal to zero the partial derivative of its profit function with respect to its own action (i.e., either quantity, $\sigma_i = q_i$, or price, $\sigma_i = p_i$):

$$\frac{\partial \pi_1}{\partial \sigma_1} = 0 \quad \text{and} \quad \frac{\partial \pi_2}{\partial \sigma_2} = 0.$$

Assuming that the second-order condition is satisfied, i.e.,

$$\pi^{ii} \equiv \frac{\partial^2 \pi_i}{\partial \sigma_i^2} < 0,$$

we obtain a unique Nash equilibrium, which we note $\{\sigma_1^*(x_1, x_2), \sigma_2^*(x_1, x_2)\}$, by solving the system of the two first-order conditions.

As we know from Chapter 3, the sign of the cross partial derivative of profit, noted π^{ij}, depends on the nature of competition. We postulate that, under quantity competition, quantities are strategic substitutes, $\pi^{ij} < 0$, whereas, under price competition, prices are strategic complements, $\pi^{ij} > 0$. In sum,

$$\pi^{ij} \equiv \frac{\partial^2 \pi_i}{\partial \sigma_i \partial \sigma_j} = \frac{\partial^2 \pi_j}{\partial \sigma_i \partial \sigma_j} \begin{cases} < 0 & \text{under quantity competition,} \\ > 0 & \text{under price competition.} \end{cases}$$

This difference will prove crucial for assessing the effect of strategic behaviour and of R&D cooperation.

18.3.1   Effects of strategic behaviour

By considering a two-stage game, we implicitly assume that firms are not able to commit to their second-stage choices (i.e., quantity or price) at the same time as they choose their R&D. As a consequence, investments in R&D are strategic in the sense that they are carried out with a view to affecting the environment in which the second-stage game is played.[e] To isolate this

---

[e] In this respect, the present model is reminiscent of the one we used in Chapter 16 to elaborate a taxonomy of entry-related strategies.

strategic incentive to invest in R&D, we contrast the results of the two-stage game with those of a hypothetic one-stage game in which firms choose simultaneously their R&D intensity and their product market actions.

We focus here on the case where firms do not cooperate at the R&D stage (i.e., firms choose their R&D expenditure independently). Hence, firm i chooses x_i to maximize its first-stage profit (which incorporates the second-stage equilibrium):

$$\tilde{\pi}_i(x_i, x_j) = \pi_i[c_i(x_i, x_j), \sigma_i^*(x_i, x_j), \sigma_j^*(x_i, x_j)] - r(x_i).$$

The first-order condition for profit maximization is given by

$$\frac{d\tilde{\pi}_i}{dx_i} = 0 \Leftrightarrow \underbrace{\frac{\partial \pi_i}{\partial c_i}\frac{\partial c_i}{\partial x_i}}_{\text{Direct effect}} + \underbrace{\frac{\partial \pi_i}{\partial \sigma_i}\frac{\partial \sigma_i^*}{\partial x_i}}_{=0} + \underbrace{\frac{\partial \pi_i}{\partial \sigma_j}\frac{d\sigma_j^*}{dx_i}}_{\text{Strategic effect}} = r'(x_i).$$

Let us decompose the latter condition. When firm i assesses the effect of increasing its R&D intensity, it first considers the *direct* or *'cost-minimizing' effect* a further cost reduction will have on its profit ($\partial \pi_i / \partial x_i$). From the production costs (18.3), we have that the direct effect is simply equal to the equilibrium second-stage quantity q^*. If firm i were non-strategic, this is the only effect that would matter for its choice. We can thus say that *in the absence of strategic behaviour and of R&D cooperation, the marginal private return to R&D per unit of output is simply the reduction in the firm's own unit costs* (i.e., 1 under our assumptions).

However, when firm i is strategic, it also anticipates the effect of its R&D choice on the subsequent product market equilibrium. There are two potential effects. A first effect should be ignored; indeed, using the envelope theorem, we know that the effect on π_i from the change in firm i's own second-stage action is nil (since σ_i is chosen so that $\partial \pi_i / \partial \sigma_i = 0$). On the other hand, the second effect is crucial. This is the *strategic effect* resulting from the combined influence of firm i's investment on firm j's second-stage action ($d\sigma_j^*/dx_i$) and of firm j's action on firm i's profit ($\partial \pi_i / \partial \sigma_j$).

As for the latter derivative, it is easy to see that firm i is hurt when firm j increases its quantity, but benefits when firm j increases its price. That is, $\partial \pi_i / \partial \sigma_j < 0$ if $\sigma_j = q_j$, while $\partial \pi_i / \partial \sigma_j > 0$ if $\sigma_j = p_j$. Assessing the sign of the former derivative is trickier as an increase in x_i reduces not only firm i's marginal cost but also firm j's (unless spillovers are nil). As both firms become tougher competitors, we understand that the net effect on firm j's second-stage decision (σ_j^*) will depend on the nature of the strategic variables and on the degree of spillovers. We thus treat quantity and price competition separately.

Let us start with quantity competition. We know from Chapter 3 that when firms produce substitutable products, quantity competition typically refers to a situation with strategic substitutability, which implies downward-sloping reaction functions. As depicted in the left panel of Figure 18.3, an increase in x_i allows firm i to move its reaction function to the right (from R_i to R_i'): because firm i has a lower marginal cost, it reacts to any firm j's quantity by producing a larger quantity than before. In the absence of spillovers ($\beta = 0$), the analysis stops here: firm j's reaction function does not move and the new equilibrium is such that firm j produces a lower quantity as a result of the increase in x_i. However, for $\beta > 0$, firm i's R&D investment also reduces firm j's marginal cost, which shifts firm j's reaction function to the right (from R_j to R_j'). As shown in the figure, if firm j's reaction function

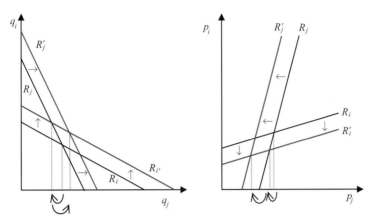

Figure 18.3 Strategic effect of R&D investments (left: quantity competition; right: price competition)

moves sufficiently outward (i.e., if spillovers are large enough), the new equilibrium is such that firm j produces a *larger* quantity than before. There exists thus a threshold value of the spillover parameter around which the sign of the strategic effect changes. We denote this threshold by $\bar{\beta}$. We show below how to derive the value of $\bar{\beta}$ in our general model. For now, we observe:

$$\text{If } \sigma_j = q_j, \text{ then } d\sigma_j^*/dx_i < 0 \text{ for } \beta < \bar{\beta} \quad \text{and} \quad d\sigma_j^*/dx_i > 0 \text{ for } \beta > \bar{\beta}.$$

From this, we conclude that the strategic effect of an increase in the R&D of one firm on its own profit is positive for small spillovers ($\beta < \bar{\beta}$) and negative for large spillovers ($\beta > \bar{\beta}$).

We repeat now the analysis for price competition. Because of strategic complementarity, reaction functions slope upward. A decrease in a firm's marginal cost allows this firm to set a lower price for any price of the rival firm, i.e., to shift its reaction functions inward (from R_i to R_i'). As illustrated in the right panel of Figure 18.3, we now have two reinforcing effects: (i) by reducing c_i, the increase in x_i shifts firm i's reaction function down and brings the equilibrium towards a lower value of p_j; (ii) by also reducing c_j (when $\beta > 0$), the increase in x_i shifts firm j's reaction function to the left (from R_j to R_j'), which decreases further firm j's equilibrium price. Hence, we conclude:

$$\text{If } \sigma_j = p_j, \text{ then } d\sigma_j^*/dx_i < 0 \text{ for all values of } \beta.$$

Recalling that $\partial \pi_i/\partial \sigma_j < 0$ if $\sigma_j = q_j$ and $\partial \pi_i/\partial \sigma_j > 0$ if $\sigma_j = p_j$, we are now in a position to sign the strategic effect.

Lesson 18.6   **The strategic effect of an increase in the R&D of one firm on its own profit is (i) positive for small spillovers ($\beta < \bar{\beta}$) and negative for large spillovers ($\beta > \bar{\beta}$) under quantity competition, (ii) always negative under price competition.**

Using the terminology introduced in Chapter 16, we can summarize the intuition behind this result as follows. Because an increase in its R&D expenditure makes the firm a tougher competitor, it is worth investing more from a strategic point of view only if tough behaviour is met by a soft response of the rival firm. This is the case under quantity competition provided that spillovers are small enough (because otherwise, the other firm also becomes a tougher competitor), and is never the case under price competition. As a corollary, if the rival reacts toughly (i.e., under price competition or under quantity competition with strong spillovers), strategic firms choose optimally to invest less in R&D than they would do were they only motivated by cost minimization. In that case, strategic behaviour leads to larger marginal costs and thus, to lower output.

Let us now show in our general setting that, under fairly general conditions, $\bar{\beta}$ lies between 0 and 1 under quantity competition, and $\bar{\beta} < 0$ under price competition (which implies that the strategic effect is always negative). Under quantity competition, $\sigma_i = q_i$ and $d\pi_i/dq_i = p_i + (dp_i/dq_i)q_i - c_i$; under price competition, $\sigma_i = p_i$ and $d\pi_i/dp_i = q_i + (dq_i/dp_i)p_i - (dq_i/dp_i)c_i$. We summarize the two cases in the following way:

$$\frac{d\pi_i}{d\sigma_i} = 0 \Leftrightarrow \frac{\partial(p_i q_i)}{\partial \sigma_i} - c_i q_\sigma = 0, i = 1, 2, \tag{18.4}$$

where $q_\sigma \equiv \partial q_i/\partial \sigma_i$ is positive (equal to one) under quantity competition and negative (equal to $\partial q_i/\partial p_i$) under price competition.

To establish the sign of the strategic effect, we totally differentiate the second-stage first-order conditions (18.4):

$$\begin{cases} \pi^{ii}d\sigma_i + \pi^{ij}d\sigma_j + q_\sigma dx_i + \beta q_\sigma dx_j = 0, \\ \pi^{ii}d\sigma_j + \pi^{ij}d\sigma_i + q_\sigma dx_j + \beta q_\sigma dx_i = 0. \end{cases} \tag{18.5}$$

In the present case, we consider an increase in R&D by firm i alone, meaning that $dx_i > 0$ and $dx_j = 0$. Solving the above system of equations for $d\sigma_j$, we obtain

$$d\sigma_j = -\frac{1}{\Delta}\left(\beta\pi^{ii} - \pi^{ij}\right)q_\sigma dx_i,$$

with $\Delta \equiv (\pi^{ii} - \pi^{ij})(\pi^{ii} + \pi^{ij})$. To guarantee the stability of the second-stage equilibrium, we assume that $-\pi^{ii} > \pi^{ij}$, or $\pi^{ii} + \pi^{ij} < 0$ (this condition is trivially satisfied under quantity competition). We also make the additional assumption that the own effect dominates the cross effect: $-\pi^{ii} > -\pi^{ij}$, or $\pi^{ii} - \pi^{ij} < 0$ (this condition is trivially satisfied under price competition). It follows from these two assumptions that $\Delta > 0$.

Hence, we can express the strategic effect as follows:

$$SE = \frac{\partial\pi_i}{\partial\sigma_j}\frac{d\sigma_j^*}{dx_i} = \left(-\frac{1}{\Delta}q_\sigma\frac{\partial\pi_i}{\partial\sigma_j}\right)(\beta\pi^{ii} - \pi^{ij}).$$

It is easy to see that the term in the first bracket is positive. Indeed, under quantity competition, $\partial\pi_i/\partial\sigma_j < 0$ and $q_\sigma = 1 > 0$, whereas under price competition, $\partial\pi_i/\partial\sigma_j > 0$ and $q_\sigma = \partial q_i/\partial p_i < 0$. The product $q_\sigma(\partial\pi_i/\partial\sigma_j)$ is thus negative and as $(-1/\Delta) < 0$, we have that the whole term is positive. We therefore have the following

$$SE > 0 \Leftrightarrow \beta\pi^{ii} - \pi^{ij} > 0 \Leftrightarrow \beta < \frac{\pi^{ij}}{\pi^{ii}} \equiv \bar{\beta}.$$

Under quantity competition, our assumptions imply that $0 < \bar{\beta} < 1$. On the other hand, under price competition, we have that $\bar{\beta} < 0$.

18.3.2   **Effects of R&D cooperation**

Suppose now that firms cooperate in their choice of R&D levels (i.e., they choose them to maximize joint profits), though they continue to compete at the second stage. For the moment, we assume that cooperation does not affect the value of the spillover parameter (we will relax this assumption below).[9] In this case, the first-order condition for joint profit maximization in the first stage is given by

$$\frac{d(\tilde{\pi}_i + \tilde{\pi}_j)}{dx_i} = 0 \Leftrightarrow \begin{vmatrix} \underbrace{\frac{\partial \pi_i}{\partial c_i}\frac{\partial c_i}{\partial x_i}}_{\text{Direct effect}} + \underbrace{\frac{\partial \pi_i}{\partial \sigma_i}\frac{\partial \sigma_i^*}{\partial x_i}}_{=0} + \underbrace{\frac{\partial \pi_i}{\partial \sigma_j}\frac{d\sigma_j^*}{dx_i}}_{\text{Strategic effect 1}} \\ + \underbrace{\frac{\partial \pi_j}{\partial c_j}\frac{\partial c_j}{\partial x_i}}_{\text{Spillover effect}} + \underbrace{\frac{\partial \pi_j}{\partial \sigma_i}\frac{d\sigma_i^*}{dx_i}}_{\text{Strategic effect 2}} + \underbrace{\frac{\partial \pi_j}{\partial \sigma_j}\frac{\partial \sigma_j^*}{\partial x_i}}_{=0} = r'(x_i). \end{vmatrix} \quad (18.6)$$

Because x_i is now chosen to maximize total profits, its effect on firm j's profit has also to be taken into account. There are three effects. First, because of spillovers, an increase in x_i affects directly firm j's profit by decreasing firm j's marginal cost. Obviously, this positive 'spillover effect' increases with the spillover parameter β. Second, a change in x_i modifies firm i's second-stage action, which in turn affects firm j's profits. One understands intuitively that this strategic effect is negative whatever the nature of competition: by investing more in R&D, firm i gains a competitive advantage over its rival; that is, firm i is able to produce more or to set a lower price in the second stage, which hurts firm j. One also understands that this negative strategic effect weakens when spillovers get stronger (since the competitors' efficiency is also enhanced). Finally, a change in x_i also affects firm j's equilibrium second-stage decision and, thereby, its profit. Yet, as firm j makes an optimal decision in the second stage, this effect can be ignored.

In sum, R&D activities in the presence of spillovers create two types of externalities. The first externality affects overall industry profits and increases with the level of spillovers; it is ignored when firms choose their R&D levels separately but is internalized when firms choose their R&D levels so as to maximize their joint profits. The second externality affects a firm's competitive advantage with respect to its rival: firms invest in R&D to become relatively more efficient than their competitors. This externality, which weakens as spillovers increase, is present when firms choose their R&D investments separately but is fully internalized when they act cooperatively. We can therefore conclude that there exists a pivotal spillover rate above which the total effect of the two externalities is positive. Indeed, if spillovers are large enough, the competitive advantage motivation for investing in R&D is weak, whereas the temptation to free-ride on the other firm's effort is high; as a result, cooperation leads to larger investments in R&D, implying further reductions in unit costs and a larger output.

Lesson 18.7   When firms behave strategically, R&D cooperation leads to more R&D when spillovers are large but to less R&D when spillovers are small.

Note that when firms do not behave strategically (i.e., when they commit to both R&D levels and second-stage actions), only the direct and the spillover effect remain in expression

(18.6). It follows that the effect of x_i on total profits is equal to $(1 + \beta) q^*$. Hence, the private and social returns to R&D coincide: cooperation fully internalizes the externality arising from R&D spillovers and is thus desirable.

Let us now derive the pivotal value of the spillover parameter in our general model. We start by assessing the second strategic effect. To this end, we use again the total differentiation of the second-stage first-order conditions given by expressions (18.5). Solving for $d\sigma_i$ this time, we have:

$$d\sigma_i = -\frac{1}{\Delta} \left(\pi^{ii} - \beta \pi^{ij} \right) q_\sigma dx_i.$$

The second strategic effect is thus given by

$$\frac{\partial \pi_j}{\partial \sigma_i} \frac{d\sigma_i^*}{dx_i} = \frac{\partial \pi_j}{\partial \sigma_i} \left(-\frac{1}{\Delta} \left(\pi^{ii} - \beta \pi^{ij} \right) q_\sigma \right) = \phi \left(\pi^{ii} - \beta \pi^{ij} \right) q^*,$$

where

$$\phi \equiv -\frac{1}{\Delta} \frac{\partial \pi_i}{\partial \sigma_j} \frac{q_\sigma}{q^*} > 0.$$

Cooperation leads to a larger private marginal return to R&D if the sum of the spillover effect and of the second strategic effect in expression (18.6) is positive, which is equivalent to

$$\beta q^* + \phi \left(\pi^{ii} - \beta \pi^{ij} \right) q^* > 0 \Leftrightarrow \beta > \bar{\beta}' \equiv \frac{-\phi \pi^{ii}}{1 - \phi \pi^{ij}}. \tag{18.7}$$

As $\phi > 0$ and $\pi^{ii} < 0$, we have that $0 < \bar{\beta}' < 1$.

As an illustration, suppose that the second stage is a Cournot duopoly and that the inverse demand is given by $p = a - q_i - q_j$. Firm i chooses q_i to maximize $\pi_i = (a - c_i - q_i - q_j)q_i$. Solving for the first-order condition, we find firm i's reaction function: $q_i(q_j) = (1/2)(a - c_i - q_j)$. By analogy, firm j's reaction function is $q_j(q_i) = (1/2)(a - c_j - q_i)$. The equilibrium quantity of firm j is then easily found as $q_j^* = (1/3)(a - 2c_j + c_i)$, and its profits are simply equal to the square of the equilibrium quantity. As $c_i = c - x_i - \beta x_j$ and $c_j = c - x_j - \beta x_i$, we can rewrite firm j's equilibrium profit as

$$\pi_j^* = \tfrac{1}{9} \left(a - c + (2 - \beta) x_j + (2\beta - 1) x_i \right)^2.$$

When it comes to choose x_i in the first stage, R&D cooperation leads to a larger value provided that an increase in x_i implies an increase in π_j^*. We see from the above expression that the condition for this is $2\beta - 1 > 0$. Hence, in this particular case, $\bar{\beta}' = 1/2$.

R&D cooperation and information sharing

We refer to the previous mode of R&D cooperation as the formation of an *R&D cartel*. One can distinguish it from the case of a *cartelized Research Joint Venture (RJV)*, in which firms not only coordinate their R&D decisions but also share their information completely so as to eliminate duplication of effort. As a result, in a cartelized RJV, the final spillover parameter β is internally set to unity. This naturally tends to make cooperation more attractive from a welfare point of view. Indeed, it turns out that *a cartelized RJV yields a superior performance compared to noncooperative R&D in all criteria of interest: propensity for R&D, firms' profits, consumer surplus, and thus social welfare.*[10]

The previous theoretical analysis leads thus to unambiguous antitrust implications: *public authorities should permit simultaneous R&D sharing and coordination of R&D decisions among firms that compete in a product market.* No direct action seems to be needed to encourage such cooperation as the firms' incentives for cooperation in R&D are clear (information sharing and coordination of R&D decisions yield higher profits); public authorities just need to provide the attending legal framework for such cooperative arrangements, which corresponds to what is currently done in the US, in the EU and in Japan, as described in Case 18.3.

Case 18.3 Antitrust provisions related to R&D cooperation

As we will make clear in the next chapter, IP generating activities suffer from three sources of market failures: externalities, indivisibilities and uncertainty. When it comes to R&D, one way to alleviate these three problems is to allow firms to form a cooperative R&D venture. As we have emphasized in this section, rival firms often exert positive externalities on one another through their research activities. Indeed, new knowledge easily spreads across firms, meaning that firms freely benefit (at least partly) from the R&D efforts of their rivals. As we have seen, these knowledge spillovers raise the prospect of free-riding and firms might be inclined to cut back their R&D spending. In response to this problem, the formation of a cooperative R&D venture allows firms to internalize the externalities and, thereby, to preserve their incentives to do R&D.

Cooperative R&D ventures are also a way to pool risk and, hence, to better manage technological and market uncertainty. Furthermore, cooperative R&D ventures might also reduce the problems stemming from indivisibilities by allowing firms to share costs, to eliminate useless duplication of R&D projects, to pool complementary skills and to exploit economies of scale.

Although cooperative R&D may be subject to contractual hazards (opportunistic behaviour, free-riding, difficulties about sharing the results, etc.), it is generally accepted that their formation is welfare-enhancing. This is why antitrust authorities tolerate this type of collaborative arrangements between firms.

In the US, the National Cooperation Act passed in 1984 allows firms to cooperate in R&D provided they remain competitors on product markets. A similar permissive antitrust attitude towards R&D cooperation is the norm in Europe and Japan. Furthermore, public policies, such as the European Framework Programmes, explicitly encourage firms to pool their R&D activites.

18.3.3   **Futher analysis of R&D cooperation**

The previous analysis can be extended in several directions, essentially with respect to (i) the nature of R&D spillovers, (ii) the design of R&D cooperation, and (iii) the potential effect of R&D cooperation on product market collusion. We briefly review here a number of those extensions.

The nature of R&D spillovers

In the setting we used, knowledge spillovers were modelled as a 'manna from heaven': firms were automatically benefiting from the other firms' R&D effort (according to the factor β). The realism of this assumption can be questioned. R&D may not only generate new information, but may also enhance the firm's ability to identify, assimilate and exploit existing information from the environment. That is, R&D also contributes to develop a stock of prior knowledge, which is called *absorptive capacity*,[11] and thereby increases a firm's ability to learn from others. In the strategic games we have considered above, introducing this additional property of R&D has two opposite effects on R&D investments: on the one hand, the firm wants to learn more from the rival firms and therefore has an incentive to raise its own R&D expenditure; yet, on the other hand, this will increase the other firms' incentive to free-ride, meaning that there will be less to learn from.

To formalize this intuition we rewrite the cost function (18.3) as follows:[12]

$$c_i(x_i, x_j) = c - x_i - B(x_i)x_j,$$

where $0 \leq B(x_i) \leq 1$ describes the proportion of R&D that spills over from firm j to firm i. In contrast with our previous formulation, the spillover rate is no longer exogenously fixed ($B(x_i) = \beta$) but is an increasing function of the firm's own investment: we assume that $B'(x_i) > 0$ to capture the idea that by investing more, firm i increases its absorptive capacity and, thereby, its ability to learn from firm j.

To evaluate the impact of this modification, let us consider a Cournot duopoly for a homogeneous product, whose inverse demand is given by $p = a - q_i - q_j$ (with $a > c$).[13] Assume also that R&D costs are given by $r(x_i) = (1/2)x_i^2$. In the second stage of the game (production stage), firm i chooses q_i to maximize

$$\pi_i = (a - q_i - q_j)q_i - (c - x_i - B(x_i)x_j)q_i.$$

From the first-order condition, we derive firm i's reaction function (where b stands for $a - c$): $q_i(q_j) = \frac{1}{2}(b - q_j + x_i + B(x_i)x_j)$. Proceeding in a similar way for firm j and solving for the system of the two reaction functions, we find the Nash equilibrium of the production stage as

$$q_i(x_i, x_j) = \frac{1}{3}[b + (2 - B(x_j))x_i + (2B(x_i) - 1)x_j].$$

Equilibrium profits are

$$\tilde{\pi}_i(x_i, x_j) = [q_i(x_i, x_j)]^2.$$

Consider now the first stage of the game (R&D stage) in the absence of cooperation. Firm i's problem is to choose the R&D level x_i that maximizes $\hat{\pi}_i(x_i, x_j) = \tilde{\pi}_i(x_i, x_j) - (1/2)x_i^2$. Using the above expressions, we can write the first-order condition as: $\partial \hat{\pi}_i / \partial x_i = 0$

if and only if

$$\tfrac{2}{9}(b + (2 - B(x_j))x_i + (2B(x_i) - 1)x_j)(2 - B(x_j) + 2B'(x_i)x_j) = x_i.$$

Assuming that firms are symmetric, we have $x_i = x_j = x$ at the symmetric equilibrium and we can rewrite the previous expression as

$$\frac{\partial \widehat{\pi}}{\partial x} = \tfrac{2}{9}(b + (1 + B(x))x)(2 - B(x) + 2B'(x)x) - x = 0$$

$$\Longleftrightarrow Vx^2 + (W - Y)x + Z = 0, \tag{18.8}$$

where $V \equiv 4(1 + B(x))B'(x)$, $W \equiv 4bB'(x)$, $Y \equiv 9 - 2(1 + B(x))(2 - B(x))$ and $Z \equiv 2b(2 - B(x))$. Because $0 \le B(x) \le 1$ and $B'(x) > 0$, we have $V, W, Y, Z > 0$.

We want to compare the equilibrium R&D investment level in the game where the spillover rate is affected by absorptive capacity effects ($B(x)$) to the game of the previous section where the spillover rate is exogenous (β). Let us denote the former equilibrium R&D level by x_a (with a for absorptive) and the latter by x_e (with e for exogeneous). Using the first-order condition (18.8), we have that x_a and x_e are respectively defined by

$$V_a x_a^2 + (W_a - Y_a)x_a + Z_a = 0 \quad \text{and} \tag{18.9}$$

$$-Y_e x_e + Z_e = 0, \tag{18.10}$$

where the second line follows from the fact that $B'(x) = 0$ if the spillover rate is exogenous (implying that $V_e = W_e = 0$). We can now show that if the spillover rate ($B(x_a)$) generated by the game with absorptive capacity effects is the same as the exogenous spillover rate (β) in the game of the previous section, then we necessarily have that $x_a > x_e$: *the presence of absorptive capacities induce larger R&D investments for a similar (ex post) spillover rate*. The proof goes as follows. If $B(x_a) = \beta$, then $Y_e = Y_a$ and $Z_e = Z_a$. Combining (18.9) and (18.10), we have $V_a x_a^2 + (W_a - Y_a)x_a + Y_a x_e = 0$, or $(V_a x_a + W_a)x_a = Y_a(x_a - x_e)$. As $(V_a x_a + W_a)x_a > 0$ and $Y_a > 0$, it necessarily follows that $x_a > x_e$. Intuitively, by imposing $B(x_a) = \beta$, we 'freeze' the traditional negative effect of spillovers on R&D investments (i.e., the free-riding effect) and we are left, in the model with absorptive capacity, with a pure *positive learning effect* of own R&D that drives up the incentive to invest.

Design of R&D cooperation

One shortcoming of the approach we followed above is that it assumed away the question of the endogenous formation of research joint ventures. Indeed, for simplicity, we have restricted attention to a duopoly. Results do not critically hinge on this assumption and one can consider an arbitrary number of firms. However, a limitation of any such analysis is that we have compared complete non-cooperation in R&D with industrywide R&D cooperation.[14] In many industries, (i) there are typically several research joint ventures competing with each other, or (ii) firms' R&D cooperation is bilateral and nonexclusive in nature (translating into situations where firms i and j, and j and k collaborate with one another, respectively, while firms i and k do not collaborate). To account for the former possibility, we can model the formation of RJVs in terms of a *coalition structure*, which is a partition of the set of firms (each firm belonging to one RJV only). To account for the latter possibility, we need to consider two-player relationships, which collectively generate a network structure.[15]

R&D cooperation and product market collusion

So far we have implicitly assumed that firms act non-cooperatively on the product market. However, a major antitrust concern is the possibility that cooperation in R&D could pave the way for, or at least increase the likelihood of, collusive behaviour in the product market. If this conjecture turns out to be true, we might have to reconsider the policy recommendation according to which R&D cooperation and information sharing should be permitted, if not encouraged. Indeed, if R&D cooperation appears to worsen product market performance, then public policy toward R&D cooperation involves a trade-off between market power and efficiency, and it is by no means clear that this trade-off will always balance out in favour of R&D cooperation. As indicated in Case 18.4, there are reasons to fear collusive behaviour on the part of firms forming R&D joint ventures.

Case 18.4 Research joint ventures and collusion[16]

May collusive behaviour be facilitated by research joint ventures (RJVs)? Answering empirically this question is extremely difficult as it requires one to isolate the impact of the returns to collusion on the decision to join an RJV from the other factors determining the decision to join the venture. Goeree and Helland (2008) have found a nice way around this difficulty. They exploit the variation in RJV formation generated by a quasi-experiment that affects the collusive benefits of an RJV while not directly affecting the research synergies associated with that venture. Their identification strategy is simple: if product market collusion is not a motivation to form an RJV then, after controlling for firm, RJV and industry characteristics, the propensity to enter into an RJV should not be impacted by changes in the antitrust policy aimed at deterring collusion in the final goods market.

The authors focus on RJVs in the US telecommunication industry. In this industry, 38% of firms are involved in at least one RJV with another direct product market rival. There is also a history of potentially collusive behaviour among firms in this industry. As for antitrust policy, it became tougher in the US in 1993 and in 1995. In 1993, the revision of the so-called 'leniency policy program' made it more attractive for cartel members to report illegal behaviour (see Chapter 14); in 1995, the Department of Justice substantially increased the penalties for antitrust violations.

After controlling for industry characteristics, RJV characteristics, firm attributes and correcting for the endogeneity of R&D, the authors find that, among telecom firms, the decision to join an RJV is impacted by the policy change in a very significant way: the revised leniency policy reduces the probability telecom firms join a given RJV by 25%.

Review questions

1. Why does a monopolist have less incentives to innovate than a perfectly competitive firm? Explain the meaning of the 'replacement effect'.

2. Why does a monopolist threatened by entry have more incentives to innovate than a potential entrant? Explain the meaning of the 'efficiency effect'.

3. Explain why firms might invest too much in R&D (from a social point of view) when they are racing to obtain a patent on an innovation.

4. Discuss the effects of strategic behaviour on firms' investments in R&D.

5. Is it a sensible policy to allow firms to coordinate their R&D decisions? Discuss.

Further reading

An important reading is the seminal article of Arrow (1962), in which he explores the problems associated with activities generating new knowledge and the influence of market structure on the incentives to innovate. For the reverse influence of innovation on market structure, see Gilbert and Newbery (1982) and their explanation of the 'efficiency effect' leading to the persistence of monopoly. Our treatment of asymmetric patent races was based on Reinganum (1983). As for the effect of strategic behaviour and cooperation on R&D decisions, the seminal paper is d'Aspremont and Jacquemin (1988). For a unified treatment of these issues (incorporating strategic substitutes and complements on the product market), see Leahy and Neary (1997).

19 Intellectual property

In the previous chapter, we focused on the positive aspects of R&D by examining the interplay between market structure and innovation. In consequence, we were not too specific about the exact regime of intellectual property (IP) protection. In this chapter, we want to adopt a more normative point of view and study how IP protection should optimally be organized. This chapter also provides the reader with a broad (and essentially non-technical) description of the realm of IP.

In Section 19.1, we describe the appropriability problem of innovation and we consider several ways to close the wedge that this problem drives between social and private rates of return from innovation. We start with the main policy instrument that has been designed to promote innovation, namely the institution of intellectual property and its legal protection (essentially through IP rights such as patents and copyrights). We explain that the main rationale of IP rights is to provide incentives to produce information and knowledge by conferring a monopoly right to the producer. We then compare this institution to other public and private responses.

In our discussion of IP rights in Section 19.1, we argue that the negative impacts that monopolies have on welfare call for limitations on the legal protection conferred by IP rights. What type of limitations? This is the question we address in Section 19.2. As innovations are mainly protected by patents, we focus on the optimal patent design. We examine two adjustable dimensions of a patent: the length and the breadth. The *length* of a patent simply refers to the duration of patent protection. The *breadth* of the patent, refers to the usage the innovator can make of the patent with respect to its competitors. In other words, the breadth of the patent defines how different another product must be in order not to infringe.

In the first two sections, IP rights are essentially seen as exclusive rights aiming at inducing innovation. In Section 19.3, we focus on another aspect of IP rights by seeing them as *transferable* rights aiming at facilitating exchange in a 'market for innovations'. Transferability is as important as exclusivity because it channels assets toward the agents who have the highest valuation for them. Patents are transferred through licensing agreements. Patent holders may also decide to group their patents within a common pool. We examine how the market for licenses and the possibility of pooling patents affect the optimal design of the IP system. This issue is of particular relevance in sectors such as software or biotechnology where innovation follows a cumulative process.

While the first three sections are centred around theoretical arguments, the last section has a more applied nature. Section 19.4 applies the previous general analyses to the specificities of the digital economy. Two topical issues are addressed: the piracy of digital products and the development of open source software.

19.1   Remedies to the appropriability problem

We start this section by describing the appropriability problem that mars the production of information and knowledge. We consider then public and private responses to this problem. The main public responses consist either in restricting the exploitation of knowledge (by instituting intellectual property and by protecting it), or in raising the expected returns of new knowledge by lowering its cost of production (through subsidization of research and patronage of artists, or by allowing putative competitors to form cooperative R&D ventures, as already described in the previous chapter). We examine these various responses in turn and we discuss their respective merits. We close this section by looking at how innovators protect their R&D investments in practice. It turns out that the legal protection of IP is often complemented by private measures.

19.1.1   Information and appropriability

What do inventions, business methods, industrial processes, novels, songs, paintings, . . . have in common? They all result from the production of *information* (or *knowledge*). The problem with activities generating information is that they suffer from the three generic sources of market failure: uncertainty, indivisibilities and externalities. As a result, these activities face a generic problem of *appropriability*, which sets them apart from other investments made by firms or individuals.

A first source of market failure in information markets is *uncertainty*. Investments in R&D involve two types of uncertainty: on top of technological uncertainty (how to make new things and how to make them work), there is also commercial uncertainty (how to make new things adopted by the consumers). For instance, it is estimated that in the US, the odds for a potential medicine to make it through the R&D pipeline and be approved for patient use are about one in 10 000.[17] The same uncertainties apply for the creation of artistic and literary work. The decisions to produce or to invest in information-generating activities are therefore necessarily mixed with decisions to bear risk. Separating the two types of decisions is often difficult because of moral hazard: it is very hard to attribute the failure of a project to bad luck or to a lack of effort (which is typically unobservable). Hence, a balance has to be found between incentives and the transfer of risk, which undermines the efficiency of the investment.

Indivisibilities are a second source of failure in information markets. The creation of new knowledge and new information involves large fixed setup costs. For instance, the innovation cost of a new molecule in the pharmaceutical industry is estimated to be 1.25 billion euros; the remake of *King Kong* by Peter Jackson has cost 170 million euros. As such activities often require the division of highly specialized labour, they are also prone to economies of scale. Finally, both knowledge and information are inherently discrete. As a result, marginal costs are generally driven below average costs, which makes marginal cost pricing economically unviable. Furthermore, there is a tendency towards monopolization of such markets.

The third source of market failure in the production of information and knowledge stems from the *public good* nature of these two goods. Producers of public goods generate many externalities and it is well known that in the presence of externalities, markets may not provide the right incentives to produce. Public goods are characterized by *nonrivalness* in consumption: the consumption of the good by one person does not prevent (rival) its consumption by another person; there is thus a potential for collective consumption. Another way to define nonrivalness is to say that a good is nonrival if for any given level of production, the marginal cost of providing it to an additional consumer is zero. This is clearly the case for knowledge and information. Think of a new idea or of a song performed in public. Public goods are said to be 'pure' when they are also *nonexcludable*, in the sense that one person cannot exclude another person from consuming the good in question. Whereas nonrivalness is an attribute of the good itself, excludability depends, at least in part, on the available technology for exclusion, and the institutional (legal) framework that permits or facilitates such technically feasible exclusion.[a]

The three sources of market failure associated with information production generate a *problem of appropriability*. That is, innovators and creators face a serious risk of appropriating only incompletely the returns from their activities. As a result, there is a general presumption that markets provide too little incentive to introduce new innovations and that the production of information and knowledge may well be insufficient from a social point of view. Economists therefore agree that governments ought to intervene to promote *dynamic efficiency*, i.e., to provide the right *incentives* to create and innovate. We turn now to various responses, both public and private, to the problem of appropriability.

19.1.2   Intellectual property protection

Intellectual property (IP) refers to the legal rights which result from intellectual activity in the industrial, scientific, literary and artistic fields. These rights attach not only to inventions, business methods, industrial processes, chemical formulae, unique names (the so-called 'industrial property branch' of IP), but also to all information products that derive their intrinsic value from creative expression, literary creation, ideas, or presentations (the so-called 'copyright branch' of IP). For instance, the text that you are currently reading, the articles and books that are referred to in this text, and the various pieces of software that have been used to produce this text are all intellectual properties.

Incentives versus use

Most countries have adopted laws to protect intellectual property. The main objective of IP law is to promote innovation and aesthetic creativity. To solve the appropriability problem, IP law intends to make knowledge or information excludable by legal means. That is, IP law grants exclusive use of the protected knowledge or creative work to the creator. Thereby, IP law provides creators with the incentives to produce new knowledge and partly solves the *underproduction* problem that would have resulted from the nonexcludability

---

[a] To understand this difference, just look at television programme services in most countries. A television signal is clearly nonrival since, once it is broadcast, the marginal cost of making the broadcast available to another user is zero. Actually, to watch terrestrial TV broadcast, all you need is TV receiving equipment. Yet, to use such equipment, you may be required by law to pay a special tax: those who fail to pay are legally – but not technologically – excluded from watching terrestrial broadcasts. On the other hand, cable TV broadcasts are made exclusive by encrypting the signal and charging for the device that allows it to be decoded. A similar distinction holds for knowledge: as we explain in this chapter, most countries have adopted laws to 'protect' intellectual property, i.e. to allow producers of IP to prevent non-payers from using it.

of knowledge. However, by granting exclusive – i.e., monopoly – rights to the creator, IP law creates an *underutilization* problem. Indeed, as the marginal cost of production is zero (knowledge and information are nonrival goods), any positive price creates a welfare-reducing rationing.

In order to strike a balance between these two conflicting problems, IP law grants exclusive rights only for a limited period of time. That is, IP law addresses the two problems sequentially. First, legal protection makes the good excludable: to enjoy the services, users have to pay royalties to the producer. Second, once the protection is over, the good falls in the public domain, which means that all users may access the good for free (i.e., at marginal cost). In sum:

> **Lesson 19.1**   IP law attempts to find the best possible compromise between dynamic efficiency considerations (how to provide the right incentives to create and innovate), and static efficiency considerations (how to promote the diffusion and use of the results of creation and innovation).

Note that dynamic efficiency calls for the broadest and longest possible protection (to maximize the flow of new knowledge creation), whereas static efficiency calls for the absence of protection (to avoid the deadweight loss of monopoly). Therefore, the balance struck by IP law is necessarily imperfect as it is impossible to reach both objectives at the same time.

Let us make the latter point more precise by considering the simple model illustrated in Figure 19.1. Consider an industry where an arbitrary number of firms produce a homogeneous good at constant marginal cost c_0. Firms are assumed to compete à la Bertrand. Therefore, at this stage, the price is equal to c_0, a quantity q_0 is sold, the consumer surplus is represented by area 1 and the producer surplus is nil. Suppose now that some firm i discovers a process innovation that reduces the marginal cost of production from c_0 to c_1. (For simplicity, we do not explicitly model the R&D cost that is associated with discovering the innovation.) We assume that the innovation is nondrastic (i.e., as defined in Chapter 18, the cost advantage generated by the innovation does not allow the innovator to escape totally from the competition of the other firms in the industry).

Absent IP protection, as knowledge is nonrival and nonexcludable, all firms would possibly have access to the innovation.[b] As a result, firm i would anticipate that the innovation would not generate any extra profit and would therefore refrain from investing in R&D. This would be detrimental for society as a more efficient production technology would not be used. By granting exclusive rights on the innovation, IP law provides firm i with incentives to innovate. Firm i becomes then the only firm producing at marginal cost c_1. Because the innovation is supposed to be nondrastic, the monopoly price corresponding to c_1 is larger than the marginal cost of the rival firms (c_0). Therefore, as we saw in Chapter 3, the equilibrium is such that all firms set a price equal to c_0 and all consumers buy from the innovator, who then

---

[b] This implicitly assumes that the innovator does not take any effort to conceal information (see the discussion of secrecy below).

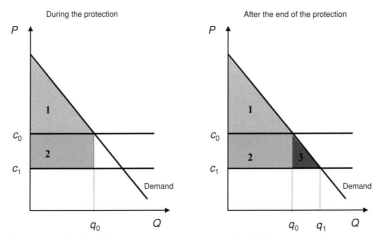

During the protection   After the end of the protection

Figure 19.1 Trade-off between dynamic and static efficiency

sells a quantity q_0.[c] The consumer surplus is still given by area 1 and social welfare is now augmented by area 2, which represents firm i's profit.

However, as long as the innovation is protected, social welfare does not reach its maximum. Indeed, from the point of view of static efficiency, the quantity sold by firm i falls short of the optimal quantity corresponding to cost c_1 (i.e., q_1). It is only when the legal protection ends that this quantity is produced: all firms have access to the new technology and the market price falls to c_1. The producer surplus is nil again but the consumer surplus now amounts to areas 1, 2 and 3. In sum, area 3 can be seen as the temporary deadweight loss society has to pay to make sure that the innovation takes place: *a temporary reduction in static efficiency enhances dynamic efficiency.*

Main IP regimes

The IP protection legislation generally distinguishes among four separate IP regimes, which are targeted at different subject matters. On the one hand, *patents, trade secrets* and *trademarks* are designed to protect industrial property (such as inventions, processes, machines, brand names, industrial designs, . . .). On the other hand, *copyrights* concern literary, musical, choreographic, dramatic and artistic works (such as novels, poems, plays, films, songs, drawings, paintings, photographs, sculptures, architectural designs, . . .).

In this chapter, we will mainly focus on patents (in Sections 19.2 and 19.3) and on copyrights (in Section 19.4).[d] Although both regimes aim at striking a balance between incentives and use, they accomplish this objective in very different manners. In short, patent law provides inventors with a strong and broad form of protection, but on a relatively short

---

[c] This assumes that in case of equal prices, consumers buy from the most efficient firm. Although there is a continuum of symmetric equilibria where all firms set a price p lying between c_1 and c_0, the one we select here is the only equilibrium that resists small perturbations (see the discussion in Chapter 3). Alternatively, we could say that the innovator sets a price one cent below c_0 and attracts all consumers because it is less expensive than the other firms.
[d] We briefly describe trade secrets below. Trademark protection is designed to protect the integrity of the commercial marketplace, rather than to promote innovation.

period of time. By contrast, copyright law affords a weaker and narrower form of protection (it merely protects expression, not the underlying ideas) but for a longer duration of time. Table 19.1 compares the two main IP regimes.[18]

Table 19.1. *Comparative overview of patent and copyright protection in the EU and in the US*

	Patent	Copyright
Requirements for protection	(EU) Novelty, inventive step, industrial use (US) Novelty, non-obviousness, utility	Originality, authorship, form of expression
Ownership	(EU) First to file (US) First to invent	Author/creator
Rights	*Bundle of rights extending to the idea*: exclusive rights against all commercial uses (make, use, sell the innovation)	*Economic and moral rights on the form of expression*: exclusive rights against copying (rights of performance, display, reproduction, derivative works)
Scope of protection	Wide	Narrow
Duration	20 years from filing	Life of author + 70 years
Costs of protection	Filing, issue, and maintenance fees; litigation costs	No filing necessary; suit requires registration; litigation costs

Patents or copyrights?

Altough the subject matters of patents and copyright are quite distinct, some innovations have elements that pertain to the two categories and it is therefore not clear whether such innovations should benefit from the short and broad protection of patents or from the long and narrow protection of copyrights. The typical example is software. Software has traditionally been protected by copyright. Over recent years, however, patent protection has been awarded to an increasing number of software. Software patents have become the norm in the US while in Europe, although the Munich Convention of 1973 excludes software from the domain of patentability, some imperfections of the law have led the European Patent Office (EPO) to award software patents. To address this ambiguity, the European Commission has put forward in 2002 a project aimed at introducing software patents. Very quickly, this project has become a major arena for policy conflicts. Supporters of the proposed directive include large software corporations such as Microsoft, IBM and Hewlett-Packard, as well as the EPO itself. Their main argument is that absent patent protection for software, thousands of jobs and inventions would be at risk in the EU. On the other hand, opponents to the proposal are to be found among free software and open source programmers (see Subsection 19.4.2 below), academics, small business groups and commercial software developers. Their argumentation is based on what they see as abuses of the software patent system in the US. They contend that although some software patents might be beneficial, the net effect of the proposed directive would be to hinder innovation and reduce competition.

In Case 19.1, we shed some light on this debate by examining the economic specificities of software, and by assessing whether the 'one-size-fits-all' tool of patent protection is appropriate given these specificities.

Case 19.1 Should software be protected by patents or by copyright?

Producers of software have to be protected not only from competitors' imitation, but also from consumers' copying. The protection against consumers' copying is the economic role of copyright. As for the protection against imitation by competitors, patents seem more appropriate. Yet, considering that software innovation involves relatively low costs compared to the private and social returns it generates, patents might confer too strong a protection from a social point of view.

The previous conclusion has to be qualified when we take into account the intrinsic *cumulativeness* of software innovation (see Subsection 19.2.2 for a complete analysis). Software innovation exhibits the two types of cumulativeness: sequentiality and complementarity. On the one hand, given that any new software is built upon previous lines of code, innovation is sequential, which calls for broad (and short) patents. On the other hand, because there are complex interdependencies between different software and that interoperability is very often a major concern, software innovations are complementary, which raises the prospect of the 'tragedy of the anticommons' when strong property rights are awarded to separate right-holders. In this respect, protection should be optimally designed so as to favour interoperability, with easy access to interfaces.

Another important feature of software is the presence of *network effects*. There are various reasons for which a software becomes more valuable for its users the more widely it is adopted. As we will explain in Chapter 20, the presence of such reinforcement mechanisms drives the competition between incompatible software towards a 'winner-takes-all' scenario: it is very likely that a single software will end up dominating its market. In such a context, one might question the necessity of supplementing this natural tendency towards monopolization with the creation of a legal monopoly resulting from strong IP rights.

An opposite argument can be proposed when invoking the *durability* of software. As software does not wear out, we recall from Chapter 10 that, according to the Coase conjecture, a software producer might not be able to price above marginal cost because it cannot commit not to decrease prices in the future. Therefore, a stronger IP protection should be granted to software producers so as to provide them with the incentives to create. However, software producers have designed tactics to counter the durability problem. For instance, producers can sell subscription instead of standalone software packages. They can also add new features that improve upon older versions in order to create a new flow of demand. Another commonly used tactic consists in 'planning the obsolescence' of older versions by decreasing compatibility and/or technical support.

Collecting the previous arguments, we realize how complex it is to assess whether patent protection should be extended to software. On the one hand, we understand how software patents could foster innovation by increasing private returns on R&D. On the other hand, we also realize that software patents could stifle innovation because they grant too strong a protection given the sequential and complementary nature of software, and because of the heavy need for interoperability. In one of the rare empirical analyses on this topic, Bessen and Hunt (2004) argue that regulatory changes that reduced the cost of software patents in the USA lead firms to patent software innovations more for strategic motives than for covering R&D expenditures. Their analysis also indicates a negative correlation between software patenting intensity and R&D intensity in the software sector.

The gradual reinforcement of IP protection

Under the initiative of the US and of Europe, *IP protection has been strengthened, broadened and harmonized internationally.* In terms of *strengthening*, in the early 1980s, legal and procedural reforms in the US provided stronger protection to holders of existing patents;[e] in Europe, the European Patent Office (EPO) granted the first European patents in 1978, but a genuine European patent (superseding national patents) is still under debate. Regarding *broadening* IP, new categories of inventions have been protected, either through an extension of patent protection (software, business methods, genetic inventions) or through the creation of 'sui generis' rights (semiconductors, databases). Finally, the TRIPS Agreement of 1994, negotiated within the framework of the World Trade Organization, represents a major advance toward the *harmonization* of IP laws; it includes a general definition of patents, which adopts US criteria and, thereby, broadens the scope of patentable inventions internationally; furthermore, the US and the EU repeatedly concluded bilateral agreements with their trading partners in order to coerce them to significantly strengthen their own IP rights regimes.

19.1.3   Subsidization and secrecy

Subsidization and secrecy are two alternative incentive mechanisms to promote innovation and aesthetic creativity, which do not entail as large a deadweight loss as IP law, but which might create other problems.

Subsidies and prizes

Governments fund technical and artistic works through in-house development, procurement through competitive bidding, research grants to universities and promising scientists, or patronage of artists. Such funding mechanisms enhance static efficiency with respect to IP protection: as there is no need to grant exclusive rights to the innovator, the innovation is in free access and no deadweight loss ensues. However, to fund research and creation, governments have to raise

---

[e] For instance, the Patent and Trademark (Bayh-Dole) Act of 1980 allows universities and other nonprofit organizations to patent discoveries made in their laboratories. Also, the Court of Appeals for the Federal Circuit was established in 1982 to harmonize patent law nationwide, which had the effect to strengthen patent protection.

taxes, which introduces distortions elsewhere in the economy and reduces static efficiency. In contrast, the patent system assigns costs to users rather than to tax payers. Moreover, there is no guarantee that subsidies achieve dynamic efficiency. Indeed, the uncertainty surrounding the social value of an innovation might yield the government to over- or underestimate the amount of subsidy and, thereby, to give too much or too little incentive. In contrast, the patent system can be implemented without requiring sensible economic information that is only privately known.

To address the latter problem, several methods are used to ensure that a prize reflects the value of the innovation. For instance, by giving the inventor the option to choose IP protection instead, the prize effectively becomes a patent *buy-out*: the inventor will enter the scheme only if the prize is at least as large as the value of the underlying patent, which constrains the prize to reflect the value. Another method consists in making the prize conditional on a verifiable performance standard, as illustrated in Case 19.2.

Case 19.2 The 'H-Prize'[19]

The H-prize was passed in May 2006 by the US House of Representatives. This national prize competition would help overcome technical challenges related to hydrogen. Modelled after the successful X Prize (which spurred the first privately funded suborbital human spaceflight in 2005), the H-prize offers prizes in three categories: (i) technological advancements (four prizes of up to $1 million awarded biennially in the categories of hydrogen production, storage, distribution and utilization); (ii) prototypes (one prize of up to $4 million awarded biennially that forces working hydrogen vehicle prototypes to meet ambitious performance goals); and (iii) transformational technologies (one grand prize consisting of a $10 million cash award).

Trade secrets

In the absence of any external mechanism, inventors might sometimes find sufficient incentives to innovate when they manage to keep their discoveries secret. Famous examples are the Michelin radial tires and the recipe for Coke, which have never been deconstructed or revealed. As long as the innovation is kept secret, information is excludable and the appropriability problem disappears. Firms may prefer to protect their discoveries through secrecy because they find that seeking a patent is, comparatively, a long and costly process. They might also wish to exploit their discoveries on a longer period than the duration of the patent. However, secrecy might be hard to keep as the risk is high that an employee (or some industrial spy) will disclose the invention, which would then become public knowledge. Trade secrets partly reduce such risk. Trade secret law protects the inventor against individuals within the laboratory or firm and those subject to contractual limitations who misappropriate proprietary information; to obtain this protection, the inventor needs merely to take reasonable steps to maintain secrecy. But, even if the costs of keeping secrets are reduced, the innovator loses all protection once the idea is released. Also, trade secrets offer no protection against independent innovations (which, by contrast, patents do).

Although secrecy makes information excludable, which solves the underproduction problem, secrecy does not solve the underutilization problem as information remains nonrival. Hence, the absence of diffusion creates a cost for society. This cost is reduced in the patent system for two reasons. First, as already explained, patent protection is limited in time: at the end of the protection, the innovation falls in the public domain. Second, patents entail a disclosure requirement: applicants must describe their invention in sufficient detail for a skilled person or team to be able to reproduce it. Knowledge is thus diffused, which fosters technical progress.

19.1.4   Protection of IP in practice

Besides the public responses designed to alleviate the appropriability problem of innovation, there also exist a number of private responses. As we have just seen, innovators might try to keep their discoveries secret. They might also take future imitation as a fact and simply rely on the (temporary) competitive advantage conferred by their innovative position. When interrogated, innovators often declare that they prefer such private measures to patents. However, the number of patents filed and granted has exploded over the last three decades. Is there a contradiction? These are the questions we address in this subsection.

Survey of innovators

Several empirical studies have attempted to assess the relative attractiveness of the different means innovators have at their disposal to protect their inventions. Interestingly, it appears that innovating firms consider trade secrets (for process innovations) and business strategies based on early-mover advantage (for product innovations) as the main means of getting returns on R&D investments and to appropriate the rents stemming from innovation. Similarly, according to a recent survey, managers claim that 'lead time, learning curves, and sales or service efforts are substantially more effective in protecting IP than patents are'.[20]

It appears thus that the appropriability problem is often better addressed through private responses than through public responses. In particular, except for the chemical and pharmaceutical sectors (see Case 19.3 below), patent protection is generally deemed as of little efficacy, especially for process innovations. We can give a number of reasons for this lack of efficacy: (i) that a patent can easily be 'invented around' by imitators, (ii) that a patent is costly to obtain and to enforce, and (iii) that innovators suffer from disclosing the information, as required by the patent.[21]

Case 19.3 Patents in the pharmaceutical sector

The three market failures we identified above are particularly acute in the pharmaceutical sector: large indivisibilities result from huge R&D fixed costs (the average cost of a new molecule is estimated at EUR 1.25 billion); the length of the R&D process and the need to get public approval for new drugs cause a lot of uncertainty (of 10 000 pharmaceutical products patented, only 10 are marketed);[22] finally, because knowledge is more science-based and more codified in the pharmaceutical sector, imitation costs are low and hence, externalities are important. It must be added that successful pharmaceutical innovations create other powerful consumption externalities as they improve public health. For all these reasons, the discrepancy between social and private returns to innovation is particularly wide in the case of pharmaceuticals and thus, absent appropriate intervention, the level of pharmaceutical innovation would undoubtedly be insufficient from a social point of view.

Does the patent-based system constitute the appropriate public intervention for the pharmaceutical sector? In terms of *dynamic efficiency*, empirical studies indicate two reasons for concluding that the patent system is relatively more efficient in the pharmaceutical sector than in other industrial sectors. First, it appears that pharmaceutical companies rely heavily on patents to appropriate the returns from their inventions.[23] Second, macroeconomic analyses also show that the pharmaceutical sector plays a leading role when looking at the patent explosion (especially in the US). Note that patents are relatively efficient in the pharmaceutical sector despite the fact that the effective patent life (i.e., the patent time remaining at the product launch) is significantly reduced for drugs. Indeed, patents in pharmaceuticals are typically applied for early in the development process; because of the length of the regulatory approval process, marketing exclusivity occurs only after a number of years. In consequence, the US, Europe and Japan have enacted patent term restoration laws.

On the other hand, the *static inefficiency* resulting from monopoly prices is worse for pharmaceuticals than for most other products. To put it bluntly, the rather abstract 'deadweight-loss of monopoly' takes here a much more concrete and tragic form, which can be measured, following the World Health Organization (WHO), in *disability-adjusted life years* (DALYs) lost.[f] Therefore, one understands why, in many developed countries, the prices of drugs are controlled and/or expenditures for drugs are covered by public or private insurance. While such interventions alleviate the static inefficiency of patents, they also distort market incentives, as potential demand levels condition research efforts. The latter consideration stresses another shortcoming of the patent-based system: as R&D priorities are decided on the basis of potential demand levels, the system provides little incentives to develop products with relatively small economic markets. What makes the matter worse is that those products are generally of great social need.[24] It thus appear that in the pharmaceutical sector, the patent-based system needs to be complemented by adequate subsidy-based approaches.

The patent explosion

In spite of what innovators declare about the relative unimportance of patents to protect their IP, the number of patent applications and grants has risen drastically over the last decades. In

---

[f] According to the World Health Organization, 'DALYs for a disease are the sum of the years of life lost due to premature mortality in the population and the years lost due to disability for incident cases of the health condition. The DALY is a health gap measure that extends the concept of potential years of life lost due to premature death to include equivalent years of "healthy" life lost in states of less than full health, broadly termed disability. One DALY represents the loss of one year of equivalent full health.'

the US, it has more than tripled between 1980 and 2001 (whereas it was practically stable over the previous two decades). A comparable trend is observed for European countries (although it began later). Although nearly all technology fields experienced growth in patenting, two technology fields contributed substantially to the overall surge in patenting: biotechnology and information and communication technologies.

However, this growth in the number of patents does not necessarily mean that the total value of innovations follows the same increasing path. Ultimately, what we would like to measure is the consumer value created by R&D spending. As long as R&D spending and patents are linked, the issue is thus to measure the private value of patents. Yet, this issue is far from simple as the private value of receiving a patent depends on the counterfactual. That is, what would happen if no patent was granted? There are four possible scenarios: either (i) the invention is not made at all, or the invention is made, but (ii) the patent is granted to a rival firm, or (iii) the invention is put in the public domain, or (iv) the invention is kept secret and not patented. Scotchmer (2004, p. 275) summarizes the main results drawn from various estimations of patent values: '(1) the values of patent rights are very dispersed, (2) the distribution of values is very skewed, with most of the value provided by a few high-earning patents, and (3) the average value of patent rights is much lower than the average R&D cost of innovation'. In Case 19.4, we discuss how the value of innovations is usually quantified.

Case 19.4 Patent indicators

Among the few available indicators of technology output, patent indicators are the most frequently used. The main *advantages* of patent indicators are the following: (i) patents have a close link to invention; (ii) patents cover a broad range of technologies; (iii) patent documents contain a rich source of information; (iv) patent data are readily available from patent offices.

However, patent indicators are also subject to some major *disadvantages*. First, because there is no standard method of calculating indicators from patent data, there is also a wide divergence in the political lessons that can be drawn from patent indicators. To solve this problem, the OECD has initiated a process to standardize these indicators. Such standardization requires a good understanding of how and why patents are taken out, of how they are administered and enforced, and of how all this changes over time. Indeed, a second disadvantage of patent indicators comes from four sources of differences in the interpretation of patent counts: (i) differences across countries in economic costs and benefits of patents, (ii) differences among technologies and sectors in the importance of patents as protection against imitation, (iii) differences among firms in propensity to patent (especially unimportant innovations), and (iv) differences in patent law over the years. A third disadvantage is that patents are an imperfect indicator of inventive output; indeed, many inventions are simply not patented (either because they are not patentable or, as we mentioned above, because inventors prefer to protect them using other methods, such as secrecy, lead time, etc).

Several attempts have been made to refine the measure of innovation given by patents. One direction consists in weighing each patent for the number of citations it generates in subsequent patents (so as to measure knowledge externalities). Another approach is to use renewal efforts or the filing of a legal opposition to the patents. It is indeed expensive for holders of European patents to renew patent protection for one year. Similarly, legal battles are costly. So, only privately valuable patents are worth renewing or opposing. Finally, useful additional information can be drawn from direct interviews of inventors.

A patent paradox?

The huge increase in patent counts seems to contradict what innovators declare about the relative unimportance of patents to protect their IP. How can we solve this so-called 'patent paradox', which has been systematically documented in the semiconductor industry?[25] For a number of reasons firms in most sectors still do bother to seek patent protection for their inventions:[26] (i) patents are relatively inexpensive to register (although they are generally costly to defend); (ii) patents can serve to measure the ouput of a firm's R&D division and, thereby, to structure compensation and incentive schemes; (iii) venture capitalists often demand that firms patent technology, both to block rivals and to have assets to sell in case the firm flounders; (iv) patents can be used as a 'trading device'.

The latter reason is confirmed by a number of surveys, which show that it is essentially large firms that resort to patent protection, and especially in complex industries (e.g., biotech, IT, telecoms, electronics and software).[g] We will return to this *patent portfolio theory* in Section 19.3. The main idea is that, in many industries, patents are more valuable when aggregated than when taken individually. Firms have thus an incentive to constitute large 'portfolios' of related patents. This is particularly true in complex industries that heavily rely on *cumulative innovations*.

19.2   Optimal patent design

In the previous section, we explained that IP law seeks a compromise between static and dynamic efficiency considerations. The two objectives are, on the one hand, to promote the diffusion and use of new innovations while, on the other hand, preserving the incentives to innovate in the first place. In this section, we study how to achieve the best possible balance between these two conflicting objectives. We focus on patents and we examine the optimal choice of two dimensions of patents, namely length and breadth.

19.2.1   Optimal patent length

The 1994 WTO's *Agreement on Trade-Related Aspects of Intellectual Property Rights* (*TRIPS*) is an attempt to narrow the gaps in the way IP rights are protected around the world, and to bring them under common international rules. The agreement specifies that patent protection must

---

[g] A survey published in *The Economist* (20 October 2005) reports the following facts: IBM now earns over $1 billion annually from its IP portfolio; HP's revenue from licensing has quadrupled in less than three years, to over $200m this year; Microsoft is on course to file 3000 patents this year, when in 1990 it received a mere 5; 54% of companies saw growth in licensing of 10–50% between 2000 and 2002; almost 75% of executives say they expect to buy as well as sell more licences over the next two to five years, and 43% expect a dramatic increase in their licensing revenue (according to a survey by McKinsey).

be available for both products and processes, in almost all fields of technology. It also describes the minimum rights that a patent owner must enjoy. In terms of patent length, the agreement says that patent protection must be available for at least 20 years. Why 20 years? Is such duration appropriate? As we saw in the previous section, the key to answer these questions is to determine the right balance between incentives (i.e., the private return on R&D investments accruing to the innovator during the duration of the patent) and use (i.e., the social benefits accruing to consumers and other firms once the patent expires and competition emerges).

To address this trade-off, we consider an innovator with a strictly convex cost function[27]

$$C(x) = \tfrac{1}{2}\phi x^2,$$

where ϕ reflects the exogenous efficiency of the existing innovation technology (the lower ϕ the more efficient the innovation technology). We assume that ϕ is large enough, so that in all circumstances $x \leq 1$ and, accordingly, x can be seen as the success probability of the innovation. That is, with probability x, the innovation is succesful and the innovator obtains the monopoly profit π^m during the life of the patent, and some competitive return $\bar{\pi}$, with $0 \leq \bar{\pi} < \pi^m$, once the patent has expired and the innovation has become available to everyone. Noting the patent length T, we can express the present discounted value (in continuous time) of the innovator's return in case of success as

$$P(T) = \int_0^T e^{-rt}\pi^m dt + \int_T^\infty e^{-rt}\bar{\pi} dt.$$

The innovator's problem is thus to choose x so as to maximize $xP - (1/2)\phi x^2$. The solution is easily found as

$$x^*(T) = P(T)/\phi.$$

As $\bar{\pi} < \pi^m$, $P(T)$ is clearly an increasing function of T, and so is $x^*(T)$: the longer the patent protection, the higher the innovator's return and, hence, his incentive to invest in R&D.

Similarly, we can express the social return on innovative effort as

$$S(T) = \int_0^T e^{-rt}W^m dt + \int_T^\infty e^{-rt}\bar{W} dt,$$

where W^m and $\bar{W}$ depict social welfare (computed as the sum of consumer surplus and industry profits) when the patent is in force and after it expires. Contrary to $P(T)$, $S(T)$ decreases with T (since $W^m < \bar{W}$), which sets the crucial distinction between the social and private return on innovation. The policymaker's task is to choose the patent length that maximizes $S(T)$, given that it correctly anticipates the innovator's profit-maximizing research intensity $x^*(T)$. That is, the policymaker's objective can be written as

$$\max_T x^*(T)S(T) - \tfrac{1}{2}\phi(x^*(T))^2.$$

Slightly rearranging terms, we can rewrite the first-order condition as

$$\underbrace{\frac{\partial x^*(T)}{\partial T}S(T)}_{\text{Marginal dynamic gain}} = \underbrace{x^*(T)\left(\phi\frac{\partial x^*(T)}{\partial T} - \frac{\partial S(T)}{\partial T}\right)}_{\text{Marginal static loss}}. \tag{19.1}$$

The latter condition illustrates the trade-off between the static and dynamic efficiency considerations facing the policymakers. The optimal patent length should be chosen so that the marginal dynamic gain of prolonged protection is equal to the marginal static loss. The marginal dynamic gain is measured by the left-hand side of (19.1), which shows how an increase in patent life encourages innovative endeavours. The marginal static loss is measured by the right-hand side of (19.1); it comprises two terms: the increased R&D cost due to the accelerated innovative effort and the decrease in consumer surplus resulting from a longer innovator's monopoly.

The main conclusion from this model is that *the optimal patent duration is finite*. There are indeed two forces that work to limit the optimal length of a patent. First, there are diminishing returns to R&D activity: because the cost function is convex, it becomes progressively more expensive to increase the probability of success and therefore, it will take progressively greater increases in T to achieve a given probability of success. The second force is discounting: the consumer benefits from the innovation will not be realized until after the patent expires and so, the larger T, the smaller the present value of those benefits.

Lesson 19.2   A patent that is unlimited in duration cannot be welfare maximizing.

The argument carries over to copyright protection. As illustrated in Case 19.5, it is exactly the framework we have just presented that was used by a number of economists to express their disagreement with the extension of the copyright term in the United States.

Case 19.5 Arguments against the extension of copyright term in the US

Voted in 1998, the Copyright Term Extension Act (CTEA, aka Sonny Bono Copyright Act) extended the duration of existing US copyrights by 20 years (i.e., to life of the author plus 70 years and for works of corporate authorship to 120 years after creation or 95 years after publication, whichever endpoint is earlier). In 1999, a group of commercial and non-commercial interests who relied on the public domain for their work (lead by Eric Eldred, an Internet publisher) challenged the constitutionality of the CTEA. In 2002, seventeen economists (among them five Nobel laureates) supported the petitioners by submitting an *amicus curiae* brief (i.e., some information voluntarily offered by a 'friend of the court' to assist the court in deciding a matter before it). The first section of the brief was entitled: 'It is highly unlikely that the economic benefits from copyright extension under the CTEA outweigh the costs.' To justify this statement, the economists used the above framework: they argued that the revenues earned during the additional 20 years of protection are so heavily discounted that they lose almost all value, while the extended protection of existing works generates immediate deadweight losses (which are even larger when taking the increased cost of creating new derivative work into account). Despite this support, the Supreme Court found against the petitioners (see Eldred *et al. vs.* Ashcroft, Attorney General, 537 U.S. 186, 2003).[28]

19.2.2   Optimal patent breadth

Fixing a finite patent duration is not the only way through which policymakers can avoid
excessive monopoly power. The extent of monopoly power can also be curbed by limiting
the *breadth* of the patent. The meaning of patent breadth is relatively vague.[h] The breadth
measures the *degree of patent protection*, but several measures have been proposed. Basically,
economists study breadth in two types of innovative environments: where the innovation is
threatened by horizontal competition, or where an innovation might be supplanted by an
improved innovation. We consider these two innovative environments in turn. We also analyse
situations where firms try to broaden the protection on a given product or process by filing
'sleeping patents' on substitutable products or processes, just to make sure that no rival will
be able to market them.

Horizontal competition

As far as horizontal competition between innovations is concerned, economists model breadth
in two ways: either in the 'product space', by defining how similar a product must be to infringe
a patent; or in the 'technology space', by defining how costly it is to find a noninfringing
substitute for the protected market. In the first interpretation, a broader patent excludes a larger
set of horizontal substitutes; in the second interpretation, a broader patent makes it more costly
to enter on the market with an alternative technology (i.e., to invent around the patent). We
simplify matters here by assuming that the innovator's profit and social welfare are functions
of patent breadth, which we measure by the parameter $b \in [0, 1]$. Accordingly, we note

$$\begin{cases} \pi(b) \text{ with } \pi(1) = \pi^m \text{ and } \pi(0) = \bar{\pi}, \\ W(b) \text{ with } W(1) = W^m \text{ and } \pi(0) = \bar{W}. \end{cases}$$

As $\pi'(b) > 0$ and $W'(b) < 0$, patent breadth exerts, like patent length, opposite effects on the
innovator's profit and on social welfare. The private and social returns on innovation can now
be rewritten as

$$P(T, b) = \int_0^T e^{-rt}\pi^m(b)\,dt + \int_T^\infty e^{-rt}\bar{\pi}\,dt,$$

$$S(T, b) = \int_0^T e^{-rt}W^m(b)\,dt + \int_T^\infty e^{-rt}\bar{W}\,dt.$$

Regarding the innovator, we just need to re-express the first-order condition as

$$x^*(T, b) = P(T, b)/\phi. \tag{19.2}$$

Totally differentiating (19.2) yields

$$\frac{dT}{db} = -\frac{\partial P/\partial b}{\partial P/\partial T} < 0, \tag{19.3}$$

which implies that *length and breadth are substitutable policy tools* with regard to innovation.

[h] The notion of patent breadth is not directly defined in the IP law. Breadth is actually a matter of interpretation. On
the one hand, the patent office will evaluate the patentability of the innovation (is the innovation – using the European
terminology – novel, inventive and industrially applicable?) and the legitimacy of the claims put forth by the patentee
along with the description of the innovation. On the other hand, courts will judge whether there is infringement.

The policymaker's task is now to find the optimal patent breadth–length mix, anticipating the innovator's optimal conduct. This problem is usually understood as the maximization of social welfare from existing innovation, constraining the supply of innovation to a predetermined level. Formally, it amounts to maximizing S with respect to T and b, fixing the innovation activity x at some required level. Doing so, we can define $T(b)$ by solving Equation (19.2) for T and express the social value of an existing innovation as a function of breadth only: $S(T(b), b)$. Differentiating the latter function with respect to b and using (19.3) gives

$$\frac{dS}{db} = \frac{\partial S}{\partial T}\frac{dT}{db} + \frac{\partial S}{\partial b} = -\frac{\partial S}{\partial T}\frac{\partial P/\partial b}{\partial P/\partial T} + \frac{\partial S}{\partial b}. \tag{19.4}$$

The optimal patent policy is determined by the sign of dS/db. There are two possible cases.

1. If $dS/db > 0$, then increasing breadth is welfare enhancing. Consequently, *the optimal patent is broad and short*: it has maximum breadth and minimum length, i.e., $b = 1$ and $T = \underline{T}$ (where $\underline{T}$ is defined as the value of T solving Equation (19.2) for $b = 1$). Using Equation (19.4) and recalling that $\partial S/\partial T$ is negative, we have that

$$\frac{dS}{db} > 0 \iff \frac{\partial P/\partial b}{\partial P/\partial T} > \frac{\partial S/\partial b}{\partial S/\partial T}, \tag{19.5}$$

which can be interpreted by saying that an increase in patent breadth stimulates investment in innovation relatively more than patent length while reducing the post-innovation welfare relatively less. It is therefore optimal to set as short a patent life as possible and to extend patent breadth correspondingly.

2. If $dS/db < 0$, then increasing breadth is welfare detrimental. Consequently, *the optimal patent is narrow and long*: it has minimum breadth and maximum length, i.e., $b = \underline{b}$ and $T = \infty$ (where $\underline{b}$ is defined as the value of b solving Equation (19.2) for $T \to \infty$).[i] In this case, reversing the sign of inequality (19.5), we have that an increase in patent breadth curbs post-innovation social welfare relatively more and accelerates innovative activity relatively less than an increase in patent life; hence, it is desirable to make a patent as narrow as possible by prolonging patent life correspondingly; this leaves the incentive to innovate unaltered but expands static social welfare.

---

[i] For the interest of the analysis, it is assumed that the minimum values $\underline{T}$ and $\underline{b}$ exist, and are positive and finite.

Sleeping patents

It is common in many industries that the same firm patents a large number of related processes or products, using only one of them and leaving the other ones 'sleeping'. For instance, according to an article published in the *Financial Times* in July 2001, IBM, Philips and Siemens were reported to use only about 40% of their portfolio of patents. Several reasons can be proposed to explain why a number of new processes or products remain under- or unexploited on firms' shelves: duplication of R&D efforts, lack of complementary assets to bring the innovation to the market, or poor fit between the innovation and the firm's objectives. Strategy considerations might be invoked as well: sleeping patents can be used by dominant firms to block entry into their market. Holding several patents all related to the same process or product would thus create a buffer of protection around the truly valuable patent.

To establish this conjecture, we use again an argument that should by now be familiar: when threatened by entry, an incumbent firm is generally willing to pay more for an innovation that will block entry than what the entrant is willing to pay for this innovation. This is the so-called 'efficiency effect' that we introduced in the previous chapter. It explains the persistence of monopoly due to preemptive patenting, and it explains here why an incumbent firm might want to patent products or processes that could threaten its monopoly position if they were owned by rival firms.

Cumulative innovations

Innovations are not only threatened by horizontal competition: they may also be supplanted by an improved innovation. One talks then of *cumulative (or sequential) innovations*. The cumulativeness of innovations can take various forms: improved quality of an existing product, reduced cost of an existing production process, or discovery of new applications of an invention. Cumulative innovations are widespread in sectors such as information technology and biotechnology.

In this context of dynamic competition, patent breadth is defined by the extent to which vertical substitutes are excluded.[j] It must be recalled here that patents have a double purpose: protect R&D investments *and* facilitate the diffusion of knowledge (other researchers will benefit from the publication of the patent; future research might also be indirectly improved as open questions can be better identified). Obviously, the latter purpose becomes even more important in the presence of cumulative innovations. This forces us to reconsider the previous analysis of the optimal patent length–breadth mix and address two additional basic questions: (i) Should the initial innovator have a right on subsequent innovations? (ii) Insofar as subsequent innovations are not necessarily substitute to the initial innovation (they use it and reproduce it), should they be considered as infringements?

Intuitively, in order to provide each innovator with the proper incentives, we would like to answer 'yes' to the first question and 'no' to the second. Indeed, as earlier innovators provide benefits to later innovators, they should be compensated for their contributions by being granted some right on subsequent innovations. Also, if all subsequent innovations were considered as infringements, later innovators would have no incentive to invest. Yet, the larger

---

[j] This notion is sometimes referred to as the *height* of a patent.

the rights granted to the initial innovator, the lower the incentives for subsequent innovators, and vice versa. The problem is thus to determine how profit should be divided between successive innovators. This is a delicate problem and, unfortunately, IP appears as a blunt instrument in that respect.

It is impossible to do justice here to the abundant, and complex, literature that has recently developed around this issue.[30] Let us just mention two lessons that Gallini and Scotchmer (2002) draw from their analysis of this literature. They first recognize that 'the complexities of cumulativeness seem to defy clear, unqualified design implications'. Nevertheless, they argue (with some caution) that *sequential innovations call for broad (and short) patents*: 'Broad patents can serve the public interest by preventing duplication of R&D costs, facilitating the development of second-generation products, and protecting early innovators who lay the foundation for later innovators.' The second lesson is drawn from the finding that *the benefits of broad patents disappear if licensing fails*; more precisely, the optimal design of the patent system for cumulative innovations hinges on the ease with which rights holders can contract among them and find a way to solve the conflicts in rights.

Therefore, we postpone the discussion on cumulative innovations to the next section, where licensing is introduced.

19.3   Patent licensing and pooling

The exclusive rights granted by IP law are also *transferable rights* (they can be transferred, licensed, rented or mortgaged to third parties). This transferability is economically very important as it ensures that innovations and artistic creations are used by the agents who value them most. Transferability is also important because it gives an additional source of profit to the innovator: the innovator can earn profit through his own working of the patent but also by licensing the patent. There are three common modes of patent licensing: (i) a royalty per unit of output produced with the patented technology, (ii) a fixed fee that is independent of the quantity produced with the patented technology, or (iii) a combination of the previous two options. The patent holder (the 'patentee') can choose among these three modes and can also decide either to allow any firm to purchase a license or to auction a limited number of licenses.

From a social viewpoint, licenses have the clear positive impact of increasing the diffusion and use of knowledge. However, one needs to evaluate the impact of licenses on the incentives to innovate. We examine this issue in two different contexts: first, when the patentee and its potential licensees are direct competitors on the product market; second, when innovations are cumulative.[k]

19.3.1   Licensing to rival firms

The question we address here is: do innovating firms have an incentive to license their patented discovery to some or all of their rivals? As we now show, the answer depends on the innovation

---

[k] In the previous chapter, we already examined the case where the licensor is not an incumbent rival. Indeed, investigating how much firms are willing to pay for an innovation (what we called the 'profit incentive') is equivalent to asking how much profits a patentee, who is outside the industry, can realize from licensing its innovation by means of a uniform royalty per unit of output.

size and on market structure. Consider first the case of *drastic (major) innovations*. Because such innovations allow the patentee to drive its competitors from the market and become a monopolist, it is intuitively clear that the patentee has no incentive to grant licenses, as this will reintroduce competition in the market and thereby, lowers its profits. This conclusion holds whether competition on the market is Cournot or Bertrand.[1]

Let us now turn to the more interesting case of *nondrastic (minor) innovations*. Suppose that there are n firms on the market, that the inverse demand is given by $p = a - Q$, and that the innovation has the effect of reducing the constant marginal cost from c (with $c < a$) to $c - x$, with $0 < x < a - c$.[m] Consider first Bertrand competition. In this case, it is easy to see that licensing gains the innovator nothing. When the innovator does not license the innovation, we saw above that its optimal conduct is to set a price just below the other firms' cost ($p = c - \varepsilon$), thereby serving the whole market and securing a margin of $(x - \varepsilon)$ on each unit sold. Alternatively, if the innovator lets any rival use the innovation, the only sensible royalty rate, r, is such that the rivals' new cost, $c - x + r$, is just below their original cost c: that is, $r = x - \varepsilon$. In this case, the licensor and its licensees share the market at price $p = c - \varepsilon$; the quantity sold is the same as in the absence of licensing; the innovator secures a margin of $(x - \varepsilon)$ on the units it sold and collects a royalty $r = x - \varepsilon$ on the units sold by the licensees. In total, the innovator achieves thus exactly the same profit as in the absence of licensing, which proves our claim.

> **Lesson 19.5** It is not profitable for an incumbent innovator to license its cost-reducing innovation to its industry rivals (i) when the innovation is drastic, or (ii) when the innovation is nondrastic and Bertrand competition prevails on the product market.

Consider next Cournot competition. We analyse the following three-stage game: in the first stage, the incumbent innovator selects a royalty rate r at which it will license its new technology; in the second stage, the other firms decide simultaneously whether or not to become licensees; in the third stage, the firms in the industry (the innovator, the licensed and unlicensed firms) engage in Cournot competition.

If the innovator decides to license its technology, it will select a royalty no larger than the cost reduction the innovation entails: $r < x$. At such a rate, every firm at stage 2 is willing to become a licensee since this reduces its marginal cost from c to $c - x + r$. Therefore, at stage 3, competition takes place among one firm with cost $c - x$ and $n - 1$ firms with cost $c - x + r$. We showed in Chapter 3 that the Cournot equilibrium quantity and profit for a typical firm k under this setting are respectively given by

$$q_k^* = \frac{1}{n+1}\left(a - nc_k + \sum_{j \neq k} c_j\right), \quad \pi_k^* = (q_k^*)^2. \tag{19.6}$$

---

[1] Even if the patentee is able to extract almost the entire licensees' profits via the royalties, the sum of oligopolists' profits is generally less than the monopoly profits.

[m] Recall that the innovation is minor as long as the post-innovation monopoly price is above the pre-innovation competitve price: $(a + c - x)/2 > c$, or $x < a - c$.

As for the innovator, its marginal cost is $c - x$ and the sum of the rivals' marginal costs is equal to $(n - 1)(c - x + r)$; as for a typical licensee, its marginal cost is $c - x + r$ and the sum of the rivals' marginal costs is equal to $(n - 2)(c - x + r) + (c - x)$. Substituting these values into Equation (19.6), we can derive the equilibrium quantity for the innovator and for the licensees respectively as

$$q^*_{inn} = \frac{a - c + x + r(n - 1)}{n + 1} \quad \text{and} \quad q^*_{lic} = \frac{a - c + x - 2r}{n + 1},$$

where $q^*_{lic} > 0$ as $r < x < a - c$. The innovator's profit is then computed as

$$\pi_{inn} = \left(q^*_{inn}\right)^2 + r(n - 1)q^*_{lic}.$$

Let us now compute the optimal royalty rate level. Deriving the innovator's profit with respect to r, we get

$$\frac{\partial \pi_{inn}}{\partial r} = \frac{(n - 1)(n + 3)}{(n + 1)^2}(a - c + x - 2r) > 0,$$

which implies that $r^* = x$.[n] Substituting $r = x$ in the expression of π_{inn}, we obtain

$$\pi^*_{inn} = \frac{(a - c)^2 + \left(2n + n^2 - 1\right)(a - c)x + x^2}{(n + 1)^2}.$$

Alternatively, the innovator can select a prohibitive royalty rate $r > x$. In such a case, no firm will accept to become a licensee and competition will take place among one firm with cost $c - x$ and $(n - 1)$ firms with cost c. Using again Equation (19.6), we can compute the innovator's profit in that case as

$$\hat{\pi}_{inn} = \frac{(a - c + nx)^2}{(n + 1)^2}.$$

Simple computations establish that

$$\pi^*_{inn} - \hat{\pi}_{inn} = \frac{(n - 1)(a - c - x)x}{n + 1} > 0,$$

which shows that the incumbent innovator gains from licensing its innovation to all its competitors.[31] The fact that $\pi^*_{inn} > \hat{\pi}_{inn}$ is easy to understand. Whether the innovator licenses its innovation at $r = x$ or whether it keeps its innovation for itself does not affect the competitive situation: in both cases, the innovator has marginal cost $c - x$ and its rivals have marginal cost c. So, the innovator makes the same (direct) profit in both situations (i.e., $\hat{\pi}_{inn}$). However, when it licenses the innovation, the innovator also collects royalties, which strictly improves its total profits.

Note that society also gains from licensing. Indeed, with $r = x$, total ouput is the same with or without licensing, so that consumers are as well off; the other $(n - 1)$ firms have the same profit but the innovator strictly increases its profit. Social welfare is thus strictly larger.

---

[n] In this case, each firm is indifferent between being or not being a licensee (as both options lead to a marginal cost of c). However, in the unique subgame-perfect equilibrium of the game, every firm chooses to be a licensee.

> **Lesson 19.6**   In the case of quantity competition on the product market, it is always profitable for an incumbent innovator to license a nondrastic cost-reducing innovation to its industry rivals. Licensing also benefits society.

19.3.2   Licensing and cumulative innovations

In Subsection 19.2.2, we noted that in the presence of cumulative innovations, the optimal design of the patent system hinges on the ease with which patentees can contract among them, in particular through licensing. To analyse the effect of licensing, it is useful to distinguish between two types of cumulativeness.

In the case of *sequential innovations*, a particular innovation leads to many second-generation innovations. For instance, the invention of the laser lead to surgical applications, spectroscopy, etc. The main problem with sequential innovations is that a patent on the first-generation innovation confers the patentee a *holdup* right over subsequent innovations. *Ex ante licensing* might alleviate this problem.

In the case of *complementary innovations*, a second-generation product requires the input of a number of different first-generation innovations. Think of firms in the electronics industry (e.g., trying to produce new peripherals to be coupled with personal computers or video game consoles) or in the biotech industry (e.g., combining patented genes to bioengineer a new crop seed). Here, the main problem, referred to as the 'tragedy of the anticommons', is that the prices are higher if they are set by independent patentees rather than jointly. *Cross-licensing* and *patent pools* may mitigate this problem.

Sequential innovations: holdup and ex ante licensing

As we noted above, an important problem that arises with sequential innovations is that of dividing the profit between innovators in a way that respects their costs. If a single pot of money has to be distributed between two innovators and most is allocated to the first firm, the second inventor's incentive for research is reduced and vice versa. A related problem concerns the distribution of rights. An early patent holder may have a claim against subsequent innovators. Anticipating the expected cost of such claims, subsequent innovators may be reluctant to invest in R&D if the commercial exploitation of their innovation depends on the holder of a previous patent. This is the classic economic problem of *holdup*.

In the first decade of this millenium (mostly in the United States), holdup has become a primary component of patent litigation and patent licensing, with the rise of so-called Non-Practicing Entities (NPEs), i.e., patent holders who license or bring suit using their patents without any intention to practice those particular patents. NPEs – which have also been dubbed *patent trolls*[o] – are accused of taking firms by surprise once they have made irreversible investments. Component-driven industries, like information technology, are particularly prone to such holdups. The problem is more acute in the United States where patent infringements

---

[o] In Scandinavian mythology, a troll is a devious creature that often lives under bridges and pesters travellers and merchants for safe passage.

can be punished through a permanent injunction (i.e., a court order against further infringement). NPEs can then use the threat of permanent injunction to extort hefty fees in licensing negotiations, or huge settlements from companies they have accused of infringing. A famous example is the $612.5 million out-of-court settlement that Research in Motion accepted to pay to NTP in 2006 to avoid the risk of its popular BlackBerry service being shut down. Because such tactics may stifle innovation in the long term, the US Supreme Court decided in 2006 to review the practice of automatically issuing a permanent injunction whenever a patent was found valid and infringed. Case 19.6 describes the case that led to this decision.

Case 19.6 MercExchange vs. eBay: a fatal blow to patent trolls?[32]

You may be familiar with eBay's online auction interface, named 'Buy It Now', that allows users to purchase items without going through the bidding process. What you may not know is that in 2001, MercExchange (a small patent-holding company) alleged that this interface infringed upon three of its patents. MercExchange prevailed in 2003 and sought an injunction to prevent eBay from continuing to use its 'Buy It Now' feature, but the District Court denied the request. The United States Court of Appeals for the Federal Circuit reversed the District Court: on top of being ordered to pay more that $25 million in damages, eBay was also required to cease using its auction interface. eBay appealed that decision all the way to the Supreme Court. In 2006, in a landmark decision, the justices ruled unanimously in eBay's favour, stating that the traditional 'four-factor test' for determining whether to issue a permanent injunction applies equally in patent cases: (1) Irreparable harm; (2) Inadequate remedies at law; (3) Balance of hardships; and (4) Public interest. In the present case, the justices found that because MercExchange did not use its patent itself, it would not be harmed if 'Buy It Now' was still offered while eBay tried to find a non-infringing substitute, and it could eventually be compensated with additional monetary damages if the infringing continued. There was thus no reason to impose a sanction as drastic as an injunction to eBay.

To illustrate the potential holdup problem with sequential innovations, we use the following simple model.[33] Suppose there are two sequential innovations, $i = 1, 2$; innovation i has (private and social) value v_i and can be produced by firm i only at an R&D cost of c_i. The sequentiality is translated by the assumption that innovation 2 can only be achieved by using the results of innovation 1; therefore, if the first innovation does not exist, nor does the second. We assume that it is socially desirable to produce the two innovations: $v_1 + v_2 > c_1 + c_2$. The question is how to design patents so as to reach the social optimum. One could think first of granting a patent for each innovation. For this option to work, it must be that $v_1 > c_1$. Otherwise, firm 1 will not find it profitable to invest in R&D and neither the first nor the second innovation will be produced.

In the latter case (i.e., if $v_1 < c_1$), we need to consider the alternative option of granting a broader (or 'deeper') patent to firm 1 so as to provide it with the incentive to produce the first innovation. That means that firm 1 would have rights on innovation 2 as well, but such a situation would put firm 2 at risk. Indeed, firm 2 can rationally anticipate to be held up: once it has sunk the R&D cost of producing the second innovation, it will be in firm 1's best interest to appropriate the total value of this innovation, v_2. Therefore, firm 2 will not be able to recoup its investment and will prefer not to invest. As a consequence, innovation 2 will not be produced. Moreover, as $v_1 < c_1$ and as v_2 does not materialize, firm 1 will have no incentive either to invest in the first innovation. We can therefore conclude the following.

> **Lesson 19.7**   **Because of the holdup problem, a broad patent covering later developments of an innovation is not more efficient than a sequence of narrow patents.**

One can use a nice metaphor to explain why the holdup problem is worst in industries where hundreds if not thousands of patents can potentially read on a given product.

> In these industries, the danger that a manufacturer will step on a land mine is all too real. The result will be that some companies avoid the mine field altogether, that is, refrain from introducing certain products for fear of holdup. Other companies will lose their corporate legs, that is, will be forced to pay royalties on patents that they could easily have invented around at an earlier stage, had they merely been aware that such a patent either existed or was pending. Of course, ultimately the expected value of these royalties must be reflected in the price of final goods.' (Shapiro, 2001, p. 126)

In a more general setting, however, it can be argued that, because of the difficulties in dividing profit, patent lives will have to be longer than if the whole sequence of innovations occurs in a single firm.[34] Then *ex ante licensing* (i.e., licensing before the second innovator sinks funds into R&D) is a way of mimicking the latter outcome. The other possibility is that licensing occurs *ex post*, i.e., after the second innovator has achieved the improvement or application of the first innovation. The difference, of course, is that the second innovator has sunk his costs at the time of the negotiation, which opens the door for opportunistic behaviour on the part of the first innovator (i.e., of holdup).[p]

In constrast, it can be argued that in the case of sequential innovations, patent protection is not as useful for encouraging innovation and might even be counterproductive.[35] This can be shown in a sequential model of innovation in which an innovator's prospective profit may actually be enhanced by competition and imitation. The idea is that the loss in revenue due to increased competition may be offset by the long-term gain of being able to share the available technologies. Open Source Software is an example that seems to fit the predictions of this model. We return to this topic in the next section.

---

[p] We expect thus more licensing agreements occurring ex ante rather than ex post in industries which are known for sequential innovation. Yet, empirical evidence suggests otherwise: Anand and Kanna (2000) found that only 5% to 6% of licensing agreements occurred ex ante in computer and electronic industries, and 23% in chemicals and pharmaceuticals. Bessen (2004) suggests that the reason could be asymmetric information: if there is sequential innovation, it is probably because the second innovator possesses private information about the profitability of a subsequent innovation that the first innovator did not have (or did not find it profitable to acquire).

Complementary innovations: cross-licensing and patent pools

If innovations are complementary, the patent system creates what Shapiro (2001) calls a *patent thicket*: 'an overlapping set of patent rights requiring that those seeking to commercialize new technology obtain licenses from multiple patentees'. The fear is that, because it is costly for firms to 'hack their way' through this dense thicket, stronger patent rights can have the perverse effect of stifling, not encouraging, innovation.

In particular, the patent system could be in danger of imposing an unnecessary drag on innovation by enabling multiple rights owners to 'tax' new products or processes. This problem is well understood since Cournot's classic work on the pricing of complements in 1838. Cournot showed that a single monopolist of several complements sets a lower price than separate monopolists, each controlling one of the goods. The intuition behind this result is simple: each individual firm ignores the positive effect that a decrease in its own price has on the demand for the other firms' products; in contrast, an integrated firm internalizes the complementarity between the products and, hence, has a further incentive to decrease prices.

This situation is sometimes referred to as the *tragedy of the anticommons* to describe the fact that when several individuals own rights of exclusion and exercise those rights, they restrict access and therefore use of common resources.[36] This is exactly what applies when multiple firms control blocking patents for a particular product or process. What Cournot (1838) shows is that not only the consumers but also the firms benefit from the 'collusive' pricing of complements. Therefore, right holders will find it profitable to coordinate their decisions, either by creating a *patent pool* or by engaging in *cross licensing*. Under a patent pool, an entire group of patents is licensed in a package, either by one of the patent holders or by a new entity established for this purpose, usually to anyone willing to pay the associated royalties. A cross license is simply an agreement between two companies that grants each the right to practise the other's patents (possibly involving fixed fees or running royalties).[q]

These forms of coordination, however, entail transaction costs and might be seen with suspicion by antitrust authorities. Regarding antitrust concerns, the previous argument suggests that package licensing is desirable for complementary patents but not for substitute patents. It can be shown that requiring pool members to be able to independently license patents matters if and only if the pool is otherwise welfare reducing, a property that allows the antitrust authorities to use this requirement to screen out unattractive pools.[37]

Patent portfolios

It appears from the previous discussion that in industries relying on cumulative innovations, firms seek to constitute portfolios of related patents, because the aggregation of these patents gives to the portfolio a value that is larger than the sum of the values of the individual patents. In other words, the more patents the merrier, because patent portfolios can be used as a 'trading device' or a 'bargaining chip'. Indeed, in the presence of patent thickets, a firm is very likely to infringe another firm's patent; then, a large portfolio provides the infringing firm with a

---

[q] A recent example of a patent pool is the MPEG-2 video compression technology. Nine companies have pooled their patents to permit one-stop shopping for makers of televisions, digital video disks and players and telecommunications equipment as well as cable, satellite and broadcast television services. Shapiro (2001) reports that broad cross licenses are the norm in markets for the design and manufacture of microprocessors.

credible threat of counter-infringement litigation. A large portfolio also improves its holder's bargaining position with other firms.

We can find here an explanation for the patent paradox that we mentioned in Section 19.1 (i.e., the combined facts that patent counts have exploded over the last decades, while innovators view patents as a secondary way to protect their investments in R&D).

19.4   Intellectual property in the digital economy

The main form of IP protection that we have considered so far in this chapter is the patent system. The patent system is designed to protect industrial property, such as inventions, processes, machines, . . . Yet, as we mentioned in Section 19.1, there is a wide range of other productions of information which suffer from the same appropriability problem as industrial innovations, but which are not covered by the patent regime. We think of the production of literary, musical, choreographic, dramatic and artistic works (such as novels, poems, plays, films, songs, drawings, paintings, photographs, sculptures, architectural designs, . . .). Such works are protected by *copyright*. Although copyrights and patents stem from the same economic rationale (absent legal protection, creators lack incentives to engage in the production of information), they strike a differerent balance between static and dynamic efficiency considerations: roughly put, the protection offered by copyright is longer but narrower than the protection offered by a patent. Copyright applies to the expression of works, in whatever mode or form, and gives authors an exclusive right over the reproduction, performance, adaptation and translation of their work. Compared to patents, this protection is weaker (as only the expression is protected, and not the underlying ideas) but it is extended over a longer period of time (nowadays, it lasts for 70 years after the author's death in both Europe and the United States).

Most of the arguments we have developed above remain useful in understanding the economics of copyright. However, the industries producing copyrighted goods, and the way people use and enjoy these goods, have recently been deeply altered by digital technology and the Internet. Because it modifies the interaction between copyright holders, technology companies and consumers, this evolution poses interesting challenges for the economic analysis of IP protection.

In this section, we build on our previous analysis and develop some new tools in order to address topical issues. We focus on music and software as these two industries have experienced the most significant change and so have dominated the public debate. Regarding the music industry, we examine the impact of end-user copying on the decisions of copyright holders, as well as on total welfare. Regarding the software industry, we complement our previous discussion about the appropriate IP regime for software (see Case 19.1 above) by examining the development of open source software.

19.4.1   Digital music and end-user piracy

Record companies claim that they are suffering huge revenue losses due to Internet piracy.[38] But in which economic environments can such a claim be substantiated? Are there other strategies that copyright owners can use to counter this new form of piracy? And, from a public policy perspective, to which extent are the social interests aligned with the interests of copyright owners?

Let us take a look at digital products.[39] They can be compressed without losing much information or quality. Thus, digital copies have a technical quality similar to the original. However, the original digital product is often bundled with other non-digital components such as a printed manual for software and printed booklet (with lyrics, pictures, song and artist information) and CD case for music CDs. This suggests that the original gives some additional value compared to the copy. In addition, there may be complementary products for which access can be controlled (examples are live concerts as complements to recorded music and customer support as a complement to software). Complementarities may allow firms to indirectly appropriate some of the rents generated through end-user copying.

In most cases, digital products also involve interactions. These interactions can be of two different natures: formal interaction for software that requires to exchange standardized/formatted information, and social interaction for music and video files about which people like to talk about with their friends. These formal and social interactions imply that there possibly exist network effects in the use of a digital product (see Chapter 20 for the definition and analysis of network effects).

Also, many digital products are complex in the sense that the amount of information required to describe them is large. As a consequence, consumers need to test them in order to correctly value them. In other words, some digital products are experience goods and a copy can be useful in providing information on their characteristics. This feature applies not only to digital products such as music CDs but also to software with a large number of commands and a large potential number of interactions with other computer components and software, etc.

Non-authorized copying of digital products can be done in two different ways: by borrowing originals from friends and family members or by downloading from the Internet. In the former case, networks of friends share the good on a small-scale basis. Then it is possible in some cases to indirectly appropriate revenue from sharing activities. The copying process only requires a storage device such as a hard-drive or a CD Recorder or any portable media device. Information on the characteristics of the copied product is easy and cheap to obtain by word-of-mouth.

In the latter case, monitoring copies from copies is arduous. However, copying using file-sharing technologies often provides a lower value than copying directly from friends for several reasons. First, users are spending time looking for and downloading files. Secondly, the digital copy lacks valuable information such as instructions on how to install the software or song lyrics. Finally, the file can be badly compressed or incomplete. Therefore, we can expect consumers to be heterogeneous with respect to the value of the original relative to the copy.

Piracy and social underprovision of originals: some basics

Suppose that a consumer can either purchase the original or she can copy at a cost $c + z(1 + x)$, where c is the marginal cost of production, x is the extent of copyright protection and z is the additional cost of making a copy, which is heterogeneous for consumers (in the absence of copyright protection). The value that consumers attach to the product depends on its quality. Because of the heterogeneity in the copying costs, for moderate prices, some consumers prefer the original while others prefer the copy. Clearly, if the firm's price is sufficiently low, copying is unattractive to all consumers. The monopolist produces a single quality and copies have the same quality as the original. However, the model can be interpreted as if the value of the original relative to the copy is heterogeneous but that the associated disutility of copying is the same for all consumers. That is, the original gives a value which is the same across consumers, while the copy gives the same value minus $z(1 + x)$. In words, the perceived quality degradation of the copy is heterogeneous.

In this model, the monopolist chooses a quality which is too low compared to the social optimum because the monopolist cannot appropriate all rents from quality improvements.[40] It can be shown that an increase in copyright protection leads to an increase in the quality offered by the monopolist provided that the density of z is increasing, i.e., there are relatively more consumers with higher than with lower copying costs. This means that the effect of underprovision favours a strict copyright enforcement. Interestingly, a stricter copyright protection does not increase the social loss due to underutilization: as the copyright protection increases, some consumers switch from the copy to the original, thus saving the copying cost that is wasteful from a social point of view.

Instead of postulating that consumers are heterogeneous with respect to their copying cost, we may want to look at an alternative model in which consumers are heterogeneous with respect to their valuation of the product itself. In the spirit of the vertical differentiation model we used in Chapter 5, a consumer derives utility $\theta s - p$ for the original, where θ is the consumer's taste parameter, distributed uniformly on the unit interval and s is the quality of the original. She derives utility $\alpha \theta s - c$ for the copy, where $1 - \alpha$ is the factor of quality depreciation and c the copying cost. Then pricing in the presence of piracy is the same as pricing against a firm pricing at c a product of quality αs. Obviously, in this setup the firm's profits decrease with the availability of digital copies.

The total effect of piracy on short-run welfare is positive because the loss in profits (from deterring or accommodating piracy) is overcompensated by an increase in consumer surplus. Lower profits, however, reduce the ex ante incentives to provide the good so that piracy leads to an inefficiently low quality of the original. Alternatively, if we do not consider incentives to invest in quality but entry incentives for originals of different mass attraction, piracy leads to less variety of originals in the market.

Socially costly copyright protection

Consider now the more elaborate problem in which copyright (or IP) protection leads to a private cost to consumers.[41] Formally, a consumer's utility takes the form $\alpha \theta s - c - x$, where x denotes the consumers' additional cost due to copyright protection (which also constitutes a social cost). Then the monopolist's profits are increasing in x, while consumer surplus is decreasing. Total surplus is initially decreasing in x and then, after reaching its minimum, is inversely U-shaped. One can then show that in the short run the socially optimal copyright protection should be set such that the monopolist optimally reacts by deterring copying. The copyrighted product is then fully protected in the sense that copies are driven out of the market. However, the monopolist has to lower its price compared to a situation of 'blockaded entry', which describes a situation in which copying is not feasible. Thus profits generated by the copyrighted product are reduced under the social optimum.

Welfare effects of piracy

Is piracy necessarily bad for originators and, in the long run, for society? The general insight from basic models with end-user piracy is that artists and their intermediaries lose from piracy whereas consumers gain in the short run. Long-run effects for society are certainly negative if piracy strongly discourages artists to produce. However, we may want to develop a more nuanced picture. Many minor artists (minor not in terms of their artistic achievements but in terms of their audience) often derive a large parts of their income from live performances and other activities but, to a much lesser extent, from the sale of recorded music. Some of these artists are also not mainly driven by profit incentives. For those artists, the presence of music piracy is likely to have a positive effect. This is because of information asymmetries in the music market (these are particularly pronounced in the traditional market environment) in which a small number of acts are heavily promoted, whereas niche artists have a hard time to find their audience. Here, the Internet with its streaming, downloading and rating possibilities increases the possibility that artists find their audience. The reverse is also true. Consumers can look around and discover music they like but would not have discovered otherwise. Overall the quality of matches between artists and consumers is improved. This tends to increase social welfare and may even be profit-increasing for the artists themselves.[42]

19.4.2   Economics of open source

Software can be transmitted in either *source code* (i.e., the code using languages such as Basic, C and Java, which could be easily interpreted and modified by programmers) or *object code* (i.e., the sequence of 0s and 1s that directly communicates with the hardware). Most commercial software vendors provide users only with object code.[r] In contrast, an open source software (OSS) is, as its name indicates, such that the source code is made available to everyone. While open source presents a way to broadly make the sources of a product publicly accessible, the open source licenses allow the authors to fine tune such access by defining users' rights on usage, modification and redistribution.[s]

Major OSS projects are nowadays competing head-to-head with commercial software vendors. For instance, *Linux* accounts (in 2007) for a 38% market share of the server operating system market and is supported by leading hardware firms (such as IBM, SUN, Compaq/HP and Siemens). Another prominent example is the open source web server *Apache*, which captured a market share of 72% by June 2005. Another success story is the open source web browser *Firefox*, which managed, very quickly after its introduction, to grab a 5% market share from Microsoft's *Internet Explorer* (the estimated market share of Firefox was 30% at the end of 2006).

The successful development of OSS projects puzzled economists. At first glance, economists would not expect that complex software could be produced through a loose form

---

[r] IP law does not require disclosure of source code: copyrights for software can be registered without fully revealing the source code and software patents typically do not include the source code.

[s] There exist a large variety of open source software licenses. The most prominent example is the popular GNU General Public License (GPL), which requires that all enhancements to the original material must also be made publicly available. Note that OSS must be distinguished from freeware and shareware (which can both be downloaded free of charge but do not allow access to the source code) and from public domain software (which is not licensed and is thus usable by everyone without constraint).

of coordination between a very large number of individual programmers, who donate their time and effort free of charge. However, this is exactly how *Linux*, *Apache* and many other OSS projects have been, and still are, developed. Consequently, a substantial and growing economics and business literature has addressed the organizational, motivational and product-structural features of OSS development.[43] We briefly examine here the roles and incentives of the various actors in the open source process.

Motivations of open source contributors

Why do top-notch programmers choose to write code that is released for free? Is such behaviour consistent with the self-interested-economic-agent paradigm? A simple cost/benefit analysis allows us to understand better what motivates programmers to participate in OSS projects. On the *cost side*, the programmers incur an opportunity cost of time (which can be measured by the monetary compensation that they could earn were they working instead for a commercial software vendor).

On the *benefit side*, several short- or long-run benefits may outweigh these costs. First, many contributors are sophisticated users who need to remove a bug or tailor the code to their specific applications; contributing to an OSS project may thus improve their performance in paid work. Second, having turned the code back to the community, they may see others improve on their modifications, increasing their private benefit further. Third, programmers may find more intrinsic pleasure and fun in contributing to a 'cool' OSS project rather than in working on a routine task set by an employer. Fourth, the delayed benefits are likely to be non-negligible. Contributions to OSS projects are indeed well recognized among peers; this provides contributors not only with ego gratification, but also with the prospect of future monetary compensation (under the form of better job offers, shares in commercial OSS companies, or future access to the venture capital market).

Finally, comparing the commercial and open source environments, it is fair to say that the former offers better current compensation, while the latter generates larger delayed rewards. There are indeed three reasons why programmers find it easier to signal a high level of competence in the open source environment: (i) the contribution of each individual can be seen by a large community of outsiders, (ii) the programmer takes full responsibility for the success of a subproject, (iii) because of the cumulative nature of software innovation, knowledge accumulated on a particular subproject can easily be transferred to another project, which increases the programmer's attractiveness for future employers.

Attitude of commercial firms

The way for-profit firms work and compete with OSS projects is much less intriguing for economists than the 'volunteer' participation of programmers is. First, a profitable business model consists in developing a proprietary market segment by offering specific expertise or support services that are complementary to an open source software (which is not appropriable in itself). For instance, Red Hat, VA Linux or Caldera package *Linux* in a user-friendly way and provide additional material such as manuals and support services. Second, commercial companies tend to allocate some of their talented staff to open source programs. This allows them to keep abreast of open source developments and so, to better know the competition and to develop an absorptive capacity (for incorporating open source ideas into commercial software and for spotting talented programmers). Third, commercial firms may compete directly with OSS providers in the same market. On the other hand, they may participate in an OSS project for strategic reasons: embracing an OSS project may preempt the development of a standard around a technology owned by a powerful rival.[t]

Furthermore, commercial software vendors may find it profitable to release some existing proprietary code, and then rely on the open source community for the ensuing development process. For this *code release* strategy to make sense, the company must be able to increase profit in a proprietary complementary segment and thereby, offset any profit that would have been made in the primary segment. This is more likely to happen when the company already lags behind its competitors in the primary segment, or when network effects and switching costs are strong (which implies, as we will see in Chapter 20, that the best-selling software captures almost the entire market). As software innovation is largely cumulative, code release may also induce further development, which could eventually benefit the initial innovator. Case 19.7 illustrates this intuition.

Case 19.7 Why share IP?[44]

For more than a decade, IBM ranks every year as number one in the list of patent filers in America (with about 3000 patents per year). That did not prevent IBM from placing a substantial number of its existing software patents into a patent 'commons' that allows open-source software developers to use the innovations and build upon them without risk of infringement. Other companies have taken similar initiatives: Nokia claimed it would not assert its patents against the inner code of Linux; Red Hat also promised to contribute to a patent commons; Computer Associates donated 14 patents for free use by the open source community; Sun Microsystems made its Solaris operating system open source. These decisions are not motivated by generosity or philanthropy. Most of these firms fear that software patent protection has become so strong that it risks undermining innovation. The whole industry (and so the firms themselves) might then suffer, unless intiatives like the patent commons are taken to help restore the balance.

Profiting from voluntary code release: a simple model

We now develop a simple model to understand when voluntary code release could be profitable.[45] We consider Cournot competition between n firms (indexed by $i = 1 \ldots n$) producing differentiated varieties. Each firm i incurs a constant marginal cost equal to c_i and

---

[t] For instance, in 2000, IBM, NEC, Intel, SGI, Dell Computer and Hewlett-Packard joined Linux companies to launch the *Open Source Development Laboratory* (OSDL) with the aim of coaxing Linux into high-end, multiprocessor machines (like mobile phones, ATM machines, ...). Naturally, Microsoft was not part of this coalition.

produces a differentiated product in quantities q_i, sold at price p_i. We use the model of horizontal product differentiation introduced in Chapter 3 where a quadratic utility function leads to the linear inverse demand schedule $p_i = a - q_i - \gamma \sum_{j \neq i} q_j$ in the region of quantities where prices are positive.[u] The parameter γ is an inverse measure of product differentiation: the lower γ the more products are differentiated; in the limit if $\gamma = 1$ products are perfect substitutes, if $\gamma = 0$ products are perfectly differentiated and as a result demands are independent. The problem of a typical firm i can be written as

$$\max_{q_i} \pi_i = (a_i - c_i - q_i - \gamma q_{-i}) q_i,$$

where q_{-i} denotes the sum of the quantities produced by all firms but firm i. From the first-order condition, we derive firm i's reaction function:

$$q_i (q_{-i}) = \tfrac{1}{2} (a_i - c_i - \gamma q_{-i}). \tag{19.7}$$

Then, summing the previous expression over all $i = 1 \ldots n$, we derive the total quantity at the Nash equilibrium, q^*, as (where $C \equiv \sum_{i=1}^{n} c_i$):

$$q^* = \tfrac{1}{2} (na - C - \gamma (n-1) q^*) \Leftrightarrow q^* = \frac{na - C}{2 + \gamma (n-1)}. \tag{19.8}$$

Combining expressions (19.7) and (19.8), one finds

$$2q_i^* = a_i - c_i - \gamma \left(\frac{na - c_i - \sum_{j \neq i} c_j}{2 + \gamma (n-1)} - q_i^* \right) \Leftrightarrow$$

$$q_i^* = \frac{(2 - \gamma)a - (2 + \gamma(n-2)) c_i + \gamma \sum_{j \neq i} c_j}{(2 - \gamma)(2 + \gamma(n-1))}.$$

From the first-order condition, it is easily seen that $\pi_i^* = (q_i^*)^2$.

In the pre-innovation stage, all firms produce at the same marginal cost: $c_i = c > 0 \ \forall i$. Suppose now that one firm, say firm 1, has developed a software innovation that has the effect of decreasing its marginal cost from $c_1 = c$ to $c_1 = c - x$ (with $0 < x < c$). If firm 1 keeps this innovation secret or patents it, it will be its sole user and, thereby, obtain a (per-period) profit equal to

$$\pi_1^{\text{secret}} = \left(\frac{(2 - \gamma)a - (2 + \gamma(n-2)) (c - x) + \gamma (n-1)c}{(2 - \gamma)(2 + \gamma(n-1))} \right)^2.$$

Alternatively, firm 1 can choose to disclose the source code of its innovation. Disclosure will entail two contrasting effects. On the one hand, the quality of the software will be enhanced thanks to the efforts of open source developers (who will find, diagnose and fix bugs, and who will add improvements and extensions). We model this positive effect by assuming that firm 1's cost will be reduced further after disclosure: its marginal cost becomes $c_1 = c - \alpha x$, with $\alpha > 1$ (and $\alpha < c/x$). On the other hand, disclosure also means that firm 1's competitors will have access to the innovation as well. We assume that after disclosure, the other firms' marginal cost becomes $c_j = c - \alpha \beta x$ ($j = 2 \ldots n$), where $0 \leq \beta \leq 1$ measures the 'generality' of firm 1's software (if $\beta = 0$, the software is completely specific to firm 1's production process and cannot usefully be employed by any other firm; if $\beta = 1$, the software

---

[u] The demand system can be obtained from the optimization problem of a representative consumer.

is completely general and yields identical benefits to all firms). Alternatively, we can interpret β as a measure of the knowledge spillovers, as we did in Section 18.1. It follows that under the disclosure strategy, firm 1 obtains a (per-period) profit equal to

$$\pi_1^{\text{disclose}} = \left(\frac{(2-\gamma)a - (2+\gamma(n-2))(c-\alpha x) + \gamma (n-1)(c-\alpha\beta x)}{(2-\gamma)(2+\gamma(n-1))} \right)^2 .$$

We now compare the two profits to assess under which conditions the firm will prefer to release the source code. Simple computations establish that

$$\pi_1^{\text{disclose}} \geq \pi_1^{\text{secret}} \iff \alpha \geq \alpha_{\min} \equiv \frac{2 + \gamma(n-2)}{2 + \gamma(n-2) - \gamma\beta(n-1)}. \tag{19.9}$$

It is clear that $\alpha_{\min} \geq 1$; it can also easily be checked that $\alpha_{\min}$ increases with γ, n and β. Therefore, condition (19.9) teaches us that the likelihood of source code release is increased by:

- lower competition on the product market (more product differentiation (lower γ) or higher concentration (lower n) reduce $\alpha_{\min}$);

- the specificity of the software for the innovating firm (a lower value of β reduces $\alpha_{\min}$);

- larger contributions from the open source community (a larger value of α).

Lesson 19.8 **Voluntary source code release is more likely when competition on the product market is low, when the software of the innovating firm is more specific and when the open source community contributes more to further software development.**

As an illustration of these effects, note that for $\gamma = 0$ (no competition) or for $\beta = 0$ (complete specificity of the software), $\alpha_{\min} = 1$ and the firm always prefers disclosure; on the other extreme, for $\gamma = \beta = 1$ (products are perfect substitutes and the software is completely general), $\alpha_{\min} = n$, meaning that disclosure is preferred only if it multiplies the software performance by a factor that is at least as large as the number of firms in the industry.

Open source vs. traditional IP incentives

The main advantage of open source with respect to the legal protection of IP is that it avoids the deadweight loss resulting from monopoly pricing. Open source therefore improves static efficiency (it also accelerates the discovery of subsequent innovations through automatic disclosure). Of course, the important question is whether it does so at the expense of dynamic efficiency. As innovators do not get any (immediate) monetary reward, incentives have to be found elsewhere. We have reviewed above the entire suite of incentives that open source comprises. What is important to note is that these various incentives have separate and distinct welfare implications: 'own use' incentives may lead to under-provision of code as benefits

conferred on third parties cannot be appropriated; 'signalling' incentives may lead programmers to invest more in projects in which they can showcase their competence, rather than
in projects with most consumer value; among the 'social psychological' incentives, those
based on extrinsic motivations (desire for reputation within the open source community,
'ego boost', 'feelings of personal efficacy', etc.) and on intrinsic motivations (creative pleasure, desire to be part of a team, satisfaction and accomplishment, ideological opposition to
proprietary software, etc.) may lead developers to partly internalize the social benefits they
confer.

It seems therefore legitimate to conclude with the following lesson:

Lesson 19.9   **Open source incentives often lead to an under-supply of goods relative to the patent
system. However, in the environments where open source works,[v] it is often superior
to the proprietary software system.**

This mitigated conclusion does not prevent public authorities throughout the world
taking measures to promote open source development to various extents. For instance, a
number of European governments encourage the use and purchase of OSS for government
use; the Chinese government even mandates the development of localized OSS projects;
Brazil's government ministries and state-run enterprises are abandoning Windows in favour of
open source software like Linux. The reasons advanced to motivate such policies are generally
cost savings, a better control over key applications and a lower reliance on commercial software
vendors.

Economic analyses have suggested that such policies supporting OSS projects are
likely to have an ambiguous effect on social welfare.[46] On the other hand, the regime of IP
protection clearly interacts with open source activity. Let us thus reopen for a moment our
previous discussion about the patentability of software. As we mentioned above, software
patents create the possibility of holding up software producers. As a result, large commercial
software vendors are acquiring large numbers of patents for purely defensive reasons, so as
to keep others' patent threats at bay. It is not clear whether the open source movement will
itself enter into a similar strategy of defensive patenting. From the outset, the answer is likely
to be negative because of the loose structure of open source communities and because of the
non-commercial objectives of most of their members. OSS projects might then be vulnerable
to software patents.[w]

---

[v] According to Maurer and Scotchmer (2006), 'open source works in environments where the knowledge created
(a) is complementary to some *other* good whose profitability is immune to imitation, such as human capital or
another proprietary product, or (b) where the motives to invent are intrinsic and have nothing to do with
appropriating value'.
[w] There are, nervertheless, a number of interesting initiatives aiming at protecting open source software from
patents. For instance, the Open Source Development Lab (OSDL) has created the *Patent Commons Project*, which
provides a central reference library and database where patent holders pledge their IP for the benefit of open source
software. The OSDL has also created a *Linux Legal Defense Fund* to defray legal expenses of Linux end users
who may become involved in litigation with patent holders on issues that affect the Linux community and
industry.

Review questions

1. Explain how IP law strikes a balance between dynamic and static efficiency considerations or, in other words, between incentives and use.

2. What is behind the so-called 'patent paradox'? How can it be explained?

3. Why isn't it optimal in terms of public policy to have patents that last forever? Discuss.

4. Does a firm have incentives to license its innovation to rival firms? Discuss.

5. What is the meaning of the 'tragedy of the anticommons'? How does this problem apply to innovations and how can it be mitigated?

6. What are the effects of end-user piracy of digital products on the producers' choices and on social welfare? Discuss.

Further reading

The seminal paper of Arrow (1962) remains a useful reading to complement this chapter. Important contributions about the optimal design of intellectual property are Nordhaus (1969) and Gilbert and Shapiro (1990). Takalo (2001) provides a nice summary of this literature. For more on the relative merits of IP protection and subsidies (and the combination of these two institutions in practice), see Chapter 8 of Scotchmer (2004). As for our treatment of IP in the digital economy, you can find more on the digital music market in Peitz and Waelbroeck (2006a), and on open source software in Lerner and Tirole (2002 and 2005b). Finally, for a less technical and more exhaustive treatment of the economics of IP, we recommend the book of Lévêque and Ménière (2004).

Notes for Part VII

1. See Maurer and Scotchmer (2004, 2006).

2. Taken from 'The meaning of XBox', *The Economist*, 24 November 2005.

3. A number of papers examine the link between various measures of competition and the incentive to innovate. See, e.g., Delbono and Denicolo (1990), Bester and Petrakis (1993) and Qiu (1997). For a comprehensive analysis within a unified framework, see Belleflamme and Vergari (2010).

4. This was stressed by Gilbert and Newbery (1982).

5. We follow here Reinganum (1983), which is itself an extension of Loury (1979) and Lee and Wilde (1980).

6. This case draws from Carson and Vaitheeswaran (2007).

7. We follow here Leahy and Neary (1997) who provide a useful synthesis and extension of this literature, with the aim of disentangling the separate influence of strategic behaviour on the one hand and R&D cooperation on the other. The idea that R&D generates incentives for firms to behave strategically has been first examined by Brander and Spencer (1983), assuming no R&D spillovers between firms and Cournot competition on the product market. Spence (1984) and Okuno-Fujiwara and Suzumura (1990) extended this analysis by considering, respectively, positive spillovers and Bertrand competition. Regarding R&D cooperation, d'Aspremont and Jacquemin (1988) presented a seminal analysis, which was then extended by, e.g., Kamien *et al.* (1992) and generalized by Amir *et al.* (2003).

8. We also assume that $r(x)$ turns to infinity as x goes to $c/2$.

9. See the seminal analysis of d'Aspremont and Jacquemin (1988).

10. See Amir *et al.* (2003) who generalize the results of Kamien *et al.* (1992).

11. See Cohen and Levinthal (1989).

12. We follow the analysis of Grunfeld (2003). For an alternative approach, see Kamien and Zang (2000).

13. This is the basic setup of d'Aspremont and Jacquemin (1988).

14. See Kamien *et al.* (1992) and Leahy and Neary (1997).

15. See Yi and Shin (2000) for the coalition approach, and Goyal and Moraga-González (2001) for the network approach.

16. This case is based on Goeree and Helland (2008).

17. These numbers are reported by PhRMA, the trade organization of the US pharmaceutical firms, on its website: www.phrma.org.

18. This table is adapted from Menell and Scotchmer (2005) and from Strowel (2005).

19. See H-Prize Act of 2006 (H.R. 5143).

20. See Anand and Galetovic (2004), which is based on a survey with 600 managers.

21. See the survey of recent studies by Caillaud (2003).

22. See OECD (2000).

23. See Mansfield (1986), Levin *et al.* (1987), Cohen *et al.* (2000) and Arora *et al.* (2003).

24. As Ridley *et al.* (2006) explain it, '[t]hree diseases with the greatest burden are HIV/AIDS, malaria, and tuberculosis. Manufacturers do invest in R&D for HIV/AIDS, because there is a market in both developed and developing countries for these therapies. There is less incentive to invest in R&D for malaria, because more than 99 percent of disability-adjusted life years (DALYs) lost to malaria are in developing countries.'

25. Hall and Ziedonis (2001) interviewed industry representatives and observed (on the period 1979–95) that (i) firms did not rely heavily on patents to appropriate returns to R&D, but (ii) their propensity to patent rose dramatically since the mid 1980s.

26. See Geroski (1995).

27. The first rigorous model explaining this fundamental trade-off was proposed by Nordhaus (1969). Since this seminal paper, there has been extensive research on the consequences of patent protection for social welfare. We summarize here the main finding of this research in a simplified framework. The exposition follows Takalo (2001).

28. See Liebowitz and Margolis (2004) for a deeper analysis of this case.

29. Using different models of R&D competition and different measures of patent breadth, a number of economists have reached opposite conclusions about the socially optimal patent length–breadth mix. Tandon (1982) and Gilbert and Shapiro (1990) call for narrow and long patents. In contrast, Gallini (1992) advocates broad and short patents, while for Nordhaus (1972), all mixes are equivalent. Klemperer (1990) provides examples of all these results. Denicolo (1996) and Takalo (2001) show that the above-mentioned rule can be applied to reconcile the seemingly contradictory policy implications drawn from a number of previous analyses.

30. The interested reader will find an excellent survey in Scotchmer (2004, Chapter 5).

31. This analysis is due to Kamien and Tauman (2002). The authors also consider two alternative modes of patent licensing: the auction method and the fixed fee method. They show that if the size of the innovation is large enough, precisely for $x > (a - c)/(n + 2)$, the incumbent innovator prefers to license its innovation by means of a royalty rather than of an auction or a fixed fee.

32. Based on Supreme Court Buries Patent Trolls, by Jessica Holzer, Forbes.com, 16 May 2006.

33. We follow here the simplified version of the Green and Scotchmer (1995) model presented by Lévêque and Ménière (2004).

34. See Green and Scotchmer (1995).

35. See Bessen and Maskin (2004).

36. Heller and Eisenberg (1998) explain why the classic complements problem of Cournot can be seen as the mirror image of the well-known tragedy of the commons (which refers to the fact that a resource – like fishing grounds or clean water – can be overused if it is not protected by property rights).

37. This issue is formally studied by Lerner and Tirole (2004) who provide a necessary and sufficient condition for a patent pool to enhance welfare.

38. For the empirical evidence see, e.g., the survey by Liebowitz (2006). In this debate an important paper that questions the record companies' claim and has been controversial is Oberholzer-Gee and Strumpf (2007).

39. A much more detailed account is given in Peitz and Waelbroeck (2006a).

40. See Novos and Waldman (1984).

41. See Yoon (2002).

42. For a formal analysis see Peitz and Waelbroeck (2006b).

43. See Rossi (2006) for a comprehensive literature survey. We follow mainly here Lerner and Tirole (2001, 2002, 2005a and b), and Maurer and Scotchmer (2006).

44. Source: An open secret: Sharing intellectual property can be more profitable than keeping it to yourself, *The Economist*, 20 October 2005.

45. This model is adapted from Harhoff *et al.* (2003).

46. See Lerner and Tirole (2005b) for more.

References for Part VII

Amir, R., Evstigneev, I. and Wooders, J. (2003). Noncooperative versus Cooperative R&D with Endogenous Spillover Rate. *Games and Economic Behavior* 42: 183–207.

Anand, B. and Galetovic, A. (2004). How Market Smarts can Protect Property Rights. *Harvard Business Review* (December): 73–79.

Anand, B. N. and Khanna, T. (2000). The Structure of Licensing Contracts. *Journal of Industrial Economics* 48: 103–135.

Arora, A., Ceccagnoli, M. and Cohen, W. C. (2003). R&D and the Patent Premium. NBER Working Paper n.9431.

Arrow, K. (1962). Economic Welfare and the Allocation of Resources for Inventions. In Nelson, R. (ed.), *The Rate and Direction of Inventive Activity*. Princeton: Princeton University Press.

Belleflamme, P. and Vergari, V. (2010). Incentives to Innovate in Oligopolies. *Manchester School*. Forthcoming.

Bessen, J. (2004). Holdup and Licensing of Cumulative Innovations with Private Information. *Economics Letters* 82: 321–326.

Bessen, J. and Hunt, R. M. (2004). An Empirical Look at Software Patents. Mimeo. Federal Reserve Bank of Philadelphia.

Bessen, J. and Maskin, E. (2004). Sequential Innovation, Patents, and Imitation. Mimeo. Boston University School of Law and Research on Innovation.

Bester, H. and Petrakis, E. (1993). The Incentives for Cost Reduction in a Differentiated Industry. *International Journal of Industrial Organization* 11: 519–534.

Brander, J. and Spencer, B. (1983). Strategic Commitment with R&D: The Symmetric Case. *Bell Journal of Economics* 14: 225–235.

Caillaud, B. (2003). La propriété Intellectuelle sur les Logiciels. In Conseil d'Analyse Economique (ed), *Propriété intellectuelle*. Paris: La Documentation Française.

Carson, I. and Vaitheeswaran, V. (2007). *Zoom: The Global Race to Fuel the Car of the Future*. Twelve Publishers.

Cohen, W. M. and Levinthal, D. A. (1989). Innovation and Learning: The Two Faces of R&D. *Economic Journal* 99: 569–596.

Cohen, W. M., Nelson, R. R. and Walsh, J. P. (2000). Protecting their Intellectual Assets: Appropriability Conditions and Why US Manufacturing Firms Patent or Not. NBER Working Paper n.7552.

Cournot, A. (1838). *Recherches sur les Principes Mathematiques de la Theorie des Richesses*. Paris: Hachette.

d'Aspremont, C. and Jacquemin, A. (1988). Cooperative and Noncooperative R&D in Duopoly with Spillovers. *American Economic Review* 78: 1133–1137. Erratum: *American Economic Review* 80 (1990): 641–642.

Delbono, F. and Denicolo, V. (1990). R&D Investment in a Symmetric and Homogeneous Oligopoly. *International Journal of Industrial Organization* 8: 297–313.

Denicolo, V. (1996). Patent Races and Optimal Patent Breadth and Length. *Journal of Industrial Economics* 44: 249–265.

Gallini, N. (1992). Patent Policy and Costly Imitation. *Rand Journal of Economics* 23: 52–63.

Gallini, N. and Scotchmer, S. (2002). Intellectual Property: When is it the Best Incentive System? *Innovation Policy and the Economy* 2: 51–77.

Geroski, P. (1995). Markets for Technology: Knowledge, Innovation and Appropriability. In Stoneman, P. (ed.), *Handbook of Economics of Innovation and Technological Change*. Oxford: Blackwell.

Gilbert, R. and Newbery, D. (1982). Preemptive Patenting and the Persistence of Monopoly. *American Economic Review* 72: 514–526.

Gilbert, R. and Shapiro, C. (1990). Optimal Patent Length and Breadth. *Rand Journal of Economics* 21: 106–112.

Goeree, M. S. and Helland, E. (2008). Do Research Joint Ventures Serve a Collusive Function? Mimeo.

Goyal, S. and Moraga-González, J. L. (2001). R&D Networks. *Rand Journal of Economics* 32: 686–707.

Green, J. and Scotchmer, S. (1995). On the Division of Profit in Sequential Innovation. *Rand Journal of Economics* 26: 131–146.

Griliches, Z. (1990). Patent Statistics as Economic Indicators: A Survey. *Journal of Economic Literature* 18: 1661–1707.

Grünfeld, L. A. (2003). Meet Me Halfway but Don't Rush: Absorptive Capacity and Strategic R&D Investment Revisited. *International Journal of Industrial Organization* 21: 1091–1109.

Hall, B. H. and Ziedonis, R. H. (2001). The Patent Paradox Revisited: An Empirical Study of Patenting in the US Semiconductor Industry, 1979–95. *Rand Journal of Economics* 32: 101–128.

Harhoff, D., Henkel, J. and von Hippel E. (2003). Profiting from Voluntary Information Spillovers: How Users Benefit by Freely Revealing their Innovations. *Research Policy* 32: 1753–1769.

Heller, M. and Eisenberg, R. S. (1998). Can Patents Deter Innovation? The Anticommons in Biomedical Research. *Science* 280: 698–701.

Kamien, M. I., Muller, E. and Zang, I. (1992). Research Joint Ventures and R&D Cartels. *American Economic Review* 82: 1293–1306.

Kamien, M. I. and Tauman, Y. (2002). Patent Licensing: The Inside Story. *The Manchester School* 70: 7–15.

Kamien, M. I. and Zang, I. (2000). Meet Me Halfway: Research Joint Ventures and Absorptive Capacity. *International Journal of Industrial Organization* 18: 995–1012.

Klemperer, P. (1990). How Broad Should the Scope of a Patent Be? *Rand Journal of Economics* 21: 113–130.

Leahy, D. and Neary, J. P. (1997). Public Policy Towards R&D in Oligopolistic Industries. *American Economic Review* 87: 642–662.

Lee, T. and Wilde, L. (1980). Market Structure and Innovation: A Reformulation. *Quarterly Journal of Economics* 94: 429–436.

Lerner, J. and Tirole, J. (2001). The Open Source Movement: Key Research Questions. *European Economic Review* 45: 819–826.

Lerner, J. and Tirole, J. (2002). Some Simple Economics of Open Source. *Journal of Industrial Economics* 50: 197–234.

Lerner, J. and Tirole, J. (2004). Efficient Patent Pools. *American Economic Review* 94: 691–711.

Lerner, J. and Tirole, J. (2005a). The Scope of Open Source Licensing. *Journal of Law, Economics and Organization* 21: 20–56.

Lerner, J. and Tirole, J. (2005b). The Economics of Technology Sharing: Open Source and Beyond. *Journal of Economic Perspectives* 19: 99–120.

Lévêque, F. and Ménière, Y. (2004). *The Economics of Patents and Copyright*. The Berkeley Electronic Press.

Levin, R. C., Klevorick, A. K., Nelson, R. R. and Winter, S. G. (1987). Appropriating the Returns from Industrial R&D. *Brookings Papers on Economic Activity*: 783–820.

Liebowitz, S. (2006). Economists Examine File-Sharing and Music Sales. In Illing, G. and Peitz, M. (eds.), *Industrial Organization and the Digital Economy*. Cambridge, MA: MIT Press.

Liebowitz, S. and Margolis, S. (2004). Seventeen Famous Economists Weigh in on Copyright: The Role of Theory, Empirics, and Network Effects. *bePress Legal Series*, Paper 397.

Loury, G.C. (1979). Market Structure and Innovation. *Quarterly Journal of Economics* 93: 395–410.

Mansfield, E. (1986). Patents and Innovation: An Empirical Study. *Management Science* 32: 173–181.

Maurer, S. M. and Scotchmer, S. (2004). Procuring Knowledge. In Libecap, G. (ed.), *Intellectual Property and Entrepreneurship: Advances in the Study of Entrepreneurship, Innovation and Growth* 15: 1–31. The Netherlands: JAI Press (Elsevier).

Maurer, S. M. and Scotchmer, S. (2006). Open Source Software: The New Intellectual Property Paradigm. In Hendersshott, T. (ed.), *Handbook of Economics and Information Systems*. The Netherlands: Elsevier.

Menell, P., and Scotchmer, S. (2005). Intellectual Property. Forthcoming in *Handbook of Law & Economics*.

Nordhaus, W. (1969). *Invention, Growth and Welfare*. Cambridge, MA: MIT Press.

Nordhaus, W. (1972). The Optimal Life of the Patent: Reply. *American Economic Review* 62: 428–431.

Novos, I. E. and Waldman, M. (1984). The Effects of Increased Copyright Protection: An Analytic Approach. *Journal of Political Economy* 92: 236–246.

Oberholzer-Gee, F. and Strumpf, K. (2007). The Effect of File Sharing on Record Sales: An Empirical Analysis. *Journal of Political Economy* 115: 1–42.

OECD (2000). Competition and Regulation Issues in the Pharmaceutical Industry. DAFFE/ CLP(2000)29.

Okuno-Fujiwara, M. and Suzumura, K. (1990). Strategic Cost-Reduction Investment and Economic Welfare. Mimeo. IER, Hitotsubashi University.

Peitz, M. and Waelbroeck, P. (2006a). Piracy of Digital Products: A Critical Review of the Theoretical Literature. *Information Economics and Policy* 18: 449–476.

Peitz, M. and Waelbroeck, P. (2006b). Why the Music Industry May Gain from Free Downloading – The Role of Sampling. *International Journal of Industrial Organization* 24: 907–913.

Qiu, L. D. (1997). On the Dynamic Efficiency of Bertrand and Cournot Equilibria. *Journal of Economic Theory* 75: 213–229.

Reinganum, J. (1983). Uncertain Innovation and the Persistence of Monopoly. *American Economic Review* 73: 741–748.

Ridley, D. B., Grabowski, H. G. and Moe, J. L. (2006). Developing Drugs for Developing Countries. *Health Affairs* 25: 313–324.

Rossi, M. A. (2006). Decoding the 'Free/Open Source (F/OSS) Software Puzzle': A Survey of Theoretical and Empirical Contributions. In Bitzer, J. and Schröder, J. P. H. (eds.), *The Economics of Open Source Software Development*. Amsterdam: Elsevier Science Publishers.

Schumpeter, J. (1943). *Capitalism, Socialism, and Democracy*. London: Unwin University Books.

Scotchmer, S. (2004). *Innovation and Incentives*. Cambridge, MA: MIT Press.

Shapiro, C. (2001). Navigating the Patent Thicket: Cross Licenses, Patent Pools, and Standard Setting. *NBER/Innovation Policy and the Economy* 1: 119–150.

Spence, M. (1984). Cost Reduction, Competition and Industry Performance. *Econometrica* 52: 101–112.

Strowel, A. (2005). The Principles and Rationale of Patent Protection. Mimeo. Facultés Saint-Louis, Brussels (Belgium).

Takalo, T. (2001). On the Optimal Patent Policy. *Finnish Economic Papers* 14: 33–40.

Tandon, P. (1982). Optimal Patents with Compulsory Licensing. *Journal of Political Economy* 90: 470–486.

Yi, S.-S. and Shin, H. (2000). Endogenous Formation of Research Coalitions with Spillovers. *International Journal of Industrial Organization* 18: 229–256.

Yoon, K. (2002). The Optimal Level of Copyright Protection. *Information Economics and Policy* 14: 327–348.

Part VIII
Networks, standards and systems

Introduction to Part VIII: Networks, standards and systems

Information products and technologies are rarely used in isolation or just for their own sake. Most of the time, they have to be combined with a number of other complementary products or technologies to provide their users with some utility. Take the example of an *instant messaging (IM) software* (like AOL Instant Messenger, Yahoo! Messenger, or Microsoft MSN, now Windows Live, Messenger). Most instant message services allow you (i) to send messages to another user across the Internet in real time, (ii) to set up individual chat rooms with people you choose to talk to, (iii) to exchange files, (iv) to check your email, and (v) to access pre-selected websites. From the description of the service, it appears clearly that the acquisition of an IM software involves a larger set of considerations than the purchase of, say, a bag of potatoes. Let us examine why.

First, the user has to look further than the present acquisition of a single product: what she really cares about is a *stream of (past and future) purchases or investments*. For example, an IM software is often bundled with a particular web browser, which makes the acquisition of the two products interdependent. Moreover, the user will have to spend some time and energy to learn to work with a particular IM software; this can be seen as an investment in some form of specific human capital. We use the term *system* to describe such a chain of complementary products.

Second, a user of an IM software will also care about *what other users are doing*. The benefits of using the software come, indeed, from two sources: first and foremost, the ability to communicate with other users (through chats and emails), and additionally, services that are either proprietary to the service provider (like information on weather, on financial market performances, etc.) or are provided by other sources (web pages for instance). What is important to stress is that *the benefits for an individual user increase with the number of other users of the software*: either directly for the communication benefits (a larger base of users directly increases the number of potential contacts any user can have via the IM software), or indirectly for the benefits related to services (a larger base of users induces providers to supply more and/or better services to be combined with the IM software, which in turn raises the attractiveness of the software). We use the term *network* to describe the community of users whose benefits are made interdependent by the nature of the product they use. By analogy, we call goods like IM software *network goods*.

In this part of the book, we want to shed light on a number of issues that are specific to the demand and supply sides of markets with network goods. A brief history of instant messaging illustrates the kind of issues we study in the next two chapters. While instant messaging actually predates the Internet, it really took off in 1996 when Mirabilis launched ICQ (shorthand for 'I Seek You'), a free IM software that anyone could use. In 1997, AOL followed suit with its own IM software, AIM; in 1998, AOL acquired Mirabilis and ICQ. Until 1999, AOL was clearly dominating the IM market, but Microsoft and Yahoo! entered the market. AIM's initial popularity remained for a while because it allowed AOL subscribers to communicate with non-members. The two competitors' products were indeed made to interface with AOL's software, but

AOL quickly shut off the access from other IM software by changing protocols in AIM. We see here two themes that we shall develop below: (1) there seems to be an early-mover advantage related to the launch of network goods; (2) entrants tend to favour compatibility, while incumbent firms tend to prefer incompatibility.

AOL's incompatibility strategy did not prevent its two main competitors from slowly gaining market shares. In 2003, AOL was estimated to serve half of the American market, with Yahoo! and Microsoft sharing the other half. However, AOL was much less present outside the United States, in contrast with Microsoft (and, with Yahoo!, although to a lesser extent). Because of network effects, MSN's worldwide popularity finally helped in the United States. AOL's initial dominance was further eroded when Microsoft and Yahoo! joined forces in 2006 to allow their users to communicate with each other on one service. We observe here two other themes that will be discussed below: (3) firms producing competing network goods often decide to form alliances in order to make their products compatible or to agree on a common standard; (4) network effects give rise to market dominance, but an initial dominant player may be displaced by a new one.

The IM market is still currently characterized by incompatibility: users have to run multiple software if they wish to use more than one of the competing networks. It must be noted, however, that various efforts have been made to reduce the need to run multiple software.[a] There have also been several attempts to create a unified standard for instant messaging.[b] Furthermore, public authorities also intervened in the instant

messaging arena. For instance, in 2002, AOL has been under increased scrutiny by the US federal government for its dominance of the market. As a condition of its merger with Time Warner, AOL was required by the Federal Communications Commission to offer interoperability with outside services should it launch any 'advanced IM' product, such as a version that includes video. We conclude by extracting two other important themes: (5) from the point of view of consumers, compatibility is desirable; this drives third parties and standard-setting organizations to devote resources to provide compatibility solutions; (6) public authorities might decide to intervene in markets with network goods.

In Chapter 20, we define more precisely the main features we observe on the demand side of network goods. We define the notion of 'network effects' and we focus on pricing decisions in the presence of such effects. We suppose first that only one network good is available. We show that several demand levels can be compatible with the same price, and we explain that the reason for this multiplicity of equilibria has to be found in a form of self-fulfilling prophecies. Based on the analysis of demand, we characterize the provision of a network good under the two extreme market structures of perfect competition and monopoly. We show that there is a tendency towards underprovision of a network good by a monopolist, and even by perfectly competitive firms. We move next to situations where consumers have to choose between incompatible network goods. We argue first that the consumers' desire for compatibility gives rise to demand-side economies of scale (or positive feedback effects) that tend to lead to a winner-take-all situation. We also put the emphasis on the coordination problems facing the consumers. These coordination problems may lead to market failures such as excess inertia, a situation whereby users fail to switch to a new network good although they would be made better off if every user switched. We then proceed to the supply side and

[a] A number of free services and open source applications have been proposed to combine various services (for instance, Trillian provides a centralized location for different IM contacts, which are shown in the same window).
[b] One of these attempts has been sponsored by the IETF (Internet Engineering Task Force), an open standard organization that develops and promotes Internet standards. Yet, to this day, all attempts to standardize the IM protocols have failed.

examine an oligopoly setting, where competing producers offer substitutable network goods. We show that pricing and capacity decisions crucially depend on the degree of compatibility between competing network goods. In particular, we argue that enhanced compatibility entails two contrasting effects: on the one hand, it expands demand, which benefits all firms; on the other hand, it reduces quality differentiation, which favours firms with small market shares at the expense of firms with large market shares.

Chapter 21 further explores the supply side of markets with network goods. Not only do firms adjust prices and capacities in the presence of network effects, but they also develop specific strategic instruments. Making products compatible or not becomes a strategic decision of paramount importance. Basically, choosing incompatibility means that one competes *for* the market, resulting in a standards war; on the other hand, choosing compatibility induces pre-market standardization and thus, competition *in* the market. In the case of a standards war, we study strategic instruments that firms may use to increase their chances of winning:

preempting rival firms by building an early installed base of users, choosing the timing of entry given the trade-off between backward compatibility and performance, and managing consumers' expectations in favour of the firm's product. We close this chapter by describing the difficulties faced by public authorities when trying to correct, or at least alleviate, the market failures that might result from network effects.

What will you learn in this part of the book?
You will get acquainted with the particular working of markets on which you are probably active consumers (software, computers, mp3 players, game consoles, and the like). You will understand that because consumers care about compatibility (between their own purchases or with the purchases of other consumers), firms have to make strategic decisions about the extent to which their products are compatible with the products of their competitors. You will also realize that the very nature of competition on these markets depends on these decisions regarding compatibility.

20 Markets with network goods

This chapter starts with a broad description of what network effects are: we distinguish between direct and indirect network effects, we compare network effects to switching costs and we report a number of empirical studies that have estimated the importance of network effects for various products (Section 20.1). We then proceed by characterizing demand and supply in network markets, looking first at a single good (Section 20.2) and next, at several incompatible goods (Section 20.3). We will see that demand decisions may lead to multiple equilibria, leading to potential coordination problems, while supply decisions crucially depend on the level of compatibility between competing goods.

20.1   Network effects

Like instant messaging software, a large majority of information products and technologies exhibit *network effects*. Loosely defined, network effects refer to the idea that, other things being equal, it is better to be connected to a bigger network. In this section, we first make this idea more precise by distinguishing between direct and indirect network effects. We then draw the similarities and differences between network effects and switching costs. Finally, we provide some empirical evidence about the strength of network effects in various markets.

20.1.1   Direct and indirect network effects

Network effects can be formally defined as follows: *a product is said to exhibit network effects if each user's utility is increasing in the number of other users of that product or of products compatible with it.* Network effects are observed on two types of markets.

- In *network* (or *communication*) *markets*, the benefit of consumers comes from the ability to communicate with other consumers via the network. In such markets, network effects are said to be *direct* and translate the fact that the more agents are present on a network, the larger are the communication opportunities, and the greater are the incentives for other agents to join this network.

- In *system markets*, products are obtained by combining different components in a complementary way (often some hardware and a variety of applications). Here, the network effects are *indirect* by nature: they refer to the fact that the more applications are available for a hardware, the greater are the incentives for consumers to purchase the system, *and* the more application writers desire writing applications for this hardware. In systems markets, the 'network' is virtual rather than physical, and the positive effect of an increase in the number of users is mediated by the availability of applications.

Examples

Obvious examples of goods exhibiting *direct* network effects are telephone, fax, email, instant messaging; less 'technological' examples are the adoption of languages (it is useful to learn English because it has become the lingua franca in many environments) or of conventions (driving is safer if everyone keeps on the same side of the road). To the extent that buyers tend to give valuable feedback and reviews, an electronic retailer such as Amazon also exhibits direct network effects.

Examples of goods exhibiting *indirect* network effects abound in the world of consumer electronics products, such as personal computers, VCR, videogame consoles, CD and DVD players. Considering the latter example, the greater the variety of movies proposed for a certain DVD format, the greater the benefit derived from the DVD player reading this particular format; in turn, the decisions of movie studios to back a particular DVD format depend on the number of consumers who adopt the compatible DVD player.[c] In general, indirect network effects are present in 'two- (or multi-) sided markets' (such as payment systems – e.g. Amex, Mastercard or Visa – and heterosexual dating clubs), which can be defined as platforms that serve two (or more) distinct groups of customers who value each other's participation or level of transaction (for instance, credit card holders' utility increases as more stores near them accept their card, and the more customers carrying the card, the more stores value it). We defer the specific analysis of situations of this sort to Chapter 22.

20.1.2   Network effects and switching costs

Like instant messaging software, many information products and technologies also exhibit *switching costs*, which refer to the idea that buyers must bear costs when they switch from one product to a functionally identical product supplied by another firm. As we discussed in Chapter 7, switching costs arise when a consumer makes investments specific to buying from a firm, so that it is more valuable to buy different goods, or goods at different dates, from that firm.[1] For information products and technologies, these specific investments are usually *physical investments* (in complementary equipment) and *informational investments* (in finding out how to use a product or about its characteristics).

The main similarity between switching costs and network effects is that they both lead consumers to value *compatibility*, though with slightly different meanings and implications. In the presence of switching costs, compatibility is understood as the ability for a consumer to take advantage of the same investment between her *own* purchases. The value consumers place on such ability is measured by the premium they are ready to pay for keeping the same product, or for staying with the same vendor. With network effects, compatibility is understood as the ability to communicate directly with, or to take advantage of the same complements

---

[c] Direct network effects are also present for these products insofar as users derive utility from sharing or exchanging software (like CDs, DVDs or computer applications).

as, *other* consumers. Here, the value placed on compatibility translates in an increase in the consumers' willingness-to-pay to join larger (physical or virtual) networks.

As a corollary of this valuation of compatibility, users of information technologies often face *lock-in*, resulting either from their own previous choices or from other consumers' choices. Such lock-in confers a potential ex post power to the sellers: in the presence of switching costs, the seller can raise its price above competitors' by an amount almost equal to the consumer's switching costs; in the presence of network effects, the larger the network, the larger the price the network owner can charge to users. As a result, the locus of competition shifts accordingly: competition largely concerns streams of products or services in the presence of switching costs, and selling to large groups of users in the presence of network effects. Competition also focuses on early adoptions: competition is fierce *ex ante* in order to reap the *ex post* rents created by the higher willingness-to-pay that consumers exhibit once they are locked-in. However, problems arise due to the incompleteness of simple sales contracts, which generally cover only present and bilateral transactions. These problems are examined in detail in the next sections.

From the previous discussion, one understands easily that when either switching costs or network effects are present, expectations and history play a key role. The importance of expectations follows from the incompleteness of contracts: as contracts fail to specify transactions which are complementary and highly relevant to the current one, it is crucial for buyers to form expectations about those transactions. This also means that history matters: because consumers value compatibility with either their own or other consumers' purchases, past choices guide future ones. Consequently, from the sellers' point of view, past market share becomes a highly valuable asset: switching costs might create a stock of locked-in consumers who can be exploited through higher prices; in the presence of network effects, a large network will tend to 'snowball' (that is, a large network creates positive expectations about its future size in a self-reinforcing way since consumers have incentives to join the network now and therefore enlarge the network tomorrow).

To conclude this comparison of switching costs and network effects, we explain in Case 20.1 why the two concepts may sometimes be hard to distinguish.

Case 20.1 Network effects: cause or consequence of switching costs?

In network markets, (direct) network effects can be seen as a *cause* of switching costs. When groups of users make sequential choices, early choices tend to commit later users, creating a form of 'collective switching costs'. Actually, with network effects, one user's investment in assets specific to the network is complementary to other (past and future) users' investments, which considerably expands the number of complementary assets and the associated lock-in. On the other hand, in system markets, (indirect) network effects may be seen as a *consequence* of switching costs. When choosing between competing systems, consumers tend to privilege the one offering the largest (current and future) availability of applications. This availability depends on the number of consumers who adopt the system in question (creating the indirect network effects) only if there are switching costs between systems, both for consumers and for application writers. These switching costs are related to the degree of compatibility between systems. If systems are compatible (meaning that applications written for one system can be 'ported' onto another system, with no loss of quality for the users, and no additional development cost for writers), switching involves no cost and a user's benefits no longer depend on the number of users adopting the system of her choice.

20.1.3   Empirical evidence on network effects

A small but growing body of work has endeavoured to quantify network effects in a variety of markets. As we have just seen, the theory predicts that the value of a good subject to network effects increases with the size of the associated network. How can one test such a proposition? The option of simply including the demand for the good as an econometric predictor of itself is fraught with difficulties: a positive coefficient could be the result of network effects, but also of correlations with unobserved taste or quality variables (at the individual level), or of herding and learning effects (from a dynamic point of view). Other methods must therefore be used. Case 20.2 illustrate some of these methods.

Case 20.2 Empirical evidence on network effects in software markets

To estimate network effects, several authors use the hedonic price approach, which is based on the hypothesis that heterogeneous goods are aggregations of characteristics. The idea is to calculate implicit marginal prices as derivatives of the hedonic price equation with respect to levels of the characteristics.[2] This method has been mainly used to test for the presence of network effects in the PC software market; the strategy is to estimate the value that different product aspects contribute to a consumer's utility and then, to calculate the implicit price of having either an installed base, or compatible products, or an established standard. Here are some of the results obtained through this method.[3]

Spreadsheet packages Based on a particular data set, consumers were found to be willing to pay a significant premium for spreadsheets that are compatible with the Lotus platform (an average of 46%) and for spreadsheets that offer links to external databases; a 1% increase in a product's installed base is associated with a 0.75% increase in its price.

Word-processing software Network effects are found to have a significant effect on prices; the price premium is more important for strong players than for the installed base of the incumbent, suggesting that consumers have non-adaptive expectation functions.

Database software The capability of executing programs written for the dominant database product yields a significant price premium; the ability to read and write data in the dominant spreadsheet format is also associated with higher prices.

Indirect network effects in system markets have also been quantified using the nested logit approach for the components, as the following case documents.

Case 20.3 Empirical evidence on network effects in systems markets using the nested logit approach

A number of papers use models comprising two main components. The first component is hardware adoption, which is represented by a nested logit model (see Chapter 5). Recall that the nested logit model deals with cases in which choices are made sequentially: typically, the consumer decides first whether to buy the hardware; if she decides to buy, she then chooses which brand to buy. The second component is software provision, which results from the interaction between software providers. The indirect network effects are then characterized by the interaction of the two components. Some results drawn from these analyses of system markets are documented here.[4]

VCRs Network effects played a significant role in the format competition between VHS and Betamax. For instance, it is estimated that (i) the value of the network effect grew from $5.6 million in 1978 to $343 million in 1986 for all US households (in constant 1978 US$), and (ii) the network advantage of VHS explains at least 70.3% to 86.8% of (the logarithm of) relative sales of VHS to Betamax in each year between 1981 and 1988.

CDs The cross-elasticity of CD player adoption with respect to the variety of CD titles is found to be significant, which indicates that there is a two-way feedback between hardware and software for compact disc players.

DVDs Complementarities between DVD player adoption and availability of content on DVD are statistically and economically significant (in 2001, a 1% increase in new DVD releases was estimated to increase DVD player sales by 0.5%, and a 1% increase in DVD player installed base was estimated to increase the number of new DVD releases by 0.19%). Moreover, the data are generally consistent with the hypothesis that the preannouncement of DIVX slowed down the adoption of DVD technology.

PDAs It is estimated that the network effect explains roughly 22% of the log-odds ratio of the sales of all Palm O/S compatible PDAs to Microsoft O/S compatible PDAs, where the remaining 78% reflects price and model features.

Video games The emphasis here is more on producers' strategies rather than on the mere estimation of network effects. It is found that introductory pricing is an effective practice at the beginning of the product cycle, and expanding software variety becomes more effective later. Estimations also show that software providers continue to exploit the installed base of hardware users after hardware demand has slowed. Regarding network effects, evidence suggests that they are asymmetric between the competitors: for a particular time period the firm with a smaller customer network (Nintendo) was found to have higher network strength than the firm with the larger customer base (Sega).

Furthermore, recent empirical work has established the significant role played by *direct network effects* in the diffusion of mobile telecommunication services. For instance, it is estimated (with 2003 German data) that in the absence of network effects, if prices remained as observed, the penetration of mobiles could be lower by at least 50%. It is also shown that even in the absence of any price differential between on-net and off-net calls, there is a form of pure network effect, as a disproportionate number of calls are on-net.[5]

20.2   Markets for a single network good

We start our analysis of network markets by assuming for simplicity that only one network good is available. Our goal is to derive the demand for a network good, taking into account the various features that we identified in the previous section, in particular that consumers' choices are interdependent and that expectations matter. We then turn to the supply side and analyse the provision of a network good, either by a competitive industry or by a monopolist.

20.2.1   Modelling the demand for a network good

A good is said to exhibit positive network effects when a consumer's willingness to pay for the good depends positively on the size of the corresponding network (i.e., on the number of consumers who purchase compatible products). The typical utility function employed in settings with network effects is of the following form:

$$U_{ij} = a_i + f_i\left(n_j^e\right),$$
(20.1)

where U_{ij} is the utility to consumer i from the use of one unit of good j (or, in other words, from belonging to network j). This utility is assumed to depend on two (additively separable) benefits. The first term (a_i) represents a *stand-alone benefit,* which comes from the immediate use of the technology (or which measures the consumer's valuation for the intrinsic quality of the technology). The second term represents the *network benefit:* under the assumptions that $f(0) = 0$ and $f_i' > 0$, we have that the network benefits are zero in a network of size zero, but increase as soon as the network is expected to expand (i.e., as n_j^e, the expected number of consumers in the network, increases). Both benefits can differ among consumers.

Modelling direct and indirect network effects

Formulation (20.1) seems particularly well suited to describe the *direct network effects* that arise in network or communication markets: there is indeed a direct link between the network size and the quality of the technology. The classic example of a direct network is a local telephone exchange (as represented by the star network of Figure 20.1). Consumer A accesses the network by purchasing a link from her location to the local switch (link AS). If consumer B has subscribed to a similar link (link BS), A and B are able to call each other. The links AS and BS can be seen as two complementary goods which, when combined, create a valuable system. If the network is comprised of n subscribers, there are $n(n-1)/2$ systems of this sort. Hence, an extra subscriber joining the network creates n new systems, which benefits all existing subscribers and is the source of the network effects.

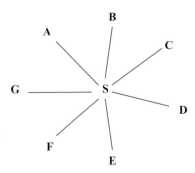

Figure 20.1 A simple star network

Expression (20.1) can also be seen as a reduced form describing settings with *indirect network effects*. In system markets, systems often consists of one unit of hardware and one unit of compatible software. Because consumers value variety, they demand multiple systems, each system combining one unit of hardware with a different variety of software. This hardware/software paradigm applies to many markets combining information technologies and information goods (for instance, consumers usually use more than one application program on their PC, listen to more than one CD on their stereo, play more than one video game on their console, ...). Hence, a consumer's utility for a particular hardware increases with the number of compatible applications available for this hardware. Letting m_j denote this number for hardware j, we have that U_{ij} depends on $g_i(m_j)$ with $g_i' > 0$. But the number (and quality) of compatible applications depends itself on and increases with the (expected) number of consumers who adopt system j (because more application developers will find it profitable to write applications as the demand for system j is expected to expand). We can therefore write $m_j = h(n_j^e)$, with $h' > 0$, and let $f_i(n_j^e) = g_i(h(n_j^e))$, which brings us back to expression (20.1).

Indirect network effects occur for a number of reasons but the general underlying interdependences are that some actions of sellers depend on the number of users of a system and that the users' utility depends on the actions taken by the sellers. Here, we will explore a number of channels. First, for a given number of sellers, their investment in quality (and pricing) may be affected by the number of active users. Users net utility in turn depends on the quality and pricing decision so that, indirectly, the number of users enters the utility function of the user. Secondly, for given quality levels, sellers have to decide whether to enter. If each seller offers a distinct product, the number of sellers determines product variety. Here, the entry decision depends on the number of active users. In turn, a user's utility depends on the number of active sellers. This argument can be made precise in a context in which each seller has monopoly power and firms are heterogeneous, e.g., with respect to their fixed cost. It can also be made precise in a context of imperfect competition with differentiated products in which sellers are homogeneous. Imperfect competition gives rise to a third mechanism. For this, one may consider e.g. homogeneous firms that compete in quantities (or capacities). Here, more sellers do not offer more variety but lead to more intense competition, which affects the utility of users through lower prices.

Let us illustrate this point through a simple example that focuses on the first channel. Consider a videogame platform, such as Sony Playstation, for which people buy video games from game developers.[d] Suppose that n consumers use Sony Playstation. Consumer i's utility comes from two sources: on the one hand from the platform itself (measured by a_i) and on the other hand, from the quality of the games that can be played on the console. The quality of games produced, s, increases with the developer's investment, x, according to the function $s(x) = 2\sqrt{x}$; the marginal cost of increasing quality is constant and equal to unity. In each of the n transactions, the developer is assumed to be able to appropriate a share λ of the benefits stemming from her investment (leaving the complementary share $(1 - \lambda)$ to the buyer). Her problem is thus to choose the investment x that maximizes $2n\lambda\sqrt{x} - x$. We compute easily that $x^* = n^2\lambda^2$ and $s(x^*) = 2n\lambda$. It follows that consumer i's utility is written as $U_i = a_i + (1 - \lambda)(2n\lambda)$, which exhibits network effects as it increases with n, the number of users of the game console.

We now turn to a more elaborate analysis of indirect network effects arising from product variety in the context of monopolistic competition. This analysis is technically more involved and can be skipped at the first reading.

Consider n consumers with preferences defined over hardware, software, and a competitively supplied outside good.[6] The timing of the game is as follows. Consumers buy the hardware in the first period, before knowing how much software is going to be available in the second period. Software producers observe the consumers' adoption decision and provide m varieties of software in period 2; we present the continuum version and therefore integrate over varieties.

Consumers have the following utility function:

$$U = q_0 + \mu \left[\left(\int_0^m q_j^\rho \, dj \right)^{\frac{1}{\rho}} \right]^\beta, \tag{20.2}$$

where q_0 is the quantity of the outside good, μ denotes the type of the consumer, and q_j the quantity of software j. As far as the utility of software is concerned, we use a CES utility function[7] to capture the idea that the level of software service increases both with the quantity consumed and the variety of software packages available for the hardware (see Chapter 3). We impose $0 < \rho < 1$ (a standard restriction in this type of model to make sure that monopolistic competition works) and $\beta < \rho$ (which implies that the marginal benefit of an extra variety of software is declining).

All consumers are endowed with income I, which they can spend either on the competitively supplied outside good (taken as a numéraire), or on the hardware sold at price $\hat{p}_h$ and each variety j of software sold at price p_j. Denoting by $E = \int_0^m p_j q_j dj$ the total expenditure on software, we can express the consumer's budget constraint as: $q_0 + \hat{p}_h + E = I$. Combining the latter expression with (20.2), we can write the consumer's indirect utility from purchasing the hardware/software combination as

$$v = I - \hat{p}_h - E + \mu \left[\left(\int_0^m q_j^\rho \, dj \right)^{\frac{1}{\rho}} \right]^\beta. \tag{20.3}$$

According to this formulation users only derive utility from a system consisting of hardware and software; in particular, the hardware does not give any stand-alone utility.

---

[d] In Chapter 22, we turn to pricing issues in such platforms.

Each variety of software is produced by a different firm. Firms operate under increasing returns to scale: the marginal cost of production is equal to c, and associated with each software variety is a fixed cost equal to f. They also operate in a monopolistic competition market structure. Recall that under monopolistic competition firms face downward-sloping demand and set price above marginal cost. However, they make zero profits in equilibrium due to free entry. That is, in this market structure, the number of firms (varieties) adjusts to make the profit of each software firm equal to zero. In particular, it is easily checked that the CES utility function implies a price elasticity of $1/(1-\rho)$ and a constant monopoly markup of $(1-\rho)/\rho$. The monopoly price for each variety j is thus $p_j = c/\rho$ and the zero-profit condition implies

$$(p_j - c)q_j - f = 0 \Leftrightarrow q_j = \frac{\rho}{1-\rho}\frac{f}{c} \equiv q.$$

Because the latter condition holds for every firm in the industry, we have that total revenues in the software industry equal total fixed costs (mf). On the other hand, total revenues also equal total expenditure by all n consumers who buy the hardware/software combination (nE). It follows that $mf = nE$, meaning that the number of software varieties is endogenously determined as $m = nE/f$. We can now plug q and m into expression (20.3) and obtain:

$$v = I - \hat{p}_h - E + \mu q^\beta \left(\frac{nE}{f}\right)^{\frac{\beta}{\rho}}$$

$$= I - \hat{p}_h - E + \mu An^\alpha E^\alpha, \tag{20.4}$$

with $\alpha \equiv \beta/\rho$ and $A \equiv q^\beta/f^\alpha$. Maximizing expression (20.4) for the optimal expenditure E on software, we find

$$E^* = (\mu\alpha An^\alpha)^{\frac{1}{1-\alpha}}. \tag{20.5}$$

Substituting (20.5) into (20.4), we obtain a consumer's indirect utility as a function of the number of consumers purchasing the hardware/software combination:

$$v = I - \hat{p}_h + \mu^{\frac{1}{1-\alpha}} Kn^{\frac{\alpha}{1-\alpha}},$$

with $K \equiv (1-\alpha)(\alpha A)^{\frac{1}{1-\alpha}}$.

Now, define $h(n) \equiv Kn^{\frac{\alpha}{1-\alpha}}$ and $\theta \equiv \mu^{\frac{1}{1-\alpha}}$ as a monotonic transformation of the consumer's type. The latter expression rewrites then as:

$$v = I + \theta h(n) - \hat{p}_h,$$

which is similar to formulation (20.1): the stand-alone benefit is the same for all consumers ($a_i = 0$ for all i), and the network benefit varies across consumers ($h_i(n) = \theta h(n)$, where θ denotes the identity (type) of consumer i). Our main insight is summarized by the following lesson.

Lesson 20.1   Indirect network effects can arise in a buyer–seller context because of the effect of consumer participation (and intensity of use) on quality, price and variety. In the reduced form consumer utility directly depends on the number of consumers.

Modelling expectations and consumers heterogeneity

Although expression (20.1) seems quite simple, its reliance on expectations about the size of the network introduces important complications. Further assumptions have to be made to model how expectations are formed. Two basic approaches have been proposed. In the *fulfilled-expectations approach*, consumers base their current purchasing decisions on their expectations about future network sizes, and attention is restricted to equilibria in which these expectations turn out to be correct (i.e., are rational). An alternative approach (which is, arguably, less satisfactory but more tractable analytically) is to eliminate all intertemporal links by assuming that consumers have *myopic expectations* and base their decisions only on actual network sizes.[e]

Let us now derive the demand for an information technology exhibiting network effects. We use the fulfilled expectations approach. To simplify the computations, we assume that network benefits increase linearly with the expected network size: $f_i(n_j^e) = v_i n_j^e$, with $v_i > 0$.[f] Moreover, as we consider for the moment the demand for a single good, we drop the technology index j. We contrast two scenarios about consumers' heterogeneity: in the first scenario, consumers differ only in their valuation of the network benefit ($a_i = a_k = a$ and $v_i \neq v_k$ for all i, k); in the second scenario, consumers differ only in their valuation of the stand-alone benefit ($a_i \neq a_k$ and $v_i = v_k = v$ for all i, k). In both scenarios, we assume that we have a continuum of consumers (of mass one) identified by a taste parameter θ which is uniformly distributed on the interval $[0, 1]$. It is the interpretation of this taste parameter that differs under the two scenarios. Case 20.4 presents examples that are best described by one scenario or by the other.

Case 20.4 Heterogeneous adopters for network goods

Most consumer electronics products are characterized by sequential adoption: there is a minority of early adopters and a majority of mainstream consumers, who usually take a wait-and-see approach. In our modelling, the early adopters can be seen as those with a large value of the parameter θ, and the mainstream consumers as those with lower values of θ. The question remains as to why early adopters are keener to adopt the new network good than other consumers: do they value more the network benefits of the good, or its stand-alone benefits?

Take the example of smartphones, like the Blackberry, which allow users to stay connected on the go with wireless access to email. The Blackberry became quickly popular among business people, who were valuing highly the possibility of reading and sending emails any time and anywhere. Non professional users only adopted the

---

[e] Another complication arises in the case of indirect network effects, as it is not clear who is forming expectations. Actually, the interdependence between the system-adoption decisions of consumers and the application-supply decision of manufacturers forces each group to form expectations about the behaviour of the other. The timing of actions is not clear either (this is known as the 'chicken-and-egg' problem). In this chapter, we abstract the latter considerations away (but we come back to it in Chapter 22).

[f] The assumption of linear network effects is convenient, and it is standard in the literature. As indicated above, for the direct network effects appearing in communication networks (like phone, fax or email networks), there is a straightforward explanation for the linear form.

Blackberry later because of their lower willingness to pay for permanent connection to emails. In this example, users seem thus to differ according to their valuation of the network benefits of the technology.

Consider next the example of high-definition television (HDTV). Indirect network effects are present here as HDTV sets become more valuable as more diverse content is broadcast in HD (and television companies have larger incentives to broadcast in HD the larger the installed base of HDTV sets). In this case, the early adopters were found among the so-called 'tech aficionados' who were primarily interested in superior picture quality, whatever the available content. As for mainstream consumers, they are still to be found: most of them take a wait-and-see approach because their lower valuation for increased picture quality does not make up for the relative lack of compatible content. As a result, content producers also wait, which slows down the take-off of HDTV. This is a perfect illustration of the 'chicken-and-egg' problem that we will further describe below. We just record here that for the case of HDTV, the heterogeneity of consumers seems to be related to the stand-alone dimension of the good.

Network effects and equilibrium network size: Heterogeneous network effects

In the first scenario, $\theta \in [0, 1]$ measures the consumer's valuation of the network effects. In particular, we write expression (20.1) as

$$U(\theta) = a + \theta vn^e. \tag{20.6}$$

The most eager consumer ($\theta = 1$) values the network benefit at vn^e, while the least eager consumer ($\theta = 0$) has a utility which does not increase with the expected size of the network; all consumers share the same valuation for the stand-alone benefit of the technology.[8]

If the technology is sold at a price p and if the expected network size is n^e, the consumer who is indifferent between purchasing the technology or not (with the utility of not using the technology being, as usual, normalized to zero) is identified by $\hat{\theta}$ such that

$$a + \hat{\theta} vn^e - p = 0 \Leftrightarrow \hat{\theta} = \frac{p - a}{vn^e}.$$

Because all consumers with a higher valuation than $\hat{\theta}$ decide to buy the technology, we will have that $n = 1 - \hat{\theta}$. Combining the latter two expressions, we can write the willingness to pay for the nth unit of the technology when n^e units are expected to be sold as

$$p(n, n^e) = (a + vn^e) - vn^e n.$$

This function decreases with n, like any well-behaved downward-sloping demand, but it increases with n^e because of the positive network effects. To find the equilibrium between these two forces, we follow the fulfilled-expectations approach: when consumers form rational expectations, the equilibrium must be such that $n = n^e$. Therefore, we define the fulfilled-expectations demand curve as

$$p(n, n) = a + vn(1 - n); \tag{20.7}$$

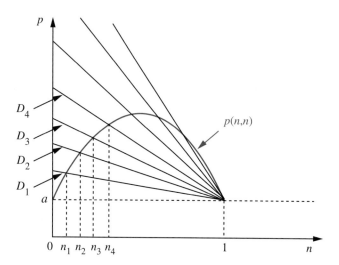

Figure 20.2 Fulfilled expectations demand when consumers value network benefits differently

the fulfilled-expectations demand curve matches each price p with those adoption levels n such that, when consumers expect adoption n, just n of them will adopt at price p.

Figure 20.2 illustrates the construction of a typical fulfilled expectations demand $p(n, n)$.[9] Each curve $D_i = p(n, n_i)$ shows the willingness to pay for a varying quantity n, given an expected network size $n^e = n_i$; at $n = n_i$, expectations are fulfilled and the point belongs to $p(n, n)$ as $p(n_i, n_i)$; thus $p(n, n)$ is obtained by collecting all such points $p(n_i, n_i)$, which gives this bell shape.

From the bell shape of the demand function, it follows that *there might exist more than one n (that is, more than one quantity or network size) that satisfies the equilibrium condition for a given price*. For instance, for any price p such that $a < p < a + v/4$, there are three network sizes consistent with this price:[g] (1) a zero size network ($n_0 = 0$), (2) a network size $n_1(p)$ at the first intersection of the horizontal through p with $p(n, n)$, and (3) a network size $n_2(p)$ at the second intersection of the horizontal through p with $p(n, n)$, with

$$n_1(p) = \tfrac{1}{2} - \sqrt{\tfrac{1}{4} - \tfrac{p-a}{v}}; \; n_2(p) = \tfrac{1}{2} + \sqrt{\tfrac{1}{4} - \tfrac{p-a}{v}}. \tag{20.8}$$

The multiplicity of equilibria follows directly from the coordination problem induced by the presence of network effects. Each equilibrium relies on *self-fulfilling prophecies*. For instance, if each consumer expects no other consumer will adopt the technology ($n^e = 0$), then each consumer is willing to pay a price no larger than $a < p$; it follows that it is a Nash equilibrium for each consumer not to join the network of technology adopters, which fulfils the expectations ($n_0 = n^e = 0$). Similarly, the other two equilibria also correspond to fulfilled expectations. In the first equilibrium, there is a positive but small number of consumers who join the network: consumers do not think that the network will be very large, so they are not willing to pay much to connect to it, and the resulting network is therefore not very large. In the second equilibrium, the same price gives rise to a larger network and the marginal consumer

---

[g] For any price larger than $a + v/4$, there exists no equilibrium with a positive n.

who connects to the network does not value it very highly (consumers with a higher valuation have already joined).

Lesson 20.2 **Due to network effects that affect consumers' utility differently, there often exist multiple consumer equilibria for the given price of the network industry.**

As multiple equilibria can occur, we need a rule to choose among them. A first solution would be to introduce some dynamic adjustment process in the model. Suppose we start at one particular equilibrium and that a little perturbation takes place; that is, either the price slightly changes or some consumers modify their decision. With such a process in mind, we argue that the small-network equilibrium, $n_1(p)$, is unstable.[10] Indeed, if the price increases slightly or if some consumers drop out, we are now, at n_1, in a situation where the demand curve lies beneath the price line. As consumers are willing to pay less than the price of the service, it seems plausible to assume that the market will contract. Repeating this logic, the eventual outcome will be that all consumers leave, which will bring the process to equilibrium n_0. Similarly, if the price is slightly reduced or if an extra consumer joins the n_1 consumers already in the network, we reach a situation where the demand curve is above the price curve. Now, as consumers are willing to pay more than the cost of the product, the market is likely to expand and it will do until it reaches equilibrium $n_2(p)$. We can extend the previous reasoning to claim that once the network reaches the size $n_1(p)$, it is virtually certain that it will reach the larger size $n_2(p)$ (since only a slight price reduction is necessary to achieve this). Accordingly, we refer to size $n_1(p)$ as a *critical mass* for the network.

Applying the thought experiment to equilibria n_0 and $n_2(p)$, we quickly come to the conclusion that both equilibria are stable. To tell which is likely to occur, we resort to the *Pareto criterion*: if, at a certain price, there exist more than one number of consumers ('quantity') that satisfies the equilibrium condition and one of these 'quantities' Pareto-dominates (i.e., makes everyone better off than) the others, consumers expect this allocation to prevail in equilibrium. In the present case, the larger n that satisfies (20.7) gives a larger value to the network good, so everyone would be better off by coordinating on this solution. Hence, we pick $n_2(p)$ when following the Pareto-criterion.

Network effects and equilibrium network size: Heterogeneous stand-alone benefits

In this alternative setting, θ measures the preference for the stand-alone benefit of the technology and expression (20.1) can be rewritten as

$$U(\theta) = \theta a + \nu n^e. \tag{20.9}$$

The most eager consumer ($\theta = 1$) values the intrinsic quality of the technology at $a > 0$, while the least eager consumer ($\theta = 0$) values it at zero; all consumers share the same valuation for the network benefit of the technology.

We proceed as above by identifying the indifferent consumer (noted $\tilde{\theta}$) for a given price p and a given expected network size n^e: $\tilde{\theta}a + \nu n^e - p = 0 \Leftrightarrow \tilde{\theta} = (p - \nu n^e)/a$. We

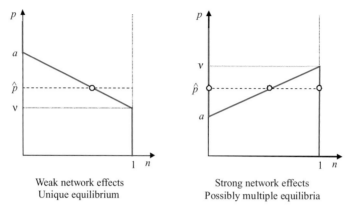

Figure 20.3 Fulfilled expectations demand when consumers value stand-alone benefits differently

note that $\tilde{\theta} \geq 0$ as long as $n^e \leq p/v$, and $\tilde{\theta} \leq 1$ as long as $n^e \geq (p - a)/v$. It follows that for a given price p and a given expected network size n^e, the actual number of consumers adopting the technology is given by

$$n(p, n^e) = \begin{cases} 0 & \text{if } n^e < (p - a)/v, \\ 1 - \frac{p - vn^e}{a} & \text{if } (p - a)/v \leq n^e \leq p/v, \\ 1 & \text{if } n^e > p/v. \end{cases} \tag{20.10}$$

We now impose fulfilled expectations: $n = n^e$. Using the demand function (20.10), we see easily that $n = n^e = 0$ if $p > a$, and $n = n^e = 1$ if $p < v$. For these two corner equilibria to coexist, the price of the technology must be such that $a < p < v$, which supposes that $v > a$. If the latter inequality is satisfied, we say that network effects are 'strong'; in such a case, the most eager consumer ($\theta = 1$) values the highest possible network benefit (which is reached when all consumers adopt the technology, $n^e = 1$) *more* than the stand-alone benefit. In the opposite case (i.e., $v < a$), we say that network effects are 'weak'.

The interior equilibrium is such that $0 < n = n^e < 1$ and is found by solving the following equation for n:

$$n = 1 - \frac{p - vn}{a} \Leftrightarrow n(p) = \frac{a - p}{a - v}. \tag{20.11}$$

In the case of *weak network effects* ($v < a$), $n(p)$ is a decreasing function of the price, and $0 < n(p) < 1$ as long as $v < p < a$. In contrast, under *strong network effects* ($v > a$), $n(p)$ is an *increasing* function of the price, and $0 < n(p) < 1$ as long as $a < p < v$.

In sum, we observe that under *weak network effects* ($v < a$), there is a *unique demand level at any given price*: $n = 0$ for $p > a$, $n = (a - p)/(a - v)$ for $v \leq p \leq a$, and $n = 1$ for $p < v$. As represented in the left panel of Figure 20.3, the fulfilled expectations demand is downward-sloping: the traditional 'law of demand' effect outweighs the network effect. Yet, the demand becomes more elastic as the network effect increases.

The case of *strong network effects* ($v > a$) offers a very different picture, as depicted on the right panel of Figure 20.3. This case looks more like what we obtained previously under the assumption of heterogeneous network effects. Indeed, for intermediate prices (i.e., $a < p < v$), three fulfilled expectations equilibria coexist: $n = 0$, $n = (p - a)/(v - a)$, and $n = 1$. As above, it can be argued that the interior equilibrium is not stable: as the equilibrium number of consumers increases with the price, a small price increase (resp. reduction) would drive the equilibrium towards full (resp. zero) participation. Among the remaining two equilibria, full participation ($n = 1$) is clearly Pareto-dominant.

> Lesson 20.3   In the presence of network effects and heterogeneous stand-alone utilities, the fulfilled expectations demand is monotone and strictly decreasing if network effects are not too strong. Otherwise, if network effects are sufficiently strong, there might exist multiple consumer equilibria for the given price of the network industry.

Looking beyond the two models

Implicit in formulation (20.1) are the assumptions that network effects are *monotonically positive* (i.e., the payoff of agent i (weakly) increases when another agent joins the network agent i belongs to, whatever the size of this network) and *anonymous* (i.e., only the number of agents joining the network matters, not their identity).

These assumptions are often made to keep models tractable, but they might prove restrictive when it comes to analyse some particular settings. First, it seems often more reasonable to consider *local* (rather than anonymous) interaction models: individuals might indeed have a higher incentive to coordinate their choice of network with people in their 'neighbourhood' than with people located 'far away' from them. For instance, people buying a mobile phone usually put more weight on being able to talk to their family and friends than on being able to call and be reached by random people and business. Similarly, it has been documented that people are more likely to buy their first home computer in areas where a high fraction of households already own computers or when a large share of their friends and family own computers.[11] Accordingly, network effects are still assumed to be monotonically positive but only *within* communities of individuals; the degree of interaction *between* communities becomes then a critical factor for assessing the overall diffusion of some particular technology (or standard, or social norm).

Second, the assumption of monotonically positive network effects might be questioned when one considers strategic concerns which possibly undermine the value attached by individuals to coordination.[12]

20.2.2   Provision of a network good

Let us now consider the supply side. We still use the setting of the previous section: a single network good is available, consumers' expectations are fulfilled at equilibrium and consumers are able to coordinate on the Pareto-dominant equilibrium in case of multiple equilibria. We suppose that there is a constant marginal cost, $c \geq 0$, to produce the network good (or to connect an extra consumer to the network). Our goal is to derive the network size that is achieved at equilibrium when the industry is perfectly competitive or when it is a monopoly. Then, comparing with the social optimum, we will assess whether network effects are a source of externalities.

Perfect competition vs. monopoly

We consider in turn the two scenarios about consumers' heterogeneity. We assume for now that there is no potential for price discrimination, which means that all consumers are charged the same flat price for the network good.

Different network benefits The inverse demand for the network good is given by expression (20.7): $p(n, n) = a + vn(1 - n)$. We assume that $c < a + v/4$ (otherwise, the market will fail altogether since $a + v/4$ is the maximum price consumers are willing to pay in the present case). Under *perfect competition*, the technology is priced at marginal cost. Recalling our previous analysis, we find that the network size at the (fulfilled-expectations, Pareto-dominant) equilibrium is $n^c = 1$ if $c \leq a$, or is given by expression (20.8) with $p = c$ for $c > a$:

$$n^c = \tfrac{1}{2} + \sqrt{\tfrac{1}{4} - \tfrac{c-a}{v}}.$$

The *monopolist* chooses the network size n to maximize

$$\pi = n(a + vn(1 - n) - c) \text{ s.t. } n \leq 1.$$

As profit is a cubic function of n, the first derivative is a quadratic function, meaning that the first-order condition admits two roots. We have indeed

$$\frac{\partial \pi}{\partial n} = a - c + 2vn - 3vn^2 = 0 \Leftrightarrow n = \tfrac{1}{3} \pm \sqrt{\tfrac{1}{9} - \tfrac{c-a}{3v}}.$$

Using the second-order condition, we easily check that the largest root corresponds to a maximum (and the lowest root to a minimum). We therefore conclude that

$$n^m = \tfrac{1}{3} + \sqrt{\tfrac{1}{9} - \tfrac{c-a}{3v}},$$

and we check that $n^m \leq 1 \Leftrightarrow c \geq a - v$. So, for $c \geq a - v$, we have an interior solution and the optimal price is computed as

$$p^m = \tfrac{1}{9}\left[3(2a + c) + v + \sqrt{v(3(a - c) + v)}\right] > c \text{ for } a - v \leq c < a + v/4.$$

Otherwise (i.e., $c < a - v$), the market is fully covered, $n^m = 1$ and $p^m = a > c$.

Different stand-alone benefits For the interest of the analysis, consider the case of *weak network effects*: $v < a$. In that case, the unique demand level is given by $n = (a - p)/(a - v)$. The inverse demand is obtained by inverting the latter expression: $p = a - (a - v)n$. We also assume that $c < a$ to ensure the existence of the market. Under perfect competition, $p = c$ and

$$n^c = \frac{a - c}{a - v} \text{ if } v < c < a, \text{ and } n^c = 1 \text{ otherwise.}$$

As for the monopolist, the maximization programme can be written as

$$\max_n \pi = n(a - (a - v)n - c) \text{ s.t. } n \leq 1.$$

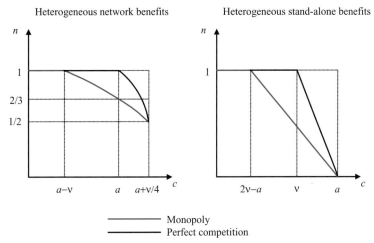

Figure 20.4 Network provision under monopoly and perfect competition

There is an interior solution as long as the solution to the first-order condition $n = (a - c)/2(a - v)$ satisfies the constraint; this is so if and only if $c \geq 2v - a$. We can thus summarize the monopolist's optimal behaviour as follows:

$$\begin{cases} \text{for } 2v - a \leq c < a: n^m = \frac{a-c}{2(a-v)}, \quad p^m = c + \frac{a-c}{2}, \\ \text{for } 0 \leq c \leq 2v - a: n^m = 1, \qquad\quad p^m = v. \end{cases}$$

A quick comparison of the perfect competition and monopoly solutions reveals that the following result obtains under the two utility specifications.

> **Lesson 20.4** **A monopolist (who cannot resort to price discrimination) supports a smaller network and charges a higher price than perfectly competitive firms.**

As depicted in Figure 20.4, when the marginal cost is sufficiently low, perfect competition and monopoly lead both to full market coverage. However, we can check that prices remain higher in the monopoly market structure. Hence, the presence of network effects does not challenge the usual conclusion that monopoly reduces welfare with respect to perfect competition. This is so despite the fact that, contrary to competitive firms, the monopolist has the ability to 'internalize' network effects. The monopolist recognizes indeed that a decrease in price improves consumers' expectations about the network size and, therefore, further increases demand.

Let us now derive the socially optimal provision of the network good. Our measure of welfare is the sum of the consumer surplus and of the suppliers' profits at the (Pareto-dominant) fulfilled expectations equilibrium; that is

$$W(n) = \int_{1-n}^{1} (U(\theta, n) - p(n, n)) \, d\theta + n(p(n, n) - c) = \int_{1-n}^{1} U(\theta, n) \, d\theta - nc.$$

The following table develops the latter expression for the two utility functions we have analysed above.

$$U(\theta, n) = \begin{cases} a + \theta vn \\ \theta a + vn \end{cases} \rightarrow W(n) = \begin{cases} n(a + vn - c) - \frac{n^2}{2} vn, \\ n(a + vn - c) - \frac{n^2}{2} a. \end{cases}$$

It is easily checked that in both cases, $W(n)$ increases with n for all $n \in [0, 1]$. Therefore, we can conclude that social welfare is maximized when all consumers join the network ($n = 1$).

Now, comparing our previous results with the social optimum, we observe the following.

Lesson 20.5   **There is a tendency towards underprovision of the network good by the monopolist, and even by perfectly competitive firms.**

We can therefore say that network effects give rise to network externalities (in the sense that network participation is insufficient at equilibrium, meaning that there are unexploited gains from trade). The source of the market failure is the following: when they adopt a good exhibiting network effects, consumers take only into account their private benefits; they fail, however, to internalize that other consumers are also made better off by their decision to 'join the network'. Moreover, when the production cost of the network good is large enough, neither a monopolist nor competitive firms manage to internalize these external effects. The resulting equilibrium network size is then smaller than social efficiency would require.

The latter explanation is relatively uncontroversial in the case of direct network effects. However, there has been a debate among researchers over whether indirect network effects also give rise to network externalities. Under some circumstances indirect network effects do indeed give rise to network externalities.[13] Referring to system markets combining hardware and software, the critical requirements are three-fold: (i) increasing returns to scale in the production of software, (ii) free entry into software, and (iii) consumer preferences for software variety. The argument goes as follows. The marginal adopter does not take into account the benefits that accrue to inframarginal adopters from the response of the software industry to an increase in hardware sales. Under increasing returns to scale and free entry into the production of differentiated software, the response to an increase in hardware sales is an increase in software variety and inframarginal consumers benefit from the latter increase.

20.3   Markets for several network goods

We now turn to situations where several competing network goods are available and consumers have to choose which good to adopt. This choice problem is relevant if firms have made products incompatible. Consumers can then try to coordinate their actions to make their choices compatible. In Subsection 20.3.1, we postulate that goods are incompatible, which implies that network effects are specific to each good (that is, the benefits of network effects only accrue to consumers purchasing the same good). For simplicity, we restrict the attention to two incompatible goods and we assume that both goods are supplied competitively (there is a large number of firms producing each good).

In Subsection 20.3.2, we turn to the supply side of the market. We address the question whether firms have an incentive to provide some degree of compatibility between products. Hence, the compatibility decision of firms can be seen as a substitute for coordination efforts among consumers.

20.3.1 Demand for incompatible network goods

The objective of this subsection is to highlight the *coordination problems* that could arise when consumers have to choose among incompatible network goods. First, we analyse a very simple model in which consumers arrive in the market sequentially; that is, in each period, a new consumer must choose between the two network goods. We show how network effects translate into a self-reinforcing process that leads to the eventual dominance of one good at the expense of the other. Second, we study another stylized model in which two users have to decide whether to keep an 'old' good or to replace it by a 'new' one. We show that the market mechanism might fail, leading either to *excess inertia* (users do not adopt the new good although they would be better off if they did so) or to *excess momentum* (users adopt the new good although they would be better off if they stuck to the old one). We also argue that such market failures are more likely when users have only incomplete information about the other users' preferences for the available technologies.

Sequential choices: self-reinforcement and lock-in

We develop a simple model to highlight the importance of historical events in the competition between incompatible network goods.[14] There are two goods exhibiting network effects, A and B.[h] Consumers differ in their valuations of the stand-alone benefits of these goods. In particular, we assume that there are two types of consumers: the 'A fans' derive larger stand-alone benefits from good A than from good B, and conversely for the 'B fans'. Adapting expression (20.9), we define the consumers' utility at some date t as in Table 20.1, where n_A^t and n_B^t are the respective numbers of consumers who have adopted good A and B up to date t, $v \geq 0$ measures the importance of network effects, $\theta_A > \theta_B$ and $\mu_B > \mu_A$ (in order to translate the idea that some consumers are A fans and others are B fans). It is assumed that consumers are myopic: they base their choice on the current network sizes, without forming expectations about future network sizes.

Table 20.1. *Consumers' utility*

	Good A	Good B
A fans	$\theta_A + vn_A^t$	$\theta_B + vn_B^t$
B fans	$\mu_A + vn_A^t$	$\mu_B + vn_B^t$

---

[h] Both goods are competitively supplied; prices are thus equal to marginal costs and, for simplicity, we assume that they are the same.

Consumers are supposed to arrive in the market sequentially. That is, in each period of time, one consumer must decide whether to adopt good A or B. We assume that which type of consumer gets to choose is random: with probability $1/2$ it is an A fan, with probability $1/2$ it is a B fan. This assumption is intended to represent random events that can occur when consumers are deciding which good to adopt. We are interested in the sequence $\{\delta^t\}$, where $\delta^t \equiv n_A^t - n_B^t$ is the difference in installed base (i.e., the current number of adopters) between goods A and B after t consumers have chosen (i.e., after t periods).

Absent network effects ($v = 0$), this is just like flipping a coin. In particular, by the law of large numbers, δ^t tends to 0 as t tends to infinity. In that case, the model is like the classic model of economics: it is ahistorical. Equilibrium is purely driven by the long-run forces of supply and demand; historical events may have a transitory effect but long-run forces will eventually bring the economy back to its equilibrium state.[i]

The presence of network effects ($v > 0$) interestingly challenges the previous result. Consider the adoption decision of the $(t + 1)$th consumer. If the consumer is an A fan, she prefers to adopt her preferred good (A) if and only if

$$\theta_A + vn_A^t \geq \theta_B + vn_B^t \Leftrightarrow \delta^t \geq \Delta_A \equiv -(\theta_A - \theta_B)/v.$$

She prefers to adopt good B otherwise. Similarly, if the consumer is a B fan, she prefers to adopt her preferred good (B) if and only if

$$\mu_B + vn_B^t \geq \mu_A + vn_A^t \Leftrightarrow \delta^t \leq \Delta_B \equiv (\mu_B - \mu_A)/v.$$

She prefers to adopt good A otherwise. By definition, $\Delta_B > 0 > \Delta_A$.

We can define three regions: (1) in region I, $\delta^t < \Delta_A$ and all consumers adopt good A; (2) in region II, $\Delta_A \leq \delta^t \leq \Delta_B$ and consumers of both types adopt their preferred good; and (3) in region III, $\delta^t > \Delta_B$ and all consumers adopt good B. The situation is depicted in Figure 20.5 where the sequence $\{\delta^t\}$ (on the vertical axis) is plotted against time (on the horizontal axis). The dynamic process starts in region II ($\Delta_A < \delta_0 = 0 < \Delta_B$). For a while, each arriving consumer chooses his or her preferred good. This is so as long as the difference δ_t stays within the band $[\Delta_A, \Delta_B]$. However, it can be shown that with probability 1, the sequence will eventually cross one or the other barrier. The process will then either be in region I or in region III where, respectively, technology A or B is unanimously adopted. At that stage, the process becomes *self-reinforcing* as every arriving consumer chooses the leading good, which in turn increases the lead of this good. Hence, the barriers Δ_A and Δ_B can be called *absorbing barriers*: once the sequence $\{\delta^t\}$ passes one of these barriers, the industry is *locked-in* to one of the goods (there is no way to go back to region II and market dominance prevails).

Despite its simplicity, this model allows us to derive a number of instructive implications. First, the model predicts that *market dominance is the long-run outcome* of competition between incompatible network goods. Second, as the evolution of the sequence $\{\delta^t\}$ in region II is random, *the long-run is determined by small historical events* and *the identity of the long-run*

---

[i] In mathematical terms, the sequence $\{\delta_t\}$ is an *ergodic* system: δ_{t+k} does not depend on δ_t if k is large enough (historical events may have an effect, but that effect vanishes as time goes by).

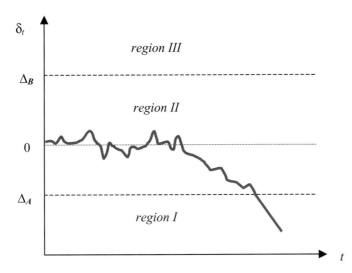

Figure 20.5 Technology adoption with network effects

winner cannot be predicted.[j] Third, *installed base matters* in this kind of competition. As we will show in the next chapter, installed base is a key strategic variable in imperfectly competitive network markets. Finally, *the market process might be inefficient*: the good preferred by the majority might not be the long-run winner, which depends on the preferences of the early movers. We therefore conclude:

Lesson 20.6   **The competition between incompatible network goods is likely to lead, in the long run, to market dominance by a single good. The dominant good cannot be predicted beforehand (it will depend on small historical events) and might not be the best available option.**

Excess inertia, excess momentum and bandwagons

To help us understand the dynamics of technology adoption in the presence of network effects, the previous model was highly simplified. In particular, it assumed that consumers were acting in a very mechanical way. Here, we reverse our focus: we simplify the dynamics but we assume that consumers are strategic, in the sense that they take other consumers' decisions into account when making their own adoption decision. Our goal is to highlight the coordination problems that network effects raise on the demand side of the market.

To keep things tractable, we consider two users who have to decide whether to keep an 'old' network good (indexed by A) or to replace it by a 'new' good (indexed by B). We study two settings in turn. In the first setting, each user knows the preferences of the other user about the two goods (complete information); in the second setting, each user knows only her own preferences (incomplete information).

[j] In mathematical terms, the first property means that the system is *non-ergodic*. As for the second property, the process is said to be *path dependent*.

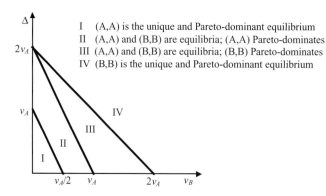

I   (A,A) is the unique and Pareto-dominant equilibrium
II   (A,A) and (B,B) are equilibria; (A,A) Pareto-dominates
III   (A,A) and (B,B) are equilibria; (B,B) Pareto-dominates
IV   (B,B) is the unique and Pareto-dominant equilibrium

Figure 20.6 Potential coordination failures in the adoption of incompatible network goods

A model with complete information For simplicity, let us assume that the two users have the same utility functions for the network goods. In particular, let $U_A = a_A + v_A n_A$ and $U_B = a_B + v_B n_B$ denote the utility a user obtains when, respectively, she keeps the old good and n_A users do so, or she adopts the new good and n_B users do so. We assume that $v_A, v_B > 0$ to capture the idea that both goods exhibit network effects. We further assume that because of technological progress, the new good is supposed to offer larger stand-alone benefits than the old one: $a_B > a_A$; we write good B's advantage as $\Delta \equiv a_B - a_A > 0$.

The two users have to decide simultaneously whether to switch to the new good or not. The game they play can be represented by the matrix of Table 20.2.

Table 20.2. *A typical coordination game*

	Old (A)	New (B)
Old (A)	$a_A + 2v_A, a_A + 2v_A$	$a_A + v_A, a_B + v_B$
New (B)	$a_B + v_B, a_A + v_A$	$a_B + 2v_B, a_B + 2v_B$

Let us first show that there cannot be an equilibrium where the two users adopt different goods. For this situation to be an equilibrium, two conditions should be fulfilled: (i) $a_A + v_A \geq a_B + 2v_B \Leftrightarrow v_A - 2v_B \geq \Delta$, and (ii) $a_B + v_B \geq a_A + 2v_A \Leftrightarrow \Delta \geq 2v_A - v_B$. For these two inequalities to be compatible, we would need $v_A - 2v_B \geq 2v_A - v_B \Leftrightarrow 0 \geq v_A + v_B$, which contradicts our initial assumption that $v_A, v_B > 0$. Therefore, we know that both users will adopt the same good at the (pure-strategy) equilibrium of the game. They both adopt the old good A if and only if $a_A + 2v_A \geq a_B + v_B \Leftrightarrow \Delta \leq 2v_A - v_B$; they both adopt the new good B if and only if $a_B + 2v_B \geq a_A + v_A \Leftrightarrow \Delta \geq v_A - 2v_B$.

As represented in Figure 20.6, there are configurations of parameters (namely areas II and III) for which the two equilibria coexist. This does not come as a surprise as we have understood by now that network effects are prone to generate multiplicity of equilibria. When analysing the market for a single network good in the previous section, we dealt with the multiplicity of equilibria by assuming that agents were able to coordinate on the Pareto-dominating equilibrium. Yet, we did not really discuss this assumption. The fact is that in practice, there is no guarantee that users will indeed manage to coordinate on the Pareto-dominant equilibrium. In the present setting, the Pareto-dominant equilibrium is the one leading to the highest total utility. That is, the new good B should be adopted if and only if $2(a_B + 2v_B) > 2(a_A + 2v_A) \Leftrightarrow \Delta > 2(v_A - v_B)$; otherwise, the old good A should be adopted.

It is now apparent from Figure 20.6 that the locus $\Delta = 2(v_A - v_B)$ separates areas II and III where, as mentioned above, the multiplicity of equilibria is observed. We can thus identify two potential coordination failures. On the one hand, in area III, there could be *excess inertia* if users coordinate on the old good although the new good should be adopted (because $\Delta > 2(v_A - v_B)$). This could occur because, although coordination on the new good would be more profitable for each user, neither of them initiates the switch by fear of not being followed. On the other hand, in area II, there could be *excess momentum* if users coordinate on the new good although the old good should be adopted (because $\Delta < 2(v_A - v_B)$). Here, coordination failure could result from the fact that both users switch by fear of being stranded alone with the old good, although it would be preferable for both of them to stick to the old good.[15]

Lesson 20.7   **Due to the coordination problem among consumers, there may be excess inertia or excess momentum in the adoption of a network good.**

Naturally, the inefficiency associated to excess inertia or excess momentum is an artefact of our assumption of simultaneous choices. In fact, if users can move sequentially, they will inevitably coordinate on the Pareto-dominating good. This is so in our simple model because users have similar preferences and complete information about these preferences. However, as we now show, excess inertia and momentum become a real possibility when each user only has incomplete information about the other user's preferences (which might conflict with hers).

A model with incomplete information Suppose now that users are uncertain as to whether they would be followed if they switched to the new good. What we want to show is that such uncertainty is likely to generate excess inertia even in a setting in which users can move sequentially. The typical situation goes like this. You would enjoy the largest benefits if you and the other user switched to the new good. However, you do not know the other user's payoff and there is thus a chance that you would not be followed in the case you initiated the switch. As you fear the low benefits you would earn if you were the only adopter of the new good, you are not willing to take the risk of moving first. Now, if the other user is just like you, both of you will wait and no one will switch, therefore failing to achieve high benefits.

Excess inertia is likely to be more acute in system markets. Indirect network effects might indeed lead to a *'chicken and egg' phenomenon*: a new hardware product fails to succeed on the market because consumers are reluctant to buy a product with no compatible programs and, at the same time, software providers do not create many programs as long as there is no installed base of hardware. Inertia results from each side's incomplete information about the preferences of the other side. The next lesson summarizes the intuition, Case 20.5 gives an example and the formal model follows. We elaborate further on this theme in Chapter 22.

Lesson 20.8 There is excess inertia when users fail to switch to a new network good although they would be made better off if every user switched. Excess inertia is more likely to happen in markets with indirect rather than direct network effects and where each user only has incomplete rather than full information about the other users' preferences (which might conflict with hers).

Case 20.5 The failure of quadraphonic sound[16]

In the early 1970s, quadraphonic sound was introduced as an alternative to stereo sound for playing audio recordings. In spite of its higher quality, quadraphonic sound failed to become the new industry standard. Although the early takeup of the technology was encouraging, the initial support quickly faded for mainly two reasons: first, because the technology was not mature enough when it was introduced, early adopters were dissatisfied; second, the technology was proposed under several incompatible formats and there was uncertainty about which version would eventually become the industry standard. Similar stories can be told about other once promising technologies that failed to displace existing competing technologies (e.g., digital cassettes, digital videos, and different versions of Teletext).

We now develop a model that formalizes the intuition presented above.[17] Because the argument relies on incomplete information and sequential moves, we need to solve the model for its perfect Bayesian Nash equilibria,[k] which makes the analysis a bit more involved.

We consider a model with two users, two network goods, two periods and incomplete information. Each user ($i = 1, 2$) is identified by her type, θ_i, which measures her valuation of network effects. In particular, a user's utility function can be written now as follows: $u_A(n_A; \theta_i) = a_A + \theta_i v_A n_A$ if user i of type θ_i adopts the old good (along with $(n_A - 1)$ other users), and $u_B(n_B; \theta_i) = a_B + \theta_i v_B n_B$ if she adopts the new good (along with $(n_B - 1)$ other users). As before, $v_A, v_B > 0$. We assume that types θ_1 and θ_2 are a priori (independently) drawn from the uniform distribution on the unit interval. Information is incomplete: each user knows her own type but is ignorant about the other user's type. The game has two periods. Each user has the opportunity to switch at time 1 or time 2 or not at all; reswitching is ruled out. Payoffs accrue at the end of date 2.

We develop a numerical example to highlight the main insights of this model. Let $a_A = 3$, $v_A = 1$, $a_B = 1$, and $v_B = 5$. Utility can be written then as:

$$\begin{cases} u_A(1;\theta_i) = 3 + \theta_i & \text{(only } i \text{ adopts old good)}, \\ u_A(2;\theta_i) = 3 + 2\theta_i & (i \text{ and } j \text{ adopt old good}), \\ u_B(1;\theta_i) = 1 + 5\theta_i & \text{(only } i \text{ adopts new good)}, \\ u_B(2;\theta_i) = 1 + 10\theta_i & (i \text{ and } j \text{ adopt new good}). \end{cases} \tag{20.12}$$

[k] See Appendix A for a definition.

The utility function (20.12) displays a number of interesting properties. First, we observe that $u_B(1; \theta_i) - u_A(2; \theta_i) = -2 + 3\theta_i$ and $u_B(2; \theta_i) - u_A(2; \theta_i) = -2 + 8\theta_i$ are both strictly increasing in θ_i; this property captures the fact that users with higher types (higher values of θ_i) are more eager to switch, both unilaterally and if the other user also switches. Second, we have that $u_B(1; 1) = 6 > u_A(2; 1) = 5$, which means that unilateral switching is worthwhile for users with a very high type (i.e., θ_i close to 1). Third, at the other end of the spectrum, we have that $u_A(1; 0) = 3 > u_B(2; 0) = 1$, which means that the very low types (i.e., θ_i close to 0) would rather remain alone with the old technology than join the other user with the new technology. Finally, $u_B(2; \theta_i) - u_A(1; \theta_i) = -2 + 9\theta_i$ is strictly increasing in θ_i: if a user with a given type prefers a combined switch to the new technology than remaining alone with the old one, then so do all users with higher types.[1]

We define a bandwagon strategy for user $i = 1, 2$ by a pair (α, β) with $0 < \alpha < \beta < 1$ such that: (i) if $\theta_i > \beta$, the user switches at time 1; (ii) if $\alpha < \theta_i \leq \beta$, the user does not switch at time 1, and then switches at time 2 if (and only if) the other user switched at time 1; and (iii) if $\theta_i \leq \alpha$, the user never switches. Then, a symmetric bandwagon equilibrium is defined to be a perfect Bayesian Nash Equilibrium in which each user plays a bandwagon strategy with the same pair (α, β).[18]

To determine the values of the cutoffs α and β, there are three 'plans of actions' to consider: pa_1: switch at time 1; pa_2: do not switch at time 1, switch at time 2 if opponent switched at time 1; pa_3: do not switch at time 1 nor at time 2.[m] Let $Eu(pa_k, \theta_i)$ be the expected utility of user i with type θ_i when it uses the plan of actions pa_k and when its opponent is using a bandwagon strategy (α, β). Table 20.3 is helpful for deriving the expected benefits for the three plans of actions: each cell indicates the outcome of the game (the first entry is user i's choice of good, and the second user j's) according to the plan of actions played by i (in row) and to the type of j (in column).

Table 20.3. *Outcomes when opponent plays a bandwagon strategy*

i's plan	$0 \leq \theta_j \leq \alpha$	$\alpha < \theta_j \leq \beta$	$\beta < \theta_j \leq 1$
pa_1	new (B), old (A)	new (B), new (B)	new (B), new (B)
pa_2	old (A), old (A)	old (A), old (A)	new (B), new (B)
pa_3	old (A), old (A)	old (A), old (A)	old (A), new (B)

[1] These properties of the utility function allow us to make an analogy between this technology choice game and a political 'bandwagon' effect: 'Politicians considering what positions to take on an issue are concerned not only with how strongly they feel about it, but perhaps also with how likely it is that their stand will become the majority view. Intuitively, we might expect vigorous opponents to oppose the issue regardless of their expectations. Staunch supporters might commit themselves without waiting to see whether it seems that theirs will become the popular view. A more "political" middle group may wait awhile to test the political waters, declaring themselves to be "for" the measure if the bandwagon begins to roll and "against" otherwise.' (Farrell and Saloner, 1985, p. 76)

[m] Actually, there is a fourth possible plan of actions, which consists in switching at time 2 if the opponent did not switch at time 1, but it is easy to show that this plan is dominated for all types at the symmetric bandwagon equilibrium.

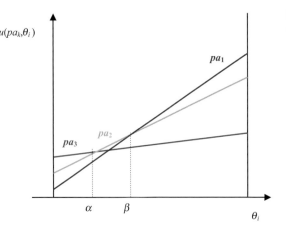

Figure 20.7 Symmetric bandwagon equilibrium

Using the uniform distribution of types, we obtain:

$$\begin{cases} Eu(pa_1, \theta_i) = \alpha u_B (1; \theta_i) + (1 - \alpha) u_B (2; \theta_i), \\ Eu(pa_2, \theta_i) = \beta u_A (2; \theta_i) + (1 - \beta) u_B (2; \theta_i), \\ Eu(pa_3, \theta_i) = \beta u_A (2; \theta_i) + (1 - \beta) u_A (1; \theta_i). \end{cases}$$

According to the bandwagon strategy, users are supposed to play according to pa_1 if their type is above β, to pa_2 if their type is between α and β, and to pa_3 if their type is below α. Therefore, a user i with type $\theta_i = \alpha$ should be indifferent between playing plans pa_2 and pa_3; similarly, a user i with type $\theta_i = \beta$ should be indifferent between playing plans pa_1 and pa_2. The former indifference condition translates as:

$$Eu(pa_2, \alpha) = Eu(pa_3, \alpha) \Leftrightarrow u_B (2; \alpha) = u_A (1; \alpha) \Leftrightarrow$$

$$1 + 10\alpha = 3 + \alpha \Leftrightarrow \alpha = 2/9.$$

The latter indifference condition can be rewritten as:

$$Eu(pa_1, \beta) = Eu(pa_2, \beta) \Leftrightarrow \beta u_A (2; \beta) = \alpha u_B (1, \beta) + (\beta - \alpha) u_B (2, \beta) \Leftrightarrow$$

$$\beta (3 + 2\beta) = \alpha (1 + 5\beta) + (\beta - \alpha)(1 + 10\beta) \Leftrightarrow \beta (2 + 5\alpha - 8\beta) = 0.$$

The latter equation admits two roots. We reject the first root ($\beta = 0$) because it is inferior to α, and we accept the second root:

$$\beta = \frac{2+5\alpha}{8} = \frac{7}{18} > \alpha = \frac{2}{9}.$$

We can now plug the values of the cutoffs into the expected benefit functions for the plans of actions pa_1 to pa_3. One checks that user i's best reply is the bandwagon strategy (α, β): that is (as illustrated in Figure 20.7), plan pa_3 yields the highest expected benefit for values of θ_i lower than α, pa_2 does so for values of θ_i between α and β and pa_1 for values of θ_i larger than β.

The symmetric bandwagon equilibrium entails symmetric excess inertia. There indeed exist pairs of types (θ_1, θ_2) such that for all $i = 1, 2$, (i) $\theta_i < \beta$ (meaning that the users do not switch) and (ii) $u_B (2; \theta_i) > u_A (2; \theta_i)$ (meaning that each user would be better off were the switch made). We check indeed that $u_B (2; \theta_i) > u_A (2; \theta_i) \Leftrightarrow 1 + 10\theta_i > 3 + 20\theta_i \Leftrightarrow \theta_i > 1/4$, and $1/4 < \beta = 7/18$. The intuition is that both users are 'fencesitters, happy to jump on the bandwagon if it gets rolling but insufficiently keen to set it rolling themselves' (Farrell and Saloner, 1985, p. 78). There is also asymmetric excess inertia; that is, situations where the switch is not made (because for some $i = 1, 2, \theta_i < \beta$) even though the sum of benefits is higher when standardization takes place on the new rather than on the old good (i.e., $u_B(2; \theta_1) + u_B(2; \theta_2) > u_A(2; \theta_1) + u_A(2; \theta_2) \Leftrightarrow \theta_1 + \theta_2 > 1/2$).

20.3.2   Oligopoly pricing and standardization

When two (or more) goods exhibiting network effects compete with one another, the issue of compatibility becomes of paramount importance. Actually, the degree of compatibility between the two goods determines the *nature of competition* between the firms sponsoring these goods. At one extreme, when goods are *incompatible*, each makes up its own network. In this case, as shown above, network effects induce a self-reinforcing process: success tends to feed success and failure to beget failure. As a result, large networks naturally become larger, and small networks smaller. Sooner or later, one good completely dominates the market and all other incompatible goods disappear. Hence, at the start of the competition process, firms really *compete for the market*: they compete for the prize of becoming the future monopolist.

The picture dramatically changes when goods are *compatible*. There is now a single network for these goods; that is, network effects are no longer limited to the adopters of a particular good (as users of compatible goods can make use of the other goods' networks and vice versa). It follows that several compatible goods may coexist, meaning that firms now *compete in the market*. As compatibility is a matter of decision, the fundamental question for firms competing in a network market is whether competition 'for the market' (i.e., between incompatible goods) will be more or less profitable than competition 'within the market' (i.e., between compatible goods). Firms can make their goods compatible through *standardization*.

In this section, we introduce a general model of competition between incompatible networks and, through comparative static exercises, we analyse how changes in compatibility affect equilibrium profits.[19] In the next chapter, we will exploit this model (referred to hereafter as the 'Katz–Shapiro model') to highlight several aspects of strategic decisions regarding compatibility and network expansion. In particular, we will analyse under which circumstances standardization is observed as an equilibrium phenomenon.

Imperfect competition with incompatible networks

The demand side of the market is modelled as in Section 20.2.1. In particular, there is a continuum of new consumers (of mass one) who are identified by a taste parameter, θ, which can take any value between 0 and 1. This parameter measures the consumer's valuation for the stand-alone benefits of a network good. As for the network benefits, we assume that all consumers value them in the same way. We formulate thus the consumer's utility as in expression (20.9): $U(\theta) = \theta a + vn^e$, with $a, v > 0$. To simplify the exposition we set $a = 1$, and following the analysis of Section 20.2.2, we assume that $v < 1/2$ to avoid full market coverage and tipping effects.

The main difference with the framework of Section 20.2.1 comes from the fact that there are now two available network goods (indexed by $i = A, B$). As discussed above, the degree of compatibility between the two goods determines the magnitude of the network effects consumers can enjoy when they adopt one or the other good: if goods are incompatible, each makes up its own network, whereas if they are perfectly compatible, there is a single 'unified' network for the two goods. In order to allow for any situation between those two extremes, we let $\gamma \in [0, 1]$ denote the level of compatibility between the two goods. If the expected size of the network of goods i and j are respectively equal to n_i^e and n_j^e, then the *actual network benefit* for a consumer adopting good i is equal to $v(n_i^e + \gamma n_j^e)$. That is, the consumer enjoys 'full' network effects from all consumers belonging to the same network as her, and also a fraction γ of the 'full' network effects from consumers belonging to the other network. This latter fraction reflects the fact that good j is only partially compatible with good i; therefore, as long as γ lies strictly between 0 and 1, the utility of an adopter of good i increases when network j expands, but to a lesser extent than if network i was expanding.[20] Case 20.6 illustrates the notion of partial compatibility.

Case 20.6 Compatibility, incompatibility and partial compatibility in telephony

Consider communication networks and suppose there are two networks A and B. These networks are compatible if a user subscribed to network A can make calls to users in network B (that is, an off-net call) at the same price as calls within the network (that is, an on-net call). Communication networks are incompatible if calls can only be made within a network.

Traditional fixed telephony typically has compatible networks. An example of an incompatible network used to be Skype. Skype is a software program that allows users to make telephone calls over the Internet. When this service was launched, users of Skype could only make calls within their community. Quickly after its launch, the program also allowed its users to place calls to landlines or cell phones. Compatibility became only partial, though, as users can call within the community free of charge but outside the community for a fee. There are many examples which have the flavour of partial compatibility. Partial compatibility means that an off-net call gives lower utility than an on-net call. This is for instance typically the case for mobile telephony in Europe, where an on-net call is cheaper than an off-net call. (Such pricing is referred to as termination-based price discrimination. We consider the regulation of termination rates in another case in Chapter 22.)

Regarding the supply side of the market, we assume that each good is produced by a separate firm (which we also index by $i = A, B$). The two firms compete for the new consumers. From past competition, each firm also already has an *installed base* of customers, noted $\beta_i \geq 0$. We assume that the installed bases are locked in previously signed contracts, whose terms cannot be changed by the firms. Letting q_i^e denote the number of new customers that a customer expects firm i to have, we can thus express the expected size of the network of good i by $n_i^e = q_i^e + \beta_i$.

We can now state that a new customer of type $\theta \in [0, 1]$ obtains a net surplus from adopting the good of firm i at price p_i equal to

$$U_i(\theta) = \theta + g_i - p_i,$$

where g_i measures the relevant expected network benefit from good i (which can also be seen as good i's 'expected quality') and is given by

$$g_i = v \left[(\beta_i + q_i^e) + \gamma \left(\beta_j + q_j^e \right) \right]. \tag{20.13}$$

Firms compete *à la Cournot* over new customers: they choose their capacities for market expansion simultaneously. Given these capacities, prices adjust at levels such that (i) consumers are indifferent between the goods offered by the two firms, and (ii) demand is equal to supply. Formally speaking, we analyse subgame perfect Nash equilibria in which consumers observe capacities before making actual consumption decisions. Since consumers have to make their choice given the choices of all other consumers in a Nash equilibrium, each consumer's beliefs about the behaviour of other consumers are confirmed.

A priori unattached customers view the two goods as perfect substitutes. Thus, if both of them attract new customers, the 'quality-adjusted prices' are the same:

$$p_A - g_A = p_B - g_B = \hat{p}. \tag{20.14}$$

The marginal customer who is indifferent between using either technology and not using any has valuation $\theta_0 + g_A - p_A = \theta_0 + g_B - p_B = 0 \Leftrightarrow \theta_0 = \hat{p}$. From the uniform distribution assumption, we obtain that the expected total number of consumers $(q_A^e + q_B^e)$ is equal to the mass of consumers with a larger valuation than θ_0 (i.e., $1 - \theta_0$). As we did in the previous sections, we focus on fulfilled-expectations equilibria, i.e., $q_A = q_A^e$ and $q_B = q_B^e$. We can therefore express the demand for technologies as:

$$q_A + q_B = 1 - \hat{p}. \tag{20.15}$$

Together, Equations (20.13), (20.14) and (20.15) determine the equilibrium prices (p_A, p_B) as functions of the capacities (q_A, q_B): for $i \neq j$,

$$\begin{aligned} p_i &= 1 - (q_i + q_j) + g_i \\ &= 1 + v(\beta_i + \gamma \beta_j) - (1 - v)q_i - (1 - \gamma v)q_j. \end{aligned} \tag{20.16}$$

Last, we will assume that firm i incurs a cost c_i per unit of good produced. Given that the profit associated with the installed base is constant, firm i chooses its capacity q_i so as to maximize its profit on new customers:

$$\pi_i = (p_i - c_i)q_i = \left[1 + v \left(\beta_i + \gamma \beta_j \right) - (1 - v)q_i - (1 - \gamma v)q_j - c_i \right] q_i.$$

Solving for the system of first-order conditions for profit maximization, one finds the following equilibrium quantities and profits: for $i \neq j = A, B$,

$$q_i^* = \frac{2(1-v)\left[1 - c_i + v\left(\beta_i + \gamma\beta_j\right)\right] - (1 - \gamma v)\left[1 - c_j + v\left(\beta_j + \gamma\beta_i\right)\right]}{4(1-v)^2 - (1-\gamma v)^2}, \tag{20.17}$$

$$\pi_i^* = (1 - v) \left(q_i^* \right)^2. \tag{20.18}$$

It is interesting to note that, other things being equal, a better compatibility between the goods of the firms has a *demand expansion effect*. As the parameter γ increases, so does total equilibrium demand:

$$q_A^* + q_B^* = \frac{2 - c_A - c_B + v(1+\gamma)(\beta_A + \beta_B)}{2(1-v)+(1-\gamma v)} \quad \text{and}$$

$$\frac{d(q_A^* + q_B^*)}{d\gamma} = \frac{2 - c_A - c_B + (\beta_A + \beta_B)(3-v)}{[2(1-v)+(1-\gamma v)]^2}v > 0.$$

It follows that consumers are made better off when compatibility increases. Indeed, consumer surplus is easily computed as

$$CS = \tfrac{1}{2}\left(q_A^* + q_B^*\right)^2. \tag{20.19}$$

Lesson 20.9   In a market with network effects and two competing networks, enhanced compatibility leads to a market expansion effect, resulting in a larger consumer surplus.

On the other hand, enhanced compatibility also entails a *quality differentiation effect*. Although new customers *a priori* view the two goods as perfect substitutes, the firm with the lowest production cost and/or the largest installed base will benefit from a better perceived relative quality, but this advantage decreases as compatibility is improved. To see this, first compute the difference between the equilibrium capacities of firms A and B:

$$q_A^* - q_B^* = \frac{c_B - c_A + v(1-\gamma)(\beta_A - \beta_B)}{2(1-v)-(1-\gamma v)}.$$

Suppose next that both firms have the same installed base, $\beta_A = \beta_B$, but that firm A has a cost advantage, $c_A < c_B$. In that case,

$$q_A^* - q_B^* = \frac{c_B - c_A}{2(1-v)-(1-\gamma v)} > 0 \quad \text{and}$$

$$\frac{d(q_A^* - q_B^*)}{d\gamma} = \frac{v(c_A - c_B)}{[2(1-v)+(1-\gamma v)]^2} < 0.$$

Consider instead that both firms have the same cost, $c_A = c_B$, but that firm A has an advantage in terms of installed base, $\beta_A > \beta_B$. Now, we have that

$$q_A^* - q_B^* = \frac{v(1-\gamma)(\beta_A - \beta_B)}{2(1-v)-(1-\gamma v)} > 0 \quad \text{and}$$

$$\frac{d(q_A^* - q_B^*)}{d\gamma} = \frac{v(1-v)(\beta_B - \beta_A)}{[2(1-v)+(1-\gamma v)]^2} < 0.$$

The following lesson summarizes our findings and the following case illustrates them.

Lesson 20.10   Enhanced compatibility reduces quality differentiation. Thus enhanced compatibility is less attractive for a firm that is more efficient or enjoys a larger installed base.

Case 20.7 Trying to build a wall to protect the bricks[21]

Chances are high that when you were a kid (or even later?), you played with Basic LEGO Bricks, i.e., the LEGO Group's standard toy building bricks that can be easily and endlessly assembled thanks to their eight bosses on the upper surface. Toy bricks can be seen as a network good: the more compatible bricks you and your friends have, the larger your building possibilities. When it was invented in the 1950s, the brick was awarded patent protection as it provided a technical solution for a technical problem and simultaneously, as it had a certain design. The last major patents covering LEGO's building blocks expired in 1978. Since then, the LEGO Group has zealously guarded its trademarks and other intellectual property (IP) rights (see Part VII for more on patents and IP rights). For instance, the Group has filed dozens of lawsuits against competitors such as Mega Bloks or Best-Lock. LEGO presented these efforts as a way to maintain a quality product. In the opinion of the competitors, LEGO was rather using IP law unfairly to extend its dominant position on the market. Clearly, what LEGO attempted was to prevent competitors from selling blocks that are compatible with the Basic LEGO Bricks. Indeed, being the incumbent on the market, LEGO enjoyed a large installed base and had a lot to lose if it had to share this installed base with its smaller competitors. However, in November 2005, LEGO failed in its attempt to enforce its trademark for the design of its building blocks in the Canadian Supreme Court, which commented its decision in the following explicit way: 'The monopoly on the bricks is over, and Mega Bloks and Lego bricks may be interchangeable in the bins of the playrooms of the nation. Dragons, castles and knights may be designed with them, without any distinction.'

Review questions

1. Define direct and indirect network effects, and illustrate with examples.

2. Explain why there often exist multiple consumer equilibria for a given price of the network industry.

3. Explain why there is a tendency towards underprovision of a network good by a monopolist, and even by perfectly competitive firms.

4. Explain why the competition between incompatible network goods is likely to lead, in the long run, to market dominance by a single good.

5. Describe what is meant by excess inertia and explain why this situation is more likely to happen in markets with indirect rather than direct network effects and where each user only has incomplete rather than full information about the other users' preferences.

Further reading

Rohlfs (1974) was the first to highlight the possibility of having several equilibrium network sizes corresponding to a single price of the network good. Economides (1996) extends Rohlfs' analysis and provides a comprehensive survey of the adoption and provision of network goods. As for the adoption of incompatible network goods, we have followed the analyses of Arthur (1989), and Farrell and Saloner (1985). Finally, our model of imperfect competition with incompatible network goods is an extension of the seminal article of Katz and Shapiro (1985), as proposed by Crémer, Rey and Tirole (2000).

21 Strategies for network goods

In the previous chapter, we analysed the consumers' adoption decision in the presence of network effects. The emphasis was on expectations, on coordination problems and on reinforcing mechanisms. We also studied the provision of network goods in various contexts and showed how prices and capacities are adjusted in the presence of network effects.

In this chapter, we want to explore further the decision making on the supply side of network markets. As a matter of fact, the particular features of demand resulting from network effects drive firms to make additional strategic choices and to develop specific strategic instruments. We start in Section 21.1 by examining firms' choices with respect to compatibility. As the competition between incompatible network goods is likely to lead to a 'winner-take-all' situation, firms have first to choose how to compete: choosing compatibility means competing *in* the market, while choosing incompatibility means competing *for* the market. We examine under which conditions one or the other situation is likely to emerge as an equilibrium.

When firms choose to compete for the market, they engage in what is called a 'standards war'. In Section 21.2, we describe and analyse a number of strategic instruments that firms can resort to in order to win such a standards war: building an installed base for preemption, choosing between backward compatibility and performance, and managing consumers' expectations in one's favour.

Finally, in Section 21.3, we discuss whether public interventions are able to correct, or at least alleviate, the market failures that may occur both on the demand and supply sides of network markets. We distinguish between *ex ante* interventions, by which the public authorities take an active part in the competition process among network goods, and *ex post* interventions, by which the public authorities do not try to influence the competition process, but aim at safeguarding it by controlling firms' conducts. We explain why both types of interventions are fraught with major difficulties.

21.1 Choosing how to compete

In this section, we analyse firms' choices with respect to compatibility. In the simple settings we consider, compatibility can only be achieved through standardization, i.e., when firms decide to adhere to a common standard and produce the same good. We first introduce a typology of the potential equilibria resulting from the firms' compatibility decisions. We then use the Katz–Shapiro model of the previous chapter to give a more precise characterization of the equilibrium outcomes under different scenarios.

A simple analysis of standardization

Suppose there are two firms (or two coalitions of firms, noted 1 and 2) that have to choose between two possible versions of a network good (noted A and B).[22] Because the two versions are assumed to be incompatible, compatibility can only be achieved through standardization, i.e., when the two firms decide to produce the same version of the good. The reduced-form payoffs from the adoption of either good are summarized in the matrix of Table 21.1:

Table 21.1. *A simple standardization game*

	A	B
A	π_1^{AA}, π_2^{AA}	π_1^{AB}, π_2^{AB}
B	π_1^{BA}, π_2^{BA}	π_1^{BB}, π_2^{BB}

The form of competition will depend on the firms' compatibility strategies. In this simple framework with two firms, there are four combinations of such strategies.

1. The two firms agree to choose one particular version of the good: we call this situation *straightforward standardization*. For instance, there is straightforward standardization on version A if (A, A) is the only Nash equilibrium of the game (i.e., if $\pi_1^{AA} > \pi_1^{BA}$, $\pi_2^{AA} > \pi_2^{AB}$, and either $\pi_1^{AB} > \pi_1^{BB}$ or $\pi_2^{BA} > \pi_2^{BB}$).

2. Firms still agree that standardization is the best option, but they disagree about what the standard should be, a situation usually referred to as the *Battle of the Sexes* (for reasons that will become clear below). Here, both (A, A) and (B, B) are Nash equilibria (i.e., $\pi_1^{AA} > \pi_1^{BA}$, $\pi_2^{AA} > \pi_2^{AB}$, $\pi_1^{BB} > \pi_1^{AB}$ and $\pi_2^{BB} > \pi_2^{BA}$), but firms rank the two equilibria differently (for instance, $\pi_1^{AA} > \pi_1^{BB}$ and $\pi_2^{BB} > \pi_2^{AA}$).

3. There is a clear competition for the market: both firms prefer to compete to become the *de facto* standard, resulting in a *standards war*. For instance, if firm 1 wants to impose version A while firm 2 wants to impose version B, then (A, B) is the only Nash equilibrium of the game (this is so if $\pi_1^{AB} > \pi_1^{BB}$, $\pi_2^{AB} > \pi_2^{AA}$, and either $\pi_1^{AA} > \pi_1^{BA}$ or $\pi_2^{BB} > \pi_2^{BA}$).

4. Firms have contrasting strategies: one firm prefers incompatibility while the other, whom Besen and Farrell (1994) call the *Pesky Little Brother*, wishes to be compatible with the rival's good. In this situation, there is no Nash equilibrium in pure-strategies (this is so, for instance, if $\pi_1^{AA} > \pi_1^{BA}$, $\pi_1^{BB} > \pi_1^{AB}$, $\pi_2^{AB} > \pi_2^{AA}$ and $\pi_2^{BA} > \pi_2^{BB}$).

The following two cases illustrate this typology. Case 21.1 shows that the market for High-Definition DVDs exhibits both cooperative standardization and a standards war, as two formats vied for market dominance and each format was jointly sponsored by separate groups of firms. Case 21.2 describes a 'pesky little brother' situation on the Digital Right Management scene.

Case 21.1 Standard battle for high-definition DVDs

At the start of the twenty-first centruy, two rival formats have long been vying to dominate the new generation of DVD: Blu-ray and HD DVD. The two technologies used blue-light lasers that increase disc capacity, allowing one disc to hold hours of HDTV-quality video. The two formats were mostly incompatible (although some hardware firms announced at some point the release of dual-format players). We were thus in the middle of a formidable standards war, akin to the VHS versus Betamax war of the early 1980s (see Case 21.4 below). Each standard was backed by a powerful coalition of firms coming from the hardware and from the content sides of the market. The main hardware firms behind Blu-ray were Sony, Panasonic, Philips, Pioneer, Dell and Apple. Behind HD DVD, one essentially found Toshiba, NEC, Microsoft and Intel. As for content producers, five of the eight major Hollywood studios had decided to support Blu-ray exclusively and only one had taken the same single-format approach with HD DVD. For a long time, each coalition seemed to stand a reasonable chance of winning the standards war. Yet, in February 2008, Toshiba announced that it would stop production of HD DVD players and recorders, thereby ending the standard battle. As reported by the BBC, 'Toshiba said the tipping point came last month when Warner Bros' followed a number of other film studios in deciding to release its movies only in the Blu-ray format.'[23]

Case 21.2 VirginMega wants Apple to open its FairPlay DRM

Digital Right Management (DRM) systems enable the copyright owner of a piece of intellectual property (such as music, video, or text) to specify what someone else can do with it. Typically, DRMs are used to offer downloads without having to worry that the user is freely distributing the file over the Web without any compensation to the copyright holder. For the distribution of digital music, Apple uses a DRM technology called Fairplay. That is, every file bought from the iTunes Store with iTunes is encoded with FairPlay; this prevents users from playing these files on other players than the Apple iPod, which is the number one digital audio player worldwide. Apple keeps Fairplay proprietary and refuses to license it to third-parties. In 2004, Virgin-Mega (the Virgin Group's French online music joint venture with media company Lagardère) claimed that Apple was guilty of anticompetitive behaviour by refusing to license *its* DRM technology. But the complaint was ruled to be short on convincing evidence, according to the French Competition Council. We can see VirginMega's move as a 'pesky little brother's' attempt to gain access (i.e., compatibility) to the large network owned by Apple (the 'big brother'). Indeed, Virgin wanted Apple to license FairPlay so it can incorporate the technology into the tracks it sells, thus making them iPod-compatible. But Apple was not keen to share.

21.1.2   A full analysis of standardization

We now use the Katz–Shapiro model of the previous chapter in order to derive endogenously the payoffs of the previous matrix. This will allow us to characterize more precisely under which circumstances each of the four combinations of strategies may arise as an equilibrium of the compatibility choice game.

The Katz–Shapiro model: a quick reminder

Two firms produce competing network goods. They compete à la Cournot for new consumers. That is, they choose their capacities for market expansion simultaneously. Given these capacities, prices adjust at levels such that (i) consumers are indifferent between the goods offered by the two firms, and (ii) demand is equal to supply. From past competition, each firm may also already have an installed base of locked-in customers, noted $\beta_i \geq 0$. Letting q_i^e denote the number of new customers that a customer expects firm i to have, we can thus express the expected size of the network of firm i by $n_i^e = q_i^e + \beta_i$. We let $\gamma \in [0, 1]$ denote the level of compatibility between the two goods. If the expected size of the network of goods i and j are respectively equal to n_i^e and n_j^e, then the actual network benefit for a consumer adopting the good produced by firm i is equal to $g_i = v(n_i^e + \gamma n_j^e) = v\left[(\beta_i + q_i^e) + \gamma (\beta_j + q_j^e)\right]$, where v measures the importance of network effects for consumers. At equilibrium, we require that consumers' expectations about network sizes be fulfilled.

Assuming that there is a continuum of consumers who differ by their valuation of the stand-alone benefits of the goods, we can derive the inverse demand functions for the two goods as follows (with $i \neq j$):

$$p_i = 1 + v \left(\beta_i + \gamma \beta_j\right) - (1 - v) q_i - (1 - \gamma v) q_j. \tag{21.1}$$

Firm i chooses its capacity q_i so as to maximize its profit on new customers $\pi_i = (p_i - c_i) q_i$, where c_i is the constant cost of producing a unit of good i. Solving for the system of first-order conditions for profit maximization, one finds the following equilibrium quantities and profits:

$$q_i^* = \frac{2(1-v)\left[1-c_i+v\left(\beta_i+\gamma\beta_j\right)\right]-(1-\gamma v)\left[1-c_j+v\left(\beta_j+\gamma\beta_i\right)\right]}{4(1-v)^2-(1-\gamma v)^2}, \tag{21.2}$$

$$\pi_i^* = (1 - v) \left(q_i^*\right)^2. \tag{21.3}$$

Equilibrium quantities exhibit the following two important properties: (i) a better compatibility between the goods of the firms has a *demand expansion effect* ($q_i^* + q_j^*$ increases with γ); (ii) enhanced compatibility also entails a *quality differentiation effect* as the advantage enjoyed by the firm with the lowest production cost and/or the largest installed base decreases as compatibility is improved.

Two extensions

Firms 1 and 2 have to choose between two possible goods, noted A and B. We make the following list of assumptions.

- Firm 1 has a preference for good A, and firm 2 for good B.[a] To translate this preference in the model, we let firm i's marginal cost of production, c_i, be equal to zero when firm i adopts its most-preferred good, and equal to $c > 0$, when it adopts its least-preferred good.

- Compatibility can only be achieved through standardization (i.e., the common adoption of the same good). In the above model, this means that $\gamma = 1$ when both firms choose good A or B, and $\gamma = 0$ when the two firms opt for different goods.

- To ease the computations, we posit that the consumers' valuation of the network effects, v, is equal to $1/4$. Furthermore, to guarantee positive quantities and prices in all situations, we assume that $\beta_i, c \in [0, 1/2)$.

- As for the firms' installed bases, we contrast two interpretations. In the *first scenario*, we introduce some asymmetry between the two firms by assuming that *only firm 1 enjoys the benefits of an existing installed base.* We want to examine how this asymmetry affects the equilibrium decisions about standardization; in particular, we address the trade-off between two contrasting effects of standardization: on the one hand, it expands the market but on the other hand, it makes the firms' products qualitatively equivalent. In the *second scenario*, we consider that *firms can benefit from a common installed base provided that they choose standardization*; if they opt for incompatibility, past users will stick to their old network good and the market for goods A and B will only be made of new users. Here, the interesting trade-off is between compatibility and performance: standardization gives access to an installed base (thereby increasing demand of new users) but raises production costs (as one of the two firms has to produce its less preferred good).

Choosing how to compete

Suppose that only firm 1 enjoys the benefits of an existing installed base: $\beta_1 = \beta > 0$ and $\beta_2 = 0$. Accordingly, we call firm 1 the 'large' firm, and firm 2, the 'small' firm. Under our previous assumptions, we use expressions (21.2) and (21.3) to derive the profit levels for the different cells of Table 21.1.

Consider first the *two cases of standardization*. When both firms adopt the same good (whether A or B), full compatibility entails that network benefits are equal to $g_1 = g_2 = \frac{1}{4}(\beta + q_1 + q_2)$. Hence, the inverse demand function is given by $p_1 = p_2 = \frac{1}{4}(4 + \beta - 3(q_1 + q_2))$. The only difference between the two firms stems from their cost function: the firm adopting its preferred good (call it i) has no unit cost, whereas the other firm (call it j) incurs a cost of c per unit. Their respective profit functions thus can be written as:

$$\pi_i = \tfrac{1}{4}\left(4 + \beta - 3(q_i + q_j)\right) q_i, \quad \text{and} \quad \pi_j = \tfrac{1}{4}\left(4 + \beta - 3(q_i + q_j)\right) q_j - c q_j.$$

From the first-order conditions for profit maximization, we derive the firms' reaction functions:

$$q_i\left(q_j\right) = \tfrac{1}{6}\left(4 + \beta - 3q_j\right) \quad \text{and} \quad q_j\left(q_i\right) = \tfrac{1}{6}\left(4\left(1 - c\right) + \beta - 3q_i\right).$$

[a] It might be the case that the firm has developed this good, or that it already uses complementary products which are compatible with it.

Solving for the previous system of equations, one finds the equilibrium capacities, which can then be used to compute the equilibrium profits:

$$q_i^* = \tfrac{1}{9}(4 + \beta + 4c) \quad \text{and} \quad q_j^* = \tfrac{1}{9}(4 + \beta - 8c)$$

$$\pi_i^* = \tfrac{1}{108}(4 + \beta + 4c)^2 = \pi_1^{AA} = \pi_2^{BB},$$

$$\pi_j^* = \tfrac{1}{108}(4 + \beta - 8c)^2 = \pi_2^{AA} = \pi_1^{BB}.$$

Consider next the *incompatibility situation* in which firm 1 adopts good B and firm 2 good A. Here, firms do not differ through costs: as they both adopt their least-preferred good, they incur the same cost ($c_1 = c_2 = c$). Yet, firms differ through network benefits: because of incompatibility, the consumers of firm 2 do not gain access to the installed base of firm 1: $g_1 = \tfrac{1}{4}(\beta + q_1)$ and $g_2 = \tfrac{1}{4}q_2$. Firms 1 and 2's profits thus can be written respectively as

$$\pi_1 = \tfrac{1}{4}(4 + \beta - 3q_1 - 4q_2)q_1 - cq_1, \quad \text{and} \quad \pi_2 = \tfrac{1}{4}(4 - 3q_2 - 4q_1)q_2 - cq_2.$$

Proceeding as above, we derive the firms' reaction functions, we solve for their intersection, and we compute the equilibrium quantities and profits:

$$q_1(q_2) = \tfrac{1}{6}(4(1 - c) + \beta - 4q_2) \quad \text{and} \quad q_2(q_1) = \tfrac{1}{6}(4(1 - c) - 4q_1),$$

$$q_1^{BA} = \tfrac{1}{10}(4(1 - c) + 3\beta) \quad \text{and} \quad q_2^{BA} = \tfrac{1}{10}(4(1 - c) - 2\beta)$$

$$\pi_1^{BA} = \tfrac{3}{400}(4(1 - c) + 3\beta)^2 \quad \text{and} \quad \pi_2^{BA} = \tfrac{3}{400}(4(1 - c) - 2\beta)^2.$$

As for the other incompatibility situation (where each firm adopts its preferred good), equilibrium profits are easily derived by setting $c = 0$ in the above expressions:

$$\pi_1^{AB} = \tfrac{3}{400}(4 + 3\beta)^2 \quad \text{and} \quad \pi_2^{AB} = \tfrac{3}{400}(4 - 2\beta)^2.$$

The results are collected in the matrix of Table 21.2.

Table 21.2. *Payoffs in standardization game – Scenario 1*

	A		B	
A	$\frac{(4+\beta+4c)^2}{108}$,	$\frac{(4+\beta-8c)^2}{108}$	$\frac{3(4+3\beta)^2}{400}$,	$\frac{3(4-2\beta)^2}{400}$
B	$\frac{3(4(1-c)+3\beta)^2}{400}$,	$\frac{3(4(1-c)-2\beta)^2}{400}$	$\frac{(4+\beta-8c)^2}{108}$,	$\frac{(4+\beta+4c)^2}{108}$

Let us now characterize the Nash equilibria in the standardization game summarized in Table 21.2. Our goal is to associate Nash equilibria to each pair of the two key parameters: c, the cost of adopting the rival's good, and β, the installed base advantage of the large firm. We start by examining the conditions for the *joint adoption of good A* to be a Nash equilibrium:

$$\begin{cases} \text{(C1)} & \pi_1^{AA} \geq \pi_1^{BA} \Leftrightarrow \beta \leq \tfrac{4}{17} + \tfrac{76}{17}c, \\ \text{(C2)} & \pi_2^{AA} \geq \pi_2^{AB} \Leftrightarrow \beta \geq -\tfrac{1}{7} + \tfrac{20}{7}c. \end{cases}$$

Similarly, for the *joint adoption of good B* to be a Nash equilibrium, we need:

$$\begin{cases} \text{(C3)} & \pi_1^{BB} \geq \pi_1^{AB} \Leftrightarrow \beta \leq \tfrac{4}{17} - \tfrac{80}{17}c, \\ \text{(C4)} & \pi_2^{BB} \geq \pi_2^{BA} \Leftrightarrow \beta \geq -\tfrac{1}{7} - \tfrac{19}{7}c. \end{cases}$$

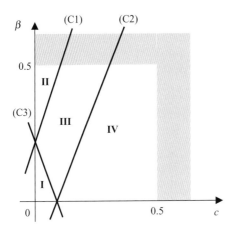

Figure 21.1 Nash equilibria (NE) in the standardization game

Area I   *AA* and *BB*: *Battle of the Sexes.*
Area II   No pure-strategy NE: *Pesky Little Brother.*
Area III *AA* : *Straightforward standardization.*
Area IV   *AB* : *Standards war.*

The conditions for the two other possible equilibria are now easily derived: for situation AB to be an equilibrium, conditions (C2) and (C3) must be simultaneously violated; for situation BA to be an equilibrium, conditions (C1) and (C4) must be simultaneously violated. Regarding the latter situation, a quick look at condition (C4) reveals that it is always met (since both c and β are assumed to be positive). We thus conclude that the situation where both firms adopt their rival's good (BA) cannot be a Nash equilibrium of the standardization game. The intuition is straightforward. When the large firm adopts good B, the small firm has all the reasons to do the same: adopting B (its most-preferred good) reduces its cost and ensures compatibility, which has the twofold positive effect of expanding demand and of giving the small firm a quality advantage over the large firm.

Figure 21.1 depicts conditions (C1)–(C3) in the (c, β) plane. Together, the three conditions delimit four areas, which correspond to the four combinations of strategies identified in our simple analysis of standardization. Let us detail them in turn.

- In *area I*, the two compatibility situations (AA and BB) are Nash equilibria in pure strategies.[b] In this area, the cost of not adopting one's preferred good and the installed base advantage of the large firm are relatively low. As a result, both firms prefer to adopt a common standard to 'going it alone'. The problem is that the firms' preferences diverge about which particular standard to choose. In game-theoretic jargon, the game has the features of the classic *Battle of the Sexes*.[c]

- In *area II*, the cost of adopting the rival's good is still very low but the installed base advantage of the large firm is now much larger. As a result, the small firm prefers compatibility more than ever. However, the large firm prefers incompatibility in

[b] There exists also an equilibrium in mixed strategies.
[c] In this classic coordination game (see Appendix A), a man and a woman are choosing between the ballet and a football game. The main concern of each is to be in the company of the other (regardless of where they go); but he prefers the ballet and she the football game (or vice versa).

order to keep the benefits of its installed base for itself. In this *Pesky Little Brother* situation, a Nash equilibrium in pure strategies fails to exist because the two firms pursue opposite compatibility strategies. (There exists, however, an equilibrium in mixed strategies, which we do not detail here.)

- In *area III*, the latter situation no longer prevails. Here, *AA* is the unique Nash equilibrium: both firms agree to standardize on technology *A* (*straightforward standardization*). The small firm is ready to incur a slightly higher cost (*c* is relatively low in this area) in order to enjoy the benefit of being compatible with the large firm's installed base. As for the large firm, the demand expansion effect dominates the quality differentiation effect as long as technology *A* is the standard (but the opposite prevails if *B* is chosen as the standard). The large firm, therefore, does not mind sharing its installed base with the small firm.

- In *area IV*, the cost of adopting the rival's technology is sufficiently high to convince both firms to compete to establish their preferred technology as the *de facto* standard. In this *standards war*, *AB* is the unique Nash equilibrium.

The previous analysis teaches us the following.

Lesson 21.1   **Pre-market standardization is more likely to emerge as an equilibrium when the parties are relatively symmetric and do not have marked preferences for a particular good. In contrast, a standards war is more likely to emerge as an equilibrium when the parties have marked (and diverging) preferences for a particular good.**

Standardization to overcome collective switching costs

Let us assume now that the installed base is made of consumers of an existing network good. As we discussed in the previous chapter, when users have the possibility of switching from an old network good to a new one, they might refrain from switching even if a collective switch would make everyone better off. This situation of excess inertia is even more likely when the new network good is offered in various incompatible versions. Users of the existing good anticipate that one of these incompatible versions will eventually dominate the market. The problem is that they are unable to predict which version is going to stay and which ones are going to disappear. As a consequence of this uncertainty, existing users prefer to wait and see, and they stick to the old network good. Because of such 'collective switching costs', the market for the new good might never take off, unless the producers agree to standardize. Indeed, if the versions of the new good are compatible with one another, users of the old good will face a lower uncertainty, lower lock-in prospects, and can expect to enjoy larger network effects if they switch to the new good. The market for high-definition DVDs described above in Case 21.1 is a perfect example of this situation: because of the technological uncertainty (and because equipment were still relatively expensive), consumers adopted a wait-and-see approach and the market for high-definition DVDs was very slow to take-off. Case 21.3 provides further evidence that excess inertia may be exarcerbated if the new technology is introduced under several incompatible versions.

Case 21.3 (In)compatibility and excess inertia in the diffusion of PCs and of mobile telephony

Koski (1999) studies the European microcomputer market between 1985 and 1994. During this period, the market for operating system was dominated by two incompatible technologies, Apple and MS-DOS operating systems, which were unable to run each other's software programs. He shows that the diffusion speed of PCs was vitally dependent on the relative order of magnitude of the network size of the two dominating operating systems: diffusion was slower in countries where Apple and MS-DOS had relatively similar market shares. A possible explanation is that the adoption of a potential user depends not only on the absolute number of the users of the technologies, but also on their adoption rates relative to one another; observing relatively similar rates would induce the user to postpone her decision, thereby causing inertia.

Gruber and Verboven (2001) and Koski and Kretchmer (2002) study the diffusion for mobile telephony (respectively for the first and the second generation). They find that standardization (leading to a reduced uncertainty as to the future dominant technology) accelerated diffusion.

In sum, because of the fear of being locked in, it is only if standardization prevails that existing users accept to migrate toward the new network good (thereby providing network benefits to new users). In the above model, we translate this situation by the following assumptions: (i) when both firms choose good A or B (implying that $\gamma = 1$), both firms share an installed base of size β, so that $\beta_1 = \beta_2 = \beta/2$; when the two firms opt for different goods (implying that $\gamma = 0$), they do not benefit from the installed base, so that $\beta_1 = \beta_2 = 0$

We can repeat the previous analysis under these new assumptions. As far as the two cases of standardization are concerned, we easily see that the results of the previous scenario carry over to the present setting (consumers of both firms have indeed access to the same installed base of size β). Consider next situation BA where each firm adopts its least preferred good; in this case, incompatibility prevails ($\gamma = 0$) and firms are symmetric: $c_i = c$, $\beta_i = 0$, and $g_i = \frac{1}{4}q_i$ for $i = 1, 2$. The profit of firm i writes as $\pi_i = \frac{1}{4}(4 - 3q_i - 4q_j)q_i - cq_i$. From the first-order condition for profit maximization, we find firm i's reaction function: $q_i(q_j) = \frac{2}{3}(1 - c - q_j)$. Invoking symmetry, we have that $q_i = q_j$ at equilibrium, which allows us to find:

$$q_1^{BA} = q_2^{BA} = \tfrac{2}{5}(1 - c) \quad \text{and} \quad \pi_1^{BA} = \pi_2^{BA} = \tfrac{3}{25}(1 - c)^2 .$$

Setting $c = 0$ in the previous expressions, we compute the equilibrium profits for case AB (which differs only by the fact that $c_1 = c_2 = 0$):

$$\pi_1^{AB} = \pi_2^{AB} = \tfrac{3}{25}.$$

We collect the results in the matrix of Table 21.3.

Table 21.3. *Payoffs in standardization game – Scenario 2*

	A	B
A	$\frac{(4+\beta+4c)^2}{108}$, $\frac{(4+\beta-8c)^2}{108}$	$\frac{3}{25}$, $\frac{3}{25}$
B	$\frac{3(1-c)^2}{25}$, $\frac{3(1-c)^2}{25}$	$\frac{(4+\beta-8c)^2}{108}$, $\frac{(4+\beta+4c)^2}{108}$

To characterize the Nash equilibria of the standardization game, we first note that

$$\pi_1^{AA} - \pi_1^{BA} = \pi_2^{BB} - \pi_2^{BA} = \frac{(38+5\beta+2c)(2+5\beta+38c)}{2700} > 0.$$

This finding implies that (as in the previous scenario) the incompatibility situation in which each firm adopts the other firm's preferred good cannot be an equilibrium. Because of the symmetry of the model, this also implies that a single condition determines whether the equilibrium involves standardization (AA or BB) or incompatibility (AB). Precisely, standardization prevails if and only if

$$\pi_2^{AA} = \pi_1^{BB} \geq \pi_1^{AB} = \pi_2^{AB} \Leftrightarrow \beta + \tfrac{2}{5} \geq 8c, \tag{21.4}$$

i.e., if taking advantage of the installed base sufficiently compensates for the cost of standardization.

Let us now examine the point of view of the new users. Recalling that the consumer surplus is computed as half the square of total equilibrium quantity, $CS = \tfrac{1}{2}(q_1^* + q_2^*)^2$, we obtain:

$$CS^{AA} = CS^{BB} = \tfrac{2}{81}(4+\beta-2c)^2 \quad \text{and} \quad CS^{AB} = \tfrac{8}{25}.$$

Hence, new users prefer standardization if and only if

$$CS^{AA} = CS^{BB} \geq CS^{AB} \Leftrightarrow \beta + \tfrac{2}{5} \geq 2c. \tag{21.5}$$

Comparing conditions (21.4) and (21.5), it is obvious that when $2c \leq \beta + 2/5 < 8c$, firms and users disagree: firms choose incompatible goods while users would be better off if standardization prevailed. The reason behind this disagreement is that firms and users view differently the trade-off between compatibility and performance: firms do not appropriate all the positive benefits they confer to users when they choose compatible goods, while users do not perceive fully the extra cost c that standardization imposes on one of the firms.

Lesson 21.2   **Consumer and producer interests in standardization may not be aligned because consumers do not perceive the full cost of standardization whereas firms cannot fully appropriate the benefits from standardization.**

21.2   Strategies in standards wars

In network markets, profit-maximizing firms have to factor in network effects in the formation of their strategies: we have indeed seen in the previous chapter how prices and capacities are adjusted in the presence of network effects. Firms also develop specific strategic instruments in network markets. We have just analysed the strategic choice of compatibility as a way to achieve a standard, i.e., the choice between pre-market standardization and a standards war.

In this section, we study strategic instruments that firms may use to increase their chances of winning a standards war. We first introduce a dynamic perspective in our analysis and consider firms' incentives to preempt their rivals by building an early installed base of users. We then analyse entry on network markets, focusing on the trade-off between compatibility and performance: it might be easier to enter the market with a good that is compatible with the existing good because it facilitates users' migration, but such backward compatibility generally decreases the quality of the new good. Finally, recalling that expectations play a critical role in users' adoption decisions, we examine different ways through which firms can manage expectations in their favour.

21.2.1   Building an installed base for preemption

In the previous section, we considered for simplicity that the installed base was given exogenously. In reality, firms have a clear interest in trying to build an installed base before their rivals. Doing so, they can benefit from an early-mover advantage, which, because of the self-reinforcing power of network effects, is likely to lead to a long-lasting domination of the market.

To illustrate this point, we use another extension of the Katz–Shapiro model. Suppose that there are two periods. In each period, there is a continuum of users (of mass one) who are identified by a taste parameter, θ, uniformly distributed between 0 and 1. In period 1, only firm 1 is active on the market, producing network good A; in period 2, firm 2 has the possibility to enter the market with network good B. The marginal costs of production are assumed to be equal to $c \in [0, 1]$ for both firms; the degree of compatibility between the two goods is given by $\gamma \in [0, 1]$. Through its first-period sales, firm 1 can constitute an installed base of users, β_1, who will be locked-in in period 2 when the new generation of users arrives on the market. Our goal is to examine the strategic choice of β_1 by firm 1.

We distinguish two scenarios according to whether or not the first generation of users derives network benefits from the consumption of good A (and of good B if it is compatible) by second-generation users (i.e., whether or not the utility of first-period users is increasing in the size of the second-period sales). We can think that 'intra-generation' network effects are direct (stemming, e.g., from the benefits of communication among users), while 'inter-generation' network effects are indirect. The nature of the latter indirect effects determines which of the two scenarios is the most appropriate. If network effects result from the existence of learning by doing or some word-of-mouth process, the second generation benefits from first-period sales but not the other way round (with learning by doing, second-period users enjoy a version of the good which has been improved through the testing or bug-fixing achieved by first-period users; under word-of-mouth, first-period consumption reveals useful information about the good, which reduces search costs for second-period users). On the other hand, if network effects result from the availability of complementary products (software, content, . . .), one can think that each generation of users benefits from consumption by the other generation, because producers of complementary products base their long-term investment decisions on their expected sales in both periods.

Early users do not benefit from later sales

Proceeding by backward induction, we first look at period 2. If firm 2 enters the market, its equilibrium quantity is found by setting $c_1 = c_2 = c$ and $\beta_2 = 0$ in expression (21.2):

$$q_2^*(\beta_1) = \frac{(1 - 2v + \gamma v)(1 - c) + v(\gamma(2 - v) - 1)\beta_1}{4(1 - v)^2 - (1 - \gamma v)^2}. \tag{21.6}$$

Naturally, firm 2 will only enter the market if $q_2^*(\beta_1) \geq 0$. From the above expression, we see that firm 2 always finds it profitable to enter when the network goods are sufficiently compatible (which implies that firm 2 takes sufficient advantage from firm 1's installed base). Indeed, $\gamma \geq 1/(2 - v)$ implies that $q_2^*(\beta_1) > 0$. Note that the latter condition is harder to meet the stronger the network effects (i.e., the larger the value of v). Otherwise, if $\gamma < 1/(2 - v)$ and goods are relatively incompatible, firm 2 enters as long as firm 1 did not build too large an installed base in period 1:

$$q_2^*(\beta_1) \geq 0 \Leftrightarrow \beta_1 \leq \tfrac{(1-2v+\gamma v)(1-c)}{v(1-\gamma(2-v))}.$$

Given the size of the first-period market, we have that $\beta_1 \leq 1$ and therefore, the latter condition is necessarily met when

$$\tfrac{(1-2v+\gamma v)(1-c)}{v(1-\gamma(2-v))} > 1 \Leftrightarrow \gamma > \tfrac{v(3-2c)-(1-c)}{v(3-c-v)},$$

which is true for $v < (1 - c)/(3 - 2c)$. Collecting the previous results, we observe that $q_2^* < 0$ if the following three conditions are met:

$$\text{(i) } v > \tfrac{1-c}{3-2c}, \quad \text{(ii) } \gamma < \tfrac{v(3-2c)-(1-c)}{v(3-c-v)} \quad \text{and} \quad \text{(iii) } \tfrac{(1-2v+\gamma v)(1-c)}{v(1-\gamma(2-v))} < \beta_1 \leq 1.$$

Stating these results in words, we record the following:

Lesson 21.3 In the market with potentially two competing networks, entry can be deterred if (i) network effects are strong enough, (ii) goods are incompatible enough, and (iii) the incumbent firm built a large enough installed base.

Firm 2's entry can even be *blockaded* for stronger network effects. Recall from Chapter 16 that entry is blockaded when the entrant stays out of the market even though the incumbent firm behaves as if there was no threat of entry. To examine this possibility, let us first derive the demand for good A in period 1. The indifferent user is identified by $\tilde{\theta} = p_{A1} - v\beta_1^e$, where p_{A1} is the price of good A in period 1 and β_1^e is the expected network size. As all users with $\theta > \tilde{\theta}$ decide to consume, we have that the actual network size is given by $\beta_1 = 1 - \tilde{\theta} = 1 - (p_{A1} - v\beta_1^e)$. Imposing fulfilled expectations, we have that $p_{A1} = 1 - (1 - v)\beta_1$. Hence, a myopic firm 1 would choose β_1 to maximize its first-period

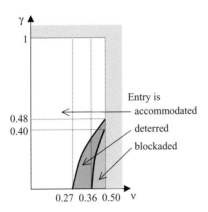

Figure 21.2 Entry deterrence through installed base building ($c = 0.4$)

profit:

$$\beta_1 \in \arg\max_{\beta_1} \left\{ (1 - (1 - v)\beta_1 - c)\beta_1 \right\} \Leftrightarrow \beta_1^m = \frac{1-c}{2(1-v)} \quad \text{and} \quad p_{A1}^m = \frac{1+c}{2}.$$

Substituting β_1^m for β_1 in firm 2's equilibrium quantity (21.6), we find that $q_2\left(\beta_1^m\right) < 0$ if the following two conditions are satisfied

$$v > 0.36 \quad \text{and} \quad \gamma < \frac{7v - 4v^2 - 2}{v(4 - 3v)}.$$

Figure 21.2 depicts the regions in the (v, γ) plane where the incumbent can blockade entry, has the opportunity to deter it, or has to accommodate it.

To complete the analysis, we suppose that network effects are not strong enough for firm 1 to be able to deter firm 2's entry. Say, $v = 1/4$. In period 1 (supposing no discounting) firm 1's problem can be written as

$$\max_{\beta_1} \Pi_1 = \left(1 - \tfrac{3}{4}\beta_1 - c\right)\beta_1 + \tfrac{3}{4}\left(\frac{4(2+\gamma)(1-c) + (6 - 4\gamma + \gamma^2)\beta_1}{(10 - \gamma)(2+\gamma)}\right)^2 \text{ s.t. } \beta_1 \le 1,$$

where the second term of the objective function is firm 1's second period profit, obtained by setting $v = 1/4$ and $c_1 = c_2 = c$ and $\beta_2 = 0$ in expression (20.18). We check that Π_1 is a concave function of β_1 and we compute the optimal installed base and price as:

$$\beta_1^*(\gamma) = \beta_1^m + \tfrac{1}{6}g(\gamma) \quad \text{and} \quad p_{A1}^*(\gamma) = p_{A1}^m - \tfrac{1}{8}g(\gamma),$$

$$\text{with } g(\gamma) \equiv \frac{(18 + 2\gamma + \gamma^2)(6 - 4\gamma + \gamma^2)}{(1+\gamma)(7-\gamma)(13+2\gamma)}(1 - c).$$

It can be checked that $g(\gamma)$ decreases with γ (see Table 21.4 for an illustration).

Table 21.4. *Installed base and penetration pricing*

$v = 0.25, c = 0$	$\beta_1^*(\gamma)$	$p_{A1}^*(\gamma)$
myopic	0.667	0.500
$\gamma = 1$	0.725	0.456
$\gamma = 0.5$	0.767	0.425
$\gamma = 0$	0.864	0.352

Lesson 21.4   The less compatible the two network goods (i.e., the lower γ), the larger the installed base built by the incumbent and the lower the price of the network good in the first period.

The latter results illustrates the tactic of *penetration pricing*, which is commonplace in network markets (and which has the same flavour as the 'bargain-then-rip-off' pricing often observed in the presence of switching costs, as shown in Chapter 7).

Early users benefit from later sales

Suppose now that the utility of first-generation users increases in the size of second-period sales. To keep things simple, assume that good B is incompatible with good A ($\gamma = 0$), and that the strength of (inter and intra-generation) network effects is still set to $\nu = 1/4$. In period 1, user θ decides to purchase good A if and only if $\theta + \frac{1}{4}\left(\beta_1^e + q_1^e\right) - p_{A1} \geq 0$, or

$$\theta \geq \tilde{\theta}_1 \equiv p_{A1} - \tfrac{1}{4}\left(\beta_1^e + q_1^e\right),$$

where, sticking with our previous notation, β_1^e and q_1^e denote the sales that firm 1 is expected to make in, respectively, period 1 and period 2. Actual sales are given by:

$$\beta_1 = 1 - \tilde{\theta}_1 \quad \text{and} \quad q_1 = \tfrac{1}{10}\left(3\beta_1 + 4 - 4c\right),$$

where the latter expression is obtained from (21.2) by setting $\nu = 1/4$, $\beta_2 = 0$, $c_1 = c_2 = c$. Imposing fulfilled expectations, $\beta_1 = \beta_1^e$ and $q_1 = q_1^e$, we combine the previous equations to derive the demand function for good A in period 1: $p_{A1} = \tfrac{1}{40}\left(44 - 27\beta_1 - 4c\right)$.

As in the previous scenario, firm 1 chooses in period 1 its capacity β_1 that maximizes its profit over the two periods (supposing no discounting and taking into account that the second-period capacities, q_1 and q_2, are the Nash-equilibrium levels derived in the second period):

$$\max_{\beta_1} \Pi_1 = \left(\tfrac{1}{40}\left(44 - 27\beta_1 - 4c\right) - c\right)\beta_1 + \tfrac{3}{4}\left(\tfrac{1}{10}\left(3\beta_1 + 4 - 4c\right)\right)^2 \text{ s.t. } \beta_1 \leq 1.$$

It can be checked that the profit function is concave, meaning that the optimal capacity is found by solving the first-order condition:

$$\beta_1 = \tfrac{256}{243}\left(1 - c\right).$$

To guarantee an interior solution (i.e., $\beta_1 < 1$), we assume that $c > 13/256 \simeq 0.05$. With the value of β_1, we can compute the capacities for goods A and B in period 2: $q_1 = \tfrac{58}{81}\left(1 - c\right)$ and $q_2 = \tfrac{46}{243}\left(1 - c\right)$. Finally, we compute firm 1's margins in periods 1 and 2:

$$p_{A1} - c = \tfrac{7}{18}\left(1 - c\right) \quad \text{and} \quad p_{A2} - c = \tfrac{29}{54}\left(1 - c\right). \tag{21.7}$$

As $29/54 > 7/18$, we observe again that firm 1 resorts to penetration pricing ($p_{A1} < p_{A2}$). However, in the present case, this increasing sequence of prices seems less attractive for firm 1. Indeed, firm 1 might prefer to set a lower price in period 2 (by selling a larger quantity) in order to generate larger (expected) network benefits for first-generation users and, thereby, larger profits in period 1. Yet, in the absence of any binding promise on the future price of good A, first-period users recognize firm 1's incentive to increase price in period 2, and thus, they take this opportunistic behaviour into account when they make their purchase decision.

We now examine how firm 1's decisions would change if it could use a credible mechanism to commit itself to a low future price (we describe later two mechanisms that could achieve this objective). With such a mechanism, firm 1 chooses both β_1 and q_1 at the start of period 1. Assuming that firm 2 can use a similar mechanism, we have that firm 2 also chooses q_2 at the start of period 1.[d] The two firms' respective problems can be written thus as:

$$\max_{\beta_1, q_1} \Pi_1 = \left(1 + \tfrac{1}{4}q_1 - \tfrac{3}{4}\beta_1 - c\right)\beta_1 + \left(1 + \tfrac{1}{4}\beta_1 - \tfrac{3}{4}q_1 - q_2 - c\right)q_1,$$

$$\max_{q_2} \Pi_2 = \left(1 - \tfrac{3}{4}q_2 - q_1 - c\right)q_2.$$

The three first-order conditions are

$$\begin{cases} \frac{\partial \Pi_1}{\partial \beta_1} = 0 \Leftrightarrow 3\beta_1 - q_1 = 2\left(1 - c\right), \\ \frac{\partial \Pi_1}{\partial q_1} = 0 \Leftrightarrow -\beta_1 + 3q_1 + 2q_2 = 2\left(1 - c\right), \\ \frac{d\Pi_2}{dq_2} = 0 \Leftrightarrow 2q_1 + 3q_2 = 2\left(1 - c\right). \end{cases}$$

The unique solution to this system is $\beta_1 = q_1 = 1 - c$ and $q_2 = 0$. It follows that firm 1 has the same margin on A in the two periods:

$$p_{A1} - c = p_{A2} - c = \tfrac{1}{2}\left(1 - c\right). \tag{21.8}$$

Let us now gauge the effect of firm 1's ability to commit. First, comparing expressions (21.7) and (21.8), we observe that *when firm 1 can commit, the first period price is higher while the second-period price is lower* (that is, firm 1 sells less in period 1 but more in period 2). Second, *commitment allows firm 1 to deter firm 2's entry* (since $q_2 = 0$ under commitment and $q_2 > 0$ otherwise). Third, computing profits in both cases, we observe that *commitment allows firm 1 to increase its profits*: $\Pi_1^{\text{com}} = (1 - c)^2 > \Pi_1^{\text{no com}} = \frac{193}{243}(1 - c)^2$.

Lesson 21.5 **If the incumbent network can commit to second-period price, it will set a higher first-period price and a lower second-period price. This strategy deters entry more effectively.**

The next question which arises naturally is how to make credible the promise of lowering price in the future. As Case 21.4 illustrates, two commitment mechanisms used in the VCR standards war are to commit to a large production of the second-generation product and

---

[d] If q_2 is chosen in period 2, firm 1 acts as a Stackelberg leader by taking 2's best-response into account. This would give firm 1 an additional advantage, which we want to abstract away here so as to focus on the impact of commitment.

to engage in licensing agreements (these two commitment strategies relate to topics addressed in Chapters 16 and 19, respectively).

Case 21.4 Commitment in the VCR standards war

The historic standards war between the two video cassette recorder (hereafter VCR) formats, Beta and VHS, provides two useful illustrations of strategic moves that played a decisive role in the competition.[24] Note first that VCR formats are subject to (indirect) network effects: as more consumers use a particular format, more movie titles for that format will be available. Although the Beta format (sponsored by Sony) had a first-mover advantage of more than a year and dominated the market for a few years, it eventually lost the standard war to the incompatible VHS format (sponsored by JVC) and exited the consumer market in 1989. The initial lead gained by Sony might be attributed to Sony's strategy of capacity commitment. When the first Beta machine was launched in 1976 (more than one year before the introduction of VHS), Sony started production on a very large scale (the annual potential output clearly exceeded the world market at that time). Though suicidal from a short-run point of view, this strategy might have important long-run benefits as larger production facilities imply a transfer of costs from the future to the present and alter pricing decisions. Sony's motivation was indeed to commit credibly to lower future prices by immediately sinking part of the production costs.

This strategy worked: the Beta format became the dominant technology and the VCR became a mass product. However, Sony's dominant position slowly eroded and in 1980, VHS managed for the first time to have the larger installed base in the US market. The more open attitude of JVC towards other VCR producers might explain this reversal of dominance. Indeed, in contrast to Sony, JVC followed a strategy aimed at forming as large a group of allies as possible, aggressively pursuing licensing agreements. Again, the rationale of such strategy might be questioned from a short-run point of view: what benefit could JVC find in surrendering to its competitors its exclusivity rights on the VHS technology? The answer is the long-term benefit of guaranteeing thereby mass production and lower prices for the technology in the future, exactly what Sony achieved in the past through capacity building.

21.2.2   **Backward compatibility and performance**

As network effects create collective switching costs, entry is typically more difficult on network markets than on traditional markets. In order to overcome this natural entry barrier, firms might be tempted to ease consumers' switching by offering a new product that is compatible with the existing one(s). However, ensuring such 'backward compatibility' often has the following downside: compatibility forces the firm to fix some characteristics of its product and, thereby, restricts its potential for horizontal, and more importantly, vertical differentiation (i.e., quality improvement or technological advancement). There is thus generally a trade-off between backward compatibility and performance. Case 21.5 perfectly illustrates this trade-off with the example of *Drupal*, 'an open source content management platform, which can support

a variety of websites ranging from personal weblogs to large community-driven websites'
(http://drupal.org).

Case 21.5 Making *Drupal* backward compatible or not?

On his blog,[25] Dries Buytaert, lead of the Drupal Project, explains the following. 'When I
first released Drupal, I chose not to preserve backward compatibility, because I was
mainly interested in getting the technology right. Preserving backward compatibility often
requires that you drag historical baggage along, and in interpreted languages like PHP, this
comes at a significant performance cost. So it was decided that we can break people's
code, but not people's data. Our mission was to make Drupal fast, small, clean and on the
bleeding-edge of technology. In the early days I focused, completely and utterly, on the
aesthetics of Drupal's code. I spent days trying to do something better, with fewer lines of
code and more elegant than elsewhere. And with me, many others.

It was the right thing to do. Over the years, we've seen a lot of innovations
happen that would not likely have happened while preserving backward compatibility (the
node system being one of the most prominent examples). Developers always had free
reign to implement their ideas in the best possible way. It is something that Drupal has in
its favor compared to many other content management systems. It's been interesting to see
how Drupal has spread and how it has grown to be more flexible and cover more niches
than many other systems. If anything, this needs to be attributed to the fact that we haven't
cared much about backward compatibility, and our single-mindedness to get the
technology right.

Of course, breaking backward compatibility has its disadvantages. Expensive
upgrade paths and frustrations due to lack of up-to-date modules being the examples that
immediately come to mind. And for many people, this matters a lot.

Unfortunately, there is no right or wrong answer here: there are both advantages
and disadvantages to backward compatibility. As a result, there will always be a tension
between the need for hassle-free upgrades and the desire to have fast, cruft-free code with
clean and flexible APIs. At the end of the day, we can't make everybody happy and it is
very important that you realize that.'

To analyse the exact nature of this trade-off, we use once again our Katz–Shapiro
model. The setting we develop here looks very much like the two-period model we used in
the previous section to examine preemption. We assume that in period 1, only firm 1 is active
on the market, producing network good A at cost $c_1 = c > 0$. Through its first-period sales,
firm 1 constitutes an installed base of users, β_1. This installed base is supposed to be locked-in
in period 2 when the new generation of users arrive on the market and when firm 2 has the
possibility to introduce network good B. The novelty here is that firm 2 can now choose the
degree of compatibility, $\gamma \in [0, 1]$, between the new good B and the existing good A.

As we pointed out above, increasing compatibility allows firm 2 to benefit more from
the network effects generated by the installed base of A-users, but has the adverse effect of
making the goods more substitutable. To add the other adverse effect of backward compatibility
that we just mentioned (i.e., the fact that compatibility decreases performance), we model the

higher performance of good B with respect to good A as a cost advantage for firm 2, but we assume that this cost advantage decreases with the degree of compatibility; to keep the model tractable, we simply assume

$$c_2 = \gamma c.$$

That is, firm 2's cost advantage is the highest when firm 2 enters with an incompatible good ($c_2 = 0 < c_1$ for $\gamma = 0$) and nil when it enters with a fully compatible good ($c_2 = c = c_1$ for $\gamma = 1$).

Using expression (21.1), we can write the price–cost margin for the two firms (recalling that, as firm 2 enters the market, it has no installed base: $\beta_2 = 0$):

$$\begin{cases} p_1 - c_1 = 1 + (v\beta_1 - c) - (q_1 + q_2) + v(q_1 + \gamma q_2), \\ p_2 - c_2 = 1 + \gamma(v\beta_1 - c) - (q_1 + q_2) + v(q_2 + \gamma q_1). \end{cases}$$

It is readily seen that for $\gamma = 1$, $p_1 - c_1 = p_2 - c_2$. That is, when firm 2 enters with a fully compatible product, the two firms are symmetric and will thus equally share the market at the Cournot equilibrium.

For $\gamma < 1$, we see that the key variable is $\Delta \equiv v\beta_1 - c$, which measures the difference between the 'installed-base effect' of full compatibility (in terms of network effects, $v\beta_1$) and the 'performance effect' of full incompatibility (in terms of cost advantage, c). Supposing that the firms choose equal capacities ($q_1 = q_2$) and that $\gamma < 1$, we have that firm 2 has a lower price–cost margin than firm 1 if $\Delta > 0$, and a higher price–cost margin if $\Delta < 0$. We would therefore expect that firm 2 prefers compatibility when $\Delta > 0$ (i.e., when the installed-base effect is larger than the performance effect) and incompatibility otherwise. However, there is a flaw in the previous reasoning, for it is wrong to assume that firms will choose equal capacities when $\gamma < 1$.

To derive properly firm 2's optimal compatibility decision, we need to compute firm 2's profit at the Cournot equilibrium and examine how this profit varies with γ. To avoid repeating the derivation of the equilibrium, we simply adapt expressions (21.2) and (21.3) by setting $\beta_2 = 0$, $c_1 = c$, $c_2 = \gamma c$ and $\Delta \equiv v\beta_1 - c$, and we find:

$$q_2^*(\gamma) = \frac{(1 - 2v + \gamma v) - (1 - 2\gamma + \gamma v)\Delta}{4(1-v)^2 - (1 - \gamma v)^2}, \qquad \pi_2^*(\gamma) = (1-v)\left(q_2^*(\gamma)\right)^2.$$

A first look at firm 2's equilibrium capacity reveals that it is always possible to find a value of γ that makes $q_2^*(\gamma) > 0$. That is, in contrast with the previous model, firm 1 is no longer able to deter firm 2's entry when firm 2 can choose the degree of backward compatibility.[e]

Let us now examine how firm 2's profit varies with γ. To simplify the computation, we set $v = 1/4$, which gives $\Delta = (\beta_1/4) - c$ and

$$\pi_2^*(\gamma) = \frac{12(2 + \gamma - (4 - 7\gamma)\Delta)^2}{(10 - \gamma)^2(2 + \gamma)^2},$$

$$\frac{d}{d\gamma}\pi_2^*(\gamma) = \frac{24(2 + \gamma - (4 - 7\gamma)\Delta)}{(10 - \gamma)^3(2 + \gamma)^3}\left((2 + \gamma)^2 + \left(172 - 8\gamma + 7\gamma^2\right)\Delta\right).$$

Suppose first that the installed-base effect is larger than the performance effect ($\Delta \geq 0$). Then, it is immediate that the first derivative is everywhere positive, meaning that firm 2's optimal choice is full compatibility: $\gamma^* = 1$.

---

[e] Indeed, q_2^* can be made positive by choosing $\gamma > 1/(2 - v)$ if $\Delta > 0$, or $\gamma < 1/(2 - v)$ if $\Delta < 0$.

Suppose now that the performance effect is larger than the installed-base effect ($\Delta < 0$). There may exist $\hat{\gamma} \in [0, 1]$ such that $d\pi_2^*(\hat{\gamma})/d\gamma = 0$. Yet, computing the second derivative of profit with respect to γ, it can easily be shown that it is everywhere positive when $\Delta < 0$, meaning that $\pi_2^*(\gamma)$ is convex in γ in that case. To find the optimal value of γ, we need thus to compare the values taken by firm 2's equilibrium profit at the extremes, $\gamma = 0$ and $\gamma = 1$. We find

$$\pi_2^*(1) - \pi_2^*(0) = \tfrac{4}{27}(\Delta + 1)^2 - \tfrac{3}{25}(2\Delta - 1)^2 = \tfrac{1}{675}(28\Delta + 1)(19 - 8\Delta).$$

As $\Delta < 0$, we have that

$$\pi_2^*(1) > \pi_2^*(0) \Leftrightarrow 28\Delta + 1 > 0 \Leftrightarrow \Delta > -\tfrac{1}{28}.$$

It follows that firm 2 still prefers to enter with a fully compatible product when the installed base is slightly dominated by the performance effect. Reversing this proposition, we conclude:

Lesson 21.6   A firm that enters a network market with a superior product makes this product incompatible with the competitor's existing inferior product only if what it gains by selling a higher-quality product is sufficiently larger than what it loses by not being compatible with the incumbent's installed base.

21.2.3   Expectations management

As we have stressed throughout this chapter, expectations are crucial in markets with network effects: when incompatible network goods compete head to head, the final outcome may heavily depend on the expectations formed by the consumers and by the producers of complementary products. One understands therefore why firms aim at strategically manipulating these expectations in their favour.

We briefly present here three commercial tactics that are largely used to manage expectations in network markets. The first tactic is simply a form of advertising that consists in portraying one's product as the inevitable winner. If a consumer is convinced by this message, and believes that so are most other consumers, then she will expect this product to generate large network effects and will therefore choose to buy it. Therefore, the advertising campaign becomes self-fulfilling as the product will indeed be the winner. This tactic is likely to work better in situations where the information about the size of installed bases is hard to obtain or to verify. For instance, the software vendor Oracle regularly runs advertisements mentioning that 98 out of Fortune 100 companies use Oracle technology.[26] The Blu-ray versus HD-DVD format war described in Case 21.1 above offers another illustration.

Case 21.6 Expectations management in the high-definition DVDs arena

One way to generate positive expectations about the future dominance of a particular standard is to trumpet the victory of the standard. This is what the backers of HD DVD and Blu-ray have been repeatedly doing. The website Reghardware.co.uk reported the following in January 2007:[27] 'The HD DVD Promotion Group proudly claimed some 175,000 HD DVD players were sold in the US by 5 January 2007. An impressive number for a totally new format, but one eclipsed by the 475,000 Blu-ray ready PlayStation 3s Sony sold in the period between the console's 17 November launch and Christmas Day.' It was also reported that firms showed a lot of optimism about future sales: 'The HD DVD Promotion Group believes its members will together have shipped 2.5m players by the end of 2007, though that figure includes the 175,000 units that have been sold already. Again, Sony's response is to point to the PS3, which it yesterday said would be in 3m homes by the end of the year.'

A similar, but more pernicious, tactic is called *FUD (Fear, Uncertainty, and Doubt)* and consists in disseminating negative (and vague) information on rival products. The idea is clearly to generate pessimistic consumer expectations about the rival products and, thereby, increase the chances of its own product to win the standards battle. Although the term FUD originated to describe misinformation tactics in the computer hardware industry (IBM being the first firm that was accused of using this tactic), the tactic has since been used more broadly, namely in the software industry as illustrated in Case 21.7.

Case 21.7 Novell sues over 'cereal box' ad campaign[28]

In 2001, in a typical FUD campaign, Microsoft sent fake cereal boxes with NetWare-to-Windows NT/2000 software inside to NetWare users. Before that, Microsoft also published a story on its website indicating that Novell was abandoning the software business in favour of consulting in light of its union with Cambridge Technology Partners. Novell reacted by slapping a lawsuit on Microsoft for 'making and distributing false and misleading statements about Novell and NetWare 6'. Examples of such statements are: 'What's the expiration date on that NetWare platform?' and 'You're left with a server platform without the full support of its manufacturer.' NetWare customers were glad to see Novell taking action, but wished the company had fought back sooner. 'If Novell was going to fight back against all the false and misleading statements Microsoft has made about Novell products, they should have started doing so 10 years ago when they had a far better product and a large market share . . . instead of turning the other cheek,' says Doug Spindler, president of the San Francisco Windows NT and NetWare User Groups.

Finally, *product preannouncement* is a salient way to manage expectations. It consists in announcing a new product well in advance of actual market availability. The objective is to deter consumers from buying (and firms from offering complementary products to) a competing, existing product. Although preannouncements are made in various industries, they have a particular bite in network markets because of the presence of collective switching costs: if some consumers delay their purchase until the preannounced product becomes available, other consumers will have an incentive to do so as well and the preannoucement will indeed freeze the sales of the competing product. It has been reported that product preannouncements are quite common in the computer software and consumer electronics industries.[f] Whether preannounce-ments do indeed affect the outcome of a standards competition largely remains an open issue.[g]

An important issue associated with such announcements is their credibility: do firms have an incentive to be truthful or to lie in their announcements? In case the announcement turns out to be (intentionally or unintentionally) false, it is common to refer to the software or hardware in question as a *vaporware*. This term has been coined to describe promised products that are significantly delayed (or sometimes even fail to emerge) or fail to live up to expectations.[h] Another issue is that product preannouncement may be a double-edged sword: the preannouncement might freeze the sales not only of the competing product, but also of the current generation of the firm's own product. Moreover, in the case of vaporware, it might deteriorate the firm's reputation.[29]

21.3   Public policy in network markets

We have seen in the previous sections that network effects may cause market failures: for instance, users may coordinate on inferior standards, or firms may fail to make their products compatible when it would be welfare-improving to do so. The next question which arises naturally is whether public interventions are able to correct, or at least alleviate, those market failures. In this section, we consider two broad types of public interventions in network markets: *ex ante* and *ex post* interventions. By *ex ante* interventions, we mean that the public authorities take an active part in the competition process among network goods, before standardization takes place. In contrast, with *ex post* interventions, the public authorities do not try to influence the competition process, but aim at safeguarding it by controlling firms' conduct. As we now discuss, these two types of interventions are fraught with major difficulties.

21.3.1   Ex ante interventions

As we have seen above, standards may emerge in two basic ways: either as the outcome of a standards war, or because of a pre-market standardization agreement. It is customary to refer to the former standards as *de facto* standards, and to the latter as *de jure* standards.

To examine how public authorities might influence *de facto* standardization, let us recall the model with sequential adoption decisions that we analysed in the previous chapter. There are two unsponsored technologies, A and B, available to consumers at zero marginal cost. In each period, one new consumer arrives in the market and buys one unit of one of the technologies. Some consumers favour technology A, some technology B; all benefit from the size of the network they link into. This model predicts that market dominance is the long-run outcome of competition between incompatible network goods: eventually, all users

---

[f] Bayus *et al.* (2001) document that only approximately 50% of 123 software products announced during the 1985–95 period were shipped within three months of the announcement date. Moreover, more than 20% of the products were first shipped more than nine months after the announcement date.

[g] With the exception of Dranove and Gandal (2003), who establish that the preannouncement of DiVX (a rival format to the emerging DVD format) slowed down the adoption of DVD technology, there is little analytical empirical work on this issue.

[h] If you want to see some of the best vaporware in the gaming industry, visit *CNET.com* at http://reviews.cnet.com/4520-9020_7-6555927-1.html (last visited: February 2009).

will adopt the same technology, whatever their intrinsic preferences. Also, the model tells us that the long-run is determined by small historical events and the identity of the long-run winner cannot be predicted.

According to David (1987), this form of path-dependence implies that public intervention in network competition faces three generic problems. There is first what he calls the *Narrow Policy Window Paradox*. As the final outcome is driven by small historical events, and especially those which take place early in the process, there exist available 'windows' for effective public policy intervention at small costs: by influencing the first users (by taxes/subsidies), it is possible to influence the whole process.[i] However, it is not easy to take advantage of these windows while they remain open, as the point at which such intervention can have maximum leverage tends to be confined towards the very beginnings of the dynamic process, and to have an uncertain but generally brief temporal duration. This exposes public authorities to a second dilemma, which David calls the *Blind Giant's Quandary*: the moment at which public authorities are likely to be the most powerful is just when they know least about which technology to prefer. Some form of counter-action might then be a remedy: by subsidizing only the lagging technology, public authorities may prevent the policy window from shutting before better information is available. Yet, such counter-action might entail social costs. Not only will some network effects remain unexploited, but when the market will eventually tip in favour of one technology, the users of the other technology will become *Technological Orphans* (in David's terminology) and be rightfully angry because their technological expectations were falsely nourished by public interventions. These orphans might lobby to have their subsidies extended or might question the credibility of public policies.

Another possibility for public authorities is to get directly involved in the *de jure* standardization process. Many standards are indeed selected by government agencies. For instance, this was done in Europe in the context of mobile telephony with the GSM standard, or in the US in the context of high-definition television. It is not clear, however, whether *de jure* standards should be preferred to *de facto* standards. On the one hand, *de jure* standards are developed through agreed, open and transparent procedures, based on a consensus of all interested parties; they present thereby a particular legitimacy and avoid the costs associated with *de facto* standards of adopting privately profitable, but socially undesirable, technologies. On the other hand, *de jure* standards suffer a major drawback: the pace of reaching them is often too slow in a context of rapid technological progress compared to the rather quick emergence of *de facto* standards.[j] Sometimes this inertia drives firms to exit the institutional process and to set up consortia to resolve standardization: a great deal of standards are indeed selected by private standard-setting organizations (SSOs).[k]

---

[i] Another possibility is to use the buying power of public administrations to influence the process. Administrations are indeed large and pivotal users of information technologies; their purchasing decisions might therefore have a significant influence on private parties' decisions. For instance, we mentioned in Chapter 19 that several countries are mandating the use of open source software in their public administrations.

[j] David and Shurmer (1996) report that the average time taken by the *de jure* standardization process to produce a standard varies from $2\frac{1}{2}$ years at the national level, through to 4–5 years regionally, and 7 years or more at the international level.

[k] There are hundreds of technology SSOs in existence. Most of them, and the work they do, are totally unknown to the general public. Some of them sometimes appear in the news, like the World Wide Web Consortium (or W3C, which develops common protocols to enable the evolution and interoperability of the Web) or the Wi-Fi Alliance (which certifies wireless products). For a list of the main SSOs, ranked by technical or industry categories, see www.consortiuminfo.org.

21.3.2   **Ex post interventions**

When public authorities refrain from intervening directly in the (*de facto* or *de jure*) standard-ization process, they still keep the possibility of controlling the process indirectly, ex post, mainly through *competition (antitrust) policy*. However, the application of competition policy becomes rather subtle in network markets. We have indeed shown in the previous sections that market share inequality and very high profitability of a top firm are natural in network markets and do not necessarily result from anticompetitive conduct. Therefore, alleged anticompeti-tive actions should not be judged against the benchmark of perfect competition, but against some 'but for' market structure with significant inequality and profits. With that in mind, the traditional limits on unilateral conduct by dominant firms, such as prohibitions on exclusive dealing and tying, can be fruitfully applied in network markets. Some conducts are also spe-cific to network markets (such as the expectations management tactics described above) and deserve careful scrutiny. For instance, Microsoft and IBM have been accused of using product preannouncement to maintain their respective dominant positions.[1]

A more complex issue is what attitude competition authorities should have with respect to cooperation in standard-setting. By and large, competition policy is not standing in the way of needed cooperation to establish compatibility standards. This does not mean, however, that this form of cooperation is immune from antitrust scrutiny. A first, fundamental, issue is the following. Allowing or not allowing cooperative standard setting amounts to choosing between two forms of competition: competition *in* the market if cooperation is allowed, or competition *for* the market if cooperation is prohibited and a standards war ensues. From a dynamic welfare perspective, it is far from clear which type of competition should be preferred as the two types have opposite costs and benefits. Indeed, competition *for* the market entails intense competition in the near term to build a decisive installed base of consumers; firms are willing to invest (in terms of price reductions and quality improvements) up to the expected flow of profits they would earn if they win the standards war. The downside is naturally that competition will disappear in the future as one firm will monopolize the market. The exact reverse prevails under competition *in* the market. As firms agree on a common standard, they will share the market, which guarantees competition in the future. However, pre-market standardization greatly reduces competition and innovation incentives in the near term. There is thus a clear trade-off: generally, competition will prevail either in the near term or in the future, but not in both. However, there are situations where cooperative standard setting increases competition at all points in time. Those are the situations where standardization is a prerequisite to overcome collective switching costs: facing incompatible network products, consumers would stick to the existing product. In that case, the front-end competition of a standards war would be in vain as none of the competing products would eventually manage to take off.

When competition authorities allow firms to cooperate in standard setting, they should nevertheless make sure that this does not lead to more harmful forms of cooperation, like

---

[1] As reported by Choi *et al.* (2006), although Microsoft announced that its DOS 5.0 would be released in the first quarter of 1991, it was not released until June 1991; it was also alleged that some of the announcements about the features were spurious. As for IBM, it was the announcement of its System/360 line of computers in the 1960s that was contentious.

price-fixing. They should also examine whether the internal rules set by the SSOs and their policies governing the disclosure and licensing of IP are not unfair with respect to some members or to outsiders. Case 21.8 reports that the European Commission is seeking to prevent the most powerful technology companies (many of which are American) from locking up standards markets.

Case 21.8 EU's inquiries in network markets

In 2006, the European Commission conducted an investigation concerning Hollywood studios. The question was whether rival manufacturers of next-generation DVDs (see Case 21.1 above) were using unfair practices to knock one another out of the standards war. The main backers of the two formats (i.e., Sony for Blu-ray and Toshiba for HD-DVD) were suspected of stifling competition through exclusive contracts with film studios and computer makers. The European Union asked Hollywood studios to reveal any dealings over high-definition DVDs with technology companies contained in email messages, faxes, PowerPoint presentations, meeting notes, internal reports and even conversations.[30] This investigation came just after the EU battle with Microsoft to open up the computer software market to greater competition. As we already described in Chapter 17, the European Commission accused Microsoft of two illegal conducts: first to unfairly promote its media player at the expense of rivals by including it in the Windows package; second, to leverage its leading position in personal computers in order to dominate the low-end server market.

Review questions

1. Discuss the conditions under which pre-market standardization is more likely to emerge as an equilibrium than a standards war.

2. Explain why consumer and producer interests in standardization may not be aligned.

3. Explain why incumbent producers of network goods may have an incentive to build an installed base of consumers through penetration pricing.

4. Describe the trade-off between backward compatibility and performance.

5. Explain how and why firms try to influence consumers' expectations in a standards war?

Further reading

The basic discussion about how to compete in network markets (i.e., competition *for* or *in* the market) comes from Besen and Farrell (1994). Although the various models presented in this chapter have been developed for the occasion, a number of papers discuss similar issues: the seminal papers of Katz and Shapiro (1985, 1986) and Farrell and Saloner (1985) analyse the link between users' adoption and firms' compatibility decisions; Farrell and Saloner (1986) study the impact of an installed base on compatibility decisions; Choi *et al.* (2006) discuss at length the issue of product preannouncement; Thum (1996) studies capacity commitment in the presence of network effects; Haan (2003) examines how vaporwares can serve as a means of entry deterrence. For a comprehensive and non-technical guide to strategies in network markets, we refer the reader to the book by Shapiro and Varian (1999). As for the public policy implications of network effects, we followed David (1987); the reader will also find a useful survey in Gandal (2002).

Notes for Part VIII

1. This definition, as well as most of the analysis in this section, comes from Farrell and Klemperer (2001).

2. See, e.g., Berndt (1991).

3. See Gandal (1994, 1995) and Brynjolfsson and Kemerer (1996) for spreadsheet packages; Gröhn (1999) for word-processing software; Harhoff and Moch (1997) for database software.

4. For VCRs, see Ohashi (2003) and Park (2004); for CDs, see Gandal, Kende and Rob (2000); for DVDs, see Dranove and Gandal (2003) and Karaca-Mandic (2004); for PDAs, see Nair *et al.* (2004); for video games, see Shankar and Bayus (2003) and Clements and Ohashi (2005).

5. See Doganoglu and Grzybowski (2006) for the first result and Birke and Swann (2006) for the second.

6. We follow here Chou and Shy (1990) and Möbius (2002), see also Nocke, Peitz and Stahl (2007).

7. As used in Dixit and Stiglitz (1977).

8. We follow here the exposition of Economides (1996).

9. This figure is adapted from Economides (1996).

10. See Rohlfs (1974).

11. See Goolsbee and Klenow (2002).

12. See Axelrod *et al.* (1995) for an illustration and Belleflamme (1998) for a model along these lines.

13. See Church, Gandal and Krause (2003).

14. We adapt here the model of Arthur (1989).

15. This terminology has been proposed by Farrell and Saloner (1985).

16. See Kretschmer (2001).

17. This model is due to Farrell and Saloner (1985).

18. Farrell and Saloner (1985) demonstrate that any equilibrium strategy is a bandwagon strategy.

19. This model is an extension of the seminal model proposed by Katz and Shapiro (1985). This extension is itself adapted from Crémer, Rey and Tirole (2000).

20. Crémer, Rey and Tirole (2000) endogenize the level of compatibility as follows. Before choosing capacities, each firm i chooses a quality γ_i for its 'side' of the compatibility between the two goods. The final level of compatibility, γ, is then equal to $\min\{\gamma_1, \gamma_2\}$.

21. Sources: Lego plays hardball with rights to bricks, by Ian Austen, *New York Times*, 3 February 2005 and IPKat weblog (http://ipkitten.blogspot.com/2005/11/lego-loses-in-canada.html).

22. This subsection is based on Besen and Farrell (1994).

23. See 'Toshiba drops out of HD DVD war' (19 February 2008), http://news.bbc.co.uk/2/hi/business/7252172.stm (last consulted February 2009).

24. See Cusumano *et al.* (1992), Thum (1996) and Ohashi (2003).

25. See http://buytaert.net/backward-compatibility; posted on 17 May 2006.

26. Example given by Koski and Kretchmer (2004).

27. See 'HD DVD, Blu-ray backers trumpet formats' victory', www.reghardware.co.uk (last consulted February 2009).

28. See Connor, Deni, *Network World*, 8 October 2001.

29. See Choi, Kristiansen and Nahm (2006) for a review of the literature that analyses preannouncements as a firm strategy.

30. See EU's DVD inquiry goes to Hollywood, *International Herald Tribune*, James Kanter and Ken Belson, 8 August 2006.

References for Part VIII

Arthur, W. B. (1989). Competing Technologies, Increasing Returns, and Lock-in By Historical Events. *Economic Journal* 99: 116–131.

Axelrod, R., Mitchell, W., Thomas, R., Scott Bennett, D. and Bruderer, E. (1995). Coalition Formation in Standard-Setting Alliances. *Management Science* 41: 1493–1508.

Bayus, B. L., Jain, S. and Rao, A. G. (2001). Truth or Consequences: An Analysis of Vaporware and New Product Announcements. *Journal of Marketing Research* 38: 3–13.

Belleflamme, P. (1998). Adoption of Network Technologies in Oligopolies. *International Journal of Industrial Organization* 16: 415–414.

Berndt, E. R. (1991). *The Practice of Econometrics: Classic and Contemporary*. Reading, MA: Addison-Wesley Pub. Co.

Besen, S. and Farrell, J. (1994). Choosing How to Compete: Strategies and Tactics in Standardization. *Journal of Economic Perspectives* 8: 117–131.

Birke, D. and Swann, G. M. P. (2006). Network Effects and the Choice of Mobile Phone Operator. *Journal of Evolutionary Economics* 16: 65–84

Brynjolfsson, E. and Kemerer, C. F. (1996). Network Externalities in Microcomputer Software: An Econometric Analysis of the Spreadsheet Market. *Management Science* 42: 1627–1647.

Choi, J. P., Kristiansen, E. G. and Nahm, J. (2006). Preannouncing Information Goods. In Illing, G. and Peitz, M. (eds.), *Industrial Organization and the Digital Economy*. Cambridge, MA: MIT Press.

Chou, C.-F. and Shy, O. (1990). Network Effects without Network Externalities. *International Journal of Industrial Organization* 8: 259–270.

Church, J., Gandal, N. and Krause, D. (2003). Indirect Network Effects and Adoption Externalities. CEPR Discussion Paper No. 3738. London.

Clements, M. and Ohashi, H. (2005). Indirect Network Effects and the Product Cycle: Video Games in the U.S., 1994–2002. *Journal of Industrial Economics* 53: 515–542.

Crémer, J., Rey, P. and Tirole, J. (2000). Connectivity in the Commercial Internet. *Journal of Industrial Economics* 48: 433–472.

Cusumano, M. A., Mylonadis, Y. and Rosenbloom, R. S. (1992). Strategic Maneuvering and Mass-Market Dynamics: The Triumph of VHS over Beta. *Business History Review* 66: 51–94.

David, P. A. (1987). Some New Standards for the Economics of Standardization in the Information Age. In Dasgupta, P. and Stoneman, P. (eds.), *Economic Policy and Technological Performance*. Cambridge: Cambridge University Press. pp. 206–239.

David, P. A. and Shurmer, M. (1996). Formal Standard-Setting for Global Telecommunications and Information Services. *Telecommunications Policy* 20: 789–815.

Dixit, A. and Stiglitz, J. (1977). Monopolistic Competition and Optimum Product Diversity. *American Economic Review* 67: 297–308.

Doganoglu, T. and Grzybowski, L. (2006). Estimating Network Effects in Mobile Telephony in Germany. Mimeo. University of Munich.

Dranove, D. and Gandal, N. (2003). The DVD vs. DIVX Standard war: Empirical Evidence of Network Effects and Preannouncement Effects. *Journal of Economics and Management Strategy* 12: 363–386.

Economides, N. (1996). The Economics of Networks. *International Journal of Industrial Organization* 16: 673–699.

Farrell, J. and Klemperer, P. (2001). Coordination and Lock-in: Competition with Switching Costs and Network Effects. Mimeo. Nuffield College, Oxford University. (Preliminary draft chapter for *Handbook of Industrial Organization*, Vol. 3).

Farrell, J. and Saloner, G. (1985). Standardization, Compatibility and Innovation. *Rand Journal of Economics* 16: 70–83.

Farrell, J. and Saloner, G. (1986). Installed Base and Compatibility: Innovation, Product Preannouncement, and Predation. *American Economic Review* 76: 940–955.

Gandal, N. (1994). Hedonic Price Indexes for Spreadsheets and an Empirical Test for Network Externalities. *Rand Journal of Economics* 25: 160–170.

Gandal, N. (1995). Competing Compatibility Standards and Network Externalities in the PC Software Market. *Review of Economics and Statistics* 77: 599–608.

Gandal, N. (2002). Compatibility, Standardization and Network Effects: Some Policy Implications. *Oxford Review of Economic Policy* 18: 80–91.

Gandal, N., Kende, M. and Rob, R. (2000). The Dynamics of Technological Adoption in Hardware/Software Systems: the Case of Compact Disc Players. *Rand Journal of Economics* 31: 43–61.

Goolsbee, A. and Klenow, P. J. (2002). Evidence on Learning and Network Externalities in the Diffusion of Home Computers. *Journal of Law and Economics* 45: 317–344.

Gröhn, A. (1999). Network Effects in PC Software: An Empirical Analysis. Mimeo, National Bureau of Economic Research, Cambridge, MA.

Gruber, H. and Verboven, F. (2001). The Evolution of Markets under Entry and Standards Regulation – the Case of Global

Mobile Telecommunications. *International Journal of Industrial Organization* 19: 1189–1212.

Haan, M. (2003). Vaporware as a Means of Entry Deterrence. *Journal of Industrial Economics* 51: 345–358.

Harhoff, D. and Moch, D. (1997). Price Indexes for PC Database Software and the Value of Code Compatibility. *Research Policy* 26: 509–520.

Karaca-Mandic, P. (2004). Network Effects in Technology Adoption: The Case of DVD Players. Mimeo. University of California at Berkeley.

Katz, M. and Shapiro, C. (1985). Network Externalities, Competition and Compatibility. *American Economic Review* 75: 424–440.

Katz, M. and Shapiro, C. (1986). Technology Adoption in the Presence of Network Externalities. *Journal of Political Economy* 95: 822–841.

Koski, H. (1999). The Installed Base Effect: Some Empirical Evidence from the Microcomputer Market. *Economics of Innovation and New Technology* 8: 273–310.

Koski, H. and Kretschmer, T. (2002). Entry, Standards and Competition: Firm Strategies and the Diffusion of Mobile Telephony. ETLA Discussion paper No. 824.

Koski, H. and Kretschmer, T. (2004). Survey on Competing in Network Industries: Firm Strategies, Market Outcomes, and Policy Implications. *Journal of Industry, Competition and Trade* 4: 5–31.

Kretschmer, T. (2001). Competition, Inertia, and Network Effects. Mimeo. London Business School and INSEAD.

Möbius, M. M. (2002). Lecture V: Network Competition - Basic Theory. Mimeo. Harvard University.

Nair, H., Chintagunta, P. and Dubé J.-P. (2004). Empirical Analysis of Indirect Network Effects in the Market for Personal Digital Assistants. *Quantitative Marketing and Economics* 2: 23–58.

Nocke, V., Peitz, M. and Stahl, K. O. (2007). Platform Ownership. *Journal of the European Economic Association* 5: 1130–1160.

Ohashi, H. (2003). The Role of Network Effects in the US VCR Market, 1978–1986. *Journal of Economics and Management Strategy* 12: 447–494.

Park, S. (2004). Quantitative Analysis of Network Externalities in Competing Technologies: The VCR Case. *Review of Economics and Statistics* 86: 937–945.

Rohlfs, J. (1974). A Theory of Interdependent Demand for a Communications Service. *Bell Journal of Economics* 5: 16–37.

Shankar, V. and Bayus, B. L. (2003). Network Effects and Competition: An Empirical Analysis of the Video Game Industry. *Strategic Management Journal* 24: 375–394.

Shapiro, C. and Varian, H. (1999). *Information Rules: A Strategic Guide to the Network Economy*. Cambridge, MA: HBS Press.

Thum, M. (1996). Network Externalities and Efficient Capacity Commitment. *Jahrbücher für Nationalökonomie und Statistik* 215: 274–286.

Part IX
Market intermediation

Introduction to Part IX: Market intermediation

Most products and services are not sold directly from the producer to the final consumer but pass through intermediaries. Intermediaries and the services they offer are the focus of this last part of the book. We distinguish between the following four major roles of intermediaries.

1. *Dealer* The intermediary buys goods or services from suppliers and resells them to buyers.

2. *Platform operator* The intermediary provides a platform where buyers and sellers (or more generally various groups of agents with complementary businesses) are able to interact.

3. *Infomediary* The intermediary acts as an information gatekeeper, or 'infomediary',[a] allowing consumers to access and process more efficiently information about prices or the match value of products and services.

4. *Trusted third-party* The intermediary acts as a certification agent by revealing information about a product's or seller's reliability or quality.

The intermediary essentially chooses whether to operate as a dealer or a platform operator. However, hybrid business models are also possible, as the well-known electronic intermediary

[a] The term infomediary is a contraction for *informational intermediary*.

Amazon nowadays exemplifies. The other two roles are complementary in nature and are often the main reason for intermediaries to be important for the functioning of markets. Amazon also fulfils these two roles, as we now detail it.

When it started in 1995, Amazon.com was a pure online *dealer*: first of books, then of music CDs, videotapes, DVDs and software, and later, of many other product categories (consumer electronics, toys and games, kitchenware, lawn and garden items, etc.). Amazon's main competitive advantage as a dealer was its ability to offer many more titles than traditional 'brick-and-mortar' dealers or mail-order businesses. In addition, it could adjust its product portfolio quickly. In 2001, taking a cue from auctioneer eBay, Amazon launched its Marketplace service that allows customers and third-party sellers to sell books, CDs, DVDs, and other products. Through this service, Amazon started to act as a *platform operator*. What made this platform successful was the large participation on its two sides: the buyer and the seller sides. Actually, each side's valuation of such a platform increases with the participation of the other side. It follows that the presence of an additional buyer creates a positive externality for all sellers active on the platform, and vice versa. The role of platform operator is precisely to internalize these external effects by controlling access and transactions on the platform. Amazon does indeed charge a commission rate based on the sale price, a transaction fee and a variable closing fee (in exchange, Amazon takes care of billing, collecting the money and crediting the seller's account).[b]

[b] Amazon also offers an alternative platform service by allowing third-party dealers to set up their own shop on Amazon, called a Z-Shop.

Amazon also acted early on as *infomediary* by allowing users to submit online product reviews and to rate products on a scale from one to five stars. It also put in place a personal recommendation system, which uses the past purchases of a consumer to identify his/her interests and the shopping history of other users with similar interests to present the consumer with items he/she is likely to want. These two services allow consumers to drastically reduce their search efforts to obtain the products they like. When the products are sold by Amazon Marketplace Sellers, consumers may question the sellers' reliability, which may undermine trade. To address this issue, Amazon plays the role of a *trusted third-party* by organizing a reputation system: consumers are invited to leave feedback on transactions; so, before making a purchase, consumers can form their opinion about the seller's reliability by viewing comments as well as one-to-five-star ratings submitted by previous buyers.

Although some intermediaries, such as Amazon, choose to fulfill the four roles, most intermediaries specialize in fewer roles. To obtain a clear understanding of each role, it is useful to analyse how intermediaries affect market outcomes by considering each role separately.

We start in Chapter 22 with the first two roles, which concern the intermediated exchange of goods and services. In this chapter, we first think of intermediaries as dealers. Their main function is to bring two or more sides of a market together and to provide a substitute to direct trade, where sellers directly sell to buyers or where a non-monetary interaction occurs in a decentralized way. We have in mind, e.g., retailers, wholesalers, or used car dealers who buy and resell goods.[c] The question of interest here is whether at least some agents may do better if they access an intermediary instead of trading in a decentralized way.

Instead of controlling the transaction price by buying and reselling products, intermediaries may simply charge for access and transactions and switch from a dealer role to a platform operator role. For instance, a department store may merely rent its shelf space. We examine the relative merits of these two business models.

We then consider platforms where users are interested not so much in the size than in the composition of the other side. This is particularly relevant if there is heterogeneity on one side that is pay-off relevant for the other side and if making selected matches is costly. This is the case for platforms provided by brokers, such as travel agents, real estate agents, insurance agents or stock brokers; but also for matching services. Such market environments may call for market segmentation at the level of the intermediary.

In the third section of Chapter 22, we focus on the platform operator role. When operating a platform, an intermediary has the ability to control the number of traders and the volume of trade of the market. In the extreme, markets may appear which hardly existed before the appearance of such an intermediary. The term 'platform' broadly refers to some basic infrastructure that must be provided to make trade or interactions possible. Examples are game platforms (in the market for video games), software operating systems (in software markets), and telephone networks (in the market for phone calls). The intermediary may also provide services which make centralized trade beneficial. For instance, eBay provides a payment system, shopping malls offer free parking and activities. All these markets can be called 'two-sided (or multi-sided) platforms' because their main function is to allow the interaction of two or more groups of users who are linked by indirect network effects, in the sense that a user's valuation of the platform increases with the participation of the other group. Basically, sellers are interested in a large number of buyers (because this increases their sales) and, at the same time, buyers are interested in many sellers

---

[c] In contrast to the analysis of vertical oligopoly in Chapter 17, price-setting power rests with the intermediary.

(because this often increases the variety of offers and, in addition, more sellers may lead to more intense competition and thus lower prices). After identifying key features of these markets, we analyse the price structure for intermediation services on a platform. We also examine the competition between intermediaries, as well as the implications for antitrust and regulation.

In Chapter 23, we turn to the other two roles of intermediaries: infomediary and trusted third-party, which both have to do with information and reputation. The role of an infomediary is to provide tools that help consumers to find, sort and organize information. As the saying goes, 'too much information kills information'. Infomediaries can alleviate this information overload. One thinks here of search engines on the Web that make price information easily accessible. Intermediaries may also install a recommender system, so as to allow consumers to perform directed search, thereby reducing their search efforts significantly. The role of trusted third-party is to certify quality. This certification may be actively pursued by the intermediary by providing quality checks. Alternatively, the intermediary may aggregate information that market participants have provided. To this end, the intermediary can put a reputation system in place. Examples are seller rating systems in Amazon MarketPlace and eBay. In these examples, it is not information by the intermediary (gathered e.g. through testing) but information by other consumers (gathered through experience) that allows consumers to make better informed choices. What we want to examine is to what extent intermediaries, through their role of trusted third-party, manage to alleviate asymmetric information problems between firms and consumers.

What will you learn in this part of the book?

You will get a deeper understanding of how a number of markets do actually work. The important finding is that many markets would not work properly, or even exist, without the activities of intermediaries. Analysing why and how these intermediaries operate is thus crucial to understanding the role of intermediaries as 'visible hands' in the functioning of markets.

You will also complement the knowledge you have acquired in the previous parts of the book as the themes we develop here are closely connected to themes explored before. First, the dealer role of intermediaries is best understood within the framework of vertically related markets, which we introduced in Chapter 17. Second, the platform operator role involves internalizing network effects and may help in solving the chicken-and-egg problem; these are issues that were already studied in Part VIII. Third, for some applications the pricing of a platform operator resembles price discrimination in the form of group pricing, which was the focus of Chapter 8. Fourth, two-sided platforms raise challenging issues for competition policy, which leads us to complement the analysis we made in Part VI. Fifth, when analysing the infomediary role, we will extend the price dispersion model of Chapter 7 by introducing an intermediary. Sixth, the trusted third-party role may alleviate asymmetric information problems, which were the focus of Part V.

22 Markets with intermediated goods

In this chapter, we consider the two roles of intermediaries that concern the trade of goods and services: the role of a dealer and the role of a platform operator.

Section 22.1 focuses on the dealer role in its simplest form: the intermediary buys and resells a product, without adding any service to the transaction. Compared to a situation where buyers and sellers interact on a decentralized market, we show that the intermediary may add value for some market participants by this simple buy and resell activity. As we will argue, the intuition for this result is that intermediation allows for a valuable self-selection of types when buyers and sellers are affected by the type of their matching partner. Intermediaries can thus find profitable opportunities to operate centralized exchanges.

What is the most profitable form of centralized exchange: buying and reselling the goods or just providing buyers and sellers with an opportunity to meet? That is, does the intermediary prefer to act as a dealer or as a platform operator who only taxes trade? We show that the picture is mixed. Decentralizing pricing leads to positive and negative effects for the intermediary.

In Section 22.2, we examine matching environments. Intermediaries providing matching services can add value by internalizing two types of externalities. First, indirect network externalities are present when agents in one group value the matching services of an intermediary all the more that the participation of the other group is large, because that increases their chances of finding their match. Second, users of matching services may care not so much about the number of matching prospects than about their identities. Here, the intermediary may control the composition of the various groups and, thereby, internalize a sorting externality.

Finally, in Section 22.3, we focus on indirect network effects on the two sides of the market and consider so-called 'two-sided platforms'. Here, the intermediary's main role is to control the access to a platform that two (or more) groups of agents use for their interaction. The main characteristic of these platforms is that users of each group value a platform all the more when it is largely used by the other group. Hence, individual decisions to affiliate with a particular platform generate indirect network effects on agents on the other side of this platform. Through a centralized operation of the platform, the intermediary may add value, and capture rents, by contributing to internalize these externalities. This is the main theme we develop in this section.

22.1 Intermediaries as dealers

As we discussed in the general introduction, Amazon.com started its business as a dealer, or retailer, by buying books from publishers and reselling them to consumers. Its business was similar to the one of 'brick-and-mortar' bookstores like Barnes & Noble, Borders or Fnac, except that it was conducted online rather than through physical stores. An immediate question is to ask why publishers and readers use the services of such intermediaries instead of trading directly with each other. Leaving aside potential explanations related to logistics, storage or inventory,[d] we show in Subsection 22.1.1 that buyers and sellers may prefer to trade via an intermediary because it improves their matching opportunities. We also described above the Marketplace service that Amazon launched in 2001. Alongside its dealer business, Amazon also started to operate a platform where third-party sellers can trade with Amazon customers. In Subsection 22.1.2, we compare these two modes of operation from the point of view of the intermediary and of the trading partners.

22.1.1   Intermediated versus nonintermediated trade

Clearly, there are many instances in which trade occurs or matches are made in the absence of intermediaries such as department stores or shopping malls. Some manufacturers sell directly to consumers and some relationships are established in the absence of intermediaries such as dating clubs. However, department stores and dating clubs exist. One may therefore ask why at least some agents appear to benefit from the use of intermediaries. This subsection looks at this issue. We start by postulating that there exists a decentralized market in which buyers and sellers interact in the absence of an intermediary. We then consider the changes in allocations and rents that arise if an intermediary enters the market.

First, consider a market which operates freely, i.e. buyers and sellers are not charged for joining. Suppose, furthermore, that buyers and sellers (or more generally, the trading partners from two populations) are randomly matched. In such a setup, we want to show that a market maker can profitably enter in order to buy and sell the product at a price difference so that he makes a profit although consumers have the possibility to participate for free in the random matching market.

Suppose that there is a large number of buyers and sellers who are heterogeneous in their type. Buyers have high valuation v_H or low valuation v_L and sellers have low costs c_L or high costs c_H. For the sake of the example, assume that both types are equally likely.[1] If a seller or buyer does not trade its surplus is normalized to zero. Furthermore, both the mass of buyers and sellers are set equal to 1. Suppose that $v_H > c_H > v_L > c_L$, so that there are positive gains from trade for all matches except for a match in which a low-valuation buyer meets a high-cost seller. In the latter case no trade takes place. Any gains from trade are assumed to be evenly split.[e] The expected net surpluses for the various agents are reported in the next table.

High-valuation buyer:	$\frac{1}{2}(v_H - \frac{c_L+c_H}{2})$
Low-valuation buyer:	$\frac{1}{4}(v_L - c_L)$
Low-cost seller:	$\frac{1}{2}\left(\frac{v_H+v_L}{2} - c_L\right)$
High-cost seller:	$\frac{1}{4}(v_H - c_H)$

---

[d] These factors are mostly relevant for the trade of physical goods; they are much less of an issue for digital goods and for services.

[e] This is the outcome under Nash bargaining according to which the joint surplus above the joint value of the outside option is evenly split.

The matching market operates in a socially inefficient way. Indeed, welfare is maximized when all high-valuation buyers interact exclusively with low-cost sellers. That is, at the first best, welfare is equal to $\frac{1}{2}(v_H - c_L)$ and the size of trade is $1/2$. In contrast, the matching market generates too much trade (the size of trade is $3/4$) and a lower welfare: $\frac{1}{4}(v_H - c_L) + \frac{1}{4}(v_H - c_H) + \frac{1}{4}(v_L - c_L) = \frac{1}{2}(v_H - c_L) - \frac{1}{4}(c_H - v_L) < \frac{1}{2}(v_H - c_L)$.

Introducing an intermediary may improve the allocation and even implement the first best in this situation. The intermediary sets profit-maximizing bid-and-ask prices (or wholesale and retail price). These prices w and p must have the property that high-valuation buyers and low-cost sellers prefer intermediated exchange and that other buyers and sellers refrain from migrating to the intermediary. Suppose therefore that all high-valuation buyers and all low-cost sellers go to the intermediary, whereas all low-valuation buyers and high-cost sellers stay in the matching market. High-valuation buyers know that they encounter only high-cost sellers in the matching market. Therefore, they are willing to pay a higher price to the intermediary as they avoid an unfavourable match in the matching market, which would only give a net surplus of $\frac{1}{2}(v_H - c_H)$. They are indifferent between the random matching market and the intermediary if $\frac{1}{2}(v_H - c_H) = v_H - p$. Similarly, low-cost sellers are indifferent between the two markets if $\frac{1}{2}(v_L - c_L) = w - c_L$. Prices that maximize the intermediary's profits are therefore

$$p = \tfrac{1}{2}(v_H + c_H) \quad \text{and} \quad w = \tfrac{1}{2}(v_L + c_L).$$

At these prices, the intermediary makes a profit equal to the bid-ask spread $p - w$ times the mass of buyer–seller pairs:

$$\tfrac{1}{2}(p - w) = \tfrac{1}{4}(v_H - v_L) + \tfrac{1}{4}(c_H - c_L).$$

Low-valuation buyers and high-cost sellers do not have an incentive to imitate the behaviour of the other type of buyers and sellers, respectively, as $v_L - p < 0$ and $w - c_H < 0$.

To summarize, we have found an equilibrium in which high-valuation buyers and low-cost sellers self-select into the intermediated market. In other words, the presence of a profit-maximizing dealer leads to endogenous sorting according to type. In our special two-type model sorting is even perfect. The intermediary makes positive profit since he offers high-valuation buyers and low-cost sellers a better deal than what the matching market provides. Here, intermediated trade improves upon the allocation in the decentralized matching market and implements the first best, because under decentralized matching socially inefficient trade takes place.

Lesson 22.1   **In the presence of a random-matching market, there are profitable opportunities for intermediaries to operate centralized exchanges since buyers and sellers are affected by the type of their matching partner and intermediation allows for self-selection of types. Intermediated trade may partially or even fully replace decentralized trade and lead to a more efficient allocation.**

In the case that every match generates gains from trade, that is $v_L > c_H$, it may seem less obvious that intermediated trade can occur. Under random matching, there are positive gains from trade for all buyer–seller pairs and the matching market in isolation operates efficiently.[2] With respect to the previous case, the expected surpluses of high-valuation buyers and low-cost sellers are unchanged, while those of low-valuation buyers and high-cost sellers are modified, as reported in the next table.

High-valuation buyer:	$\frac{1}{2}(v_H - \frac{c_L+c_H}{2})$
Low-valuation buyer:	$\frac{1}{2}(v_L - \frac{c_L+c_H}{2})$
Low-cost seller:	$\frac{1}{2}(\frac{v_H+v_L}{2} - c_L)$
High-cost seller:	$\frac{1}{2}(\frac{v_H+v_L}{2} - c_H)$

Suppose that for prices p and w, all high-valuation buyers and all low-cost sellers go to the intermediary. Then the expected gain for a high-valuation buyer at the matching market is $\frac{1}{2}(v_H - c_H)$. Similarly, the expected gain for a low-cost seller is $\frac{1}{2}(v_L - c_L)$. If $p = v_H - \frac{1}{2}(v_H - c_H) = \frac{1}{2}(v_H + c_H)$ and $w = c_L + \frac{1}{2}(v_L - c_L) = \frac{1}{2}(v_L + c_L)$, high-valuation buyers and low-cost sellers do not have an incentive to deviate. Neither do low-valuation buyers and high-cost sellers. In particular, they strictly prefer to go to the free random-matching market. For a low-valuation buyer the incentive constraint reads

$$\frac{1}{2}(v_L - c_H) > v_L - p.$$

This becomes

$$\frac{1}{2}(v_L - c_H) > v_L - v_H + \frac{1}{2}(v_H - c_H) = \frac{1}{2}(v_L - c_H) - \frac{1}{2}(v_H - v_L),$$

which is clearly satisfied. Similarly for the high-cost seller. Hence, the intermediary makes profits $\frac{1}{2}(p - w) = \frac{1}{4}(v_H - v_L) + \frac{1}{4}(c_H - c_L)$. Here, intermediation does not affect the number of items traded. However, it leads to endogenous sorting so that high-cost types only find low-valuation partners in the matching market.

> **Lesson 22.2** In the presence of a random-matching market, intermediaries may profitably operate centralized exchanges even if the matching market in isolation operates efficiently. Intermediation then leads to market segmentation.

We may ask whether buyers and sellers are better off under intermediation. Clearly, low-valuation buyers and high-cost sellers are necessarily worse off since the pool of possible trading partners deteriorates. Interestingly, in our model, high-valuation buyers and low-cost sellers are also necessarily worse off since, due to segmentation, the expected utility from going to the matching market is less than in a world in which only decentralized trade exists.

22.1.2 Dealer versus pure platform operator

In the previous subsection, we assumed that the intermediary buys and sells goods. However, in many markets, the intermediary has the choice whether he controls the transaction price or whether he simply charges for access and transactions. For instance a department store may set prices on both sides of the market (presuming it has the price-setting power on both sides) or

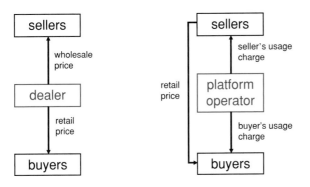

Figure 22.1 Intermediaries' business models: dealer and platform operator

merely rent its shelf space, as some retailers such as Walmart have been reported to be partly doing. What are the relative merits of these two business models?

To answer this question, we focus on the organization of the exchange of goods between sellers and buyers and abstract from other roles that intermediaries often fulfil (we say more on that later). We compare the two polar forms of such intermediated exchanges. In the first case, the intermediary acts as a *dealer* (or retailer) in the sense that it buys the goods from the sellers and resells them to the buyers (as in the previous subsection). Here, the pricing is centralized in the hands of the intermediary. In the second case, the intermediary does not take control of the sellers' goods but simply offers buyers and sellers access to a *platform* (or marketplace) on which they can interact as they please. Here, pricing is decentralized to the market participants and the platform taxes trade.

Figure 22.1 illustrates the two business models; the arrow points at the price-taking party. In the basic platform operator model, it is irrelevant which side of the market has to bear the usage fee. We can therefore restrict attention to the case in which sellers have to pay the usage fee. Note also that we assume that sellers have the price-setting power. In procurement problems the situation may be the reverse: buyers may have price-setting power. An analogous analysis applies to this alternative situation.

We develop a simple model to show that buyer–seller relationships differ markedly in the two business models with, in general, ambiguous results on intermediary's profits and volume of trade. We discuss additional factors that affect the success of these two business models. Case 22.1 illustrates that dealers, platform operators, and hybrid forms exist in different parts of the digital economy.

Case 22.1 Dealers and platform operators in the digital economy[3]

The two forms of intermediation we consider in this section can be seen as the two extreme points of a whole spectrum. Internet intermediaries may occupy different positions along this spectrum. For instance, eBay appears to be very close to the platform end of the spectrum, as its major role is to put buyers and sellers in contact and to tax trade on the platform. At the other extreme used to be Apple's iTunes Music Store. Apple acted as a dealer as it acquires from the music publishers the right to distribute their songs to the users; it repackages the songs with its own digital rights management (DRM) system and sells them under its own price policy (in the US traditionally $0.99 per song). It thus fixed prices on both sides of the market and took a cut. Its decision to allow publishers to choose between a small menu of different prices is a step toward decentralized pricing. A hybrid form is Amazon. It originally acted only as a dealer (presuming that it could dictate the price on the seller side). However, nowadays it also offers 'Amazon Marketplace', which allows other sellers than Amazon to use the platform to sell their goods. These sellers are then charged for transactions. This means that Amazon has decentralized pricing for parts of the transactions that occur via the platform.

Modelling framework

Suppose that there is a unit mass of sellers and a unit mass of buyers. Each seller produces a totally differentiated good at a constant unit cost c, which is assumed to be uniformly distributed over $[0, 1]$. (Alternatively, we can think of a single seller with unknown cost c.) Buyers have unit demand for each good; they buy if they are offered a price below or equal to their reservation price v, which is also assumed to be uniformly distributed over $[0, 1]$. For simplicity, the intermediary does not incur any variable cost. For the two intermediary roles that we consider, we assume for simplicity that all sales have to go through the intermediary; that is, we rule out direct exchanges between unaffiliated sellers and consumers.

Dealer intermediation

Suppose, first, that the intermediary acts as a dealer who makes *take-it-or-leave-it offers* to both sides of the market. That is, the intermediary buys the goods from the sellers and sells them to the buyers. It seeks to maximize its profit by setting a retail price or 'ask price' p for the buyers and a wholesale price or 'bid price' $(p - P)$ for the sellers.[4] Here, the transaction fee P corresponds to the *bid–ask spread*. According to our previous notation, $w = p - P$. We are considering the situation in which, at stage 1, the intermediary sets prices p and P and, at stage 2, buyers and sellers simultaneously decide which product to buy or to sell. (The same outcome obtains if one side of the market moves first.) Given these prices, the indifferent buyer is identified by $\underline{v} = p$ and the indifferent seller by $\bar{c} = p - P$. Under dealer intermediation, all active sellers obtain the same retail price p.

The dealer cannot distinguish between the different types of buyers and sellers because buyer and seller types are assumed to be private information. This leads, as we will see, to socially insufficient trade since the intermediary exerts its monopoly power on both sides of the market.

Given prices p and P, we obtain the number of participating buyers and sellers as the result of the participation decision buyers and sellers take at stage 2. For the uniform distribution, they are given by $n_b = 1 - p$ and $n_s = p - P$. Therefore, the total quantity exchanged is equal to $n_s n_b = (1 - p)(p - P)$ and the intermediary's problem can be written as

$$\max_{p,P} \Pi = P(1 - p)(p - P).$$

The first-order conditions are

$$\begin{cases} \frac{\partial}{\partial p} \Pi = P(P - 2p + 1) = 0, \\ \frac{\partial}{\partial P} \Pi = (1 - p)(p - 2P) = 0. \end{cases}$$

As $P = 0$ and/or $p = 1$ yield zero profit, the profit-maximizing prices are easily found as (where the superscript D stands for 'dealer')

$$p^D = \tfrac{2}{3}, \quad \text{and} \quad P^D = \tfrac{1}{3}. \tag{22.1}$$

Thus buyers pay the retail price $p^D = 2/3$ and sellers receive the wholesale price $p^D - P^D = 1/3$. It follows that $n_s^D = n_b^D = 1/3$ and that the intermediary achieves a profit of

$$\Pi^D = \tfrac{1}{27}. \tag{22.2}$$

Platform intermediation and decentralized pricing

Suppose now that the intermediary stops buying from sellers in order to resell to buyers, but lets buyers and sellers interact on its platform (or marketplace). Instead of fixing bid and ask prices, the intermediary then sets a transaction fee, P, on each unit exchanged on the platform. We assume, without any loss of generality, that the transaction fee is entirely borne by the sellers.[f] The timing of the game is as follows: first the intermediary sets P; next agents on one side of the market choose the retail price p for the goods and finally, agents on the other side of the market decide to participate or not. There are thus two cases to consider according to whether the sellers or the buyers have the price-setting power.

Sellers set the price At the last stage, buyers decide to purchase if their reservation price is larger than the price p set by the sellers. Therefore, each seller faces a demand $q(p) = 1 - p$ for its product. Moving to the second stage, we have that a seller with unit cost c chooses its price p to maximize $\pi_s = (p - c - P)(1 - p)$. The profit-maximizing price is easily found as

$$p(c) = \tfrac{1+P}{2} + \tfrac{c}{2}.$$

Only the sellers who can make a profit will participate in the market, i.e., the sellers such that $p(c) \geq c + P$ or, equivalently,

$$c \leq 1 - P = \bar{c}.$$

We can now compute the total quantity that will be exchanged on the market as:

$$Q = \int_0^{\bar{c}} (1 - p(c))\, dc = \int_0^{1-P} \tfrac{1}{2}(1 - c - P)\, dc = \tfrac{1}{4}(1 - P)^2,$$

which is the same as in the dealer market with $P^D = 1/3$. Hence profit and trading volume must be the same in the two settings. We comment on this below.

To complete the analysis, we note that, at the first stage of the game, the intermediary chooses P to maximize $\Pi = P\tfrac{1}{4}(1 - P)^2$. The optimal transaction fee and profit are (note that the superscript O stands for 'platform operator'):

$$P^O = \tfrac{1}{3}, \tag{22.3}$$

$$\Pi^O = \tfrac{1}{27}. \tag{22.4}$$

---

[f] It is easy to show that the results are invariant to the specific split of the fee between buyers and sellers.

Buyers set the price We also briefly consider the situation that buyers set the price p, which is the mirror image of the previous case. Then only sellers such that $p > c + P$ accept to participate. That is, each buyer faces a supply equal to $p - P$ and hence, chooses p to maximize $u_b = (v - p)(p - P)$ under the constraint that $p \leq v$. The unconstrained price is equal to $p(v) = (v + P)/2$, which satisfies the constraint as long as $v \geq P$. We can now compute the total quantity that will be exchanged on the market as

$$Q = \int_P^1 (p(v) - P)\, dv = \int_P^1 \tfrac{1}{2}(v - P)\, dv = \tfrac{1}{4}(1 - P)^2,$$

which is the same volume of trade as in the case where sellers have market power. The intermediary's problem is thus unchanged, and expressions (22.3) and (22.4) give the intermediary's optimal transaction fee and profit.

Dealer vs. platform operator

Comparing expressions (22.2) and (22.4), we observe that, in the special case of the uniform distribution, *the intermediary is indifferent between the two forms of intermediation* as they both yield the same profit: $\Pi^D = \Pi^O = 1/27$. Expressions (22.1) and (22.3) indeed reveal that *the optimal bid–ask spread is equal to the optimal transaction fee*: $P^D = P^O = 1/3$. Also *the volume of trade in the two cases* is the same, $n_s^D n_b^D = Q^O = 1/9$. In other words, the intermediary achieves the same profit whether it buys the sellers' goods and resells them at a higher price to the buyers, or it lets sellers and buyers freely interact on its platform but taxes the transactions.

What is going on? Since in the present model the price p is decentralized, sellers can condition their retail price on their cost type. This is a mixed blessing, both for the intermediary and for society. Given P, we note that sellers now exert monopoly power over buyers. This implies that sellers charge a markup over costs. In the dealer setting, a positive markup arises for inframarginal sellers since the intermediary cannot price discriminate; however, sellers cannot exert market power since the price is set by the intermediary. Suppose that $P = 1/3$, which is the profit-maximizing spread set by a dealer. Given this price, we observe that any seller with $c > 0$ sets a price strictly above $2/3$. Thus, due to monopoly power, consumers face a higher retail price from all sellers except the one with type $c = 0$. This reduces transactions and is bad for welfare. However, there is a countervailing effect since decentralized price setting allows less efficient sellers to trade and make positive profit. Take a seller with costs $c = 1/3 + \varepsilon$. This seller would not participate in the dealer model. However, facing the same profit margin of the intermediary P, it can set a price $p > P + c$ and make positive profit. In our specific example, these two countervailing effects cancel out so that profits and trading volume are the same under centralized and decentralized trade.

For general distributions, this equivalence results does not hold. Already in the present special case, we observe that *seller and buyer decisions do not coincide in the two environments*. Also, surplus on both sides is affected. Under bid and ask prices, every seller with cost lower than $1/3$ sells to all buyers with valuation larger than $2/3$. As Figure 22.2 illustrates, all buyer–seller pairs in the shaded area trade. With a transaction fee and market power on the sellers' side, the participating sellers have a cost between 0 and $\bar{c} = 1 - P^O = 2/3$. A seller of type

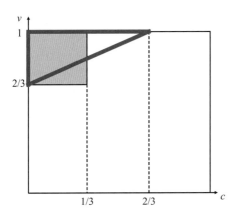

Figure 22.2 Equilibrium trade under dealer and platform intermediation

c sells at price $p\,(c) = 2/3 + c/2$, to all buyers v between $p(c) \geq 2/3$ and $1.$[g] Figure 22.2 depicts these equilibrium transactions between buyer–seller pairs: if the intermediary chooses the pure platform role, all buyer–seller pairs in the triangle trade.

In spite of these differences, *the two options are equivalent from a welfare point of view.* We indeed check that

$$W^D = \int_0^{\frac{1}{3}} \left(\int_{\frac{2}{3}}^1 (v - c)\,dv \right) dc = \tfrac{2}{27},$$

$$W^O = \int_0^{\frac{2}{3}} \left(\int_{\frac{2}{3}+\frac{c}{2}}^1 (v - c)\,dv \right) dc = \int_{\frac{1}{3}}^1 \left(\int_0^{\frac{v}{2}-\frac{1}{6}} (v - c)\,dc \right) dv = \tfrac{2}{27}.$$

We summarize our main insights in the following lesson.

Lesson 22.3   Suppose that an intermediary's only role is to organize the exchange of goods between sellers and buyers. If the intermediary acts as a dealer (i.e., buys and resells goods), trade is socially insufficient because the intermediary exerts monopoly power on both sides of the market. If the intermediary acts as a platform operator and only taxes trade while sellers set the retail price p, sellers condition their offer on their cost type and exert monopoly power over buyers. This tends to lead to higher prices but more sellers participating. In general, it is ambiguous under which role the intermediary makes higher profits and transaction volumes are higher.

For a number of reasons which are outside our setting, intermediaries may prefer one role over the other. We saw the intermediary simply as a prerequisite for transactions to take place but it did not add any value to the transactions otherwise. Naturally, as already discussed above, there are many instances where the intermediary does add value to the transactions. Then, the added value may differ according to whether the intermediary acts as a dealer or

[g] When market power is on the buyers' side, participating buyers have a valuation between $1/3$ and 1, and they buy at $p\,(v) = 1/6 + v/2$, which varies between $1/3$ and $2/3$, meaning that participating sellers have a cost between 0 and $1/3$.

as a platform operator. For instance, if buyers and sellers face a fixed cost to trade, potential participants on one side of the market have to consider the participation decisions on the other side and indirect network effects come into play. This may lead the intermediary to prefer the dealer role as it runs the risk of not being able to initiate buyers' and sellers' participation under the platform role. Indeed, as we discuss below, if each side of the market values a larger participation of the other side (e.g., because buyers value variety, which increases with sellers' participation), pessimistic expectations may lead to a situation where each side waits for the other side to move first and finally, nobody joins the platform. Acting as a dealer might then be helpful to solve the underlying coordination problem and 'break' these pessimistic expectations. The evolving business model of Amazon is indicative in this respect: Amazon started as a dealer and thus avoided the expectation coordination problem. Since then it has partly switched to the platform model since it has assured market participation.

   Another simplifying assumption of our setting is that the intermediary does not incur any variable cost. Clearly, the sources of costs may differ in the two business models: inventory and storage costs are incurred by dealers but not by platform operators; the reverse applies for information processing costs (i.e., costs of bringing buyers and sellers together, or of monitoring the transactions).[5]

   Independent of the role of the intermediary, there are other reasons why intermediaries exist and why their number is limited. The underlying force is again network effects. One important reason (which is orthogonal to our formal analysis) is that large markets provide more liquidity, a property which risk-averse market participants appreciate.[6] Intermediaries who control transactions on such markets can then charge positive transaction fees provided that trading via more than one intermediary is costly. This argument supports the fact that most shares are predominantly traded at one stock exchange. The issue of 'liquidity' in a different sense arises also in some matching markets: a more liquid market increases the probability of a successful match. We turn to such markets in the next section.

   In other markets, the reason for the existence of one dominant intermediary is that intermediaries carrying a large number of products, say shops in a shopping mall, provide more variety and lower prices (due to more intense competition between shops) to consumers and thus become more attractive in the eyes of the consumers. Consumers may stop to trade on alternative platforms if it is costly for them to establish a link to other platforms. This allows intermediaries to charge for transactions (and access) on their platform. The general argument is that network effects tend to lead to a concentrated market for intermediation services. We turn to the analysis of this issue in Section 22.3 with the analysis of intermediation in two-sided platforms.

22.2   Intermediaries as matchmakers

In this section, we turn to intermediaries that operate matching markets and contrast two different matching environments. The first environment has the feature that agents in one group value the matching services of an intermediary all the more when the participation of the other group is large because a large pool is more likely to lead to a successful match. Think, e.g., of business-to-business (B2B) electronic marketplaces. On these virtual meeting places, buyers and sellers can search for each other in order to conduct transactions. Business analysts report that the main motivation for firms to join a B2B marketplace is to enlarge their portfolio of potential trading partners.[7] The matching environment thus generates indirect network effects. This will lead to trade on only one platform. We provide a formal analysis of price competition between nondifferentiated intermediaries: we establish that indirect network effects lead to a winner-takes-all situation when intermediaries are homogeneous. In this context, we also explore the so-called 'divide-and-conquer' strategy, which appears as the key pricing strategy that intermediaries use in such situations.

In the second matching environment, users of matching services do not care so much about the number of matching prospects than about the characteristics of their trading partner.[h] This is the case, for example, in markets such as job search, dating or real estate. Another type of externality therefore arises: by joining an intermediary, an agent affects the welfare of agents in the other group by changing the composition, and hence the quality, of the pool of participants in its own group. As intermediaries are now defined not only by the size but also by the quality of the pool of participants, endogenous vertical differentiation may outweigh the indirect network effects and allow multiple intermediaries to coexist at equilibrium. In the second part of this section, we formally show that such coexistence is indeed possible, even in the absence of horizontal differentiation.

22.2.1   Divide-and-conquer strategies

Consider a population of buyers and a population of sellers (denoted by subscript b for buyers and subscript s for sellers, respectively), each consisting of a continuum of mass one.[8] Each agent has a unique trading partner in the other population, whom he can find only by using the matching services of an intermediary. There exist two intermediaries (noted $i = 1, 2$). If two matching partners have registered with the same intermediary, the probability of finding each other is equal to $0 < \lambda \leq 1$. Therefore, if a number n_b of buyers register with an intermediary, the probability for a seller to find her match through this intermediary is equal to $\lambda n_b \in [0, 1]$. Gains from trade in case of a successful match are normalized to one and are supposed to be equally shared between the trading partners following some efficient bargaining process.

The intermediaries compete à la Bertrand with two possible types of prices: registration fees M_k^i and a transaction fee P^i, with $i = 1, 2$ and $k = s, b$. Note that because of our assumptions (namely, constant gains from trade and efficient bargaining), transaction fees are non-distortionary and therefore, it is only the total fee that matters (i.e., $P^i = P_s^i + P_b^i$) and not the way it is split between the trading partners (i.e., the particular values of P_s^i and P_b^i). The net surplus to be shared between matched partners becomes $1 - P^i$.

We want to characterize the equilibria of the game in which the intermediaries first simultaneously set their price structure, and then agents choose which intermediary (if any)

---

[h] Nonintermediated trade under random matching in Section 22.1 also had this feature. Different from that model, we postulate here that there are complementarities in buyer and seller types. We need this key property to obtain sorting in the present model.

to register with. It is assumed that agents can register with at most one intermediary and that their utility is equal to zero if they do not register with any. The expected utilities for a buyer and for a seller when registering with intermediary i along with n_b^i buyers and n_s^i sellers are respectively equal to

$$U_b^i = n_s^i \lambda \tfrac{1}{2} \left(1 - P^i\right) - M_b^i,$$
$$U_s^i = n_b^i \lambda \tfrac{1}{2} \left(1 - P^i\right) - M_s^i.$$

Intermediary i's profits when attracting n_b^i buyers and n_s^i sellers are computed as

$$\Pi^i = \sum_{k=s,b} n_k^i \left(M_k^i - C_k\right) + \lambda n_b^i n_s^i P^i,$$

where C_b and C_s are the constant costs an intermediary incurs when providing services to one buyer and one seller, respectively.[i] An equilibrium in this game is a pair of price structures, $\left(M_b^1, M_s^1, P^1\right)$ and $\left(M_b^2, M_s^2, P^2\right)$, such that intermediaries maximize their profits and agents have no incentive to modify their registration decision.

We now show that *any equilibrium in the game involves a single active intermediary with zero profits.*[9] To understand this result, suppose that all agents register with, say, intermediary 1. For this situation to be an equilibrium, it must be that no pricing strategy allows intermediary 2 to earn a positive profit when agents hold pessimistic beliefs against 2 (i.e., after any price deviation by 2, agents coordinate on a distribution of agents across intermediaries that yields minimal profits for 2). Facing such pessimistic beliefs, intermediary 2 can only resort to a *'divide-and-conquer'* strategy. That is, 2 must first 'divide' by subsidizing one group (say buyers) to convince them to join; the subsidy, $-M_b^2$, must then satisfy: $-M_b^2 > \lambda\tfrac{1}{2}(1 - P^1) - M_b^1$ (the left-hand side is the utility buyers enjoy if they register with 2, holding the pessimistic belief that no seller will come along; the right-hand side is the utility they enjoy when staying with intermediary 1). If the latter condition is met, the participation of all buyers is obtained, which creates a bandwagon effect that allows 2 to 'conquer' all sellers (independently of their beliefs). The migration by all buyers and sellers generates maximal aggregate surplus $\lambda - C_b - C_s$, which intermediary 2 can capture by setting the transaction fee at its maximal level ($P^2 = 1$).

So, for such divide-and-conquer strategy not to be profitable, 2 must not be able to recoup the subsidy paid to buyers by taxing away aggregate surplus once all agents have migrated. Therefore, in equilibrium, agents must receive the total surplus and intermediary 1 cannot make a strictly positive profit. Intermediary 1 is constrained to design the following pricing strategy: subsidize full participation, charge the maximal transaction fee ($P^1 = 1$) and make zero profit ($M_b^1 + M_s^1 = C_b + C_s - \lambda$).

Alternatively, we could consider a sequential game with an incumbent intermediary 1 and a potential entrant 2. The previous result would then be interpreted as follows: the incumbent intermediary manages to monopolize the market but has to forego all profits in order to deter entry.[10]

---

[i] We assume that intermediation is efficient, in the sense that when all agents register with the same intermediary, total gains from trade are larger than total costs ($\lambda > C_s + C_b$).

22.2.2   **Sorting by an intermediary in a matching market**

In the previous model, agents on both market sides were supposed to be identical other than looking for a unique match in the other group. Hence, all that mattered for an agent when deciding to join a particular matchmaker was the expected number of agents on the other side joining the same matchmaker, as it defined the probability to find his or her match. Affiliation decisions affected the size of a group, thereby creating an indirect network externality.

We now take a different approach by assuming that agents within each group have heterogeneous types (or qualities) and are randomly matched with the agents of the other group who have joined the same matchmaker as them. We also assume that each agent's valuation increases when matched with an agent of higher quality.[11] Markets which fit that pattern are, e.g., job, dating or real estate markets; note, however, that, in reality, matching is in many instances *not* random. Here, it is not the expected size (since matching is random) but the expected quality of the pool of participants that affects an agent's decision to join a particular matchmaker. Because affiliation decisions affect the composition of the pool of participants, they create a *sorting externality*.

The model

We continue to consider a population of buyers and a population of sellers, each consisting of a continuum of mass one. Agents in each group are identified by a heterogeneous one-dimensional characteristic, which we call their 'type' (or 'quality'). For simplicity, we assume that the two sides are completely symmetric: on each side, types θ_s and θ_b are uniformly (and independently) distributed on the interval $[a, b]$, with $0 < a < b < \infty$.[12] Two intermediaries, or 'matchmakers', offer the same matching services to the two groups of agents (there is no horizontal differentiation between the two services). The matchmakers are assumed to be unable to observe types of agents and to price discriminate among the two groups. Their only price instrument is a uniform access or membership fee: $M_s^i = M_b^i \equiv M_i$ ($i = 1, 2$).

Given M_1 and M_2, agents simultaneously choose to use either matchmaker 1's or matchmaker 2's services (joint use of the two services is ruled out, i.e. we impose so-called singlehoming), or refrain from participating in the matching market (in which case their utility is normalized to zero). In each matching market, agents are randomly pairwise matched. This means that the probability that a buyer (resp. seller) of some type meets a seller (resp. buyer) whose type is in some set equals the proportion of participating sellers (resp. buyers) whose type belongs to that set. The match between a buyer of type β and a seller of type σ produces a value of $\beta\sigma$ to both of them. This means that types on the two sides are complementary and the socially efficient outcome would be to have fully assortative matching, i.e. in our symmetric setting $\beta = \sigma$. Let β_i and σ_i ($i = 1, 2$) define the expected type (i.e., the average quality) of, respectively, buyers and sellers participating in the matching market created by intermediary i. Then the utility of a buyer of type β and a seller of type σ using the services of matchmaker i are respectively given by $\beta\sigma_i - M_i$ and $\sigma\beta_i - M_i$.

The objective of each matchmaker is to maximize the sum of membership fees collected from buyers and sellers (to simplify, we assume that the matching process is costless: $C_b = C_s = 0$). We assume that the two matchmakers choose their price sequentially, with matchmaker 1 being (for some unmodelled reason) the price leader. We look then at pure-strategy (subgame perfect) equilibria of the following game: in stage 1, matchmaker 1 sets its price M_1; in stage 2, matchmaker 2 observes M_1 and sets its price M_2; in stage 3, given M_1 and M_2, buyers and sellers simultaneously choose which matchmaker to register with. This sequential-move game will allow us to identify intuitive conditions for the two matchmakers to coexist at equilibrium and to understand the sorting role of prices.[13]

Two matchmakers coexist at equilibrium

Since the two matchmakers are pure Bertrand competitors (recall that they offer homogeneous matching services), it may seem surprising that they may both manage to attract subsets of buyers and sellers and to achieve positive profits at equilibrium. To understand how it can be so, we first note that the assumption of a random-matching technology implies the absence of any indirect network effect (and hence of the reinforcing mechanisms leading to monopolization that we described in the previous model). Second, marginal cost pricing may be avoided here because prices may allow agents to sort themselves. As agents have private information about their type, they self-select into matching markets based on the prices and on their expectation of the quality of the pool of participants from the other group. In consequence, if one matchmaker sets a price equal to marginal cost (i.e. zero under our assumptions), the other matchmaker still has the possibility of charging a higher price and earn strictly positive profits by attracting the types willing to pay more to be matched with higher types (whom they rationally expect to participate for the very same reason).[j]

Now, for the two matchmakers to be active at equilibrium, matchmaker 2 should not find it profitable to use the latter strategy to drive out matchmaker 1. By charging an appropriately higher price than M_1, matchmaker 2 could provide a higher-quality market that would induce highest types to leave matchmaker 1, thereby inducing lower types to follow suit until no single agent stays with matchmaker 1. This so-called strategy of 'overtaking' is made possible by the sorting role of prices. The coexistence of the two matchmakers at equilibrium supposes thus that the first mover manages to survive overtaking. To do so, matchmaker 1 must choose a sufficiently low price to induce matchmaker 2 to prefer the creation of a second, more exclusive, matching market over the strategy of overtaking, which would drive matchmaker 1 out of business. As we now show, this possibility exists as long as agents in both groups are heterogeneous enough, in the sense that the distribution of types is 'sufficiently diffused'.

---

[j] There is thus a form of vertical product differentiation that emerges between intermediaries. This differentiation is endogenous: the quality of the matching services does not result from an exogenous initial choice of the firms (as we assumed in Chapter 5), but follows endogenously from the choice of prices that, in turn, determine the participation decisions of the agents and hence, the expected quality of the match (which results from the composition of the pools of participants).

Suppose there is full participation (hence a must be sufficiently large) and that there is sufficient type heterogeneity (as we will see, we need $b > 3a$). Supposing that the two conditions are met, we analyze matchmaker 2's best response given an M_1 which fulfils $0 < M_1 < a^2$. Like in any price competition, matchmaker 2 could think of undercutting its rival by setting $M_2 < M_1$. However, one can show that even with a zero price, matchmaker 2 would not be able to undercut matchmaker 1 because it is more attractive to stay with the pool of matchmaker 1 given that the worst types would be the first to deviate. Thus consider the possibility that matchmaker 2 overtakes by setting a higher price. We have to show that for $M_1 > 0$ but still small, it is not profit-maximizing for matchmaker 2 to drive matchmaker 1 completely out of the market, which would give zero profit to matchmaker 1. For $M_2 > M_1$, agents in each group can be divided into two segments: types lying between a and $\widehat{\theta}$ join matchmaker 1 and types lying between $\widehat{\theta}$ and b join matchmaker 2. It follows that the average type of agents (buyers or sellers) joining matchmaker 1 is computed as $m_1 = \frac{1}{2}(a + \widehat{\theta})$. Similarly, the average type for matchmaker 2 is given by $m_2 = \frac{1}{2}(\widehat{\theta} + b)$. We can identify the type $\widehat{\theta}$ who is indifferent between joining one or the other matchmaker as follows:

$$\widehat{\theta}m_1 - M_1 = \widehat{\theta}m_2 - M_2 \Leftrightarrow \widehat{\theta} = 2\frac{M_2 - M_1}{b - a}.$$

Note that agents of the lowest type a strictly prefer joining matchmaker 1 over not participating if $am_1 = \frac{1}{2}a(a + \widehat{\theta}) > M_1$; a sufficient condition is $a^2 > M_1$. Matchmaker 2 then chooses M_2 to maximize

$$\Pi_2 = M_2 \frac{2}{b - a}\left(b - 2\frac{M_2 - M_1}{b - a}\right) \text{ s.t. } \widehat{\theta}(M_2) = 2\frac{M_2 - M_1}{b - a} \geq a.$$

Ignoring the constraint and given M_1, we compute the profit-maximizing membership fee as $M_2^* = \frac{1}{4}(2M_1 + b(b - a))$. We then observe that only higher types join matchmaker 2,

$$\widehat{\theta}(M_2^*) = \frac{b(b - a) - 2M_1}{2(b - a)} > a \Leftrightarrow M_1 < \frac{1}{2}(b - 2a)(b - a) \equiv \bar{M}_1.$$

Moreover, we note that $a^2 < \bar{M}_1$ is equivalent to $b > 3a$. Hence, for some $M_1 > 0$ matchmaker 1 cannot be completely driven out of the market and matchmaker 1 will set M_1^* with this property. This gives the main lesson from our analysis.

Lesson 22.5 Suppose that two intermediaries offer similar random matching services to two groups of heterogeneous agents and that each agent's valuation increases when matched with an agent of higher quality. Due to the sorting role of prices, two matchmakers competing through membership fees may coexist at the equilibrium of a sequential move game as long as the distribution of types is sufficiently diffused; the matchmaker who moves first survives with strictly positive profits.

22.3   Intermediaries as two-sided platforms

In this section, we examine situations with two groups of agents who may interact through one or several intermediaries and who prefer a larger pool of trading partners. Thus the interaction between the two groups exhibits indirect network effects: agents of one group are better off when the number of agents in the other group increases. Think of, for instance, payment systems organized around credit cards: the more merchants accept a particular card, the higher the benefits for consumers carrying this card, and vice versa. Similarly, users enjoy a computer operating system (OS) with a large variety of software, and developers prefer to write software for an OS with a large base of users. And so it goes in other so-called *two-sided (or multi-sided) platforms* such as video-game consoles, shopping malls, real-estate agents, etc. On such platforms, intermediaries have to design pricing strategies to induce agents on both sides to participate. The competition between intermediaries is therefore also affected by the agents' ability to register or not with more than one platform. Antitrust evaluations have to be carefully adapted to the particular market environment.

Before we address the latter three issues, we introduce some terminology and notation that we will use throughout this section. To fix ideas, and because it is consistent with most of the cases we analyse, we refer to the two groups of agents as *sellers* and *buyers*, and identify them with subscripts s and b, respectively. Intermediaries operate a *marketplace* or a *platform*, the two words being used interchangeably. When two intermediaries are present, we identify them by superscripts 1, 2. As for the prices intermediaries charge for their services, we distinguish between *membership (or access) fees* (which correspond to a fixed access or registration charge) and *transaction (or usage) fees* (which correspond to variable usage fees): M_k^i and P_k^i denote, respectively, the membership fee and the transaction fee that intermediary i charges to an agent of group $k \in \{s, b\}$.

22.3.1   The price structure for intermediation services

We consider a market with positive indirect network effects of the form that the presence of more agents on one side of the market increases the utility of agents on the other side of the market. If agents on each side are heterogeneous, they will make different consumption choices. Those with a high opportunity cost to participate will stay away, whereas those with a low opportunity cost to participate will join.

For simplicity, let us first consider the case of a monopoly platform, which operates under zero marginal costs. Then price equal to marginal costs means that the use of the platform is free. If access of the platform were subsidized on one side, additional participants on this side of the market would join. Because of positive indirect network effects, participants on the other side would obtain a higher utility. Consequently, more consumers would join on the other side. This leads to positive feedback. The socially optimal access or membership fees involve subsidization of both sides of the market. Clearly, also a for-profit platform internalizes the existence of network effects but maximizes profits. Nevertheless, there are important differences between privately and socially optimal membership fees.

Before analysing the profit-maximizing price structure of an intermediary who sets membership fees, consider the case that the intermediary sets only usage fees. We note that if buyers and sellers internalize a change in the price structure in their contractual relationship the structure of usage prices is neutral and only the total level of the usage fee matters, i.e. the way in which the total usage fee $P = P_s + P_b$ is split among buyer and seller is irrelevant. However, in the opposite case, the structure of usage fees is not neutral.

To better understand this issue, it is useful to take a look at the credit card industry, as done in Case 22.2. In the credit card industry in which the no-surcharge rule holds, we can analyse a model in which the surplus of buyers and sellers depends on the participation and intensity of use on the other side and in which the transaction price that applies to one side of the market is fully borne by this side.[k]

Case 22.2 The 'no surcharge rule' in the credit card industry

In the credit card industry, a credit card constitutes a payment system that is used by some buyers to pay sellers. It is useful to distinguish two groups of buyers, those who only pay in cash and those who only pay by credit card. In a very simplified representation of the credit card industry, there is a single credit card company that represents the intermediary. This intermediary can charge a price per transaction (here we ignore the possibility of charging membership fees). Suppose that the seller has to set the same retail price for cash and non-cash buyers (this is the so-called no-surcharge rule). Then not only the total price of a transaction but the structure of this usage fee matters. In particular, if the share of buyers who buy in cash is large, the seller will approximately only consider these buyers when setting the retail price. If, on the contrary, the seller is allowed to charge different prices for the two groups of buyers, it is irrelevant whether buyers or sellers have to pay the usage fee if a transaction is made using a card; only the total price of a transaction matters. Thus, to have a meaningful analysis of the price structure in the credit card industry, we have to consider market environments in which the no-surcharge rule applies.

We now turn to the price structure of membership fees and abstract from usage fees. Then the intermediary has two price instruments: the membership fee on the buyer side and the membership fee on the seller side. Suppose that a single intermediary hosts a number of sellers that sell independent products on a single platform. All buyers who access the intermediary's platform have the same demand at each seller. Thus each seller has a seller–buyer relationship with each buyer and each buyer has a seller–buyer relationship with each seller. Suppose furthermore that in a seller–buyer relationship, prices or terms of transaction are independent of the membership fee that applies to buyers and sellers. We provide two alternative justifications for this assumption. First, suppose buyers have a demand for one unit from each seller. Then seller and buyer may engage in bilateral bargaining once they meet on the intermediary's platform. At this point, the membership fees are already paid and thus sunk; therefore they do not affect the bargaining outcome. Secondly, membership fees do not affect transaction prices if the price-setting power exclusively rests with the seller and buyers

---

[k] Rochet and Tirole (2006) define as two-sided market a market in which the price structure for usage is not neutral. It is important to note that the answer to the question whether a particular market is a two-sided market in the above sense may depend on the rules which are enforced by antitrust authorities, as in the case of the no-surcharge rule.

have variable demand for each product. In particular, suppose that the seller faces downward-sloping demand by each buyer, $q(p)$ and has constant marginal costs of production c. Then independent of the number of active buyers and sellers, the seller will set its monopoly price $p^m = \arg\max_p (p - c)q(p)$ (presuming that the monopoly problem is well-defined). Denote monopoly profit by $\pi = (p^m - c)q(p^m)$ and net surplus by $u = \int_{p^m}^{\infty} q(p)dp$.

Each seller makes a profit per buyer of π and each buyer derives utility u per seller. Then the surplus of a seller who joins the platform (gross of any fixed costs) is $v_s = n_b\pi - M_s$, where n_b is the number of buyers on the platform and M_s is the membership fee for sellers. Similarly, the surplus of a buyer who joins the platform is $v_b = n_s u - M_b$, where n_s is the number of sellers on the platform and M_b is the membership fee for buyers. The number of buyers and sellers on the platform is determined by a free-entry condition. Buyers have heterogeneous opportunity costs of joining the platform. Thus the lower the membership fee, the larger the number of buyers who join, everything else equal. We capture this relationship by writing the number of buyers on the platform as a function of the buyers' surplus, $n_b = N_b(v_b)$. Similarly, we express the number of sellers on the platform as a function of the sellers' surplus, $n_s = N_s(v_s)$.

The intermediary is assumed to incur a constant cost per buyer, C_b, and a constant cost per seller, C_s. Its profits are therefore $\Pi = n_s(M_s - C_s) + n_b(M_b - C_b)$. Note that membership fees induce a surplus v_b for each buyer and a surplus v_s for each seller.[14] Using the definitions of v_b and v_s, we can express membership fees as functions of surpluses, $M_s = N_b(v_b)\pi - v_s$ and $M_b = N_s(v_s)u - v_b$. Thus the intermediary's profit as a function of the surpluses offered to buyers and sellers is

$$\Pi(v_s, v_b) = (N_b(v_b)\pi - v_s - C_s)N_s(v_s) + (N_s(v_s)u - v_b - C_b)N_b(v_b).$$

First-order conditions for profit maximization are

$$\begin{cases} \frac{\partial\Pi}{\partial v_s} = (N_b(v_b)\pi - v_s - C_s)N_s'(v_s) - N_s(v_s) + N_s'(v_s)u N_b(v_b) = 0, \\ \frac{\partial\Pi}{\partial v_b} = N_b'(v_b)\pi N_s(v_s) - N_b(v_b) + (N_s(v_s)u - v_b - C_b)N_b'(v_b) = 0. \end{cases}$$

This can be written as

$$\begin{cases} (M_s - C_s)N_s'(v_s) - N_s(v_s) + N_s'(v_s)u N_b(v_b) = 0, \\ N_b'(v_b)\pi N_s(v_s) - N_b(v_b) + (M_b - C_b)N_b'(v_b) = 0. \end{cases}$$

Hence, profit-maximizing membership fees satisfy

$$M_s = C_s - un_b + \frac{N_s(v_s)}{N_s'(v_s)}, \quad \text{and} \quad M_b = C_b - \pi n_s + \frac{N_b(v_b)}{N_b'(v_b)}.$$

Monopoly prices are equal to the cost of providing access adjusted *downward* by the external benefit exerted on the other side of the market, and adjusted *upward* by a factor related to the sensitivity of participation on the platform. Note that for a given number of participants on the other side of the market, the demand elasticities for access can be expressed as

$$\eta_s(M_s|n_b) = M_s\frac{N_s'(n_b\pi - M_s)}{N_s(n_b\pi - M_s)} \quad \text{and} \quad \eta_b(M_b|n_s) = M_b\frac{N_b'(n_s u - M_b)}{N_b(n_s u - M_b)}.$$

We can thus rewrite the equation for profit-maximizing membership fees as

$$\frac{M_s - (C_s - un_b)}{M_s} = \frac{1}{\eta_s(M_s | n_b)},$$ (22.5)

$$\frac{M_b - (C_b - \pi n_s)}{M_b} = \frac{1}{\eta_b(M_b | n_s)}.$$ (22.6)

This formula is similar to the monopoly pricing formula (or Lerner index) derived in Chapter 3. Since the intermediary has monopoly power on both sides of the market, the formula now applies to buyers and sellers. Furthermore, the monopoly intermediary internalizes indirect network externalities. This is reflected by the downward adjustment of the cost by the external benefit buyers exert on sellers, un_b, in the pricing formula for the sellers' membership fees and, similarly, by the external benefit sellers exert on buyers, πn_s, in the pricing formula for the buyers' membership fees. We observe that markups are set as if there were lower costs $C_s - un_b$ and $C_b - \pi n_s$, respectively.

In the special case that elasticities are constant and of the same size on both sides of the market and that costs for granting access are the same, the group which exerts the larger external benefit enjoys the lower membership fee. This membership fee may even be zero or negative – that is, one side of the market receives a payment for joining. The main insight of our analysis is stated in the next lesson and illustrated in Case 22.3.

Lesson 22.6 In a market with a single intermediary who charges membership fees, the side of the market which exerts the larger external benefit on the other tends to face lower membership fees. A profit-maximizing intermediary may subsidize one side of the market so as to generate a higher volume of trade and thus, higher profits on the other side of the market.

Case 22.3 Pricing access to night clubs

If you have started this book as part of a course, you are likely to finish soon and may think of celebrating a successful final exam by dancing the night away. If you consider going to a discotheque you are likely to observe gender-specific prices: women pay a lower entrance fee and sometimes can enter for free. For instance, if you were to go to a night club in Johannesburg, South Africa during April 2007, the Voodoo Lounge would charge a cover charge of SAR 200 for men but only SAR 100 for women on Fridays and Saturdays. The same ratio applies to Catwalk, Fourways, where men pay entrance fees SAR 100, while women pay only SAR 50. In relative terms, somewhat more attractive to men is the Manhattan Club which charged an entrance fees of SAR 70 for men and of SAR 60 for women. Two other hot spots were Café Vacca Matta with an entrance fee of SAR 60 for men and SAR 40 for women and Panache Café with an entrance fee of SAR 50 for men and SAR 30 for women.[15] While these clubs certainly do not operate in isolation, they all are apparently concerned about the gender balance.

Having studied price discrimination in Part IV, you may merely explain this phenomenon by different price elasticities for men and women. However, a deeper insight can be obtained taking into account indirect network effects. Even if men and women have the same willingness to pay for a visit to a disco, a profit-maximizing disco may charge different prices to men and women. As a matter of fact, the disco can be seen as an intermediary in a matching market with indirect network effects: the utility functions of men and women depend positively on the number of visitors of the opposite sex. If men are more responsive to the number of women than women to the number of men, the profit-maximizing price structure has the property that women pay less than men.

So far we have derived the privately optimal price structure of the intermediary. We can compare this outcome with the socially optimal pricing structure. Total welfare as the unweighted sum of surpluses is $W = \Pi(v_s, v_b) + PS(v_s) + CS(v_b)$, where PS is the aggregate surplus of sellers and CS the aggregate surplus of buyers. Note that PS satisfies $PS'(v_s) = N_s(v_s)$ and CS satisfies $CS'(v_b) = N_b(v_b)$. Welfare maximization leads to individual surplus

$$v_s = (u + \pi)n_b - C_s \quad \text{and} \quad v_b = (u + \pi)n_s - C_b.$$

The membership fees that implement the welfare-maximizing solution satisfy

$$M_s = C_s - un_b \quad \text{and} \quad M_b = C_b - \pi n_s.$$

In words, welfare-maximizing sellers' membership fees are equal to the cost of providing access to a seller minus the external benefit a seller exerts on buyers (which is the number of buyers, n_b, times the utility each buyer receives u). Comparing the profit-maximizing to the welfare-maximizing solution, we observe that the intermediary correctly internalizes the indirect network effects that are present in the market, but, due to his monopoly position, he charges a premium for access on both sides of the market, which depends on how strongly participation reacts to the level of the membership fee.

Lesson 22.7   **The welfare-maximizing membership fee for an agent on one side of the platform is equal to the cost of providing access to this agent decreased by the external benefit that this agent exerts on agents on the other side of the platform. These fees are lower than the fees a monopoly intermediary would charge.**

22.3.2   Competing intermediaries

Our analysis so far in this section was concerned with monopoly intermediaries. How does competition between intermediaries change the picture? We know from Chapter 20 that, with indirect network effects, a winner-takes-all situation can emerge. In the previous section, we obtained answers to this question in a matching market. Our main goal in this section is to shed some light on this question in two-sided markets with indirect network effects and differentiation between intermediaries. In particular, we want to see under which conditions more than one intermediary can survive with strictly positive profits. We first address this issue in environments where agents can only access a single intermediary; this is called singlehoming.

We show that monopolization by a single intermediary is more likely the stronger the indirect network effects and the more similar the marketplaces are. We than analyse situations with so-called multihoming: some agents have the opportunity to register simultaneously with different intermediaries.

A model of platform competition

In Section 22.3.1, we analysed the pricing by a single intermediary. We now extend this analysis to a market in which two intermediaries compete with each other for buyers and sellers. For the moment, we consider environments where buyers and sellers are restricted to visit only one intermediary (we will consider below cases where they may decide to visit both intermediaries). That is, we assume here that both sides singlehome. This appears to be the first natural extension of the monopoly setting we have analyzed. Furthermore, this is also a reasonable approximation of a number of real-life situations, as illustrated in Case 22.4.

Case 22.4 Singlehoming environments

Singlehoming environments in the real world can be motivated by indivisibilities and limited resources, or by contractual restrictions. The former applies to certain real-world market places where buyers and sellers can physically locate in only one of them (flea and farmer markets come to mind). For the latter, we find more examples. For instance, taxi companies in Germany sign exclusive contracts with taxi call centres. There also appears to be little multihoming on the consumer side. Similarly, some employment agencies for temporary work can be characterized by singlehoming on both sides of the market. It is less clear to which extent video game platforms can be approximated by two-sided singlehoming. Some gamers have more than one platform and leading game developers nowadays develop the same game for different platforms. Hagiu and Lee (2007) state that prominent video game publishers have the vast majority of their hit games present on all major video game consoles. For instance, Evans and Schmalensee (2008) report that Electronic Arts, a leading game developer, released its games for the Nintendo, Microsoft and Sony platforms. However, Clements and Ohashi (2005) considering an earlier generation of game platforms report that only 17% of titles in their sample was available on multiple platforms. Also, it has been claimed that the market for certain specialized magazines, where the magazine serves as the platform and advertisers and readers constitute the two sides of the market, can be described as a market on which both sides singlehome (see Kaiser and Wright, 2006). In addition, many media markets have the property that content is exclusive. If content providers sell their content to consumers while the media platform only charges for the services it offers, we are also in a situation where both sides singlehome (provided that consumers singlehome in these markets).

As before, there are two sides of the market, the buyer side and the seller side. Each seller and each buyer goes to either one of the two platforms 1 and 2.[16] Suppose that each side is of mass 1, so that the total number of buyers adds up to 1, $n_b^1 + n_b^2 = 1$, and also the total number of sellers adds up to one, $n_s^1 + n_s^2 = 1$. A buyer at platform i buys one unit from each seller at the same platform. Hence, using otherwise the same setup as in the previous analysis of a monopoly intermediary, buyer and seller surpluses gross of any opportunity cost of visiting a platform are

$$v_s^i = n_b^i \pi - M_s^i \quad \text{and} \quad v_b^i = n_s^i u - M_b^i,$$

where M_b^i and M_s^i are the membership fees set by intermediary i. Suppose sellers and buyers are uniformly distributed on the unit interval and that platforms are located at the extreme point of the unit interval. We furthermore assume that participation is sufficiently attractive such that all buyers and sellers participate in the market. Sellers and buyers are assumed to incur an opportunity cost of visiting a platform that increases linearly in distance at rates τ_b and τ_s, respectively. For both sides of the market, we thus obtain the standard Hotelling specification,

$$n_s^i = \frac{1}{2} + \frac{v_s^i - v_b^i}{2\tau_s} \quad \text{and} \quad n_b^i = \frac{1}{2} + \frac{v_b^i - v_s^i}{2\tau_b}.$$

Using the expressions for buyer and seller surplus and the facts that $n_b^j = 1 - n_b^i$, and $n_s^j = 1 - n_s^i$, we obtain the following expressions for the numbers of buyers and sellers at the two platforms:

$$\begin{cases} n_s^i\left(n_b^i\right) = \frac{1}{2} + \frac{1}{2\tau_s}\left[(2n_b^i - 1)\pi - (M_s^i - M_s^j)\right], \\ n_b^i\left(n_s^i\right) = \frac{1}{2} + \frac{1}{2\tau_b}\left[(2n_s^i - 1)u - (M_b^i - M_b^j)\right]. \end{cases} \tag{22.7}$$

Looking at the first line, we observe that, for given membership fees, an additional buyer attracts π/τ_s additional sellers (i.e., $\partial n_s^i/\partial n_b^i = \pi/\tau_s$). Similarly, looking at the second line, we see that an additional seller attracts u/τ_b additional buyers.

Combining these two findings, we see that the indirect network effects on each side of the market are measured by the ratio $u\pi/\tau_b\tau_s$. The strength of the indirect network effects determines the number of active intermediaries at equilibrium. In particular, two intermediaries cannot be active if the indirect network effects are too strong with respect to the degree of horizontal differentiation.[1]

To exclude this possibility, we require that $u\pi/\tau_b\tau_s < 1$, or equivalently that $\tau_b\tau_s > u\pi$, i.e., that the opportunity costs τ_b and τ_s (which measure the perceived horizontal differentiation between the two platforms) be sufficiently large with respect to the gains from trade u and π (which measure the indirect network effects). We can then solve the implicit expressions (22.7) for the number of buyers and sellers to obtain the following formulas:

$$n_s^i = \frac{1}{2} + \frac{\pi(M_b^j - M_b^i) + \tau_b(M_s^j - M_s^i)}{2(\tau_b\tau_s - u\pi)},$$

$$n_b^i = \frac{1}{2} + \frac{u(M_s^j - M_s^i) + \tau_s(M_b^j - M_b^i)}{2(\tau_b\tau_s - u\pi)}.$$

Under the assumption that $\tau_b\tau_s > u\pi$, we see that the number of sellers (resp. buyers) at one platform decreases with the membership fee that sellers (resp. buyers) have to pay on this platform (i.e., n_s^i decreases with M_s^i, and n_b^i with M_b^i). Interestingly, we also see that the number of sellers (resp. buyers) at one platform decreases with the membership fee *buyers*

---

[1] As we have seen in the previous section, homogeneous matchmakers who compete in prices make zero profits and only one of them is active.

(resp. *sellers*) have to pay on this platform (i.e., n_s^i decreases with M_b^i, and n_b^i with M_s^i). The latter effect is due to the indirect network effects.[m]

We can now turn to the resolution of the intermediaries' pricing game.[n] Assuming as before that the intermediary's cost per buyer is C_b and per seller is C_s, we can write platform i's profit as

$$\Pi^i = (M_s^i - C_s)\left(\frac{1}{2} + \frac{\pi(M_b^j - M_b^i) + \tau_b(M_s^j - M_s^i)}{2(\tau_b\tau_s - u\pi)}\right)$$

$$+ (M_b^i - C_b)\left(\frac{1}{2} + \frac{u(M_s^j - M_s^i) + \tau_s(M_b^j - M_b^i)}{2(\tau_b\tau_s - u\pi)}\right).$$

The two intermediaries simultaneously choose membership fees on both sides of the market. First-order conditions of profit maximization in a symmetric equilibrium, i.e. $M_s^1 = M_s^2 \equiv M_s$ and $M_b^1 = M_b^2 \equiv M_b$, can be written as

$$\begin{cases} M_s = C_s + \tau_s - \frac{u}{\tau_b}(\pi + M_b - C_b), \\ M_b = C_b + \tau_b - \frac{\pi}{\tau_s}(u + M_s - C_s). \end{cases}$$

The equilibrium membership fee for the sellers is equal to marginal costs plus the product-differentiation term as in the standard Hotelling model, adjusted downward by the term $\frac{u}{\tau_b}(\pi + M_b - C_b)$. Recall that each additional seller attracts u/τ_b additional buyers. These additional buyers allow the intermediary to extract π per seller without affecting the sellers' surplus. In addition, each of the additional u/τ_b buyers gives a profit of $M_b - C_b$ to the seller. Thus $\frac{u}{\tau_b}(\pi + M_b - C_b)$ represents the value of an additional buyer to the intermediary. The higher this value, the more aggressive the price setting among intermediaries. The same holds on the buyers' side.

Solving the system of first-order conditions gives explicit expressions for equilibrium membership fees:

$$\begin{cases} M_s = C_s + \tau_s - u, \\ M_b = C_b + \tau_b - \pi. \end{cases}$$

These expressions are particularly simple because a price reduction by one intermediary does not lead to any market expansion, but only to an increase in its share of buyers and sellers (this is due to the Hotelling specification). We observe that the side of the market that exerts a strong indirect network effect on the other tends to be subsidized. Also the side of the market with little product differentiation tends to pay a lower price. This confirms our qualitative result obtained with a single intermediary according to which the side of the market with more elastic participation tends to pay lower membership fees. In the special case in which u and π are determined through bilateral bargaining between buyer and seller we observe that a gain in bargaining power (across all buyer–seller pairs) is more than offset by the intermediaries' increase of membership fees.

---

[m] For stronger indirect network effects, i.e. for $u\pi > \tau_b\tau_s$, the number of agents on one platform would be an *increasing* function of the membership fee that these agents pay on this platform. This naturally creates tipping effects and leads to a winner-takes-all situation (as explained in Chapter 20).

[n] To make sure that the second-order conditions are satisfied in the maximization programmes of this game, we impose a slightly more restrictive condition than $\tau_b\tau_s > u\pi$, namely $4\tau_s\tau_b > (u + \pi)^2$.

If both intermediaries are active, they make positive profits

$$\Pi^i = \tfrac{1}{2}(\tau_b + \tau_s - u - \pi).$$

These profits are increasing in the degree of product differentiation on both sides of the market and decreasing in the buyers' and sellers' surplus for each transaction, i.e., the size of indirect network effects.

To evaluate the effect of competition on the level of membership fees, we compare the equilibrium expression obtained here with the expressions obtained under monopoly. Given that both intermediaries set the same prices, the intermediaries' elasticities of the number of buyers and sellers with respect to membership fees are $\eta_b = M_b/\tau_b$ and $\eta_s = M_s/\tau_s$, respectively. Hence, equilibrium membership fees can be expressed as

$$\frac{M_s - (C_s - 2n_b u)}{M_s} = \frac{1}{\eta_s},$$

$$\frac{M_b - (C_b - 2n_s \pi)}{M_b} = \frac{1}{\eta_b}.$$

Compared to the formula with a single intermediary – i.e., expressions (22.5) and (22.6) – we observe that the membership fee on one side is reduced twice as strongly in the size of the indirect network effect exerted by the other side, which is measured by u. To understand the difference between monopoly intermediation and intermediation under competition, note that the effect of a lost seller on the intermediaries profit is more pronounced under competition. Under competition, this lost seller joins the competitor's platform and thus makes it more difficult to keep the same number of buyers. The membership fee paid by buyers has thus to be reduced twice as much under competition to keep the number of buyers constant. The same logic holds for a change in the number of buyers.

> **Lesson 22.8** In a market in which buyers and sellers join either one of two intermediaries, membership fees react more strongly on network effects than in a market with a single intermediary.

The effects of multihoming

We have focused so far on environments where buyers and sellers singlehome, i.e., use at most one platform. In other environments, multihoming may be attractive and feasible. For instance, buyers may go to both intermediaries because this gives them a larger selection of products if sellers are restricted to visit only one platform. On the other hand, sellers may visit both platforms to reach all potential buyers if buyers visit only one platform. In both cases, one side of the market visits both platforms (i.e., multihomes) and the other one visits one platform (i.e., singlehomes). It should be clear that if one side multihomes, there are no gains for the other side to multihome as well. Thus at most one side multihomes.° Case 22.5 gives a number of examples of platforms with multihoming.

Case 22.5 Multihoming environments[17]

Multihoming on the seller side *Media platforms*: viewers tend to watch a single programme at a time, whereas firms can place advertising in various programmes that are shown simultaneously (similarly for newspapers and magazines). *Shopping platforms*: shoppers tend to visit a single shopping mall whereas chains can open stores in various shopping malls. *Computer operating systems (OS)*: users typically use a single OS but, as analysed by Lerner (2002), developers tend to develop software for various OS. *Credit cards*: most merchants accept credit cards from several platforms; many consumers carry multiple credit cards but Rysman (2007) reports that most of them seem to use a favourite card most often.

Multihoming on the buyer side *Flea markets*: every Sunday morning, there are two flea markets in Brussels; their locations are sufficiently close for consumers to be able to visit both on the same morning; however, sellers are not mobile and stay put on a single market. *Shopping platforms*: owner-managed shops may set up in only one of the shopping areas, but consumers may be able to make it to both areas for their shopping. *In general*: such situations arise in cases in which sellers sign exclusivity contracts with platforms but where buyers are not restricted to singlehome.

To understand how multihoming may affect the results that we have derived so far, we focus on situations where sellers multihome and buyers singlehome. Here, a seller lost to one platform is not a seller gained by the other platform. Thus intermediaries have to be more concerned with losing buyers. This suggests that although one might naively think that those agents that have the ability to access various platforms simultaneously are at an advantage compared to those who cannot, actually the opposite reasoning is true once the pricing by the intermediaries is taken into account. Intermediaries compete fiercely for buyers, this tends to lead to low and possibly even negative prices for buyers accessing the platform but prices above costs for the seller side.

Compared to the situation with a single intermediary this suggests that competition may distort prices and may actually lead to a price structure that is further away from the socially optimal one than if a single intermediary was granted exclusive rights.

We extend our previous model with a single intermediary to two competing inter-mediaries and include heterogeneous sellers who can access both platforms.[18] The number of sellers on platform i is determined according to a function N_s^i that depends on the number of buyers who visit the platform and on the membership fee that sellers are charged:

$$n_s^i = N_s^i(n_b^i, M_s^i).$$

° However, participants on one side may be heterogeneous so that some multihome whereas others do not. In this case, the same may happen on the other side.

Hidden behind this formulation is the heterogeneity of sellers. Suppose for instance that sellers have heterogeneous fixed costs of establishing their business. In particular, if these fixed costs are distributed uniformly on some interval, then N_s^i is linear in the membership fee M_s^i. In general, N_s^i is decreasing in M_s^i and increasing in n_b^i. Clearly, a seller's decision to join platform i is not affected by its decision whether to join the other platform j.[p]

An intermediary's revenue on the seller side is $n_s^i M_s^i = N_s^i(n_b^i, M_s^i) M_s^i$. Since, for a given number of buyers on platform i, the membership fee on the seller side uniquely determines the number of sellers, we can write *revenues on the seller side* as a function of n_b^i and n_s^i, denoted by $R_s^i(n_b^i, n_s^i)$.

Concerning the buyer side, it is again useful to think of platforms offering net utilities to buyers (excluding heterogeneous transportation costs or other sources of heterogeneity). The utility of buyers for visiting platform i is $v_b^i = u(n_s^i) - M_b^i$.[q] If u is increasing, the seller side exerts a positive indirect network effect on buyers, otherwise the indirect network effect is negative.[r] The number of buyers on platform i is a function of the net utilities offered to buyers by the different platforms: $n_b^i = N_b^i(v_b^i, v_b^j)$, which increases in the first argument and decreases in the second (a particular case is the linear Hotelling specification that we used in the previous model).

Each platform maximizes its profits

$$\Pi^i = n_b^i(M_b^i - C_b) + n_s^i(M_s^i - C_s)$$
$$= N_b^i(v_b^i, v_b^j)(M_b^i - C_b) + R_s^i(n_b^i, n_s^i) - n_s^i C_s$$

where, as above, C_b and C_s are the platform's cost per buyer and per seller, respectively. The intermediary can vary n_s^i and M_b^i to keep the net surplus constant, $u(n_s^i) - M_b^i = \bar{v}_b^i$. Substituting M_b^i by $u(n_s^i) - \bar{v}_b^i$, we can write profits as

$$\Pi^i = N_b^i(v_b^i, v_b^j)(u(n_s^i) - \bar{v}_b^i - C_b) + R_s^i(n_b^i, n_s^i) - n_s^i C_s.$$

For a given number of buyers, each platform is in a monopoly position with respect to sellers. Therefore, suppose that platform i attracts n_b^i buyers to whom it offers a utility $\bar{v}_b^i$. Then each platform maximizes profits with respect to M_b^i and n_s^i holding buyers' net utility constant at $\bar{v}_b^i$. Given $n_b^i = \bar{n}_b^i$, platform i decides to take in the number n_s^{i*} of sellers where

$$n_s^{i*} = \arg\max_{n_s} \bar{n}_b^i(u(n_s)) + R_s^i(\bar{n}_b^i, n_s) - n_s C_s.$$

Changes in the intermediary's profit coincide with changes in the combined buyers' and intermediary's surplus (for a given number of buyers) and the sellers' interests are effectively ignored. Hence, for any given number of buyers, the number of sellers is less than what is socially desirable. If platforms are symmetric, each has an equilibrium market share of $1/2$ on the buyer side. Hence, platforms set a membership fee on the seller side which is too high from a welfare perspective. (The corresponding equilibrium membership fee for sellers satisfies $n_s^{i*} = N_s^i(\bar{n}_b^i, M_s^{i*})$.)

---

[p] Formally, the model is therefore equivalent to a model with three sides, sellers that can only access platform 1, sellers that can only access platform 2 and buyers that access either platform.
[q] For example, $u(n_s^i) = n_s^i u$ as has been assumed in some models above.
[r] Taking the example of a media platform, advertisers (i.e., the sellers) exert a negative externality on the readers (i.e., the buyers) if readers dislike advertisements.

> **Lesson 22.9** In a market with competing intermediaries in which sellers can set up shops at both intermediaries, the sellers' surplus is ignored in the pricing decisions of the intermediary. For any given number of buyers, the intermediary maximizes the joint surplus between buyers and the intermediary itself.

Since buyers are valuable to extract profits on the seller side, platforms tend to compete fiercely for buyers whereas they milk sellers. This may even lead to membership fees below costs on the buyer side. Clearly, if buyers rather than sellers can go to more than one intermediary, the whole story has to be reversed.

22.3.3   Implications for antitrust and regulation

As we have shown in the previous sections, the nature of two-sided platform markets affects the forms of competition that can take place on and among platforms. For instance, the presence of strong indirect network effects increases the risks of monopolization or of dominance. Also, because intermediaries operate on different sides of the same market, they tend to act as multiproduct firms and use cross-subsidization to exploit complementarities. The resulting price structures may then look like price discrimination or unfair competition. Hence, multi-sided platforms seem to be prone to raise the suspicion of competition authorities. At the same time, the presence of network effects indicates that less concentration may decrease welfare, as the benefits for all agents may be larger if they all interact on the same platform. It must also be noted that many platforms operate in sectors that are subject to specific modes of regulation, either because they use physical networks organizing the transport of information (such as the Internet, telecommunication and credit card networks) or because their activities are centred around information goods, for which intellectual property laws apply.

Recently, several antitrust actions in the US and in Europe have been related to intermediation platforms. For instance, the European Commission questioned the structure of interchange fees among banks in card payment networks such as Visa and MasterCard.[s] Also, Microsoft has been the focus of much attention from competition authorities on both sides of the Atlantic, and high-profile merger cases have been investigated in media industries (e.g., AOL and Time Warner). A recurring theme in these cases concerns the implications platform intermediation can have on the application of competition laws and on various modes of regulation. As we discuss below, the main risk regulators and competition authorities face when dealing with cases involving intermediation platforms is to apply a conventional 'one-sided' logic where a multi-sided logic is called for. This is true for the definition of the market, for the assessment of market power, for the analysis of unilateral and coordinated conduct and for the design of regulation.[19]

Definition of the relevant market

The definition of the relevant market is a prerequisite to identify the competitive constraints that a firm faces, and thereby to provide a framework for competition policy. In Chapter 2,

---

[s] The interchange fee is the percent of the transaction that a bank that acquires a transaction has to pay to the bank that issued the credit card.

we described the *hypothetical monopolist test* that US and European competition authorities now commonly use to identify the closest substitutes to a given product or service. Recall that this test defines as the relevant market the smallest product group such that a hypothetical monopolist controlling that product group could profitably sustain a *SSNIP*, that is a *small but significant non-transitory increase in price* (in practice, a 5 to 10% price increase over one year).

A number of difficulties arise when extending this test to intermediation markets. The first difficulty has to do with the price or prices that the hypothetical monopolist should be thought of as raising. An intermediary sets (at least) two prices and we have seen in the previous two sections that profits are determined by both the price level and the price structure. Different scenarios can then be envisioned to perform a SSNIP test. The hypothetical monopoly intermediary could be thought of as raising (i) the sum of prices while optimally adjusting the price structure, (ii) all prices together while keeping the price structure fixed, (iii) each of the prices separately allowing the other prices to be adjusted optimally, or (iv) each of the various prices while keeping the other prices fixed.[20]

Second, as intermediaries internalize the indirect network effects between the various groups that they serve, the profit function of a hypothetical monopoly intermediary incorporates the profits made on the various sides of the platform. The question arises then of which feedbacks from one side to the other should be taken into account when simulating a SSNIP on one side of the platform. Our previous analysis suggests that we should look at what happens to profits on all sides of the platform. Whether taking all feedbacks into account should lead to a larger definition of the market remains, however, a matter of debate, as illustrated in Case 22.6.

Case 22.6 Market definition for satellite radio services[21]

In February 2007, the two US satellite digital radio services (SDARS), Sirius and XM, announced that they had agreed to merge. To go through, the merger had to be approved by the antitrust division of the US Department of Justice (DoJ) and by the Federal Communications Commission (FCC). It appeared immediately that the decisions would crucially depend on how the relevant market would be defined. If SDARS constituted the relevant market, the horizontal combination of these two companies would amount to a merger to monopoly and would certainly be blocked. But if the market was defined as including other forms of broadcast (such as terrestrial broadcast or streaming radio via the Internet), it was more likely that the merger would go through.

A one-sided logic would simply ask whether SDARS consumers perceive, say, terrestrial broadcast radio to be reasonably interchangeable for SDARS. The answer would probably be negative. Yet, a multi-sided logic would acknowledge the fact that XM and Sirius compete with other broadcasters not only for subscribers but also for content producers and for advertisers. The fact that Sirius spent $500 million over five years to sign up the very popular Howard Stern Show seems to indicate that it is the content side of the market that holds market power, and that the platforms have to compete fiercely to have the right to distribute that content. XM and Sirius also argued that the opposition of the National Association of Broadcasters (NAB) to the merger was evidence that SDARS compete with broadcast radio; the NAB was concerned that the merger would divert advertising dollars away from radio stations. These arguments may have reached the DoJ and the FCC since they approved the merger in June 2008.

Exercise of unilateral market power

In platform markets, following a one-sided approach may lead to an over-estimation of market power and its potential anti-competitive effects. Competition authorities should thus adopt a multi-sided approach. Doing so, they should first recognize that *in intermediation markets, the efficient price structure must not reflect the cost structure*. Intermediaries are indeed primarily concerned with getting the different sides of the market on board to make the platform operate efficiently. Therefore, it is the intensity of the indirect network effects that determines the prices and not so much the relative costs of serving each group of users. Typically, as stated in Lesson 22.6, prices tend to be lower on the market side that exerts a stronger externality on the other side. Also, as stated in Lesson 22.9, prices tend to be higher on the side that multihomes and lower on the side that singlehomes. It follows that the usual Lerner index is no longer an appropriate measure of market power; as we have suggested in the previous section, this index has to be adapted to take the indirect network effects into account. Another consequence is that cost-based regulation is doomed to failure in such markets.

A second implication of the multi-sided approach is the two-fold realization that *prices above marginal cost do not necessarily indicate market power, nor do prices below marginal cost necessarily indicate predation.* As just stressed, asymmetric price structures are common on two-sided platforms as they help getting the different groups of users on board. In particular, negative margins (i.e., subsidies) may be necessary to overcome the chicken-and-egg problem by convincing agents of one group to join the platform when they hold pessimistic expectations about the participation of the other group. The losses on that side of the market must then be recouped through larger margins on the other side. Alleged excessive market power or predation must then be assessed by looking at the entire price structure, taking into account the relationships between the different groups of users.

By the same token, *it is wrong to think that multi-sided platforms exhibit cross-subsidization.* One would be tempted to say that if users on one side of the platform receive services below marginal cost, then they must be receiving a cross-subsidy from users on the other side. Here, however, the difficulty lies in identifying what services are exactly provided to the two sides. Take the example of a free newspaper. Does the distribution of the newspaper free of charge (although the marginal cost, however small it may be, is positive) imply that readers receive a cross-subsidy from advertisers? If so, advertisers should be better off if the price of advertising space was reduced and compensated by an increase in the price of the newspaper. But this is far from clear insofar as even a small newspaper price could discourage most of the potential readers, which would seriously deteriorate the advertisers' situation. As illustrated by this example, likening an asymmetric price structure to cross-subsidization amounts to neglecting the fact that participation on one side raises the value of participation on the other side.

Even the effects of competition have to be reconsidered. Contrary to what a one-sided logic suggests, *an increase in competition in multi-sided markets does not necessarily lead to a more efficient or balanced price structure*. Indeed, if one admits that the price structure is more governed by the necessity to balance the incentives of the various groups, there is no reason to believe that the welfare-maximizing price structure differs in any fundamental way from the structure that a monopoly intermediary would adopt. As shown in Lesson 22.7, both the welfare maximizing and the monopoly membership fees for an agent on one side of the platform decrease with the external benefit that this agent exerts on agents on the other side of the platform. Similarly, even if more competition may lower the sum of the prices charged on the various groups, there is no reason why the relative difference between these prices should decrease. Actually, Lesson 22.8 suggests the opposite as, in singlehoming environments, membership fees react more strongly on indirect network effects when going from one to two intermediaries; competition would thus increase the asymmetry of prices. On the other hand, our analysis of multihoming environments shows that competition may increase or reduce asymmetry in the price structure depending on which side of the market multihomes.

Finally, *the potential anticompetitive effects of exclusive contracts have to be reconsidered under a multi-sided approach*. As we have seen in Chapter 17, the Chicago School questioned the alleged anticompetitive nature of exclusive contracts by arguing that consumers remain free not to agree to exclusivity. Hence, if consumers agree to sign exclusive contracts, it means that they expect larger benefits than costs from dealing with a single firm, meaning that the contracts do not harm competition. This argument can be challenged in multi-sided markets when taking the effects on all sides of the market into account.[t] It might be the case that consumers on one side benefit (at least in the short run) from exclusivity but fail to realize that exclusive contracts help the platform gain market power on the other side, thereby reducing the welfare of consumers on the other side. In the long run, all consumers may then suffer from exclusive contracts as these contracts could be used by one platform to exclude competitors. But even if this possibility exists, the welfare consequences of exclusive contracts are ambiguous, as illustrated by Case 22.7, which estimates the impact of exclusive contracting in the videogame industry.

Case 22.7 Exclusive contracting in the videogame industry[22]

Videogame consoles can be seen as two-sided platforms that link game developers to end-users. The so called 'sixth generation' of videogame consoles were in use during the period 2000–5. Sony was the first-mover in 2000 with its Playstation 2 (PS2) console. Nintendo and Microsoft followed suit one year later by releasing the Gamecube (GC) and Xbox consoles, respectively. During the whole period, Sony maintained its lead by selling almost double the number of consoles as both its competitors combined.

While hardware devices are provided by a single firm, videogame software is produced by a large number of firms that develop and publish games (Sony, Nintendo and

[t] In Chapter 17, we showed that the Chicago School argument has some shortcomings in traditional 'one-sided' markets as well.

Microsoft also produce their own titles that are exclusive to their platform). What is important to note is that games developed for one console are incompatible with other consoles; the 'portability' to another console supposes that another version of the software be developed, which entails non-negligible costs (up to a few million dollars). Hence, third-party software developers make a highly strategic decision when they choose for which platform to develop. They face the following trade-off: portability (i.e., the release of a game on multiple platforms) means a larger audience but higher costs; conversely, exclusivity means lower costs but a narrower audience. As for exclusivity, several options are possible: the developer can either make the title exclusive on a voluntary basis, or enter into a publishing agreement with the console manufacturer, or sell the game (or even the entire studio) outright.

Lee (2008) develops a framework for analysing the adoption decisions of end users and software developers for competing videogame consoles. He applies this framework to empirically measure the impact of exclusive vertical arrangements between console providers and game developers on the competitive structure of the industry in the United States. The main finding is that these exclusive arrangements were pro-competitive because they benefited Nintendo and Microsoft (the smaller entrant platforms) at the expense of Sony (the incumbent). If exclusive arrangements had been prohibited, the entrants would have been reduced to a lower market share as high-quality videogame titles would have been primarily developed for the PS2 and its large installed base, before being ported (if at all) to the GC and the Xbox. In other words, exclusivity allowed entrant platforms to solve the 'chicken-and-egg' coordination problem and break into an established market: by preventing some third-party developers from also supporting Sony, Nintendo and Microsoft gained a competitive advantage and sparked the positive-reinforcing dynamics of indirect network effects in their favour, thereby enhancing platform competition.

Mergers and coordinated practices

How should *mergers* in intermediation markets be assessed? A first important step in the merger assessment is the definition of the relevant market, as already discussed above. Case 22.6 illustrated that the recognition of the multi-sided nature of the provision of satellite digital radio services may have led antitrust authorities to a broad market definition and to the approval of the Sirius–XM merger. Once the market is defined, the multi-sided features of the market (in particular, the indirect network effects) have to be assessed. If they are not the predominant aspect of the market, nothing precludes mergers from being analysed under the traditional one-sided logic (as has often been done for, e.g., supermarket mergers). In any case, there is no reason to abandon the one-sided framework altogether, not only because mergers raise many of the same concerns in one-sided and in multi-sided environments, but also because many of the same concepts and tools can be applied in the two environments. Nevertheless, mergers in intermediation markets can raise specific competitive concerns, as illustrated in Case 22.8.

Case 22.8 The Travelport/Worldspan EC case[23]

In August 2007, the European Commission cleared the merger of Travelport (Galileo) and Worldspan, two operators of Global Distribution Systems (or GDS, i.e., computerized systems through which airlines, hotels, or car rental companies can distribute their products to travel agents), unconditionally. The Commission defined the relevant market narrowly as the market for electronic travel distribution services through a GDS. The merger had the effect of reducing the number of suppliers on this market from four to three (i.e., Galileo/Worldspan, Sabre and Amadeus). The Commission recognized the two-sided nature of GDS platforms, with important indirect network effects between the two sides, namely travel service providers (essentially, airlines) and travel agents. As airlines multihome and travel agents singlehome, GDS platforms compete hard to expand their installed base of travel agents and end up subsidizing them. In its assessment of the potential unilateral effects of the merger, the Commission added to the usual one-sided concerns (namely higher prices – or lower subsidies – for travel agents) concerns about so-called 'vertical cross-market effects'. With Galileo/Worldspan becoming an unavoidable gateway for airlines to reach a substantial part of end-consumers (40 to 80% in various Member States), the merger would improve the bargaining position of the parties vis à vis airlines. The Commission therefore feared that airlines would pay higher prices after the merger. However, the parties argued that these effects were unlikely to materialize because airlines have strong bargaining tools that they could use to induce travel agents to switch GDS (by withdrawing selective content and imposing surcharges) and thereby, to prevent the merged entity from imposing a price increase. The Commission followed that argument.

Regarding coordinated practices, such as *cartels* and *price-fixing*, two comments are in order when taking multi-sided features into account. First, cartels are likely to be harder to sustain in two-sided environments as prices need to be coordinated on both sides of the market: market power on one side is not enough as supracompetitive profits on one side will be competed away on the other side. Second, some forms of price-fixing may enhance efficiency instead of reducing it. For instance, in the NaBanco v. Visa case,[24] US courts found that the collective setting of the interchange fee helped to internalize the indirect network externalities between cardholders and merchants, and eliminated the need for costly bilateral negotiations.

Regulation

Concerning regulation, the first point we want to stress is that *regulating prices on a platform may not be competitively neutral*. Regulation of some firms is said to be competitively neutral if it does not give an advantage to their rival unregulated firms. In normal industries, regulation is likely to be competitively neutral if the market is sufficiently competitive. For instance, if one firm is forced to lower its price, that will not allow rival firms to attract customers more easily; in fact, competition will drive rival firms to lower their price too. This reasoning no longer applies in multi-sided markets as forcing a platform to reduce (or raise) its price on one side of its business may not drive its rival(s) to do the same. Take the example of heterosexual night clubs described above in Case 22.3. In some jurisdictions, asymmetric price structures in night clubs are considered as sexual discrimination and therefore banned. Imagine that club *A* faces such a ban while club *B*, which is located in a different but neighbouring jurisdiction, does not. If the regulated club *A* stops subsidizing women, will the rival unregulated club *B* follow suit? Probably not. Why would club *B* implement a suboptimal price structure? Club *B* is likely to continue subsidizing women so as to attract more of them and thereby, to attract more men (even if prices for men may be lower in club *A* because of the regulation). Hence, club *B* will gain an advantage meaning that the regulation is not competitively neutral.

A second point regarding regulation in platform markets is that *it is not clear whether regulating platform prices eventually benefits end users.* For instance, consider once more interchange fees on credit cards. In 2003, the Reserve Bank of Australia decided to reduce these fees by almost half. The impacts of this decision on the various sides of the market have been estimated as follows:[25] issuers recovered between 30 and 40 per cent of the loss of interchange fees; merchants benefited from lower fees; yet, those benefits did not seem to have been substantially passed on to their customers. In total, there was relatively little evidence (two years after) that the intervention had affected the volume of card transactions in Australia. Case 22.9 provides another illustration by describing the impact of regulatory intervention to cut termination rates of calls from fixed lines to mobile phones.

Case 22.9 The waterbed effect in mobile telephony[26]

Fixed-to-mobile telecommunications networks can be represented as two-sided platforms with a singlehoming side (mobile subscribers wish to join at most one mobile operator) and a multihoming side (callers on the fixed telephone networks wish to call mobile subscribers of all operators). As explained above, intermediaries on such platforms set low prices on the singlehoming side and high prices on the multihoming one. In the present case, a mobile operator, even if competing against other mobile operators, has an incentive to set high fixed-to-mobile termination rates (MTRs) as it holds a monopoly over delivering calls to its subscribers. Such conduct provided justification for regulatory intervention in several countries to cut MTRs. However, reducing the level of termination charges may increase the level of prices for mobile subscribers on the other side of the platform. This potential phenomenon has been called the 'waterbed' effect.

Genakos and Valletti (2007) analyse the impact of MTR regulation on prices and profit margins on a set of mobile operators across more than twenty countries during the last decade. To identify and quantify the waterbed effect, they use quarterly frequency data and employ panel data techniques that control for unobserved time-invariant country-operator characteristics and general time trends. Their estimates suggest that although regulation reduced termination rates by about ten per cent, this also led to a ten per cent increase in mobile outgoing prices. However, the analysis also provides evidence that the waterbed effect is not full: mobile firms have suffered from cuts in MTR as they tend to keep part of termination rents instead of passing them on to their customers. Finally, the analysis reveals that the waterbed effect is stronger the more intense competition is in markets with high levels of market penetration and high termination rates.

We close with the following rather vague, general lesson.

Lesson 22.10   **To be effective, regulation and antitrust assessment must be based on an accurate understanding of the way each market operates. In this respect, it is crucial to recognize the possible multi-sided aspects of a market; sticking to a one-sided logic may lead to erroneous decisions.**

Review questions

1. Why do buyers and sellers sometimes prefer to trade via a dealer rather than in a decentralized way?

2. Taking the viewpoint of an intermediary, compare two polar business models for market intermediation: the dealer model (buying and reselling goods) and the platform model (providing a marketplace where affiliated sellers can sell directly to affiliated buyers).

3. Describe the sorting role of the prices set by intermediaries in matching markets.

4. How do intermediaries set the price structure on two-sided platforms?

5. Why do intermediaries in two-sided industries tend to achieve high profits on the multihoming side but to dissipate these profits through competition on the singlehoming side?

Further reading

Our comparison of intermediated and nonintermediated trade is inspired by Spulber (1999) and Bose and Pingle (1995). More generally, Spulber's book provides a comprehensive look at the role of firms as intermediaries in a variety of contexts. Our analysis of matching markets follows Caillaud and Jullien (2003) and Damiano and Li (2008). Most of our analysis of two-sided platforms draws from Armstrong (2006). Jullien (2005) and Rochet and Tirole (2006) propose useful road maps to the recent literature in industrial organization that examines such platforms; instructive case studies can be found, e.g., in Evans (2003). As for the implications of two-sided platforms for antitrust, we refer you to Wright (2004) and Evans and Schmalensee (2008).

23 Information and reputation in intermediated product markets

Intermediation can play an important role in the process through which consumers obtain information. Section 23.1 deals with a number of situations where consumers can access and process information more efficiently if they use the services of an intermediary. First, we consider situations in which consumers may suffer from information overload and in which an information gatekeeper is valuable for consumers. Second, we analyse the role of gatekeepers who provide price information in search markets. Third, we turn to the possibility that the intermediary, through the installation of a recommender system, allows consumers to perform directed search. This potentially allows consumers to drastically reduce their search efforts to obtain the products they like.

In Section 23.2, we turn to asymmetric information problems. We first analyse whether and how an intermediary can alleviate asymmetric information problems between firms and consumers. Possibly, the intermediary can act as a certifier. There is, however, the risk that the intermediary simply extracts rents from the market without providing any services. We then turn to the analysis of reputation systems where it is not the intermediary's information disclosure but the previous experience of other consumers that allows consumers to make better informed choices, thereby alleviating asymmetric information problems.

23.1 Intermediation and information

Intermediaries that act as information distributors play an increasingly important role, since consumers are limited in their capability to process information. In this section we take a look at consumers with limited information-processing capabilities and the role of 'infomediaries' in this context. Instead of relying on an infomediary as a filtering device, consumers may do the filtering themselves. This can be interpreted as an open access platform from which a consumer has to (randomly) pick some of the information that is provided.

23.1.1 Information overload

Consumers have to be selective when it comes to processing information. This is a critical issue for marketing departments at firms. They have to figure out how they can raise the consumers' attention to their ads. They can increase the chance of being successful by targeting particular media that address consumers who tend to be more interested in the particular product. Consumers may then have a larger attention span for such media because they anticipate the expected benefit.

In such a market, firms as advertisers compete for the limited attention span of consumers. Consumers, who lack sophisticated selection mechanisms for competing messages, select randomly and adjust their attention span to the expected quality of the match. In this environment, firms are assumed not to be competitors in the marketplace. However, due to the limited consumer attention span, they compete with each other for the consumers' attention. We develop a simple model in which the total number of messages sent by firms and processed by consumers is endogenous.[27] We derive information overload as an equilibrium outcome. It relies on participation decisions by firms and on the decision by the consumer as to how many messages to process.

Various network effects are at work in this model. First, there is a direct negative network effect between firms because additional messages increase the information overload and thus decrease the probability of a given sender to be sampled. Second, there is a positive indirect effect from receiver to sender because more processed messages generate surplus on the firm side. Third, there is an indirect effect from receiver to sender of ambiguous sign because the expected surplus per firm typically depends on the number of active firms.

Suppose there is a large number of firms that decide whether or not to send a message to a particular consumer. In total there are then n active firms. This number is determined by a free-entry condition. Denote by $\pi(\theta)$ the profit a firm of type θ makes when selling to the consumer. The firms are ordered such that π is weakly decreasing in θ. If the consumer randomly selects ϕ messages, the probability for a particular firm to be sampled is ϕ/n. Sending a message costs γ (with $\pi(0) > \gamma$). Thus, under free entry, there is a marginal type $\theta^* = n$ which satisfies

$$\pi(\theta^*)\frac{\phi}{n} - \gamma = 0. \tag{23.1}$$

All firms of type $\theta < \theta^* = n$ send a message, while all others do not. The consumer decides to sample and process ϕ messages. Each message gives an expected surplus gross of any sampling and information-processing costs equal to $\int_0^{\theta^*} s(\theta)d\theta$. Since the consumer incurs a cost for sampling and processing, she may not sample and process all messages that have been sent. In this case, she solves the problem

$$\max_\phi \frac{\phi}{n} \int_0^{\theta^*} s(\theta)d\theta - C(\phi),$$

where s is the net surplus derived after consuming the product and C is the increasing and convex sampling cost. The first-order condition of utility maximization can be written as

$$\frac{1}{n} \int_0^n s(\theta)d\theta = C'(\phi).$$

This determines the attention span ϕ as a function of the number of messages sent, as long as $\phi \leq n$. Denote the expected surplus with n active firms by $s^e(n) = \frac{1}{n}\int_0^n s(\theta)d\theta$. Then the attention span is

$$\phi(n) = \min\{n, C'^{-1}(s^e(n))\}. \tag{23.2}$$

Equations (23.1) and (23.2) then determine the equilibrium under free access. As a special case, consider the situation that all firms achieve the same profit π_0 (which has to be greater than γ). In this case, the free-entry condition can be rewritten as $n = \pi_0\phi/\gamma$. Suppose

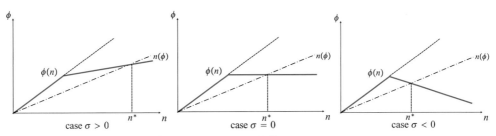

Figure 23.1 Information overload on an open access platform

furthermore that C takes the form $C(\phi) = c\phi^2/2$ and that $s(\theta) = s_0 + 2\sigma\theta$, where $s_0 > 0$. Then the expected surplus is $s^e(n) = s_0 + \frac{1}{n}\int_0^n 2\sigma\theta d\theta = s_0 + \sigma n$. The attention span then is $\phi(n) = (s_0 + \sigma n)/c$. Assuming that $c\gamma > \sigma\pi_0$, equilibrium values are

$$n^* = \frac{\pi_0 s_0}{c\gamma - \sigma\pi_0},$$

$$\phi^* = \frac{\gamma s_0}{c\gamma - \sigma\pi_0}.$$

We observe that $n^* > \phi^*$ so that there is information overload.

Lesson 23.1   **When consumers incur costs when sampling and processing information, there may be information overload in equilibrium: consumers sample fewer messages than they have received.**

The particular shape of the function determining the attention span depends, in particular, on the sign of σ. Figure 23.1 characterizes equations (23.1) and (23.2) for the special case proposed above. Note that for $\sigma = 0$, the total number of messages does not affect the expected surplus from sampling. Therefore, even if the free-entry condition for firms changes, the consumer does not change her attention span (of course, provided that $\gamma < \pi_0$).

However, if $\sigma < 0$, the consumer reacts to a reduction of the number of sent messages by increasing her attention span because of an improvement of the average quality of the match between firm and consumer (since π_0 is constant in this specification, the corresponding increase of the surplus is fully absorbed by the consumer). Suppose that the free-entry condition leads to a rotation of $n(\phi)$ as depicted in Figure 23.2. In particular, if the cost of sending a message is increased, the function $n(\phi)$ rotates 'downward' (beware that the dependent variable is on the horizontal axis), say from n_1 to n_2. This implies that the number of sent messages goes down in equilibrium and that the consumer increases her attention span. Here, due to the higher cost of sending messages, unwanted messages never make it into the mailbox of the consumer and are therefore never selected. This makes the consumer willing to read more of the messages that are sent to her.

This points to the beneficial role of an information gatekeeper in this market. Here, the information gatekeeper simply has to charge a price to firms sending out messages. A profit-maximizing information gatekeeper prices in such a way that the information overload

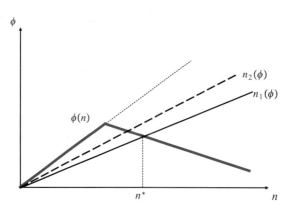

Figure 23.2 Information overload and the role of an information gatekeeper

is avoided. The consumer is better off and would even be willing to pay for the service the information gatekeeper provides.

Lesson 23.2 **An information gatekeeper who increases the cost of sending messages can avoid the information overload in the market.**

Alternatively, if the consumer can charge herself, she may also be able to avoid information overload. A very crude measure to avoid unsolicited messages is to register on a do-not-call-list.

23.1.2   'Infomediaries' and competition in search markets

In the search models presented in Chapter 7, it was assumed that firms do not have to incur any cost to convey price information to the consumers. In contrast, in the informative advertising models presented in Chapter 6, we assumed that each firm had to devote resources if it wanted to advertise its price. Somewhere in between these two extremes are situations where the information acquisition and diffusion process is mediated by a profit-maximizing information gatekeeper or clearing house, which can charge both sides of the market for its services. That is, firms pay the clearing house to advertise their price and consumers pay to gain access to the list of prices posted at the clearing house. Many newspapers and online price-comparison search engines fit this description. Clearing houses of this sort can be seen as intermediaries or platforms working in a two-sided market. Our objective in this subsection is to complement the previous consumer search models by endogenizing the 'infomediation' process.

We slightly modify the pure price dispersion model presented in Chapter 7 in the following way.[28] Suppose there are two local markets. On each market, there is a single firm and a unit mass of consumers. The two firms sell identical products at a constant marginal cost which, for simplicity, is supposed to equal zero (the cost of delivering goods to consumers is also zero). Each consumer has a demand function $q(p) = 2 - p$. The two local markets are completely segmented: consumers in local market i only have access to firm i. Therefore, the expected profits of firm i when it charges a price p to consumers in its local market is $\pi(p) = p(2 - p)$; the monopoly price is easily computed as $p^m = 1$. It costs a consumer

$0 < z < 1/2$ to visit a local store. The assumption that $z < 1/2$ ensures that a consumer who is charged the monopoly price p^m obtains sufficient surplus to make a visit worthwhile. The consumer surplus at some price p is indeed computed as $v(p) = \frac{1}{2}(2-p)^2$; hence, $v(p^m) - z = 1/2 - z > 0$.

The Internet makes it possible for an intermediary to open a virtual marketplace and, thereby, eliminate geographic boundaries between the two local markets. In the absence of such a virtual marketplace, each firm simply charges the monopoly price to all of its local consumers to earn profits of $\pi(1) = 1$. In contrast, the creation of a virtual marketplace allows firms and consumers to globally transmit and access price information. The intermediary runs the flows of information by charging an access fee, $M_s \geq 0$, to firms posting their price on the website, and a subscription fee, $M_b \geq 0$, to consumers accessing price information from the website.

We analyse the following game: in the first stage, the intermediary announces the fees M_s and M_b; in the second stage, given the fees, consumers decide whether or not to subscribe to the website; firms choose their price for the product and decide whether or not to post it on the website; finally, consumers shop. We solve the game for its symmetric subgame perfect equilibria.

Proceeding backward, we start by characterizing *optimal shopping by consumers*. We want to prove the following result: *(1) Nonsubscribing consumers visit and purchase from their local firm. Subscribing consumers (2a) first visit the website and (2b) purchase at the lowest price available there. (2c) If no price is listed, they visit and purchase from their local firm.* Part (1) is obvious because nonsubscribing consumers earn sufficient surplus to cover the cost of their physical visit: for all $p \leq p^m$, $v(p) \geq v(p^m) > z$. Part (2a) is obvious as well because visiting the website costs nothing (once the subscription fee is paid). What subscribing consumers do next depends on whether at least one price is listed on the website. If no price is listed, the previous reasoning applies and subscribing consumers visit and purchase from their local firm. On the other hand, if at least one price is listed, part (2b) applies: the optimal conduct is to purchase at the lowest available price on the website. This conduct is clearly optimal when the subscriber observes the ad of her local firm (say i) on the website, for it saves her the cost z of physically visiting the firm. On the other hand, if only firm j has posted its price on the website, the subscriber needs to decide whether it is worth paying z to obtain an additional price quote from her local firm i. Letting $G(p)$ denote the equilibrium consumer beliefs about firm i's price when it does not post its price, we can express the condition as follows:

$$\int_0^{p_j} (v(t) - v(p_j)) dG(t) \geq z.$$

Define $\bar{p}$ as the value of p_j for which the previous equation holds with equality. Then, given the consumers' decision rule, firm i will not charge prices below $\bar{p}$ when it does not post its price. This implies that for any $G(\cdot)$ consistent with equilibrium pricing,

$$\int_0^{\bar{p}} (v(t) - v(\bar{p})) dG(t) = 0,$$

which cannot be true given the way we defined $\bar{p}$. We therefore have a contradiction, which establishes part (2b).

We turn now to *firms' pricing and posting decisions*. Suppose that in each local market, a fraction $\lambda^I > 0$ of consumers subscribe to the website (in total, there are thus $2\lambda^I$ subscribers). Suppose, also, that each firm posts its price with probability α, and the posted price has an atomless cumulative distribution function $F(p)$. Let us first derive the expected profits of a *nonposting firm*. Such a firm will only attract customers residing in its locale. It will attract all local customers if no price is listed on the website (which occurs with probability $1 - \alpha$) or only the share $(1 - \lambda^I)$ of local consumers who do not subscribe (which occurs with probability α). In any case, the firm will optimally set the monopoly price $p^m = 1$. The expected profits are thus computed as (where the superscript N stands for 'nonposting'):

$$E\pi_i^N = (1 - \alpha) + \alpha \left(1 - \lambda^I\right) = 1 - \alpha\lambda^I. \tag{23.3}$$

Consider now a *posting firm* i. Whatever the decision of firm j, firm i pays the access fee M_s, and makes a profit $\pi(p_i)$ on its $\lambda^U \equiv 1 - \lambda^I$ nonsubscribing local consumers. The profits firm i collects from the $2\lambda^I$ subscribing consumers depends on the other firm's decision. With probability $(1 - \alpha)$, firm j does not post its price and firm i makes a profit $\pi(p_i)$ on all subscribers. On the other hand, with probability α, firm j also posts its price p_j and firm i only sells if it has posted the lowest price: i.e., if $p_j \geq p_i$, which occurs with probability $1 - F(p_i)$. Collecting these results and considering a price $p_i = p$, we compute the expected profits of a posting firm as:

$$\begin{aligned} E\pi_i^P &= \lambda^U \pi(p) + 2\lambda^I [(1 - \alpha) + \alpha(1 - F(p))] \pi(p) - M_s \\ &= \left(1 + \lambda^I\right) \pi(p) - 2\alpha\lambda^I F(p)\pi(p) - M_s. \end{aligned} \tag{23.4}$$

In order for F in the previous equation to be part of a symmetric Nash equilibrium, firm i's expected profit must be constant for all prices in the support of F. And in order for firms to randomize between posting price or not at equilibrium, we must have that the expected profits from posting price p must equal the expected profits from not posting and charging the monopoly price. Equating (23.3) and (23.4) and solving for F yields a candidate for the distribution of posted prices in a symmetric equilibrium (recalling that $\pi(p) = p(2 - p)$):

$$F(p) = \frac{\left(1 + \lambda^I\right) p(2 - p) + \alpha\lambda^I - 1 - M_s}{2\alpha\lambda^I p(2 - p)}. \tag{23.5}$$

To find the support of F, set $F(p_0) = 0$ in Equation (23.5) and solve to get

$$p_0 = \frac{1}{1 + \lambda^I} \left(1 + \lambda^I - \sqrt{\left(1 + \lambda^I\right)\left(\lambda^I - M_s + \alpha\lambda^I\right)}\right),$$

with $0 < p_0 < 1$. As $\pi(p) = p(2 - p)$ is continuous and increasing up to $p^m = 1$, $F(p)$ is increasing and is thus an atomless distribution with support $[p_0, 1]$. At the monopoly price, we must have that $F(1) = 1$. Imposing this and recalling that $\pi(p^m) = 1$, we can rewrite Equation (23.4) as $E\pi_i^P = (1 + \lambda^I) - 2\alpha\lambda^I - M_s$. Equating the latter expected profits to expression (23.3) yields a firm's propensity to post its price:

$$\alpha^* = \max\left\{0, 1 - \left(M_s/\lambda^I\right)\right\}.$$

Therefore, firms' posting decisions can be summarized as follows. *When access fees are not too high ($M_s < \lambda^I$), firms are indifferent between posting and not posting their price, and earn expected profits of* $E\pi_i^N = E\pi_i^P = 1 - \lambda^I + M_s$. *In contrast, when $M_s > \lambda^I$, firms do not find it profitable to post their price and equilibrium expected profits are* $E\pi_i^N = 1 > E\pi_i^P$.

Posted prices (which are in the interval between p_0 and 1) are always lower than nonposted prices (which are equal to $p^m = 1$). Because the virtual marketplace eliminates geographical distance, each firm can use it to steal business from its distant rival. However, to do so, the firm must randomly select both the timing of posting prices (i.e., $\alpha^* \in (0, 1)$) and the level of 'discount' (i.e., $1 - F(p)$) to 'confuse' the rival firm and prevent it from undercutting systematically the posted price. As a result, *price dispersion is observed at the equilibrium.*

We are now in a position to analyse *consumers' subscription decisions*. Given the subscription fee M_b, the proportion of other subscribing consumers $2\lambda^I$, and the posting strategy of firms (α, F), each consumer decides optimally whether or not to subscribe. A *subscribing consumer* faces the following potential prices and costs: (i) with probability α^2, both firms post their price and the price is the lower of two draws from the price distribution F; (ii) with probability $(1 - \alpha)^2$, neither firm posts a price and the consumer has to pay the monopoly price, plus the physical visit cost z; (iii) with the remaining probability, only one firm posts its price, which is a draw from F. In any case, the subscription fee M_b is incurred. Collecting terms and denoting by $h_2(p)$ the density of the lowest price in two draws from F, we can express the expected surplus of a subscriber as:[a]

$$V^I = \alpha^2 \int_{p_0}^1 v(p) h_2(p) \, dp + 2\alpha (1 - \alpha) \int_{p_0}^1 v(p) \, dF(p)$$
$$+ (1 - \alpha)^2 \left(\tfrac{1}{2} - z\right) - M_b.$$

A *nonsubscribing consumer* saves the subscription fee but incurs the physical visit cost z and does not benefit from comparison shopping on the website. With probability α, her local firm posts its price and the price distribution is thus F; with probability $(1 - \alpha)$, the local firm does not post its price and charges $p^m = 1$. Hence, the expected surplus of a nonsubscriber is computed as:

$$V^U = \alpha \int_{p_0}^1 v(p) \, dF(p) + (1 - \alpha) \tfrac{1}{2} - z.$$

Let us denote by $\beta(M_s, \lambda^I)$ the value of M_b that solves the equation $V^I = V^U$. That is, $\beta(M_s, \lambda^I)$ corresponds to the maximum amount a consumer would be willing to pay for a subscription when the firms' access fee is M_s and a fraction λ^I of consumers in each locale subscribe. In the case where all consumers subscribe ($\lambda^I = 1$), each consumer is willing to pay up to $M_b^*(M_s) \equiv \beta(M_s, 1)$ for a subscription.

At the second stage of the game, when the intermediary sets an access fee $M_s \in [0, 1]$ and a subscription fee $M_b \in \left[0, M_b^*(M_s)\right]$, three equilibria are possible. (i) *Inactive market for information*: no consumer subscribes ($\lambda^I = 0$) and no firm posts its price ($\alpha^* = 0$). (ii) *Active market for information with partial consumer participation*: in each locale, a fraction

---

[a] It can be shown that $h_2(p) = 2(1 - F(p)) f(p)$.

$\lambda^I \in (M_s, 1)$ of consumers subscribe, where λ^I solves $\beta(M_s, \lambda^I) = M_b$, and each firm posts its price with probability $\alpha^* = (\lambda^I - M_s)/\lambda^I$. (iii) *Active market for information with full consumer participation*: all consumers subscribe ($\lambda^I = 1$) and each firm posts its price with probability $\alpha^* = 1 - M_s$. Note that the latter two equilibria exhibit price dispersion, but prices are more competitive with full consumer participation. The creation of a virtual marketplace results in lower average prices for consumers, larger consumer surplus and lower profits. This is all the more true if consumer participation is large.

We finally examine the *intermediary's fee-setting decision*. We assume that the only cost to the intermediary of establishing a virtual marketplace is a fixed setup cost, K. The intermediary's problem is to maximize expected revenues from fees less the fixed setup cost:

$$\max_{M_s, M_b} E\Pi = 2\alpha M_s + 2\lambda^I M_b - K.$$

The intermediary faces the following 'chicken-and-egg' problem: to increase the willingness to pay of one group, the intermediary needs to raise the participation of the other group, but he can only do so by lowering the fee that he charges to this other group. Here, a larger consumer participation forces firms to post prices more intensively. It turns out that for a given access fee, the increased revenues stemming from firms (due to their larger posting intensity) more than offset the loss in revenues stemming from consumers (due to the initial reduction of the subscription fee). Therefore, *the intermediary finds it profitable to reduce the subscription fee so as to induce full consumer participation*.

Collecting the previous results, we can draw the following lesson.

Lesson 23.3   Equilibrium price dispersion persists in an environment with optimizing consumers, firms and a monopoly infomediary organizing a virtual marketplace, because it is costly for firms to advertise prices on the website. All consumers choose to subscribe and are 'fully informed' in the sense that they buy from the cheapest firm on the virtual marketplace. Despite this fact, firms earn positive profits at equilibrium. The creation of the marketplace results in lower average prices, greater surplus for consumers and lower profits for firms.

As shown by the previous analysis, firms are ambivalent about posting their price on the website. For sure, they make higher profits when the services of the infomediary are not available. Yet, when the website exists and consumers subscribe to it, both firms are willing to pay to post their price because they would suffer if only the price of the rival was posted on the website.

There also exist intermediaries who collect themselves the price information of various firms and let consumers freely access this information. Such intermediaries base their business models on advertising rather than on the collection of fees from the participants. As Case 23.1 illustrates, similar mixed feelings on the part of firms are witnessed in such situations: often the same firms that publicly denounce those websites which publish leaked price information are, at the same time, themselves an important source of the leaks.

The day after Thanksgiving, the so-called Black Friday, is one of the biggest shopping days of the year in the United States. On that day, most retailers organize important sales. Information about retail sales were traditionally published in scattered newspaper circulars. But the Internet made it possible to organize this information into a single database, thereby making it easier for consumers to compare prices of particular items. The tradition is thus nowadays to surf the web for advance information about Black Friday sales on sites such as BFads.net or Gottadeal.com, which publish prices online ahead of the release dates set by the retailers. This practice does not seem to please large retail chains, which have repeatedly tried to put an end to it by threatening legal action. The main fear of these retailers is that the leaked information tips off their competitors. However, it turns out that despite the protests, it is often the retailers themselves that leak the information. As evidence, the website BFads.net made public an email it received from an employee of Pacific Sunwear who was worried because the site did not immediately post a circular from his company; the employee wrote: 'I haven't seen our Black Friday deals on your site yet, so I am sending it again.'

23.1.3   Information and recommendation networks

Helped by the improved access to information through the Internet, consumers can easily evaluate, locate and purchase a wide range of products. In particular, recommender software, sampling tools, and search engines enable consumers to find products that match their tastes. An important question is how these changes affect the sales distribution of existing products and, eventually, how this affects the provision of variety. Of particular interest is the performance of niche products, i.e., products with a small market potential. It has been argued that niche products are doing relatively better under the new technologies so that the tail of the sales distribution becomes thicker (and longer). This hypothesis has been dubbed the 'long tail'.[30]

Of particular importance for the analysis of the long tail hypothesis are recommender systems or recommendation networks that allow consumers to learn from the experience of others. An example is the consumer reviews that sites like Amazon put together. This is similar to 'word-of-mouth' in the traditional world, where friends and colleagues make recommendations. However, while such word-of-mouth communication can be argued to be of importance in local markets, it cannot provide the richness of information that recommender systems provide. Recommender systems can provide additional information that otherwise would be difficult to observe.

The first issue we want to investigate is whether reviews from fellow users matter for consumer purchasing decisions. In particular, we want to know whether positive reviews increase sales and negative reviews decrease sales. Reviews relay information that is provided by fellow users who do not receive a monetary payment for their services. We may call this 'community content', which becomes a public good for the community. Similarly to other public goods (such as goods provided by the open source movement; see Chapter 19), one may wonder why consumers have an incentive to place their reviews for free, e.g., on the Amazon or Barnes & Noble site. However, there are clearly non-monetary incentives (reviewers are identified and can be rated) as well as the need to communicate one's experience or knowledge. To the extent that experiences are subjective (reflecting particular tastes), the question is how valuable a review is, given that there may be a large taste heterogeneity. This matters even if the review is sincere. Here, by actually reading the review (and not simply looking at the summary statistics), the consumer may disentangle match value from objective quality characteristics and even be able to figure out whether the reviewer has similar tastes.

A separate question is whether the online retailer has an incentive to establish such a recommender system. In particular, it loses control of the content created and other retailers may be able to free-ride on the content that is provided. With respect to the first point, it can be remarked that a retailer who offers a wide selection of different products has little to fear from negative reviews for particular products. The reviews that arrive may actually allow him to better manage warehouse stocks (and to make better recommendations to potential buyers). With respect to the second point, there appears to be no evidence that large retailers use reviews from rival retailers.

There are few questions that theory can answer. It must be empirical analyses that provide answers to the impact of reviews on sales. One such study, which sheds some light on the role of reviews by other consumers on product sales, is presented in Case 23.2.

Case 23.2 Book reviews on Amazon and Barnes & Noble in the US

Chevalier and Mayzlin (2006) analyse the effect of book reviews on sales patterns of the two leading online booksellers in the US (at that point in time), Amazon and Barnes & Noble. Both offer buyers the possibility of posting book reviews on their site. The central question of the study is whether an additional negative report on e.g. Amazon leads to a fall of sales at Amazon relative to the sales at Barnes & Noble. If the answer is 'yes', this means that book reviews carry relevant information that affect sales. To answer this question, Chevalier and Mayzlin use the 'differences-in-differences' approach, i.e., they take differences between the relative sales of the book at the two retailers to control for possible effects of unobserved book characteristics on book sales and reviews. Data were publicly available: they cover a random selection of book titles with certain characteristics in three short periods, two-day periods in May and August 2003 and May 2004.

Chevalier and Mayzlin regress the natural logarithm of the sales rank of book i at retailer j (which serves as a proxy for sales) on a number of variables including fixed effects, prices at Amazon and Barnes & Nobles, and the share of positive reviews (5 star reviews) as well as the share of negative reviews (1 star reviews). In the regression formula, i stands for the particular book and $j = A, B$ for the identity of the internet retailer. The econometric model is

$$\log(rank_i^j) = v_i + \mu_i^j + \alpha^j \log(p_i^j) + \gamma^j \log p_i^{-j} + X\Gamma^j + S\Pi^j + \varepsilon_i^j$$

where v_i is the retailer fixed effect, μ_i^j is the book-retailer fixed effect, p_i^j is the price of book i at retailer j and p_i^{-j} the price of the book at the competing retailer. Of key interest are variables in X which measure the availability and content of reviews. The variable S measures the type of shipping. Taking differences between retailers gives an equation with

$\log(rank_i^A) - \log(rank_i^B)$ on the left-hand side. To control for book-retailer fixed effects ($\mu_i^A \neq \mu_i^B$), differences over time are also taken (referred to by Δ). The differences-in-differences then take the form of the following equation:

$$\Delta[\log(rank_i^A) - \log(rank_i^B)] = \beta^A \Delta \log(p_i^A) + \beta^B \Delta \log(p_i^B)$$
$$+ \Delta X\Gamma + \Delta S\Pi + \Delta \varepsilon_i$$

where $\beta^A = \alpha^A - \gamma^B$ and correspondingly for B. All other variables are self-explanatory.

Chevalier and Mayzlin show that an additional positive review for a particular book at one retailer leads to an increase in the sales of this book at that retailer relative to the other. There is also some evidence that an additional negative review is more powerful in decreasing book sales than an additional positive review is in increasing sales (measured by the sales rank). The fact that also the length of reviews matters suggests that buyers do not only use summary statistics but actually take a look at the reviews; this also suggests that they take the content of the review explicitly into account (perhaps to evaluate how much to trust a particular review or because there is uncertainty with respect to the fit of the match, which is consumer-specific).

While the above recommender system is based on subjective product valuations, other recommender systems use historic click and purchasing data. Since the latter document actual choices of other consumers, they are potentially more powerful and indeed more complete than consumer reviews.

Let us consider the role of popularity information, i.e., information that displays how often a product has been purchased in relative terms. For this purpose, we present a particularly simple model, which focuses on consumer behaviour and treats firm behaviour as exogenous, in particular the prices of all products are fixed. Consumers know in advance whether some product features fit their taste but are not fully informed about a quality dimension of the product. Here, a recommender system reporting popularity of a product may provide valuable information to consumers.

The model

Suppose that consumers face a choice problem to buy one unit of two products offered by two different sellers; they may buy none, one, or both products. Prices are fixed throughout the analysis. With probability $\lambda > 1/2$, a consumer thinks more highly of product 1 than of product 2. Otherwise products are independent. Product 1 can be called a mass market product and product 2, a niche product. A product of high quality that provides the wrong match is assumed to give net utility $v_H = 1$ and a product of low quality, $v_L = 0$. A product with the right match gives the previous net utilities augmented by t. These utilities are gross of the opportunity cost z a consumer incurs visiting a seller (e.g., clicking onto its website). A consumer knows her match value and receives a noisy private signal about quality. The noisy quality signal may come from noisy information in the public domain such as publicly revealed tests. The ex ante probability of high quality is assumed to be $1/2$. The probability that the signal provides the correct information is ρ, which, for the signal to be informative but noisy, lies between $1/2$ and 1. Hence, with a positive signal realization, the posterior belief that the product is of high quality is ρ. It follows that if a consumer who prefers product i receives a high-quality signal and buys from seller j, she obtains expected utility $U_{Hg} \equiv \rho + t - z$ if $i = j$ and $U_{Hb} \equiv \rho - z$ if $i \neq j$. Correspondingly, with a low-quality signal expected utility is $U_{Lg} \equiv (1 - \rho) + t - z$ if $i = j$ and $U_{Lb} \equiv (1 - \rho) - z$ if $i \neq j$. Table 23.1 displays the four possible levels of expected utility.

Table 23.1. *Expected utility according to signal and match*

	Good match	Bad match
High-quality signal	$U_{Hg} \equiv \rho + t - z$	$U_{Hb} \equiv \rho - z$
Low-quality signal	$U_{Lg} \equiv (1 - \rho) + t - z$	$U_{Lb} \equiv (1 - \rho) - z$

For a given match, $\rho > 1/2$ implies that the consumer is better off with a high-quality signal: $U_{Hk} > U_{Bk}$ for $k = g, b$. Also, for a given signal, $t > 0$ implies that the consumer prefers to have a good match: $U_{Kg} > U_{Kb}$ for $K = H, L$. What is unclear is how the consumer balances the quality of the match with the quality of the signal. The consumer finds the quality of the match more important if $U_{Lg} > U_{Hb}$, which means that the consumer is better off with a low-quality signal and a good match than with a high-quality signal and a bad match. This is so if $1 + t > 2\rho$. Otherwise, the quality of the signal weighs more than the quality of the match. We distinguish these two cases in our analysis.

Product choice of a single consumer

A consumer buys the product independently of the signal realization and match value if $U_{Lb} > 0$, i.e., the opportunity cost of visiting a seller is sufficiently small, $z < z_{Lb} \equiv 1 - \rho$. By contrast, if the opportunity cost is too large, the consumer will never buy. This is the case if $U_{Hg} < 0$ or, equivalently, $z > z_{Hg} \equiv \rho + t$. Hence, we focus on the intermediate range where $z \in [z_{Lb}, z_{Hg}]$. A product with a good match but a low-quality signal is bought if $U_{Lg} \geq 0$, or, equivalently, $z \leq z_{Lg} \equiv 1 - \rho + t$. A product with a bad match but a high-quality signal is bought if $U_{Hb} \geq 0$ or $z \leq z_{Hb} \equiv \rho$.

As indicated above, two scenarios are possible. In the first scenario, the quality of the match is seen as more important by the consumer; the inequality $U_{Lg} > U_{Hb} \Leftrightarrow z_{Lg} > z_{Hb}$ holds, which is equivalent to $1 + t > 2\rho$. For this scenario to apply, consumer tastes must be sufficiently heterogeneous (t large) and signals sufficiently noisy (ρ sufficiently small). In the second scenario, it is the quality of the signal that matters more; we have $U_{Lg} < U_{Hb} \Leftrightarrow z_{Lg} < z_{Hb}$. For this scenario to apply, consumer tastes must be sufficiently homogeneous (t small) and signals sufficiently informative (ρ sufficiently large). Consumer choice can thus be fully described depending on whether $z_{Lg} > z_{Hb}$ or the reverse inequality holds.

For $z_{Lg} > z_{Hb}$, we obtain that a product is bought by a consumer who does not observe a low-quality signal and a bad match if $z \in (z_{Lb}, z_{Hb})$, it is bought by a consumer who observes a good match if $z \in (z_{Hb}, z_{Lg})$, and it is bought by a consumer who observes a good match and a high-quality signal if $z \in (z_{Lg}, z_{Hg})$. For $z_{Lg} < z_{Hb}$, we obtain that a product is bought

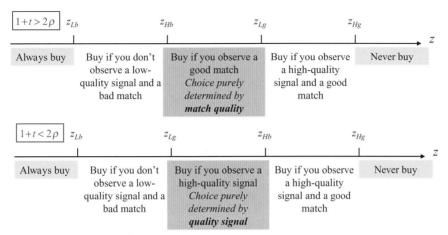

Figure 23.3 Product choice of a single consumer

by a consumer who neither observes a low-quality signal nor a bad match if $z \in (z_{Lb}, z_{Lg})$, it is bought by a consumer who does not observe a low-quality signal if $z \in (z_{Lg}, z_{Hb})$, and it is bought by a consumers who observes a good match and a high-quality signal if $z \in (z_{Hb}, z_{Hg})$. Interestingly, in the first scenario if $z \in (z_{Hb}, z_{Lg})$ consumer choice is purely determined by the match quality whereas in the second scenario, if $z \in (z_{Lg}, z_{Hb})$, consumer choice is purely determined by the signal realization. Figure 23.3 summarizes the consumer's decision in the two cases.

Recommender system

Let us first focus on the two intermediary cases (i.e., the middle areas in Figure 23.3) and introduce a recommender system that provides popularity information. For a recommender system to have any impact, we at least need another consumer who makes her choice after obtaining the information that is generated from the choices of the first consumer. The recommender system here simply reports the choices of the first consumer. The second consumer knows that parameter of the model but neither knows the signal realization nor the type of the first consumer. We assume that all random variables are i.i.d. across consumers (concerning the quality signal, this is conditional on true quality).

   In the first case, where $z \in (z_{Hb}, z_{Lg})$, the choice of the first consumer does not reveal anything about her private signal. Hence, the recommender system does not contain any valuable information for the second consumer. In the second case, where $z \in (z_{Lg}, z_{Hb})$, the choice made by the first consumer is solely determined by the signal realization. The second consumer will then use the information provided by the recommender system to update her beliefs: she updates her quality perception upward if a particular product has been bought (purchase data) or if the seller has been visited (click data). This implies that a previous visit or purchase increases the chance of subsequent visits and purchases. Here, the recommender system favours the sale of high-quality products.

   To analyse whether a recommender system favours mass market products or niche products, we have to consider the remaining cases of interest, namely $z \in (z_{Lb}, \min\{z_{Hb}, z_{Lg}\})$ and $z \in (\max\{z_{Hb}, z_{Lg}\}, z_{Hg})$. The former case is characterized by a relatively low cost of visiting sellers. Here, a consumer who observes a good match with a particular product always visits the corresponding seller. The seller of the product with a bad match is only visited in case of a high-quality information. This implies that click and purchase data still contain some useful information for the second consumer. The second consumer knows whether she has a taste for the niche product or the mass market product. Hence, if she has a taste for the niche product, she knows that it is unlikely that the first consumer had the same taste. Therefore, it is quite likely that the visit or purchase by the first consumer was driven by a positive realization of the quality signal. The opposite reasoning applies to a consumer who has a taste for the mass market product. Here, click and purchasing data are less informative. This implies that sellers of niche products benefit more from information on visits or purchases.

In the latter case where $z \in (\max\{z_{Hb}, z_{Lg}\}, z_{Hg})$, information on a *lack* of visits or purchases hurts the seller of the mass market product more. While niche sellers are at a disadvantage matching consumer tastes, this disadvantage becomes an asset when it comes to consumer inferences about product quality. It increases the benefit due to favourable popularity information and reduces the loss due to unfavourable popularity information.[31]

Lesson 23.4   **A recommender system based on product popularity often affects mass market and niche products differently. Niche sellers compared to mass market sellers tend to benefit more from the information released through the recommender system.**

A prominent mix of various recommender systems is in place at Amazon.com. Perhaps the most prominent example (at least in product categories in which consumers do not search among product substitutes) is that, when listing a particular product, Amazon recommends other products consumers have purchased together with the displayed product. The economics of such a recommender system are different from a system that merely reports the popularity of products. It allows consumers to discover products that serve similar tastes and thus is likely to produce good matches at low search costs. Such a recommender system is based on previous sales and appears to be particularly useful for consumer decision making for products that enjoy complementary relationships. It implies that products that have no or limited sales will receive little attention. This reasoning suggests that recommender systems may work against the long tail, an argument in contrast to the view that people discover better matches on recommender systems. The latter view is based on the observation that consumers with very special tastes more easily find products that provide a good match to their tastes, so that they do not need to resort to very popular products or buy at random. However, these two views are not necessarily contradictory. While the long tail story refers to the diversity of aggregate sales, the discovery of better matches refers to diversity at the individual level. It might well be the case that people discover better matches through recommender systems but that they discover products which are already rather popular in the whole population. Hence, sales data in the presence of recommender systems may show more concentration at the aggregate level.[32]

While this is an interesting insight, empirical analyses will have to show whether recommender systems indeed lead to more concentrated sales or whether the directed search, which is inherent in recommender systems, reduces search costs of users to the extent that they feel more encouraged to search out from known products they like, with the effect that diversity also increases at the aggregate level. Indeed, as can be formally shown, if the consumer population is characterized by taste heterogeneity, a recommender system that provides personalized recommendations may lead to a 'longer' tail in the aggregate, meaning that less popular products receive a larger share of sales after the introduction of a recommender systems.[33] A likely outcome then is that more niche products will be put on the market and that product variety in the market therefore increases. The following case sheds some light on the empirics.[34]

Case 23.3 Copurchase links on Amazon.com and the long tail

Oesterreicher-Singer and Sundararajan (2008) collected a large data set starting in 2005 of more than 250 000 books from more than 1400 categories sold on Amazon.com. They restrict their analysis to categories with more than 100 books. This leaves them with more than 200 categories. On all books, they obtain detailed daily information, including copurchase links, i.e., information on titles that other consumers bought together with the product in question (and which Amazon prominently communicates to consumers). These copurchase links exploit possible demand complementarities. Since these links arise from actual purchases and not statements by consumers, they can be seen as providing reliable information about what other consumers like. By reporting these links, Amazon essentially provides a personalized shelf for each consumer depending on what she was looking at last. This allows consumers to perform a directed search based on their starting point.

   The question then is whether and how these copurchase links affect sales. In particular, the question is: which products make relative gains in such a recommendation network? Are these the products who already have mass appeal (because they are linked to other products) or rather niche products? To answer this question, one must measure the strength of the links that point to a particular product. For this it is important to count the number of links pointing to a product as well as the popularity of the products from which a link originates. Hence, a web page receives a high ranking if the web pages of many other products point to it or if highly ranked pages point to it. This is measured by a weighted page rank which is based on Google's initial algorithm. The authors also construct the Gini-coefficient for each product category as a measure of demand diversity within a category. They regress this measure of demand diversity on the page rank (averaged within a category), together with a number of other variables. In their 30-day sample, they find that categories with a higher page rank are associated with a significantly lower Gini coefficient. This means that in a product category in which on average recommendations play an important role, niche products within this category do relatively better in terms of sales, whereas popular products perform relatively worse than in a product category where this is not the case. This is evidence in support of the theory of the long tail.[35]

A different type of recommendation network concerns the perceived quality of a particular seller. In this case, the reputation of the seller (or the intermediary who facilitates the trade) matters. We will turn to this issue in the next section.

23.2   Intermediation and reputation

If consumers cannot observe the quality or reliability of products before purchase, firms of low quality have an incentive to mimic high-quality firms and firms that choose quality have an incentive to underprovide quality. In Chapters 12 and 13, we have analysed environments in which market participants can overcome this information problem. However, in many real-world markets, the efforts required by a firm to overcome the associated adverse selection or moral hazard problem can be substantial to the effect that the firm may refrain from engaging in the effort with all the well-known consequences. If a firm still deems the effort worthwhile, it has to substantially distort some of its decisions and use resources. Both are privately and socially costly. The presence of third parties which act as information intermediaries may alleviate this problem.

In the previous section, we have analysed information intermediaries that reveal price information or facilitate information on the match value of products; in this section, we will analyse information intermediaries who reveal information about a product's or seller's reliability or quality. Guides such as the *Guide Michelin* may be seen as such information intermediaries. Also, the rating system provided by Amazon for the sellers in Amazon Marketplace plays the role of an information intermediary. These two examples differ in the sense that *Guide Michelin* actively collects and processes information, whereas Amazon only aggregates the information provided by buyers.

We first focus on information intermediaries such as *Guide Michelin*. Here, the intermediary is an expert who has better information than individual consumers. This advantage of the intermediary can be explained by scale and scope effects. Suppose there are many potential buyers and just one intermediary. For the sake of the argument, suppose that by spending effort e a party can evaluate the quality of all products in the market. Each individual consumer typically buys only a small subset of the products available and thus obtains direct experience on a restricted set (even when including word-of-mouth between consumers who know each other). In contrast, an intermediary may have more scale and thus more experience. Also, an intermediary is often permanently around whereas a consumer only buys in particular moments in time. Then, if the intermediary provides this effort e, his costs per unit are relatively small but possibly prohibitive if exerted by buyers. The intermediary may then reveal his information to consumers. This is beneficial for him if he can charge consumers for his role. We present a simple model in which we implicitly assume that it is prohibitively costly for consumers to obtain directly information about product quality but where the intermediary acts as a certifier.

23.2.1   Certifying intermediaries

We analyse here two models with a monopoly intermediary. Although the assumptions of the two models differ only slightly, the results they lead to stand in sharp contrast. We end this subsection by discussing in which environment intermediaries are more likely to play a certifying role.

A model with two product qualities

Consider a market with a continuum of sellers of mass n_s and a continuum of buyers of mass n_b.[36] Buyers have unit demand for each product. Each seller can offer its product with high or low quality. The cost of high and low quality are denoted by c_H and c_L, respectively. Producing high quality is assumed to be more costly than producing low quality, $c_H > c_L$. Consumers are willing to pay v_H for high quality and v_L for low quality. They do not observe the product quality. Thus we have a moral hazard problem.

If firms cannot reveal or signal their quality, firms may have no incentive to actually produce high quality and the market then only provides low quality. Suppose that firms can certify or brand their products such that they have no incentive to deviate to low quality (for an explicit analysis of branding, see Chapter 13). Such branding or certification is assumed to come at a cost per buyer $\psi > 0$. Since firms sell independent products, we can restrict for the moment the analysis to a single seller.

We consider the following game: first, the firm chooses its quality and spends the associated production cost; second, it decides whether or not to certify quality. If it certifies, it incurs a cost ψ at this point. Consumers observe whether a product has been certified by the firm but otherwise do not observe the quality. They form beliefs about the quality of the product and then decide whether to purchase. If the firm does not certify, it is not trusted by consumers. Hence, they believe the product to be of low quality. The associated profit of a low-quality firm is $v_L - c_L$. If the firm certifies, it reveals that it is of high quality. The associated profit is $v_H - c_H - \psi$. Hence, a firm brands or certifies its product if $v_H - c_H - \psi > v_L - c_L$. If this inequality is violated, it offers low quality.

Let us now introduce an intermediary. The intermediary is assumed to be an expert who perfectly observes the quality of each product. As explained earlier in this section, the superior information of the intermediary comes from the fact that the intermediary operates on a much larger scale. Therefore, the efforts required to obtain information on the product quality are small for the intermediary but possibly prohibitive for individual buyers.

The intermediary charges a commission P for providing certification and the firms sell directly to consumers. Our result about the certification role of the intermediary would remain the same if the intermediary bought and sold products, as would be the case in retailing. This commission is announced at the beginning of the game. Then firms choose quality. They also decide whether or not to certify and whether or not to apply to sell via the intermediary. The intermediary then decides which products to take in. Finally, consumers buy the product in random order. Consumers learn the quality of each product immediately after purchase. Thus they can condition the expected quality of a product sold by the intermediary on the quality that has previously been observed at the same intermediary. The economic mechanism that gives the intermediary the role as a certifier will be that not only the seller but also the intermediary will be blamed for any deficiencies in product quality. Since the intermediary repeatedly interacts with consumers, he has a strong incentive to preserve his reputation.

We construct a perfect Bayesian equilibrium in which all firms provide high quality and sell through the intermediary. The intermediary then becomes a bearer of reputation and effectively certifies the quality. Note that the only thing the intermediary has to do is to reject low-quality applicants, no further communication between intermediary and consumer is needed. Clearly, a firm that certifies independently is believed to be of high quality. The intermediary becomes a bearer of reputation because a product sold through the intermediary is believed to be of high quality by a consumer unless he previously experienced low quality of some other product sold through the intermediary. A deviation to low quality is not profitable for a firm because the intermediary would reject such a product even if the firm is trying to bribe the intermediary by offering a higher payment. The intermediary does not want to jeopardize his reputation.

Recall that a firm that sells independently high quality and certifies makes profit $v_H - c_H - \psi$. Alternatively, if it chose low quality, it would make profit $v_L - c_L$. We first consider the situation where low quality is provided in a nonintermediated market, i.e., $v_L - c_L > v_H - c_H - \psi$. Hence, in order to give any incentive for a seller to produce high quality, the intermediary's commission must satisfy $v_H - c_H - P \geq v_L - c_L$. The maximal commission that respects this constraint is $\overline{P} \equiv (v_H - c_H) - (v_L - c_L)$, which is positive if and only if it is socially efficient to have high quality under full information. Take $\overline{P}$ as given. We have to check that, given the commission $\overline{P}$, no seller has an incentive to deviate and produce low quality. Such a deviation can only be profitable if this product is still sold through the intermediary. If the intermediary admits such a low-quality seller, this seller would make profit $v_H - c_L - P$ which is clearly greater than if it produced high quality. The critical argument then is to show that the intermediary will reject low quality. Everything else equal, an additional seller leads to a positive marginal profit $n_b P$, where n_b is the number of buyers. However, this will lead consumers to revise their beliefs for other products. On average, consumers will still have to make half their purchases after buying one particular product. By accepting one low-quality product, the intermediary would lose half of its revenues. Clearly one additional sale per consumer cannot overcompensate for not being able to sell on average half of the portfolio of products to every consumer. Consequently, the intermediary rejects a low-quality product. To summarize, the moral hazard problem is solved and the intermediary proves himself to be trustworthy.

> **Lesson 23.5**   In the presence of asymmetric information about product quality, intermediaries can become bearers of reputation. Consumers buy through a trusted intermediary, who effectively certifies quality to consumers.

The intermediary is also active if independent sellers can solve the moral hazard problem themselves, albeit at a cost ψ, i.e., $v_L - c_L < v_H - c_H - \psi$. In this case the intermediary can set the commission at a level up to $P = \psi$. The argument then follows the one above. Here, intermediated trade saves society the cost $n_b n_s \psi$.

In many product markets, some strong seller brands are present that do not rely on the certification of an intermediary. Our analysis can easily be modified to account for this observation. For this, we would need to introduce some heterogeneity, e.g., in a seller's certification, which is unobserved by other market participants. Then, the intermediary charges a commission such that firms with high certification costs sell through the intermediary whereas firms with low certification costs sell independently their branded product.

The argument in the above model has been that the intermediary with the role of a certifier provides incentives for firms to invest in quality. Instead of this moral hazard environment, we may prefer to look at an adverse selection environment, where firms have private information about product quality. However, the intermediary has an inspection technology that allows it to also obtain this information. Here, the intermediary screens between high- and low-quality products: it denies access to low-quality products provided that the rents obtained from selling high quality under full information are larger than the rents which are obtained when selling a mix of high and low quality. Alternatively, if it allows for access, it may provide more detailed information through rating. One example is the information provided by tour operators on hotel quality, as illustrated in Case 23.4.

Case 23.4 Quality certification by UK tour operators

Clerides, Nearchou and Pashardes (2008) collected data on 380 hotels in the Mediterranean. These hotels were picked by the four big tour operators in the UK that offer package holidays (containing at least flight and hotel). Since the degree of substitutability between such package holidays and, e.g., long-haul trips appears to be small, we may exclusively focus on this market segment.

The market segment for package holidays to the Mediterranean is highly concentrated (the four largest tour operators had a market share of more than 85%). The products they offer (sun and beach) are relatively homogeneous across countries, which allows for a meaningful cross-country comparison. A further advantage of focusing on this market segment is that a large number of destinations per country is available.

Consumers who book such a package holiday typically face a large degree of uncertainty with respect to the quality of the hotels. They may rely on the rating provided by national rating agencies whose task is to assess the hotel quality and rate hotels according to a five-point star system. The rating may however contain a national bias (different requirements across countries) and may be misleading even within the country because it may neglect criteria which are important to consumers but not reflected by the rating. Here, tour operators may step in and provide their own ratings of the different hotels based on customer feedback and their own assessment of the facility. Are these ratings by tour operators trustworthy? Since tour operators are unconstrained in their ratings, they may systematically upgrade the rating of hotels in order to justify higher prices (in particular, they may upgrade those which give them higher profit margins). However, the theory on reputation suggests that tour operators do not gain from deliberately misleading consumers. While such deviating behaviour may have short-term benefits, the long-run loss of reputation may be too large.[b]

The empirical analysis by Clerides, Nearchou and Pashardes suggests that the ratings of tour operators serve two purposes. First, they serve to streamline different rating

---

[b] Recall the analysis from Chapter 13.

standards across countries, thus making rating comparable across countries. Second, tour operators assess quality differently than national rating agencies, which leads to reversals of the ordering among hotels even within countries. They apparently use additional 'soft' information that is not used by national rating agencies but that is useful for consumers. Hence, operators become certifying intermediaries even though a public rating system is already in place.

A model with a continuum of product qualities

While certification works well in the previous simple model, we should be careful with any claim that full information disclosure also results in other market environments. In particular, we want to take a look at our model assumption that products can only be of either high or low quality, which is not the case, e.g., in the case of hotel ratings.[37] Suppose instead that consumer valuations are between v_L and v_H, and that quality is drawn from some distribution function that is continuous and strictly increasing on its support; e.g., take the uniform distribution on [0, 1]. We also set all costs equal to zero.[c]

In such a setting, we first consider the situation where the intermediary maximizes its profit with respect to P with the requirement that the intermediary fully discloses the quality of the sellers unless it takes in all sellers. Full information disclosure can be of the form that the intermediary undertakes precise quality tests, the outcome of which is fully disclosed to consumers. The intermediary collects profits from the provision of his certification service. As a result, the intermediary fully solves the asymmetric information problem for those products that are traded via the intermediary. However, due to its market power, the intermediary sells fewer products than the total number under full information. The intermediary has an incentive to play the role of a certifier if the only alternative is not to reveal quality, in which case the intermediary would not earn any profit.

The timing is as follows: at stage 1 the intermediary sets his price P and commits to an information disclosure policy.[d] At stage 2, after observing the intermediary's decision, the firms decide whether to pay P and offer their products for sale via the intermediary. If they do so, they submit their product for testing. Afterwards, consumers observe P, an information disclosure policy, whether the product was tested and the (truthful) information disclosure by the intermediary. At the last stage, consumers bid for the product (alternatively, the seller makes a take-it-or-leave-it offer): consumers bid their true expected valuations so that consumers, in expectations, have zero rents. Note that bidding also takes place if the product is directly sold by the seller.

If some seller types do not sell through the intermediary, these are the rather low quality types. Suppose there is some seller type $\widehat{v}$ who is indifferent. Then in the uniform distribution example, since all seller types between 0 and $\widehat{v}$ would sell directly, the expected quality of those sellers is $\widehat{v}/2$, which is the profit any seller then makes. The indifferent type $\widehat{v}$ thus must satisfy the following condition: the profit when selling via the intermediary,

---

[c] Since we are in an adverse selection environment, we no longer need the assumption that higher quality entails higher costs.

[d] Assuming commitment is a short-cut for explicitly modelling reputation concerns of the intermediary. For explicit models of reputation, see Chapter 13.

$\widehat{v} - P$, must be equal to the profit when selling directly, $\widehat{v}/2$, which is equivalent to $\widehat{v} = 2P$. Hence, the intermediary's demand at price P is $1 - 2P$ for $P < 1/2$ and zero for $P \geq 1/2$. The intermediary thus maximizes $P(1 - 2P)$ and the profit-maximizing certification fee is $P = 1/4$. It follows that seller types between $1/2$ and 1 sell through the intermediary, and the intermediary makes profit $1/8$. This shows that the intermediary is better off with this full disclosure policy than with no information disclosure.

An important extension is to allow for a richer set of disclosure policies. We still postulate that the intermediary observes the seller type after testing and that he is committed to his announced disclosure policy. However, the intermediary may only disclose that the true type belongs to some interval. In the extreme, if this is the full $[0, 1]$-interval, the disclosure policy is uninformative. It is easy to see that given such a larger set of disclosure policies, *a full disclosure policy cannot be optimal for the intermediary*. Take the full disclosure policy and $P = 1/4$. If instead the intermediary announces that he will only tell whether the true type is in $[0, 1/2)$ or in $[1/2, 1]$, consumers expect that a seller trading through the intermediary will be on average of type $3/4$ and will bid accordingly. This implies that a seller of type $1/2$ would make profit $3/4 - P$ if selling through the intermediary, while it still makes profit $1/4$ if it were selling separately. This implies that the intermediary can raise the certification fee and still serve the same demand. Therefore, full disclosure cannot be profit-maximizing.

Actually, the intermediary may provide even less information. The argument is that the intermediary can make the interval for low types smaller. Denote the threshold by $\widetilde{v}$. This reduces the expected quality of sellers who sell independently (conditional expectation). As $\widetilde{v}$ converges to zero, the conditional expectation also converges to zero. This implies that firms who sell independently obtain zero profit. The conditional expectation for those above the threshold converges to the unconditional expectation. This implies that the intermediary can set $P = Ev$, which is $1/2$ in our example and almost all sellers sell through the intermediary (all except the lowest type). This allows the intermediary to extract all the surplus from the market without any information being disclosed. Firms pay P and sell through the intermediary to avoid being perceived as lowest quality. Interestingly, under a general condition on the type distribution (that includes the uniform distribution), this is the unique equilibrium outcome. The intermediary extracts all rents and does not alleviate the asymmetric information problem. This provides us with a drastically different lesson from the previous one.

Lesson 23.6   **A certifying monopoly intermediary may disclose essentially no information on product quality and still extract all expected rents from the market.**

Discussion

Where does this leave us? In the model with a continuum of product qualities, we assumed that there are benefits from trade for all seller types. If we introduce unit costs higher than the valuation for the lowest type, or negative valuations (e.g., because products are unsafe), we can rediscover a positive role for the certifying intermediary. Here, the intermediary certifies that product valuation is above unit cost. This means that the intermediary certifies that a product is in accordance with a minimum quality standard. This policy is welfare-improving compared to a world without certification. Note that with a minimum quality standard, the communication between intermediary and consumers can be minimal. The fact that a firm sells separately contains the message that this firm does not meet the minimum quality standard.

Competition between intermediaries helps in this world. Return to the case in which there are positive gains from trade for all seller types. Then with two or more intermediaries, there are always equilibria with full information disclosure. Suppose there was little information disclosure in equilibrium. Then each intermediary has an incentive to provide full disclosure. Bertrand competition between intermediaries then does the rest: there is full disclosure by at least two intermediaries and certification fees are set at zero.

23.2.2   Reputation systems

In many markets, consumers buy only once or at least infrequently so that their experiences concerning previous consumption on their own do not provide a sufficient restraint for sellers not to deviate from high quality. In this case, communication between consumers can maintain seller reputation so that the moral hazard problem is solved. An important issue for a firm that wants to operate in such a market is how it can facilitate communication between consumers. By using an appropriately designed reputation system, it may convince consumers that it cannot profitably deviate from high-quality provision because such a deviation is communicated to other consumers who can then punish the firm.

The reputation of sellers on trading platforms is easily observed through summary statistics and may guide consumer choices. Such reputation systems can be seen as the digitization of word-of-mouth about a seller's quality characteristics which are not easily observable prior to purchase.[38] A number of studies have considered the online auction platform eBay and the effect of seller reputation on price and transaction volume. Until recently eBay had the peculiarity that sellers could retaliate in case of negative valuations (because feedbacks were immediately displayed, leaving time for reactions) and buyers seemed to care. This made the eBay feedbacks highly biased towards positive ratings. It also meant that a single negative rating could possibly have a strong negative impact for the seller. An unbiased approach was chosen by Amazon on its Amazon Marketplace, where third-party retailers offer their products. Buyers can rate these retailers after a transaction is completed. However, buyers cannot be rated; indeed there is little reason to evaluate a buyer since the payment is made at the moment of purchase; this is different from the eBay auction platform where the buyer may not, or only with delay, pay the price to the seller.

Reputation in electronic markets is summarized by a reputation profile. Typically, such a profile contains the number of transactions the seller has successfully completed, a summary of ratings from buyers who have completed transactions with the seller in the past, and a list of textual feedback provided by these buyers. A concrete example, given in Case 23.5, is the reputation system in place on Amazon marketplace.[39]

Case 23.5 Reputation on Amazon Marketplace

Consider the reputation system on Amazon Marketplace. While different studies analysing various auction and shopping sites do not find unambiguous evidence using simple summary statistics, one reason may be that reputation is not one-dimensional and different buyers care for different quality dimensions. If this is the case, buyers may pay particular attention to the text feedback that is given by previous buyers. Take for instance the sale of packaged consumer software. Some buyers may be particularly concerned about packaging, others may be particularly interested in fast delivery. Here, text messages can be checked that contain qualifiers along these and other dimensions. In an empirical analysis, text mining techniques can be used to find out about the dimensions in which sellers built up a particular track record. This information can be used in the regression analysis by constructing a scoring function that assigns pricing premium scores in each dimension. Ghose, Ipeirotis and Sundararajan (2006) isolate the extent to which the information provided by previous buyers in the text feedback for a particular seller affects its pricing. Features that turned out to be statistically significant for a particular dataset about the transaction of packaged consumer software are, e.g., the seller's responsiveness to queries, the quality of customer service, product quality, and misrepresentation of the product. All these features may contain adverse selection and moral hazard properties. If a sufficient number of buyers is willing to pay large enough price premia for particular features, the adverse selection and moral hazard problem is solved for these features.

A first simple insight into the role of reputation systems is to reconsider the branding argument that was formalized in Part V.[40] In particular, suppose that a single seller offers one unit in each of two periods. Consumers are willing to pay r for high quality and 0 for low quality. There are two populations of consumers, a period-1 population that is only active in period 1 and a period-2 population that is only active in period 2. The firm commits to its quality at the beginning of the game and incurs a unit cost $c < r$ for high quality. Consumers face an asymmetric information problem and only learn quality after purchase. Clearly, if period-2 consumers do not observe the performance of the product in period 1, they must form beliefs over the likelihood that high quality is provided. Period-1 consumers do not have information to start with. Since a low-quality firm has always an incentive to mimic the high-quality firm, high quality is not provided.

Introduce a reputation system that allows period-1 consumers to report observed quality to period 2-consumers. Suppose that the period-1 consumer who purchased the product truthfully reports the observed quality. We note that, in terms of monetary benefits, a period-1 consumer does not have an incentive to post reports since she will not be active in period 2 (presuming that she has positive opportunity cost of time). However, we resort to a behavioural justification: we postulate that consumers want it to be known how the product has performed so that fellow consumers can make informed decisions. With a reputation system in place and period-1 consumers actively using it, a high-quality firm is in period 2 in a very different position compared to a low-quality firm. It can obtain a revenue of r per consumer whereas the low-quality firm cannot make any positive revenue. This possibly affects the incentive to choose high quality. In period 1 a high-quality firm incurs higher costs c. However, in the presence of a reputation system it makes a higher benefit of the size $r - c$ per consumer compared to a low-quality firm. Hence, if $r > 2c$ the establishment of a reputation system solves the moral hazard problem. Alternatively, if the firm faces an adverse selection rather than a moral hazard problem, a similar argument can be made: then a reputation system can possibly solve the adverse selection problem. In both cases, firms gain from the existence of such reputation systems (in the adverse selection case only the high-quality firm) so that an intermediary that offers such reputation systems can make profits from them.

Lesson 23.7 Reputation systems can solve asymmetric information problems between firms and consumers and are thus valuable for firms.

Let us now turn to a market such as eBay on which price is determined through an auction.[41] We will uncover a role for reputation systems even if all consumers are informed before purchase. The role of the reputation system then is to guide consumers to the more valuable products. Suppose that it is too costly for consumers to become active in more than one auction. Hence, before taking part in an auction, consumers have to select the auction they want to participate in. We consider an environment in which consumers cannot coordinate their actions. Consequently, some sellers will not sell and some buyers will not find supplies because they are in competition with another buyer. In such a context, we introduce quality uncertainty at the ex ante stage. However, as already mentioned above, we postulate that in the auction itself, all asymmetric information has disappeared so that consumers pay their true valuation if they are not alone in the auction (this means that *buyers* behave like Bertrand competitors).

Suppose that there is a continuum of buyers with unit demand and a continuum of sellers with unit supply in each of two periods. Buyers are active for one period only, whereas sellers sell one unit in each period. For simplicity, suppose that in each period, the two groups are of equal size, which is set equal to 1. Seller i can be of high or low quality, $s_i \in \{s_L, s_H\}$. To make our analysis as simple as possible, we assume that observing the quality in period 1 leads to perfect revelation of the quality in period 2. Consumers are willing to pay s_H for high quality and s_L for low quality, costs are zero. A share $\lambda \in (0, 1)$ of sellers is of high quality. Hence, if consumers do not know the seller's quality they are willing to pay $s^e \equiv \lambda s_H + (1 - \lambda)s_L$.

In period 1 sellers can announce their quality (which may be true or false). Period-1 consumers then decide which firm to visit. They observe the true product quality of that firm and then place their bid. In period 2, consumers possibly obtain information about product quality thanks to the reputation system. Then period-2 consumers decide which firm to visit, observe the true product quality of the chosen firm and then place their bid. Assuming a second-price auction, according to which the bidder with the highest bid pays the second highest bid, consumers bid their true valuation. Since consumers are homogeneous, they obtain zero rents if more than one bidder shows up. Otherwise, if they are the only bidder, they obtain the product at zero price. Hence, if consumers knew the product quality ex ante, more would go to high-quality firms because they lead to a higher surplus in case no other bidder shows up.

High-quality firms have a weakly better reputation than low-quality firms. Denote the expected quality of a pronounced high-quality firm in period t by $\widehat{s}_H^t$; analogously for a low-quality firm. We must have $\widehat{s}_H^t \geq \widehat{s}_L^t$. In equilibrium, consumers must be indifferent between firms that enjoy a good reputation and those that do not. If firms separate into two segments, a perceived high-quality segment with market share β^t and a perceived low-quality segment with market share $1 - \beta^t$, we must have that $\beta^t \widehat{s}_H^t + (1 - \beta^t)\widehat{s}_L^t = \lambda s_H + (1 - \lambda)s_L = s^e$. This is equivalent to $\widehat{s}_H^t = [s^e - (1 - \beta^t)\widehat{s}_L^t]/\beta^t$. Suppose that a share of consumers turn to reputed firms and another share turn to non-reputed firms in period t. The market tightness is defined as the number of consumers per firm; in the high-quality segment, this is denoted by ϕ_H^t, and in the low-quality segment by ϕ_L^t. Hence $\beta^t \phi_H^t$ is the share of consumers in the high-quality segment and we must have that the shares in both segments add up to 1, i.e. $\beta^t \phi_H^t + (1 - \beta^t)\phi_L^t = 1$ or, equivalently, $\phi_H^t = [1 - (1 - \beta^t)\phi_L^t]/\beta^t$.

It can be shown that the probability of being the only bidder for a firm's product is $\exp\{-\phi\}$ in a market with tightness ϕ. The probability that there is at least one buyer is $1 - \exp\{-\phi\};$[42] the probability that there is more than one buyer is $\mu(\phi) \equiv 1 - \exp\{-\phi\} - \phi \exp\{-\phi\}$. Hence, a firm with quality s makes expected profit $\mu(\phi)s$ in a market with tightness ϕ. The expected utility of a consumer visiting a firm in a segment with tightness ϕ is $\exp(-\phi)\widehat{s}$ when she expects quality $\widehat{s}$.

Let us first see what happens in the absence of any information that consumers may extract. In this case consumers can only randomize over all firms and the market has tightness 1. Consumers have expected quality s^e. A share $1 - \exp(-1)$ of firms receive at least one consumer. Hence, the expected welfare is $\exp(-1)s^e$ per period.

Next we analyse the situation in which consumers can distinguish the two market segments. Here we only analyse equilibria in which some consumers will go to the low-quality segment.[43] Since buyers are homogeneous, the indifference condition reads $\widehat{s}_H^t \exp(-\phi_H^t) = \widehat{s}_L^t \exp(-\phi_L^t)$. Substituting the expression for ϕ_H^t, we can write ϕ_L^t as a function of β^t, $\widehat{s}_L^t$, and $\widehat{s}_H^t$, namely $\phi_L^t = 1 - \beta^t \ln(\widehat{s}_H^t/\widehat{s}_L^t)$.

What is then the role of a reputation system? With a reputation system that reports types (i.e., first-period qualities), a seller with a low-quality product in period 1 acquires a bad reputation in the second period. Period-2 consumers know that the product is of low quality even before selecting the firm. Hence, $\widehat{s}_L^2 = s_L$ and $\widehat{s}_H^2 = s_H$. Hence, more consumers will go to the reputed segment than the non-reputed segment. This increases welfare compared to the situation without a reputation system. The statement in the first period is meaningless and thus does not contain any information.

Alternatively, one can consider a reputation system that honours honest announcements in period 1. If a good reputation comes from an honest announcement and not from high quality, some low-quality firms may prefer to announce their low-quality before period 1. This implies that there are separate segments already in period 1. However, the honest low-quality firms can use their reputation to obtain higher profits in period 2. Installing a reputation system for honesty is welfare-improving as well.[44]

To summarize, both reputation systems allow consumers to direct their visits toward high-quality firms. Our general conclusion is given in the following lesson.

> **Lesson 23.8**   Reputation systems that reveal information (about product quality or the honesty of previous claims) help consumers to identify which seller type they will visit in an auction. This leads to a partial separation of firm types: high-quality firms tend to receive more visits than firms with low quality. The introduction of a reputation system is welfare-increasing.

Our analysis suggests that intermediaries may be able to attract more traffic by installing a reputation system. Such a system may then allow the intermediary to charge for its services and thus make a profit from resolving asymmetric information problems. Case 23.6 closes this section with an account of two analyses of eBay's reputation system.

Case 23.6 Reputation on eBay

eBay's reputation system has received quite some attention in empirical work. Most studies analyse reputation effects with the help of cross-section regressions.[45] These, however, have the potential problem of unobserved seller heterogeneity. Here, we discuss two alternative approaches.

Resnick *et al.* (2006) conduct a controlled field experiment. An established seller offers identical postcards under his name and under a new name. They find that buyers are willing to pay a premium to firms with a longer history, for comparable rates of favourable ratings. In particular they find that consumers pay an 8% premium when purchasing from a seller with 2000 positive feedbacks and 1 negative instead of a seller with only 10 positive feedbacks and no negatives.

Cabral and Hortaçsu (2008) estimate reputation effects making use of panel data. They postulate that the frequency of buyer feedback is a good proxy for the frequency of actual transactions and that the nature of the feedback is a good proxy for the degree of buyer satisfaction. While in particular the first assumption may be criticized, they provide statistical tests according to which the likelihood of feedback appears to be uncorrelated with a variety of seller characteristics. The panel data of seller histories make it possible to consider how buyers react to changes in reputation and how sellers strategically react to the reputation system.

The empirical findings suggest that negative responses have a strong and significantly negative effect on seller profits: when a seller first receives negative feedback, his weekly sales growth rate falls from plus 5% to minus 8%. Cabral and Hortaçsu also find that a seller is more likely to exit the lower his reputation and that, just before exiting, sellers receive more negative responses than their average. This is compatible with sellers spending their reputation before exiting.

Review questions

1. How can consumers react to information overload?

2. What is the role of an information gatekeeper in a search market?

3. How do recommendation networks affect sales?

4. In which situations are intermediaries bearers of reputation?

5. Do sellers benefit from the presence of a reputation system on Amazon MarketPlace? Provide a detailed answer.

Further reading

This chapter contains an arguably more idiosyncratic mix of topics and models compared to the rest of the book. Our analysis of information overload is based on Anderson and de Palma (2007). The analysis of information gatekeepers follows Baye and Morgan (2001). We then follow Tucker and Zhang (2008) and present their simple model of consumer choice in the presence of a recommender system. Our formal analysis of certifying intermediaries is partly inspired by Biglaiser (1993). We then base our analysis on Lizzeri (1999). The formal analysis of the role of a reputation system follows Kennes and Schiff (2007).

Notes for Part IX

1. The example is similar to Spulber (1999). However, part of his analysis and conclusions are not correct (see the next endnote). A related analysis in which also the nonintermediated market operates efficiently can be found in Bose and Pingle (1995). See also Gehrig (1993) and Rust and Hall (2003).

2. Spulber (1999) wrongly claims that in such an environment there is no role for a market maker. On page xxi he writes: 'It is easy to demonstrate that there are no prices at which a monopoly intermediary is profitable.' Yet, the illustration following this claim is not correct.

3. These examples come from Hagiu (2006).

4. Spulber (1999, Chapter 7) analyses the same model.

5. See Hagiu (2006) for a model that takes some of these factors into account.

6. See Pagano (1989).

7. The business literature stresses that 'liquidity' is essential for the success of B2B marketplaces: 'To succeed, [neutral] e-hubs must attract both buyers and sellers quickly, creating liquidity at both ends' (Kaplan and Sawhney, 2000); 'the first pillar of e-marketplace success is building liquidity' (Brunn et al., 2002).

8. This model is adapted from Caillaud and Jullien (2003).

9. This is socially desirable because efficiency requires all agents to register with the same intermediary (because of network effects).

10. Caillaud and Jullien (2001, 2003) show that when transaction fees are not feasible, there may exist equilibria with a single active intermediary and positive profits.

11. We follow here Damiano and Li (2008).

12. Damiano and Li (2008) consider, more generally, any distribution function with a non-increasing density function and a non-decreasing hazard rate function. Their results also hold for $a = 0$ and/or $b = \infty$.

13. If the two matchmakers set their registration fee simultaneously, Damiano and Li (2008) show that the only coexistence equilibria are in mixed strategies; it is harder to obtain clear insights from the analysis of such equilibria.

14. The analysis follows Armstrong (2006, Section 3).

15. This information is reported in Holland (2007).

16. The analysis is based on Armstrong (2006).

17. Some of these examples come from Evans (2003), Evans and Schmalensse (2008) and Armstrong (2006). Other examples come from our own research.

18. Again, we follow Armstrong (2006).

19. We follow here Wright (2004) and Evans and Schmalensee (2008).

20. Filistrucchi (2008) discusses the design and implementation of a SSNIP test for media markets. He suggests that the test be run by raising each of the two prices separately allowing each time the other price to be adjusted. He also suggests that profits on both sides of the market and all feedbacks should be taken into account.

21. This case draws from Wallsten (2007), Knowledge@Wharton (2007) and Sidak and Singer (2008).

22. This case draws from Lee (2008).

23. This case draws from RBB Economics (2008).

24. National Bancard Corp. v. Visa U.S.A., Inc., 779 F.2d 592 (11th Cir. 1986).

25. This case is based on Genakos and Valletti (2007).

26. See Chang et al. (2005).

27. The analysis is based on Anderson and de Palma (2007). At various points, we make simplifying assumptions, which also allow us to provide explicit solutions.

28. We present here a simplified version of Baye and Morgan (2001).

29. This case is based on 'U.S. retailers working with Web sites to lift post-Thanksgiving sales' (by Michael Barbaro, International Herald Tribune, 20 November 2007) and 'Some retailers try to suppress Web scoops on prices' (by Randall Ross, International Herald Tribune, 18 November 2007).

30. This term has been popularized by Anderson (2006). For a short informal account of some of the underlying forces see, e.g., Brynjolfsson, Hu, and Smith (2006).

31. For a formal analysis, see Tucker and Zhang (2008). An interesting question which we do not analyse here is the possibility of rational herding. This is a situation in which consumers ignore their private information and fully rely on the aggregate information provided by the system. This means that learning stops at some point. A seminal paper on rational herding is Banerjee (1992). Tucker and Zhang (2008) also address herding in the present context.

32. This point is made in the numerical analyses of Fleder and Hosanagar (2008). However, in their model the recommendation network essentially provides information about the popularity of a product and does not allow for more fine-tuned recommendations.

33. See Hervas-Drane (2008) for a formal analysis.

34. Other interesting empirical work has been done by Brynjolfsson, Hu and Simester (2007), Oberholzer-Gee and Elberse (2007) and Tucker and Zhang (2008). Brynjolfsson, Hu, and Simester (2007) compare online and offline retailing with each other and find that onlines sales are more dispersed. While compatible with the hypothesis that recommender networks lead to more dispersed sales, other explanations can be given.

Oberholzer-Gee and Elberse (2007), comparing DVD sales in 2005 to those in 2000, find that the tail has got longer in 2005. However, they also find that a few blockbusters enjoy even more sales; this is like a superstar effect. Again the role of recommender systems is not explicit. Tucker and Zhang (2008) use data from a website that lists wedding services vendors and show in their field experiment that, at the margin, popularity information tends to be more valuable for niche products.

35. To take into account possible unobserved heterogeneity in the data, Oesterreicher-Singer and Sundararajan (2008) also construct a panel data set. The estimation results are confirmed with panel data techniques.

36. The analysis is inspired by Biglaiser (1993), Biglaiser and Friedman (1994) and Chu and Chu (1994).

37. The following arguments are due to Lizzeri (1999). For a related analysis with moral hazard, see Albano and Lizzeri (2001).

38. See Dellarocas (2003) for a discussion.

39. See, e.g., Resnick *et al.* (2000).

40. This is a simplified version of the base model with independent selling that was used to analyse the role of umbrella branding.

41. In this book we did not include auction models into the analysis and rather focused on markets in which consumers see posted prices. However, the Cournot model can be interpreted as a market in which a welfare-maximizing auctioneer sells a given quantity to consumers. Given the prominence of eBay and the relative simplicity of the model, we consider here a model in which all sellers auction off their product. The analysis is based on Kennes and Schiff (2007). This auction model cannot be rephrased as a price-setting model because the prevailing price here depends on the number of bidders and is stochastic.

42. This function is an urn-ball matching function. It approximates the probability that an urn contains at least one ball if each of m balls is randomly placed in one of n urns, where m/n is constant and m large. For a derivation of such matching functions, we refer to Montgomery (1991) and Peters (1991).

43. To exclude situations in which all buyers are better off to visit only one segment, i.e., $f_H = 1/\beta$ and $f_L = 0$, we must have $\widehat{s}_H \exp(-1/\beta) < \widehat{s}_L$.

44. It is in general unclear which of the two reputation systems is superior.

45. See, e.g., Melnik and Alm (2002), Resnick and Zeckhauser (2002).

References for Part IX

Albano, G. and Lizzeri, A. (2001). Strategic Certification and the Provision of Quality. *International Economic Review* 42: 267–283.

Anderson, C. (2006). *The Long Tail: Why the Future of Business Is Selling Less of More*. New York: Hyperion Press.

Anderson, S. P. and de Palma, A. (2007). Information Congestion: Open Access in a Two-Sided Market. Mimeo.

Armstrong, M. (2006). Competition in Two-Sided Markets. *Rand Journal of Economics* 37: 668–691.

Banerjee, A. V. (1992). A Simple Model of Herd Behavior. *Quarterly Journal of Economics* 107: 797–817.

Baye, M. and Morgan, J. (2001). Information Gatekeepers on the Internet and the Competitiveness of Homogeneous Product Markets. *American Economic Review* 91: 454–474.

Biglaiser, G. (1993). Middlemen as Experts. *Rand Journal of Economics* 24: 212–223.

Biglaiser, G. and Friedman, J. W. (1994). Middlemen as Guarantors of Quality. *International Journal of Industrial Organization* 12: 509–531.

Bose, G. and Pingle, M. (1995). Stores. *Economic Theory* 6: 251–262.

Brunn, P., Jensen, M. and Skovgaard, J. (2002). e-Marketplaces: Crafting a Winning Strategy. *European Management Journal* 20: 286–298.

Brynjolfsson, E., Hu, Y. and Simester, D. (2007). Goodbye Pareto Principle, Hello Long Tail: The Effect of Search Costs on the Concentration of Product Sales. Mimeo.

Brynjolfsson, E., Hu, Y. J. and Smith, M. D. (2006). From Niches to Riches: Anatomy of the Long Tail, *Sloan Management Review* 47: 67–71.

Cabral, L. and Hortaçsu, A. (2008). The Dynamics of Seller Reputation: The Case of eBay. Forthcoming in *Journal of Industrial Economics*.

Caillaud, B. and Jullien, B. (2001). Competing Cybermediaries. *European Economic Review (Papers and Proceedings)* 45: 797–808.

Caillaud, B. and Jullien, B. (2003). Chicken & Egg: Competition among Intermediation Service Providers. *Rand Journal of Economics* 34: 309–328.

Chang, H., Evans, D. and Garcia-Swartz, D. (2005). The Effect of Regulatory Intervention in Two-Sided Markets: An Assessment of Interchange-Fee Capping in Australia. *Review of Network Economics* 4: 328–358.

Chevalier, J. and Mayzlin, D. (2006). The Effect of Word of Mouth on Sales: Online Book Reviews. *Journal of Marketing Research* 43: 345–354.

Chu, W. and Chu, W. (1994). Signaling Quality by Selling Through a Reputable Retailer: An Example of Renting the Reputation of Another Agent. *Marketing Science* 13: 177–189.

Clements, M. and Ohashi, H. (2005). Indirect Network Effects and the Product Cycle: Video Games in the U.S., 1994–2002. *Journal of Industrial Economics* 53: 515–542.

Clerides, S., Nearchou, P. and Pashardes, P. (2008). Intermediaries as Quality Assessors: Tour Operators in the Travel Industry. *International Journal of Industrial Organization* 26: 372–392.

Damiano, E. and Li, H. (2008). Competing Matchmaking. *Journal of the European Economic Association* 6: 789–818.

Dellarocas, C. (2003). The Digitalization of Word of Mouth: Promises and Challenges of Online Reputation Systems. *Management Science* 49: 1407–1425.

Evans, D. (2003). Some Empirical Aspects of Multi-sided Platform Industries. *Review of Network Economics* 2: 191–209.

Evans, D. and Schmalensee, R. (2008). Markets with Two-Sided Platforms. *Issues in Competition Law and Policy (ABA Section of Antitrust Law)* 1: 667–693.

Filistrucchi, L. (2008). A SSNIP Test for Two-Sided Markets: The Case of Media. Mimeo.

Fleder, D. and Hosanagar, K. (2008). Blockbuster Culture's Next Rise or Fall: The Impact of Recommender Systems on Sales Diversity. Forthcoming in *Management Science*.

Gehrig, T. (1993). Intermediation in Search Markets. *Journal of Economics and Management Strategy* 2: 97–120.

Genakos, C. and Valletti, T. (2007). Testing the Waterbed Effect in Mobile Telephony. Mimeo.

Ghose, A., Ipeirotis, P. G. and Sundararajan, A. (2006). The Dimensions of Reputation in Electronic Markets. Mimeo.

Hagiu, A. (2006). Merchant or Two-Sided Platform? *Review of Network Economics* 6: 115–133.

Hagiu, A. and Lee, R. (2007). Exclusivity and Control. Mimeo.

Hervas-Drane, A. (2008). Word of Mouth and Recommender Systems: A Theory of the Long Tail. Mimeo.

Holland, M. (2007). Two-Sided Markets: A Challenge to Competition Policy? Mimeo.

Jullien, B. (2005). Two-Sided Markets and Electronic Intermediaries. *CESifo Economic Studies* 51: 235–262.

Kaiser, U. and Wright, J. (2006). Price Structure in Two-sided Markets: Evidence from the Magazine Industry. *International Journal of Industrial Organization* 24: 1–28.

Kaplan, S., and Sawhney, M. (2000). E-hubs: The New B2B Marketplaces. *Harvard Business Review* 78(3): 97–106.

Kennes, J. and Schiff, A. (2007). Simple Reputation Systems. *Scandinavian Journal of Economics* 109: 71–91.

Knowledge@Wharton (2007). Sirius and XM: Can Two Archrivals Sing the Same Tune? Mimeo.

Lee, R. S. (2008). Vertical Integration and Exclusivity in Platform and Two-Sided Markets. Mimeo. New York University.

Lerner, J. (2002). Did Microsoft Deter Software Innovation? Mimeo.

Lizzeri, A. (1999). Information Revelation and Certification Intermediaries. *Rand Journal of Economics* 30: 214–231.

Melnik, M. I. and Alm, J. (2002). Does a Seller's eCommerce Reputation Matter? Evidence from eBay Auctions. *Journal of Industrial Economics* 50: 337–350.

Montgomery, James D. (1991). Equilibrium Wage Dispersion and Interindustry Wage Differentials. *Quarterly Journal of Economics* 106: 163–179.

Oberholzer-Gee, F. and Elberse, A. (2007). Superstars and Underdogs: An Examination of the Long Tail Phenomenon in Video Sales. Mimeo.

Oestreicher-Singer, G. and Sundararajan, A. (2008). Recommendation Networks and the Long Tail of Electronic Commerce. Mimeo.

Pagano, M. (1989). Trading Volume and Asset Liquidity. *Quarterly Journal of Economics* 104: 255–274.

Peters, M. (1991). Ex Ante Price Offers in Matching Games: Non–Steady States. *Econometrica* 59: 1425–1454.

RBB Economics (2008). Two Sides to Every Story? Lessons from the Travelport/Worldspan EC case. *RBB Brief* 25: 1–4.

Resnick, P., Kuwabara, K., Zeckhauser, R. and Friedman, E. (2000). Reputation systems. Communications of ACM 43(12) 45–48.

Resnick, P., Zeckhauser, R., Swanson, J. and Lockwood, K. (2006) The Value of Reputation on eBay: A Controlled Experiment. *Experimental Economics* 9: 79–101.

Resnick, P. and Zeckhauser, R. (2002). Trust Among Strangers in Internet Transactions: Empirical Analysis of eBay's Reputation System. In Baye, M. (ed.), *The Economics of the Internet and E-Commerce*. Volume 11 of Advances in Applied Microeconomics. Amsterdam: Elsevier Science. pp. 127–157.

Rochet, J.-C. and Tirole, J. (2003). Platform Competition in Two-Sided Markets. *Journal of the European Economic Association* 1: 990–1024.

Rochet, J.-C. and Tirole, J. (2006). Two-Sided Markets: A Progress Report. *Rand Journal of Economics* 37: 645–667.

Rust, J. and Hall, G. (2003). Middlemen versus Market Makers: A Theory of Competitive Exchange. *Journal of Political Economy* 111: 353–403.

Rysman, M. (2007). An Empirical Analysis of Credit Card Usage. *Journal of Industrial Economics* 55: 1–36.

Sidak, J. G. and Singer, H. J. (2008). Evaluating Market Power with Two-Sided Demand and Preemptive Offers to Dissipate Monopoly Rent: Lessons for High-Technology Industries from the Proposed Merger of XM and Sirius Satellite Radio. *Journal of Competition Law and Economics* 4: 697–751.

Spulber, D. (1999). *Market Microstructure. Intermediaries and the Theory of the Firm*. Cambridge: Cambridge University Press.

Tucker, C. and Zhang, J. (2008). How Does Popularity Information Affect Choices? Theory and a Field Experiment. Mimeo.

Wallsten, C. (2007). Comments to the Federal Communications Commission – Antitrust, Two-Sided Markets, and Platform Competition: The Case of the XM-Sirius Merger. Mimeo.

Wright, J. (2004). One-sided Logic in Two-sided Markets. *Review of Network Economics* 3: 44–64.

Appendix A
Game theory

Game theory is the formal analysis of decision making in situations of strategic interactions. A game can be formalized in two different ways, in its normal form and in its extensive form. We start with one-shot simultaneous move games, which are best analysed in their normal form.

A.1   Games in normal form and Nash equilibrium

Normal form games

A *normal form game* consists of a set of players N and, for each player $i \in N$, a set of feasible actions X_i, and a payoff function π_i, which gives a profit or payoff for each feasible profile of actions, $\pi_i(x_i, x_{-i})$. Here x_i denotes the player's action and $x_{-i} = (x_1, \ldots, x_{i-1}, x_{i+1}, \ldots x_n)$ the other players' action profile. Examples for such actions are prices or quantities set by firms. A normal form game can thus be written as $\{N, (X_i, \pi_i(\cdot))_{i=1,\ldots,n}\}$. We say that $x_i \in X_i$ is a pure strategy. A mixed strategy $\sigma_i \in \Sigma_i$ is a probability distribution over X_i. Strategy σ_i is called a best response for player i to his rivals' strategies σ_{-i} if

$$\pi_i(\sigma_i, \sigma_{-i}) \geq \pi_i(\sigma'_i, \sigma_{-i}) \quad \text{for all} \quad \sigma'_i \in \Sigma_i.$$

Rationalizable strategies

Strategy σ_i is never a best response if there is no σ_{-i} for which σ_i is a best response. Suppose that all players are rational, i.e., they maximize their payoff function. It implies that it cannot be best for a player to choose a strategy that is never a weak best response. In the prisoner's dilemma, the property that all players are rational implies that player 1 chooses B and player 2 chooses R. The following table provides the normal form representation of the prisoner's dilemma with $d > a > b > c$. The matrix reports the payoffs for player 1 and player 2 for all possible strategy profiles.

		Player 2	
		L	R
Player 1	T	a, a	c, d
	B	d, c	b, b^*

Suppose furthermore that all players know that all players are rational and that all know that all know that all players are rational and so on until infinity. This assumption on the knowledge of rationality at all levels of understanding is called *common knowledge of rationality*. It implies that players only choose strategies that survive the process of iterative elimination of strategies that are never a weak best response. Such strategies are called *rationalizable*. Games with strategic complementarities (i.e., supermodular games) possess nice properties of the set of rationalizable strategies. However, we typically require a consistency of actions that is not implied by rationalizability.

Nash equilibrium

A strategy profile x^* constitutes a pure-strategy *Nash equilibrium* of the game $\{N, (X_i, \pi_i(\cdot))_{i=1,\ldots,n}\}$ if for every $i \in N$,

$$\pi_i(x_i^*, x_{-i}^*) \geq \pi_i(x_i, x_{-i}^*) \quad \text{for all} \quad x_i \in X_i.$$

For an alternative definition, we define the *best response correspondence* of player i, b_i, as containing those actions which lead to the highest payoff for given choices of the other players (denoted by x_{-i}):

$$b_i(x_{-i}) \equiv \{x_i \in X_i \mid \pi_i(x_i, x_{-i}) \geq \pi_i(x_i', x_{-i}) \quad \text{for all} \quad x_i' \in X_i\}.$$

Then, the strategy profile x^* is a (pure strategy) Nash equilibrium if and only if

$$x_i^* \in b_i(x_{-i}^*) \quad \text{for all} \quad i \in N.$$

In words, a Nash equilibrium is a situation in which all players choose mutual best responses. This means that they hold consistent conjectures or beliefs about the play of other players. This is in contrast to rationalizable strategies according to which beliefs are not necessarily mutually consistent. Note that Nash equilibrium can be the result of a self-enforcing agreement. If players can reach nonbinding agreements, they should reach the agreement to play an action profile that constitutes a Nash equilibrium.

Mixed-strategy equilibrium

To analyse situations in which players can choose not only among pure strategies but can also mix between various strategies (and thus choose a non-degenerate mixed strategy), we consider the notion of mixed-strategy equilibrium. A mixed strategy profile $\sigma^* = (\sigma_1^*, \ldots, \sigma_n^*) \in \Sigma_1 \times \cdots \times \Sigma_n$ constitutes a (mixed-strategy) Nash equilibrium of a normal form game with mixed strategies if for every player $i \in N$,

$$\pi_i(\sigma_i^*, \sigma_{-i}^*) \geq \pi_i(\sigma_i, \sigma_{-i}^*) \quad \text{for all} \quad \sigma_i \in \Sigma_i.$$

Note that any pure strategy that is played with positive probability in equilibrium must yield the same payoff. Otherwise, a deviation would be profitable. Finding mixed-strategy equilibria is in general quite cumbersome. However, we can use the following property of an equilibrium mixed-strategy profile σ^*: $\pi_i(x_i, \sigma_{-i}^*) = \pi_i(x_i', \sigma_{-i}^*)$ for all $x_i, x_i' \in X_i^+$ and $\pi_i(x_i, x_{-i}^*) \geq \pi_i(x_i', x_{-i}^*)$ for all $x_i \in X_i^+$ and all $x_i' \notin X_i^+$. Here X_i^+ denotes the set of pure strategies that are played with strictly positive likelihood in equilibrium.

Finite games

We distinguish between finite and continuous games. Suppose first that the game is finite, meaning that each player's strategy set consists of a finite number of possible actions. Note that a pure-strategy equilibrium may fail to exist already in simple 2×2 (2 players, two strategies) games. If an equilibrium exists, multiple pure-strategy equilibria may exist. Hence, when analysing such games, the issues of existence and uniqueness have to be addressed. A simple example that illustrates the possibility of multiple equilibria is the battle of the sexes in which two pure-strategy equilibria exist and in which the two players do not agree on which equilibrium is the most preferred. Given numbers a, b, c, d, e, f with $a, b > c, d, e, f$, the normal form representation of the battle of the sexes is:

Player 2

		L	R
Player 1	U	a^*, b^*	c, d
	D	e, f	b^*, a^*

Indicating with a $*$ the best responses of each player, we observe that both (U, L) and (D, R) are pure-strategy equilibria.

With respect to mixed-strategy equilibria, we note that any finite game must have at least one mixed-strategy equilibrium (which may be degenerate in the sense that it coincides with the pure-strategy equilibrium). Hence, the problem that a mixed-strategy equilibrium may not exist does not arise: *any finite game has a mixed-strategy equilibrium*. We also note that any pure-strategy equilibrium in the game with pure actions must be an equilibrium in the game with mixed actions, in the sense that the degenerate probability distribution that assigns probability 1 to the pure strategy in question constitutes a mixed-strategy Nash equilibrium.

Continuous games

Suppose now that each player's strategy is a real number; thus we are in a continuous game. Suppose furthermore that there is a lower and an upper bound for each player's strategy, $X_i = [\underline{x}_i, \overline{x}_i]$ (e.g., in a price-setting game, an upper bound would be a price with the property that demand is necessarily zero at this or a higher price level, independently of the action of other players). Then a sufficient condition for the existence of a Nash equilibrium in pure strategies is that the payoff function π_i is quasi-concave in x_i and continuous in x for all players i. The payoff function π_i is quasi-concave in x_i if it is single-peaked. Assuming continuous differentiability of the profit function, an interior (pure-strategy) Nash equilibrium is characterized by the solution to the system of first-order conditions

$$\frac{\partial \pi_i(x_i, x_{-i})}{\partial x_i} = 0 \quad \text{for all} \quad i \in N.$$

An extension to a higher-dimensional strategy space is obvious (for instance, the strategy space is two-dimensional if firms have to choose simultaneously advertising and price).

A mixed strategy in a continuous game is a probability distribution over the set of pure strategies. Characterizing mixed-strategy equilibria in continuous games can be quite demanding and involves solving differential equations. In a particular model, we analyse such equilibria in Chapter 7.

A.2   Games in extensive form and subgame perfection

Extensive-form games

Many games have the feature that players make their decisions at different points in time. Such dynamic situations are typically better approached as games presented in their extensive form. The extensive form representation of a game specifies a number of things: (1) the players in the game (this possibly includes a player called Nature to include the situation in which some external event occurs with a particular probability and some players have to make decisions before the uncertainty is resolved); (2) when each player has to make a decision; (3) what decisions each player can make whenever it is his or her turn; (4) what each player knows about the other players' decisions which were made before; (5) the payoffs of each player for each combination of decisions that can possibly be chosen by the players. A formal definition of an extensive form game would take us much time; see Mas-Colell, Whinston and Green (1995).

A game in extensive form starts at an *initial decision node* at which player i makes a decision. Each of the possible choices by player i is represented by a *branch*. At the end of each branch is another decision node at which some other player j has to make a choice; again, each choice is represented by a branch. This is continued until no more choices are made and the end of the game is reached, represented by *terminal nodes*. At each terminal node, we list the players' payoffs arising from the sequence of decisions leading to that terminal node. The set of all decision nodes between which a player cannot distinguish are called an *information set*.

Games of perfect information

A special class of games are *games of perfect information*. In such games, all players know in which decision node they are when making a choice. In other words, in games of perfect information, each information set contains exactly one decision node.

As an example of a game of perfect information, consider a simplified Stackelberg game with demand $P(q) = 0$ for $q > 2$, $P(q) = 1/2$ for $q \in (1, 2]$, and $P(q) = 1$ for $p \in (0, 1]$. Marginal costs are assumed to be equal to zero. Each of the two players can choose either high output $q_H = 3/2$ or low output $q_L = 1/4$. Profits are $\pi_i(q_H, q_H) = 0$, $\pi_i(q_L, q_L) = 1/2$, $\pi_i(q_H, q_L) = 3/4$ and $\pi_i(q_L, q_H) = 1/4$. Suppose firm 1 sets the quantity before firm 2. Thus we are considering a 2-stage game in which, at stage 1, firm 1 chooses its quantity $q_1 \in \{q_L, q_H\}$ and, at stage 2, firm 2 chooses its quantity $q_2 \in \{q_L, q_H\}$. Games in extensive form are often represented by game trees. The game tree for our example is depicted in Figure A.1 (where, at each terminal node, firm 1's payoff is written above firm 2's payoff).

Using simple reasoning, it is clear that if firm 1 chose q_L, firm 2 would choose q_H and if firm 1 chose q_H firm 2 would choose q_L. If firm 1 anticipates these choices of firm 2 (which it does if it knows that firm 2 maximizes profit), it will choose q_H if it maximizes its profit. Because players know exactly where they are in the game tree whenever they have to make a decision (i.e., their information set at each point of decision contains a single element), we can use the *backward induction procedure* to obtain a unique prediction of the outcome of the game (as long as payoffs of each player are different across the different end nodes of the game).

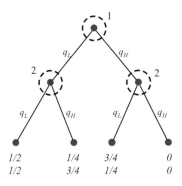

Alternatively, we can consider the normal-form representation of this game. Strategies are

$$X_1 = \{q_L, q_H\},$$

$$X_2 = \{q_L|q_L \wedge q_L|q_H, q_L|q_L \wedge q_H|q_H, q_H|q_L \wedge q_L|q_H, q_H|q_L \wedge q_H|q_H\}.$$

Firm 1 only has one decision node and can choose between two actions at this node; therefore, firm 1 has two strategies: firm 1's strategy q_L is denoted by L and the strategy q_H by H. As for firm 2, it has two decision nodes and two possible actions at each node; that makes 4 (2×2) strategies for firm 2: firm 2's strategy $q_L|q_L \wedge q_L|q_H$ is denoted by LL, $q_L|q_L \wedge q_H|q_H$ by LH, $q_H|q_L \wedge q_L|q_H$ by HL and $q_H|q_L \wedge q_H|q_H$ by HH. Note that strategies are contingent plans that tell the player what to decide at each decision node where the player is called upon to play. The normal-form representation of the game is then

		Firm 2			
		LL	LH	HL	HH
Firm 1	L	1/2, 1/2	1/2*, 1/2	1/4, 3/4*	1/4*, 3/4*
	H	3/4*, 1/4*	0, 0	3/4*, 1/4*	0, 0

We observe that this game form has three pure-strategy Nash equilibria, (H, LL), (H, HL) and (L, HH). The second of these three equilibria, (H, HL), is also the outcome of our previous reasoning. The other two equilibria, however, can be criticized as unreasonable because they involve non-credible threats by firm 2: in (H, LL), firm 2 threatens to choose q_L if firm 1 has chosen q_L, which is not credible; similarly, in (L, HH), firm 2 threatens to choose q_H if firm 1 has chosen q_H, which is not credible either. We can exclude such non-credible threats by the backward induction procedure that was exemplified above. The general result is the following: *Every finite game of perfect information has a pure-strategy equilibrium that can be derived through backward induction. If no player has the same payoffs at any two terminal nodes, there exists a unique Nash equilibrium that can be derived through backward induction.* This is Zermelo's theorem.

Subgame perfect Nash equilibrium

We want to exclude non-credible threats not only in games of perfect information but more generally in any multi-stage game. To do so, we first have to introduce the notion of a *subgame*.

A subgame in an extensive-form game (1) begins at a decision node that is the only decision node of the information set it belongs to (i.e. at the beginning of a subgame, the player who is about to decide knows where he is in the game) and (2) includes those and only those decision and terminal nodes that follow the decision node at which the subgame starts. In addition, we require that if we take any information set that contains a decision node in the subgame, all decision nodes contained in this information set must belong to the subgame. In the game tree, this means that a subgame cannot cut information sets.

To exclude non-credible threats, we have to require that a Nash equilibrium of the whole game induces a Nash equilibrium in each of its subgames. The corresponding equilibrium concept is that of a *subgame perfect Nash equilibrium (SPNE)*. Let us define this a bit more formally. Denote an extensive-form game by Γ_E. A strategy profile s^* in an n-player extensive form game Γ_E is defined to be a SPNE if it induces a Nash equilibrium in every subgame of Γ_E. The following result holds. *Consider an extensive form game Γ_E and some subgame Γ_E^S of Γ_E. Suppose that strategy profile s^{s*} is an SPNE in subgame Γ_E^S. Let $\hat{\Gamma}_E$ be the reduced game formed by replacing subgame Γ_E^S by a terminal node with payoffs equal to those arising from play of s^{s*}. Then, (1) in any SPNE s^* of Γ_E in which s^{s*} is an SPNE of Γ_E^S, players' reduced strategies $\hat{s}^*$ of s^* in the reduced game $\hat{\Gamma}_E$ constitute an SPNE of $\hat{\Gamma}_E$ and (2) if $\hat{s}^*$ is an SPNE of $\hat{\Gamma}_E$, then the strategy profile s^* that specifies the moves in s^{s*} at information sets belonging to Γ_E^S and that specifies the moves as described by $\hat{s}^*$ at information sets not belonging to Γ_E^S is an SPNE of Γ_E.*

For games with a finite number of stages (of perfect or imperfect information), we can generalize the backward induction procedure from above that is only useful for games of perfect information. The generalized backward induction procedure works as follows.

1. Identify all Nash equilibria of the final subgames (those that have no other subgames nested within).

2. Select one Nash equilibrium in each of those subgames and derive the reduced extensive form in which the subgames are replaced by the equilibrium payoffs in the selected Nash equilibrium of those subgames.

3. Repeat steps 1 and 2 for the reduced game until this procedure provides a path of play from the initial node to a terminal node of the game.

The outcome of this generalized backward induction procedure gives all subgame perfect Nash equilibria of the game. We make use of this result repeatedly in the book. Note however that the procedure is not useful, e.g., in infinitely repeated games. Infinitely repeated games are analysed in Chapter 14.

A.3   Static asymmetric information games and Bayesian Nash equilibrium

So far, we have ignored the possibility that some players may possess private information, i.e., payoff-relevant information that is not available to other players. To analyse such situations of *incomplete information*, we consider Bayesian games as games in which Nature chooses the state of the world $\omega \in \Omega$, which is only partially revealed to players. Formally, suppose $\theta_i \in \Theta_i$ is a random variable chosen by Nature. The realization θ_i is only observed by player i. We say that player i is of type θ_i. For instance, the type may reflect a firm's cost type, which may be unobservable for other players. Players have common knowledge of the type distribution; this is a joint probability distribution of the θ_i's, denoted by $\rho(\theta_1, \ldots, \theta_n)$. Payoff functions π_i then depend on the actions $x \in X$ and the realization of types $\theta \in \Theta$. Hence, a Bayesian game in normal form consists of the type space Θ, the prior probability distribution ρ, the set of players N, a strategy set X_i and a payoff function π_i for each player $i \in N$.

Suppose there is a finite number of types θ_i for each player. Then all players share common prior probabilities $\rho(\theta_1, \ldots, \theta_n)$. Player i observes his or her type θ_i so that his or her beliefs are the conditional probability $\rho(\theta_{-i}|\theta_i)$. Note that the conditioning does not affect beliefs if the own type realization does not provide information of the type distribution of the other players. This is for instance the case if types are drawn independently from some type distribution that applies to all players. Observing θ_i, player i has expected payoff

$$\sum_{\theta_{-i} \in \Theta_{-i}} \rho(\theta_{-i}|\theta_i)\pi_i(x_i, s_{-i}(\theta_{-i}), (\theta_i, \theta_{-i}))$$

if he chooses x_i and the other players follow decision rules (or strategies) $s_j(\theta_j)$, $j \neq i$. Hence, observing θ_i, player i chooses

$$s_i^*(\theta_i) \in \arg\max_{x_i \in X_i} \sum_{\theta_{-i} \in \Theta_{-i}} \rho(\theta_{-i}|\theta_i)\pi_i(x_i, s_{-i}^*(\theta_{-i}), (\theta_i, \theta_{-i}))$$

in a *Bayesian Nash equilibrium*.

It is straightforward to see that Bayesian Nash equilibrium is formally the same concept as Nash equilibrium. Since each type occurs with positive probability, the above formulation is equivalent to the following ex ante formulation that solves for all types of each player i,

$$s_i^*(.) \in \arg\max_{s_i(.) \in X_i^{\Theta_i}} \sum_{\theta_i \in \Theta_i} \sum_{\theta_{-i} \in \Theta_{-i}} \rho(\theta_i|\theta_{-i})\pi_i(s_i(\theta_i), s_{-i}^*(\theta_{-i}), (\theta_i, \theta_{-i})), \qquad (A.1)$$

with $X_i^{\Theta_i}$ denoting the space of pure strategies.

Hence, a Bayesian Nash equilibrium for the Bayesian game is a strategy profile $(s_1^*(.), \ldots, s_n^*(.))$ that constitutes a Nash equilibrium of game in normal form with strategy sets $X_i^{\Theta_i}$ and payoff functions

$$\tilde{\pi}_i(s_1(.), \ldots, s_n(.)) = \sum_{\theta_i \in \Theta_i} \sum_{\theta_{-i} \in \Theta_{-i}} \rho(\theta_i, \theta_{-i})\pi_i(s_i(\theta_i), s_{-i}(\theta_{-i}), (\theta_i, \theta_{-i})),$$

which are the (ex ante) expected payoffs of each player. That is, for all $i \in N$, (A.1) is satisfied.

A.4   Dynamic asymmetric information games and perfect Bayesian Nash equilibrium

In static games of incomplete information, the beliefs of uninformed players are easy to specify: players know the probability distribution that Nature uses to assign types, and their private information about their type possibly allows them to update their beliefs. However, since their decisions are being made simultaneously they cannot base their beliefs on decisions of other players. Things change in dynamic games of incomplete information, where players make their decisions at different points in time. Here, before making a decision, uninformed players have the opportunity to use the observation of other players' previous decisions to update their beliefs from the initial probability distribution used by Nature. In such contexts, we want to refine Nash equilibrium by requiring that beliefs are formed optimally given decisions, while decisions are made optimally given beliefs. This defines intuitively the concept of perfect Bayesian Nash equilibrium (PBNE).

Perfect Bayesian Nash equilibrium

To give a more precise definition of PBNE, we need to introduce three additional notions. First, we define a *belief system* as an assignment of probabilities to every node in the game such that the sum of probabilities in any information set is 1. Second, we say that a strategy profile is *sequentially rational* at a particular information set for a particular belief system if and only if the expected payoff of the player who has the move at that information set is maximal given the strategies played by all the other players. A strategy profile is sequentially rational for a particular belief system if it satisfies this requirement for every information set. Third, a belief system is *consistent* for a given strategy profile if and only if the probability assigned by the system to every node is computed as the probability of that node being reached given the strategy profile, i.e., players use Bayes' rule. We can then define a perfect Bayesian equilibrium as *a strategy profile and a belief system such that the strategies are sequentially rational given the belief system and the belief system is consistent, wherever possible, given the strategy profile.* A more detailed definition is given in the context of signalling games below.

In the definition, the phrase 'wherever possible' deserves some explanation. Bayes' rule can be applied to compute beliefs at information sets that are *on the equilibrium path*, i.e., that can be reached with positive probability given the players' equilibrium strategies. Off the equilibrium path, beliefs are also determined by Bayes' rule and the players' equilibrium strategies, where this is possible. Still, in many games this does not impose many restrictions giving rise to a large set of equilibria. Several approaches have been proposed for ruling out unreasonable off-the-equilibrium-path beliefs. Some equilibrium refinements of PBNE restrict the players' beliefs about moves off the equilibrium path to the set of those types only for which the observed off-equilibrium move could have been worthwhile. In the context of signalling games studied below, the most commonly used refinement is the so-called *intuitive criterion*. Since we avoid issues of equilibrium selection in this book, we do not describe this or other refinements.

Signalling games

Signalling games form a class of dynamic games of incomplete information. In signalling games, an informed player takes an action which serves as a signal to an uninformed player: the latter can use the signal to update her beliefs about the informed player's unknown type. For simplicity, we consider a finite type space Θ.

The timing of the game is thus as follows. At stage 1, the type $\theta \in \Theta$ of player 1 is realized with probability $\rho(\theta)$; this probability distribution is common knowledge. The realized type θ is privately observed by player 1. At stage 2, player 1 chooses his strategy x_1. This is then publicly observed. At stage 2, player 2 updates her beliefs on player 1's type based on x_1 and makes her decision x_2. Payoffs are denoted by $\pi_i(x_1, x_2, \theta)$, $i = 1, 2$.

A PBNE in a signalling game consists of player 1's strategy $x_1^*(\theta)$ that assigns a decision x_1 to each possible type of player 1, player 2's strategy $x_2^*(x_1)$ that assigns a decision x_2 to each possible choice of player 2, and posterior beliefs of player 2 $\mu(\theta|x_1)$ that assign probabilities to each type for any given choice of player 1, x_1. To be a PBNE the following requirements have to be fulfilled: (1) posterior beliefs are a probability distribution over types, $\sum_{\theta \in \Theta} \mu(\theta|x_1) = 1$; (2) player 2 maximizes her payoff given her beliefs, i.e. $x_2^*(x_1) = \arg\max_{x_2 \in X_2} \sum_{\theta \in \Theta} \mu(\theta|x_1)\pi_2(x_1, x_2, \theta)$; (3) player 1 maximizes his payoff given player 2's equilibrium strategy $x_2^*(x_1)$, i.e. $x_1^*(\theta) = \arg\max_{x_1 \in X_1} \pi_1(x_1, x_2^*(x_1), \theta)$; (4) for each choice $x_1 \in X_1$ and types that player 2 considers compatible with this choice of player 1, $\theta \in \tilde{\Theta}(x_1)$, posterior beliefs $\rho(\theta)$ are formed according to Bayes' rule, i.e., $\mu(\theta|x_1) = \rho(\theta)/(\sum_{\theta \in \tilde{\Theta}(x_1)} \rho(\theta))$.

In such games we distinguish between two types of PBNE, separating and pooling equilibria (there is possibly a third type, so-called hybrid equilibria, which we do not consider here). A *separating equilibrium* is such that different types of the informed player send signals from disjoint subsets of the set of available signals. The uninformed player is then able to deduce the informed player's type based on the signal sent. In contrast, in a *pooling equilibrium*, all informed player types take the same action. The uninformed player is therefore unable to extract information from this action and does not update her prior beliefs. We analyse signalling games for instance in Part V.

Further reading

A good introduction into standard concepts of game theory is Gibbons (1992). Also, Mas-Colell, Whinston and Green (1995) provide a good coverage of the standard material. For an advanced treatment, see Fudenberg and Tirole (1991).

Appendix B
Competition policy

Throughout the book, we have described a number of situations where firms might restrict competition in their attempt to increase their market power at the expense of their competitors and/or of consumers: collusive agreements in Chapter 14, welfare-reducing horizontal mergers in Chapter 15, predatory behaviour in Chapter 16 and exclusionary practices in Chapter 17. To assess whether such conducts are detrimental or not, we measured their effects on economic welfare. That allowed us to show that not all restrictions to competition are detrimental (think of the vertical restraints that we discussed in Chapter 17). But in the case they are, we were forced to recognize that market forces are not always sufficient to curb market power and reduce prices, implying that public intervention, namely *competition policy*, may be desirable.

Competition policy (or antitrust policy, as it is called in the US) can be broadly defined (following Motta, 2004, p. 30) as 'the set of policies and laws which ensure that competition in the marketplace is not restricted in a such a way as to reduce economic welfare'. In this appendix, our aim is to complement our previous analyses by giving a broad description of competition policy. We start by offering a brief historical perspective to understand where competition policy comes from (Section B.1). Then, focusing on the European Union and the United States, we describe the relevant laws and link economics issues (exclusion, collusion, merger etc.) to the particular laws (Section B.2). We proceed finally to a comparison of legal practice on the two sides of the Atlantic. There exist important differences between the EU and the US, but practices seem to converge nowadays (Section B.3).

B.1   A brief historical perspective

Competition policy was introduced in North America at the end of the nineteenth century and then spread across the rest of the world very gradually. Most European countries, as well as Japan, adopted competition policies in the mid twentieth century. Other countries followed suit only recently in order to comply with regional agreements (such as the adhesion to the EU for Eastern European countries) or with multilateral agreements (such as the membership of the WTO), or simply as part of a move towards a more market-oriented economic system (as was the case for a number of South-East Asian and Latin-American countries). To understand why some countries adopted competition policies earlier than others, it is useful to take a historical perspective. Indeed, competition laws have often been designed and enforced in response to particular economic, social or political contexts and, sometimes, with quite different objectives in mind than economic efficiency.[1]

In the United States, the large improvements in transportation and communication at the end of the nineteenth century entailed cascade effects that eventually led to the introduction of competition policy: the constitution of a single market drove firms to exploit economies of scale and scope in order to reduce their costs; this increased competition, resulting in a succession of price wars; to stabilize prices, dominant firms reacted by forming cartels and so-called 'trusts';[a] competitors, downstream firms and consumers got hurt in the process and lobbied to have antitrust laws passed in many US States; finally, a federal law, the *Sherman Act*, was adopted in 1890. This act prohibits price agreements among competitors *per se* and covers monopolization practices by individual firms. Yet, it does not cover mergers, to which firms increasingly resorted in the early twentieth century as a way to coordinate prices. As a response, antitrust legislation was extended, through the *Clayton Act* of 1914, to cover mergers capable of reducing competition. In 1936, the *Robinson-Patman Act* amended the provisions of the Clayton Act on price discrimination. We detail these three acts in the next section.

It is instructive to observe that US antitrust laws have not always been enforced with the same intensity. In the period between the two world wars, a coalition between business and politics was regulating the economy instead of leaving it governed by market forces. This resulted in a more lenient enforcement of antitrust laws. For instance, in the aftermath of the Great Depression of 1929, some price-fixing agreements were tolerated as a necessary evil to allow badly affected industries to survive.[b] In contrast, the period between the end of WWII and the mid 1970s was marked by an intense antitrust activity, which was perhaps more motivated, in accordance with the dominant economic thinking of the time, by an activism against large firms than by efficiency considerations. In this period, antitrust policy was mainly guided by the early industrial organization known as the structure–conduct–performance (SCP) approach, following the work of economists like Chamberlin and Mason in the so-called Harvard School.

The end of the 1970s and the 1980s witnessed another swing of the pendulum. As we describe below (see Section B.3), the so-called Chicago School heavily criticized the previous interventionist approach to business practices and mergers, and advocated the explicit recognition of the efficiencies that can be brought by such practices. This view gained support by antitrust agencies and judges, who started to adopt a laissez-faire approach. This squared well not only with the dominant view of the period that market forces should freely select the more efficient firms, but also with the need to restore the competitiveness of US firms abroad. Finally, the recent years have been characterized by a median position between the extremes of the two previous periods. Noticeable is the introduction of a leniency policy in order to strengthen the fight against cartels (see Chapter 15).

In the European Union, competition laws exist at the national and the supra-national level. We mainly deal here with the supra-national laws, introduced by the Treaty of Rome in 1957. As for the national laws, they are nowadays largely modelled on the EU laws. For most European countries, these are the first proper competition laws. However, the United Kingdom and Germany have a longer history in this matter, which is worth mentioning.

In the United Kingdom, competition laws were first introduced in 1919 in an attempt to curb prices after WWI; they were then amended after WWII with another objective in mind, namely reducing unemployment through competition in the marketplace. The various acts that were passed before the major reform of 1998 (inspired by the EU legislation) were characterized

---

[a] Trusts were created in the following way: the companies in one industry convinced their shareholders to convey their shares to a board of trustees, in exchange for dividend-paying certificates. Although the companies were not merging, they were nevertheless able to eliminate the competition between them.

[b] The financial crisis of 2008 inspired similar policies. For instance, on 30 September 2008, the Irish government passed an emergency legislation that allowed for competition law to be set aside to allow bank mergers, if deemed necessary to protect the stability of the financial system (see *Irish Times*, 1 October 2008, 'Bill allows State to take stake in any financial institution given aid', by Collins, S., Carswell, S., and Hennessy, M.).

by a lack not only of clear objectives, but also of enforcement tools. As for Germany, in the early twentieth century, cartels were not only permitted but were even enforceable in courts, as they were seen as an instrument to stabilize prices (and as the priority was given to the freedom of contracting). It is only under the pressure of hyper-inflation, in 1923, that a Cartel Law was introduced. However, the law was not enforced with great vigor as close cooperation between firms and mergers were seen as a powerful way to create 'national champions' that were better equipped to compete on foreign markets. The break up of these powerful industrial groups was part of the motivation behind the imposition of competition laws in Germany by the Allies after WWII.[c]

At the same period, the US sought to transplant their antitrust notions to other European countries as well. These attempts were first received rather coldly as several forms of corporatist state interventionism were still prevalent at the time (such as planification in France, nationalization of heavy industries in the UK or social market economy in Germany). However, a first supra-national competition law was adopted in 1951 within the Treaty of Paris, which created the European Community for Steel and Coal (ECSC). In Article 65, the Treaty of Paris prohibited agreements and concerted practices that aimed to 'prevent, restrict, or distort the normal operation of competition' within the Community and in Article 66, it forbade 'unauthorized concentrations'.

In 1957, the six member states of the ECSC (i.e., France, Germany, Italy and the three Benelux states) signed the Treaty of Rome, which founded the European Economic Community (EEC). As we detail in the next section, the Treaty of Rome deals with competition issues mainly in Articles 85 and 86 (and also enunciates the logic of free competition in a number of other articles).[d] It is important to note that, in both treaties, competition legislation was adopted in conjunction with trade liberalization within the community. Indeed, the common European competition laws have always been an important vehicle not only for economic efficiency, but also for market integration. This distinguishes the EU from the US and partly explains why divergences still exist between competition laws on the two sides of the Atlantic (see Section B.3).

After the entry into force of the Treaty of Rome and up to the 1980s, the member states modified their existing laws or adopted new ones in order to harmonize them with European law. At the supra-national level, the Merger regulation was adopted in 1989 in order to fill the gap left by the Treaty of Rome (which did not explicitly consider mergers).

B.2   Competition laws

In this section, we present the main texts in which the competition legislation is contained, first in the United States and then, in the European Union.[2] Given the importance of case law (or judicial precedent) and the longer antitrust tradition in the US, we also briefly review a number of landmark cases that have moulded the US antitrust policy.[3]

---

[c] The same applied to Japan.

[d] The current consolidated version of the EC Treaty is the Nice Treaty, which was signed in 2001 and came into force in 2003. It amended the Maastricht Treaty (or the Treaty on European Union) and the Treaty of Rome (or the Treaty establishing the European Community). Articles 85 and 86 of the Treaty of Rome are now numbered 81 and 82 in the current version.

B.2.1   **Antitrust legislation in the United States**

Legislation

The cornerstone of US antitrust policy is contained in the two first sections of the *Sherman Antitrust Act* of 1890. The Sherman Act outlaws 'every contract, combination, or conspiracy in restraint of trade' (Section 1), and any 'monopolization, attempted monopolization, or conspiracy or combination to monopolize' (Section 2). As clarified by the Supreme Court, not every restraint of trade is prohibited, only those that are unreasonable. On the other hand, certain acts are *per se* violations of the Sherman Act (meaning that no defence or justification is allowed) because they are considered so harmful to competition. These include plain arrangements among competing firms to fix prices, divide markets, or rig bids. Although most enforcement actions are civil, the Sherman Act is also a criminal law and individuals and businesses that violate it may be prosecuted by the Department of Justice (DOJ) and incur severe penalties.

The *Clayton Act* of 1914 addresses specific practices that the Sherman Act does not clearly prohibit, especially mergers. In Section 7, it prohibits mergers and acquisitions where the effect 'may be substantially to lessen competition, or to tend to create a monopoly'. In 1992, the FTC and the DOJ have developed *horizontal merger guidelines* that set out the agencies' analytical framework for assessing merger proposals (the Guidelines were revised in 1997). The Clayton Act was amended in 1936 by the *Robinson-Patman Act* to ban certain practices of price discrimination. It was amended again in 1976 by the *Hart-Scott-Rodino Antitrust Improvements Act* to require companies planning large mergers or acquisitions to notify the government of their plans in advance.

The *Federal Trade Commission Act* of 1914 established the Federal Trade Commission (FTC) as a separate enforcement agency for antitrust violations. It bans 'unfair methods of competition' and 'unfair or deceptive acts or practices'. The FTC enforces the Clayton and Federal Trade Commission Acts as well as a number of other antitrust and consumer-protection laws. Although the FTC does not technically enforce the Sherman Act, it can bring cases under the FTC Act against the same kinds of activities that violate the Sherman Act (as the Supreme Court decided that all violations of the Sherman Act also violate the FTC Act).

Landmark cases

The first two major cases tried under Section 1 of the Sherman Act are *Trans-Missouri Freight Association* (1897) and *Addyston Pipe and Steel* (1897). In both cases, a group of firms was found guilty of fixing prices (eighteen railroad companies in the former case, and six producers of cast-iron pipe in the latter). These two cases clearly established that all collusive agreements are per se illegal. The strict enforcement of Section 2 (monopolization) only started with the famous *Standard Oil* case in 1911. The Standard Oil Company was a trust created by J. D. Rockfeller. The Supreme Court found that it had illegally monopolized the petroleum refining industry (through discriminatory price cuts aimed at excluding rivals and a number of acquisitions of minor companies). As a corrective measure, the company was split into thirty-four separate companies. In the same year, the *American Tobacco* trust was also dismantled (the company had been created in 1890 through the consolidation of five separate entities and by 1910, it had swallowed a large number of minor competitors so as to control about 80% of the tobacco market).

In 1920, the *U.S. Steel* decision had a major impact on the US antitrust policy. In that decision, the Supreme Court made it clear that what matters is not the mere fact of being a monopoly but how a firm has obtained monopoly power and how it uses it. It was not sufficient to show that U.S. Steel had a large market share; what had to be shown was the exploitation of monopoly power or an intent to monopolize. This decision triggered the development of industrial economics tools allowing analysts to infer illegal behaviour from structural features of the markets. One major instance where the Supreme Court used such inference is the *Alcoa* case (1945). Alcoa was found guilty of monopolization in the aluminum ingot market although there was no overt evidence of business intent; Alcoa's size and market behaviour (in particular, the building of excessive capacity that was deemed to deter entry) was seen as sufficient to prove monopolization (and the intent of it). Compared to the U.S. Steel decision, the Alcoa decision swung the pendulum towards a more activist antitrust policy. This trend was confirmed by a number of merger decisions. For instance, in *Brown Shoe* (1962), the Supreme Court disallowed a merger between two firms that together would have had only 5% of the national shoe market. However, by the late 1970s, many analysts felt that decisions such as Brown Shoe were excessive. Under the influence of the Chicago School (which we describe in the next section), the Supreme Court decided in the *General Dynamics* case (1974) to reject the government's efforts to block a large merger. The decision was justified on grounds of efficiencies and of the disciplining force of new entrants. Also indicative of a less-interventionist antitrust policy is the *GTE-Sylvania* case (1977), which established that non-price vertical restraints should be subject to a rule of reason.

B.2.2   Competition legislation in the European Union

EU Competition legislation is mainly contained in Articles 81 and 82 of the Treaty of the European Community (or EC Treaty).

Article 81 deals with cartels and restrictive vertical agreements. Prohibited are 'all agreements between undertakings, decisions by associations of undertakings and concerted practices which may affect trade between Member States and which have as their object or effect the prevention, restriction or distortion of competition within the common market'. The most obvious example of illegal conduct infringing Article 81 is a cartel between competitors (which may involve price-fixing or market sharing).

Article 82 deals with firms that have a dominant market share and abuse that position ('abuse of dominant position'). Under Article 82, firms with a dominant position are imposed a special responsibility to conduct themselves appropriately; for instance, they cannot use price discrimination or exclusive dealing to the detriment of certain parties. The Commission is empowered by the Treaty to apply the prohibition rules of Articles 81 and 82, and enjoys a number of investigative powers to that end. It may also impose fines on firms that violate EU competition rules.

Article 82 has also been extended to cover mergers, acquisitions and joint ventures. The latest *Merger regulation* (known by the abbreviation *139/2004/EC*) covers mergers going beyond the national borders of any one Member State and where the annual turnover of the merging firms exceeds specified thresholds in terms of global and European sales. The merging firms (no matter where in the world they have their registered office, headquarters, activities or production facilities) have to notify the proposed merger to the Commission, which must then examine whether it would significantly impede effective competition in the EU. If the Commission finds that a proposed merger could distort competition, the parties may still commit to taking action to correct this likely effect.

B.3   Competition policy in the EU and in the US

In this section, we illustrate some of the main differences that exist between US and EU competition policy. We also argue that these differences tend to decrease nowadays, meaning that competition policies on the two sides of the Atlantic are on a converging path.

To illustrate the discrepancies in approach and standards between US antitrust and EU competition law, we refer to a specific case, namely the *Virgin/British Airways* cases that were defended in the US and in the EU around 2000. Case B.1 shows that the same facts (i.e., a loyalty scheme put in place by a dominant firm) actually led to completely opposite conclusions. In short, in the US, British Airways was not found guilty of any restraint of trade or attempted monopolization in violation of the Sherman Act, whereas in the EU, British Airways was found guilty of having abused its dominant position in violation of Article 82 of the EC Treaty.[4]

Case B.1 Virgin/British Airways cases

The dispute between Virgin and British Airways (BA) centred around incentive schemes that BA provided for travel agents in the UK. In that period, travel agents were making profits by taking a commission on the tickets they bought from the airlines and sold to the travellers. BA promoted its ticket sales by offering travel agents additional financial incentives on top of the standard commissions if they sold more of its tickets. As BA was the dominant purchaser of air travel agency services in the UK (with about 40% market share, its competitors having less than 10%), Virgin complained (before the European Commission in 1993 and before a US court in 1994) that BA's scheme was anticompetitive and predatory because it was reducing the travel agents' incentives to sell tickets of competing airlines.

The complaint was rejected in the US on the ground that Virgin had failed to demonstrate any adverse effects on competition (such as increased prices, reduced quantity or quality). It was indeed stressed that what matters in such cases is the harm to competition rather than the harm to a specific competitor. Anyway, the appeals court stated, Virgin could not even claim to be harmed as it was economically successful (in 1995 Virgin had even become market leader on the London–New York route).

In contrast, for the European Commission, whether BA's scheme had a significant effect on competition was basically irrelevant. In accordance with previous similar cases, the Commission followed the principle that a dominant firm is not allowed to offer discounts to encourage loyalty (it can only do it for efficiency reasons, such as cost savings from large orders). That is, once a dominant position is established, this type of conduct by the dominant firm is condemned per se. This analysis was not questioned by the fact that BA's competitors had been gaining market shares in UK despite BA's scheme. The Commission indeed stated that 'it can only be assumed that competitors would have had more success in the absence of the abusive scheme'. (*Virgin/British Airways*, para. 107)

It is not only discount or loyalty schemes that receive diverging treatments under US and EU competition approaches. In other business practices such as predatory or excessive prices, bundling and tying, US antitrust is generally less interventionist than the European Commission. Also, mergers are more likely to be allowed in the US than in the EU.

The historical perspective that we outlined in Section B.1 can help us understand why these differences arise. As we noticed, one of the main goals of US antitrust law since its beginnings was to protect competition and prevent monopolies in the interest of consumers. On the other hand, from the late 1950s on, the European Commission saw strict competition policy as a vehicle for market integration. It must indeed be kept in mind that national European markets were formerly protected by trade barriers, resulting in significantly more local dominant positions than in the United States. The different history of the European business environment explains thus partly the more interventionist or legalistic approach of competition policy in the EU.

What also partly explains the divergent approaches is the larger involvement of professional economists in the review of competition cases in the US than in the EU. The importance of economic analysis in US antitrust has been significantly increased by the Chicago School in the 1970s and 1980s, and later by 'post-Chicago' theories of industrial organization rooted in game theory (that is, the theories presented in this book). Starting from the premise that markets tend to lead to efficient outcomes if left unrestricted, the proponents of the Chicago School (i.e., lawyer-economists such as Robert Bork, Harold Demsetz, Richard Posner and George Stigler) recommended not to exaggerate market imperfections and to look instead at the potential welfare-enhancing efficiency effects resulting from higher concentration, mergers, vertical arrangements and other conducts that used to be seen as anticompetitive per se.[5]

Even if later developments in the theory of industrial organization have complemented and sometimes challenged the Chicago theories, the Chicago ideas have exerted a deep influence on US antitrust by forming the basis for a set of 'ground rules' for antitrust law that are still largely prevalent nowadays. The major rule is probably that the ultimate objective of antitrust law is consumer welfare; competition is only an intermediate goal, which may sometimes be traded off against efficiencies (such as synergies resulting from a merger). We find here the basic argument behind the US judgment in the Virgin/British Airways case, which can be summarized by the following popular phrase: 'competition policy should protect competition, not competitors'. As a corollary, assessment under a rule of reason should be preferred to per se prohibition for many practices and agreements, in particular nonhorizontal ones.[6]

As for the EU, it is only recently that economics has become more important in competition policy and practice. Looking at judgments and the reasoning that supports them, and considering the evolution of the legal framework and policy statements, it appears clearly that economic insights, both theoretical and empirical, play an increasing role. Another illustration of the increased emphasis on the compatibility of EU competition policy with economic learning was the appointment in 2003 of a Chief Competition Economist in Directorate General for Competition of the European Commission.

As reported by Neven (2006, p. 746), over the last twenty years, economic analysis has had a strong impact on the following areas: '(1) the analysis of agreements between firms, in particular vertical agreements under Article 81, has increasingly focused on effects; (2) the assessment of competition has moved away from the formal notion of dominance towards effective competition; (3) the analysis of the factors that determine effective competition has become more sophisticated, in particular regarding the definition of the relevant markets, bidding markets, the proximity of competitors' position and buyer power; (4) the concept of collective dominance has been progressively developed in terms of the theory of collusion in repeated interactions; (5) quantitative methods have become more important; (6) enforcement procedures, like the leniency programmes, which find some foundation in economic analysis, have been implemented'.

In conclusion, it seems fair to state that EU competition law is currently moving closer toward US antitrust, even though some differences remain.

Further reading

Motta (2004) and Buccirossi (2008) draw a detailed picture of the state of the art in the theory of competition policy. For a discussion of US cases see Kwoka and White (2009). A number of interesting European cases are analysed in Lyons (2009); for a detailed documentation of a large number of European cases see Russo *et al.* (2009).

Notes for Appendices

1. This section draws on Motta (2004, Chapter 1) and Resch (2005).

2. For more detailed information, see the websites of the Federal Trade Commission and of the European Commission, respectively at www.ftc.gov/bc/antitrust and ec.europa.eu/comm/competition/index.html.

3. For more information see Kwoka and White (2009).

4. We follow here the analysis of Niels and ten Kate (2004). The exact references of the two cases are the following. For the US:

Virgin Atlantic Airways LTD v. British Airways PLC, 257 F.3d 256 (2d Cir. 2001). In the EU: Case COMP/D-2/34.780, Virgin/British Airways, O.J. (L 30/1), 4 February 2000.

5. For a deeper account of the Chicago School's influence and a comparison with other schools of thought, see, e.g., Welch and Greaney (2005).

6. See Niels and ten Kate (2004, pp. 9–10) for a more detailed description of these ground rules.

References for Appendices

Buccirossi, P. (ed.) (2008). *Handbook of Antitrust Economics*. Cambridge, MA: MIT Press.

Fudenberg, D. and Tirole, J. (1991). *Game Theory.* Cambridge, MA: MIT Press.

Gibbons, R. (1992). *Game Theory for Applied Economists*. Princeton: Princeton University Press. [In Europe published as: *A Primer in Game Theory*. Hertfordshire: Harvester Wheatsheaf.]

Kwoka, J. E. Jr. and White, L. (eds.) (2009). *The Antitrust Revolution: Economics, Competition, and Policy.* 5th Edition. Oxford: Oxford University Press.

Lyons, B. (ed.) (2009). *Cases in European Competition Policy: The Economic Analysis.* Cambridge: Cambridge University Press.

Mas-Colell, A., Whinston, M. D. and Green, J. R. (1995). *Microeconomic Theory.* Oxford: Oxford University Press.

Motta, M. (2004). *Competition Policy. Theory and Practice*. Cambridge: Cambridge University Press.

Neven, D. (2006). Competition Economics and Antitrust in Europe. *Economic Policy*, October: 741–791.

Niels, G. and ten Kate, A. (2004). Introduction: Antitrust in the U.S. and the EU – Converging or Diverging Paths? *Antitrust Bulletin* (Spring/Summer): 1–27.

Resch, A. (2005). Phases of Competition Policy in Europe. Mimeo. Institute of European Studies.

Russo, F., Schinkel, M. P., Günster, A. and Carree, M. (2009). *European Commission Decisions on Competition: Landmark Antitrust and Merger Cases from an Economic Point of View*. Forthcoming at Cambridge University Press.

Welch, P. J. and Greaney, T. L. (2005). Alternative Economic Approaches to Antitrust Enforcement. In Oppenheimer, M. and Mercuro, N. (eds.)., *Law and Economics: Alternative Economic Approaches to Legal and Regulatory Issues*. Armonk, New York: M. E. Sharpe.

Index